THE POEMS OF ALEXANDER POPE: VOLUME I

The Poems of Alexander Pope is a multi-volume edition of the poetry of Alexander Pope (1688–1744) resulting from a thorough reappraisal of his work, from composition through to reception. The annotations and headnotes are full and informative, and the layout is designed to enable the reader to navigate easily between the poems, the record of variants and the editorial commentary. The poems are presented in chronological order of publication, with original capitalisation, italicisation, punctuation and spelling preserved. A record of variants to each poem illustrates the changes Pope made in subsequent editions, and full editorial annotation sets the poems in appropriate literary, historical and cultural contexts.

This volume contains the poetry that appeared between 1709 and 1714, including the *Pastorals* and the 'Rape of the Locke'. Much of the publication history of these poems shows Pope collaborating with the major writers and publishers of his time, as might be expected of a writer whose preparation for a literary career was so meticulous. But Pope was also beginning to establish himself on his own account, publishing (at first anonymously) a substantial statement of ideas, *An Essay on Criticism*. Another separate pamphlet, *Windsor-Forest*, constituted his distinctive contribution to the heavy freight of 'Peace' poems prompted by the Treaty of Utrecht. In all, the poems presented in this volume reveal an engagement with the literary and publishing industry that is at once amenable and independent.

Julian Ferraro is a Senior Lecturer in the Department of English, University of Liverpool, UK. He works chiefly on seventeenth- and early eighteenth-century poetry, particularly satire, and on twentieth-century and contemporary literature and culture, particularly pictorial narrative, the relationship between literature and architecture, and the literary representation of money. He has published many articles on Alexander Pope, with a particular focus on his manuscripts, together with articles on subjects ranging from Joseph Conrad to contemporary comics.

Paul Baines is Professor in the Department of English, University of Liverpool, UK. He works chiefly on literature and culture in the long eighteenth century, especially satire, crime and the book trade. His main publications are *The House of Forgery in Eighteenth-Century Britain* (1999), *The Complete Critical Guide to Alexander Pope* (2000), *Five Romantic Plays 1768–1821* (co-edited with Edward Burns, 2000), *Edmund Curll, Bookseller* (with Pat Rogers, 2007) and *The Collected Writings of Edward Rushton* (2014).

LONGMAN ANNOTATED ENGLISH POETS

General Editors: Paul Hammond and David Hopkins
Previous General Editors: F. W. Bateson and John Barnard

The Poems of Shelley, Vols 1–4
Edited by Michael Rossington, Jack Donovan and Kelvin Everest

The Poems of Andrew Marvell
(Revised Edition)
Edited by Nigel Smith

Spenser: The Fairie Queene
(Revised Second Edition)
Edited by A. C. Hamilton

Tennyson: A Selected Edition
(Revised Edition)
Edited by Christopher Ricks

Blake: The Complete Poems
(Revised Third Edition)
Edited by W. H. Stevenson

Dryden: Selected Poems
Edited by Paul Hammond and David Hopkins

The Poems of Alexander Pope, Volume Three
Edited by Valerie Rumbold

The Complete Poems of John Donne
Edited by Robin Robbins

Robert Browning: Selected Poems
Edited by John Woolford, Daniel Karlin and Joseph Phelan

The Complete Poems of Shakespeare
Edited by Cathy Shrank and Raphael Lyne

The Poems of Alexander Pope, Volume One
Edited by Julian Ferraro and Paul Baines

For more information about the series, please visit: www.routledge.com/Longman-Annotated-English-Poets/book-series/LAEP

THE POEMS OF
ALEXANDER POPE

– Volume I –

EDITED BY
JULIAN FERRARO AND PAUL BAINES

LONDON AND NEW YORK

First published in paperback 2024

First published 2019
by Routledge
4 Park Square, Milton Park, Abingdon, Oxon OX14 4RN

and by Routledge
605 Third Avenue, New York, NY 10158

Routledge is an imprint of the Taylor & Francis Group, an informa business

© 2019, 2024 selection and editorial matter, Julian Ferraro and Paul Baine; individual chapters, the contributors

The right of Julian Ferraro and Paul Baines to be identified as the authors of the editorial material, and of the authors for their individual chapters, has been asserted in accordance with sections 77 and 78 of the Copyright, Designs and Patents Act 1988.

All rights reserved. No part of this book may be reprinted or reproduced or utilised in any form or by any electronic, mechanical, or other means, now known or hereafter invented, including photocopying and recording, or in any information storage or retrieval system, without permission in writing from the publishers.

Trademark notice: Product or corporate names may be trademarks or registered trademarks, and are used only for identification and explanation without intent to infringe.

Publisher's Note
The publisher has gone to great lengths to ensure the quality of this reprint but points out that some imperfections in the original copies may be apparent.

British Library Cataloguing-in-Publication Data
A catalogue record for this book is available from the British Library

Library of Congress Cataloging-in-Publication Data
A catalog record for this book has been requested

ISBN: 978-0-582-42341-1 (hbk)
ISBN: 978-1-03-283680-5 (pbk)
ISBN: 978-1-315-76118-3 (ebk)

DOI: 10.4324/9781315761183

Typeset in New Baskerville and Minion
by Swales & Willis Ltd, Exeter, Devon, UK

Contents

Note by the General Editors	vii
Chronology of Pope's Life and Publications	viii
Preface	xvi
Acknowledgements	xxvi

1	January and May (1709)	1
2	The Episode of Sarpedon (1709)	60
	Appendix	92
3	*Pastorals* (1709)	103
	Appendix I	164
	Appendix II: A Discourse on Pastoral Poetry	168
4	*An Essay on Criticism* (1711)	184
	Appendix I	290
	Appendix II	291
5	Lines from *The Critical Specimen* (1711)	293
6	Sapho to Phaon (1712)	301
7	Messiah (1712)	329
8	The First Book of Statius his Thebais (1712)	353
9	The Fable of Vertumnus and Pomona (1712)	424
10	To a Young Lady, with the Works of Voiture (1712)	439
11	On Silence (1712)	451
12	To the Author of a Poem, intitled, Successio (1712)	463
13	Verses design'd to be prefix'd to Mr. Lintott's Miscellany (1712)	469
14	The Rape of the Locke (1712)	477
15	On a Fan of the Author's Design (1712)	521
16	*Windsor-Forest* (1713)	528
17	Prologue to *Cato* (1713)	593
18	*Ode for Musick* (1713)	610
19	The Gardens of Alcinous (1713)	633

20	Epigram upon Two or Three (1713)	642
21	The Wife of Bath Her Prologue (1713)	648
22	Prologue, Design'd for Mr. D —— 's Last Play (1713)	685
23	The Arrival of Ulysses in Ithaca (1713)	693

Bibliography 715
Indexes of Titles and First Lines 750

Note by the General Editors

The Longman Annotated English Poets series was launched in 1965 with the publication of Kenneth Allott's edition of *The Poems of Matthew Arnold*. F. W. Bateson wrote then that the 'new series is the first designed to provide university students and teachers, and the general reader with complete and fully annotated editions of the major English poets'. That remains the aim of the series, and Bateson's original vision of its policy remains essentially the same. Its 'concern is primarily with the *meaning* of the extant texts in their various contexts'.

Accordingly, the annotation which the various editors provide ranges from the glossing of obscure words and references to the evocation of the cultural, social, and political contexts within which the poems were created and first received. The editions draw on recent scholarship but also embody the fruits of the editors' own new research. The aim, in so far as this is possible through the medium of editorial annotation, is to place the modern reader in a position which approximates to that enjoyed by the poems' first audience.

The treatment of the text has varied pragmatically from edition to edition; some have provided modernised texts where the original conventions of spelling and punctuation were likely to create problems for a reader, whereas others, including this edition of Pope, retain the original accidentals – the spelling, punctuation, italics, and capitals. The rationale for not modernising the accidentals of Pope's poems is that Pope himself took great care over such details, albeit changing his mind about how he wanted his texts to appear in the course of his career. Since these details are expressive elements of Pope's texts, it has been decided to retain them.

We hope that this new edition of Pope's poetry will enable a new generation of readers to appreciate the rich diversity of his work, and the subtle and complex commentary on Pope's world which it provides.

Paul Hammond
David Hopkins

Chronology of Pope's Life and Publications

For further detail see Reginald Berry, *A Pope Chronology* (1988), and for a full biography, Maynard Mack, *Alexander Pope: A Life* (1985).

1688 (21 May) Alexander Pope (AP) born in Plough Court, Lombard Street, in the City of London to a Catholic merchant of the same name and his second wife Edith.
(5 November) William of Orange arrives at Torbay; the Catholic James II abandons the throne and goes into exile in France (22 December); 'Glorious Revolution' results in the enthronement of William and his wife Mary, James's daughter; both are Protestants.
1689 War with France begins.
The Whig Thomas Shadwell (1640–92) replaces the Tory and Catholic John Dryden (1631–1700) as Poet Laureate.
1690 (15 June) Martha Blount born at Mapledurham House, near Reading.
(1 July) William III's army defeats James II's forces at Battle of the Boyne in Ireland, ending rebellion there.
1692 AP's family moves to Hammersmith, perhaps in order to comply with legislation requiring Catholics to vacate the environs of London and Westminster.
(May–June) French fleet, supporting the claim of James II to the throne, defeated at La Hogue.
(October; dated 1693) Dryden publishes English version of the *Satires* of Juvenal.
1693 'National Debt' system of public finance inaugurated.
1694 (27 July) Bank of England founded.
(28 December) Death of Queen Mary.
1695 Sir Richard Blackmore, *Prince Arthur*.
1696 AP begins education under tutors at various clandestine Catholic schools.
1697 Peace of Ryswick ends war between Britain, France, Spain and the Netherlands.
(July) Dryden publishes English translation of the *Works of Virgil*.
(November) Dryden's *Alexander's Feast* performed.
1698 Whitehill House at Binfield, in Windsor Forest area, acquired by Pope's father through family connections.
1699 Samuel Garth, *The Dispensary*.
1700 Family in residence at Binfield, giving AP a base for reading, walking in Windsor Forest and occasionally visiting London.
(1 May) Death of John Dryden, shortly after publication of *Fables Ancient and Modern* (March).
1701 Act of Settlement comes into force, outlawing accession of Catholics to British throne, providing for the accession of the Electors of Hanover in the event that Anne, the immediate heir, dies without issue (her longest-surviving son having died in 1700).
John Dennis, *Advancement and Reformation of Modern Poetry*.

1702 (8 March) Death of William III and accession of Queen Anne, the last monarch of the Stuart line (James II's second daughter).

(15 May) Beginning of War of Spanish Succession (to 1713) with British forces under the command of the Duke of Marlborough.

1704 Jonathan Swift, *A Tale of a Tub*; Dennis, *The Grounds of Criticism in Poetry*.

(13 August) British forces defeat the French at the Battle of Blenheim, leading eventually to the construction of Blenheim Palace, near Woodstock in Oxfordshire. Much celebrated in verse, e.g. Joseph Addison, *The Campaign* (14 December).

1705 first surviving letters of AP, to the dramatist William Wycherley. Early poems composed. Literary friendships with John Sheffield (Duke of Buckinghamshire), William Walsh, Sir William Trumbull, and William Congreve.

1706 (20 April) Tonson solicits manuscript of AP's *Pastorals* for publication.

(23 May) British victory at Ramillies.

1707 (6 March) Union of England and Scotland.

AP probably meets the Blount sisters, Teresa and Martha, in Catholic circles; also friendly with Henry Cromwell.

1708 (16 March) Death of Walsh.

(11 July) British victory at Oudenarde.

1709 (12 April) Richard Steele begins publishing *The Tatler*.

(2 May) AP begins publishing career in *Poetical Miscellanies: The Sixth Part*: 'January and May', 'The Episode of Sarpedon', and *Pastorals*.

(2 June) Nicholas Rowe's edition of *The Works of Shakespeare*.

(11 September) British victory at Malplaquet.

1710 (27 February) Trial of High-Church clergyman Henry Sacheverell begins.

(5 April) 'An Act for the Encouragement of Learning', later known as the first 'Copyright Act' because it formally conferred intellectual ownership rights on authors, becomes law.

(28 April) Death of Thomas Betterton, actor and friend of AP.

Cooling of friendship with Wycherley, after dispute about AP's revisions to Wycherley's poems.

(August) Following a general election, a Tory ministry led by Robert Harley and Henry St John, with Swift as main political writer, begins to negotiate the end of the war.

1711 (1 March) *The Spectator*, by Addison and Steele, commences.

(15 May) AP publishes (anonymously) *An Essay on Criticism*, initiating lifelong controversy with the poet and critic John Dennis (*Reflections*, 20 June) but eliciting some praise from Addison in the *Spectator* (20 December).

(May) Harley created Earl of Oxford.

AP becomes friendly with John Gay.

(27 November) Swift, *Conduct of the Allies*.

(31 December) Marlborough falls from power after accusations of ambition and peculation.

1712 (March–July) Dr John Arbuthnot, *History of John Bull*.

(18 March) AP's version of 'Sapho to Phaon' published in the eighth edition of Tonson's *Ovid's Epistles, Translated by Several Hands*.

AP contributes 'Messiah', various prose pieces, and 'Upon a Fan' to *The Spectator*.

(20 May) AP contributes seven poems, including 'The First Book of Statius his Thebais' and the two-canto 'Rape of the Locke', to *Miscellaneous Poems by Several Hands*, published by Bernard Lintot.

(July) Henry St John created Viscount Bolingbroke.

(28 October) Thomas Tickell, *On the Prospect of Peace*.

1713 (January) Gay's *Rural Sports* dedicated to AP.

(7 March) AP publishes *Windsor-Forest* in celebration of the imminent Treaty of Utrecht (31 March) which formally ends the War of Spanish Succession. The poem is admired by Swift, soon a close literary associate.

(12 March) Steele commences *The Guardian*; AP contributes essays including mock praise of Ambrose Philips' *Pastorals*, 27 April, and ending with 'Gardens of Alcinous' essay in September.

(14 April) Addison's *Cato* first performed with Prologue by AP.

(12 May) Gay's *Wife of Bath* first performed, with 'Epilogue' perhaps in part by Pope.

(16 July) AP's *Ode for Musick* published.

AP studies painting with Charles Jervas, later the addressee of an *Epistle* (March 1716).

(October) AP issues subscription proposals for a translation of Homer's *Iliad*.

(29 December) AP's 'Wife of Bath Her Prologue' and 'The Arrival of Ulysses' published in Steele's *Poetical Miscellanies*.

1714 AP moves in the circle of Tory-inclined satirists and wits, including Swift, Gay, and Arbuthnot, sometimes known as the 'Scriblerus Club'.

(2 March) AP publishes expanded five-canto version of *The Rape of the Lock*.

(23 March) Agreement with Lintot for translation of *The Iliad*.

(6 April) Charles Gildon attacks AP in *A New Rehearsal*.

(14 April) Gay, *Shepherd's Week*.

(27 July) Harley loses political role as Lord Treasurer.

(1 August) Death of Queen Anne; accession of George I, first of the Hanoverian kings (crowned 20 October), ushering in dominance of Whigs.

AP writes 'Epistle to Miss Blount . . . After the Coronation'.

1715 (1 February) AP publishes *The Temple of Fame*.

(27 March) Bolingbroke avoids arrest by fleeing to exile in France, becoming Secretary of State to the Pretender.

(25 April) AP publishes hoax *A Key to the Lock*.

(6 June) First instalment of the *Iliad* translation, published by Lintot two days before Tickell's rival version published by Tonson.

(16 June) Harley committed to the Tower of London.

(July) AP begins friendship with Lady Mary Wortley Montagu.

(August) Rowe appointed Poet Laureate.

(September) Serious Jacobite rising begins; completely suppressed by February 1716.

(31 December) Death of Wycherley.

1716 (26 January) Gay, *Trivia*.

(22 March) Second instalment of AP's *Iliad* translation.

(26 March) Rogue publisher Edmund Curll publishes *Court Poems*, unauthorised material attributed to Gay, Montagu and AP; in revenge, AP spikes Curll's drink with emetic and publishes hoax pamphlets embellishing the results.

(March–April) Because of renewed pressure on Catholics, AP's family leaves Binfield and moves to Chiswick, under the protection of the Earl of Burlington.

(May) serious attacks on AP: Oldmixon, *The Catholick Poet*; Dennis, *A True Character of Mr. Pope*.

(August) AP begins correspondence with Montagu, who accompanies her husband on a diplomatic mission to the Ottoman Empire.

1717 (16 January) First performance of *Three Hours After Marriage*, a controversial comedy co-written by Gay, Arbuthnot and AP.

(3 June) Third instalment of the *Iliad* translation and one volume of *Works*, including new work such as 'Eloisa to Abelard' and 'Verses [later Elegy] to the Memory of an Unfortunate Lady', and an important 'Preface'.

(13 July) AP publishes anonymously edited miscellany, *Poems on Several Occasions*, including at least 15 of his own poems.

(23 October) AP's father dies suddenly; estate passes to AP. Atterbury makes a formal attempt to convert AP to the Church of England; AP responds with a dignified refusal.

1718 (18 January) Death of Garth.

(15 February) AP attacks Colley Cibber in *A Clue to the Comedy of the Non-Juror*.

(10 April) AP attacked by Charles Gildon in *Memoirs of Wycherley*.

(14 June) Fourth instalment of *Iliad* translation

Using the profits from Homer, AP leases property at Twickenham and begins to remodel the house as a Palladian villa and to create a garden and grotto.

(2 October) Montagu arrives back in London.

(24 October) Death of poet and friend Thomas Parnell.

1719 (March) AP moves to Twickenham house.

(17 June) Death of Addison.

1720 (c. 12 April) AP publishes a further prose lampoon against Curll.

(12 May) *Iliad* translation completed with two further volumes.

(August–October) Stock-market crash known as the South-Sea Bubble ruins many; AP less badly affected.

1721 (24 February) Duke of Buckinghamshire, AP's early patron, dies.

(21 May) AP agrees to edit Shakespeare for Tonson.

(September) AP's *Epistle to Addison* prefixed to Tickell's edition of Addison's *Works*.

(12 December) AP publishes edition of the *Poems* of Parnell with his own 'Epistle to Oxford' prefixed.

Rise of Sir Robert Walpole as First Lord of the Treasury or 'Prime Minister'.

1722 AP occupied with work on Shakespeare edition and on translation of the *Odyssey*.

(16 June) Marlborough dies; funeral conducted by Atterbury, Bishop of Rochester, who is shortly afterwards arrested for treason (August).

1723 (24 January) AP publishes edition of *Works* of the Duke of Buckinghamshire; in the heightened atmosphere of Jacobite conspiracy the edition is seized and censored.

(8 May) AP gives testimony at Atterbury's trial; Atterbury ordered into exile (16 May; leaves 19 June).

(23 May) Bolingbroke returns from exile with partial pardon, later settling at Dawley Farm, Uxbridge (March 1725).

(19 June) Atterbury goes into exile in France.

1724 (21 May) Death of Harley.

Swift, *Drapier's Letters* against cheap copper coinage in Ireland.

AP's work on Shakespeare edition and *Odyssey* translation nears completion.

1725 (12 March) Tonson publishes AP's edition of *The Works of Shakespear*.

(23 April) The first instalment of his *Odyssey* translation published, again by Lintot; rumours circulate about the extent of the collaboration with William Broome and Elijah Fenton.

1726 (March) Lewis Theobald attacks AP's scholarship in *Shakespeare Restored*.

(June) *Odyssey* translation completed with the partially acknowledged help of Fenton and Broome. AP awarded £200 from Civil List.

(June) Joseph Spence publishes critique of AP's *Odyssey* which later leads to friendship.

(July) Curll publishes *Miscellanea. In Two Volumes*, including several early letters and other poems and documents by AP, without authority.

(September) AP seriously injured in coaching accident.

AP spends much time with Swift, visiting from Ireland to oversee covert publication of *Gulliver's Travels* (28 October).

(December) *The Craftsman*, an opposition journal, begins.

1727 (April–September) Swift visits again, the last time the two men will meet.

(11 June) Death of George I and accession of George II.

(22 June) AP and Swift publish two volumes of *Miscellanies*.

1728 (29 January) Gay's *The Beggar's Opera* begins hugely successful run.

(8 March) AP and Swift, 'Volume the Last' of *Miscellanies*, including 'Peri Bathous: or, Martinus Scriblerus His Treatise of the Art of Sinking in Poetry', provoking further attacks on AP.

(18 May) First version of *The Dunciad* published, with Theobald as 'hero'.

(28 March) Curll publishes *Compleat Key to the Dunciad*, the first of dozens of entries in the controversy.

1729 (19 January) Death of Congreve.

(3 April) Gay's *Polly*, banned sequel to *Beggar's Opera*, published.

(12 March) Advance copy of AP's *The Dunciad Variorum*, complete with mock-scholarly apparatus, notes and appendices, presented by Walpole to the King and Queen (published 10 April). Renewed controversy, including *The Curliad* (30 April) and *Pope Alexander's Supremacy and Infallibility Examin'd* (13 May).

(1 September) Death of Steele.

(October) AP begins depositing correspondence in the Harley library.

(November) Publishes and suppresses second volume of Wycherley's *Posthumous Works* against Theobald's edition of 1728.

1730 (26 January) Edward Young, *Two Epistles to Mr. Pope*.
(28 February) James Thomson's *Sophonisba* first performed, with 'Prologue' by AP.
The *Grub-street Journal*, a satirical newspaper aligned with AP's views, begins publishing (to 1737); attacks James Moore Smythe, one of AP's antagonists (11 June). One of the publishers is Lawton Gilliver, whom AP uses as agent for much of his work in the following decade.
(14 June) AP dines with Walpole.
(6 July) The *Ode for Musick* performed at Cambridge in a new version with score by Matthew Greene.
(3 December) Appointment of Colley Cibber, actor and playwright, as Poet Laureate.
1731 AP in poor health; makes several visits around the country to friends such as Bolingbroke and Lord Cobham.
(13 December) AP publishes the *Epistle to Burlington*, originally *An Epistle to the Right Honourable Richard Earl of Burlington*, subtitled *Of Taste*. Attacked on the grounds of ungrateful satire against the Duke of Chandos in the character of Timon, which AP denies.
1732 Richard Bentley's edition of *Paradise Lost*.
(4 March) Death of Atterbury.
(4 October) AP and Swift publish fourth and last volume, labelled 'The Third Volume', of *Miscellanies*.
(4 December) Death of Gay; AP a pall-bearer at the funeral in Westminster Abbey (23 December).
1733 (15 January) First version of the *Epistle to Bathurst*, originally titled *Of the Use of Riches*.
(15 February) AP begins publishing the poems collectively known as the *Imitations of Horace*, continuing to 1738: *The First Satire of the Second Book of Horace, Imitated*.
(20 February) First Epistle of the *Essay on Man* published anonymously (second, 29 March; third, 8 May); unwittingly praised by several enemies of AP.
(9 March) AP attacked by *Verses Address'd to the Imitator of Horace*, apparently co-authored by Montagu and John, Baron Hervey.
(March) Walpole's Excise scheme introduced and withdrawn.
(7 June) Death of AP's mother. AP recuperates at the houses of Burlington, Bathurst, Cobham and other friends.
(11 October) AP begins covert manoeuvres to induce Curll to publish his correspondence.
(5 November) AP's modernisation of John Donne's fourth satire.
(10 November) AP attacked by Hervey in *An Epistle from a Nobleman*; AP composes but does not publish a prose reply.
(18 December) AP provides a 'Prologue' for a benefit performance on behalf of Dennis.
1734 (16 January) AP publishes *Epistle to ... Cobham*.
(24 January) Fourth and final 'Epistle' of the *Essay on Man* (complete edition, 2 May).
(27 November) Swift begins publishing an edition of his *Works* in Dublin.

(21 December) AP publishes (anonymously) *Sober Advice from Horace* 'Imitated in the Manner of Mr. Pope'.

1735 (2 January) AP publishes *An Epistle from Mr. Pope to Dr Arbuthnot*.

(8 February) AP's *Of the Characters of Women: An Epistle to a Lady*, addressed to Martha Blount without naming her.

(27 February) Death of Arbuthnot.

(23 April) AP issues a second volume of *Works*.

(12 May) Curll publishes an unauthorised edition of AP's *Letters*; AP protests, while surreptitiously encouraging the venture. Curll is questioned by the House of Lords but released and publishes several more volumes along similar lines.

1736 (3 February) Death of Bernard Lintot, AP's former publisher (3 February).

AP anxiously attempting to reclaim his letters from the increasingly ill Swift, among others.

1737 (28 April) AP publishes *The Second Epistle of the Second Book of Horace*.

(25 May) AP, the so-called *Epistle to Augustus*, properly *The First Epistle of the Second Book of Horace Imitated*.

(19 May) Official edition of AP's *Letters*.

(20 November) Death of Queen Caroline; AP friendly with the Prince of Wales and his alternative 'Patriot' court.

1738 (23 January) AP publishes the *Sixth Epistle of the First Book of Horace Imitated*.

(c. 13 May) Samuel Johnson's poem *London* published; AP approves of it.

(16 May, 18 July) AP's *Epilogue to the Satires* appears in two 'Dialogues', originally under the title *One Thousand Seven Hundred and Thirty-Eight*, concluding the Horatian series.

(21 July) While AP dines with Bolingbroke, some windows of his house are smashed, amidst sustained political attacks on the satires.

Essay on Man translated into French and attacked (1738) by a Swiss theologian, prompting a defence of its orthodoxy by William Warburton (1738–39).

1739 (11 January) Collected edition of the Horatian poems.

(February) AP begins corresponding with Warburton.

(April) Bolingbroke leaves for France once more.

(July) 'War of Jenkins' Ear', against Spanish trading practices, begins.

(3 November) Death of Jervas.

1740 (23 April) AP meets Warburton, who becomes a close supporter and editorial advisor. Extensive decoration of grotto using minerals supplied from Cornwall by an admirer, William Borlase, and by the wealthy supporter Ralph Allen at Bath. Increasing health problems and medical treatment, including surgery.

1741 (16 April) AP publishes the collectively authored *Memoirs of Martinus Scriblerus*.

(4–17 June) AP sues Curll, successfully, over literary property issues; Curll immediately pirates an edition of Swift's letters.

1742 (2 February) Resignation of Walpole; becomes Earl of Orford.

(10 March) AP publishes *The New Dunciad*, i.e., book IV.

(20 May) Swift is formally declared incapable of responsible action and committed to the care of guardians.

(24 July) Cibber publishes a *Letter ... to Mr. Pope*, containing several highly embarrassing anecdotes about AP.

1743 (15 February) Cibber publishes a *Second Letter*.

(29 October) AP publishes *The Dunciad in Four Books*, replacing the earlier hero, Theobald, with Cibber.

(12 December) Spence witnesses AP's will (12 December).

1744 (19 January) Cibber publishes final scurrilous pamphlet.

(February) George II revives rule against Catholics living in London as rumours of Jacobite invasion increase.

AP attempts to edit his works with commentary by Warburton.

(10 April) AP writes final couplet, on the fate of his dog Bounce.

(c. 1 May) AP circulates 'deathbed' edition of *Four Ethic Epistles*.

(30 May) AP dies, in the presence of several friends; buried in Twickenham parish church (5 June).

(14 June) AP's will proved; the bulk of his estate goes to Martha Blount, with Warburton as his literary executor and other literary property bequeathed to Bolingbroke.

1745 (18 March) Walpole dies.

(July) Final significant Jacobite rising begins with French support (crushed 1746).

(19 October) Swift dies in Dublin.

1751 Warburton publishes nine-volume edition of AP's *Works*.

Preface

The Longman Annotated English Poets edition of Pope presents for the first time the complete canon of Pope's original verse in the order of its first printed publication. The present volume is the first of five, and includes the poems published up to and including 1713. Volume II will include the poems published between 1714 and 1727; volume III (edited by Valerie Rumbold, and published in 2007) contains the 1728 *Dunciad* and 1729 *Dunciad Variorum*; volume IV will include the poems published between 1730 and 1735; and volume V will include those published between 1736 and 1744 (together with an appendix containing posthumously published poems).

Pope's poetry offers particular challenges to would-be editors. From the very beginning of his career in print he demonstrated an unusual level of interest in, and exercised an unusual level of control over, the dissemination of his texts. These facts are further complicated by Pope's somewhat liminal position. In some ways he was the epitome of the successful eighteenth-century professional writer – fully exploiting the possibilities of the burgeoning market for print and, thanks to new copyright procedures, becoming, to all intents and purposes, his own publisher in the latter half of his career. At the same time, he can be seen as akin to the coterie poets of the seventeenth century, circulating his poems in elaborate manuscript copies among a select group of privileged readers.

Pope was a writer for whom (occasionally radical) revision was, in the case of some of his poems, a process ended only by death, and in whose work rejected readings remain susceptible to reinstatement in subsequent incarnations of a 'finished' text. Yet, paradoxically, he is also a writer who lavished attention on the visual form of his work in both manuscript and print to convey a sense of the text on paper that is almost monumental. His exquisite manuscript fair copies carefully imitate the layout of a printed page – often down to the painstaking imitation of type – and letters to his printers show a concern for layout, ornament and even the quality of the ink, and care taken in 'working off' the sheets to 'preserve the blackness of the Letter' (*Corr.* I.217).

The current 'standard' edition of Pope, the Twickenham Edition, begun in the 1930s and completed in the 1960s, is one of the high-water marks of twentieth-century editing. It set new standards for accuracy and thoroughness of collation and is notable, for the most part, for the clarity with which it sets out the sometimes labyrinthine textual history of Pope's poems. However, as has long been recognised, the Twickenham Pope is not without its problems. Each of the editors adopted a slightly different approach to the text of the poems in the volume for which they were responsible. Broadly speaking, however, the Twickenham Pope presents an eclectic text based on the first edition, or 'the earliest for which it may be confidently asserted that Pope was responsible' (*TE* I.vi–vii), incorporating any of Pope's subsequent 'corrections' in a form modified to accord with the typography of the first edition. In this way the reader is presented with a mixture of the poet's first intentions in typographic form and last intentions in terms of the words actually used. As the work of David Foxon, Jim McLaverty and others has made clear, this version of the Greg/Bowers distinction between 'accidental' and 'substantive' variants is a problematic one in handling the presentation of Pope's verse, not least because the text that often results is one that was never published by Pope and one which would have looked strange to him and his contemporaries.

Surviving proofs from various stages in his career show Pope attending to the use of capitals and italics as well as making verbal emendations. But it is not simply a case of him 'perfecting' his text. Unlike Dryden, for instance, Pope was intimately involved in the creation of various 'monumental' collections of his verse. The two great collections of *Works*, published in 1717 and 1735, were followed by a succession of subsequent editions, in a variety of formats, incorporating newly published poems. There is considerable variety in typographic practice between these editions, suggesting perhaps that Pope had a sense that the form in which his poems appeared should depend on the format, and cost, of a given edition (or at least that this form should accord with prevailing fashions for various formats within the marketplace). Similarly, verbal revisions sometimes suggest a desire to choose his moment for introducing particular lines rather than a teleological process of 'correction'. The portrait of 'Sporus' in the *Epistle to Arbuthnot*, for instance, is considerably ruder about its thinly disguised target, Lord Hervey, in the version printed in the 1735 *Works* than it is in the first edition of the previous year. However, the more offensive lines in the portrait of 'Sporus' were not newly composed but retrieved from the earlier manuscript and 'smuggled' into the text of the poem in the later edition, when it formed part of a larger collection.

Jerome McGann makes a distinction between the 'poem' as 'the locus of a specific process of production … and consumption' and the 'work' which comprehends the global set of all … the poems that have emerged in the literary production and reproduction processes' (McGann 1991: 32). Pope's persistent revision of the texts and typography of the published versions of his poems and his inclusion of textual variants – from manuscripts and earlier printed editions – as part of a critical apparatus, underlines the need to consider his poetic output as 'works' in just this sense – as Maynard Mack, who was responsible for the *Essay on Man* volume of the Twickenham Edition, put it: 'the typical Pope poem is a work-in-progress' (Mack 1984: 16).

The Longman Annotated Pope is the first complete edition of Pope to dispense with the thematic grouping that Pope first introduced in his collected editions of 1717 and 1735 and which has been followed, in various forms, by the editions of Warburton (1751), Warton (1797), Elwin and Courthope (1871–79) and the Twickenham (1939–69). The primary focus of the Longman Annotated Pope, above the editorial line, is on his poems as they were first available to readers and thus with the specific material forms that contributed to their meaning for those readers. To that end the copy texts for all poems are the first printed editions, with texts presented in full and with as little modernisation as possible, retaining original spelling, capitalisation and italicisation. Aspects of presentation, design and typography are discussed where relevant in the editorial commentary.

The following editorial emendations have been applied throughout: obvious typographical errors have been silently corrected; short 's's have been supplied for long; punctuation has been set in roman type, as appropriate, rather than the occasional italic of the copy texts, and spaces between words and pieces of punctuation have been closed;

double inverted commas have been changed to single and repeated inverted commas at the beginning of lines of direct speech have been dispensed with, while closing inverted commas have been inserted; digraphs have been separated and abbreviations for 'et cetera' that use unfamiliar characters have been modernised. Asterisks and obeli, and other special designs used in the original text to indicate the presence of a footnote have not been reproduced; instead Pope's original notes are cued by line number and presented immediately below the copy text. Editorial judgement has been applied to the form of plural and singular genitives on a case-by-case basis. On occasion the textual record has suggested that a problematic instance might fall under the category of obvious misprint; however, variations can also indicate fluidity in eighteenth-century orthographic practice. When the meaning is clear, and the form of the copy text is at odds with that meaning, the text has been emended silently – otherwise, original readings have been retained and any subsequent authorial revisions recorded as textual variants.

With the exception of obvious typographical errors, all verbal variants from subsequent authorised editions are presented in the textual apparatus in the typographic form in which they are first introduced. The record of changes to punctuation is limited to significant variants. This category necessarily requires the exercise of editorial judgement. Broadly speaking, if a change in punctuation clearly affects meaning or emphasis it has been recorded. The introduction of commas within lines has presented a particular problem in this regard, as it can change or clarify meaning or emphasis, but recording such changes individually in an apparatus does not really allow the reader to appreciate their overall effect. Variations in typography and orthography have not been recorded, except as a consequence of the recording of verbal variants.

In the Preface to Volume I of the Twickenham edition, John Butt explained the decision of the editors to preclude treatment of all but a few of the surviving autograph manuscripts on grounds of space and because 'their readings belong to the partially formed, prenatal history of the poems; they were provisional only, liable to rejection, and frequently in fact rejected'. However, a significant number of the surviving autograph manuscripts of Pope's poems are fair copies prepared for, and circulated among, a particular readership. As such, they represent, at least to a certain point, a 'finished' form of those poems. Of the poems presented in the current volume, the manuscripts of the *Pastorals*, 'The Episode of Sarpedon', *The Essay on Criticism*, *Windsor-Forest* and 'Sapho to Phaon' fall into this category. Frequently these fair copies underwent a further round of revision before the first printing of the poem or in some cases afterwards, as a result of 'paper-sparing' Pope's habit of retaining and returning to his original manuscripts throughout his career. Where fair-copy manuscripts survive, the text that forms the first version of the poem recoverable from the manuscript has been identified and treated as a discrete state of the poem. Significant variants have been collated from this version of the text alone. For the sake of clarity and economy of space, the apparatus does not record any variants that derive from subsequent revision of the manuscripts. It is not part of the scope of the current edition to represent Pope's process of composition in full. Once a fair-copy text has become a working manuscript, it becomes impossible to record all variant readings, deletions, substitutions, re-orderings and the like in a textual apparatus.

Of the 23 items included in this volume, 14 were first published in some form of poetical miscellany, which had become the proving ground for new writers, alongside established talents, since the publisher Jacob Tonson the elder and the Poet Laureate (as he then was) John Dryden had instituted an influential and much-imitated series with *Miscellany Poems* in 1684. The first three poems certainly of Pope's authorship to reach print appeared in the last volume in the series, *Poetical Miscellanies: The Sixth Part*, published on 2 May 1709. At the other end of the present volume stand three poems published in *Poetical Miscellanies*, edited by Richard Steele, again for the Tonson imprint, as a sort of extension to the main series. This was dated 1714 but published on 29 December 1713. Items 8–14 were published by Bernard Lintot in a rival miscellany, possibly edited or in some less formal way overseen by Pope himself: *Miscellaneous Poems and Translations*, which came out in May 1712. Another item, 'Sapho to Phaon', was commissioned by Tonson as an addition to the eighth edition of *Ovid's Epistles, Translated by Several Hands* (1712). Four items (7, 15, 17, 19) first appeared in *The Spectator* and *The Guardian*, journals run by Steele and Joseph Addison, leading figures on the Whig side of the literary marketplace in these years; Pope also cut his teeth as a prose writer in these periodicals. Steele was also responsible for commissioning the *Ode for Musick*, a rare foray (for Pope) into the ode form and published as a separate pamphlet by Lintot in 1713. Addison, meanwhile, requested the 'Prologue' for his contentious play *Cato*, performed to houses which were packed (in every sense) in April 1713; it was published soon after the first performance in *The Guardian*, as well as with copies of the play itself.

These items show Pope collaborating with the major writers and publishers of his time, as might be expected of a writer whose preparation for a literary career was so meticulous. But Pope was also beginning to establish himself on his own account, publishing (at first anonymously) a substantial statement of ideas, *An Essay on Criticism*, through a much more obscure figure, the Catholic bookseller William Lewis, in 1711. Another separate pamphlet, *Windsor-Forest*, constituted his distinctive contribution to the heavy freight of 'Peace' poems prompted by the Treaty of Utrecht, ending the long-running War of Spanish Succession. This was published by Lintot, who would go on to be the agent for Pope's hugely successful translation of Homer's *Iliad*, for which subscription proposals were being issued just as the last poems of the present volume were published. Lintot would also publish his first self-edited *Works* of 1717. In all, the poems presented in this volume reveal an engagement with the literary and publishing industry that is at once amenable and independent.

The year 1714 would begin with the revised, five-canto *Rape of the Lock*, which would cement Pope's reputation as the most inventive and provocative poet of his day; but the period 1709–13 had already established him as a poet of extraordinary ability and tonal range. The shortest piece in this volume is a seven-line epigram; the longest, the 864-line version of the first book of Statius' *Thebaid*. The *Miscellany* format, with its polite encouragement of a mingled commerce of letters and a diversity of styles and modes, was well adapted for Pope, who chose his contributions to showcase the variety of his abilities and interests. *Poetical Miscellanies: The Sixth Part* contains Pope's modernisation of Chaucer's risqué 'Merchant's Tale', an unimpeachably serious (and politically resonant) extract from Homer's *Iliad* and the almost free-standing set of *Pastorals*, demonstrating the young poet's abilities in racy English narrative verse, sober classical translation and neoclassical genre poetry. The version of Ovid's *Heroides* in which Sappho complains of abandonment to her lover Phaon gives Pope an opportunity to explore female desire in terms of pathos. The seven certain contributions to Lintot's *Miscellaneous Poems and Translations* begin with the sustained intensity of Statius' Oedipal epic and conclude with mock-heroic in the shape of 'The Rape of the Locke'. 'Vertumnus and Pomona' presents a lighter story of seduction from Ovid; 'To a Young Lady' observes contemporary social mores with sympathetic gallantry; early imitations of other poets ('On Silence', 'To the Author of a Poem, intitled, Successio') take us closer to Pope's familiar identity as politically allusive satirist. 'Verses design'd to be prefix'd to Mr. Lintott's Miscellany' cheerfully mocks the publisher himself, suggesting early practice at literary flyting and the contempt for booksellers which would come to feature so prominently in *The Dunciad*. Items in periodicals include the millenarian eclogue 'Messiah', the amorous address of 'On a Fan', the vexedly British 'Prologue' for Addison's *Cato* and the suggestive Homeric episode 'The Gardens of Alcinous'. For Steele's *Poetical Miscellanies*, Pope returned to Chaucer with another story of marital discord and illicit sexual fulfilment, and to Homer, this time in the symbolic episode from the *Odyssey* in which the exiled hero returns to reclaim his kingdom and his wife; there was also a mildly mischievous 'Prologue', notionally on behalf of the fading London playwright Thomas D'Urfey.

In many of these pieces, Pope was, like other authors, competing with the culturally dominant if politically sidelined figure of Dryden, who had died in 1700. Pope's *Ode for Musick* was the only serious rival, in contemporary critical opinion, to Dryden's *Alexander's Feast*. Dryden's last volume, *Fables Ancient and Modern* (1700) contained modernising revisions of Chaucer and translations from Ovid, and indeed a version of the first book of Homer's *Iliad*. Pope's Homer translations have every appearance of staking a claim to the territory left vacant by Dryden's death. But the two major poems published separately, the *Essay on Criticism* and *Windsor-Forest*, also show dramatic internal contrasts in tone and a determined attempt to establish an independent poetic identity, though each shows the influence of Dryden's critical power and covert political allegiances. The *Essay* was an attempt at ecumenical harmonisation of criticism and poetry, bearing the general aspiration of early eighteenth-century poetry to embody 'What oft was *Thought*, but ne'er before *Exprest*', and yet its occasional satirical inflections brought Pope his first taste of literary controversy, in the furiously hostile response from the poet and critic John Dennis, and prompted his own first venture into the rougher world of anonymous prose parody and satire in *The Critical Specimen*. *Windsor-Forest* was a long-meditated poem on the area of Britain in which he had grown up, completed and redirected to take its place amid a deluge of 'Peace' poems, but its in some ways hazardous political engagement (celebrating the Golden Age of the already-fading Queen Anne, ignoring the military commander the Duke of Marlborough) presented a highly distinctive poetic practice as the reign of the Stuarts began to draw to a close. It also suggested that Pope was prepared to burn some of his literary bridges: as party-political lines hardened as a result of the Treaty of Utrecht, his friendships with Swift, Gay, Parnell and Arbuthnot, the satirically inclined writers sometimes referred to as the 'Scriblerus Club' and strongly aligned with the Tory ministry of Robert Harley, had begun to eclipse his closeness to Steele and Whig circles. He remained on reasonable terms with less doctrinaire Whigs such as Garth and Rowe, but the accession of the Hanoverians in 1714 and what Pope construed as Addison's treachery in relation to the *Iliad* translation in 1715 would at least temporarily erode his freedom of association further.

To lay the poems out in chronological sequence in their original textual forms as the present volume does is to tell a particular kind of story (one which otherwise requires consultation of three separate volumes of the Twickenham Edition and a certain amount of textual reconstruction). This is not the only possible sequencing, of course. Pope's preparation for the life of an author was, as noted, unusually careful and less driven by commercial need than in the case of many of his contemporaries. He lived during his teenage years (see Chronology) in the family home at Binfield, an enclave in the Windsor Forest area, using his father's library to read widely in British, European and classical literature and criticism. When he began to write he did so under the eyes of a politically disparate (from Whig to Jacobite) but politely protective set of literary guardians: John Sheffield, William Walsh, William Congreve, Samuel Garth, William Trumbull and several others. These men vetted his compositions and provided critical suggestions and authority. He corresponded with Wycherley, a dramatist from a former age, whose poems he tried to revise, not always very successfully, and swapped rakish banter and comic Ovidian verse with Henry Cromwell. Many of his ideas and experiences were recounted in letters to John Caryll, head of Pope's local branch of the beleaguered Catholic gentry. It was a long apprenticeship, helping Pope to enter the world of professional literary authorship with confident aplomb in 1709 and producing enduring habits of self-scrutiny.

Much of what Pope published between 1709 and 1713 was thus originally written at least a decade earlier, circulated amongst friends, critics and literary guardians for comment and then polished, revised and released as opportunity arose or circumstances prompted. (Other pieces were written very quickly, for an occasion, as in the case of the *Ode for Musick*.) Pope had written a great deal more that remained to be released, overtly or covertly, by arrangement with publishers or by accidental transfer of manuscripts, over the course of the rest of his life, and beyond. Pope oversaw the publication of some of his own juvenilia, imitations and translations in the *Works* of 1717 and 1735, often with conflicting statements about the dates of their composition. Edmund Curll, the brash interloping publisher who came (usefully, in some respects) to represent for Pope all that was corrupt about the commercial publishing industry, saw to some major disclosures in the decade immediately following the pieces in this volume. Much of the compositional chronology of Pope's career can be partially reconstructed from mentions in the *Correspondence*, comments to his friend Joseph Spence and other sources. We have attempted to give a succinct account of what is known about the composition of the poems Pope published and the material witnesses to his practices in the Headnotes to each poem, without embarking on what would necessarily be a fragmentary and uncertain account of the chronology of everything he wrote up to the end of 1713: the volume presents the oeuvre of the poet as he emerged into the world of print. Headnotes also contain accounts of the main formal models and literary sources of each item. A final section describes the situation of each work at the intersection of several contextual fields: personal, political, social, linguistic, commercial, artistic and religious, as particularly relevant in each case, and includes, where possible, evidence of its early reception.

These poems represent a canon that is not really in doubt, though some items, such as the 'Prologue, Design'd for Mr. D—'s last Play', may well be of composite authorship. Several items ascribed to Pope at various times have been omitted, and reasons are given in the Headnotes to relevant or adjacent poems. In 1711 Dennis accused Pope of having written the commendatory poem on the *Pastorals*, published in the name of Wycherley in the same volume of *Poetical Miscellanies*; the claim (much repeated thereafter) is not really a serious one, but the status of the poem is discussed in the Headnote to the *Pastorals*. Items sometimes attributed to Pope in Lintot's *Miscellaneous Poems and Translations*, but not included here, are discussed in the Headnote to 'The First Book of Statius his Thebais', the first item in that collection; the 'Epilogue' to Gay's *Wife of Bath*, which contains material close to Pope's 'Wife of Bath Her Prologue', is discussed in the Headnote to that poem.

Other items have simply lacked any confirming evidence or general scholarly consent. In 1977, for example, David Nokes reported the discovery of the initials 'A. P.' written in Pope's hand in his copy of *A New Collection of Poems Relating to State Affairs* (1705), after the title of a four-line political epigram, 'On the Death of the Queen and Marshall Luxemburgh':

> Behold, *Dutch* Prince, here lye th' unconquer'd Pair,
> Who knew your Strength in Love, your Strength in War!
> Unequal Match, to both no Conquest gains,
> No Trophy of your Love or War remains.

The second couplet has been struck out, as if proprietorially (though that is not the only possible explanation). Nokes argued that this was in fact Pope's first published poem, on the grounds that it contains animus against William III of the kind later found in *Windsor-Forest*, and speculated that William Walsh, who was already praising Pope's abilities as a writer of pastorals to Wycherley in April 1705, might have been responsible for its insertion in the volume, which contains a further poem signalled as Walsh's by Pope's annotation (see further Headnote to 'Messiah'). It would be possible to suggest that the aligned presence of 'Unequal', 'Conquest' and 'Trophy', all of which appear in *The Rape of the Lock* in the context of mock-heroic conflation of the military and the sexual, helps to confirm the link, though mock-heroic language naturally attracts words of that sort of epic register. The poem is reprinted in Mack's finding list of Pope's books (1982: 436) and the annotation confirmed, without further comment. The attribution has been tentatively accepted by Howard Erskine-Hill (1996: 64) and with more conviction by Joseph Hone (2015b) in his detailed article about the politics of Pope's early (and in some cases lost) writing before the *Poetical Miscellanies* which launched Pope's 'official' career in 1709. On the other hand, it is unlikely that Walsh, a Whig MP, would have encouraged what was essentially a Jacobite epigram in his young protégé; in any case Walsh's own poem had been widely printed before 1705, and there is no evidence he had any say in the selection of the poems in the volume which Pope owned, which was full of anti-Williamite sentiment. Pope would have been six at the time of the deaths which are the focus of the poem, which would be precocious indeed if it were written close to the events, and about 17 when it was published, a decade after they occurred, and a full four years before anything else emerged. He does not otherwise mention the duc de Luxembourg or ever revert to or reclaim the poem other than by these initials, entered at an unknown date for a purpose which is not transparent. The poem reappears, in slightly variant text, in volume I of *A Collection of Epigrams* (1735), no. 400, again with no attribution. On balance, there has not seemed enough confirmatory evidence to identify the item as clearly by Pope, and it is not edited here.

Amongst other signs of Pope's intention to establish himself as a kind of self-evidently classic author is his habit of self-annotation, sometimes for the purpose of drawing attention to an allusion or translation, and sometimes (increasingly so, over the course of his career) to illustrate the current text of a poem by comparison with some former version, as if he was always in the process of producing his own 'variorum' edition. To an extent unparalleled in previous literary history, he achieved a form of self-publication over his own commentary: the mock-annotation in *The Dunciad Variorum* is only partly a joke. (This aspect is registered in the page layout of the present volume, as explained below.) Pope was, however, as that poem reminds us, constantly subject to hostile as well as benign critique, and one of the chief weapons at the disposal of his literary enemies was the identification of borrowings or thefts from earlier authors, particularly in works which involve dialogue with many disparate sources, ancient and modern, such as the *Essay on Criticism* or *Windsor-Forest*. While literary imitation and allusion were a recognised method of composition in Pope's time, accusations of plagiarism were already beginning to be damaging to authors. After his death, critical review and editing of Pope by Warton, Johnson and Wakefield continued to amass points of origin and imitation, and, while this was not in itself necessarily hostile, the process encouraged later writers to downgrade Pope on the score of the new virtue of originality. Nineteenth-century editions from Bowles to Elwin-Courthope continued to generate lists of sources, often to show how Pope had done damage to whatever he had absorbed. The Twickenham editors, better versed in and more sympathetic to the literary practices of Pope's own day, nonetheless searched meticulously and found still more material to cite. Short articles illustrating Pope's borrowings were a mainstay of *Notes and Queries* for much of the twentieth century and longer studies (in particular Brower 1959 and Mason 1987) cemented Pope's reputation as the 'Poet of Allusion'. Two substantial books by Pat Rogers (2004; 2005a) which reconstruct the intellectual and artistic cultures Pope calls upon in *Windsor-Forest* offer a vast resource for the study of Pope's transformative attitude to pre-existing materials; the process continues and, indeed, we contribute something to it in our Commentary.

It is not, however, possible or indeed worthwhile to record every phrasal resemblance to an earlier writer that has ever been noted in relation to these poems, and we have concentrated our attention on material where it seems an allusion is part of Pope's point or where it appears helpful to present contextual material as a way to reconstruct meaning. We have explained, where necessary, Pope's own annotations on these and other issues and have recorded comments made by his contemporaries about particular lines, images or allusions, as this constitutes evidence of reception. Where an earlier instance of a phrase or image helps to explain the range of Pope's possible meaning or usage, we have noted this, especially where the usage is no longer current. We have also recorded such earlier instances where they help to establish the available register or tone of a phrase (epic, comic, pathetic and so forth), whether Pope's own usage is then in accord with it or at variance with it. We have drawn heavily on the materials collected by previous editors, especially the Twickenham scholars, as well as undertaking our own investigations. In most cases, we have quoted versions of earlier texts that were or could have been available to Pope, rather than from modernised editions, using the nearest available section numbering, act or scene division, canto or stanza number, and page number, or signature; some early texts, such as Dryden's *Works of Virgil* (1697) and John Oldmixon's *Amores Britannici* (1703) supply their own line-numbering, which we have adopted here. For ease of reference, however, we have also given modern lineation or similar reference where convenient modern editions of the early text exist, though the quotation itself is normally as Pope would have seen it. Where we can be certain that Pope owned a particular edition of a poem or book, we have noted this. We have also sometimes noted where Pope revisits his own phrase in later writings, either seriously (as often in the Homer translations) or by inversion or transformation (in the satires). Many of the positions, images and values advanced in poems of relative security, such as the *Essay on Criticism* and *Windsor-Forest*, for example, return, inverted or besmirched, to haunt the *The Dunciad* and the Horatian poems of the 1730s. References to poems by Pope other than those in the present volume or volume 3 of this edition are to the text and lineation of the Twickenham edition. Definitions for words are often initially based on Samuel Johnson's *Dictionary of the English Language* (1755) as Johnson was certainly Pope's most intelligent contemporary reader; he often included phrases from these poems as part of his definitions. Further definitions are given from *OED* as necessary.

We have treated the poems neutrally in providing commentary on them. The annotation in the Twickenham edition varies markedly between types of poem. The *Pastorals*, the *Essay on Criticism* and *Windsor-Forest*, constituting a particular type of intellectually serious early-career canon for many scholars, are very heavily annotated in volumes I and II of Twickenham. Those regarded as 'Minor Poems' (volume VI) commonly have little or no annotation, though that volume contains some very substantial items. Thus many of the poems in the present volume have previously received little or no explanatory commentary. Translations from Statius, Ovid and Chaucer, however sizeable in themselves, and 'Imitations' of earlier English writers, have likewise not seemed to previous editors to merit much commentary. Mindful of the resurgence of interest in translation, classical reception and literary imitation over the past 25 years, we have taken the view that such poems do in fact require a similar level of explication, not only in terms of the local meanings of unfamiliar words, phrases and ideas, but in relation to the significance of the changes, omissions and additions Pope makes to his sources and, where relevant, his reading of the versions of previous translators. It being no longer possible to regard Latin, still less Greek, as the common currency of Pope's readers, we have translated all quotations from classical sources as literally as possible or quoted translations Pope could have read in the form he could have read them where these are helpful.

The Longman Annotated Pope is designed for the practical needs of twenty-first-century readers, with a page layout that provides for ease of navigation amid complex multiple layers of text. The page is divided by a full rule: above it is Pope's text, set in Baskerville, and below it is editorial commentary, set in double columns in Minion. The upper portion of the page thus contains the verse and, where present, the authorial annotation found in the copy text. Where there are variants – both in verse and authorial annotation – from later authorised editions, these are also placed above the full rule, following the readings of the copy text, and clearly separated from it by a short rule on the left. Variants in Pope's annotation appear first, cued by line number followed by the letter n, and are separated from verse variants by a single line space. This visual coding is designed to ease the reader's progress from page to page and minimise the danger of confusing copy text with variants or, worse, Pope's annotation with that of his editors.

Acknowledgements

Work on this edition has been supported by periods of research leave awarded by the Department of English, University of Liverpool, and also by periods of research leave funded by the British Academy, the Arts and Humanities Research Council and the University of Liverpool; we are most grateful for the extended opportunities for the close study of Pope's texts and contexts provided in this manner. We have benefited from the wisdom and acumen of many colleagues, inside and outside our home institution, during the preparation of this volume; in particular we would like to thank Pat Rogers, Claude Rawson, Jim McLaverty, Valerie Rumbold, Kelvin Everest, Greg Lynall, Michael Davies, Jill Rudd, Matthew Bradley, Elaine Hobby, Paul Davis, Maynard Mack and Howard Erskine-Hill.

To the general editors past and present, John Barnard, Paul Hammond and David Hopkins, we owe a deep debt of gratitude for their continued belief in and support of the project and their assiduous attention to the details of both text and commentary. For all errors that remain, we take full responsibility.

We also wish to thank the reading room staff of the British Library, the Bodleian Library, Cambridge University Library, William Andrews Clark Memorial Library, Houghton Library, Huntington Library, Pierpont Morgan Library, Washington University Library, and the Special Collections and Archives division of the University of Liverpool Library for prompt and helpful assistance in all matters pertaining to manuscript materials and early printed books.

Editions of this kind incur a hidden debt in the case of those closest to the editors, and we would like here to thank, finally and above all, Katy Hooper and Maryam Khosravi for their patient interest in the poetry of Pope's early years.

> But *those attain'd*, we tremble to survey
> The growing Labours of the lengthen'd Way,
> Th' *increasing* Prospect *tires* our wandring Eyes,
> Hills peep o'er Hills, and *Alps* on *Alps* arise!

1
JANUARY AND MAY
(1709)

Editors' Headnote

Composition and publication

'January and May' was first published on 2 May 1709. Pope offered slightly conflicting accounts of the period of composition. The 'Advertisement' to the 1736 *Works* suggests a date for the translation – together with the 'Wife of Bath Her Prologue' – during a period of self-improvement and precocious practice in versification shortly after the publication of Dryden's *Fables Ancient and Modern* in 1700: 'Mr *Dryden's Fables* came out about that time, which occasion'd the Translations from *Chaucer*'. However, the note Pope attached to the poem itself in 1736 states, 'This Translation was done at sixteen or seventeen Years of Age', which would suggest 1704–5. Pope's copy of Thomas Speght's 1598 edition of *The Workes of our Antient and Learned English Poet, Geffrey Chavcer, newly Printed* survives in the library of Hartlebury Castle; it has an autograph inscription of the flyleaf recording it as a gift from Gabriel Young, a neighbour and former owner of Whitehill House, the Pope family home at Binfield (see further Headnote to *Windsor Forest*): 'Ex Libris | ALEXANDRI POPEI: | Ac è Dono | GABRIELIS YOUNG 1701' (Mack 1982: 179). This was most likely the text, therefore, from which Pope made his versions of Chaucer. The translation would seem to have been substantially completed, and in his mind, by the time of Pope's letter on aspects of English versification to his friend and mentor, the critic and poet William Walsh, dated (if the date is reliable) 22 October 1706; Pope quotes what became line 302 as an illustration of the desirability of avoiding hiatus (*Corr.*, I.24).

The receipt for payment for the 'Tale of Chaucer' and 'Eclogues' (i.e. *Pastorals*) is reproduced in Sherburn (1934: opp. 85). It is dated 4 March 1707/8 and states that Pope received from Jacob Tonson ten guineas for the combined poems, reckoning this to total 'ab^t one thousand and 2 hundred lines' (actually 1210 lines, giving a remuneration rate of a little over 2*d* per line). The Tonson firm (the senior Jacob and his nephew the younger Jacob) had been courting Pope for the *Pastorals* since 1706. 'January and May' was first published, together with the *Pastorals* and the 'Episode of Sarpedon', in the last volume of the series of miscellanies started by Dryden and Tonson in the 1680s, *Poetical Miscellanies: The Sixth Part*. Pope's name was given in full at the head of his poem, which occupies pp. 177–224 of the volume; the pagination of the volume as a whole is irregular because of a change of plan in the printing of the volume. There is a gap in pagination between pp. 172 and 177, where 'January and May' starts; the numbering of pp. 221–4 is repeated, with a false catch-word ('Believe') at the foot of p. 224. This is puzzling, since no line in the poem begins with the word 'Believe'. Further details of the printing of the volume will be found in the Headnote to the *Pastorals*.

Text

The text presented here is from the first edition of 1709. Revision is largely confined to three later texts: the *Works* of 1717 shows widespread revision with the excision of two couplets, while further minor verbal revisions occur in 1736 and 1741. The various extant texts of 'January and May' are referred to in the apparatus as follows:

1709: *Poetical Miscellanies: The Sixth Part*, octavo (Griffith 1)

1717: *Works*, quarto (Griffith 79)

1736: *Works*, vol.III, octavo (Griffith 417, 418)

1741: *Works*, vol.I, part 2, octavo (Griffith 521)

1745: *Works*, vol.I, part 2, octavo (Griffith 611)

1751: *Works*, ed. Warburton, vol.II, octavo (Griffith 644)

Models and sources

As noted, the edition in which Pope read Chaucer was *The Workes of our Antient and Learned English Poet, Geffrey Chavcer, newly Printed* (1598). Though a poor edition by modern standards, it represented at least an appreciative effort at establishing the complete text and canon of a revered author, and it proudly (if with some exaggeration) offered a number of 'additions', including Chaucer's 'Portraiture and Progenie shewed', his 'Life collected', 'Arguments to euery Booke gathered', a glossary of 'Old and obscure words explaned', and some explanatory glossing or 'Difficulties opened'. It was edited by Thomas Speght and printed by Adam Islip to form what was clearly a high-status book. Speght dedicated it to Sir Robert Cecil in terms which recalled the dedication of a previous volume of Chaucer to Henry VIII. As well as his own reverential account of Chaucer, Speght included a letter from the dramatist Francis Beaumont, whom he knew from Cambridge days. Beaumont's letter was an important defence of Chaucer as a creator of comic characters, not least because Beaumont offered a reason for Chaucer's bawdy: not only was this not out of line with the 'vncleane wantonnesse' of the Latin poets normally taught in schools, it was precisely appropriate to the characterisation within Chaucer's human comedy, his attempt 'to describe all men liuing in those days', with, in some cases, their 'filthie delights'.

Speght's volume was reprinted with a different text in 1602; Pope may have owned a copy of this edition also (Mack 1982: 401 suggests the ownership signature is 'late'). The 1602 text was reissued in 1687, the last black-letter version of Chaucer to be produced.

There were a few translations and loose imitations under the label 'Chaucer' following Speght's editions, such as William Painter's *Chaucer New Painted* (1623), a verse narrative of distantly Chaucerian character. In 1665 Richard Brathwait published *A Comment upon the Two Tales of our Ancient, Renovvned, and Ever-Living Poet Sr Jeffray Chaucer, Knight* which, however inaccurate its sense of Chaucer's personal dignities, is of importance as Dryden and Pope fairly certainly knew of it: one of its 'Tales' is the Wife of Bath's, together with her 'Prologue'. The other glossed and 'commented' tale is the 'Miller's Tale', suggesting renewed Restoration interest in the bawdy aspects of medieval literature. Brathwait commended Chaucer 'for his Rich Fancy, Pregnant Invention, and Present Composure'. Chaucer's name was variously taken in vain by 'a lover of antiquity' who published in 1672 *Chaucer's Ghoast, or, A Piece of Antiquity Containing Twelve Pleasant Fables of Ovid* 'penn'd after the Ancient Manner of writing in England, which makes them prove mock-poems to the present poetry'; 'Chaucer Junior', author of a jest-book, *Canterbury Tales Composed for the Entertainment of all Ingenious Young Men* which appeared in the same year as the last folio Chaucer reprint (1687); and the 'Nobody' (perhaps William Pittis) who issued a short book of verse jests in 1701 called *Canterbury Tales, Rendered into Familiar Verse*. (Pittis is also credited with *Chaucer's Whims*, a 1701 collection of Tory-inclined satirical verse.) 'Chaucer' was therefore well represented in Pope's time as a teller of humorous, human tales and invited light, ribald or satiric opportunism.

The public reputation and private reading of Chaucer since 1400 have been extensively documented (e.g. Spurgeon 1914; Brewer 1978). The main issues in the period leading up to Dryden's and Pope's versions were Chaucer's metre (which appeared often to lack a full syllabic count), the obsolescence of much of the diction, and the 'low' or obscene nature of the comedy. In 1694 Joseph Addison gave a cheerfully unsympathetic view of Chaucer in his 'Account of the Greatest English Poets', 9–16, *Annual Miscellany: For the Year 1694*, p. 318:

> ... *Chaucer* first, a merry *Bard*, arose;
> And many a Story told in Rhime and Prose.
> But Age has Rusted what the *Poet* writ,
> Worn out his Language, and obscur'd his Wit:
> In vain he jests in his unpolish'd strain,
> And tries to make his Readers laugh in vain.

In July 1699 Dryden wrote to Samuel Pepys to thank him for the suggestion that he look at the character of Chaucer's Parson, from the *Canterbury Tales* (Ward 1942: 1156). The following year his *Fables Ancient and Modern* was published by Tonson, including not only 'The Character of a Good Parson', from Chaucer, but the full-scale Chaucerian versions 'Palamon and Arcite' (from 'The Knight's Tale'), 'The Cock and the Fox' (from 'The Nun's Priest's Tale'), 'The Flower and the Leaf' (then attributed to Chaucer), and 'The Wife of Bath her Tale', interspersed with versions of Ovid, Boccaccio, Homer and some original poems. There was an important appendix of nearly all the Chaucerian source-text, the first in modern typeface, allowing comparison between original and version but also showing what Chaucer would look like without the black letter. (See further Hammond and Hopkins V, 1995–2005.)

Like most seventeenth-century poets, Dryden had been aware both of Chaucer as the originator of 'English' poetry and of the obsolescence of his vocabulary and obscurity of his metre. In the Preface to his *Fables*, Dryden explains his choices and sums up the value of Chaucer at the end of his own career. He states that 'From *Chaucer* the Purity of the *English* Tongue began', venerating him as 'the Father of *English* poetry'. To some extent he could be considered a sort of English Homer: 'He is a perpetual Fountain of good Sense; learn'd in all Sciences; and therefore speaks properly on all Subjects'. Dryden cites the favourable opinions of Spenser and of the Earl of Leicester against the negative verdict of Abraham Cowley; he compares Chaucer's tales favourably with those of Ovid (as more natural) and tells how he 'resolved to put their Merits to the Trial, by turning some of the *Canterbury* Tales into our Language, as it is now refined'. Dryden had no time for those who held 'a certain Veneration due to his old Language' or considered it 'little less than Profanation and Sacrilege to alter it'. In addition, the 'Verse of *Chaucer*, I confess, is not Harmonious to us'; it had 'the rude Sweetness of a *Scotch* Tune in it, which is natural and pleasing', but it was simply impossible to scan the metre correctly in the modern way. '*Chaucer*, I confess, is a rough Diamond, and must first be polish'd e'er he shines'. Dryden therefore omitted anything he considered unnecessary or undignified; added connective material as he saw fit; and used a modern vocabulary, inflected by wide allusion to poets both classical and modern.

Dryden saw the chief value of Chaucer as quasi-dramatic, a matter of vivid characterisation in narrative: 'I see ... all the Pilgrims in the *Canterbury* Tales, their Humours, their Features, and the very Dress, as distinctly as if I had supp'd with them at the *Tabard* in *Southwark* ... '. Chaucer must have been

> a Man of a most wonderful comprehensive Nature, because ... he has taken into the Compass of his *Canterbury Tales* the various Manners and Humours ... of the whole *English* Nation, in his Age. ... The Matter and Manner of their Tales, and of their Telling, are so suited to their different Educations, Humours, and Callings, that each of them would be improper in any other Mouth ... here is God's Plenty. We have our Fore-fathers and Great Grand-dames all before us, as they were in *Chaucer's* Days.

Aware of Chaucer's reputation for bawdy, and having been recently attacked for the immoral tendency of his own work by Jeremy Collier, Dryden made a strategic claim to have avoided any 'Immorality or Profaneness' and to have chosen for his treatment only 'such Fables ... as contain in each of them some instructive Moral'. He makes a point of what he is missing out on moral grounds:

> If I had desir'd more to please than to instruct, the *Reve*, the *Miller*, the *Shipman*, the *Merchant*, the *Sumner*, and above all, the *Wife of Bathe*, in the Prologue to her Tale, would have procur'd me as many Friends and Readers, as there are *Beaux* and Ladies of Pleasure in the Town. (*Fables*, sig. *C1)

In particular, he dare not 'adventure on' the Wife of Bath's 'Prologue', 'because 'tis too licentious'. Pope would respond to at least two of these challenges as he looked for a striking entry to the world of professional authorship.

Context

The process of modernising Chaucer elicited both praise (e.g. Jabez Hughes's *Verses Occasion'd by Reading Mr. Dryden's Fables*, 1721; dedicated to Pope's friend John Sheffield, Duke of Buckinghamshire, and written, according to 'To the Reader', in 1706 or 1707) and sneering (e.g. William Harison's *Woodstock Park*, 1706, p. 4). But there is little doubt that Dryden's version had an energising effect on the earlier poet's reputation and accessibility for the coming century. Pope certainly owned at some point Dryden's *Fables* (Mack 1982: 410; there is no annotation and no date of acquisition), but Gabriel Young's gift of the 1598 Speght edition gave him the materials for a lifelong interest in the full range of Chaucer's text (see Rumbold 1983). Pope's copy of Chaucer arrived at Hartlebury Castle via the ownership of Bishop Richard Hurd, who acquired it on the death of one of Pope's executors, Bishop William Warburton. The volume is briefly described in Nokes (1976), and more fully in Mack (1979, and 1982: 401, items 36 and 36a). Pope's marginalia show him indexing the book for characteristic descriptive and allegorical passages. From this evidence, Pope certainly read, at one point or another, *The Canterbury Tales*, *The Romaunt of the Rose*, the translation of Boethius, the 'Assemble of Fowles' [i.e. *The Parliament of Fowls*], as well as *The Court of Love*, and *The Plowman's Tale*, both then attributed to Chaucer. *The Merchant's Tale*, from which 'January and May' is derived, and which occupies fols. 27–32^v, has no marginal markings at all, however. Speght's text differs markedly from that of modern editions, in innumerable small instances of phrasing, wording and spelling, but more importantly in two passages of bawdy description, fol. 32–32^v, dropped from modern texts (see notes to 744–51 and 770–71; for further expurgation cf. note to 684–5). As Pope was reading Chaucer in a different version from that known to modern readers, we have quoted from his source in making comparisons; but since Speght has no lineation, we have provided line numbers from the modern Riverside edition for ease of reference, although Riverside lineates from the larger fragments, so the 'Merchant's Tale' begins at 1245. Pope's 1709 paragraphing has been matched to the source passages in Chaucer, and further correspondences, differences, additions and cuts have been noted where significant.

Chaucer was certainly Pope's favourite pre-Spenserian author (for brief comments on other medieval authors see *OAC*, I.179–80). As well as his own further imitations ('The Wife of Bath Her Prologue, from Chaucer', 1713; *The Temple of Fame*, 1715; the short bawdy invention 'A Tale of Chaucer', not published until 1727, and not acknowledged even then, though probably written before 1709), Pope made several comments and allusions to the poet. These references are by no means all positive, and Pope alludes to standard problems such as obsolescence of language (*Essay on Criticism*, 483–4). His 'Receit to make an Epic Poem' (*Guardian* 78, 10 June 1713; *PW*, I.115–20) makes satirical use of Chaucer glossaries such as Speght's in the ironic promotion of archaic vocabulary. In the *Epistle to Augustus* (1737) Pope claims it as a mark of cultural desolation that 'Chaucer's worst ribaldry is learn'd by rote' (37; at 97n he criticises Spenser's affected use of Chaucerian 'unequal measures' and archaic vocabulary). In private, however, he was less guarded. On 26 September 1723 he recommended Chaucer's visionary descriptions as a model for Judith Cowper's writing (though his model was the inauthentic 'The Flower and the Leaf'; *Corr.*, II.202). To his friend, critic, and recorder of conversation Joseph Spence, he was unambiguous: Addison's characterisation of Chaucer's failed humour, referred to above, was 'diametrically opposite to the truth' (*OAC*, I.74; December 1730). Pope remarked, echoing Dryden (*OAC*, I.179; May 1730): 'I read Chaucer still with as much pleasure as almost any of our poets. He is a master of manners and of description, and the first tale-teller in the true enlivened natural way'. In 1736 he still saw Chaucer, Spenser, Milton and Dryden as the 'great landmarks' of English poetry (*OAC*, I.178). Pope's last-known verse couplet, in a letter to Orrery, 10 April 1744 (*Corr.*, IV.517) on the death of Bounce the dog, alludes affectionately to Chaucer. At Pope's own death a few weeks later, 'a Chausor in a black frame' was found in 'the little parlour' of his house. This was perhaps by Jonathan Richardson, or even by Pope himself; Spence had seen a 'grave old Chaucer of his drawing from Occleve' of Pope's drawing. Pope was himself depicted as in the line of Chaucer, Spenser and Milton, and indeed in one case actually as Chaucer (Mack 1969: 255, 311, and plates 47, 50).

While the *Pastorals* was undoubtedly Tonson's main target in the recruitment of Pope (see Headnote to *Pastorals*), the ability of the young man to supply other types of material in place of the lost Dryden, poetic father of the series of *Miscellanies* of which the 1709 volume was the final instalment, was surely a strong motive also. Dryden wrote at the height, and end, of his freelance career, while Pope was just ready, after long preparation, to set out; accordingly, the deal struck worked out at twopence a line rather than the sixpence a line Dryden had agreed on in his final contract (Hammond and Hopkins V.34, 1995–2005). Dryden had issued, in the *Fables*, a translation of the first book of Homer's *Iliad* as a kind of specimen for a complete translation, another challenge picked up by Pope, in the 'Episode of Sarpedon', and before long in the actual translation of the whole, for which he contracted, however, with Tonson's rival Bernard Lintot. *Poetical Miscellanies: The Sixth Part* (1709) was fronted by the *Pastorals* of Ambrose Philips; then followed a translation of Lucan, book IX, by Pope's future friend Nicholas Rowe, and a paraphrase upon Psalm 104 by Joseph Trapp, before Pope's 'January and May'. There were contributions from writers Pope would come to admire or commune with, among them Anne Finch and Jonathan Swift, as well as existing friends and advisors such as William Wycherley, Samuel Garth and John Sheffield, Duke of Normanby (see further Headnote to *Pastorals*).

Chaucer's 'The Merchant's Tale' consists, in modern editions, of 1173 lines (excluding the 'Prologue', which is not part of Pope's poem, and the 'Epilogue' or exchange with the Host, which is not present in Speght). Pope's 'January and May', in its first incarnation, came to 824 lines (later reduced to 820). The scale of Pope's cutting is somewhat greater than these figures suggest, because Speght includes at least twelve lines of sexually explicit description of the encounter between May and Damian which are omitted as inauthentic in modern editions. Additionally, many of Pope's 824 lines are additions to the source narrative. Overall, Pope's versions are different from Dryden's in this respect, as Dryden tends to expand and supply, where Pope tends to condense and focus (for modern studies of Dryden's versions of Chaucer see especially Mason 1975 and 2007, and for succinct comparison of Pope's methods with Dryden's, Mason 2005). Pope regularly cuts several types of material, including much reference to scholastic authorities (Seneca, Theophrastus, Constantin, Marcian). While he retains a few obsolete words or senses (see notes to e.g. 13 and 704) he cuts much of Chaucer's Merchant's homely colloquialism (see notes to e.g. 204–5, 391). Pope has cut much of the bawdy. The scenes in January and May's bedroom, and up the pear tree, are notably less explicit in Pope than in Chaucer (especially in the version of Chaucer that Pope read), though there is a good deal of supplementary, covert suggestiveness in Pope's representation of May's sexual motivations. Pope has taken out 'low' moments, such as the scene where May tears up Damian's note and disposes of it in the privy. Instead Pope adopts a diction which, as the notes illustrate, derives from the high tradition of Milton or Dryden's epic (or sometimes mock-epic) mode or was felt suitable for use in that way, since Pope recalled a lot of his own phrasing here in later work, notably *The Rape of the Lock* and the Homer translations. Layers of allusion, whether to Milton (431) or Boccaccio (375, 385) or more pervasively to Dryden's versions of Chaucer, are often not merely echoes but a way of producing ironic contrast, as when characters adopt the speech patterns of contemporary comedy (439, 774). Thus there is an almost fully formed mock-heroic posture in Pope's first publication. This is intensified by other kinds of cut: Pope omits cross references to other elements in the structure of the *Canterbury Tales*; there is no prologue, no epilogue with the Host commenting on marriage matters, no cross-referencing to the Wife of Bath or the other tales in what is sometimes now called 'the marriage group'. This is designed as a stand-alone satiric tale. There is almost no sense of the Merchant as a characterised narrator, which is perhaps why Pope has given the poem a title based on the main characters: in the same way that Dryden had largely edited out the Wife of Bath's characteristic presence in her 'Tale' apart from a brief allusion to her 'Prologue' at the very end, Pope has either removed or radically truncated the interjections in which Chaucer has his Merchant narrator make direct comment on the action or addresses to the company, leaving only the occasional suave address to the ladies from a more independent satirical position. Other cuts tend this way: there is less psychological analysis in Pope's presentation of January's marriage debate, Damian's frustrated desire or May's dilemma, and more incisive satiric inflection. May flagrantly excuses her behaviour up the tree to January in both Chaucer and Pope, but Pope's May does it with some extended fake weeping (787–92) for which there is small warrant in Chaucer but plenty in contemporary comedy (see further Mason 2005: 433).

Pope's letter to Walsh 22 October 1706 (*Corr.*, I.24; the letter is perhaps a later reconstruction by Pope) shows how the Chaucer imitation was at work in his mind as an instance of rhythmic experimentation (he quotes line 302):

> To come to the *Hiatus*, or Gap between two words which is caus'd by two Vowels opening on each other ... I think the rule in this case is either to use the *Cæsura*, or admit the *Hiatus*, just as the Ear is least shock'd by either: For the *Cæsura* sometimes offends the Ear more than the *Hiatus* itself, and our language is naturally overcharg'd with Consonants: As for example; If in this Verse,
>
> *The Old have Int'rest ever in their Eye,*
>
> we should say, to avoid the Hiatus,
>
> *But th' Old have Int'rest —*

Pope heroic couplets are more often end-stopped than in Chaucer and have much more obvious use of antithesis: particular examples can be found at 47–8, 186–9, 238–41, and 504–7, where the less structured pathways of thought and decision of Chaucer's characters are tightly and efficiently rounded up and presented for display in Pope's. (Wimsatt 1994 analyses the metrical and syntactic differences between Pope's couplets and Chaucer's.) Pope reflects Dryden's style in being freer with his triplets and his Alexandrines than he would ever be again, but the essentials of his own couplet art are already present.

The poem itself did not attract much specific attention in the eighteenth century. Lines 461–66 were quoted with approval, if not of a straightforward kind (see Commentary), in a *Guardian* essay on 15 April 1713; and Mack (1985: 799) records the impression made on at least one female admirer, 'Amica', during Pope's lifetime. Warton (1782: 70) had been sufficiently impressed with Pope's versions to wish that he had tried one of the more emotionally rich tales, or *Troilus and Criseyde*. The efforts of Dryden and Pope combined certainly rendered 'imitation' a valid literary model, and bawdy Chaucerian material became more acceptable. Arthur Maynwaring's 'The Court of Love, A Tale from Chaucer', appeared in 1709 (slightly later than *Poetical Miscellanies*), in Ovid's *Art of Love*, a book probably owned and annotated by Pope (see note to 381–2). Pope's friend, the actor and dramatist Thomas Betterton, who had died in 1710, left behind some manuscript versions of the notoriously bawdy 'Tale' of the Reeve, as well as of the 'General Prologue', which Pope finished or perhaps more than finished: these were published (as 'The Miller of Trompington' and 'Chaucer's Characters') in *Miscellaneous Poems and Translations* (1712), alongside Pope's 'Rape of the Locke' and other poems (for the publication and authorship question see Sherburn 1934: 50; Ault 1949: 27–48; Foxon 1991: 34; McLaverty 2001: 15–20). This also contained 'An Imitation of Chaucer' using obsolete diction. Samuel Cobb's *The Carpenter of Oxford* (1712), a version of 'The Miller's Tale', was published with two further 'imitations' of Chaucer by Matthew Prior. John Smith's *Poems on Several Occasions* (1713) also contained a version of the Miller's Tale. *The Miller of Trompington*, a further (anonymous) version of 'The Reeve's Tale' in light octosyllabics, appeared in 1715 (for further examples see Bowden 1991). In 1716, following Pope's more sober take on poetic lineage in *The Temple of Fame* (1715), based on book III of Chaucer's *Hous of Fame*, proposals for a new full edition of Chaucer were published; the edition itself, by John Urry, was published by Lintot in 1721, inaugurating a new era of Chaucer scholarship (see Alderson and Henderson 1970).

The 'argument' added in the 1602 reprint of Speght's *Workes* (fol. 26) reads 'Old January marrieth young May, and for his vnequall match, receiueth a foule reward', suggesting that a lack of sympathy for the deceived husband was part of its received cultural significance, *EC*'s outrage at Pope's flippant disregard for sexual morality and religious decency notwithstanding. The young wife/old husband problem was a stock device of the Restoration comedy that Pope knew, and that there was never much in the way of sympathy for the Januarys of the world after Wycherley's *The Country Wife*; *TE* (II.7) points to the tradition of the 'indecently comic moral tale' on the same theme in two of the *Miscellaneous Poetical Novels* (1705). Pope's desire to appear urbane and amorously knowledgeable is well evidenced in his letters of this period to Cromwell and Wycherley, and in early poems he chose not to publish, such as 'Rondeau' and the imitations of the Earl of Dorset, 'Artimesia' and 'Phryne' (see Griffin 1978: 39–42). Mack (1985: 123–9) reads the poem as an opportunity for the young man to display mastery of sexual comedy and of the ways of wayward women within a culture which dooms them to arranged marriages. It has also been seen as an early experiment in aligning an unauthorised satiric poetry with the guile of the subordinate female (Morsberger 1993) and as a commentary on issues of female sovereignty and the politics of conciliation, marital and otherwise, in the context of Queen Anne's reign (Smallwood 2015).

Mack speculates that Pope's family might have been embarrassed by Pope's choice of model, but in the *Works* of 1717 he compounded the offence, if any, by commissioning a headpiece illustration for 'January and May' which shows her climbing the tree for her encounter with Damian (reproduced in Foxon 1991: 87). There is also a suggestive Initial 'T'. As McLaverty (2001: 73) points out, the quality of the illustration endorses the status of the work and the deliberate nature of what Pope was doing. Pope did not however choose to supply Chaucerian originals for 'January and May' in the 1735–36 *Works* in the manner of the more dignified *Temple of Fame* (McLaverty 2001: 240); this omission was partly supplied in volume II of Warton's 1797 edition, so that 'the reader may form a judgment of Pope's many improvements and alterations' (109).

JANUARY and *MAY*;
OR, THE
Merchant's Tale:
FROM
CHAUCER.
By Mr. *ALEXANDER POPE.*

THERE liv'd in *Lombardy*, as Authors write,
In Days of old, a wise and worthy Knight;
Of gentle Manners, as of gen'rous Race,

Title, n. *1736–51: This Translation was done at sixteen or seventeen Years of Age.*

Half-title. added *1717–51:* JANUARY AND MAY.

1–8. Chaucer, 1245–51.

1. *TE* suggests Pope's first line aligns itself with the opening of Dryden's 'The Cock and the Fox', *Fables Ancient and Modern* (1700), p. 223: 'There liv'd, as Authors tell, in Days of Yore . . .'.

   as Authors write: As *TE* notes, this is Pope's version of Chaucer's customary deference to written authority, but not from the *Merchant's Tale* itself.

2. Days of old: translating 'Whylome'; *TE* notes that Dryden, 'Palamon and Arcite: or, The Knight's Tale', I.1, uses the same substitution.

   wise and worthy: 'worthy', according to Chaucer's Merchant (1246, fol. 27^r), who later describes him as 'so wise' in an ironic coda to January's praise of marriage (1266, fol. 27^v).

3–4. Mostly Pope's addition.

3. gentle: 'well born; well descended; ancient, though not noble' (*SJ*), cf. May's claim in 595. The word is used 14 times in the poem, more often in the modern sense of softness of manner.

   gen'rous: 'not of mean birth; of good extraction' (*SJ*); it can also mean 'strong; vigorous'.

   Race: family. The phrase is not in Chaucer; perhaps recalled from Dryden, 'The Wife of Bath her Tale', 455, *Fables*, p. 495, where the crone offers to make the unwilling knight 'Father of a generous Race', though Dryden himself might have recollected Tate, *The Second Part of Absalom and Achitophel*, 1085 (1682), p. 32: 'Then Death unworthy seized a gen'rous Race'. Pope reused his phrase in his translation of Homer's *Iliad*, VIII.227. Cf. 181.

Blest with much Sense, more Riches, and some Grace.
5 Yet led astray by *Venus* soft Delights,
He cou'd not rule his Carnal Appetites;
For long ago, let Priests say what they cou'd,
Weak, sinful Laymen were but Flesh and Blood.

But in due Time, when Sixty Years were o'er,
10 He vow'd to lead that Vicious Life no more.
Whether pure Holiness inspir'd his Mind,
Or Dotage turn'd his Brain, is hard to find;
But his high Courage prick'd him forth to wed,
And try the Pleasures of a lawful Bed.
15 This was his nightly Dream, his daily Care,
And to the Heav'nly Pow'rs his constant Pray'r,

---

6. *1717–51:* He scarce could rule some idle appetites:
10. that: *1717–51:* this

---

4. much . . . more . . . some: a construction of discrimination not present in Chaucer.

Sense: here and generally in the poem with the positive meaning of 'wisdom' or 'intelligence'; the sly contrast between January's mental and commercial endowments indicate that he has more money than sense. For Pope's complex understanding of 'sense', see Headnote to *Essay on Criticism*. Later (174) it indicates sensuality, or the 'bodely delite | On women, there as was his appetite', which the Merchant (1249–50, fo. 27) ascribes to January and which Pope characterises in the next lines.

Grace: probably here 'virtue; effect of God's influence' (*SJ*); cf. 125.

5. Venus: Roman goddess of 'soft Delights', i.e. of sexual love; cf. 330.

6. Carnal: Pope's revision slightly tones down the sexual directness, already reduced from the source. Cf. 310, where both physical and spiritual versions of love are specified.

7–8. Pope's addition, following the pervasive anti-clerical satire of Dryden (e.g. the opening of *Absalom and Achitophel*, 1–2 (1681)).

8. Laymen: Chaucer has 'these foles that ben seculeres' (1251, fol. 27ʳ); Pope's irony is more tolerant.

9–18. Chaucer 1252–60; Pope then omits 1261–6.

10. Vicious: 'devoted to vice' (*SJ*), i.e. fornication; not in Chaucer.

12. Dotage: 'Loss of understanding; imbecility of mind; deliriousness' (*SJ*), commonly associated with old age; Chaucer's word (1253).

13. Courage: Chaucer's 'great corage' (1254), in the sense of sexual ardour; cf. Chaucer 1759. Pope uses the word ambiguously at 170, and again in the Chaucerian sense at 333. Pope's other usages of the word are in the main in the straightforward heroic sense. *OED* sense 3e dates the sense of 'sexual vigour and inclination' as obsolete from 1615.

prick'd: spurred, but the sexual sense confirms the type of 'courage'. Not in Chaucer.

15. Chaucer (1256, fol. 27ᵛ): 'day and night he doth all that he can', expanded perhaps by reminiscence of Dryden, 'Dido to Aeneas', 28, *Ovid's Epistles, Translated by Several Hands* (1680), p. 217: 'Their daily longing, and their nightly dream'. Cf. also 'Sapho to Phaon', 144; *Essay on Criticism*, 126; 'The First Book of Statius his Thebais', 446.

16. Heav'nly Pow'rs: Pope's mock-epic periphrasis for Chaucer's 'our lord' (1258); generally Pope uses some variant of this periphrasis throughout the poem. Pope later used the particular phrase without irony in his Homer translations (e.g. *Iliad,* II.314, VII.47).

Once, e're he dy'd, to taste the blissful Life
Of a kind Husband, and a loving Wife.

These Thoughts he fortify'd with Reasons still,
20 (For none want Reasons to confirm their Will)
Grave Authors say, and witty Poets sing,
That honest Wedlock is a glorious Thing:
But Depth of Judgment most in him appears,
Who wisely weds in his maturer Years.
25 Then let him chuse a Damsel young and fair,
To bless his Age, and bring a worthy Heir;
To sooth his Cares, and free from Noise and Strife
Conduct him gently to the Verge of Life.
Let sinful Batchelors their Woes deplore;
30 Full well they merit all they feel, and more:
Unaw'd by Precepts, Human or Divine,
Like Birds and Beasts, promiscuously they join:
Nor know to make the present Blessing last,
To hope the future, or esteem the past;

---

18. kind: benevolent, loving; cf. 336, and (in relation to women), 304 and 502.

19-20. Pope's addition.

20. want: lack.

21-42. Chaucer 1267-92 (with omissions).

21-2. *TE* notes that this couplet, 21-2, resembles Dryden's 'The Wife of Bath her Tale', 464-5, *Fables*, p. 496: 'Philosophers have said, and Poets sing, | That a glad Poverty's an honest Thing'. In Chaucer (1267) the assertion is phrased as that of the Merchant narrator, though he seems to speak ironically. It is unclear who (character or narrator) voices the subsequent passage in praise of marriage (Chaucer 1267-1392; see Benson 1988: 885). In Pope's narrative the reasoning appears to be aligned with January's 'weighty Motives' (77) and the narrator is not sufficiently characterised to be intrusive.

28. Verge of Life: *TE* notes that this is not in Chaucer and suggests Pope was recollecting Chaucer 1401, fol. 28^r, 'on the pittes brinke'; cf. also 88 below. The phrase 'Verge of Life' is common, but Pope may recall John Pomfret's popular poem *The Choice*, 156 (1700), p. 8, where the poet chooses a kind female relation (explicitly not a wife) to look after him when he has 'approach'd the Verge of Life'. The 'Life/Strife' rhyme is also found in Dryden, 'Baucis and Philemon', 171-2, in the context of a contented marriage.

29. deplore: lament.

31-5. Largely Pope's addition, though Chaucer has 'They liue but as birdes or bestes' at 1281, fol. 27^v.

32. promiscuously: cf. Dryden, *Absalom and Achitophel*, 5-6 (1681), p. 1: 'When Nature prompted, and no law denied | Promiscuous use of Concubine and Bride'; and Dryden, *Aureng-Zebe*, IV (1676), p. 51: 'Promiscuous Love is Nature's general Law' (part of a dialogue of illicit sexual approach). A less salubrious model for the phrase is Rochester, 'A Ramble in St James's Park', 32, 'And here promiscuously they swive' (the reading of the early manuscripts, though *Poems on Several Occasions* (1680), p. 15 has 'promiscuously they strive'; the poem was not included in the 1696 edition which Pope owned).

35	But vainly boast the Joys they never try'd,
	And find divulg'd the Secrets they wou'd hide.
	The marry'd Man may bear his Yoke with Ease,
	Secure at once himself and Heav'n to please;
	And pass his inoffensive Hours away,
40	In Bliss all Night, and Innocence all Day:
	Tho' Fortune change, his constant Spouse remains,
	Augments his Joys, or mitigates his Pains.
	But what so pure, which envious Tongues will spare?
	Some wicked Wits have libell'd all the Fair:
45	With matchless Impudence they stile a Wife
	The dear-bought Curse and lawful Plague of Life:
	A Bosome Serpent, a Domestick Evil,
	A Night-Invasion, and a Mid-day Devil.
	Let not the Wise these slandrous Words regard,
50	But curse the Bones of ev'ry lying Bard.
	All other Goods by Fortune's Hand are giv'n,
	A Wife is the peculiar Gift of Heav'n:
	Vain Fortune's Favours, never at a Stay,
	Like flitting Shadows, pass, and glide away;

---

43. **spare?:** *1745:* spare,
51. *1751:* no new paragraph
54. **flitting:** *1717–51:* empty

---

35. TE cites Dryden, 'The First Book of Ovid's Metamorphoses', 644, *Examen Poeticum* (1693), p. 41: 'and hates the Joys she never try'd' (Daphne resisting the advances of Apollo).
39-40. Pope's addition, based on Chaucer's 'Liueth a life blisfully' (1284, fol. 27ᵛ).
43-50. Chaucer 1293-304, much condensed, and then omitting 1305-10. Chaucer's Merchant cites particularly the views of Theophrastus, known as the author of an attack on marriage, and referred to also in the Wife of Bath's 'Prologue' (671 in Chaucer; cf. 86-99 in Pope's version); Pope shifts the ground from scholasticism to a 'lying Bard'.
46. TE compares Dryden, 'The First Book of Homer's *Ilias*', 752, *Fables*, p. 217 (Zeus rebuking Hera): 'My Household Curse, my lawful Plague'.
47-8. These two-word phrases to identify bad wives are all Pope's invention, loosely based on January's paraphrase of Theophrastus.
51-8. Chaucer 1311-18, then omitting 1319-24.
52. ***peculiar:*** particular; cf. 'The Wife of Bath Her Prologue', 160.
53. ***at a Stay:*** still, stable; for the usage cf. Dryden, *The Medall*, 46 (1682), p. 4: 'Yet still he found his Fortune at a stay', and 'Of the Pythagorean Philosophy', 268, *Fables*, p. 513: 'For Time no more than Streams, is at a stay'.
54. ***flitting Shadows:*** Chaucer's January envisages other possessions, emanating from Fortune, 'That passen, as a shadow on a wall' (1315, fol. 27ᵛ). Lady Chudleigh uses the phrase 'flitting Shadows' of fame, 'The Resolve', 3, *Poems on Several Occasions* (1703), p. 104.

55   One solid Comfort, our Eternal Wife,
     Abundantly supplies us all our Life:
     This Blessing lasts, (if those who try, say true)
     As long as Heart can wish — and longer too.

     Our Grandsire *Adam*, e'er of *Eve* possest,
60   Alone, and ev'n in Paradise, unblest,
     With mournful Looks the blissful Scenes survey'd,
     And wander'd in the solitary Shade:
     The Maker saw, took pity, and bestow'd
     Woman, the last, the best Reserve of God.

65   A Wife! ah gentle Deities, can he
     That has a Wife, e'er feel Adversity?
     Wou'd Men but follow what the Sex advise,
     All things wou'd prosper, all the World grow wise.
     'Twas by *Rebecca*'s Aid that *Jacob* won

---

64. Reserve: *1736–51:* reserv'd

---

55. *solid Comfort*: cf. 80, 562.

   ***Eternal Wife*:** TE cites Dryden's version of Persius, II.29: 'But my Eternal Wife!' *Satires of Decimus Junius Juvenalis* (1693), p. 22, where the invocation is however a complaint, not a reminder of comfort.

58. Chaucer's January senses (1317–18, fol. 27ᵛ) that a wife 'woll last and in thin house endure | Well lenger than thee list [pleases you] parauenture'.

59–64. Chaucer 1325–9, then largely omitting 1330–55, consisting largely of enthusiastic imaginings about the fidelity, obedience, and helpfulness of a wife. Pope's January thinks only of the 'helpmeet' idea set out in Genesis 2, not of the subsequent Fall (Genesis 3).

62. *solitary Shade*: a common setting for reflection in seventeenth-century poetry. Chaucer's phrasing is more robust: Adam is 'alone bely naked' (1326, fol. 27ᵛ).

64. Pope's addition. Milton's Adam addresses Eve as 'Heav'n's last best gift' in *Paradise Lost*, V.19.

   Reserve: 'store kept untouched, or undiscovered' (*SJ*); a possession held back.

65–6. Chaucer 1338–9.

65. *gentle Deities*: Chaucer's Merchant (1337, fol. 27ᵛ) invoked 'saint Mary'; an instance of Pope's shifting the ground slightly towards mock-heroic language.

67–8. Chaucer 1356–61, much condensed.

67. *the Sex*: the female sex.

69–76. Chaucer 1362–74; Pope changes the order of examples slightly, then omits Chaucer 1375–92, which include quotations from Seneca and Cato and the Merchant's own comments.

69. Rebecca ... Jacob: Genesis 27 tells how Rebecca, wife of Isaac, disguises their younger son Jacob to win the paternal blessing due to the elder son Esau – at best an ambivalent example of maternal rather than spousal advice, since the husband is directly deceived, as Chaucer shows in greater detail. See further 312.

70	His Father's Blessing from an Elder Son:
	Abusive *Nabal* ow'd his forfeit Life
	To the wise Conduct of a prudent Wife:
	Heroick *Judeth*, as the Scriptures show,
	Preserv'd the *Jews*, and slew th' *Assyrian* Foe:
75	At *Hester's* Suit, the Persecuting Sword
	Was sheath'd, and *Israel* liv'd to bless the Lord.
	These weighty Motives *January* the Sage
	Maturely ponder'd in his riper Age;
	And charm'd with virtuous Joys, and sober Life,
80	Wou'd try that Christian Comfort, call'd a Wife:
	His Friends were summon'd, on a Point so nice,

---

73. the Scriptures: *1717–51:* old *Hebrews*

71-2. Nabal: I Samuel 25 tells how Abigail (named in Chaucer but not in Pope) intercedes beguilingly on behalf of her husband, Nabal, when David seeks revenge upon him for his rudeness to his messengers. However, since Nabal dies shortly afterwards and David proceeds to marry Abigail, this is another somewhat ambiguous model of wifely devotion.

72. prudent Wife: Abigail is described as 'the wise and prudent wife of base Naball' in *The Glory of Women, or a Looking Glass for Ladies*, translated from Cornelius Agrippa by Hugh Crompton (1652), p. 11. Cf. Pope's 'Wife of Bath Her Prologue', 190-1.

73-4. Judeth: The book of Judith, xi–xiii, narrates how Judith saves the Israelites by cutting off the head of Holofernes ('th' Assyrian Foe') while he sleeps, drunk; she has distracted him at the siege of Bethulia with sexual promise and the 'Heroick' act is a form of resourceful deceit.

Scriptures: Judith, as a deuterocanonical book, was not included in the King James version; but it was in the pre-Reformation Bible of Chaucer's church, and in the Bibles of Pope's Catholic church. This is perhaps the reason behind Pope's revision, but 'old Hebrews' also suggests Dryden, *Absalom and Achitophel*, 440 (1681), p. 14: 'some dull Hebrew ballad'. Cf. 688.

75-6. Hester: the (canonical) book of Esther narrates how the Jewish wife of the Persian king Ahasuerus saves her people and her kinsman Mordecai from a vengeful vizier, Haman, not without some subsequent personal advantage, rounding off a series of examples which January can be seen to have slightly misread. Chaucer later (1744-5) compares May's complacency as a wife to Hester's; cf. 345-6 below.

77-84. Chaucer 1393-8.

80. Christian Comfort: Pope's addition; cf. 55, 562. The phrase perhaps reflects the third reason for marriage according to the service set out in the Church of England's *Book of Common Prayer* (1693), sig. Bbb[r]: it is ordained for 'the mutual society, help and comfort, that the one ought to have of the other'.

81. TE cites Dryden's version of Juvenal, *Satires*, VI.639, *Satires of Juvenal*, p. 114: 'The rest are summon'd, on a point so nice' (the context there is a female-only discussion of hairdressing).

nice: 'requiring scrupulous exactness' (*SJ*).

> To pass their Judgment, and to give Advice;
> But fix'd before, and well resolv'd was he,
> (As Men that ask Advice are wont to be.)
>
> 85 My Friends, he cry'd, (and cast a mournful Look
> Around the Room, and sigh'd before he spoke:)
> Beneath the Weight of threescore Years I bend,
> And worn with Cares, am hastning to my End;
> How I have liv'd, alas you know too well,
> 90 In worldly Follies, which I blush to tell;
> But gracious Heav'n has op'd my Eyes at last,
> With due Regret I view my Vices past,
> And as the Precept of the Church decrees,
> Will take a Wife, and live in Holy Ease.
> 95 But since by Counsel all things shou'd be done,
> And many Heads are wiser still than one;
> Chuse you for me, who best shall be content
> When my Desire's approv'd by your Consent.
>
> One Caution yet is needful to be told,
> 100 To guide your Choice; This Wife must not be old:

83–4. Chaucer does not make this narrative comment, but implies that January's mind is made up later, at 1408–9, fol. 28ʳ: 'I pray you shapeth for my mariage | All sodainly, for I woll nat abide [delay]'.

85–98. Chaucer 1399–414.

85–6. Pope's January is more theatrical in his address than Chaucer's, who merely begins with 'face sad'.

87. Chaucer 1400, fol. 28ʳ: 'I am hoore and old'. January is over sixty in Chaucer and Pope; Pope's phrasing here suggests recollection of the biblical limit of life, 'threescore years and ten' (Psalms 90:10)

88. See 28n. *TE* compares Dryden's poem 'To my Dear Friend Mr. Congreve', 66, Congreve, *The Double Dealer* (1694), a3ʳ: 'Already I am worn with Cares and Age'.

90. worldly Follies: Pope's January shows more tendency to boast about his sinful exploits than Chaucer's.

91. my Eyes: an instance of 'hiatus'; cf. *Essay on Criticism*, 348 and Commentary, and 258 and 504 below.

93. Pope recollects his source's earlier deliberation: 'Mariage is a full great sacrament' (1319, fol. 27ᵛ). The supposed 'precept' of the church is selected from such pronouncements as Paul, 1 Corinthians 7:9: 'But if they cannot contain, let them marry; for it is better to marry than to burn'.

94. Holy Ease: an ambiguous phrase, meaning religiously sanctioned comfort to January but a concept often found in anti-clerical satire from Chaucer onwards; Dryden had mentioned this aspect of Chaucer in his own preface to *Fables Ancient and Modern.* Cf. Ozell's version of Boileau's *Lutrin* (1708), p. 8: 'Dissolv'd in Ease the Holy Sluggard lay'.

99–112. Chaucer 1415–30.

100. In modern texts, Chaucer's January sets the limit of his prospective wife's age at twenty (1417), but 'fiftene' is the age given in Speght.

There goes a Saying, and 'twas wisely said,
Old Fish at Table, but young Flesh in Bed.
My Soul abhors the tastless, dry Embrace,
Of a stale Virgin with a Winter Face;
105 In that cold Season Love but treats his Guest
With Beanstraw, and tough Forage, at the best.
No crafty Widows shall approach my Bed,
Those are too wise for Batchelors to wed;
As subtle Clerks by many Schools are made,
110 Twice-marry'd Dames are Mistresses o' th' Trade:
But young and tender Virgins, rul'd with Ease,
We form like Wax, and mold them as we please.

Conceive me Sirs, nor take my Sense amiss,
'Tis what concerns my Soul's Eternal Bliss;
115 Since if I found no Pleasure in my Spouse,
As Flesh is frail, and who (God help me) knows?
Then shou'd I live in lewd Adultery,
And sink downright to *Satan* when I die.
Or were I curst with an unfruitful Bed,

---

101. **wisely:** *1717–51:* shrewdly

---

102. Chaucer 1418, fol. 28ʳ: 'Old fish and yong flesh woll I haue fain'; Pope's antithesis is more illustrative. The phrase is proverbial (F236 in Whiting 1968). Chaucer's January extends the list of metaphorical delicacies much further.

106. Chaucer 1422, fol. 28ʳ: 'It nis but Beanstraw and great forage', i.e. winter fodder for livestock.

107. **crafty Widows:** 'old widowes' who 'connen [know] so moch craft' (Chaucer, 1423–4, fol. 28ʳ), exemplified by Chaucer's own Wife of Bath (cf. 305 and 310 of Pope's version of her Prologue), and by Restoration comedies such as his friend Thomas Betterton's *The Amorous Widow* (1706). Chaucer's reference (1424) to 'Wades bote', a deeply obscure crux, is omitted by Pope.

109. **subtle Clerks... Schools:** close to Chaucer, 1427–8; for Pope's other early comments on 'schools' see *Essay on Criticism*, 26, 441.

112. The 'wax' image is in Chaucer (1430, fol. 28ʳ): 'Right as men may warm Waxe with hands plie'. It returns to haunt January when his wife takes the impressions of his private key in wax (514).

113–26. Chaucer 1431–56.

113. **Conceive:** understand.

116. **Flesh is frail:** not in Chaucer; more normally, 'the flesh is weak', Matthew 26:41. It connotes here a susceptibility to sexual sin.

119. **unfruitful Bed:** By the end of the tale, January's wife is (by her own account) pregnant with an heir. Chaucer's January specifically states that he is trying to produce an heir to prevent his 'heritage' from falling into 'straunge hondes' (1439–40, fol. 28ʳ), but also (1449–50, Pope's 120-1) to honour God.

	The righteous End were lost for which I wed,
120	
	To raise up Seed t' adore the Pow'rs above,
	And not for Pleasure only, or for Love.
	Think not I dote; 'tis Time to take a Wife,
	When vig'rous Blood forbids a chaster Life:
125	Those that are blest with Store of Grace Divine
	May live like Saints, by Heav'ns Consent, and mine.
	And since I speak of Wedlock, let me say,
	As, thank my Stars, in modest Truth I may,
	My Limbs are active, still I'm sound at Heart,
130	And a new Vigour springs in ev'ry Part.
	Think not my Virtue lost, tho' Time has shed
	These rev'rend Honours on my Hoary Head;
	Thus Trees are crown'd with Blossoms white as Snow,
	The Vital Sap then rising from below:

---

121. t' adore: *1717–51:* to bless

---

123. dote: 'to have the intellect impaired by age or passion; to be delirious' (*SJ*); Chaucer's word (1441). Cf. 'dotage', 12.

125. Grace Divine: One would need special 'grace' from God to be able to live in chastity; cf. 4. Pope's addition, along with 126.

126. Saints: not in Chaucer. The word was commonly used in seventeenth-century satire as a form of mockery against Puritans and others who aspired to extreme holiness.

127–38. Chaucer 1457–68.

127–8. *TE* compares Dryden, 'The Cock and the Fox', 616–17, *Fables*, p. 246: 'But since I speak of Singing let me say, | As with an upright Heart I safely may' (the words of the beguiling fox).

128. Stars: In Chaucer, 1457, January thanks God.

131. Virtue: in the Latinate sense of 'manly power' rather than moral rectitude; cf. Chaucer's January's claim that he has bodily strength to do 'all that a man belongeth to' (1459).

132. rev'rend Honours: venerable white hair, from the Latin 'honores', literally 'honours' in the civic sense but metaphorically beauties or ornaments, sometimes used in epic to signify hair, as in Virgil, *Aeneid*, X.172 in Dryden's translation, *Works of Virgil* (1697), p. 503, of Jove: 'And shook the sacred Honours of his Head'. Dryden used the same line, again of Zeus, in his version of 'The First Book of Homer's Ilias', *Fables*, p. 215. Pope uses the word thus in *Iliad*, XV.45, XVII.229 and XIX.414. Wasserman (1966) locates many instances of 'honores capitis', 'honours of the head' in Statius, *Sylvae*, I.2 and 113, etc. As *TE* notes, Dryden had parodied the usage in *Mac Flecknoe*, 134, *Miscellany Poems* (1684), p. 7: 'The *Syre* then shook the honours of his head'. For its use in relation to female hair cf. 'Rape of the Locke', II.53, and Commentary.

135 Old as I am, my lusty Limbs appear
    Like Winter Greens, that flourish all the Year.
    Now Sirs you know to what I stand inclin'd,
    Let ev'ry Friend with Freedom speak his Mind.

    He said; the rest in diff'rent Parts divide,
140 The knotty Point was urg'd on ev'ry Side;
    Marriage, the Theme on which they all declaim'd,
    Some prais'd with Wit, and some with Reason blam'd.
    'Till, what with Proofs, Objections, and Replies,
    Each wond'rous positive, and wondrous wise;

---

140. **ev'ry:** *1717–51:* either

133-6. The simile is longer in Chaucer (1461-6). For Pope's phrasing TE compares Dryden, 'The Flower and the Leaf: or, the Lady in the Arbour', 583-4, *Fables*, p. 404: 'Ev'n when the vital Sap retreats below, | Ev'n when the hoary Head is hid in Snow'. An earlier version of the image is in John Harrington, *A Pindarick Ode upon the Death of his Late Sacred Majesty King Charles II* (1685), 13-16: 'The Trees seem to refuse to grow, | Naked and Shievering on the Plain, | The Roots the Vital Sap retain, | To spend in Melting Tears below.'

135. **Old as I am:** cf. Dryden, 'Cymon and Iphigenia', 1, *Fables*, p. 541: 'Old as I am, for Ladies Love unfit' (Dryden's addition).

136. **Winter Greens:** evergreens; cf. Cotton, *Wonders of the Peake*, 1426-7 (1681), p. 83, where the phrase indicates yew, holly and box. Chaucer mentions 'Laurell' (1466, fol. 28ʳ), an evergreen tree or shrub with more obviously noble connotations.

138. Chaucer's January (1468, fol. 28ʳ) asks directly for agreement, not free comment: 'I pray you to my will ye woll assent'.

139-46. Chaucer 1469-77.

139-40. TE compares Addison, 'The Birth of Bacchus', 7-8, from Ovid, *Metamorphoses*, III, *Poetical Miscellanies: The Fifth Part* (1704), p. 528: 'The Hearers into diff'rent Parts divide, | And Reasons are produc'd on either Side'. In Chaucer (1473, fol. 28ʳ) the process of 'altercacioun' goes on 'all day'.

139. **He said:** an 'epic' (or mock-epic) way of indicating the end of a speech, imitated from Homer; not in Chaucer. Cf. Dryden, *Absalom and Achitophel*, 1026 (at the end of David's speech), and Pope, 'Episode of Sarpedon', 53; 'The First Book of Statius his Thebais', 348; 'Rape of the Locke', II.39 and 90.

140. **knotty Point:** Pope's addition; he may remember the phrase from the parody in section IX of Swift's *Tale of a Tub* (1704), p. 170; the narrator 'proceeds to unravel this knotty Point' with a comic page of lacunae and asterisks. The phrase is common in restoration drama and occurs in relation to a discussion of marriage issues in Thomas Rymer, *A Short View of Tragedy* (1692), p. 105. Pope remembered the phrase in *The Second Epistle of the Second Book of Horace Imitated*, 58: 'But knottier Points we knew not half so well . . .', and *Epistle to Bathurst*, 337.

144. Pope's addition.

145 There fell betwixt his Brothers a Debate,
   Placebo This was call'd, and *Justin* That.

    First to the Knight *Placebo* thus begun,
   (Mild were his Looks, and pleasing was his Tone)
   Such Prudence, Sir, in all your Words appears,
150 As plainly proves, Experience dwells with Years:
   Yet you pursue sage *Solomon*'s Advice,
   To work by Counsel when Affairs are nice:
   But, with the Wiseman's Leave, I must protest,
   So may my Soul arrive at Ease and Rest,
155 As still I hold your own Advice the best.

    Sir, I have liv'd a Courtier all my Days,
   And study'd Men, their Manners, and their Ways;
   And have observ'd this useful Maxim still,
   To let my Betters always have their Will.
160 Nay, if my Lord affirm'd that Black was White,
   My Word was this; *Your Honour's in the right.*

---

145. **betwixt:** *1717–51:* between
150. **Years::** *1717–51:* years!

---

146. **Placebo ... Justin:** Chaucer's names (Chaucer normally has 'Justinus' for 'Justin'). Placebo is Latin for 'I will please', indicating intentional flattery, and Chaucer's editors (Benson 1988: 886) suggest in view of January's age a further allusion to the text of an antiphon used in the service of Vespers for the dead. 'Justinus' perhaps recalls Justin Martyr, a theologian martyred in 165 AD, though he is not connected with any known debate on marriage and the name may merely suggest 'just' advice (cf. 181).
147–55. Chaucer 1478–90, with many omissions.
148. Pope's addition.
151. **Solomon:** the wise judge of the Bible, after being granted 'discernment' at his own request and as the special gift of heaven (1 Kings 3–10). See also Proverbs, 19:20: 'Hear counsel, and receive instruction, that thou mayest be wise in thy latter end' (the book of Proverbs is often ascribed to Solomon). See further 635–42 and 673–87 below.
152. **nice:** cf. 81.
156–75. Chaucer 1491–518. *TE* comments that in this speech Pope 'exchanges [Chaucer's] irony for direct satire and so needs to turn back at l. 166'.
156. **Courtier:** the first instance in Pope of a word which would often have ironic connotations for him. Chaucer has 'court man' (1492, fol. 28ᵛ). Though Pope uses the word without irony in some of his later epitaphs, the instance here is closer to 'Rape of the Locke', II.164.
157. Echoing Cowley, 'The Country Mouse', 37, *Verses, Written upon Several Occasions* (1663), p. 39: 'You should see Towns, and Manners know, and men' (for an extended contextual study of Cowley's poem see Hopkins 2010: 55–87).
160. **Black ... White:** not in Chaucer.

JANUARY AND MAY (1709) 21

      Th' assuming Wit, who deems himself so wise
      As his mistaken Patron to advise,
      Let him not dare to vent his dang'rous Thought;
165 A Noble Fool was never in a Fault.
      This Sir affects not you, whose ev'ry Word
      Is weigh'd with Judgment, and befits a Lord:
      Your Will is mine; and is (I will maintain)
      Pleasing to God, and shou'd be so to Man;
170 At least, your Courage all the World must praise,
      Who dare to wed in your declining Days.
      Indulge the Vigour of your mounting Blood,
      And let grey Fools be Indolently good;
      Who past all Pleasure, damn the Joys of Sense,
175 With rev'rend Dulness, and grave Impotence.

      Justin, who silent sate, and heard the Man,
      Thus, with a Philosophick Frown, began.

      A Heathen Author, of the first Degree,
      (Who, tho' not *Faith*, had *Sense* as well as We)

---

162. *assuming:* presumptuous (cf. *SJ*, where to 'assume' is 'to be arrogant; to claim more than is due'). Chaucer (1503, fol. 28ᵛ) has Placebo denounce any courtier who dares 'presume' to know better than his master.

  Wit: witty person, clever intellectual or poet; cf. 189, and *Essay on Criticism*, 36–40; also Defoe, *The Dyet of Poland*, II (1705), p. 43: 'A finish'd Coxcomb, with Assuming Wit'.

165. *Noble Fool:* cf. *Essay on Criticism*, 421–4. Chaucer's Placebo (1498–9) says that as a social inferior he accepts that his lord will know better than he.

170. *Courage:* poised between the sense of 'bravery' and 'sexual ardour' (see 13, 333; Chaucer 1513).

171. *declining Days:* cf. 'The First Book of Statius his Thebais', 540.

172–5. Pope's addition. Chaucer's Placebo (1516, fol. 28ᵛ) warns January that 'Your hart hongeth on a joly pin' ('is cheerfully tuned', perhaps with a sexual suggestion).

173. *Indolently good:* i.e. good because not performing any activity at all, good or bad.

174. *Joys of Sense:* cf. the final line of Chudleigh, 'A Dialogue between Alexis and Astrea', *Poems on Several Occasions*, p. 39, where Astrea condemns 'the mean Joys of Sense', meaning sensuality.

175. *rev'rend Dulness...grave Impotence:* figures of religious or moral authority who condemn sexual energy now that they do not have any; cf. 'The Wife of Bath Her Prologue', 369–76.

176–215. Chaucer 1519–65.

177. *Philosophick Frown:* Pope's addition. Chaucer's Justinus merely listens and answers (1519–20). 'Philosophick' here indicates an austere and sceptical world view, the frown appropriate to the sober mind of the thinker; cf. 630.

178. *Heathen Author:* Chaucer (1523, fol. 28ᵛ) identifies the source as 'Seneck', i.e. Seneca the Younger, d. 65 AD; the reference is to his moral treatise *De Beneficiis* ('Of Benefits').

179. *Sense:* here, good sense, wisdom: Chaucer's 'wordes wise' (1523, fol. 28ᵛ). Cf. 4. The mention of *Faith* is Pope's addition (but see 219).

180 Bid us be certain our Concerns to trust
To those of gen'rous Principles, and just.
The Venture's greater, I'll presume to say,
To give your Person than your Goods away:
And therefore, Sir, as you regard your Rest,
185 First learn your Lady's Qualities at least:
Whether she's chast or rampant, proud or civil;
Meek as a Saint, or haughty as the Devil;
Whether an easie, fond, insipid *Fool*,
Or such a *Wit* as no Man e'er can rule?
190 'Tis true, Perfection none must hope to find
In all this World, much less in Womankind;
But if her Virtues prove the larger Share,
Bless the kind Fates, and think your Fortune rare.
Ah gentle Sir, take Warning of a Friend,
195 Who knows too well the State you thus commend;
And, spight of all its Praises, must declare,
All he can find is Bondage, Cost, and Care.

---

180. **Bid:** *1717–51:* Bids
188. **insipid:** *1717–51:* familiar
196. **its:** *1736–51:* his

---

181. gen'rous: perhaps with overtones of 'noble' (cf. 3), but the Chaucerian passage (1527–9) contains much about gifts and giving.

182. Venture: 'a hazard; an undertaking of chance and danger' (*SJ*). There is a perhaps a suggestion of a merchant's sense of risk. Not in Chaucer, though there is much talk of the transfer of goods at this point.

186–9. Pope makes neat antitheses out of Chaucer's varied list of possible problems (1533–6).

186. rampant: 'exuberant; overgrowing restraint' (*SJ*), here perhaps in a sexual sense (*OED* sense 3, which cites a number of instances in relation to female sexual behaviour from the decade before Pope's poem). Chaucer's Justinus does not warn January about a wife's potential lustfulness at this point, but cf. 210–13 below.

186–7. The 'civil/Devil' rhyme appears acceptable in the poetry of the period; e.g. Dryden, *Absalom and Achitophel*, 557–8, and Pope's *Rape of the Lock*, IV.127–8.

188. fond: 'foolish; silly, indiscreet; imprudent; injudicious' (*SJ*); cf. 'The Wife of Bath Her Prologue', 58.

189. Wit: witty person, as in 162; here especially one of bold self-confidence. That a wife should be a wit is not among the possible problems identified in Chaucer's equivalent speech, and the identity was much less commonly associated with women; cf. however a play by 'W. M.', ridiculing *The Female Wits*, i.e. three prominent women dramatists, acted and published in 1704, and a poem of the same title had appeared in Behn's *Miscellany, Being a Collection of Poems* (1685).

196. spight of: in spite of.

197. Bondage: slavery. Pope adds this to Chaucer's 'but cost and care' (1547, fol. 28^v). *TE* notes that the phrase 'cost and care' is also in Dryden's 'The Secular Masque', 69.

        Heav'n knows, I shed full many a private Tear,
        And sigh in Silence, lest the World shou'd hear:
200   While all my Friends applaud my blissful Life,
        And swear no Mortal's happier in a Wife;
        Demure and chast as any Vestal Nun,
        The meekest Creature that beholds the Sun!
        But, by th' Immortal Pow'rs, I feel the Pain,
205   And he that smarts has Reason to complain.
        Do what you list, for me; you must be sage,
        And cautious sure; for Wisdom is in Age:
        But, at these Years, to venture on the Fair!
        By him, who made the Ocean, Earth, and Air,
210   To please a Wife when her Occasions call,
        Wou'd busie the most Vig'rous of us all.
        And trust me, Sir, the chastest you can chuse
        Will ask Observance, and exact her Dues.
        If what I speak my noble Lord offend,
215   My tedious Sermon here is at an End.

        'Tis well, 'tis wondrous well, the Knight replies,
        Most worthy Kinsman, faith, you're mighty wise!

---

202. Vestal: originally one of the virgins charged with maintaining the temple of Vesta (goddess of chastity) in Rome. Pope's addition.

204-5. Chaucer (1553, fol. 28ᵛ) has the colloquial: 'But I wot best, where wringeth me my shoe'; cf. 'The Wife of Bath Her Prologue', 239-40.

206. list: please (cf. quotation in 58n).

207. Wisdom is in Age: TE points out the phrase echoes Dryden, 'The Wife of Bath her Tale', 236, *Fables,* p. 487: 'Then tell your Pain: For Wisdom is in Age' (the crone, offering advice to the guilty knight).

208. the Fair: the 'fair sex', women.

210-13. Chaucer's Justinus warns January in similar terms, but with more of a suggestion that the wife will seek satisfaction elsewhere and that a husband will struggle to keep her to himself (1359-63).

213. Observance: duty (more normally of a religious kind). Chaucer (1564) uses the same word for a wife's sense of sexual rights (Pope's 'exact her Dues'); cf. 386.

214-15. Pope's addition. Chaucer's Justinus merely breaks off at this point with a wish that January 'be not euill apaied' (1565, fol. 28ᵛ).

215. tedious Sermon: an unwelcomely long lecture in Church; cf. the 'long Sermon' delivered to the unhappy knight by his crone wife in Dryden, 'The Wife of Bath her Tale', 509, *Fables,* p. 497.

216-21. Chaucer 1566-71. TE notes that Pope's January uses irony to counter Justin, whereas Chaucer's January is more openly and colloquially scornful. The ironic use of 'wondrous' (not in Chaucer) echoes 144 above.

217. Kinsman: In Chaucer, Placebo and Justin are 'brethren two' (1475, fol. 28ʳ) and both address January as a brother, but this may not indicate actual blood kinship. See, however, 299-304.

>   We, Sirs, are Fools; and must resign the Cause
>   To heathnish Authors, Proverbs, and old Saws.
> 220   He spoke; and turn'd, with Scorn, another way —
>   What does my Friend, my dear *Placebo* say?
>
>   I say, quoth he, by Heav'n the Man's to blame,
>   Who ventures Sacred Marriage to defame.
>   At this, the Council broke without Delay;
> 225   Each, in his own Opinion, went his Way;
>   With full Consent, that all Disputes appeas'd,
>   The Knight should marry, when and where he pleas'd.
>
>   Who now but *January* exults with Joy?
>   The Charms of Wedlock all his Soul imploy:
> 230   Each Nymph by turns his wav'ring Mind possest,
>   And reign'd the short-liv'd Tyrant of his Breast;
>   While Fancy pictur'd ev'ry lively Part,
>   And each bright Image wander'd in his Heart.
>   Thus, in some publick *Forum* fix'd on high,

---

220. 1717–51: He spoke with scorn, and turn'd another way; —
223. 1717–51: To slander wives, and wedlock's holy name.
224. **broke:** *1717–51:* rose,
233. **in:** *1717–51:* o'er

---

219. heathnish: Chaucer's January (1568–9, fol. 28ᵛ) objects to the 'schoole termes' (rhetorical language) of Seneca, not the lack of approved faith (but see 179): 'I count it not worth a pannier of herbes'.
  old Saws: antiquated moral tags.
222–7. Chaucer 1572–6.
225. in his own Opinion: Pope's insertion, rendering ironic the 'full Consent' of 226 (based on Chaucer 1575, fol. 28ᵛ, the debaters having 'assented fully' to January's plan).
228–49. Chaucer 1577–604.
228. *TE* notes that 228 is phrased as imitation of Dryden's 'Palamon and Arcite', II.426, *Fables*, p. 40: 'Who now but *Palamon* exults with Joy?' as an addition to the Chaucerian source.
229. Condensed from the 'High fantasie and curiousnesse' which impress January's 'soule' in Chaucer 1577–9, fol. 28ᵛ.

230. Nymph: 'a goddess of the woods, meadows, or waters'; usually in Pope, 'A lady. In poetry' (*SJ*).
  wav'ring Mind: perhaps in parody of the habit of religious self-examination, e.g. Francis Quarles, *Emblemes*, IV.6 (1643), p. 190, commenting on Romans, 7:23: 'I know the nature of my wav'ring mind; | I know the frailty of my fleshly will'. The succession of reigning beauties may receive some reinforcement from the parade of women in Cowley, 'The Chronicle', including the rhyme and idea at 52–3, *Poems . . . Written by A. Cowley* (1656), p. 23: 'Thousand worse *Passions* then possest | The *Interregnum* of my brest'.
232. lively Part: a more sexual image than Chaucer's 'fair shappe' (1580, fol. 28ᵛ).
234. Forum: the Roman market place and central civic space. In Chaucer (1583, fol. 28ᵛ) the image is of a 'comen market place'.

235   A Mirrour shows the Figures moving by;
　　　　Still one by one, in swift Succession, pass
　　　　The gliding Shadows o'er the polish'd Glass.
　　　　This Lady's Charms the Nicest cou'd not blame,
　　　　But vile Suspicions had aspers'd her Fame;
240   That was with Sense, but not with Virtue blest;
　　　　And one had Grace, yet wanted all the rest.
　　　　Thus doubting long what Nymph he shou'd obey,
　　　　He fix'd at last upon the youthful *May*.
　　　　Her Faults he knew not, Love is always blind,
245   But ev'ry Charm revolv'd within his Mind:
　　　　Her tender Age, her Form divinely Fair,
　　　　Her easie Motion, her attractive Air,
　　　　Her sweet Behaviour, her enchanting Face,
　　　　Her moving Softness, and majestick Grace.

250   　Much in his Prudence did our Knight rejoice,
　　　　And thought no Mortal cou'd dispute this Choice:
　　　　Once more in haste he summon'd ev'ry Friend,
　　　　And told them all, their Pains were at an End.
　　　　Heav'n, that (said he) inspir'd me first to wed,

---

241. **yet:** *1717–51:* that
251. **this:** *1741–51:* his

236–41. Chaucer 1589–93.
238. Nicest: most exactingly particular, most fastidious; cf. 81, 152.
239. aspers'd: maligned.
　　Fame: reputation (in sexual sense; 'bad name' in Chaucer, 1593, fol. 29ʳ); cf. 593; 'To a Young Lady, with the Works of Voiture, 35–6'; 'On Silence', 27; etc.
240. Sense: here probably 'good sense', as in 4.
244. Love is blind also in Chaucer (1598).
245–9. Pope's January concentrates on visual appearance; in Chaucer (1603–4, fol. 29ʳ) January finds that as well as sexual attractiveness she is also (perhaps ironically, as it turns out) endowed with 'wise gouernance', 'gentilnesse' and 'sadnesse' [seriousness].

245. *TE* notes that in Chaucer (1599, fol. 29ʳ) January is performing this mental review 'whan that he was in his bedd ibrought'.
246–9. Replacing Chaucer's set of virtues, 1601–4. *TE* detects the influence of 'Delia. A Pastoral Eclogue . . . ', e.g. 43–6, *Poetical Miscellanies: The Fifth Part* (1704), p. 612, by Pope's friend and adviser William Walsh: 'What Lover in his Mistress hopes to find | A Form so lovely, with so bright a Mind? | *Doris* may boast a Face divinely Fair, | But wants thy Shape, thy Motions, and thy Air.'
250–7. Chaucer 1605–22.
250–1. Chaucer's January decides in addition that the 'wit' [intelligence] of all his friends is 'so bad' that nobody could oppose the choice (1608–9, fol. 29ʳ).

255   Provides a Consort worthy of my Bed;
         Let none oppose th' Election, since on this
         Depends my Quiet, and my future Bliss.

         A Dame there is, the Darling of my Eyes,
         Young, beauteous, artless, innocent and wise;
260   Chaste tho' not rich; and tho' not nobly born,
         Of honest Parents, and may serve my Turn.
         Her will I wed, if gracious Heav'n so please;
         To pass my Age in Sanctity and Ease:
         And thank the Pow'rs, I may possess alone
265   The lovely Prize, and share my Bliss with none!
         If you, my Friends, this Virgin can procure,
         My Joys are full, my Happiness is sure.

         One only Doubt remains; Full oft I've heard
         By Casuists grave, and deep Divines averr'd;
270   That 'tis too much for Human Race to know
         The Bliss of Heav'n above, and Earth below.
         Now shou'd the Nuptial Pleasures prove so great,
         To match the Blessings of the future State,
         Those endless Joys were ill exchang'd for these;

---

256. Election: choice, decision.
258-67. Chaucer 1623-33.
258. Dame: cf. 110; a term 'still used in poetry for women of rank' (*SJ*); 'Rape of the Locke', I.19.
　　my Eyes: cf. Commentary to 91.
261. honest Parents: in Chaucer (1625, fol. 29ʳ) May's family is 'of small degre', i.e. of low rank.
　　serve my Turn: satisfy my needs. Not in Chaucer. Warton comments: 'one of Dryden's familiar colloquial terms, happily used'. *TE* compares Dryden, 'The Wife of Bath her Tale', 320, *Fables*, p. 491: 'And nothing but the Man would serve her turn' (where the crone holds the knight against his will to the marriage debt) and Spenser, *Faerie Queene*, I.vi.22, where a 'forlorne mayd' who 'did with loues longing burne' seeks her lover 'to serue her turn'. Pope used a similar phrase in similar circumstances in 'The Wife of Bath Her Prologue', 28-9 and 295; cf. Henry Higden, *A Modern Essay on the Tenth Satyr of Juvenal* (1687), p. 55: 'Marriage can only serve her turn'.
264-5. possess . . . Prize: recalled by Pope in *Rape of the Lock*, II.44.
268-75. Chaucer, 1634-54, very much condensed; Chaucer's January extends his theological doubts much further.
269. Casuists: writers on cases of law or conscience, normally from a religious perspective; cf. 'Rape of the Locke', II.167.
　　deep Divines: wise theologians. Both types of thinker are recalled with irony in Pope's *Epistle to Bathurst*, 2, 204. Neither type of scholar is mentioned in Chaucer; January has merely 'heard' these objections (1637, fol. 29ʳ). In his letter to Cromwell, 27 April 1708 (*Corr.*, I.48), Pope mocks 'deep Divines, profound Casuists, grave Philosophers' and their interminable writings.

275 Then clear this Doubt, and set my Mind at ease.

This *Justin* heard, nor cou'd his Spleen controul,
Touch'd to the Quick, and tickl'd at the Soul.
Sir Knight, he cry'd, if this be all you dread,
Heav'n put it past your Doubt whene'er you wed,
280 And to my fervent Pray'rs so far consent,
That e'er the Rites are o'er, you may repent!
Good Heav'n no doubt the nuptial State approves,
Since it chastises still what best it loves.
Then be not, Sir, abandon'd to Despair;
285 Seek, and perhaps you'll find, among the Fair,
One, that may do your Business to a Hair;
Not ev'n in Wish, your Happiness delay,
But prove the Scourge to lash you on your Way:
Then to the Skies your mounting Soul shall go,
290 Swift as an Arrow soaring from the Bow!
Provided still, you moderate your Joy,
Nor in your Pleasures all your Might imploy,
Let Reason's Rule your strong Desires abate,
Nor please too lavishly your gentle Mate.
295 Old Wives there are, of Judgment most acute,
Who solve these Questions beyond all Dispute;

276-98. Chaucer 1655-88.

276. Spleen: here, 'anger; spite; ill humour' (*SJ*). For a short contemporary essay on the spleen, characterised as 'a nice and exceptious Temper', see Jeremy Collier, *Miscellanies upon Moral Subjects* (1695), pp. 34-40, and for its use in poetry of the time see Griffin (1990). Pope would explore the female version of spleen (hysteria) in Canto IV of *The Rape of the Lock*.

277. tickl'd: irritated. Chaucer's Justinus (1655-6, fol. 29ʳ) 'hated' January's 'folie' but answered 'in his iaperye' [buffoonery].

282-6. Pope's addition.

283. Cf. Dryden, 'Prologue' to Dryden and Lee, *The Duke of Guise*, 26 (1683), A3ᵛ: 'To show you love Him much, chastise Him more'.

286. do your Business: euphemism, like 'serve my Turn' at 261.

  to a Hair: precisely, with complete exactness; Aden (1978: 65) sees this as a bawdy pun, in the spirit of 'The Rape of the Locke', II.19-20.

288-9. Chaucer, 1671-2 (fol. 29ʳ): 'She may by Goddes meane & Goddes whip | Than shall your soule up to heauen skip'. Pope recalled his phrasing at *Odyssey*, XVIII.388: 'The scourge, the scourge shall lash thee into sense'.

291. still: however.

293. Cf. Dryden, 'The Wife of Bath her Tale', 363, *Fables*, p. 492: 'If not your Wife, let Reasons Rule persuade' (the crone to the knight).

295. Old Wives: Chaucer (1685-7) makes explicit reference here to the Wife of Bath's comments on marriage; her 'Prologue' and 'Tale' are placed before 'The Merchant's Tale' in modern editions, but Pope would have found them immediately after it in Speght, and it is sometimes thought that the Merchant's Tale was originally designed to be told by the Wife.

296. solve: resolve.

Consult with those, and be of better Chear;
Marry, do Penance, and dismiss your Fear.

So said they rose, nor more the Work delay'd;
300   The Match was offer'd, the Proposals made:
The Parents, you may think, wou'd soon comply;
The Old have Int'rest ever in their Eye:
Nor was it hard to move the Lady's Mind;
When Fortune favours still the Fair are kind.

305   I pass each previous Settlement and Deed,
Too long for me to write, or you to read;
Nor will with quaint Impertinence display
The Pomp, the Pageantry, the proud Array.
The Time approach'd, to Church the Parties went,
310   At once with carnal and devout Intent:
Forth came the Priest, and bade th' obedient Wife

---

298. Pope's addition, based on Chaucer's 1665-7.

299-304. Corresponding to Chaucer 1689-95, fol. 29^r, but largely invented; in Chaucer the marriage is more intricately agreed 'by wise and slie treate' [bargaining], apparently by the joint management of Justinus and Placebo. There is nothing specific about the views of May's family in Chaucer.

302. For Pope's citation of this line in his letter to Walsh, 22 October 1706 (*Corr.*, I.24), see Headnote.

304. Fortune: connected with 'Int'rest' (302) or financial advantage, beneath the conspicuous sense of Fortune as a supernatural force.

   still: always.

   kind: willing, favourably disposed (often with a sexual sense in women, as in 502); cf. 'Autumn', 52. These elements are not in 'The Merchant's Tale' at this point, but Pope may recall Chaucer's 'The Knight's Tale', 2682, where it is said that in general women 'folowen all the fauour of fortune'.

305-14. Chaucer 1696-708.

305. pass: omit; cf. note to 308.

306. Pope's addition, condensed from Chaucer 1696-7.

307. quaint Impertinence: probably recalling Garth, *The Dispensary*, V, sixth edition (1706), p. 82: 'Whilst one *Assassin* his learn'd Collegue tires | With quaint Impertinence...'. Pope's 'quaint' is 'minutely, superfluously exact' (*SJ*), though in the 'Merchant's Tale' Chaucer uses it to mean 'deceitful' ('poison queint', 2061, fol. 31^r); elsewhere in Chaucer it occurs often as a noun with an obscene pun. Cf. 'The Wife of Bath Her Prologue', 259, in reference to female appetite, and otherwise only in *The Dunciad*, IV.52, attached to the 'Harlot form' of Opera.

   Impertinence: 'troublesomeness; intrusion' (*SJ*).

308. TE compares Dryden, 'Palamon and Arcite', I.14, *Fables*, p. 2: 'I pass their warlike Pomp, their proud Array'. Dryden uses the phrase at least three further times in that book, and cf. Milton, *Samson Agonistes*, 345 (1671), p. 27: 'Armies rank't in proud array'.

   proud: 'grand; lofty; splendid; magnificent' (*SJ*). Pope recalls the phrase thus in his translation of Homer, *Odyssey*, XXIII.131, 140.

310. In Chaucer they go to church simply 'to receiue the holy Sacrament' (1701-2, fol. 29^v).

Like *Sarah* and *Rebecca* lead her Life:
Then pray'd the Pow'rs the fruitful Bed to bless,
And made all sure enough with Holiness.

315   And now the Palace Gates are open'd wide, ⎫
    The Guests appear in Order, Side by Side,   ⎬
    And, plac'd in State, the Bridegroom and the Bride. ⎭
    Expensive Dainties load the plenteous Boards,
    The best Luxurious *Italy* affords:
320   The breathing Flute's soft Notes are heard around,
    And the shrill Trumpets mix their Silver Sound;
    The vaulted Roofs with ecchoing Musick ring,
    These touch the vocal Stops, and those the trembling String.
    Not thus *Amphion* tun'd the warbling Lyre,

---

312. **and:** *1717–51:* or
318–19. *1717–51:* omitted

---

312. **Sarah ... Rebecca:** Chaucer 1704. Sarah was the wife of Abraham and Rebecca of Isaac: Genesis 17–27 and, for Sarah as a model of spousal rectitude, 1 Peter 3:6. For Rebecca see also above, 69–79.

315–27. Chaucer, 1709–21.

315. **Palace:** Chaucer also locates the feast in a 'paleies' (1712, fol. 29ᵛ).

318. **Expensive Dainties:** Chaucer (1714, fol. 29ᵛ) has 'The moste deintes of all Itaile'.

    Boards: tables or side-boards.

320–3. Chaucer (1715–19, fol. 29ᵛ) has less exactly identified 'instruments' and 'minstralcie'.

321. **Silver Sound:** normally in poetry 'soft of voice' (*SJ*), here echoing Dryden's 'Palamon and Arcite', III.85, *Fables*, p. 52 (describing the voice of Emetrius, military companion of Arcite): 'Loud as a Trumpet, with a Silver Sound', i.e. deriving a metallic quality from the instrument that makes the noise; cf. however *Rape of the Lock*, I.18: 'The press'd Watch return'd a silver Sound'. In Dryden's 'The Cock and the Fox', 619, the fox flatters Chanticleer by using the phrase to describe his singing; in *Iliad*, I.775 and XVIII.574, Pope associates 'silver Sound' with music.

322. **vaulted Roofs:** a phrase used several times in similar context by Dryden, e.g. *Alexander's Feast*, 36 (1697) and 'Cymon and Iphigenia', 580, *Fables*, p. 562: 'Sweet Voices mix'd with instrumental Sounds | Ascend the vaulted Roof, the vaulted Roof rebounds'. Recalled by Pope in *Rape of the Lock*, V.104 and in *Odyssey* XX.222.

323. **vocal Stops:** the fingerholes of woodwind instruments such as flutes.

    trembling String: of a harp or lyre, as in 'Sapho to Phaon', 235. The line is an Alexandrine; cf. 808, and *Essay on Criticism*, 359.

324. **Amphion:** so in Chaucer, 1716, though Pope omits Chaucer's other mythical musician, Orpheus, at this point. Amphion was king of Thebes and supposedly built the city by charming the stones together with his lyre, an event to which Pope refers in *The Temple of Fame*, 85–6, and 'The First Book of Statius his Thebais', 11–12; cf. also *Ode for Musick*, 35^6 variant.

    warbling: cf. 'Spring', 26; *Ode for Musick*, 6, and 466 below. A 'warbling Lute' is associated with amorous pursuits in a verison of Gallus, *Elegia*, I, *Poetical Miscellanies: The Sixth Part*, p. 368.

325   Nor *Joab* the sounding Clarion cou'd inspire,
             Nor fierce *Theodamas*, whose sprightly Strain
             Cou'd swell the Soul to Rage, and fire the Martial Train.

             Bacchus himself, the Nuptial Feast to grace,
             (So Poets sing) was present on the Place;
330   And lovely *Venus*, Goddess of Delight,
             Shook high her flaming Torch, in open Sight,
             And danc'd around, and smil'd on ev'ry Knight:
             Pleas'd her best Servant wou'd his Courage try,
             No less in Wedlock than in Liberty.
335   Full many an Age old *Hymen* had not spy'd
             So kind a Bridegroom, or so bright a Bride.
             Ye Bards! renown'd among the tuneful Throng
             For gentle Lays, and joyous Nuptial Song;
             Think not your softest Numbers can display

---

325. Joab: Chaucer, 1719; one of David's military commanders, associated with the martial trumpet or 'sounding Clarion' or trumpet (2 Samuel, 2:28, 18:16, 20:22).

  Clarion: 'a trumpet; a wind instrument of war' (*SJ*); used of the trumpet of good and bad fame, in Pope's *Temple of Fame*, 327 and 402.

  inspire: blow into, as in 'Spring', 11, and *Ode for Musick*, 325.

326. Theodamas: Chaucer, 1720–1; mentioned in Statius, *Thebais*, VIII.275–347 and X.160–553, as an augur whose prayers for the besieging Argive army were succeeded by trumpet calls, rather than as himself a trumpeter.

327. Another Alexandrine; cf. 323. *TE* compares Dryden, *Alexander's Feast*, 160 (1697), p. 7, also an Alexandrine (within an irregular stanza), where the flute and lyre music of Timotheus 'Cou'd swell the Soul to rage, or kindle soft Desire'.

328–42. Chaucer 1722–41.

328–9. Bacchus: Greek god of wine, which in Chaucer's account (1722) he 'skinketh [pours] all about'.

330. Venus: previously invoked at 5. *TE* compares Dryden, 'The Cock and the Fox', 687, *Fables*, p. 249: 'Ah blissful *Venus*, Goddess of Delight'.

333. Courage: cf. 13, 170, but here clearly a form of sexual strength; Chaucer, 1725.

335. Hymen: god of marriage. Also in Chaucer, 1730–1, fol. 29^v, where however the 'God of wedding' sees only the joy of the 'wedded man'.

337–42. Chaucer, 1732–41, fol. 29^v, instructs one poet only, 'Marcian', to 'Hold thou thy peace' on grounds of incapacity to describe the wedding. Pope omits Chaucer's description of Martianus Capella's fifth-century Latin allegorical poem *De Nuptiis Philologiae et Mercurii* (On the Marriage of Philology and Mercury).

338. Lays: songs.

  Nuptial Song: hymn celebrating marriage, or 'epithalamium', of which Pope would have known several notable examples e.g. Spenser, *Epithalamion* (1595). Cf. also Ephelia's 'A Nuptial Song', *Female Poems on Several Occasions* (1682), p. 112, and Dryden, 'The Wife of Bath her Tale', 339, where the narrator omits the 'Nuptial Song' of the apparently embarrassing wedding of knight and crone.

339. softest Numbers: gentlest verses (cf. *Essay on Criticism*, 340), inappropriate to the sexual fervour implied by 341–2.

340   The matchless Glories of this blissful Day;
The Joys are such, as far transcend your Rage,
When tender Youth has wedded stooping Age.

        The beauteous Dame sate smiling at the Board,
And darted am'rous Glances at her Lord;
345   Not *Hester*'s self, whose Charms the *Hebrews* sing,
E're look'd so lovely on her *Persian* King:
Bright as the rising Sun, in Summer's Day,
And fresh and blooming as the Month of *May*!
The joyful Knight survey'd her by his Side,
350   Nor envy'd *Paris* with the *Spartan* Bride:
Still as his Mind revolv'd with vast Delight
Th' entrancing Raptures of th' approaching Night;
Restless he sate, invoking ev'ry Pow'r
To speed his Bliss, and haste the happy Hour.
355   Mean time the vig'rous Dancers beat the Ground,

341–2. Morsberger (1993: 12) glosses: 'though on one level [Pope] refers to the "poetic fire" or "rage to write," on another level rage over the marriage of youth and age can be taken literally'.

342. stooping Age: the phrasing of the line is very close to Chaucer's 1738 (fol. 29ᵛ): 'Whan tender youth hath wedded stouping age', but Pope uses it as a closing line for the paragraph, whereas Chaucer uses it to introduce an interjection from the Merchant (1739–41) challenging the audience to dispute the accuracy of his description by trying such a marriage themselves. Pope recalled the phrase in *Iliad*, XX.472 ('*Priam*'s stooping age').

343–58. Chaucer 1742–71 (with many omissions).

344. darted am'rous Glances: conventional behaviour; cf. e.g. Thomas Carew, 'Song. Conquest by Flight', 10, *Poems* (1640), p. 23: 'Young men fly, when beautie darts | Amorous glances at your hearts'.

345. Hester: Chaucer, 1744–5; see above, 75–6.

348. Cf. Sarah Fyge Egerton, 'To Philaster', 9, *Poems on Several Occasions* (1703), p. 34: 'As fresh and blooming as the new-born day'.

349–50. The scene in Dryden, *Alexander's Feast*, 9–10 (1697) p. 1, perhaps supplies Pope's rhyme here: 'The Lovely *Thais* by his side, | Sate like a blooming *Eastern* Bride'.

350. Spartan Bride: Helen, abducted by the Trojan prince Paris, precipitating the Trojan war; Pope recalled the phrase 'Spartan Bride' for Helen in his translation of Homer, *Iliad*, VII.429. At this point Pope omits Chaucer 1755–61, in which January worries that his sexual fervour ('All my corage, it is so sharpe and kene') will prove too much for May, a worry the narrative does not bear out.

351. revolv'd: considered, turned over.

353–4. TE compares Dryden's 'The Fable of Iphis and Ianthe', 151–2, *Examen Poeticum*, p. 79: 'Invoking *Hymen*'s Name and *Juno*'s Pow'r, | To speed the work, and haste the happy hour'.

355. Dancers beat the Ground: In Chaucer, 'men dauncen' (1768, fol. 29ᵛ). TE cites Milton, 'A Mask', 143, *Poems* (1645), p. 81: 'Com, knit hands, and beat the ground'; but it is a common, classically-derived image.

And Songs were sung, and Healths went nimbly round;
With od'rous Spices they perfum'd the Place,
And Mirth and Pleasure shone in ev'ry Face.

Damian alone, of all the Menial Train,
360 Sad in the midst of Triumphs, sigh'd for Pain;
Damian alone, the Knight's obsequious Squire,
Consum'd at Heart, and fed a secret Fire.
His lovely Mistress all his Soul possest,
He look'd, he languish'd, and cou'd find no Rest:
365 His Task perform'd, he sadly went his Way,
Fell on his Bed, and loath'd the Light of Day.
There let him lye, 'till the relenting Dame
Weep in her turn, and waste in equal Flame.

The weary Sun, as Learned Poets write,
370 Forsook th' *Horizon,* and roll'd down the Light;
While glitt'ring Stars his absent Beams supply,
And Night's dark Mantle overspread the Sky.

---

356. **Healths went nimbly:** *1717–51:* flowing bowls went
364. **find:** *1717–51:* take
367. **the:** *1736–51:* his

---

356. ***Healths:*** toasts wishing good health; Pope's revision is a clarification. Cf. Tate, *Syphilis* (1686), p. 66: 'Bowls of sparkling wine go nimbly round'; and Robert Gould, 'The Twelfth of June', *Works* (1709), II.402: 'And the great *Health* goes nimbly round' (published 17 March 1709; *Daily Courant*).
359–68. Chaucer 1772–82.
361. ***obsequious:*** 'obedient; compliant' (*SJ*), not apparently having at this date the *OED* sense of 'unduly or servilely compliant' (2a). In Chaucer, the 'squier' merely 'carfe before the knight many a daie' (1773, fol. 29ᵛ). Cf. 609.
362. TE cites Dryden, 'The First Book of Ovid's Metamorphoses', 668–9, *Examen Poeticum,* p. 43: 'So burns the God, consuming in desire, | And feeding in his Breast a fruitless Fire'; cf. also Dryden's version of *Aeneid,* IV.4, *Works of Virgil* (1697), p. 296:

'and fann the secret Fire'; but these are divine or heroic instances.
367–8. Pope condenses much of Chaucer's description of Damian's amorous response to the sight of May (1774–9). Pope also omits Chaucer 1783–94, in which the Merchant exclaims about the perils of hidden desire and warns of Damian's cuckolding of his master.
369–74. Chaucer 1795–1804.
369. **as Learned Poets write:** Pope's addition (cf. 1); perhaps a slightly ironic gesture towards Chaucer's more astronomical description of the setting sun (1795–9). Chaucer had written a treatise on the astrolabe, which was in the Speght edition; for Pope's interest in astronomy see *Windsor-Forest,* 243n.
370. **roll'd down:** epic phrasing: cf. Dryden, *Aeneid,* II.330, *Works of Virgil* (1697), p. 244: 'Mean time the rapid Heav'ns rowl'd down the Light'.

Then rose the Guests; and as the time requir'd,
Each paid his Thanks, and decently retir'd.

375   The Foe once gone, our Knight wou'd strait undress,
So keen he was, and eager to possess:
But first thought fit th' Assistance to receive,
Which grave Physicians scruple not to give;
Satyrion near, with hot *Eringo's* stood,
380   *Cantharides*, to fire the boiling Blood,
Whose Use old Bards describe in luscious Rhymes,
And Criticks learn'd explain to Modern Times.

---

375. **wou'd strait:** *1717–51:* prepar'd t'
380. **boiling:** *1717–51:* lazy

---

374. **decently:** in the manner required by decorum. Chaucer's January (1815, fol. 30ʳ) requests that the house be emptied in 'curteis wise'.

375–82. Chaucer 1805–12.

375. **The Foe once gone:** everyone else having left. TE finds the exact phrase and a 'similar' context in Dryden, 'Sigismonda and Guiscardo', 173. In Dryden's version of Boccaccio's tale, the context is of love between a squire and the daughter of his master; the 'Foe' is the priest, called in to conduct the marriage ceremony with unseemly haste. The tale ends in the death of both lovers.

376. **eager to possess:** not in Chaucer; cf. 264 and 497.

377–82. Chaucer's January (1807–12, fol. 30ʳ) drinks 'Ipocras, clareie, and vernage | Of spices hote, to encrease his corage', a recipe of cordials and wines explicitly based on the writings of a 'cursed monke, dan Constantine' (Constantinus Africanus, 1015–87), in *De Coitu* ('Of sexual intercourse').

378. **grave Physicians:** cf. Garth, *The Dispensary*, V, sixth edition (1706), p. 82: 'the solemn State | Of grave *Physicians*'.

379–80. **Satyrion ... Eringo's ... Cantharides:** aphrodisiacs. *Satyrion* is a type of orchid, thought in ancient medicine to act as a male aphrodisiac; *Eringo* is the root of the sea holly (*Eryingium maritimum*); and *Cantharides* is a genus of beetle-type insects commonly known as Spanish Fly. Their properties were widely mentioned in drama: e.g. satyrion is in Thomas Otway, *The Souldier's Fortune*, V.ii (1681), p. 67; cantharides in Beaumont and Fletcher's *Phylaster*, IV.i (1620), p. 41; Fletcher, *The Elder Brother* IV.iv (1637), sig. H2ʳ, has eringoes and cantharides as a recipe for priapism; eringoes are also mentioned in Shakespeare, *Merry Wives of Windsor*, V.v.20. See also John Greenfield, *A Treatise of the Safe, Internal Use of Cantharides in the Practice of Physick* (1706). Pope acknowledges a receipt of 'Oysters and Eringo-roots' as a possible 'provocative' in a letter to John Morley, 13 December 1722 (*Corr.*, II.148).

380. **boiling:** proleptic adjective, i.e. the blood will 'boil' as an effect of the fiery drug. Pope took out the syntactic oddity in revisions from *1717* onwards.

381–2. Pope's addition.

381. **luscious Rhymes:** erotic verse.

382. **Criticks learn'd:** TE suggests that Pope was thinking of Ovid's *Ars Amandi*, published in a scholarly edition in Paris in 1660; some of the notes to this were added to a translation of *Ovid's Art of Love. In three books* published by Tonson in 1709,

> By this the Sheets were spread, the Bride undrest,
> The Room was sprinkl'd, and the Bed was blest.
385 What next ensu'd beseems not me to say;
> 'Tis sung, he labour'd 'till the dawning Day,
> Then briskly sprung from Bed, with Heart so light,
> As all were nothing he had done by Night;
> And supt his Cordial as he sate upright:
390 He kiss'd his balmy Spouse, with wanton Play,
> And feebly sung a lusty Roundelay:

---

389. **supt**: *1717:* supp'd; *1736–51:* sipp'd

---

which identified the 'several eminent hands' or translators as Pope's friend Congreve, Dryden, Tate, Charles Hopkins and others. What are thought to be Pope's marginalia, reproduced in the *European Magazine* (October 1787, 261), and described again by Mack (1982: 433–4), suggest close critical attention to the work, but there would have to have been pre-publication access to it for any influence to operate (*Poetical Miscellanies* was published 2 May 1709, the Ovid not until July: *London Gazette* 16 July, *Daily Courant* 22 July). Book II.459–74 of this translation inveighs against aphrodisiacs, among them '*Eringo's* hot salacious root'; the notes (pp. 167–8) discuss a version of satyrion.

At this point Pope omits Chaucer 1813–17, an aspect already covered in Pope's 373–4.

383–93. Chaucer 1818–65, very much condensed.

383. By this: by this time. In Chaucer, the 'bride was brought to bed as still as ston' (1818, fol. 30ʳ).

384. sprinkl'd: probably with holy water. The detail is not in Chaucer, though the bed is 'with the priest iblessed' (1819).

385. *TE* compares Dryden, 'Sigismonda and Guiscardo', 170, *Fables*, p. 129: 'What Thoughts he had, beseems not me to say'; in Dryden's version of Boccaccio's tale, this line pertains to the priest, hastily marrying the lovers; the 'thoughts' are impure ones. Pope omits here 1821–41, in which Chaucer's January explains to May his plans for the night of consummation and the legal and moral situation of their sex life; he also omits Chaucer's comic detail of January's prickly beard against May's soft face.

386. labour'd: 'laboureth' in Chaucer (1842, fol. 30ʳ). Cf. 'Work', 475. Pope was fond of this type of joke: cf. his *Roman Catholick Version of the First Psalm* (1716), 5–8: 'To Please her shall her Husband strive | With all his Main and Might, | And in her Love shall Exercise | Himself both Day and Night'. Cf. the euphemism 'toyling and moyling' for sexual activity in Wycherley, *The Country-Wife*, IV.i (1675), p. 70.

387. briskly: Chaucer's 'He was all coltish, and full of ragerie, | And full of gergon [jargon] as is flecked Pie [magpie]' (1847–8, fol. 30ʳ).

388. Pope's addition.

389. Cordial: 'a medicine that increases the force of the heart, or quickens the circulation' (*SJ*). Chaucer's January (1843, fol. 30ʳ) imbibes a 'soppe of fine clarre' (bread soaked in wine), a less obviously medicinal restorative.

390. balmy: scented, fragrant; not in Chaucer.

391. feebly: in Chaucer (1845, fol. 30ʳ), he sings 'full loud and clere', but this is modified quickly (1850): 'While that he sang, so chaunteth he & craketh' [croaks].

Then on the Couch his weary Limbs he cast;
For ev'ry Labour must have Rest at last.

But anxious Cares the pensive Squire opprest,
395 Sleep fled his Eyes, and Peace forsook his Breast;
The raging Flames that in his Bosome dwell,
He wanted Art to hide, and Means to tell.
Yet hoping Time th' Occasion might betray,
Compos'd a Sonnet to the lovely *May*;
400 Which writ and folded, with the nicest Art,
He wrapt in Silk, and laid upon his Heart.

When now the fourth revolving Day was run,
('Twas *June*, and *Cancer* had receiv'd the Sun)
Forth from her Chamber came the beauteous Bride,

---

lusty Roundelay: bawdy song. Chaucer does not say what January sings. May's reaction is not recorded by Pope. Chaucer's Merchant claims not to know ('God wot what May thought in her hert', 1851, fol. 30ʳ) but goes on to assert 'She praiseth [valued] not his playing worth a Bene' (1854), to close a sharply-detailed description of January's aged appearance in his night-shirt from her point of view (1852-4).

393. Rest at last: Chaucer 1855. Chaucer's Merchant goes on to make it clear (1859-65) that rest at this point, for May also, is in accordance with God's natural ordinances.

394-401. Chaucer 1875-84. Pope has omitted Chaucer 1866-1874, in which the Merchant addresses Damian with a vivid warning not to risk speaking to May.

394. anxious Cares: a poetic commonplace, recalled by Pope in 'Rape of the Locke', II.1, also alluding to Dryden, *Aeneid*, IV.1, *Works of Virgil* (1697), p. 296: 'But anxious Cares already seiz'd the Queen'.

pensive: 'sorrowfully thoughtful; ... mournfully serious; melancholy' (*SJ*). See Mason (1972: 51) for discussion of the particular strength of the word in Pope's translations of Homer, where it occurs frequently; and cf. 'The Rape of the Locke', II.1, and 'The Arrival of Ulysses in Ithaca', 68.

397. wanted: lacked. The line, with 398, is Pope's addition.

398. betray: reveal, discover.

399. Sonnet: a little song or 'small poem' (*SJ*), rather than necessarily the 14-line form normally understood by the term. Cf. *Essay on Criticism*, 420. Chaucer, 1881, fol. 30ʳ, has 'a complaint or a lay'.

400. nicest Art: most careful skill.

401. In Chaucer, 1884, Damian puts the poem in a silk purse hanging from his shirt.

402-19. Chaucer 1885-940, with many omissions.

402. fourth revolving Day: Chaucer had already indicated, 1860-1 that May would follow the custom of brides to stay in the bedchamber until the fourth day after marriage; it is emphasised again at 1885-92, with a certain apparent impatience at the convention.

403. For the phrasing, TE compares Dryden, 'Palamon and Arcite', II.10, *Fables*, p. 26: '*May* within the *Twins* receiv'd the Sun'. Pope calculates the month as June on the basis of astronomical details in Chaucer (1885-7) in which the moon was in Taurus on the day of the marriage but has passed to Cancer by the time May emerges from retreat. Cf. the use of astronomy in *Pastorals*, e.g. 'Spring', 102.

405   The good old Knight mov'd slowly by her Side.
      High Mass was sung; they feasted in the Hall;
      The Servants round stood ready at their Call.
      The Squire alone was absent from the Board,
      And much his Sickness griev'd his worthy Lord,
410   Who pray'd his Spouse, attended by her Train,
      To visit *Damian*, and divert his Pain.
      Th' obliging Dames obey'd with one Consent;
      They left the Hall, and to his Lodging went;
      The Female Tribe surround him as he lay,
415   And close beside him sate the gentle *May*:
      Where, as she try'd his Pulse, he softly drew
      A speaking Sigh, and cast a mournful View;
      Then gave his Bill, and brib'd the Pow'rs Divine
      With secret Vows, to favour his Design.

---

417. **speaking:** *1736–51:* heaving

---

405. TE compares Dryden, 'Wife of Bath her Tale', 346, *Fables*, p. 492: 'The good old Wife lay smiling by his Side', there a grotesque parody of marital union. Pope's 'slowly' is not in Chaucer; he and May are both 'As fresh as is the bright Somers day' (1896, fol. 30ʳ).

406. High Mass: Chaucer 1894. This appears to be Pope's only mention in poetry of the main event of Roman Catholic worship, apart from the ironic instance in *The Fourth Satire of Dr. John Donne*, 15–16.

408–11. Chaucer (1897–931) gives a much longer account of January's concern for his (as he thinks) discreet, thrifty and able servant, with open condemnation from the Merchant as narrator.

410–11. In Chaucer (1925–6, fol. 30ᵛ) January instructs May to say that he will visit Damian himself after resting, meanwhile sending May with her 'women all' (1921), i.e. Pope's 'Train' and 'Female Tribe' (414).

416. try'd his Pulse: Chaucer's May merely comforts Damian 'as goodly as she may' (1935, fol. 30ᵛ).

417. speaking: meaningful. Chaucer's Damian 'sighed wonders depe and sore' (1940, fol. 30ᵛ).

418. Bill: billet, short letter ('written paper of any kind'; *SJ*). Chaucer (1937, fol. 30ᵛ) uses the same word, indicating that this is not the sonnet of Pope's 399 but a note in which 'he had written all his will' (1938).

418–19. brib'd the Pow'rs Divine: In Chaucer (1941–3) Damian pleads in a whisper to May not to give him away. For the mock-heroic appeal to divine assistance cf. the travesty-sacrifice in 'Rape of the Locke', I.51–64. After 419 Pope omits Chaucer 1941–54, which shows the whispered words of Damian to May and her return to January, who kisses her but falls asleep; she reads Damian's letter before tearing it to bits and disposing of it in the privy.

420   Who studies now but discontented *May*?
       On her soft Couch uneasily she lay:
       The lumpish Husband snor'd away the Night,
       'Till Coughs awak'd him near the Morning Light.
       What then he did, I not presume to tell,
425   Nor if she thought her self in Heav'n or Hell.
       Honest and dull, in Nuptial Bed they lay,
       'Till the Bell toll'd, and All arose to Pray.

       Were it by forceful Destiny decreed,
       Or did from Chance, or Nature's Pow'r proceed,
430   Or that some Star, with Aspect kind to Love,
       Shed its selectest Influence from above;
       Whatever was the Cause, the tender Dame
       Felt the first Motions of an infant Flame;
       She took th' Impressions of the Love-sick Squire,
435   And wasted in the soft, infectious Fire.

---

424. **I:** *1736–51:* I'll
434. **She took:** *1717–51:* Receiv'd

420-7. Chaucer 1955–66.

420. studies: thinks hard. *SJ* has (s.v. 'Study' as an intransitive verb) 'to think with very close attention; to muse'; *OED* 2d has 'to debate with oneself, deliberate, consider'. Chaucer, 1955, has 'Who studieth now but fair fresh May'.

422. lumpish Husband: not in Chaucer (1956). Pope may have recalled the image from a poem attribution to William Shippen, *Moderation Display'd* (1704), p. 13: 'Whilst her dull Husband, senseless of her Charms, | Lies lumpish in her soft encircling Arms'. The word 'lumpish' is used to described mankind in general in Dryden, 'The Cock and the Fox', 461.

423. The cough detail is in Chaucer (1957).

424-5. Similar to Chaucer's 'How that he wrought, I dare nat to you tell | Or wheder she thought it paradise or hell' (1962–3, fol. 30ᵛ), but the Merchant has implied that May has no choice in the matter (1958–61).

426. Honest: faithful. Pope's addition.

427. In Chaucer, 1966, the specific service is evensong; Pope's phrasing suppresses the idea that they have been in bed for much of the day.

428-35. Chaucer 1967–86, with many omissions.

428-9. *TE* compares Dryden, 'Palamon and Arcite', II.11, *Fables*, p. 26: 'Were it by Chance, or forceful Destiny' (referring to Palamon's escape from prison).

431. selectest Influence: a wry allusion to the passage in Milton, *Paradise Lost*, VIII.511–13 (1674), p. 208, in which Adam recalls the consummation of his relationship with Eve: 'all Heav'n, | And happie Constellations on that houre | Shed thir selectest influence'. Chaucer (1969–71, fol. 30ᵛ) has a 'constellacion, that in soch estate | The heuen stood, that tyme fortunate | (Was for to put a bill of Uenus werkes) . . . '.

434. Impressions: also Chaucer's word (1978, fol. 30ᵛ), though his phrase 'impression . . . Of pite [pity], on this sicke Damian' has a different sense from Pope's, which appears to mean here 'Image fixed in the mind' (*SJ*).

435. wasted: wasted away, became weak. The line is Pope's addition. At this point Pope omits Chaucer 1982–5, May's internal reasonings about her desire for Damian.

Ye Fair draw near, let *May*'s Example move
Your gentle Minds to pity those who love!
Had some fierce Tyrant in her stead been found,
The poor Adorer sure had hang'd or drown'd:
440   But she, your Sexes Mirrour, free from Pride,
Was much too meek to prove a Homicide.

    But to my Tale: Some Sages have defin'd
Pleasure the Sov'reign Bliss of Humankind:
Our Knight (who study'd much, we may suppose)
445   Deriv'd this high Philosophy from Those;
For, like a Prince, he bore the vast Expence
Of lavish Pomp, and proud Magnificence:
His House was stately, his Retinue gay,
Large was his Train, and gorgeous his Array.

---

436. 1751: no new paragraph
445. **this:** *1736–51:* his

436–41. Chaucer 1987–94; but Chaucer's Merchant advises his whole audience (not just maidens) to take note of this example of humane womanhood.

437. Equivalent to Chaucer, 1986, fol. 30ᵛ: 'Lo pite renneth sone in gentle hert'; an image found in many other places in Chaucer, though normally not with the sexual consequences of this tale, where it acts as an ironic gloss on May's self-persuasion. Pope quotes a version of the line, actually from Dryden's 'Palamon and Arcite', II.331–2, in his letter to Cromwell, 24 July 1711 (*Corr.*, I.130).

439. poor Adorer: an attitudinal cliché of romance, e.g. Congreve, *The Double Dealer*, IV.ii.18 (1694), p. 45.

440–1. The Pride/Homicide rhyme is Chaucer's (1993–4, fol. 30ᵛ). The idea fuses the courtly love convention that a woman can 'kill' a man by rejecting him (as in *The Rape of the Lock*) with the possibility that a servant making advances to his master's wife might actually be killed.

440. your Sexes Mirrour: a model of female conduct (ironically); not in Chaucer.

At this point Pope omits Chaucer 1995–2020, which shows May reading Damian's poem and responding with an explicit letter of sexual consent which she puts under his pillow, causing him to recover and present himself, elaborately groomed and complaisant, for normal duty.

442–57. Chaucer 2021–35.

442. Sages: 'clerkes' (scholars, or possibly clergy) in the equivalent line in Chaucer (2021, fol. 30ᵛ). The reference is to the Epicurean doctrine that pleasure is the measure of human happiness, but in its philosophical development by several 'sages', the doctrine was more concerned to overcome pain by equanimity of mind than to pursue sensual pleasures on the hedonistic model of January; Pope's 'high Philosophy' (445) is ironic.

447. proud Magnificence: cf. John Oldmixon, *Amores Britannici*, III.89 (1703), p. 64: '*Hampton*'s proud Magnificence'. Pope's details are more extravagant than Chaucer's, though his January's 'housing' and 'aray' is 'To his degre ... made as a kinges' (2026–7).

448. Retinue: company or followers; essentially the same as 'Train' (449). The metre suggests a stress on the middle syllable.

    gay: 'fine; showy' (*SJ*).

449. gorgeous: 'Fine; splendid; glittering in various colours; showy; magnificent' (*SJ*).

450 His spacious Garden, made to yield to none,
Was compass'd round with Walls of solid Stone;
Priapus cou'd not half describe the Grace
(Tho' God of Gardens) of this charming Place:
A Place to tire the rambling Wits of *France*
455 In long Descriptions, and exceed *Romance*;
Enough to shame the boldest Bard that sings
Of painted Meadows, and of purling Springs.

Full in the Center of this Spot of Ground,
A Crystal Fountain spread its Streams around,
460 Its fruitful Banks with verdant Lawrels crown'd:

---

456. **boldest:** *1717–51:* gentlest
458. **this Spot of:** *1717–51:* the flow'ry
460. **Its:** *1717–51:* The

450-1. Pope's version of the garden is made more pointedly fortified than Chaucer's more straightforward: 'He had a garden walled all with stone' (2029, fol. 31ʳ). Cf. the walled garden in 'Vertumnus and Pomona', 3-4 and 19, and 'The Gardens of Alcinous', 1-4.

452-3. **Priapus ... Gardens:** Priapus was the Greek god of gardens, but also of fertility; cf. 'Vertumnus and Pomona', 23. In Chaucer (2034-5) the reference to Priapus comes after the mention of romance (see next note).

454-5. Chaucer's reference (2032-3) is specifically to the early French poem the *Romaunt of the Rose*, which Pope is known to have read in Chaucer's version (see Headnote); Pope's phrasing here, however, suggests reference to the notoriously long seventeenth-century French romances which he mocked elsewhere; cf. Commentary to 'Rape of the Locke', I.54, and *The First Epistle of the Second Book of Horace, Imitated*, 146. Pope's notes to his translation of the *Iliad* make many references to the modern conventions of Romance. His letter to Cromwell of 11 July 1709 (*Corr.*, I.66-9), mocks his own narrative as having the 'Air of a Romance'; cf. also his letters to the Blount sisters, between 7 and 13 September 1714 and to Martha Blount, between 14 and 29 November 1716 (*Corr.*, I.252-3 and 375-6).

456. The substitution of 'gentlest' for 'boldest' in *1717* is probably intended to confirm the insipidity of Addison (see note to next line).

457. Pope uses 'purling' (to 'purl' is 'to flow with a gentle noise', *SJ*) in relation to rills and streams (though not springs) as an obviously ironic cliché in the *Essay on Man*, I.204; cf. also *Essay on Criticism*, 353-6. The 'boldest Bard' in Pope's sights here is, as suggested by *TE*, Addison, 'A Letter from Italy', 320-1, *Poetical Miscellanies: The Fifth Part* (1704), p. 12: 'My humble Verse demands a softer Theme, | A painted Meadow or a purling Stream'; Pope parodies these lines in the *Epistle to Arbuthnot*, 149-50.

458-66. Chaucer 2036-41.

459-60. Chaucer has a well rather than a fountain (2036-7), though Pope's further phrasing suggests a natural spring rather than an elaborate water feature.

459. **Crystal:** 'bright; clear; transparent' (*SJ*); a favourite early adjective of Pope's: cf. 'The Episode of Sarpedon', 326; 'Summer', 27; 'Winter', 21; *Essay on Criticism*, 355; *Windsor-Forest*, 374.

About this Spring (if ancient Fame say true)
The dapper Elves their Moonlight Sports pursue;
Their Pigmy King, and little Fairy Queen,
In circling Dances gambol'd on the Green,
465 While tuneful Sprights a merry Consort made,
And Airy Musick warbled thro' the Shade.

Hither the Noble Lord wou'd oft repair
(His Scene of Pleasure, and peculiar Care)
For this, he kept it lock'd, and always bore
470 The Silver Key that op'd the Garden Door.
To this sweet Place, in Summer's sultry Heat,

---

465. **Consort:** *1751:* concert
467. **Lord:** *1717–51:* knight
469. **kept it lock'd:** *1717–51:* held it dear
470. **op'd:** *1717–51:* lock'd

461–6. In an essay on pastoral in *The Guardian*, no. 30, 15 April 1713, Thomas Tickell praises these lines as an instance of native mythology: 'The Theology of the ancient Pastoral is so very pretty, that it were pity entirely to change it; but I think that part only is to be retained which is universally known, and the rest to be made up out of our own rustical Superstition of Hob-thrushes, Fairies, Goblins and Witches. The Fairies are capable of being made very entertaining Persons, as they are described by several of our Poets, and particularly by Mr. *Pope*'. This was, implicitly, an assault on Pope's normal classicising practice; for the debate see Headnote to *Pastorals*. In *The Spectator*, no. 419, 1 July 1712, Addison had more generally enthused about the 'Fairie way of Writing', developing a (misquoted) phrase of Dryden's from the 'Epistle Dedicatory' to *King Arthur: or, the British Worthy* (1691).

461. Fame: report.

462. dapper Elves: In Chaucer (2038–41) the supernatural figures are the more august Pluto and Proserpine, king and queen of the classical underworld, though they disport themselves in much the same way. Pope draws on the folklore elements used by Milton in 'A Mask', 117-19, *Poems*, p. 80: 'And on the Tawny Sands and Shelves, | Trip the pert Fairies and the dapper Elves; | By dimpled Brook, and Fountain brim . . .' *TE* cites also Dryden, 'The Wife of Bath her Tale', 3-4, *Fables*, p. 479: 'The King of Elfs and little Fairy Queen | Gamboll'd on Heaths, and danc'd on ev'ry Green'.

465. Sprights: spirits.

 Consort: musical group, normally associated in the seventeenth century with instruments such as viols; clarified in the late revision.

466. warbled: cf. 324.

467–76. Chaucer 2042-52. Warton (*Works of Pope*, II.130) especially commended this section: '[Pope] has no where copied the free and easy versification and the narrative style of Dryden's Fables so happily as in this pleasant tale'.

468. peculiar Care: cf. 52, and 'The First Book of Statius his Thebais', 406 and Commentary. Dryden uses the phrase in 'Baucis and Philemon', 198.

He us'd from Noise and Business to retreat;
And here in Dalliance spend the livelong Day,
Solus cum Sola, with his sprightly *May.*
475 For whate'er Work was undischarg'd a-bed,
In this fair Garden he perform'd and sped.

Thus many a Day, with Ease and Plenty blest,
Our gen'rous Knight his gentle Dame possest:
But ah! what Mortal lives of Bliss secure,
480 How short a Space our Worldly Joys endure?
O Fortune, fair, like all thy treach'rous Kind,
But faithless still, and wav'ring as the Wind!
O painted Monster form'd Mankind to cheat
With pleasing Poison, and with soft Deceit!

---

476. *1717–51:* The duteous knight in this fair garden sped.
477–78. *1717–51:* omitted

---

474. Solus cum Sola: 'he alone with her alone'. Not in Chaucer, who has 'no wight but they two' (2050, fol. 31ʳ). The phrase (from a proverbial joke about the expected behaviour of a man and woman alone together) is no doubt recalled from Dryden's 'The Cock and the Fox', 90, where it is the theme of the cock Chanticleer's amorous singing to and about Dame Partlet; see further Hammond and Hopkins (V.337). Pope uses it almost contemporaneously with the publication of the poem in a letter to Cromwell, 7 May 1709 (*Corr.,* I.57), to make insinuations about Cromwell's private walks 'with Sapho'.

475–6. Closely modelled, including the rhymes, on Chaucer 2051–2, though 'Work' is Pope's addition; cf. 386.

476. perform'd: Chaucer's word; perhaps dropped after 1709, along with 477–8, as slightly too obviously sexual.

sped: succeeded in, finished; also Chaucer's word (2052, fol. 31ʳ).

477–88. Chaucer 2053–72, greatly condensed.

477. Ease and Plenty: recalling Pomfret, *The Choice,* 155 (1700), p. 8: 'Thus I'd in Pleasure, Ease and Plenty live'.

478. Chaucer does not emphasise the sexual 'possession' of May in this way: 'Liued this January and this fresh May' (2054).

479–84. Pope uses some of Chaucer's images (2057–64) but Chaucer's main comparison, between Fortune and a deceiving but deadly Scorpion, is omitted. Pope's January has himself already contrasted the benefits of a constant wife (41, 51–3) with the mutable gifts of fortune, following Chaucer (1314). Pope's Justin is more sceptical about the chances of January's 'Fortune' being worth having (193), and cf. the narrator's intervention at 304. Pope would have known also Dryden's version of Horace, *Odes,* III.29, the ninth stanza of which meditates on the inconstancy of Fortune, characterised as a vacillating prostitute. The fickleness of Fortune is a major theme of Pope's more serious imitation of Chaucer, *The Temple of Fame* (1715): 296, 454, 518.

482. wav'ring... Wind: cf. 'The Wife of Bath Her Prologue', 398.

483. painted: disguised. Condensed from Chaucer, 2062–3, fol. 31ʳ: 'O monster, that so sodainly canst peint | Thy gifts, under the hew of stedfastnesse'.

485   This aged *January*, this worthy Knight,
        Amidst his Ease, Enjoyment and Delight,
        Struck blind by thee, resigns his Days to Grief,
        And calls on Death, the Wretches last Relief.

        The Rage of Jealousie then seiz'd his Mind,
490   For much he fear'd the Faith of Womankind.
        His Wife, not suffer'd from his Side to stray,
        Was Captive kept; he watch'd her Night and Day,
        Abridg'd her Pleasures, and confin'd her Sway.
        Full oft in Tears did hapless *May* complain,
495   And sigh'd for Woe, but sigh'd and wept in vain;
        She look'd on *Damian* with a Lover's Eye,
        For oh, 'twas fix'd, she must possess or die!
        Nor less Impatience vex'd her Am'rous Squire,
        Wild with Delay, and burning with Desire.
500   Watch'd as she was, yet cou'd not He refrain
        By secret Writing to disclose his Pain,

---

485. 1717–51: This rich, this am'rous, venerable knight,
486. **Enjoyment:** *1717–51:* his solace
495. **for Woe,:** *1717–51:* full oft';
500. **not He:** *1736–51:* he not

487–8. TE compares Dryden, 'Palamon and Arcite', I.416–17, *Fables*, p. 16: 'Nor Art, nor Natures Hand can ease my Grief, | Nothing but Death, the Wretches last Relief' (Arcite's words).

489–503. Chaucer 2073–106, greatly condensed. Chaucer's catalogue of January's fears and his surveillance methods is more extensive than Pope's.

489. TE compares Dryden, 'Palamon and Arcite', I.464, *Fables*, p. 18: 'The Rage of Jealousie then fir'd his Soul' (speaking of Palamon).

490. **Faith:** faithfulness, especially in a sexual sense. EC censures Pope for omitting 'one of the deeper and more solemn touches which [he] systematically rejected' at this point, i.e. January's eventual patient acceptance of his plight, 'after a moneth or tway' (Chaucer 2081–2, fol. 31ʳ).

493. **Abridg'd:** reduced, limited.
    Sway: power, control.

494–7. Cf. Chaucer 2092–6, in which May's emotional torment is given slightly more extended attention. The genuine sighing and weeping here contrast with the theatrical performances beginning at 580–1.

497. TE suggests the influence of Dryden's 'Cinyras and Myrrha' from Ovid, *Metamorphoses*, X.231, *Fables*, p. 181: 'She stood resolv'd or to possess, or die' (a line close to Sandys's version; see Hammond and Hopkins, V.278). In that story the guilty desire is of a daughter for her father.

499. Pope's substitution for Chaucer 2098–9, fol. 31ʳ, in which Damian is rather 'the sorowfullest man | That ever was'. Pope recalled his phrasing at *Iliad*, V.173: 'Wild with Delay, and more enrag'd by Pain'.

The Dame by Signs reveal'd her kind Intent,
'Till both were conscious what each other meant.

Ah gentle Knight, what wou'd thy Eyes avail,
505 Tho' they cou'd see as far as Ships can sail?
'Tis better sure, when Blind, deceiv'd to be,
Than be deluded when a Man can see!

Argus himself, so cautious and so wise,
Was overwatch'd, for all his hundred Eyes:
510 So many an honest Husband may, 'tis known,
Who, wisely, never thinks the Case his own.

The Dame at last, by Diligence and Care,
Procur'd the Key her Knight was wont to bear;
She took the Wards in Wax before the Fire,
515 And gave th' Impression to the trusty Squire.
By means of this, some Wonder shall appear,
Which in due Place and Season, you may hear.

Well sung sweet *Ovid*, in the Days of yore,

---

502. kind: cf. 304.
504-7. Chaucer 2107-10.
504. thy Eyes: cf. Commentary to 91.
506-7. Chaucer says it is 'as good' to be deceived when blind as when sighted: there is no real difference. Pope makes the latter state comparatively worse.
508-11. Chaucer 2111-15.
508. Argus: In some versions of the myth, Argus or Argos was one of Jupiter's sons, by Niobe, and endowed with a variable number of extra eyes and the ability to live without sleep. He was tasked by Zeus' wife Hera with watching over Io, who had been turned into a heifer by Zeus, at whose instigation Hermes tricked Argos into sleep and then killed him. Argos' eyes were placed in the tail of the peacock. The story was best known from Ovid, *Metamorphoses*, I.668-723; Chaucer mentions it in the Wife of Bath's 'Prologue', 357-61, in the context of illicit sexual activity. Pope omits it in his version of the 'Prologue'

but refers to the story in 'The First Book of Statius his Thebais', 355, and in the notes to *Dunciad Variorum*, II.342.
509. overwatch'd: to 'overwatch' is 'to subdue with long want of rest' (*SJ*), citing Dryden's 'Ceyx and Alcyone', 344-5, *Fables*, p. 374: 'the lazy Monarch overwatch'd | Down from his propping Elbow drops his Head'.
512-17. Chaucer 2116-24.
514. Wards: indentations of the key, which fit the projections inside the lock.
515. trusty: The squire's trustworthiness is now directed towards May, not January; Pope's addition (cf. 540).
518-23. Chaucer 2125-31.
518. sweet **Ovid:** The 'sweetness' of Ovid was a critical commonplace, but Pope probably recalls it from Dryden's 'To the Earl of Roscommon, on his Excellent Essay on Translated Verse' (printed with Roscommon's poem in 1685), 59. Chaucer (2125, fol. 31ʳ) has 'noble Ouid'.

What Sleight is that, which Love will not explore?
520   And *Pyramus* and *Thisbe* plainly show
The Feats, true Lovers when they list, can do:
Tho' watch'd, and captive, yet in spight of all,
They found the Art of Kissing thro' a Wall.

But now no longer from our Tale to stray;
525   It happ'd, that once upon a Summer's Day,
Our noble Knight was urg'd to Am'rous Play:
He rais'd his Spouse e'er Matin Bell was rung;
And thus his Morning Canticle he sung.

Awake my Love, disclose thy radiant Eyes;
530   Arise my Wife, my beauteous Lady rise!
Hear how the Doves with pensive Notes complain,
And in soft Murmurs tell the Trees their Pain;
The Winter's past, the Clouds and Tempests fly,
The Sun adorns the Fields, and brightens all the Sky.
535   Fair without Spot, whose ev'ry charming Part

---

526. **noble:** *1717–51:* rev'rend
533. **Tempests:** *1751:* tempest

---

519. **Sleight:** trick, stratagem. Chaucer has the same word (2126 and 2131).

520. **Pyramus *and* Thisbe:** also in Chaucer (2128), who found the story in Ovid, *Metamorphoses*, IV.55–166, where it forms a template for love tragically thwarted by family divisions. Chaucer's *Legend of Good Women* also contains a version of Thisbe's story.

523. Chaucer (2130, fol. 31ʳ) has the lovers 'rowning' or whispering through the wall. The phrase 'the Art of Kissing' occurs in Dryden, *The Kind Keeper*, I.i (1680), p. 3, but Pope is probably using it humorously as a hybrid between the Ovidian *Ars Amandi* and the burlesque version of the story in Act V of Shakespeare's *Midsummer Night's Dream*, in which the wall that parts the lovers is a speaking character. In Ovid (and in Shakespeare) the lovers do not actually manage to kiss each other.

524–8. Chaucer 2132–7. In Chaucer it is early June.

526. **urg'd:** in Chaucer (2135, fol. 31ʳ) the desire to visit the garden is prompted by the 'eggyng of his wife'.

527. **Matin Bell:** the bell for matins, the early morning service; not in Chaucer.

528. **Canticle:** small song, 'used generally for a song in scripture' (*SJ*), commonly associated a hymn of praise such as the Te Deum or Magnificat. Not in Chaucer, where January 'seith' his words to May.

529–38. Chaucer 2138–48.

529. ***Awake my Love:*** probably echoing Spenser, *Epithalamion*, 74 (1595), p. 195: 'Wake now my loue, awake' and generally (in keeping with the 'Canticle'), the biblical Song of Solomon or Song of Songs, Chaucer's source in this section, 2138, fol. 31ᵛ: 'Rise up my wife, my loue, my lady fre[e]'.

535. **ev'ry charming Part:** Chaucer's January explicitly praises May's eyes and breasts (2141–2).

My Bosome wounds, and captivates my Heart,
Come, and in mutual Pleasures let's engage,
Joy of my Life, and Comfort of my Age!

This heard, to *Damian* strait a Sign she made
540 To haste before; the gentle Squire obey'd:
Secret, and undescry'd, he took his Way,
And ambush'd close behind an Arbour lay.

It was not long e'er *January* came,
And Hand in Hand, with him, his lovely Dame;
545 Blind as he was, not doubting All was sure,
He turn'd the Key, and made the Gate secure.

Here let us walk, he said, observ'd by none,
Conscious of Pleasures to the World unknown:
So may my Soul have Joy, as thou, my Wife,
550 Art far the dearest Solace of my Life;
And rather wou'd I chuse, by Heav'n above,
To die this Instant, than to lose thy Love.
Reflect what Truth was in my Passion shown,
When Un-endow'd, I took thee for my own,
555 And sought no Treasure but thy Heart alone.
Old as I am, and now depriv'd of Sight,
While thou art faithful to thy own true Knight,
Nor Age, nor Blindness, rob me of Delight.

---

538. Age!: *1717–51:* age.
557. While: *1751:* Whilst

---

538. After the equivalent conclusion in Chaucer, the Merchant coolly remarks: 'Such old leud [unlearned or ignorant] words used he' (2149, fol. 31ᵛ), a judgment omitted by Pope.
539-42. Chaucer 2150–55.
540. gentle: here perhaps 'meek' (cf. 3, 595).
542. ambush'd: 'lying in wait' (*SJ*).
543-6. Chaucer 2156–9.
547-60. Chaucer 2160–9.
548. *TE* compares Dryden, 'The Flower and the Leaf', 142–3, *Fables*, p. 388: 'Single, and conscious to my Self alone, | Of Pleasures to th' excluded World unknown'; the narrator in that poem is quietly enjoying a vision of the Lady in a private arbour in a fairy world.
552. Chaucer's January would rather 'dien on a knife' than 'the[e] offend, dere true wife' (2163–4, fol. 31ᵛ).
554. Un-endow'd: without a dowry. Chaucer's January points out that he took her 'Nat for couetise ... But onely for the loue I had to the[e]' (2166–7, fol. 31ᵛ). For the financial status of Pope's May, see 260–1, 301–4.
556. Old as I am: cf. 135.
557-60. Chaucer (2169, fol. 31ᵛ) has January merely ask May 'Be to me true'.
557. *TE* compares Dryden, 'The Cock and the Fox', 414, *Fables*, p. 239: 'While thou art constant to thy own true Knight', the words of the cock Chanticleer to the hen Dame Partlet,

Each other Loss with Patience I can bear,
560 The Loss of thee is what I only fear.

Consider then, my Lady and my Wife,
The solid Comforts of a virtuous Life.
As first, the Love of Christ himself you gain;
Next, your own Honour undefil'd maintain;
565 And lastly that which sure your Mind must move,
My whole Estate shall gratifie your Love:
Make your own Terms; and e'er to Morrow's Sun
Displays his Light, by Heav'ns it shall be done.
I seal the Contract with a holy Kiss,
570 And will perform, by this—my Dear, and this.—
Have Comfort, Spouse, nor think thy Lord unkind;
'Tis Love, not Jealousie, that fires my Mind.
For when thy Beauty does my Thoughts engage,
And join'd to that, my own unequal Age;

568. **Heav'ns:** *1717–51:* heav'n
573. **Beauty does my:** *1717–51:* charms my sober
574. **that:** *1717–51:* them

which thus come to Pope as already parodic. 'True knight' (not in Chaucer) is often in context a comic phrase: see e.g. Falstaff's letter to Mistress Page in Shakespeare, *The Merry Wives of Windsor*, II.i.20.

559–60. For the syntactic positioning of 'only' TE compares Dryden's 'The Last Parting of Hector and Andromache', 107, *Examen Poeticum*, p. 463: 'But loss of Honour is my only Fear'. See also his 'Fable of Acis, Polyphemus, and Galatea' (from Ovid, *Metamorphoses*, XIII), 97–8 (*ibid.*, p. 90): 'All other faults with patience I can bear, | But swiftness is the Vice I only fear'. Pope nowhere else uses this formulation. The sense of loss perhaps parodies Adam's fear about Eve, *Paradise Lost*, IX.896–916.

561–78. Chaucer 2170–84.

562. **solid Comforts:** not in Chaucer. These 'comforts', derived from a 'virtuous Life', are normally religious, centred on the scriptural promise of salvation: e.g. Robert Jenison, *Solid Comforts for Sound Christians* (1641). Cf. the earlier uses at 55, 80. In both Pope and Chaucer, January rapidly notes the love of Christ and reputation for virtue before arriving at May's financial gain ('Estate', Pope 565; 'heritage', Chaucer 2172, fol. 31ᵛ) as her chief inducement to chastity. The phrasing may recall, ironically, Rochester, 'A Letter from Artemisia in the Town, to Cloe in the Country', 220–1, *Poems on Several Occasions* (1696), p. 75: 'With an Estate, no Wit, and a young Wife: | The solid Comforts of a Coxcomb's Life'.

569. TE compares Dryden, 'The Wife of Bath, her Tale', 524, *Fables*, p. 498, where the seemingly foul wife, having won control, proposes to 'seal the Bargain with a Friendly Kiss'.

570. **this . . . this:** kisses (Chaucer 2176, but not enacted there).

572. TE points out that Chaucer's January admits that he is jealous (2177).

573. The revision excises the ancillary expletive 'does', in line with Pope's later sense that such props bring a line down; cf. *Essay on Criticism*, 349.

575　　From thy dear Side I have no Pow'r to part,
　　　　Such secret Transports warm my melting Heart.
　　　　For who that once possest those Heav'nly Charms,
　　　　Cou'd live one Moment, absent from thy Arms?

　　　　He ceas'd, and *May* with sober Grace reply'd;
580　　Weak was her Voice, as while she spoke she cry'd.
　　　　Heav'n knows, (with that a tender Sigh she drew)
　　　　I have a Soul to save as well as You;
　　　　And, what no less you to my Charge commend,
　　　　My dearest Honour, will to Death defend.
585　　To you in holy Church I gave my Hand,
　　　　And join'd my Heart, in Wedlock's sacred Band:
　　　　Yet after this, if you distrust my Care,
　　　　Then hear, my Lord, and witness what I swear.

　　　　First may the yawning Earth her Bosome rend,
590　　And let me hence to Hell alive descend;
　　　　Or die the Death I dread no less than Hell,
　　　　Sow'd in a Sack, and plung'd into a Well:
　　　　E'er I my Fame by one lewd Act disgrace,
　　　　Or once renounce the Honour of my Race.
595　　For know, Sir Knight, of gentle Blood I came,
　　　　I loath a Whore, and startle at the Name.

---

579. **sober:** *1717–51:* modest

---

576. **secret Transports:** cf. 'The First Book of Statius his Thebais', 579.
579–88. Chaucer 2185–94.
579. **sober Grace:** probably recalling by way of parody the ideal lady's address in Dryden, 'Flower and the Leaf', 178, though it is a common phrase. Chaucer's May (2186, fol. 31ᵛ) answers 'Benignely' (graciously), but cf. Commentary on May's 'sadnesse', 245–9 above. The insertion of 'modest' in the revision is perhaps more obviously ironic by this stage.
580. TE compares Dryden, 'The First Book of Homer's Ilias', 570, *Fables*, p. 210: 'Sigh'd ere she spoke, and while she spoke she cry'd;' in Dryden it is a goddess speaking. Pope adds the sighing to his source; cf. 494–7n and 670n.

589–90. Added by Pope. Rudat (1984) notes that the extravagant oath is based on the epic protestation of Dido in Virgil, *Aeneid*, IV, in Dryden's version, IV.32–3, *Works of Virgil* (1697), p. 297: 'But first let yawning Earth a Passage rend; | And let me through the dark Abyss descend'. The phrase 'yawning earth' is also used twice in Sandys's version of Ovid's *Metamorphoses*, XIII and XV (1632), pp. 433 and 497.
591–602. Chaucer 2195–206.
592. Chaucer's May specifies being drowned in a river, also in a sack (2200–1, fol. 31ᵛ).
593. **Fame:** reputation (for chastity); cf. 239.
595. **gentle Blood:** noble rank; cf. 3.
596. **Whore:** Chaucer's May does not use this word, but declares (2202, fol. 31ᵛ) 'I am a gentil woman and no wench'.

But jealous Men on their own Crimes reflect,
And learn from thence their Ladies to suspect:
Else why these needless Cautions, Sir, to me?
600 These Doubts and Fears of Female Constancy?
This Chime still rings in ev'ry Lady's Ear,
The only Strain a Wife must hope to hear.

Thus while she spoke, a sidelong Glance she cast,
Where *Damian* kneeling, rev'renc'd as she past.
605 She saw him watch the Motions of her Eye,
And singled out a Pear-Tree planted nigh:
'Twas charg'd with Fruit that made a goodly Show,
And hung with dangling Pears was ev'ry Bough.
Thither th' obsequious Squire address'd his Pace,
610 And climbing, in the Summit took his Place:
The Knight and Lady walk'd beneath in View,
Where let us leave them, and our Tale pursue.

---

599. **me?:** *1745–51:* me;
600. **Constancy?:** *1751:* constancy!
604. **rev'renc'd:** *1717–51:* worshipp'd

---

startle: shrink from, be startled by; commonly used in this intransitive sense in Pope's time. *TE* compares Garth, *Dispensary*, VI, sixth edition (1706), p. 114, speaking of female desire: 'They like the Thing, That startle at the Name'.
601. ***Chime:*** repeated sound, as of a bell. Chaucer (2204) has 'reprofe'.
602. ***Strain:*** refrain, repeated phrase.
603–12. Chaucer 2207–18, with omissions.
603. ***sidelong Glance:*** a calculated gesture perhaps recalled from Dryden, *Aureng-Zebe*, III (1676), p. 46: 'She darted from her eyes a sidelong glance'; Dryden's translation of Persius, *Satires*, III.224, *Satires of Juvenal* (1693), p. 41, has the phrase 'when she casts on thee a sidelong glance' (speaking of a 'tempting Harlot'). Chaucer's May simply 'saw' Damian (2207, fol. 31ᵛ). The nature of the 'glance' here signals a change from May's behaviour in 344.

604. ***rev'renc'd*** did reverence, i.e. bowed, as to a religious figure. Pope's addition: Chaucer's Damian 'Sate in the bussh' (2208, fol. 31ᵛ). *TE* suggests the influence of Milton, 'A Mask', 301, *Poems* (1645), p. 88, on the revised line: 'And as I past, I worshipt'.
605. ***Motions . . . Eye:*** Chaucer's May signs with her fingers (2209). Pope may recall Dryden, *The Hind and the Panther*, I.533 (1687), p. 30: 'Watching the motions of her Patron's eye', or, in more amorous context, Chudleigh, 'The Inquiry', 164, *Poems on Several Occasions* (1703), p. 111: 'And watch the Motions of your Eye'. In Chaucer (2212–16) there is a pre-rehearsed sequence of signs for the assignation.
608. ***dangling Pears:*** In Chaucer (2211, fol. 31ᵛ) the (pear) tree is 'charged . . . with frute', but Pope's image is more suggestive.
609. ***obsequious:*** cf. 361.

'Twas now the Season when the glorious Sun
His Heav'nly Progress thro' the *Twins* had run;
615 And *Jove*, Exalted, his mild Influence yields,
To glad the Glebe, and paint the flow'ry Fields.
Clear was the Day, and *Phoebus* rising bright,
Had streak'd the Azure Firmament with Light;
He pierc'd the glitt'ring Clouds with golden Streams,
620 And warm'd the Womb of Earth with Genial Beams.

It so befel, in that fair Morning-tide,
The Fairies sported on the Garden's Side,
And, in the midst, the Monarch and his Bride.
So featly tripp'd the light-foot Ladies round,
625 The Knights so nimbly o'er the Greensword bound,
That scarce they bent the Flow'rs, or touch'd the Ground.

***623*. the Monarch:** *1717–1751:* their Monarch

***613–20*.** Chaucer 2219–24; Pope gives less astronomy and more climatic details of colour and warmth.

***613–15*.** The sun is leaving the constellation Gemini; in Chaucer (2222) it is still within that sign. Cf. 402–3 and Commentary.

615. Exalted: In Chaucer (2223–4, fol. 31ᵛ), this has a more strictly astronomical force, as Phoebus (the sun) is in Gemini, 'But litle fro his declinacion, | The causer of Jouis exaltacion'. 'Jove' is the planet Jupiter; cf. 813.

***616*.** TE compares Dryden, 'The Flower and the Leaf', 6, *Fables*, p. 383: 'To glad the Ground, and paint the Fields with Flow'rs'; cf. also 'Palamon and Arcite', II.56: 'And nature's ready Pencil paints the Flow'rs'. Chaucer has the sun 'gladen euery flour', 2221, fol. 31ᵛ. Cf. also 'Spring', 28.

Glebe: 'Turf, soil, ground' (*SJ*).

620. Genial: 'that contributes to propagation' (*SJ*), a faintly sexual image (following the 'Womb of Earth'); essentially Pope's addition.

***621–30*.** Chaucer 2225–36.

***624–8*.** Pope's invention, based in part on Dryden's 'The Wife of Bath her Tale', 215–18,

Fables, p. 487: 'He saw a Quire of Ladies in a round, | That featly footing seem'd to skim the Ground: | Thus dancing Hand in Hand, so light they were, | He knew not where they trod, on Earth or Air'. In Chaucer, Pluto, Proserpine and the company do not dance. Chaucer (2232) makes reference to the Latin author Claudian, fourth-century AD author of *The Rape of Proserpine*, as a source for the original story of Proserpine's abduction, which is not part of Pope's conception of the fairy element here.

624. featly: 'neatly; nimbly; dextrously' (*SJ*); TE suggests comparison with Shakespeare, *Tempest*, I.ii.381: 'foot it featly'.

light-foot: TE finds the phrase in Renaissance versions of fairy-writing such as Spenser, *Shepheardes Calendar*, 'June', 26; also in Michael Drayton, 'Henry Howard Earl of Surrey to the Lady Geraldine', 201, *The Barron's Warrs . . . With England's Heroical Epistles* (1603), fol. 89ᵛ: 'Where light-foote Fayries sport at prison base'.

625. Greensword: i.e. greensward.

***626*.** A miniature version of Virgil's Camilla: cf. *Essay on Criticism*, 373, and Commentary.

The Dances ended, all the Fairy Train
For Pinks and Daisies search'd the flow'ry Plain;
While on a Bank reclin'd of rising Green,
630   Thus, with a Frown, the King bespoke his Queen.

'Tis too apparent, argue what you can,
The Treachery you Women use to Man:
A thousand Authors have this Truth made out,
And sad Experience leaves no room for Doubt.

635   Heav'n rest thy Spirit, noble *Solomon*,
A wiser Monarch never saw the Sun:
All Wealth, all Honours, the supreme Degree
Of Earthly Bliss, was well bestow'd on thee!
For sagely hast thou said; Of all Mankind,
640   One only just, and righteous, hope to find:
But should'st thou search the spacious World around,
Yet one good Woman were not to be found.

Thus says the King who knew your Wickedness;
The Son of *Sirach* testifies no less.
645   So may some Wildfire on your Bodies fall,
Or some devouring Plague consume you all,

---

642. **were:** *1736-51:* is

---

628. Pinks: carnations. In Chaucer, Prosperpine gathers unspecified flowers.
630. Frown: cf. 177.
   bespoke: addressed.
631-4. Chaucer 2237-41.
633. thousand Authors: in Chaucer (2240, fol. 31ᵛ), Pluto alleges 'Ten hundred thousand' witnesses to his point.
635-42. Chaucer 2242-8.
635. Solomon: cf. 151.
642. Chaucer 2247-8, fol. 31ᵛ-32ʳ: 'Among a thousand men yet fonde I one | But of all women fonde I neuer none', indicating more clearly that the reference is to Ecclesiastes 7:28: 'one man among a thousand haue I found, but a woman among all those haue I not found'.
643-50. Chaucer 2249-57.

644. Son of Sirach: Jesus ben Sira, reputed author of the deuterocanonical book Ecclesiasticus, which contains much conventional scepticism about women's fidelity, amid some rather more balanced views than the King suggests here.
645. Wildfire: another name for St Anthony's Fire or erysipelas, an inflammatory skin disease. Chaucer (2252, fol. 32ʳ) has 'wilde fire'.
646. devouring Plague: *TE* compares Dryden, 'The Wife of Bath her Tale', 545, *Fables*, p. 499: 'And some devouring Plague pursue their Lives'; the couplet (the end of the poem) continues: 'Who will not well be govern'd by their Wives', altering the force of the recollection here towards Pope's own conclusion (823-4).

As well you view the Leacher in the Tree,
And well this Honourable Knight you see:
But since he's blind and old, (a helpless Case)
650 His Squire shall cuckold him before your Face.

Now, by my own dread Majesty I swear,
And by this awful Scepter which I bear,
No impious Wretch shall 'scape unpunish'd long,
That in my Presence offers such a Wrong.
655 I will this Instant undeceive the Knight,
And, in the very Act, restore his Sight:
And set the Strumpet here in open View,
A Warning to these Ladies, and to You,
And all the faithless Sex, for ever to be true.

660 And will you so, reply'd the Queen, indeed?
Now, by my Mother's Soul, it is decreed,
She shall not want an Answer at her Need.
For her, and for her Daughters I'll ingage,
And all the Sex in each succeeding Age,
665 None shall want Arts to varnish an Offence,
And fortify their Crimes with Confidence.
Nay, were they taken in a strict Embrace,
Seen with both Eyes, and seiz'd upon the Place,
They need no more but to protest, and swear,
670 Breath a soft Sigh, and drop a tender Tear;

---

665. **None shall want Arts:** *1717–51:* Art shall be theirs
668. **seiz'd upon:** *1717–51:* pinion'd on
669. **They need no more but:** *1717–51:* All they shall need is

---

647. *Leacher:* lecher; Chaucer's word (2257, fol. 32ʳ).
651–9. Chaucer 2258–63.
652. *awful:* awe-inspiring, hallowed. This 'Scepter' is not in Chaucer, and the dignified preamble to 654 is largely Pope's addition.
657. *Strumpet:* not in Chaucer, though he does refer to May's 'harlotry' (2262).
658–9. Pope's addition; Chaucer's Pluto seems more concerned with warning January about his wife and women in general.
660–72. Chaucer 2264–75; and cf. 'The Wife of Bath Her Prologue', 70–3.
662. She shall not lack a response when she needs one.
663. *ingage:* pledge.
665. *want:* lack, be short of.
    varnish: gloss over.
666. *fortify:* defend.
667. *strict:* close.
668. *seiz'd upon the Place:* taken or arrested at the scene, as the revision, 'pinion'd', confirms.
670. Echoing Congreve, *The Tears of Amaryllis for Amyntas*, 169 (1703), p. 8: 'Give a soft Sigh, and drop a tender Tear'. Pope recalled the latter phrase in non-parodic context

'Till their wise Husbands, gull'd by Arts like these,
Grow gentle, tractable, and tame as Geese.

What tho' this sland'rous *Jew*, this *Solomon*,
Call'd Women Fools, and knew full many a one?
675 The wiser Wits of later Times declare
How virtuous, chast, and constant, Women are.
Witness the Martyrs, who resign'd their Breath,
Serene in Torments, unconcern'd in Death;
And witness next, what *Roman* Authors tell,
680 How *Arria, Portia,* and *Lucretia* fell.

But since the Sacred Leaves to All are free,
And Men interpret *Texts*, why shou'd not We?

---

674. **one?:** *1751:* one;
676. **virtuous, chast, and constant:** *1717–51:* constant, chast, and virtuous

---

in e.g. *Iliad,* III.186. Lines 787–92 show the effect in full ironic detail, but May has already shown herself capable of theatrical sighing and weeping at 580–1.

672. **tractable:** 'docile; compliant...governable' (*SJ*).

Geese: Chaucer's queen (2275, fol. 32ʳ) also makes this comparison.

673–80. Chaucer 2276–85.

673–4. Cf. Pope's version of 'The Wife of Bath Her Prologue', 21–2, where Solomon's multiple marriages are brought into the debate.

678. Pope's addition. Having been educated, covertly, as a Catholic, he perhaps had a stronger sense than most Anglicans of the traditions of female martyrology.

680. Pope adds these examples of Chaucer's unspecified 'Romain iestes' (*gestae,* actions) (2284, fol. 32ʳ), of a kind which Chaucer elsewhere narrated in *The Legend of Good Women*; they are all virtuous suicides.

Arria: the Elder, wife of A. Caecina Paestus, ordered by the Emperor Claudius to commit suicide because of his involvement in a conspiracy (AD 42); when he was unable to do it, she stabbed herself to give him an example and handed the knife back, saying it did not hurt; the story was told at length in George Rivers, *The Heroinae* (1639), and Chudleigh, 'The Resolution', 147–73, *Poems on Several Occasions,* pp. 50–1.

Portia: daughter of M. Porcius Cato, wife from 45 BC of Marcus Junius Brutus, one of the assassins of Julius Caesar. She stabbed herself in the thigh to show that she could resist torture and could be trusted by the conspirators; in some accounts she committed suicide in 43 BC after Brutus left for Greece. The main classical source was Plutarch's *Life of Brutus*; she is also a character in Shakespeare's *Julius Caesar*.

Lucretia: The Roman historian Livy (I.57–60) tells how Lucretia, wife of Brutus, was raped by Sextus, son of Tarquinius Superbus, and though guiltless, committed suicide, instigating the expulsion of the kings from Rome. The story was well known, not least from Chaucer's own *Legend of Good Women*, as well as Shakespeare's poem *The Rape of Lucrece* (1593); see Donaldson (1982).

681–2. Pope's addition, perhaps recalling the Wife of Bath's radical attitude to her husband's interpretation of theological doctrine (413–18, in Pope's version), and picking up the previously omitted 2276, fol. 32ʳ, of Chaucer: 'What recketh me of [what do I care for] your auctoritees?'

By this no more was meant, than to have shown,
That Sovereign Goodness dwells in *Him* alone
685 Who only *Is*, and is but only *One*.
But grant the worst; shall Women then be weigh'd
By ev'ry Word that *Solomon* has said?
What tho' this King (as *Hebrew* Story boasts)
Built a fair Temple to the Lord of Hosts;
690 He ceas'd at last his Maker to adore,
And did as much for Idol Gods, or more.
Beware what lavish Praises you confer
On a rank Leacher, and Idolater,
Whose Reign Indulgent God, says Holy Writ,
695 Did but for *David*'s Righteous Sake permit;
David, the Monarch after Heav'ns own Mind,
Who lov'd our Sex, and honour'd all our Kind.

Well, I'm a Woman, and as such must speak;
Silence wou'd swell me, and my Heart wou'd break.
700 Know then, I scorn your dull Authorities,
Your idle Wits, and all their Learned Lies.
By Heav'n, those Authors are our Sexe's Foes,
Whom, in our Right, I must, and will oppose.

Nay, (quoth the King) dear Madam be not wroth;
705 I yield it up; but since I gave my Oath,

---

688. Hebrew: 1717–51: ancient

---

681. Sacred Leaves: scripture; cf. Pope's 'Messiah', 11.
683–97. Chaucer 2286–304.
684–5. Chaucer 2289–90, fol. 32ʳ: 'that in souerayn bounte | Nys non but God, that sitteth in trinite'. The line about the Trinity is not now regarded as Chaucer's and does not appear in modern editions. Pope's version avoids any mention of the Trinity, a highly problematic area of theology in his time; he absorbs Proserpine's mention (2291) of 'God that nis but one'.
688. The substitution of 'ancient' for '*Hebrew*' perhaps accentuates dismissiveness towards scriptural 'authority'.
689–92. The building of the temple is described in 1 Kings 6–8; Solomon's persuasion towards false gods (by his wives, an element not mentioned by the Queen) is in chapter 11.

693. Leacher: lecher, as in 647 (and Chaucer 2298); the King's wife uses his own word against his authority figure.
696. Pope's phrasing echoes Dryden's carefully modulated account of King David's sexual profligacy in *Absalom and Achitophel*, 7 (1681), p. 1: 'Then *Israel*'s Monarch, after Heavens own Heart . . . '.
698–703. Chaucer 2305–10.
698–9. Cf. 'The Wife of Bath Her Prologue', 276.
701. idle: 'Trifling; of no importance' (*SJ*).
704–8. Chaucer 2311–15; the King's partial climbdown prefigures January's own submission to his wife's explanation at the end of the tale.
704. Madam: Chaucer, 2311, fol. 32ʳ, has 'Dame'.
   wroth: 'Angry' (*SJ*, who regarded it as 'out of use' in 1755); it is Chaucer's word.

That this much-injur'd Knight again shou'd see;
It must be done—I am a King, said he,
And one, whose Faith has ever sacred been.

And so has mine, (she said)—I am a Queen!
710 Her Answer she shall have, I undertake;
And thus an End of all Dispute I make:
Try when you list; and you shall find, my Lord,
It is not in our Sex to break our Word.

We leave them here in this Heroick Strain,
715 And to the Knight our Story turns again,
That in the Garden, with his lovely *May*,
Sung merrier than the Cuckow or the Jay:
This was his Song; Oh kind and constant be,
Constant and kind I'll ever prove to thee.

720 Thus singing as he went, at last he drew
By easie Steps, to where the Pear-Tree grew:
The longing Dame look'd up, and spy'd her Love
Full fairly perch'd among the Boughs above.
She stopp'd, and sighing, Oh good Gods, she cry'd,
725 What Pangs, what sudden Shoots distend my Side?
O for that tempting Fruit, so fresh, so green;
Help, for the Love of Heav'ns immortal Queen!
Help dearest Lord, and save at once the Life
Of thy poor Infant, and thy longing Wife!

---

709. **Queen!:** *1736–45:* Queen; *1751:* Queen:
716. **That:** *1717–51:* Who

---

706. The 'much-injur'd Knight' is Pope's addition.
708. Stronger than Chaucer's 'I am a king, it set me not to lye' ['it is not proper for me to lie'] (2315, fol. 32ʳ).
709-13. Chaucer 2316–19. Smallwood (2015: 116) suggests an emphasis here on contemporary issues of female sovereignty under Queen Anne.
710. Pope's phrasing is almost exactly Chaucer's (2317, fol. 32ʳ).
713. An irony added by Pope; Chaucer's Queen merely agrees not to argue any more.

714-19. Chaucer 2320–3; 714 is Pope's addition.
714. *Heroick:* slightly mocking; cf. 73.
717. *Cuckow . . . Jay:* Chaucer (2322, fol. 32ʳ) has 'the Popingay', or parrot; Pope's cuckoo signals cuckoldry.
720-29. Chaucer 2324–37.
722. Pope's addition.
726. *tempting Fruit:* Pope's addition, overtly aligning the event with Eve's transgression in the Garden of Eden (Genesis 3). Cf. 608.
729. *poor Infant:* Chaucer's May refers less explicitly (2335, fol. 32ʳ) to her 'plite' (plight, i.e. pregnancy) as the explanation for her intense appetite for fruit.

730	Sore sigh'd the Knight, to hear his Lady's Cry,
	But cou'd not climb, and had no Servant nigh,
	Old as he was, and void of Eye-sight too,
	What cou'd, alas, the helpless Husband do?
	And must I languish then (she said) and die,
735	Yet view the lovely Fruit before my Eye?
	At least, kind Sir, for Charity's sweet sake,
	Vouchsafe the Bole between your Arms to take;
	Then from your Back I might ascend the Tree;
	Do you but stoop, and leave the rest to me.
740	With all my Soul, he thus reply'd again;
	I'd spend my dearest Blood to ease thy Pain.
	This said, his Back against the Trunk he bent;
	She seiz'd a Twig, and up the Tree she went.
	Now prove your Patience, gentle Ladies all,
745	Nor let on me your heavy Anger fall:
	'Tis Truth I tell, tho' not in Phrase refin'd;
	Tho' blunt my Tale, yet honest is my Mind.
	What Feats the Lady in the Tree might do,
	I pass, as Gambols never known to you:
750	But sure it was a merrier Fit, she swore,
	Than in her Life she ever felt before.

---

733. **the:** *1741–51:* a
737. **Bole:** *1717–51:* trunk
742. **This said:** *1717–51:* With that
744. **all,:** *1717–51:* all!

730–9. Chaucer 2338–45.
733. TE finds a model for the phrasing in Addison's 'Phaeton's Sisters Transform'd into Trees', 47 (427 of Addison's translation of Ovid, *Metamorphoses*, II): 'What cou'd alas! the weeping Mother do?' but Addison's initial text in *Poetical Miscellanies: The Fifth Part* (1704), lacks this segment, which appears to have been added in the collective 1717 translation of the *Metamorphoses*, and its composition date is uncertain; see Guthkelch (1914: I.62).
737. Bole: the trunk of the tree, clarified in the revision of *1717*.

740–3. Chaucer 2346–9. This scene is prominently illustrated in the headpiece to the poem in Pope's *Works* of 1717.
744–51. Chaucer 2350–3. Chaucer's merchant apologises to the ladies in the audience but does not draw a polite veil over the actual consummation. In Speght's edition, fol. 32^r–32^v, between 2353 and 2354 of modern lineated text, come a further eight lines of highly explicit description of the coupling. These lines are not now regarded as Chaucer's and do not appear in modern editions.
749. Gambols: frolics.
750–1. Perhaps the closest part of this passage to Speght's text (fol. 32^v): 'She said it

In that nice Moment, lo! the wondring Knight
Look'd out, and stood restor'd to sudden Sight.
Strait on the Tree his eager Eyes he bent,
755 As one whose Thoughts were on his Spouse intent;
But when he saw his Bosome-Wife so drest,
His Rage was such, as cannot be exprest:
Not frantick Mothers when their Infants die,
With such loud Clamours rend the vaulted Skie:
760 He cry'd, he roar'd, he rag'd, he tore his Hair;
Death! Hell! and Furies! what dost Thou do there?

What ails my Lord? the trembling Dame reply'd;
I thought your Patience had been better try'd:
Is this your Love, ungrateful and unkind,
765 This my Reward, for having cur'd the Blind?
Why was I taught to make my Husband see,
By Strugling with a Man upon a Tree?
Did I for this the Pow'r of Magick prove?

---

759. such loud: *1717–51:* louder
760. rag'd: *1717–51:* storm'd

---

was the meriest fit | That euer in her life she was at yet'. Pope suppresses what he took to be Chaucer's May's open contempt for January's feeble abilities ('He may nat swiue worth a leke'). Cf. also Pope's 'Wife of Bath Her Prologue', 23.

750. Fit: exciting experience, paroxysm.

752-61. Chaucer 2354-67. In Chaucer, it is made explicit that Pluto has given January back his sight.

752. nice: delicate.
   wondring: amazed (Pope's addition).

756. drest: perhaps simply a reference to her state of undress, but in Chaucer, 2361-2, fol. 32ᵛ, January sees that 'Damian his wife had dressed | In such manere...', where 'dressed' means 'treated'.

757. Also inexpressible in Chaucer, except 'if I would speke uncurtesly' (2363, fol. 32ᵛ).

758-61. The syntax of this ranting, equivalent to Chaucer 2364-7, prefigures Belinda's mock-heroic grief in 'Rape of the Locke', I.119-20; see also the comic outburst 'Furies, death and rage!' of *Epistle to Dr Arbuthnot*, 57.

759. loud Clamours: a common phrase in poetry, but normally from epic: cf. Dryden, *Aeneid*, XI.222-3, and later, Pope, *Iliad*, XVII.118, and XV.404.

   rend the vaulted Skie: similarly epic, as in Dryden's version of the *Aeneid*, XI.221, and XII.1344; and 'Palamon and Arcite', III.582. Recalled by Pope, *Odyssey*, VIII.404, and XVIII.119.

760. TE compares Dryden, 'Palamon and Arcite', I.523, *Fables*, p. 20: 'He roar'd, he beat his Breast, he tore his Hair'.

762-9. Chaucer 2368-75.

768. Magick: Chaucer's May does not mention magic but does present the encounter as something she was 'taught' (2372, fol. 32ᵛ) as a cure for blindness.
   prove: try.

Unhappy Wife, whose Crime was too much Love!
770   If this be Strugling, by this holy Light,
'Tis Strugling with a Vengeance, (quoth the Knight:)
So Heav'n preserve the Sight it has restor'd,
As with these Eyes I plainly saw thee whor'd;
Whor'd by my Slave—Perfidious Wretch! may Hell
775   As surely seize thee, as I saw too well.

Guard me, good Angels! cry'd the gentle *May*,
Pray Heav'n, this Magick work the proper Way:
Alas, my Lord, 'tis certain, cou'd you see,
You ne'er had us'd these killing Words to me.
780   So help me Fates, as 'tis no perfect Sight,
But some faint Glimm'ring of a doubtful Light.

What I have said, quoth he, I must maintain;
For, by th' Immortal Pow'rs, it *seem'd* too plain —
By all those Pow'rs, some Frenzy seiz'd your Mind,
785   (Reply'd the Dame:) Are these the Thanks I find?
Wretch that I am, that e'er I was so Kind!

---

778. **Lord,:** *1717–51:* love!
784. 1741–51: new paragraph

---

769. TE cites Dryden's 'Dido to Aeneas' (from the seventh of Ovid's *Heroides*), 176, *Ovid's Epistles, Translated* (1680), p. 225: 'Who know no Crime but too much Love of thee'. An ironic reminiscence of heroic grief.

770–5. Chaucer 2376–9.

770–1. In Speght's edition, fol. 32ᵛ, between 2376 and 2377 of modern lineation, a further four lines of January's outrage give highly explicit details of what he has witnessed. January also suggests that May's pregnancy is the result of adultery: 'It is no wonder though thy bely swell'; cf. 820.

772. Pope's addition, partly based on Chaucer 2385.

774. **Slave:** vassal, servant.
    Perfidious Wretch!: an exceedingly common utterance in drama, giving January a further histrionic twist; cf. Congreve, *Way of the World*, IV.i.443 (1700); Vanbrugh, *The False Friend*, V.1 (1702), p. 51; these comic moments themselves parody the bluster of tragic instances, e.g. John Dennis's in *Rinaldo and Armida*, IV (1699), p. 45.

776–81. Chaucer 2380–3.

780. **So help me Fates:** not in Chaucer.

782–6. Chaucer 2384–9.

783–4. Pope also adds 'th' Immortal Pow'rs'; Chaucer's January thanks God for his restored sight (2385, fol. 32ᵛ).

784. **Frenzy:** Chaucer's May (2387, fol. 32ᵛ) tells January 'Ye mase ye mase, good sir' [you are stunned].

786. **Kind:** here, more in the modern sense of 'benevolent', 'generously inclined' (to January', but perhaps recalling ironically the senses suggested in 304, 502. It is however Chaucer's word (2389).

She said; a rising Sigh express'd her Woe,
The ready Tears apace began to flow,
And as they fell, she wip'd from either Eye
790   The Drops, (for Women when they list, can cry.)

The Knight was touch'd, and in his Looks appear'd
Signs of Remorse, while thus his Spouse he chear'd:
Madam, 'tis past, and my short Anger o'er;
Come down, and vex your tender Heart no more:
795   Excuse me, Dear, if ought amiss was said,
For, on my Soul, amends shall soon be made:
Let my Repentance your Forgiveness draw,
By Heav'n, I swore but what I *thought* I saw.

Ah my lov'd Lord! 'twas much unkind (she cry'd)
800   On bare *Suspicion* thus to treat your Bride;
But 'till your Sight's establish'd, for a while,
Imperfect Objects may your Sense beguile:
Thus when from Sleep we first our Eyes display,
The Balls seem wounded with the piercing Ray,
805   And dusky Vapors rise, and intercept the Day:
So just recov'ring from the Shades of Night,
Your swimming Eyes are drunk with sudden Light,
Strange Phantoms dance around, and skim before your Sight.

---

804. **seem:** *1736–51:* are

787–92. The sentimental act, and response, are Pope's addition, bearing out the pattern predicted by the queen at 670. TE suggests a model for January's reaction from a less ironic context in Dryden, 'Palamon and Arcite', I.93, *Fables*, p. 4: 'The Prince was touch'd, his Tears began to flow'.

793–8. Chaucer 2390–5, omitting some picturesque sexual detail in 2394–5.

796. **amends ... made:** cf. Dryden, 'The Wife of Bath her Tale', 364, *Fables*, p. 492: 'Name but my Fault, amends shall soon be made' (the crone to her reluctantly wedded knight).

799–800. Pope's substitution for Chaucer 2396.

799. **much unkind:** TE finds an echo from Dryden, 'The Wife of Bath her Tale', 359, *Fables*, p. 492: 'Believe me my lov'd Lord, 'tis much unkind' (the crone to the reluctant knight).

801–8. Chaucer 2397–2406.

802. **Imperfect Objects:** cf. Garth, *Dispensary*, IV, sixth edition (1706), p. 68: 'Imperfect Objects tell the doubtful Day'. Chaucer's May suggests an awakening man would not see a 'thing ... parfitely' (2398–9).

Sense: perception.

803. **display:** uncover (by opening the eyelids).

804. **Balls:** eyeballs.

piercing Ray: recalling, with some irony in the present context, the blind Milton's long personal invocation to light in the opening of *Paradise Lost*, III.24.

806. **Shades of Night:** recalling the final words of book IV of *Paradise Lost*.

807. **swimming Eyes:** dizzy vision; common in 'high' genres, e.g. Dryden, *Aeneid*, V.1113, and IX.594; Pope reuses it in his version of the *Iliad*, XXII.598.

808. An Alexandrine; cf. 323, 327.

Then Sir be cautious, nor too rashly deem;
810 Heav'n knows, how seldom things are what they seem!
Consult your Reason, and you soon shall find,
'Twas You were jealous, not your Wife unkind:
Jove ne'er spoke Oracle more true than this,
None judge so wrong as those who think amiss.

815 With that, she leap'd into her Lord's Embrace,
With well-dissembl'd Virtue in her Face:
He hugg'd her close, and kiss'd her o'er and o'er,
Disturb'd with Doubts and Jealousies no more:
Both, pleas'd and blest, renew'd their mutual Vows,
820 A fruitful Wife, and a believing Spouse.

Thus ends our Tale, whose Moral next to make,
Let all wise Husbands hence Example take;
And pray, to crown the Pleasures of their Lives,
To be so well deluded by their Wives.

---

823. **Pleasures:** *1736–51:* pleasure

Strange Phantoms: Pope re-used this phrase in the 'Cave of Spleen' episode in *Rape of the Lock*, IV.40.

809–14. Chaucer 2407–10; 812–13 are Pope's addition.

812. **unkind:** unnatural, undutiful; a euphemism for unfaithful.

813. **Jove:** Roman version of Zeus or Jupiter, king of the Gods in Greek mythology; cf. 615.

814. Cf. *Essay on Criticism*, 6.

815–17. Chaucer 2411–15.

816. Pope's addition. Cf. Commentary to 'Arrival of Ulysses in Ithaca', 172.

817. Chaucer 2413; Pope omits a further proprietorial detail: 'And on her wombe he stroketh her ful softe' (2414, fol. 32^v).

818–24. All Pope's addition; Chaucer's Merchant ends his tale more abruptly with a blessing (2416–18), after which, in Speght, the Wife of Bath follows directly. In modern texts, the Host makes some remarks about the 'sleightes and subtilitees' of wives (2419–40), reminding readers of the context of this tale amongst others on the theme of marriage.

820. **fruitful:** pregnant. The ironic balance of the line perhaps suggests recollection of January's suspicions about the parentage of the child; cf. 770–1, Commentary.

823–4. TE finds a model for Pope's 'moral' in section IX of Swift's *Tale of a Tub* (1704), p. 171), where the hack recommends the '*Possession of being well Deceived*' as a recipe for happiness. Swift's hack is himself quoting a long tradition: see the edition by Marcus Walsh (2010), p. 437, for sources, including Rochester, 'Letter from Artemisia', 115: 'The perfect Joy of being well deceaved'. For an analogue in Erasmus' *Praise of Folly*, on the wisdom of turning a blind eye, see Smallwood (2015). The rhyme and rhythm surely recall the tongue in cheek 'moral' ending of Dryden's 'The Wife of Bath her Tale'; cf. Commentary to 646 above.

2
THE EPISODE OF SARPEDON
(1709)

Editors' Headnote

Composition and publication

'The Episode of Sarpedon' was first published on 2 May 1709. According to Spence, in the last year of his life Pope described himself as having been 'nursed up in Homer and Virgil' (*OAC*, I.83), with his first exposure to Homer coming from John Ogilby's translation of the *Iliad* (1660): 'Ogilby's translation of Homer was one of the first large poems that ever Mr. Pope read, and he still spoke of the pleasure it then gave him, with a sort of rapture, only on reflecting on it'. 'It was that great edition with pictures. I was then about eight years old' (*OAC*, I.14). Ogilby does not have a plate illustrating the death of Sarpedon, though there is one, opposite p. 263, showing the fight at the gate. This late recollection is in contrast to the disparaging mention of Ogilby made in *The Dunciad Variorum*, I.121 and 258.

Writing to William Broome on 16 June 1715, Pope suggested that Homer 'was the first author that made me catch the itch of poetry' (*Corr.*, I.297), and Spence records Pope's recollection that, at the age of twelve, he 'wrote a kind of play' consisting of 'a number of speeches from the *Iliad*, tacked together with verses of my own' (*OAC*, I.15). By this time Pope also seems to have begun to read Homer in Greek, rather than in English translation: Spence records the testimony of William Mannock – the family priest in the household of Pope's brother-in-law, Charles Rackett – that Pope 'set to learning Latin and Greek by himself [at] about twelve' (*OAC*, I.12). In August 1730, Pope told Jonathan Richardson that in 1701 he

> applyd himself so Diligently as to be able to Translate into Verse, within 2 or 3 Years, many Passages of Homer, Virgil, Ovid, Statius, and the most eminent Latin & Greek Poets, some of which (tho since corrected) have been printed.
> (Sherburn 1958a: 346).

A letter purporting to date from 1706 to his critic-mentor, William Walsh, approves of Homer's use of sound to suggest sense (Pope to Walsh, 22 October 1706: *Corr.*, I.22–23), though this may be a partial fabrication from a later letter to Cromwell,

25 November 1710. On 18 September 1707, Sir William Trumbull wrote to his nephew, Ralph Bridges, about Pope's project of translating Homer, claiming that

> Little Pope is returned from Mr. Walsh's; and resolves to go on with translating of Homer. He has begun with some Pieces taken out here & there according to his Fancy; and what I have seen, I think . . . they are very well don.
> (Sherburn 1958a: 343)

On 11 March 1708, Pope sent Bridges, a clergyman and minor scholar, a draft of the poem, asking him 'to compare with the Original Greek and to give me your sincere opinion of, in regard to the Fidelity of the Version'; and to 'mark any places where you find I have mistaken my Author, & give me the reason' (Sherburn 1958b: 395). Bridges returned 'a few loose pieces of Paper' containing his remarks via Trumbull on 29 March (Sherburn 1958a: 344). Eleven sheets of Bridges's queries and suggestions, together with Pope's responses, sometimes deferential and sometimes critically robust, are preserved, together with the manuscripts of the poem, in the British Library (Add. MS 4809, fols 194–9). See Appendix for a full transcription of this material.

Jacob Tonson had received 'January and May' and the *Pastorals* from Pope on 4 March 1708, and in his 11 March letter to Bridges Pope wrote of the 'Episode', 'if I publish it, it must be within a month or a little more'. On 5 April Pope again wrote to Bridges, thanking him for 'the speed, with which you Dischargd so troublesome a Task' (*Corr.*, I.43), and on 9 April, Trumbull urged Pope to 'send this presently to be added to the Miscellanies', adding his hope that 'it will come time enough for that purpose' (*Corr.*, I.46). In the event, publication of the sixth volume of the *Poetical Miscellanies* was delayed, and the 'Episode of Sarpedon' was first published on 2 May 1709, the second of Pope's contributions to the volume, after 'January and May' and before the *Pastorals*. At pp. 301–23, it was sandwiched between poems by John Sheffield, Earl of Mulgrave, and Dr Samuel Garth, both friends of Pope's. The receipt Pope received from Tonson for the poem is in the Pierpont Morgan Library: 'Jan. 13. 1708/9. Receivd of Mr Tonson 3 Guineas for a Translation of the Episode of Sarpedon, printed in ye 6th pt of Miscellany Poems. A. Pope' (reproduced in Sherburn 1934: opp. 85).

An autograph copy of the 'Episode', which appears to have been designed to serve as the printer's copy for the 1709 publication, is held in the British Library, incorporated into the manuscript of Pope's later translation of the whole of the *Iliad* (Add. MS 4807, fols 201–7 and Add. MS 4808, fols 19–23). The manuscript has instructions for typography in the margin of each of the prose 'arguments' introducing the two sections, and the second section has marginal instructions for page-breaks. The first of these is marked '317' and corresponds to p. 317 of *Poetical Miscellanies*. The indications for breaks at the third, fourth and fifth pages are each out of place by two lines of verse. The mark '(x)' on the title page of the manuscript corresponds to the signature of the sheet on which the title page is printed in 1709. With the exception of fol. 205 recto and verso, the numbers at the bottom left-hand of each page correspond to the original number of lines of verse printed on that page.

The text of the manuscript reveals two stages of revision. Several lines have been thoroughly erased and replaced by neatly written alternatives, indicating revisions that were made before the 1709 printing. The second round of revision introduces changes made when the 'Episode' was incorporated into the translation of the whole of the *Iliad*, revealing that, from the start of his career in print, Pope retained his manuscripts and returned to them when he came to revise his poems for publication in subsequent editions.

Text

The text presented here is taken from the first edition of 1709. The original spelling, capitalisation and italicisation are preserved. A second edition appeared in 1716, in *The Sixth Part of Miscellany Poems*, showing just two emendations, one of which – the correction of the misprint at line 334 – has been incorporated in the text of the present edition.

The whole of books XII and XVI subsequently appeared in Volumes III (1717) and IV (1718) of Pope's *Iliad* translation, and the two parts of the 'Episode' were revised to reflect their incorporation into the translation of the poem as a whole. Although the revisions that Pope made at this point do not relate to the 'Episode' as a separate poem, they have been recorded in the apparatus. One revision that Pope made at this point is worth highlighting, because it further highlights the political resonance latent in the 'Episode of Sarpedon'. In the 'Episode' lines 292–3 – 'Thus fell the King; and laid on Earth Supine, | Before his Chariot stretch'd his Form divine' – are preceded by this simile:

> Then as the stately Pine, or Poplar tall,
> Hewn for the Mast of some great Admiral,
> Nods, groans, and reels, 'till with a crackling Sound
> It sinks, and spreads its Honours on the Ground.

For the publication of book XVI of the *Iliad* translation in 1718, Pope revised the first three lines as follows:

> Then, as the Mountain Oak, or Poplar tall,
> Or Pine (fit Mast for some great Admiral)
> Nods to the Axe, till with a groaning Sound

The words 'Oak' – δρῦς – and 'axes' – πελέκεσσι – are in the Greek text (482, 484), but Homer makes no reference in the lines that follow to 'the King' or 'his Form divine'. The wording of the description of Sarpedon's death is a formulaic one in Homer. Lines 489–93 of book XIII of the *Iliad*, describing the death of Asius, are identical to lines 582–6 of book XVI, which Pope translates here. Pope does not, however, translate the two passages in the same way. In book XIII Asius 'Groans to the oft heav'd Axe, with many a Wound', and Pope does not create the juxtaposition with 'Thus fell the King' – instead he has 'So sunk proud Asius'. In the context of the 'Episode', Pope refashions his formulaic material to create an altogether different resonance. The juxtaposition, resulting from these revisions, of 'Nods to the Axe', the 'Oak' – a conventional symbol of Stuart monarchy – and 'Thus fell the King', might be taken to recall the execution of Charles I and the Civil War application given to the speech of Sarpedon to his kinsman Glaucus earlier in the 'Episode' by Sir John Denham in his translation, published in his *Poems* (1668), pp. 78–9. 'Nods to the Axe' in particular seems to allude to Charles's fabled nonchalance before his executioners. (For more detailed discussion of the significance of these textual revisions, see Ferraro 1993a.)

Significant manuscript readings recoverable from the first version of the poem in the fair copy that forms the basis of the surviving British Library material have been recorded in the textual apparatus. The various extant texts of the 'Episode of Sarpedon' are referred to in the apparatus as follows:

MS: 'The Episode of Sarpedon' (British Library, Add. MS 4807, ff. 201–7v, and 4808, ff. 19–23; *IELM* PoA 194 and 195)

1709: *Poetical Miscellanies: The Sixth Part*, octavo (Griffith 1)

1716: *The Sixth Part of Miscellany Poems*, doudecimo (Griffith 61)

1717: *The Iliad of Homer*, vol.III, quarto (Griffith 75)

1718: *The Iliad of Homer*, vol.IV, quarto (Griffith 93)

Models and sources

At various times, Pope owned many books connected with Homer: a Paris edition of the *Iliad* (1554); George Chapman's version of the *Iliad* (1611); a Leiden edition of both epics (1656); Thomas Hobbes's translation (1686 edition); an Amsterdam edition of the whole works (1707, acquired 1714); Anne Dacier's French translation (1711, acquired 1714); and Joshua Barnes's Cambridge edition of the two epics (1711, given to him by the Earl of Halifax in 1714); (Mack 1982: 414–18, items 83–89). The full translations of Homer that Pope knew well were those by Chapman (*The Iliads of Homer Prince of Poets*, 1611), Ogilby (*Homer His Iliads Translated*, 1660), and Hobbes (*Homers Iliads in English*, 1676). The sections of Homer, in conventional modern lineation, on which Pope drew are: XII.290–471; XVI.419–505 and 666–83. The sections of the translations relevant to Pope's poem are: Chapman, pp. 165–8 (book XII), 226–8 and 231 (book XVI); Ogilby, pp. 272–8 (book XII), 360–2 and 367 (book XVI); Hobbes, pp. 179–83 (book XII), 246–8 and 252–3 (book XVI). Both Chapman (p. 165) and Ogilby (p. 272) have marginal notes signalling the high status and significance of the character and speech of Sarpedon. Pope was most disparaging of Hobbes's version, telling Spence: 'There are several passages . . . which, if they had been writ on purpose to ridicule that poet, would have done very well' (*OAC*, I.193, no. 451); he parodied it at *Dunciad Variorum*, II.88.

Pope was certainly strongly aware also of Dryden's translation of the first book of the *Iliad*, printed in that poet's last book, *Fables Ancient and Modern* (1700), as a sort of calling card for the full translation which, in the event, it would fall to Pope to produce; the 'Episode of Sarpedon' was the first and perhaps the most serious of Pope's preliminary claims on the territory (see also 'The Gardens of Alcinous' and 'The Arrival of Ulysses in Ithaca', in this volume). Pope's language shows an awareness of Dryden's epic register from the book I sample and from the complete translation of Virgil's *Aeneid* in *The Works of Virgil* (1697). Segments of Homer translated for this kind of display were less common in the miscellany tradition than translations from Horace and other Latin poets, but among the examples Pope would have known are excerpts such as the 'Last Parting of Hector and Andromache', translated by Dryden, in *Examen Poeticum* (1693), a poem which Erskine-Hill (1996: 60–2) suggests acted additionally as a model of political coding. That volume included two further sections relating to the death of Hector translated by Pope's friend Congreve; and in the *Annual Miscellany: For the year 1694*, Dryden published Thomas Yalden's 'Patroclus's Request to Achilles for his Arms' from *Iliad*, XVI, an item which fills in part of the gap left in Pope's narrative. The label 'Episode' was surprisingly rare as a title of a poetic piece, though it was common enough in criticism (e.g. in *The Whole Critical Works of Monsieur Rapin*, 1705, I.153, 151, 183, speaking specifically of Homer and Virgil). Pope later used it satirically in his 'Receit to make an Epic Poem', *Guardian*, no. 78, 10 June 1714. It had been used as a title by Dryden in 'The Entire Episode of Nisus and Euryalus, translated from the 5th. and 9th books of Virgils Aeneids' (in *Sylvae*, 1685) which also provided a model for a single narrative 'episode', drawn together from different books of an epic, to complete an arc from heroic aspiration through to noble death.

Pope's direct model for Sarpedon's speech, Sir John Denham's version, was much reprinted in Denham's works from 1668 onwards (e.g. in 1703 and 1709) and was itself a 'Miscellany' item, e.g. *Miscellany Poems: The First Part*, third edition (1702), pp. 188–9. Peter Anthony Motteux's longer version, 'The Speech of Sarpedon to Glaucus. Translated, or rather Imitated, from Book XII. of Homer's Iliads', was printed in *The Muses Mercury: or Monthly Miscellany*, I (1707), pp. 69–70. It is likely that Pope knew of Motteux's version, because the issue in which it was published contained contributions by Dryden and Wycherley, and Pope referred to the journal itself in a letter to Cromwell in 1709 (Ferraro 1993a: 17n). Pope was dismissive about Motteux, whereas Denham remained a conspicuous hero (see Headnote to *Windsor-Forest*). The equivalent passage in Homer is 19 hexameter lines (XII.310–328). Denham takes 28 lines of heroic couplets (with a half-line acting as a sort of title) to translate Sarpedon's speech; Pope also takes 28. Motteux produces 54 lines in couplets.

Overall, Pope's 349 pentameter lines are generated from 277 of Homer's hexameters, though Pope also drops a few short passages and images. Pope's expansion is well within the model set by Dryden's 'The First Book of Homer's *Ilias*', which consists of 815 lines of pentameter couplets, derived from 611 of Homer's hexameters. Chapman's 247 lines are 14 syllables long, and overall roughly equal to Pope in extent. Ogilby takes 294 lines of heroic couplets; Hobbes is the trimmest of all, with 259 alternately rhyming pentameter lines covering the sequence.

Context

While not so extensively worked over and polished by the advice of friends and mentors as the *Pastorals* were, the 'Episode of Sarpedon' had something of the same careful pre-publication scrutiny and coterie circulation, suggesting careful planning and long-term ambition to demonstrate capability. (There appears to be much less of this in the case of 'January and May'.) The foundational aesthetic standing of Homer for Pope was already clear enough; much of what he writes in his letter to Bridges of 5 April 1708 (*Corr.*, I.43–4) later found its way into the 'Preface' to his full translation of the *Iliad* (1715). As well as commenting on the 'deviations' in his version inspired by the authoritative but misleading example of Chapman and Hobbes, and his willingness to alter his own expressions even where he has 'Mr Dryden's Example for each of them', he expatiates upon 'the original Beauties of *Homer*' in terms of 'the Invention and Design', and most of all

> the Manners, (which include all the speeches, as being no other than the Representations of each Person's Manners by his words:) and then in that Rapture and Fire, which carries you away with him, with that wonderfull Force, that no man who has a true Poetical spirit is Master of himself, while he reads him.

He goes on:

> The great Beauty of Homer's Language, as I take it, consists in that noble simplicity, which runs through all his works; (and yet his diction, contrary to what one would imagine consistent with simplicity, is at the same time very Copious.)

The character of Sarpedon, on whom Pope inserted a very long note at XVI.512 of the full translation (equivalent to 209 of the 'Episode'), was presented as matching these literary aspects:

> This Hero is by Birth superior to all the Chiefs of either side, being the only Son of *Jupiter* engaged in this War. His Qualities are no way unworthy his Descent, since he every where appears equal in Valour, Prudence, and Eloquence, to the most admired Heroes: Nor are these Excellences blemish'd with any of those Defects with which the most distinguishing Characters of the Poem are stain'd. So that the nicest Criticks cannot find any thing to offend their Delicacy, but must be obliged to own the Manners of this Hero perfect. His Valour is neither rash nor boisterous; his Prudence neither timorous nor tricking; and his Eloquence neither talkative nor boasting. He never reproaches the living, or insults the dead: but appears uniform thro' his Conduct in the War, acted with the same generous Sentiments that engaged him in it, having no Interest in the Quarrel but to succour his Allies in Distress. This noble Life is ended with a Death as glorious; for in his last Moments he has no other Concern, but for the Honour of his Friends, and the Event of the Day.

Pope's own phrasing, in the endeavour to replicate Homer's 'noble simplicity', suggests, of course, Dryden, and to a much lesser extent Milton, but also some of the civic poetry and would-be epic of Pope's time, still in the midst of a long war and its attendant panegyrics. Pope uses the long Alexandrine line many times, a feature about which he was to become more sceptical (see *Essay on Criticism*, 359); he is already highly given to antithesis (e.g. 83–4, where he makes a four-square couplet out of a single line of Homer); and he omits details which might be thought 'low', such as the familiar epithet πέπον (see Commentary at 43) and the simile of the old woman and her spinning (see Commentary at 166–72). For further extended appraisals of Pope's engagement with his models see especially Sowerby (2006: 230–46) and Hopkins (2010: 299–310). Homer was never a neutral object of 'literary' appreciation. The royalism implied by Chapman was superseded by Ogilby's version, Pope's childhood favourite, which appeared as an avowedly Royalist book, published in the year of the Restoration and dedicated to Charles II, explicitly co-opting Homer to Charles's cause: Homer was '*a most constant Asserter of the Divine right of* Princes *and Monarchical Government*' (Dedication). Of the other translators, Hobbes was better known as a theorist of sovereignty than as a poet; Denham had been a Royalist exile; Motteux was a Whig-leaning Huguenot refugee to Britain. Each brought a direct political perspective to the translation of a famous speech about kingly courage and virtue. Ferraro (1993a) shows in detail how Pope's mixed allusions to Denham's 'royalist Civil War poem' and Motteux's 'Williamite polemic' allow him to situate the narrative of Sarpedon's doomed heroism in the context of ongoing if covert debate about the 'situation leading up to the overthrow of Charles I and to the eventual accession of William III' (24). See further Commentary at 15–16, 35–42, 150, 316.

THE
EPISODE
OF
SARPEDON,

Translated from the
Twelfth and *Sixteenth* BOOKS
OF
HOMER's ILIADS.

By Mr. *ALEXANDER POPE.*

The ARGUMENT.

Sarpedon, *the Son of* Jupiter, *commanded the* Lycians *who came to the Aid of* Troy. *In the first Battel when* Diomed *had put the* Trojans *to flight, he incourag'd* Hector *to rally, and signaliz'd himself by the Death of* Tlepolemus. *Afterwards when the* Greeks *had rais'd a Fortification to cover their Fleet, which the* Trojans *endeavour'd to overthrow, this Prince was the Occasion of effecting it. He incites* Glaucus *to second him in this Action by an admirable Speech, which has been render'd in English by Sir* John Denham; *after whom the Translator had not the Vanity to attempt it for any other reason, than that the Episode must have been very imperfect without so Noble a part of it.*

Title. Episode: 'An incidental narrative, or digression in a poem, separable from the main subject, yet rising naturally from it' (*SJ*); see Headnote.

Argument. Son: by Laodameia, daughter of Bellerephon, according to Homer: later accounts make Europa the mother (cf. 'The First Book of Statius his Thebais', 7, Commentary).

Jupiter: Zeus, king of the classical gods in Greek mythology, also referred to as Jove.

Lycians: allies of the Trojans, from Lycia, a mountain region of Asia Minor.

Diomed: Diomedes, one of the chief Greek warriors.

Hector: eldest son of Priam, King of Troy, and chief warrior of the Trojans.

Tlepolemus: son of Herakles, and a Greek warrior from Rhodes; his death is described at *Iliad*, V.628–69.

Glaucus: son of Hippolochus, cousin of Sarpedon, and another of the Lycian leaders at Troy; subsequently killed during the fighting over the body of Achilles (outside the *Iliad* narrative).

Denham: For Sir John Denham's version of the speech, published in his *Poems and Translations* (1668), pp. 78–9, see Headnote. See also Appendix for Pope's request to Bridges for advice about whether to make this kind of acknowledgement.

        THus *Hector*, great in Arms, contends in vain
           To fix the Fortune of the fatal Plain,
    Nor *Troy* cou'd conquer, nor the *Greeks* wou'd yield,
    'Till bold *Sarpedon* rush'd into the Field;
5   For Mighty *Jove* inspir'd with Martial Flame
    His God-like Son, and urg'd him on to Fame.
    In Arms he shines, conspicuous from afar,
    And bears aloft his ample Shield in Air,
    Within whose Orb the thick Bull-hides were roll'd,
10   Pondrous with Brass, and bound with ductile Gold;
    And while two pointed Jav'lins arm his Hands,
    Majestick moves along, and leads his *Lycian* Bands.

    So prest with Hunger, from the Mountain's Brow,

1–2. 1717: Thus God-like *Hector* and his Troops contend
              To force the Ramparts, and the Gates to rend;
4. bold . . . into: *1717:* great *Sarpedon* tow'r'd amid
6. God-like: *1717:* matchless

1–208. Drawn from Homer, XII.290–471 (where book XII ends).

2. fix: determine.

   Fortune: fate, victory; cf. 85.

   fatal Plain: a cliché of the war poetry of Pope's early life, e.g. John Dennis, *Britannia Triumphans* (1704), p. 50; Addison, *The Campaign* (1705), p. 19; but also found in earlier military epics, e.g. Dryden, *Aeneid*, X.1045, *Works of Virgil* (1697), p. 529: 'Like Death attends thee on this fatal Plain'. The line has no basis in Homer.

3. Nor: neither.

4. In the full translation of the *Iliad*, at XII.348, Pope adds a note from the commentator Eustathius on the 'Abundance of Pomp' with which Homer introduces Sarpedon.

5. Martial Flame: a phrase of which Blackmore appears to have been very fond: e.g. *King Arthur*, II and VII (1697), pp. 55 and 177. Cf. also 'The First Book of Statius his Thebais', 716.

7. Pope's invention.

8. ample Shield: cf. Milton, *Paradise Lost*, VI.255 (1674), p. 153, where Satan wields a similarly circular 'ample Shield' during the war in heaven; perhaps recalling Chapman's identical phrase in *The Iliads of Homer Prince of Poets*, XI.35 (1611), p. 143. Also used in Dryden's version of Virgil, *Aeneid*, e.g. V.471, *Works of Virgil*, p. 341, it entered the stock vocabulary of Pope's full *Iliad* translation, e.g. IV.534.

9. Orb: circular rim.

10. Pondrous with Brass: a possible echo of 'The Play-House. A Satyr', by T. E. Gent', in *A Pacquet from Parnassus* (1702), p. 20, where the phrase describes a fake crown worn by an actor.

   ductile: 'easy to be drawn out into length' (*SJ*); Pope later used the word parodically in *The Dunciad Variorum*, I.62.

11. Jav'lins: spears.

12. Majestick moves along: TE cites Dryden's *Aeneid*, I.225, *Works of Virgil*, p. 208 (of Poseidon): 'Majestick moves along, and awful Peace maintains'. The line is Pope's invention.

13–16. For Pope's discussion of this simile with Bridges see Appendix. In the full *Iliad*, XII.357, Pope adds a note by Dacier comparing the simile with a passage in Isaiah 31:4, where God is compared to a lion.

Descends a Lion on the Flocks below;
15   So stalks the Lordly Savage o'er the Plain,
    In sullen Majesty, and stern Disdain:
    In vain loud Mastives bay him from afar,
    And Shepherds gaul him with an Iron War;
    Regardless, furious, he pursues his way;
20   He foams, he roars, he rends the panting Prey.

        Resolv'd alike, Divine *Sarpedon* glows
    With gen'rous Rage, that drives him on the Foes.
    He views the Tow'rs, and meditates their Fall;
    To sure Destruction dooms the *Grecian* Wall;
25   Then casting on his Friend an ardent Look,
    Fir'd with the Thirst of Glory, thus he spoke.

---

24. the *Grecian*: *1717:* th' aspiring

15–16. These lines are Pope's addition to the simile; the regal lordliness is perhaps suggested by Ogilby, *Homer His Iliads Translated* (1660), p. 273, where the lion is the 'Forest King'.

15. Savage: cf. 297, and Commentary to *Windsor-Forest*, 57.

17. Mastives: i.e. guard-dogs.
   bay: bark at.

18. gaul: gall, prod.
   Iron War: defensive weapons (Ogilby, p. 273, has 'Pikes and Prongs'). Pope might have had a sense of the phrase as mildly mock-heroic, from Dryden's use of it in his version of Virgil, *Georgics*, I.232, *Works of Virgil*, p. 56, where it refers to garden implements used against weeds; Luke Milbourne protested about the wording in his *Notes on Dryden's Virgil* (1698), pp. 119–20. Cf. the straightforwardly military context of Robert Pricket, *A Souldiers wish unto his Soveraigne Lord King James* (1603), sig. A4ʳ: 'A Soldiers hand made rough with Iron warre'.

20. panting Prey: cf. Dryden, *King Arthur*, II (1691), p. 19, where a lamb is the 'panting Prey' of a hungry lion; added to the original, as Pope acknowledges to Bridges (Appendix). Homer (XII.305–6) makes it clear that the lion himself risks death, as does Chapman, XII.307, p. 165: 'and either snatch, a prey, or be a prey'; Ogilby, p. 273: 'Eeither [*sic*] a Prey, or Death upon a Launce'.

21–6. Pope has greatly expanded the build-up here from Homer's XII.307–9; see Appendix for Pope's discussion of drafts of this passage.

22. gen'rous: noble; cf. 'January and May', 3, and Commentary. For 'gen'rous Rage' in military context cf. e.g. Dryden, 'Palamon and Arcite', I.117, *Fables Ancient and Modern* (1700), p. 5; Pope reused the phrase in 'The First Book of Statius his Thebais', 714.

23. meditates . . . Fall: cf. *Windsor-Forest*, 102; 'Rape of the Locke', I.47.

26–52. In Homer the speech lasts 19 lines, or 20 counting the introductory line (XII.309–328). See Headnote for comment on this speech, which Pope translated in competitive homage to Denham's version; his mock-heroic version of it, spoken by Clarissa, was added to Canto V of *The Rape of the Lock* in 1717. In his full *Iliad* version, at XII.371, Pope adds a composite note on the high morality of this heroic example.

Why boast we, *Glaucus*, our extended Reign,
Where *Xanthus'* Streams enrich the *Lycian* Plain?
Our num'rous Herds that range each fruitful Field,
30   And Hills where Vines their Purple Harvest yield?
Our foaming Bowls with gen'rous *Nectar* crown'd,
Our Feasts enhanc'd with Musick's sprightly Sound?
Why on those Shores are we with Joy survey'd,
Admir'd as Heroes, and as Gods obey'd?
35   Unless great Acts superior Merit prove,
And Vindicate the bounteous Pow'rs above:
'Tis ours, the Dignity They give, to grace;
The first in Valour, as the first in Place:
That while with wondring Eyes our Martial Bands

---

28. Plain?: MS: Plain;
29. each: *1717:* the
31. gen'rous: *1717:* purer
33. those: *1716:* these
39. while: *1717:* when

---

27. In Homer (XII.310), Sarpedon asks rather why he and Glaucus τετιμήμεσθα ('have been honoured') by their possessions; and (313) why νεμόμεσθα ('we have we been allotted') them. Both are passive verbs: they have done nothing to gain their kingdoms. Motteux, 'The Speech of Sarpedon to Glaucus', *The Muses Mercury: or Monthly Miscellany*, I (1707), pp. 69–70, has the pair 'indulg'd by Fate'; Denham, p. 78, 'why is our Pomp, our Power?'; Chapman, 311 (1611), p. 165: 'why are we honord more'; Hobbes, *Homers Iliads in English* (1676), p. 179: 'what cause . . . is there . . . | That we . . . more honor'd are'. Most of the adjectives used to describe the possessions in these lines ('numerous', 'fruitful', 'generous', 'sprightly') are Pope's addition to the Greek.
  Reign: Bridges questioned the use of 'Reign' in the sense of 'realm' and Pope responded that the usage was Dryden's; see Appendix.
28. Xanthus: a river in Lycia.
29. fruitful Field: cf. Isaiah 29:17: 'Lebanon shall be turned into a fruitful field'. Recalled by Pope in 'Winter', 47.

31. Nectar: normally the drink of eternal life, as ambrosia (328) is the food. Cf. Blackmore, *Eliza*, V (1705), p. 147: 'their Goblets crown'd | With gen'rous Nectar'. In Homer (XII.311) Sarpedon refers merely to 'full cups' (πλείοις δεπάεσσιν); Chapman, 312–13, p. 165, has 'greater store . . . | Of cups'; Denham, p. 78: 'the rich Grape'; Ogilby, p. 273: 'large Goblets crown'd'; Hobbes, p. 179: 'best wine'; Motteux, p. 69: 'Rich Grapes profusely bleed'.
32. sprightly Sound: The phrase has no basis in Homer, and there is no music in the other translations, but Denham, p. 78, has 'Musick charms their ears'.
33–4. Cf. Denham, 10–11, p. 78, 'Why as we pass, do those on *Xanthus* shore, | As Gods behold us, and as Gods adore?' The syntactic antithesis is not present in Homer or in other translations. Motteux, p. 69, has: 'We seem the Gods, and humble Crouds the Slaves'; Ogilby, p. 273: 'like their Gods ador'd'.
35–42. Homer's emphasis is more straightforwardly on material and pragmatic aspects of kingship and on impressing the

40   Behold our Deeds transcending our Commands,
     Such, they may cry, deserve the Sov'reign State,
     Whom those that Envy dare not Imitate!
     Cou'd all our Care elude the greedy Grave,
     Which claims no less the Fearful than the Brave,

---

43. **greedy:** *1717:* gloomy

---

soldiers. Ferraro (1993a: 16) notes how in Pope 'Homer's material benefits of kingship become theoretical rights and responsibilities'; there is no direct link in Homer between the privileges of rank and being seen to fight well, though the link may be understood. For further analysis see Hopkins (2010: 299–310). Chapman, 320–1, p. 166, has 'these are right | Our kings, our Rulers; these deserve to eate and drinke the best'; Chapman is followed by Denham, 14–15, p. 79, but in a more abstract way: 'These are They | Deserve the Greatness'; Ogilby, p. 273: 'Fighting in Front the Fury of the Day | ... | Our Princes no unworthy Leaders are'; Hobbes, p. 179: 'our Princes have | More honour, since they are of greater might'; and Motteux, p. 69: 'Men fit to lead, and worthy to be Kings'. Homer (XII.318-19) has only: οὐ μὰν ἀκλεέες Λυκίην κάτα κοιρανέουσιν | ἡμέτεροι βασιλῆες ('Not ingloriously they rule through Lycia | Our kings'). Motteux, p. 69, is 'almost Republican' (Ferraro 1993a: 19) in canvassing the possibility that royalty might be scorned as useless: 'No idle Monarchs, no luxurious Drones, | The State's Disease, or Lumber of their Thrones'. His heavily-emphasised point, appropriate to the Williamite and emerging Hanoverian context, is that monarchs have to earn their titles by conspicuous action rather than mere inheritance.

36. Vindicate: as Brower (1959: 111) notes, this alludes to Milton's intention to 'justifie the wayes of God to men', *Paradise Lost*, I.26, which Pope later alluded to further using the same verb: 'But vindicate the ways of God to Man', *Essay on Man*, I.16. Ferraro (1993a: 19) points out that Motteux, p. 70, has 'justifie their Title by their Worth' at this point.

37. grace: used here 'to convey at once the idea of worldly distinction ... and a sense of the religious significance of kingship' (Ferraro 1993a: 21).

38. first ... first: Ferraro (1993a: 20) compares Motteux's political version (p. 69): 'The First in Valour, as in Rank the first'; the phrase also resembles Oldmixon, *Amores Britannici*, V.83 (1703), p. 103: 'The first in Valour he, by Birth the first'. The antithesis has no basis in Homer.

40. Cf. Chapman, 322–3, p. 166: 'These ... Do more then they command to do'; Denham, 17, p. 79, 'what they act, transcends what they command', i.e. the leaders do more than they are asking the soldiers to do, and are therefore worthy of their positions. Homer (XII.321) has merely Λυκίοισι μέτα πρώτοισι μάχονται ('they fight with the frontline Lycians').

42. Pope omits here Homer's references to the food and drink that the leaders consume, focusing only on their valour.

43-6. See Pope's discussion with Bridges about this section and various versions of it, Appendix 1.

43. In the full translation, XII.387, Pope paraphrases notes from Eustathius and Dacier on the particular moral utility of the sentiment here. Homer's line begins with an endearment, πέπον, literally 'sun-ripened', but always metaphorical in Homer: 'kind, mild, gentle'. Pope omits it again at 302 (Homer, XVI.492), though he quotes the Greek line in the exchange with Bridges

45 For Lust of Fame I shou'd not vainly dare
    In fighting Fields, nor urge thy Soul to War.
    But since, alas, ignoble Age must come,
    Disease, and Death's inexorable Doom;
    The Life which others pay, let Us bestow,
50 And give to Fame what we to Nature owe;
    Brave, tho' we fall; and honour'd, if we live;
    Or let us Glory gain, or Glory give!

    He said, his Words the list'ning Chief inspire
    With equal Warmth, and rouze the Warrior's Fire;
55 The Troops pursue their Leaders with Delight,
    Rush to the Foe, and claim the promis'd Fight.

---

51. **tho':** MS: if

(Appendix); Denham, 18, p. 79, registers it with 'oh friend', as does Chapman, 323, p. 166, who has 'dear friend' at the second instance. Ogilby has 'my dear *Glaucus*' the first time (p. 273) and omits it the second time; Hobbes omits it both times; Motteux, p. 70, has 'Noble Friend'.

greedy Grave: Ferraro (1993a: 22) observes that Spenser uses this phrase, *Faerie Queene*, I.ix.33, where the cave of Despair is 'like a greedie graue', and again at II.ii.24; it is also very common in seventeenth-century religious verse. It has no basis in Homer, who simply has εἰ μὲν γὰρ πόλεμον περὶ τόνδε φυγόντε | αἰεὶ δὴ μέλλοιμεν ἀγήρω τ' ἀθανάτω τε | ἔσσεσθ' ('if, surviving this war, we two were always to be ageless and undying'; XII.322-4).

45-6. TE cites Dryden, *Aeneid*, VIII.685, *Works of Virgil*, p. 454: 'In fighting Fields from you shall learn to dare'. Ferraro (1993a: 22) suggests recollection of Motteux, p. 70: 'Or urge his Friend undauntedly to dare?' The phrase 'fighting fields' occurs at least six times in Dryden's version of the *Aeneid*; there is no exact equivalent in Homer.

45. **Lust of Fame:** not in Homer. The 'fierce lust | Of fame' is attacked in Henry Vaughan, 'Ivvenal's Tenth Satyre Translated', 230-1, *Poems* (1646), p. 64, and praised in Henry Denne, *A Poem on the Taking of Namur, by His Majesty* (1695), p. 7: 'The Lust of Fame provokes their noble Rage'.

48. **inexorable Doom:** Brower (1959: 109) locates the source of this in Dryden, *Georgics*, III.111, *Works of Virgil*, p. 99, translating Virgil's *inexorabile fatum*; Thomas May had used the same phrase at the same point in *Virgil's Georgicks Englished* (1628), p. 77.

49-51. All these antithetical clauses are Pope's invention, in part based on the syntax of Denham's lines 23-6; Motteux, p. 70, has a cumulative series of 'Since' clauses at this point.

52. TE compares Hobbes, p. 179: 'And either honour gain or honour give'. Homer has ἠέ τῳ εὖχος ὀρέξομεν ἠέ τις ἡμῖν ('whether we hand fame to someone, or someone [hands it] to us'; XII. 328); Ogilby, p. 274, has 'And Glory give, or purchase from the Foe'; Motteux, p. 70: 'And endless Fame or purchase or bestow'.

53-6. A very free expansion of Homer's 329-30.

53. **He said:** epic phrasing based on Homer's conventional ὣς ἔφατ' ('so he spoke'), XII.329. Cf. 'January and May', 139; 'The First Book of Statius his Thebais', 348.

55. **pursue:** follow.

Menestheus from on high the Storm beheld,
Threat'ning the Fort, and black'ning in the Field;
Around the Walls he gaz'd, to view from far
60   What Aid appear'd t' avert th' approaching War,
And saw where *Teucer* with th' *Ajaces* stood,
Insatiate of the Fight, and prodigal of Blood.
In vain he calls, the Din of Helms and Shields
Rings to the Skies, and ecchoes thro' the Fields,
65   The Gates resound, the Brazen Hinges fly,
While each is bent to conquer or to die.
Then thus to *Thoos*; — Hence with speed (he said)
And urge the bold *Ajaces* to our Aid;
Their Strength united best may help to bear
70   The bloody Labours of the doubtful War:

---

62. *1717:* Of Fight insatiate, prodigal of Blood.
65–6. *1717:* The brazen Hinges fly, the Walls resound,
    Heav'n trembles, roar the Mountains, thunders all the Ground.
67. *1717:* new paragraph

---

57. Menestheus: Greek warrior, son of Peteos, leader of troops from Athens, famous for his battle-cry, but viewed, alongside Odysseus, as hanging back from battle at *Iliad* IV.327–31. Pope omits Homer's indication that he 'shuddered at' (ῥίγησ') the sight of the Trojans (XII.331), where Chapman, 335, p. 166, has 'his haire stood vp on end' and Hobbes, p. 180, has him 'terribly afraid'. He is however μεγαθύμου ('great-hearted'), on Ajax's arrival at XII.373, an instance omitted by Pope at the relevant moment, 90–1, below.

Storm: not in Homer at this point; Ogilby, p. 274, has a 'gather'd Tempest'. Cf. 92.

58. TE cites Dryden, *Aeneid*, IX.40, *Works of Virgil*, p. 465: 'Blackning the Fields, and thickning thro' the Skies'. There is no 'black'ning' in Homer.

60. War: 'forces; army. Poetically' (*SJ*, citing Milton, *Paradise Lost*, XII.213–14: 'the Waves return, | And overwhelm thir Warr').

61. Teucer: Teukros, one of the most prominent archers among the Greeks (see 75), half-brother to Ajax (see 81).

Ajaces: the two heroes called Ajax (Aias): Ajax son of Telamon or the 'greater Ajax', King of Salamis, and Ajax son of Oileus; referred to as the 'Aiaces' in Chapman; 'Ajaxes' in Ogilby and Hobbes; Αἴαντε δύω (grammatically a 'dual', stressing twinship) in Homer, XII.335.

62. Insatiate of the Fight: literally from Homer, XII.335, πολέμου ἀκορήτω.

prodigal of Blood: cf. Chudleigh, 'The Resolution', 279, *Poems on Several Occasions* (1703), p. 55: 'Her valiant Sons, who prodigal of Blood' (speaking of Homer's Greeks); not in Homer.

63. Helms: helmets.

65. Brazen Hinges: not in Homer, and probably recalled from Dryden, *Aeneid*, I.631, *Works of Virgil*, p. 220: 'The lofty Doors on brazen Hinges sound'; Dryden uses similar phrasing several times in the *Aeneid* translation. Cf. also 193 below.

66. Pope's addition.

67. Thoos: clearly a herald (cf. 77), and signalled as such in Homer and in Ogilby, though Hobbes, p. 180, calls him a 'Squire'.

70. bloody Labours: a phrase from contemporary war poetry, e.g. Thomas Yalden, *On the Conquest of Namur*, st. 13 (1695), p. 9: 'Amidst the bloody Labours of the Field'.

Hither the *Lycian* Princes bend their Course,
The best and bravest of the *Trojan* Force.
But if too fiercely, there, the Foes contend,
Let *Telamon* at least our Tow'rs defend,
75 And *Teucer* haste, with his unerring Bow,
To share the Danger, and repel the Foe.

Swift as the Word, the Herald speeds along
The lofty Ramparts, through the Warlike Throng,
And finds the Heroes, bath'd in Sweat and Gore,
80 Oppos'd in Combate on the dusty Shore.
Strait to the Fort great *Ajax* turn'd his Care,
And thus bespoke his Brothers of the War:
Now valiant *Lycomede*, exert your Might,

---

71. **Princes bend:** MS: Chiefs direct
72. **Trojan:** *1717:* hostile
78. **Warlike:** *1717:* martial
80^1. *1717:* Ye valiant Leaders of our warlike Bands!
  Your Aid (said *Thoos*) *Peteus*' Son demands,
  Your Strength, united, best may help to bear
  The bloody Labours of the doubtful War:
  Thither the *Lycian* Princes bend their Course,
  The best and bravest of the hostile Force.
  But if too fiercely, here, the Foes contend,
  At least, let *Telamon* those Tow'rs defend,
  And *Teucer* haste, with his unerring Bow,
  To share the Danger, and repell the Foe.

---

  doubtful: of uncertain result. The phrase 'doubtful War', which has no equivalent in Homer, comes very near the start of Dryden's version of the *Aeneid*, I.5, among other instances; TE cites particularly Dryden, *Aeneid*, X.1090, *Works of Virgil*, p. 530: 'And dauntless undertook the doubtful War'.
74. **Telamon:** father of both Teucer and the 'greater' Ajax (cf. 81); at this point in Homer it is clearly Ajax who is summoned, but Chapman also refers to him as 'Telamon'; Ogilby and Hobbes use 'Telamonius'.
75. **unerring Bow:** probably recalled from Dryden, *Aeneid*, XII.580, *Works of Virgil*, p. 595 (referring to Apollo).
76. Pope's addition.
77. **Swift . . . Word:** Pope's addition.
78. **lofty Ramparts:** this phrase occurs in a parallel military context in Thomas Ross, *The Second Punic War Between Hannibal, and the Romanes*, XVII (1661), p. 493.
79. **bath'd . . . Gore:** not in Homer.
81. At this point in Homer, XII.354–63, Thoos repeats his instructions from Menestheus more or less as already heard; Pope omits from the 'Episode', but includes the version at **80^1 variant** in his full translation of Book XII in 1717.
83. **Lycomede:** Lycomedes, a Boeotian warrior; perhaps adapted to fit the trisyllabic name within the metre.

And brave *Oïleus*, prove your Force in Fight:
85 To you I trust the Fortune of the Field,
'Till by this Arm the Foe shall be repell'd;
That done, expect me to compleat the Day:
Then, with his Sev'nfold Shield, he strode away.
With equal Steps bold *Teucer* prest the Shore,
90 Whose fatal Bow the strong *Pandion* bore.
High on the Walls appear'd the *Lycian* Pow'rs,
Like some black Tempest gath'ring round the Tow'rs;
The *Greeks* oppress'd, their utmost Force unite,
Prepar'd to labour in th' unequal Fight;
95 The War begins; mix'd Shouts and Groans arise;
Tumultuous Clamour mounts, and thickens in the Skies.
Fierce *Ajax* first th' advancing Host invades,
And sends the brave *Epicles* to the Shades,
Sarpedon's Friend; Across the Warrior's Way,
100 Rent from the Walls, a Rocky Fragment lay;
In modern Ages not the strongest Swain
Cou'd heave th' unwieldy Burthen from the Plain:
He poiz'd, and swung it round; then tost on high,

---

95. begins;: *1717:* renews,

---

84. Oïleus: King of Lokris and father of the 'lesser' Ajax, the hero who is addressed here (the Greek is Ὀϊλιάδην ('son of Oileus'), XII.365).
85. Fortune . . . Field: cf. 2.
87. compleat: finish, see through.
88. Sev'nfold Shield: Ajax's iconic shield, made of seven-fold ox-hides, not actually mentioned by Homer at this point (XII.370), but recalled from book VII: see Pope's VII.267–8 for the description. Pope parodies this epithet in *Rape of the Lock*, II.119, speaking of a petticoat as 'that sev'nfold Fence'.
90. fatal: death-dealing.
    Pandion: a Greek warrior. In the full translation, *Iliad*, XII.444, Pope inserts a note from Eustathius explaining what he perceived as the oddity of having someone carry Teucer's bow.
92. black Tempest: Homer's ἐρεμνῇ λαίλαπι ('dark thunder-shower'), XII.375.

94. unequal Fight: Pope's addition. The phrase occurs several times in Dryden's version of the *Aeneid*: e.g. II.508, 577, etc.; Pope recalled it ironically in 'Rape of the Locke', II.132, and returned it to epic usage in his version of the *Odyssey*: XVI.276 and XVIII.39.
96. thickens: cf. Commentary to 58.
97. invades: attacks.
98. Epicles: Epikles, a warrior on the Trojan side, mentioned only this once in Homer.
100. Rocky Fragment: cf. Blackmore, *King Arthur*, XII (1697), p. 340: 'And heav'd a mighty Rocky Fragment up'. In the full translation, *Iliad* XII.454, Pope adds a note from Eustathius observing that there is a parallel with Hector's throwing of a rock (at 183–96), but that Homer makes the Greek warrior able to perform the deed without the help of Zeus.
101. Swain: peasant, rustic.
103. poiz'd: balanced.

It flew with Force, and labour'd up the Sky;
105　Full on the *Lycian*'s Helmet thundring down,
　　The pondrous Ruin crush'd his batter'd Crown.
　　As skilful Divers from some Airy Steep
　　Headlong descend, and shoot into the Deep,
　　So falls *Epicles*; then in Groans expires,
110　And murm'ring from the Corps th' unwilling Soul retires.

　　While to the Ramparts daring *Glaucus* drew,
　　From *Teucer*'s Hand a winged Arrow flew,
　　The bearded Shaft the destin'd Passage found,
　　And on his naked Arm inflicts a Wound.
115　The Chief who fear'd some Foe's insulting Boast
　　Might stop the Progress of his warlike Host,
　　Conceal'd the Wound, and leaping from his Height,
　　Retir'd reluctant from th' unfinish'd Fight.
　　Divine *Sarpedon* with Regret beheld
120　Disabl'd *Glaucus* slowly quit the Field;
　　His beating Breast with gen'rous Ardour glows,
　　He springs to Fight, and flies upon the Foes.

---

110. 1717: And murm'ring to the Shades the Soul retires.
119. MS: With deep Regret the *Lycian* King beheld

---

104. labour'd . . . Sky: not in Homer.
107-8. This simile is much expanded from Homer's more basic ἀρνευτῆρι ἐοικώς, XII.385, rendered by Hobbes, p. 181, as 'like a diver'. The Greek word normally means 'acrobat'; Ogilby, p. 275, refers to a 'Tumbler'. Ogilby has a marginal note referring, among other material, to ancient descriptions of the behaviour of diving dolphins which might have influenced Pope's phrasing: 'holding their wind as a string, they spring and shoot forth their bodies as an Arrow'. A diving bird is another possible model for the image.
107. Airy Steep: high cliff.
110. An Alexandrine: cf. *Essay on Criticism*, 359; there are four further examples in the poem (198, 208, 272, 299).
113-14. For the acceptability of this rhyme cf. 'Sapho to Phaon', 129-30 and Commentary.

Pope re-used it in his version of Homer, *Iliad*, V.103-4.
113. bearded: feathered (see 137), or perhaps barbed.
　　destin'd: fated (because the bow is unerring). The line is Pope's invention.
115. insulting: cf. Ogilby, p. 275: 'Least at his Hurt the insulting Foe should scoff'. Cf. also 316. 'Insult' carries the Latin sense of 'triumph'.
119-20. For Pope's brief discussion of these lines and variations, see Appendix.
121. gen'rous: 'Noble of mind; magnanimous; open of heart' (*SJ*). Pope quotes this line in his own notes to *Dunciad Variorum* (1729), II.175. The phrase 'gen'rous ardour' might be recalled from Nisus's words in Dryden, *Aeneid*, IX.237, *Works of Virgil*, p. 471: 'A gen'rous ardour boils within my Breast'.
122. Pope's invention.

Alcmaon first was doom'd his Force to feel,
Deep in his Breast he plung'd the pointed Steel,
125 Then from the yawning Wound with Fury tore
The Spear, pursu'd by gushing Streams of Gore;
Down sinks the Warrior, with a thundring Sound,
His Brazen Armour rings against the Ground.

Swift to the Battlement the Victor flies,
130 Tugs with full Force, and ev'ry Nerve applies;
It shakes; the pondrous Stones disjoynted yield;
The rowling Ruins smoak along the Field.
A mighty Breach appears, the Walls lye bare,
And like a Deluge rushes in the War.
135 At once bold *Teucer* draws the twanging Bow,
And *Ajax* sends his Jav'lin at the Foe;
Fix'd in his Belt the feather'd Weapon stood,
And thro' his Buckler drove the trembling Wood;
But *Jove* was present in the dire Debate,
140 To shield his Off-spring, and avert his Fate.
The Prince gave back; not meditating Flight,
But urging Vengeance and severer Fight;
Then rais'd with Hope, and fir'd with Glory's Charms,
His fainting Squadrons to new Fury warms.

---

143. **Hope:** *1717:* Hopes

---

123. **Alcmaon:** Alkmaon, a Greek warrior.
127. **thundring:** as in Ogilby, p. 275: 'His Armour ratling like a Thunder crack', rather than Homer, where the armour merely βράχε ('rattled'), XII.396.
129–34. See Pope's discussion with Bridges about this section, Appendix.
130. **Nerve:** muscle, sinew. The image is Pope's addition.
132. **smoak:** Here, to smoke is 'to move very fast, so as to raise dust like smoke' (*SJ*). The whole line is Pope's addition.
134. **War:** i.e. the army, as in 60. Pope's addition; in Homer, XII.399, Sarpedon has πολέεσσι δὲ θῆκε κέλευθον ('made a path for many').

137. feather'd Weapon: Teucer's arrow.
138. Buckler: shield 'buckled' to the arm.
139. dire: 'dreadful; dismal' (*SJ*), from Latin 'dirus' ('dreadful, terrible'). Pope used the phrase 'dire Debate' as a periphrasis for battle many times in the *Iliad* translation, e.g. III. 321, 398; he might have recalled it from Dryden's *Aeneid*, e.g. I.396, II.981.
141. gave back: retreated slightly. Ogilby, p. 276, uses the same phrase.
142. severer: fiercer.
143–4. See Pope's revision of these lines in discussion; Appendix.
143. Glory's Charms: cf. Blackmore, *Eliza*, II (1705), p. 49: 'Our noble Youth inspir'd with Glory's Charms'. Cf. *Ode for Musick*, 44.

145   O where, ye *Lycians*, is the Strength you boast,
       Your former Fame, and ancient Virtue lost?
       The Breach lyes open, but your Chief in vain
       Attempts alone the guarded Pass to gain:
       Unite, and soon that Hostile Fleet shall fall,
150   The Force of pow'rful Union conquers All.

          This just Rebuke inflam'd the *Lycian* Crew,
       They join, they thicken, and th' Assault renew;
       Unmov'd, th' embody'd *Greeks* their Fury dare,
       And fix'd support the Weight of all the War:
155   Nor cou'd the *Greeks* repell the *Lycian* Pow'rs,
       Nor the bold *Lycians* force the *Grecian* Tow'rs.
       As on the Confines of adjoyning Grounds,
       Two stubborn Swains with Blows dispute their Bounds;
       They tugg, they sweat; but neither gain, nor yield,
160   One Foot, one Inch, of the contended Field:
       Thus obstinate to Death, they fight, they fall;
       Nor these can keep, nor those can win the Wall:

---

145. **boast,:** *1717:* boast?
147. **your Chief:** MS: I strive
148. **Attempts alone:** MS: With single Strength

---

146. Pope's addition.
150. The phrasing perhaps glances at the 'Union' of England and Scotland in 1707, one of the justifications for which was greater military strength in resisting invasion. Chapman, 404, p. 167, has 'the noble worke, of many, hath no match'; Ogilby, p. 276: 'With many Hands it will be better done'; Hobbes, p. 181: 'For many hands much better are than one', all close to Homer. See further Ferraro (1993a: 23) and Commentary to 'Spring', 89.
151. **just Rebuke:** perhaps recalled from Milton, *Paradise Lost*, IX.10: 'Anger and just rebuke, and judgment giv'n'. Chapman, 405, p. 167, has 'just rebuke' at this point, however. Pope discussed this and the ensuing few lines with Bridges; see Appendix.
153. **embody'd:** united in a body. *TE* compares Milton, *Paradise Lost*, I.574 (1674), p. 19: 'imbodied force'.

dare: brave, defy.
154. i.e. 'and standing firm, [the Greeks] bear the pressure of the whole fight'.
155-6. Pope's couplet is condensed from four lines of Homer (XII.417-20), whereas Ogilby, p. 276, and Hobbes, p. 181, both give the idea an equivalent set of four lines.
156. force: overpower, take.
157-60. See Pope's discussion of the simile with Bridges, Appendix. In the full translation, *Iliad* XII.511, Pope adds Eustathius's note commending the justness and effectiveness of the simile.
157. *TE* compares Hobbes, p. 182, 'As two men on the Confines of their ground'.
158. **stubborn Swains:** cf. 101. Homer, XII.421, has simply δύ' ἀνέρε ('two men'); Ogilby, p .276, calls the contestants 'Farmers'.
160. **contended:** disputed (cf. 1); Hobbes, p. 182, has 'Contending earnestly about their bound'.

Their Manly Breasts are pierc'd with many a Wound,
Loud Strokes are heard, and ratling Arms resound,
165   The copious Slaughter covers all the Shore,
And the high Ramparts drop with Human Gore.

As when two Scales are charg'd with doubtful Loads,
From side to side the trembling Balance nods,
'Till poiz'd aloft, the resting Beam suspends
170   Each equal Weight, nor this, nor that descends.
So Conquest loth for either to declare,
Levels her Wings, and hov'ring hangs in Air.
'Till *Hector* came, to whose Superior Might
Jove ow'd the Glory of the destin'd Fight.
175   Fierce as a Whirlwind, up the Walls he flies,
And fires his Host with loud repeated Cries:
Advance ye *Trojans*, lend your valiant Hands,
Haste to the Fleet, and toss the blazing Brands!
They hear, they run, and gath'ring at his Call,

168^9. 1717: (While some laborious Matron, just and poor,
  With nice Exactness weighs her woolly Store)
171–4. 1717: So stood the War, till *Hector*'s matchless Might
  With Fates prevailing, turn'd the Scale of Fight.

165–6. See Appendix for discussion of the appropriate 'simplicity' here.

166–72. Pope's simile is based on Homer's XII.433–6, but Homer's simile involves a γυνὴ χερνῆτις ἀληθής ('an honest woman manual labourer'; a 'Spinster poore and iust' in Chapman, 426, p. 168, similarly in Ogilby, simply a 'woman' in Hobbes, p. 182) balancing out wool in order to earn as much as possible for her family, an image Pope suppresses here, no doubt as insufficiently epic. Ogilby's marginal note, p. 277, stresses the importance of this 'rich *Simile*' and relates the ancient tradition that it concerned Homer's own mother. A second note on the same page gives further details of the economic practices featured. In the full translation, *Iliad*, XII.523, Pope partially relented and featured a 'laborious Matron, just and poor', inserting the note from Eustathius from which Ogilby derived his comment. See further commentary on Pope's indecision in Sowerby (2006: 243).

167. doubtful Loads: loads of virtually equal weight.

171. Conquest: Pope's version of 'Victory', the winged goddess known in Greek as Νίκη (Nike); but not so personified, or even mentioned, in Homer at this point. Pope might recall the opening of the sixth book of Chapman's *Iliad*, VI, p. 83: 'conquest, with doubtful wings', also not based on Homer.

173–4. Unless Pope is using 'owe' abnormally to mean 'confer ownership on', this is an odd reversal of Homer's logic: at XII.437 Homer says simply that Zeus κῦδος ὑπέρτερον Ἕκτορι δῶκε ('gave the highest glory to Hector'). Ogilby, p. 277, renders this: 'Till *Jove* that Honour did to *Hector* grant'.

173. Superior Might: Pope discussed this phrase with Bridges: see Appendix.

178. blazing Brands: burning torches.

80   THE EPISODE OF SARPEDON (1709)

180   Raise scaling Engines, and ascend the Wall:
      Around the Works a Wood of glitt'ring Spears
      Shoots up, and All the rising Host appears.
      A pondrous Stone bold *Hector* heav'd to throw,
      Pointed above, and rough and gross below:
185   Not two strong Men th' enormous Weight cou'd raise,
      Such Men as live in these degen'rate Days.
      Yet this, as easie as a Swain wou'd bear
      The snowy Fleece; he tost, and shook in Air:
      For *Jove* upheld, and lighten'd of its Load
190   Th' unwieldy Rock, the Labour of a God.
      Thus arm'd, before the folded Gates he came,
      Of massy Substance and stupendous Frame,
      With Iron Bars and brazen Hinges strong,
      On lofty Beams of solid Timber hung.
195   Then thundring thro' the Planks, with forceful Sway,
      Drives the sharp Rock; the solid Beams give way,
      The Folds are shatter'd, from the crackling Door

---

183. MS: The Chief advancing heav'd a Stone to throw,
187. **wou'd:** *1717:* could

---

180. scaling Engines: movable towers and ladders used in siege warfare; Chapman, 436, p. 168, has 'skaling ladders'. These are not in Homer (or Ogilby, or Hobbes) at this point: the warriors break through and clamber over by sheer force. In the full translation, *Iliad*, XII.483, Pope inserts Eustathius's note indicating that the action suggests that 'this Wall of the *Greeks* was not higher than a tall Man'.

181. glitt'ring Spears: TE compares Milton, *Paradise Lost*, I.547 (1674), p. 18: 'A Forrest huge of Spears'. This kind of phrasing was much favoured by Blackmore, e.g. *King Arthur*, IV (1697), p. 100: 'Lances, Swords and Woods of glitt'ring Spears'.

183. pondrous: very heavy.

184. gross: thick and bulky.

186. these degen'rate Days: Ogilby has a marginal note here (p. 277) on Homer's conventional idea of the former strength of mankind. In the full translation, *Iliad*, XII.455, Pope inserts Dacier's note on the issue of whether this comparison can be used to date the Homeric poems. Pope parodies the idea in *The Dunciad Variorum*, II.35–6: 'But such a bulk as no twelve bards could raise, | Twelve starveling bards of these degen'rate days'.

191. folded Gates: Homer's adjective (XII.455) is δικλίδας ('double-folding').

192. stupendous: 'wonderful; amazing; astonishing' (*SJ*).

193. brazen Hinges: cf. 65.

195–6. Pope omits Homer's detail (XII.458) of Hector planting his feet well apart to steady his position ('Fixing his Feet to re-enforce his Hands', Ogilby, p. 277).

197. crackling: splintering, corresponding to Homer's μέγα δ' ἀμφὶ πύλαι μύκον ('great creaking around the gates'), XII.460. Cf. 290. Chapman, 445, p. 168, has 'all the gates did cracke'.

>   Leap the resounding Bars, the flying Hinges roar.
>   Now rushing in the furious Chief appears,
> 200 Gloomy as Night, and shakes two shining Spears;
>   A dreadful Gleam from his bright Armour came,
>   And from his Eye-balls flash'd the living Flame:
>   He moves a God, resistless in his Course,
>   And seems a Match for more than Mortal Force.
> 205 Then pouring after, thro' the gaping Space
>   A Tide of *Trojans* flows, and fills the Place;
>   The *Greeks* behold, they tremble, and they fly,
>   The Shore is heap'd with Death, and Tumult rends the Sky.

---

199. **the furious Chief appears,:** MS: with two refulgent Spears;
200. MS: Brandish'd in Air, the gloomy Chief appears;
200^1. MS: Fierce as a black tempestuous Night, that brings
    Th' [   ] Thunder on its dusky Wings.

---

198. An Alexandrine, cf. 110; TE suggests an attempt to make sound echo sense; 'resounding' and 'roar' have no equivalent in Homer.

200. TE compares *Paradise Lost*, II.670-2, 'black it stood as Night... | And shook a dreadful Dart'. Homer describes Hector as νυκτὶ θοῇ ἀτάλαντος ὑπώπια, 'equal in countenance to swift-descending night' (XII.463), but otherwise says only that he held two spears (XII.464-5).

201. dreadful Gleam: cf. Dryden, 'Palamon and Arcite', II.244-5, *Fables*, p. 34: 'Like Lightning flam'd their Fauchions to and fro, | And shot a dreadful Gleam'.

203. resistless: irresistible; cf. Dryden, *Aeneid*, XII.546, *Works of Virgil*, p. 594: 'So where resistless *Turnus* takes his Course' (the ensuing rhyme word is 'force', as with 204 here). Cf. also *Essay on Criticism*, 215, and 'The First Book of Statius his Thebais', 270.

204. Homer (XII.465-6) says that οὔ κέν τίς μιν ἐρύκακεν ... | νόσφι θεῶν ('no-one could have restrained him except gods'), more closely rendered by Chapman and Hobbes. Pope also enhances Hector's sole power by omitting at this point his direct command to the other warriors to follow him (Homer, XII.467-8).

208. An Alexandrine (cf. 110).

Connection of the foregoing with the following Part.

The Wall being forc'd by Hector, *an obstinate Battel was fought before the Ships, one of which was set on fire by the* Trojans. Patroclus *thereupon obtaining of* Achilles *to lead out the* Myrmidons *to the Assistance of the* Greeks, *made a great Slaughter of the Enemy, 'till he was oppos'd by* Sarpedon. *The Combate betwixt these Two, and the Death of the latter, with the Grief of* Jupiter *for his Son, are describ'd in the ensuing Translation, from the Sixteenth Book of the* Iliads.

<pre>
        WHEN now the Chief his valiant Friends beheld
210   Grov'ling in Dust, and gasping on the Field,
        With this Reproach his flying Host he warms,
        Oh Stain to Honour! oh Disgrace of Arms!
        Forsake, inglorious, the contended Plain;
        This Hand unaided shall the War sustain:
215   The Task be mine the Hero's Strength to try,
        Who mows whole Troops, and makes whole Armies fly.

        He said, and leap'd from off his lofty Car;
        Patroclus lights, and sternly waits the War.
</pre>

---

209. **the Chief his valiant:** *1718: Sarpedon* his brave
212. **of:** *1718:* to
215. **the:** *1718:* this
216. **whole Armies:** *1718:* an Army
217. 1718: He spake; and speaking, leaps from off the Car;

Connection. *Patroclus:* the closest companion of *Achilles*, foremost of the Greek warriors; when Achilles withdrew from fighting because of a personal slight from the overall commander of the expedition, Agamemnon, Patroclus, in desperation, borrowed his armour and led out his troops (the *Myrmidons*). After wreaking much vengeful havoc on the Trojans, Patroclus kills Sarpedon and is then in turn killed by Hector, in the latter half of book XVI of the *Iliad*, bringing Achilles back into the war in the subsequent books; Achilles then kills Hector. The intervening books, XIII–XV, continue the story of the battle and the machinations of the warring Gods on behalf of their own favoured sides, as well as describing Patroclus's conversation with Achilles and his preparations for war.
209–321. Drawn from Homer, XVI.419–505.

209. At XVI.512 of the full translation, Pope inserted a very substantial note containing a 'Sketch of some Particulars which constitute a Character the most faultless and amiable in the whole Iliad'; see Headnote. The note goes on to suggest that Sarpedon's heroic death at this point foreshadows the fall of Hector and subsequently of Troy itself.
211. flying: retreating.
warms: to warm is to 'heat mentally, to make vehement' (*SJ*).
214–16. Largely Pope's invention, 214 perhaps recalling, as *TE* suggests, Dryden's *Aeneid*, XII.27, *Works of Virgil*, p. 579: 'This Arm unaided shall assert your Right' (Turnus speaking).
217. lofty Car: chariot; the phrase is used by Dryden, *Aeneid*, XI.962.
218. Originally Pope wrote 'The Greek descends', but Bridges objected that nobody

As when two Vulturs on the Mountain's Height
220   Stoop with their sounding Pinions to the Fight;
They cuff, they tear, they raise a screaming Cry;
The Desart ecchoes, and the Rocks reply:
The Warriors thus oppos'd in Arms engage,
With equal Valour, and with equal Rage.

225   *Jove* view'd the Combate, whose Event foreseen,
He thus bespoke his Sister and his Queen.
The Hour draws on; the Destinies ordain,
My God-like Son shall press the *Phrygian* Plain:
Already on the Verge of Death he stands,

---

220. their sounding: *1718:* re-sounding
223–4. MS: With equal Rage, descending on the Plain
    The warring Chiefs a dubious Fight maintain.
224. Valour: *1718:* Clamours
228. God-like: MS: valiant

---

would know which Greek (see Appendix). Homer names Patroclus at this point (XVI.427), as do Ogilby and Hobbes (but not Chapman).

219. Vulturs: in the full translation, at XVI.522, Pope inserts a note from Eustathius on the propriety of the simile and the details of the description.

220. Stoop: a term used in falconry to indicate the 'fall of a bird upon his prey' (*SJ*). In Homer the vultures ὄρουσαν ('darted'), towards each other.

    sounding Pinions: resounding wings. *TE* compares Garth, *Dispensary*, VI, sixth edition (1706), p. 99, describing (in mock-heroic vein) Jove's eagle: 'Stoops on his sounding Pinions from above'. Pope's imagery is more extended than Homer's (XVI.428–9), as is the case in Chapman's version (p. 226), but he drops some ornithological detail, as Brower (1959: 115) observes: γαμψώνυχες ἀγκυλοχεῖλαι ('crooked-clawed, hook-beaked'), is omitted; in Homer the warriors are κεκλήγοντες as they attack, the vultures κλάζοντε, both from κλάζω, 'shriek' or 'yell', an etymological link lost in translation.

221. cuff: 'strike with talons' (*SJ*).
222. Pope's addition.
224 MS, dubious: 'doubtful' in the sense of 70 and 168. Pope evidently struggled with the phrasing of this section; see the discussion with Bridges, Appendix.

226. Sister ... Queen: Hera: wife of Zeus, and like him, the child of Kronos and his sister Rhea. The phrasing recalls Dryden, 'Palamon and Arcite', I.107, *Fables*, p. 5: 'But left his Sister and his Queen behind'; but there the phrase indicates different women. Chapman, XVI.410, p. 227, and Hobbes, p. 247, both have 'wife and sister' here. In Homer, literally, 'of the same father [and] sharer of the bed' (κασιγνήτην ἄλοχόν, XVI.432). Cf. 'The First Book of Statius his Thebais', 366.

227. Destinies: 'fate' or 'fates' in most translations, corresponding to Homer's μοῖρ[α] (XVI.434; share, fate, lot).

228 and MS. The epithet Homer's Zeus actually uses here (XVI.433) is 'dearest of men' (φίλτατον ἀνδρῶν).

    press: lie heavily on.

Phrygian: in antiquity Phrygia was a large area of Asia Minor (roughly equivalent to modern Turkey), of which Troy was a city region.

229. Verge of Death: probably a deliberate allusion to Dryden, *Aeneid*, X.664, *Works of Virgil*, p. 518: 'And stands already on the Verge of Death', since the words are Jove's, recalling the death of Sarpedon while speaking of the imminent death of Turnus (more of the passage is quoted in the Commentary at 239–43 below).

230   His Life is ow'd to fierce *Patroclus*' Hands.
        What Passions in a Parent's Breast debate!
        Say, shall I snatch him from Impending Fate;
        And send him safe to *Lycia*, distant far
        From all the Dangers and the Toils of War;
235   Or to his Doom my bravest Off-spring yield,
        And fatten, with Celestial Blood, the Field?

        Then thus the Goddess with the radiant Eyes:
        What Words are these, O Sov'reign of the Skies?
        Short is the Date prescrib'd to Mortal Man;
240   Shall *Jove*, for one, extend the narrow Span,
        Whose Bounds were fix'd before his Race began?
        How many Sons of Gods, foredoom'd to Death,
        Before proud *Ilion* must resign their Breath!

---

235. **my bravest Off-spring:** MS: th' unhappy Warrior

---

231. The indication of the troubles of a 'Parent's Breast' here is not in Homer, who has at XVI.435 what Brower (1959: 122) takes to be the more personal inwardness of διχθὰ δέ μοι κραδίη μέμονε φρεσὶν ὁρμαίνοντι ('my split heart yearns within me as I turn this over in mind').

232. The phrasing is mentioned in the discussion with Bridges, Appendix. At the corresponding point (XVI.535) in the full translation, Pope inserted a long note beginning: 'It appears by this Passage, that *Homer* was of Opinion, that the Power of God could over-rule Fate or Destiny'. He controverts the opposite opinion of Dryden (based on a quotation about the death of Sarpedon in book X of Virgil's *Aeneid*, cited below in the commentary to 239–43), and asserts that Homer's view is demonstrated here by Zeus's 'Doubt and Deliberation in this Place.... *Homer*'s Opinion at least, as to the Dispensations of God to Man, has ever seem'd to me very clear, and distinctly agreeable to Truth'. Cf. 'The First Book of Statius his Thebais', 299.

236. Pope's substitution for Homer's ὑπὸ χερσὶ Μενοιτιάδαο δαμάσσω ('or let him be beaten by the son of Menoetius'), i.e. Patroclus, XVI.438.

237. **radiant Eyes:** In Homer, Hera is actually (XII.439) βοῶπις ('ox-eyed'), i.e. with very large eyes, a term of beauty for Homer but omitted by all the translators. Pope defended Homer's use of characteristic epithets as appropriate and significant in his own day, but inadmissible in translation, except where 'they derive an additional Beauty from the Occasions on which they are employed'; 'Preface' to the *Iliad* (1715), sig. F1r, *PW*, I. 248–9.

239–43. TE compares Dryden's *Aeneid*, X.657–61, *Works of Virgil*, p. 517 (Jove speaking): 'Short bounds of Life are set to Mortal Man, | 'Tis Vertues work alone to stretch the narrow Span. | So many Sons of Gods in bloody Flight, | Around the Walls of *Troy*, have lost the Light: | My own *Sarpedon* fell beneath his Foe ...'. Cf. also Commentary to *Essay on Criticism*, 477.

243. **Ilion:** Troy.

Were thine exempt, Debate wou'd rise above,
245 And murm'ring Pow'rs condemn their partial *Jove*.
Give the bold Chief a glorious Fate in Fight;
And when th' ascending Soul has wing'd her Flight,
Let *Sleep* and *Death* convey, by thy Command,
The breathless Body to his Native Land.
250 His Friends and People, to his future Praise,
A Marble Tomb and Pyramid shall raise,
And lasting Honours to his Ashes give;
His Fame ('tis all the Dead can have!) shall live.

She said; the Cloud-Compeller overcome,
255 Assents to Fate, and ratifies the Doom.
Then, touch'd with Grief, the weeping Heav'ns distill'd
A Show'r of Blood o'er all the fatal Field.

---

246. **bold:** MS: brave

244–5. The potential for political allusion here seems to have been largely passed over. Hobbes, p. 247, has Hera warn Zeus: 'take heed how you offend the State', and Ogilby's Hera cautions him (p. 360) not to over-use his 'Prerogative', in 1660 a highly loaded term because of its association with royal power.

248. Sleep *and* Death: so in Homer (XVI.454, order reversed): θάνατόν...καὶ...ὕπνον; described further, 344–5 below. In his full translation, XVI.551, Pope inserts a note, based on Dacier's commentary, relating to ancient funeral customs and the Lycian cult of Sarpedon. In Pope's later note, to 831 of the full translation, he calls Sleep and Death 'imaginary Deities', but they are referred to as 'terrible gods' (δεινοὶ θεοί) in a description of them by Hesiod, *Theogony*, 758–66.

249. breathless *Body*: The phrase is used at least four times in Dryden's version of the *Aeneid*, e.g. VI.318, *Works of Virgil*, p. 371 (opposite an engraving showing the scene).

251. *Pyramid*: In Homer this is a στήλη, an inscribed or decorated stone slab used as a memorial marker. Chapman, 425, p. 227, has 'columne'; Ogilby, p. 361, an '*Obelisk*'; Hobbes omits it (but see 333).

253. TE compares Dryden, *Aeneid*, VII.6, *Works of Virgil*, p. 400: 'Thy Name ('tis all a Ghost can have) remains'. At 457 Homer's Hera declares more flatly (of the monument, not of any 'fame') τὸ γὰρ γέρας ἐστὶ θανόντων ('For that is the due of the dead').

254. *Cloud-Compeller*: standard Homeric epithet of Zeus (νεφεληγερέτα), 'cloud-compelling' or 'cloud-gathering'; hence Pope's ironic use of it in relation to Dulness, *Dunciad Variorum*, I.77: 'the cloud-compelling Queen'. At this point in the original (XVI.458), however, Homer has πατὴρ ἀνδρῶν τε θεῶν τε ('father of gods and men') as his epithet for Zeus, which Brower (1959:123) takes to be more appropriate in the context of the impending loss of the son. Pope's chosen epithet returns, this time matching Homer, at 322. Pope's substitution at this point may relate to the 'Show'r of Blood' about to fall from the sky.

257. *Show'r of Blood*: At the corresponding point in the full translation (XVI.560) Pope inserts a note on this meteorological phenomenon, following Ogilby, who has a marginal note (p. 361) based on Eustathius. Pope sides with the view that such things were caused by a cloud of red insects, resembling blood.

The God, his Eyes averting from the Plain,
Laments his Son, predestin'd to be slain,
260 Far from the *Lycian* Shores, his happy Native Reign.

Now met in Arms the Combatants appear,
Each heav'd the Shield, and pois'd the lifted Spear:
From strong *Patroclus*' Hand the Jav'lin fled,
And pass'd the Groin of valiant *Thrasymed*,
265 The Nerves unbrac'd no more his Bulk sustain,
He falls, and falling, bites the bloody Plain.
Two sounding Darts the *Lycian* Leader threw,
The first aloof with erring Fury flew,
The next more fatal pierc'd *Achilles*' Steed,
270 The gen'rous *Pedasus*, of *Theban* Breed;
Fix'd in the Shoulder's Joint, he reel'd around;
Rowl'd in the bloody Dust, and paw'd the slipp'ry Ground.
His sudden Fall the entangled Harness broke;
Each Axle groan'd; the bounding Chariot shook;
275 When bold *Automedon*, to disengage
The starting Coursers, and restrain their Rage,
Divides the Traces with his Sword, and freed
Th' incumber'd Chariot from the dying Steed:
The rest move on, obedient to the Rein;
280 The Car rowls slowly o'er the dusty Plain.

---

261. **Combatants:** MS: warring Kings
269. 1718: The next transpierc'd *Achilles*' mortal Steed,
274. 1718: Each Axle crackled, and the Chariot shook:

---

264. **Thrasymed:** Thrasymedes, son of Nestor (XVI.321), specifically in Homer (XVI.463-5) a servant of Sarpedon's.
265. **Nerves:** cf. 130.
267. **sounding:** cf. 220.
268. **aloof:** at some distance.
270. **Pedasus:** horse of Achilles, won by him at the siege of Thebes; 'mortal' (revised version) by comparison with two other horses of Achilles, both immortal. At XVI.572 of the full translation Pope inserted a facetious note responding to Eustathius's contention that as a gelding Pedasus could not be immortal.
272. An Alexandrine; cf. 110.
274. **Each Axle groan'd:** Ogilby, p. 361: 'The Axell groans'.
275. **Automedon:** Achilles' charioteer.
276. **starting:** excited, animated.
  Coursers: horses.
  Rage: eagerness.
277. **Traces:** part of the harness holding the horses together; cf. 'Autumn', 62.

THE EPISODE OF SARPEDON (1709) 87

   The towring Chiefs to fiercer Fight advance,
   And first *Sarpedon* tost his weighty Lance,
   Which o'er the Warrior's Shoulder took its Course,
   And spent, in empty Air, its dying Force.
285 Not so *Patroclus* never-erring Dart;
   Aim'd at his Breast, it pierc'd the mortal Part
   Where the strong Fibres bind the solid Heart.
   Then as the stately Pine, or Poplar tall,
   Hewn for the Mast of some great Admiral,
290 Nods, groans, and reels, 'till with a crackling Sound
   It sinks, and spreads its Honours on the Ground;
   Thus fell the King; and laid on Earth Supine,
   Before his Chariot stretch'd his Form divine:
   He grasp'd the Dust, distain'd with streaming Gore,
295 And, pale in Death, lay groaning on the Shore.
   So lyes a Bull beneath the Lion's Paws,

---

281. **The towring Chiefs:** MS: The Chiefs oppos'd
282. **tost:** *1718:* whirl'd
288–90. 1718: Then, as the Mountain Oak, or Poplar tall,
   Or Pine (fit Mast for some great Admiral)
   Nods to the Axe, till with a groaning Sound
292. **Thus:** MS: So

281–321. Sowerby (2006: 238–40) focuses on Pope's expansions of Homer in this passage.

284. dying Force: Dryden has a similar phrase in *Aeneid*, X. 1116, but in that instance the javelin thrust hits its target. There is no equivalent in Homer.

285–7. See Pope's discussion with Bridges of the phrasing here, Appendix.

285. Dart: spear.

287. TE compares Chapman, 445, p. 227: 'where life's strings, close about the solid hart' (the rhyme word is 'part' in Chapman). Cf. also Ogilby, p. 361: 'The trembling Fibers peirc'd which guard his Heart'. In Homer, Patroclus hits the φρένες ... ἀμφ' ἀδινὸν κῆρ ('the midriff round the throbbing heart'); cf. 318–21 below.

289. Mast ... Admiral: already imitated in Milton, *Paradise Lost*, I.292–4 (1674), p. 11 (of Satan): 'His Spear, to equal which the tallest Pine | Hewn on *Norwegian* hills, to be the Mast | Of some great Ammiral, were but a wand'. In Homer the tree falls merely as ship's timber (νήϊον), cut down for that purpose by carpenters or τέκτονες ἄνδρες (483–4). See Headnote for the political undercurrent here.

290. crackling: cf. 197.

291. Honours: leaves, from the sense of 'ornament; decoration' (*SJ*); cf. 'Winter', 32, and *Windsor-Forest*, 219.

294. distain'd ... Gore: cf. 'The First Book of Statius his Thebais', 113 and Commentary.

296–9. Homer, XVI.487–9. Brower (1959: 116) observes that Pope has omitted Homer's more pastoral and local detail and intensified the savagery and bloodiness of the simile.

While the grim Savage grinds with foamy Jaws
The trembling Limbs, and sucks the smoking Blood;
Deep Groans and hollow Roars rebellow thro' the Wood.

300   Then to the Leader of the *Lycian* Band,
The dying Chief address'd his last Command.
Glaucus, be bold, Thy Task be first to dare
The glorious Dangers of destructive War,
To lead my Troops, to combate at their Head,
305   Incite the Living, and supply the Dead.
Tell 'em, I charg'd them with my latest Breath,
Not unreveng'd to bear *Sarpedon*'s Death.
What Grief, what Shame must *Glaucus* undergo,
If these spoil'd Arms adorn a *Grecian* Foe?
310   Then as a Friend, and as a Warrior, fight;
Defend my Corps, and conquer in my Right;
That taught by great Examples, All may try
Like thee to vanquish, or like me to die.

He ceas'd; the Fates supprest his lab'ring Breath,
315   And his Eyes darken'd with the Shades of Death:

---

309. **If**: MS: Shou'd

---

297. ***Savage:*** i.e. the lion of the simile. Cf. Commentary to 15.
298. ***smoking:*** steaming.
299. An Alexandrine, cf. 110.
   rebellow: to 'bellow in return' (*SJ*), a term specifically applied to bulls in e.g. Spenser, *Faerie Queene*, IV.x.46 'The raging Buls rebellow through the wood'.
302–13. This dying speech is particularly recommended for study by Pope in his long note to the corresponding line, 605, of the full translation, on the grounds that it is 'made up of noble Sentiments, and fully answering the Character of this brave and generous Prince, which he preserves in his last Moments'. It contains much that Pope invented, such as 305–6 and 311–13 (see further Sowerby 2006: 238–9 on Pope's endeavours to enhance congruity between the earlier speech to Glaucus and this dying speech).
302. For the form of address, see commentary on 43.
305. TE compares Dryden, *Aeneid*, IX.1052, *Works of Virgil*, p. 495: 'To save the living, and revenge the dead'.
   supply: replace.
306–7. Pope's addition.
306. ***latest:*** last.
309. ***spoil'd Arms:*** despoiled weapons and armour, appropriated as a prize by the enemy, as in Dryden, 'The Twelfth Book of Ovid his Metamorphoses', 616, *Fables*, p. 442: 'the spoil'd Arms of slain *Halesus*'.
311–13. Sowerby (2005: 160) observes that Pope's Sarpedon 'almost becomes a spokesman for Renaissance literary theory' in proposing 'great Examples' for others to imitate.

Th' insulting Victor with Disdain bestrode
The prostrate Prince, and on his Bosom trod;
Then drew the Weapon from his panting Heart,
The reeking Fibres clinging to the Dart;
320   From the wide Wound gush'd out a Stream of Blood,
And the Soul issu'd in the Purple Flood.

Then thus to *Phoebus*, in the Realms above,
Spoke from his Throne the Cloud-compelling *Jove*:
Descend my *Phoebus*, on the *Phrygian* Plain,
325   And from the Fight convey *Sarpedon* slain;
Then bathe his Body in the crystal Flood,

---

317. **Prince:** MS: Chief
321^2. 1718 has an additional 184 lines here.

---

316. insulting Victor: cf. 115 above. Pope might have recalled this phrase from Sandys, *Ouid's Metamorphosis Englished*, III (1632), p. 82, and Dryden uses it twice in his version of 'The Twelfth Book of Ovid his Metamorphoses', 190, 441, *Fables*, pp. 426, 435; for the idea in parody see also 'Rape of the Locke', II.142. Sowerby (2006: 239) argues that 'insulting' carries something of the Latin sense 'to leap at or on' as well its modern meaning. This image, 316-17, is a considerable modification of Homer, where Patroclus is described as λὰξ ἐν στήθεσι βαίνων ('going with his heel on the chest') in order to lever the spear out. The image of a 'prostrate Prince' is politically suggestive: it is not in Homer. Pope comments on Patroclus's pause in the note on his full translation, XVI.605.

318-21. Homer, XVI.504-5: ἐκ χροὸς ἕλκε δόρυ, προτὶ δὲ φρένες αὐτῷ ἕποντο: | τοῖο δ' ἅμα ψυχήν τε καὶ ἔγχεος ἐξέρυσ' αἰχμήν: ('he drew the spear from the body, the midriff came with it; he had drawn out his soul at the same time as the point of the spear'). Homer's 'φρένες' means the midriff, but also the heart, the parts about the heart, and in some respects the seat of thought, will and feeling. Chapman, 467, p. 228, has Patroclus draw out 'the filme and strings of his yet-panting hart'; the spear in Hobbes, p. 248, has 'pieces of the Midriff sticking to't'. Cf. 287.

319. reeking: steaming.

321. Purple Flood: Pope's addition; Motteux has this phrase in his version of Sarpedon's speech, p. 70. Cf. Ogilby, p. 362: 'His soul in Purple issuing on the Point'.

322-49. Based on Homer, XVI.666-83. In the gap (506-665), the fighting has continued, with Glaucus inspired by Sarpedon's death to pray to Apollo, successfully, to have his wound healed; there is much ensuing slaughter. The Greeks have, meanwhile, managed to strip Sarpedon's armour in precisely the way he feared.

322-3. The sublime and regal details are supplied by Pope: in Homer, Zeus merely Ἀπόλλωνα προσέφη, ('addressed Apollo').

322. Phoebus: Apollo (cf. 336), son of Zeus, sun-god but also god of medicine and healing.

326. crystal Flood: in Homer, Apollo is directed to clean up the body in a flowing river (λοῦσον ποταμοῖο ῥοῆσι). Chapman, 615, p. 231: 'cleare floud'; Ogilby, p. 367: 'Christall Brook'. Dryden uses the phrase 'crystal flood' widely, e.g. *Aeneid*, VII.1082 and IX.26, and for Pope's use of the adjective cf. 'January and May', 459; 'Summer', 27; 'Winter', 21; *Essay on Criticism*, 355; and *Windsor-Forest*, 374.

With Dust dishonour'd, and deform'd with Blood:
O'er all his Limbs *Ambrosial* Odours shed,
And with Celestial Robes adorn the mighty Dead.
330 Those Honours paid, his sacred Corps bequeath
To the soft Arms of silent *Sleep* and *Death*;
They to his Friends the mournful Charge shall bear;
His Friends a Tomb and Pyramid shall rear;
These unavailing Rites he may receive,
335 These, after Death, are All a God can give!

Apollo bows, and from Mount *Ida*'s Height
Swift to the Field precipitates his Flight;
Thence, from the War, the breathless Hero bore,
Veil'd in a Cloud, to silver *Simois* Shore:
340 There bath'd his honourable Wounds, and drest
His Manly Members in th' Immortal Vest,

---

329. **mighty:** *1718:* omitted
330. **Those Honours paid:** *1718:* Those Rites discharg'd
334. **unavailing:** *1709:* unvailing
334–5. 1718: What Honours Mortals after Death receive,
    Those unavailing Honours we may give!

---

327. **deform'd with Blood:** for 'deform' SJ has both 'disfigure' and 'dishonour'. Pope's phrase had been much used by Blackmore, e.g. *King Arthur*, VII (1697), p. 184: 'With Brains bespatter'd, and deform'd with Blood'. There is no equivalent in Homer.

328. **Ambrosial:** Homer, XVI.670, χρῖσόν τ' ἀμβροσίῃ, rendered by Ogilby, p. 367: 'with *Ambrosia* . . . | Anoynt him'. Ambrosia means 'undying'; it is the food of immortality, normally reserved for the Gods, used sometimes as embalming ointment. Cf. 'Nectar' (31). Pope parodies the idea in *The Dunciad Variorum*, II.80. The phrase 'ambrosial odours' is probably recalled from Milton, *Paradise Lost*, II.245.

329. **Celestial Robes:** cf. 341. Chapman, 617, p. 231: 'diuine weeds'; Hobbes, p. 252: 'immortal garment', equivalent to Homer's ἄμβροτα εἵματα (XII.670 and 680); Ogilby, 'heavenly weeds' (p. 367). Cf. 341 below.

331–5. Pope's variation on his version of Hera's lines at 250–3. In Homer the two sets of lines (XVI.671–5, and XVI.454–7), are closer verbally, and the final pair are identical.

331. **soft Arms:** Pope's addition.

333. **Pyramid:** cf. 251. Here Hobbes, p. 252, has 'Pillar', and Ogilby, p. 367, '*Obeliske*'.

336–49. Apollo's mission (XVI.679–83) almost exactly duplicates his instructions from Zeus (XVI.660–73); Pope varies the phrasing considerably.

336. **Ida:** mountain range stretching through Phrygia to the plain of Troy, sometimes regarded as a seat of the Gods.

337. **precipitates his Flight:** hastens down. *TE* compares Dryden, *Aeneid*, VIII.565, *Works of Virgil*, p. 450 (of Vulcan): 'Through the brown Air precipitates his Flight'. Dryden used the phrase many times in the Virgil translations.

339. **Simois:** river which rises on Mt Ida and flows across the Trojan plain towards the Scamander.

341. **Members:** limbs.

And with Perfumes of sweet *Ambrosial* Dews,
Restores his Freshness, and his Form renews.
Then *Sleep* and *Death*, two Twins of winged Race,
345 Of matchless Swiftness, but of silent Pace,
Receiv'd *Sarpedon*, at the God's Command,
And in a Moment reach'd the *Lycian* Land;
The Corps amidst his weeping Friends they laid,
Where endless Honours wait the Sacred Shade.

Vest: vestment, 'an outer garment' (*SJ*); cf. 329 above. Homer repeats his exact phrase, but Pope varies it.

342. Ambrosial Dews: cf. 328, and the mock-heroic description in Garth, *The Dispensary*, sixth edition, VI (1706), p. 112: 'Ambrosial Dews descend...'.

344. Twins: so in Homer, XVI.682: διδυμάοσιν. Chapman, 618, p. 231, has 'twins'; Hobbes, p. 252, 'sisters'. In the 'Commentarius' section at the end of book XVI in Chapman's version, and in the margin at this point in Ogilby's translation, p. 367, there are notes on the propriety, in ancient culture, of having Sleep and Death take over care of the corpse and on Eustathius's contention that in Lycia there was no real funeral but an empty ceremony; at XVI.831 of the full translation Pope inserts a note further discussing this contention, concluding: 'it is probable the Poet intended only to represent the Death of this favourite Son of *Jupiter*, and one of his most amiable Characters, in a gentle and agreeable View, without any Circumstances of Dread or Horror; intimating by this Fiction, that he was delivered out of all the Tumults and Miseries of Life by two imaginary Deities, *Sleep* and *Death*, who alone can give Mankind Ease and Exemption from their Misfortunes'.

348-9. Without equivalent in Homer.

349. Shade: ghost, spirit. 'Sacred shade' is usually used in poetry of landscape, e.g. Dryden, *Aeneid*, VIII.359 and XII.1111, but here the sense of the human spirit must predominate; it is used of Virgil's posthumous spirit in Tate's *Syphilis* (1686), p. 36.

APPENDIX.

The surviving manuscript material relating to the 'Episode of Sarpedon' held in the British Library (Add MS 4807, fols 201–7^v and Add MS 4808, fols 19–23) includes the following exchanges between Pope and Ralph Bridges (Add MS 4807, fols 194–9). A transcription, based on the Percy Transcripts in the Bodleian Library, was published by an anonymous correspondent in Vol. XI (June 1787) of the *European Magazine and London Review*, and some of the exchanges are reproduced in *TE* I, 354–5. Julian Ferraro's 'Rising into Light' (unpublished PhD thesis, Cambridge University, 1993b) transcribes the original manuscript, together with the previously unpublished manuscript of the 'Episode' itself.

Pope evidently sent Bridges a manuscript of an earlier draft of the poem for comment and Bridges seems to have marked lines and passages in the manuscript and cued these either to comments in the margins or on six separate sheets of paper. Pope has then either used the cropped margins or the separate sheets to fill in relevant lines from the original draft and quotations from the original Greek, together with his responses to Bridges's comments. These seem then to have been returned to Bridges to form the basis of further discussion between the two men. The laborious process revealed by the exchanges with Bridges are evidence both of the pains that Pope took to anticipate criticism of his translation on the grounds of its fidelity, and of his confidence in asserting the primacy of English poetic precedent (particularly that of Dryden) and faithfulness to the spirit of Homer over strict fidelity.

Bridges's comments are reproduced in bold, Pope's responses in plain type. In the one instance in which a specific passage is not clearly indicated in the manuscript, the lines of the 'Episode' to which it refers have been supplied in square brackets.

194. ~~(1)~~

    Homer, Iliad. M. line 298.

    Βη ρ ιμζυ ϖ τε λεϖν- &c – yᵉ whole simile
    – And while two pointed Javelins arm his hands,
    Majestic moves along, and leads his Lycian Bands.
    So fill'd with sullen Rage & stern Disdain,
    The Lordly Lion stalks across the Plain, &c.

x   **This Simile you seem to have apply'd to yᵉ verses above; whereas according to Homer the Lines below are to be applyd to it.** Pray give me your opinion of yᵉ 2 lines below wᶜʰ I have added to yᵉ end of yᵉ simile & be pleased to read Homer once more in this place, for he seems to me to connect yᵉ simile both wᵗʰ wᵗ goes before & wᵗ follows.

---

    x He foams, he roars, he rends the panting Prey.
x   **This is not in y.ᵉ Original.** I own this is added to yᵉ original; would it be better thus? He rushes to yᵉ Prey.?
"Being resolv'd (says o.ʳ Auth.ʳ) to get "his Prey, or be wounded in y.ᵉ attempt. Not that he is actually master of it.

ϕ   The two first of the following lines are added to clear yᵉ comparison, according to y.ʳ Sense of it. They immediatly follow yᵉ Simile. – He foams, he roars, he rushes to the Prey.
    Thus to the Fort Divine Sarpedon goes,
    Thus fix'd on Death, or Conquest, dares the Foes;
    O'erlooks the Tow'rs, and Meditates their Fall,
    To sure Destruction dooms th' aspiring Wall:
    Then casting on his Friend an Ardent Look,
    Fir'd with the Thirst of Glory, thus he spoke. &c –

(2)
− **Extended**[x] <u>Reign</u>.

**x I question not, but you have good
Autority for using that word so.**
    x   Mr Dryden's, in several places.

---

flows along
the Plain[x] **or some such word that is more
agreable to y.ᵉ plainess requird in a Speech.**
    The Lines, as they are now corrected, & made
nearer to ye sence of Homer, are these.
    Why boast
    Where
    Our
    And
    Why
    Admir'd
I wish you had read Sr. John Denham's Transla
tion of this Speech wᵗʰ mine (wᶜʰ is printed in his Po
ems). Do you think it will not be necessary I shou'd
make some Apology to yᵉ World, in yᵉ Argument or other
wise, for attempting the Speech after that Author?

195. ~~(3)~~
  1 The opposition betwixt Renown & Immorta
  :lity to me seems not to be exact.
  What think you of <u>Disgrace</u> or <u>old Age</u> ?
2 Alter these. This is Homer's Sense.
"At y.ᵗ rate, (Says Sarpedon) I my self w.ᵈ never
"be y.ᵉ foremost in Battle, nor w.ᵈ I ever desire
"You to engage in war.

---

3. Leave out these two lines

4.   Lets   both

5. Leave out these lines also. – If I
mistake not, the six only do sufficiently &
very well express the sense of the three
verses in Homer.

      See overleaf.

(4)
      Hom. Il. M. lin. 322. beginning –
          Ω πεπον ει μεν γαρ πολεμον – &c –
1. 2.   The Verses were thus when you objected to 'em.
        Cou'd we, by Flight, elude the Fates Decree,
        1 Or change Renown for Immortality,
        2 What glorious Madman then wou'd vainly dare
        In fighting Fields, or urge thy Soul to War?
Do you approve of this Alteration?
        Cou'd all our Care elude the Fate's Decree,
X   Or flight secure our Immortality,
        For Lust of Fame I wou'd not vainly dare
        In fighting Fields, nor urge thy Soul to War,
           Or of this?
        Cou'd we, by Flight, elude the Fate's Decree,
        Fame were well lost for Immortality,
        Nor shou'd I then for Lust of Glory dare
        In fighting Fields, or urge thy Soul to War.
              <u>But since &c</u>
Is the sense of either of these clear enough? is there no
objection to ye Second line of the first of these Alterations
mark'd thus x In short wch do you like best, or do
you like none?

---

                two

3. You would have ~~these~~^ lines here left out, wch there
is a necessity of keeping in to clear ye Sense, as when
we meet I will show you.

5. These two Lines I have left out, as you advise.

196. ~~(5)~~

Hom. Il. M. line 390.
x Αψ^δ   απο   τειχεος αλτο   λαθων.–   He secretly retires
from yᵉ Lines. – That's all Homer says of him.

---

x Wᵗʰ deep regret the Lycian King beheld
His Friend retreating, and his Troops repelld.
x   **It does not appear in Homer that
Glaucus' Troops retreated with him. I rather
believe yᵉ contrary.**   Altered thus.
        With deep regret the Lycian King beheld
        Disabled Glaucus slowly quit the Field.

(6)
    Hom. Iliad M. line 397. beginning -
    Σαρπηδων δ αρ επαλξιν ελων
    x   **πολεεσσι   δε θηκε κελευθον**
    "And opens a way for a multitude to enter.
    This I think ought to be put in another verse,
    & added to ye two excell.t lines above.
Do you approve them thus altogether?

        Swift to the Battlement the Victor flies,
        Tugs with full force, & ev'ry Nerve applies;
        It shakes; the pond'rous Stones disjointed yield;
        The rowling Ruins smoak along the Field.
   x   A mighty Breach appears, the walls lie bare,
        And, like a Deluge, rushes in the War. – .

---

   x   Hom. Iliad. M. line 406. Χωρησεν δ αρα τυτθον επαλξιος –
"Then turning to his Lycian Troops he
"thus encourages them. – That's what Homer
says. – By all means alter those lines.
        The lines objected to were these –
With his own fires his fainting Troops he warms,
Revives their Rage, and animates their Arms.
        Will the following do?
Then rais'd with Hope, and fir'd with Glory's charms
His fainting Squadrons with these words he warms.
               &c.
(For you will find Homer mentioning in this place the Hopes Sarpedon had of gaining Glory in this Battle – <u>επει οι θυμος εελπετο κυδO αρεαθαι</u>.)

197. ~~(7)~~

Ilias lib. 12. M. beginning at the 413th line,
    Ως εφαθ, οι δε ανακτO υποδδεισαντες ομοκλην
This just Reproach inflam'd the Lycian Crew,
They join, they thicken, and th' Assault renew;

Unmov'd, th' embodied Greeks their Fury dare,^{bear}
And fix'd,   the Weight of All the War;

<u>As</u> on the Confines of adjoyning Grounds,
Two stubborn Swains with Blows dispute their Bounds;
They tug, they sweat, but neither gain, nor yield,
One Foot, one Inch, of the contended Field.
x <u>Thus</u> obstinate alike, they fight, they fall;
Nor these can keep, nor those can win the Wall.
Their manly Breasts are piercd with many a wound,
Loud strokes are heard, & ratling Arms resound - &c.

x   **Unless You compleat the Comparison,**
with a <u>Thus</u>; Y.^r Readers will be at a loss
to distinguish, whether you mean ye Swains
in ye simile, or ye Troops engagd in Fight.
        See the whole Passage, (as it is altred) above – The
1. 3. 4. 5. 6. lines are newly altered –

(8)
The Trench is fill'd,
    x – ^ the Tow'rs are cover'd oer

With copious Slaughter, and with floods of Gore.
X That is not agreable to Homer's Simplicity.
But however it may doe.   Or this?
        The copious Slaughter covers all the Shore,
        And the high Rampires drop wth human Gore.

– x Superior might.
x   **You need not alter that.** (It was only marked as having been twice us'd in this Translation, ye other has been since put out, so this stands.)

———————

198. ~~(10)~~

x The Greek descends –
**x Patroclus must be mentiond here expressly
by name, or y.ᵉ readers left to guess
who this Greek is.**
        Patroclus lights, and sternly waits the War.

---

x With equal clamours issuing on the Ground
x by all means change that Verse
I cou'd have been glad to have known what it was you
objected to in this verse. Whether to yᵉ Expression, Issuing
on yᵉ Ground, (wᶜʰ Mʳ Dryd. uses) or to yᵉ Clamours,
wᶜʰ makes a pᵗ of yᵉ Simile in Homer? I do not well
know how to alter it, till you tell me. Is this better
or worse?
        ~~alighting~~ on the Plain,
With equal Rage, descending on the Ground,
        The warrior Kings a dubious Fight maintain.
Fought the fierce Kings, & wound return'd for wound.
It is yᵉ simile of the Vulturs in yᵉ 16th Iliad, line, 428
Οι δ ωστ αιγυπιοι γαμψωνυχες αγκυλοχειλαι
Πετρη εφ υψηλη μεγαλα κλαζοντε μαχονται,
Ωs οι κεκληγοντες επ αλληλοισιν ορουσαν.

---

x Impending Fate.
  **x I see no reason for any alteration
there.** (Twas markd only on accᵗ of having been
us'd in another place, & is to remain here)

[ll. 238–53]
**x You need not alter this. To do you
Justice here, once for all: you have an
admirable Talent in Turning Homer's
Speeches, w.ᶜʰ I always thought the
best & most difficult part of Him.**

(11)   199.

 x **by all means alter that.** (M[r] Dryden
led me into it. Virg. Aen. 12. The Lance drove on, &
      bore along the Death.)
x This was the following expression:
  Not so Patroclus deadly Spear; that sung
  <u>Thro' cleaving Skies, & bore the Death along</u>
  Aim'd at his Brest, it piercd the Mortal Part
  Where the strings close around the solid Heart.
Do you approve of this Alteration? which is nearer
the words of y[e] original than y[e] former
  Not so the Greek's inevitable Dart,
  Which pierc'd his Breast, & found the mortal p[t]
  Where the strings close around the solid Heart.

Sir, I observe you have made very few Remarks
on this second Part of the Episode of Sarpedon, &
fear it was want of Time, not want of seeing
the faults, that caus'd it to pass wth fewer blots
than the other.

3
PASTORALS
(1709)

Editors' Headnote

Composition and publication

The *Pastorals* were first published on 2 May 1709. In a note at the head of the surviving fair-copy manuscript, Pope states that the poems were first written in 1704 and circulated amongst a select group of patrons, poets and critics:

> This Copy is that w[ch] past thro y[e] hands of M[r] Walsh, M[r] Congreve, M[r] Mainwaring, Dr. Garth, M[r] Granville, M[r] Southern, Sr H. Sheers, Sr W. Trumbull, L[d]. Halifax, L[d] Wharton, Marq. of Dorchest[r]. D. of Bucks. &c. Only y[e] 3rd Eclog was written since some of these saw y[e] other 3. w[ch] were written as they here stand wth y[e] Essay [i.e. 'A Discourse on Pastoral Poetry', reproduced in Appendix II below], anno 1704. – Aetat. meae, 16./The Alterations from this Copy were upon y[e] Objections of some of these, or my own.

There are some discrepancies in Pope's accounts elsewhere of the early readers of the *Pastorals*, but it is significant that almost all had been associated in some way with Dryden (see *OAC*, II.616–18). Elsewhere, Pope was at pains to stress both this early date of composition (the half title in the *Works* of 1717 reads 'Written in the Year 1704') and the help he received to refine these 'green Essays' (to Wycherley, 25 March 1705, *Corr.*, I.5), as well as the care he had taken to polish the verse: 'There is scarce any work of mine in which the versification was more laboured than in my *Pastorals*' (*OAC*, I.175).

On 20 April 1706 Jacob Tonson the younger wrote to Pope seeking to publish the 'pastoral' he had lately seen 'in mr. Walsh's & mr Congreves hands, which is extreamly ffine & is generally approv'd off by the best Judges in poetry' (*Corr.*, I.17; and see Bernard 2015: 157, where the younger Tonson is identified as the contact). On 28 October 1707 Ralph Bridges told his uncle, Sir William Trumbull (see further below) that Pope 'designs in the Spring to print & publish his Pastorals' (Sherburn 1958a: 343). It was not until 4 March 1707/8, however, that Pope received from Tonson the sum of ten guineas 'for ye Tale of Chaucer, and the Eclogues' (Sherburn 1934: opp. 85). In the course of these two years, Pope made several rounds of revision, one stage of which is preserved along with the manuscript in a series of exchanges with Walsh reproduced in Appendix I below. Pope's updating of the poem's one topical allusion suggests that this process went on well into 1707. In the manuscript, the lines '*Say Daphnis, say, what Region canst thou find,* | *In which by Thistles, Lilies are outshin'd?*' might be taken to refer to the defeat of the French at Blenheim on 13 August 1704. In his exchanges with Walsh, Pope arrives at a new version which might be taken as an allusion to the re-design of the Royal Arms of England, approved by Queen Anne on 6 March 1706, in which the Scottish emblem took pride of place from the French Lily: 'Nay tell me first, in what more happy Fields | The *Thistle* springs, to which the *Lilly* yields?' ('Spring', 89–90). There is also some evidence (Foxon 1991: 22) to suggest that Pope was enabled by Tonson to undertake a final round of revision in proof before, on 2 May 1709, the *Pastorals* were finally published as the last item in *Poetical Miscellanies: The Sixth Part*. Tonson had begun his series of *Poetical Miscellanies* in 1684 claiming, in later editions, that they were 'Publish'd by Mr. Dryden'. Each of the first four volumes opened with a hundred or so pages of Dryden's verse, supplemented with the work of other writers, and, as such, they can be seen to provide a model for Pope's later venture with Lintot. In the sixth volume, Pope's *Pastorals* share pride of place with those of Ambrose Philips (c. 1675–1749), the status of both poets' work emphasised by the use of superior paper for Philips's poem and Pope's 'January and May' along with separate title pages for both sets of *Pastorals* (Foxon 1991: 18–23). In a letter to Ralph Bridges of 28 May 1709, Pope makes explicit his somewhat equivocal sense of the rite of passage involved in the printed publication of his work through the commercial offices of the book trade:

> I guess you perceive by this time, on a Review of my Part of the Book, that Manuscripts, like Pictures, tho ordinary enough, may be thought tolerable when shown for a Rarity; & that tis with false Wit as with false Jewells, those may pass unsuspected in a private Cabinet, which would be of small account in the Shop.

In the same letter he goes on compare in ironic terms his 'obscure State' as 'a private Scribbler before' with his new-found status 'after . . . being erected into an Author and created an Eminent Hand by Jacob, who makes Poets as Kings sometimes make Knights, for Money, and not for their Honour' (Sherburn 1958b: 395–6).

For a full-length study of the genesis and compositional development of the *Pastorals*, see Prest (1977).

Text

The text presented here is taken from the first edition of 1709. For the sake of clarity, manuscript variants are recorded in the form in which they first appear, with subsequent stages of revision recorded and discussed in the Commentary, only when they are of particular interest. Beyond the first edition, significant revision is confined to three later texts, the *Works* of 1717, 1736 and 1751, which also embody considerable expansions in the explicatory apparatus, as well as the addition of the 'Discourse on Pastoral Poetry', the short essay on the subject matter, major writers and appropriate language of pastoral which was probably written before 1705 but not published until 1717 (see Appendix II; also printed in *PW*, I.297–302, and *TE*, I.23–33). Pope's notes were first included in the *Works* of 1736. The various extant texts of the *Pastorals* are referred to in the apparatus as follows:

> MS: 'First Copy of the Pastorals' and 'Alterations to the Pastoralls' (reproduced in Prest 1977, Mack 1980 and 1984; *IELM* PoA 273 and 274)
>
> *1709*: *Poetical Miscellanies: The Sixth Part*, octavo (Griffith 1)
>
> *1716*: *The Sixth Part of Miscellany Poems*, duodecimo (Griffith 61)
>
> *1717*: *Works*, quarto (Griffith 79)
>
> *1736*: *Works*, vol.I, octavo (Griffith 413, 414)
>
> *1740*: *Works*, vol.I, part I, octavo (Griffith 510)
>
> *1751*: *Works*, vol.I, octavo (Griffith 643)

Models and sources

In his *Dictionary* (1755), Samuel Johnson defined 'pastoral' as 'A poem in which any action or passion is represented by its effect upon a country life, or according to the common practice in which speakers take upon them the character of shepherds'. In support, Johnson cited a passage from Pope's 'Discourse on Pastoral Poetry.' So far as Pope was concerned, pastoral as a genre originated with Theocritus, a Sicilian poet of the early third century BC who worked at the court of Alexandria around 270 BC. He was the author of some highly varied poems in Greek, traditionally thirty in number though not all now reckoned authentic, later known as *Idyllia* or 'vignettes'. Among the poems are some sufficiently rural in scope (notably the earlier ones in the sequence) to have established the formal characteristics of the genre as later understood, such as the shepherd's love complaint, the repeated refrain, the lament for the dead shepherd-poet, and the antiphonal singing contest between shepherds celebrating their rival loves and competing for a suitable prize. 'Arcadia', later the name for a generalised pastoral utopia, was the name of an area of Southern Greece from which many settlers had arrived in Sicily; 'Doric' was their dialect of Greek, used by Theocritus as a literary device for the entertainment of the sophisticated Alexandrian court rather than as an example of 'natural' pastoral dialect as such. (His basic metre was Homeric hexameter.) Theocritus had two notable successors writing in Greek at least a century later: Bion (late second century BC), whose lament for the dying Adonis formed an extended model of pastoral elegy; and Moschus (mid-second century BC), whose elegy for Bion established the pastoral elegy as specifically appropriate for a dead poet (see Schenck 1988); these were each translated into English (via French) by John Oldham (1653–83), and a further version from Moschus was published in *Examen Poeticum* in 1693. The wide European influence of Theocritus is described in Rosenmayer (1969). *Sixe Idillia: that is, sixe small, or petty poems, or aeglogues, chosen out of the right famous Sicilian poet Theocritus, and translated into English verse*, appeared in 1588 and translations from the third and eleventh Idylls, by Dryden and Richard Duke, appeared in *Miscellany Poems* in 1684. Five further translations, some by William Bowles, were published in *Sylvae* in 1685. Pope owned a copy of the fuller translation by Thomas Creech, *The Idylliums of Theocritus* (1684) (Mack 1982: 443, item 158).

Virgil (Publius Vergilius Maro, 70–19 BC) was author of ten hugely influential pastoral poems originally known as *Bucolica* (literally, 'things pertaining to herdsmen') and latterly as *Eclogae* or eclogues ('selections'). These were in some instances closely based on Theocritus, but with a strong admixture of contemporary detail drawn from Virgil's own experience as a landowner dispossessed in civil war. Virgil's eclogues also featured more high-minded and noble rural figures than the fishermen, threshers and goatherds (not to mention the Cyclops) populating the world of Theocritus. The poems were school text exercises, and had been translated several times, including a several-hands version in *Miscellany Poems* (1684) and most recently by Dryden in *The Works of Virgil* (1697); Pope bought a copy of the 1709 edition of this in 1710 (Mack 1982: 459, item 171). The great majority of Pope's own notes on his allusions and imitations in these poems signal his homage to Virgil. 'Messiah' (1712) would be his Christianised version of Virgil's fourth *Eclogue* (see Headnote to that poem for further details of the reception and translation of Virgil's pastoral poems).

The earlier exponents of pastoral in English, such as Alexander Barclay and Barnaby Googe, used the form partly for satiric purposes, pitting the simple living of the countryside against the religious corruptions of the town. Pastoral verse (and drama and prose) was enormously popular during the English Renaissance, eliciting sequences and versions from Samuel Daniel, Phineas Fletcher, William Browne, and Michael Drayton, and a popular anthology, *England's Helicon* (1600). Pope's major English model was Edmund Spenser, an early favourite author of his (*OAC*, I.19), whose *Shepheardes Calender*, in twelve '*Aeglogues*' (one for each month, to some extent prefiguring Pope's seasonal emphasis and elaborate scheme of time–age parallels), appeared in 1579; at some point Pope owned a copy of the 1611 folio collection Spenser's works (Mack 1982: 441–2, item 153). While calling on classical models, Spenser represented an anglicising form of pastoral, with a greater sense of local rather than classical landscape and lore, and especially by use of provincial and supposedly rustic dialect, in imitation of the Doric of Theocritus. His pastorals were also unusually varied in stanzaic and metrical terms. They contained a considerable amount of Protestant-leaning political and religious comment by way of allegory, an element retained in Milton's influential pastoral elegy 'Lycidas' (published in an anthology of elegies for Edward King in 1638) but increasingly suppressed in later seventeenth-century versions of pastoral. Spenser also developed the tradition of adopting a pastoral soubriquet, in his case 'Colin Clout', and of using pastoral identities in elegising dead poets ('Astrophel', for Sir Philip Sidney). That pastoral could embody a serious allegory or disguised commentary on some higher matter, and was thus not really about rural life at all, was accepted by both Sidney (in the *Defence of Poesie*, 1595) and George Puttenham in *The Art of English Poesie* (1589).

Pastoral scenes were also common in Baroque art, such as Nicolas Poussin's *Four Seasons* series (painted 1660-4; for comparison with Pope's poems see Melchiori 1963). The genre remained popular among restoration poets and was modified and parodied by, among others, Andrew Marvell; John Wilmot, Earl of Rochester; and Aphra Behn, in the case of the latter two with a marked increase in overt sexual content. Pastoral remained one of the approved generic opportunities for emerging women authors of the period, sometimes in imitation of Pope (see Messenger 2001). The Dryden-Tonson series of *Miscellanies*, beginning with *Miscellany Poems* in 1684, usually included some examples of the form, and Pope's mentor William Walsh contributed a closing pastoral elegy (alluded to by Pope in 'Winter') to *Poetical Miscellanies: The Fifth Part* (1704). The inclusion of Pope's pastorals in Tonson's 1709 *Poetical Miscellanies: The Sixth Part* was therefore natural enough, though Dryden himself, Pope's model for so many other genres, largely avoided it outside the Virgil translations.

For general treatments of the genre see Alpers (1996).

Context

As Congleton (1952) shows, in the later seventeenth century Pastoral became a subject of extensive critical debate in France and England. The view that Pastoral should be an idealised recreation of an idyllic 'Golden Age' was espoused by the French critic René Rapin (1621-86), in a substantial Latin preface ('Dissertatio De Carmine Pastorali') to his own pastorals (*Eclogae Sacrae*, 1659). The essay, freighted with much classical quotation and scholarly reference from the Renaissance onwards, was translated into English by Thomas Creech (1659-1700) to accompany his version of Theocritus (1684). On the assumption that pastoral had once been the authentic literary expression of early shepherd-kings and had therefore worth and dignity, Rapin sought to derive from the practice of Theocritus and (especially) Virgil a coherent Aristotelian schema of rules for a genre about which ancient critics were silent. An alternative view, termed 'rationalistic' by Congleton, was proposed by Bernard le Bovier de Fontenelle (1657-1757) in his *Discours sur la Nature de l'Eglogue* (1688), a treatise translated Peter Anthony Motteux (1663-1718) and published as 'Of Pastorals' in le Bossu's *Treatise of the Epic Poem* (1695), pp. 277-95. A new edition of Fontenelle's own *Poesies Pastorales* appeared in 1707. Fontenelle's view stressed the beneficial psychological effects of a literature devoted to a confessedly imaginary innocence and tranquillity rather than fidelity to polite classical models or a historically implausible Golden Age. Fontenelle recommended abstention from allegory, symbolism and satire in pastoral, concentration on the easy passion of love, and active suppression of the hardships of agrarian life, in favour of a fabricated dream-image of rural peace and innocent leisure in which the shepherd-figure himself was not even really necessary. Fontenelle's essay was regarded as one of the first blasts of the trumpet of the 'Moderns' against the 'Ancients', and Knightly Chetwood (1650–1720) provided a robust defence of the original authenticity of pastoral, and of the literary authority of Virgil, in his 'Preface' to Dryden's translation of the *Eclogues* in the *Works of Virgil* (1697).

There was in Britain a marked decrease in the political significance of pastoral, consonant with the views of Fontenelle, but it continued to be used to 'figure' some state events, particularly in the form of pastoral elegies, despite the complaints of critics such as William Coward (*Licentia Poetica Discuss'd*, 1709: 69–70). Pope's 'Discourse on Pastoral Poetry', not published with the poems but included as a sort of 'Preface' to them in the *Works* of 1717 (see Appendix II), provides a summary theoretical position which attempts to select a critical consensus from Rapin, Fontenelle and Chetwood. There was, in practice, much to agree on. For Pope, Pastoral has three main characteristics: 'simplicity, brevity and delicacy; the two first of which render an eclogue natural, and the last delightful'. Metre should, as Rapin suggests, be heroic, but 'the smoothest, the most easy and flowing imaginable'. Pastoral, Pope theorises in his 'Discourse',

> is an image of what they call the Golden age. So that we are not to describe our shepherds as shepherds at this day really are, but as they may be conceiv'd then to have been; when a notion of quality was annex'd to that name, and the best of men follow'd the employment.

In fact, not even this notion of a historical origin for pastoral is really necessary for Pope. 'Knowledge in rural affairs' may be useful, if skilfully deployed; but Pope follows Fontenelle in arguing that pastoral is not about 'real' countryside at all, whether historical or contemporary, but constitutes a pleasureable Arcadian fantasy. To sustain this it is necessary to 'use some illusion to render a Pastoral delightful; and this consists in exposing the best side only of a shepherd's life, and in concealing its miseries'. Of his models, Pope finds that Virgil succeeds most fully. Pope adheres to Rapin's view that pastoral ought to be written in 'heroic' measure, and censures Spenser's varying metrical experiments on that account, just as he dislikes Spenser's use of obsolete words and provincialisms as low and inadequate as an equivalent to Theocritus's Doric. He also disapproves of Spenser's allegorical use of Pastoral, preferring again an innocent version of 'Nature'. Theocritus's own great fault is that 'his swains are sometimes abusive and immodest, and perhaps too much inclining to rusticity'. Virgil refines on Theocritus in all ways, albeit at the loss of some 'simplicity'. The *Pastorals* themselves embody some attempt to include something of Spenser's specific Englishness alongside Virgil's classical Arcadia; but although Pope wrote of the English landscape on the basis of his life in Binfield, in Windsor Forest, and although he used some English flower names in the poems, his use of heroic couplets against Spenser's varied metres, and classical literary names rather than Spenserian rustic ones, signalled Pope's essentially Virgilian aspirations.

Those aspirations were carefully nurtured. Pope's published note, invocations of writers in the poems themselves, and annotation on the manuscript itself about the poem's draft circulation all serve to signal an unusually high degree of conscious intention behind the *Pastorals*. His elaborate pre-publication preparations implicated an entire phalanx of established writers and noble patrons (the categories not necessarily distinct) to act as guard of honour to his first publication. Sir William Trumbull (1639-1716) was a MP and diplomat, and an early mentor and patron of Pope; he had been Secretary of State from 1695 but in 1697 was manoeuvred into resigning and lived thereafter at Easthampstead, Berkshire, near the Pope family home at Binfield. (Pope's account of their days reading and riding in Windsor Forest is in *OAC*, I.31.) Pope dates the friendship from before 1704; the earliest correspondence is Trumbull to Pope, 15 June 1706, *Corr.*, I.17. William Walsh (1663-1708) was a poet and critic, celebrated by Dryden, and another early friend and mentor of Pope's (*OAC*, I.31-2), celebrated also in *Essay on Criticism*, 730; Walsh apparently desired the acquaintance of Pope after Wycherley sent him the *Pastorals* manuscript in 1705 (*Corr.*, I.7, 20 April 1705). Samuel Garth (1661-1719), a respected physician and Fellow of the Royal Society, was a member of Dryden's circle and the author of the popular mock-heroic poem *The Dispensary* (1699), on a squabble between doctors and apothecaries, a major influence on Pope, especially in *The Rape of the Lock*. A poem by Garth appeared at pp. 324-6 of the volume of *Miscellanies* in which the *Pastorals* appeared. From 1717 he was dedicatee of 'Summer'. William Wycherley (1641-1715), a poet and dramatist, was Pope's 'first poet-friend' (*OAC*, I.32), his earliest known correspondent, and dedicatee of 'Autumn', a favour returned in his commendatory poem for Pope in the same volume. George Granville, first Baron Lansdowne (1666-1735), was a poet and Tory politician, and later dedicatee of Pope's *Windsor-Forest* (1713), the '*Granville* the polite' of the *Epistle to Dr Arbuthnot* (135). Charles Montagu, first Earl of Halifax (1661-1715), was a politician and literary patron, later a strong supporter of Pope's translation of *The Iliad*. John, Baron Somers (1651-1716), was a lawyer, statesman and literary patron, and dedicatee of Jonathan Swift's *Tale of a Tub* (1704). Arthur Maynwaring or Mainwaring (1668-1712), was a writer and politician, formerly a supporter of the exiled James II and his descendants, later a writer in the Whig interest (for Pope's awareness of this change see *OAC*, I.203, item 475).

On the manuscript itself Pope noted some more eminent men who had been consulted: William Congreve (1670-1729), poet and dramatist, a lasting friend of Pope's and later dedicatee of Pope's *Iliad* translation; 'Southern', probably Thomas Southerne (1660-1746), a popular dramatist; 'Sir H. Sheers', probably Sir Henry Sheres (1641-1710), military engineer and poet; 'Ld Wharton', i.e. Thomas, first Marquess of Wharton (1648-1715), Whig politician; 'Marq. of Dorchester', i.e. Evelyn Pierrepoint, first Duke of Kingston (c. 1667-1726), created Marquess of Dorchester in 1706, and father of Pope's friend and later antagonist Lady Mary Wortley Montagu; 'D. of Bucks', i.e. John Sheffield, first Duke of Buckinghamshire (1648-1721), Jacobite courtier and poet, celebrated in the *Essay on Criticism* (see Commentary to 540 and 725 of that poem). These names represent cross-party interests and probably have as much to do with gaining social and political influence as literary judgment. Nonetheless the exchanges with Walsh in particular (see Appendix I) show an extraordinary degree of attention to verbal 'correctness' and other literary matters such as imitation and allusion.

Since the example of Virgil, whose *Eclogues* were succeeded by the didactic poem on agricultural subjects known as the *Georgics*, and finally by the epic of the founding of Rome, the *Aeneid*, pastoral had had the potential to act as a signal for high poetic ambition, which is certainly one reason why Pope announces his allusions so clearly. Spenser's progress from the pastoral *Shepheardes Calender* to the quasi-epic *Faerie Queene* described a similar trajectory, and Milton's pastoral elegy 'Lycidas' (1638) could be seen to have announced his intentions towards future epic (*Paradise Lost*, 1667). At pp. 253–6 of the *Poetical Miscellanies* appeared Wycherley's commendatory poem 'To my Friend, Mr. Pope, on his Pastorals', praising Pope for having rediscovered 'the long-lost Graces of Simplicity' in an appropriate literary dialect, and predicting that he would soon, like his model Virgil, 'take a higher Flight'. A further poem, 'To Mr Pope. By Another Hand' (pp. 257–61), noted Pope's ability to move from pastoral to the heroic verse of the 'Episode of Sarpedon'. Each emphasise aspects of Pastoral that Pope himself highlights in his 'Discourse'. (John Dennis, in his *Reflections* on the *Essay on Criticism* (1711: 29–30), claimed Pope wrote Wycherley's poem himself, a charge then repeated at least twice by Charles Gildon and addressed by Pope in his suppressed edition of Wycherley's letters in 1729; for documentation see Elias 1977, and for Wycherley's admiring letters on the *Pastorals* before publication, including reference to his own 'damn'd Compliment in Verse', see *Corr.*, I.49–50.) Pellicer (2008) cites an unpublished poem by Basil Kennett of 1710 which indicates that Pope's *Pastorals* had already been seen to lay claim to the wider political and poetic landscape of Sir John Denham's *Cooper's Hill*, even before *Windsor-Forest* (in some ways Pope's equivalent of Virgil's stepping stone to epic, *The Georgics*) made it obvious.

Trumbull and Bridges received their copies of the book with due courtesy in early May (Sherburn 1958a: 344). Wycherley repeatedly insisted to Pope that his 'portion' of the book was judged the best by 'Coffee-house Wits' and 'Criticks' (18 and 26 May 1709; *Corr.*, I.58–63). However, Pope's entry into print was offset by a competitor who also had powerful supporters. The first forty-eight pages of the volume were occupied by Six 'Pastorals, by Mr. [Ambrose] Phillips'. Four of these had already appeared in *Oxford and Cambridge Miscellany Poems* (1708). These were populated with Spenserian characters such as Lobbin, Thenot, Colinet, Cuddy and Hobbinol, and used English folklore rather than classical mythology, together with some Spenserian diction. They also had, like Pope's, an epigraph from Virgil on a divisional title page, and used heroic couplets as Pope did, so Virgilian aspiration was by no means abandoned. Philips (1674–1749) had also supplied a two-page 'Preface' on the pastoral genre and the pleasures of country life. Pope expressed careful and moderate praise of Philips's pastorals to Henry Cromwell, 28 October 1710 (*Corr.* I.100–1), but it was clear that the antagonistic singing contest which pastorals themselves dramatise internally was already happening between the two young poets. Spenser's pastoral *alter ego* 'Colin Clout' hangs his pastoral pipe on a tree at the end of 'December', offering the chance for later poets to pick up the role of England's pastoralist, and Philips noted the image in his fourth Pastoral. He also noted in his 'Preface' that 'Virgil *and* Spencer [sic] *made use of it as a Prelude to* Heroick Poetry' (*Miscellanies*, sig. B2r); the fifth Pastoral, which has a starring role for Colin Clout, sets out his own stall. Steele had praised Philips's poems, without mentioning Pope's, in *The Tatler*, no. 12, 7 May 1709; further praise came in *The Spectator*, no. 223, 15 November 1711, and 400, 9 June. In no. 523, 30 October, Joseph Addison praised Philips's *Pastorals* as a model of modern poetry's ability to dispense with classical mythology and 'all the Tribe of rural Deities' (such as Pope had included). In April 1713 Philips was lauded, probably by Addison's protégé Thomas Tickell (for the authorship see Stephens 1982: 626), in a series of gently amusing essays in *The Guardian* (nos. 22, 23, 28, 30, 32; 6–17 April), for his anglicisation of the pastoral genre through naturalistic local detail and rural dialect; the series concluded by putting him forward as the modern 'son' of Spenser and Theocritus in this regard, in contrast to the ancient 'neoclassical' type of pastoral associated with Virgil – and with Pope, who is not mentioned at all, except for some praise of the 'dapper Elves' passage, 461–6 of 'January and May', in no. 30. Pope was on the verge of setting out to translate Homer's *Iliad* to complete the advance to epic status also signalled by the high national claim of *Windsor-Forest* (1713), and he felt himself insulted on both personal and critical grounds. By this point there was certainly some additional political animus in this exchange, since Philips was associated with the Whig group led by Addison and Steele, with whom Pope was by then on strained terms, and Philips's *Pastorals* had, as Patterson (1987: 206–14) notes, discreet but clear Whig allegiances, their 'naturalistic' surface notwithstanding (see further Aden 1978: 61–3; Santesso 2004; Williams 2015: 127–32).

Rather than mount an open attack, Pope quietly continued Tickell's sequence of *Guardian* essays by sending in an essay on the same theme, supposedly in praise of Philips as 'the eldest Born of *Spencer*' but actually a brilliantly ironic demolition of Philips's '*beautiful Rusticity*' as low and inane (*Guardian*, no. 40, published on the same day as Addison's *Cato*, with Pope's 'Prologue', 27 April 1713; *PW*, I.97–106). Steele's failure to note the irony has never been fully explained, but was probably no more than hurried inadvertence; see Stephens (1982: 640). In this essay Pope observes, ostensibly as a negative criticism, his own careful artistic adherence to balanced Aristotelian unities of seasons, times and scenes. (For modern analysis of these aspects as evidence of Pope's aspirations as a craftsman-artist see Battestin 1969, and Rogers 1980, which uses the near-correspondence of the main segments of the poems to a 366-line, leap-year pattern as a starting-point for a discussion of the aesthetic patterning and structure of the sequence as a whole.) Pope further notes the extent to which the poems of Theocritus and Virgil actually exceed the generic limits of Pastoral, and concludes by apologising for not developing the critique of his own poems, on the grounds that they are, like Virgil's, 'by no means *Pastorals*, but *something Better*'. The incident was the beginning of a lasting antagonism, based as much on political and personal issues as critical positions, which were neither as separate nor as stable as is sometimes assumed, as Lund (2009) shows in a careful study of the sometimes contradictory critical underpinning and ambiguous intentions of Pope's two essays on Pastoral. John Gay's *The Shepherd's Week* (1714), a series of six mock eclogues apparently burlesquing the rusticity of Philips's new English style of pastoral, may have been intended as a continuation of the war, since Gay had become friendly with Pope. Gay's series, however, has generally been found to have a lighter and more affectionate touch than Pope's parody, and to possess more rural naturalism than Pope would perhaps have espoused. In his life of Gay (1781) Johnson commented that 'These Pastorals became popular, and were read with delight, as just representations of rural manners and occupations, by those who had no interest in the rivalry of the poets, nor knowledge of the critical dispute' (Lonsdale, III.96)

Keener (1974:19) writes that Pope's *Pastorals* are the last written in English

> to which the poet could seriously hope that reality might attach itself as it had to equivalent poems by Spenser and Milton, Virgil, and the ancients. Pope's are the last pastorals we have wherein Renaissance myth and convention may not seem patently unnatural.

But Pope's own critical essays, and their sources in Rapin and Fontenelle, indicate that any element of 'reality' was already a long-lost cause. Joseph Trapp, discoursing 'De Poemate Pastorali' in 1715, argued that the genre was now far too remote from modern life to be convincing, and that Virgil's poems were better than those of Theocritus because (as Pope had partly argued) they were not really pastorals at all (*Praelectiones Poeticae*, II (1715) 76–89; translated into English, 1742). During the later eighteenth century the Virgilian-inspired form as Pope used it certainly came to seem artificial, bookish and insufficiently attentive to 'natural' or local landscape. There were no more essays after Pope's in defence of neoclassical pastorals. Philips's neo-Theocritan model, however, continued to garner critical praise from writers such as Charles Gildon (c.1665–1724) in his *Complete Art of Poetry* (1718; I.157) and John Hughes (c. 1678–1720) in his edition of Spenser (1715: I.civ). Thomas Purney's two pastoral collections of 1716–17, and his *Full Enquiry into the True Nature of Pastoral* (1717) ploughed a similar furrow, and it could be said that this shift towards a specifically English pastoral landscape eventually fed into other notionally 'realistic' developments – the dominance of the topographical poem, estate literature, and British Georgic, to which Pope would make his own distinctive contributions.

Joseph Warton, in the first full-length critical study of Pope, the *Essay* of 1756 (pp. 4–10), considered the poems as awkwardly hybridising English scenes with classical tropes, deficient in originality, derivative in imagery and lacking personal feeling (for suggestive analysis of covert biographical expression in the poems, however, see Stephanson 1991). Samuel Johnson demolished the claims of most pastoral theories in *Rambler*, no. 37, 24 July 1750, and in his devastating account of the insincerity of Milton's 'Lycidas': as a pastoral it was 'easy, vulgar, and therefore disgusting' (Lonsdale, I.278–9). His account of Pope's *Pastorals*, is, however, perversely generous, as he defends Pope against Warton's charge of a lack of imagination.

To charge these Pastorals with want of invention, is to require what never was intended. The imitations are so ambitiously frequent, that the writer evidently means rather to shew his literature than his wit. It is surely sufficient for an author of sixteen not only to be able to copy the poems of antiquity with judicious selection, but to have obtained sufficient power of language, and skill in metre, to exhibit a series of versification, which had in English poetry no precedent, nor has since had an imitation.

(Lonsdale, IV.66.)

PASTORALS.
BY
Mr. *ALEXANDER POPE.*

Rura mihi, & rigui placeant in vallibus amnes,
Flumina amen, sylvasque, Inglorius!
Virg.

Title. *1717-51:* PASTORALS, | with a | DISCOURSE on *PASTORAL.* | Written in the Year 1704.

Epigraph. From Virgil, *Georgics* II. 485–6: 'May I find pleasure in the countryside and in the streams which flow unfailingly through the valleys; may I love rivers and woods, remote from glory.' Cf. the comment on Trumbull, 'Spring', 8.

SPRING.

The First Pastoral,

OR

DAMON.

Inscrib'd to Sir WILLIAM TRUMBULL.

SPRING, n. *1736–51:* These Pastorals were written at the age of sixteen, and then past thro' the hands of Mr. *Walsh,* Mr. *Wycherley,* G. *Granville,* afterwards Lord *Lansdown,* Sir *William Trumbal,* Dr. *Garth,* Lord *Halifax,* Lord *Somers,* Mr. *Mainwaring,* and others. [*1751:* All these gave our Author the greatest encouragement, and particularly Mr. *Walsh* (whom Mr. Dryden, in his Postscript to Virgil, calls the best critic of his age.) "The Author (says he) seems to have a particular genius for this kind of Poetry, and a judgment that much exceeds his years. He has taken very freely from the Ancients. But what he has mixed of his own with theirs is in no way inferior to what he has taken from them. It is not flattery at all to say that Virgil had written nothing so good at his Age. His Preface is very judicious and learned." *Letter to Mr. Wycherley, Ap.* 1705. The Lord Lansdown about the same time, mentioning the youth of our Poet, says (in a printed Letter of the Character of Mr. Wycherley) "that if he goes on as he has begun in the Pastoral way, as Virgil first tried his strength, we may hope to see English Poetry vie with the Roman," etc.] Notwithstanding the early time of their production, the Author esteem'd these as the most correct in the versification, and musical in the numbers, of all his works. The reason for his labouring them into so much softness, was, that this sort of poetry derives almost its whole beauty from a natural ease of thought and smoothness of verse; whereas that of most other kinds consists in the Strength and fulness of both. In a Letter of his to Mr. *Walsh* about this time, we find an enumeration of several Niceties in Versification, which perhaps have never been strictly observ'd in any *English* poem, except in these Pastorals. They were not printed till 1709.

Sir WILLIAM TRUMBULL, n. *1751:* Sir *William Trumbal.*] Our Author's friendship with this gentleman commenced at very unequal years; he was under sixteen, but Sir William above sixty, and had lately resign'd his employment of Secretary of State to King William.

Half-title. MS: *SPRING:* | *The First Pastorall;* | OR | DAMON.; *1717–43: SPRING.* | THE | FIRST PASTORAL. | TO | Sir *WILLIAM TRUMBAL.;* *1751:* SPRING. | THE | FIRST PASTORAL, | OR, | DAMON. | To Sir WILLIAM TRUMBAL.

Pope's general note. For the individuals named, see Headnote.

others: Pope named several other literary supporters on the manuscript: for these see Headnote.

Dryden: an early favourite writer of Pope's (*OAC,* I. 19), who praised Walsh as the 'best Critick of our Nation' in the Postscript to his translation of Virgil's *Aeneid, The Works*

of Virgil... translated... by Mr. Dryden (1697), p. 622.

Letter to Mr. Wycherley: Walsh to Wycherley, 20 April 1705, *Corr.,* I.7, a slightly different text from Pope's here. The 'Preface' is the 'Discourse on Pastoral Poetry' (Appendix II) which Pope printed before the *Pastorals* in his *Works* of 1717; Pope asked Walsh's advice about the 'liberty of Borrowing', for

FIrst in these Fields I try the Sylvan Strains,
Nor blush to sport on *Windsor*'s blissful Plains:

1, n. 1736–51: *Prima Syracsio dignata est Indere versu*
Nostra nec erubuit sylvas habitare Thalia.

This is the general Exordium and opening of the Pastorals, in imitation of the 6th of *Virgil*, which some have therefore not improbably thought to have been the first originally. In the beginnings of the other three Pastorals, he imitates expressly those [*1751:* which now stand first] of the three chief Poets in this kind, *Theocritus, Virgil, Spenser,* [*1751: Spencer, Virgil, Theocritus,*]

> *A Shepherd's Boy (he seeks no better name) –*
> *Beneath the shade of a spreading Beach displays, –*
> *Thyrsis, the Musick of that murm'ring Spring, –*

are manifestly imitations of

> *A Shepherd's Boy (no better do him call) –*
> *Tityre, tu patulæ recumbans sub tegmine fagi.*
> Αδυ τι το ψιθυρισμα και α πιτυξ, αιπολε, τηνα –

1. try: MS: *sing*
2. blissful: MS: *peaceful*

---

which Walsh defends him here, in a letter of 2 July 1706, and Walsh replied reassuringly on 20 July and 9 September (*Corr.*, I.19–22), though he acknowledged that some people had commented adversely on the extent of the imitations.
Virgil: See Headnote.
Lansdown: from *The Genuine Works in Verse and Prose, of the Right Honourable George Granville, Lord Landsowne*, 2 vols (1732), I.437; for Virgil's movement from pastoral to epic, see Headnote.
Letter ... to Mr. Walsh: Pope's correspondence with Walsh on these topics dates (according to Pope) from 24 June 1706 (*Corr.*, I.18).
SPRING. In his parodic essay on pastoral in the *Guardian*, no. 40, 27 April 1713 (*PW*, I.97–106), Pope compared this pastoral with Philips's sixth. The singing contest is a common element of pastorals, e.g. Theocritus, *Idylls*, V and IX; Virgil, *Eclogues*, III and VII; Spenser, 'August'.
Title. *DAMON*: conventional pastoral name, used by Virgil in *Eclogues*, III and VIII, and in several English pastorals, such as Marvell's 'Damon the Mower' and Walsh's third eclogue.
Dedication. For Trumbull, see Headnote.
1. Pope later quoted his own line pointedly at the end of *Windsor-Forest*, 431–2.
First: Pope is the first poet to celebrate this place in this way; also a signal that the *Pastorals* are an effort preliminary to greater, epic work.
these Fields: the fields of the Windsor Forest area, a park, with mixed woodland, clearings and grazing.
Sylvan: of woodland, a conventional epithet derived from Latin 'silva', woods, as in the epigraph.
Strains: of melody, i.e. songs, poetry.
1 Pope's note. Virgil, *Eclogues*, VI.1–2: 'Our Thalia first held it worthy to sport with Syracusan verse, and did not blush to inhabit woodlands'. Thalia is the Muse of comedy and of pastoral; Syracuse was the major city of Sicily, home of Theocritus; Virgil is saying that his earliest poetry was pastoral.

Fair *Thames* flow gently from thy sacred Spring,
While on thy Banks *Sicilian* Muses sing;
5   Let Vernal Airs thro' trembling Osiers play,
And *Albion*'s Cliffs resound the Rural Lay.

You, that too Wise for Pride, too Good for Pow'r,
Enjoy the Glory to be Great no more,

---

other ... he: i.e. Pope's the next three pastorals, the opening lines of which Pope then quotes.

Theocritus: the earliest pastoral author; see Headnote.

Virgil: see Headnote.

Spenser: see Headnote; the Spenser line is from Spenser's *Shepheardes Calender* (1579), 'Januarie', 1; 'Beneath the shade' translates the opening of Virgil, *Eclogues*, I.1: 'Titryus, lying beneath the cover of a spreading beech'; 'Thyrsis, the Musick ... ' is modelled on Theocritus, *Idylls*, I.1: 'The whispering sound is sweet, and the pine tree, o goatherd'.

1 **MS.** Pope, unhappy with the repeated 's' sounds, suggested the greater propriety of 'try', which Walsh thought an improvement; see Appendix I.

2. **Nor blush ... Plains:** Pope adopts Virgil's own defiant stance from *Eclogues*, VI.1–2. TE compares Dryden's version, *Works of Virgil*, p. 26: 'I First transferr'd to *Rome Sicilian* Strains: | Nor blush'd the *Dorick* Muse to dwell on *Mantuan* Plains'.

sport: play.

Windsor: Windsor Forest. For a succinct account of Pope's home landscape see Rogers (2010), pp. 7–50.

3. sacred Spring: The Thames, to be more elaborately celebrated in *Windsor-Forest*, rises near Cirencester; but Pope's invocation suggests the sacred springs associated with the classical Muses or goddesses of arts invoked in the next line. TE compares the refrain of Spenser, *Prothalamion* (1596): 'Sweete *Themmes* runne softly, till I end my Song'.

4. **Sicilian:** Theocritus was from Sicily.

Muses: In Greek mythology, goddesses of the various arts, nine in number, invoked as inspirational figures in poetry.

5. **Vernal Airs:** the breezes of Spring, suggesting inspiration or music.

trembling Osiers: willows vibrating in the wind. Wakefield compares Milton, *Paradise Regain'd*, II.26 (1671), p. 29: 'Where winds with Reeds, and Osiers whisp'ring play'; and Dryden, 'Theodore and Honoria', 79, *Fables Ancient and Modern* (1700), p. 260: 'The Winds, within the quiv'ring Branches plaid'. TE adds Milton, *Paradise Lost*, IV.264–6 (1674), p. 93: ' ... aires, vernal aires, | Breathing the smell of field and grove, attune | The trembling leaves ... '

6. Wakefield compares Roscommon, *An Essay on Translated Verse*, 18–19 (1684), p. 2: '*Theocritus* do's now to *Vs* belong; | And *Albion*'s *Rocks* repeat his *Rural Song*'.

Albion: conventional poetic name for Britain and a signal of Pope's transference of the classical genre to a British locale; cf. *Windsor-Forest*, 106.

Cliffs: the landscape of the island as a whole, or perhaps the cliffs along the south coast, rather than the moderate hills around Windsor.

Lay: song, poem.

7. **You:** Trumbull. The earliest of Pope's many invocations of the virtue of not being in political power. Lashmore-Davies (2009) transcribes Trumbull's essay on plain living from a letter dated 4 August 1708.

8. Glory ... no more: it is more glorious to retire from political power than exert it. The words recall the 'inglorius' of the Latin epigraph. Wakefield compares Lucan,

And carrying with you all the World can boast,
10   To all the World Illustriously are lost!
O let my Muse her slender Reed inspire,
'Till in your Native Shades You tune the Lyre:
So when the Nightingale to Rest removes,
The Thrush may chant to the forsaken Groves,
15   But, charm'd to Silence, listens while She sings,
And all th' Aerial Audience clap their Wings.

12, n. *1736–51: In your native shades.*] Sir *W. Trumbal* was born in *Windsor*-Forest, to which he retreated after he had resign'd the post of Secretary of State to King *William* III.

7–16. MS: omitted

VIII.493–5: 'Exeat aula, | qui volt esse pius. Virtus et summa potestas | non coeunt.' ('Let he who wishes to maintain his integrity leave the court. Virtue and the highest power do not go together.')

9. all the World can boast: in terms of intellectual knowledge, rather than wealth. *EC* compares Waller, *The Maid's Tragedy Alter'd* (1690), p. 45: 'Happy is she that from the World retires, | And carrys with her what the World admires.'

11. slender Reed: the traditional reed pipe of pastoral poetry, perhaps alluding also to Pope's slight physique; cf. 'Summer', 39. *TE* compares Virgil, *Eclogues*, VI.8: 'agrestem tenui meditabor harundine Musam' ('I will try the rural Muse with a thin reed').

inspire: punning on the (now archaic) literal sense, to blow into; cf. 'Summer', 40; 'January and May', 325; *Ode for Musick*, 2.

12. Native Shades: the protecting or sheltering environment of Windsor Forest, where, as Pope's note indicates, Trumbull was born and where he lived (see Headnote, and *Windsor-Forest*, 255–6).

tune the Lyre: i.e. Pope's pastoral verse will inspire Trumbull to more epic verse achievements. Cf. 'Summer', 43. For the phrase cf. 'January and May', 324.

13. Nightingale: conventionally associated with the purest song and a conventional figure of the poet; Southerne (see Headnote) nicknamed Pope the 'little nightingale' (Mack 1985: 97). Pope commented on Philips's use of previous examples of the figure in his *Guardian* no. 40 essay on Pastoral, *PW*, I.99. Pope tactfully figures himself as the imitating and inferior Thrush (line 14) to Trumbull's nightingale. See also 26 below.

14. Groves: stands of trees, often associated with a sacred retreat.

16. Aerial Audience: the other birds. This image was singled out by Concanen in *A Supplement to the Profund* (1728), p.12, as incongruously drawn from the theatre; in his copy (see Mack 1982: 403) Pope wrote 'Dryden' in the margin against the comment; *TE* construes this as an allusion to the final couplet of 'Verses to Her Highness the Duchess [of York]', in *Annus Mirabilis* (1667), sig. a3ʳ: 'Each Poet of the air her Glory sings, | And round him the pleas'd Audience clap their Wings'.

> *Daphnis* and *Strephon* to the Shades retir'd,
> Both warm'd by Love, and by the Muse inspir'd;
> Fresh as the Morn, and as the Season fair,
20   In flow'ry *Vales* they fed their fleecy Care;

17–22, n. 1736–51: The Scene of this Pastoral a Vally, the Time the Morning. It stood originally thus;
> Daphnis *and* Strephon *to the shades retir'd,*
> *Both warn'd by Love, and by the Muse inspir'd;*
> *Fresh as the morn, and as the season fair,*
> *In flow'ry vales they fed their fleecy care;*
> *And while* Aurora *gilds the mountain's side,*
> *Thus* Daphnis *spoke, and* Strephon *thus reply'd.*

17–21. MS: Daphnis *and* Strephon *led their Flocks along,*
> *Both fam'd for Love, and both renown'd in Song;*
> *Fresh as the Morn, and as the Season fair,*
> *In flow'ry Plains they fed their fleecy Care;*
> *And while Aurora gilds the Mountains Side,*

1736–51:   Soon as the flocks shook off the nightly dews,
> Two Swains, whom Love kept wakeful, and the Muse,
> Pour'd o'er the whitening vale their fleecy care,
> Fresh as the morn, and as the season fair:
> The dawn now blushing on the mountain's side,

---

17. Daphnis . . . Strephon: conventional pastoral names. 'Daphnis' is the subject of Theocritus, *Idylls*, I and XXVII, and of Virgil, *Eclogues*, V. The name had also been in common use since the Hellenic romance *Daphnis and Chloe* (see *OAC*, I.265). Rochester had written 'A Pastoral Dialogue, Between Alexis and Strephon', and 'Strephon' was used as an elegiac codename for Rochester by Aphra Behn in her poem 'To Mr Creech (Under the Name of Daphnis) On His Excellent Translation of Lucretius', in her *Poems upon Several Occasions* (1684).

17–21 variant. Pour'd . . . vale: the vale 'whitens' as the white sheep cover it; alternatively, the whitening occurs as the sun rises. Wakefield suggests the derivation of some images in the later variant lines from Congreve, *The Tears of Amaryllis for Amyntas*, 5–6 (1703), p. 1: 'When woolly Flocks their bleating Cries renew, | And from their fleecy Sides first shake the silver Dew'.

19. Fresh . . . Morn: Wakefield compares Dryden, 'Palamon and Arcite', I.182, *Fables*, p. 8: 'Fresh as the Month, and as the Morning fair'.

20. fleecy Care: flock of sheep, the creatures they care for; cf. 'Messiah', 47, and Pope's translation of *Iliad*, XIII.622.

And while *Aurora* gilds the Mountain's Side,
Thus *Daphnis* spoke, and *Strephon* thus reply'd.

DAPHNIS.

Hear how the Birds, on ev'ry bloomy Spray,
With joyous Musick wake the dawning Day!
25   Why sit we mute, when early Linnets sing,
When warbling *Philomel* salutes the Spring?

23. **Birds:** MS: Larks
25. **Linnets:** MS: Turtles

21. Aurora: Roman version of the Greek goddess of dawn, Eos.

Mountain: TE cites *OED*'s explanation that the word might mean an elevation 'of moderate altitude' in the eighteenth century, but this is based on quotations from 1765 and 1773; *SJ* in 1755 has 'a large hill; a vast protuberance of the earth'. The word recurs in a similar context several times in the *Pastorals*, e.g. 'Summer', 37; 'Autumn', 16; and 'Winter', 89, as well as *Windsor-Forest*, 35, 87, etc.

22. spoke ... reply'd: Wakefield compares Virgil, *Eclogues*, VII.20: 'hos Corydon, illos referebat in ordine Thyrsis' ('These [verses] Corydon [sang], those Thyrsis returned in order'). The dialogue form, often presented as a contest, was a basic convention within pastoral; see e.g. Virgil, *Eclogues*, III, which has carved bowls and a heifer as prizes in the competition. Theocritus' first *Idyll* has a carved cup which had long been a focus of literary astonishment (see Pope's comment in his 'Discourse on Pastoral Poetry', Appendix II, 76). Spenser's version of the convention comes in 'August'. In Philips's sixth *Pastoral*, the prize is an oboe. For extended commentary on the bowl as a central image for the aesthetic order of the *Pastorals* as a whole, see Battestin (1969) and Rogers (1980); the latter explores its resemblance to a miniaturised version of Achilles's allegorical shield from *Iliad*, XVIII.

23. bloomy Spray: Wakefield compares the first line of Milton, Sonnet I, *Poems of Mr. John Milton* (1645), p. 44: 'O Nightingale, that on yon bloomy Spray'.

23 **MS. Larks:** cf. 'Autumn', 45; 'Winter', 53.

24. dawning Day: Wakefield compares Congreve, *Tears of Amaryllis*, 3–4 (1703), p. 1: 'When grateful Birds prepare their Thanks to pay, | And warble Hymns to hail the dawning Day'. For the rhyme in this couplet cf. Pope's 'January and May', 385–6.

25. Wakefield cites Waller, 'Chloris and Hilas', 1–2, *Poems, &c.* (1645), p. 157: '*Hilas*, oh *Hilas*! why sit we mute, | Now that each Bird saluteth the Spring?'

25 **MS. Turtles:** see 'Summer', 52; 'Autumn', 19.

26. Philomel: poetic name for nightingale (cf. 13), more normally signalling musical melancholy, as at 'Winter', 78. The allusion is to the story of Philomela, raped and mutilated by her brother in law Tereus; see the cancelled lines of 'Summer', 67–8, and 'Sapho to Phaon', 176. Concanen objected to the impropriety of calling an English bird by a classical name (*Supplement to the Profund*, p. 13); Pope noted 'Spenser' in the margin of the pamphlet, as 'Philomele' appears at 'Nouember', 141, a line quoted in Pope's *Guardian* no. 40 essay on Pastoral, *PW*, I.100. The phrase 'warbling Philomel' is fairly common in verse, e.g. Nicholas Billingsley, 'The World's Infancy', V, *Kosmobrephia, or, The Infancy of the World* (1658), p. 33.

salutes: greets, hails in song.

Why sit we sad, when *Phosphor* shines so clear,
And lavish Nature paints the Purple Year?

STREPHON.

Sing then, and *Damon* shall attend the Strain,
30   While yon slow Oxen turn the furrow'd Plain.
Here on green Banks the blushing Vio'lets glow;
Here Western Winds on breathing Roses blow.
I'll stake my Lamb that near the Fountain plays,
And from the Brink his dancing Shade surveys.

***34, n.** 1736–51:* The first reading was,
 And his own Image from the bank surveys.

31. MS: *There the pale* Primrose *and the* Vi'let *grow*;
 1751: Here the bright crocus and blue vi'let glow;
32. MS: *There Western Winds on Beds of* Roses *blow*.
33. my: *1736–51:* yon'
34. MS: *And his own Image from the Bank surveys.*

---

27. **Phosphor:** In Greek mythology, Phosphorus is the sun of Eos or Dawn (see 21), and personifies the morning star, i.e. the planet Venus, visible around sunrise.
28. **lavish Nature:** Wakefield compares Dryden, 'The Cock and the Fox', 456, *Fables*, p. 240: 'How lavish Nature has adorn'd the Year'; *TE* adds Dryden's version of Virgil, *Eclogues*, VII.76, 'And lavish Nature laughs', in a section marked by a comma in Pope's copy (Mack 1982: 459, item 171). Spenser uses the phrase in 'Muiotpotmos', 163.
 paints: colours brightly; cf. 'January and May', 616.
 Purple: Warburton suggests 'the Latin sense of the brightest, most vivid colouring in general, not of that specific tint so called', exemplified in Dryden's translation of Virgil, *Eclogues*, II.62, *Works of Virgil*, p. 8: 'With all the Glories of the Purple Spring'; Dryden uses 'Purple Spring' again at V.91 and IX.53. In poetry, according to *SJ*, 'purple' means 'red'. Cf. Thomas Stanley, 'Venus Vigils', *Poems* (1651), p. 73: '*She* paints the purple colour'd year'. For Pope's observation of colour see Ault (1949: 68–100).
29. **attend:** listen to.
30. **Oxen . . . Plain:** Actual agricultural labour in the *Pastorals* is rare, and Pope's view was that it had to be so: 'We must . . . use some illusion to render a Pastoral delightful; and this consists in exposing the best side only of a shepherd's life, and in concealing its miseries'; 'A Discourse on Pastoral Poetry', Appendix II. For his comic view of rustic farmworkers, see *Guardian*, no. 40.
31. **blushing:** i.e. fully coloured (violets are blue or mauve), without the connotation of embarrassment as in 2. Cf. 'Summer', 75. The violet, like the 'primrose' of the MS and the 'crocus' of the 1751 reading, is perhaps a sign of the Englishness of the landscape; cf. 42 below. *EC* criticises Pope for having flowers of different seasons blooming together in the variant, a fault which Pope pointed out in Philips in *Guardian*, no. 40.
32. **Western Winds:** regarded as gentle and often personified as Zephyrs ('Winter', 49).
 breathing: fragrant, exhaling scent. *TE* compares Milton, 'Arcades', 32, *Poems* (1645), p. 53: 'breathing Roses of the Wood'; *Paradise Lost*, II.244–5 and IX.193; 'Messiah', 24; *Rape of the Lock*, I.134.
33. **stake:** bet, wager, in the singing competition (as in Virgil, *Eclogues*, III).
 Fountain: spring.
34. **dancing Shade:** unsteady reflection or shadow.

DAPHNIS.

35 And I this Bowl, where wanton Ivy twines,
And swelling Clusters bend the curling Vines:
Four Figures rising from the Work appear,
The various Seasons of the rowling Year;

35–6, n. *1736–51: Lenta quibus torno facili superaddita vitis,*
      Diffusos edera vestit pallenti corymbos. Virg.
36, n. *1736–51: And Clusters lurk beneath the curling vines.*
38, n. *1736–51: The various Seasons.*] The Subject of these Pastorals engraven on the bowl is not without its propriety. The Shepherd's hesitation at the name of the *Zodiac*, imitates that in *Virgil*,
    — *Et quis fuit alter?*
Descripsit radio totam qui gentibus orbem.

36. swelling clusters bend: MS: *Clusters lurk beneath*

---

34 MS. Walsh approved Pope's alternative reading in MS; see Appendix I.

35–40. Pope cited these lines to suggest his command of descriptive verse in contrast to Philips in *Guardian*, no. 40, *PW*, I.102.

35–6 Pope's note. Virgil, *Eclogues*, III.38–9: 'on which a supple vine laid on by a skilful chisel clothes the clusters spread by the pale ivy'. *TE* compares Spenser, 'August', 29–30: 'And ouer them spred a goodly wild vine, | Entrailed with a wanton Yuie twine'.

35. wanton: appearing to grow loosely or luxuriantly, a sense common in Pope, e.g. 'Vertumnus and Pomona', 21. See quotation from Spenser in previous note, and 53–6 below.

36. Clusters: of grapes; cf. 'Autumn', 74, and, among many possible sources for the phrase 'swelling Clusters', Garth, *Dispensary*, IV, sixth edition (1706), p. 70: 'The Vine undress'd her swelling Clusters bears'. Cf. also 'Vertumnus and Pomona', 60.

 curling Vines: Pope recycled the image in his translation of Homer, *Iliad*, VI.166: 'With curling Vines and twisted Ivy bound'; almost the whole line is re-used in 'Vertumnus and Pomona', 60.

37. rising: carved in relief, standing out from the surface. Wakefield compares Dryden's version of Virgil, *Aeneid*, VIII.835, *Works of Virgil*, p. 458: 'And *Roman* Triumphs rising on the Gold'; *TE* compares further 'The First Book of Statius his Thebais', 636.

38. rowling: indicating the turning of the earth and succession of the seasons, the subject of the four *Pastorals* as a whole, represented by the 'figures' of 37.

38 Pope's note. Virgil, *Eclogues*, III.40–1: 'And who was the other one, who marked out the whole celestial sphere for mankind with a rod?' *EC* compares Dryden's version, 59–62, *Works of Virgil*, p. 12: 'The Lids are Ivy, Grapes in clusters lurk, | Beneath the Carving of the curious Work. | Two Figures on the sides emboss'd appear; | *Conon*, and what's his Name who made the Sphere, | And shew'd the Seasons of the sliding Year'.

 TE identifies the second astronomer as Eudoxus of Cnidus (c. 390–c.340 BC). *TE* also notes the phrase 'various Seasons of the year' in Thomas Creech's translation of the same

> And what is That, which binds the Radiant Sky,
40 Where twelve bright Signs in beauteous Order lye?

> *DAMON.*

> Then sing by turns, by turns the Muses sing,
> Now Hawthorns blossom, now the Daisies spring,
> Now Leaves the Trees, and Flow'rs adorn the Ground;
> Begin, the Vales shall Echo to the Sound.

41, n. 1736–51: Then sing by turns.] Literally from *Virgil,*
Alternis dicetis, amant alterna Camoenae:
Et nunc omnis ager, nunc omnis parturit arbos,
Nunc frondent sylvae, nunc formosissimus annus.

40. bright: MS, *1751: fair*
44. Echo to the Sound: *1736–51:* ev'ry note rebound

passage, *Miscellany Poems* (1684), p. 24, and Dryden's version of Virgil, *Georgics*, I.349, *Works of Virgil*, p. 59: 'And the four Quarters of the rolling Year'. Cf. the 'Discourse', Appendix II, 36 variant, on ancient shepherds and astronomy.

39–40. Wakefield compares Dryden's translation of Virgil, *Georgics*, I.328–9, *Works of Virgil*, p. 59: 'And cross their limits cut a sloping way, | Which the twelve Signs in beauteous order sway'. Cf. also Blackmore, *Prince Arthur*, II. (1695), p. 40: 'The Sphears in tuneful Measures Roll above, | And Heav'n's bright Orbs in beauteous Order move'. Cf. also 'Gardens of Alcinous', 27. Johnson, *Rambler*, no. 37, 24 July 1750, objected to the falsity of a pastoral figure who did not recognise the Zodiac.

41 Pope's note. Virgil, *Eclogues*, III.59, 56–7 (Pope reorders the lines in his quotation): 'Sing alternately: the Muses love singing by turns. Even now each field, each tree is budding; now the woods are in leaf, now the year is at its most beautiful'.

42. Hawthorns ... Daisies: further 'English' natural history

43. Flow'rs ... Ground: cf. *Windsor-Forest*, 38.

44 variant. Wakefield compares Dryden's version of Virgil, *Eclogues*, X.10–11, *Works of Virgil*, p. 45: 'The vocal Grove shall answer to the Sound, | And Echo, from the Vales, the tuneful Voice rebound'.

45. EC compares Virgil, *Eclogues*, VII.21–3: 'aut mihi carmen, | quale meo Codro, concedite (proxima Phoebi | versibus ille facit)' ('or allow me to make a song, the same kind as you allowed my Codrus, next to Phoebus in poetry').

Phoebus: one of the names of Apollo, Greek god of poetry.

Delia: conventional name of an ideal poetic maiden, used for example in Virgil, *Eclogues*, III and VII (and in 'On a Fan of the Author's Design', 3); see note on 'Alexis', 'Summer'. For Walsh's 'Delia' see note to title of 'Winter'. Pope originally had 'Chloris', a similarly conventional name, in mind; see Appendix I.

STREPHON.

45   Inspire me *Phoebus*, in my *Delia*'s Praise,
With *Waller*'s Strains, or *Granville*'s moving Lays!
A Milk-white Bull shall at your Altars stand,
That threats a Fight, and spurns the rising Sand.

DAPHNIS.

O Love! for *Sylvia* let me gain the Prize,
50   And make my Tongue victorious as her Eyes;

46, n. *1736–51: Granville –*] *George Granville, afterwards Lord Lansdown, known for his Poems, most of which he compos'd very young, and propos'd Waller as his model.*
47, n. *1736–51: A milk-white Bull.*] Virg. – *Pascite taurum,*
    Qui cornu petat, & pedibus jam spargat arenam.

45–48. MS: *Ye Fountain* Nymphs, *propitious to the Swain,*
    Now grant me Phaebus *or* Alexis *Strain*:
    My fairest Bull *shall at your Altars stand,*
    With butting Horns, and Heels y.ᵗ spurn the Sand.
49–52. MS: Pan, *let my Numbers equal* Strephon'*s Lays,*
    Of Parian *Stone thy* Statue *will I raise*;
    But if I conquer, and augment my Fold,
    Thy Parian Statue *shall be chang'd to* Gold.

---

45 MS. Fountain Nymphs: mythological water spirits.

46. Waller: Edmund Waller (1606–87), courtier and poet, one of Pope's earliest favourite authors (*OAC*, I.19, item 43, and see further I.196, items 455–7), of whose lyric style Pope produced several imitations in his youth and who was generally regarded as a poet of great technical smoothness; see *Essay on Criticism*, 364, and 'On a Fan of the Author's Design', Headnote.

Granville: For George Granville, first Baron Lansdowne, see Headnote.

Lays: songs.

46 MS. *Alexis* Strain: Cf. 'Winter', 11.

47–8. i.e. for sacrifice to Apollo in gratitude for victory.

47–8 Pope's note. Virgil, *Eclogues*, III.86–7: 'feed up a bull, which can already attack with his horn and scatter the sand with his hooves'. Wakefield compares Dryden's version of Virgil, *Aeneid*, IX.859 and 862, *Works of Virgil*, p. 489: 'A now-white Steer, before thy Altar led ... | And dares the Fight, and spurns the yellow Sands'; Dryden has a 'Milk white Steed' as a sacrificial victim in the first scene of *King Arthur, or, The British Worthy* (1691), p. 7.

48. spurns: kicks with his hooves, as in Dryden's 'To the Earl of Roscommon', 67, in Roscommon's *Essay on Translated Verse* (1684), sig. A2ʳ: 'Muse feed the Bull that spurns the yellow sand'.

49. Love: i.e. Eros or Cupid, god of Love.

Sylvia: conventional name of ideal poetic nymph; cf. 'Rape of the Locke', I.55.

49 MS. Numbers: metre; cf. 'January and May', 339, and *Essay on Criticism*, 340.

50. victorious ... Eyes: the conventional poetic idea that a woman's eyes 'conquer' her male lover.

50 MS. Parian Stone: fine white marble from the island of Paros, much used in sculpture.

No Lambs or Sheep for Victims I'll impart,
Thy Victim, Love, shall be the Shepherd's Heart.

STREPHON.

Me gentle *Delia* beckons from the Plain,
Then hid in Shades, eludes her eager Swain;
55   But feigns a Laugh, to see me search around,
And by that Laugh the willing Fair is found.

DAPHNIS.

The sprightly *Sylvia* trips along the Green,
She runs, but hopes she does not run unseen,

58, n. *1736–51: She runs, but hopes.*] Imitation of *Virgil,
Malo me Galatea petit, lasciva puella,
Et fugit ad salices, sed se cupit ante videri.*

53. gentle *Delia*: MS: *lovely* Sylvia
54. MS: *Then hides in Shades from her deluded Swain*
57. The sprightly *Sylvia*: MS: *Coy* Amaryllis

---

51. *Victims*: sacrificial victims, like Strephon's bull.
   ***impart*:** grant, hand over.
53–6. For Pope's queries to Walsh about the wording of this stanza see Appendix I; for the original 'lovely' of 53 Pope considered 'wanton', perhaps suggested by Virgil's 'lasciva', which can mean 'playful' or 'lascivious'; but Walsh told him that the word when 'apply'd to a woman is equivocal & therefore not proper'. Cf. 35. Sandys noted that 'Lasciviousness' was 'Hieroglyphically presented by ivy' in a note to his *Ovid's Metamorphosis Englished*, VI (1632), p. 204. The word 'wanton' appears eight times in Milton's *Paradise Lost*, with several shades of meaning; Pope had used it of 'Ivy' in line 35, and cf. 'January and May', 390; 'Vertumnus and Pomona', 21; 'Sapho to Phaon', 85–6; *Windsor-Forest*, 78.
53–60. Pope quoted these lines to suggest his superior 'knack of Versifying' over a similar exchange in one of Philips's *Pastorals* in his *Guardian*, no. 40.
54. *Shades*: shadows.
56. *willing Fair*: cf. Dryden's version of Virgil, *Eclogues*, VIII.36, *Works of Virgil*, p. 36: 'he weds the willing Fair'; for the broader idea, *EC* compares 34–7 of Dryden's translation of Horace, *Carmina*, I.ix.21–4, *Sylvae* (1685), p. 126: 'The half unwilling willing kiss, | The laugh that guides thee to the mark, | When the kind Nymph wou'd coyness feign, | And hides but to be found again'.
57 MS. *Amaryllis*: a recurrent name in Virgil's pastorals, e.g. *Eclogues*, I.
58 Pope's note. Virgil, *Eclogues*, III.64–5: 'Galatea, flirtatious girl, pelts me with an apple, and runs to the willows, and hopes to be seen before [she gets there]'. *TE* suggests the influence of Dryden's version of the lines, *Works of Virgil*, p. 13: 'With pelted Fruit, me *Galatea* plyes; | Then tripping to the Woods the Wanton hies: | And wishes to be seen, before she flies.'

126　　　　　　　　　　　PASTORALS (1709)

   While a kind Glance at her Pursuer flies,
60 How much at variance are her Feet and Eyes!

       STREPHON.

  O'er Golden Sands let rich *Pactolus* flow,
  And Trees weep Amber on the Banks of *Po*;

61, n. *1736–51:* It stood thus at first,
   Let *rich* Iberia *golden fleeces boast,*
   Her purple wool the proud Assyrian *coast;*
   Blest Thames*'s shores, &c.*

61–76. MS: *Go flow'ry Wreath, and let my Sylvia know,*
   Compar'd to thine, how bright her Beauties show;
   Then dye; and dying, teach the lovely Maid,
   How soon the brightest Beauties are decay'd.
      Daphnis.
   Go tuneful Bird, that pleas'd the Woods so long;
   Of Amaryllis *learn a sweeter Song;*
   To Heav'n, arising, then her Notes convey,
   For Heav'n alone is worthy such a Lay.

---

59. kind: loving, amorously encouraging; cf. 'Autumn', 52.

61–4. For similar aspiration and rivalry between English and classical localities see *Windsor-Forest*, 355–60. Wakefield identifies a possible source for the contrast in Denham, *Cooper's Hill*, 165–8, *Poems and Translations* (1668), p. 11: 'Though with those streams he no resemblance hold, | Whose foam is Amber, and their Gravel Gold; | His genuine, and less guilty wealth t' explore, | Search not his bottom, but survey his shore.'

61. Pactolus: river of ancient Lydia, now modern Turkey, once famous for the presence of the gold amalgam known as electrum; the mythological King Midas was supposed to have cleansed himself of the 'golden touch' there, according to Ovid, *Metamorphoses* XI.140–4.

61 MS. flow'ry Wreath: a developed version of the image appears in 'Summer', 55–7.

61–2 Pope's note. In the manuscript these lines stood at 67–8, and the contrast that occupies 61–8 of the 1709 text was at 67–74.

 rich *Iberia* . . . fleeces: the Spanish order of the Golden Fleece, not the story of Jason and the Argonauts: the traditional location of that golden fleece was Colchis, at the eastern end of the Black Sea.

 purple . . . Assyrian: *TE* notes that Assyria was anciently confused with Tyre, the source of the imperial purple dye. For the reference to Assyrian wool *TE* cites Virgil, *Georgics*, II.465: 'alba neque Assyrio fucatur lana veneno' ('if the white wool is not dipped in Assyrian dye').

62. Trees weep Amber: The trees exude resin or sap which becomes fossilised as amber; cf. 'Autumn', 38, and *Windsor-Forest*, 30, 391.

 Po: Italian river identified with the mythological river Eridanus, on the bank of which Phaeton (son of the sun god Helios)

> Blest *Thames*'s Shores the brightest Beauties yield,
> Feed here my Lambs, I'll seek no distant Field.
>
> DAPHNIS.
>
> 65 Celestial *Venus* haunts *Idalia*'s Groves,
> *Diana Cynthus, Ceres Hybla* loves;
> If *Windsor*-Shades delight the matchless Maid,
> *Cynthus* and *Hybla* yield to *Windsor*-Shade.
>
> STREPHON.
>
> All Nature mourns, the Skies relent in Show'rs,

69, n. *1736–51: All nature mourns]*
  Virg. *Aret ager, vitio moriens sitit aëris herba,* &c.
  Phyllidis adventu nostrae nemus omne virebit –

69–72. n. *1736–51:* These verses were thus at first;

  All nature mourns, the birds their songs deny,
  Nor wasted brooks the thirsty flow'rs supply;
  If Delia *smile, the flow'rs begin to spring,*
  The brooks to murmur, and the birds to sing.

---

crashed when thrown from the heavens; Phaeton's weeping sisters were turned into trees, and their tears hardened into amber. The story is alluded to in Virgil, *Eclogues*, VI.62–3, but as *TE* notes, Pope's allusion is more directly to Ovid, *Metamporphoses*, II.329–66, esp. 364–5: 'inde fluunt lacrimae, stillataque sole rigescunt | de ramis electra novis' ('their tears flow thence, and dropped from young branches, harden in the sun as amber').

65–8. *EC* suggests this quatrain recalls Virgil, *Eclogues*, VII.61–4 and 67–8, and, as a model for Pope's syntax, suggest a translation by Thomas Adams in *Miscellany Poems* (1684), p. 59 of second sequence: '*Bacchus* the Vine, the Laurel *Phoebus* loves, | Fair *Venus* cherishes the myrtle Groves, | *Phillis* the Hazels loves, while *Phillis* loves that Tree, | Myrtles and Lawrels of less fame shall be.'

65. haunts: frequents, is often present in.
  Idalia: town in Cyprus, which was strongly associated with worship of Aphrodite.

66. Diana Cynthus, Ceres Hybla loves: Diana was the Roman version of the Greek goddess Artemis, associated with hunting, wild nature, childbirth and the moon (see *Windsor-Forest* 160, 198), and was reputedly born on Mount Cynthus, on the island of Delos. Ceres was the Roman version of the Greek goddess Demeter, associated with fertility of the soil; Hybla is a Sicilian mountain known for the production of herbs and honey (Virgil, *Eclogues*, VII.37). Each goddess 'loves' her proper home. The MS reading of this stanza (see variants at 84^5) has 'Aetna' for Hybla; Ceres' Greek original, Demeter, was supposed to have lit her torches at Mount Etna, the volcano on Sicily, in her search for her abducted daughter, Persephone. See also 'Autumn', 91, and 'Sapho to Phaon', 12.

67–8. Windsor-Shades: the shaded landscape of the Windsor Forest area, shortly to be celebrated in *Windsor-Forest*, especially 1–42.

69. Cf. Congreve, *The Mourning Muse of Alexis*, 167 (1695), p. 8: 'All Nature Mourns; the Flouds and Rocks deplore'.

  relent: 'melt; to grow moist' (*SJ*, citing this line).

70 Hush'd are the Birds, and clos'd the drooping Flow'rs;
If *Delia* smile, the Flow'rs begin to spring,
The Skies to brighten, and the Birds to sing.

DAPHNIS.

All Nature laughs, the Groves fresh Honours wear,
The Sun's mild Lustre warms the vital Air;
75 If *Sylvia* smile, new Glories gild the Shore,
And vanquish'd Nature seems to charm no more.

STREPHON.

In Spring the Fields, in Autumn Hills I love,
At Morn the Plains, at Noon the shady Grove;
But *Delia* always; forc'd from *Delia*'s Sight,
80 Nor Plains at Morn, nor Groves at Noon delight.

DAPHNIS.

Sylvia's like Autumn ripe, yet mild as *May*,
More bright than Noon, yet fresh as early Day,

---

73. fresh Honours wear: *1736–51:* are fresh and fair
75. smile: *1717–51:* smiles
77. Spring: MS: May
79. Delia: MS: Sylvia
   forc'd from *Delia*'s: *1736–51:* absent from her
81. Sylvia's: MS: *My Love's*

---

69 Pope's note. Virgil, *Eclogues*, VII.57, 59: 'The field is parched, the grass is thirsty, dying from the taint of the air'.

71-2. Wakefield compares Addison's epilogue for Granville's *The British Enchanters* (1706), sig. [A]2ᵛ: 'The Desart smiles; the Woods begin to grow, | The Birds to warble, and the Springs to flow'.

73. laughs: in the figurative sense of appearing 'favourable, pleasant, or fertile' (*SJ*).

   Honours: leaves; the usage is classical, following the Latin 'honores'. Cf. 'Episode of Sarpedon', 291; 'Winter', 32; *Windsor-Forest*, 219, and Commentary.

75-6. For Pope's experiments on these lines and Walsh's comments, see Appendix I.

76. vanquish'd: nature's 'smile' is less 'charming' than Sylvia's.

77-84. Pope cited these lines as part of his own contest with Philips in the *Guardian*, no. 40: *PW*, I.100-1.

77 MS. May: at no point in the published set of poems does Pope name an actual month.

80. delight: The verb applies to both 'Plains' and 'Groves' and the understood object is 'me'.

81-2. Wakefield identifies Pope's source as Cowley, *Davideis*, III.553-4, *Poems... Written By A. Cowley* (1656), p. 96: 'Hot as ripe *Noon*, sweet as the *blooming Day*, | Like *Iuly* furious, but more fair then *May*.'

Ev'n Spring displeases, when she shines not here,
But blest with her, 'tis Spring throughout the Year.

STREPHON.

85 Say, Shepherd, say, in what glad Soil appears
   A wondrous *Tree* that Sacred *Monarchs* bears?
   Tell me but this, and I'll disclaim the Prize,
   And give the Conquest to thy *Sylvia*'s Eyes.

86, n. 1736–51: A wond'rous Tree that sacred Monarchs bears.] An allusion to the Royal Oak, in which *Charles* the second [*1751:* II.] had been hid from the pursuit after the battle of *Worcester.*

83. **shines:** MS: *stays*
84^5. MS: *Let rich* Iberia *Golden Fleeces boast,*
   Her Purple Wool the proud Assyrian Coast;
   Fair Thames's Shores the brightest Beauties yield;
   Feed here my Lambs, I'l seek no distant Field.
      Daphnis.
   Celestial Venus *haunts* Idalia*'s Groves,*
   Diana Cynthus, Ceres Aetna *loves;*
   If Windsor *Shades delight the matchless Maid,*
   Cynthus *and* Aetna *stoop to* Windsor *Shade.*
85–90. MS: *Say* Daphnis, *say, what Region canst thou find,*
   In which by Thistles, Lilies *are outshin'd?*
   If all thy Skill *can make the Meaning known,*
   The Prize, *the Victor's* Prize, *shall be thy own.*
      Daphnis.
   Nay tell me first, in what new Grove appears
   A wondrous Tree that sacred Monarchs bears?
85. **Shepherd:** *1751: Daphnis*

85–6. Warton (1756: 8–9) objected to this riddle as savouring 'of pun, and puerile conceit'.
85. ***glad Soil:*** happy or blessed land or place.
86. ***wondrous* Tree:** As Pope's note indicates, this is an allusion to the 'Boscobel Oak', in which Charles II is supposed to have hidden from Parliamentarian forces after defeat at the Battle of Worcester, 6 September 1651; cf. *Windsor-Forest*, 219. The anniversary of Charles's restoration was celebrated as Oak-Apple Day. 'Sacred *Monarchs*' is a strong statement of divine-right theory, more possible for Pope under the Stuart Anne than it would have been under William III or the Georges. See further Headnote to *Windsor-Forest*.

130   PASTORALS (1709)

DAPHNIS.

    Nay tell me first, in what more happy Fields
90   The *Thistle* springs, to which the *Lilly* yields?
    And then a nobler Prize I will resign,
    For *Sylvia*, charming *Sylvia* shall be thine.

DAMON.

    Cease to contend, for (*Daphnis*) I decree
    The Bowl to *Strephon*, and the Lamb to thee:
95   Blest Swains, whose Nymphs in ev'ry Grace excell;

90, n. *1736–51: The Thistle springs, to which the Lilly yields,*] alludes to the Device of the *Scots* Monarchs, the *Thistle*, worn by Queen *Anne*; and to the Arms of *France*, the *Fleur de Lys*. The two Riddles are in imitation of those in *Virg. Ecl.* 3.

    Dic quibus in terris inscripti nomina Regum
    Nascuntur Flores, *& Phyllida solus habebis* [*1751: habeto*].

93. MS: *I've heard enough; and* Daphnis, *I decree*

89–90. Pope offered Walsh two versions of this couplet: see Appendix I.

89. happy Fields: cf. the 'glad Soil' of 85. 'Field' can also mean a heraldic field ('the surface of a shield', *SJ*; *OED*, sense 17a), as on the Royal Arms of England, where from 1707, after the Act of Union between England and Scotland, the quartering was altered to reflect the new status of Scotland, with France removed to the less important second quarter. The thistle had been a national symbol (though not heraldic in this instance) of Scotland since the thirteenth century; the '*Lilly*' or fleur-de-lis was the heraldic emblem of France (cf. *Windsor-Forest*, 304). *TE* (I.40) notes in addition that Queen Anne had revived the Order of the Thistle in 1703. The Order was founded by the exiled James II, Anne's father, and thus had some Jacobite resonances (Aden 1978: 63; Santesso 2004). Pope's note on the symbolism suggests the submission of France to Britain; the two countries had been at war for most of Pope's life, and he would celebrate the end of the War of Spanish Succession in *Windsor-Forest*. Cf. 'Rape of the Locke', I.71 and Commentary. *TE* (I.40) suggests the riddle alludes specifically to the British victory at Blenheim in 1704. The reference to Virgil is *Eclogues*, III.106–7: 'tell me in what lands are born flowers inscribed with the names of kings, and you may have Phyllis to yourself'. *EC* cites Dryden's expanded version, 163–6, *Works of Virgil*, p. 16: 'Nay tell me first, in what new Region springs | A Flow'r, that bears inscrib'd the names of Kings: | And thou shalt gain a Present as Divine | As *Phoebus* self, for *Phillis* shall be thine'.

95. Nymphs: conventional poetic and mythological female spirits of the countryside, often used as a poetic label for women, as here for Sylvia and Delia. Addison, who may have assisted Philips in writing his *Pastorals* (*OAC*, I.67), praised Philips for abandoning this type of 'superstitious mythology' in *The Spectator*, no. 523, 30 October 1712; Pope ironically repeated the

Blest Nymphs, whose Swains those Graces sing so well!
Now rise, and haste to yonder Woodbine Bow'rs,
A soft Retreat from sudden vernal Show'rs;
The Turf with rural Dainties shall be Crown'd,
100   While opening Blooms diffuse their Sweets around.
For see! the gath'ring Flocks to Shelter tend,
And from the *Pleiads* fruitful Show'rs descend.

99, n. *1736–51:* was originally,

> The turf with country dainties shall be spread,
> And trees with twining branches shade your head.

99. Crown'd: MS: spread
100. MS: *And twining Trees with Branches shade y.^r Head.*

---

praise in his *Guardian* no. 40 essay, *PW*, I.104, noting that Philips had not used 'the Words *Nymph, Dryad, Naiad, Fawn, Cupid,* or *Satyr*' in his *Pastorals*. Pope used them all in the *Pastorals* except 'Fawn', which, however, appears at 'Vertumnus and Pomona', 21.

97. Woodbine: honeysuckle, a twining and fragrant woodland plant.

99. Dainties: delicacies. Pope reused the phrase 'rural Dainties' in his version of *The Odyssey*, IV.110. For the phrase 'twining branches', in the second line of the alternative reading given in his note, cf. 'Vertumnus and Pomona', 61.

100. opening: beginning to bloom, as in 'Autumn', 37, and 'The Garden', Pope's juvenile imitation of Cowley, 3: 'Where opening *Roses* breathing sweets diffuse'.

Sweets: perfumes.

101. tend: make their way.

102. Pleiads: Pleiades, a group of stars in the constellation Taurus. The rising of this constellation in the morning occurred in April and was associated with Spring rains, the 'fruitful Show'rs' of the same line, which also refers to the identification of the Pleiades with the seven daughters of Atlas, transformed to stars because of their sorrow at the fate of their father. Pope uses constellations again in this manner at 'Summer', 21; 'Autumn', 72; 'Winter', 85; and cf. the astronomical aspects of 'January and May', 402–3, 609–16, and *Windsor-Forest*, 243.

SUMMER.

The Second Pastoral,

OR

ALEXIS.

A Faithful Swain, whom Love had taught to sing,
Bewail'd his Fate beside a silver Spring;

1–4, n. 1736–51: VER 1, 2, 3, 4. were thus printed in the first edition;

A faithful swain, whom Love had taught to sing,
Bewail'd his Fate beside a silver spring;
Where gentle Thames *his winding waters leads,*
Thro' verdant forests, and thro' flow'ry meads.

Title. MS: *SUMMER:* | *The Second Pastoral,* | OR | ALEXIS.; *1717–43:* SUMMER. | THE | SECOND PASTORAL. | To Dr. GARTH.; *1751:* SUMMER. | THE | SECOND PASTORAL, | OR ALEXIS. | To Dr. GARTH.
1–2. MS, *1736–51: A Shepherd's Boy (he seeks no better Name)*
Led forth his Flocks along the silver Thame;

SUMMER. In the parodic *Guardian*, no. 40, Pope suggested comparing this pastoral with Philips's first: *PW*, I.102. The love complaint is a common type of pastoral: e.g. Virgil, *Eclogues*, II, VIII, X; Spenser, 'Januarie' and 'June'. *TE* (I. 44) points out that the eleventh of Theocritus' *Idylls*, the complaint of the Cyclops Polyphemus, is addressed to a physician. In 1717 'Summer' was dedicated to Samuel Garth; see title variant and 9.

Title. *ALEXIS*: conventional pastoral name, as in Virgil, *Eclogues*, II, where Alexis is the youth beloved of Corydon, and VII; also Congreve, *The Mourning Muse of Alexis* (1695), a pastoral elegy for Queen Mary. In 'A Pastoral Dialogue, Between Two Shepherdesses. By the Author of the Poem on the Spleen' [Anne Finch], Alexis is found lamenting his love for Delia (in the same volume of *Poetical Miscellanies* as Pope's *Pastorals*). Several commentators speculate on the personal resonance of the name for Pope (e.g. Battestin 1969; Mack 1982: 381–2; Stephanson 1991).

1–4 MS and variants. Shepherd's . . . Name: See Pope's note to 'Spring', 1: the first line overtly recalls the opening lines of Spenser's *The Shepheardes Calender* (1579): 'A Shepeheards boye (no better doe him call,) | . . . Led forth his flock'; cf. 39 and Pope's note to 'Spring', 1, and Commentary there.

Thame: the Thames itself, rather than the tributary Thame which joins it near Dorchester-on-Thames (cf. *Windsor-Forest*, 338).

quiv'ring shade: cf. *Windsor-Forest*, 135.

1–2. Pope presented Walsh with the reading of the manuscript and two further options for the first line: see Appendix I.

>   Where gentle *Thames* his winding Waters leads
>   Thro' verdant Forests, and thro' flow'ry Meads.
> 5   There while he mourn'd, the Streams forgot to flow,
>   The Flocks around a dumb Compassion show,
>   The *Naiads* wept in ev'ry Watry Bow'r,
>   And *Jove* consented in a silent Show'r.
>
>   Accept, O *Garth*, the Muse's early Lays,

3, n. 1736–51: The Scene of this Pastoral by the River's side; suitable to the heat of the season; the Time, Noon.

8, n. 1736–51: And Jove *consented.*] Virg. *Jupiter & laeto descendet plurimus imbri.*

9, n. 1736–51: Dr. *Samuel Garth,* Author of the *Dispensary,* was one of the first friends of the author, whose acquaintance with him began at fourteen or fifteen. Their friendship continu'd from the year 1703, to 1718, which was that of his death.

3–4. MS: *There to the Winds he plain'd his hapless Love,*
       And Amaryllis *filled the* Vocal Grove.

   1736–51: Where dancing sun-beams on the waters play'd,
             And verdant alders form'd a quiv'ring shade.

5–7. MS: *For him, the Lambs a dumb Compassion show,*
          The list'ning Streams forget a while to flow;
          Relenting Naids *wept in ev'ry Bow'r,*

5. There while: *1751:* Soft as
9–12. MS: omitted

---

3. winding Waters: a common phrase, but probably recalled from Dryden's version of Virgil, *Georgics*, III.22, *Works of Virgil*, p. 97: 'And Reeds defend the winding Waters Brink'. Cf. *Windsor-Forest*, 298 and Commentary.

3 Pope's note. Cf. Pope's note at 'Spring', 17–22.

5. forgot: cf. Virgil, *Eclogues*, VIII.4: 'et mutata suos requierunt flumina cursus' ('And the changed rivers abandoned their courses'). EC cites also Garth, *Dispensary*, IV, sixth edition (1706), p. 64: 'The Banks of *Rhine* a pleas'd Attention show, | And Silver *Sequana* forgets to flow'. Pope returns to the idea at 84.

6. dumb Compassion: EC compares Congreve, *The Tears of Amaryllis*, 14 (1703), p. 2: 'And dumb Distress and new Compassion shew'.

7–8. Pope presented a version of this couplet to Walsh: see Appendix I.

7. Naiads: in classical mythology and poetry, water nymphs.

Bow'r: 'an arbour; a sheltered place covered with green trees, twined and bent' (*SJ*), as in 'Spring' 97; Pope imagines an underwater version of this. See quotation in Commentary at 51 below.

8. Jove: one of the names of the supreme god in classical mythology (in Greek, Zeus; in Roman, Jupiter), whose 'consent' is normally given by a nod (see Pope's translation of Homer, *Iliad*, I.680–7). His 'silent Show'r' here indicates sympathetic weeping in the form of rain; cf. 'The Episode of Sarpedon', 256–7.

8 Pope's note. Virgil, *Eclogues*, VII.60: 'and Jupiter shall descend plentifully in a joyful shower of rain'.

9. Garth: see Headnote. In 1717, when Pope contributed to the translation of Ovid's *Metamorphoses* that Garth was editing, Pope formally dedicated this pastoral to him (see textual notes).

Lays: songs.

10   That adds this Wreath of Ivy to thy Bays;
       Hear what from Love unpractis'd Hearts endure,
       From Love, the sole Disease thou canst not cure!

       Ye shady Beeches, and ye cooling Streams,
       Defence from *Phoebus*, not from *Cupid*'s Beams;
15   To you I mourn; nor to the Deaf I sing,
       The Woods shall answer, and their Echo ring.
       Ev'n Hills and Rocks attend my doleful Lay,
       Why art thou prouder and more hard than they?
       The bleating Sheep with my Complaints agree,

15, n. *1736–51:* – *Nor to the deaf I sing* –] *Non canimus surdis, respondent omnia sylvae.* Virg.
16, n. *1736–51: The woods shall answer, and their echo ring,* is a line out of *Spenser's Epithalamion.*

14. Phoebus: *1751:* Phoebus'
17. Ev'n: MS, *1736–51:* The
19. MS: *And with my Cries the bleating Flocks agree,*

---

10. Ivy ... Bays: versions of honouring the poet with a crown of leaves; see *Essay on Criticism*, 709. Pope adds an additional crown of ivy, Garth's own efforts having already crowned him with bays (laurel). TE cites Virgil, *Eclogues*, VIII.11–13, and 17–18 of Dryden's translation, *Works of Virgil*, p. 35: 'Amidst thy Laurels let this Ivy twine, | Thine was my earliest Muse ...'; and Dryden, 'To the Memory of Mr. Oldham', 24, *Works of Mr. John Oldham* (1684), 'Remains', sig. A4ʳ: 'Thy Brows with Ivy, and with Laurels bound'.

11. unpractis'd: inexperienced, unskilled, therefore also uncalculating, sincere.

12. cure: alluding to Garth's profession as doctor. Wakefield identifies a source in the opening of Theocritus, *Idylls*, XI, the love-complaint of the Cyclops Polyphemus, also addressed to a physician. In Creech's *Idylliums of Theocritus* (1684), p. 62: 'IN vain, *Learn'd Sir,* in vain is all your Art, | There is no *Physick* for a wounded heart; | No Herb can ease, no Salve the Pain remove, | There is no cure for the disease of Love | Beside the *Muses* ...'

14. Phoebus: cf. 'Spring', 45.
   Cupid: cf. 'Spring', 49.

15 Pope's note. Virgil, *Eclogues*, X. 8: 'We are not singing to the deaf: all the woods respond'. Wakefield cites the version by Ogilby, 9–10, *Works of Publius Virgilius Maro* (1654), p. 55: 'Nor to the deaf do we our numbers sing, | Since woods in answering us with echoes ring'.

16 Pope's note. Each stanza of Spenser's *Epithalamion* (1595) concludes with a variant of this line, e.g. 'The woods shall to me answer and my Eccho ring'.

18. thou: addressing the beloved, whereas the previous 'you' (15) must be the 'shady Beeches' and 'cooling Streams' of 13.

19. Complaints: in the literary sense, common in amatory lyric and pastoral, of songs of lament; e.g. Shakespeare, 'A Lover's Complaint', in the *Sonnets* (1609). Cf. 'Autumn', 3, 58; 'Winter', 77.

20   They parch'd with Heat, and I inflam'd by thee.
      The sultry *Sirius* burns the thirsty Plains,
      While in thy Heart Eternal Winter reigns.

      Where are ye Muses, in what Lawn or Grove,
      While your *Alexis* pines in hopeless Love?
25   In those fair Fields where Sacred *Isis* glides,
      Or else where *Cam* his winding Vales divides?

23, n. *1736–51: Where stray ye Muses, &c.*]

Quae nemora, aut qui vos saltus habuere, puellae
Naiades, indigno cum Gallus amore periret?
Nam neque Parnassi vobis juga, nam neque Pindi
Ulla moram fecere, neque Aonia Aganippe.
                                    Virg. out of *Theoc.*

22. While: MS: *But*
23. are: *1717–51:* stray
26. winding Vales: MS: *Laurel-Banks*

---

20. Cf. Dryden's translation of Virgil, *Eclogues*, II.14, *Works of Virgil*, p. 6: 'They fry'd with Heat, and I with fierce Desire'.

21. Sirius: a bright star in the constellation Canis Major or 'the Great Dog', hence known as the dog star; associated since classical times with high summer, excessive heat and illness. Cf. 'The First Book of Statius His Thebais', 748; 'On the Statue of Cleopatra', 64; and *Epistle to Dr Arbuthnot*, 3. For the scientific background in Pope's time see Nicolson and Rousseau (1968: 280–1). For similar uses of constellations see 'Spring', 102; 'Autumn', 72; 'Winter', 85.

thirsty: parched by drought.

22. Eternal Winter: The phrase is common in poetry: e.g. Congreve, *Tears of Amaryllis*, 57 (1703), p. 4. For 'winter' as emotional coldness, EC compares Spenser, 'Januarie', 25: 'Such rage as winters, reigneth in my heart'. Cf. also Thomas Randolph, 'A Pastoral Courtship', *Poems* (1652), p. 106: 'But that which only moves my smart, | Is to see winter in thy heart'.

23. Lawn: a clearing in a wood; cf. *Windsor-Forest*, 21, and Commentary.

23 Pope's note. Virgil, *Eclogues*, X.9–12: 'What groves or what glades did you inhabit, young Naiads, when Gallus was perishing with an undeserving love? For no ridge or Parnassus or of Pindus, no Aonian Aganippe, caused you delay'. Wakefield cites Ogilby's version, *Works of Publius Virgilius Maro* (1654), p. 55: 'Say *Naiades* where were you, in what Grove, | Or Lawn, when *Gallus* fell by ill-match'd love'; and Milton, 'Lycidas', 50–1, *Poems* (1645), p. 59: 'Where were ye Nymphs when the remorseless deep | Clos'd o're the head of your lov'd *Lycidas*?' The reference to Theocritus is to *Idylls*, I.65–7; in Creech's *Idylliums*, p. 5: 'Where were you *Nymphs*? Where did the *Nymphs* reside, | Where were you then when *Daphnis* pin'd and dy'd?'

25-6. For the image, Wakefield compares Addison, *The Campaign*, 323–4 (1705), p. 16: 'Or where the *Sein* her flow'ry Fields divides, | Or where the *Loire* through winding Vineyards glides'. Cf. 'Winter', 3.

　　　　As in the Crystal Spring I view my Face,
　　　　Fresh rising Blushes paint the watry Glass;
　　　　But since those Graces please thy Sight no more,
30　　　I'll shun the Fountains which I sought before.
　　　　Once I was skill'd in ev'ry Herb that grew,
　　　　And ev'ry Plant that drinks the Morning Dew;
　　　　Ah wretched Shepherd, what avails thy Art,
　　　　To cure thy Lambs, but not to heal thy Heart!

27, n. *1736–51: Oft in the crystal spring I cast a view,*
　　　　　　　　And equal'd Hylas, *if the glass be true;*
　　　　　　　　But since those graces meet my eyes no more,
　　　　　　　　I shun, &c.
Virgil *again from the* Cyclops *of* Theocritus,
　　　　　　　　nuper me in litore vidi
　　　　　　　　Cum placidum ventis staret mare, non ego Daphnim
　　　　　　　　Judice te, metuam, si nunquam fallat imago.

27–29. MS: *Oft' in the Spring I cast a careful View,*
　　　　　　　And rival'd Daphnis, *if the Glass be true;*
　　　　　　　But now those Graces meet my Eyes no more,
29. Sight: *1736–51:* eyes
30. I'll: MS, *1717–51:* I

---

25. Sacred Isis: the name sometimes given to the section of the Thames that runs through Oxford; cf. *Windsor-Forest*, 337–8.

26. Cam: the river that runs through the relatively flat ground of Cambridge: Pope's landscape is more metaphorically suggestive than strictly accurate.

27. Crystal: 'bright; clear; transparent' (*SJ*); cf. 'January and May', 459; 'Episode of Sarpedon', 326; 'Winter', 21; *Essay on Criticism*, 355; *Windsor-Forest*, 374. The spring (or stream) is used as a mirror ('watry Glass'), perhaps in an allusion to the myth of Narcissus or Milton's story of Eve's fascination with her own image (*Paradise Lost*, IV.460–76).

27 Pope's note. For Hylas see Commentary on the title of 'Autumn'. Virgil, *Eclogues*, II.25–7: 'recently I saw myself on the shore when the sea stood calm from the winds; if you were the judge, I would not fear Daphnis, if the reflection never lies'. The further reference is to Theocritus, *Idylls*, XI.

28. rising Blushes: the colour in Alexis' cheeks, visible in the reflection, caused by strong sexual emotion.

29. Graces: pleasing features.

30. Fountains: springs or streams.

31–4. Cf. 12; as a shepherd Alexis uses herbal medicine to care for his flock. Wakefield compares Milton, 'Il Penseroso', 172, *Poems* (1645), p. 44: 'And every Herb that sips the dew' (cf. 69 below). Pope recalled the image in his *Iliad*, XI.877.

34. Wakefield cites Ovid, *Metamorphoses*, I. 522–4: 'et herbarum subiecta potentia nobis. | ei mihi, quod nullis amor est sanabilis herbis | nec prosunt domino, quae prosunt omnibus, artes;' ('and the powers of herbs are subject to us; alas, that love is curable by no herbs and the arts which help all others cannot help their master').

35   Let other Swains attend the Rural Care,
          Feed fairer Flocks, or richer Fleeces share;
          But nigh that Mountain let me tune my Lays,
          Embrace my Love, and bind my Brows with Bays.
          That Flute is mine which *Colin*'s tuneful Breath
40   Inspir'd when living, and bequeath'd in Death;
          He said; *Alexis*, take this Pipe, the same
          That taught the Groves my *Rosalinda*'s Name –

39, n. *1736–51: Colin.*] The name taken by *Spenser* in his Eclogues, where his mistress is celebrated under that of *Rosalinda.*

40, n. *1736–51:* [*1751:* bequeath'd in death; etc.]] *Virg. Ecl.* 2.

  Est mihi disparibus septem compacta cicutis
  Fistula, Damaetas dono mihi quam dedit olim.
  Ex dixit moriens, Te nunc habet ista secundum.

35. other Swains: MS: *those who list*
36. share;: *1751:* sheer:
37. that: MS: *this*; *1736–51:* yon'
39–41. MS: *Of slender Reeds a tuneful Flute I have,*
              The tuneful Flute, which dying Colin gave;
              And said, Alexis, *take this Pipe, the same:*

---

35. Rural Care: the shepherd's task of tending the sheep, a rare example of labour in the *Pastorals.* Wakefield identifies a source in Theocritus, *Idylls,* VIII.53–6.

36. share: shear (cf. 1751 reading in the textual apparatus), possibly pronounced to rhyme with 'care' in Pope's day.

39–40. Pope presented Walsh with a different version of this couplet; see Appendix I.

39. Flute: a reed pipe, conventional image of pastoral music; see Commentary at 'Spring', 11.

Colin: As Pope's note indicates, this alludes to Spenser's pastoral name, 'Colin Clout', in the *Shepheardes Calender*; Rosalinda is the mistress. Thomas Lodge's *Rosalynde* (1590) and Shakespeare's *As You Like It* (1600) also use the name for a pastoral mistress, as does Philips in his first and sixth pastorals. For the rivalry over the succession of pastoral poets, see Headnote. In handing the pipe to Alexis in 41, a clear signal of the succession is given.

40. Inspir'd: punning on the literal sense of 'inspiration', to breathe into; cf. 'Spring', 11.

40 Pope's note. Virgil, *Eclogues,* II. 36–8: 'I have a pipe, fixed together from seven hemlock stalks of different lengths, which Damoetas once gave me for a gift. And he said, dying, this now has you as second [owner]'.

42. taught . . . Name: i.e. by repeating the name aloud; cf. 'Winter', 43. Wakefield cites Virgil, *Eclogues,* I.5: 'formosam resonare doces Amaryllida silvas' ('you teach the woods to resound beautiful Amaryllis'). TE compares the translation by John, Lord Caryll (d. 1711; uncle of Pope's closest Catholic friend John Caryll senior), in *Miscellany Poems* (1684), 6: 'And every Grove learns *Amarillis* name'.

Yet soon the Reeds shall hang on yonder Tree,
For ever silent, since despis'd by thee.
45 O were I made by some transforming Pow'r,
The Captive Bird that sings within thy Bow'r!
Then might my Voice thy list'ning Ears employ,
And I those Kisses he receives, enjoy.

And yet my Numbers please the rural Throng,
50 Rough *Satyrs* dance, and *Pan* applauds the Song:
The Nymphs forsaking ev'ry Cave and Spring,
Their early Fruit, and milk-white Turtles bring;

---

43. **Yet soon:** MS: *But soon*; *1717–51:* But now
44–6. MS: *If once their Music sounds not sweet to thee.*
       Some pitying God *command me to be made*
       The Bird *that sings within thy secret Shade*:
49. **rural:** MS: *Sylvan*
50. **applauds:** MS: *attends*
51. **The:** MS: *And*
52–4. MS: *Of Fruits and Turtles rural Presents bring*:
       Ah wanton Nymphs, *your rural Gifts are vain*;
       My Amaryllis *wins them all again*!

---

43. Reeds: the reed pipe or flute, as in 39. At this point Alexis speaks once more in his own voice, lamenting the unresponsiveness of his love to his music. For the hanging of the reed on the tree see 39. Lyres, also a symbol of poetic art ('Spring', 12), are hung on trees in *Windsor-Forest*, 274.

45–6. For Pope's alternative version of this couplet, presented to Walsh, see Appendix I.

45. transforming Pow'r: of the kind exemplified throughout Ovid's *Metamorphoses*. TE cites Dryden's translation of Theocritus, *Idylls*, III.28–9, *Miscellany Poems* (1684), p. 236: 'Some God transform me by his Heavenly pow'r | Ev'n to a *Bee* to buzz within your Bow'r'.

46. Captive Bird: a songbird in a cage.

49–50. EC cites Dryden's translation of Virgil, *Eclogues*, VI.42–3, *Works of Virgil*, p. 27: 'He rais'd his voice; and soon a num'rous throng | Of tripping Satyrs crowded to the Song'. For line 49 Wakefield compares Virgil, *Eclogues*, IX.33–4: 'me quoque dicunt | vatem pastores' ('the shepherds call me a poet also').

49. Numbers: verses; cf. *Essay on Criticism*, 340, and Commentary.

50. Satyrs: originally in Greek mythology, wild and semi-bestial companions of Dionysus, god of wine; also associated with Nature and fertility rites, hence 'Rough ... dance'. TE suggests a reminiscence of Milton, 'Lycidas', 34, *Poems* (1645), p. 58: 'Rough *Satyrs* danc'd'. See also Commentary at 'Spring', 96.

Pan: god of shepherds and wild nature, who features in Theocritus, *Idylls*, I; Virgil, *Eclogues*, II and X; and Spenser, 'Januarie', 17, and throughout 'December'; cf. *Windsor-Forest*, 37, 181.

51. EC compares Spenser, 'The Mourning Muse of Thestylis', 1–2, *Colin Clouts Come Home Againe* (1595), sig. G3ʳ: 'Come forth ye Nymphes come forth, forsake your watry bowres, | Forsake your mossy caues'; but very similar imagery occurs in 'Aprill', 37–9, in the *Shepheardes Calender*.

52–3. EC suggests a source for the giving of gifts by appreciative nymphs in Spenser, *Astrophel*, 47–8, *Colin Clouts Come Home*

SUMMER 139

Each am'rous Nymph prefers her Gifts in vain,
On you their Gifts are all bestow'd again!
55   For you the Swains the fairest Flow'rs design,
And in one Garland all their Beauties join;
Accept the Wreath which You deserve alone,
In whom all Beauties are compriz'd in One.

See what Delights in Sylvan Scenes appear!
60   Descending Gods have found *Elysium* here.
In Woods bright *Venus* with *Adonis* stray'd,
And chast *Diana* haunts the Forest Shade.

---

55. fairest: MS: *choicest*
57. the: MS: *a*
58. compriz'd: MS: *combin'd*
59–60. MS: (no new paragraph)
    Nor Scorn a Shepherd; Heav' ns Immortal Pow'rs
    For Sylvan *Scenes have left their blissful Bow'rs*;
61. bright: MS: *fair*

Againe, sig. F1ʳ: 'And brought him presents, flowers if it were prime, | Or mellow fruit if it were haruest time'.

52. Turtles: turtle-doves, traditional symbol of loving companionship, as in Song of Solomon 2:12; cf. 'Sapho to Phaon', 43.

53. prefers: 'prefer' in the sense of 'present ceremoniously' or 'offer solemnly' (*SJ*).

54. bestow'd again: i.e. Alexis gives to his beloved all the gifts given to him by the Nymphs, as Colin forwards the gifts of Hobbinol to Rosalind, in Spenser, 'Januarye', 57–60.

55-6. The rhyming of 'join' with 'design' was acceptable in Pope's time and may indicate the pronunciation 'jine'; cf. John Tutchin, *The Apostates* (1701), p. 8: 'For tho to feast the *Hero's* they did join, | Against the *Parliament* was the Design'.

55. design: work into a design (the 'Wreath' of 56).

59. Sylvan Scenes: cf. 'Spring', 1, and Commentary. Pope's phrase perhaps echoes Dryden's 'To the Pious Memory of the Accomplisht Young Lady Mrs. Anne Killigrew', 108, *Examen Poeticum* (1693), p. 358: 'The *Sylvan* Scenes of Herds and Flocks'; Dryden also uses it in his version of the *Aeneid*, III.34.

60. Elysium: in classical mythology, a place of abode for distinguished or virtuous souls after death.

60 Pope's note. Virgil, *Eclogues*, II.60: 'the Gods have also lived in woods', and X.18: 'Even beautiful Adonis has fed sheep by rivers'.

61. Venus ... Adonis: The tragic story of Venus' love for the mortal youth Adonis was mentioned in Theocritus, *Idylls*, III; *Idyll* XV describes the Adonis festival. Pope would have known the story from this and other allusions, e.g. Virgil, *Eclogues*, X and Ovid, *Metamorphoses*, X.519–739, and from Shakespeare's elaborate narrative poem *Venus and Adonis* (1592). He probably knew Oldham's 'Lamentation for Adonis', published in Oldham's *Some New Pieces* (1681), modelled on the first *Idyll* of the Theocritan imitator Bion.

62. chast: chaste.

Come lovely Nymph, and bless the silent Hours,
When Swains from Sheering seek their nightly Bow'rs;
65   When weary Reapers quit the sultry Field,
And crown'd with Corn, their Thanks to *Ceres* yield.
This harmless Grove no lurking Viper hides,
But in my Breast the Serpent Love abides.
Here Bees from Blossoms sip the rosie Dew,

60, n. *1736–51: Descending Gods have found* Elysium *here.*]
 – *Habitarunt Dî quoque sylvas* – Virg.
 Et formosus oves ad flumina pavit Adonis. Idem.

63–86. MS: *Oh deign a while to bless our humble Seats,*
 Our mossie Fountains, and our Green Retreats.
 This harmless Grove no lurking Viper hides,
 But Love the Serpent in my Breast abides.
 Here Tereus *mourns, and* Itys *tells his Pain;*
 Of Progne *they, and I of you complain.*
 Here Bees from Blossomes sip the rosie Dew,
 But your Alexis *knows no Sweet but You.*

 Come lovely Maid, and crown the silent Hours,
 When Swains from Shearing *seek their nightly Bow'rs;*
 When weary Reapers *leave the sultry Field,*
 And crown'd with Corn, *their Thanks to* Ceres *yield.*
 While to the Groves your Presence you deny,
 Our Flow'rs are faded, and our Floods are dry;
 Tho' with'ring Herbs lay dying on the Plain,
 At your Return, they shall be green again.
 In shady Forests *I may waste my Days,*
 Invoke the Muses, and proclaim your Praise;
 Your Praise in Songs the Birds to Heav'n shall bear,
 And Wolves grow milder when the Sound they hear.

---

64. Sheering: shearing.
65. Wakefield suggests a source in Virgil, *Eclogues*, II.10: 'rapido fessis messoribus aestu', translated by Ogilby, *Works of Publius Virgilius Maro* (1654), p. 7, as 'And for the Reapers, tir'd with sultry heats'.
66. crown'd with Corn: apparently suggesting that reapers wore crowns of plaited corn in ceremonial worship of Ceres, for whom see 'Spring', 66.
67-8 MS. An allusion to the story of Philomela; see 'Spring', 26, and Commentary.
67. lurking Viper: Wakefield compares Virgil, *Eclogues*, III.93: 'latet anguis in herba' ('a snake lurks in the grass'); there is perhaps for Pope's audience also a suggestion of the serpent (68) who lurked in the Garden of Eden; see variant to 'Spring', 36.
69. TE compares Dryden's translation of Virgil, *Georgics*, IV.76, *Works of Virgil*, p. 124, speaking of bees: 'They skim the Floods, and sip the purple Flow'rs', and of *Eclogues*, I.110, *ibid.*, p. 5: 'No more my Sheep shall sip the Morning Dew'. Cf. the quotation in Commentary to 31–4.
 rosie Dew: nectar.

70   But your *Alexis* knows no Sweet but you.
      Some God conduct you to these blissful Seats,
      The mossie Fountains, and the Green Retreats!
      Where-e'er you walk, cool Gales shall fan the Glade,
      Trees, where you sit, shall crowd into a Shade,
75   Where-e'er you tread, the blushing Flow'rs shall rise,
      And all things flourish where you turn your Eyes.
      Oh! how I long with you to pass my Days,
      Invoke the Muses, and resound your Praise;

79–80, n. *1736–51: Your praise the tuneful birds to heav' n shall bear,*
                    And list'ning wolves grow milder as they hear.
   [*1751:* So the verses were originally written. But the author, young as he was, soon found the absurdity which *Spenser* himself overlooked, of introducing Wolves into England.]

63–86. (cont.)
   Such magick Musick dwells within your Name,
   The Voice of Orpheus *no such pow'r cou'd claim*;
   Had you then liv'd, when he the Forests drew,
   The Trees and Orpheus *both had follow'd You.*

   But see, the Southing Sun displays his Beams;
   See Tity'rus *leads his Herd to Silver Streams*;

70. Sweet: *1751:* sweets
71. *1736–51:* Oh deign to visit our forsaken seats,
78. Praise;: *1736–51:* praise!

---

70. Sweet: pleasing sweetness, analogous to the nectar sought by the bees.

71–6. Pope offered Walsh several different versions of these lines; see Appendix I.

71. blissful Seats: Milton uses 'blissful seat' of Paradise twice: *Paradise Lost*, I.5 and III.527.

72. mossie Fountains: Milton has 'mossie Fountain' in *Paradise Regain'd*, II.184, but it is there a place of sexual ambush. Cf. Pope, 'Messiah', 3.

   Green Retreats: cf. Addison, 'A Letter from Italy', 148, *Poetical Miscellanies: The Fifth Part* (1704), p. 5, 'Or cover me in *Umbria*'s Green Retreats' and Fenton, 'The Dream', 1, *Oxford and Cambridge Miscellany Poems* (1708), p. 174: 'To green Retreats, that shade the Muses stream'.

73–6. These lines were interpolated into George Frederick Handel's oratorio *Semele* (1744), based on an opera of that title by Pope's friend William Congreve (see Headnote), first printed in 1710; Pope's passage was probably interpolated by Newburgh Hamilton. *TE* collects several of analogues for the general idea of this passage, including most prominently the opening speech of Ben Jonson, *The Sad Shepherd* (from the *Workes*, 1641, vol. 2), and Waller, 'At Pens-hurst', 11–16 (*Poems, &c.*, p. 23) with an origin in stories of the birth of Aphrodite (Hesiod, *Theogony*, 118–200), whose footsteps produced the growth of grass. Jones (2010) argues that Pope is competitively alluding both to Waller and to Waller's source in Ovid, *Metamorphoses*, X.86–106, where the central figure is Orpheus the poet (see 81).

73. Gales: a poeticism for 'breezes', common in Pope; cf. 'Autumn', 17; 'On a Fan of the Author's Design', 5; etc.

75. blushing: colourful; cf. 'Spring', 31.

77. Wakefield cites Virgil, *Eclogues*, X.43, 'hic ipso tecum consumerer aevo' ('here with you I would wear away through age itself').

78. i.e. compose poetry in praise of the beloved.

>   Your Praise the Birds shall chant in ev'ry Grove,
> 80 And Winds shall waft it to the Pow'rs above.
>   But wou'd you sing, and rival *Orpheus* Strain,
>   The wondring Forests soon shou'd dance again,
>   The moving Mountains hear the pow'rful Call,
>   And headlong Streams hang list'ning in their Fall!
>
> 85   But see, the Shepherds shun the Noon-day Heat,
>   The lowing Herds to murm'ring Brooks retreat,
>   To closer Shades the panting Flocks remove,

80, n. *1736–51: And Winds shall waft –*]

> Partem aliquam, venti, divúm referatis ad aures!
> Virg.

81. Orpheus: *1717–51: Orpheus'*

79–80 variants. Eight of the monthly eclogues in Spenser's *Shepheardes Calender* contain references to wolves, the greatest concentration being in 'September'. *TE* points out that in that poem (151-3) Hobbinol notes that wolves have not been seen recently. Wolves may not have been quite extinct in Britain in Spenser's time, and may have survived in Scotland even into Pope's day. See also 'Autumn', 90, variant. In his *Guardian* no. 40 essay on Pastoral, Pope makes fun of Philips for introducing wolves into his first pastoral; *PW*, I.99. Cf. also *Winsdor-Forest*, 72, and Commentary.

80 Pope's note. Virgil, *Eclogues*, III.73: 'Winds, carry some part to the ears of the gods'. Wakefield compares 90 of Creech's translation: 'Winds bear their Musick to the Gods above'.

81–4. Cf. 'Messiah', 26.

81. rival Orpheus Strain: compete with the singing of Orpheus, offspring of Apollo and a Muse, legendary poet of early Greece and standard reference point for the dark mysteries of poetic imagination. He was supposed to have been able to make trees and mountains move to the music of the lyre, hence the images in 82-4. Cf. 'To the Author of a Poem, intitled, Successio', 9.

82. dance again: *TE* compares Virgil, *Eclogues*, III.46: 'Orpheaque in medio posuit silvasque sequentis', and the translation of (among others) Ogilby, 'Where *Orpheus* 'midst the dancing woods is set'.

83. moving: moved by the music.

84. headlong Streams: waterfalls. Wakefield cites Lucan, *De Bello Civili*, VI.472-3: 'De rupe pependit | abscisa fixus torrens' ('the immobile waterfall hangs from the precipice') and many possible intermediate analogues, including Congreve, *The Tears of Amaryllis*, 19 (1703), p. 2: 'And rapid Rivers listen'd at their Source'. Bowles cites Oldham, 'Bion', 40, *Some New Pieces*, p. 75: 'For which the list'ning streams forgot to run'. For the image cf. also 'The First Book of Statius his Thebais', 500.

85-92. *TE* suggests close modelling on the final lines of Virgil, *Eclogues*, II, as signalled in Pope's note to 88.

Ye Gods! and is there no Relief for Love?
But soon the Sun with milder Rays descends
90   To the cool Ocean, where his Journey ends;
On me Love's fiercer Flames for ever prey,
By Night he scorches, as he burns by Day.

88, n. *1736–51*: [*1751: Ye Gods, etc.*]]
  Me tamen urit amor, quis enim modus adsit amori?
  Id.
91, n. *1736–51: Me love inflames, nor will his fires allay.*

91. MS: *Me Love inflames, nor will his Fires allay,*

---

87. **closer Shades:** deeper shelter from the sun. **panting:** short of breath in hot weather.
88 **Pope's note.** Virgil, *Eclogues*, II. 68: 'Love burns me, however, for what limit can there be to love?' Wakefield suggests a source in Dryden's translation, 99-100: 'Cool Breezes now the raging Heats remove; | Ah, cruel Heaven! that made no Cure for Love!'.
91 **Pope's note.** To 'allay' is 'to quiet; to pacify; to repress' (*SJ*).

AUTUMN.

The Third Pastoral,

OR

HYLAS and AEGON.

To W. WYCHERLEY, *Esq*;

B Eneath the Shade a spreading Beech displays,
Hylas and *Aegon* sung their Rural Lays;
To whose Complaints the list'ning Forests bend,
While one his Mistress mourns, and one his Friend:

AUTUMN, *n. 1736–51:* This Pastoral consists of two parts, like the 8th of *Virgil*: The Scene, a Hill; the Time, at Sun-set.

Title. MS: *AUTUMN.* | *The Third Pastoral,* | OR | HYLAS and AEGON.; *1717–43: AUTUMN.* | THE | THIRD PASTORAL. | To Mr. *WYCHERLEY.*; *1751:* AUTUMN. | THE | THIRD PASTORAL, | OR | HYLAS and AEGON. | To Mr. WYCHERLEY.

3–4. *1736–51:* This mourn'd a faithless, that an absent Love,
        And *Delia*'s name, and *Doris* fill'd the Grove.

AUTUMN. *TE* (I. 45) suggests general sources for this pastoral in Virgil, *Eclogues*, VIII, and Theocritus, *Idylls*, II and III.

    Pope's note. For the time scheme, see Pope's notes at 'Spring', 17, and 'Winter', 89, and Commentary.

Title. *HYLAS and AEGON:* In Greek mythology, Hylas was the name of Herakles' companion, who was seduced into a spring and drowned by water-nymphs who had fallen in love with him; the story is told in Theocritus, *Idylls*, XIII, and mentioned in Virgil, *Eclogues*, VI.44; Pope travesties the story in the mud-diving contest in *The Dunciad* (1728), II.300 (see Rumbold 2007, Commentary on II.58 and 271-2). The name appears in Waller's lyric dialogue, 'Chloris and Hylas'; the name *Aegon* appears in Theocritus, *Idylls*, IV, and Virgil, *Eclogues*, III and IV.

Dedication. *To* W. *WYCHERLEY:* William Wycherley, comic dramatist and poet, with whom Pope enjoyed a strong early literary friendship and correspondence; see Headnote and Commentary to Pope's general note.

1. Wakefield compares Dryden's version of Virgil, *Eclogues*, I.1, 'Beneath the Shade which Beechen Boughs diffuse'; Pope's note to 'Spring', 1, points out the allusion to Virgil.

    displays: causes to be observed or perceived (*OED*, sense 4b); perhaps also unfurls, expands or spreads out (*OED*, sense 1a), i.e. the branches frame to view the shade they are providing. Pope used the phrase in the latter sense in his version of the *Odyssey*, XII.347: 'Then while the night displays her awful shade'.

2. *Lays:* songs.

3. *list'ning . . . bend:* EC compares Oldham, 'Bion', 41, *Some New Pieces*, p. 75: 'And Trees lean'd their attentive branches down'. Cf. also 'Summer', 74.

4. *Mistress . . . Friend:* For Pope's later erasure of the homoerotic suggestion that the love for the friend is equivalent to love for the mistress, see Commentary at 18.

5   Ye *Mantuan* Nymphs, your sacred Succour bring;
       Hylas and *Aegon*'s Rural Lays I sing.

       Thou, whom the Nine with *Plautus*' Wit inspire,
       The Art of *Terence*, and *Menander*'s Fire;
       Whose Sense instructs us, and whose Humour charms,
10   Whose Judgment sways us, and whose Rapture warms!

7, n. 1751: Thou, whom the Nine] Mr. Wycherley, a famous Author of Comedies; of which the most celebrated were the *Plain-Dealer* and *Country-Wife*. He was a writer of infinite spirit, satire, and wit. The only objection made to him was that he had too much. However he was followed in the same way by Mr. Congreve; tho' with a little more correctness.

5. MS: *Ye* Nymphs *of* Thames, *your kind Assistance bring,*
7–12. MS: omitted
10. Rapture: *1736–51:* spirit

3–4 variant. Doris: conventional poetic name for shepherdess or nymph.

   fill'd the Grove: Wakefield compares Dryden's version of Virgil, *Eclogues*, I.6, *Works of Virgil*, p. 1: 'And *Amarillis* fills the shady Groves'. Cf. also *Windsor-Forest*, 296.

5. Mantuan *Nymphs*: Virgil, Pope's pastoral model, was reputedly born near Mantua (now Mantova) in Cisalpine Gaul; Pope invokes the aid of the nature spirits that attended Virgil, whose own *Eclogues* I and X celebrate his Mantuan connections.

   sacred Succour: Pope reused the phrase in his version of Homer, *Iliad*, V.149: 'Now, Goddess, now, thy sacred Succour yield'.

7 Pope's note. *The Plain-Dealer* was first performed in 1676, *The Country-Wife* in 1675. For Congreve, see Headnote, and 'Summer', 73–7. On the excess wit of Wycherley, see Commentary to *Essay on Criticism*, 80–1, 306–7.

7. the Nine: Muses.

   Plautus: Titus Maccius Plautus, Roman comic playwright, c. 254–184 BC. Wycherley's plays were all comedies.

8. Terence: Publius Terentius Afer, Roman comic playwright, 195 or 185–159 BC, generally regarded as more naturalistic, urbane and humane than Plautus.

Menander: Greek comic dramatist, c.343–292 BC, whose plays were mined for plots by both Plautus and Terence. Warburton in a long note argues that Pope was alluding to a description of Terence, attributed to Julius Caesar in Suetonius' biography of Terence, in which Terence was said to lack the 'vis Comica' or 'comic strength' of Menander. The Caesar story is recalled in Dryden, *Of Dramatick Poesie* (1668), pp. 13–14.

9. Sense: meaning, doctrine, morality; analogous to 'Judgment', 10, as 'Humour' is to 'Rapture'; the principle is that poetry should combine the 'utile' with the 'dulci', the useful with the pleasing (Horace, *Epistola ad Pisones* or *Ars Poetica*, 343). These terms receive more elaborate discussion in the *Essay on Criticism*.

10. Rapture: 'uncommon heat of imagination' (*SJ*). TE approves the textual change to 'spirit' on the grounds that 'rapture' was inappropriate for Wycherley. Pope used the word repeatedly in his commendation of Homer in the Preface to his translation of *The Iliad* (1715), as well as commonly in the Homer translations themselves. Cf. also *Essay on Criticism*, 239, and *One Thousand Seven Hundred and Thirty Eight*, 3, speaking of himself: 'You grow *correct* that once with Rapture writ'.

Attend the Muse, tho' low her Numbers be,
She sings of Friendship, and she sings to thee.

The setting Sun now shone serenely bright,
And fleecy Clouds were streak'd with Purple Light;
15   When tuneful *Hylas* with melodious Moan
Taught Rocks to weep, and made the *Mountains* groan.

Go gentle Gales, and bear my Sighs away!
To *Thyrsis* Ear the tender Notes convey!

11–12. 1736–51: Oh, skill'd in Nature! see the hearts of Swains,
   Their artless passions, and their tender pains.
13. **The setting Sun now shone:** MS: *Now Golden* Phaebus *sett*; *1717–51:* Now setting *Phoebus* shone
16. MS: *Made Vales resound and hollow Mountains groan.*
17. **gentle . . . Sighs:** MS: *whispring . . . Plaints*
18. **Thyrsis . . . convey!:** *1736–51: Delia's . . .* convey.

---

11. Attend: pay heed to.

   low . . . Numbers: humble in rhythm and versification; cf. 'Spring', 49–52 MS, and Commentary.

11–12 variant. skill'd in Nature: i.e. Wycherley is skilled in understanding and representing human nature on stage and will thus understand the emotions of the shepherds. *TE* cites Lansdowne's 'A Character of Mr. Wycherley', in Abel Boyer, *Letters of Wit, Politicks and Morality* (1701), p. 255, in which Wycherley is praised for his 'strickt Enquiries into Nature' and 'close Observations upon the several Humours, Manners, Sentiments, and Affections of Men'.

   artless: natural, unsophisticated; cf. 'Summer', 11.

14. fleecy Clouds: *TE* cites Milton, 'Il Penseroso', 72, *Poems* (1645), p. 40: 'Stooping through a fleecy cloud'.

15. melodious Moan: song of lament.

16. For the phrasing, Wakefield cites Waller, 'To my Lord Admirall', 11–12, *Poems, &c.*, p. 40: '*Euridice*, for whom his num'rous moan | Makes list'ning trees, and salvage mountains groan'.

17. Hylas begins to speak here. *TE* suggests the refrain deliberately echoes the opening line of Waller's Song 'Goe lovely Rose', *Poems, &c.*, p. 89. The repetition of 17 here at 23, 31, etc., is in keeping with the use of refrains in e.g. Theocritus, *Idylls*, I; Virgil, *Eclogues*, VIII. Cf. also 'Sapho to Phaon', 207–8.

   Gales: cf. 'Summer' 73.

18. Thyrsis: conventional pastoral name, used in e.g. Theocritus, *Idylls*, I; Virgil, *Eclogues*, VII, and in 'Winter'.

   Notes: musical notes.

18 variant. Delia: Pope dropped the male lover Thyrsis for the female Delia, another conventional name (see 'Spring', 45), in 1736, presumably to tone down the homoerotic aspects of the poem. Virgil's *Eclogues* commonly celebrate love between men, especially Corydon and Alexis in *Eclogues*, II, and in Spenser's 'Januarie', Hobbinol is devoted to Colin Clout. In the *Guardian*, no. 40, Pope had identified '*Corydon*'s criminal Passion for *Alexis*' as inappropriate to the innocent world of pastoral (*PW*, I.97), but with an irony designed to suggest that Virgil's *Eclogues*, and his own, were superior to such narrow formal rules.

　　　　　As some sad Turtle his lost Love deplores,
20　　　And with deep Murmurs fills the sounding Shores;
　　　　　Thus, far from *Thyrsis,* to the Winds I mourn,
　　　　　Alike unheard, unpity'd, and forlorn.

　　　　　Go gentle Gales, and bear my Sighs along!
　　　　　For him the feather'd Quires neglect their Song;
25　　　For him the Lymes their pleasing Shades deny;
　　　　　For him the Lillies hang their heads and dye.
　　　　　Ye Flow'rs that droop, forsaken by the Spring,
　　　　　Ye Birds, that left by Summer, cease to sing,
　　　　　Ye Trees that fade when Autumn-Heats remove,
30　　　Say, is not Absence Death to those who love?

　　　　　Go gentle Gales, and bear my Sighs away!
　　　　　Curs'd be the Fields that cause my *Thyrsis'* Stay:
　　　　　Fade ev'ry Blossom, wither ev'ry Tree,
　　　　　Dye ev'ry Flow'r, and perish All, but He.
35　　　What have I said? — where-e'er my *Thyrsis* flies,

---

19. his: MS: *her*
21. Thyrsis: 1736–51: *Delia*
21–2. MS: *Thus to the Groves, the Fields, and Floods I mourn,*
　　　　Like her deserted, and like her forlorn.
23. gentle ... Sighs: MS: *whispring ... Plaints*
24–6. him: 1736–51: *her,*
27. droop, forsaken by the: MS: *languish when forsook by*
28. left by Summer, cease: MS: *cease when Summer's past*
30. who: MS: *that*
31. gentle ... Sighs: MS: *whispring ... Plaints*
32. Thyrsis': 1736–51: *Delia's*
34. He: 1736–51: *she*
35. — where-e'er my Thyrsis flies: MS: *Where e'er my friend remains*; 1736–51: *where'er my Delia flies*

---

19. Turtle: dove, as in 'Summer', 52.
　　deplores: laments (in song).
20. Murmurs: the song of the turtle-dove; 'murmur' can also mean 'to grumble; to utter secret and sullen discontent' (*SJ*). EC comments that the Latin name, 'turtur', mimics the sad and 'monotonous' call of the bird.
　　sounding: resounding, echoing; cf. *Essay on Criticism,* 369.
24. feather'd Quires: songbirds.
25. Lymes ... deny: the lime trees shedding leaves in grief.
29. remove: depart.
30. Wakefield compares Sidney, 'The Ladd Philisides', in *The Countess of Pembrokes Arcadia*, III (1593), p. 197: 'Say all, & I with them | Absence is death, or worse, to them that loue'.
33. EC compares Congreve, *Mourning Muse of Alexis,* 80 (1695), p. 5: 'Fade all ye Flowers, and wither all ye Woods'.

  Let Spring attend, and sudden Flow'rs arise;
  Let opening Roses knotted Oaks adorn,
  And liquid Amber drop from ev'ry Thorn.

  Go gentle Gales, and bear my Sighs along!
40 The Birds shall cease to tune their Ev'ning Song,
  The Winds to breathe, the waving Woods to move,
  And Streams to murmur, e'er I cease to love.
  Not bubling Fountains to the thirsty Swain,

37, n. 1736–51:   *Aurea durae*
  Mala ferent quercus, narcisso floreat alnus,
  Pinguia corticibus sudant electra myricae.
        Virg. Ecl. 8.

43, n. 1736–51: *Quale sopor fessis in gramine, quale per aestum*
    Dulcis acqua saliente sitim restinguere rivo.
          Ecl. 5.

36. MS: *Let Flow'rs and Blossoms purple all the Plains*:
39. gentle ... Sighs: MS: *whispring ... Plaints*
42^3. MS: *With him thro' Lybia's burning plains I'll go,*
   On Alpine *Mountains tread th' Eternal Snow*;
   Yet feel no Heat but what our Loves impart,
   And dread no Coldness but in Thyrsis *Heart.*
   Go whispring Gales and bear my Plaints away
   Come Thyrsis, *come, ah why this long Delay*!

37–8. Wakefield cites a number of sources for the idea and the imagery, among them the anonymous version of Theocritus, *Idylls*, I, in *Sylvae* (1685), p. 364: 'On Brambles now let Violets be born, | And op'ning Roses blush on ev'ry Thorn'; Walsh's third eclogue, 'Damon', 51–2, *Letters and Poems* (1692), p. 119: 'Upon hard Oaks let blushing Peaches grow, | And from the Brambles, liquid Amber flow'; and 33–6 of Dryden's translation of Virgil's *Eclogues*, VIII, *Works of Virgil*, p. 18: 'Unlabour'd Harvests shall the Fields adorn, | And cluster'd Grapes shall blush on every Thorn. | The knotted Oaks shall show'rs of Honey weep, | And through the Matted Grass the liquid gold shall creep.'
37. opening: cf. 'Spring', 100.
knotted: with rough bark.
Oaks: see 'Spring', 86, and Commentary.
37 Pope's note. Virgil, *Eclogues*, VIII.52–4: 'Let tough oaks bear golden apples, let alder flower with narcissus, let tamarisks sweat rich amber from their bark'.
38. liquid Amber: sap, resin (see 'Spring', 62 and Commentary). The idea is that nature should produce sweetness out of roughness wherever Thyrsis is.
40. tune: sing.
42. Streams ... murmur: see 'Summer', 86.
43. Fountains: streams or springs.
43 Pope's note. Virgil, *Eclogues*, V.46–7: 'Like sleep on grass to the weary, like quenching thirst in a leaping stream of sweet water'.

Not balmy Sleep to Lab'rers faint with Pain,
45 Not Show'rs to Larks, nor Sunshine to the Bee,
Are half so charming as thy Sight to me.

Go gentle Gales, and bear my Sighs away!
Come, *Thyrsis*, come; ah why this long Delay?
Thro' Rocks and Caves the name of *Thyrsis* sounds,
50 *Thyrsis*, each Cave and ecchoing Rock rebounds.
Ye Pow'rs, what pleasing Frensie sooths my Mind!
Do Lovers dream, or is my Shepherd kind?
He comes, my Shepherd comes! — now cease my Lay,
And cease ye Gales to bear my Sighs away!

55 Next *Aegon* sung, while *Windsor* Groves admir'd;
Rehearse, ye Muses, what your selves inspir'd.

Resound ye Hills, resound my mournful Strain!
Of perjur'd *Doris*, dying I'll complain:

52, n. *1736–51: An qui amant, ipsi sibi somnia fingunt?*
Id. 8.

45. nor: *1736–51:* or
46^7. MS: *But see, my* Thyrsis *comes! now cease my Song,*
  And cease, ye Gales, to bear my Plaints along.
48–50. Thyrsis: *1736–51: Delia*
52. Shepherd: *1736–51: Delia*
53. He . . . Shepherd: *1736–51:* She . . . *Delia*
55. while: MS: *and*
56. your selves: *1736–51:* yourselves
58. Doris: MS: Phillis
  I'll complain:: *1717–51:* I complain!

---

44. Pain: labour.
51. Frensie: frenzy, madness. Wakefield compares the 'amabilis insania' ('pleasing madness') of Horace, *Odes*, III.iv.5–6.
52. kind: in the sense of reciprocating love or attraction; cf. 'Spring', 59.
52 Pope's note. Virgil, *Eclogues*, VIII.108: 'or do those who love invent their own dreams?'
53–4. EC cites Virgil, *Eclogues*, VIII.109, 'parcite, ab urbe venit, iam parcite, carmina, Daphnis' ('cease, songs, now cease, Daphnis comes from the city').

55. Windsor: see 'Spring', 2.
  admir'd: marvelled.
56. Rehearse: repeat.
57. Aegon's refrain (65, 71, 77, 96) corresponds to Hylas' (see 23).
  Strain: song.
58. complain: cf. 3 above, and 'Summer', 19. Wakefield cites 26 and 29 of Dryden's translation of Virgil, *Eclogues*, VIII. *Works of Virgil*, p. 36: 'While I my *Nisa*'s perjur'd Faith deplore . . . | Yet shall my dying Breath to Heav'n complain'.

Here where the *Mountains* less'ning as they rise,
60 Lose the low Vales, and steal into the Skies.
While lab'ring Oxen, spent with Toil and Heat,
In their loose Traces from the Field retreat;
While curling Smokes from Village-Tops are seen,
And the fleet Shades glide o'er the dusky Green.

65 Resound ye Hills, resound my mournful Lay!
Beneath yon Poplar oft we past the Day:
Oft on the Rind I carv'd her Am'rous Vows,
While She with Garlands grac'd the bending Boughs:
The Garlands fade, the Vows are worn away;
70 So dies her Love, and so my Hopes decay.

Resound ye Hills, resound my mournful Strain!
Now bright *Arcturus* glads the teeming Grain,

64, n. 1736–40: And the fleet shades fly gliding o'er the green.

61. **spent:** MS: *tir'd*
64. **glide o'er the dusky:** MS: *fly gliding o'er the*
66. **yon:** MS: *this*
67. **the:** MS: *this*
68. **grac'd:** MS, *1736–51: hung*

59–60. Perhaps an early thought towards the 'Alps' simile, *Essay on Criticism*, 228–35.
60. Lose: leave behind.
61–2. Wakefield compares Milton, 'A Mask', 290–1, *Poems* (1645), p. 88: 'Two such I saw, what time the labour'd Oxe | In his loose traces from the furrow came'. TE adds 95–8 of Dryden's translation of Virgil, *Eclogues* (expanding Virgil's 66–7), *Works of Virgil*, p. 9: 'See from afar the Fields no longer smoke, | The sweating Steers unharnass'd from the Yoke, | Bring, as in Triumph, back the crooked Plough; | The Shadows lengthen as the Sun goes Low.'
63. Village-Tops: the chimneys on the cottages in the village. Wakefield cites Virgil, *Eclogues*, I.82: 'et iam summa procul villarum culmina fumant' ('and now the high tops of the villages smoke'). TE notes in addition the translation of this eclogue by John, Lord Caryll, in *Miscellany Poems* (1684), p. 9 of separate sequence: 'And curling smoak from Village tops ascends'.
64. fleet: swift-moving.
Shades: shadows.
67–8. Wakefield compares Virgil, *Eclogues*, X.53–5: 'tenerisque meos incidere amores | arboribus' ('to engrave my loves on tender trees'), and TE notes Stafford's translation, in *Miscellany Poems* (1684), p. 84: 'On smoothest rinds of Trees, I'le carve my woe'.
67. Rind: bark.
72. Arcturus: the main star in the constellation Boötes; the rise of the constellation in September was anciently associated with a period of rainfall which here 'glads' or irrigates the 'teeming Grain', i.e. the unharvested cereal crop; see also 'The First Book

> Now Golden Fruits on loaded Branches shine,
> And grateful Clusters swell with floods of Wine;
> 75 Now blushing Berries paint the fertile Grove;
> Just Gods! shall all things yield Returns but Love?
>
> Resound ye Hills, resound my mournful Lay!
> The Shepherds cry, 'Thy Flocks are left a Prey —
> Ah! what avails it me, the Flocks to keep,
> 80 Who lost my Heart while I preserv'd my Sheep.
> *Pan* came, and ask'd, what Magick caus'd my Smart,
> Or what *Ill Eyes* malignant Glances dart?
> What Eyes but hers, alas, have Pow'r on me!
> Oh mighty Love, what Magick is like thee!
>
> 85 Resound ye Hills, resound my mournful Strains!
> I'll fly from Shepherds, Flocks, and flow'ry Plains. —

82, n. *1736–51: Or what ill eyes.*]

Nescio quis teneros oculus mihi fascinat agnos.

83, n. *1736–51: What eyes but hers, alas, have pow'er on me!*
Oh mighty Love! what magic is like thee!

75. fertile: MS, *1717–51:* yellow
78. a Prey – : MS: *to stray.*
79. the: MS: *my*
81. MS: Pan *comes & asks, what Magick works my Smart,*
83. on me: *1717–51:* to move
84. *1717–51:* And is there magic but what dwells in love?

---

of Statius his Thebais', 521; *Windsor-Forest,* 53, 119. For similar uses of constellations see 'Spring', 102, 'Summer', 21, and 'Winter', 85. *TE* suggests Virgil, *Georgics,* I.68 and 204 as a source for Arcturus; for 'teeming Grain' cf. Dryden's version of Virgil, *Georgics,* I.156, *Works of Virgil,* p. 54: 'to swell the teeming Grain', and also of *Eclogues,* V.53, *ibid.,* p. 22.
74. grateful: 'pleasing; acceptable; delightful; delicious' (*SJ,* citing this line).
  Clusters: cf. 'Spring', 36. Pope himself later cultivated vines in his garden at Twickenham. Cf. also the vines in 'Gardens of Alcinous', 17–25.
75. blushing: reddening; cf. 'Summer', 75.

  paint: colour; cf. 'Spring', 28, and *Windsor-Forest,* 38.
81. Pan: see 'Summer', 50, and Commentary.
  Smart: pain. Wakefield compares Virgil, *Eclogues,* X.26: 'Pan deus Arcadiae venit' ('the god Pan came to Arcadia'), and 21: 'omnes "unde amor iste" rogant "tibi?"' ('everyone asked "whence this love to you?"').
82. Ill Eyes: the evil eye of witchcraft.
82 Pope's note. Virgil, *Eclogues,* III.103: 'an unknown eye bewitches my young lambs'. Wakefield compares 158-9 of Dryden's translation, *Works of Virgil,* p. 16: 'What magick has bewitch'd the woolly Dams, | And what ill Eyes beheld the tender Lambs?'

From Shepherds, Flocks, and Plains, I may remove,
Forsake Mankind, and all the World — but Love!
I know thee Love! wild as the raging Main,
90   More fell than Tygers on the *Lybian* Plain;
Thou wert from *Aetna*'s burning Entrails torn,
Got by fierce Whirlwinds, and in Thunder born!

Resound ye Hills, resound my mournful Lay!
Farewell ye Woods! adieu the Light of Day!
95   One Leap from yonder Cliff shall end my Pains.
No more ye Hills, no more resound my Strains!

89, n. *1736–51: Nunc scio quid fit amor, duris in cotibus illum,* &c.

89. wild as the raging Main: MS: *on desart Mountains bred*; *1751:* on foreign mountains bred
90. MS, *1751: Wolves gave thee suck, and savage Tygers fed*;
94. MS: *To Shades unknown Death summons me away*:
94^5. MS: *See where yon Mountains, less'ning as they rise,*
            Swell o'er the Vales, and steal into the Skies;
95. MS: *One Leap from thence shall finish all my Pain*:
96. Strains!: MS: *Strain.*

---

89. Main: ocean.
89 Pope's note. Virgil, *Eclogues*, VIII.43: 'Now I know what Love is; on jagged crags [Tmaros bore] him ... '. Wakefield compares Stafford's version in *Miscellany Poems* (1684), p. 63 of separate sequence: 'I know thee, Love; on Mountains thou wert bred, | And *Thracian* Rocks thy infant fury fed', as well as Dryden's, 60–1, *Works of Virgil*, p. 37: 'I know thee, Love; in Desarts thou wert bred, | And at the Dugs of Salvage Tygers fed'. *TE* suggests several other possible mediations for the images, which derive from Theocritus, *Idylls*, III.15–17. Johnson, *Rambler*, no. 37, 24 July 1750, objected to the image in both Virgil and Pope as not derived from rural life.
90. fell: savage.
   Lybian Plain: the deserts of Northern Africa.
90 MS. Wolves ... suck: suckled, nourished, as in the myth of the foundation of Rome in which Romulus and Remus were suckled by a she-wolf; here with the implication that the savagery of the wolf is passed on to Love. See also 'Summer', 79–80, and Commentary.
91. Aetna: Etna, volcanic mountain on Sicily, mentioned by Theocritus in several *Idylls* (I, IX, XI); hence the 'burning Entrails' or molten inner workings. See Commentary at 'Spring', 66 and at 'Sapho to Phaon', 12.
92. Wakefield compares Dryden's translation of Ovid, *Heroides*, VII (Dido to Aeneas), 40, *Ovid's Epistles Translated by Several Hands* (1680), p. 218: 'Got by the winds, and in a Tempest born'.
95. end my Pains: i.e. in suicide, in a manner presaged also in Pope's 'Sapho to Phaon', 188–208, and its classical sources. In his *Guardian* no. 40 essay, Pope noted that Virgil, *Eclogues*, VIII, 'introduces a Shepherd whom an inviting Precipice tempts to Self-Murder'; *PW*, I.97. Wakefield notes the allusion is to 58–60 of that poem: 'vivite silvae; | praeceps aerii specula de montis in undas | deferar' ('live, woods: I shall throw myself headlong from the high watchtower on the mountains into the waves'); and 84 and 86 of Dryden's

    Thus sung the Shepherds till th' Approach of Night,
    The Skies yet blushing with departing Light,
    When falling Dews with Spangles deck'd the Glade,
100 And the low Sun had lengthen'd ev'ry Shade.

---

translation, *Works of Virgil*, p. 38: 'From yon high Cliff I plunge into the Main... And cease, my silent Flute, the sweet *Maenalian* Strain'. *TE* adds Walsh, 'Damon', 63-4, *Letters and Poems*, p. 120: 'This Leap shall put an end to all my Pains. | *Now cease, my Muse, now cease th'* Arcadian *Strains*'.

97–100. For the alternative versions of these lines offered to Walsh see Appendix I.
99. deck'd: adorned.
100. Wakefield cites Virgil, *Eclogues*, II.67, and 98 of Dryden's translation, *Works of Virgil*, p. 9: 'The Shadows lengthen as the Sun goes Low'.

WINTER.

The Fourth Pastoral,

OR

DAPHNE.

To the MEMORY of a Fair Young LADY.

LYCIDAS.

THyrsis, the Musick of that murm'ring Spring
Is not so mournful as the Strains you sing,

***Young LADY, n.** 1736–51:* This Lady was [*1751:* of an ancient family in Yorkshire, and] particularly admired by the Author's friend Mr. *Walsh*, who having celebrated her in a Pastoral Elegy, desired his friend to do the same. [*1751:* same, as appears from one of his Letters, dated Sept. 9, 1706. "Your last Eclogue being on the same subject with mine on Mrs. Tempest's death, I should take it very kindly in you to give it a little turn as if it were to the memory of the same lady."] Her death happening [*1751:* having happened] on the night of the great storm in 1702 [*1751:* 1703], gave a propriety to this eclogue, which in its general turn alludes to it. The Scene of this Pastoral lies in a grove, the time at midnight.

Title. MS: WINTER: | *The Fourth Pastorall*; | OR | DAPHNE.; *1717–43:* WINTER. | THE | FOURTH PASTORAL. | To the Memory of Mrs. TEMPEST.; *1751:* WINTER. | THE | FOURTH PASTORAL, | OR| DAPHNE. | To the Memory of Mrs. TEMPEST.
LYCIDAS. MS: *Meliboeus* (and so throughout)

WINTER. Pope's favourite pastoral, according to Warburton; Spence thought 'Messiah' was his 'own favourite of them all' (see *OAC*, I.175). In the *Guardian*, no. 40, Pope suggested comparing this pastoral with Philips's fourth (*PW*, I.102). The pastoral elegy is another standard form, beginning at the very start with Theocritus, *Idylls*, I, a lament for Daphnis, the supposed founder of pastoral song, and IV; Bion, *Idylls*, I (see 'Summer', 61 and Commentary); Moschus' lament for the death of Bion; Virgil, *Eclogues*, V; Spenser, 'Nouember', and *Astrophel*; Milton, 'Lycidas', and more recent examples by Walsh and Congreve, cited below in the notes. Walsh himself died in 1708 and there may be some sense of a displaced elegy for Pope's mentor.

Variant dedication. *Mrs. Tempest:* For what is known of Henrietta Tempest (1686–1703) and her connection with the poem through Walsh see Rogers (2005b). Walsh's 'Delia. A Pastoral Eclogue; Lamenting the Death of Mrs. Tempest, Who dy'd upon the Day of the Late Storm', had appeared in *Poetical Miscellanies: The Fifth Part* (1704), pp. 609–16. See Walsh to Pope, 9 Sept 1706, *Corr.*, I.22, which is phrased slightly differently from the extract given by Pope. The storm took place on the night of 26 November 1703, and its most influential literary product was Daniel Defoe's *The Storm* (1704), which itself included a Virgilian 'Pastoral, Occasion'd by the Late Violent Storm'. Pope's poem does not actually include any

Nor Rivers winding thro' the Vales below,
So sweetly warble, or so smoothly flow.
5   Now sleeping Flocks on their soft Fleeces lye,
The Moon, serene in Glory, mounts the Sky,
While silent Birds forget their tuneful Lays,
Oh sing of *Daphne*'s Fate, and *Daphne*'s praise!

5–6, n. 1736–51: In the warm folds the tender flocks remain,
                  The cattle slumber on the silent plain,
                  While silent birds neglect their tuneful lays,
                  Let us, dear Thyrsis, *sing of* Daphne *'s praise.*

3. MS: *Nor these soft Streams that wash the Vale below,*
5–6. MS: *Now in warm Folds the tender Flock remains;*
           The Cattle slumber on the silent Plains;
7. **silent:** MS: sleeping
8. MS: *Let us, dear* Thyrsis, *sing of* Daphne' *s Praise.*

---

images of the storm, but rather concentrates on a symbolic 'death of the year'. Pope's note on time emphasises his overall scheme: see Pope's note at 'Spring', 17, and 89 below.

DAPHNE: conventional pastoral name for a nymph or shepherdess, but also in Greek mythology a virgin huntress, the object of sexual attention from Apollo, to escape which she was transformed into the Laurel tree (botanical name 'Daphne') which was thus associated with Apollo as god of poetry; cf. 'Summer', 10, and below, 20; 'Sapho to Phaon', 28. Battestin (1969) argues that Daphne represents, by allusion to the pastoral poet-shepherd Daphnis, a principle of artistic power and order.

LYCIDAS: conventional pastoral name, used by Bion in *Idylls*, II, Virgil in *Eclogues*, IX, and by Milton in his pastoral elegy 'Lycidas'.

MS. Meliboeus: conventional pastoral name, adopted from Virgil, *Eclogues*, VII, perhaps dropped in favour of Milton's specifically elegiac figure.

1. **Thyrsis:** conventional pastoral name for a shepherd; cf. 'Autumn', 18.

murm'ring Spring: cf. 57 below, 'Summer', 86 and 'Autumn', 42. Pope's note to 'Spring', 1, signals that this line is a deliberate imitation of Theocritus, *Idylls*, I.1. Wakefield compares Theocritus, *Idylls*, I.9–10 in the translation by Creech, *Idylliums* (1684), p. 2: 'And, *Sheapherd*, sweeter Notes thy Pipe do fill | Than murmuring springs that roul from yonder hill'.

2. Strains: songs.

3–4. The comparative 'flow' of song and river is echoed in 13–14. Wakefield compares 131 of Dryden's translation of Virgil, *Eclogues*, V.131, *Works of Virgil*, p. 24: 'Nor winding Streams that through the Valley glide'.

4. warble: 'utter musically' (*SJ*).

5–8. Pope showed Walsh a reading of these lines similar to the version in his own note, with concern about the word 'remain[s]'. He gave Walsh three further versions of the lines but Walsh was unhappy with all of them, hence the completely different version Pope actually printed; Appendix I.

6. mounts the Sky: rises.

7. Lays: songs.

THYRSIS.

    Behold the *Groves* that shine with silver Frost,
10   Their Beauty wither'd, and their Verdure lost.
    Here shall I try the sweet *Alexis'* Strain,
    That call'd the list'ning *Dryads* to the Plain?
    Thames heard the Numbers as he flow'd along,
    And bade his Willows learn the moving Song.

LYCIDAS.

15   So may kind Rains their vital Moisture yield,
    And swell the future Harvest of thy Field!
    Begin; this Charge the dying *Daphne* gave,
    And said; 'Ye Shepherds, sing around my Grave.'
    Sing, while beside the shaded Tomb I mourn,
20   And with fresh Bays her Rural Shrine adorn.

THYRSIS.

    Ye gentle *Muses* leave your Crystal Spring,

13, n. 1736–51: Thames *heard.*]

    Audiit Eurotas, jussitque ediscere lauros. Virg.

9. Groves: MS: *Trees*
10. MS: *Whose Arms are wither'd, and whose Leaves are lost;*
12. Dryads to the: MS: *Fawns from ev'ry*
16. thy Field!: *1740–51:* the field.
18. Grave.: *1717–51:* grave!
19. beside the shaded: MS: *in Tears upon the*

---

10. Verdure: green colouring; cf. 'verdant', 'Summer', 4, and below, 37.

11. Alexis' Strain: cf. 'Spring', 45–8, MS. Here a reference to Congreve's *The Mourning Muse of Alexis* (1695). EC points out that the couplet is modelled on a similar allusion in Garth, *Dispensary*, IV, sixth edition (1706), p. 64: 'As tuneful C[on]greve trys his rural Strains, | *Pan* quits the Woods, the list'ning Fawns the Plains'. EC also cites Dryden's translation of Virgil, *Eclogues*, VI.100, *Works of Virgil*, p. 29: 'And call'd the Mountain Ashes to the Plain'. Alexis is also the name of the main character of 'Summer'.

12. Dryads: female tree spirits or nymphs, in Greek mythology and poetry, here attracted from the woods to the plains by Alexis' song.

13 Pope's note. Virgil, *Eclogues*, VI.83: 'Eurotas heard, and commanded his laurels to learn [the song] by heart'.

14. Willows: used as a symbol of mourning in *Windsor-Forest*, 274.

15–16. The sympathetic weeping of nature will enrich future crops.

17. Charge: command. EC cites Virgil, *Eclogues*, V.41: 'mandat fieri sibi talia Daphnis' ('Daphnis demands such things be done for him').

20. Bays: laurel, symbol of poetic achievement; see note on the title 'Daphne'.

21–2. TE compares the refrain of Oldham, 'Bion', *Some New Pieces*, pp. 73–87: '*Come all ye* Muses, *come, adorn the Shepherd's Herse | With never-fading Garlands, never-dying Verse*'.

Let *Nymphs* and *Sylvans* Cypress Garlands bring;
Ye weeping *Loves*, the Stream with Myrtles hide,
And break your Bows, as when *Adonis* dy'd;
25   And with your Golden Darts, now useless grown,
Inscribe a Verse on this relenting Stone:
'Let Nature change, let Heav'n and Earth deplore,
Fair *Daphne*'s dead, and Love is now no more!'

'Tis done, and Nature's various Charms decay;

23, n. *1736–51: — Inducite fontibus umbras —*
Et tumulum facite, & tumulo superaddite carmen.

27. let Heav'n: MS: *and Heav'n*
29. various Charms decay;: MS: *chang'd, since you are gone,*

---

21. Crystal Spring: cf. 'Summer', 27, and cross-references.

22. Sylvans: woodland spirits; cf. 1 above, and 'Vertumnus and Pomona', 20.

Cypress: 'sad cypress' was a symbol of funerals, as in Shakespeare, *Twelfth Night*, II.iv.51, and Spenser, *The Shepheardes Calender*, 'Nouember', 145: 'Now bale full boughes of Cypres doen aduance'.

23. Loves: cupids, cherubs, as in *Windsor-Forest*, 293.

Myrtles: shrub associated with Aphrodite (Venus), goddess of love; cf. 'Messiah', 74, and Commentary to 'Spring', 65–8; also 'To a Young Lady, with the Works of Voiture', 73, and *Ode for Musick*, 78–9.

23 Pope's note. Virgil, *Eclogues*, V.40: 'draw shades across the springs', and 42: 'build a tomb, and put the song on the tomb'. Wakefield compares Dryden's translation, 61–2, *Works of Virgil*, p. 22: 'With Cypress Boughs the Crystal Fountains hide, | And softly let the running Waters glide'.

24 Bows . . . Adonis: the traditional bow and arrow of love, associated with Cupid (the Roman version of the Greek Eros), son of Venus, to whose tragic love for Adonis Pope refers in 'Summer', 61. Wakefield cites the broken bow of Cupid in Ovid's elegy for Tibullus (*Amores*, III.ix.7–8) and Bion, *Idylls*, I.80–2; TE compares the breaking of arrows and bows in Oldham's 'Lamentation for Adonis, Imitated out of the Greek of Bion of Smyrna', 169–70.

25. Darts: arrows.

26. relenting: The stone is not so hard (metaphorically as well as literally) as to resist an inscription for Daphne; cf. 'Spring', 69.

27. deplore: lament.

27–8. The lines are in quotation marks because this is a paraphrase from Walsh's own eclogue, 'Delia', *Poetical Miscellanies: The Fifth Part*, p. 613: 'Now, Shepherds, now lament! and now deplore! | Delia is dead, and Beauty is no more!' TE cites also Congreve, *Mourning Muse of Alexis*, 167–8, (1695), p. 8: 'All Nature Mourns; the Flouds and Rocks deplore, | And cry with me, PASTORA is no more!' Durant (1971: 482) observes that this is 'the first of Pope's uses of the biblical "Let there be light"'; (Genesis 1:3).

29–30. Pope offered Walsh two different versions of these lines; see Appendix I.

30   See gloomy Clouds obscure the chearful Day!
     Now hung with Pearls the dropping Trees appear,
     Their faded Honours scatter'd on her Bier.
     See, where on Earth the flow'ry Glories lye,
     With her they flourish'd, and with her they dye.
35   Ah what avail the Beauties Nature wore?
     Fair *Daphne*'s dead, and Beauty's now no more!

     For her, the Flocks refuse their verdant Food,
     Nor thirsty Heifers seek the gliding Flood.
     The silver Swans her hapless Fate bemoan,

38, n. 1736–51: For her the flocks the dewy herbs disdain,
  Nor hungry heifers graze the tender plain.

30. MS: *Behold, the Clouds have put their Mourning on*:
31. **dropping Trees:** MS: *weeping Groves*
32. MS: *And cast their faded Honours on your Bier.*
33. **See, where:** MS: *Behold*
34. **her . . . her:** MS: *You . . . You*
36. **Beauty's now:** *1717–51:* beauty is
37–8. MS: *For You the Flocks their Grassy Fare disdain,*
  Nor hungry Heyfars crop the tender Plain:
38. **Nor . . . seek:** *1751:* The . . . shun
39. **her:** MS: *your*

---

30. **obscure:** make dark.
31. **Pearls:** dew, imagined as the jewelled, sympathetic tears of nature.

  dropping: i.e. dripping, weeping, but with a suggestion of 'drooping'. Wakefield compares Dryden, 'On the Death of Amyntas', 1–2, *Miscellany Poems: The Fifth Part*, p. 16: ''Twas on a Joyless and a Gloomy Morn, | Wet was the Grass, and hung with Pearls the Thorn'; *TE* cites also Dryden's translation of Virgil, *Eclogues*, X.20, *Works of Virgil*, p. 45: 'And hung with humid Pearls the lowly Shrub appears'.

32. **Honours:** leaves, which crown the tree; cf. 'Spring', 73, etc. Pope may recall the last line of Dryden's 'First Book of Ovid's Metamorphoses', *Examen Poeticum* (1693), p. 49, where Daphne, transformed into a laurel, 'shook the shady Honours of her Head'.

  TE derives the image from Oldham, 'Bion', 64, *Some New Pieces*, p. 76: 'Trees drop their Leaves to dress thy Funeral'.

37–8. Wakefield compares Spenser, *Colin Clouts Come Home Againe*, 26, (1595), sig. A3ᵛ: 'And all their flocks from feeding to refraine'; *EC* compares Spenser, 'Nouember', 133 (1579), fol. 46: 'The feeble flocks in field refuse their former foode'; and Dryden's version of Virgil's *Eclogues*, V.38–9.

38 **Pope's note. Herbs:** not culinary or medicinal plants, as in 'Summer', 31–4, but vegetation or fodder in general.

39–40. Birds of mourning, understood to signal their own death in song (cf. *Essay on Criticism*, 452^3 MS; 'Rape of the Locke', II. 121; *Windsor-Forest*, 273–4); a pastoral convention known (and disputed) from classical times. Wakefield cites Oldham,

40   In sadder Notes than when they sing their own.
        Eccho no more the rural Song rebounds,
        Her Name alone the mournful *Eccho* sounds,
        Her Name with Pleasure once she taught the Shore,
        Now *Daphne*'s dead, and Pleasure is no more!

45   No grateful Dews descend from Ev'ning Skies,
        Nor Morning Odours from the Flow'rs arise.
        No rich Perfumes refresh the fruitful Field,
        Nor fragrant Herbs their native Incense yield.
        The balmy *Zephyrs*, silent since her Death,
50   Lament the Ceasing of a sweeter Breath.
        Th' industrious Bees neglect their Golden Store;

---

40. **In sadder Notes:** MS: *With sadder Notes,;* 1736–51: In notes more sad
41–2. MS, 1736–51: *In gloomy Caves sweet* Echo *silent lies,*
         Silent, or only to your [1736–51: her] *Name replies*:
43. **Her:** MS: *Your*
45. **No grateful:** MS: *No more soft*
47. **fruitful:** MS: *fertile*
48. MS: *Which but for You, did all its Incense yield*:
49. **her:** MS: *your*
51. **Golden:** MS: *fragrant*

'Bion', 25–8, *Some New Pieces*, pp. 74–5: 'Ye gentle Swans... In doleful notes the heavy loss bewail, | Such as you sing at your own Funeral'.

39. **silver:** a common poetic colouring for swans, e.g. in Orlando Gibbons's madrigal *The Silver Swan* (1612).

41–2. **Eccho:** in classical mythology a nymph who fell in love with Narcissus (cf. *Summer*, 26) and who dwindled to a mere echo of the utterances of others. The story is told in Ovid, *Metamorphoses*, III.359–401; TE cites 394, 'solis ex illo vivit in antris' ('after that she lives in lonely caves') as the source of analogues cited by Wakefield, e.g. Milton, 'A Mask', 229, *Poems* (1645), p. 94: 'Sweet Echo, sweetest Nymph that liv'st unseen'; Cowley, 'Eccho', 5–6, *Poems* (1656), p. 40: 'Ah gentle *Nymph* who lik'st so well, | In hollow, *solitary* Caves to dwell', and Oldham, 'Bion', 60, *Some New Pieces*, p. 76: 'Sad *Eccho* too does in deep silence moan'.

41. **rebounds:** in transitive sense, to bounce something back (*OED*, sense 3c).

43. **taught the Shore:** i.e. Daphne's name was echoed round the shore. Cf. 'Summer', 42.

45. **grateful:** cf. 'Autumn', 74.

48. This version of the line was deemed 'better' by Walsh than the alternatives that Pope showed him; Appendix I.

49–50. **Zephyrs:** the west winds, traditionally 'balmy' or soothing (cf. 'Autumn,' 44), as in 'Spring', 32, in contrast to Boreas, the harsh north wind, 87. Cf. 'Sapho to Phaon', 83, MS; *Essay on Criticism*, 367.

50. **Lament the Ceasing:** Wakefield compares Oldham, 'Bion', 115–16, *Some New Pieces*, p. 79: 'Fair *Galatea* too laments thy death, | Laments the ceasing of thy tuneful breath'.

51–2. Wakefield compares Oldham, 'Bion', 69–72, *Some New Pieces*, p. 77: 'The painful Bees neglect their wonted toil: | Alas! what boots it now their Hives to store | With the rich spoils of every plunder'd Flower, | When thou, that was all sweetness, art no more?'

Fair *Daphne*'s dead, and Sweetness is no more!

No more the mounting Larks, while *Daphne* sings,
Shall list'ning in mid Air suspend their Wings;
55   No more the Nightingales repeat her Lays,
Or hush'd with Wonder, hearken from the Sprays:
No more the Streams their Murmurs shall forbear,
A sweeter Musick than their own to hear,
But tell the Reeds, and tell the vocal Shore,
60   Fair *Daphne*'s dead, and Musick is no more!

Her Fate is whisper'd by the gentle Breeze,
And told in Sighs to all the trembling Trees;
The trembling Trees, in ev'ry Plain and Wood,
Her Fate remurmur to the silver Flood;
65   The silver Flood, so lately calm, appears
Swell'd with new Passion, and o'erflows with Tears;

53–54. MS: *No more the Wolves, when You your Numbers try,*
   Shall cease to follow, and the Lambs to fly:
55. Nightingales repeat: MS, *1751: birds shall imitate*
56. hush'd with Wonder: MS: *charm'd to Silence*
61. Her: MS: *Your*
64. Her: MS: *Your*
66. new Passion: MS: *this Sorrow*

---

52. Rogers (2006: 579) suggests that the line might recall the aromatic leaves of the laurel, the tree into which Daphne was turned in Ovid, *Metamorphoses*, I.452–567.
54. suspend: hold still. Skylarks hover but do not of course stop flapping their wings.
55. *Nightingales:* cf. 78 and 'Spring', 13, 26.
57. *Murmurs:* cf. 'Summer', 86.
59. *vocal Shore:* vocal because of the sound of the action of waves on it.
61–2. Pope later mocked the conventional nature of the rhyme in this couplet in *Essay on Criticism*, 353–4; see Commentary there.
62. *trembling:* cf. 'Spring', 5.
64. remurmur: 'to utter back in murmurs: to repeat in low, hoarse sounds' (*SJ*, citing this line only). A recent coinage; *OED* cites nothing earlier than 1697, and quotes this line of Pope as the earliest instance of the specific sense: 'To repeat (sounds, words, etc.) in a murmur; to murmur (something) repeatedly'. Wakefield cites Dryden's translation of Virgil, *Aeneid*, VII.1041–2, *Works of Virgil*, p. 431: 'Yet his untimely Fate, th' *Angitian* Woods | In sighs remurmur'd, to the *Fucine* Floods'. Cf. also 'The First Book of Statius his Thebais', 166.
   silver Flood: sparkling river; cf. 38.
65–6. Wakefield cites Ovid, *Metamorphoses*, XI.47–8: 'lacrimis quoque flumina dicunt | increvisse suis' ('they say also rivers swelled with their own tears'). *TE* adds, amongst other suggestions, Oldham, 'Lamentation for Adonis', 64–5, *Some New Pieces*, p. 91: 'The Rivers too, as if they would deplore | His death, with grief swell higher than before'.

The Winds and Trees and Floods her Death deplore,
Daphne, our Grief! our Glory now no more!

But see! where *Daphne* wondring mounts on high,
70 Above the Clouds, above the Starry Sky.
Eternal Beauties grace the shining Scene,
Fields ever fresh, and Groves for ever green!
There, while You rest in *Amaranthine* Bow'rs,
Or from those Meads select unfading Flow'rs,
75 Behold us kindly who your Name implore,
Daphne, our Goddess, and our Grief no more!

LYCIDAS.

How all things listen, while thy Muse complains!

69–70, n. 1736–51: *miratur limen Olympi,*
Sub pedibusque vidit nubes & sydera Daphnis. Virg.

67. Her: MS: y^r.
68. our Glory now: MS: *and our Delight*
77–84. MS: *Thy Songs, dear* Thyrsis, *more delight my Mind,*
Than the soft Whisper of the breathing Wind;
Or whisp'ring Groves, when some expiring Breeze
Pants on the Leaves, and Trembles in the Trees!
When teeming Ewes increase my fleecy Breed,
To Thee, bright Daphne, *oft' a Lamb shall bleed.*
While Vapours rise, and driving Snows descend,
Thy Honor, Name, and Praise, shall never end!

---

67. deplore: cf. 27.
69–70 Pope's note. Virgil, *Eclogues*, V. 56–7: 'Daphnis is amazed at the threshold of Olympus, and sees the clouds and stars beneath his feet'. Wakefield cites Dryden's translation, 86–7, *Works of Virgil*, p. 23: 'Daphnis, the Guest of Heav'n, with wondring Eyes, | Views in the Milky Way, the starry Skies'. Boire (1977) cites Spenser, 'Nouember', 188–9, *Shepheardes Calender* (1579), fol. 47: 'Fayre fieldes and pleasaunt layes there bene, | The fieldes ay fresh, the grasse ay greene'.
69–72. The transfiguration of Daphne prefigures that of Belinda's tress at the end of 'The Rape of the Locke', II.172–3. Pope adopted a more sceptical attitude to such transformations in his mock-essay on Pastoral in *Guardian*, no. 40.
72. fresh ... green: Pope later reproduced this image in drastically ironic fashion in *Dunciad* (1728), II.136.
73. Amaranthine: the amaranthus flower, sometimes known as 'Love Lies Bleeding': 'In poetry it is sometimes an imaginary flower, supposed, according to its name, never to fade' (*SJ*); hence the 'unfading Flow'rs' of 74. Cf. *Ode for Musick*, 75.
Bow'rs: cf. 'Summer', 7. *TE* compares Milton, *Paradise Lost*, XI.78–9 (1674), p. 288: 'thir blissful Bowrs | Of *Amarantin* Shade'.
77. while ... complains: while your poetry laments.

> Such Silence waits on *Philomela*'s Strains,
> In some still Ev'ning, when the whisp'ring Breeze
> 80 Pants on the Leaves, and dies upon the Trees.
> To thee, bright Goddess, oft a Lamb shall bleed,
> If teeming Ewes encrease my fleecy Breed.
> While Plants their Shade, or Flow'rs their Odours give,
> Thy Name, thy Honour, and thy Praise shall live!
>
> *THYRSIS.*
>
> 85 See pale *Orion* sheds unwholsome Dews,
> Arise, the Pines a noxious Shade diffuse;
> Sharp *Boreas* blows, and Nature feels Decay,

81, n. 1736–51:   *illius aram*
           Saepe tener nostris ab ovilibus imbuet agnus. Virg.
86, n. 1736–51: *solet esse gravis cantantibus umbra,*
           Juniperi gravis umbra —   Virg.

85. See pale *Orion*: MS, *1751: But see*, Orion

---

78. Philomela: name for the nightingale; see Commentary to 'Spring', 26; 'Sapho to Phaon', 176–8; 'The Wife of Bath Her Prologue', 212.

80. Pants . . . dies: There is perhaps a sexual suggestion to these words; cf. *Essay on Criticism*, 541, and *Windsor-Forest*, 194. But cf. also 'Summer', 87.

81. Lamb . . . bleed: Lycidas offers a regular sacrifice of a lamb to Daphne to mark the increase of his flock.

81 Pope's note. Virgil, *Eclogues*, I.7–8: 'often shall a young lamb from our sheepfolds stain his altar' (i.e. with sacrificial blood). Wakefield cites Dryden's translation, 9–10, *Works of Virgil*, p. 1: 'The tender Firstlings of my Woolly breed | Shall on his holy Altar often bleed'.

82. teeming: producing many offspring; cf. 'Autumn', 72, and *Essay on Criticism*, 424. Pope used the word in this sense in his translation of the *Iliad*, XI.825, but satirically in the phrase 'a teeming Mistress', *Epistle to a Lady*, 72.

83–4. *TE* cites Virgil, *Eclogues*, V.76–8: 'dum iuga montis aper, fluvios dum piscis amabit, | dumque thymo pascentur apes, dum rore cicadae, | semper honos nomenque tuum laudesque manebunt.' ('While the boar likes the mountain heights, and the fish likes the rivers, while bees feed on thyme and cicadas on dew, forever your honour, name and praise shall remain'.) Pope parodies this kind of utterance in 'Rape of the Locke', I. 127–34.

85. Orion: constellation named after the legendary hunter and giant; its rise was associated with a change to stormy weather. For similar uses of constellations see 'Spring', 102; 'Summer', 21; 'Autumn', 72.

86. noxious: poisonous. Since Daphne's transfiguration 'shade', which normally in the *Pastorals* connotes protection, has acquired unsympathetic connotations.

86 Pope's note. Virgil, *Eclogues*, X.75–6: 'the shade is often harmful to singers; the shade of the Juniper is harmful'. Wakefield cites Dryden's translation, 110–12, *Works of Virgil*, p. 48: ' . . . hoarseness oft invades | The Singer's Voice, who sings beneath the Shades. | From Juniper, unwholesom Dews distill . . .'

87. Boreas: the fierce, cold North wind, opposed to Zephyr (49). Cf. also 'Lines from *The Critical Specimen*', I.3; 'The First Book of Statius his Thebais', 267.

>   Time conquers All, and We must Time obey.
>   Adieu ye *Vales,* ye *Mountains, Streams* and *Groves,*
> 90   Adieu ye Shepherds rural *Lays* and *Loves,*
>   Adieu my Flocks, farewell ye *Sylvan* Crew,
>   *Daphne* farewell, and all the World adieu!
>
>   FINIS.

89–92, n. 1736–51: These four last lines allude to the several *Subjects* of the four Pastorals, and to the several *Scenes* of them, particularised before in each.

89. MS: *Adieu ye Rivers, Plains, and conscious Groves;*

---

88. Time conquers All: Battestin (1969: 200) notes the conspicuous shift from Virgil's well-known motto, 'omnia vincit Amor' ('Love conquers all'), *Eclogues*, X.69. See also Ovid, *Metamorphoses*, XV.234, 'tempus edax rerum' ('time the devourer of things').

89–92 Pope's note. Pope's concluding comment in the 'Discourse' (Appendix II) states his intention to produce a structured model of life in his quartet. *TE* notes that the final six lines of Spenser's 'December' (which reviewed the periods of human life), constituted a summary of *The Shepheardes Calender*.

91–2. Wakefield compares Dryden's version of Virgil's *Eclogues*, I.111–12 (greatly expanding line 77 of Virgil's poem), *Works of Virgil*, p. 5: 'No more my Song shall please the Rural Crue: | Adieu, my tuneful Pipe! and all the World, adieu'; and Walsh, 'Damon', *Letters and Poems*, p. 119: 'Adieu, ye Flocks, no more shall I pursue! | Adieu, ye Groves, a long, a long Adieu!'

91. Sylvan Crew: the other shepherds, or rural dwellers; cf. 22.

APPENDIX I.

The surviving manuscript of the *Pastorals* includes two sheets with the following queries and proposals for revisions, on recto and verso, sent by Pope to William Walsh, probably in the late spring of 1707 (Mack 1984, 20). Walsh's responses are reproduced in bold. Where Pope has interlineated alternative readings, these are contained in square brackets.

Alterations to the Pastoralls:
(The Solutions of the Queries are written by Mr Walsh.)

Past. 1. lin. 1.   First in these Fields I <u>sing</u> the Sylvan Strains,
                   Nor blush to sport on Windsor's <u>peaceful</u> Plains;
                   Fair Thames flow gently from thy sacred Spring,
                   While on thy Banks Sicilian Muses <u>sing</u>.

Objection.   That the letter is hunted too much – Sing the Sylvan – Peaceful Plains –
             and that the word <u>Sing</u> is us'd two lines after, Sicilian Muses Sing.
Alteration.   First in these Fields I <u>try</u> the Sylvan Strains,
              Nor blush to sport on Windsor's <u>happy</u> Plains. &c.;
Quere. If <u>Try</u> be not properer in relation to First; as, we first attempt a thing; and more modest? And if <u>Happy</u> be not more than <u>Peaceful</u>?

Try is better than sing – <u>Happy</u> does not sound right, ye first Syllable being short, perhaps you may find a better word than Peaceful as Flowry

---

Past. 1. lin. 23.   I'll stake my Lamb that near the Fountain plays,
                    And <u>his</u> <u>own</u> <u>Image</u> from the Brink surveys.
Or, And from the Brink <u>his</u> <u>dancing</u> <u>Shade</u> surveys.
Quere. Which of these 2 lines is better? **The second**

Past.1.lin.43   *Me <u>lovely</u> Chloris beckons from the Plain,*
                  Then <u>hides</u> in Shades <u>from</u> <u>her</u> <u>deluded</u> <u>Swain</u>;
                  But feigns a Laugh to see me search around,
                  And by that Laugh the willing Fair is found.
Objection. That <u>hides</u> without the Accusative <u>herself</u> is not good English, and that <u>from her deluded Swain</u> is needless.
Alteration.   Me <u>wanton</u> Chloris beckons from the Plain,
              Then <u>hid</u> in Shades, <u>eludes</u> <u>her</u> <u>eager</u> Swain; &c.
Quere. If <u>wanton</u> be more significant than <u>lovely</u>: if <u>Eludes</u> be properer in this case than <u>deluded</u>: If <u>eager</u> be an expressive Epithet to the Swain who searches for his Mistress?—**Wanton apply'd to a woman is equivocal & therefore not proper—Eludes is properer than deluded. Eager is very well**

Past.1.lin.57   If Sylvia smile, she brightens all the Shore,
                         The <u>Sun's</u> <u>outshin'd</u>, and Nature charms no more.
Quere. Whether to say the Sun <u>is</u> outshin'd, is be too bold & Hyperbolical? **For Pastoral it is**
If it shou'd ~~not~~ be soften'd with <u>seems</u>; Do you approve any of these Alterations
                         If Sylvia smile, she brightens all the Shore,
Quere which of
these three?   All Nature <u>seems outshind</u>, and charms no more.
                         or, Light <u>seems outshind</u>, and Nature charms no more.
                         Or, And vanquishd Nature <u>seems</u> to <u>shine</u> no more.
The last of these I like best

Past.1.lin.81.   Nay tell me first what Region canst thou find,
                         In which by Thistles Lillies are outshin'd?
           Or, Nay tell me first in what ˣmore happy Fields   x This Epithet refers
                 The Thistle springs to which the Lilly yields?   To something going before
Quere. Which of these Couplets are better express'd and better Numbers? And whether it's better here to use Thistle or Thistles, Lilly or Lillies, Singular or Plural? (Alluding to ye Arms of Scotland & France)
The second Couplet is best; & singular, I think better than Plural

---

Past.2.lin.1.   A Shepherds Boy (he seeks no better Name)
                         Led forth his Flocks along the silver Thame.
Objection. against the Parenthesis (he seeks no better Name)
Quere. Wou'd it be anything better to say (he loves that humble Name) or thus:
                         A Shepherds Boy, (who sung for Love, not Fame)
           or, A Shepherds Boy, who fed an Am'rous Flame,
                         Led forth his Flocks along the silver Thame.
Quere which of all these is best, or are none of them good?
The first is Spensers way, & I think better than the others.

Past.2.lin.7.   Relenting Naiads wept in ev'ry <u>Bow'r</u>,
                         And Jove <u>consented</u> in a silent Show'r.
Objection. That the Naiads weeping in Bowers is not so proper being Water Nymphs. and that the word <u>consented</u> is doubted by some to whom I have shown these verses.
Alteration.   The Naiads wept in ev'ry <u>watry Bow'r,</u>
                         And Jove <u>relented</u> in a silent Show'r.
Quere Which of these Couplets you like best? — ~~The First~~ **Upon yᵉ second thoughts I think the second is best.**

Past.2.lin.35.   Of slender Reeds a tuneful Flute I have,
                         The tuneful Flute which dying Colin gave.

Objection. That the first line is too much transpos'd from the natural Order of ye words: and that the Rhyme is unharmonious.

Alteration.   That Flute is mine which Colin's tuneful Breath
                Inspir'd when living, and bequeath'd in Death.

Quere. Which of these is best? — **The second**

Past.2.lin.41.   Some pitying God permit me to be made
                   The Bird that sings beneath thy Mirtle Shade:
                   Then might my Voice thy listning Ears employ,
                   & I those Kisses he receives, enjoy.
             Or, Oh, were I made by some transforming Pow'r
                   The Captive Bird that sings within thy Bow'r! Then might — &c.

The Epithet Captive seems necessary to explain the Thought, on account of those Kisses in ye last line.

Quere. If these be better than the other? **The second are best, for tis not enough to permitt you to bee made, but to make you**

Past.2.lin.67.   Oh deign to grace our happy rural Seats,
                   Our mossy Fountains, and our Green Retreats:
                   While you y^r Presence to the Groves deny,
                   Our flow'rs are faded, and our Brooks are dry;
                   Tho' withring Herbs lay dying on the Plain,
                   At y^r Return they shall be green again.
             Or, Oh deign to grace our happy Rural Seats,
                   Our mossy Fountains, & our green Retreats:
                 x Winds, where you walk, shall gently fann the Glade,
                   [Or, Where'er you walk, fresh Gales shall fan ye Glade,]
                   Trees, where you sit, shall crowd into a Shade,
                 x Flow'rs, where you tread, in painted Pride shall rise
                   [or Where'er you tread, the purple flow'rs shall rise,]
                   And all things flourish where you turn your Eyes!

Quere. Which of these you like better?
The second, with the alterations on ye side. [in square brackets]

Past.4.lin.5.   Now in warm folds the tender Flock remains,
                  The Cattle slumber on the silent Plains,
                  While sleeping Birds forget their tuneful lays,
                  Let us, dear Thyrsis, sing in Delias [Daphne's] Praise.

Objection to the word remains:
I do not know whether these following be better or no, & desire y^r opinion.

                    Now while the Groves in Cynthia's Beams are drest
                    And folded Flocks on their soft Fleeces rest;
                    While sleeping Birds —
                    Or, While Cynthia tips with silver all the Grove^s,
                    [Or, While the bright Moon wth silver tips ye Gro]
                    And scarce the Winds the topmost Branches move; & c.
                    not a Breeze   quiv'ring   moves
I think ye last best but might not even y^t bee mended?

Past.4.lin.29.   Tis done, and Nature's chang'd since you are gone,
                   Behold the clouds have put their Mourning on.
                   Or, Tis done, and Nature's various Charms decay,
                   See sable Clouds eclypse the chearful Day.
Quere. Which of these is the better? — **Clouds put in mourning is too conceited**
                                        for Pastoral: the second is better & the
                                        thick or the dark I like better than sable

---

Past.4.lin.39.   No rich Perfumes refresh the fruitful Field,
                   Which, but for you, did all its Incense yield.
                         for y^r sake
Quere, Will the second line be better'd by being altred thus?
                   No rich Perfumes refresh the fruitful field,
                   Nor fragrant Herbs their native Incense yield.
                   The second is better

Pas.3.lin.91.   Thus sung the Swains, while Day yet strove with Night,
                   And Heav'n yet ^{x} languished with departing light;
                   When falling Dews with Spangles deck'd the Glade,
                   And the low Sun had lengthened ev'ry Shade.
x Quere, if languish be a proper word? **x Not very proper**
Objection. That to mention the Sunsett after Twilight (Day yet strove wth Night) is
improper, Is the following Alteration any thing better?
                   Thus sung the Swains while Day yet strove w:th Night,
                   The Sky still blushing wth departing light;
                   When falling Dews with Spangles deck'd the Glade,
                   And the brown Evening lengthen'd evry Shade.
Tis not ye Evening but ye Suns being low y^t lengthens ye Shades. otherwise ye second pleases mee best.

APPENDIX II.

A DISCOURSE ON *PASTORAL POETRY.*

    THERE are not, I believe, a greater number of any sort of verses than of those which are called Pastorals, nor a smaller, than of those which are truly so. It therefore seems necessary to give some account of this kind of Poem, and it is my design to comprize in this short paper the
5 substance of those numerous dissertations the Criticks have made on the subject, without omitting any of their rules in my own favour. You will also find some points reconciled, about which they seem to differ, and a few remarks which I think have escaped their observation.

    The original of Poetry is ascribed to that age which succeeded the

---

Title, n. 1751: Written at sixteen years of age.

Title. MS: AN | ESSAY | ON | PASTORAL.
1–8. MS: omitted
9. **Poetry is ascribed to that age:** MS: *Poesie is attributed to that Age of Innocence*

The 'Discourse' was first printed in the *Works* of 1717. Pope's fair-copy MS was circulated amongst the same readership as the MS of the poem (see Headnote).

5. ***numerous dissertations:*** notably René Rapin, 'Dissertatio De Carmine Pastorali', attached to his own *Eclogae Sacrae* (1659), cited here in translation from 'A Treatise De Carmine Pastorali', added to Thomas Creech's translation of *The Idylliums of Theocritus with Rapin's Discourse of Pastorals* (1684), pp. 1–68; Bernard le Bovier de Fontenelle, *Discours sur la nature de l'eglogue* (1688), translated by Peter Anthony Motteux as 'Of Pastorals' in *Monsieur Bossu's Treatise of the Epic Poem* (1695), pp. 277–95; Knightly Chetwood, 'Preface to the Pastorals' in Dryden's *Works of Virgil* (1697), sig. ***–*****2. See further Congleton (1952).

9–10. In accordance with Rapin, 'Treatise', pp. 14–15, citing the authority of Hesiod and Lucretius: 'Pastorals were the invention of the simplicity and innocence of that Golden

creation of the world: And as the keeping of flocks seems to have been the first employment of mankind, the most ancient sort of poetry was probably pastoral. 'Tis natural to imagine, that the leisure of those ancient shepherds requiring some diversion, none was so proper to that solitary life as singing; and that in their songs they took occasion to celebrate their own felicity. From hence a Poem was invented, and afterwards improv'd to a perfect image of that happy time; which by giving us an esteem for the virtues of a former age, might recommend them to the present. And since the life of shepherds was attended with more tranquillity than any other rural employment, the Poets chose to introduce their Persons, from whom it receiv'd the name of Pastoral.

12, n. pastoral.] MS, *1751:* Fontanelle's *Discourse of* [*1751: Disc. on*] *Pastorals.*

10. **keeping . . . seems:** MS: *Feeding . . . appears*
12. **'Tis:** MS: *It is*
13. **requiring:** MS: *requir'd*; *1751:* admitting and inviting
   diversion, none: MS: *Diversion*; & *none*
13–14. **solitary life:** *1751:* solitary and sedentary life
14. **singing; and that in their:** MS: Singing. *These Songs were adapted to their present Circumstances; & in these*
16. **giving:** MS: *infusing into*
17. **them:** MS: *the same*
18. **shepherds:** MS *a* Shepherd
18. **more:** MS *most*
19. **than any other rural employment:** MS: omitted
19–20. **chose to introduce:** MS: *retain'd*

---

age, if there was ever any such, or certainly of that time which succeeded the beginning of the World . . . the Manners of the first Men were so plain and simple, that we may easily derive both the innocent imployment of Shepherds, and Pastorals from them'.

12 Pope's note. Fontenelle, 'Of Pastorals', p. 277: 'Of all kinds of Poetry the Pastoral is probably the most Ancient, as the keeping of Flocks was one of the first Employments which Men took up. 'Tis very likely that these primitive Shepherds, amidst the Tranquility and Leisure which they enjoy'd, bethought themselves of singing their Pleasures and their Loves'. Similar views are expressed by Rapin, 'Treatise', p. 2; Chetwood, 'Preface', sig. ***; and Tickell, in *Guardian*, no. 22, 6 April 1713.

16. perfect . . . time: Rapin, 'Treatise', p. 5, praises the 'lowly simplicity of a Sheapards Life' as 'a perfect image of the state of Innocence, of that golden Age, that blessed time, when Sincerity and Innocence, Peace, Ease, and Plenty inhabited the Plains'.

20. Pastoral: i.e., from the Latin 'pastor', a shepherd or herdsman.

A Pastoral is an imitation of the action of a shepherd; the form of this imitation is dramatic, or narrative, or mix'd of both; the fable simple, the manners not too polite nor too rustic: The thoughts are plain, yet admit a little quickness and passion, but that short and flowing: The

---

22, n. mix'd of both] MS: Heinsius, *Not. in* Theocr. Idyll.; *1751:* Heinsius in Theocr.
  fable simple] MS: Hor. Ar. Poet. *vers.* 23
    Denique sit, quod vis, simplex duntaxat, & unum.
23, variant, n. Golden Age] MS: Rapin, *de Carm. pastor. p.* 2.

21. shepherd; the: MS, *1751:* Shepherd, *or* One considered under that Character. *The*
22. dramatic, or narrative: MS: Dramatick, Narrative
  of both: MS: omitted
23. nor too: MS *nor yet too*
  The thoughts are plain,: MS: *In Order to a just Preservation of which, they are represented according to the Genius of the Golden Age. Comfortable to the Manners, the* Thoughts *are plain and pure;*

---

21. Pope's definition resembles that in Rapin, 'Treatise', p. 19: '*the imitation of the Action of a Sheapard, or of one taken under that Character*', but Rapin goes on to specify the example of Gallus, 'a man of great quality in Rome', appearing in pastoral guise in Virgil's tenth *Eclogue*. Chetwood, 'Preface to the Pastorals', sig. ***ᵛ, confirms that 'Pastoral is the *imitation of a Shepherd consider'd under that Character*' but like Pope does not venture into the corollary given by Rapin.

22. Pope's note. Heinsius: Daniel Heinsius (1580–1655), classical scholar at Leiden, editor of a text of Theocritus and the other Greek 'bucolic' poets published in 1603; an edition of Theocritus with notes from Heinsius and other scholars was published at Oxford in 1699. For his influence in England see Sellin (1968). Rapin paraphrases Heinsius's notes on Theocritus in 'Treatise', p. 29: '*the Character of* Bucolicks *is a mixture of all sorts of Characters, Dramatick, Narrative, or mixt*'. Pope referred lightly to Heinsius's scholarly expertise in letters to Cromwell of 12 or 13 July 1707 and 24 June 1710, *Corr.*, I.26, 90, and more pointedly in *Guardian*, no. 40, 27 April 1713, in mocking Philips. For the possibility that the reference is to the son, Nicolaas Heinsius (1620–81), who edited Virgil in 1664 and commented on pastoral theories in the 'Vita' attached to its various reprints, see Stephens (1982: 641).

Hor. Ar. Poet.: Horace, *Epistola ad Pisones*, commonly known as *Ars Poetica*, 23: 'to sum up, let [the poem] be what you wish, but let it be essentially single and unified'.

22. the fable simple: Rapin, 'Treatise', p. 31, writes that the 'Fable', in order that 'it might be agreeable to the Person it treats of . . . must be plain and simple'.

23. too rustic: Rapin, cited in Pope's note, rules out 'rusticity' and 'Clownish' elements in Pastoral in the 'Treatise', p. 33; but he also excludes 'too much Neatness' and anything 'too Courtly'. Pope deemed Philips's *Pastorals* to be too rustic; hence his parody of Spenserian names and provincial speech and habits of thought in *The Guardian*, no. 40.

23 MS variant. Genius: spirit, character.
  Comfortable: i.e. conformable, appropriate.
23–4. thoughts . . . passion: Rapin, 'Treatise', pp. 34–5, declares that the 'Thought . . . must be plain and pure' and yet have 'some quickness of Passion'.

25   expression humble, yet as pure as the language will afford; neat, but not florid; easy, and yet lively. In short, the fable, manners, thoughts, and expressions, are full of the greatest simplicity in nature.

The complete character of this poem consists in simplicity, brevity, and delicacy; the two first of which render an eclogue
30   natural, and the last delightful.

If we would copy Nature, it may be useful to take this consideration along with us, that pastoral is an image of what they call the Golden age. So that we are not to describe our shepherds as shepherds at this day really are, but as they may be conceiv'd then to have been; when a

---

28, n. simplicity] 1751: Rapin *de Carm. Past. p.* 2.

26. florid ... and: MS: *exquisit ... but*
31. would: MS: *design to*
   consideration: 1751: Idea
32. is an image of what they call: MS: *properly belongs to*
34–5. a notion ... and: 1736a–51: omitted

---

25. humble ... pure: Rapin, 'Treatise', p. 35: 'Let the Expression be plain and easy, but elegant and neat, and the purest which the language will afford'.

28. Rapin, 'Treatise', p. 37: 'as Simplicity was the principal vertue of that Age, so ... the Fable, Manners, Thought, and Expression ought to be full of the most innocent simplicity imaginable'.

28. simplicity: Tickell discussed at length the necessity of 'Simplicity' in Pastoral in the *Guardian*, no. 23, 7 April 1713. In Pope's *Guardian*, no. 40, in the course of a mock argument suggesting Virgil's *Eclogues*, and his own, are not really pastoral, this point is repeated with irony: 'As Simplicity is the distinguishing Characteristick of Pastoral ... the Simplicity proper to the Country', and so on. See also 115 below.

28 Pope's note. Indicating 'The Second Part' of Rapin's 'Treatise'; here, p. 44, where Rapin commends three virtues in Pastoral: '*Simplicity* of Thought and expression: *Shortness* of Periods full of sense and spirit: and the *Delicacy* of a most elegant ravishing unaffected neatness'.

31. copy Nature: cf. *Essay on Criticism*, 141.

32. Golden age: see Rapin as cited in Commentary to 12 and 15–16 above, and *Essay on Criticism*, 479–80, and Commentary. The return of the Golden Age is predicted by Virgil's fourth eclogue: see 'Messiah', Headnote. Pope's ludicrous ballad in contrived rustic Dorsetshire dialect, in *Guardian*, no. 40, is predicated ironically on 'that *Innocence of the Golden Age*, so necessary to be observed by all Writers of Pastoral'.

33–5. Rapin, 'Treatise', p. 37, citing Synesius, *Encomium on Baldness*, declares Pastoral is the proper genre of the Golden Age because 'Poetry fashions its subject as Men imagine it should be, and not as really it is'. Fontenelle repeatedly insists that pastoral does not please by reflecting 'real Shepherds' but an idea of tranquil simplicity; 'Of Pastorals', pp. 278–80.

35   notion of quality was annex'd to that name, and the best of men follow'd the employment. To carry this resemblance yet farther, that Air of piety to the Gods should shine thro' the Poem, which so visibly appears in all the works of antiquity: And it ought to preserve some relish of the old way of writing; the connections should be loose, the narrations and

---

37, n. Poem] MS: Preface *to the* Pastorals *in* Dryd. Virg.

35. that: MS: *the*
36. the employment: MS: *that Employment*
    farther, that Air: MS, *1751: farther, it wou'd not be amiss to give the Shepherds some Skill in* Astrology [*1751:* astronomy], *as far as it may be useful to that sort of Life. And an Air*
37–8. should shine . . . antiquity: MS: *which is so visibly diffus'd thro' all the Works of Antiquity, shou'd shine throughout the Poem.*
38. And it: MS: *Above all, a* Pastoral
39. old: MS: Ancient
    writing; the: MS: *Writing. For which Reason the*
    connections: *1751:* connection

---

35. quality: i.e., higher class, 'superiority of birth or station' (*SJ*), as in the segment of Rapin, cited in Commentary at 21 above. Rapin lists biblical shepherd-kings and asserts that in the 'golden Age' every man was a shepherd; 'Treatise', pp. 2–3, 3–4. Chetwood, 'Preface to the Pastorals', sig. ***v–***2, in the course of an argument about the ancient association of husbandry with 'Quality', states: '*It is commonly known, that the Founders of three the most renown'd Monarchies in the World, were Shepherds*', and declares that kings in Homer were 'Shepherds *of the* People' who all understood how to raise sheep.

37–8. piety . . . Poem. Pope's MS note indicates a source in Chetwood's first rule for Pastoral, 'Preface to the Pastorals', sig. ****v: '*that an air of Piety upon all occasions should be maintain'd in the whole Poem*', citing the practice of Homer and Virgil.

36 MS variant. Skill in *Astrology:* TE suggests that this point, which does not appear to be drawn from Rapin or Fontenelle, may be prompted by Dryden's identification of Virgil as 'an exact astronomer' in the 'Dedication' of the translation of the *Aeneid, Works of Virgil*, sig. (a)2ʳ. Pope ensures that the element occurs in each of his *Pastorals*: 'Spring', 38–40, 102; 'Summer', 21; 'Autumn', 72; 'Winter', 85.

39. old way of writing: Chetwood's sixth rule, 'Preface to the Pastorals', sig. *****: '*as the Style ought to be natural, clear, and elegant, it should have some peculiar relish of the Ancient Fashion of Writing*'.

   connections: from the same rule: 'Nor ought the Connexions and Transitions to be very strict, and regular'.

40　descriptions short, and the periods concise. Yet it is not sufficient that the sentences only be brief, the whole Eclogue should be so too. For we cannot suppose Poetry to have been the business of the ancient shepherds, but their recreation at more vacant hours.

45　But with a respect to the present age, nothing conduces to make these composures natural, than when some Knowledge in rural affairs is discover'd. This may be made to appear rather done by chance than on design, and sometimes is best shewn by inference; lest by too much study to seem natural, we destroy the delight. For what is inviting in this sort of poetry (as *Fontenelle* observes) proceeds not so much

---

40, n. concise] MS, *1751:* Rapin, *Reflexions* [*1751: Reflex.*] sur *l'Art Poet. d'Arist. p.* 2. *refl.* 27.
46, n. discover'd] MS, *1751* Preface [*1751: Pref.*] to Virg. Past. *in* Dryd. Virg.

---

40. short: MS: *little*
　　concise: MS: *short*
42. Poetry to: MS, *1751: Poetry in those days to*
42–3. the ancient shepherds: MS, *1751: Men*
43. recreation at: MS: *recreation us'd at*
46. to: MS: omitted
48. destroy the: *1751* destroy that easy simplicity from whence arises the
49. sort of: MS: omitted
　　(as *Fontenelle* observes): MS, *1736–51:* omitted

---

40. periods: sentences; cf. the passage of Rapin cited at 26 above.
40. Pope's note. See Thomas Rymer's translation of Rapin's *Reflections on Aristotle's Treatise of Poesie* (1674), p. 135, of eclogues: 'Narrations are short, *Descriptions* little'. Rapin, 'Treatise', p. 64, writes: '*Pastoral* may sometimes admit plain, but not long *Narrations*'.
40–1. The requirement of overall brevity constitutes, for Chetwood, 'Another Rule omitted by P. Rapine ... *that not only the Sentences should be* short, *and* smart ... *but that the whole piece should be so too*'; 'Preface to the Pastorals', sig. *****. In fact Rapin commends 'brevity' as a virtue in 'Treatise', pp. 41–2.
42–3. business ... recreation: TE compares Chetwood, 'Preface to the Pastorals', sig.

*****: '*For Poetry and Pastime was not the Business of Mens Lives in those days, but only their seasonable Recreation after necessary Labours*'.
45. composures: compositions. Pope rarely uses the word in this sense otherwise, and may as TE suggests have learned it from Creech's translation of Rapin's 'Treatise', where it occurs at least thirteen times; Motteux uses it three times in his version of Fontenelle, 'Of Pastorals'; Chetwood not at all.
46 Pope's note. Chetwood's fifth rule, 'Preface to the Pastorals', sig. *****v: '*the Writer should shew in his Compositions, some competent skill of the Subject matter, that which makes the Character of the Persons introduc'd*'.

50 from the Idea of a country life itself, as from that of its Tranquillity. We must therefore use some illusion to render a Pastoral delightful; and this consists in exposing the best side only of a shepherd's life, and in concealing its miseries. Nor is it enough to introduce shepherds discoursing together, but a regard must be had to the
55 subject; that it contain some particular beauty in itself, and that it be different in every Eclogue. Besides, in each of them a design'd scene or prospect is to be presented to our view, which should likewise have its variety. This Variety is obtain'd in a great degree by frequent comparisons, drawn from the most agreeable objects of the country;

53, n. miseries] MS, *1751:* Fontanelle's *Discourse* [*1751: Disc.*] *of* Pastorals.
58, n. variety] MS, *1751: See the foremention'd* Preface.

50. **of a . . . Tranquillity:** *1751:* of that business, as of the tranquility of a country life
51. **We . . . :** MS, *1751: new paragraph*
54. **together, but:** *1751:* together in a natural way; but
55. **subject; that:** MS: Subject. *First, that*
   and that: MS: *and secondly, that*
56. **each:** MS: *ev'ry one*
57. **view,:** MS: *Eyes;*
57–8 **likewise have:** MS: *also charm by its*
58. **This Variety:** MS: *This Grace*
59. **of:** MS: *in*

---

53 Pope's note. Fontenelle, 'Of Pastorals', p. 284: 'The Illusion and at the same time the pleasingness of Pastorals therefore consists in exposing to the Eye only the Tranquility of a Shepherd's Life, and in dissembling or concealing its meanness, as also in showing only its Innocence and hiding its Miseries'. Tickell, in *Guardian*, no. 22, endorses this view.

56–7. design'd scene: *TE* cites Chetwood's Third Rule, 'Preface to the Pastorals', sig. *****: '*That there should be some Ordonnance, some Design, or little Plot, which may deserve the Title of a Pastoral* Scene', citing the practice of Virgil.

58. Variety: the MS note signals a source in Chetwood, 'Preface to the Pastorals', sig. *****: the '*Fourth Rule, and of great importance in this delicate sort of Writing, is, that there be choice diversity of Subjects; that the* Eclogues, *like a Beautiful Prospect, should Charm by its Variety*'. Chetwood then tabulates the differing subjects of Virgil's *Eclogues*.

58–9. frequent comparisons: as advised in Rapin, 'Treatise', p. 66: 'your *Comparisons* must be frequent' and taken from 'such things, as the Shepherds must be familiarly acquainted with'.

60   by interrogations to things inanimate; by beautiful digressions, but those short; sometimes by insisting a little on circumstances; and lastly by elegant turns on the words, which render the numbers extremely sweet and pleasing. As for the numbers themselves, tho' they are properly of the heroic measure, they
65   should be the smoothest, the most easy and flowing imaginable.

65, n. imaginable] MS: Rapin, *de Carm. pastor. Pt. 3.*

60. **inanimate; by:** MS: *inanimate, in which the* Delicacy *of* Pastoral *is chiefly compriz'd: by*
61. **insisting:** MS: *enlarging*
64. **tho':** MS: omitted
64–5. **they should be:** MS: *but*

---

60. interrogations ... inanimate: addresses or questions to elements of the landscape and objects such as pipes. For examples from Pope's own *Pastorals*, see 'Summer', 13; 'Autumn', 27–9, 54, 57; 'Winter', 91. Pope does not use 'interrogation' in this sense otherwise and probably derives it, as *TE* suggests, from Rapin, 'Treatise', p. 62: 'short Interrogations made to *inanimate Beings*'.

61. insisting ... circumstances: Fontenelle, 'Of Pastorals', pp. 291–2, discusses the psychology of a reader's interest in 'circumstances', particularly in relation to stories of love and jealousy.

62. turns on the words: cf. *Essay on Criticism*, 391 and Commentary, and the ironic passage quoted from *Guardian*, no. 40, there.

63. numbers: versification and metre; cf. *Essay on Criticism*, 340, and Commentary.

 sweet and pleasing: Rapin, 'Treatise', p. 66, commends '*repetitions*' and 'doublings of some words', which, 'luckily plac'd ... make the Numbers extream sweet, and the turns ravishing and delightful'. An example in Pope's own *Pastorals* might be 'Spring', 65–8. At the very end of his life, Pope commented to Spence: 'There is a sweetness that is the distinguishing character of pastoral versification. The fourth and fifth syllables, and the last but two, are chiefly to be minded, and one must tune each line over in one's head to try whether they go right or not' (*OAC*, I.176, item 402, 5–7 April 1744). Earlier, in 1730, he had remarked that 'Virgil's Eclogues in particular are the sweetest poems in the world' (*ibid.*, item 403).

64. heroic measure: the hexameter, or, in English verse, the iambic pentameter line used by Dryden and Pope in their translations from classical epic, as opposed to song-like 'lyric' forms (see 102). Rapin, 'Treatise', p. 63 (in 'The Third Part', as in Pope's note), points to the authority of Theocritus, despite some examples of non-heroic meter, and Virgil, who 'useth no Numbers but *Heroick*'; but Rapin also advises that the verses should be 'not so strong and sounding as in *Epicks*'. Chetwood sets out examples of metrically similar lines from each of Virgil's three main genres to show the different effects that can be appropriately achieved ('Preface to the Pastorals', sig. *****[v]). To Spence, Pope said that 'Though Virgil in his pastorals has sometimes six or eight lines together that are epic, I have been so scrupulous as scarce ever to admit above two together, even in the *Messiah*'; *OAC*, I.176, item. 401 (5–7 April 1744).

It is by rules like these that we ought to judge of Pastoral. And since the instructions given for any art are to be deliver'd as that art is in perfection, they must of necessity be deriv'd from those in whom it is acknowledg'd so to be. 'Tis therefore from the practice of *Theocritus* and *Virgil,* (the only undisputed authors of Pastoral) that the Criticks have drawn the foregoing notions concerning it.

Theocritus excells all others in nature and simplicity. The subjects of his *Idyllia* are purely pastoral, but he is not so exact in his persons, having introduced Reapers and fishermen as well as shepherds. He is apt to be long in his descriptions, of which that of

---

74, n. Reapers] MS, *1751:* ΘΕΡΙΣΤΑΙ *Idyl.* 10. *And,* 'ΑΛΙΕΙΣ *Idyl.* 21.

66. these that: MS: *these, which are but Nature reduc'd to Method, that*
68. of necessity: MS: omitted
69. is acknowledg'd: MS: *is generally acknowledg'd*
70. undisputed: MS: *uncontested*
71. the foregoing: MS: *these useful*
71–2. it. Theocritus: MS: *it. Perhaps a Word of those Poets in this place may not be impertinent.* Theocritus
73. his: MS: *the*
74. as well as: MS: *among his*
75. be long: *1736a–51:* be too long

---

66. rules: the 'Third Part' of Rapin's 'Treatise' (cited in Pope's note to 58) is subtitled '*Rules for Writing* Pastorals'.
67–9. Rapin, 'Treatise', pp. 52–3: 'For all the Rules that are to be given of any Art, are to be given of it as excellent, and perfect, and therefore ought to be taken from them in whom it is so'.
70. Theocritus *and* Virgil: the 'Fathers of Pastoral', according to Rapin, 'Treatise', p. 52; see Headnote. Tickell makes a comparison between the two writers in the *Guardian*, no. 28, mostly in favour of Theocritus.
72. Theocritus *excells:* Rapin, 'Treatise', p. 38, writing of 'simplicity', states that '*Theocritus* excells *Virgil* in this'.
73. Idyllia: the name by which the poems of Theocritus were known in antiquity and in translation, e.g. *Sixe Idillia* (1588) and Creech's translation, *The Idylliums of Theocritus, with Rapin's Discourse of Pastorals* (1684), which Pope owned (Mack 1982: 443, item 158). An Idyll is a 'small short poem' (*SJ*), not necessarily in pastoral mode. In *Guardian*, no. 40, Pope limits the pastoral 'Idyllia' of Theocritus to eleven; Rapin, citing Servius and Heinsius, had limited the number to ten ('Treatise', pp. 26–7).
74 Pope's note. The Greek words mean 'reapers' and 'fishers' respectively and the references to *Idylls* 10 and 21 are correct; the text of 21 is corrupt and the poem is not now regarded as the work of Theocritus. Pope mentions the work of reapers at 'Summer', 65. Both Rapin, 'Treatise', pp. 27–8, and Fontenelle, 'Of Pastorals', p. 283, exclude from Pastoral any form of rural labourer who is not a shepherd.

the Cup in the first pastoral is a remarkable instance. In the manners he seems a little defective, for his swains are sometimes abusive and immodest, and perhaps too much inclining to rusticity; for instance, in his fourth and fifth *Idyllia*. But 'tis enough that all others learn'd their excellencies from him, and that his Dialect alone has a secret charm in it which no other could ever attain.

Virgil who copies *Theocritus*, refines upon his original: and in all points where Judgment has the principal part, is much superior to his master. Tho' some of his subjects are not pastoral in themselves, but only seem to be such; they have a wonderful variety in them which the *Greek*

78, n. rusticity] MS: Idyl. 4. & 5.
82, n. original] MS Rapin *Reflex. on Arist. p̃. 2. ref.* 27.

76. **pastoral:** MS: *Idyll*
79. **for instance . . . Idyllia:** MS omitted
82. **Virgil . . . and:** MS: *is certainly the Copy, but then he is such an one as equals his Original.*
83. **has . . . part:** is principally concerned, he *1751*
  part, is: MS: *Part, he is*
84. **seem:** MS: *appear*

---

76. **Cup:** *Idylls*, I.25–60. Rapin draws attention to the 'long immoderate description' of the Cup (and the 'prudent Moderation' of Virgil in this respect) in 'Treatise', p. 65; Fontenelle, 'Of Pastorals', p. 292, declares that it 'somewhat exceeds the Bounds'. Pope's equivalent is the bowl in 'Spring', 35–40.

78 **Pope's note.** Fontenelle, 'Of Pastorals', p. 278–9, finds fault with the fifth *Idyll*, amongst others, for the 'gross Clownishness' of the squabble between Comatas and Lacon; the fourth *Idyll* contains much rural banter about cattle and some salacious gossip. Rapin finds Theocritus sometimes 'faulty' in his depiction of rural 'Manners' and in 'making his Shepherds too sharp, and abusive to one another'; 'Treatise', p. 67.

80. **Dialect:** Doric; see 110.

81. **secret charm:** cf. Dryden's 'Dedication' of the Pastorals, *Works of Virgil*, sig. A2: 'I must confess that the Boorish Dialect of Theocritus *has a secret charm in it, which the* Roman *Language cannot imitate*'. Tickell commends the inimitable 'Softness of the *Dorick* Dialect' in the *Guardian*, no. 28, 13 April 1713.

82 **Pope's note.** Rapin, *Reflections on Aristotle's Treatise of Poesie*, p. 135: '*Theocritus* is more sweet, more natural, more delicate, by the character of the *Greek* Tongue. *Virgil* is more judicious, more exact, more regular, more modest, by the character of his own *Wit*, and by the *Genius* of the Latin Tongue. *Theocritus* hath more of all the graces that make the ordinary beauty of *Poetry*; *Virgil* has more of *good sense*, more vigor, more nobleness, more modesty. . . . *Theocritus* is the Original, *Virgil* is only the Copy: though some things he hath Copied so happily, that they equal the Original in many places'. See also next note.

85. **wonderful variety:** Pope's note refers to the passage of Chetwood's 'Preface to the Pastorals' cited in Commentary at 59 above; Virgil is '*admirable in this Point, and far surpasses* Theocritus, *as he does every where, when Judgment and Contrivance have the principal part*'. See also previous note.

was a stranger to. He exceeds him in regularity and brevity, and falls short of him in nothing but simplicity and propriety of style; the first of which perhaps was the fault of his age, and the last of his language.

Among the moderns, their success has been greatest who have most endeavour'd to make these ancients their pattern. The most considerable Genius appears in the famous *Tasso*, and our *Spenser*. *Tasso* in his *Aminta* has as far excell'd all the Pastoral writers, as in his *Gierusalemme* he has outdone the Epic Poets of his country. But as this piece seems to have been the original of a new sort of poem, the

---

86, n. stranger to] MS: *Preface to the* Eclogues *in* Dryd. *Virg. 1751:* Rapin *Refl. on Arist. part* ii. *refl. xxvii. – Pref. to the Ecl. in Dryden's Virg.*

86. was a: MS: *was utterly a*
  brevity, and: MS: *Brevity, and is perfect in the Manners. And*
88. perhaps: MS: omitted
89. has: MS: *is said to have*
92. writers: MS: *Poets of his Nation*
93. Epic Poets of his country: MS: Epicks
94. seems to have been: MS: *was*

---

88. Rapin, 'Treatise', p. 36, declares that is was 'much harder for the *Latines* to write *Pastorals*, than for the *Greeks*; because the *Latines* had not some *Dialects* peculiar to the Country, and others to the City, as the *Greeks* had; Beside the *Latine* Language ... is not capable of the neatness which is necessary to Bucolicks, no, that is the peculiar priviledge of the *Greeks*'.

89. For the pitting of ancients against moderns in critical discourse in Pope's time, see *Essay on Criticism*, 328 and Commentary. TE cites Walsh's letter to Pope, 20 July 1706, *Corr.*, I.20: 'The best of the modern Poets ... are those that have the nearest copied the Ancients'. Tickell's essay in the *Guardian*, no. 30, 15 April 1713, sets out 'wherein the Knowledge of Antiquity may be serviceable' before showing where a writer 'may lawfully deviate from the Ancients'.

92. Tasso ... Aminta: Torquato Tasso (1544–95), author of the pastoral play *Aminta*, written for the court of Ferrara in 1573 and translated by Henry Reynolds as *Torquato Tassos Aminta Englisht* in 1628; also by John Dancer as *Aminta: the Famous Pastoral* in 1660. A version by John Oldmixon was acted at the Theatre Royal in 1698 and a parallel Italian–English edition of Tasso's text was issued at Oxford in about 1701. Fontenelle, 'Of Pastorals', p. 289, rated *Aminta* 'the best Thing that *Italy* has produc'd in the Pastoral kind'. Rapin, 'Treatise', p. 31, censured Tasso and the Italian writers of pastoral comedy (see 95, Commentary) because their shepherds were too elegant and courtly. Dryden ranked Spenser above Tasso in the 'Dedication' of the *Pastorals*, at the point cited in Commentary at 102 below.

93. Gierusalemme: i.e. *Gerusalemme Liberata*, an epic on the First Crusade written in 1581 and translated as *Godfrey of Bulloigne, or the Recouerie of Hierusalem* by Richard Carew in 1594 and under a similar title by Edward Fairfax in 1600.

95   Pastoral Comedy, in *Italy*, it cannot so well be consider'd as a copy
       of the ancients. *Spenser*'s *Calender*, in Mr. *Dryden*'s opinion, is the most
       complete work of this kind which any Nation has produc'd ever since
       the time of *Virgil*. Not but he may be thought imperfect in some few
       points. His Eclogues are somewhat too long, if we compare them with

---

98, n. Virgil] MS, *1751:* Dedication *to* Virgil's *Eclogs.* [*1751: Virg. Ecl.*]

95. **consider'd as:** MS: *thought*
96. **ancients. *Spenser*'s:** MS: *Ancients. I shall then proceed to* Spencer *whose*
97. **kind:** MS: *sort,*
98. **Not but:** *1751:* Not that but
98. **he may be thought:** MS: *he seems*
99. **somewhat:** generally
99–101. **if we . . . before him:** MS: *Some often contain two hundred Lines, and others considerably exceed that Number*

---

95. ***Pastoral Comedy, in* Italy:** such as Battista Guarini's *Il Pastor Fido* (1585), translated by Sir Richard Fanshawe as *The Faithful Shepherd* (1648), and Guidubaldo Buonarelli's *Filli di Sciro*, translated by 'J. S. Gent.' in 1655. Walsh tried to persuade Pope to write a pastoral comedy on these models, an idea Pope courteously declined on the grounds that the 'Taste of our Age will not relish a Poem of that sort'; see Walsh to Pope, 24 June 1706, and Pope's response, 2 July, *Corr.*, I.18-19, for Pope's extended thoughts on the sub-genre. Tickell comments on Italian pastoral comedy in the *Guardian*, no. 28.

95–6. **copy of the ancients:** Classical pastoral did involve non-verse forms, e.g. in the prose romance *Daphnis and Chloe*, attributed to 'Longus' (see 'Spring', 17 and Commentary); but there were no pastoral comedies of the type Pope is referring to.

Spenser's Calender: *The Shepheardes Calender Conteyning twelue Aeglogues proportionable to the twelue monethes* (1579). See next note.

98 **Pope's note.** Dryden's 'Dedication' of the *Pastorals, Works of Virgil*, sig. A2: '*Our own Nation has produc'd a third Poet in this kind, not inferiour to the two former. For the Shepherd's Kalendar of* Spencer, *is not to be match'd in any Modern Language*'.

99. **somewhat too long:** the longest of Spenser's twelve eclogues is May (317 lines, excluding emblems); the shortest is January (78 lines); the mean average is 184 lines. Virgil's ten eclogues range from 63 to 111 lines, with an average of just under 83 lines. Theocritus ranges from 8 to 281 lines, but some of the poems are incomplete and not all are 'pastoral'. Pope's four *Pastorals*, in this first version, average 96.5 lines, ranging only between 92–102 (for the significance of the actual numbers, see Rogers 1980). Cf. the comment on brevity at 41–3, and Commentary: Chetwood, in the passage cited there, goes on to chide Virgil for occasional excess in this respect.

100   the ancients. He is sometimes too allegorical, and treats of matters of religion in a pastoral style as *Mantuan* had done before him. He has employ'd the Lyric measure, which is contrary to the practice of the old Poets. His Stanza is not still the same, nor always well chosen. This last may be the reason his expression is sometimes not
105   concise enough: for the Tetrastic has oblig'd him to extend his sense to the length of four lines, which would have been more closely confin'd in the Couplet.

---

103. **old Poets:** MS: *Ancients*
104. **sometimes:** MS: *often*
105. **extend:** MS: *spin out*
106. **length:** MS: *Compass*
   would have: MS: *had*

100-1. ***matters of religion:*** e.g. the allegorical 'Maye', which sets Protestant against Catholic 'pastors', and 'Julye' and 'September'. Because 'pastor' also meant 'priest', or 'shepherd of a flock' in the religious sense of 'pastoral care', the allegory was very well understood. Pope introduced some obvious political imagery in 'Spring', 85-90.

Mantuan: Baptista Spagnuoli Mantuanus (1448-1516), a monk at the Carmelite monastery in Mantua, author of ten Latin religious-allegorical eclogues published in *Adulescentia, seu, Bucloica* (often published for the use of schools throughout the sixteenth and seventeenth centuries in England); two of these were adapted as vehicles of political satire by Alexander Barclay, c. 1520 and full translations were made by George Turberville, *The Eglogs of the Poet B. Mantuan Carmelitan* (1567) and by Thomas Harvey, *The Bucolicks of Baptist Mantuan* (1655). The last Latin edition in England is dated 1707. Rapin and Fontenelle both censure Mantuan for being too 'clownish' and rough: 'Treatise', p. 33; 'Of Pastorals', pp. 280. Fontenelle also objects to the religious allegory, pp. 287-8.

102. ***Lyric measure:*** Theocritus and Virgil both write in hexameter verse; Spenser uses several different metres, among them the iambic pentameter that Pope uses, alongside much shorter, 'lyric' metres in stanza form. The lyre as a symbol of song occurs at 'Spring', 12.

105. ***Tetrastic:*** 'an epigram or stanza of four verses' (*SJ*, citing Pope's remark). Pope perhaps echoes Rymer's strictures against D'Avenant's *Gondibert* in the 'Preface' to his translation of *Rapin's Reflections on Aristotle's Treatise of Poesie* (1674), sig. a1: 'he obliges himself to stretch every period to the end of four lines. Thus the sense ... is either not discern'd, or found not sufficient for one just Verse, which is sprinkl'd on the whole *tetrastick*'. Dryden, in the dedicatory epistle normally known as the 'Discourse Concerning the Original and Progress of Satire', in *The Satires of Decimus Junius Juvenalis* (1693), p. viii, criticises Spenser for 'his Obsolete Language, and the ill choice of his Stanza' (in *The Faerie Queene*) on similar grounds, but goes on to praise Spenser's invention within these constraints.

In the manners, thoughts, and characters, he comes near
Theocritus himself; tho' notwithstanding all the care he has taken,
110   he is certainly inferior in his Dialect: For the *Doric* had its beauty
and propriety in the time of *Theocritus*; it was used in part of *Greece*,
and frequent in the mouths of many of the greatest persons;
whereas the old *English* and country phrases of *Spenser* were either
entirely obsolete, or spoken only by people of the basest condition.
115   As there is a difference betwixt simplicity and rusticity, so the
expression of simple thoughts should be plain, but not clownish.
The addition he has made of a Calendar to his Eclogues is very

---

108. **In:** MS: *For*
108–9. **near *Theocritus*:** *1751:* near to Theocritus
110–16. **For the *Doric* . . . clownish:** MS: omitted
114. **basest:** *1736a–51:* lowest
117–18. **very beautiful::** MS: *beautiful in the highest Degree.*

---

110. **Doric:** one of the many localised forms of the Greek language, originally associated with areas of 'Dorian' occupation such as the Peloponnese, certain islands including Crete, and Asia Minor; by the time of Theocritus, one of many literary dialects used for certain effects in some genres, and not in fact the only dialect in use in the *Idylls*. For Dryden's usage of 'the *Dorick* Muse' see his version of Virgil's sixth *Eclogue*, cited in Commentary to 'Spring', 2. Like most commentators, Dryden assumed that Doric was the actual spoken dialect of Theocritus' Sicily, though he is less prone than Pope to render it a 'noble' speech: 'Even his Dorick Dialect has an incomparable sweetness in its Clownishness, like a fair Shepherdess in her Country Russet, talking in a *Yorkshire* Tone'; 'Preface' to *Sylvae* (1685), sig. a6. In the 'Dedication' of his translation of the *Eclogues*, *Works of Virgil*, sig. A2, he commends Spenser's imitation of Doric based on 'Northern' and Chaucerian English.

114. **basest condition:** lowest social class and occupation.

115. **simplicity and rusticity:** cf. 23. Pope who discussed the virtues of simplicity in pastoral comedy in his response to Walsh, mentioned in Commentary to 99 above. But in *Guardian*, no. 40, simplicity becomes rusticity, no doubt following Tickell's praise of the 'pretty Rusticity' of Spenser and Philips in *Guardian*, no. 30 (rusticity is also a virtue in no. 32, 17 April 1713). Pope lavished ironic praise on the '*beautiful Rusticity*' of some trite verses from Philips's *Pastorals* in *Guardian*, no. 40, as well as pretending to wonder why Virgil 'had not imitated the Rusticity of the *Doric*'. In his mocking poem 'To Eustace Budgell, Esq. on his Translation of the Characters of Theophrastus' (unpublished prior to *TE*, VI.123), Pope suggests that Budgell has drawn the characters from his acquaintance in Addison's circle: 'The *Rustic Lout* so like a Brute, | Was *Philips*'s beyond Dispute'.

116. **plain . . . clownish:** *TE* compares Rapin, 'Treatise', p. 58: 'for though the Thought ought to be rustick, and such as is suitable to a Shepherd, yet it ought not to be Clownish'. Among *SJ*'s definitions of 'clownish' are: 'coarse; rough; rugged; uncivil; ill-bred; ill-mannered'.

beautiful: since by this, besides that general moral of innocence and simplicity, which is common to other authors of pastoral, he has one peculiar to himself; he compares human Life to the several Seasons, and at once exposes to his readers a view of the great and little worlds, in their various changes and aspects. Yet the scrupulous division of his Pastorals into Months, has oblig'd him either to repeat the same description, in other words, for three months together; or when it was exhausted before, entirely to omit it: whence it comes to pass that some of his Eclogues (as the sixth, eighth, and tenth for example) have nothing but their Titles to distinguish them. The reason is evident, because the year has not that variety in it to furnish every month with a particular description, as it may every season.

Of the following Eclogues I shall only say, that these four comprehend all the subjects which the Critics upon *Theocritus* and *Virgil* will allow to be fit for pastoral: That they have as much variety of description, in respect of the several seasons, as *Spenser*'s: That in order

---

118. **since:** MS: *For*
    that: MS, *1751: the*
119. **of pastoral:** MS: omitted
120. **human Life:** MS: *the Life of Man*
122. **changes and aspects:** MS: *Aspects and Conditions*
122–3. **Yet . . . to repeat:** MS [new paragraph]: '*Twas from hence I took my first Design of the following Eclogues. For looking upon* Spencer *as the Father of English Pastoral, I thought myself unworthy to be esteem'd even the meanest of his Sons, unless I bore some Resemblance of him. But as it happens with degenerate Offspring, not only to recede from y*ᵉ *Virtues, but dwindle from the Bulk of their Ancestors; So I have copy'd* Spencer *in* Miniature, *and reduc'd his twelve* Months *into Four* Seasons. *For his Choice of the former, has either oblig'd him to repeat*
125–40. **whence . . . imitate:** MS: omitted

---

120. **compares . . . Seasons:** cf. Pope's note to 'Winter', 89–92 and Commentary.
125-40 **variant.** The MS of the 'Discourse' is incomplete. It ends with the catchword 'Whence', suggesting the loss of at least some version of this concluding paragraph.

128. **variety:** TE suggests that Addison's critique of the lack of 'suprize and variety' consequent on Hesiod's month-by-month methods in his *Georgics* (now generally known as *Works and Days*), influences Pope's thinking here; see 'An Essay on the Georgics', in Dryden's *Works of Virgil*, sig. ¶¶.

to add to this variety, the several times of the day are observ'd, the rural
employments in each season or time of day, and the rural scenes or
places proper to such employments; not without some regard to the
several ages of man, and the different passions proper to each age.
    But after all, if they have any merit, it is to be attributed to some
good old Authors, whose works as I had leisure to study, so I hope
I have not wanted care to imitate.

134–5. rural employments: generally, the 'fleecy Care', or 'Rural Care', i.e. the rearing of sheep, as in 'Spring', 20 and 'Summer', 35; in Pope's *Pastorals* there are only rare and oblique mentions of cattle-herding ('Spring', 30) and periodic jobs such as sheep-shearing and reaping ('Summer', 64–5). More specific details emerge in the parody pastoral of *Guardian*, no. 40, and in Gay's *The Shepherd's Week* (see Headnote to *Pastorals*).

4

AN ESSAY ON CRITICISM
(1711)

Editors' Headnote

Composition and publication

An Essay on Criticism was first published on 15 May 1711. In a note on the title page of the autograph manuscript that served as the printer's copy of the poem, Pope claimed that it was 'Written in the year 1709', a statement repeated in the half-title of the poem in the 1717 *Works* and all subsequent editions. In his editorial note to the letter on versification sent to Walsh, dated 22 October 1706, Pope re-asserted this date: 'Mr. *Walsh* died at 49 Years old, in the Year 1708. The Year after, Mr. Pope writ the *Essay on Criticism* . . .' (*Corr.* I.25n; the letter itself may be a fabrication based on a letter to Henry Cromwell of 25 November 1710). Spence records Pope's clear statement: 'My *Essay on Criticism* was writ in 1709 and published in 1711, which is as little time as ever I let anything of mine lay by me' (*OAC*, I.41, no. 98, 1736). On other occasions, however, Pope suggested to Spence that he had shown a copy of the poem to Walsh in 1706 (*OAC*, I.31, no. 72, June 1739) or that he had written the poem 'two or three years before it was printed' (*OAC*, I.42, no. 99, 18–21 January 1743) and Jonathan Richardson Jr. claimed that 'Mr. P. told me himself that yᵉ Essay on Criticism was indeed written 1707, tho' said 1709 by mistake' (*OAC*, I.42, no. 98n). *TE* cites the possible allusion to a sermon preached by Dr White Kennett on 5 September 1707 as evidence that this part of the poem, at least, was written after that date; see Commentary to 550). In October 1708, Ralph Bridges described an encounter with Pope in a letter to Trumbull: 'Near the Temple met "little Pope." He would walk with me from thence to the farther end of St. James's Park, and all that way he plied me with criticisms and scraps of poetry' (*TE*, I.202). Altogether, it seems most likely that the poem's genesis was spread over several years. In February– March 1735 Pope told Spence, 'I wrote the *Essay on Criticism* fast, for I had digested all the matter in prose before I began upon it in verse' (*OAC*, I.45, no. 107) and it is perhaps this distinction that accounts for his divergent accounts of the poem's composition.

The manuscript that was used as printer's copy is in the Bodleian Library. The state of the manuscript suggest that Pope made some revisions in proof before the poem's appearance in print (Schmitz 1962: 9–11; Mack 1982: 336–7). Pope's first separately published work, the *Essay* was entered in the Stationers' Register on 11 May 1711, and published anonymously four days later. Pope seems to have sold the copyright to the publisher, William Lewis (a Catholic, and named as an old schoolfriend of Pope's by John Nichols, *Literary Anecdotes*, III.646 and VIII.168), for a period of five years because, on 17 July 1716, Lintot paid Pope a further £15 for the copyright (Foxon 1991: 23, 251). There are two versions of the imprint on variant title pages of the first edition – one listing the copyright-holder only, the other adding a list of publishers or subscribing booksellers (W. Taylor, T. Osborn and J. Graves; Foxon 1991: 10–11). One thousand copies of the first edition were printed in the quarto format normal for a critical pamphlet; a second edition in octavo, acknowledging Pope's authorship on a new title page, followed on 27 November 1712 (post-dated 1713), with a third edition in duodecimo in 1713, though the first remained in print until at least 1718. Foxon (1991: 23) suggests that this third edition was produced primarily to follow the new fashion for Elzevier types – it shows only one substantive revision (at l.609). As with the *Pastorals*, a further sheet of autograph notes (transcribed in Appendix II) survives, alongside the fair-copy manuscript of the *Essay*. This material shows Pope trying out revisions in response to criticism of the newly published poem, principally that of John Dennis (see below).

As often, it is difficult to draw a clear line between composition and publication. Between 1711 and 1744 Pope returned several times to the *Essay*, making rounds of revision and adding an expanding apparatus of notes and textual variants culled, in most cases, from the original manuscript. The manuscript provides evidence – in the form of notes to his amanuensis, Jonathan Richardson Jr. – of two distinct plans for harvesting this material. Pope's first instruction was for an extensive collation and recording of variants:

> Insert in ye Head of Alt[erations] whatever verses in this poem are [ ] as omitted in all ye printed Editions. & also whatever lines appear up[on compa]rison to be alterd from ye 1st printed Editions So [ ] & wt are thus markd x & underlind.

This ambitious task has been struck out and replaced by a more manageable instruction to: 'Transcribe from this only what is directly markd under & has ye word Transcribe at ye side.' For further discussion of the 'afterlife' of the manuscript, see Schmitz (1962: 9–23).

Text

The text presented here is taken from the first edition of 1711; this is marked by the extensive use of italic for emphasis. This is repeated in the second edition, but reduced in the third and absent from the 1717 *Works*. The *Essay* is the only one of Pope's poems to use italic in this way; McLaverty (2001: 8–9) suggests that Creech's translation of Horace's *Art of Poetry* served as a model in this respect. At the heart of the manuscript material of the *Essay on Criticism* is a handsome fair copy, which represents, as Schmitz (1962: 23) suggests, 'a finished poem and also a poem in transition'. Substantive variant readings from this text of the poem are recorded in the apparatus in the form in which they first appear in the fair copy: no attempt has been made to record the often complex subsequent revisions that Pope made in the manuscript. Beyond the first edition, significant verbal revision is confined to four later texts, the third edition of 1713 and the *Works* of 1717, 1736 and 1744, which also embody expansions in editorial apparatus (particularly the recording of variant readings), as does the *Works* of 1751. The survival of the manuscript, together with the plethora of subsequent editions of the *Essay*, makes clear the care Pope (and his various printers) took over the typographic form of the poem in different formats; employing more 'directive' italicisation in the pocket editions of the *Works*, while moving towards a cleaner, more 'classical' typography in larger format editions (Foxon 1991: 28–31, 162–183). The various extant texts of the *Essay on Criticism* referred to in the apparatus are as follows:

MS: 'An Essay on Criticism' (Bodleian Library, MS Eng.poet.c.1, ff. 1-15; reproduced in Schmitz 1962; *IELM* PoA 160)

1711: *An Essay on Criticism*, First Edition, quarto (Griffith 2)

1713a: Second Edition, octavo (Griffith 8)

1713b: Third Edition, duodecimo (Griffith 26)

1717: *Works*, quarto (Griffith 79)

1722: *Miscellaneous Poems and Translations*, vol.I, duodecimo (Griffith 35)

1727: *Miscellany Poems*, vol.I, duodecimo (Griffith 192)

1736a: *Works*, vol.I, octavo (Griffith 413)

1736b: *Works*, vol.I, octavo (Griffith 414)

1744: *An Essay on Criticism*, quarto (Griffith 590)

1751: *Works*, vol.I, octavo (Griffith 643)

Models and sources

Lady Mary Wortley Montagu told Spence (in 1741): 'I admired Mr. Pope's *Essay on Criticism* at first very much, because I had not then read any of the ancient critics and did not know that it was all stolen' (*OAC*, I.304, item 745). Pope himself told Spence that between the ages of 13 and 21 he 'went through all the best critics', among other wide reading (*OAC*, I.20, item 44). The process of noting Pope's allusions, imitations and echoes of previous poets and critics began with Pope's own notes to the poem (signalling allegiances) and with Dennis's hostile *Reflections* of 1711 (signalling thefts and misreadings). The poem has since been well served by source-hunters and *TE*'s commentary is rich in the history of the ideas and images that Pope calls on. We have quoted the most significant illustrative material and added to it as necessary for the explication of the range of Pope's possible meanings, but have not attempted to reproduce all the possible sources, parallels and analogues collected in and since *TE*.

In the poem Pope identified models in three categories, classical, French and English, and in two genres: the formal, systematic treatise in prose and the more loosely constructed, 'conversational' verse essay. Pope cites Aristotle (384–322 BC) directly at 88 and 648–53, without quoting his treatise, the *Poetics*, the surviving portion of which discusses the ethical importance, psychological effects and practical details, of tragedy and epic. It was the oldest extant literary-critical treatise and of the highest authority for Pope's period as a source of literary 'Rules', particularly as mediated through European theorists such as René Rapin, *Réflexions sur la Poétique d'Aristotle* (1674). This had been translated by Thomas Rymer as *Reflections on Aristotle's Treatise of Poesie Containing the Necessary, Rational, and Universal Rules for Epick, Dramatick, and the Other Sorts of Poetry* (1674; reprinted 1694). Aristotle's treatise was edited by James Upton at Cambridge in 1696 and an anonymous translation of it appeared in 1705.

Quintilian, praised at 672 of the poem and cited repeatedly in Pope's notes, was the Roman rhetorician Marcus Fabius Quintilianus (first century AD), author of a twelve-book *Institutio Oratoria*, a manual on the education of the public speaker. Pope owned a Dutch edition of 1665 (Mack 1982: 437); there was a significant new edition by Edmund Gibson at Oxford in 1693. 'Quintilian [was] a particular favourite with Mr. Pope', according to Spence (*OAC*, I. 20, 231). Quintilian covered many literary topics, and his view that the purpose of education was to promote humane culture forms the basis of Pope's poem; Quintero (1992: 19–39) suggests that the poem is structured as a six-part classical oration based on Quntilian's templates for 'deliberative and forensic speeches'.

Pope also highlighted a Greek treatise of the first century AD, ΠΕΡΙ ΥΨΟΥΣ (*Peri Hypsous*), known as *On the Sublime*, ascribed uncertainly to 'Longinus', which analysed the 'high' style associated with 'sublimity' and the power of extraordinary moments of imaginative passion, as opposed to routine correctness. Longinus's concern with the emotive effects of language is celebrated in the poem at 678–83 and is visibly influential on matters of artistic achievement at 142–61. There was an edition of Longinus at Oxford in 1636, and a translation into English by John Hall in 1652, but it was the translation into French by Nicolas Boileau-Despréaux (1674) which marked its emergence as a major theoretical work: Dryden began to absorb it soon after Boileau's translation. English versions appeared in 1680 (*A Treatise of the Loftiness or Elegancy of Speech*) and 1698 (*An Essay upon Sublime*), with one by Leonard Welsted, later Pope's enemy, in 1712. Pope later parodied Longinus with his mock treatise, 'Peri Bathous, or Martinus Scriblerus His Treatise of the Art of Sinking in Poetry', first printed in the so-called 'Last' volume of the Pope–Swift *Miscellanies* (1728; dated 1727). (For the connection between sublimity and satire in Pope's circle, see Noggle (2001) and Fanning (2005)).

An alternative version of literary authority was offered by the enormously influential *Epistola ad Pisones*, commonly known as the *Ars Poetica*, of Horace (Quintus Horatius Flaccus, 65–8 BC). Like Aristotle's *Poetics*, on which it was regarded as a sort of commentary, it was ostensibly concerned with dramatic representation, but its comments on nature, language, decorum and design were taken as authoritative precepts for all branches of literature. A translation by Ben Jonson was published in his 1640 *Workes* as *Q. Horatius Flaccus: His Art of Poetry*; it was further translated by the Earl of

Roscommon as *Horace's Art of Poetry* (1680) and by John Oldham in *Some New Pieces* (1681). Pope, who owned the Jonson translation, as well as several editions of the Latin original (Mack 1982: 419, items 90–2), commented to Spence: 'Horace's *Art of Poetry* was probably only fragments of what he designed. It wants the regularity that flows from the following a plan, and there are several passages in it that are hints only of a larger design' (*OAC*, I.227). Jonathan Richardson Jr., censuring Warburton for trying to promote the 'regularity' of Pope's *Essay on Criticism*, declared that Pope 'spoke of it always, as an "irregular collection of thoughts, thrown together as they offered themselves, as *Horace's Art of Poetry* was," he said, "and written in imitation of that irregularity," which he even admired, and said was beautiful'; *Richardsoniana* (1776), p. 264. Horace is praised at 658–69, but he is alluded to throughout; he was one model of the critic (and poet) as man of good sense and breeding, and the notion that Horace's verse embodied the precepts of the *Ars Poetica* underlay Pope's own poem.

Pope also cites Persius (Aulus Persius Flaccus, 34–62 AD) and Petronius, author of the episodic story known as the *Satyricon*, generally identified in Pope's day with Gaius Petronius Arbiter (d. 66 AD), described by the historian Tacitus (*Annals*, XVI.17) as a witty, polished courtier and hedonistic intimate of the emperor Nero. Mediating between ancient and modern was Marcus Hieronymus Vida (c. 1480–1566), whose *Poeticorum Libri Tres*, containing a verse art of poetry (*De Arte Poetica*), had been edited by Basil Kennett at Oxford in 1701. Pope later commended Christopher Pitt's 1725 English version (*Corr.*, II.383), which absorbed some of Pope's phrasing. Pope sent Cromwell some examples from Vida illustrating the sound/sense principle (see Commentary to 366), on 25 November 1710 (*Corr.*, I.107) and his edition of *Selecta Poemata Italorum Qui Latine Scripserunt* (1740) contained work by Vida, including one of the sources for *The Rape of the Lock*. Hopkins and Mackillop (1976) suggest that Pope's encomium at 707–11 was relatively fresh and in part responsible for reviving Vida's reputation.

In detailing the revival of literature after the Renaissance, Pope states 'But *Critic Learning* flourish'd most in *France*' (715). His early epic *Alcander* was written after 'the French Criticks', according to his recollection in 1730 (Sherburn 1958a: 346). These included Dominique Bouhours, rated 'the most penetrating of all the *French* Criticks' by Addison in *The Spectator*, no. 62, 11 May 1711, on the basis of two works, *Les Entretiens D'Ariste at D'Eugène* (1671) and *La Manière de Bien Penser dans les Ouvrages d'Esprit* (1687), the latter recently translated as *The Art of Criticism: or, the Method of Making a Right Judgment upon Subjects of Wit and Learning* (1705). Boileau's translation of Longinus appeared in the same year as his verse *L'Art Poetique* (1674), itself translated by Sir William Soames and John Dryden as *The Art of Poetry* (1683); Pope owned and annotated a copy of this translation and other works by Boileau (Mack 1982: 399, items 24–6). Boileau is mentioned, not altogether warmly, at 717. Pope also knew René Le Bossu's *Traité du Poëme Epique* (1675), a systematic account of the underlying rules of epic, translated as *Monsieur Bossu's Treatise of the Epick Poem* (1695). Pope alludes slightly to Le Bossu at 116, but praised his work in the 'Preface' to his translation of *The Iliad* and appended an account of epic summarised from Le Bossu to his translation of *The Odyssey*. In addition to his essay on Aristotle's *Poetics*, René Rapin wrote several critical works, including a notable comparison between Homer and Virgil, which appeared in a two-volume translation, *The Whole Critical Works of Monsieur Rapin* (1706).

These critics were absorbed into English literary culture through practising poets and dramatists such as Dryden and Dennis. Allusions and coincidences of thought in the poem suggest that Pope had read several of Dryden's most substantial essays: 'The Author's Apology for Heroique Poetry and Poetic Licence' (in *The State of Innocence*, 1677); 'The Grounds of Criticism in Tragedy' (the 'Preface' to *Troilus and Cressida*, 1679); 'A Discourse concerning the Original and Progress of Satire', the dedicatory epistle to his translation of the *Satires* of Persius and Juvenal (1693); the 'Dedication' of *Examen Poeticum* (1693); the 'Dedication' of his translation of Virgil's *Aeneid* (in *The Works of Virgil*, 1697); and the 'Preface' to *Fables Ancient and Modern* (1700).

Rymer's translation of Rapin's *Reflections on Aristotle's Treatise of Poesie* (1674) came with a polemical preface castigating the ignorance of English writers in relation to 'the fundamental Rules and Laws of *Aristotle*' (sig. A6ᵛ). Rymer's insistence on 'poetic justice' and preference for the three 'unities' of time, place and action, supposedly derived from Aristotle but actually largely codified by French dramatists such as Pierre Corneille, were strong influences on all literary theory of the Restoration period. Dennis, who responded to Rymer with *The Impartial Critick* (1693), began his own major phase of literary theory with two ambitious prose works, *The Advancement and Reformation of Modern Poetry* (1701), and *The Grounds of Criticism in Poetry* (1704), the latter promising 'some New Discoveries never made before, requisite for the Writing and Judging of poems Surely'. Both treatises contained extensive treatments of 'the Rules'; both made much of the Longinian sublime and urged the model of Milton in the Christian application of it. Pope would also have been aware of Dennis's nationalistic analysis of French critical regulation, in contradistinction to British wit and liberty, in the 'Epistle Dedicatory' (to Pope's friend John Sheffield) of *Advancement and Reformation*. Alongside these prose statements of English critical principles came several on the model of the verse 'essay'. In the *Dictionary*, Johnson defines 'essay' as an 'attempt' or 'endeavour', 'a loose sally of the mind; an irregular indigested piece; not a regular and orderly composition'. Dryden's conversational *Of Dramatick Poesie* (1668) was 'an essay' in this sense. Pope's title was initially intended to align his poem with some well-known poems, on the Horatian model, of advice about writing by aristocratic writers of the Restoration (the abstract of the 'Contents' of the *Essay*, added from 1736 onwards, was intended to give the poem more of the coherence of a prose treatise). One was *An Essay upon Poetry* (1682), by John Sheffield, Earl of Mulgrave and later Duke of Buckinghamshire (1648–1721), patron of Dryden, dedicatee of Dryden's translation of Virgil's *Aeneid* (1697) and one of the sponsors of Pope's *Pastorals*. Sheffield, whose posthumous *Works* Pope would edit, was also credited with *An Essay upon Satyr* (c. 1680), another verse treatise widely reprinted, e.g in the volume of *Poems Relating to State Affairs* (1705), which Pope owned and annotated (Mack 1982: 435); Pope thought Dryden had a hand in this. Another was *An Essay on Translated Verse* (1684), by Wentworth Dillon, Earl of Roscommon (1637–85), accompanied by a celebratory poem from Dryden. Sheffield's and Roscommon's essays expressed strong aspirations for British verse; both had recently been reprinted in pirated editions (1709). Pope praises Roscommon at 726–9 and Sheffield in a variant to the same point in later editions. Another patron of his, George Granville, wrote 'Concerning Unnatural Flights in Poetry' in *A New Miscellany of Original Poems, on Several Occasions* (1701), pp. 311–22; with its defence of just proportion against the 'monstrous' extravagances of the imagination and its praise for the reforming authority of Sheffield and Roscommon, this further facilitated Pope's poem; it was retitled 'An Essay Upon Unnatural Flights in Poetry' in Lansdowne's *Poems* (1712). Pope knew Addison's 'An Account of the Greatest English Poets', published in *The Annual Miscellany: For the Year 1694* (1694), and Samuel Cobb's *Poetae Britannici* (1700; revised as 'Of Poetry' in Cobb's *Poems on Several Occasions*, 1707), each of which offered poetic histories of British verse. William Coward's *Licentia Poetica Discuss'd* (1709), a poem about poetry, came with a commendatory poem by Pope's future friend John Gay. Pope was also greatly interested in artistic theory and practice, especially in respect of design and perspective, and had certainly read Dryden's translation, *De Arte Graphica. The Art of Painting* (1695), from the French of Charles-Alphonse Dufresnoy, with Dryden's prefatory 'Parallel betwixt Poetry and Painting'.

Collections of the kinds of critical essay Pope was drawing on can be found in Spingarn (1908–9) and Womersley (1997); Nisbet and Rawson (1997) offer overviews of the history of critical writing in the Restoration and eighteenth century.

Context

Pope's poem foregrounds on certain key themes and concepts inherited from these sources and analogues.

Nature is mentioned 23 times in the poem, principally as the '*Source*, and *End*, and *Test* of *Art*' at 68–91. In his *Dictionary*, Johnson summarised various meanings of the term 'which occurs so frequently, with significations so various, and so difficultly defined', on the basis of Robert Boyle's *Free Enquiry into the Vulgarly Receiv'd Notion of Nature* (1686). While Pope's use of 'Nature' in the *Pastorals* corresponds to the more limited and modern sense of the external world of landscape and the non-human, in the *Essay on Criticism*, 'Nature' is heavily laden with ethical meaning. The idea of 'following' nature as a rule for life was classical in origin (e.g. Cicero, *De Officiis*, I.xxviii.10) and picked up in standard sources such as *The Art of Poetry*, translated by Dryden and Soames, III.358 (1683), p. 49: 'To study Nature be your only care'; Walsh told Pope, 9 September 1706 (*Corr.*, I.21): 'you are certainly in the right, that in all Writings whatsoever (not Poetry only) *Nature* is to be follow'd'. *The Spectator*, no. 404 (13 June 1712), assigned to Pope by Ault (*PW*, I.37–41), refers to the oracle that directs Cicero to follow nature as his study, and Pope's note to line 300 cites Quintilian's exhortation, 'Naturam intueamur, hanc sequamur' ('let us contemplate nature and let us follow her'). A broadly conceived 'Nature' had been a dominant aesthetic paradigm from Renaissance neo-Platonism onwards as in Sir William D'Avenant's definition in the Preface to *Gondibert* (1651), p. 7: Nature 'is the onely visible power, and operation of God'. As Dennis put it in *The Advancement and Reformation of Poetry*, sig. A8^v (Hooker

1939–43, I. 202): 'Nature ... is nothing but that Rule and Order, and Harmony, which we find in the visible Creation' (for further discussion see Savage 1988). In attacking Pope's *Essay*, Dennis asserted that to Horace 'nature' meant 'human Life, and the manners of Men' but only in the Platonic or ideal sense of 'that innate Original, and that universal Idea, which the Creator has fix'd in the minds of ev'ry reasonable Creature' (*Reflections, Critical and Satyrical*, p. 31, Hooker 1939–43, I.418).

If Nature is the fundamental order of the cosmos in Pope's poem, **Wit** is the fundamental quality of the creative mind. In the course of an extensive discussion, Dryden argued that 'The composition of all Poems is or ought to be of wit ... Wit written, is that which is well defin'd, the happy result of thought, or product of that imagination' ('An Account of the Ensuing Poem', in *Annus Mirabilis* (1667), sig. A7ᵛ). Robert Wolseley, defending the Earl of Rochester's 'universal Genius' and 'unbounded Fancy', defines 'poetical Wit' as '*a true and lively expression of Nature*', meaning 'not only ... all sorts of material Objects and every species of Substance whatsoever, but also general Notions and abstracted Truths, such as exist only in the Minds of men and in the property and relation of things one to another' ('Preface', to *Valentinian, A Tragedy: As tis alter'd by the late Earl of Rochester*, 1685; Spingarn 1908–9, III.21). Pope studied Rochester's wry comments on the tendency of everyone to be happy with their own share of 'wit', annotating lines from 'An Epistolary Essay from M. G. to O. B.' in his 1696 copy of Rochester's *Poems* with a reference to Descartes's *Discourse of Method* (Mack 1982: 438). In the poem, Pope uses 'Wit' to encompass both 'Imagination', which appears only once in the poem (58), and 'Fancy' (twice: 653 and 670). It is the most charged keyword of the poem, occurring 49 times, 13 of them in rhyming position, spread relatively evenly through the poem (every sixteen lines on average, according to Empson's classic 1950 article). *OED* sense 1, 'the seat of consciousness or thought', was largely obsolete by Pope's time, but Johnson gives the 'original signification' of the word as 'powers of the mind' in 1755. Johnson also gives 'imagination; quickness of fancy', 'sense; judgment', and 'invention; ingenuity' as possible meanings and equivalences. These senses, corresponding variously to *OED* sense 2, 'the faculty of thinking in general', 5a, 'Good or great mental capacity; intellectual ability; genius, talent, cleverness', and 7, 'Quickness of intellect or liveliness of fancy, with capacity of apt expression', were all still current, among many other nuances. Sense 8a, 'That quality of speech or writing which consists in the apt association of thought and expression, calculated to surprise and delight by its unexpectedness ... later always with reference to the utterance of brilliant or sparkling things in an amusing way', close to the modern sense, is present but not necessarily dominant in Pope's usage. Empson's article, which tabulates Pope's various senses, argues that 'there is not a single use of the word in the whole poem in which the idea of a joke is quite out of sight'. However this may be, Wit constitutes Pope's essential category of creative intelligence and its artistic manifestations in writers and their productions. A 'wit' was also to Johnson a 'man of fancy' and 'man of genius', a usage which accounts for 13 of the instances of the word in the poem. It can also mean a literary product such as a poem, as well as the quality that produces it or is displayed by it; at line 728, and perhaps elsewhere, it appears to mean the total creative production of a given culture, as in Gay's survey, *The Present State of Wit*, also published in 1711. Pope's first recorded letter, to the ageing poet William Wycherley, himself certainly a 'wit' of the old school (26 December 1704, *Corr.*, I.2) defines true wit as 'a perfect Conception, with an easy Delivery'; and he returned to the matter repeatedly: see Commentary to 300–1. In 1733–4 he was planning an essay 'Of the Use of Wit' (*OAC*, I.132–3).

Often conventionally opposed to 'Wit', **Judgment** occurs 13 times in the poem. In Pope's period the need for the secondary faculty of judgment to curb the primary force of wit (or invention, or imagination) was routinely stressed; the opposition appears throughout Dryden's *Of Dramatick Poesie*. In the *Essay upon Poetry*, 36 (1682), p. 3, Sheffield writes 'So without Judgment, Fancy is but mad'; and Sir William Temple subjects 'the heat of Invention and liveliness of Wit' to 'the coldness of good Sense and soundness of Judgment', in 'Of Poetry', *Miscellanea . . . The Second Part* (1690), p. 294. In 'On the Excellent Poems of my most Worthy Friend', in Thomas Flatman, *Poems and Songs* (1674), sig. A7ʳ, Charles Cotton declares 'Nor is it *all*, to have a share of *wit*, | There must be *judgment too* to manage it'; and likewise John Cutts, 'To the Dutchess of Monmouth', *Poetical Exercises* (1687), p. 40: 'Nature to some has giv'n an active Wit, | But hardly Sense enough to manage it'. In the chapter 'Of Discerning, and other Operations of the Mind' (book II, chapter XI, 1690, p. 68) of John Locke's *An Essay Concerning Humane Understanding* Locke unequivocally separates the two operations:

> For *Wit* lying most in the assemblage of *Ideas*, and putting those together with quickness and variety, wherein can be found any resemblance or congruity, thereby to make up pleasant Pictures, and agreeable Visions in the Fancy: *Iudgment*, on the contrary, lies quite on the other side, in separating carefully *Ideas* one from another, wherein can be found the least difference, thereby to avoid being misled by Similitude, and by affinity to take one thing for another.

(For discussion of Locke in relation to Pope's ideas see Vermeule 1998). This opposition underlies the querulous response of Wycherley to Pope's attempts to prune and curb his over-fluent productions: Wycherley declared the 'sprightliness of Wit' despises the dullness of method (22 November 1707; *Corr.*, I.33). However, as Johnson's definition of 'wit' shows, the word can itself mean 'sense' and 'judgment', and the categories were easily blurred: Shadwell wrote in the 'Preface' to *The Humorists* (1671), sig. a3ʳ: 'judgment does . . . comprehend wit, for no man can have that who has not wit'. La Rochefoucauld argued, in *Moral Maxims and Reflections* (1694, no. 98):

> The making a Difference between *Wit* and *Judgment*, is a *Vulgar Error*. The *Judgment* is nothing else, but the *Exceeding Brightness* of the *Wit*, which, like *Light*, pierces into the very *Bottom of Things*, observes all that ought to be observed there, and Discovers what seemed to be past any bodies finding out. From whence we must conclude that the *Energy* and *Extension* of this *Light* of the *Wit*, is the very thing, that produces all those effects, usually ascrib'd to the *Judgment*.

Wit and Judgment were both facets of **Genius**, which occurs five times in the poem. In the *Essay upon Poetry*, 20-4 (1682), p. 2, Sheffield called genius 'the Soul' of a work,

> A Spirit which inspires the work throughout,
> As that of Nature moves this World about;
> A heat that glows in every word that's writ,
> That's something of Divine, and more than Wit;

Dryden declared,

> A happy *Genius* is the gift of Nature: it depends on the influence of the Stars say the *Astrologers*, on the Organs of the Body say the *Naturalists*; 'tis the particular gift of Heaven say the *Divines*, both *Christians* and *Heathens*. How to improve it many Books can teach us; how to obtain it none; that nothing can be done without it all agree.
>
> ('Preface of the Translator' in *De Arte Graphica* (1695), p. xxxiv)

Temple spoke of 'that Elevation of Genius, which can never be produced by any Art or Study, by Pains or by Industry ... and therefore is agreed by all, to be the pure and free Gift of Heaven or of Nature'; he thought no nation had 'so much true Genius' as the English, meaning 'Sharpness of Wit', 'Pleasantness of Humor', 'Range of Fancy', and 'Penetration of Thought or Depth of Reflection'; 'Of Poetry', *Miscellanea . . . The Second Part*, pp. 292-3, 335. Pope's usage seems to combine the sense, now almost obsolete, of 'characteristic disposition; inclination; bent, turn or temper of mind' (*OED*, sense 3) and 'natural ability or capacity; quality of mind; the special endowments which fit a man for his peculiar work' (sense 4), with 'native intellectual power of an exalted type ... instinctive and extraordinary capacity for imaginative creation' (sense 5), although *OED* suggests this latter only developed later in the eighteenth century. Pope's 'Preface' to his 1717 *Works* uses the term freely (*PW*, I.289-96) and in his letters to Judith Cowper, 18 October 1722 (*Corr.*, II.138) and to Swift, 17 August 1736 (*Corr.*, IV.28), Pope asserts the inborn nature of genius.

Taste, the inbuilt faculty of the critic as wit is of the poet, occurs five times, four in the familiar modern sense related to aesthetic appreciation. This meaning, 'The sense of what is appropriate, harmonious, or beautiful; *esp.* discernment and appreciation of the beautiful in nature or art; *spec.* the faculty of perceiving ... what is excellent in art, literature, and the like', was relatively modern, dating from 1671 according to *OED* sense 8a. Dennis's *A Large Account of the Taste in Poetry, and the Causes of the Degeneracy of it*, dedicated to Granville, appeared in 1702. In *Spectator*, no. 409, 29 June 1712, Addison proposed 'Rules ... how we may acquire that fine Taste of Writing, which is so much talked of among the Polite World', as if it were a new phenomenon. 'Of Taste' was the original subtitle of Pope's *Epistle to Burlington* (1731). In that poem (41-4), Pope prioritised another quality of the critical mind:

> Something there is, more needful than Expence,
> And something previous ev'n to Taste—'tis *Sense*:
> Good Sense, which only is the gift of Heav'n,
> And tho' no science, fairly worth the seven:

Sense is used 23 times in the *Essay on Criticism*, nine times as a rhyme word. Pope had previously declared it an attribute of Wycherley in 'Autumn', 9. Among Johnson's definitions are 'understanding; strength of natural reason; reasonable meaning; opinion; notion; judgment; consciousness; conviction; moral perception'; the word thus indicates both the content, argument or meaning of literary texts and the intelligence with which literature is read and understood. Morris (1984: 296–321) elaborates Pope's concept of the poet as man of sense and of sense as incorporating a mode of gentlemanly candour in conversation, writing, and other social interchanges.

Though Pope invokes these terms as part of a shared cultural vocabulary, avoiding definitions on the supposition that the reader already knows what they mean, they were hardly matters of uniform agreement. Hooker (1951) presents much material from the Restoration period to show that 'Wit' was under prolonged ethical attack during the period leading up to Pope's reaffirmation of its primacy literary force. Cowley's Ode 'Of Wit' (*Poems . . . Written by A. Cowley*, 1656, pp. 2–4) discerned true wit as the mystical 'soul' or ordering principle of art and false wit as puns, quibbles, and verbal ornament, while Rochester's 'Satyr against [Reason and] Mankind' contains a brief, fractious dialogue with an imaginary clergyman who attacks 'this gibeing jingling knack call'd *Wit*' and longs 'to lash it in some sharp Essay' (48–55; *Poems on Several Occasions* (1680), p. 8). In 1690 Locke was signalling a deep distrust of literary language (the expression of wit) as at best ornamental and pleasure-seeking and at worst delusory and artificial, good 'for nothing else, but to insinuate wrong *Ideas*, move the Passions, and thereby mislead the Judgment; and so indeed are perfect cheat' [*sic*]; *Essay Concerning Humane Understanding*, book III, chapter 10 (1690), p. 251. In its power to combine images not 'naturally' combinable, and in its association with the loose social world of Restoration theatre, it could be aligned with aristocratic privilege, pleasure and irrationality rather than truth, learning, or utility. In 1700 Blackmore published his bitterly sober *Satyr against Wit*, partly in response to the wit of Pope's friend Samuel Garth, whose mock-heroic poem *The Dispensary* (1699) had offended him, initiating a controversy between a middle-class professional ethos of business and probity, against an older order of wit and licence. In Blackmore's estimation the 'Plague of Wit' was ruinously corrupting the nation's work ethic, standards of learning, and virtue. *TE* cites serious defences of wit's ability to find truths beyond the superficial from some surprising sources, including the clergyman Joseph Glanville's *An Essay Concerning Preaching* (1678, reissued 1703):

> true Wit is a perfection in our Faculties, chiefly in the Understanding, and Imagination; Wit in the Understanding is a Sagacity to find out the Nature, Relations, and Consequences of things; Wit in the Imagination, is a quickness in the phancy to give things proper Images.
>
> (pp. 71–2)

It was thus useful for divines speaking in public. In 'A Whip for the Droll', *Saducismus Triumphatus* (1700), pp. 4–5, Glanvill defended wit's associative powers, calling it: 'a Faculty to dive into the depth of things, to find out their Causes and Relatives, Consonancies and Disagreements, and to make fit, useful, and unobvious Applications of their respective Relations and Dependencies'. Pope's future friend Francis Atterbury had likewise preached recently of wit as 'a certain uncommon Reach and Vivacity of Thought ... very fit to be employ'd in the Search of Truth, and very capable of assisting us to discern and embrace it'; *Fourteen Sermons* (1708), p. 158. Discussions of this element of wit were also undertaken by Addison in *The Spectator*, nos. 58 to 63, 7–12 May 1711. The Earl of Shaftesbury's *Sensus Communis: an Essay on the Freedom of Wit and Humour* (1709) was published as part of his optimistic programme for free-minded public discussions as a stimulus to human betterment. Pope's exploration of wit is thus less a neutral reminder of what everybody knew than a particular balancing of contradictory elements from one of the major critical debates of the late seventeenth century.

In 1711 there were no authoritative institutions of literary criticism; there had been proposals for an English Academy, but English literature was not routinely studied in universities. Joseph Trapp, Oxford's first Professor of Poetry (prompting the *Praelectiones Poeticae*, the first of which also came out in 1711) has been cited as the first 'professional' literary critic (Patey 1997a: 10). There were no formal literary reviews of a regular kind before *The Monthly Review* (founded 1749). *The Tatler* and *The Spectator* carried occasional literary essays; the latter ran essays on popular ballads on 21 and 25 May 1711, just after the appearance of Pope's poem, which was itself praised by Addison in the same journal later in the year. But nobody was a professional critic in the modern sense: all critical acts were freelance. 'Criticism' was itself a relatively recent word in the modern sense in which Pope uses it. *OED* dates this sense (2), 'The art of estimating the qualities and character of literary or artistic work; the function or work of a critic' to Dryden's 'Author's Apology for Heroique Poetry', prefaced to *The State of Innocence* (1677), sig. b1^v: 'Criticism, as it was first instituted by *Aristotle*, was meant a Standard of judging well', a sentiment recalled by Pope's opening line. *OED* sense 1, 'the passing of unfavourable judgement; fault-finding, censure' dates from somewhat earlier, and Dryden, speaking as a dramatist whose income depended on the approval of paying audiences, was arguing that literary culture had recently become infected with needlessly combative review, by 'Illiterate, Censorious, and Detracting people, who, thus qualified, set up for Critiques'. Virtually all of the considerable body of commentary and position-taking that led Samuel Johnson to regard Dryden as 'the father of English criticism' (Lonsdale, II.118) appeared as prefaces or dedications to plays, poems and collections, often in response to hostile critiques by others. As he put it in the 'Dedication' to *Examen Poeticum* (1693), sig. A4^r: 'the corruption of a Poet, is the Generation of a Critick' (meaning 'Critick in the general acceptation of this Age'). In his 'Life of Lucian', posthumously published in *The Works of Lucian* (1711), I.50–1, he writes, '*Criticism*, is now become mere Hang-man's Work, and meddles only with the Faults of Authors'. Against the generous (gentleman) poet was now set a new breed of enviously hostile critics, operating through pamphlets, gossip in coffee houses, and hissing in the theatre.

Rymer remarks, in the 'Preface' to his translation of *Rapin's Reflections on Aristotle's Treatise of Poesie* (1674), sig. A3^v, that until 'late years *England* was as free from Criticks, as it is from *Wolves*', a suggestive formulation. Rymer goes on: 'this priviledge, whatever extraordinary Talent it requires, is now usurped by the most ignorant: and they who are least acquainted with the game, are aptest to bark at every thing that comes in their way'. Swift devotes section III of *A Tale of a Tub* (1704) to a mock dissertation on the malignity and crassness of modern critics, and his characterisation of Criticism as a malign deity in the *Battle of the Books* foreshadows Pope's own Goddess of Dulness. Swift is echoed in Cobb's 'A Discourse on Criticism and the Liberty of Writing', *Poems on Several Occasions* (1707), sig. A4^v: 'Criticism, which was formerly the Art of judging well, is now become the pure Effect of Spleen, Passion and Self-conceit'. As for the 'rules' of critics, these were useful only as an educational tool for young minds which can be cast off in favour of 'free, generous and manly Spirit' of adult wit. *The Tatler*, no. 165, 29 April 1710, contained a caricature of that 'importunate, empty, and conceited animal . . . generally known by the name of a Critic', a fool who has read only a few passages of French theorists. The same journal had commented (no. 29, 14 June 1709) on the opposition between the Wit and the Critic: 'These two gentlemen are great opponents on all occasions, not discerning that they are the nearest each other, in temper and talents, of any two classes of men in the world'. Shaftesbury's *Soliloquy; or, Advice to an Author* (1710) was an attempt to deny that the opposition between critic and author was in any sense fundamental or natural, and Pope's poem occupies a similar ground of optimistic consensus.

Pope read and annotated *The Tragedies of the Last Age* (Mack 1982: 438–9), and told Spence that Rymer was 'a learned and strict critic' (*OAC*, I.205, item 480). But Rymer himself was partly responsible for the controversial divide between poets and critics: he was not a practising dramatist and his polemic against the failure of English writers to comply with neoclassical prescriptions, in *The Tragedies of the Last Age Considered* (1677) and *A Short View of Tragedy* (1692), was bitter and contemptuous, provoking the opposition of writers such as Wycherley and Dryden (Zimansky 1956: 193–4); Dryden's 'Heads of an Answer to Rymer', in which he traded interpretations of Aristotle with the critic, was sketched in 1677 but published in 1711, in Tonson's edition of the *Works* of Beaumont and Fletcher. Rymer's critical diatribe resurfaced in different guise in the late 1690s when dramatists such as Dryden, Vanbrugh, Congreve, Dennis and Wycherley were excoriated for their failure to observe decorum of various kinds in Jeremy Collier's *Short View of the Immorality and Profaneness of the English Stage* (1698). Dozens of rejoinders were published, including many by the dramatists attacked. There are signs at several points that Pope drew on the moral content of such treatises, but also had Collier's over-literal and extra-literary critical prurience at the edge of his vision.

Another critical controversy underlying Pope's zestfully urbane pronouncements is the conflict between proponents of classical and modern culture. Dryden's *Of Dramatick Poesie* was a carefully balanced discussion of the relative strengths of modern drama compared with ancient, and Dennis's essays contrast the achievements of the ancients in tragedy with the progress made by moderns in sciences and other forms of knowledge. Some writers openly welcomed a new era: Farquhar playfully dismissed the relevance of Aristotle to English comedy in his 'Discourse upon Comedy' in *Love and Business* (1702) while in *Licentia Poetica Discuss'd* (1709) Coward was freely critical of any rules based on the practice of the ancients. A modern 'querelle' amongst French cultural commentators had been sparked in 1687 when Charles Perrault read out his poem, *Le Siècle de Louis le Grand*, to the Académie Française; his celebration of the achievements of the moderns caused an uproar, Boileau demanding that the reading be halted. The year of Pope's birth saw many of the key publications of the debate: the first volume of Charles P. Perrault's *Parallele des Anciens et des Modernes* (4 volumes, 1688–96), and Bernard le Bovier de Fontenelle's *Digression Sur les Anciens et les Modernes* in his *Poésies Pastorales* (1688). Sir William Temple's essays on 'Ancient and Modern Learning' and 'Of Poetry', published in his *Miscellanea* (1690), which defended the ancients, were criticised for their nostalgia and inaccuracy by William Wotton, in his *Reflections upon Ancient and Modern Learning* (1694) and Richard Bentley in his *Dissertation upon the Epistles of Phalaris* (1697). These critics in turn were regarded as pedantic and mechanistic the gentleman authors of Pope's circle; amongst much other controversial literature, Swift's *Tale of a Tub* and *Battle of the Books* (1704), in the latter of which Homer slays Perrault, fed heavily on the controversy.

The historical context incorporates also a political one. This can be over-simplified, in that Dennis and Blackmore were both Whigs yet implacably antagonistic to each other, and most Whig theorists were happy to praise Dryden's talents despite his obvious Tory-Jacobite leanings. Nonetheless, Pope's poem was published during the Tory ascendancy which eventually brought the long-running War of Spanish Succession to the end celebrated in *Windsor-Forest*, and his airy dismissal of 'Parties . . . of *State*' (457) belongs to his one period of political confidence. Pope was freer for the moment to ignore panegyrics on the victories of the Duke of Marlborough, routinely issued by writers like Blackmore, whose *Advice to the Poets* (1706) constituted an *Ars Poetica* stressing the suitability of Marlborough's wars for Miltonic-sublime verse. Coward's *Licentia Poetica Discuss'd* constituted another, somewhat more maverick, Whig argument, with notes on Marlborough and other commanders and a 'political essay' on contemporary factions as an appendix. Womersley (1997: xxxi–xxxviii) sees Pope's poem as an 'eloquent rearguard action' against an emerging Whig critical theory, and Williams (2005: 37–43) reads it as strongly aligned with Tory critics such as Sheffield, Roscommon and Dryden, against Whigs such as Dennis, whose elevation of the republican Milton as the rule-transcending poet of the sublime is in marked contrast to Pope's erasure of the great British 'modern'. On the other hand, the poem's values of harmony, decency and moderation, are linked less to any obvious Tory agenda than to the moralised polite culture promoted in the Whiggish periodicals (to which Pope contributed) of Addison and Steele.

Pope's poem entered a critical arena which was often riven by bitter public and personal controversy. Its predominant mode might be called eclectic, or synthetic, in the sense of attempting to combine disparate elements. There had been many prose treatises of criticism and many verse arts of poetry, but no significant *verse* arts of *criticism*:

Pope's own poem was a deliberate hybrid, seeking to reconcile poetry and criticism, prose and verse, nature and art, wit and judgment, rules and licence, restraint and liberation, ancient and modern, Whig and Tory, Catholic and Protestant, in often paradoxical comparisons. Pope, who commented freely on the negative aspects of contemporary critical practice in the 'Preface' to his *Works* of 1717 and (perhaps) in an essay in *The Guardian*, no. 12, 25 March 1713 (*PW*, I.88–92, 289–96; the authorship is not certain), registered the discontents of criticism fully in the poem itself, asking 'Where's the man' who can balance the seemingly opposite characteristics of the ideal critic (634–45); it then exemplifies him, through patterned sequences of qualities in the closing lines (730–45) in Pope's recently deceased friend William Walsh, the innermost member of the close coterie who read the *Pastorals* before publication, with whom he had discussed many of the issues in the *Essay*. Dryden's published view, in the 'Postscript' to his translation of the *Works of Virgil* (1697), p. 622, that Walsh was 'without flattery . . . the best Critick of our Nation' was based less on the tiny amount of critical discourse that Walsh actually published than on his manner of candid and non-partisan private judgement. The poem closes with Pope's own self-characterisation as a humble representative of similar virtues.

The dominant way of thinking about Pope's poem in modern times has been as a kind of masterful negotiation between competing claims of various kinds, amounting for some to a proto-Romantic unity of conception (e.g. Spacks 1970; Morris 1984: 47–74). The early reception of the poem suggests that its conciliatory balances were not quickly appreciated, and that for some it contained more satire than was consonant with its 'humane' ethos. Several lines in the first published text upset some of Pope's Roman Catholic friends, precipitating some heart-searching discussion with John Caryll throughout the summer of 1711. On 18 June (*Corr*., I.118–19), Pope told Caryll,

> I will set before me that excellent example of that great man and great saint, Erasmus, who in the midst of calumny proceeded with all the calmness of innocence, the unrevenging spirit of primitive Christianity! However I would advise them to suffer the mention of him [at 696] to pass unregarded least I should be forced to . . . vindicate so great a light of our Church from the malice of past times and the ignorance of the present, in a language which may extend farther than that in which the trifle about criticism is written.

On 19 July (*Corr*., I.128) he continued:

> What these . . . are really angry at is that a man whom their tribe oppressed and persecuted . . . should be vindicated after a whole age of obloquy, by one of their own people who is free and bold enough to utter a generous truth in behalf of the dead.

On 25 June (*Corr*. I.122), Pope explained to Caryll that Thomas Southcott, a Benedictine father, had expressed concerns about the view of monks given in 694–5:

> The only difference between us in relation to the monks is, that he thinks most sorts of learning *flourish'd* among 'em, and I am of opinion that only some sort of learning was barely *kept alive* by 'em. He believes the most natural and obvious sense of [694] will be thought meant of learning in general, and I fancy it will be understood only, as 'tis meant, of polite learning, criticism, poetry, &c., which is the only learning concerned in the subject of the *Essay*.

On 19 July (*Corr.*, I.127–8), Pope insisted that the superstition he identified was an undeniable historical fact, that the line 'does in no sort reflect upon the present Catholics, who are free from it'. In the same letter he had to defend line 429:

> an ordinary man would imagine the author plainly declared against these schismatics for quitting the true faith out of contempt of the understanding of some few of its believers. But these believers are called *Dull*, and because I say that *These schismatics think some believers dull*, therefore these charitable well-disposed interpreters of my meaning say that *I think all believers dull*.

Lines 397–8, on sects, were likewise taken badly: in the 18 June letter (*Corr*, I.118–19), Pope emphasises that his simile concludes at line 398 with the full stop, and that

> the censure of damning here lies not on our Church unless they will call our Church one small sect. And the cautious words *by each man*, manifestly show it a general reflection on all such ... who entertain such narrow and limited notions of the mercy of the Almighty, which the reformed ministers of the presbyterians are as guilty of as any people living.

He also commented: 'what follows, *meanly they seek &c.*, speaks only of wit, which is meant by *that Blessing, that Sun*', and pointed out that the 'they' of 399 refers not to Catholics but to 'those criticks there spoken of, who are partial to some particular set of writers, to the prejudice of all others'.

Writing to Caryll on these matters on 19 July (*Corr.*, I.128), Pope defended the controversial points in the poem so far as his own 'conscience' was concerned, yet offered in 'friendship' to 'recant and alter whatever you please in case of a Second Edition'. (For revisions see Commentary to 397–8, 429–30, 692–9, 730; opposition was still evident when Pope wrote to Caryll on 8 November 1712; *Corr.*, I.150–2). Pope also spoke with some disappointment of the poem as 'a treatise ... which not one gentleman in a three score even of a liberal education can understand', which hardly suggests broad cultural authority. Warton (*Works of Pope*, I.xviii) quoted Lewis (the bookseller-publisher) as saying that the poem 'lay many days in his shop, unnoticed and unread', until Pope 'packed up and directed twenty copies to several great men', after which its reputation grew. It is not clear if Pope knew of an anonymous eighty-line poem of extravagant praise, 'To Mr — on his *Essay Upon Criticism*', published between the first and second editions, which is transcribed and analysed in Hammond (1985). Pope's poem was prominently welcomed as a 'Master-piece in its kind' by Addison in *The Spectator*, no. 253, 20 December 1711; Pope at first thought the praise came from Steele (exchanges of 30 December 1711 and 20 January 1712, *Corr.*, I.139-41). Addison noted Pope's allegiances to the poetic essays of Sheffield and Roscommon and praised its informal Horatian manner. However, Addison's remarks on the poem came in an essay on envy and detraction (also subjects within the poem), and his approval of it was introduced by a rebuke for Pope's unkind mockery of Dennis, who by then had produced his own incontinently furious response.

Dennis was a relic of the late Restoration theatre, who had known Dryden, Wycherley, Congreve, Walsh, Sheffield and Cromwell, before Pope arrived. His *Letters upon Several Occasions* (1696) included correspondence on literary matters from Dryden (including an important response to Rymer), Wycherley and Congreve. He had established himself as a critic by responding to Rymer and Collier and he had formulated an ideal of gentlemanly criticism not very dissimilar to Pope's in his *A Large Account of the Taste in Poetry* (1702). However, by February 1709, when the failure of his tragedy *Appius and Virginia* handed Pope his figleaf of a codename (588-90), Dennis's career was in obvious decline and he had become himself a type of the hostile, obsessive, impotent critic, his grandiose plans for reforming British poetry unfulfilled. His friendship with Richard Steele collapsed in 1710; early in 1711 he began discerning in in *The Tatler* and *The Spectator* many concealed attacks on his own failings. He took especially personally an attack in *Spectator*, no. 40, 16 April 1711, on the theory of poetic justice, publishing his aggrieved response in *An Essay on the Genius and Writings of Shakespeare* (1712). In January 1711 he had been lampooned as the dictatorial critic Dyphthong in Act II of Charles Johnson's comedy *The Generous Husband*, and was therefore ready-primed when Pope, to him an upstart interloper who had published very little, poked fun.

Pope perhaps joked about Dennis in a verse letter to Cromwell in July 1707: 'And for a Butcher's well-fed Daughter | Great *D—s* roar'd, like Ox at Slaughter' (*Corr.*, I.27); and Wycherley expressed a grievance against him in a letter of 11 August 1709 (*Corr.*, I.69); his Whiggish battle poems were no doubt a factor. But Dennis complained, with some justice, about being attacked 'without any manner of Provocation on my side, and attack'd in my Person, instead of my Writings' in his *Reflections Critical and Satyrical, upon a late Rhapsody, call'd, An Essay upon Criticism*, the first of the major attacks on Pope, published on 20 June 1711 (advertised in the *Daily Courant*, and in *The Spectator*, 29 June). He repaid Pope's slight with interest in a blistering account of Pope's physique, literary pretension and hypocrisy. The *Essay* itself was subjected to a hostile close reading, much longer than the poem itself, discovering absurdities and errors on every page. It also identified a strong vein of Jacobite propaganda in Pope's account of cultural history of the seventeenth century (535-54) and other places.

Pope commented to Spence, 'When I heard for the first time that Dennis had writ against me, it gave me some pain, but it was quite over as soon as I came to look into his book and found he was in such a passion' (*OAC*, I.42). Lintot had sent Pope a pre-publication copy, and Pope immediately began a process of revision, writing with studied nonchalance to Caryll on 25 June 1711: 'I send you Mr Dennis's Remarks on the *Essay*, which equally abound in just criticisms and fine railleries: the few observations in my hand in the margin are what only a morning's leisure permitted to make purely for you perusal' (*Corr.*, I.121). He had initially thought a Windsor Forest oak cudgel was the appropriate response, but protested that he would have withdrawn the vignette had he known that Dennis was 'persecuted by fortune', as the 'Preface' to the *Reflections* claimed. (The vignette was not withdrawn.) In any case, he could not 'conceive what ground he has for [so] excessive a resentment, nor imagine how those three lines can be call'd a reflection on his person, which only describe him subject to a little to colour and stare on some occasions'. But he resolved, taking his own advice at 217, to 'Make use of ev'ry *Friend*—and ev'ry *Foe*', to 'make my enemy do me a kindness where he meant an injury, and so serve instead of a friend' (*ibid.*, and see further the letter to Caryll of 2 August, expressing an intention to make no response; *Corr.*, I.131-2 and Pope to Sir William Trumbull, 10 August 1711; Sherburn 1958b: 397). His notes in the light of Dennis's comments are listed in the Commentary and Appendix (see further the analysis in Guerinot 1969: 7-11). But battle was now joined: *The Critical Specimen* (1711; see Headnote to 'Lines from *The Critical Specimen*'), a mock proposal for a vast critical treatise containing 'The History of the Renown'd *Rinaldo Furioso*, Critick of the Woful Countenance', and several hits at Dennis's particular obsessions, was Pope's covert response to Dennis. Gay's 'Dedication' to his farce *The Mohocks* (1712) was decidedly on Pope's side. Pope told Caryll on 19 November 1712 that Dennis's pamphlet had made him 'very heartily merry in two minutes time' (*Corr.*, I.155), but after Dennis's attack on Addison's *Cato* (see Pope's 'Prologue to *Cato*' in this volume), the merriment took the further form of *The Narrative of Dr. Robert Norris* (*PW*, I.1-18, 153-68). These hostilities continued at least as far as *The Dunciad Variorum* (1729), which in darkly parodic ways drew on the aspirations of the *Essay on Criticism*.

The *Essay on Criticism* was translated into French three times in Pope's lifetime: in 1713, 1717, and 1730 (see France 1988); Pope thanked the first translator, Anthony Hamilton, in a high-spirited letter of 10 October 1713 (*Corr*, I.192-3). In the *Works* of 1751 Warburton attempted to demonstrate its perfect intellectual coherence by means of an elaborate commentary (I.135-211). Warton (1756: 100) detected something 'partial and invidious' in Addison's review in *The Spectator*, and argued that the poem had much more 'just integrity' and 'lucid order' than Addison would allow it. In addition, though the *Essay* fell exactly into that category of 'didactic' poetry which Warton generally thought not of the highest poetic ambition, he declared that the poem was far more original than Addison had suggested: 'though on a beaten subject, [it] abounds in many new remarks, and original rules, as well as in many happy and beautiful illustrations, and applications of the old ones'. Warton was 'amazed to find such a knowledge of the world, such a maturity of judgment, and such a penetration into human nature ... in so very young a writer' (1756: 101). In his general estimation, Warton was followed by Johnson, both in his review of Warton's book (*Literary Magazine*, I, 1756, 35-8) and in his *Life* of Pope, where he found that the poem 'displays such extent of comprehension, such nicety of distinction, such acquaintance with mankind, and such knowledge both of ancient and modern learning, as are not often attained by the maturest age and longest experience'. Johnson, however, reasserted the 'informal' reading of the poem, suggesting that Warburton had 'discovered in it such order and connection as was not perceived by Addison, nor, as is said, intended by the author' (Lonsdale, IV.6, 8).

AN ESSAY ON *CRITICISM.*

————Si quid novisti rectius istis,
Candidus imperti; si non, his utere mecum.
                                             HORAT.

Title. added *1717–51*: Written in the Year 1709.
Epigraph. *1736a–51*: omitted

Epigraph. Horace, *Epistles*, I.vi.67–8: 'if you know anything better than these precepts, honestly pass them on; if not, follow these with me'. Horace is speaking of general rules for living. Pope's own 'Imitation' of this poem appeared in 1738; the final four lines of that poem expand the motto.

AN
ESSAY
ON
CRITICISM.

    'TIS hard to say, if greater Want of Skill
    Appear in *Writing* or in *Judging* ill;
But, of the two, less dang'rous is th' Offence,
To tire our *Patience*, than mis-lead our *Sense*:
5   Some few in *that*, but Numbers err in *this*,
Ten Censure wrong for one who Writes amiss;
A *Fool* might once *himself* alone expose,
Now *One* in *Verse* makes many more in *Prose*.

1-2. TE compares Sheffield, *Essay upon Poetry*, 1-2 (1682), p. 1: 'Of Things in which Mankind does most excell, | Nature's chief Master-piece is writing well'; and Dryden's definition of criticism as originally 'a Standard of judging well', from 'The Authors Apology for Heroique Poetry; and Poetique Licence', in *The State of Innocence* (1677), sig. b1ᵛ. The title page of Dennis's *The Grounds of Criticism in Poetry* (1704) promises 'some New Discoveries never made before, requisite for the Writing and Judging of Poems surely'. Pope immediately draws attention to the potential for doing it badly.

4. **Sense:** For the range of meanings see Headnote: Context.

6. Cf. 'January and May', 814.
   Censure: judge, criticise in public. Cf. Rochester, 'An Epistolary Essay from *M. G.* to *O. B.* upon Their Mutual Poems', 87-8, *Poems, (&c.) on Several Occasions* (1696), p. 84: ''tis two to one | Whene'er they censure they'll be in the wrong'. (Pope owned this edition and marked this poem: Mack 1982: 437-8, item 144). *OED* regards the senses 1 ('to estimate, judge of, pass judgment on, criticize, judge') and 3 ('to form or give an opinion') as passing into obsolescence in Pope's day; *SJ*, in 1755, has only the negative senses 'to blame; to brand publicly ... to condemn by a judicial sentence', corresponding to *OED*'s sense 5: 'To pronounce an adverse judgement on, express disapproval of, criticize unfavourably; to find fault with, blame, condemn'.

7-8. **Fool ... Prose:** In his manuscript notes, Pope noted 'Fool, let it not be usd so often' (see Appendix). In the first version of the poem the word appears 16 times; for alterations and suppressions see textual notes to 32, 34, 600. *TE* compares Dryden's 'Epilogue' to *All for Love*, 5-6 (1678), p. 79: 'We wonder how the Devil this diff'rence grows, | Betwixt our Fools in Verse, and yours in Prose'.

'Tis with our *Judgments* as our *Watches,* none
10   Go just *alike,* yet each believes his own.
                In *Poets* as true *Genius* is but rare,
                True *Taste* as seldom is the *Critick*'s Share;
                Both must alike from Heav'n derive their Light,
                These *born* to Judge, as well as those to Write.
15   Let such teach others who themselves excell,
                And *censure freely* who have *written well.*

15.] De Pictore, Sculptore, Fictore, nisi Artifex judicare non potest, Pliny.

15, n. MS, *1713a–51:* Qui scribit artificiosè, ab aliis commodè scripta facile intelligere poterit. Cic. ad Herenn. lib. 4.

15. 1727–32: new paragraph

9–10. *TE* compares Sir John Suckling, 'Epilogue' to *Aglaura*, 6–8 (1638), p. 38: 'But as when an authentique Watch is showne, | Each man windes up, and rectifies his owne, | So in our verie Judgements…'. For watches cf. also 'Rape of the Locke', I.18.

9. Judgments: For the range of senses see Headnote: Context.

11–12. *TE* compares Saint-Evremond, 'Some Observations upon the Tast and Judgment of the French', *The Works of Mr. de St. Evremont*, 2 vols (1700), I.166: 'Since good Judges are as rare as good Authors; since 'tis as difficult to find Judgment in one, as Genius in the other'.

11. Genius: For this critical term, see Headnote: Context. The phrase 'true genius' recurs in the 'Atticus' portrait, *Epistle to Dr Arbuthnot*, 194.

12. Taste: For this central aesthetic category, see Headnote: Context.

   Share: endowment, natural gift.

13. Light: reason, intelligence. *TE* compares the anonymous translation of Roger de Piles, *The Art of Painting* (1706), pp. 9–10: '*Genius therefore is that Light of the Mind, which conducts us to the end by the most easy Means*'.

14. born to Judge: *TE* cites Charles Gildon's 'An Apology for Poetry', in *Miscellaneous Letters and Essays, on Several Subjects* (1694), p. 14: 'A Poet derives the honor of that Name from his *Nature* and *Genius*, not from his *Art*; *This* every Scholar has, *That* none but the Darling of Heav'n and Nature. This may be acquir'd by a Studious Pedant, That must be born…for *Poeta nascitur non fit*', i.e., 'the poet is born, not made.'

   Another conventional tag, 'orator fit, poeta nascitur' ('an orator is made, a poet is born'), distinguishes the innate talent of the poet from the learned skills of the prose writer. Pope suggests rather that critical and poetic arts equally require innate talent.

15 Pope's note. Pliny, *Epistles*, I.x.4: 'Concerning a painter, a sculptor, or an image-maker, unless a man is himself an artist, he cannot judge'; Cicero, *Ad Herennium*, IV.iv.7: 'whoever writes skilfully will be able to discern what has been properly written by others'. The attribution of *Ad Herennium* to Cicero is no longer generally accepted.

15–16. Let such … written well: *TE* compares the opening sentence of Addison's essay in *The Tatler*, no. 239, 19 October

> *Authors* are partial to their *Wit*, 'tis true,
> But are not *Criticks* to their *Judgment* too?
> Yet if we look more closely, we shall find
20 Most have the *Seeds* of Judgment in their Mind;
> Nature affords at least a *glimm'ring Light*;
> The *Lines*, tho' touch'd but faintly, are drawn right.

20.] Omnes tacito quodam sensu, sine ulla arte, aut ratione, quae sint in artibus ac rationibus recta ac prava dijudicant. Cic. de Orat. lib. 3.

1710: 'It is ridiculous for any man to criticize on the works of another, who has not distinguished himself by his own performances'; also Dryden's 'Preface' to *All for Love* (1692 edition), sig. B2ʳ: 'Poets themselves are the most proper, though I conclude not the only Criticks'. Cf. also Dennis's 'Epistle Dedicatory' in *The Advancement and Reformation of Modern Poetry* (1701), sig. A2ᵛ, Hooker, I.197: 'there never was a great Poet in the World, who was not an accomplish'd Critick'. But in his *Reflections Critical and Satyrical* (1711), p. 2, Hooker, I.398-9, Dennis was incensed by Pope's precept, 'which is denied by matter of Fact, and by the Experience of above Two thousand Years', i.e. many of Pope's critical authorities (Aristotle, Quintilian, Longinus) were not poets. Pope himself had published only three items before this one.

17. *TE* cites Dryden's translation of the first satire of Persius, 113, *Satires of Juvenal* (1693), p. 9 of second sequence: 'All Authours, to their own defects, are blind'.

Wit: perhaps the most important word in the poem; see Headnote: Context.

19-22. Brower (1959: 197) connects the imagery to Milton, *Paradise Lost*, II.1034-7 (1674), p. 58: 'But now at last the sacred influence | Of light appears, and from the walls of Heav'n | Shoots farr into the bosom of dim Night | A glimmering dawn...'

***20* Pope's note.** Cicero, *De Oratore*, III.50(195): 'Everyone judges between things that are straight and things that are crooked in arts and sciences, without possessing any art or science, through some hidden sense'. *TE* compares Dryden's dedicatory epistle, usually known as 'A Discourse Concerning the Original and Progress of Satire', in *Satires of Juvenal*, p. xvii: 'Mankind, even the most Barbarous have the seeds of Poetry implanted in them'.

21. Nature: another keyword of the poem; see Headnote: Context.

22. Lines: an outline or initial sketch, as in the development of the metaphor, 23-5. Similar analogies are found in classical literary criticism, e.g. Aristotle, *Poetics*, 1450b; *TE* cites the anonymous translation, *Aristotle's Art of Poetry* (1705), p. 73: 'For, if the finest Colours were mix't on a Cloath confusedly and without order, it would not give so much pleasure, as the simple Sketches of a Draught'. For Pope's own studies as a painter in this connection see Ault (1949: 75-6).

>   But as the slightest Sketch, if justly trac'd,
>   Is by ill *Colouring* but the more disgrac'd,
> 25 So by *false Learning* is *good Sense* defac'd;

25, n. MS, *1744–51: Plus sine Doctrina Prudentia, quam sine prudentia valet Doctrina.* Quintil.
  MS: *Adolescentulos existimo in Scholis stultissimos fieri, qui nil ex his quae in usu habemus, aut audiunt, aut vident.* Petronius.

25^6, n. *1736–51:* Between Verse 25 and 26, were these lines, [*1744–51:* since omitted by the author:]
>   Many are spoil'd by that pedantic throng,
>   Who with great pains teach youth to reason wrong.
>   Tutors, like Virtuoso's, oft inclin'd
>   By strange transfusion to improve the mind,
>   Draw off the sense we have, to pour in new;
>   Which yet with all their skill, they ne'er could do.

25^6. MS: (*Good Sense*, which only is the Gift of Heav'n,
>   And tho no *Science*, yet is worth the *Sev'n*.)
>   Many are spoil'd by that *Pedantic* Throng,
>   Who, with great Pains, teach Youth to reason wrong.
>   *Tutors* like *Virtuoso's*, oft, inclin'd
>   By strange *Transfusion* to improve the Mind,
>   Draw off the Sense we have, to pour in *new*,
>   Which yet, with all their Skill, they ne'r cou'd do.

---

24. disgrac'd: in the now obsolete sense of 'disgrace', *OED*, sense 1: 'To undo or mar the grace of; to deprive of (outward) grace; to disfigure'; cf. also the poem's stress on artistic grace, 145, etc.

25 Pope's note. Quintilian, *Institutio Oratoria*, VI.v.11: 'Good sense without learning is worth more than learning without good sense'. Pope has compressed and rephrased Quintilian's sentence. Petronius, *Satyricon*, I.i: 'I reckon that young men become extremely stupid in schools, because they see and hear nothing of those matters that we ordinarily deal with'.

25^6 MS. Good Sense ... Sev'n: The seven 'liberal arts' of medieval schooling: grammar, rhetoric, and dialectic (or logic), making up the 'trivium', and arithmetic, geometry, astronomy and music, the 'quadrivium'. For '*Science*' see note to 60. Pope later used this discarded couplet in the *Epistle to Burlington*, 43–4.

Pedantic *Throng*: teachers and academics; an early indication of Pope's scepticism towards institutional education, developed throughout the fourth book of the *Dunciad* (esp. 189ff). For his own relatively informal education and study, see *OAC*, I.8–13, 21–2.

Tutors: at university, or a private tutor in a noble family.

Virtuoso's: A virtuoso is 'a man skilled in antique or natural curiosities' (*SJ*). For Pope (several of whose friends were collectors), it normally meant connoisseurs, men who study, to the point of obsession, some small subject; since Thomas Shadwell's comedy *The Virtuoso* (1676), which Pope had read (*OAC*, I.205–6), this kind of scholar was a ready object of satire, pursued by Pope and his collaborators in their play *Three Hours after Marriage* (1717), *The Memoirs of Martinus Scriblerus* (1742), and in the fourth book of *The Dunciad*.

Some are bewilder'd in the Maze of Schools,
And some made *Coxcombs* Nature meant but *Fools.*
In search of *Wit* these lose their *common Sense,*
And then turn Criticks in their own Defence.
30   Those hate as *Rivals* all that write; and others
But envy *Wits,* as *Eunuchs* envy *Lovers.*

---

26. Some are bewilder'd: MS: Thus some are *wilder'd*
28. these: MS: some
30. Those: *1727–32:* Some
30–1. *1736a–51:* Each burns alike, who can, or cannot write,
    Or with a Rival's, or an Eunuch's spite.

Transfusion: the pouring of liquid from one vessel to another. *TE* follows a long tradition in stating that Pope refers specifically to blood transfusion, the focus of Royal Society experiments since the 1660s; Nicolson and Rousseau (1968: 90–3) supply additional contextual material, and see Daniel Baker, 'Death', *Poems on Several Occasions* (1697), p. 94: 'The Blood that issu'd from my Saviour's Side | By strange Transfusion fill'd each Vein...'. But the metaphor, as with 'draw off' and 'pour' in the next line, comes from chemistry in general, as in Denham's preface to *The Destruction of Troy* (1656), sig. A3ʳ, speaking of translation: 'Poesie is of so subtile a spirit, that in pouring out of one Language into another, it will all evaporate; and if a new spirit be not added in the transfusion, there will remain nothing but a *Caput mortuum*'. Denham's comparison was quoted in William Wotton, *Reflections upon Ancient and Modern Learning* (1694), p. 54.

26. Maze of Schools: confusingly competitive schools of philosophical or religious doctrine; for Pope's scepticism on 'the wresting of commentators or the additions of schoolmen' see *OAC,* I.135.

27. Coxcombs: A coxcomb is 'a fop; a superficial pretender to knowledge or accomplishments' (*SJ,* citing this line). Cf. Rochester, 'A Letter from Artemisia in the Town to Chloe in the Country', 159, *Poems (&c.),* p. 72: 'God never made a Coxcomb worth a Groat'. (This poem was marked by Pope in his copy; Mack 1982: 438.) Pope discussed coxcombs and fools with Wycherley in letters of 23 June and 26 October 1705 (*Corr.,* I.9, 11. 28); see also the discussion in *The Spectator,* no. 404, 13 June 1712, previously ascribed to Budgell, but which Ault attributes to Pope on grounds of verbal similarity to the *Essay* (*PW,* I.37–41): 'Nature:... has sometimes made a Fool, but a Coxcomb is always of a Man's own making, by applying his Talents otherwise than Nature designed'.

29. turn Criticks ... Defence: *EC* compares Dryden, *The Medall,* 51 (1682), p. 4: 'The Wretch turn'd loyal in his own defence'; and his 'Prologue' to *Amphitryon.* 14–15 (1690), sig. A4ʳ: 'And Wits turn Blockheads in their own defence'. Much of Dryden's critical work was prompted by hostile critiques; see Headnote: Models and sources.

30–1. Rivals ... Eunuchs: The power to write is aligned with sexual potency, one of the underlying metaphors of the poem: cf. 103–5, 433–4, etc. *EC* compares Rochester's 'Epilogue' to Charles D'Avenant's *Circe* (1677), sig. I2ʳ: '"Twas Impotence did first this Vice begin, | Fooles censure Wit, as Old men raile of Sin', and Dryden, 'Prologue' to *The Second Part*

All *Fools* have still an Itching to deride,
And fain *wou'd* be upon the *Laughing Side*:
If *Maevius* Scribble in *Apollo*'s spight,
35   There are, who *judge* still *worse* than he can *write*.
   Some have at first for *Wits*, then *Poets* past,
Turn'd *Criticks* next, and prov'd plain *Fools* at last;
Some neither can for *Wits* nor *Criticks* pass,
As heavy Mules are neither *Horse* nor *Ass*.

---

32. Fools: *1717–32:* such
33^4. MS: Tho' such with Reason Men of Sense abhor,
   Fool against Fool is barb'rous *Civil War*;
34. in *Apollo*'s spight: MS: and the *City Knight*

---

of *The Conquest of Granada*, 1–2 (1672), p. 71: 'They who write Ill, and they who ne'r durst write, | Turn Critiques, out of meer Revenge and Spight'. Brower (1959: 196) derives the variant phrasing from Horace, *Epistles*, II. i. 117: 'scribimus indocti doctique poemata passim' ('skilled and unskilled, we all write poems, without distinction'). The nearest line (180) in Pope's 1737 version, *The First Epistle of the Second Book of Horace*, reads 'And call for Pen and Ink to show our Wit'.
31. Wits: the first instance of the word as 'man of wit'; see Headnote: Context.
32. Itching: pathological urge, echoing the phrase 'insanabile cacoethes scribendi', 'incurable compulsion to write', derived from Juvenal, *Satires*, VII.51–2.
33^4 MS. Pope used a version of this couplet in *The Dunciad* (1728), III.145–6.
34–5. EC cites Dryden's translation of Persius, I.98–9, *Satires of Juvenal*, p. 9: 'Such little Elegies as Nobles Write; | Who wou'd be Poets, in *Apollo*'s spight.'
34. Maevius: contemporary of the Roman writers Virgil and Horace, known only through their references to him as an incompetent scribbler (e.g. Virgil, *Eclogues*, III.90; Horace, *Epodes*, X.2); a standard name for poor writer; cf. 'To the Author of a Poem, intitled, Successio', 19.
Scribble: derogatory term for writing, recalled in the name of the anti-hero of Pope's group of satirists, Martinus Scriblerus; cf. 598.
Apollo: God of Poetry in Greek mythology.
spight: 'in spite of' Apollo's standards and rules.
34 MS. City Knight: a man advanced by commerce, as opposed to a traditional landed gentleman (cf. *The Second Satire of the Second Book of Horace Imitated*, 178); Pope perhaps has Blackmore (see Commentary to 464) in mind.
36–7. According to Pope's *Narrative of Dr. Robert Norris* (1713), *PW*, I.166, Dennis, 'coming to these two Lines ... flung down the Book in a terrible Fury, and cried out, *By G—he means Me*'.
39. Mules: hybrid of horse and donkey, used as beast of burden, and infertile; both suggestions are in play here.

40   Those half-learn'd Witlings, num'rous in our Isle,
     As half-form'd Insects on the Banks of *Nile*;
     Unfinish'd Things, one knows not what to call,
     Their Generation's so *equivocal*:
     To tell 'em, wou'd a *hundred Tongues* require,
45   Or *one vain Wit's*, that wou'd a hundred tire.

---

42. one knows not: MS: which none know
45. wou'd: *1713a–51:* might

---

40. Witlings: 'pretender to wit; a man of petty smartness' (*SJ*, citing this line); cf. 'The Rape of the Locke', II.114, and *Epistle to Dr Arbuthnot*, 223. It was a recent word: OED cites nothing earlier than Dryden's 'Prologue' to Persius, I.16, *Satires of Juvenal*, p. 3. Cf. Abel Boyer, *The English Theophrastus; or, the Manners of the Age* (1702), p. 6: 'There are many impertinent witlings at Wills', i.e. at the coffee-house where Dryden and other wits congregated.

41. Insects: 'Insect' could be used of 'any thing small or contemptible' (*SJ*). TE compares Dryden's view of critics in the 'Dedication' of *Examen Poeticum* (1693), sig. A4ʳ, as 'another sort of Insects, more venomous than the former'. Cf. also Blackmore, *A Satyr Against Wit* (1700), p. 3: 'Fierce Insect-Wits draw out their noisy Swarms'. The image of the writer as insect would recur in *The Dunciad* (1728), I.47–50, and cf. *Epistle to Dr Arbuthnot*, 169–70. The critic Dypthong, a caricature of Dennis, is introduced as a 'Paper-worm ... an Insect that was born only to suck the Poison of Books ... a Maggot bred in Books', in Charles Johnson, *The Generous Husband*, II (1711), pp. 17, 21.

Nile: When it flooded, the river Nile was supposed to breed insects and other creatures by a, spontaneous process: Ovid, *Metamorphoses*, I.423–37.

43. Generation's ... equivocal: *SJ* cites Pope's line under 'equivocal', giving the sense 'uncertain; doubtful; happening different ways'. OED cites Benjamin Stillingfleet, *Origines Sacrae* (1662), I.iv.§9, referring to the reproduction of plants and animals without parents. The phrase, common in both science and satire, often indicated hybridity. TE compares Dorset, 'A Faithful Catalogue of our most Eminent Ninnies', 178–9, *Works of ... Rochester and Roscommon* (1709), II. 54: 'With foul Corruption sure he first was fed, | And by equivocal Generation bred'. Fairer (1984: 177) cites Josuah Sylvester, *Du Bartas His Diuine Weekes and Workes ... Translated*, The Second Day of the First Week (1621), p. 39: 'As on the edges of som standing Lake ... | The foamy slime, it self transformeth oft | To green half-Tadpoles, ... | Half-dead, half-liuing; half a frog, half-mud.'

44–5. To number ('tell') all the insect-wits would require a hundred speakers, or one talkative enough to out-chatter a hundred other people. EC cites Dryden's translation of Persius, V.36–7, *Satires of Juvenal*, p. 61: 'For this a hundred Voices I desire; | To tell thee what an hundred Tongues wou'd tire'. Pope recalled the phrase in epic context: 'To count them all, demands a thousand Tongues', *Iliad*, II.580 (Pope's translation); Homer's number was ten.

>   But *you* who seek to *give* and *merit* Fame,
>   And justly bear a Critick's noble Name,
>   Be sure *your self* and your own *Reach* to know,
>   How far your *Genius*, *Taste*, and *Learning* go;
> 50   Launch not beyond your Depth, but be discreet,
>   And mark *that Point* where Sense and Dulness *meet.*
>   Nature to all things fix'd the Limits fit,
>   And wisely curb'd proud Man's pretending Wit:

---

48. **Be sure:** MS: First learn
51. **mark:** MS: know
52. 1744–51: new paragraph

---

46. Aden (1978: 101) compares Lansdowne, 'An Essay Upon Unnatural Flights in Poetry', *A New Miscellany of Original Poems, on Several Occasions* (1701), p. 317: 'Who seek from Poetry, a lasting Name, | May in their Lessons, learn the road to Fame'.

48–9. TE compares Horace, *Ars Poetica*, 38–40 : 'sumite materiam vestries, qui scribitis, aequam | viribus et versate diu, quid ferre recusent, | quid valueant umeri.' ('You writers, take a subject which matches your strength, and ponder for a long time what your shoulders can and cannot bear'.) TE also cites passages glossing Horace's advice in Vida, *De Arte Poetica*, I.39–40, and Boileau, *L'Art Poetique*, I.12.

48. your self ... know: The injunction γνωθι σεαυτόν ('know thyself'), inscribed in the Temple of Apollo at Delphi, is quoted as a divine injunction by Juvenal, *Satires*, XI.27; also well known in the Latin form 'nosce teipsum', as in the poem of that title by Sir John Davies (1599). Pope restated it in *Essay on Man* (1733–4), II.1–2.

Reach: 'limit of faculties' (*SJ*, citing this line). Cf. Roscommon, *Essay on Translated Verse*, 71–2 (1684), p. 5: 'The first great work, (a Task perform'd by few) | Is, that *your self* may to *your self* be True'; the subsequent lines exhort intense self-analysis.

50. discreet: 'prudent; circumspect; cautious; sober ... not hardily adventurous' (*SJ*).

51. Sense ... Dulness: 'sense' (see Headnote: Context) is intelligence and reason, aligned with Wit and Nature, 'dulness' is the stupidity which lies beyond the limits of one's mental capabilities. This is Pope's earliest use of 'dulness', a major feature of later satire, especially *The Dunciad*, but he had been editing a poem by Wycherley on the subject (see Pope to Wycherley, 26 October 1705 and 20 November 1707, and Wycherley's reply, 22 November, *Corr.*, I.11, 31–3), and it was already a prominent term in satires such as Dryden's *Mac Flecknoe* (1682). Cf. also 'On Silence', 19.

53. pretending Wit: aspirational intelligence, of the kind displayed by Adam, and 'curb'd' by the angel Raphael's advice to 'be lowlie wise', in Milton's *Paradise Lost*, VIII.159–78 (1674), p. 198. To 'pretend' is to claim something beyond what is allotted. Pope revisited the limits of knowledge, and the desire to exceed it, in the *Essay on Man*, especially Epistle I. Cf. also 'On Silence', 12–13. For a possible faint hint of the defeat of 'the Pretender', i.e. the Stuart claimant to the throne, and other political reference points in the passage to 68, see Winn (2014: 560–1).

As on the *Land* while *here* the *Ocean* gains,
55 In *other Parts* it leaves wide sandy Plains;
Thus in the *Soul* while *Memory* prevails,
The solid Pow'r of *Understanding* fails;
Where Beams of warm *Imagination* play,
The *Memory*'s soft Figures melt away.
60 One *Science* only will one *Genius* fit;
So *vast* is Art, so *narrow* Human Wit:
Not only bounded to *peculiar Arts*,
But ev'n in *those*, confin'd to *single Parts*.
Like Kings we lose the Conquests gain'd before,
65 By vain Ambition still t' extend them more:

---

63. ev'n: *1713a–15:* oft
65. t' extend: *1717–51:* to make

54–9. The simile in these lines was belaboured as incoherent in Dennis's *Reflections*, p. 8, Hooker, I.402.

54–5. TE compares Addison's translation of Lucan, *De Bello Civili*, I.409-11, in *Remarks on Several Parts of Italy, &c.* (1705), p. 115: 'Wash'd with successive Seas, the doubtful Strand | By turns is Ocean, and by turns is Land'.

56–9. When the mind ('Soul') is engaged in the act of remembering, it is unable to think analytically; similarly, the imagination is more powerfully vivid than the images ('soft Figures') conjured by memory. On the sentiment, TE compares Temple, 'Essay Upon the Ancient and Modern Learning', *Miscellanea. ... The Second Part*, p. 53: 'few Men or none excel in all Faculties of Mind. A great Memory may fail of Invention, both may want Judgment to Digest or Apply, what they Remember or Invent'; and Locke, *An Essay Concerning Humane Understanding*, II.xi.2 (1690), p. 68, on the 'common Observation, That Men who have a great deal of Wit, and prompt Memories, have not always the clearest Judgment, or deepest Reason'.

58. Imagination: see Commentary to 653.

60–4. Dennis censured these lines as 'wrong... absurd ... false ... abominable', *Reflections*, p. 9, Hooker, I.403, with sufficient cogency for Pope to make a minor amendment. See Appendix.

60. Science ... Genius: individual minds can excel in only one form of knowledge; 'science' in Pope's time referred to a wider range of disciplines than it does now; see Nicolson and Rousseau (1968: 88–9). TE compares Sheffield, *Essay upon Poetry*, 342 (1682), p. 21: 'Who can all Sciences exactly know?' But see also Rymer, 'Preface' to his translation of Rapin's *Reflections on Aristotle's Treatise of Poesie* (1674), sig. A8ᵛ: 'Although a Poet is oblig'd to know all Arts and Sciences, yet he ought discreetly to manage this knowledge'.

61. Wakefield notes that the line recalls the phrase 'ars longa, vita brevis', 'Art is long, life is short', traditionally ascribed to the early Greek physician Hippocrates in the reverse form Ὁ βίος βραχύς, ἡ δὲ τέχνη μακρή' ('life is short, but art is long'). 'Art' refers to the whole spectrum of artistic endeavour.

62. peculiar Arts: single kinds of intellectual activity.

63. single Parts: particular aspects.

64–5. TE cites the example of the expansionist Charles XII of Sweden, defeated at Poltawa (1709), and the image of Charles X of Sweden in Dryden's *Astraea Redux*, 9–10

Each might his *sev'ral Province* well command,
Wou'd all but *stoop* to what they *understand*.
   First follow NATURE, and your Judgment frame
By her just Standard, which is still the same:
70   *Unerring Nature*, still divinely bright,
One *clear, unchang'd*, and *Universal* Light,
Life, Force, and Beauty, must to all impart,
At once the *Source*, and *End*, and *Test* of *Art*.

(1660), p. 5: 'Th 'Ambitious *Swede* like restless Billowes tost, | On this hand gaining what on that he lost'. Pope may also be thinking generally of the War of Spanish Succession, which after a string of victories for the British under the Duke of Marlborough, most recently at Malplaquet (1709), had begun to falter and which the Tory administration was trying to bring to the end celebrated in Pope's *Windsor-Forest* (1713). Marlborough's position had weakened considerably during 1710, though he was not dismissed until December 1711. For the possibility that Pope was reflecting on political wrangles of the time see Winn (2014: 565).

66. sev'ral: different, distinct.

67. stoop: condescend, return to an appropriate level; Pope later claimed that he 'stoop'd to Truth, and moralis'd his song'; *Epistle to Dr. Arbuthnot*, 341.

68–9. 'frame' means 'To regulate; to adjust'; 'To form to any rule or method by study or precept'; 'to form and digest by thought' (*SJ*). Plowden (1983: 61) derives the couplet from Manilius, *Astronomica*, I.520-1, translated (alongside Lucretius) by Thomas Creech (1700), p. 22: 'Its course it urges on, and keeps its Frame, | And still will be, because 'twas still the same'.

68. *NATURE*: For the concept, see Headnote: Context. Dennis attacked lines 68–73 as 'one continued Absurdity', *Reflections*, p. 9, Hooker, I.403, but his criticism was largely ignored in Pope's revisions to this passage. Pope's wording in this passage is surprisingly close to the unorthodox form of divinity known as 'natural religion', e.g. Timothy Nourse, *A Discourse of Natural and Reveal'd Religion ... or, The Light of Nature, a Guide to Divine Truth* (1691).

69. still: always. Cf. Dryden, 'The Preface of the Translator, with A Parallel, of Poetry and Painting', *De Arte Graphica* (1695), p. xxviii: 'the way to please being to imitate Nature ... Nature is still the same in all Ages, and can never be contrary to her self'. Queen Anne's motto, echoing that of Elizabeth I, was 'semper eadem', 'always the same'.

70–1. bright ... Light: like the 'Light' of heaven, 13. Wakefield cites Roscommon, *Essay on Translated Verse*, 193-4 (1684), p. 13: '*Truth* still is *One*; *Truth* is Divinely bright, | No cloudy *Doubts* obscure her Native Light'.

73. End: the purpose, the final idea. *EC* cites the Soames–Dryden translation of Boileau, *Art of Poetry*, I.37-8 (1683), p. 3: 'Love Reason then: and let what e're you Write | Borrow from her its Beauty, Force, and Light'. *TE* also cites Boileau's translation of Longinus, 'Traité du Sublime', in *Oeuvres Diverses* (1701), p. 18, in which nature is 'la baze, le principe, & le premier fondement' ('the base, the principle, and the foundation') of all artistic production. Savage (1988) cites Sir Thomas Pope Blount's anthology *De Re Poetica* (1694), p. 239: '*Virgil* ought to be the Pattern, Rule, Beginning and End of all *Poetical* Imitation'. Dennis calls Nature 'the foundation and basis' of all art in *The Advancement and Reformation of Poetry*, p. 115, Hooker, I.245.

That *Art* is best which most resembles *Her*,
75   Which still *presides*, yet never does *Appear*;
In some fair Body thus the sprightly Soul
With Spirits feeds, with Vigour fills the whole,
Each Motion guides, and ev'ry Nerve sustains;
It self unseen, but in th' *Effects*, remains.

74–5. *1717–51:* Art from that fund each just supply provides,
  Works without show, and without pomp presides:
76. the sprightly: *1717–32:* the secret; *1736a–51:* th' informing

---

74–5. TE cites Dryden, 'A Parallel, of Poetry and Painting', *De Arte Graphica*, p. xxxi: 'To imitate Nature well in whatsoever Subject, is the perfection of *both arts*; and that *Picture* and that *Poem* which comes nearest to the resemblance of Nature is the best'. Pope's couplet was criticised by Dennis as commonplace, *Reflections*, p. 10, Hooker, I.404, and Pope revised it, but probably merely to remove the expletive 'does'.

74–5 variant. *just supply:* correct amount.
   show: display.
   pomp: elaborate ceremony; cf. 'Rape of the Locke', II.59.

74. Her: Nature, normally personified as female following the gender of the Latin noun 'natura'.

75. presides: in the manner of a judge directing a court.
   never does **Appear:** as in the Roman poet Ovid, 'si latet ars, prodest' (*Ars Amatoria*, II.313), 'it is better if art remains hidden', i.e. the most accomplished technique will be invisible. The tag 'ars est celare artem', 'art should hide art', quoted e.g. by Dryden in *Of Dramatick Poesie* (1668), p. 59, is of unknown origin.

76–9. In *Reflections*, pp. 10–11, Hooker, I.404, Dennis claimed that this simile contradicted lines 56–7. TE compares Sheffield, *Essay upon Poetry*, 20–5 (1682), p. 2: 'Without a Genius too, for that's the Soul; | A Spirit which inspires the work throughout, | As that of Nature moves this World about; | A heat that glows in every word that's writ, | That's something of Divine, and more than Wit; | It self unseen, yet all things by it shown.'

76. sprightly: spirited, spiritual, hence the 'spirits' or vital fluids of 77; cf. 'Rape of the Locke', I.25. The soul inhabits and pervades the body's 'form', invisibly ('unseen', 79) performing the functions described in 77–9; the soul is to the body as nature is to a work of art.

76 variant. *informing:* giving form and character to. *TE* suggests that the alteration was made because 'sprightly' 'soul' and 'spirits' (77) were too similar in meaning.

77. Wakefield cites Dryden's translation of Virgil's *Aeneid*, VI.983–4, *Works of Virgil* (1697), p. 391: '... one Common Soul | Inspires, and feeds, and animates the whole'.
   Spirits: Pope probably has the ancient concept of bodily 'humours' in mind here; see note to 211. He is describing the interaction of the immaterial soul and the corporeal body, a subject of extensive scientific and theological debate; see Porter (2003).

79. Wakefield cites Ovid, *Metamorphoses*, IV.287: 'causa latet, vis est notissima fontis' ('the cause is secret but the effect is obvious').

80   There are whom Heav'n has blest with store of Wit,
     Yet want as much again to manage it;
     For *Wit* and *Judgment* ever are at strife,
     Tho' meant each other's Aid, like *Man* and *Wife*.
     'Tis more to *guide* than *spur* the Muse's Steed;
85   Restrain his Fury, than provoke his Speed;
     The winged Courser, like a gen'rous Horse,
     Shows most true Mettle when you *check* his Course.

80–1. 1744–51: Some, to whom Heav'n in wit has been profuse,
      Want as much more, to turn it to its use;
82. ever: *1744–51:* often

80-1. Dennis denounced this as outright nonsense (*Reflections*, p. 11, Hooker, I.404–5), and it was also attacked in Concanen, *Supplement to the Profund* (1728), p. 11: 'Any one may perceive that the Writer meant *Judgment* should manage *Wit*; but as it stands, it's *Pert*, and that's to be preferr'd to all other Considerations'. Cf. Pope's comments on the relative wit and judgement of Wycherley and Congreve in his annotation to 'Autumn', 7, and for material suggesting that in contemporary critical thinking, Judgment could be part of Wit, see Headnote: Context, to the present poem. Pope's eventual alteration of the line preserves the apparent paradox.

82. TE cites Rymer's translation of Rapin, *Reflections on Aristotle's Treatise of Poesie*, p. 2: 'as Judgment without Wit is cold and heavy, so Wit without Judgment is blind and extravagant'.

83. Man *and* Wife: Pope does not specify which is the representative of wit and which of judgement. Cf. Dennis to Wycherley, 30 October 1695, *Letters upon Several Occasions* (1696), p. 45, Hooker, II.383, defining 'man of wit': 'a man like you, Sir, ... in whom Fancy and Judgment are like a well-match'd Pair; the first like an extraordinary Wife, that appears always Beautiful, and always Charming, yet is at all times Decent, and at all times Chast; the Second like a Prudent and well-bred Husband, whose very Sway shews his Complaisance, and whose very Indulgence shews his Authority'.

84–7. TE notes that the metaphor of bridle and spur, corresponding to judgment and wit, is found in Longinus, *Peri Hypsous*, II.3 ('as often as the spur is used, so often is the bridle necessary') and in Quintilian, *Instituto Oratoria*, X.iii.10. The image of human mentality as a wild horse straining against control is found earlier, e.g. in Plato's *Phaedrus*. TE cites further the phrasing of Boileau's translation of Longinus, and Ben Jonson's 'Explorata: or, Discoveries': 'Yet when wee thinke wee have got the faculty, it is even then good to resist it, as to give a Horse a check sometimes with bit, which does not so much stop his course, as stirre his mettle'; *Workes of Beniamin Ionson* (1640), II.104. Wakefield compares Waller's 'Of this Translation and of the Use of Poetry', in Roscommon's translation of Horace's *Art of Poetry*, 11–12 (1680), sig. A4ʳ: 'Direct us how, to back the winged Horse, | Favour his flight, and moderate his force'. See also 151, and Pope's parody of the idea in 'Lines from *The Critical Specimen*' and 'To the Author of a Poem, intitled, Successio', 3.

84. Muse: one of the nine goddesses of arts in Greek mythology, and thus a personification of poetry.

86. winged: wingèd, to fill out the metre.

   gen'rous: when used of animals, 'spritely; daring; courageous' (*SJ*); possessed of strength and 'Mettle', 87.

87. Mettle: 'spirit; sprightliness; courage' (*SJ*, citing this line).

> Those RULES of old *discover'd*, not *devis'd*,
> Are *Nature* still, but *Nature Methodiz'd*;
> 90   *Nature*, like *Monarchy*, is but restrain'd
> By the same Laws which first *herself* ordain'd.
> First Learned *Greece* just Precepts did indite,
> When to repress, and when indulge our Flight:

---

90. Monarchy: *1744–51:* Liberty
92. *1717–51:* Hear how learn'd *Greece* her useful rules indites,
93. Flight:: *1717–51:* flights!

---

88. RULES: the critical precepts derived ultimately from Aristotle's *Poetics* (see Headnote: Models and sources.

discover'd ... devis'd: critics formulated the rules by discovering the governing hand of nature within the best literary works: to 'devise' rules would be arbitrary invention.

89. Methodiz'd: reduced to system; see Pope to Wycherley, 29 November 1707 (*Corr.*, I.34): 'To *methodize* in your Case ...'. TE compares Rymer's translation of Rapin's *Reflections on Aristotle's Treatise of Poesie*, p. 16: 'these Rules well considered one shall find them to be made onely to reduce Nature into method ... They are founded upon *good sense*, and sound Reason, rather than on authority'. TE suggests the mediating influence of Dryden's absorption of these phrases in the 'Preface' to *Troilus and Cressida* (1679). Pope's discussion of the 'rules' continues to 164; for Dennis's objections to Pope's characterisation of them see *Reflections*, pp. 6–7, Hooker, I.401, and for Dennis's own earlier characterisation of the rules of Aristotle as 'nothing but Nature and Good Sence reduc'd to a Method', see *The Impartial Critick* (1693), p. 49, Hooker I.39. Savage (1988) cites also Laurence Echard's view, in *Terence's Comedies Made English* (1699), 'Preface', p. xviii, that the rules were '*pure Nature only Methodiz'd*'.

90–1. Kingship is restrained by the laws which it has itself instituted; an elegant solution to the major political question of the preceding century (see 165). For the phrasing TE cites Cowley, 'Inconstancy', 21, *Poems ... Written by A. Cowley* (1656), p. 11 (speaking of Nature): 'For 'twere to break the *Laws* her self has made', and for the politics, Dryden, *The Medall*, 139–40 (1682), p. 9, speaking of kings: 'Already they have lost their best defence, | The benefit of Laws, which they dispence'.

90 variant. Liberty: this late variant was advanced in a note to *The Dunciad* (1743), IV.181–2, possibly by Pope's editor Warburton, before its incorporation in 1744–51. It marks a shift towards the 'contract' theory of social organisation; cf. 551–2 below.

92. Learned: learnèd, well-versed in scholarship.
indite: dictate, set down.

93. repress ... indulge: Cf. *Windsor-Forest*, 19–20.

Flight: the imaginative flight of poetry; cf. the parody of this in the second set of 'Lines from *The Critical Specimen*' and 'To the Author of a Poem, intitled, Successio', 15–18.

High on *Parnassus'* Top her Sons she show'd,
95   And pointed out those arduous Paths they trod,
Held from afar, aloft, th' Immortal Prize,
And urg'd the rest by equal Steps to rise;
From great *Examples useful Rules* were giv'n;
She drew from *them* what they deriv'd from *Heav'n*,
100 The gen'rous Critick *fann'd* the *Poet's Fire*,
And taught the World, *with Reason* to *Admire*.
Then Criticism the Muses Handmaid prov'd,

98, n. MS, *1717–51: Nec enim artibus editis factum est ut argumenta inveniremus, sed dicta sunt omnia antequam praeciperentur, mox ea scriptores observata & collecta ediderunt.* Quintilian.

94. **on *Parnassus*':** MS: on the *Parnassu's*
98. 1717–51: Just precepts thus from great examples giv'n,
99. **Heav'n,:** MS: Heav'n.
102. **Muses:** *1717–22:* Muse's

---

94. **Parnassus:** mountain in Greece, sacred to the Muses and hence a metaphor for high achievement in poetry.
  her Sons: the successful poets of Greece.
  show'd: displayed.
94–5. **show'd ... trod:** apparently an acceptable rhyme at this period; cf. Dryden, 'Palamon and Arcite', II.45–6, where 'rode' rhymes with 'trod'.
96. **Prize:** fame, explored at length in Pope's *Temple of Fame* (1715, but written c. 1712). Wakefield compares the Soames–Dryden translation of Boileau, *Art of Poetry*, IV.229 (1683), p. 66: 'And afar off hold up the glorious prize'.
97. ***equal Steps:*** the same route.
98 **Pope's note.** Quintilian, *Institutio Oratoria*, V.x.120: 'For it is not from previously published textbooks that we produce arguments; all things were said before they were laid down as precepts; after that writers published the things they had observed and collected.'
98–9. Greece summarises as the 'just Precepts' (92) of literary criticism the rules which the 'great Examples' (in poetic history) have 'deriv'd from Heav'n'.
100–6. For Dennis's hostile misreading of these lines see *Reflections*, p. 5, Hooker, I.400–1. Wakefield compares Dryden's 'Dedication' of *Examen Poeticum*, sig. A4ᵛ, where Dryden laments that ancient critics were 'Defendors of Poets' but modern ones were their enemies, 'Wits of the Second Order ... subservient to the Fame of Writers'.
100. **gen'rous:** not in the sense used at 87 but in the modern sense, 'liberal, munificent' (*SJ*); Johnson also notes, however, that it means 'Not of mean birth; of good extraction' and 'Noble of mind', a class-based sense which may be in play here. Cf. 'January and May', 3.
101. **Admire:** wonder at; cf. 203.
102. ***Muses Handmaid:*** *TE* finds this a 'clever turn on Philosophia Theologiae ancilla' ('philosophy is the maidservant of theology'), a precept associated with Aquinas (see 445–6). Samuel Cobb, 'Of Poetry', *Poems on Several Occasions* (1707), p. 191, calls French literature 'the Handmaid of the *English* Muse'.

To dress her Charms, and make her more belov'd;
But following Wits from that Intention stray'd;
105 Who cou'd not win the Mistress, woo'd the Maid:
Set up themselves, and drove a *sep'rate* Trade:
Against the Poets *their own Arms* they turn'd,
Sure to hate most the Men from whom they *learn'd*.
So modern *Pothecaries*, taught the Art
110 By *Doctor's Bills* to play the *Doctor's Part*,
Bold in the Practice of *mistaken Rules*,
Prescribe, apply, and call their *Masters Fools*.
Some on the Leaves of ancient Authors prey,
Nor Time nor Moths e'er spoil'd so much as they:

---

106. *1736a–51:* omitted

104–5. Cf. Cobb, 'A Discourse on Criticism and the Liberty of Writing', *Poems* (1707), sig. A5ʳ: '*some Persons, who would be Poets, which they cannot be, become Criticks which they can be*'; Cobb attributes the remark to St Evremont, but it also recalls Dryden's 'the corruption of a Poet, is the Generation of a critic', 'Dedication' of *Examen Poeticum* (1693), sig. A4ʳ.

105. Pope's early correspondence with rakish figures such as Wycherley and Henry Cromwell encouraged this kind of association; e.g. Pope to Cromwell, of the Blount sisters, 21 December 1711 (*Corr.*, I.137–8): 'How gladly wou'd I give all I am worth, that is to say, my *Pastorals* for *one* of their *Maidenheads*, & my *Essay* for the other? I wou'd lay out all my *Poetry* in *Love*; an *Original* for a *Lady*, & a *Translation* for a *Waiting Maid*!' See further Wycherley to Pope, 7 April 1705; Pope to Cromwell, 18 March 1708; Wycherley to Pope, 13 and 18 May 1708; Pope to Cromwell, 20 July 1710 and 12 November 1711 (*Corr.*, I.6–7, 42, 50–1, 92, 135).

106. **Trade:** a slighting allusion to the idea of the professional critic, a tradesman laboriously 'driving' his business, as opposed to the aristocratic poet; cf. Commentary to 589.

107–8. Cf. Dryden, 'Dedication' of *Examen Poeticum*, sig. A4ᵛ: 'Are our Auxiliary Forces turned our Enemies?' 108 is a line of monosyllables; see 229 and 350.

109. **Pothecaries:** apothecaries or pharmacists, socially inferior to physicians, hence envious of the masters whose prescriptions ('*Bills*', 110) they ignorantly mimic as critics envy poets. Garth, later dedicatee of 'Summer', was a physician and poet and his much-reprinted mock-epic *The Dispensary* (1699), referred to here at 622, was based on a quarrel between the physicians and the apothecaries.

112. **apply:** treat with potions. TE compares Garth, *Dispensary*, II.107–8, sixth edition (1706), p. 22: apothecaries are 'Bold to Prescribe, and busie to Apply'.

113–14. A hostile reference to scholarly editing of the kind performed by Richard Bentley (1662–1742), as in his controversial edition of Horace (1711), which Pope would attack fiercely in *The Dunciad* and elsewhere.

115 Some dryly plain, without Invention's Aid,
    Write dull *Receits* how Poems may be made:
    These lost the Sense, their Learning to display,
    And those explain'd the Meaning quite away.
       You then whose Judgment the right Course wou'd steer,
120 Know well each Ancient's proper *Character*,
    His *Fable, Subject, Scope* in ev'ry Page,
    Religion, Country, Genius of his *Age*:

---

117. **lost:** *1736a–43:* lose; *1744–51:* leave
  the: *1727–32:* their
118. **explain'd:** *1736a–51:* explain

115-16. Dennis opined that Pope would have included Aristotle in the category if he were a modern; *Reflections*, p. 6, Hooker, I.401.

115. **Invention:** 'the act or power of producing something new' (*SJ*). Cf. 'imagination', 58, and 'fancy', 653. For Pope, Homer 'is universally allow'd to have had the greatest Invention of any Writer whatever' ('Preface' to *The Iliad, PW*, I.223). Johnson specified the *Essay* as proof of Pope's own '*Invention* . . . by which extrinsick and adventitious and embellishments and illustrations are connected with a known subject' (Lonsdale, IV.78).

116. **Receits:** recipes. In a letter to Caryll, 23 June 1713 (*Corr.*, I.180), Pope acknowledged the squib known as 'A Receit to Make an Epic Poem' (*Guardian*, no. 78, 10 June 1713; *PW*, I.115–20), a parody of works such as Le Bossu's tightly-structured *Traité du Poëme épique* (1675; see Headnote: Models and sources); it was reprinted as chapter xv of 'Peri Bathous' (*PW*, II.228–33). *TE* suggests that Pope may also have been thinking of writers such as Charles Gildon and John Oldmixon, reproducing French critical sources, but neither had published much in that line by 1711; Pope's target might have been Blackmore's prefaces to his modern epics, *Prince Arthur* (1695) and *King Arthur* (1697).

117. Cf. 25 above.

118. Cf. the academic's boast in *Dunciad*, IV.251-2: 'For thee explain a thing till all men doubt it, | And write about it, Goddess, and about it.'

120-2. EC cites the Soames–Dryden translation of Boileau, *Art of Poetry*, III.110 (1683), p. 35: 'Keep to each man his proper Character. | Of Countryes and of Times the humors know; | From diff'rent Climates, diff'ring Customs grow.'

120. **Ancient:** classical author: 'those that lived in old time were called *ancients*, as opposed to the moderns' (*SJ*).

Character: combining *OED* sense 9, 'The aggregate of the distinctive features of any thing; essential peculiarity; nature, style', with sense 11, 'The sum of the moral and mental qualities which distinguish an individual'. *TE* cites the English version of Roger de Piles, *The Art of Painting* (1706), p. 52: 'Character consists then in the manner in which the Painter thinks Things. 'Tis the Seal that distinguishes his Works from those of other Men, and which imprints on them the lively Image of his Mind'.

121. **Fable:** main plot.
  Scope: range of subject matter and intention.

122. **Genius:** the spirit or character of his times (as opposed to individual creative genius, 11, 49, 60). For discussion of the issue of contextual understanding in relation to Pope's poem see Smallwood (2004).

Without all these at once before your Eyes,
You may *Confound,* but never *Criticize.*
125 Be *Homer's* Works your *Study,* and *Delight,*
Read them by Day, and meditate by Night,

124, n. 1736a–43: Between Verse 124 and 125: [*1744–51: Cavil you may, but never criticize*] The author after this verse originally inserted the following, which he has however omitted in all the editions:]

> Zoilus, *had these been known, without a name*
> *Had dy'd, and* Perault *ne'er been damn'd to fame;*
> *The sense of sound Antiquity had reign'd,*
> *And sacred* Homer *yet been unprophan'd.*
> *None e'er had thought his comprehensive mind*
> *To modern Customs, modern Rules confin'd;*
> *Who for all Ages writ and all Mankind.*

124. **You may Confound:** *1713a–51: Cavil* you may
124^5. MS*: Zoilus,* had these been known, without a Name
  Had dy'd, and *Perault* ne'er been *damn'd to Fame;*
  The Sense of sound Antiquity had reign'd;
  And Sacred *Homer* yet been unprophan'd.
  None e'er had thought His Comprehensive Mind
  To modern Customs, modern Rules confin'd,
  Who for All Ages writ, and All Mankind!
125. **Homer's:** MS: his great

123–4. EC compares Roscommon, *Essay on Translated Verse,* 195–6 (1684), p. 13: 'While in your *Thoughts* you find the *least* Debate, | You may *Confound,* but *never* can *Translate*'.
124. **Confound:** confuse, put in disorder.
124 variant. **Cavil:** object frivolously. TE cites Dryden, 'Preface' to *Sylvae* (1685), sig. a4ᵛ: *'to arraign a Man is one thing, and to cavil at him is another'.* Cf. also Dennis, *The Impartial Critick* (1693), p. 27, Hooker, I.33: 'a Caviller can never esteem any thing perfect'.
124^5 MS. **Zoilus:** see 466 and note.
  Perault: Charles Perrault (1628–1703), whose *Parallèle des Anciens et des Modernes* (1688–92) rated modern writers above ancient and thus initiated the 'Querelle'; see Headnote: Context.
  damn'd to Fame: condemned to notoriety (by Boileau, in Perrault's case); Pope returned to this phrase in *The Dunciad* (1728), III.158 and *Essay on Man* (1733–4), IV.284.
  All Ages . . . All Mankind: TE compares Jonson's commendatory poem in the first folio edition of Shakespeare (1623), 'To the Memory of . . . William Shakespeare', 43, 'He was not of an age, but for all time!'
125. **Homer:** supposed author of the two foundational epics of Greek antiquity, the *Iliad* and the *Odyssey.* Pope had read Homer as a child in the translations by John Ogilby (1660 and 1665); see *OAC,* I.11, 14–15, 20, 26, and Headnote to 'The 'Episode of Sarpedon'. Pope spent two major periods, 1713–16 and 1722–6, on versions of *The Iliad* and *The Odyssey,* but he was discussing the problems of translating Homer as early as the letter to Ralph Bridges of 5 April 1708 (*Corr.,* I.43). Pope's Preface to *The Iliad* translation (1715; *PW,* I.221–56) was the other major critical statement of his

Thence form your Judgment, thence your Notions bring,
And trace the Muses *upward* to their *Spring*;
Still with *It self compar'd*, his *Text* peruse;
130   And let your *Comment* be the *Mantuan Muse*.

---

127. **Notions:** *1744–51:* maxims
130. **And:** *1736a–43:* Or

---

early career. Thomas Parnell's 'Essay on the Life, Writings and Learning of Homer', published in the first volume of Pope's translation of the *Iliad*, was prepared by Pope on what he told Spence were very uncertain materials (*OAC*, I.83–4). The original integrity of the Homeric texts was already doubted by radical scholars such as Bentley (see Commentary at 113–14; Patey 1997b: 53–6).

Study . . . Delight: in accordance with the principle that poetry should mix 'dulce' with 'utile', the pleasing with the useful, a phrase deriving from Horace, *Ars Poetica*, 343.

126. meditate: reflect on them. Wakefield compares Horace, *Ars Poetica*, 268–9: 'vos exemplaria Graeca | nocturna versate manu, versate diurna', translated by Roscommon (1680), p. 19, as 'Consider well the Greek Originals, | Read them by day, and think of them by night', with an added gloss from Vida, *De Arte Poetica*, I. 409–11. *TE* further cites the first psalm, in Tate and Brady, *A New Version of the Psalms of David* (1696), p. 3: 'But makes the perfect Law of God | His Bus'ness and Delight; | Devoutly reads therein by Day, | And meditates by Night.' (Pope's *Roman Catholick Version of the First Psalm*, 1716, was a smutty parody of this version.) Cf. also 'Sapho to Phaon', 144.

127. Notions: precepts and working rules of criticism.

127 variant. maxims: succinctly-expressed general principles; Pope had repeatedly suggested to Wycherley that his verses would be better phrased as prose maxims (e.g. *Corr.*, I.34, 86–7). The model for maxims of this kind was the Duc de La Rochefoucauld.

128. trace . . . Spring: The *Iliad* and the *Odyssey* themselves both open with invocations to the Muse. Wakefield compares Dryden's translation of Virgil, *Georgics*, IV.408, *Works of Virgil*, p. 134: 'And upward follow Fame's immortal Spring'.

129. Cf. Roscommon, *Essay on Translated Verse*, 186 (1684), p. 12: 'Consult your *Author*, with *Himself* compar'd'.

130. Comment: commentary, guide; cf. Dryden, *Of Dramatick Poesie*, p. 10, where Horace's *Ars Poetica* is described as an 'excellent Comment' on Aristotle's *Poetics*.

Mantuan Muse: Virgil (70–19 BC), reputedly born at Mantua (see note to 'Autumn', 5), regarded as a 'comment' or commentary on Homer because his twelve-book *Aeneid* was conspicuously modelled on the Greek epics. The linkage of Homer and Virgil was a standard one, e.g. the translation of Rapin's 'A Comparison of Homer and Virgil', *The Whole Critical Works of Monsieur Rapin*, 2 vols (1706), I.116–210, and Dryden's 'Preface' to *Fables Ancient and Modern* (1700), sig. *A2ᵛ–*B1ᵛ. Pope's 'Preface' to his translation of the *Iliad* (*PW*, I.223–56), contains his own sustained critical comparison.

AN ESSAY ON CRITICISM (1711) 221

When first great *Maro* in his boundless Mind
A Work t' outlast Immortal *Rome* design'd,
Perhaps he seem'd *above* the Critick's Law,

131, n. 1736a–43: When first great Maro *in his boundless mind*
   A work t' outlast Immortal Rome design'd.
   1713a–51: [*1751:* When first young Maro, *etc.*]] Virgil, Eclog. 6. *Cum canerem Reges &*
   Proelia, Cynthius aurem Vellit —
   1744–51: It is a tradition preserved by *Servius*, that *Virgil* began with writing a poem of
   the *Alban* and *Roman* affairs; which he found above his years, and descended first to
   imitate *Theocritus* on rural subjects, and afterwards to copy *Homer* in Heroic poetry.

131. **great:** *1713a–51:* young
131–2. 1713a–43:   When first young *Maro* sung of *Kings* and *Wars*,
             Ere warning *Phoebus* touch'd his trembling Ears,

---

131. great Maro: Virgil's full name was Publius Vergilius Maro. For a full-length discussion of Pope's fable of young Maro, the identity between Homer and Nature as objects of imitation, and the history of the idea, see Savage (1988).

132. outlast Immortal Rome: a deliberate hyperbole, perhaps based on Horace's claim (*Odes*, III.30) to have constructed, by his poetry, 'monumentum aere perennius', 'a monument more lasting than bronze'. For the 'eternal Reign' of Rome see 'The First Book of Statius his Thebais', 33. Dennis ridiculed Pope's formulation here, *Reflections*, p. 8, Hooker I.402, and in his manuscript memoranda Pope writes 'alter ye seeming Incosistency' (see Appendix), hence the variant couplet. The words 'Arms and ye Man', which Pope experimented with at the same time, translate the opening of Virgil's *Aeneid*, 'arma virumque'.

131 Pope's note. Virgil, *Eclogues*, VI.3–4, in Dryden's translation, 3–5, *Works of Virgil*, p. 26: 'But when I try'd her [the Muse's] tender Voice, too young; | And fighting Kings, and bloody Battels sung, | Apollo check'd my pride...'. Having imitated Virgil's *Eclogues* in his *Pastorals*, this extended appreciation of the Roman poet in his epic guise suggests Pope's own ambitions.

Servius: grammarian of the 4th century AD, author of a commentary on Virgil;

Savage (1988: 87) notes that Pope has streamlined what Servius and Donatus, a supplementary commentator, say about Virgil's abandoned early work on epic themes, which is more ambiguous than Pope's summary indicates. The variant story is also mentioned by Wotton, *Reflections upon Ancient and Modern Learning* (1694), p. 35.

Alban: of Alba Longa, early city state situated near modern Castle Gandolfo, supposedly destroyed by the ascendant Rome in the seventh century BC.

Theocritus: see Headnote to *Pastorals*.

131–2 variant. Phoebus: Apollo, god of Poetry (see 34). Pope's variant couplet contained an echo ('trembling ears') from Milton, 'Lycidas', 77, *Poems of Mr. John Milton* (1645), p. 60, as well as a strained rhyme. The idea of trembling ears was satirically related to the loss of ears in the pillory for sedition, and thus inappropriate to the young Virgil: see e.g. *The Dunciad* (1728), II.127. Cf. 201.

133. TE compares Addison's comments on Milton in 'An Account of the Greatest English Poets', *Annual Miscellany: For the Year 1694* (1694), p. 322: 'Bold, and sublime, my whole attention draws, | And seems above the Criticks nicer laws'. Cf. also the quotation from Dryden in the note to 136, which has the same rhyme as Addison.

                    And but from *Nature's Fountains* scorn'd to draw:
135   But when t' examine ev'ry Part he came,
                    Nature and *Homer* were, he found, the *same*:
                    Convinc'd, amaz'd, he checkt the bold Design,
                    And did his Work to Rules as strict confine,
                    As if the *Stagyrite* o'erlook'd each Line.
140   Learn hence for Ancient *Rules* a just Esteem;
                    To copy *Nature* is to copy *Them.*
                            Some Beauties yet, no Precepts can declare,
                    For there's a *Happiness* as well as *Care.*
                    Musick resembles *Poetry*, in each
145   Are *nameless Graces* which no Methods teach,
                    And which a *Master-Hand* alone can reach.

138, n. 1736a–43: And did his work to rules as strict confine.

137. checkt: *1717–51:* checks
138. *1717–51:* And rules as strict his labour'd work confine,
142. MS: Yet are there Beauties that no Rules declare,
143. For: MS: And

---

134. but: except.
   Nature's Fountains: a traditional image of nature as the source of art.
136. *TE* compares Dryden's 'Prologue' to his adaptation of *The Tempest*, 7–8 (1670), sig. A4ʳ (of Shakespeare): 'He Monarch-like gave those his subjects law, | And is that Nature which they paint and draw'.
137. Convinc'd: cf. Dryden, 'Pygmalion and the Statue', 90, *Fables*, p. 168: 'Convinced, o'erjoyed, his studied Thanks and Praise'.
   checkt: cf. 84–7; Virgil confines his 'bold Design' within the limits imposed by Homer or Nature.
139. Stagyrite: Aristotle (see 88), born at the Macedonian city of Stagira.
   o'erlook'd: oversaw, corrected.
141. copy Nature: cf. 'Discourse on Pastoral Poetry', *Pastorals*, Appendix II, 31.
142. declare: *OED*, sense 1: 'to clear up, explain, expound, interpret, elucidate'.
143. Happiness: unpredictable brilliance (from 'happen'), as opposed to 'Care' or careful labour. *TE* cites D'Avenant's Preface to *Gondibert* (1651), p. 19: '*Wit* is the laborious, and the lucky resultances of thought, having towards its excellence (as we say of the strokes of Painting) as well a happiness as care'. *TE* further suggests the origin of the phrase as a whole is the 'curiosa felicitas' or 'careful good fortune' attributed to Horace by Petronius, *Satyricon*, 118. See also Dryden's 'Preface' to *Sylvae*, sig. a6ᵛ–a7ʳ, where Horace's own 'happiness' of phrasing is linked to 'curiosa felicitas' ('careful good fortune') and 'feliciter audet' ('he dares luckily'), from Horace, *Epistles*, II.i.166.
144–6. Warton compares Sir Francis Bacon, 'Of Beauty', Essay XLIII of *The Essays, or Councils, Civil and Moral* (1625), p. 252: 'a Painter, may make a better Face, than euer was; But he must doe it by a kinde of Felicity, (as a Musician that maketh an excellent Air in Musick) And not by Rule'.
145. nameless Graces: see note to 156. *EC* compares Rymer's translation of Rapin,

If, where the *Rules* not far enough extend,
(Since Rules were made but to promote their End)
Some Lucky LICENCE answers to the full
150   Th' Intent propos'd, *that Licence* is a *Rule.*
Thus *Pegasus,* a nearer way to take,
May boldly deviate from the common Track.

147.] Neque tam sancta sunt ista Praecepta, sed hoc quicquid est, Utilitas excogitavit; Non negabo autem sic utile esse plerunque; verum si eadem illa nobis aliud suadebit utilitas, hanc, relictis magistrorum autoritatibus, sequemur. Quintil. l. 2. cap. 13.

147, n. Neque tam sancta: 1744–51: Neque enim rogationibus plebisue scitis sancta

148. **answers:** *1751:* answer
153–4. 1744–51: follows l.161

Reflections on Aristotle's Treatise of Poesie (1674), p. 57: 'Yet is there in *Poetry,* as in other Arts, certain things that *cannot be expressed,* which are (as it were) *mysteries.* There are no precepts, to teach the hidden *graces,* the insensible *charms,* and all that secret *power* of *Poetry* which passes to the heart...'. Ault (*PW,* I.xlvi) thought Pope had coined the phrase 'nameless Graces' and used its occurrence in *The Spectator,* no. 292, 4 February 1712, to argue for Pope's authorship of the paper. But the phrase occurs much earlier, in e.g. 'Ode 13. of the First Book of Horace' in Tate's *Poems by Several Hands, and on Several Occasions* (1685), p. 88.
147 **Pope's note.** Quintilian, *Institutio Oratoria,* II.xiii.6–7: 'For these precepts are not inviolable, like a law or decree of the people; rather, usefulness has devised whatever it contains. I will not deny, moreover, that it is for the most part useful... but truly, if that same usefulness persuades us otherwise, then we will follow usefulness, leaving behind the authority of teachers.' Pope's 1744 text is more accurate than the earlier one.
149. **Lucky LICENCE:** *TE* compares the anonymous English translation of Roger de Piles, *The Art of Painting* (1706), pp. 39–40 'The *Licences* are so necessary, that all Arts admit of them; they are Literally against the *Rules,* but when we come to explain our selves, we shall shew they assist them, if they are made use of *à Propos....* There are none but great *Genius*'s who are above Rules, and who know when to make use ingeniously of the *Licences...*'. Dryden discussed the subject in 'The Author's Apology for Heroique Poetry; and Poetic Licence', in *The State of Innocence* (1677), and cf. Coward's critical poem *Licentia Poetica Discuss'd* (1709). For 'lucky' cf. also Dryden on Shakespeare, *Of Dramatick Poesie,* p. 47: 'All the Images of Nature were still present to him, and he drew them not laboriously, but luckily'.
151. **Pegasus:** mythological winged horse, responsible for creating the Hippocrene spring on Mount Helicon, in Greece, near sites sacred to the Muses; an embodiment of imaginative 'flights'. Cf. Pope's 'Lines from *The Critical Specimen*', II.1. In the engraved headpiece to the *Essay on Criticism* in Pope's *Works* of 1717, Pegasus is visibly in flight.

Great Wits sometimes may *gloriously offend*,
And *rise* to *Faults* true Criticks *dare not mend*;
155   From *vulgar Bounds* with *brave Disorder* part,
And *snatch* a *Grace* beyond the Reach of Art,
Which, without passing thro' the *Judgment*, gains
The *Heart*, and all its End *at once* attains.
In *Prospects*, thus, some *Objects* please our Eyes,
160   Which *out of* Nature's *common Order* rise,
The shapeless *Rock*, or hanging *Precipice*.

153-5. In *The Grounds of Criticism in Poetry*, sig. b1^v-b2^r, Hooker, I. 333, Dennis praised Milton for daring to 'break thro' the Rules of Aristotle' and declared *Paradise Lost* to be less 'against the rules' than 'above them all'. Dryden refused to apologise for disregarding the 'unity' of time in the 'Preface' to *Don Sebastian* (1690), sig. a2^v, arguing that 'to gain a greater Beauty, 'tis lawful for a Poet to supersede a less'.

153. Wakefield compares Dryden, *Aureng-Zebe*, IV.i.115 (1676), p. 51: 'Mean Soul! and dar'st not gloriously offend?'

155. Wakefield compares the Soames–Dryden translation of Boileau, *Art of Poetry*, II.76-7: 'Her generous stile at random oft will part, | And by a brave disorder shows her Art'; and IV.76-9: ''Tis he will tell you, to what noble height | A generous Muse may sometimes take her flight; | When, too much fetter'd with the Rules of Art, | May from her stricter Bounds and Limits part.'

156. snatch: suggesting Prometheus' theft of fire from Zeus.

Grace: beautiful touch, as in 145; something that mere labour could not achieve. *TE* cites the anonymous English version of de Piles, *The Art of Painting* (1706), p. 8, where Grace is '*what pleases, and gains the Heart, without concerning it self with the Understanding*', whereas Beauty is produced 'by the Rules only'. See also Dryden, 'Preface' to *An Evening's Love* (1671), sig. a4^v: 'Judgement, indeed, is necessary in him [the poet]; but 'tis fancy that gives the life touches, and the secret graces to it'. Monk (1944) cites abundant contextual material on this idea that Pope would have known, from Quintilian and Cicero, Castiglione's *Book of the Courtier* (1528; English translation by Thomas Hoby, 1561), Renaissance art criticism, and the unpredictable 'je ne sais quoi' discussed in Bouhours, *Les Entretiens d'Ariste et de Eugène* (1671).

159. **Prospects:** landscapes or landscape paintings.

161. hanging: overhanging. Pope is describing the pleasure, inexplicable by the normal rules of 'nature', to be occasionally found in 'unnatural' but powerful objects of magnificence, a feature of 'sublime' aesthetics. *EC* compares Thomas Sprat, 'An Account of the Life and Writings of Mr Abraham Cowley', *Works of Mr. Abraham Cowley* (1668), sig. b1^v: 'He knew that in diverting mens minds, there should be the same variety observ'd as in the prospects of their Eyes: where a Rock, a Precipice, or a rising Wave, is often more delightful than a smooth, even ground, or a calm Sea'. *TE* cites Dennis's observation from *Advancement and Reformation of Poetry*, sig. a1^v-a2^r, Hooker, I.202-3, that as the 'Harmony of Universal Nature' can include apparent irregularities, so poems may display things 'seemingly against Reason' which are actually 'perfectly regular' as part of 'a great and a just Design'.

AN ESSAY ON CRITICISM (1711)

But Care in Poetry must still be had,
It asks *Discretion* ev'n in *running Mad*;
And tho' the *Ancients* thus their *Rules* invade,
165 (As *Kings* dispense with *Laws* Themselves have made)
Moderns, beware! Or if you must offend
Against the *Precept,* ne'er transgress its *End,*
Let it be seldom, and compell'd by Need,
And have, at least, *Their Precedent* to plead.
170 The Critick else proceeds without Remorse,
Seizes your Fame, and puts his Laws in force.

162–3. 1744–51: omitted
164. **And:** *1744–51:* But
168. **Let it be:** MS: Do it but

---

163. Cf. Dryden, *Absalom and Achitophel,* 163-4 (1681), p. 6: 'Great Wits are sure to Madness near ally'd; | And thin Partitions do their Bounds divide', loosely calling on the more positive classical concept of 'furor poeticus', the 'poetic madness' of quasi-divine inspiration. Wakefield compares Horace, *Satires,* II.iii.271: 'insanire ... certa ratione modoque', 'to go mad by fixed rule and method'. TE compares Rymer's translation of Rapin's *Reflections on Aristotle's Treatise of Poesie* (1674), p. 6: "Tis in no wise true, what most believe, That some little mixture of Madness goes to make up the character of a Poet: for though his Discourse ought in some manner to resemble that of one inspir'd: yet his mind must always be serene, that he may discern when to *let his Muse run mad,* and when to govern his Transports'.

164. **invade:** violate.

165. Cf. 90–1. TE compares Dryden's 'Dedication' of his translation of Virgil's *Aeneid,* in *Works of Virgil,* (1697), sig. c3ᵛ: Virgil 'might make this *Anacronism,* by superseding the mechanick Rules of Poetry, for the same Reason, that a Monarch may dispense with, or suspend his own Laws, when he finds it necessary so to do'; and Knightly Chetwood's 'Preface' to Dryden's translation of the Virgil's *Pastorals* (1697), sig. ****2ᵛ : 'extraordinary *Genius*'s have a sort of Prerogative, which may dispence them from Laws, binding to *Subject-Wits*'. Dennis objected to Pope's phrasing: 'Thus is this Essayer for a double Dispensing Power in Kings and ancient Authors, and is for making the Moderns doubly Slaves, Slaves in their Actions, and Slaves in their Writings'; *Reflections,* p. 14, Hooker, I.406. For Dennis, a loyal adherent of the Whig settlement of 1688, the 'dispensing power' was 'set on foot on purpose to introduce Popery' (*ibid.,* p. 27, Hooker, I.415).

168–9. TE compares Horace, *Ars Poetica,* 51-3: 'dabiturque licentia sumpta pudenter: | et nova fictaque nuper habebunt verba fidem, si | Graeco fonte cadent parce detorta.' 'Licence taken modestly will be granted: and words, though new and recently coined, will gain trust if they come from a Greek source and are drawn sparingly'. For the phrasing of 168 cf. Roscommon's translation, p. 5: 'So it be seldom and discreetly done'. Horace is talking about the coinage of new words, not poetic licence generally.

169. **Precedent:** with 'plead', the term suggests the legal sense of a previous example presented in a court, prefiguring the imagery of 171.

171. **Seizes:** impounds or takes possession of, like a bailiff with a warrant.
Fame: reputation.

I know there are, to whose presumptuous Thoughts
Those *Freer Beauties*, ev'n in *Them*, seem Faults:
Some Figures *monstrous* and *mis-shap'd* appear,
175   Consider'd *singly*, or beheld too *near*,
Which, but *proportion'd* to their *Light*, or *Place*,
Due Distance *reconciles* to Form and Grace.
A prudent Chief not always must display
His Pow'rs in *equal Ranks*, and *fair Array*,

173^4. MS: The boldest Strokes of Art we may despise,
   View'd in *false Lights*, with *undiscerning Eyes*.

172-83. TE suggests Pope derives this idea from Rymer's translation of Rapin, *Reflections on Aristotle's Treatise of Poesie* (1674), pp. 66-7, recommending that poets deliberately leave certain aspects of their 'great works' unpolished, as 'studied *negligences*' heighten 'what is finish'd'. TE also cites Pope's letter to Walsh, 2 July 1706 (*Corr.*, I.18-19) in which Pope espoused the view that 'Some parts ought to be lower than the rest'.

172-3. TE shows that the Thoughts/Faults rhyme was acceptable in Pope's day, citing Roscommon, *Essay on Translated Verse*, 324-5 (1684), p. 20: '*Absur'd Expressions, crude, Abortive Thoughts,* | All the lewd *Legion* of *Exploded fau'ts*'. The rhyme (in the singular) is repeated at 423-4 below.

173. Freer Beauties: examples of 'Grace', 156. 'Beauties' and 'faults' were the conventional opposed terms of critical discourse in Pope's day; see Spingarn (1908-9: I.xcviii-c).

173-6. TE compares the anonymous translation of Longinus, *An Essay Upon Sublime* (1698), pp. 82-3: ''Tis just so with a Discourse, as 'tis with a natural Body, whose beauty rises from the union, and just proportion of every part: and tho' each limb by it self has nothing graceful, yet jointed together they form a most beauteous frame'.

174. Figures: both rhetorical 'figures' or literary expressions and shapes in visual art. **monstrous . . . mis-shap'd:** like the rocks of 159-61, here requiring to be viewed within a whole design, 176-7. Cf. 248-9.

176. TE cites Horace, *Ars Poetica*, 361-3: 'Ut pictura poesis: erit quae, si propius stes, | te capiat magis, et quaedam, si longius abstes. | haec amat obscurum, volet haec sub luce videri' ('A poem is like a picture: one will capture you more if you stand nearer, another if you stand further away; this one loves the shade; this other wants to be seen in the light'.) TE further cites the Soames-Dryden translation of Boileau, *Art of Poetry*, I.177-8 (1683), p. 11: 'Each Object must be fix'd in the due place, | And diff'ring parts have Corresponding Grace'.

178-81. TE suggests that thise analogy is from Quintilian, *Institutio Oratoria*, II.xiii.3.

179. Pow'rs: troops, forces.

   equal Ranks . . . fair Array: conspicuous order, recalling the military metaphors of 64-5, but cf. also 'The Gardens of Alcinous', 17. TE compares Oldham, 'A Letter from the Country to a Friend in Town', 194-5, *Some New Pieces* (1681), p. 128: '. . . the conduct of my words, when they | March in due ranks, are set in just array'.

180   But with th' *Occasion* and the *Place* comply,
       Oft *hide* his Force, nay seem sometimes to *Fly*.
       Those are but *Stratagems* which *Errors* seem,
       Nor is it *Homer Nods*, but *We* that *Dream*.
       Still green with Bays each *ancient* Altar stands,

183, n. MS, *1744–51: Modeste & circumspecto judicio de tantis viris pronunciandum est, ne (quod plerisque accidit) damnent quae [1744–51: quod] non intelligunt. Ac si necesse est in alteram errare partem, omnia eorum legentibus placere, quam multa displicere maluerim.* Quintil.

181. **Oft *hide*:** *1713a–51:* Conceal
    seem sometimes: MS: sometimes seem
182. **are but:** *1713a–51:* oft are
183^4. MS: In *Sacred Writ* where Difficulties rise,
    'Tis safer far to *fear* than *criticize*.
184. *1713a–51:* new paragraph

---

181. **Fly:** flee. Cf. Wesley, *Marlborough* (1705), p. 8, speaking of British troops: 'Press'd by your *Numbers*, did they *seem* to *fly*'.

182. In his manuscript notes Pope tried a different variant: 'Those may be Stratagems – ' (Appendix).

    Stratagems: a stratagem is 'a trick by which some advantage is obtained' (*SJ*, citing this line). The word had been popularised by George Farquhar's successful comedy, *The Beaux Stratagem* (1707). Johnson recorded that Pope '*hardly drank tea without a stratagem*' (Lonsdale, IV.56). Cf. 'Rape of the Locke', I.100; 'Wife of Bath Her Prologue', 163.

182–3. TE cites Roscommon, *Essay on Translated Verse*, 330–1 (1684), p. 21: 'For I mistake, or far the greatest Part | Of what some call *Neglect* was *study'd Art*'.

183. **Homer Nods:** occasional slips or errors in the Homeric epics: Roscommon, *Essay on Translated Verse*, 139–44, offers and retracts the suggestion that Homer sometimes snores as well as nods. In the *Reflections*, p. 15, Hooker, I.407, Dennis objected that Pope's line contradicted its source in Horace's *Ars Poetica*, 359, 'indignor quandoque bonus dormitat Homerus' ('I am offended whenever good Homer gets drowsy'), a line alluded to by Quintilian just before the passage cited by Pope (note to 180 above). Dryden paraphrases chapters 27 and 33 of Longinus on this issue in 'The Authors Apology for Heroique Poetry', *State of Innocence*, sig. b2ʳ: 'I could . . . find out some blemishes in *Homer* . . . but . . . they are little Mistakes, or rather Negligences, which have escap'd his pen in the fervor of his writing; the sublimity of his spirit carries it with me against his carelessness'. Cobb, 'Discourse on Criticism', *Poems* (1707), sig. A6ʳ, also defends Homer's occasional '*Sleepiness*' as trivial and by preferring Homeric rapture to the safety and dullness of rules. Pope experimented with several variants (see Appendix), but left the line unchanged, though the force of 182 was softened.

183 **Pope's note.** Quintilian, *Institutio Oratoria*, X.i.26: 'one must pronounce on such men with modest and circumspect judgment, to avoid what happens to many people, who condemn what they do not understand. But if it is necessary to err on one or other side, I would rather everything [of the classic authors] pleased readers than many things displeased [them]'.

183^4 **MS. Sacred Writ:** the Bible, focus of intense textual scrutiny, some of it from

185 Above the reach of *Sacrilegious* Hands,
Secure from *Flames*, from *Envy's* fiercer Rage,
Destructive *War*, and all-devouring *Age*.
See, from *each Clime* the Learn'd their Incense bring;
Hear, in *all Tongues* Triumphant *Paeans* ring!

---

187. **all devouring:** *1744–51:* all-involving
189. **Triumphant:** *1713a–51:* consenting

---

scholars such as Bentley (see 113–14), some from freethinkers such as Anthony Collins (1676–1729). Dryden's *Religio Laici* (1682) had in part been a response to the questions opened by Richard Simon's work on the text of the Bible. Pope omitted the potentially dangerous reference to the Bible as literature, but retained a holy tinge to the next two lines.

184–91. In the *Reflections*, pp. 3 and 32, Hooker I.399 and 418–19, cited this passage as evidence of Pope's 'servile Deference ... to the Ancients', linking it to 164–6. Pope provided an illustration of a poet bowing at the altars of Homer and Virgil as the engraved headpiece for the *Essay on Criticism* in his *Works*, 1717. TE sees the passage as in the spirit of emulation recommended by Longinus, chapter 11, citing the anonymous 1698 English translation, *An Essay upon Sublime*, p. 33: 'Thus the Majesty of the Old Writers is breath'd from their works, like Celestial blasts from so many *Tripods*, into the Souls of their Imitators. And the very dullest, and most unfit for Inspiration, are transported by a Prophetick Spirit, which is none of their own'. Cf. 'Prologue, Design'd for Mr. D—y's last Play', 9–16.

184. **Bays:** laurel leaves, bound into a wreath to crown successful poets because of its association with Apollo, god of poetry; cf. 'Summer', 10, and 701 and 709 below. Cf. D'Avenant, *Poem, to the Kings Most Sacred Majesty* (1663), p. 3, on poets in general: 'even their *Bays* cannot continue Green'.

Altar: religious reverence due to ancient authors which cannot be destroyed by worldly ('Sacrilegious', 185) forces. Wakefield cites Roscommon, 'Epilogue to *Alexander the Great*: 'Secur'd by higher Pow'rs, exalted stands | Above the reach of Sacrilegious Hands', but we have not located a published text of this earlier than *Poems by the Earl of Roscomon* (1717), p. 140–1.

186–7. Warburton's 1744 note explains this couplet as a composite allusion to 'The destruction of the Alexandrian and Palatine libraries by fire; the fiercer rage of Zoilus and Maevius ... against Wit; the irruption of the Barbarians into the empire; and the long reign of Ignorance and Superstition in the cloisters'. For Zoilus see 466 and for Maevius see 34. Plowden (1983: 61), locates a model in Manilius, *Astronomica*, I.522–3, translated by Creech (1700), p. 22, commenting on the order of the universe: 'It stands secure from *Time*'s devouring Rage, | For 'tis a *God*, nor can it change with Age'.

187. ***all-devouring* Age:** Warburton contends that this means 'the long reign of ignorance and superstition in the cloisters', but Pope seems to mean simply time, as in Ovid, *Metamorphoses*, XV.234: 'tempus edax rerum', 'Time the devourer of [all] things'. Cf. the opening line of Pope's 'To Mr. Addison, Occasioned by his Dialogue on Medals': 'See the wild Waste of all-devouring years'.

187 variant. *all-involving:* phrases similar to this are used throughout Pope's translation of the *Iliad* (e.g. V.594), calling on the Latinate sense of 'rolling in' or enveloping; Dulness also 'involves' the Dunces in this way, *Dunciad* IV.82 and 248.

190	In Praise so just, let ev'ry Voice be join'd,
	And fill the *Gen'ral Chorus* of *Mankind*!
	Hail *Bards Triumphant*! born in *happier* Days;
	Immortal Heirs of *Universal* Praise!
	Whose Honours with Increase of Ages *grow*,
195	As Streams roll down, *enlarging* as they flow!
	Nations *unborn* your mighty Names shall sound,
	And Worlds applaud that must not yet be *found*!
	Oh may some Spark of *your* Coelestial Fire
	The last, the meanest of your Sons inspire,
200	(That with weak Wings, from far, pursues your Flights;
	Glows while he *reads*, but *trembles* as he *writes*)
	To teach vain Wits that Science *little known*,

---

192. MS: Hail happy *Heroes*! born in *better Days*;
200. **with:** *1713a–51:* on
202. **that:** *1713a–51:* a

189–91. TE cites Sheffield, *Essay upon Poetry*, 323–4 (1682), p. 20: 'Nature's whole strength united; endless fame, | And universal shouts attend their name'.

189. Paeans: hymns of praise, derived from the worship of Apollo.

189 variant. consenting: (a) agreeing, in harmony (b) confirming. 'Triumphant' was removed because of its recurrence at 192; Pope noted the repetition in his manuscript notes (see Appendix).

190–1. 'join'd' could be pronounced 'jined' in Pope's day, and hence rhyme with 'mankind'; see the six further instances below: 349–50, 363–4, 525–6, 565–6, 672–3, 690–1 and *Essay on Man*, I.219–20.

192. Wakefield compares Cowley, 'On the Death of Mr. Crashaw', 59–60, *Poems* (1656), p. 30: 'Hail, *Bard Triumphant*! and some care bestow | On us, the *Poets Militant* below!' and Virgil, *Aeneid*, VI.649: 'magnanimi heroes nati melioribus annis' ('Greathearted heroes, born in better days'). *EC* cites Dryden, *Religio Laici*, 80 (1682), p. 6: 'Those Gyant Wits, in happyer Ages born', and Vida, *De Arte Poetica*, II.286: 'Autoresque alii nati felicibus annis' ('And authors born in other, lucky years').

194–5. According to Spence (*OAC*, I.18, item 41), Pope salvaged this couplet from his abandoned juvenile epic, *Alcander, Prince of Rhodes*.

194. Increase of Ages: a sort of compound interest ('Increase') by which critical praise stimulates more of the same.

196–7. Wakefield compares Cowley, *Davideis*, II.833, *Poems* (1656), p. 63: 'Round the whole earth his dreaded name shall sound, | And reach to *Worlds*, that must not yet be *found*'. Cf. also Milton, *Paradise Lost*, IV.663 (1674), p. 104, '...to Nations yet unborn'.

198–9. Wakefield cites Dryden's translation of Virgil, *Aeneid*, VII.52, *Works of Virgil*, p. 401: 'Now, *Erato*, thy Poet's Mind inspire, | And fill his Soul with thy Coelestial Fire'. Womersley (1997: 381) compares Roscommon, *Essay on Translated Verse*, 173–4 (1684), p. 12: 'Hail, mighty *MARO*! may that Sacred Name, | Kindle *my* Breast with *thy caelestial Flame*'.

199. last . . . Sons: Pope himself.

201. trembles: cf. MS variant to 131–2. Pope may recall George Sandys, *Ovid's Metamorphosis English'd*, IX (1632), p. 312: 'then fits her trembling hands to write'.

202. Science: cf. 60.

> T' *admire* Superior Sense, and *doubt* their own!
> OF all the Causes which conspire to blind
205 Man's erring Judgment, and misguide the Mind,
> What the weak Head with strongest Byass rules,
> Is *Pride*, the *never-failing Vice of Fools*.
> Whatever Nature has in *Worth* deny'd,
> She gives in large Recruits of *needful Pride*;
210 For as in *Bodies*, thus in *Souls*, we find
> What wants in *Blood* and *Spirits*, swell'd with *Wind*;
> Pride, where Wit fails, steps in to our Defence,
> And fills up all the *mighty Void* of *Sense*!
> If once right Reason drives *that Cloud* away,

204–5. Jones (2005: 271–2), finds an influence in Philemon Holland's 1603 translation of Plutarch's *Moralia* ('Of Moral Vertue', p. 75): 'as touching judgement, some erre more, some lesse'.

204. conspire to blind: cf. 342.

206. Byass: in the game of bowls, the weighted side of the bowl which causes it to roll along a curved line. Cf. Dryden, *Mac Flecknoe*, 189–90, *Miscellany Poems* (1684), p. 10: 'This is that boasted Byas of thy mind, | By which one way, to dullness, 'tis inclin'd'. Pope had commented on Wycherley's use of a similar image in his poem on Dulness in a letter of 20 November 1707 (*Corr.*, I.31).

207. Pride was the great crime of Satan in Milton's *Paradise Lost*, and would be the great human fault according to Pope's *Essay on Man*, I.123: 'In Pride, in reas'ning Pride, our error lies'.

208–9. EC cites Oldham's translation of Ovid, *Amores*, II.x, 33–4, *Poems, and Translations* (1683), p. 112: 'What Nature has in Bulk to me denied, | In Sinews and in vigor is supplied'. *TE* adds Temple, 'Upon the Ancient and Modern Learning', *Miscellanea. . . . The Second Part*, p. 55: Man's 'Pride is greater than his Ignorance, and what he wants in Knowledge he supplies by Sufficiency'. Walls (2008) glosses, 'where folly is innate (and, perhaps, incorrigible), pride is inevitable', and finds a source for the image in the *Moriae Encomium* of Erasmus (see 696 below), citing the translation (by White Kennett), *Witt against Wisdom, or, A Panegyrick upon Folly* (1683), p. 28: 'And O the incomparable contrivance of Nature, who has ordered all things in so even a method, that where ever she has been less bountiful in her gifts, there she makes it up with a larger dose of self-love'.

209. Recruits: 'supply of any thing wasted' (*SJ*); Johnson reproves Pope for using it 'less properly' here to mean 'a substitute to something wanting'.

210–11. Bodies . . . Wind: an analogy from physiology (cf. 76–7); Pope is alluding to the mind-body analogy explored ironically by Swift in *The Mechanical Operation of the Spirit* (1704), with a comic suggestion of flatulence.

212–13. TE compares Roscommon, *Essay on Translated Verse*, 161–2 (1684), p. 11: '*Pride* (of all others the most *dangerous* Fau't) | Proceeds from *Ignorance*, and want of *Thought*'. Pope's image was remade satirically in *The Dunciad* (1728), I.19–20: 'Keen, hollow winds howl thro' the bleak recess, | Emblem of music caus'd by emptiness'.

214. right Reason: a phrase used in a quasi-technical sense by moral philosophers of the seventeenth century, corresponding to the *orthos logos* of Aristotelian ethics, and more loosely by Dryden, 'Discourse Concerning . . . Satire', *Satires of Juvenal*, p. ii: 'Good

215   *Truth* breaks upon us with *resistless Day*;
Trust not your self; but your Defects to know,
Make use of ev'ry *Friend* — and ev'ry *Foe*.
A *little Learning* is a dang'rous Thing;
Drink deep, or taste not the *Pierian* Spring:
220   There *shallow Draughts* intoxicate the Brain,
And drinking *largely* sobers us again.
Fir'd with the Charms fair *Science* does impart,
In *fearless Youth* we tempt the Heights of Art;
While from the bounded *Level* of our Mind,

---

222. *1717–51:* Fir'd at first sight with what the Muse imparts,
223. Art;: *1717–51:* Arts,

Nature, by which I mean Beneficence and Candor, is the Product of right Reason'; cf. pp. xxxiii and xliv, and 'Of the Pythagorean Philosophy', 221. The phrase is used at least five times in Dennis, *Remarks upon a Book entitled Prince Arthur* (1696). Cf. Milton, *Paradise Lost*, XII.83–5 (1674), p. 316: 'true Libertie | Is lost, which alwayes with right Reason dwells | Twinn'd'; and Pope's own use of the phrase in 'The Wife of Bath Her Prologue, from Chaucer', 193, and footnote to *Odyssey*, XIX.247, quoting Plutarch on Ulysses, who had 'completely subjected all his faculties to right reason'.

215. resistless: irresistible; cf. 'Messiah', 98; 'The First Book of Statius his Thebais', 270.

217. Foe: *TE* compares the Soames–Dryden translation of Boileau, *Art of Poetry*, I.186–8 (1683), p. 12: 'But find You faithful Friends that will reprove, | That on your Works may look with careful Eyes, | And of your Faults be zealous Enemies.' In his letter to Trumbull, 10 August 1711 (Sherburn 1958b: 397), he asks to be shown where Dennis 'has hitt any blotts in my Essay? that I make my profit ev'n of an Enemy, thro' the assistance of so good a Friend'.

218. *TE* compares Pope's 'Thoughts on Various Subjects', V, *PW*, II.151: 'Learning is like Mercury, one of the most powerful and excellent things in the world in skilful hands; in unskilful, the most mischievous'.

219. Pierian: of Pieria, a district of Macedonia in Greece, near Mount Olympus; the Muses were worshipped here, and hence the Pierian Spring is a fount of poetic wisdom. Southall (1988) cites Drayton, 'To my most dearly-loved friend Henry Reynolds', in *The Battaile of Agincourt* (1631), p. 293: Ben Jonson 'had drunke deepe of the *Pierian* spring'. Cf. George Chapman's continuation of Marlowe's *Hero and Leander*, III.189–91 (1598), sig. F4^v–G1^r: 'Of his free soule, whose liuing subject stood | Vp to the chin in the Pierian flood, | And drunk to me halfe this Musaean story'; and Samuel Sheppard, 'Third Pastoral', in *Epigrams* (1651), p. 250: 'He that his worth would truely sing, | Must quaffe the whole *Pierian* spring'. Cf. the allegory of drinking from the spring of Helicon in Swift's *Battle of the Books*, Walsh (2010), p. 162.

220. shallow Draughts: light drinking, as opposed to drinking '*largely*', or heavily. *TE* compares Bacon, 'Of Atheism', no. XVI of *The Essays* (1625), p. 90: 'a little Philosophy inclineth Mans Mind to *Atheisme*; but depth in Philosophy, bringeth Mens Mindes about to *Religion*'.

223. fearless Youth: Wakefield compares Virgil, *Georgics*, IV.565, 'audax iuventa', 'bold youth'.

    tempt: attempt. Wakefield compares Dryden, *The State of Innocence*, I.i. (1678), p. 5: 'Nor need we tempt those heights which Angels keep'.

225 *Short Views* we take, nor see the *Lengths behind*,
But *more advanc'd*, survey with strange Surprize
New, distant Scenes of *endless* Science rise!
So pleas'd at first, the towring *Alps* we try,
Mount o'er the Vales, and seem to tread the Sky;
230 Th' Eternal Snows appear already past,

228, n. 1736a–43, 1751: So pleas'd at first the tow'ring Alps *to try,*
 Fill'd with ideas of fair Italy,
 The traveller beholds with chearful eyes
 The less'ning vales, and seems to tread the skies.

226. **survey:** *1713a–51:* behold
227^8. MS: Much we begin to *doubt*, and much to *fear*;
 Our Sight *less trusting*, as we see *more clear*.
228. **we:** MS: to
229^30. MS: Fill'd with Ideas of fair Italy,
 The Traveller beholds, with chearful eyes,
 The less'ning Vales, and seems to tread the Skies;

---

225. Short Views: the phrase occurs in a number of aggressive critical writings of the late seventeenth century, e.g. Rymer, *A Short View of Tragedy* (1692), and Collier, *A Short View of the Immorality and Profaneness of the English Stage* (1698). Cf. 290.
 Lengths: distances requiring to be travelled.
226. survey: in his manuscript notes (see Appendix) Pope suggested the change to 'behold' because 'survey' was used soon after (at 232, then 238).
228-35. towring Alps: cf. 'Autumn', 59–60. Pope's simile, partially reprised in *The Temple of Fame*, 53–60 (and cf. 'Eloisa to Abelard', 290), was cited by Johnson as 'the best that English poetry can show – that in which the most exact resemblance is traced between things in appearance utterly unrelated to each other' (Lonsdale, IV.68-9). Wakefield derived it from a passage in William Drummond, 'An Hymn of the Fairest Faire', *Flowres of Sion* (1623), p. 33, in which a pilgrim imagines he is near his journey's end 'Till mounting some tall Mountaine hee doe finde, | More hights before him than hee left behinde'. *TE* suggests an origin in the passage describing Hannibal's crossing of the Alps in Silius Italicus, *Punica*, III.528-35, translated in Addison's *Remarks on Several Part of Italy* (1705), pp. 427: 'From Steep to Steep the Troops advanc'd with Pain, | In hopes at last the topmost Cliff to gain; | But still by new Ascents the Mountain grew, | And a fresh Toil presented to their View.' Gay's commendatory poem 'To the Learned Ingenious Author', in Coward's *Licentia Poetica Discuss'd* (1709), sig. C2^r, had given an extended simile in which Coward's rules led the aspiring poet smoothly to the summit of Parnassus, and Pope may be countering such facile optimism here.
228 Pope's note and 229^30 MS. Mack (1982: 335) suggests that Pope compressed the phrase because 'fair Italy' suggested the world of renaissance or baroque art rather than the classic ground of Latin literature, and that it fitted better in its eventual home, the 'Epistle to Jervas', 25–6.
229. A monosyllabic line; see 350.
230. Eternal Snows: the snow in the high mountain ranges, which does not melt.

And the first *Clouds* and *Mountains* seem the last:
But *those attain'd*, we tremble to survey
The growing Labours of the lengthen'd Way,
Th' *increasing* Prospect *tires* our wandring Eyes,
235   Hills peep o'er Hills, and *Alps* on *Alps* arise!
     A perfect Judge will *read* each Work of Wit
With the same Spirit that its Author *writ*,
Survey the *Whole*, nor seek slight Faults to find;
Where *Nature moves*, and *Rapture warms* the Mind;
240   Nor lose, for that malignant dull Delight,
The *gen'rous Pleasure* to be charm'd with Wit.

236.] Diligenter legendum est, ac poene ad scribendi sollicitudinem: Nec per partes modo scrutanda sunt omnia, sed perlectus liber utique ex Integro resumendus. Quintilian.

---

232. **we tremble:** MS: he trembles
234. **our:** MS: his
237. **Spirit that:** MS: Taste with which

---

234. **Prospect:** see Commentary to 159–61.
235. For the phrasing cf. 'The Gardens of Alcinous', 14.
236. **Pope's note.** Quintilian, *Institutio Oratoria*, X.i.20: 'It is necessary to read thoroughly, with almost as much care as in writing, and to examine everything, not just part by part; once we have read it through we must take up a book again from the beginning'. The proposition had been reduced to absurdity in the 'Preface' to Swift's *Tale of a Tub* (1704), p. 18: 'Whatever Reader desires to have a thorow Comprehension of an Author's Thoughts, cannot take a better Method, than by putting himself into the Circumstances and Posture of Life, that the Writer was in, upon every important Passage as it flowed from his Pen', with a list of the material features of the tract's composition (garret, hunger, illness, poverty) to facilitate identification with the author.
238. TE cites Dryden's 'Preface' to *Sylvae*, sig. a4ᵛ: 'True judgment in Poetry, like that in Painting, takes a view of the whole together, whether it be good or not; and where the beauties are more than the Faults, concludes for the Poet against the little Judge'. Osborn notes that Pope discussed this issue with Spence in 1730 and inserted a similar idea in the revised 'Preface' to his *Works* of 1736 (*OAC*, I.169).
239. **Rapture:** 'uncommon heat of imagination' (*SJ*), and a key term of praise in Pope's 'Preface' to *The Iliad* (*PW*, I.221–56). Cf. also 391 below; Pope's comment on Wycherley in 'Autumn', 10.
240. **Nor lose:** The sense is still governed by the 'will' of 236.
   malignant dull Delight: the seeking of slight faults (238). Variants on the phrase 'dull delight' occur widely, e.g. Oldham, 'Upon the Works of Ben. Iohnson', 115, *Poems, and Translations* (1683), p. 76: 'The gaping Rabbles dull delight'.
240–1. The Delight/Wit rhyme appears to be rare.
241. **gen'rous:** cf. 100.

But in such Lays as neither *ebb*, nor *flow*,
Correctly cold, and *regularly low*,
That Shunning Faults, one quiet *Tenour* keep;
245 We cannot *blame* indeed—but we may *sleep*.
In Wit, as Nature, what affects our Hearts
Is not th' Exactness of peculiar Parts;
'Tis not a *Lip*, or *Eye*, we Beauty call,
But the joint Force and full *Result* of *all*.
250 Thus when we view some well-proportion'd Dome,

242-5. For Horace on the negative effects of playing safe see *Ars Poetica*, 265-8; also Longinus, 'On the Sublime', section 33. *EC* compares the Soames–Dryden translation of Boileau, *Art of Poetry*, I.71-2 (1683), p. 5: 'A frozen Stile, that neither Ebs or Flows, | Instead of pleasing, makes us gape and doze'. *TE* cites *A New Session of the Poets* (1700), p. 6, aimed at Blackmore: 'In which thy Rhymes a constant Cadence keep, | At once they make us smile, and make us sleep'. Cf. Dryden, 'A Parallel, Of Painting and Poetry', *De Arte Graphica*, pp. liv–lv: 'A work may be over-wrought as well as under-wrought: too much Labour often takes away the Spirit by adding to the polishing, so that there remains nothing but a dull correctness, a piece without any considerable Faults, but with few Beauties'. Cf. Walsh to Pope, 9 September 1706 (*Corr.*, I.21): 'a Man may correct his Verses till he takes away the true Spirit of them; especially if he submits to the correction of some who pass for great Critics, by mechanical Rules, and never enter into the true Design and Genius of an Author'.

243. **Correctly cold:** *TE* cites an anonymous elegy on Oldham, from *Sylvae* (1685), p. 472: 'But sweated not to be correctly dull'.

244. **Tenour:** (a) constant mode; (b) general sense or argument.

247. **peculiar:** particular.

248-9. Cf. 173-6 above. *TE* cites, among many possible analogues, Denham's 'Out of an Epigram of Martial', 8, *Poems and Translations* (1668), p. 80: ''Tis not Cheeks, nor Lips nor Eyes, | That I prize' and Christopher Codrington's prefatory poem to Garth's *Dispensary*, sixth edition (1706), sig. A4^v: 'I wou'd a Poet, like a Mistress, try, | Not by her Hair, her Hand, her Nose, her Eye; | But by some Nameless Pow'r, to give me Joy.' In *Of Dramatick Poesie*, pp. 18-19, Dryden criticises those dramatic 'Imitations of Nature' which are 'so narrow as if they had imitated onely an Eye or an Hand, and did not dare to venture on the lines of a Face, or the Proportion of a Body'. Lansdowne's 'An Essay Upon Unnatural Flights in Poetry', *New Miscellany*, p. 311, opens: 'As when some Image, of a charming Face, | In living Paint, An Artist tries to trace...'. Cf. the human body as the proper measure of perspective, *The Dunciad*, IV.233-8.

250-5. Pope's 'reasoning of the eye' in relation to architectural proportions is recorded by Spence (*OAC*, I.235, items 557-8).

250. **Dome:** cf. 'Rape of the Locke', II.139; and *Windsor-Forest* 322, where Pope perhaps uses 'dome' to indicate 'church', as in the Italian, 'duomo'. Here, the classical architecture of ancient Rome and neo-classical imitations; the actual 'Dome' is probably St Peter's. *TE* cites Addison's views of such architecture in *Remarks on Several Parts of Italy* (1705), pp. 174-5: 'The Proportions are so very well observ'd, that nothing appears to an Advantage, or distinguishes it self above the rest. It seems neither extreamly high, nor long, nor broad, because it is all of 'em in a just Equality'.

(The *World's* just Wonder, and ev'n *thine* O *Rome*!)
No single Parts unequally surprize;
All comes *united* to th' admiring Eyes;
No monstrous Height, or Breadth, or Length appear;
255 The *Whole* at once is *Bold*, and *Regular*.
   Whoever thinks a faultless Piece to see,
Thinks what ne'er was, nor is, nor e'er shall be.
In ev'ry Work regard the *Writer's End*,
Since none can compass more than they *Intend*;

---

254. **or . . . or:** MS: nor . . . nor
259. **oft the:** *1717–51:* sometimes

---

251. just Wonder: cf. 101.
254. monstrous: out of the order of regularity or nature; cf. 174. Horace's *Ars Poetica* opens by denouncing a series of absurd and 'unnatural' images possible in art and poetry; Lansdowne condemns the 'monstrous Births' of unfettered imagination in 'An Essay Upon Unnatural Flights in Poetry', *New Miscellany*, p. 312.
255. **Bold,** *and* **Regular:** combining observance of the rules with imaginative licence and imagination, 'bold' in *OED* sense 7, 'showing daring, vigour, or licence of conception, or expression; vigorous, striking'. TE cites Wycherley, 'To Mr. Pope, on his Pastorals', 19, *Poetical Miscellanies: The Sixth Part* (1709), p. 254: 'Your Strains are Regularly Bold'. Cf. also Rymer's translation of Rapin, *Reflections on Aristotle's Treatise of Poetry* (1674), p. 50, commending 'those wise and judicious boldnesses that Poesie demands'. Cf. also 'To a Young Lady, with the Works of Voiture', 26.
256–7. TE notes that Sheffield had rejected the 'vulgar error' of aiming at perfect characters on stage in *Essay upon Poetry*, 232–5 (1682), p. 15: 'There's no such thing in Nature, and you'l draw | A faultless Monster which the world ne're saw'. TE also cites the English translation of La Bruyère, *The Characters, or the Manners of the Age*, third edition (1702),

p. 13: 'What a prodigious difference is there between a fine Piece, and one that's Regular and Perfect! I question whether there is any of the last kind, it being less difficult for a rare Genius to hit upon the Great and Sublime, than to avoid all Errors'. Cf. Cobb, 'Discourse on Criticism', *Poems* (1707), sig. A4ᵛ: 'Nothing is perfect in every Part. He that expects to see any thing so, must have patience till *Dooms-day*'; and Pope's 'Preface' to his *Works* (1717): 'Every one acknowledges, it would be a wild notion to expect perfection in any work of man' (*PW*, I.289).
257. Wakefield cites Dryden's 'Of the Pythagorean Philosophy', 654, *Fables*, p. 527: 'Greater than what e'er was, or is, or e'er shall be'. The sequence also recalls the doxology at the end of each psalm in the liturgy as defined (in Britain) by the *Book of Common Prayer* (1708): 'as it was in the beginning, is now, and ever shall be'; and also Milton, *Paradise Lost*, IV.24–6 (1674), p. 86: 'the bitter memorie | Of what he was, what is, and what must be | Worse'.
258. **End:** intention, cf. 73. TE compares Pope's 'Postscript' to his translation of *The Odyssey*, *PW*, II.51: 'the first principle of Criticism . . . is to consider the nature of the piece, and the intent of its author'.
259. compass: 'to obtain; to procure; to attain; to have in the power' (*SJ*, citing this line).

260 　　And if the *Means* be just, the *Conduct* true,
　　　　Applause, in spite of trivial Faults, is due.
　　　　As Men of Breeding, oft the Men of Wit,
　　　　T' avoid *great Errors*, must the *less* commit,
　　　　Neglect the Rules each *Verbal Critick* lays,
265 　　For *not* to know some Trifles, is a Praise.
　　　　Most Criticks, fond of some subservient Art,
　　　　Still make the *Whole* depend upon a *Part*,
　　　　They talk of *Principles*, but Parts they prize,
　　　　And All to one lov'd Folly Sacrifice.
270 　　　　Once on a time, *La Mancha*'s Knight, they say,
　　　　A certain *Bard* encountring on the Way,

---

268. **Parts they:** *1717–51:* notions

260–1. EC cites Horace, *Ars Poetica*, 351–2: 'verum ubi plura nitent in carmine, non ego paucis | offendar maculis' ('where in truth many things shine in a poem, I would not myself be offended at small blemishes'), quoted by Dryden in his 'Dedication' of the *Aeneid*, *Works of Virgil*, sig. c1ᵛ. TE compares Dryden, 'The Authors Apology for Heroique Poetry', *State of Innocence*, sig. b1ᵛ: 'If the Design, the Conduct, the Thoughts, and the Expressions of a POEM, be generally such as proceed from a true Genius of Poetry, the Critique ought to pass his judgment in favor of the Author'.

260. **Means ... Conduct:** mode of expression and handling of the idea and material.

262–3. TE compares Horace, *Ars Poetica*, 31: 'in vitium ducit culpae fuga, si caret arte' ('running away from fault leads into worse imperfection, if there is a lack of art').

262–5. To adhere scrupulously to the rules of the '*Verbal Critick*' would diminish spirit. *OED* cites Pope's line 264 as the earliest example of 'verbal critic', defined as 'interested in, attending to, the mere words of a literary composition'. TE compares Rymer's Preface to his translation of Rapin's *Reflections on Aristotle's Treatise of Poesie* (1674), sig. a8ᵛ–b1ʳ: 'What has been noted, rather concerns the Niceties of *Poetry*, than any the little trifles of *Grammar*'; Wakefield refers to Quintilian, *Institutio Oratoria*, I.viii.21: 'Ex quo mihi inter virtutes grammatici habebitur, aliqua nescire' ('On which account I shall esteem it one excellence of a grammarian, to be ignorant of some things'). Pope's hostility to minutely focused textual scholarship (cf. 113–14) continued through his career (e.g. *Dunciad*, IV.203–38) and occasioned David Mallet's *Of Verbal Criticism: An Epistle to Mr. Pope* (1733). Erasmus (below, 696) was Pope model of humane scholarship (*OAC*, I.242).

270. **La Mancha's Knight:** the hero of Miguel de Cervantes's influential novel, *Don Quixote de la Mancha* (1605–15), most recently translated into English (1700–12) by Peter Anthony Motteux; Pope's library contained the first four volumes of this (Mack 1982: 400–1). The story summarised here is from *A Continuation of the Comical History of the most Ingenious Knight, Don Quixote De la Mancha*, by 'Don Alonzo Fernandez de Avellaneda', translated by Captain John Stevens (1705), pp. 164–6 (book III, chapter x). The passage was reprinted in Warton's edition and Appendix C of *TE*, I.484–6. See also Pope's *Critical Specimen* (*PW*, I.5), where the '*false* Cervantes' is mentioned.

271. **Bard:** deliberately archaic or poetic term for 'poet', used in 192 as a straightforward term of praise, but here mocking the egocentricity of the poet in question.

Discours'd in Terms as just, with Looks as Sage,
As e'er cou'd *D——s*, of the Laws o' th' Stage;
Concluding all were desp'rate Sots and Fools,
275   That durst depart from *Aristotle*'s Rules.
Our Author, happy in a Judge so nice,
Produc'd his Play, and beg'd the Knight's Advice,
Made him observe the *Subject* and the *Plot*,
The *Manners, Passions, Unities*, what not?
280   All which, exact to *Rule* were brought about,
Were but a *Combate in the Lists* left out.
What! Leave the Combate out? Exclaims the Knight;
Yes, or we must renounce the *Stagyrite*.
Not so by Heav'n (he answers in a Rage)
285   *Knights, Squires, and Steeds, must enter on the Stage.*
The Stage can ne'er so vast a Throng contain.
Then build a New, or act it in a Plain.

---

273. D—— s: 1717–51: Dennis
the Laws o' th' Stage: *1727–32:* th' *Athenian* stage; *1744–51:* the Grecian stage
272. **That:** *1736a–51:* Who
286. 1744–51: So vast a throng the stage can ne'er contain.
287^8. MS: *In all besides let* Aristotle *sway,*
       But Knighthood's Sacred, and he must give way.

---

273. D—s: Dennis, as the name was spelled out from 1717 onwards. Pope had included 'Great *D—s*', roaring 'like ox at slaughter', in doggerel written to Cromwell in July 1707; *Corr.*, I.27. Pope refers to Dennis's critical essays, especially *The Grounds of Criticism in Poetry* (1704), but exaggerates the extent to which Dennis was unthinkingly committed to the neo-Aristotelian 'Laws'. The change to 'Grecian stage' reflects Dennis's repeated admiration for 'the Virtue and Greatness of the Ancient Tragedy'; *Grounds of Criticism in Poetry*, sig. A7^r, Hooker, I. 332–4.
274. Sots: idiots.
275. Aristotle's Rules: see 88.
276. nice: 'accurate in judgment to a minute exactness' (*SJ*, citing this line).
278–9. Aspects of drama treated in Aristotle's *Poetics* or in the neoclassical commentaries derived from it.

279. Manners: behaviour of the characters, likeness to human nature.
Passions: emotions represented in the characters.
Unities: The limitations of time, place, and action, confining action to one location and a realistic natural time scheme, were a controversial aspect of neoclassical dramatic theory, partly because Shakespeare ignored them. Aristotle's *Poetics* does not specify rules about the 'unities'; Pope would have known Dryden's sceptical discussion of the issue in *Of Dramatick Poesie*, and cf. 'To a Young Lady, with the Works of Voiture', 28.
281. Combate in the Lists: a large-scale jousting tournament of the kind dear to the chivalric Quixote, hence overbalancing his devotion to neoclassical principles.
283. Stagyrite: Aristotle; see 139.

238 AN ESSAY ON CRITICISM (1711)

> Thus Criticks, of less *Judgment* than *Caprice*,
> *Curious*, not *Knowing*, not *exact*, but *nice*,
290 Form *short Ideas*; and offend in *Arts*
> (As most in *Manners*) by a *Love to Parts*.
> Some to *Conceit* alone their Taste confine,
> And glitt'ring Thoughts struck out at ev'ry Line;
> Pleas'd with a Work where nothing's just or fit;
295 One *glaring Chaos* and *wild Heap of Wit*:
> Poets like Painters, thus, unskill'd to trace

289, *n*. MS: *Est & alter, non quidem Doctus, sed Curiosus, qui plus docet quam scit.* Petronius.

292. *1713b–16, 1727–51:* new paragraph

---

288. Caprice: 'Freak; fancy; whim; sudden change of humour' (*SJ*, citing this line).

289. Curious: inquisitive, contrasted with 'knowing' or knowledgeable; the capricious critic follows a line of enquiry but never establishes real knowledge.

  ***not* exact, *but* nice:** contrasting real acumen with over-delicate concentration on minor particulars ('nice'). Southall (1988) suggests the Latin word 'nescius', 'not knowing', from which 'nice' derives, is in play here.

289 Pope's note. Petronius, *Satyricon*, 46: 'there's another boy, not indeed learned, but inquisitive, who teaches more than he knows'.

290. short Ideas: cf. the '*Short Views*' of 225.

292. Conceit: *SJ* cites this line to define 'conceit' as 'sentiment, as distinguished from imagery'; but the word usually suggests a strained, extended metaphor, like those denigrated by critics in 'metaphysical' poets such as Cowley; see Dryden's 'Preface' to *Fables*, sig. B2ʳ, and Pope's letter to Walsh, 2 July 1706 (*Corr.*, I.19): '*Conceit* is to Nature what *Paint* is to Beauty; it is not only needless, but impairs what it wou'd improve'; Walsh's reply of 9 September 1706 (*Corr.*, I.21), cautions against 'being fond of *Similies*, *Conceits*, and what they call saying *Fine Things*'. Pope annotated a line in Rochester's *Poems* (1696) with the phrase 'Indecent poor conceit' (Mack 1982: 438).

293. glitt'ring Thoughts: superficially attractive ideas. Pope described the verse of Richard Crashaw (c. 1612–49) as consisting of 'only pretty conceptions, fine metaphors, glitt'ring expressions'; to Cromwell, 17 December 1710 (*Corr.*, I.110). *TE* compares Addison, 'An Account of the Greatest English Poets', 36–7, *Annual Miscellany: For the Year 1694*, p. 320: 'One glitt'ring Thought no sooner strikes our Eyes | With silent wonder, but new wonders rise'.

295. glaring Chaos: cosmic 'Chaos' is most familiar from book II of Milton's *Paradise Lost*; but see also 'Rape of the Locke', II.37; *Windsor-Forest*, 13; and *The Dunciad* (1728), I.43.

296–9. It is harder to imitate 'naked Nature and the living Grace' than in is to paint inanimate objects such as costumes and jewellery; poets 'hide with ornaments' (stylistic features) their inability to reproduce nature. For 'Grace' see 156 and Commentary. Dennis objected to these lines as both tautologous and nonsensical; *Reflections*, p. 13, Hooker, I.405–6. *TE* cites Dryden's 'A Parallel, of Poetry and Painting', p. xlviii: 'Thus in *Poetry*, the *Expression* is that which charms the *Reader*, and beautifies the Design, which is onely the *Out-lines* of the Fables.... If [the design] be vicious ... the cost of *Colouring* is thrown away upon it. 'Tis an ugly woman in a rich

>   The *naked Nature* and the *living Grace*,
>   With *Gold* and *Jewels* cover ev'ry Part,
>   And hide with *Ornaments* their *Want of Art.*
> 300 *True Wit* is *Nature* to Advantage drest,
>   What oft was *Thought*, but ne'er before *Exprest*,
>   *Something*, whose Truth convinc'd at Sight we find,
>   That gives us back the Image of our Mind:

300.] *Naturam intueamur, hanc sequamur; Id facillimè accipiunt animi quod agnoscunt.* Quintil. lib. 8. c. 3.

---

301. before: *1713a–51:* so well
303^4. MS: *Justly* to *think*; and *readily express*;
   A *full Conception*; and *brought forth* with *Ease.*

Habit set out with Jewels'. TE also cites Cowley, 'Of Wit', st. 5, *Poems* (1656), p. 3: 'Yet 'tis not to adorn, and gild each part; | That shows more *Cost*, then *Art*. | *Jewels* at *Nose* and *Lips* but ill appear; | Rather than *all things Wit*, let *none* be there.'

300-1. In his 'Apology for Heroique Poetry', *State of Innocence*, sig. c2ᵛ, Dryden offers 'the definition of Wit ... is only this: That it is a propriety of Thoughts and Words; or ... Thoughts and Words elegantly adapted to the Subject'. Cf. Pope to Wycherley, 26 December 1704 (*Corr*, I.2): 'True Wit I believe, may be defin'd a Justness of Thought, and a Facility of Expression; or (in the Midwives phrase) a perfect Conception, with an easy Delivery'; cf. the variant to 303. Also Pope to Walsh, 2 July 1706 (*Corr.*, I.19): 'it seems not so much the Perfection of Sense, to say things that have *never* been said before, as to express those *best* that have been said *oftenest*'. TE further cites Walsh to Pope, September 1706 (*Corr.*, I.22): 'As for what you say of Expression: 'tis indeed the same thing to Wit, as Dress is to Beauty'. Addison, praising Pope's poem in *The Spectator*, no. 253, 20 December 1711, alludes to Boileau's 'Preface' to his *Works*, suggesting 'that Wit and fine Writing doth not consist so much in advancing things that are new, as in giving things that are known an agreeable Turn';

EC quotes the passage from *Oeuvres Diverses* (1701), where Boileau defines 'une pensée neuve, brillante, extraordinaire' ('a new, brilliant and extraordinary thought') as: 'une pensée qui a dû venir à tout le monde, & que quelqu'un s'avise le premier d'exprimer. ... une chose qui chacun pensoit, & qu'il la dit d'une manière vive, fine & nouvelle' ('a thought which must have come to everyone, and someone decides to express for the first time ... a thing which everyone thinks, and which he says in a lively, subtle and new manner').

300 Pope's note. Quintilian, *Institutio Oratoria*, VIII.iii.71: 'let us contemplate nature and let us follow her; minds accept most easily the things which they recognise'. Pope omits a half-sentence on eloquence from the passage.

302-3. TE sees this as a Platonic or 'ideal' tenet, citing the anonymous translation of de Piles, *Art of Painting* (1706), p. 1: 'the Painter must regard *Visible Nature* as his object. He must have an Image of her in his Mind, not only as he happens to see her in particular Subjects, but as she ought to be in her self'.

303^4 MS. Conception ... Ease: suggesting pregnancy and labour, a common metaphor for literary creation; cf. the letter cited above, Commentary to 300–1.

As Shades more sweetly recommend the Light,
305 So modest Plainness sets off sprightly Wit:
For *Works* may have more *Wit* than does 'em good,
As *Bodies* perish through Excess of *Blood*.
Others for *Language* all their Care express,
And value *Books*, as Women *Men*, for *Dress*:
310 Their Praise is still— *The Stile is excellent*:
The *Sense*, they humbly take upon Content.
Words are like *Leaves*; and where they most abound,
Much *Fruit* of *Sense* beneath is rarely found.
False Eloquence, like the *Prismatic Glass*,
315 Its gawdy Colours spreads on *ev'ry place*;
The Face of Nature we no more Survey,
All glares *alike*, without *Distinction* gay:

312, n. MS: *Est etiam in quibusdam Turba inanium verborum, qui dum comnmunem loquendi morem reformidant, ducti specie nitoris, circumeunt omnia copiosa Loquacitate.* Quintilian.

---

304. Shades: shadows or shading in art; 'recommend' in the sense of emphasising the virtues of.

305. Cf. Roscommon, *Essay on Translated Verse* (1685 version), p. 15: 'For truth shines brightest through the plainest dress'.

306-7. Cf. 76-7 and 210-11. Wakefield compares Shakespeare, *Hamlet*, IV.vii.117-18: 'for goodness, growing to a plurisy, | Dies in his own too-much'. Pope is probably thinking of a physiology of 'humours' in which the body was thought to be composed of four kinds of chemical in balance, any of which could predominate and cause disease. Boyer reported of Wycherley's play *The Plain-Dealer* (1677): 'The only Fault that has been found it it, is its being too full of *Wit*'; *Letters of Wit, Politicks, and Morality* (1701), p. 217. Pope may once more have been thinking of the problems of excess encountered during the revision of Wycherley's poems; cf. his note to 'Autumn', 7.

309. Mack (1977-8) suggests a personal slant to this idea, prompted by Pope's difficulties with women.

311. Sense: meaning, moral content.

take upon Content: take the meaning as a given, without question.

312 Pope's note. Quintilian, *Institutio Oratoria*, VIII.ii.17: 'In some writers there is a crowd of empty words; these writers, while they dread the common way of speaking, are misled by an appearance of brilliance and wrap everything up in copious long-windedness'. *TE* cites a further passage from *Institutio Oratoria*, VIII.23 and Horace, *Ars Poetica*, 60-2, likening words to leaves, which die and are replaced by new.

314. Prismatic Glass: as used by Newton in the famous optical experiment to split light into the 'gawdy Colours' (315) of the visible spectrum. See Nicolson and Rousseau (1968: 269-70) for Pope's possible acquaintance with Newton's *Opticks* (1704). The pure light of intelligence (cf. 13, and the 'unchanging Sun' of 318) is broken up by 'false eloquence' into meaningless variations. Pope deployed similar imagery for the false 'fools-colours' of Dulness; *The Dunciad* (1728), I.67-72.

317. glares: to glare is 'to shine ostentatiously, or with too much laboured lustre' (*SJ*); cf. 'To a Young Lady, with the Works of Voiture', 53.

gay: lively, bright, entertaining, perhaps with the sense of 'showy' (*SJ*); cf. *ibid.*, 1, and 'The Wife of Bath Her Prologue, from Chaucer', 75.

But true *Expression*, like th' unchanging *Sun*, ⎫
Clears, and *improves* whate'er it shines upon, ⎬
320   It *gilds* all Objects, but it *alters* none.   ⎭
Expression is the *Dress* of *Thought*, and still
Appears more *decent* as more *suitable*;
A vile Conceit in pompous Style exprest,
Is like a Clown in regal Purple drest;
325   For diff'rent *Styles* with diff'rent *Subjects* sort,
As several Garbs with Country, Town, and Court.
Some by *Old Words* to Fame have made Pretence;

327.] Abolita & abrogata retinere, insolentiae cujusdam est, & frivolae in parvis jactantiae. Quintil. lib. I. c. 6.
Opus est ut Verba a vetustate repetita neque crebra sint, neque manifesta, quia nil est odiosius affectatione, nec utique ab ultimis repetita temporibus. Oratio, cujus summa virtus est perspicuitas, quam sit vitiosa si egeat interprete? Ergo ut novorum optima erunt maximè vetera, ita veterum maximè nova. Idem.

---

323. **Style:** *1713a–51:* Words
327. 1727–32: new paragraph

318–19. Dennis, *Reflections*, p. 13, Hooker, I.406, detected this as stolen from Sheffield's *Essay on Poetry*, 12 (1682), p. 2: 'True Wit is everlasting, like the Sun'.
319. Clears: clarifies.
320. gilds: covers with gold.
321. Dress *of* Thought: continuing the metaphor of 297–8. *EC* compares Dryden, 'Preface' to *All for Love* (1678), sig. B1ᵛ: 'expressions ... are a modest cloathing of our thoughts, as Breeches and Petticoats are of our Bodies'. *TE* adds Dryden's 'A Parallel, of Poetry and Painting', *De Arte Graphica*, p. liv, words are 'the cloathing of the Thought'. See also Dryden's 'Preface' to *Albion and Albanius* (1685), sig. A2ʳ: 'Propriety of Words, is the cloathing of those thoughts, with such Expressions as are naturally proper to them'.
322. decent: cf. 'modest plainness', 305. A much stronger moral term then than now; *SJ* gives 'becoming; fit; suitable... grave; not gaudy; not ostentatious... not wanton; not immodest' as possible meanings. The Latin 'decens' can also mean 'well-formed, attractive'.
323. pompous: highly ceremonial; cf. 74–5 variant.
324. Clown: rustic or yokel. The contrast is between the low rank of the person and the high rank implied by the 'regal purple' (regal because it was the colour of the emperor's toga in imperial Rome). *TE* compares Wycherley, 'To Mr. Pope, on his Pastorals', 30–1: 'But the true Measure of the Shepherd's Wit | Shou'd, like his Garb, be for the Country fit'.
325. sort: (verb) consort, fit, suit.
326. *TE* cites Hobbes, 'The Answer ... to Sir Will. D'Avenant's Preface', *Gondibert* (1651), pp. 52–3: 'the Poets ... have lodg'd themselves in the three Regions of mankind, *Court*, *Citie*, and *Countrey* ... From hence have proceeded three sorts of Poesie, *Heroique*, *Scommatique*, and *Pastoral*', that is, epic, satiric and pastoral, three genres of paramount importance to Pope's own career.
327. Pretence: claim.

Ancients in *Phrase*, meer Moderns in their *Sense*!
Such *labour'd Nothings*, in so *strange* a Style,
330 *Amaze* th' unlearn'd, and make the Learned *Smile*.
Unlucky, as *Fungoso* in the Play,
These Sparks with aukward Vanity display
What the Fine Gentlemen wore *Yesterday*!
And but so mimick ancient Wits at best,
335 As Apes our Grandsires in their *Doublets drest.*
In *Words*, as *Fashions*, the same Rule will hold;
Alike Fantastick, if *too New*, or *Old*;

331.] Ben. Johnson's *Every Man in his Humour.*

331, n. **Ben:** *1744–51: See* Ben

333. **Gentlemen:** *1736a–51:* Gentleman

---

327. TE suggests a possible hit at Ambrose Philips (see Headnote to *Pastorals*), which might be strengthened by the presence of a pastoral 'Clown' in 324. Pope criticised the obsolescence of Spenser's diction in his 'Discourse on Pastoral Poetry' (see *Pastorals*, Appendix II).

327. Pope's note. Quintilian, *Institutio Oratoria*, I.vi.20: 'to retain things that have been destroyed and removed is a kind of arrogance, a worthless boasting about trivial matters'; and 39–41: 'it is necessary that words recalled from antiquity should not be crowded together nor too obvious, since nothing is more loathsome than affectation, and they should certainly not be recalled from the earliest times. How corrupt is speech, of which the highest virtue is clarity, if it requires a translator? Therefore, just as the best of new words will be those that are oldest, so the best of old words will be those that are newest'. The second quotation has been heavily condensed from a passage from which Pope omits Quintilian's praise of the majestic sound of old words. Dryden had defended the limited reanimation of old words in 'Discourse Concerning ... Satire', *Satires of Juvenal*, p. viii.

328. Ancients ... Moderns: For the context of the 'querelle' between the proponents of ancient learning and modern science, see Headnote: Context.

331. Fungoso: a would-be courtier, in Jonson's *Every Man Out of His Humour* (1600); Pope's note is slightly incorrect. EC suggests that he took the reference from Dryden's dedicatory epistle to Sir Charles Sedley in *The Assignation* (1673), sig. A5[r]: 'like *Fungoso* in the Play, who follows the Fashion at a distance'. Pope owned and annotated a 1692 edition of *The Works of Ben Jonson* (Mack 1982: 420); for his reading of Jonson, see Fairer (2007).

332. Sparks: lightweight men of fashion; a term 'commonly used in contempt' (*SJ*).

334–5. Manage to mimic ancient wits only successfully enough to look like monkeys dressed in the clothes of our grandfathers ('grandsires'), in the manner of the performing monkeys used by mountebanks and other showmen.

335. Doublets: type of 'double' waistcoat, long out of fashion by Pope's time.

Be not the *first* by whom the *New* are try'd,
Nor yet the *last* to lay the *Old* aside.
340   But most by *Numbers* judge a Poet's Song,
And *smooth* or *rough*, with such, is *right* or *wrong*;
In the bright *Muse* tho' thousand *Charms* conspire,
Her *Voice* is all these tuneful Fools admire,
Who haunt *Parnassus* but to please their Ear,
345   Not mend their Minds; as some to *Church* repair,
Not for the *Doctrine*, but the *Musick* there.

340.] Quis populi sermo est? quis enim? nisi carmina molli Nunc demum numero fluere, ut per laeve severos Effugit junctura ungues: scit tendere versum, Non secus ac si oculo rubricam dirigat uno. Persius, Sat. i.

---

341. **such:** MS, *1717–51:* them

336–9. Dennis, *Reflections*, pp. 15–16, Hooker I.407, saw this passage as a contradiction of Horace (*Ars Poetica*, 48–53), who appears to countenance the coinage of new words, provided it is done from Greek, and sparingly. Dennis also declared the couplet an insult to Dryden, 'for never any one was a greater Coiner than he'. Dryden defended his own coinages in 'An Account of the Ensuing Poem', *Annus Mirabilis* (1667), sig. a1[r], and elsewhere. TE points out Dryden's own recommendations of the Horatian model, 'not to be too hasty in receiving of words: but rather to stay till Custome has made them familiar to us'; 'Defence of the Epilogue', in *The Conquest of Granada* (1672), p. 168. Cf. also 'Discourse Concerning ... Satire', *Satires of Juvenal*, pp. viii–ix: 'unnecessary Coynage, as well as unnecessary Revival, runs into Affectation'.

340. Numbers: metre, versification; cf. 'January and May', 339, and Dryden, 'Preface' to *Tyrannick Love* (1670), sig. A5[r]: 'I have not everywhere observed the equality of numbers, in my Verse ... because I would not have my sense a slave to syllables'. Dryden also argued that 'Versification, and Numbers, are the greatest Pleasures of Poetry'; 'Discourse Concerning ... Satire', *Satires of Juvenal*, p. xxxviii.

340 Pope's note. Persius, *Satires*, I.63–6: 'What is the common talk of the people? What indeed, unless that songs now at last flow with a soft rhythm, so that the joint allows the strictest nails to glide lightly over. Our poet knows how to stretch a verse line, just as if he were aligning a plumbline with one eye.'

341. smooth ... rough: regularity or irregularity of metre; discussed further in 362–74, and see the treatment in Coward, *Licentia Poetica Discuss'd* (1709), pp. 53–4. The modernisations of Chaucer made by Dryden and Pope (and of Donne by Pope) were designed to smooth out irregularities of metre.

342. bright Muse: see Commentary to 84; 'bright' because identified with the 'light' of reason and nature (cf. 13).

    thousand: a thousand; the 'a' is omitted in order to fit the 'numbers'.

    conspire: agree or work together, or 'breathe together', in the then still current Latinate sense, for which cf. 204, 'Rape of the Locke', I.37, and Dryden, *Britannia Rediviva*, 154 (1688), p. 7: 'The airy Atoms did in Plagues conspire' and 320, p. 13: 'Let Angels voices, with their harps conspire'.

343. Voice: the 'numbers' or mere sound of the verse.

    tuneful: interested only in the 'tune' or 'music' of the poetry.

344. haunt: loiter around.

    Parnassus: see Commentary to 94.

345. repair: resort, go.

> These *Equal Syllables* alone require,
> Tho' oft the Ear the *open Vowels* tire,
> While *Expletives* their feeble Aid *do* join,
> 350 And ten low Words oft creep in one dull Line,

348.] Fugiemus crebras vocalium concursiones, quae vastam atque hiantem orationem reddunt. Cic. ad Herenn. lib. 4. *Vide etiam* Quintil. lib. 9. c. 4.

---

347. Equal Syllables: syllables of the same length or stress. *TE* suggests Pope alludes to the policy of Cowley in 'The Resurrection', st. 2, *Poems* (1656), p. 21, and its attendant faults: 'All hand in hand do decently advance, | And to my *Song* with smooth and equal measures dance'. Cf. Roscommon, *Essay on Translated Verse*, 226–9 (1684), p. 15: '*Vowels and Accents, Regularly plac'd* | On *even Syllables* (and still the *Last*) | Tho all imaginable *Faults* abound, | Will never want the *Pageantry* of *Sound.*' For understanding of syllabic length see the chapter 'Of Numbers', in James Greenwood, *An Essay Towards a Practical English Grammar* (1711).

348. Pope imitates the effect by producing a line dominated by 'open Vowels', that is, pairs of words of which one ends and the next begins with a vowel. Normally Pope avoided such features by eliding one vowel, as in 330, 374, etc. Dryden discusses this problem in the 'Dedication' of *Examen Poeticum*, sig. B3.

348 Pope's note. Cicero, *Ad Herennium*, IV.xii.18: 'let us avoid frequent repetitions of vowels, which make the style rough and gaping'; Pope also refers to Quintilian's extensive discussion, *Institutio Oratoria*, IX.iv.33. He quoted these passages in discussing the issue of 'hiatus' in his letter to Walsh, 22 October 1706, *Corr*, I.24–5. Cf. Commentary to 'January and May', 91, and 'Messiah', 84.

349. Expletives: small extra words, such as the 'do' conspicuously inserted in this line, whose function is to fill in a metrical gap (but cf. the 'did' in 92). Coward inveighed against them in *Licentia Poetica Discuss'd* (1709), p. 59. In a letter which discusses many of the issues in this section of the poem, Pope told Cromwell, 25 November 1710 (*Corr.*, I.107), 'I wou'd except against all Expletives in Verse, as Do before Verbs plural, or ev'n too frequent use of Did & Does, to change the Termination of the Rhime; all these being against the usual manner of Speech & meer fillers up of unnecessary syllables'. *TE* notes that Pope used many such expletives in the first text of the *Essay*, removing several in revision. Cf. 'Vertumnus and Pomona', 122 variant; 'The First Book of Statius his Thebais', 158; 'To a Young Lady, with the Works of Voiture', 9.

350. A line showing the effect Pope is condemning; but cf. 108 and 229. In the letter to Walsh just cited, Pope comments '*Monosyllable-Lines*, unless very artfully manag'd, are stiff, or languishing: but may be beautiful to express Melancholy, Slowness, or Labour'. *TE* compares Dryden, *Of Dramatick Poesie*, p. 4: 'a very Leveller in Poetry, he creeps along with ten little words in every line, and helps out his Numbers with *For to,* and *Vnto,* and all the pretty Expletives he can find, till he draggs them to the end of another line'. *TE* also notes that Dryden confessed that '"Tis possible ... though it rarely happens, that a Verse of Monosyllables may sound harmoniously'; 'Dedication' of the *Aeneid*, *Works of Virgil*, sig. e4^v. In his own notes to the translation, p. 635, Dryden pointed out instances of his deliberate use of monosyllabic lines for imitative purposes. Warton cites Quintilian's objections to multiple monosyllables, *Institutio Oratoria*, IX.iv.42. See also Atterbury's 'Preface' to *The Second Part of Mr. Waller's Poems* (1690), sig. A6^r, which identifies monosyllables, 'when they come together in any cluster' as 'certainly the most harsh untunable things in the World'.

AN ESSAY ON CRITICISM (1711)   245

>   While they ring round the same *unvary'd Chimes*,
>   With sure Returns of still *expected Rhymes*.
>   Where-e'er you find the *cooling Western Breeze*,
>   In the next Line, it *whispers thro' the Trees*;
> 355   If *Chrystal Streams with pleasing Murmurs creep*,
>   The Reader's threaten'd (not in vain) with *Sleep*.
>   Then, at the *last*, and *only* Couplet fraught
>   With some *unmeaning* Thing they call a *Thought*,
>   A *needless Alexandrine* ends the Song,
> 360   That like a wounded Snake, drags its slow length along.

---

351. ring round: as in a peal of bells ('Chimes').

351-2. In the letter cited in the Commentary to 349, Pope comments 'I wou'd except against ... The Repeating the Same Rhimes within 4 or 6 lines of each other: which tire the Ear with too much of the like Sound'. *TE* compares Atterbury, 'Preface' to *The Second Part of Mr. Waller's Poems*, sig. A7^r: 'He had a fine Ear, and knew how quickly that Sense was cloy'd by the same round of chiming Words still returning upon it'.

353-6. *EC* finds a model for this italicising of clichés in 37-42 of Boileau's second *Satire*, a practice followed also in translation, e.g. *The Second, Fourth, and Seventh Satyres of Monsieur Boileau Imitated* (1696), pp. 2-5.

353-4. Wakefield notes that Garth altered a breeze/trees rhyme in *The Dispensary* in the seventh edition (1714) after this comment from Pope; it had opened canto II of the sixth edition (1706). Pope himself had used it in the *Pastorals* (e.g. 'Winter', 61-2) and cf. 'Eloisa to Abelard', 159-60. See also *Essay on Man*, I.271-2. Wakefield compares Dryden's translation of the *Aeneid*, VI.955-6, *Works of Virgil*, p. 390: 'A sep'rate Grove, thro' which a gentle Breeze | Plays with a passing Breath, and whispers thro' the Trees', among other analogues; it occurred three times in Behn's *Poems upon Several Occasions* (1684) alone.

355-6. *TE* compares Charles Hopkins, 'The Story of Ceyx and Halcyone', *Epistolary Poems* (1694), p.75: 'Her easie Streams with pleasing Murmurs creep, | At once inviting, and assisting sleep'; and Wycherley, 'To Mr. Pope, on his Pastorals': 'So purling Streams with even Murmurs creep, | And hush the heavy Hearers into Sleep'.

355. Pope uses these stock landscape terms in *Pastorals*: 'crystal', 'Summer', 27; 'Winter', 21; 'murmur', 'Autumn', 20, 42; 'Winter', 57, 64. See also *Windsor-Forest*, 374 ('chrystal') and 200, 204 ('murmur').

356. Cf. 245. This prefigures the closing narcolepsy of the second book of *The Dunciad*.

357. fraught: laden, endowed. In his manuscript notes Pope experimented with an alternative line: 'At the last Couplett, which alone is fraught', but made no change to the published versions (see Appendix).

359. Alexandrine: a line consisting of twelve syllables, exemplified in line 360; there is another instance, more imitative of its subject, at 374. *TE* cites Cowley's defence of the imitative function of such lines in *Davideis*, book 1, note 25, *Poems* (1656), pp. 32-3; Coward, *Licentia Poetica Discuss'd* (1709), p. 55, recommends their usage be limited to the closing of verse paragraphs. Pope used three such lines in 'Messiah', including one describing a snake (82); cf. also 'January and May', 323, 808; 'Sapho to Phaon', 211, etc.

360. Wakefield compares Dryden, *Annus Mirabilis*, st. 123 (1667), p. 32: 'So glides some trodden Serpent on the Grass, | And long behind his wounded vollume trails'. Dryden's note cites Virgil, *Georgics* III.423-4, on a threatened snake: 'cum medii nexus extremaeque agmina caudae | solvuntur, tardosque trahit sinus ultimus orbis' ('while

> Leave such to tune their own dull Rhimes, and know
> What's *roundly smooth*, or *languishingly slow*;
> And praise the *Easie Vigor* of a Line,
> Where *Denham*'s Strength, and *Waller*'s Sweetness join.
> 365 'Tis not enough no Harshness gives Offence,

364^5. 1717–51: True ease in writing comes from art, not chance,
As those move easiest who have learn'd to dance.

---

its coiling middle and the column of its tail's end are loosened, its last fold drags in its slow coils'). In the letter cited in Commentary to 349, Pope deplored the 'too frequent use of Alexandrines, which are never graceful but [when] there is some Majesty added to the Verse by 'em, or when there cannot be [found] a Word in 'em but what is absolutely needfull'.

361. EC compares the Soames–Dryden version of Boileau's *Art of Poetry*, IV.52 (1683), p. 57: 'Those Tuneful Readers of their own dull Rhymes'.

362. Parodic: 'roundly' is used as an example of 'smooth' sound, 'languishingly' of 'slow'.

363–4. Dennis, *Reflections*, p. 17, Hooker, I.408, maintained that this couplet was inconsistent with the admiration of Homer expressed at 125–30.

363. Easie: smooth, unstrained.

364. Denham ... Waller: Sir John Denham (1615–69), royalist author of the topographical poem *Cooper's Hill* (1643), a model for Pope's *Windsor-Forest*, and of a version of Homer referred to in Pope's 'Argument' to the 'Episode of Sarpedon'; Edmund Waller (1606–87), poet and politician, a favourite poet, of whose style Pope produced several early imitations; see Commentary to 'Spring', 46. Atterbury's 'Preface' to *The Second Part of Mr. Waller's Poems* (1690) credits Waller with reforming English verse in the direction of smoothness. Pope confirmed his view of Waller's 'sweetness' to Spence (*OAC*, I.176). *TE* notes that Waller's talent for joining 'easie Words with pleasing Numbers' was celebrated in the Soames–Dryden version of Boileau's *Art of Poetry*, I.136 (1683), p. 9, and that Dryden coupled Waller with Denham in *Of Dramatick Poesie*, p. 7: 'they can produce ... nothing so even, sweet, and flowing, as Mr. *Waller*; nothing so Majestique, so correct, as Sir *Iohn Denham*'. *TE* also cites Henry Hall, 'To the Memory of John Dryden', *Luctus Britannici* (1700), p. 19: 'More smooth than *Waller*, or than *Denham* strong!' Jones (2010: 9) provides a wider list of similar pairings and mixtures, e.g. Prior's 'Dedication' of his *Poems on Several Occasions* (1709), p. vi, praising Dorset's 'Mixture of Delicacy and Strength ... They convey the Wit of *Petronius* in the Softness of *Tibullus*'.

364^5 variant. This famous couplet was later quoted, with slight variation, in Pope's *The Second Epistle of the Second Book of Horace Imitated*, 178–9. Aden (1978: 46) cites 'An Essay Upon Satyr', *The Fourth (and Last) Collection of Poems, Satyrs, Songs, etc.* (1689), p. 26: 'As Men aim rightest when they shoot in jest' (variously ascribed to Dryden and to Sheffield, but accepted as the latter's work in Pope's 1723 edition of Sheffield's *Works*, I.114). For further comments on 'Ease in Writing' see the two essays in *The Guardian*, 25 and 28 March 1713, attributed to Pope by Ault (*PW*, I.88–96), and 'The Wife of Bath Her Prologue, from Chaucer', 96.

365–6. Cf. Pope to Cromwell, 25 November, 1710 (*Corr.*, I.107): 'It is not enough that nothing offends the Ear ... but a good Poet will adapt the very Sounds, as well as Words, to the Things he treats of. So that there is ... a Style of Sound: As in describing a gliding

The *Sound* must seem an *Eccho* to the *Sense*.
Soft is the Strain when *Zephyr* gently blows,
And the *smooth Stream* in *smoother Numbers* flows;
But when loud Surges lash the sounding Shore,
370 The hoarse, rough *Verse* shou'd like the *Torrent* roar.

---

369. Surges: *1717–32:* billows

---

stream the Numbers shou'd run easy & flowing, in describing a rough Torrent or Deluge, sonorous & swelling'. Pope recommends Homer and Virgil as masters of the effect, and cites Vida's *De Arte Poetica* (III.367); see also his 'Preface' to *The Iliad* (*PW*, I.249). He made similar remarks in the letter to Walsh dated 22 October 1706, *Corr.*, I.22, and commented later on his own practice to Spence (*OAC*, I.18, 173–4). Wycherley commends Pope's 'Sense improv'd by Sound' in 'To Mr. Pope, on his Pastorals', 5–6. TE compares Dryden's 'Preface' to *Sylvae*, sig. A5, on Virgil: 'His Verse is every where sounding the very thing in your Ears, whose sence it bears'.

365. TE suggests an echo of Garth, *Dispensary*, IV, sixth edition (1706), p. 63: 'Harsh Words, tho' pertinent, uncouth appear, | None please the Fancy, who offend the Ear', and finds a source for this in Boileau, *L'Art Poetique*, I.112–13.

366. Cf. Roscommon, *Essay on Translated Verse*, 345 (1684), p. 22: 'The *sound* is still a *Comment* to the *Sense*'. Mannheimer (2008) links the phrasing to a Jonson's 'Eupheme; or, the Fair Fame', 39–40: 'And, though the sound were parted thence, | Still left an Eccho in the Sense'. For Pope's relation to 'phonetic iconicity' see Alderson (1996) and for the controversy on 'sound enactment' stirred by Pope's contentions, Terry (1999). Jones (2005: 1–3, 24–6, 64–8), links Pope's line to Ovid's story of Echo and Narcissus (*Metamorphoses*, III.341–510), and to debates about linguistic signs deriving from the Plato's Socratic dialogue *Cratylus*. On the linguistic principle illustrated in the following lines see further MacMahon (2007).

367–70. TE notes that Pope recalls lines from the Soames–Dryden translation of Boileau's *Art of Poetry*, I.167–70 (1683), p. 11, with greater emphasis on sound quality: 'More pleas'd we are to see a River lead | His gentle Streams along a flow'ry Mead, | Than from high Banks to hear loud Torrents roar, | With foamy Waters on a Muddy Shore.'

367. Strain: tune, music, sound.

Zephyr: the west wind; see 'Winter', 49–50, and 'Sapho to Phaon', 83.

369–70. Warburton cites Vida, *De Art Poetica*, III.388–91 as Pope's source: Tunc longe sale saxa sonant, tunc et freta ventis | incipiunt agitata tumescere: littore fluctus | illidunt rauco, atque refracta remurmurat unda | ad scopulos, cumulo insequitur praeruptus aquae mons.' ('Then the rocks resound to the wide sea, then the seas whipped up by the winds begin to swell: breakers dash against the rough-sounding shore, and the broken wave murmurs on the rocks, an overhanging mountain of water rolls in'.)

369. sounding: resounding; cf. 'Autumn', 20. TE compares Garth, *Dispensary*, V.5, sixth edition (1706), p. 75: 'The Surges gently dash against the Shoar'; and Milton, *Paradise Lost*, II.660–1 (1674), p. 47: 'the Sea that Parts | Calabria from the hoarce *Trinacrian* shore'.

> When *Ajax* strives, some Rock's vast Weight to throw,
> The Line too *labours*, and the Words move *slow*;
> Not so, when swift *Camilla* scours the Plain,
> Flies o'er th' unbending Corn, and skims along the Main.
> 375   Hear how *Timotheus*' various Lays surprize,
> And bid Alternate Passions fall and rise!

375.] Alexander's *Feast, or the Power of Musick; An Ode by Mr.* Dryden.

375, n. Alexander's: *1744–51: See* Alexander's

374. Corn: MS: Ears
375. various: *1736a–51:* vary'd

371–2. Warburton compares Vida, *De Arte Poetica*, III.415–17: 'Atque adeo, siquid geritur molimine magno, | adde moram, et periter tecum quoque verba laborent | segnia...' ('And therefore, if anything that requires great effort is to be managed, delay, and let your sluggish works labout as much as you'). *TE* adds III.375: 'ille autem membris, ac mole ignavus ingens | incedit tardo molimine subsidendo' ('that one, however, huge of limb and slothful in weight, goes slowly, subsiding with effort').

371. Ajax: hero in Greek mythology, whose colossal strength features prominently in the *Iliad*; in the 'Episode of Sarpedon', 97–106, Ajax kills Sarpedon's friend Epikles by hurling a rock at him. He fells the Trojan hero Hector in a similar way; Pope's *Iliad*, VII.320–6.

373. Camilla: a Volscian princess and warrior whose astounding speed is mentioned in Virgil's *Aeneid* (VII.803–11; XI.539–828); cf. Commentary to 'Rape of the Locke', II.140. In Dryden's translation of the first passage (VII.1200–3, *Works of Virgil*, p. 433), Camilla 'Outstrip'd the Winds in speed upon the Plain, | Flew o're the Fields, nor hurt the bearded Grain: | She swept the Seas, and, as she skim'd along, | Her flying Feet unbath'd on Billows hung.'
scours: To scour is to 'pass swiftly over' (*SJ*, citing this line); cf. 'Arrival of Ulysses in Ithaca', 9. On 11 May 1738 Aaron Hill wrote to Pope to suggest that the word produced an incorrect impression amidst a series of imitative effects, but Pope ignored his suggested redrafting; *Corr.*, IV.97.

374. An Alexandrine; see Commentary to 359.
unbending: Camilla moves so fast she does not even touch the corn.
skims: 'to pass lightly; to glide along' (*SJ*, citing this line).
Main: ocean.

375 Pope's note. *Alexander's Feast* (1697), by Dryden, celebrates Timotheus, a poet and musician from Miletus, Ionia, c. 450–360 BC, writer of many kinds of song ('various Lays'); according to Dryden's poem, he attempted imitative effects in his music. Pope commends Dryden's poem as an example of the sound/sense theory in his letter to Cromwell, 25 November 1710 (*Corr.*, I.108). Pope's *Ode for Musick*, which pursued similar effects, was often compared to Dryden's. Cf. also 'Prologue to *Cato*', 6.

376. Wakefield compares John Hughes, *The Court of Neptune* (1700), p. 3: 'Beholds th' alternate Billows fall and rise'; *TE* adds Prior, 'Presented to the King, at his Arrival in Holland...', 4, *Poems on Several Occasions* (1709), p. 95: 'And bid alternate Empires rise and fall'. Cf. Garth, *Dispensary*, V, sixth edition (1706), p. 83: 'Thus sometimes Joy prevail'd, and sometimes Fear; | And Tears and Smiles alternate Passions were'.

While, at each Change, the Son of *Lybian Jove*
Now *burns* with Glory, and then *melts* with Love;
Now his *fierce* Eyes with *sparkling Fury* glow;
380   Now *Sighs* steal out, and *Tears begin to flow.*
Persians and *Greeks* like *Turns of Nature found,*
And the *World's Victor* stood subdu'd by *Sound*!
The Pow'r of Musick all our Hearts allow;
And what *Timotheus* was, is *Dryden* now.
385   Avoid *Extreams*; and shun the Fault of such,
Who still are pleas'd *too little,* or *too much.*
At ev'ry Trifle scorn to take Offence,
That always shows *Great Pride,* or *Little Sense*;
Those *Heads* as *Stomachs* are not sure the best
390   Which nauseate all, and nothing can digest.

---

378. **then:** MS: *now*

---

377. Lybian Jove: Ammon, an Egyptian god identified by the Greeks with Zeus ('Jove'). The 'Alexander' of Dryden's poem was Alexander the Great (356–323 BC), who conquered Syria and Egypt, visited the oracle of Zeus Ammon in the Libyan desert, and was proclaimed as Ammon's son. *TE* compares Milton, *Paradise Lost,* IV.276–7 (1674), p. 93: '. . . where old *Cham,* | Whom Gentiles *Ammon* call and *Lybian Jove*'. Pope pursued the history in his note to *The Temple of Fame* (1715), 152–3. Pope showed his sense of the ironic coincidence with his own name in a letter to Caryll, 25 January 1711: 'I appear not the great Alexander Mr Caryll is so civil to, but that little Alexander the women laugh at' (*Corr.,* I.114); see also to Wycherley, 23 June 1705 (*Corr.,* I.9).

378. burns: in response to martial music.
    melts: in response to a love song. *TE* compares Dryden, *Alexander's Feast,* 158–60 (1697), p. 7: 'to his breathing Flute, | And sounding Lyre, | Cou'd swell the Soul to rage, or kindle soft Desire'.

380. *TE* compares Dryden, *Alexander's Feast,* 87–8, p. 4: 'And, now and then, a Sigh he stole; | And Tears began to flow.'

381. Persians *and* Greeks: implacable enemies, united in aesthetic sympathy.

Turns of Nature: emotional responses.

382. subdu'd: (a) made quiet, (b) conquered. *TE* compares Dryden, *Alexander's Feast,* 115, p. 5: 'The vanquish'd Victor sunk upon her Breast'.

384. Dryden: *TE* notes the identification between Dryden and Timotheus in the anonymous elegy 'To the Memory of . . . John Dryden', st. 4, *Luctus Britannici* (1700), pp. 13–15: 'Not Fam'd *Timotheus* could with greater ease | Command our Anger, or our Wrath appease:'.

385–94. A statement of one of Pope's major aesthetic themes, balance between extremes. Cf. also Commentary to 696 below.

385–6. Aden (1978: 48) discerns the influence of Defoe, *The True-Born Englishman,* 461–2 (1701), p. 9: 'Their strong Aversion to Behaviour's such, | They alwise talk too little or too much'.

387. Trifle: cf. the attitude towards Homer's blemishes at 183 and the dismissal of 'trivial Faults', 261.

390. nauseate: are nauseated by. Cf. Dennis, *The Grounds of Criticism in Poetry,* 'The Proposal', Hooker, I.328: 'Others are so squeamish, that they like nothing, and value themselves even upon that too; that is, upon the sickliness and unsoundness of their Minds; because he who likes nothing tastes nothing'.

Yet let not each gay *Turn* thy Rapture move,
For Fools *Admire*, but Men of Sense *Approve*;
As things seem *large* which we thro' *Mists* descry,
Dulness is ever apt to *Magnify*.
395 Some the *French* Writers, some our *own* despise;
The *Ancients* only, or the *Moderns* prize:

---

391. 1727–32: new paragraph
  gay *Turn*: MS: small *Trait*
395. **the *French*:** *1744–51:* foreign

---

391. Turn: perhaps recalling the 'turns of nature' of 381. *TE* glosses 'turn' as an 'iterative or echoing pattern of words', citing the authority of Dryden, who discusses turns as elements of the style of Waller, Denham, Cowley and Ovid in the 'Discourse Concerning ... Satire', *Satires of Juvenal*, pp. l–li. For the Ovid connection see also 'Sapho to Phaon', 45–8, Commentary. It could also mean simply 'the manner of adjusting the words of a sentence' (*SJ*), as in 'the easie Turn of the Words', Pope, *Guardian*, no. 40 (*PW*, I.103), or the 'elegant turns on the words, which render the numbers extremely sweet and pleasing', 'A Discourse on Pastoral Poetry' (see *Pastorals*, Appendix II, 62–3).
  Rapture: cf. 239 and Commentary.
392. Pope has used versions of 'admire' in a positive sense at 101, 203 and 253, and with a more negative suggestion at 343; here he alludes to the opening, 'nil admirari' ('admire nothing'), of a poem by Horace of which he later produced a version: *The Sixth Epistle of the First Book of Horace Imitated* (1738). Cf. his remark to Spence in 1739: '*Nil admirari* is as true in relation to our opinion of authors as it is in morality' (*OAC*, I.147). On 13 October 1746 Aaron Hill recounted to Samuel Richardson that Pope was fond of repeating this line, 'drawn from a mistaken hint in Horace', and that he had reproved him for its 'arrogance, and want of truth in nature'; *Correspondence of Samuel Richardson* (1804), I.112–13. *EC* cites Horace, *Ars Poetica*, 455–6: 'vesanum tetigisse timent fugientque poetam | qui sapient; agitant pueri incautique sequuntur' ('men who are wise fear to touch a crazy poet, and run away; incautious boys follow and irritate him'), and the version by Creech, *The Odes, Satyrs, and Epistles of Horace Done into English* (1684), p. 569: 'Men of Sense retire, | The Boys abuse, and only Fools admire'. *TE* adds the English translation of La Bruyère, *The Characters*, third edition (1702), p. 15, speaking of an author: 'A Fool may sometimes admire him, but then 'tis but a Fool: And a Man of Sense has in him the Seeds of all Truths and all Sentiments ... He admires little, it being chiefly his Province to approve'.
393. descry: detect, examine, discover, especially at a distance.
394. Dulness: cf. 51, and *The Dunciad* (1728) I.67–72. *TE* compares Sir Robert Howard, 'To the Reader', in *The Great Favourite* (1668), sig. a1ᵛ, referring to the sun: 'But when descended and grown low, its oblique shining renders the shaddow larger than the substance, and gives the deceiv'd person a wrong measure of his own proportion'.
395. *TE* suggests that Pope made the late shift to 'foreign' when the importance of French criticism had waned in Britain. While French critical theory continued to emerge, there was also a considerable body of English criticism and less sense of indebtedness to French models by the time of Pope's death; see Sambrook (1997). The *Essay on Criticism* itself was translated into French by Anthony Hamilton in 1713; see Headnote: Context.
396. Cf. Commentary to 327–8.

AN ESSAY ON CRITICISM (1711)

      Thus *Wit*, like *Faith*, by each Man is apply'd
      To *one small Sect*, and All are *damn'd beside*.
      Meanly they seek the Blessing to confine,
400   And force *that Sun* but on a *Part* to Shine;
      Which not alone the *Southern Wit* sublimes,
      But ripens Spirits in cold *Northern Climes*;
      Which from the first has shone on *Ages past*,
      Enlights the *present*, and shall warm the *last*:
405   (Tho' *each* may feel *Increases* and *Decays*,

397–8. *1713a–43:* in parentheses
405–6. *1744-51:* parentheses omitted

397–8. *TE* compares Cowley, 'To Sir William Davenant', 27–8, *Poems* (1656), p. 25: 'Some men their *Fancies* like their *Faith* derive, | And think all Ill but that which *Rome* does give'. *TE* also cites Rapin's view that the Egyptians had clearer insight because they were 'not yet Corrupted by a multitude of different Opinions, nor Biass'd by the Partiality of particular Sects'; *Whole Critical Works of Rapin* (1706), I.10. Pope argues that faith is not confined to one 'sect', Anglican, Catholic, or Calvinist. For the offence these lines caused to Pope's Catholic circle, see Headnote : Context; the insertion of parentheses round the couplet in 1713 clarified the point. See also Pope's memorandum at this point (Appendix), and *Essay on Man*, III.305–6: 'For Modes of Faith let graceless zealots fight; | His can't be wrong whose life is in the right'.

399–400. Wakefield suggests this alludes to Matthew 5:45, 'your father ... in heauen ... maketh his sunne to rise on the euill and on the good'; cf. 'Rape of the Locke', I.30.

399. Blessing: The 'blessing' is the endowment of wit, but the word is prompted by the religious comparison.

400. Sun: the light of reason and wit; cf. 13, 318–20.

401–2. *TE* indicates that Pope here 'repudiates the ancient idea that climate might impose limitations on the minds and works of men', and cites Dryden, 'Prologue' to *Aureng-Zebe*, 33–4 (1675), sig. a2^r: 'And Wit in Northern Climates will not blow, | Except like *Orange-trees*, 'tis hous'd from Snow'. For 'Northern' cf. 714 below, and 'Rape of the Locke', II.71.

401. sublimes: with 'ripens', 402, this develops a metaphor from alchemy, since the sun was anciently thought to ripen gold within in the earth. *SJ* cites this line in defining the metaphorical sense of the verb: 'To exalt; to heighten; to improve'. *OED* suggests that 'sublime' can mean to 'cause (the juices of a plant) to rise, and thereby rarefy and purify them', with 'ripens' therefore suggesting fruit.

403–4. The phrasing 'ages past ... present ... last' recalls the liturgical formula alluded to in 257 and links the light of reason to God's unvarying providential care of the world.

   Enlights: illuminates.

405. Increases *and* Decays: *EC* cites Sir Robert Howard, 'Against the Fear of Death', 12, *Examen Poeticum*, p. 118: 'And neither gives encrease, nor brings decay'. The antithesis is a standard one; e.g. Aphra Behn, 'The Reflection', 45–6, *Poems on Several Occasions* (1684), p. 85: 'For as my Kindling Flames increase, | Yours glimmeringly decay'; and 'The Counsel', 15, *ibid.*, p. 90: 'If Love increase, and Youth decay'.

        And see now *clearer* and now *darker Days*)
        Regard not then if Wit be *Old* or *New*,
        But blame the *False*, and value still the *True*.
           Some ne'er advance a Judgment of their own,
410   But *catch* the *spreading Notion* of the Town;
        They reason and conclude by *Precedent*,
        And own *stale Nonsense* which they ne'er invent.
        Some judge of Author's *Names*, not *Works*, and then
        Nor praise nor damn the *Writings*, but the *Men*.
415   Of all this *Servile Herd* the worst is He
        That in *proud Dulness* joins with *Quality*,
        A constant Critick at the Great-man's Board,
        To *fetch and carry* Nonsense for my Lord.
        What *woful stuff* this Madrigal wou'd be,

---

408. **blame:** MS: damn
413. **Author's:** *1717–51:* authors
414. **damn:** MS, *1717–51:* blame
415. *1727–32:* new paragraph

---

406. **darker:** suggests 'dark ages', the period after the collapse of Roman dominance and before the recovery of classical learning in the Renaissance; cf. 686–9 below.

410. **spreading Notion:** Wakefield notes that the image suggests infection and compares *Epistle to Dr. Arbuthnot*, 224: 'To spread about the Itch of Verse and Praise'. Pope perhaps thinks of the newly popular methods of spreading gossip and talk such as the coffee house.

411. **by Precedent:** by what has gone before, by previous judgements of a critical 'court'; 'reason . . . conclude . . . *Precedent*' suggests a process of critical judgment which is as lifeless as a legal verdict. Cf. 169–71.

413. *Author's* **Names:** hence perhaps Pope's preference for anonymity in the publication of some of his early works, including this poem.

414. **damn:** condemn; cf. 398, and 124^5 MS. For 'damn' in this critical sense see 'Prologue Design'd for Mr. D—'s last Play', 3–4.

415. **Servile Herd:** cf. Horace, *Epistles*, I.xix.19, 'o imitatores, servum pecus' ('o imitators, slavish herd').

416. **Quality:** 'persons of high rank' (*SJ*), here used satirically.

417. Great-man's Board: the nobleman's table, where the critic, a hapless relic of the Roman 'client' system, hopes to get fed.

418. **fetch and carry** *Nonsense:* criticism as a menial servant to aristocratic appetite. Pope would develop this portrait of client–patron relations in the *Epistle to Dr Arbuthnot*, 231–48; at 226 of the same poem Pope denies he has ever been one 'To fetch and carry Sing-song up and down'. *TE* also cites 'Sandys's Ghost', 19–20: 'To fetch and carry, in his Mouth, | The Works of all the Muses'; and cf. *Epistle to Bathurst*, 72. Cf. Edward Ward, *The Dissenting Hypocrite* (1704), p. 18: '. . . Will Fetch and Carry any Matter | That may the *easy Church* bespatter'.

419. **this Madrigal:** a popular poem or 'any light airy short song' (*SJ*), not the polyphonic vocal form. Dennis attacked Pope as 'an eternal Writer of Amorous Pastoral Madrigals'; *Reflections*, p. 29, Hooker, I.416. Wycherley repeatedly slighted the poems that Pope was trying to help him edit as his 'madrigals': to Pope, 24 January 1705, 22 March 1706, 28 February 1708 (*Corr.*, I.3, 15, 41). Pope refers with amusement to the

420 In some starv'd Hackny Sonneteer, or me?
     But let a *Lord* once own the *happy Lines,*
     How the *Wit brightens*! How the *Style refines*!
     Before *his* sacred Name flies ev'ry Fault,
     And each *exalted* Stanza *teems* with *Thought*!
425   The *Vulgar* thus through *Imitation* err;
     As oft the *Learn'd* by being *Singular*;
     So much they scorn the Crowd, that if the Throng
     By *Chance* go right, they *purposely* go wrong;
     So Schismatics the *dull Believers* quit,

---

420. MS: In Sing-song *D——y, Oldmixon,* or *me?*
421. **a *Lord* once:** *1727–32:* his Lordship
428^9. MS: And while to *Thoughts refin'd* they make pretence,
         Hate all that's *common,* ev'n to *common Sense.*
429. **dull:** *1713a–51:* plain

---

trifling production of 'quaint Madrigalls' in a letter to Anthony Englefield, 8 August 1707 (Sherburn 1958b: 394).

420. **Hackny:** hireling, originally used of horses and coaches. An early instance of Pope's image of the professional poet as penniless and hungry, as developed most fully in *The Dunciad* and the *Epistle to Dr. Arbuthnot*; also of Pope's ironic self-deprecation, though even as he associates himself with the hackney author, he makes himself syntactically distinct.

Sonneteer: 'a small poet, in contempt' (*SJ*). *TE* compares Dryden, 'Preface' to *All for Love* (1678), sig. B2ʳ: 'Our little Sonnettieers ... have too narrow Souls to judge of Poetry'.

420 MS. **D——y:** Thomas D'Urfey (?1653–1723), dramatist and song-writer; see 'Prologue, Design'd for Mr. D–'s last Play'. Cf. 620.

Oldmixon: John Oldmixon (1672/3–1742), Whig historian and writer, later a bitter enemy of Pope's. This is apparently Pope's earliest blow against him; he later wrote a prose *Essay on Criticism* (1728).

421–4. *TE* compares Horace, *Ars Poetica,* 382–4: 'qui nescit versus tamen audit fingere. quidni? | liber et ingenuus, praesertim census equestrem | summam nummorum vitioque remotus ab omni'.

('A man who knows nothing nonetheless dares to make verses. Why not? He is free and free-born, and most of all, is rated, in money, at the rank of a knight; he is far from every fault.')

421. **own:** acknowledge.

happy Lines: 'happy' because the Lord has acknowledged them and also because the flattering critic now spies felicities in them (as opposed to the genuine 'Happiness' of 142).

422. **Wit brightens:** recalling, in ironic diminution, the ideas of 400–4.

424. **teems:** is full, as in pregnancy (cf. Commentary to 'Winter', 82).

425. **Vulgar:** uneducated people, specifically here in opposition to 'Learn'd'.

426–8. *TE* compares Jonson, 'Explorata: or, Discoveries', *Workes* (1640), II.98: 'These men erre not by chance, but knowingly and willingly; they are like men that affect a fashion by themselves, have some singularity in a Ruffe, Cloake, or Hat-band ... and set a marke upon themselves'.

429. **Schismatics:** adherents of religious sects that have seceded from orthodox doctrines (cf. 397–8). The stress is on the first syllable. Another line taken badly by Pope's Catholic friends: see Headnote: Context. The change to 'plain' is proposed in Pope's manuscript notes (Appendix).

430 And are but damn'd for having *too much Wit.*
   Some praise at Morning what they blame at Night;
   But always think the *last* Opinion *right.*
   A Muse by these is like a Mistress us'd,
   This hour she's *idoliz'd*, the next *abus'd*,
435 While their weak Heads, like Towns unfortify'd,
   'Twixt Sense and Nonsense daily change their Side.
   Ask them the Cause; *They're wiser still*, they say;
   And still to Morrow's wiser than to Day.
   We think our *Fathers* Fools, so *wise* we grow;
440 Our *wiser Sons*, no doubt, will think *us* so.
   Once *School-Divines* our zealous Isle o'erspread;
   Who knew most *Sentences* was *deepest read*;

---

431. **blame:** MS: damn
441. **our:** *1713a–51:* this

431–2. On 20 November 1717 Pope told Francis Atterbury that at the age of fourteen (c.1702) he had found in his father's library 'a collection of all that had been written on both sides in the reign of King James the second: I warm'd my head with them, and the consequence was, that I found my self a Papist and a Protestant by turns, according to the last book I read' (*Corr.*, I.453–4).

433–4. Cf. 31 and 102–5, where Pope has already hinted at this sexualised comparison; and 502 below. A coarser version of the idea is found in Rochester, 'A Satyr Against [Reason and] Mankind', 37–8, *Poems, (&c.)*, p. 88: 'For *Wits* are treated just like *Common Whores*; | First they're enjoy'd, and then kickt out of *Doores*' (another poem marked by Pope in his copy: Mack 1982: 438.)

435. ***Towns unfortify'd:*** Cities still regularly had defensive walls around them, as the events of the War of Spanish Succession, still not quite concluded at this date, reminded Pope's readers; cf. *Windsor-Forest*, 106–10.

436. ***change their Side:*** a reminder of shifting allegiances during the same war.

437–8. TE compares Thomas Hobbes, 'The Answer of Mr. Hobbes to Sr. Will. D'Avenant's Preface Before Gondibert', *Gondibert* (1651), pp. 63–4: 'there is no reason for any man to think himself wiser to day than yesterday, which does not equally convince he shall be wiser to morrow than to day'.

441. **School-Divines:** academic theologians.
   zealous: fervently religious. 'Zeal' had been associated with Puritans and Dryden repeatedly associates it with hypocritical Whig factionalism in *Absalom and Achitophel*, but Pope here means a clergyman obsessively devoted to book-learning as opposed to actual piety. Pope told Caryll on 19 July 1711 that when he explained some of the objections to the *Essay* to Mrs Nelson, she assured him 'I had said nothing which a zealous Catholic need to disown: and I've cause to know that that lady's fault ... is not want of zeal' (*Corr.*, I.127). Cf. 680 and 732.

442. **Sentences:** in the Latin sense, 'sententiae', 'opinions' or 'maxims'; specifically, a reference to handbooks of religious statements such as Peter Lombard's *Sententiarum Libri Quatuor* (written c. 1150), which, Pope suggests, obviated the need for wide and deep reading and stimulated needless controversy.

Faith, Gospel, All, seem'd made to be *disputed*,
And none had *Sense enough to be Confuted.*
445   *Scotists* and *Thomists*, now, in Peace remain,
Amidst their *kindred Cobwebs* in *Duck-Lane.*
If *Faith* it self has *diff'rent Dresses* worn,
What wonder *Modes* in *Wit* shou'd take their Turn?
Oft, leaving what is Natural and fit,

446, n. *1736a–51: Duck-lane.*] A place where old and second-hand books were sold formerly, near *Smithfield.*

448, n. *1736a–43, 1751:* Between Verse 449 and 450;

The rhyming Clowns that gladded Shakespear*'s age,*
No more with crambo entertain the stage.
Who now in Anagrams their Patron praise,
Or sing their Mistress in Acrostic lays?
Ev'n pulpits pleas'd with merry puns of yore;
Now all are banish'd to the Hibernian *shore!*
Thus leaving what was natural and fit,
The current folly prov'd their ready wit;
And authors thought their reputation safe,
Which liv'd as long as fools were pleas'd to laugh.

443-4. Pope moves the vexed questions of religious debate to the safer ground of pre-Reformation disputes.

445-6. Scotists *and* Thomists: adherents to the doctrines of the Franciscan Duns Scotus (c.1265-1308) and the Dominican Thomas Aquinas (c.1224-74). Writing to Caryll of 19 July 1711 (*Corr*, I.126), Pope adduces the same opposition to exemplify pointless sectarian divisions. John Pomfret's poem *Reason* (1700) directs many barbs against Aquinas, Duns Scotus, and 'the noisie Jargon of the Schools' (p. 5). *TE* cites Cowley's comparison of 'the Distinctions of the Schoolmen' to cobwebs, from note 3 to 'Life and Fame', 4-6, *Poems* (1656), p. 40. Southall (1988) cites Bacon, *Advancement of Learning*, IV.1 (1640), p. 30, attacking the schoolmen's '*Cobwebs of Learning*, indeed admirable for fineness of thred and worke, but of no Substance and Profit'.

446. Duck-Lane: in Little Britain, near Smithfield, the region of London where *The Dunciad*, which partly owes its title to Duns, is set; see Rogers (1972: 256-7).

Oldham, 'A Satyr . . . Dissuading the Author from the Study of Poetry', 105, *Poems, and Translations* (1683), p. 170, drew attention to the second-hand bookshops of the area; cf. also Garth, *The Dispensary*, IV, sixth edition (1706), p. 59: 'Refuse of Fairs, and Gleanings of *Duck-Lane*'. The cobwebs of learning are 'kindred' with those of bookstalls because the books are unread.

448. Modes: fashions.

448 Pope's note. Clowns: see Commentary to 324.

crambo: a game in which players must 'cap' a verse from one player with a rhyming line of their own; it is played in Shakespeare's *Love's Labour's Lost*, IV.iii.

Acrostic: verse in which the initial letters of the lines spell out a name; with '*Anagrams*' and '*Puns*', a kind of debased use of language game, one of the problematic types of 'wit' identified by Locke and Addison; see Headnote: Context. *TE* cites Cowley, 'Of Wit', st. 6, *Poems* (1656), p. 3: 'In which who finds out *Wit*, the same may see | In *Anagrams* and *Acrostiques Poetrie*';

450   The *current Folly* proves our *ready Wit,*
      And Authors think their Reputation safe,
      Which lives as long as *Fools* are pleas'd to *Laugh.*
         Some valuing those of their own *Side,* or *Mind,*
      Still make themselves the measure of Mankind;
455   Fondly we think we honour Merit then,
      When we but praise *Our selves* in *Other Men.*
      Parties in *Wit* attend on those of *State,*

450. **our ready:** *1736a–51:* the ready
452^3. MS: The *Rhyming Clowns* that gladded *Shakespear's* Age,
         No more with *Crambo* entertain the Stage.
         Who now in *Anagrams* their Patron praise,
         Or sing their Mistress in *Acrostic* Lays?
         Ev'n Pulpits pleas'd with *merry Puns* of yore;
         Now All are banish'd to th' *Hibernian* Shore!
         And thither soon soft *Op'ra* shall repair,
         Convey'd by *Sw*—— *y* to his native Air,
         There languishing a while prolong its Breath,
         Till, like a Swan, it *sings* itself to Death.
457–8. MS: To be spoke *ill* of, may *good Works* befall,
         But those are *bad* of which *none speak at all.*

and Dryden, consigning Shadwell to 'Some peacefull Province in Acrostick Land', *Mac Flecknoe,* 206, *Miscellany Poems* (1684), p. 10.

Hibernian: Irish; cf. Dennis, *Reflections,* p. 20, Hooker, I.411: 'Is not this a Figure frequently employ'd in *Hibernian* Land?' EC argued that Pope had written these lines after Addison's *Spectator,* no. 63, 12 May 1711, which appeared the day after Pope's poem; McLaverty (2001: 238) suggests that any influence was probably the other way round.

452^3. **MS.** *soft* **Op'ra:** An early example of Pope's vexed engagement with the recent development of opera, often regarded as effeminate ('soft') by contemporaries, here in the satiric key that would later feature in *The Dunciad,* IV.45–70; cf. also 'Prologue to Cato', 42. Dennis had attacked it in *An Essay on the Opera's After the Italian Manner* (1706) and it was a theme of his *Reflections* on Pope's poem (e.g. p. 1); Pope jokes about this in *The Critical Specimen* (1711; *PW,* I.14–15).

Sw—y: Owen Swiney or Swiny (1676–1754), Irish theatre manager, active in London opera from 1706. *TE* (I.200 and 289) suggests Pope is alluding to the failure of opera seasons in 1709–10.

native Air: punning on operatic 'aria' and Sweeney's homeland.

Swan . . . Death: In folklore swans were supposed to sing just before they died; see 'Winter', 39–40, and *Windsor-Forest,* 273–4.

455. **Fondly:** vainly, in self-deceit.

457. **Parties in Wit:** intellectual factions, in the manner of political parties ('those of State'). At this point Pope was still on relatively friendly literary terms with the Whig writers Addison and Steele; during 1713, as divisions hardened, he increasingly aligned himself with Tories such as Swift and Harley. See Headnote to *Windsor-Forest,* and for the phrasing, cf. 'Rape of the Locke', II.98; *Ode for Musick,* 35.

AN ESSAY ON CRITICISM (1711) 257

    And publick Faction doubles private Hate.
    Pride, Malice, Folly, against *Dryden* rose,
460   In various Shapes of *Parsons, Criticks, Beaus*;
    But *Sense* surviv'd, when *merry Jests* were past;
    For rising Merit will *buoy up* at last.
    Might he return, and bless once more our Eyes,
    New *Bl*—— *s* and new *M*—— *s* must arise;

---

464. Bl—— *s*: *1713a–16:* S—— *s; 1717–51: Blackmores*
    M—— *s:* MS, *1713a–16: M*—— *ns; 1717–22, 1736a–51: Milbourns; 1727–32: Milbournes*

---

459. Pride: recalling 207.

Dryden: *TE* notes Pope's first surviving letter, to Wycherley, 26 December 1704 (*Corr,* I.1), commenting on attacks on Dryden: 'I suppose those Injuries were begun by the Violence of Party'. Dryden was subjected to many attacks on literary and political grounds, in a manner Pope strongly identified with (Appendix VI to *The Dunciad Variorum* charts the similarity). Dryden's conversion to Catholicism in 1685, and the events of 1688-9, in which the Catholic King James II was replaced by the Protestant William and Mary, exacerbated the position. Cf. Addison's *Spectator,* no. 125, 24 July 1711, on the effects of party divisions.

460. Parsons: possibly an allusion to the Rev. Jeremy Collier (see Commentary to 225) whose *Short View* targeted Dryden amongst many others, and the Rev. Luke Milbourne (see 464).

Criticks: *TE* cites rival dramatists such as Shadwell and Settle (a major character in *The Dunciad*), as well as Blackmore (see 464 and Commentary) and Gerard Langbaine, whose *Account of the English Dramatick Poets* (1691) contained a long account accusing Dryden of systematic plagiarism.

Beaus: men of fashion, as in 'The Rape of the Locke'. According to Dennis's *Reflections,* p. 28, Hooker, I.416, Pope's critic-friend Walsh was 'a Beau'. *TE* sees the line as a reference to George Villiers, Duke of Buckingham, co-author of *The Rehearsal* (1671), which lampooned Dryden's heroic dramas as pompous and bombastic, and Rochester, who attacked Dryden in 'An Allusion to Horace'. But these were aristocrats rather than 'beaus' and Pope probably had a more general model of complacent, fashionable antagonism in mind.

461. merry Jests: low mockery of Dryden; the phrase also suggests Restoration joke books such as *England's Merry Jester* (1693).

463. Might he return: Dryden had died in 1700; Pope supposedly saw him once (*OAC,* I.25 and II.611-12).

    bless . . . Eyes: Wakefield cites Dryden's translation of Virgil, *Georgics,* IV.729, *Works of Virgil,* p. 144: 'But she return'd no more, to bless his longing Eyes'.

464. Bl—s . . . M—s: as the variants confirm, these figures are Sir Richard Blackmore (1654-1729), who attacked Dryden as an 'old, revolted, unbelieving Bard' in his *Prince Arthur,* VI (1695), p. 167, and Luke Milbourne (1649-1720), a high-church clergyman whose *Notes on Dryden's Virgil* (1698) excoriated Dryden's work, in disappointment at his own failed translation and in vengeance for the poet's satirical comments on Anglican priests. Dryden responded in the conclusion of his 'Preface' to *Fables; TE* points out his use of the phrase 'lest some future *Milbourn* should arise', sig. C2ᵛ. Dennis's *Remarks on a Book, Entitul'd Prince Arthur* (1696) attacked Blackmore and praised Dryden.

464 variant. Pope's substitution of 'S——s' indicates Shadwell, Dryden's antagonist in the 1670s, hero of *Mac Flecknoe,* and the man who, as a loyal Protestant, replaced him as poet laureate in 1688. From 1713 to 1716 Pope was on reasonable terms

465   Nay shou'd great *Homer* lift his awful Head,
        Zoilus again would start up from the Dead.
        Envy will *Merit* as its *Shade* pursue,
        But like a Shadow, proves the *Substance* too;
        For envy'd Wit, like *Sol* Eclips'd, makes known
470   Th' *opposing Body*'s Grossness, not its *own*.
        When first that Sun too powerful Beams displays,
        It draws up Vapours which obscure its Rays;
        But ev'n those Clouds at last adorn its Way,
        Reflect new Glories, and augment the Day.
475   Be thou the *first* true Merit to befriend;

---

467. **as:** MS: like
468. **too;:** *1717–51:* true.
469–74. MS: *Wit*, as the *Sun*, such pow'rful Beams displays,
        It draws up Vapours that obscure its Rays,
        And all those *Clouds* that did at first invade
        The *rising Light*, and interpos'd a Shade,
        When once transpierc'd with its prevailing Ray;
        Reflect its Glories, and augment the Day.

---

with Blackmore, but the first volume of Blackmore's *Essays upon Several Subjects* (1716), published by Edmund Curll, attacked Swift for his impiety and obscenity, leading Pope to restore Blackmore's name. Ault (1949: 255–6) describes the quarrel.

465. **Homer:** see Commentary to 125.
    awful: awe-inspiring.
466. **Zoilus:** philosopher and grammarian of Amphipolis, Macedonia, of the fourth century BC, author of a lost treatise against the poetry of Homer, sometimes known as *Homeromastix*, 'The Scourge of Homer', in which he listed the poet's faults; a byword for malicious criticism of great writers, mentioned in Dryden's 'Dedication' of *Examen Poeticum*, sig. A4ᵛ, and in Swift's 'Digression Concerning Criticks', *Tale of a Tub*, III (1704), p. 76. Parnell added a 'Life of Zoilus' to his translation of a burlesque Homeric poem, *Battle of the Frogs and Mice*, in 1717, probably with Pope's help and certainly with Dennis in mind. Cf. 124^5 MS.
    start up from the Dead: in blasphemous parody of Christ's resurrection miracles.

467. **Shade:** shadow.
467–70. Wit, or creative intelligence is like the sun ('Sol' is Latin for sun, as in 'Rape of the Locke', I.13). Envy is insubstantial in itself but proves the real substance of the 'Merit' which casts the shadow. TE compares Sheffield, *Essay upon Poetry*, 12–14 (1682), p. 2: 'True Wit is everlasting, like the Sun; | Which though sometimes beneath a cloud retir'd, | Breaks out again and is by all admir'd.' Cf. also the passage from Howard cited in the commentary to line 394 above. Péti (2012) discerns an allusion to the description of Satan in Milton, *Paradise Lost*, I.594–7 (1674), p. 20 (amongst several possible models): 'As when the Sun new ris'n | Looks through the Horizontal misty Air | Shorn of his Beams, or from behind the Moon | In dim Eclips disastrous twilight sheds'.
475–6. Dennis criticised Pope for contradicting the spirit of these lines by being late in the day for his praise of Dryden at 459–60; *Reflections*, p. 28, Hooker, I.416. Pope was 12 when Dryden died.

His Praise is lost, who stays till *All* commend;
Short is the Date, alas, of *Modern Rhymes*;
And 'tis but just to let 'em live *betimes*.
No longer now that Golden Age appears,
480   When *Patriarch-Wits* surviv'd a *thousand Years*;
Now Length of *Fame* (our *second* Life) is lost,
And bare Threescore is all ev'n That can boast:
Our Sons their Father's *failing Language* see,
And such as *Chaucer* is, shall *Dryden* be.

---

483. **Father's:** *1736a–51:* fathers

---

476. stays: pauses, waits. TE compares Erasmus' citation of Seneca, *De Beneficiis*, II.i.2: 'Ingratum est beneficium quod diu inter dantis manus haesit' ('unpleasing is the gift which has been fixed for a long time in the hands of the giver').

477. Date: lifespan. TE compares Dryden, *Absalom and Achitophel*, 847 (1681), p. 26: 'Short is the date of all Immoderate Worth' (altered to 'Immoderate Fame' in the second edition, p. 23), and Pope's 'Episode of Sarpedon', 239.

478. betimes: before it is too late.

479-80. The 'Golden Age' is normally associated with an age of innocence in Greek mythology, celebrated by writers such as Hesiod. In his 'Discourse of Pastoral Poetry', Pope declares that 'pastoral is an image of what they call the Golden age' (see *Pastorals*, Appendix II); in *The Dunciad Variorum*, I.26, he parodies the idea with an 'age of Lead'. In the early books of the Bible, patriarchs like Methuselah lived for several hundred years. Dryden discussed the common idea that the present is weak in comparison with the past in *Of Dramatick Poesie*.

481-4. Dennis found 'two or three Absurdities' in these lines; *Reflections*, p. 18, Hooker, I.409-10.

481. Length of Fame: duration of reputation; cf. Wycherley to Pope, 1 April 1710, (*Corr.* I.80): 'no friend can do more for this Friend than preserving his Reputation ... since by preserving his Life, he can only make him live about threescore or fourscore Years; but by preserving his Reputation, he can make him live as long as the World lasts'.

Pope resumes the theme, which is influenced by the Homeric concept of posthumous heroic fame, in 'Prologue, Design'd for Mr. D—'s last Play'; *The Temple of Fame* (1715), esp. 505-8; *Essay on Man* (1733-4), IV.237-8; and *The First Epistle of the Second Book of Horace Imitated* (1737).

482. bare Threescore: barely sixty years, even shorter than the standard biblical lifespan of threescore years and ten. Pope notes in his manuscript notes, 'bare threescore, wh if it were, & threescore years is all –' (see Appendix). Cf. *The Dunciad* (1728), II.263, where Dennis asks plaintively 'And am I now *threescore?*'

boast: claim.

484. Chaucer: the earliest English poet generally cited by Pope and his contemporaries. See Headnotes to 'January and May' and 'The Wife of Bath Her Prologue'. Chaucer's modernisation of 'English' in his own day was the subject of admiring criticism by Rymer, *A Short View of Tragedy* (1693), pp. 73-8, and by Pope in his annotation to Rymer's *The Tragedies of the Last Age* (Mack 1982: 439). Dryden commented on Chaucer's obsolete diction in the 'Preface' to his *Fables*, sig. B1; Temple observed the evanescence of modern, compared with ancient, languages, in his 'Essay Upon the Ancient and Modern

485   So when the faithful *Pencil* has design'd
       Some *fair Idea* of the Master's Mind,
       Where a *new World* leaps out at his command,
       And ready Nature waits upon his Hand;
       When the ripe Colours *soften* and *unite*,
490   And sweetly *melt* into just Shade and Light,
       When mellowing Time does full Perfection give,
       And each Bold Figure just begins to *Live*;

---

486. fair: 1717–51: bright
491. **Time does:** 1717–51: years their

Learning', in *Miscellanea . . . The Second Part* (1690). Pope emphasised the point in the 'Preface' to his *Works*, 1717 (*PW*, I.293), and later began collecting literary 'authorities' for an English dictionary (*OAC*, I.170–1). In his notes Pope considered an alternative prophecy: 'Such as Chaucer is, <u>may</u> Dryden be'. *TE* suggests the influence of Waller, 'Of English Verse', st. 5, *Poems, &c.* (1686), p. 237: '*Chaucer* his Sense can only boast | The glory of his Numbers lost'.

485–94. As in 22–5, a metaphor from painting, an art in which Pope had considerable practical interest from 1705 onwards. Warton (1756: 157) compares Pope's phrasing with Dryden's prophecy to the artist Sir Godfrey Kneller that time 'with his ready Pencil' and 'ripening hand' will 'Add every Grace, which Time alone can grant; | To future Ages shall your Fame convey; | And give more Beauties, than he takes away' ('To Sir Godfrey Kneller', 174–81, *Annual Miscellany: For the Year 1694*, p. 99); but Dryden's verses comment on the permanence granted to Kneller's 'pencil' by time, whereas Pope predicts the opposite phenomenon. *TE* suggests also the influence of Addison, 'An Account of the Greatest English Poets', 30–1, *Annual Miscellany: For the Year 1694*, p. 319: 'But when we look too near, the Shades decay, | And all the pleasing Lan-skip fades away'. Aden (1978: 101) sees the passage as indebted to the opening of Lansdowne's 'Essay Upon Unnatural Flights in Poetry' (cf. Commentary to 248–9).

485. faithful: accurate.

486. fair Idea: beautiful form or shape, alluding to the Platonic doctrine of 'Ideas' as the highest manifestation of reality; for Pope's reading of Plato see *OAC*, I.226.

Master: artist, here a godlike creator, able to conjure a 'new World' by 'command' (487), that is, by drawing it.

488. waits upon: serves, in the manner of a servant.

489. ripe: prepared, ready, softened.

489–90. The artistic process of blending light and shade into a unified whole.

491. mellowing Time: cf. Dryden, 'To the Memory of Mr. Oldham', 20–1, *Works of Mr. John Oldham* (1684), sig. A4^r of second sequence: 'and maturing time | But mellows what we write'.

492. Bold Figure: distinct person, human character; 'figure' also means a rhetorical flourish at 174, and cf. the 'bold Design' of 137. Pope remembered the phrase in his translation of passage describing the decorated shield of Achilles, *Iliad*, XVIII.626: 'And each bold Figure seem'd to live, or die' (an addition to the Greek text).

	The *treach'rous Colours* in few Years decay,
	And all the bright Creation fades away!
495	Unhappy *Wit*, like most mistaken Things,
	Repays not half that *Envy* which it brings;
	In *Youth* alone its empty Praise we boast,
	But soon the Short-liv'd Vanity is lost!
	Like some fair *Flow'r* that in the *Spring* does rise,
500	And gaily Blooms, but ev'n in blooming *Dies*.
	What is this *Wit* that does our Cares employ?
	The Owner's Wife, that *other Men* enjoy,
	The more his *Trouble* as the more *admir'd*;

493, n. 1736a–43: The treach'rous colours in few years decay.
499, n. 1736a–43: Like some fair flow'r that in the spring does rise.

493. in few Years decay: MS: all at once decay; *1717–51:* the fair art betray
496. Repays not half: *1713a–51:* Attones not for
499. that in the *Spring* does rise: *1717–51:* the early spring supplies
500. And: *1717–51:* That
501. that does: *1713a–16:* which does; *1717–51:* which must
503. *1713a–16:* 'Tis most our *Trouble* when 'tis most *admir'd*;
  1717–32: Still most our trouble when the most admir'd;
  1736a–43: The most our trouble still when most admir'd;
  1744–51: Then most our trouble still when most admir'd,

---

493. treach'rous Colours: pigments betray the artist by fading (emphasised in the variant)' cf. *Windsor-Forest*, 305. Cf. Pope to Cromwell, 12 November 1711 (*Corr.*, I.135): 'We grasp some more beautifull Idea in our Brain, than our Endeavors to express it can set to the view of others; & still do but labour to fall short of our first Imagination. The gay Colouring which Fancy gave to our Design at the first transient glance we had of it, goes off in the Execution; like those various Figures in the gilded Clouds, which while we gaze long upon, to seperate [sic] the Parts of each imaginary Image, the whole faints before the Eye, & decays into Confusion'.
495. Unhappy: unfortunate.
  mistaken: misunderstood. Hooker (1951) sees this passage as based on Pope's experiences with Wycherley's poem on Dullness and 'the *unhappiness* of Wit', as detailed in Pope's letter to Wycherley, 20 November 1707, *Corr.*, I.31-2.

497-8. Mason (1974) identifies Pope's source as Dryden's translation of Virgil, *Georgics*, III.108-9, *Works of Virgil*, p. 99: 'In Youth alone, unhappy Mortals live; | But ah! the mighty Bliss is fugitive'.
499. This monosyllabic line contains the expletive 'does'; cf. Commentary to 349-50.
500. gaily: colourfully, brightly; cf. 317.
501. our Cares employ: engage our anxious attention.
502. The metaphor recalls the imagery of 102-5 and 433-4. 'Enjoy', in relation to 'Wife', carries a sexual connotation, suggesting the cuckolding of a hapless husband, unable to control her behaviour and reputation. See also Pope to Caryll, 23 June 1713, *Corr.*, I.179: 'an author who is once come upon the town like a whore that's come upon the town is enjoyed without being thanked for the pleasure, and sometimes ill treated, even by those very persons who first debauched him'.
503. admir'd: see Commentary to 101 and 392.

Where *wanted,* scorn'd, and envy'd where *acquir'd;*
505 Maintain'd with *Pains,* but forfeited with *Ease;*
Sure *some* to *vex,* but never *all* to *please;*
'Tis what the *Vicious fear,* the *Virtuous shun;*
By *Fools* 'tis *hated,* and by *Knaves undone!*
Too much does *Wit* from *Ign'rance* undergo,
510 Ah let not *Learning* too commence its Foe!
Of *old,* those found *Rewards* who cou'd *excel,*
And such were *Prais'd* who but *endeavour'd well:*
Tho' *Triumphs* were to *Gen'rals* only due,

504–5. 1713a–43: The more we give, the more is still requir'd:
   The Fame with Pains we gain, but lose with Ease;
 1744–51: And still the more we give, the more requir'd;
   Whose fame with pains we guard, but lose with ease,
509. **Too much does *Wit*:** *1717–51:* If wit so much
510^11. MS: Learning and Wit were *Friends* design'd by Heav'n,
   Those *Arms* to *guard* it, not to *wound,* were giv'n.
511. **those found:** MS: such met; *1713a–51:* those met
512. **such:** MS: those
   who: *1713a–16:* as

---

504. **wanted:** lacking. 501–4, and this phrase in particular, inspired scorn in Dennis's *Reflections,* p. 20, Hooker, I.411: 'how can Wit be scorn'd where it is not?' In his manuscript notes, Pope noted this as 'to be alterd' because of Dennis's objections (see Appendix). In his letter to Caryll, 25 June 1711 Pope admitted 'What he observes . . . was objected to by yourself . . . and had been mended but for the haste of the press' (*Corr.,* I.121). The textual variants indicate how much Pope struggled with these lines.

504–5 variant. **Fame:** literary fame (cf. 170, 481) and the 'reputation' of the married woman, easily lost by sexual indiscretion; cf. 'January and May', 239, 593.

505. **Pains:** careful efforts.

506. **Sure:** certain.

507–8. Wit is feared by the vicious and the foolish because it exposes them, shunned by the virtuous because of its licentious reputation, and 'undone' (again carrying a sexual connotation) by 'Knaves' (rogues) using it for immoral purposes.

509–10. TE notes that Blackmore had asserted, in *Satyr against Wit,* pp. 6–8, that 'the *Mob* of Wits' was hostile to learning and virtue: 'Wit does our Schools and Colleges invade, | And has of Letters vast Destruction made'.

510^11 MS. **Those Arms:** the weapons of learning; cf. 107–8 and 674.

511–12. EC notes that the same rhyme is found in Dryden, 'Prologue, to the University of Oxford', 27–8, *Miscellany Poems* (1684), p. 274: 'Be kind to Wit, which but endeavours well, | And, where you judge, presumes not to excel'. Cf. Dryden's 'To the Earl of Roscomon. . .', 37–8, in Roscommon's *Essay on Translated Verse* (1684), sig. A1ᵛ: 'That he, who but arrives to copy well, | Unguided will advance; unknowing will excel'. Pope later travestied the rhyme in *The Dunciad* (1728), II.255–6.

513. **Triumphs:** formal state processions as staged by Roman generals after victorious campaigns. Cf. Pope's comparison of writers to generals, to Caryll, 2 August 1711 (*Corr.,* I.132): 'I have read that t'was a

Crowns were reserv'd to grace the *Soldiers* too.
515 *Now* those that reach *Parnassus*' lofty Crown
Employ their Pains to spurn some others down;
And while Self-Love each jealous Writer rules,
Contending Wits become the *Sport of Fools*:
But still the *Worst* with most Regret commend,
520 And each *Ill Author* is as bad a *Friend*.
To what base Ends, and by what abject Ways,
Are Mortals urg'd by *Sacred Lust of Praise*?
Ah ne'er so *dire* a *Thirst of Glory* boast,
Nor in the *Critick* let the *Man* be lost!
525 *Good-Nature* and *Good-Sense* must ever join;
To Err is *Humane*; to Forgive, *Divine*.

---

515. **those that:** *1713a–51:* they who
520. **And:** *1713a–51:* For
522. **by:** *1717–51:* thro'

---

custom among the Romans, while the general rode in triumph, to have slaves in the streets that railed at him and reproached him; to put him in mind that tho' his services were in the main approved & rewarded, yet he had still faults enough to keep him humble'. See also 'Prologue to *Cato*', 33.

514. **Crowns:** various kinds of 'corona' or wreath awarded to Roman soldiers showing particular bravery, such as scaling an enemy wall ('corona muralis') or saving a soldier's life ('corona civica'). Ancient poets of genius are like the generals, and poets who merely tried hard without achieving a major success are the crowned soldiers, with criticism as the Roman state which awards trophies. The competitive modern situation is shown in 515–18: poets who scale Parnassus attack rather than help their fellows. *EC* compares the Soames–Dryden translation of Boileau's *Art of Poetry*, IV.110–17 (1683), p. 60: 'But above all, base Jealousies avoid, | In which detracting Poets are employ'd ... | Base Rivals, who true Wit and Merit hate, | Caballing still against it with the Great, | Maliciously aspire to gain Renown | By standing up, and pulling others down.'

516. spurn: kick away.

521. abject: 'mean and despicable' (*SJ*, citing this line).

522. **Sacred Lust:** *TE* cites the Latin 'sacer' as accursed, 'sacred' to an infernal deity, and compares 'The First Book of Statius his Thebais', 178, and *Temple of Fame*, 522. This is *OED* sense 6, exemplified by Dryden, 'The Cock and the Fox', 254, *Fables*, p. 232: 'For sacred hunger of my Gold I die'. Pope uses 'sacred' ironically at 423 and ambiguously at 553, as well as in its familiar sense of 'holy' at 625 and 183^4, MS variant. Otherwise perhaps a deliberate paradox: those driven by the love of praise see their pursuit as in some way divine.

524. **Critick ... Man:** A spirit of humanity should not be abandoned in criticism

525. TE compares Dryden, 'Discourse Concerning ... Satire', *Satires of Juvenal*, p. ii: 'Good Sence and good Nature, are never separated'.

526. **Humane:** a permissible spelling of 'human', cited by *OED* as illustration for sense 2, 'Of, relating to, or characteristic of humans as distinguished from God or gods; secular, not divine; ... mundane, worldly;

> But if in Noble Minds some Dregs remain,
> Not yet purg'd off, of Spleen and sow'r Disdain,
> Discharge that Rage on more Provoking Crimes,
> 530 Nor fear a Dearth in these Flagitious Times.
> No Pardon vile *Obscenity* should find,
> Tho' *Wit* and *Art* conspire to move your Mind;
> But *Dulness* with *Obscenity* must prove
> As Shameful sure as *Impotence* in *Love*.

527. *1727–51:* new paragraph

---

imperfect, fallible'. In his other early poems, such as 'January and May', and normally elsewhere, Pope spells 'human' in the modern way; as he did not alter this instance, he may have intended some additional suggestion here. See also 639. Rogers (2006: 584) compares Plautus, *Mercator*, II.ii.46, 'Humanum errare est, humanun autem ignoscere est' ('it is human to err, but it is human to excuse'); and cf. Eusden, 'Hero and Leander', *Poetical Miscellanies: The Sixth Part* (1709), p. 600: 'And what we fancy Human, is Divine'.

Divine: because of the model of God's mercy in Christian thought.

527. Dregs: residue after distillation, or remains of grape skin in wine (cf. 546, 610).

527-8. Pope alludes once more to a theory of humours; as any imbalance of bodily chemicals must be 'purged', so any critical tendency to bad temper should be directed against 'more provoking crimes'. 'Spleen' is here 'Anger; spite; ill humour' rather than 'melancholy; hypochondriacal vapours' (*SJ*).

530. Flagitious: wicked, shameful. Cf. 'The VI. Ode of the Third Book of Horace', 21–2, *Miscellany Poems* (1684), p. 200: 'First, those Flagitious times, | (Pregnant with unknown Crimes)', and 'The First Book of Statius his Thebais', 107.

531. *TE* compares Sheffield, *Essay upon Poetry*, 80–1 (1682), p. 6: 'Here, as in all things else, is most unfit | Bawdry barefac'd, that poor pretence to Wit', and Roscommon, *An Essay on Translated Verse*, 113–14 (1685 version), p. 8: '*Immodest words* admit of no defence; | For want of *Decency*, is want of *Sense*'. Sheffield was attacking Rochester, who was defended against this '*old thread-bare Saying among unthinking half-witted People*' by Wolseley in his 'Preface' to Rochester's version of Fletcher's *Valentinian* (1685) (Spingarn 1908-9, III.15). Roscommon's line was quoted approvingly in Blackmore's *Satyr against Wit* (1700), p. 13, and Dennis praised Sheffield's campaign against obscenity in his *Advancement and Reformation of Poetry*, sig. A4ᵛ, Hooker, I.198. Cf. also Dryden, 'Preface' to *Sylvae*, sig. a3ᵛ, defending his translation of obscene sections of Lucretius: ''Tis most certain that barefac'd Bawdery is the poorest pretence to wit imaginable'; and Coward's long discussion, *Licentia Poetica Discuss'd* (1709), p. 41. Pope had already begun experimenting covertly with innuendo-laden verses, many of them later brought to light by Curll; see e.g. Pope to Cromwell, 24 June 1710, *Corr.* I.90.

532. *conspire:* see Commentary to 342.

534. Impotence *in* Love: Pope may be thinking of Rochester's well-known poem on the subject, 'The Imperfect Enjoyment', printed in editions from 1680 onwards (but not in the 1696 edition Pope owned); a different poem on the theme, under the same title, had appeared in 1707 in Curll's edition of Rochester's *Works*. Curll published a series of divorce cases known as *Cases of Impotency*, beginning with *The Case of Insufficiency Discuss'd* (1711).

535   In the fat Age of Pleasure, Wealth, and Ease,
      Sprung the rank Weed, and thriv'd with large Increase;
      When *Love* was all an easie Monarch's Care;
      Seldom at *Council*, never in a *War*.
      Jilts rul'd the State, and Statesmen *Farces* writ;
540   Nay *Wits* had *Pensions*, and *young Lords* had *Wit*:

---

535. fat: opulent, prosperous.

536. rank: strong-growing, fruitful, luxuriant, strongly-scented, or rancid. 'Rank weed' was a very common poetic metaphor; among possible analogues TE cites Roscommon, *Essay on Translated Verse*, 65–6 (1684), p. 5: 'The Soil intended for *Pierian seeds* | Must be well *purg'd* from *rank Pedantic Weeds*', and Shakespeare, *Hamlet*, III.iv.151–2, 'And do not spread the compost on the weeds | To make them ranker'. Hamlet has already (I.ii.135–7) protested that nature is 'an unweeded garden | That grows to seed: things rank and gross in nature | Possess it merely'.

large Increase: literally, many offspring, taking a cue from Charles II, alluded to in the next line; metaphorically, many imitators, as in Dryden's parody, *Mac Flecknoe*, 8, *Miscellany Poems* (1684), p. 1: 'blest with issue of a large increase'.

537. easie Monarch: the promiscuous Charles II (ruled 1660–85); while 'ease' is normally a virtue in the poem (cf. 363, 661 and 671), Charles represents self-indulgence and lack of control. The dispraise of Charles is in contrast to the tributes in the Soames–Dryden version of Boileau's *Art of Poetry*. Dennis, who had contrasted the literary abilities of audiences in Charles's reign with those of a later age in the 'Epistle Dedicatory' (to Granville) of *The Comical Gallant* (1702, Hooker, I.291–4), objected to Pope's account of Charles's reign as a 'Libel'; *Reflections*, p. 22, Hooker, I.412–15. Spence, having remarked to Pope 'I wonder how Horace could say such coarse, obscene things in so polite an age', recorded Pope's response: ''Tis really a wonder, though 'twas the same with us in Charles the Second's time, or rather worse. However, it was not above five or six years, even in that witty reign, that it passed for wit as the saying wicked things does among some now ... the greatest wonder is that it should not have been worn out long ago by the sour reign of King William, the decent one of Queen Anne, and the foolish ones ... ever since; but the prevailing notion of genteelness consisting in freedom and ease has led many to a total neglect of decency, either in their words or behaviour'. (*OAC*, I.227)

538. Council: either the Privy Council or parliament, with the latter of which Charles had a notoriously fractious relationship. Charles led an army to defeat in the battle of Worcester, 1651, but though his 'early valor' was celebrated by Dryden in *Astraea Redux* (1660) he took no direct role in any of the European wars of his reign.

539. Jilts: 'a name of contempt for a woman' (*SJ*, citing this line), i.e. women of dubious character, especially in sexual terms: cf. Behn's story, *The Fair Jilt* (1688). Charles's mistresses, especially Barbara Villiers, Duchess of Cleveland, and Louise de Kéroualle, Duchess of Portsmouth, were widely alleged to wield disproportionate power; Rochester mocked the situation in poems such as 'A Satyr on Charles II'.

Statesmen Farces writ: probably meaning the Duke of Buckingham (see Commentary to 460).

540. Wits *had* Pensions: Some writers (in particular, Dryden, as Poet Laureate and Historiographer Royal) had state salaries. The abrupt shift in argument, to suggest that Charles's dissolute court had its merits, was noted by Dennis, who pointed out (*Reflections*, pp. 22–4, Hooker, I.412–13) that many writers, including Wycherley,

The Fair sate panting at a *Courtier's Play*,
And not a Mask went *un-improv'd* away:
The modest Fan was lifted up no more,
And Virgins *smil'd* at what they *blush'd* before—
545 The following Licence of a Foreign Reign

---

were insufficiently rewarded by aristocrats. Pope was offered a pension in 1714 by Lord Halifax (*Corr.*, I.271 and *OAC*, I.99).

young Lords had Wit: cf. the seventeenth-century 'Mob of Gentlemen who wrote with Ease', in Pope's *The First Epistle of the Second Book of Horace, Imitated*, 108. Privately, Pope thought of such men as 'holiday writers – as gentlemen that diverted themselves now and then with poetry, rather than as poets'; *OAC*, I.201–2. As well as Buckingham and Rochester, Pope could have meant Sir Charles Sedley (c.1639–1701) and Charles Sackville, Earl of Dorset (1643–1706); he produced two early imitations of Dorset's lyric style, 'Artimesia' and 'Phryne'. Dennis reproved Pope for his irreverence: 'his particular Pique seems to be at People of Quality, for whom he appears to have a very great Contempt'; *Reflections*, p. 25, Hooker, I.414. Pope's insouciant response is in his letter to Caryll, 25 June 1711, *Corr.*, I.123, where he speaks of Lord Petre, model for the hero of 'The Rape of the Locke', as 'one of those young lords that have wit in our days!'

541. The Fair: the fair sex, a woman or women generally.

sate: sat.

panting: responding emotionally (with a suggestion of heightened sexual feeling; cf. 'Winter', 80).

Courtier's Play: *TE* cites plays by Sedley; Sir Robert Howard, politician and playwright, and Dryden's brother-in-law, is another possibility. 'Play' also carried some sexual connotation.

542. Mask: A woman wearing a mask or 'vizard', commonly to increase freedom of behaviour. In 1704 an attempt was made to 'reform all other indecencies and abuses of the stage' by an edict of Queen Anne, reported in *The Daily Courant* of 24 January 1704, specifying that 'no Woman be Allowe'd or Presume to wear a Vizard-Mask in either of the Theatres'.

un-improv'd: initially suggests that drama 'improved' the minds of women, but the italics emphasise irony: what the masked women learned was bad behaviour.

543. modest Fan: Women of rank carried fans to shield themselves from inappropriate gazing and to block offensive sights. Fans could also serve as flirtatious props, as satirised in *The Tatler*, no. 52, 9 August 1709, and 239, 19 October 1710; cf. 'The Rape of the Locke', I.81, and 'On a Fan of the Author's Design'.

544. The modest virgin blush was proverbial: e.g. Tate, *Panacea: A Poem Upon Tea*, II (1700), p.24: 'A rosie Blush adorns her Virgin-Face'. Cf. Cowley, 'Of Wit', st. 6, *Poems* (1656), p. 3: 'Much less can that have any place | At which a *Virgin* hides her face'. See Pope's flirtatious letter to Martha Blount, accompanying the volume in which 'The Rape of the Locke' was first published: 'wherein (they tell me) are some things that may be dangerous to be lookd upon; however I think You may venture, tho' you shou'd Blush for it, since Blushing becomes you the best of any Lady in England, and then the most dangerous thing to be lookd upon is Yourself' (25 May 1712, *Corr.*, I.143).

545. Licence: licentiousness; closer to the negative sense of 685 than the positive one of 149–50. A glance at the policy of toleration towards protestant dissenters introduced by the 'Foreign Reign', the Dutch William of Orange, after the revolution of 1688. Dennis objected to the imputation in *Reflections*, p. 27, Hooker, I.415.

>   Did all the Dregs of bold *Socinus* drain;
>   Then *first* the *Belgian Morals* were extoll'd;
>   We their *Religion* had, and they our *Gold*:
>   Then Unbelieving Priests reform'd the Nation,
> 550 And taught more *Pleasant* Methods of Salvation;

549, n. 1736a–51: The Author has omitted two lines which stood here, as containing a National Reflection, which in his stricter judgment he could not but disapprove, on any People whatever.

547–8. 1736a–51: omitted

---

546. **bold:** rash and damagingly uncompromising, as at 111, rather than in the positive senses of 137 and elsewhere; *TE* cites Dryden, *Religio Laici*, 312 (1682), p. 20: 'the bold *Socinian*'.

Socinus: Laelius Socinus, or Lelio Sozzini (1525-62), who promulgated controversial doctrines, such as the denial of the divinity of Christ, of the atonement for sin through Christ's sacrifice, and of the sacred quality of the sacraments. Pope's early lifetime was marked by bitter theological controversy on these issues. Dennis thought Milton 'a little tainted with Socinianism' (*Grounds of Criticism in Poetry*, p. 36, Hooker, I.345). John Edwards's four-volume *Preservative Against Socinianism* (1693-1703) and Henry Sacheverell's inflammatory sermon *The Perils of False Brethren* (1709) were recent conservative attacks on the heresy; Sacheverell blamed toleration of protestant dissent for promoting '*Atheism, Deism, Tritheism, Socinianism*'. The Toleration Act did not in fact extend to such heresies and in 1697-8 William's parliament passed *An Act for the more Effectual Suppressing of Blasphemy and Profaneness*, explicitly outlawing denial of the Trinity. Whiston, whose lectures on astronomy would captivate Pope, had been dismissed from his Cambridge professorship for heterodoxy of this kind in 1710. Pope jokingly aligned his friend Walsh with Socinianism in a letter to Swift (8 December 1713, *Corr.*, I.200).

547. **Belgian Morals:** 'Belgian' refers to the low countries or Netherlands; a further hit at the (Dutch) William of Orange.

548. Pope associates subversive theology with Dutch Protestantism. The trade wars with the Dutch which had marked Charles II's reign (forming the scenic backdrop of Dryden's *Of Dramatick Poesie*) were supplanted by English involvement in William's European wars, which, some alleged, benefited city financiers at the expense of the landed interest. Aden (1978: 108) comments that this couplet summarises the 'Tory case against the Dutch alliance during the War'. Womersley (1997: xxxiii) argues that the later omission of the couplet (see Pope's note to 549) coincides with Pope's self-alignment with the Patriot opposition to Sir Robert Walpole, much of which was devoted to the 1688 settlement; McLaverty (2001: 238) suggests that the omission has more to do with refinement of tone.

549. **Unbelieving Priests:** clergyman lacking secure faith, especially those of a 'latitudinarian' outlook, such as Gilbert Burnet (1643-1715), Bishop of Salisbury, a supporter of William and object of much ridicule from Pope's circle.

reform'd: recalling the Protestant Reformation under Henry VIII, applied ironically to an undemanding religious tolerance. Burnet's controversial *History of the Reformation of the Church of England* (begun in 1679), perhaps prompted 'reform'd'; *TE* suggests that Pope is suggesting also Burnet's 're-forming' of English history and statehood.

Where Heav'ns Free Subjects might their *Rights* dispute,
Lest God himself shou'd seem too *Absolute*.
Pulpits their *Sacred Satire* learn'd to spare,
And Vice *admir'd* to find a *Flatt'rer there!*
555 Encourag'd thus, Witt's *Titans* brav'd the Skies,
And the Press groan'd with Licenc'd *Blasphemies* —

---

550. **Pleasant ... Salvation:** a reference to White Kennett (1660–1728), whose funeral sermon for William Cavendish, Duke of Devonshire (1641–1707) appeared to suggest that aristocrats were more likely to make successful deathbed repentances than people of lower class; he was installed in 1708 as Dean of Peterborough, at the instigation of Devonshire's heir. *TE* notes that Sacheverell's *Perils of False Brethren* (1709), p. 10, alludes to Kennett's sermon: 'If to *Flatter* both the *Dead* and the *Living* in their *Vices*, and to tell the World, that if they have *Wit*, and *Money* enough they need no *Repentance*, and that only *Fools* and *Beggars* can be *Damn'd*...'. John Dunton's *The Hazard of a Death-bed Repentance* (1708) was a much-reprinted riposte to Kennett. Pope returned to the incident in *The Second Epistle of the Second Book of Horace Imitated*, 220–1.

551–2. An allusion to Whig political theory, according to which civil society derived from the union of individuals whose voice was the source of political sovereignty, as opposed to Tory or patriarchal theory, which derived sovereignty from God's commission to Adam to rule over his family, and thus stressed the Divine Right of Kings (cf. 656–7). Dryden addressed similar divisions in *Absalom and Achitophel* (1681), and the political faultlines reopened in 1710 with the impeachment of Sacheverell for attacking Whigs and dissenters. Pope appears to suggest that Whig clergymen taught that individuals could negotiate the terms of their obedience to God, a view heretical under any Christian denomination.

553. **Sacred Satire:** stern religious commentary against vice. For 'Sacred' see Commentary to 423 and 522.

554. **admir'd:** was surprised (cf. 392).

555. **Titans:** in Greek mythology, an early race of primitive, godlike giants, offspring of Heaven and Earth, who overthrew their father; hence 'brav'd the Skies', i.e. defied Heaven. Roscommon, *An Essay on Translated Verse*, 155 (1684), p. 11, refers to '*Rebel-Titan's sacrilegious Crime*'. *TE* suggests the allusion is to freethinkers, challenging heaven with blasphemous publications, and also compares James Drake's attack on Blackmore, 'To Dr. Garth', in *Commendatory Verses, on the Author of the Two Arthurs* (1700), p. 20: 'Whose tow'ring Non-sense braves the very Skies'; cf. also Lady Mary Chudleigh's lines on books in *Essays upon Several Subjects* (1710), p. 236, where inspired readers 'like the Giants, brave the Skies'.

556. **Licenc'd:** Until 1695 government licensers were appointed to read works before publication to check for seditious material in advance. The Licensing Acts had also attempted to restrict the number of printing presses. Pope may mean that William's licensers were happy to pass blasphemous works, or that the lapse of the Act meant that anything was 'licensed'. *TE* suggests John Toland's *Christianity Not Mysterious* (1696) as a typical beneficiary of the supposed new laxity. Swift's *Tale of a Tub* (1704) included a satiric account of the growth in controversial publishing after 1695; the 'Apology' in the fifth edition (1710), sig. A3ʳ, referred obliquely to Francis Gastrell's *The Principles of Deism Truly Represented and Set in a Clear Light*, in which a Sceptic and a Deist discuss the uses of witty profanity in furthering their blasphemous cause (second edition, 1709, p. 56). For regulation of the

These Monsters, Criticks! with your Darts engage,
Here point your Thunder, and exhaust your Rage!
Yet shun their Fault, who, *Scandalously nice,*
560   Will needs *mistake* an Author *into Vice;*
All seems Infected that th' Infected spy,
As all looks yellow to the Jaundic'd Eye.

Learn then what MORALS Criticks ought to show,
For 'tis but half a *Judge's Task,* to *Know.*
565   'Tis not enough, Wit, Art, and Learning join;

---

558. **exhaust:** MS: discharge
565. **Wit, Art and Learning:** *1744–51:* taste, judgment, learning,

---

press in Pope's time see Downie (1979). Abel Boyer's 'Licentious Writers Check'd', in his *History of the Reign of Queen Anne, Digested into Annals. Year the Fifth* (1707), pp. 486–9, provided a list of recent post-publication prosecutions.

557. **Monsters:** (a) 'something out of the common order of nature'; (b) 'something horrible for deformity, wickedness, or mischief' (*SJ*). Cf. 'The First Book of Statius his Thebais', 705, 719, etc.; the word is very common in Pope's translations of Homer.

   Darts: arrows or spears, metaphorically weapons of criticism; cf. 107–8.

558. **Thunder:** Zeus, king of the gods in Greek mythology, was known as the 'thunderer' and punished people by hurling thunderbolts, as in Pope's translation of Homer's *Iliad,* V.559–60: 'The Wretch would brave high Heav'ns immortal Sire, | His triple Thunder, and his Bolts of Fire'. Cf. also 'The First Book of Statius his Thebais', 109–10, and 'Rape of the Locke', II.108.

559. **Scandalously nice:** pruriently fastidious, finding sexual suggestions where none is intended.

560. **mistake** *an Author:* OED cites this couplet for definition 4a of 'mistake': 'To misunderstand the meaning of (a person); to attach a wrong meaning to the words or actions of (a person)'. *TE* notes that in his 'Preface' to *Fables,* sig. D2ʳ, Dryden, after confessing that Collier (see commentary to 225, 460) had justly censured some of his work for obscenity, complained that he had also 'interpreted my Words into Blasphemy and Baudry, of which they were not guilty'.

562. **Jaundic'd:** affected by jaundice, a liver disease causing yellowing of skin; a metaphor for an inclination to find fault with everything. *EC* compares Creech's translation of *Lucretius his Six Books of Epicurean Philosophy* (1700), p. 112: 'Besides, whatever *Iaundice* Eyes do view, | Look pale as well as those, and yellow too'. Cf. also Dryden, 'Palamon and Arcite', 1097–8, *Fables,* p. 42: 'And Jealousie suffus'd, with Jaundice in her Eyes; | Discolouring all she view'd, in Tawney dress'd'. Rymer comments on the critic's eye: 'it often happens, that this eye is so distorted by envy or ill nature, that it sees nothing aright'; 'Preface' to his translation of Rapin's *Reflections on Aristotle's Treatise of Poesie,* sig. A3ʳ.

563. **show:** display in personal conduct, as well as point out in literary texts.

565 **variant.** *TE* suggests that the very late revision moves the discussion away from qualities appropriate to the poet towards those particular to the critic. Having introduced 'Judgment' here, Pope then substituted 'Sense' to avoid duplicating that word in 567. Foxon (1991: 178) plausibly suggests that the 1744 changes in this line and 567 are due to the influence of Warburton.

>   In all you speak, let Truth and Candor shine:
>   That not alone what to your *Judgment*'s due,
>   All may allow; but seek your *Friendship* too.
>   Be *silent* always when you *doubt* your Sense;
> 570 *Speak* when you're *sure*, yet speak with *Diffidence*;
>   Some positive persisting Fops we know,
>   That, if *once wrong*, will needs be *always so*;
>   But you, with Pleasure own your Errors past,
>   And make each Day a *Critick* on the last.
> 575   'Tis not enough your Counsel still be *true*,
>   *Blunt Truths* more Mischief than *nice Falshoods* do;
>   Men must be *taught* as if you taught them *not*;
>   And Things *ne'er known* propos'd as Things *forgot*.

---

567. Judgment's: 1744–51: sense is
570. 1713a–51: And speak, tho' sure, with seeming Diffidence:
571. **persisting:** MS: abandon'd
572. **That:** *1744–51:* Who
576. **Mischief:** *1727–32:* mischiefs
578. **ne'er known:** *1717–51:* unknown

---

566. Candor: 'sweetness of temper; purity of mind; openness; ingenuity; kindness' (*SJ*). Dryden finds it a quality of several of his literary noblemen dedicatees, e.g. the Earl of Dorset, 'Discourse Concerning ... Satire', *Satires of Juvenal*, p. xv. In *Of Dramatic Poesie*, p. 56, Dryden commends Horace for combining severity with 'candour' in judgment.
568. allow: acknowledge.
569–70. Dennis complained that the first line of this couplet was 'very impertinent' and the second 'very wrong', *Reflections*, p. 21, Hooker, I. 411. In his manuscript notes, Pope wrote 'alter ye Inconsi[stenc]y', hence the 1713a variant (see Appendix).
570. Diffidence: cf. 629–30. In the 'Atticus' portrait (written c. 1716 but not published until 1722), Pope chided Addison for extending this ostensibly modest behaviour into malignity; see also *Epistle to Dr. Arbuthnot*, 188–209.
571. positive: 'dogmatical; ready to lay down notions with confidence; stubborn in opinion' (*SJ*, citing this passage).

Fops: men 'of small understanding and much ostentation ... fond of show, dress and flutter' (*SJ*). Cf. 'Rape of the Locke', II.22.
572. will needs be: must be, insist on being.
574. Critick: critique, critical account. Cf. Pope to Cromwell, 20 July 1710: 'the more a man advances in understanding, he becomes the more every day a critic upon himself' (*Corr.*, I.92).
577–8. This proposal resembles the gentlemanly commerce of letters advocated by Addison and Steele, the critic acting as a friend within a social group, rather than an expert acting from above. Pope's ideas on critical tact had undergone some tempering from the experience of helping the irascible Wycherley edit his poems, the subject of many letters from 1705 onwards (see in particular *Corr.*, I.13, 15–16, and *OAC*, I.35). Pope and Cromwell exchanged more straightforward comment on each other's work, and Pope thanked Congreve publicly for similar offices in relation to the Homer translation (*PW*, I.253). See also Headnotes

Without *Good Breeding, Truth* is not approv'd,
580   *That* only makes *Superior* Sense *belov'd.*
         Be Niggards of Advice on no Pretence;
      For the *worst Avarice* is that of *Sense*:
      With mean Complacence ne'er betray your Trust,
      Nor be so *Civil* as to prove *Unjust*;
585   Fear not the Anger of the Wise to raise;
      Those best can *bear Reproof,* who *merit Praise.*
         'Twere well, might Criticks still this Freedom take;
      But *Appius* reddens at each Word you speak,
      And stares, *Tremendous*! with a *threatning Eye,*

589, n. *1744–51:* This picture was taken to himself by *John Dennis,* a furious old Critic by profession, who, upon no other provocation, wrote against this Essay and its author, in a manner perfectly lunatic: For, as to the mention made of him in v. 270. he took it as a Compliment, and said it was treacherously meant to cause him to overlook this *Abuse of his Person.*

579. not approv'd,: *1717–51:* disapprov'd;
588. Appius: MS: D ——

---

to *Pastorals,* 'The Episode of Sarpedon', 'Sapho to Phaon' and 'The First Book of Statius his Thebais'.

579. Good Breeding: polite bearing and behaviour; how this might work in practice is indicated at 634-45.

580. That *only*: that alone.

581. Niggards: SJ, citing Pope's line, defines 'niggard' as 'a miser; a curmudgeon; a sordid, avaricious, parsimonious fellow'. Pope's usage is similar to Shakespeare, *Macbeth,* IV.iii.181: 'Be not a niggard of your speech'.

583. Complacence: OED sense 3, 'disposition to please, oblige, or comply with the wishes of others; complaisance': here an unworthy willingness to please.

588. Appius: Pope's codename for Dennis, from his tragedy *Appius and Virginia* which failed at Drury Lane in February 1709. The MS variant 'D——s' confirms the obvious, despite Pope's disingenuous disavowal (see his note to 589).

589. stares: *EC* cites Steele, *The Theatre,* 12 (9 February 1720), on Dennis's personal habit: 'he starts, stares, and looks round him at every Promotion, or rather Jerk of his Person forward'; but Steele was writing nine years after Pope. The 'most learned manner of *Frowning* . . . with the *whole Art of Staring*' is listed as part of Chapter 23 of Pope's response to Dennis in *The Critical Specimen, PW,* I.15. See the letter to Caryll, 25 June 1711, *Corr.,* I.121, cited in the Headnote: Context.

Tremendous: 'Dreadful; horrible; astonishingly terrible' (*SJ,* citing *Tatler,* no. 57, 20 August 1709: 'the Priest celebrates some Mysteries which they call holy, sacred, and tremendous'). *TE* notes that Dennis's use of the word had already been satirised by Thomas Cheek in the 'Prologue' to Abel Boyer's *Achilles* (1700), and that in *A Comparison Between the Two Stages* (1702), p. 37, the author (possibly Gildon) notes of Dennis's *Iphigenia* (1700) that 'there were many TREMENDOUS things in't; but if there be any thing of Tragedy in't it lies in that word, for he is so fond of it, he had rather use it in every Page, than slay his belov'd *Iphigenia*'. The word appears four times in the play. Dennis also used it in poems such as

590   Like some fierce *Tyrant* in *Old Tapestry*!
       Fear most to tax an *Honourable* Fool,
       Whose Right it is, *uncensur'd* to be dull;
       Such without *Wit* are Poets when they please,
       As without *Learning* they can take *Degrees*.
595   Leave dang'rous *Truths* to unsuccessful *Satyrs*,
       And *Flattery* to *fulsome Dedicators*,

---

591. 1727–32: new paragraph

Britannia Triumphans (1704), p. 66, and *The Battle of Ramillia* (1706), pp. 5, 103. It was scarcely used by Dryden, but it clearly signified 'sublime' content: Blackmore used it six times in *Prince Arthur* (1695) and four in *King Arthur* (1697), and Pope would use the word without irony twelve times in the *Iliad* translation and nine in the *Odyssey*. In Act I of their co-authored play, *Three Hours after Marriage* (1717), p. 18, Gay, Pope and Arbuthnot caricature Dennis as Sir Tremendous, 'the greatest Critick of our Age'.

589 Pope's note. by profession: by his own estimation or public identification. There were no professional critics of the modern kind, but insofar as Dennis was a critic and writer working within a commercial literary system, he was antipathetic to Pope's gentlemanly, independent model; cf. 106 and Commentary.

590. Tyrant ... Tapestry: cf. 'Rape of the Locke', II.7. Narrative wall-hangings on biblical or mythological subjects were common in aristocratic houses; Pope knew Flemish examples at Hampton Court. The 'shaggy Tap'stry' of *Dunciad Variorum*, II.135 is also prefigured here. Wakefield cites Donne's fourth *Satyre*, 225–6, *Poems, by J. D.* (1633), p. 344: 'And though his Face be as ill | As theirs which in old hangings whip Christ'. Pope's *The Fourth Satire of Dr John Donne Versified*, 266–7, reads: 'And with a Face as red, and as awry, | As *Herod*'s Hang-dogs in old Tapestry', confirming the legitimacy of the rhyme.

591. tax: take to task, criticise.

   Honourable *Fool*: foolish nobleman; cf. 415–24.

594. Degrees: university degrees, sometimes awarded to members of noble families attending Oxford and Cambridge without very strict academic requirements. As a Catholic, Pope could not enter either British university, though he was later offered (and declined) an honorary doctorate from Oxford.

595. dang'rous Truths: the honesty that might infringe the law of seditious libel, a pressing concern throughout Pope's later career as a satirist; see his imaginary legal advice to himself in *The First Satire of the Second Book of Horace Imitated*, 143–8.

   Satyrs: i.e. satires. The pronunciation was less distant from the rhyme sound in Pope's time.

596. Dedicators: literary productions were commonly equipped with a flattering dedication to a nobleman in a bid for patronage. Dryden's critical essays usually took the form of dedicatory epistles to noblemen, whereas Pope generally dedicated work to fellow-writers or other figures of middling rank; the *Essay* has no dedication at all. (Cf. however *Windsor-Forest*.) See the essay on dedications in *The Guardian*, no. 4, 16 March 1713, attributed to Pope by Ault (*PW*, I.76–82). In *The Dunciad* (1728), II.179–92 and *Epistle to Dr. Arbuthnot*, 231–48, Pope caricatures the dedication process. On Pope and patronage in the period see Griffin (1996: chapter 6).

AN ESSAY ON CRITICISM (1711)

      Whom, when they *Praise*, the World believes no more,
      Than when they promise to give *Scribling* o'er.
      'Tis best sometimes your Censure to restrain,
600 And *charitably* let dull Fools be *vain*:
      Your Silence there is better than your *Spite*,
      For who can *rail* so long as they can *write*?
      Still humming on, their old dull Course they keep,
      And *lash'd* so long, like *Tops*, are lash'd *asleep*.
605 *False Steps* but help them to renew the Race,
      As after *Stumbling*, Jades will *mend* their Pace.
      What Crouds of these, impenitently bold,
      In *Sounds* and jingling *Syllables* grown old,
      Still *run on* Poets in a raging Vein,
610 Ev'n to the Dregs and *Squeezings* of the *Brain*;

---

600. dull Fools: *1713a–51:* the Dull
603. old dull: *1713a–51:* drowzy
609. raging: *1713b–16:* frantick

---

598. Cf. Pope's *The First Epistle of the Second Book of Horace*, 177–8. Johnson records that Pope himself often made this kind of unconvincing gesture; Lonsdale, IV.35–6.
    Scribling: See Commentary to 34.
602. rail *so long as*: complain noisily for as much time as. *EC* compares the 'Essay Upon Satyre' ascribed to Sheffield (see 364^5. variant), 71, *Fourth (and Last) Collection of Poems* . . . (1689), p. 26: 'But who can Rail as long as he can Sleep?' Cf. also Ward, *The Fourth Part of Vulgus Britannicus: or, The British Hudibras*, XI (1710), p. 119: 'These arm'd with *Impudence* and *Spite*, | Began to *Rail*, that is, to *Write*'.
603–4. Spinning tops were kept going by a small cord whip; at high speed the top appeared stationary. *EC* compares the last lines of 'Epilogue Written by a Person of Honour' to Dryden's *Secret-Love* (1668), p. 68: 'But 'tother day I heard this rhyming Fop | Say Criticks were the Whips, and he the Top; | For, as a Top spins best the more you baste her, | So ev'ry lash you give, he writes the faster.' *TE* adds Congreve, *The Old Bachelour*, I.i (1693), p. 8: 'should he seem to rouse, 'tis but well lashing him, and he will sleep like a Top'.
605. False Steps: a stumble.
    renew the Race: Pope later makes Curll do this in *The Dunciad* (1728), II.53–88.
606. Jades: worn-out horses, who may stumble but then pick up speed. Cf. e.g. Cotton, 'The Litany', st. vii, *Poems on Several Occasions* (1689), p. 479: 'a kicking, stumbling Jade'.
607. impenitently bold: Here, as in 111 and 546, 'bold' indicates brazen confidence, like that of a hardened criminal, as opposed to the courage it denotes at 137, 152, etc.
608. Sounds *and jingling* Syllables: the dead matter of language; for 'jingling' cf. *The Dunciad* (1743), IV.162. The word was often associated with rhyme, as in Milton's fierce defence of 'The Verse' of *Paradise Lost* (1674) against '*the jingling sound of like endings*' (sig. A4ʳ), and see 'Lines from *The Critical Specimen*'. II.1, Commentary.
610. Squeezings: Wakefield compares Dryden, *Aureng-Zebe*, II.i.230 (1676), p. 21: 'The dregs and droppings of enervate Love'. *TE* compares Oldham, 'Satyr II', 25, *Satyrs upon the Jesuits* (1681), p. 25: 'With all the

>   Strain out the last, dull droppings of their Sense,
>   And Rhyme with all the *Rage* of *Impotence*!
>   Such shameless *Bards* we have; and yet 'tis true,
>   There are as mad, abandon'd *Criticks* too.
> 615   The Bookful Blockhead, ignorantly read,
>   With *Loads of Learned Lumber* in his Head,
>   With his own Tongue still edifies his Ears,
>   And always *List' ning to Himself* appears.
>   All Books he reads, and all he reads assails,

615.] Nihil pejus est iis, qui paullum aliquid ultra primas litteras progressi, falsam sibi scientiae persuasionem induerunt: Nam & cedere praecipiendi peritis indignantur, & velut jure quodam potestatis, quo ferè hoc hominum genus intumescit, imperiosi, atque interim saevientes, Stultitiam suam perdocent. Quintil. lib. I. ch. I.

---

613. MS: But if Incorrigible *Bards* we view,
615. **Blockhead, ignorantly:** MS: Dunce, unprofitably

---

dregs and squeesings of his rage'. By adding 'Strain' and 'droppings' Pope confirms the metaphor as one of bodily excrement, another prefiguring of *The Dunciad*. Cf. the constipated poet of *Epistle to Dr Arbuthnot*, 182, who 'strains from hard-bound brains eight lines a-year'.

612. **Rage ... Impotence:** TE notes the long tradition by which Pope is held to be alluding to Wycherley here, though the syntax is clearly plural. Wycherley himself apparently praised the poem, and Pope was 'highly in his favour' in late 1711 (Cromwell to Pope, 26 October 1711, *Corr.*, I.134). TE suggests the image derives from Dryden's 'Epilogue' to *The Conquest of Granada*, first part, 14–16 (1672), p. 69: 'But elder wits are like old Lovers curst; | Who, when the vigor of their youth is spent, | Still grow more fond as they grow impotent.' Cf. also Rochester, 'The Imperfect Enjoyment', 30, *Poems on Several Occasions* (1680), p. 29: 'And *Rage*, at last, confirms me impotent'.

614. Cf. Ward, *A Journey to H[ell]*, part II, VI.37 (1700), p. 9: 'Thus did the Partial Criticks all run Mad'.

615. **Bookful:** 'Full of notions gleaned from books; crowded with undigested knowledge' (*SJ*, citing this passage); perhaps Pope's coinage.

615 **Pope's note.** Quintilian, *Institutio Oratoria*, I.i.8: 'Nothing is worse than those who having gone a little way beyond the alphabet have taken on a deluded notion of their real knowledge. For they regard it as an indignity to submit to the processes of instruction, and as if endowed with a certain right of power, with which this type of person generally swells up, imperiously and sometimes savagely indoctrinate [others] with their own stupidity'. There is a similar attack in Vida, *De Arte Poetica*, II.191–202. The passage prefigures Pope's assault on scholarship in *The Dunciad* (1728), I.106–16.

616. **Lumber:** 'Any thing useless or cumbersome; any thing of more bulk than value' (*SJ*). Garth uses it of a worthless library in *The Dispensary* IV.119, 132, sixth edition (1706), pp. 58–9; and cf. Tate, *A Monumental Poem in Memory of the Right Honourable Sir George Treby Kt.* (1701), p. 10: 'And Learning's *Library* from Loads of Rev'rend Lumber freed'.

620   From *Dryden's Fables* down to *D —— y*'s *Tales.*
      With *him*, most Authors steal their Works, or buy;
      Garth did not write his own *Dispensary*.
      Name a new *Play*, and *he's* the Poet's *Friend*,
      Nay show'd his Faults — but when wou'd Poets mend?
625   No Place so Sacred from such Fops is barr'd,
      Nor is *Paul's Church* more safe than *Paul's Church-yard*:

622, n. *1744–51:* A common slander at that time in prejudice of that deserving author. Our poet did him this justice, when that slander most prevail'd; and it is now (perhaps the sooner for this very verse) dead and forgotten.

626, n. *1736a–43, 1751:* Between Verse 625 and 626;

In vain you shrug, and sweat, and strive to fly,
These know no Manners, but in Poetry:
They'll stop a hungry Chaplain in his Grace,
To treat of Unities of Time and Place.

620. D —— y's: MS, *1727–51: Durfy*'s
626^7. MS: They'l stop a hungry Chaplain at his Grace,
         To treat of Unities of *Time* and *Place*:
         In vain you shrug, and sweat, and strive to fly;
         These know no *Manners* but in *Poetry*:

---

620. Dryden's Fables: Dryden' *Fables Ancient and Modern* appeared in 1700 and provided Pope with a model of imitation followed in his early Chaucer versions.

D——y's Tales: Thomas D'Urfey (see 420 MS variant) published *Tales, Tragical and Comical* (1704) and *Stories, Moral and Comical* (1707), the first avowedly modelled on Dryden's *Fables*, according to the opening of the 'Preface', hence Pope's pointed contrast between high and low forms of literature. TE notes the model of Blackmore, *Satyr Against Wit*, p. 9: 'From *D—fy*'s, or from Poet *D—n—*'s Plays'.

621. Pope may be thinking of the obsessive detection of plagiarism practised by Langbaine (see Commentary to 460).

622. See Commentary to 109–12.

622 Pope's note. In his *Satyr Against Wit*, p. 13, Blackmore claims that 'Felonious *G—* pursuing this Design, | Smuggles *French* Wit, as others Silks and Wine'; that is, he modelled *The Dispensary* on Boileau's *Le Lutrin*

(1674). The general charge was maintained in John Lacy's *The Steeleids* (1714).

626. Paul's Church: St Paul's Cathedral, commissioned from Sir Christopher Wren in 1668 after the Great Fire of London destroyed the medieval cathedral, finally completed in 1710.

Paul's Church-yard: The churchyard of St Paul's had been a centre of the book trade for at least a century, and was hence known as a haunt of literary hangers-on and a loitering place for idle adventurers: Chapter IV of Thomas Dekker, *The Guls Horne-book* (1609), pp. 17–22, has satirical instructions on 'How a Gallant should behaue himself in Powles-walkes', and Thomas Nashe, in *Pierce Penilesse His Supplication to the Devil* (1592), sig. A3ᵛ, has his 'careless malecontent' wander about St Paul's looking for food, money and companionship.

626 variant and Pope's note. Grace: The chaplain is interrupted in giving the grace before a meal by the critic whose idea of

>   Nay, run to *Altars*; there they'll talk you dead;
>   For *Fools* rush in where *Angels* fear to tread.
>   Distrustful *Sense* with modest Caution speaks;
> 630   It still *looks home*, and *short Excursions* makes;
>   But ratling *Nonsense* in full *Vollies* breaks;
>   And never shock'd, and never turn'd aside,
>   *Bursts out*, resistless, with a thundring Tyde!
>   But where's the Man, who Counsel *can* bestow,
> 635   Still *pleas'd* to *teach*, and yet not *proud* to *know*?
>   Unbiass'd, or by *Favour* or by *Spite*;
>   Not *dully prepossest*, or *blindly right*;
>   Tho' Learn'd, well-bred; and tho' well-bred, sincere;
>   Modestly bold, and Humanly severe?
> 640   Who to a *Friend* his Faults can freely show,

---

627. run: *1713a–51:* fly
637. or: *1744–51:* nor

'time and place' is focused only on the unities of neoclassical dramatic theory.

627–8. For the idea Warton cites Boileau, *L'Art Poetique*, IV.53–8, the two last lines closest to Pope: 'Il n'est temple si saint, des anges respecté, | Qui soit contre sa muse un lieu de sûreté' ('There is no temple so sacred, respected of angels, which is a place of safety against his muse').

627. Altars: notionally a place of sanctuary, granting protection from pursuit.

   talk you dead: Wakefield compares Horace, *Ars Poetica*, 475, 'occiditque legendo' ('and kills by reading'). For the phrase cf. Nathaniel Lee, *Gloriana*, III.i (1676), p. 23: 'Methinks already thou hast talk'd 'em dead'.

628. Cf. Donne, 'Obsequies to the Lord Harrington's Brother', 99–100, *Poems, by J. D.* (1663), p. 143: 'For, they all vertues paths in that pace tread, | As Angells goe, and know, and as men read'.

630. short Excursions: cf. Commentary to 739. Wakefield cites Virgil, *Georgics*, IV.194: 'excursusque brevis temptant' and Dryden's translation (283), *Works of Virgil*, p. 130 (speaking of bees): 'Nor Forrage far, but short Excursions make'.

637. dully prepossest: stupidly prejudiced.
   blindly right: dogmatic and blinkered.

638. TE compares Roscommon, *Essay on Translated Verse*, 69–70 (1684), p. 5: 'For none have been, with *Admiration*, read, | But who (beside their *Learning*) were *Well-bred*', and Pope, 'To a Young Lady, with the Works of Voiture', 8. Pope's 'though' suggests that learning can generate uncivil behaviour; in the ideal critic learning is joined to good breeding.

639. Modestly bold: cf. Motteux, 'To Mr. Samuel Wesley ... ', 81–2, in Wesley's *The Life of Christ* (1693), sig. c4[r]: 'happier thy Essay, | Modest yet bold'; 'Modestly Bold' describes a woman's intelligence in John Pomfret, 'Strephon's Love for Delia Justify'd', *Miscellany Poems on Several Occasions*, second edition (1707), p. 55.

   Humanly severe: perhaps simply 'humanely' (cf. 526); or, 'one's severity should be a human one and not that which measures faults by superhuman standards' (Southall 1988).

640. Wakefield cites the Soames–Dryden translation of Boileau, *Art of Poetry*, I.200 (1683), p. 12: 'A Faithful Friend is careful of your

>   And gladly praise the Merit of a *Foe*?
>   Blest with a *Taste* exact, yet unconfin'd;
>   A *Knowledge* both of *Books* and *Humankind*;
>   *Gen'rous Converse*, a *Soul* exempt from *Pride*;
> 645 And *Love to Praise*, with *Reason* on his Side?
>   Such once were *Criticks*, such the Happy *Few*,
>   *Athens* and *Rome* in better Ages knew.
>   The mighty *Stagyrite* first left the Shore,
>   Spread all his Sails, and durst the Deeps explore;
> 650 He steer'd securely, and discover'd far,

---

642. **Blest with:** MS: Who boasts
647^8. MS: Such did of old *Poetic Laws* impart,
      And what till then was *Fury*, turn'd to *Art*.
649^50. MS: That bold *Columbus* of the Realms of Wit,
      Whose *first Discov'ry's* not exceeded *yet*;
650. MS: Who steer'd so *safely*, and advanc'd so *far*,

Fame, | And freely will your heedless Errors blame'. *TE* cites also Horace, *Ars Poetica*, 445-52, for characterisation of the friendly critic. Cf. 660 below, and Pope to Wycherley, 20 November 1707: 'The repeated permissions you give me of dealing freely with you, will (I hope) excuse what I have done; for . . . I have not spar'd you when I thought Severity would do you a kindness. . .'; and Wycherley to Pope, 28 February 1708 and 11 April 1710 (*Corr.*, I.32, 40, 82-3).

642. **unconfin'd:** not limited or narrow.

644. **Converse:** 'Conversation; manner of discoursing in familiar life' (*SJ*, citing this passage). In place of *TE*'s 'well-bred intercourse', Southall (1988) glosses: 'conversation free from meanness or smallness of mind or character'. *TE* cites Knightly Chetwood, 'To the Earl of Roscomon', in Roscommon's *Essay on Translated Verse* (1684), sig. a1^r: '*Wit, reading, judgment, conversation, art,* | A *head* well *ballanc'd*, and a *generous heart*', and Dryden's 'Defence of the Epilogue', in *The Conquest of Granada*, on the subject of polite and courtly conversation. Cf. also 'To a Young Lady, with the Works of Voiture', 7.

647. **Athens *and* Rome:** centres of the Greek and Roman civilisation of 'better ages', the classical past; represented by Aristotle and Horace respectively.

648-51. *TE* cites many models for this comparison between geographical and intellectual exploration, including Chetwood, 'To the Earl of Roscomon', in Roscommon's *Essay on Translated Verse* (1684), sig. a1^v: 'Hoist Sail, bold Writers, *search, discover far,* | You have a *Compass* for a *Polar-Star*'; and Oldham, 'Upon the Works of Ben. Iohnson', 22, *Poems, and Translations* (1683), p. 70: 'By that we may Wit's vast, and trackless Ocean try, | Content no longer, as before, | Dully to coast along the shore'. The successful voyage of discovery recalls the less complete journey of the 'Alps' simile, 228-35. There is an implicit reference to Homer's voyage-narrative, the *Odyssey*, signalled in 651. Cf. also Dryden, 'To my Honoured Friend Dr. Charleton', in Charleton's *Chorea Gigantum* (1663), sig. b1^r, on Columbus as the first to challenge the 'Tyranny' of 'the *Stagirite*' and his world-view.

Led by the Light of the *Maeonian Star.*
Not only *Nature* did his Laws obey,
But *Fancy*'s boundless Empire own'd his Sway.
Poets, a *Race* long unconfin'd and free,

651, n. *1736a–51:* Between Verse 650 and 651; [*1744–51:* Between v. 646 and 647. I found the following lines, since supprest by the author:

> *That bold* Columbus *of the realms of wit,*
> *Whose first discov' ry's not exceeded yet.*
> *Led by the light of the Maeonian Star,*
> *He steer'd securely, and discover'd far.*]
> *He when all Nature was subdu'd before,*
> *Like his great pupil, sigh'd, and long'd for more:*
> *Fancy's wild regions yet unvanquish'd lay,*
> *A boundless empire, and that own'd no sway.*
> *Poets, &c.*

651^2. MS: He, when *all Nature* was subdu'd before,
    Like his great Pupill sigh'd, and long'd for *more.*
    Fancy's wild Regions yet unvanquish'd lay,
    (A *boundless* Empire, and that own'd no Sway).
652–3. *1713a–51:* omitted

---

651. Maeonian Star: Homer; Maionia was a name for the early kingdom of Lydia in Asia Minor, one of the supposed birthplaces of Homer, who was, additionally, sometimes said to be the son of 'Maeon'; cf. 'blind *Maeonides*', Milton, *Paradise Lost*, III.35 (1674), p. 62.

651 MS and Pope's note. Aristotle's pupil, Alexander the Great (see 377) is supposed to have wept when he found there were no more worlds to conquer; Aristotle is conceived to 'sigh' because he has subdued the whole of Nature to his Rules. Hence his appearance in the MS as Columbus, 'discoverer' of the Americas. *TE* compares Cowley, 'The Motto', 27–30, *Poems* (1656), p. 2: 'Welcome, great *Stagirite*, and teach me now | All I was born to know. | Thy *Scholars victories* thou dost far out-doe; | *He* conquer'd th' *Earth*, the whole *World* you.' Sidney, in *The Defence of Poesie* (1595), sig. G3ᵛ, remarks: 'This *Alexander*, left his Schoolemaister liuing *Aristotle* behinde him, but tooke dead *Homer* with him'.

652–3. Dennis (*Reflections*, p. 22, Hooker, I.412) objected to the 'blasphemy' of the couplet, perhaps occasioning Pope's later omission of it.

653. Fancy: 'Imagination' (*SJ*); similar to 'Invention' (115), and partly equivalent to 'wit' in its widest sense. 'Imagination' occurs only once in the poem (58). Fairer (1984: 1–5) presents abundant evidence to suggest that while writers of Pope's period were aware that distinctions might be drawn between fancy, imagination, and invention, as in Dryden's 'Preface' to *Annus Mirabilis*, in practice the terms were used interchangeably to denote a range of mental phenomena. It was not until significantly after the death of Pope that 'fancy' was fully differentiated as a secondary, less creative faculty than the Imagination.

654–5. Cf. Dryden, *Absalom and Achitophel*, 51–2 (1681), p. 3: 'These *Adam*-wits, too fortunately free, | Began to dream they wanted libertie'.

655   Still fond and proud of *Savage Liberty*,
       Receiv'd his Rules, and stood convinc'd 'twas fit
       Who conquer'd *Nature*, shou'd preside o'er *Wit*.
         Horace still charms with graceful Negligence,
       And without Method *talks* us into Sense,
660   Does like a *Friend* familiarly convey
       The *truest Notions* in the *easiest way*.
       He, who Supream in Judgment, as in Wit,

---

655. **Does:** *1717–51:* Will
656. **Rules:** *1713a–51:* Laws

---

655. Savage Liberty: uncivilised freedom, normally with a political inference, as in Ward's comments on the origins of monarchy, *Modern Religion and Ancient Loyalty* (1699), p. 10: 'Thus chang'd for Humane Safety Savage Liberty', and similarly on William I in Sir Walter Ralegh's *Introduction to a Breviary of the History of England* (1693), p. 7: 'the State then seem'd ... to lose little, besides their Savage Liberty, being reduced to a Civil Subjection'.

656–7. The 'Rules' (cf. 88) governing poetry are equivalent to the 'Laws' (652) by which Aristotle has 'conquer'd Nature', in his works on physics, zoology, and other subjects, whose authority Dennis questioned in *Reflections*, p. 22, Hooker, I.412. Pope's lines suggest an accommodation between contract-based and patriarchal theories of government (cf. 551–2).

658. Horace: Roman poet, author of *Ars Poetica*; see Headnote: Models and sources.

Negligence: 'graceful' (cf. Commentary to 156) because Horace avoids pedantry, extremes of opinion, and dogmatism. TE notes that the phrase 'graceful negligence' is used of verse by Oldham, 'A Letter from the Country to a Friend in Town', 49, *Some New Pieces* (1681), p. 120, and (in a different context) by Dryden, 'Palamon and Arcite', III.73. Cf. also Addison, writing of Charles Montagu, 'Account of the Greatest English Poets', 138–9, *Annual Miscellany: For the Year 1694*, p. 326: 'Now negligently Graceful he unrein's | His verse, and writes in loose Familiar strains'. Garth, *Dispensary*, I, sixth edition (1706), p. 8, has Sloth declare: 'Thro' my Indulgence, Mortals hourly share | A grateful Negligence, and Ease from Care', an ironic rewriting of the idea. Cf. also 'The Rape of the Locke', I.31.

659. without Method ... Sense: cf. 'methodis'd', 89. Horace writes a 'familiar' poem, embodying the conversational model, rather than a formally structured prose treatise such as Dennis's (or Aristotle's); see Headnote: Context. TE cites Dryden's likening of his own 'loose proceeding' to Horace's *Ars Poetica*, in which 'he observes no Method that I can trace'; 'Dedication' of the *Aeneid*, *Works of Virgil*, sig. a3ᵛ. Cf. however Oldham's 'Horace his Art of Poetry', 73, *Some New Pieces* (1681), p. 7, which recommends having a 'method to dispose his Sense', and the 'clearest *Method*' Pope ascribes to Quintilian, 673 below.

661. easiest: smoothest, most graceful; another sign of well-bred confidence and the avoidance of conflict.

662. TE cites Dryden's 'Prologue' to *Oedipus*, 4 (1682), sig. A4ʳ, of Socrates and Sophocles: 'Supreme in Wisdom one, and one in Wit'.

Might boldly censure, as he boldly writ,
Yet *judg'd* with *Coolness* tho' he sung with *Fire*;
665 His *Precepts* teach but what his *Works* inspire.
Our Criticks take a contrary Extream,
They *judge* with *Fury*, but they *write* with *Fle'me*:
Nor suffers *Horace* more in wrong *Translations*
By *Wits*, than *Criticks* in as wrong *Quotations*.
670 Fancy and Art in gay *Petronius* please,
The *Scholar's Learning*, and the *Courtier's Ease*.

670, variant, n. *1713a–43, 1751:* Dionysius *of* Halicarnassus.

669^70. *1713a–51:* See *Dionysius Homer's* Thoughts refine,
And call new Beauties forth from ev'ry Line!
670. please: *1736a–43:* meet
671. and: *1713a–51:* with
    Ease: *1736a–43:* wit

---

663. boldy censure: cf. Sir Robert Howard, 'Prologue' to *The Great Favourite* (1668), sig. a2ʳ: 'Why, then deliver him from you that sit | And boldly Censure, what, you have not Wit'.

663–8. Dennis considered these lines as in contradiction to Pope's praise of Longinus' warmth at 678–83 (*Reflections*, p. 17, Hooker, I.409). Pope experimented with alternatives but decided against alteration; see Appendix.

667. Fle'me: phlegm, 'the watery humour of the body, which, when it predominates, is supposed to produce sluggishness or dullness' (*SJ*, citing this line). The spelling was of earlier origin than 'phlegm' but still in use. In *Reflections*, p. 17, Hooker, I.409, Dennis noted that this line recalls Roscommon, *Essay on Translated Verse*, 300–1 (1684), p. 19: 'Thus make the *proper Use* of each *Extream*, | And *write* with *fury* but *correct* with *Phleam*', which confirms the pronunciation at this date. Roscommon advises authors to write passionately but revise soberly, whereas Pope attacks critics who judge passionately but write torpidly.

668. Translations: versions included those by Creech, *The Odes, Satyrs and Epistles of Horace* (1684), which Pope quoted derisively in *The Sixth Epistle of the First Book of Horace Imitated* (1738), 1–4. McLaverty (2001: 8–9), suggests that Pope's use of italics to emphasise didactic points in this poem might derive from Creech's version of Horace's *Ars Poetica*. Pope may have in mind the fashion for 'imitating' Horace, rather than directly translating him, as in Rochester's 'Allusion to Horace'.

669^70 variant. Dionysius of Halicarnassus, first century BC Greek historian and commentator on rhetoric and style in Augustan Rome. Pope refers to Dionysius' appreciation of Homer's use of sound/sense echoes in a letter to Addison, 20 October 1714, *Corr.*, I.264, and in the 'Preface' to the *Iliad* (*PW*, I.235); he is cited throughout the notes to his Homer translations.

669. than Criticks: than by critics, who quote Horace erroneously. See Pope to Caryll, 25 June 1711: 'The manner in which Mr. D. [Dennis] takes to pieces several particular lines detached from their natural places, may show how easy it is to any one to give a new sense, or a new nonsense, to what the author intended, or not intended' (*Corr*, I.122).

670–1. *TE* notes the recurrence of the please/ease rhyme at 676–7 and the textual variants later introduced to obviate the difficulty.

670. gay: 'Airy; cheerful; merry; frolick' (*SJ*).

Petronius: See Headnote: Models and sources, and Pope's notes to 25 and 289. The

In grave *Quintilian*'s copious Work we find
The justest *Rules*, and clearest *Method* join'd;
Thus *useful Arms* in Magazines we place,
675   All rang'd in *Order*, and dispos'd with *Grace*,
Nor thus alone the Curious Eye to please,
But to be *found*, when Need requires, with Ease.
The *Muses* sure *Longinus* did inspire,
And blest *their Critick* with a *Poet's Fire*.

678, n. 1736a–43: The Muses *sure* Longinus *did inspire.*

676–7. 1744–51: But less to please the eye, than arm the hand,
    Still fit for use, and ready at command.
678. 1717–51: Thee, bold *Longinus*! all the Nine inspire,
679. **blest:** *1717–51:* bless

---

mention of Petronius offended Warton, since the *Satyricon* was better known for its satire and obscenity (it had been reissued in 1709 by Curll partly for that reason), and Johnson, agreeing with Warton (*Literary Magazine*, I, 1756, pp. 36–9) doubted that Pope had even read Petronius. But *TE* cites the 'Advertisement' to Rymer's translation of Rapin's *Reflections on Aristotle's Treatise of Poesie*, sig. b3: '*Petronius* (whom no man of modesty dares name, unless on the account of those directions he gave for writing) amongst the Ordures of his *Satyre*, gives certain precepts for *Poetry* that are admirable'. Dryden thought him 'the greatest Wit perhaps of all the *Romans*', 'Dedication' of *Examen Poeticum*, sig. A5ʳ; and the 'most elegant, and one of the most judicious Authors of the Latin tongue'; 'Of Heroique Playes', in *The Conquest of Granada*, sig a3ᵛ. A summary of views of Petronius is given in Sir Thomas Pope Blount, *De Re Poetica* (1694), pp. 164–8. Pope's characterisation again presents a combination of qualities that might otherwise be thought contradictory.

672. **grave Quintilian:** 'grave' (serious) balances 'gay' (670). For Marcus Fabius Quintilianus (c. 35–95 AD), see Headnote: Models and sources.

674. **Arms . . . Magazines:** rules and methods arranged not for ornament but for use when necessary (675–8); picking up the metaphor of MS variant after 510, and cf. 107–8, 557. *TE* notes this as one of Quintilian's own metaphors (e.g. *Institutio Oratoria*, II.i.12, VII.x.14).

675. **Grace:** cf. Commentary to 156.

676. **Curious:** cf. 289, but here suggesting the sense of a private museum of curiosities of the type popular amongst noblemen from the Renaissance onwards.

678. **Longinus:** Greek literary theorist; see Headnote: Models and sources.

678 **variant.** Warton (1797: I.256) argued that the 'abrupt address' of the revised line 'is more spirited and striking, and more suitable to the character of the person addressed, than if he had coldly spoken of him in the third person, as it stood in the first edition'. *TE* notes Pope's dropping of the expletive 'did' (cf. 349).

679. Longinus wrote his (prose) treatise with (poetic) imagination.

their: Longinus is chosen by the Muses.

Fire: cf. 664; a term of high praise in Pope's 'Preface' to *The Iliad*; see *PW*, I.225.

680   An ardent *Judge*, that Zealous in his Trust,
          With *Warmth* gives Sentence, yet is always *Just*;
          Whose *own Example* strengthens all his Laws,
          And *Is himself* that great *Sublime* he draws.
          Thus long succeeding Criticks justly reign'd,
685   *Licence* repress'd, and *useful Laws* ordain'd;
          Learning and *Rome* alike in Empire grew,
          And *Arts* still *follow'd* where her *Eagles flew*;
          From the same Foes, at last, both felt their Doom,
          And the same Age saw *Learning* fall, and *Rome*.

---

680. **that:** *1713a–51:* who

---

680. ardent: burning, passionate.
    Zealous: admirably keen and conscientious; more positive than the 'zealous' of 441. Cf. 732.

681. With Warmth: suggesting passionate engagement rather than anger.
    Sentence: 'opinion' or critical view, but within the sequence of legal metaphors here Longinus is compared to a judge giving verdict in a trial.

682. Example ... Laws: cf. Thomas Blount, *The Academy of Eloquence* (1656), p. 35: 'Evarchus *making his life the example of his laws*'.

683. Sublime: 'The grand or lofty style. The *sublime* is a Gallicism, but now naturalized' (*SJ*, citing this line). For Longinus' treatise and its reception in English see Headnote: Models and sources. The word occurs only here in the poem, perhaps a sign of Pope's chariness about an aesthetic category associated strongly with Dennis. For the idea, Wakefield cites Boileau's 'Preface' to his translation of Longinus, *Oeuvres Diverses* (1701), 3–4: 'Souvent il fait la figure qu'il enseigne; & en parlant du Sublime, il est lui-mesme très-sublime' ('often he makes the figure that he teaches; and in speaking of the sublime, he is himself perfectly sublime'). Wakefield also cites Dryden's 'Prologue' to *The Tempest*, 7–8 (quoted in Commentary to 136).

684–95. Erskine-Hill (1981) compares this 'myth of usurpation' to the more obviously political version of it in *Windsor-Forest*, 43–92.

685. Licence: cf. 149–50, 545, 556. Pope experimented with an alternative line: 'Licence represt, and sacred Laws maintaind', then wrote '-quere of this'; but made no textual change (see Appendix).

    useful Laws: recalling 'useful Rules', 98. *TE* compares Chetwood, 'To the Earl of Roscomon, On his Excellent Poem', in Roscommon's *Essay on Translated Verse* (1684), sig. A3ᵛ: 'There wanted one who *license* cou'd restrain, | Make *Civil Laws* o're *Barbarous Usage* reign'.

686. Empire: the period of Roman history beginning 27 BC.

687. Eagles: symbol on the Roman army standard; cf. 'The First Book of Statius his Thebais', 24. *TE* compares Denham, 'The Progress of Learning', 51–2, *Poems and Translations* (1668), p. 175: 'Then wheresoe're her Conquering Eagles fled, | Arts, Learning, and Civility were spread', and the last line of Dennis, 'Preface' to *Miscellanies in Verse and Prose* (1693), sig. b2ᵛ, Hooker, I.10: 'Arts and Empire in Civiliz'd Nations have generally flourish'd together'.

689. Rome: perhaps pronounced to rhyme with 'Doom', though at 250–1 Pope uses the 'modern' pronunciation; cf. the passage of Dryden cited in commentary to 728 below.

690 With *Tyranny*, then *Superstition* join'd,
 As that the *Body*, this enslav'd the *Mind*;
 All was *Believ'd*, but nothing *understood*,
 And to be *dull* was constru'd to be *good*;
 A *second* Deluge Learning thus o'er-run,
695 And the *Monks* finish'd what the *Goths* begun.
 At length, *Erasmus*, that *great, injur'd* Name,

692, n. 1736a–43: All was believ'd, but nothing understood;
 1736a–51: Between Verse 692 and 693 [*1744–51:* the author omitted these two,];

  Vain Wits and Critics were no more allow'd,
  When none but Saints had licence to be proud.

692. **All:** *1713a–51:* Much
  nothing: *1713a–51:* little
693^4. MS: *Vain Wits* and *Criticks* were no more allow'd,
  When none but *Saints* had *Licence* to be *proud*;

---

690. The dark ages (cf. 698) which followed the final fall of the Roman Empire in the fifth century AD.

692 variant. Pope's textual change to the softer antithesis of 'Much' and 'little' as opposed to 'All' and 'nothing' was made in the context of the opposition from his Catholic circle; for the revision see also Appendix.

692 Pope's note. Saints: a hostile term for puritans and dissenters, mocking their supposed claims to special holiness; Pope appears to align medieval monks with the perceived arrogance of seventeenth-century sects.

693. dull: mentally inert; cf. 429–30.
constru'd: interpreted as, understood.

694. second *Deluge*: Noah's flood being the first; a metaphor for ignorance, prefiguring the apocalyptic imagery of *The Dunciad*.

695. Monks . . . Goths: The 'Goths' were the northern tribes who overran the Roman empire, aligned with 'Tyranny'; the Monks embody the pre-Reformation church, representing 'Superstition'. Cf. *The Dunciad Variorum* (1729), III.75–104, for a developed image of this cultural disaster. *TE* compares Dryden, 'To the Earl of Roscomon', 15–16, in Roscommon's *Essay on Translated Verse* (1684), sig. A1^r: 'But *Italy*, reviving from the trance | Of *Vandal, Goth,* and *Monkish* Ignorance', which picked up Roscommon's comment on the monks in 'unlearned Times', *Essay on Translated Verse*, 370–1. For quarrels amongst Catholics about this line, see Headnote: Context.

696. Erasmus: Desiderius Erasmus (1466–1536), humanist scholar and Roman Catholic priest, important for Pope because he 'had held to one side and yet seen it critically, had attacked its abuses, and yet remained loyal to the Roman Catholic Church'; Erskine-Hill (1975: 66–7). For Pope's responses to objections to his characterisation of Erasmus, see Headnote: Context. Pope later insisted he was 'Like good *Erasmus* in an honest Mean, | In Moderation placing all my Glory', *The First Satire of the Second Book of Horace Imitated*, 66–7. Pope bequeathed Bolingbroke eleven volumes of Erasmus from his own library (*PW*, II.506).

(The *Glory* of the Priesthood, and the *Shame*!)
Stemm'd the *wild Torrent* of a *barb'rous Age*,
And drove those *Holy Vandals* off the Stage.
700   But see! each *Muse*, in *Leo's* Golden Days,
Starts from her Trance, and trims her wither'd Bays!
Rome's ancient *Genius*, o'er its *Ruins* spread,
Shakes off the *Dust*, and rears his rev'rend Head!
Then *Sculpture* and her *Sister-Arts* revive;
705   *Stones* leap'd to *Form*, and *Rocks* began to *live*;

---

697. Glory ... Shame: Wakefield cites Oldham's 'A Satyr... Dissuading the Author from the Study of Poetry', 176, *Poems, and Translations* (1683), p. 173, which makes Samuel Butler 'The Glory and the Scandal of the Age'. But Pope's antithesis was in wide use: e.g. Cobb, *Poetae Britannici* (1700), p. 5: '*Homer* is *Greece's* Glory and her Shame'.

698. Stemm'd: dammed.

699. Holy Vandals: The Vandals were another Northern Germanic tribe, associated with the fall of (civilised) Rome. Pope used the phrase 'holy Vandals' of Catholics who objected to his characterisation of the monks; to Caryll, 19 July 1711 (*Corr.*, I.126).

700. Leo: Leo X, Giovanni de' Medici (1475–1521), Pope from 1513 to 1521 and a noted patron of artists such as Michelangelo and Raphael. Cf. Pope's translation from Castiglione, 'On the Statue of Cleopatra, made into a fountain by Leo the Tenth', esp. 43–4: 'But thou great *Leo*! in whose *golden* days | Revive the honours of *Rome's* ancient praise'. Wakefield compares this section to Dryden, 'To Sir Godfrey Kneller', 45–9 and 57–60, *Annual Miscellany: For the Year 1694*, pp. 90–1: '*Rome* rais'd not Art, but barely kept alive; | And with Old *Greece*, unequally did strive: | Till *Goths* and *Vandals*, a rude *Northern* Race, | Did all the matchless Monuments deface. | Then all the Muses in one ruine lye ... | Long time the Sister Arts, in Iron sleep, | A heavy Sabbath did supinely keep; | At length, in *Raphael's* Age, at once they rise; | Stretch all their Limbs, and open all their Eyes.' *TE* cites also line 95: 'And *Raphael* did with *Leo's* Gold abound'. Dryden praised Leo's patronage of art and poetry in 'Discourse Concerning ... Satire', *Satires of Juvenal*, p. vi. Leo was, however, the Pope who excommunicated the Protestant hero Martin Luther so there may be an added tinge to the praise.

701. Starts: wakes up; cf. 466, and the passage from Dryden cited in commentary to 695.

trims ... Bays: repairs the crown of laurel or bay (awarded to successful poets), which had 'wither'd' during the dark ages. See Commentary to 184.

702. Genius: presiding spirit, recalling the classical idea of the 'genius loci' ('genius of the place'); cf. 'Sapho to Phaon', 184.

Ruins: the literal ruins of Rome, invariably visited on the 'Grand Tour' by British aristocrats, and the metaphorical ruins of classical culture.

703. *TE* compares Dryden, *Threnodia Augustalis*, 514 (1685), p. 25: 'Th' asserted Ocean rears his reverend Head'; cf. also *Windsor-Forest*, 328.

705. Alluding to the ability of mythological poets such as Amphion to move rocks into architecture by music, as at the building of Thebes. For Amphion, *TE* suggests sources in Horace, *Ars Poetica* 394–6, and Ovid, *Metamorphoses* XV.418–35. For 'Leap'd to form', Wakefield compares Dryden, *Religio Laici*, 18–19 (1682), p. 2: 'Or various *Atom's* interfering Dance | Leapt into *Form*', and for the rocks, Addison, 'A Letter from Italy', 144, *Poetical Miscellanies: The Fifth Part* (1704), p. 10: 'Or teach their animated *Rocks* to live'. Pope writes of sculpted rocks that appear to live in *The Temple of Fame*, 73–4, 218–19.

With *sweeter Notes* each *rising Temple* rung;
A *Raphael* painted, and a *Vida* sung!
Immortal *Vida*! on whose honour'd Brow
The Poet's *Bays* and Critick's *Ivy* grow:
710   *Cremona* now shall ever boast thy Name,
As next in Place to *Mantua*, next in Fame!
But soon by Impious Arms from *Latium* chas'd,
Their *ancient Bounds* the banish'd Muses past;

707.] M. Hieronymus Vida, *an excellent* Latin *Poet, who writ an Art of Poetry in Verse.*

707, n. Vida: *1713b–16: Vida, of* Cremona
1713a–43: He flourish'd in the time of Leo *the Tenth.*

---

706. sweeter Notes: church music. Leo X promoted liturgical music, but *TE* suggests that Pope is thinking of its later revival under Palestrina after the Council of Trent, 1563.

rising Temple: a church in the process of being built, called 'Temple' to align it with classical religions; cf. *Windsor-Forest*, 375–6 and Commentary.

707. Raphael: Raphael Santi (1483–1520), preeminent artist of Leo's reign, and a model for imitation for all artists of Pope's day. Cf. the passage of Dryden quoted in Commentary to 700. Raphael was mentioned by Pope in an early letter of uncertain date to an unknown addressee (*Corr.*, I.4).

Vida: Marcus Hieronymus Vida (c.1490–1566), Latin poet and theorist; for the status of his *De Arte Poetica* in the early eighteenth century, see Headnote: Models and sources.

709. Bays ... Ivy: cf. 'Summer', 10. 'Bays' is the laurel wreath (cf. 184, 701) awarded to emperors, sporting victors, and poets. Since Petrarch it had been the traditional metaphorical crown for poets; see Woodman (1990) for Pope's fascination with the idea. The crown of Ivy had been associated since the time of Virgil (*Eclogues*, VII.25) and Horace (*Odes*, I.i.29–30) with poets; Wimsatt (1965: 51–4) reproduces two portraits of Pope wearing an ivy wreath. *TE* notes that ivy crowns were associated with scholars and learned men in the Renaissance. Sometimes the crowns were mixed, to indicate the presence of 'genius' (bays) and 'art' (ivy); cf. Dryden, 'To the Memory of Mr. Oldham', 24, *Works of Mr. John Oldham* (1684), sig. A4[r] of second sequence: 'Thy Brows with Ivy, and with Laurels bound'. *TE* suggests that ivy was associated with poets because it needed the support of a stronger tree (patronage) and that as a metaphor for criticism ivy might be suggest reliance on the pre-eminence of poetry (bays), as in Dryden, 'Dedication' of *Examen Poeticum*, sig. A5[r], speaking of hostile critics, 'Does the Ivy undermine the Oke, which supports its weakness?' John Dart, *A Poem on Chaucer and his Writings* (1722), p. iv (addressing Pope's friend Atterbury) differentiated 'The Critic's Ivy, and the Poet's Bays'; but Pope was attacked for what was seen as a mistake by Concanen in *A Supplement to the Profund* (1728), pp.13–14. See further *Dunciad* (1728), III.45–6, and Trapp (1958).

710. Cremona: town in Italy, birthplace of Vida.

711. Mantua: see 129. The proximity of Cremona to Mantua was noted by Virgil himself (*Eclogues*, IX.28) and by Basil Kennett in the 'Preface' to Vida's *Poeticorum Libri Tres* (1701).

712. Impious Arms: specifically, the forces of the Emperor Charles V, who sacked Rome in 1527. For the idea cf. the '*Sacrilegious* Hands' of 185, and 'The First Book of Statius his Thebais', e.g. 2.

Latium: district of central Italy in which Rome is situated.

713. past: passed.

Thence Arts o'er all the *Northern World* advance;
715 But *Critic Learning* flourish'd most in *France*.
The *Rules*, a Nation born to serve, obeys,
And *Boileau* still in Right of *Horace* sways.
But *we*, brave *Britains, Foreign Laws* despis'd,
And kept *unconquer'd*, and *unciviliz'd*,
720 Fierce for the *Liberties of Wit*, and bold,
We still defy'd the *Romans*, as *of old*.
Yet *some* there were, among the *sounder Few*
Of those who *less presum'd*, and *better knew*,
Who durst assert the *juster Ancient Cause*,

---

718. *1727–32:* new paragraph
    Britains: *1717–51:* Britons

---

715. French sources: Rapin, Boileau, and le Bossu: see Headnote: Models and sources.

716. born to serve: The obedience of the French to an autocratic system of rule under Louis XIV was a cliché of British patriotism. TE compares Dryden, 'Dedication' of *Examen Poeticum*, sig. A8ʳ: 'They follow the Ancients too servilely, in the Mechanick Rules, and we assume too much Licence to our selves, in keeping them only in view, at too great a distance'; and Gildon, 'Some Reflections on Mr. *Rymer's Short View of Tragedy'*, *Miscellaneous Letters and Essays* (1694), p. 91: 'the *French*, whose *Genius*, as well as Language, is not strong enough to rise to the Majesty of Poetry, are easier reduc'd within the Discipline of Rules, and have perhaps of late Years, more exactly observ'd 'em. Yet I never yet met with any Englishman, who wou'd preferr their Poetry to ours'.
Cf. also Wotton, *Reflections upon Ancient and Modern Learning* (1694), p. 53: 'their late Criticks are always setting Rules, and telling Men what must be done, and what omitted, if they would be Poets'. Dennis's 'Epistle Dedicatory' to *The Advancement and Reformation of Modern Poetry* was on similar lines. Cf. also 'Prologue to *Cato*', 42.

717. Boileau: Nicholas Boileau-Despréaux, critic and poet, whose *L'Art Poétique* (1674) was a major model for Pope's *Essay*; see Headnote: Models and sources.

    sways: To sway is 'to govern; to rule; to overpower; to influence' (*SJ*): Boileau governs where Horace ought to. *TE* notes that in *L'Art Poétique*, Boileau explicitly claimed to be Horace's advocate and that Dryden had referred to Boileau as a 'living *Horace*' in the 'Discourse Concerning . . . Satire', *Satires of Juvenal*, p. vii, though he was there writing about Boileau's talents as a satirist.

718–21. Weinbrot (2005: chapter 9) sees this as a defiant rewriting of Boileau's slavishly royalist 'ethic of regulation' (p. 227) in favour of a libertarian aesthetic appropriate to a constitutional monarchy. The British love of 'liberty' was as much a commonplace as French subservience; cf. Coward, *Licentia Poetica Discuss'd* (1709), p. 2: 'Bred up in Liberty the BRITON cries, | The vain *Rule-Givers* I may well despise'. Pope suggests that this gave British writing a noble independence, but also rendered it 'unciviliz'd'. Cf. Pope's *The First Epistle of the Second Book of Augustus Imitated*, 263–75.

721. defy'd the Romans: Britain had been invaded by a Roman army under Julius Caesar in 55 and 54 BC, and more fully subdued in a further invasion of AD 42, against localised resistance.

725 And here *restor'd* Wit's *Fundamental Laws.*
   Such was *Roscomon* — not more *learn'd* than *good,*
   With Manners gen'rous as his Noble Blood;
   To him the Wit of *Greece* and *Rome* was known,
   And ev'ry Author's *Merit,* but his own.
730 Such late was *Walsh,* — the Muses Judge and Friend,

725^6, variant, n. 1717–43, 1751: Essay on Poetry, by the Duke of Buckingham.

725^6. 1717–51: Such was the Muse, whose rules and practice tell,
   Nature's chief master-piece is writing well.
726–9. MS: *Such,* Learn'd and modest, not more great than good,
   With Manners gen'rous as his noble Blood,
   E're Saints impatient snatch'd him to the Sky,
   Roscomon was; and such is *Normanby.*
730. **Muses:** *1717–51:* Muse's
730–1. MS: Such late was *Walsh,* – nor canst thou, Muse, offend,
   Next these to name the Muses Judge and Friend;
   Who free from *envious Censure, partial Praise,*
   Show'd *Ancient Candour* in *malicious Days,*

---

725. restor'd ... Laws: laws more true to nature than the 'Foreign Laws' of 718. *TE* cites Dryden, 'Dedication' of the *Aeneid, Works of Virgil,* sig. a3ʳ: 'A Native of *Parnassus,* and bred up in the Studies of its Fundamental Laws'. See also Rymer's 'Preface' to his translation of Rapin's *Reflections on Aristotle's Treatise of Poesie,* sig. A6ᵛ: 'these fundamental Rules and Laws of *Aristotle*'. Perhaps also a covert political reference, since 'restore' was a keyword in Jacobite circles, following the various attempts to 'restore' James II and his descendants to the throne after the 1688 revolution. See Commentary to 165 and 545, and to 'Rape of the Locke', II.148.

725 variant. The italicised line is from Sheffield's *Essay upon Poetry,* 2; see commentary to 1–2.

726. Roscomon: Wentworth Dillon, fourth Earl of Roscommon; see Headnote: Models and sources. A model of the poet whose moral status is as high as his critical judgment. Pope singles out Roscommon for his purity amid the corruption of the court in *The First Epistle of the Second Book of Horace, Imitated,* 213–14.

726–9 MS. John Sheffield, Earl of Mulgrave and Duke of Normanby; see Headnote: Models and sources. Pope's careful note tones down the Duke's Jacobitism.

728. Wit: here, the canon of classical literature. *TE* cites Dryden, 'To the Earl of Roscomon', 26–9, in *Roscommon's Essay on Translated Verse* (1684), sig. A1ᵛ: 'The Wit of *Greece,* the Gravity of *Rome* | Appear exalted in the *Brittish* Loome; | The Muses Empire is restor'd agen, | In *Charles* his Reign, and by *Roscomon*'s Pen.'

730. Walsh: William Walsh, an early friend and mentor of Pope's; see Headnote to *Pastorals*

>   Who justly knew to blame or to commend;
>   To Failings *mild*, but *zealous* for Desert;
>   The *clearest Head*, and the *sincerest Heart*.
>   This humble Praise, lamented *Shade*! receive,
> 735 This Praise at least a grateful Muse may give!
>   The Muse, whose early Voice you taught to Sing,
>   Prescrib'd her Heights, and prun'd her tender Wing,
>   (Her Guide now lost) no more attempts to *rise*,
>   But in low Numbers short Excursions tries:

---

735. **MS:** The least, yet all a grateful Muse can give!
736. **The:** MS: That

---

and to this poem. See further Pope to Caryll, 19 July 1711, *Corr.*, I.128, responding robustly to Catholic objections here: 'Others you know, were as angry that I mentioned Mr. Walsh with honour, who, as he never refused to any one of merit, of any party, the praise due to him, so honestly deserved it from all others of never so different interest or sentiments'. Dennis, who claimed to have known Walsh as a 'learned, candid, judicious, gentleman', attacked Pope for citing his authority (*Reflections*, p. 28, Hooker, I.416). Boyce (1962) sees the passage as modelled on Horace's tribute to Quintilius Varus, 'vir bonus et prudens' ('a good and sensible man') whose practice as a critical friend is applauded in 438–52 of the *Ars Poetica*.

732. **Desert:** merit; often rhymed with 'heart' in seventeenth-century poetry.

734. **lamented Shade:** Walsh died in 1708 and Pope 'lamented' him in his 'Memorial List', in an edition of Virgil: 'a wise critic, friend, and good man' (*EC.*, I.ix).

735. **grateful:** with reference to Walsh's patronage and encouragement in the production of the *Pastorals*.

736. i.e. Walsh curbed Pope's early poetic enthusiasms.

736–7. TE compares Welsted, 'To the Duke of Buckingham, on his Essay on Poetry', 1–2: 'Here the Young Muse instructed how to sing, | Forms for the distant Flight her tender Wing', but the date of Welsted's poem is uncertain; it is quoted here from Roscommon's *Poems on Several Occasions* (1714), p. 154. Edgecombe (2005) suggests a source for this passage in Horace's deferential praise of another poet in *Odes*, IV.2.

739. **low Numbers:** modest metres, cf. 340 and 350. TE compares Dryden's translation of Persius, I.232, *Satires of Juvenal*, p. 14: 'Did crafty *Horace* his low Numbers joyn'. Cf. also Walsh, 'Eclogue II', *Letters and Poems* (1692), p. 113: 'Strives in low Numbers, such as Shepherds use'.

short Excursions: cf. 630; *SJ* cites this passage to define 'excursion': 'The act of deviating from the stated or settled path; a ramble'. TE compares Dryden, 'Epilogue', 11–14, *Miscellany Poems* (1684), p. 292: 'Your *Ben* and *Fletcher* in their first young flight | Did no *Volpone*, no *Arbaces* write. | But hopp'd about, and short excursions made | From Bough to Bough, as if they were afraid'. Smallwood (2004: 89) considers it an allusion to Dryden's translation of Ovid's 'Ceyx and Alcyone', 474–6, *Fables*, p. 379: 'A Bird new-made about the Banks she plies, | Not far from Shore; and short Excursions tries; | Nor seeks in Air her humble Flight to raise'.

740   Content, if hence th' Unlearn'd their Wants may view,
      The Learn'd reflect on what before they knew:
      Careless of *Censure*, nor too fond of *Fame*,
      Still pleas'd to *praise*, yet not afraid to *blame*,
      Averse alike to *Flatter*, or *Offend*,
745   Not *free* from Faults, nor yet too vain to *mend*.

FINIS.

---

742. **nor:** *1736b–43:* not

---

742. **Careless of:** indifferent to.
742-3. TE cites Dryden, *Religio Laici*, 452 (1682), p. 28: 'Yet neither Praise expect, nor Censure fear'.
745. TE cites the final lines of the Soames–Dryden translation of Boileau, *Art of Poetry* (1683), p. 67: 'Apter to blame, than knowing how to mend; | A sharp, but yet a necessary Friend'. Svetich (2000) suggests the final rhyme recalls also the opening of Puck's 'Epilogue', in Shakespeare, *A Midsummer Night's Dream*: 'If we shadows have offended, | Think but this, and all is mended'.

APPENDIX I.

The surviving manuscript of the *Essay on Criticism* includes the following sheet of notes in which Pope can be seen experimenting with possible revisions of various lines. The page numbers after Dennis's name refer to his *Reflections*; the remainder to Pope's pagination of the manuscript of the *Essay*. This transcription attempts to give a sense, as far as possible, of the appearance and ordering of the manuscript. For a facsimile, see Schmitz (1962: 84).

p.   ~~Be silent always w^n y^n doubt y^r sence. – Dennis p. 21.~~
     ~~Speak w^n youre sure, yet speak wth diffidence. Alter ye Inconsi[stenc]y~~

p.   A Work t'outlast immortal Rome – alter ye seeming Incosistecy.

W^n first his voice ye youthful Maro tryd Eer Phebus touchd his ear & checkd his pride

      W^n first great Maro sung of Kings & Wars
      Eer warning Phebus touchd his trembling Ears,
      Perhaps –

                             Perhaps – & – but – nature – each line
                               ~~His boundless soul perhaps disdaind~~
      Arms and ye Man then rung ye World around, & Rome commencd Imortal at ye sound
                               †Learn hence for ancient rules – To –
                               † Some beauties yet

~~p. 23. Nay fly to Altars~~
~~p. 8. Triumphant Paeans – and again – 3 lines off – Bards Triumphant~~
~~p. 9. lin. 9. read it thus – But more advancd behold wth strange surprise~~
        on acc^t of ~~survey~~ being usd after
~~p. 24. Wit & Faith   nihili~~
                /ye 2 lines left out
      ~~Where wanted scornd – of Wit – to be alterd – See Dennis p. 20~~
~~not to be altered) Horace, judgd wth Coolness - & Longin wth Fire.) Supreme alike in judgm^t~~
                               He boldly censurd & he boldly writ
                               He judgd wth Spirit as he sung
~~bare threescor, wth if it were, & threescore years is all =~~

p. 4.   – one Science – So vast is art – not only – But oft in those,   stet sic
                                     Those may be stratagems
      ~~Such as Chaucer is, may Dryden be.~~   And   less often than
      x Fool, let it not be usd so often.   ~~Nor Homer nods so often as we dream~~
      x Licence represt, and sacred Laws maintaind – quaere of this.
      x Much was believd, but little understood.
      x Schismatics y^e <u>plain</u> believers quitt
                        & speak   yet speak
        x – ~~w^n you doubt y^r Sense, Tho sure, wth seeming diffidence –~~
      x At the last Couplett, which alone is fraught –

APPENDIX II.

In the Works of 1736 Pope added the following table of contents after the title page of *An Essay on Criticism*. It introduced the poem in all subsequent editions to 1751.

THE
CONTENTS
OF THE
ESSAY on CRITICISM.

PART I.

1. [*1744–51: Introduction.*]
 THAT 'tis as great a fault to judge ill, as to write ill, and a more dangerous one to the public. [*1744–51:* v 1.]
2. The variety of men's Tastes; of a true Taste, how rare to be found. [*1744–51: That a true Taste is as rare to be found, as a true Genius,* v 9 to 18.].
3. That most men are born with some Taste, but spoil'd by false Education. [*1744–51:* v 19 to 25.]
4. The Multitude of Critics, and causes of 'em [*1744–51:* them, v 26 to 45.]
5. That we are to study our own Taste, and know the Limits of it. [*1744–51:* v 46 to 67.]
6. Nature the best guide of Judgment [*1744–51:* v 68 to 87.]
7. Improv'd by Art, and Rules, which are but methodiz'd Nature. [*1744–51:* v 88.]
8. Rules deriv'd from the Practice of the ancient Poets. [*1744–51: v id.* to 110.]
9. That therefore the ancients are necessary to be study'd by a Critic, particularly Homer and Virgil [*1744–51:* v 120 to 138.]
10. Of Licenses, and the use of 'em [*1744–51: them*] by the Ancients [*1744–51:* v 140 to 180.]
11. Reverence due to the Ancients, and praise of 'em [*1744–51:* them, v 181, &c.]

PART II. Ver. 204 [*1744–51:* 203], &c.

Causes hindering a true Judgment. 1. Pride. [*1744–51:* v 208.] 2. Imperfect Learning. [*1744–51:* v 215.] 3. Judging by parts, and not by the whole: [*1744–51:* v 233 *to* 288.] Critics in Wit, Language, Versification, only. [*1744–51:* v 288. 305. 339, &c.] 4. Being too hard to please, or too apt to admire. [*1744–51:* v 384.] 5. [*1744–51: Partiality — too*] Too much Love to a Sect, — to the Ancients or Moderns. [*1744–51:* v 394.] 6. Prejudice or Prevention [*1744–51:* v 408.] 7. Singularity. [*1744–51:* v 424.] 8. Inconstancy. [*1744–51:* v 430.] 9. Partiality [*1744–51: Party Spirit,* v 452, &c.] 10. Envy. [*1744–51:* v 466.] Against Envy, and in praise of Good-nature. [*1744–51:* v 508, &c.] When Severity is chiefly to be used by Critics? [*1744–51:* v 526, &c.] Against Immorality and Obscenity. [*1744–51: omitted*]

PART III. Ver. 565 [*1744–51:* 560], &c.
Rules for the Conduct of Manners in a Critic. [*1744–51:* 1.] Candour, [*1744–51:* v 563.] Modesty, [*1744–51:* v 566.] Good-breeding, [*1744–51:* v 572.] Sincerity, and Freedom of Advice. [*1744–51:* v 578. 2] When one's Counsel is to be restrained? [*1744–51:* v 584.] Character of an incorrigible Poet. [*1744–51:* v 600.] – And of an impertinent Critic. [*1744–51:* v 610, &c.] The [*1744–51:* omitted] Character of a good Critic. [*1744–51:* v 629.] The History of Criticism, and Characters of the best Critics. *Aristotle,* [*1744–51:* v 645.] *Horace,* [*1744–51:* v 653.] *Dionysius,* [*1744–51:* v 665.] *Petronius,* [*1744–51:* v 667.] *Quintilian,* [*1744–51:* v 670.] *Longinus.* [*1744–51:* v 675.] Of the Decay of Criticism, and its Revival. – *Erasmus,* [*1744–51:* v 693.] *Vida,* [*1744–51:* v 705.] *Boileau,* [*1744–51:* v 714.] Lord *Roscommon,* &c —— [*1744–51:* v 725.] Conclusion.

5
LINES FROM *THE CRITICAL SPECIMEN*
(1711)

Editors' Headnote

Composition and publication

No composition or publication details for this piece are firmly known; the imprint of the anonymous 16-page prose pamphlet entitled *The Critical Specimen*, in which the two passages of verse appear is 'London: Printed in the Year, 1711', a normal imprint for surreptitious publishing, and no advertisement for it has been found. Only five copies are known to survive, but even this low figure suggests that it was actually published to the extent of being circulated. It was not reprinted or collected or ever mentioned or acknowledged by Pope, and was first ascribed to him by Ault, in *PW*, I.ix–xviii, an attribution now routinely accepted (e.g. *TE*, VI.79–80). It is the earliest dated of Pope's prose works. The humour of the pamphlet is characteristic of the parodic vein Pope would develop in prose works of this decade, both in papers in the *Spectator* and the *Guardian* and in pamphlets against Edmund Curll; and the attack on Dennis in relation to the *Essay on Criticism* very strongly suggests Pope's involvement. Dennis's *Reflections, Satyrical and Critical, upon a late Rhapsody call'd, An Essay upon Criticism* (1711), published 20 June 1711 (see Headnote to *Essay on Criticism*), had made Pope rethink a few lines, but had also stimulated other kinds of response, some of which he shared with John Caryll during discussion of the poem and its aftermath during 1711. Though he professed that Dennis's book made him 'very heartily merry in two minutes time' (to Caryll, 19 November 1712, *Corr.*, I.155), he recalled Dennis's wounding image of him as a 'hunch-back'd Toad' into the period of composition of *The Dunciad*, and its inclusion and inversion in *The Critical Specimen* point convincingly to his authorship of the pamphlet and the verses it includes. Reference is also made in the pamphlet to 'A Contention in Civility and good Breeding between the Critick and a little Gentleman of W—r F—t, in which the little Gentleman had some Advantage' (*PW*, I.16–17), which is very pointedly aligned with Pope's own viewpoint. There are no very obvious other candidates for its authorship, though it is just possible that John Gay, whom Pope became friendly with around 1711, had some involvement.

Text

The text is that of *1711*; there were no further printings in Pope's lifetime.

Models and sources

Subscription proposals were becoming more popular after 1700, normally for large-scale scholarly endeavours, and indeed often came with a 'specimen', as for example in *Proposals for Printing by Subscription Monsieur Bayle's Historical and Critical Dictionary* (c. 1705); Pope's own proposals for the translation of Homer's *Iliad* are not known to survive in their original form, but date from late 1713. *The Critical Specimen* bears a lavish internal title: *A Specimen of A Treatise in Folio, to be printed by Subscription, Entitutled, The Mirror of Criticisme: Or, The History of the Renown'd Rinaldo Furioso, Critick of the Woful Countenance*, thereby managing to allude insultingly both to Dennis's own play *Rinaldo and Armida* (1699) and to Handel's highly successful opera *Rinaldo*, partly based on the same story; first performed in February 1711, it was an example of the form Dennis had denounced as dangerously corrupting in his *Essay on the Opera's after the Italian Manner* (1706). A further allusion is to the maddened hero of Ariosto's episodic renaissance romance *Orlando Furioso*, source material also for 'The Rape of the Locke' (II.159). Dennis's delusions (as presented in the pamphlet) about his own grand status as the restorer of criticism and poetry are consonant with the comic narrative of Cervantes' *Don Quixote*, a favourite text among Pope's acquaintance; he had satirised Dennis's supposedly unmoderated adherence to the rules of Aristotle in the 'Quixote' episode of the *Essay on Criticism* (270–87), and the main 'Specimen' explicitly offers 'a further Comparison of the Renown'd *Rinaldo Furioso* . . . and the valiant Restorer of Chivalry Don *Quixote de la Mancha*'. Swift had parodied the deluded narrative of a modern 'hack' author in *A Tale of a Tub* (1704) and his use of anonymous Grub-Street publication modes (in squibs such as the Bickerstaff hoaxes of 1708–9) also lies behind this identity-theft burlesque.

Context

Pope's pamphlet pays back Dennis's *ad hominem* critique of the *Essay on Criticism* (see Headnote to that poem, and for further biographical detail, Mack 1985: 177–84), but also contrives to extend his original provocation by mocking the grandiose scheme of cultural authority advanced by Dennis in *The Grounds of Criticism in Poetry* (1704), which, at 176 pages, had been published as 'preliminary to a larger work'. Dennis's own drearily Miltonic blank verse is the other main target (on this see further Terry 1993). Dennis's book set out a plan to establish rules and methods for literary criticism and presented a 'Specimen' critique of Milton and other poets in 'heroic' vein, after the 'Proposal' itself. It was uncommon to publish literary criticism by subscription, and Dennis listed only 77 subscribers to his project, including Pope's friends Walsh and

Garth; a postscript set out the failure of the subscription to match the ambition of the original plan. Nothing further had emerged by 1711, and the project remained unfulfilled. Pope's burlesque contains 35 ludicrous summary chapters and other features designed to parody the format and objectives of Dennis's book, as well as its supposed obsession with Longinian sublimity and mechanistic accounts of the 'Enthusiastick Passions' (*Grounds of Criticism*, chapter IV, pp. 16–21). That the pamphlet responds to the *Reflections* is further signalled by the title of Chapter 2, containing 'some Reflections *very Critical and Satyrical, but nothing to the Purpose*'.

The first set of verses constitutes a 'Simile' within 'A Specimen of the Preface', produced by the putative author of the *Critical Specimen* to show off the talents he had originally proposed to develop more largely in a verse epic on the life of Dennis (a task eventually carried out in parody in Thomas Parnell's caustic 'Life of Zoilus', attached to *Homer's Battle of the Frogs and Mice*, 1717). Pope's *Essay on Criticism* had abounded in similes small and large, to several of which Dennis had taken a sledgehammer in the *Reflections* (e.g. pp. 8–13). Pope had discussed and defended some of them in his letters to Caryll during June and July 1711 (*Corr*, I.117–29). Similes in epic were always on the verge of unintended self-parody, and modern would-be sublime attempts would constitute a rich resource for the Scriblerian 'Peri Bathous; or, Martinus Scriblerus His Treatise of the Art of Sinking in Poetry', from *Miscellanies. The Last Volume* (1728, dated 1727). Pope ridicules Dennis's own similes on the first page of the 'Specimen of the Preface'. In the parodic verses themselves Pope echoes either actual epic images or modern aspirant epic poets such as Blackmore, and Dennis himself, with a constant effect of comic over-reaching. Pope cheerfully turns Dennis's comment on his hunchbacked form into a full-dress over-extended simile in which the toad becomes a type of malign, toxic critic, '*frowning and swelling with Anger and Resentment, as ready to burst with Passion*'. These lines constitute Pope's earliest published piece of unrhymed verse, significantly in comedic context.

The second set of verses is drawn from the sample 'Chapter, 4th', in which it is supposedly uttered by the child Dennis in a fantasy ride on a hobby-horse: 'He fancy'd that he was now mounted on *Pegasus*, and that he had travelled several Leagues through the Air towards Mount *Parnassus*; during his Imaginary Flight, he was heard to repeat with great vehemence the following Rhapsody'. A 'rhapsody' was what Dennis had dismissively called Pope's *Essay on Criticism*, indicating what he presented as its lack of connection and organisation; it was among several terms of abuse he would reuse against Pope's work in *Remarks upon Several Passages in the Preliminaries to the Dunciad* (1729). Pope's inversion of the term puts it in one sense closer to its potentially more positive meaning of a vision driven by poetic enthusiasm; but actually the 'rhapsody' is delusional bombast, a one-sentence 'flight' of the imagination appropriate only to early childhood, not the Miltonic grandeur it emulates. Pope viewed Dennis's critical works as overwritten and pompous in style, and his championing of Longinus, the classical authority for the concept of the sublime, is portrayed in the burlesque as obsessional rather than balanced (the desired perspective of the *Essay on Criticism*).

The pamphlet as a whole shows strong elements of Menippean or mixed-form satire of a kind much developed by the 'Scriblerian' group (Sherburn 1934: 93–4 and Aden 1978: 111–14; Sherburn is not convinced by the attribution to Pope). Further assault on Dennis from Pope's group came in John Gay's first play, *The Mohocks* (1712), which mocked the critic in a dedicatory epistle and parody-Miltonic speeches. A further prose sketch, *The Narrative of Dr. Robert Norris* (1713), anonymous but virtually certainly by Pope, prompted by Dennis's virulent response to Addison's *Cato* (for which Pope had written the 'Prologue', below), extended the battle, which flared up periodically almost until Dennis's death in 1734.

Lines from *The Critical Specimen.*

I

So on *Maeotis*' Marsh, (where Reeds and Rushes
Hide the deceitful Ground, whose waving Heads
Oft' bend to *Auster*'s blasts, or *Boreas*' Rage,
The Haunt of the voracious *Stork* or *Bittern*,

---

1. **Maeotis'** *Marsh:* classical name for an area situated at the edge of what is now the Sea of Azov, where the Don flows out between modern Ukraine and Russia; mentioned in antiquity as a marsh, typifying extreme desolation (e.g. Virgil, *Georgics*, III.349–50, translated by Dryden, III.543, *Works of Virgil*, p. 112, as 'the bleak *Meotian* Strand'); it features in Satan's view of Earth, *Paradise Lost*, IX.77–8, and Pope recalled it ironically in *The Dunciad* (1728), III.79.

Reeds and Rushes: an epic echo of Chapman's *The Iliads of Homer*, XXI.348–9 (1611), p. 294: 'sea-grasse reeds, | And rushes...'.

2. **deceitful Ground:** perhaps recalling the landscape of Rochester's 'Satyr against [Reason and] Mankind', 14–15, *Poems on Several Occasions* (1696), p. 87: 'Pathless, and dangerous, wand'ring ways, it takes, | Through Errours fenny Bogs, and thorny Brakes'. Milton locates a similarly fatal landscape in *Paradise Lost*, IX.638–42 (1674), p. 233, just before the Fall: 'some evil Spirit attends | Hovering and blazing with delusive Light, | Misleads th' amaz'd Night-wanderer from his way | To Boggs and Mires, and oft through Pond or Poole, | There swallow'd up and lost, from succour farr.'

waving Heads: cf. Charles Cotton, *Wonders of the Peake*, 412–13 (1681), p. 25: 'the sedg, which scarcely in their beds | Confess a Current by their waving heads'.

3. **Auster ... Boreas:** respectively, the south wind, mentioned in 'The First Book of Statius his Thebais', 492–3 and Pope's *Iliad*, V.1058–9, as a bringer of disease; and the fierce north wind, also mentioned in 'The First Book of Statius his Thebais', 267, as an element in a simile. Cf. also 'Winter', 87, and Pope's letter to Caryll, 21 December 1712 (*Corr.*, I.166), which contains four lines of a translation of a simile from the *Iliad*, beginning 'As when the freezing blasts of Boreas blow', later incorporated in *Iliad*, XIX.380–3. A parody of 'the Cumbrous style' in 'Peri Bathous' (1728), chapter 12, contains lines alluding to 'Boreas rude breath', probably written by Pope (*PW*, II.223). The winds are added by Pope in his *The Second Satire of Dr. John Donne, Dean of St. Paul's, Versifyed*, 61–2: 'Language, which *Boreas* might to *Auster* hold, | More rough than forty *Germans* when they scold'.

4. **voracious Stork:** Pope uses the stork as an emblem of exploration in *Essay on Man*, III.105–6, but is here thinking of the fable of King Stork, who eats all the frogs who have desired to have a monarch; see Joseph Jackson, *A New Translation of Aesop's Fables* (1708), pp. 37–8. Pope recalled the fable (in a slightly different version) in the conclusion of book I of *The Dunciad*. Pope only uses 'voracious' otherwise in the Homer translations.

Bittern: regarded as a bird of ill omen because of its 'booming' cry and desolate habitat; see e.g. William Cartwright,

5   Where, or the *Crane*, Foe to *Pygmaean* Race,
     Or Ravenous *Corm'rants* shake their flabby Wings,
     And from soak'd Plumes disperse a briny Show'r,
     Or spread their feather'd Sails against the Beams,
     Or, of the Rising or *Meridian* Sun)
10   A baneful *Hunch-back'd Toad*, with look Maligne,

10.] THE Author has been very just in the Application of this Simile, though he has not dealt so ingeniously with Mankind as to own that he took the Hint from Mr. *Dennis*'s Critical and Satyrical Reflections. *vid.* Crit. and Sat. Reflections.

'Sadness', 17–18, *Comedies, Tragi-Comedies, with other Poems* (1651), p. 221: 'The Bittern on a Reed I hear | Pipes my Elegy'. Chaucer mentions the bird's peculiar cry in 'The Wife of Bath's Tale', 972–3: 'as a bitore bombleth in the mire'. In the King James version of the Bible, the bittern is associated with desolation following the destruction of towns (Isaiah 14:23 and 34:11; Zephaniah 2:14), and cf. Blackmore, an example of the would-be sublime poet, *A Paraphrase on part of the xivth Chapter of Isaiah*: 'The lonesome Bittern shall possess | This Fenny Seat, this Reedy Wilderness', and *The xxxivth Chapter of Isaiah. Paraphras'd*, both in *A Paraphrase on the Book of Job* (1700), pp. 257 and 262. Pope had probably read Dennis's own *Britannia Triumphans* (1704), in which (p. 11) Dennis addresses the Danube, after Marlborough's Blenheim victory: 'Thou like a *Bittern* through thy doleful Reeds | Complaind'st in sullen and moody Groans'.

5. Crane ... Pygmaean Race: cf. Pope's translation of Homer, *Iliad*, III.7–10: 'To warmer Seas the Cranes embody'd fly, | With Noise, and Order, thro' the mid-way Sky; | To Pygmy-Nations Wounds and Death they bring, | And all the War descends upon the Wing.' There is a comment on the simile (likening the cranes to the Trojan army) in the note to that section, which finds the comparison 'no less exact than surprising'. The battle, which was described in classical natural history writings, was also established as a motif in classical art. Milton mentions it in *Paradise Lost*, I.574–6; Sir Thomas Browne discusses it sceptically in *Pseudodoxia Epidemica*, fourth edition (1672), IV.ix, pp. 241–4; it forms the frontispiece to Joshua Barnes, *Gerania* (1675). Pope refers jokingly to the story, and its application to men of his size, in his letter to Cromwell, 24 June 1710 (*Corr.*, I.89). Addison's Latin mock-heroic poem on the subject, *Pygmaeogeranomachia*, along the lines of the classical *Battle of the Frogs and the Mice*, dated from his student days, and was the subject of many later translations, but it is not clear whether Pope could have known of it. See Addison's *Poems on Several Occasions* (1719), pp. 25–50.

6. Corm'rants: alluding to the cormorant's habit of spreading its wings to dry after diving for fish. For its reputation as gluttonous see Pope, *Odyssey*, I.207. The cormorant was one of the disguises of Satan entering Milton's Eden (*Paradise Lost*, IV.196), a passage referred to in Pope's notes to *Iliad* VII.48 and XIV.395.

6. flabby: 'Soft; not firm; easily shaking or yielding to the touch' (*SJ*). Not common in poetry other than in satire, but Pope might be recalling Blackmore, *Prince Arthur*, V (1695), p. 129: 'Last, sluggish *Auster*, to his Den with wet | And flabby Wings, does heavily retreat'.

9. Meridian: midday.

10. Hunch-back'd Toad: Pope's note accurately recalls Dennis's insult: 'As there is no Creature in Nature so venomous, there is nothing so stupid and so impotent as a hunch-back'd Toad...'; *Reflections Critical and Satyrical* (1711), p. 26. Pope recalled the words once more in his note to *The Dunciad Variorum*, I.104.

Glares on some Traveller's unwary steps,
Whether by Chance, or by Misfortune led
To tread those dark unwholesome, misty Fens,
Rage strait Collects his Venom all at once,
15   And swells his bloated Corps to largest size.

II

Fly Pegasaean *Steed, thy Rider bear,*
To breath the Sweets of pure Parnassian *Air,*

1.] The Author has Made the *Critick* Speak his *Rhapsody* in Rhime, which seems to deviate from his Character, but this, in my Opinion, wants no Excuse, since it was before he had taken the Bells off his *Hobby-Horse.*

---

13. misty Fens: probably a reminiscence of Satan's journey in *Paradise Lost*, II.621, over 'Rocks, Caves, Lakes, Fens, Bogs, Dens, and shades of death', or Blackmore's version of something similarly Satanic in *Prince Arthur*, V (1695), p. 139: 'Last the slow Powers come from their misty Dens, | That rule the *Marshes, Lakes,* and stagnant *Fens*'.

14. Venom: Toads were considered venomous; see note to 10, and *Paradise Lost*, IV. 800–9, where Satan, disguised as a toad, attempts to 'poison' Eve's ear by 'inspiring venom', an image later recalled in Pope's *Epistle to Dr Arbuthnot*, 319–20. Dennis had also written (*Reflections*, p. 26), 'there is a great deal of Venom in this little Gentleman's Temper'.

1 Pope's note. Dennis's earlier poetry, such as *The Court of Death* (1695) had used rhyme extensively, but in the preface to *The Monument* (1702), his verse elegy for William III, Dennis defended his 'patriotic' use of unrhymed verse by allusion to Milton's use of it. His later poetry, such as *Britannia Triumphans* (1704) was normally unrhymed, in line with Milton's antipathy to the 'modern bondage of rhyming' and the 'jingling sound of like endings' in his prefatory note on 'The Verse' in the second edition of *Paradise Lost* (1674). Andrew Marvell's commendatory poem 'On Paradise Lost', 45–8, added to that edition, had (though itself in rhyme) sided against 'tinkling Rhime' as a device of poor poets who would tire 'like a Pack-horse ... without his Bells'. Pope, whose allegiance was already to rhymed couplets, wrote to Caryll, 20 September 1713 and 13 July 1714 (*Corr.*, I.191 and 236), in terms which lightly associate poetry with the 'gingling' of bells on a horse's harness. After the verses, Pope writes that it occurred to Dennis that he had never 'read in *Milton,* or any of the Ancients, that *Pegasus* wore *Bells*; upon which, he in a very great rage tore the *Bells* from his Hobby-Horse, wisely imagining *Pegasus* to be like Millers Horse, that while he listned to their gingling he slacken'd his Pace, and he has rid him without *Bells* ever since'.

Pegasaean Steed: For the association of the winged horse Pegasus with the Muses and poetic inspiration, see *Essay on Criticism*, 151–2; also 93 and 200 for imaginative 'flight'. Pope would have found plenty of models of the debased horse of sublimity in his early reading; e.g. 'On Mr E—H— Upon His B— P—', 19–20: 'Thy stumbling Founder'd *Jade,* can Trot as high, | As any other *Pegasus,* can fly'; Rochester, *Poems on Several Occasions* (1680), pp. 19–20 (now attributed to the Earl of Dorset; see 'To the Author of a Poem, intitled, Successio', Headnote).

2. Parnassian: of Parnassus, the Greek mountain sacred in classical mythology to the Muses; cf. *Essay on Criticism*, 94, 344, 515. 'Parnassian' is otherwise used by

>   *Aloft I'm swiftly born, methinks I rise,*
>   *And with my Head* Sublime *can reach the Sky.*
> 5   *Large Gulps of* Aganippe's *streams I'll draw,*
>   *And give to Modern Writers* Classic *Law,*
>   *In* Grecian Buskins *Tragedy shall Mourn,*
>   *And to its* Ancient *Mirth the* Comic Sock *return.*

4.] Sublimi feriam Sydera Vertice. vid. Hor.

Pope only ironically, e.g. the 'proud Parnassian sneer' of the chief Dunce, *Dunciad Variorum*, II.5.

4 Pope's note. Horace, *Odes*, I.i.36: 'I shall reach the stars with my uplifted head'. In Horace, reaching the sky depends upon the judgement of others; for Pope's Dennis it is achieved by his own efforts (and fantasy).

Sublime: the principle concept of Dennis's aesthetic, e.g. *The Advancement and Reformation of Modern Poetry* (1701), pp. 70–7; *The Grounds of Criticism in Poetry* (1704), pp. 78–87. The sublime, relatively recently emerged as a critical category with the rediscovery of Longinus in the late seventeenth century, featured in the *Essay on Criticism* (678–83) in lines which Dennis attacked (*Reflections*, p. 18).

5. Aganippe: spring on the lower slopes of Mt Helicon, sacred to the Muses, supposedly a source of inspiration; see 'Summer', 23 and Commentary.

6. Classic Law: Dennis's *Grounds of Criticism* proposed (p. 4) 'That Poetry is to be Established, by laying down Rules'; cf. *Essay on Criticism*, 274–5. Dennis had in *Advancement and Reformation of Poetry* referred to the 'Rules' by which ancient Greek dramatists had operated as an essential aspect of the 'reformation' of the stage, but in that sense Pope's *Essay* might be construed as being more reliant than Dennis on 'Classic *Law*', a point made by Dennis himself in the *Reflections*.

7. Buskins: high boot or 'cothurnus' of classical Greek tragic actors.

8. Comic Sock: the corresponding 'low' footwear ('soccus') of actors in classical comedy: *SJ* cites Dryden, *Mac Flecknoe*, 79–80, *Miscellany Poems* (1684), p. 5: 'Great *Fletcher* never treads in Buskins here, | Nor greater *Johnson* [Ben Jonson] dares in Socks appear'. Pope's last line is an Alexandrine, for which see *Essay on Criticism*, 359.

6
SAPHO TO PHAON
(1712)

Editors' Headnote

Composition and publication

'Sapho to Phaon' was first published in March (before 18 March, according to an advertisement in *The Spectator*), 1712. As with many of Pope's early poems there is evidence of a considerable gap between first composition and publication. A note in Pope's hand on the cover page of the autograph fair-copy manuscript of 'Sapho to Phaon' in the Pierpont Morgan Library indicates that the poem was 'Written first 1707'. This would place the first composition of the poem in the same period in which Pope began his translation of Statius. There are no references to the poem in Pope's correspondence until 14 June 1709 when Wycherley wrote to Pope: 'I find by your Letter to Mr Cromwell, you have dispos'd of the Sappho, (you promis'd me,) to him, so that you have a mind to give me Jealously, but it is rather of your Friendship, than of the Love of your Sappho, since he refus'd, to let me see your last Letter to him' (*Corr.*, I.65). However, there is a particular concentration of familiar mentions of Ovid in Pope's letters to Cromwell of 1710 (e.g. 10 April, 17 May, 21 August, 12 October, 25 November; *Corr.*, I.81–105; and see Pope to Caryll, 25 January 1711, *Corr.*, I.113). Traffic was two-way: Pope commented on Cromwell's version of one of Ovid's elegies in a letter of 20 July 1710 (*Corr.*, I.92).

TE (I. 340–1) suggests that the surviving manuscript of 'Sapho to Phaon' can be dated to 1711 or early 1712. *EC* (I.90) records a note made by Jonathan Richardson Jr in his copy of the 1717 *Works* in which he describes the manuscript as 'written out elegantly . . . to show friends, with their remarks in the margin' and acknowledges the notice Pope took of such criticism – 'the present reading for the most part the effect of them'. The manuscript bears witness to two rounds of critical scrutiny: marginal comments in Pope's hand record the opinions of an unidentified reader, while a series of comments in Latin along the right-hand margin have been attributed to Cromwell (*TE*, I.340–1; Mack 1984: 72).

An abridged translation of 'Sapho To Phaon' by the minor Restoration court wit (and satiric target of Rochester), Sir Carr Scrope (1639–80) had been the opening item in *Ovid's Epistles, Translated by Several Hands*, published by Jacob Tonson in 1680, one of his first ventures in collective literary translation. In an advertisement in the eighth edition (1712) Tonson states that, because the greater part of the poem had been omitted by Scrope, he had '*sollicited an entire new Version of that Epistle, to render the whole Book compleat.*' The note goes on to explain that '*The Author of it will have me acquaint the Reader, that it was undertaken on that account only, and not out of any suppos'd defect in what that Gentleman had done.'* While Pope was evidently ready to oblige Tonson by working his existing drafts into a piece that could be used to enhance an already-distinguished collection, he was already shifting his allegiance by working with Bernard Lintot to bring out *Miscellany Poems* a couple of months later.

Text

ESTC has three entries for the eighth edition of *Ovid's Epistles, Translated By Several Hands* (1712) – T61462 (BL 1489.ff.8), T61463 (BL 76.e.15), and N69030 (Kenneth Spencer Library, University of Kansas). *TE* adopted T61463 as copy text, identifying 'And' at line 257 as a misprint and emending it to 'Ah' on the authority of the manuscript. However, both T61462 and N69030 (which are textually identical) read 'Ah' at this point. There is further evidence to suggest that there were two distinct states of the volume. ESTC mistakenly says T61462 has the catchword 'Commu-' on B1^v: in fact this occurs on B1^r, with 'Genius' on B1^v, which is also the case in N69030. In T61463, B1^r has 'Com-' while B6^r reads 'Un-', whereas T61462 and N69030 have 'Ungentle'. T61462 and N69030 both close line 168 of the poem with a period – 'well!' – whereas T61463 has a comma, leaving an awkward connection with the lines that follow.

The text here presented is taken from the version embodied in T61462 and N69030, which, while it might possibly be the second state, has the more reliable text and has been designated *1712a* in the apparatus below. All substantive variant readings from the first version of the poem in the manuscript fair copy have been recorded in the textual apparatus. For the sake of clarity, manuscript variants are recorded in the form in which they first appear, with subsequent stages of revision recorded and discussed in the editorial commentary when they are of particular interest. Beyond the first edition, revision is confined to two later texts, the *Works* of 1717 and 1736. In 1717, Pope gave 'Sapho to Phaon' the extra impetus of a section title and an engraved headpiece illustration; in 1736 he printed the Latin text at the foot of the page. The various extant texts of 'Sapho to Phaon' are referred to in the apparatus as follows:

MS: 'Sapho to Phaon' (Pierpont Morgan Library, MA 349; reproduced in Mack 1984; *IELM* PoA 297)

1712a: *Ovid's Epistles . . . By Several Hands*, octavo (Griffith 4, ESTC T61462 and N69030)

1712b: *Ovid's Epistles . . . By Several Hands*, octavo (Griffith 4, ESTC T61463)

1717: *Works* quarto (Griffith 79)

1736a: *Works*, vol.III, octavo (Griffith 417)

1736b: *Works*, vol.III, octavo (Griffith 418)

1741: *Works*, vol.I, part ii, octavo (Griffith 521)

1751: *Works*, vol.II, octavo (Griffith 644)

Models and sources

Sappho, the most celebrated female writer of antiquity, was born on the Greek island of Lesbos in the latter half of the seventh century BC. The biographical evidence is very uncertain and fragmentary. Sappho's love for the ferryman Phaon, rendered beautiful by the goddess Aphrodite, and the legend that Sappho committed suicide from the promontory on the Ionian island of Leucas, derive from much later sources, and have no relation to what little survives of the poetry. She was an important if ambivalent figure of identification for post-Renaissance women writers and a perennial object of literary fascination to male ones in Britain (for studies of her status and significance in wider context see e.g. Lipking 1988; Rainbolt 1997; Reynolds 2003). Of nine books of lyric poetry mentioned in ancient sources, only one complete poem and some sizeable fragments survived the classical era. At some point Pope owned *Carminum Poetarum Novem, Lyricae Poeseōs Principum, Fragmenta* (Heidelberg, 1598), which included pieces by Sappho (Mack 1982: 434, item 134). She was known from two items in particular. Her incomplete poem of thwarted and anxious love, preserved in Longinus' treatise *On the Sublime* and known also through a freely extended Latin adaptation by Catullus (no. LI, 'Ille mi par esse deo uidetur'), was particularly influential. It prompted many translations, e.g. by William Bowles in Nahum Tate's *Poems by Several Hands* (1685), p.8, and in some editions of Dryden's *Sylvae*; via Boileau and by a 'Lady of Quality' in Behn's *Miscellany, Being a Collection of Poems* (1685), p. 212. Addison printed a translation of Sappho's 'Hymn to Aphrodite', by Pope's enemy Ambrose Philips, in *The Spectator*, no. 223, 15 November 1711, with a short account of the Ovidian version of the story; Philips's version of the other poem, together with Catullus' Latin and Boileau's French version, appeared in no. 229, 22 November 1711, an additional prompt for Pope, perhaps. Addison followed this up with an uneasily admiring account of Sappho, culminating in a mock bill of mortality from the 'Lover's Leap' at Apollo's temple at Leucas, including the fate of Sappho and her brother, in no. 233, 27 November 1711. In writing to Steele (c. 15 December 1712, *Corr*, I.159–60) with the first version of his lyric 'The Dying Christian to his Soul', Pope claims to have had the 'fragment of Sappho' in his mind as a lyric model. The first ode of the fourth book of Horace's *Odes*, a hymn to Venus, was in some ways a reworking of Sappho's address to Aphrodite and was the only complete Horace lyric Pope imitated (in 1727).

Literary views of Sappho were heavily influenced by the *Heroides* of Ovid (Publius Ovidius Naso, 43 BC–AD 17). The collection, probably dating from around 15 BC, contains 21 verse letters mostly from legendary female characters to absent male lovers (Penelope to Ulysses, Dido to Aeneas, etc.); the authorship of no. XV, from Sappho to Phaon, remains doubtful because of its absence from or unusual position in several manuscripts, but it continues to be referred to as Ovid's in default of other likely candidates, and Pope certainly regarded it as authentic. The last six epistles consist of reciprocal letters between male and female lovers. The Dutch scholar Daniel Heinsius had published an influential edition of the *Heroides* in 1652; Pope owned a copy of Ovid's *Opera Omnia* edited by Cornelius Schrevel (Leiden, 1662), but it is not known when this was acquired (Mack 1982: 432–3, item 128). Further editions of

Heroides as a separate work appeared in 1658, 1675, 1686 and at Cambridge in 1705. Translations of the *Heroides* into English, in varying states of completeness, began with George Turberville's *The Heroycall Epistles of the Learned Poet Publius Ouidius Naso, in English Verse* (1567; much reprinted to 1600), followed by *Ovid's Heroicall Epistles. English'd by W. S.* (Wye Saltonstall, 1636; reprinted seven times to 1695) and *Ovids Heroical Epistles, Englished by Iohn Sherburne* (1639). There is no particular evidence that Pope knew these, popular as they were, but they were used by the translators of the version put together in 1680 by the publisher Jacob Tonson with a 'Preface' and contributions by Dryden. This contained work by Dryden, Nahum Tate, Thomas Flatman, Thomas Otway, Elkanah Settle and Aphra Behn, whose loose 'Paraphrase' of 'Oenone to Paris' (pp. 97–116) appears to have influenced Pope's poem. Scrope's truncated version of 'Sappho to Phaon' opened the volume (pp. 1–7). The book's first appearance prompted a burlesque, perhaps by Mathew Stevenson, called *The Wits Paraphrased; or, Paraphrase upon Paraphrase* (1680). A comic version of five epistles had already appeared in Alexander Radcliffe, *Ovidius Exulans or Ovid Travestie* (1673, reprinted several times to 1705), and Radcliffe responded to Stevenson with *Ovid Travestie, A Burlesque upon Several of Ovid's Epistles* (1680), also published by Tonson. By 1712, the Tonson 'Several Hands' collection had become the standard version, with Pope sufficiently eminent to contribute his full account of the Sappho epistle. Accounts of the significance of the 1680 volume and its relation to earlier versions are given in Tissol (2005: 204–7) and Gillespie (1988). For a succinct introduction to Ovid's varied reception history in the period see Hopkins (2012), and for a particular account of the *Heroides* in Pope's time see Trickett (1988).

Other versions of the story included John Lyly's allegorical play for child actors *Sapho and Phao* (1584), involving the machinations of Venus and Cupid, and William Bosworth's *The Chast and Lost Lovers Lively Shadowed* (1651). An Ovidian epistle, 'Sappho to Philaenis', appeared in John Donne's posthumous *Poems* of 1633; this extends the story post-Phaon and returns Sappho to the love of women in a wittily erotic puzzle about verse, sexuality and fame. *The Passion of Sappho, and Feast of Alexander* (the former by William Harison, the latter by Dryden) were set to music by Thomas Clayton and performed in 1711 (24 May) at York Buildings (see Headnote to *Ode for Musick*). A supplementary tradition of Ovidian amorous epistle translated to British characters had emerged with Michael Drayton's *England's Heroical Epistles* (1597); these were still popular into the eighteenth century, and had received an update in John Oldmixon's *Amores Britannici* (1703). David Crauford's similar collection, *Ovidius Britannicus* (1703), includes a conciliatory verse epistle from Phaon to Sappho. Pope's future co-author Elijah Fenton produced a new translation of 'Sappho to Phaon. A Love Epistle', published a few months after Pope's poem in *Miscellaneous Poems and Translations* (May 1712); in his *Poems on Several Occasions* (1717), he added a response from Phaon. It is possible, given Pope's involvement with the 1712 volume, that he saw Fenton's poem in advance of his own final text, but there is no direct evidence of this.

Ovidian translations of a suavely libertine kind, especially from the *Amores* and the *Metamorphoses*, were a staple part of the Dryden–Tonson *Miscellanies* and of rival series during the 1680s and 1690s, and Dryden's own *Fables Ancient and Modern* (1700) contained more prominent examples. The 1680 *Ovid's Epistles* was an inaugural text for a model of collaborative, gentlemanly authorship, displaying a variety of styles and viewpoints. Dryden's 'Preface' identifies some of the key elements of Ovid's reputation in the period: wit, sweetness, sympathetic feeling, non-moralistic emphasis on sexual passion which nonetheless contrives to be not bawdy:

> But of the general Character of Women which is Modesty, he has taken a most becoming care; for his amorous Expressions go no further than virtue may allow, and therefore may be read, as he intended them, by Matrons without a blush.
>
> (sig. A7ᵛ)

Dryden also took the opportunity to issue guidance on different types of translation – metaphrase (word for word), paraphrase (a looser version, retaining spirit rather than letter) and imitation (a freer, more independent poem, not really a translation at all), giving his own preference for paraphrase, clearly also Pope's own preference at this point. Pope had certainly practised the imitation of Ovid as part of his poetic self-education (cf. 'The Fable of Vertumnus and Pomona'), though much of this work was lost. Despite Spence's disdain (*OAC*, I.233) Pope retained a lifelong love of Ovid.

Context

Ovid's *Heroides* XV, 'Sappho Phaoni', consists of 220 lines in elegiac metre. Turberville's version takes 226 lines, alternately of 12 and 14 syllables, in couplets, perhaps in an attempt to give a sense of the Latin metre. Saltonstall produces 240 lines in heroic couplets, Sherburne 220 lines of the same verse, thus matching Ovid line for line; his is probably the closest version, or 'metaphrase' in Dryden's taxonomy. Scrope's 1680 version is drastically cut to 97 lines in heroic couplets. Fenton's version consisted of 230 lines of heroic couplets. Pope's, at 259 lines, is by far the most expansive. The two travesty versions, Stevenson's in 1680 and Radcliffe's in 1673, are both cut, to 135 (of octosyllabics) and 112 lines (of heroic couplets) respectively. Stevenson and Radcliffe both transplant the lovers to the insalubrious environs of tavern and brothel in something like Restoration London (Sappho threatening alternately to hang herself or throw herself out of a garret window), and do not appear likely to have much influenced Pope's serious version verbally, except by way of an example of vulgarity to avoid. It may be noteworthy, however, that Radcliffe's Sappho refers to herself as 'crooked', one of the words often used to describe Pope (by, among others, himself) and her stature as the short (see 39) but world-beating poet, in emotional distress, probably had some biographical resonance for Pope.

Saltonstall comments on the emotional tenor of the poem: 'And in this Epistle *Ovid* hath most lively expresst the soft and amorous affections of love'; Harison's poem in

1711 was based on Ovid's epistle, and was intended to display in convenient form 'all the Thoughts that can arise in the Mind of a neglected Woman who has given up her Honour'. Pope was less censorious about such things in his early work. After the May of 'January and May', Sappho (or 'Sapho' as Pope calls her) was the next in Pope's sequence of sympathetically-conceived women who depart from sexual conventions, leading up to the 'Unfortunate Lady' and the notional writer of 'Eloisa to Abelard', which mimics 'Sapho to Phaon' in many respects as it develops and transforms the Ovidian epistle form. As with 'Eloisa', it is tempting to read into the display of sexual longing some personal motivation, particularly given Sappho's complaint that her ability as a writer does not bring her the love she craves, but there is little direct evidence to adduce. For discussion of Pope's possible identification with passionate female figures, and the ambivalently dignifying and constraining aspects of this as a representation of female gender, see Mack (1982: 380–3) and Rumbold (1989: 90–1). It is at least surely significant that Pope chose (or at least agreed) to imitate the one epistle in the *Heroides* which is in the name of a historical individual, and a writer at that.

As often in the early translations, Pope opted for a tone of high elegance; some of the phrasing would later return reworked in more ironic vein. Pope is much less colloquial than the early translators, and he has suppressed various trivialities and some sexual content (see Commentary at 19, 25, 44, 76, 101, 168); other aspects are cut for less obvious reasons (33, 80, 197, 249). The expansions and additions are normally in the interests of heightening the emotional tone; the more significant of these paraphrase-type inventions are noted (see Commentary to e.g. 15–16, 26, 30, 35–6, 86, 98, etc.). Dryden had commented on Ovid's love of the so-called 'turn' or artful verbal trick, often involving repetition with variation and sometimes felt to be contextually inappropriate, as the 'darling Sin which he wou'd not be perswaded to reform' (Dryden's dedicatory epistle, to Pope's friend John Sheffield, of his version of *The Aeneid*, in *Works of Virgil*, 1697, sig. e2ᵛ). Following Dryden, Pope made strenuous efforts to mimic these effects, including the one cited by Dryden in the essay known as the 'Discourse Concerning the Original and Progress of Satire', in *The Satires of Decimus Junius Juvenalis* (1693), p. li, as 'extraordinary' (see Commentary to 45–8).

Just as 'Phaon' was used in popular songs of the Restoration period as a convenient identity for a beautiful young man, 'Sappho' appears in lyric poetry of Robert Herrick among others as a codename for a desirable woman; Wycherley wrote a poem, 'To the Sappho of the Age' in his *Miscellany Poems* (1704), pp. 191–2. Steele used the name satirically for a female wit in *The Tatler*, no. 6, 23 April 1709. Pope and Cromwell had been using 'Sappho' as a gallant code-name for female companions and poets, including (probably) Elizabeth Thomas and Pope's neighbour Mrs Nelson, since 1708 (see e.g. Pope to Cromwell, 18 March 1708 and 21 December 1711; *Corr.*, I.42, 137–8). Pope used the name slightingly for a female poet in a letter to John Caryll, c. February 1713 (*Corr.*, I.173), more flatteringly in his 'Impromptu to Lady Winchilsea' (written 1714, published 1741), in his letter to Lady Mary Wortley Montagu c. 1720 (*Corr.*, II.22) and in the epigrammatic 'Verses to Mrs Judith Cowper' (18 October 1722, *Corr.* II.138-9). By the 1730s Pope was using the name to connote a sexually wanton and diseased woman, perhaps with reference to Lady Mary Wortley Montagu (e.g. *An Epistle to Lady*, 25–6; *Epistle to Dr Arbuthnot*, 101, 369).

The manuscript of Pope's poem contains many inscriptions in a hand normally thought to be Cromwell's, alongside Pope's record of his own revisions and comments from 'X'. Those (many) that read simply 'pulchrè', 'benè', 'bellè', 'optimè' (beautiful; good; lovely; very good) have not normally been noted in this Commentary, but instances are signalled where a change has been made as a result of marginal criticism or where discussion has evidently taken place.

SAPHO to *PHAON*.
Wholly Translated.
By Mr. *POPE*.

<blockquote>

SAY, lovely Youth, that dost my Heart command,
Can *Phaon*'s Eyes forget his *Sapho*'s Hand?
Must then her Name the wretched Writer prove?
To thy Remembrance lost, as to thy Love!
5   Ask not the cause that I new Numbers chuse,
The Lute neglected, and the Lyric Muse;
Love taught my Tears in sadder Notes to flow,
And tun'd my Heart to Elegies of Woe.

</blockquote>

Title. 1717–41 SAPHO | TO | PHAON. | FROM | OVID.; *1751:* SAPPHO | TO | PHAON.
3. prove?: MS: prove,
4. Love!: MS: Love?
6. MS: These mournful Numbers suit a mournful Muse;

---

1. *Say, lovely Youth:* Wakefield compares Behn, 'A Paraphrase upon Ovid's Oenone to Paris', 231, *Ovid's Epistles, Translated by Several Hands* (1680), p. 111: 'Say, lovely Youth, why wou'dst thou thus betray'. *TE* points out the phrase in Scrope, 11, p. 2, 'Ah lovely Youth! . . .'. The line has no basis in Ovid.

3. *wretched Writer:* Pope recalled the phrase in his note to I.101 of *The Dunciad Variorum*, but there the 'wretched' indicates the poor quality of professional writing, whereas here it refers to the unhappiness of a 'private' letter-writer. Ovid refers simply to the hand 'auctoris' ('of the author').

4. Pope's addition, a 'turn' or figure of speech in Ovid's manner. For 'turns' see Headnote, and *Essay on Criticism*, 391.

5. *Numbers:* poetic metres; cf. *Essay on Criticism*, 340 and Commentary, and also 230 and 244 below. Ovid refers to 'alterna . . . carmina' (5–6; 'alternate songs'), i.e. elegiac metre (consisting of alternating hexameter and pentameter couplets) rather that the 'Lyric Muse' (6), the 'Sapphic' metre for which she was known. For Turberville's attempt at a version of elegiac metre in *The Heroycall Epistles of the Learned Poet Publius Ouidius Naso, in English Verse* (1567) see Headnote.

6. *Lute:* The lute post-dates Ovid; used by Pope as it was often the instrument chosen to accompany song.

   Lyric Muse: lyric metre, song form; Ovid, 8, mentions a lyre.

8. *Elegies.* Technically a reference to the specific Latin metre in which Ovid is writing (see 5), but the mournful connotation was also present in Ovid.

I burn, I burn, as when thro' ripen'd Corn
10   By driving Winds the spreading Flames are born!
Phaon to *Aetna*'s scorching Fields retires,
While I consume with more than *Aetna*'s Fires!
No more my Soul a Charm in Musick finds,
Musick has Charms alone for peaceful Minds:
15   Soft Scenes of Solitude no more can please,
Love enters there, and I'm my own Disease:
No more the *Lesbian* Dames my Passion move,

---

9. thro' ripened corn: MS: fierce Whirlwinds raise
10. MS: The spreading Flames, and crackling Harvests blaze.
11. scorching: MS: distant
12. While I consume: MS: Me, Love consumes
17. No more the *Lesbian* Dames: MS: The *Lesbian* Dames no more

---

9-10. Wakefield compares Scrope, 5-6, p. 1: 'I burn, I burn, like kindled Fields of Corn, | When by the driving Winds the flames are born'; the sense is quite close to Ovid, 5-6. This couplet resulted from consultation (see MS variants): 'Benè, at melius Scroop ni fallor' ('good, but Scroop is better unless I am mistaken'); 'X would alter to – standing corn' (MS).
10. born: i.e. borne, carried.
12. consume with: am consumed by.
    Aetna: Etna, a volcano on Sicily; cf. 'Spring', 66, and 'Autumn', 91.
13-14. Wakefield compares Scrope, 5-6, p. 2: 'My Muse and Lute can now no longer please, | They are th' Employments of a mind at ease'. Rogers (2006) suggests a reminiscence of the opening line of Congreve's play *The Mourning Bride* (1697): 'Music has Charms to soothe a savage Breast'. In Ovid (13), Sappho's interest in music is more specifically about the 'songs I might join to well-arranged strings' ('dispositis quae iungam carmina nervis'). Another disagreement between the early readers: 'Pulchrè – at rectius Scroop' ('beautiful – but Scroop more correct'); 'X thinks mine best' (MS).
15-16. Pope's invention, as TE observes, introducing 'a note of solitary melancholy which has no precedent either in Ovid or Scrope'. At this point Scrope does have his own melancholy addition: 'Wand'ring from Thought to Thought I sit alone' (7, *Ovid's Epistles*, p. 2), a line modelled on Rochester's 'Satyr against [Reason and] Mankind', 18, *Poems on Several Occasions* (1696), p. 87: 'Stumbling from thought to thought, falls headlong down', and recalled ironically in *The Dunciad Variorum,* I.112: 'Sinking from thought to thought, a vast profound!'. The MS shows extensive reworking at this point.
17. Lesbian *Dames*: women of Lesbos, a large island in the Aegean, Sappho's birthplace. The term 'Lesbian' is not listed in its modern association with female homosexuality by *OED* before 1890, but the content of the poem indicates that the modern resonance of the word was at least partially available to both writers. A cryptic marginal comment, perhaps from Cromwell, deleted, indicates the sexual suggestion was problematic: 'Ah! rimis Lascivè innuat[.] Licet se esse Tribadem non tamen profitetur' ('Ah! through the cracks he hints at something lubricious. It's possible she's a Tribade [Lesbian], but it's not to be openly stated').

Once the dear Objects of my guilty Love;
All other Loves are lost in only thine,
20 Ah Youth ungrateful to a Flame like mine!
Whom wou'd not all those blooming Charms surprize,
Those heav'nly Looks, and dear deluding Eyes?
The Harp and Bow wou'd you like *Phoebus* bear,
A brighter *Phoebus, Phaon* might appear;
25 Wou'd you with Ivy wreath your flowing Hair,

18^9. MS: No more I sigh for *Amythone*'s Charms,
  No more I melt in *Athys* circling Arms,
19–20. MS: All other Loves are lost in thine alone,
  This once-divided Heart is all thy own.
21. **all those blooming Charms:** MS: that resistless Youth

---

18. guilty Love: in Ovid (19) there is a textual crux in the manuscripts, which offer either 'hic sine crimine' ('here without incurring censure') or 'non sine crimine' ('not without incurring censure'). The former reading is sometimes taken by modern editors as an attempt to tone down the sexual content of the relationships described. Saltonstall, *Ovid's Heroicall Epistles. English'd by W. S.* (1636), and Scrope omit this; Turberville, p. 109, renders it 'shame ylaid aside'; Sherburne, *Ovids Heroical Epistles* (1639), p. 138, refers to 'my sins'.

19. All other Loves: Ovid 15–19 names three female individuals, including one (Athys) of the two named in Pope's MS variant text, but also more loosely the 'Pyrrhiades Methymniadesve puellae' ('girls of Pyrrha and Methymna'), and 'aliae centum' ('a hundred others'), as no longer of interest; Pope has generalised and softened this troop of lovers. Scrope makes a similar cut, whereas the earlier translators retain more of Ovid's detail.

20. Pope's substitution for Ovid 20, 'improbe, multarum quod fuit, unus habes' ('shameless one, what once belonged to many, you hold alone').
ungrateful: not responding to cultivation (*OED*, sense 1c); Pope almost certainly recalls Dryden's line about the infertile wife of 'David' (Charles II) in *Absalom and Achitophel*, 12 (1681), p. 1: 'A Soil ungrateful to the Tiller's care'.

21. blooming: TE notes that Scrope uses the same adjective in 12 (p. 2) of his version, 'blooming years and beauty'.

22. dear deluding Eyes: TE cites Scrope, 64, p. 5: 'dear deluding Vision' (from a different section of the poem); cf. also Samuel Wesley, *The Life of... Christ*, IV (1693), p. 134 (speaking of Salome): 'The same fair Face and false deluding Eyes'; John Hopkins, 'A Lady to her Lover', 42, *Amasia* (1700), p. 101: 'Curse his false Tongue, and his deluding Eyes'; and Pope's 'Eloisa to Abelard', 283. Ovid (22) has Sappho complain slightly differently that Phaon's appearance is 'oculis insidiosa meis' ('treacherous to my eyes').

23. Phoebus: Apollo, Greek god of poetry (the 'Harp') and also an infallible archer (the 'Bow'); also god of the sun, hence perhaps 'brighter' in 24, where Ovid has 'manifestus Apollo', 'a clear Apollo'.

25. In Ovid (24) Phaon can become Bacchus (see next line) if horns are added to his head (because Bacchus was in some iconic representations a horned god), a suggestion suppressed by Pope, perhaps because of the conventional association with cuckoldry in his time. Retained by Turberville, Saltsontall and Sherburne, but not Scrope.

Not *Bacchus* self with *Phaon* cou'd compare:
Yet *Phoebus* lov'd, and *Bacchus* felt the Flame,
One *Daphne* warm'd, and one the *Cretan* Dame;
Nymphs that in Verse no more cou'd rival me,
30   Than ev'n those Gods contend in Charms with thee.
The Muses teach me all their softest Lays,
And the wide World resounds with *Sapho*'s Praise.
Tho' great *Alcaeus* more sublimely sings,
And strikes with bolder Rage the sounding Strings,
35   No less Renown attends the moving Lyre,
Which *Cupid* tunes, and *Venus* does inspire.
To me what Nature has in Charms deny'd

---

36. 1717–51: Which *Venus* tunes, and all her Loves inspire.

---

26. Bacchus: Greek cult and later Roman name for Dionysus, son of Zeus and Greek god of wine and revels (cf. 159 variant), associated with ivy wreaths in ritual practices (cf. 'Messiah', 23). TE remarks that Pope expands the compliment from Ovid's bare 'Bacchus eris', 'you will be Bacchus', and notes that Ovid elsewhere refers to him as the most beautiful of the gods (*Metamorphoses*, IV.18–19).

28. Daphne: virgin huntress desired by Apollo, turned into a laurel tree to avoid rape by him (cf. Commentary to *Windsor-Forest*, 198–200, and the title character of 'Winter'); the story is told in Ovid, *Metamorphoses*, I.452–567.

   warm'd: sexually aroused.

   Cretan Dame: Ariadne, daughter of Minos and Pasiphae, rescued (in some versions of myth) by Bacchus after being deserted on Naxos by Theseus, whom she had helped to kill the Minotaur on Crete. In Ovid (25) she is referred to as 'Cnosida', i.e. from Knossos on Crete.

29–30. Ovid (26) has Sappho remark that these women could not write poetry, but the comparison in Pope's 30 is his own addition. TE remarks that Ariadne was not strictly speaking a 'nymph' (as Daphne was) and compares 65; but Pope's usage of the term was often fairly loose. Line 30 is marked 'paraphr. pulchra' ('beautiful paraphrase') in MS.

31. Lays: songs. The sense is close to Ovid's 'blandissima carmina' (27; 'most softly alluring songs').

33. Alcaeus: lyric poet, also from Lesbos, born c. 620 BC, and so an older contemporary of Sappho; in some ancient traditions, actually her lover and rival of Phaon, as well as political co-conspirator. Pope has cut Ovid's description (29) of Alcaeus as 'consors patriaeque lyraeque' ('fellow in homeland and poetry') and added 'great'. Turberville retains a version of Ovid 29, as does Sherburne; cut by Saltonstall and Scrope.

34. Rage: passion; cf. *Windsor-Forest*, 289. Ovid's Sappho (30) says that Alcaeus 'grandius ... sonet' ('makes a grander sound'), i.e. writes on more public, masculine themes. The line is marked 'pulchra paraphrasis' ('beautiful paraphrase') on the MS.

35. moving Lyre: For the actual instrument cf. *Ode for Musick*, 3; here a metaphor for emotionally inspiring verse. This line and the next are Pope's addition.

36. Cupid: son of Venus, the Roman goddess of sexual love; cf. 70, 101.

37–42. Pope could hardly have avoided reflecting on his own situation here, as a notoriously diminutive poet with aspirations for lasting poetic fame; see Headnote.

Is well by Wit's more lasting Charms supply'd.
Tho' short my Stature, yet my Name extends
40   To Heav'n it self, and Earth's remotest Ends.
Brown as I am, an *Aethiopian* Dame
Inspir'd young *Perseus* with a gen'rous Flame.
Turtles and Doves of diff'ring Hues, unite,
And glossy Jett is pair'd with shining White.
45   If to no Charms thou wilt thy Heart resign,
But such as merit, such as equal thine,

---

38. **Charms:** *1736b–51:* Flames
39. **yet my Name extends:** MS: my Immortal Name
40. MS: To Heav'n extends, and thro' the Globe my Fame.
41. **an *Aethiopian* Dame:** MS: the beauteous *Aethiop* mov'd
42. MS: Great *Perseus* heart; he saw, admir'd, and lov'd.

---

38. **Wit:** poetry, creativity, intelligence; see Headnote to *Essay on Criticism*. TE likens the phrasing here to 205–6 of that poem. Saltonstall, *Ovid's Heroicall Epistles*, fifth edition (1663), p. 167 and Sherburne, p. 138, use the same noun to translate Ovid's 'ingeni[um]' (32, 'inner talent'; Turberville, p. 110, has 'goodnesse of the braine'). The 'more lasting Charms' are Pope's invention.

39. **short ... Stature:** Ovid, 33, has 'brevis', 'short'. Robinson (1963: 35–6) records the suggestion that Sappho's name might be a pun on a Doric variant of the word ψῆφος (psephos), a small pebble.

40. **Heav'n:** not in Ovid.
    remotest Ends: translating 'terras ... omnes' ('all lands'), 33. Normally a biblical or epic phrase, e.g. Sandys, 'Psalme XCVIII', 12, *A Paraphrase vpon the Divine Poems* (1638), p. 119: 'To Earths remotest Ends'. Ovid (34) has Sappho more defiantly measure herself by the extent of her name: 'mensuram nominis ipsa fero'.

41. **Brown:** dark-skinned; in Ovid (35), Sappho confesses she is not 'candida' (white, fair, bright).
    Aethiopian Dame: Ovid (36) names Andromeda, daughter of Cepheus and Cassiopeia, rules of the Ethiopians; she was rescued from a sea monster by Perseus (42), son of Zeus by Danae, who then married her. 'Aethiop' was a common adjective for a dark-skinned woman, e.g. Shakespeare, *Love's Labours Lost*, IV.iii.114–15: 'Jove would sweare, Juno but an Aethiop were'. In Ovid she is 'patriae fusca colore suae' ('dusky with the colour of her homeland'). This line was altered after the comment 'minus placent' ('these please less') on MS.

43–4. The rhyme and idea are recalled, in parody, in *Rape of the Lock*, I.135–6.

43. **Turtles:** turtle doves ('turtur', Ovid, 38), related to ordinary doves but a different colour (brown in Turberville, p. 110; black in Saltonstall, p. 167 and Sherburne, p. 138, following Ovid's 'niger'). Cf. 'Summer', 52. The line is marked 'pulchrè non rectè' ('beautiful not correct'), on MS.

44. **Jett:** i.e. jet, a fossilised black resin used in jewellery. Ovid's contrast is less extreme: the dark turtle dove mates with a 'viridi ... ave', a green bird (thought to refer to a parrot; 'Popingay' in Turberville, p. 110; 'green Parret' in Saltonstall, p. 167; 'gay Iay' [jay] in Sherburne, p. 138).

45–8. Ovid's phrasing (39–40) results in a witty repetition: 'si, nisi quae facie poterit

By none alas! by none thou can'st be mov'd,
Phaon alone by *Phaon* must be lov'd!
Yet once thy *Sapho* cou'd thy Cares employ,
50   Once in her Arms you center'd all your Joy:
Still all those Joys to my Remembrance move,
For oh! how vast a Memory has Love?
My Musick, then, you cou'd for ever hear,
And all my Words were Musick to your Ear.
55   You stop'd with Kisses my inchanting Tongue,
And found my Kisses sweeter than my Song.
In all I pleas'd, but most in what was best;
And the last Joy was dearer than the rest.
Then with each Word, each Glance, each Motion fir'd,
60   You still enjoy'd, and yet you still desir'd,

49–50. MS: Yet once ev'n I, neglected I, had Charms,
          Once all thy joys were centrd in these Arms:
51. *1741–51:* No time the dear remembrance can remove,
55. MS: Kisses you snatch'd, & stop'd my charming Tongue,

---

te digna videri, | nulla futura tua est, nulla futura tua est' ('if, unless a girl can be seen to be worthy of you in appearance, no girl is to be yours, no girl is to be yours'). *TE* notes that Dryden had cited these lines in his prefatory discourse 'On the Original and Progress of Satire', in *Satires of Decimus Junius Juvenalis* (1693), p. li, as an 'extraordinary turn upon the words', and suggests that Pope's attempt to imitate the effect is further stimulated by Scrope's attempt at a 'turn', 13–14, p. 2: 'If none but equal Charms thy heart can bind, | Then to thy self alone thou must be kind'. The MS is endorsed 'Magis Poeticè quam Scroop' ('more poetical than Scroop'), here. The earlier translations all opt for simpler phrasing.

48. Pope's invention, a 'turn' of his own.
49–56. Loosely paraphrasing Ovid 41–5, with the various elements reordered. The MS is marked 'minus ad rem etiam et Scroop' ('still less to the matter even than Scroop').
51–2. 'melius Scroop' ('Scroop better', or possibly 'better than Scroop'), MS, but also 'Pulchrè' at 52. Scrope, 17–18, p. 2, has 'A thousand tender things to mind I call, | For they who truly Love remember all'.
54. 'Paraph: ut et Scroop' ('paraphrase: so Scroop also'), MS. Scrope, 19, p. 2, has 'Delighted with the Musick of my Tongue'.
55. inchanting Tongue: not in Ovid. *TE* suggests the influence of Scrope, 21, p. 2: 'And snatching Kisses, stop'd me as I sung', which is closer to Ovid's 'oscula cantanti tu mihi rapta dabas' ('you used to give stolen kisses to me as I sang').
56. 'Bellè – etiam Scroop' ('beautiful – as Scroop'), MS; see previous note.
57. *TE* notes that the line is monosyllabic, a rarity in Pope, but duplicated at 108–9 below (cf. *Essay on Criticism*, 350).
58. last Joy: Ovid 46, 'amoris opus' (the 'work of love'). *TE* compares the phrasing to Dryden's translation of Ovid, *Elegies*, II.xix.18, *Miscellany Poems* (1684), p. 141: 'How every kiss was dearer than the last!' 'Bellè – etiam Scroop' ('beautiful – as Scroop'), MS; Scrope, 23, p. 3: 'The earnest of the coming joyes of Love'.
60. Pope's invention, another 'turn'.

Till all dissolving in the Trance we lay,
And in tumultuous Raptures dy'd away.
The fair *Sicilians* now thy Soul inflame;
Why was I born, ye Gods, a *Lesbian* Dame?
65 But ah beware, *Sicilian* Nymphs! nor boast
That wandring Heart which I so lately lost;
Nor be with all those tempting Words abus'd,
Those tempting Words were all to *Sapho* us'd.
And you that rule *Sicilia*'s happy Plains,
70 Have pity, *Venus*, on your Poet's Pains!
Shall Fortune still in one sad Tenor run,
And still increase the Woes so soon begun?
Enur'd to Sorrows from my tender Years,
My Parent's Ashes drank my early Tears.
75 My Brother next, neglecting Wealth and Fame,

---

61. MS: Both warm'd at once, at once entranc'd we lay,
65. MS: *Ye fair Sicilians*, ah be warn'd, nor boast
72. **so soon:** MS: it has
73. **Sorrows:** *1736b–51:* Sorrow
75–6. MS: My ruin'd Brother trades from Shore to Shore,
    And gains, as basely as he lost before:

61–2. TE finds Pope indebted to Scrope, 26–7, p. 3: "Till both expiring with tumultuous Joys, | A gentle Faintness did our Limbs surprize'. The sense is close to Ovid, 49–50. The MS shows some hesitation and deletion at this point.

61. **dissolving:** normal code in Restoration verse for orgasm (as with 'melt', 106); cf. Rochester, 'The Imperfect Enjoyment', 10, 15, etc. Ovid (49) has 'confusa voluptas' ('sexual pleasure poured [or 'mixed'] together').

63. **Sicilians:** Ovid's Sappho calls these young women Phaon's 'nova praeda' ('new prey') (51), occasioning a marginal comment, 'minus rectè' ('less correct'), against Pope's version on the MS.

65–6. TE suggests the influence of Scrope, 28–9, p. 3: 'Beware, *Sicilian* Ladies, Ah! beware | How you receive my faithless Wanderer'. Ovid's 'erronem' (53; 'wandering one'), lies behind the image. The revision to the MS line was made after a marginal comment, 'remittite – minus recte' ('restore – less correct').

67–8. 'rectè – melius quam Scroop' ('correct – better than Scroop'), MS.

70. **Venus:** 'Erycina', one of Venus' epithets, in Ovid (57), from the temple of Venus on Mt Eryx in Sicily.

71. **Tenor:** 'general course or drift', but also 'a sound in musick' (*SJ*); Ovid (59) has 'tenorem' ('continued course'). Recalled in Pope's *Iliad*, VI.520: 'So shall my Days in one sad Tenor run' (Andromache to Hector).

74. **Parent's Ashes:** Ovid, 61–2: 'parentis... ossa' ('bones of a parent'). The Latin does not specify a father; Saltonstall assumes that father is meant, while Turberville and Sherburne indicate both parents.

75. **Brother.** Pope tried a number of versions of this passage, as MS variants witness, but in the end he, like Scrope, cut Ovid's 65–8, a section on the character and history of the brother (later named Charaxus) which shows that the brother is seeking to restore

Ignobly burn'd in a destructive Flame.
An Infant Daughter late my Griefs increast,
And all a Mother's Cares distract my Breast.
Alas, what more could Fate it self impose,
80   But Thee, the last and greatest of my Woes?
No more my Robes in waving Purple flow,
Nor on my Hand the sparkling Diamonds glow,
No more my Locks in Ringlets curl'd diffuse
The costly Sweetness of *Arabian* Dews,
85   Nor Braids of Gold the vary'd Tresses bind,
That fly disorder'd with the wanton Wind:

76^7. MS: Me too he hates, advis'd by me in vain,
      So fatal 'tis to be sincere and plain!
77–8. MS: An Infant now my hapless Fortune shares,
      And this sad Breast feels all a Mother's Cares.
79. **Alas, what more:** MS: What heavier ill
83. **in Ringlets curl'd:** MS: by Zephyrs fann'd
86. **with:** MS: to

---

an ill-gotten and lazily lost fortune through bad means at sea (Saltonstall and Sherburne both specify piracy, Turberville, p. 111, says more ambiguously that he 'plies the slyding seas with Ore'); he also hates Sappho for dutifully warning him of his danger. The omission has the odd effect of making Sappho's daughter look like the product of the brother's 'destructive Flame', whereas in Ovid (63) he is 'meretricis captus amore' ('captive of a prostitute's love'), versions of which are given by all the early translators. According to the Greek historian Herodotus (II.135), Charaxus ransomed a prostitute, Rhodopis, from Naucratis in Egypt, hence Sappho's accusations. The MS is marked at this point '2 priores versus Scroop pulcherrimi' ('two previous lines most beautiful [of] Scroop').
77–8. the rhyme was apparently acceptable, probably as an eye-rhyme; cf. Spenser, *Faerie Queene*, V.vi.39, Dryden, 'Sigismonda and Guiscardo', 57–8.
78–9. Pope's invention.
79–80. 'minus placent' ('[these] please less'); 'X likes 'em'; MS.

80. **last and greatest:** merely 'ultima' ('last'), in Ovid (71); recalled by Pope in *The First Epistle of the Second Book of Horace, Imitated*, 281: 'The last and greatest Art, the Art to blot' (referring to self-editing by writers). Cf. also 'Arrival of Ulysses in Ithaca', 187. At this point Pope omits Ovid 72, 'our [=my] boat is not driven by its own wind'; retained in Turberville and Sherburne, cut by Saltonstall.
81–6. Pope's description is more ornate and elaborate than Ovid's (73–6).
81. **waving Purple:** 'Purple' normally signifies royal array. Ovid's Sappho says only that she is dressed in 'veste ... vili' (a 'worthless garment'; cf 'My vesture is but vile', Turberville, p. 111ᵛ).
83 MS. **Zephyrs:** gentle west winds (cf. 244–5 and Commentary); cf. 'Winter', 49, and *Essay on Criticism*, 367.
84. **Arabian Dews:** distilled perfumes; cf. *Rape of the Lock*, I.134. Ovid, 76, has 'Arabum ... dona' ('gifts from Arabia').
86. **wanton:** See Commentary to 'Spring', 53–6, and 'Vertumnus and Pomona', 21. In Ovid (73), Sappho draws attention only

> For whom shou'd *Sapho* use such Arts as these?
> He's gone, whom only she desir'd to please!
> *Cupid*'s light Darts my tender Bosom move,
90 Still is there cause for *Sapho* still to love:
> So from my Birth the *Sisters* fix'd my Doom,
> And gave to *Venus* all my Life to come;
> Or while my Muse in melting Notes complains,
> My Heart relents, and answers to my Strains.
95 By Charms like thine which all my Soul have won,
> Who might not — ah! who wou'd not be undone?
> For those, *Aurora Cephalus* might scorn,
> And with fresh Blushes paint the conscious Morn.
> For those might *Cynthia* lengthen *Phaon*'s Sleep,

---

89. MS: My tender Heart the slightest Darts can move;
90. there: *1736b:* their
93–4. MS: Or taught to feel what first my Muse did feign,
    My [   ] Heart beats Measure to my Strain
94. *1717–51:* My beating [*1736a–51:* yielding] heart keeps measure to my strains.
95. thine: MS: these
96. MS: Alas! who might not, wou'd not be undone?

---

to her hair lying 'collo sparsi sine lege' ('on [my] neck, dispersed without order'). Scrope, 32, p. 3, expands this to 'Loose to the Winds I let my flowing Hair'. The MS comment is 'Pulchre – Scroop minus placent' ('Beautiful – Scrope's lines please less'). Another remark, '2 – Tres versus' ('2 – three verses'), probably refers to Scrope's triplet against Pope's couplet at this point.

87–8. TE suggests the influence of Scrope, 35–6, p. 3: 'For whom alas! should now my Art be shown? | The only Man I car'd to please is gone'; the sense is fairly close to Ovid, 77–8. 'Benè – melius quam Scroop' ('good – better than Scroop'), MS.

88. only: i.e. Phaon is the only one she desired to please, as in Scrope's version.

90. Still . . . still: closely imitating the 'turn' in Ovid (80), 'et semper causa est, cur ego semper amem' ('and still there is reason, why I still should love').

91. Sisters: the three Fates, who in classical mythology spin, assign the length of and cut the thread of life.
   Doom: destiny, fate.

93–4. The revision from MS was made in response to the comment 'Pulchrè – hi magis placent' ('beautiful – these please more').

93. complains: laments; cf. 131, 157, 178, and e.g. 'Summer', 19 and 'Autumn', 57

94. Strains: songs, verses.

97. Aurora Cephalus: For Cephalus, a Greek hunter, see Headnote to 'On a Fan of the Author's Design'; in a different version of his story, Aurora, Roman goddess of the dawn, abducts him to be her lover.

98. Pope's addition.
   conscious: OED sense 1, 'having guilty knowledge of', an obsolete or literary sense, probably modelled here on Dryden's usage, e.g. in the similar context of 'Amaryllis', 6–7, *Miscellany Poems* (1684), p. 235: 'Ah beauteous Nymph, can you forget your Love, | The conscious *Grottos*, and the shady Grove'.

99. Cynthia: alternative name for Artemis or Diana; cf. *Windsor-Forest*, 198. Both were associated with the moon. In Ovid (89) the name is Phoebe (so in Turberville, Saltonstall and Sherburne), loosely used as a female (lunar) version of the sun god, Phoebus Apollo.

100	And bid *Endymion* nightly tend his Sheep.
	Venus for those had rapt thee to the Skies,
	But *Mars* on thee might look with *Venus*' Eyes.
	O scarce a Youth, yet scarce a tender Boy!
	O useful Time for Lovers to employ!
105	Pride of thy Age, and Glory of thy Race,
	Come to these Arms, and melt in this Embrace!
	The Vows you never will return, receive;
	And take at least the Love thou wilt not give.
	See, while I write, my Words are lost in Tears;
110	The less my Sense, the more my Love appears.
	Sure 'twas not much to bid one kind Adieu,
	(At least to feign was never hard to you)
	Farewel my Lesbian *Love!* you might have said,
	Or coldly thus, *Farewel oh* Lesbian *Maid!*

100. **bid:** MS: let
107–8. MS: Thy Love I ask not to forsaken me
All that I ask is but to doat on thee.
108. **thou wilt:** *1717–51:* you will
109. MS: I write and weep; see Words are lost in Tears!
111. **bid:** MS: give
112. **you):** *1712b:* you.)
114. **Or thus, at least:** MS: *Farewell oh Lesbian Maid!*

---

100. **Endymion:** mortal shepherd beloved and abducted by the moon goddess Selene, and kept asleep by her in a cave on Mt Latmus. A surviving fragment (199) of the historical Sappho alludes to the story, which was also well known in English verse, e.g. in Michael Drayton's *Endimion and Phoebe* (1595), later rewritten as 'The Man in the Moone', and in John Lyly's play *Endimion, the Man in the Moon* (1591).

101. Pope (along with Sherburne) omits Venus' mode of transport (91), 'curro...eburno': 'Iuorie Wagon' (Turberville, p. 112), 'Ivory Chariot' (Saltonstall, p. 169).

102. **Mars:** Roman god of war, notoriously caught in an affair with Venus. The suggestion of Mars' possible homosexual attraction to Phaon is in Ovid and all the early translations.

106. **melt:** euphemism for orgasm; cf. 61, and Rochester, 'The Imperfect Enjoyment', 16. Pope's addition.

107–8. The final words probably do not indicate contemporary pronunciation but form a convenient antithesis; common in Dryden, e.g. 'Helen to Paris', 184–5, 'Cymon and Iphigenia', 491–2.

108–9. TE notes that these lines are again monosyllabic; cf. 57.

108. 'Scroop melius hic' ('Scroop better here'), MS; Scrope, 38, p. 3: 'Thy Love I ask not, do but suffer mine'.

109. Ovid (97–8) speaks of 'multa litura' ('many a blot'), formed by 'lacrimis... obortis' ('tears that spring'), obscuring the text of the letter.

110. **Sense:** meaning. The image of this line is Pope's idea. 'Bella paraphrasis' ('beautiful paraphrase'), MS.

112. Pope's addition, as the MS commentator recognised: 'The Parenthesis is an – interpolatio'.

113–14. The subtle adjustment of the second of these lines is Pope's addition.

115   No Tear did you, no parting Kiss receive,
       Nor knew I then how much I was to grieve.
       No Gift on thee thy *Sapho* cou'd confer,
       And Wrongs and Woes were all you left with her.
       No Charge I gave you, and no Charge cou'd give,
120   But this; *Be mindful of our Loves, and live.*
       Now by the Nine, those Pow'rs ador'd by me,
       And Love, the God that ever waits on thee,
       When first I heard (from whom I hardly knew)
       That you were fled, and all my Joys with you,
125   Like some sad Statue, speechless, pale, I stood;
       Grief chill'd my Breast, and stop'd my freezing Blood;
       No Sigh to rise, no Tear had pow'r to flow;
       Fix'd in a stupid Lethargy of Woe.
       But when its way th' impetuous Passion found,

---

115. **did you:** MS: didst thou
117. 1717–51: No lover's gift your *Sapho* could confer,
117–18. MS: No Pledge you left me, faithless and unkind!
             Nothing wth me, but Wrongs, was left behind.
119. **you:** MS: thee
121. **those:** MS: the
126. MS: A sudden Damp crept cold along my Blood;
129. MS: But when impetuous Grief its Passage found,

115–16. 'melius quam Scroop' ('better than Scroop'), MS. Scrope does not have an exact equivalent at this point.

117–18 MS. Described as 'jejunè fla[t] & ill Expres[t]' in the MS comments, hence Pope's experiments.

120. The 'love/live' wordplay is Pope's; Ovid's Sappho (106) merely wishes not to be forgotten. Marked 'Melius qu[am] Scroop', MS, but Scrope has no equivalent.

121. **the Nine:** the Muses, goddesses of poetry and arts.

125. **sad Statue:** TE notes this is not in Ovid (110–11, where Sappho merely says she was unable to cry or speak for some time) and cites Behn, 'A Paraphrase', 216, *Ovid's Epistles*, p. 110: 'sad Statue of Despair'. Pope's 'On the Statue of Cleopatra' was not published until 1717, but written about 1710.

126–8. Much expanded from Ovid, 112. Marked 'magis Poeticè ... quam Scroop' ('more poetical than Scroop'), MS. The commentator also reminds Pope of Ovid's Latin, 'adstrictum ... frigore' ('constricted by cold').

128. **stupid:** OED sense 1(a), now obsolete: 'Having one's faculties deadened or dulled; in a state of stupor, stupefied, stunned; esp. *hyperbolically*, stunned with surprise, grief, etc.'. Scrope, 45, p. 4, has: 'Speechless and stupid'.

Lethargy of Woe: perhaps recalled from the second line of Dryden's *Threnodia Augustalis* (1685), p. 1: 'Sure there's a Lethargy in mighty Woe'.

129–30. The rhyme is extremely common in Pope's time and was apparently acceptable, probably as an eye-rhyme rather than in actual pronunciation; cf. in similar context e.g. Dryden, 'Palamon and Arcite', I. 272–3, *Fables Ancient and Modern* (1700), p. 11: 'The fatal Dart a ready Passage found, | And

130   I rend my Tresses, and my Breasts I wound,
      I rave, then weep, I curse, and then complain,
      Now swell to Rage, now melt in Tears again.
      Not fiercer Pangs distract the mournful Dame,
      Whose first-born Infant feeds the Fun'ral Flame.
135   My scornful Brother with a Smile appears,
      Insults my Woes, and triumphs in my Tears,
      His hated Image ever haunts my Eyes,
      And *why this Grief? thy Daughter lives*; he cries.
      Stung with my Love, and furious with Despair,
140   All torn my Garments, and my Bosom bare,
      My Woes, thy Crimes, I to the World proclaim;
      Such inconsistent Things are Love and Shame!
      'Tis thou art all my Care, and my Delight,
      My daily Longing, and my Dream by Night:

---

130. **Breasts:** MS, *1717–51:* Breast
134. **first-born Infant:** MS: only Offspring
135. **Smile:** MS: Frown
136. **Woes:** MS: Rage
140. MS: My Robes all torn, my wounded Bosome bare,
143–4. MS: Thou art, at once, my Anguish and Delight,
         Care of my Day, and Phantom of my Night:

---

deep within his Heart infix'd the Wound' (describing Arcite's first sight of Emily). Cf. also 'The Episode of Sarpedon', 113–14 and 'On a Fan of the Author's Design', 7–8.

130–4. Cf. the parody of this sort of emotional display in 'Rape of the Locke', II.4–10 (*Rape of the Lock*, III.155–60).

131–2. Mostly Pope's addition. Marked 'melius quam Scroop' ('better than Scroop'), MS.

133–4. Ovid 115–16. 'Bella Paraphrasis' ('beautiful paraphrase'), MS.

134. **first-born Infant:** TE notes that Ovid (115–16) does not specify a first-born child, whereas Scrope, 50, p. 4, has 'her only Son'. Cf. the MS variant, in response to the comment 'Scroop fere melius' ('Scroop much better'). Turberville, p. 113, has 'her Babe his Corps'; Saltonstall, p. 169, 'the burial of a son'; Sherburne, p. 141, has 'her child'.

135. In Ovid (117) the brother is named Charaxus; so in Turberville and Sherburne, but not Saltonstall; cut in Scrope.

136. **Insults:** triumphs over; cf. 'Episode of Sarpedon', 115 and 316, and Commentary.

139–42. TE observes that Pope has reordered and expanded Ovid 121–2 in order create a pair of couplets ending on a pointed comparison; Ovid has 'pudor atque amor' ('shame and love'), but in the middle of a line. Lines 139 and 141 have no real basis in Ovid. Scrope, 51–3, p. 4, similarly ends his pointed triplet with 'So ill alas! do Love and Shame agree!', whereas the earlier translators all use the love/shame opposition but keep closer to Ovid's order. 'Pulchra Amplificatio – et recta' ('Lovely amplification – and correct'), MS.

143–54. This section was revisited for the account of Eloisa's erotic dreams in 'Eloisa to Abelard', 223–40, which includes a number of the same images, antitheses, and rhymes.

144. **daily Longing:** EC note the resemblance to Dryden's translation of *Heroides*, VII, 'Dido to Aeneas', 28, *Ovid's Epistles*, p. 217: 'Their daily longing, and their nightly

145   O Night more pleasing than the brightest Day,
      When Fancy gives what Absence takes away,
      And drest in all its visionary Charms,
      Restores my fair Deserter to my Arms!
      Then round your Neck in wanton Wreaths I twine,
150   Then you, methinks, as fondly circle mine:
      A thousand tender Words, I hear and speak;
      A thousand melting Kisses, give, and take:
      Then fiercer Joys — I blush to mention these,
      Yet while I blush, confess how much they please!
155   But when with Day the sweet Delusions fly,

---

149. **your:** MS: thy
   wanton Wreaths: MS: Am'rous Folds
150^1. MS: Thy Kisses, then, thy Words my Soul indear;
           Glow on my Lips, and murmur in my Ear:
152. **take::** MS: take!
153. **I blush:** MS: alas
154. MS: I blush, yet blushing, own how much they please!

---

dream'. Cf. also 'January and May', 15; *Essay on Criticism*, 126; and 'The First Book of Statius', 446. In Ovid (124), Sappho speaks of 'somnia formoso candidiora die' ('dreams brighter than the beautiful day').

146–8. Much expanded from Ovid's 125.

147. **visionary Charms:** in early works ('Verses to the Memory of an Unfortunate Lady', 4, and throughout the Homer translations), Pope tends to use 'visionary' sympathetically, of an imaginative insight which has emotional value or meaning. *SJ*'s neutral sense is 'Imaginary; not real; seen in a dream; perceived by the imagination only'; the more negative definition, 'Affected by phantoms; disposed to receive impressions on the imagination', applies more to Pope's usage in *The Dunciad Variorum* (e.g. his note to II.314), though *SJ* also quotes 'Eloisa to Abelard', 162, for this meaning. For the phrase cf. Oldmixon, 'King Richard II. to Queen Isabel', *Amores Britannici*, V.39 (1703), p. 101: 'I view with Joy, thy visionary charms'.

148. **fair Deserter:** the phrase is found (in a very different context, and of a woman) in an anonymous poem, 'The Confederacy', in *Poems on Affairs of State* (1703), II.249. Not in Ovid.

149. **wanton Wreaths:** not in Ovid. For the use of 'wanton' in relation to female sexuality see Commentary at 'Spring', 35 and 53–6.

150–1 MS. 'quaere si delend[a]' ('query whether these are to be deleted'), MS.

151–2. The rhyme was common and acceptable in Pope's time.

153. Ovid's Sappho does not exactly blush, but says (133): 'ulteriora pudet narrare' ('what things came next it shames [me] to tell'). Turberville, p. 113ᵛ, has 'I blush to tell the reast that followes'; Sherburne, p. 141, 'The rest I shame to speak'; Scrope, 61, p. 5: 'shame forbids to tell'. The MS comment is 'longè praestas Scroop – meo judicio' ('Scroop far pre-eminent [or possibly, 'excelling Scroop greatly'] – in my judgment'), MS.

And all things wake to Life and Joy, but I,
As if once more forsaken, I complain,
And close my Eyes, to dream of you again.
Then frantick rise, and like some Fury rove
160   Thro' lonely Plains, and thro' the silent Grove,
As if the silent Grove, and lonely Plains
That knew my Pleasures, cou'd relieve my Pains.
I view the *Grotto*, once the Scene of Love,
The Rocks around, the hanging Roofs above,
165   Which charm'd me more, with Native Moss o'ergrown,
Than *Phrygian* Marble or the *Parian* Stone.

---

157. MS: I dread the Light of cruel Heav'n to view,
158. **to dream of you again:** MS: again to dream of you
159. MS: Then like some raging *Bacchanal* I rove,
160. **silent:** MS: conscious
164. **Rocks around:** MS: Moss below
165. **Which:** *1717–51:* That
    MS: Where the rude Rock more charm'd my sight alone

157–9 **MS.** In response to MS comment '(Paraphrasis nimia et vereor, ne abire.)', '(Paraphrase excessive, and I fear that it deviates)'.

158. Not in Ovid. *TE* suggests the influence of Scrope's version, 64–5, p. 5: 'The dear deluding Vision to retain, | I lay me down, and try to sleep again', but behind that, and the moment in Alexander Radcliffe's *Ovid Travestie* (1681), p. 6, 'I turn to Sleep only to Dream again', lies Caliban's phrase in Shakespeare, *The Tempest*, III.ii.154–5: 'when I wak'd, | I cried to dream again'.

159. **Fury:** one of the Erinyes or implacable female avengers of Greek mythology; cf. 'The First Book of Statius his Thebais', Argument, 4. In Ovid, 'furialis Enyo' ('maddening Enyo'), 139, but there is a crux in the Ovidian manuscripts at this point and various editors proposed different solutions; hence Turberville, p. 114, and Sherburne, p. 141, have '*Erichtho*'. Pope generalises the identity.

159 **MS. Bacchanal:** the feasts of Bacchus (cf. 26) were associated with wild female behaviour. Scrope uses the phrase 'frantick Bacchanal' at this point, 67, p. 5. '– praestat: ni fallor' ('excellent: unless I am mistaken'), against the variant, MS.

161–2. The verbal repetition mimics Ovid's (137).

163. **Grotto:** 'A cavern or cave made for coolness. It is not used properly of a dark horrid cavern' (*SJ*); i.e. a grotto was constructed, like the one Pope began delving under his Twickenham house after 1719, not the natural feature, as signalled by 'Native Moss' (165) and the absence of building stone. Cf. however 'Arrival of Ulysses in Ithaca', 33. In Ovid (141) Sappho visits 'antra', caves. See also the 'conscious *Grottos*' mentioned by Dryden, Commentary, 98 above. 'Melius quam Scroop' ('better than Scroop'), MS; Scrope, 71, p. 5: 'And view the melancholy *Grotto* round'.

164. **hanging Roofs:** in Ovid (141) the caves are 'scabro pendentia tofo' ('hung with rough rock').

165. Pope's addition.

166. **Phrygian Marble:** Phrygia was a large area of what was known as Asia Minor, roughly western central Anatolia.

>   I find the Shades that did our Joys conceal,
>   Not Him, who made me love those Shades so well!
>   Here the prest Herbs with bending tops betray
> 170 Where oft entwin'd in am'rous Folds we lay;
>   I kiss that Earth which once was prest by you,
>   And all with Tears the with'ring Herbs bedew.
>   For thee the fading Trees appear to mourn,
>   And Birds defer their Songs till thy Return:

167–8. MS: I find the Grove, beneath whose gloomy Shade
    Our panting Limbs on springing Flow'rs were laid;
1717–51: I find the shades that veil'd our joys before,
    But, *Phaon* gone, those shades delight no more.
168. **well!**: *1712b:* well,
168^9. MS: But Thee I find not; Thee I seek alone!
    Not Flow'rs nor Shades delight, now thou art gone!
170. MS: Where to our Weight the willing Earth gave way;

Parian *Stone*: fine white marble from Paros, an island in the Cyclades. A large fragment of the so-called *marmor parium*, or Parian Marble, a *stele* inscribed with chronicles originally set up at Paros, had been in England since 1627 and what remains of it after damage is now in the Ashmolean Museum at Oxford. The stone is the source of the story of Sappho's own exile in Sicily. Ovid (142) has 'Mygdonii marmoris instar' ('an image of Mygdonian marble'); Mygdonia was an area of Thrace, later under the sway of Macedonia.

167–8. The repetition of 'Shades' mimics Ovid's repetition of 'silvam' ... 'silvaeque', 143–5.

167–8 MS. 'minus placent' ('these please less'), MS; a further deleted note on the MS reminds Pope that 'Flowr's' do not feature in Ovid and he should 'alter this 3rd line'.

168. Pope omits Ovid's 146, indicating that the ground was of low monetary value except for Phaon's presence as 'dos' ('gift' or 'dowry'). Turberville, p. 114: 'The place is but a filthie soyle, the place his dowre was hee'. Cut also by Saltonstall and Scrope.

169–72. The idea and some of the phrasing recalls Behn, 'A Paraphrase', 181–7, where Behn seems to be drawing on the imagery of this letter, XV.147–50, rather than the appropriate (V) epistle of *Heroides*.

169. **prest Herbs:** wild plants; literally from Ovid (147), 'pressas ... herbas', though Ovid appears to mean grass here (Sherburne, p. 142: 'grasse declining by our burthens prest').

170 MS. Altered in response to 'minùs placent ferè melius Scroop' ('these please less much better Scroop'), MS. Scrope, 74–5, p. 6: 'But when I spy the bank, whose grassy bed | Retains the print our weary bodies made'.

171–2. Pope has deleted his own MS comment, 'his 3rd line better than my 2^{d}', but it is not clear which lines he is referring to; Scrope, 76–7, p. 6, reads: 'On thy forsaken side I lay me down, | And with a shower of tears the place I drown'.

173. The mourning tree (appearing to weep by shedding its leaves) is a staple of Ovidian fiction. *TE* aligns Pope's image with Scrope's, 78–9, but it is fairly close to Ovid's 151 in sense.

174. An expansion of Ovid, 152: 'nullae dulce queruntur aves' ('no birds complain sweetly').

175　Night shades the Groves, and all in Silence lye,
　　　All, but the mournful *Philomel* and I,
　　　With mournful *Philomel* I join my Strain,
　　　Of *Tereus* she, of *Phaon* I complain.
　　　　A Spring there is, whose Silver Waters show
180　Clear as a Glass, the shining Sands below;
　　　A flow'ry *Lotos* spreads its Arms above,
　　　Shades all the Banks, and seems it self a Grove;
　　　Eternal Greens the mossie Margin grace,
　　　Watch'd by the Sylvan *Genius* of the Place.
185　Here as I lay, and swell'd with Tears the Flood,

---

176. Philomel: MS: Nightingale
177. MS: With her I wake, with her I joyn my Strain;
182. **Shades all the Banks:** MS: The Shaded Streams

---

175. A rendering of Ovid, 156, out of sequence.

176. mournful **Philomel:** There are many deleted efforts in the MS at this point. Ovid (154) refers more obliquely to the 'Daulian bird' ('Daulias ales') who sings of Itys; in most versions of the story this is Procne, mother of Itys, whom she killed as an act of revenge against her husband, Tereus, when he raped her sister Philomela. The sisters were turned into a swallow and a nightingale, with latterly Philomela being strongly identified with the nightingale and thus producing a song of female lamentation (Milton's 'most musicall, most melancholy' bird, 'Il Penseroso', 62, *Poems of Mr. John Milton* (1645), p. 39). The story is told in Ovid's *Metamorphoses*, VI.424–674, but without specifying which sister is turned into which bird. Pope has a long note based on Eustathius about the story and its problematic identifications in his translation of Homer, *Odyssey*, XIX.605. Of the early translators only Sherburne renders this passage of *Heroides* closely. *TE* hazards that Pope was misled by Scrope, 81, p. 6, who gives a similar image of 'mournful *Philomel*' and also constructs a general 'night' scene, whereas Ovid merely compares the silence with that of night. Cf. 'Spring', 26; 'Winter', 78; 'The Wife of Bath Her Prologue', 212.

177. Pope's addition.

179. In Ovid (157) the spring is 'sacer' ('sacred'); only Sherburne renders this.

180. The 'shining Sands' are Pope's addition, though Ovid (157) has 'nitidus' ('shining'), of the spring itself.

181. **Lotos:** so in Ovid (159). *TE* notes the phrase 'watry Lotos' in 'The Fable of Dryope', 21, and asserts that this is not the water-lily plant associated with forgetfulness (e.g. in Homer, *Odyssey*, IX.82–104) but a small North African tree or shrub.

183. Margin: verge.

184. Sylvan: woodland.

　Genius . . . Place: the classical concept of 'genius loci', the spirit that protects a place (cf. Pope's *Epistle to Burlington*, 57); stronger than in Ovid, who has (158) 'hunc multi numen habere putant' ('many think a spirit inhabits this [place]').

185. *TE* notes that the idea is Pope's addition, and a common conceit of verse of the time, though dismissed as extravagant by *EC*; cf. *Windsor-Forest*, 208, and the translation by John Cooper of 'Oenone to Paris', 45–6, in *Ovid's Epistles*, sixth edition (1701), p. 78: 'You wept, and on my Eyes you gazing stood, | Whose falling Tears increas'd the briny Flood'.

	Before my Sight a Watry Virgin stood,
	She stood and cry'd, 'O you that love in vain!
	Fly hence; and seek the far *Leucadian* Main;
	There stands a Rock from whose impending Steep
190	*Apollo*'s Fane surveys the rolling Deep;
	There injur'd Lovers, leaping from above,
	Their Flames extinguish, and forget to love.
	Deucalion once with hopeless Fury burn'd,
	In vain he lov'd, relentless *Pyrrha* scorn'd;
195	But when from hence he plung'd into the Main,
	Deucalion scorn'd, and *Pyrrha* lov'd in vain.
	Haste *Sapho*, haste, from high *Leucadia* throw
	Thy wretched Weight, nor dread the Deeps below!'

---

188. **far:** *1736a–51:* fair

---

186. **Watry Virgin:** in Ovid (162), specifically a Naiad or female water-spirit; so rendered by Saltonstall and Sherburne, while Turberville invents an avatar of Phaon to give the message. TE notes the phrase 'wat'ry Virgins' in Dryden's *Georgics*, I.43, *Works of Virgil* (1697), p. 50.

188. **Leucadian Main:** ocean waters round the island of Leucas in the Ionian Sea. In Ovid (164–6), Sappho is told to seek a region called Ambracia, on the west coast of Greece, an area of sea called Actium, and then Leucadia: Pope streamlines the detail, as do Saltonstall and Scrope.

189. **impending Steep:** overhanging cliff (roughly 600 m high).

190. **Fane:** temple. Ovid does not mention a temple as such, but has Phoebus (Apollo) himself overlook the ocean (165). Rendered literally in Turberville and Sherburne, and cut by Saltonstall. The site has remains of a temple.

191–2. TE notes that Addison had written humorously of this Lovers' Leap and of Sappho's own end, in the form of a mock bill of mortality, in *Spectator*, no. 233, 27 November 1711; a contemporary summary of the stories about the promontory and Sappho's appearance at it was in the English version of Pierre Bayle's *An Historical and Critical Dictionary*, 4 vols (1710), III.1921–2, in the article 'Leucas'. Pope's addition. On the MS there is a partially deleted comment about the possible deletion of tautology, overruled by 'X likes it' and 'stent' ('let them stand'), against these lines.

192. **forget:** cease; relinquish the compulsion.

193. **Deucalion:** equivalent to Noah in classical mythology, whose story is told in Ovid, *Metamorphoses*, I.313–415; son of Prometheus and builder of a chest which protects him and Pyrrha his wife (194) from Zeus' flood. Ovid (167–70) and all the early translators say only that Deucalion was cured of his unrequited passion, not that Pyrrha was inflicted with it.

194. In the MS a deleted comment against this or possibly the next line: 'non liquet' ('does not flow').

197. Pope here omits Ovid's 'hanc legem locus ille tenet' (171; 'that place maintains this law' or 'This place that vertue keepes', Sherburne, p. 142). Saltonstall and Scrope also cut it.

198. **wretched Weight:** a common image in literary suicide threats, e.g. Samuel Pick, 'A Madrigall', 9–10, *Festum Uoluptatis* (1639), p. 17: 'There will I headlong throw | This wretched weight this heape of miserie'.

She spoke, and vanish'd with the Voice — I rise,
200 And silent Tears fall trickling from my Eyes.
I go, ye Nymphs! those Rocks and Seas to prove;
How much I fear, but ah! how much I love?
I go, ye Nymphs! where furious Love inspires:
Let Female Fears submit to Female Fires!
205 To Rocks and Seas I fly from *Phaon*'s Hate,
And hope from Seas and Rocks a milder Fate.
Ye gentle Gales, beneath my Body blow,
And softly lay me on the Waves below!
And thou, kind *Love*, my sinking Limbs sustain,
210 Spread thy soft Wings, and waft me o'er the Main,
Nor let a Lover's Death the guiltless Flood profane!
On *Phoebus* Shrine my Harp I'll then bestow,
And this Inscription shall be plac'd below.
'Here She who sung, to Him that did inspire,
215 *Sapho* to *Phoebus* consecrates her Lyre,
What suits with *Sapho*, *Phoebus* suits with thee;
The Gift, the Giver, and the God agree.'

---

200. **And silent Tears fall:** MS: The big round Drops run
201. **Rocks and Seas:** MS: Seas and Rocks
202. **ah!:** MS: oh,
205. **Rocks and Seas:** MS: Seas and Rocks
206. **Seas and Rocks:** MS: Rocks and Seas
213. **plac'd:** MS: read

---

201. prove: try, attempt, experience.
201 MS. 'priori loco sint' ('let them be in the former place'), MS.
204–6. Pope's addition.
206. milder Fate: ironically recalled by Pope in *First Satire of the Second Book of Horace Imitated*, 83–4: 'From furious *Sappho* scarce a milder Fate, | P-x'd by her Love, or libell'd by her Hate'. By that time 'Sappho' normally represented Lady Mary Wortley Montagu in Pope's satires. The phrase is probably recalled here from a similar sequence in Waller, 'At Pens-hurst', 41–4, *Poems &c* (1645), p. 39: 'Ah cruell Nymph, from whom her humble swaine | Flyes for reliefe unto the raging maine! | And from the winds and tempests doth expect | A milder fate then from her cold neglect!'

207–8. According to Warton (1797) II.19, 'These two lines have been quoted as being the most smooth and mellifluous in our language'. Wakefield suggests a source in the final lines of Dryden, *Annus Mirabilis* (1666), p. 77: 'A constant Trade-wind will securely blow, | And gently lay us on the Spicy shore'. Cf. the refrain of 'Autumn', 17, 23 (etc.) and Commentary there.
211. Flood: sea. The line is an Alexandrine; cf. *Essay on Criticism*, 359 and Commentary.
212. Harp: Ovid (181) has 'chelyn', the tortoise-shell forming the soundbox of the lyre.
216. suits: The repetition in Ovid (184), is 'convenit illa mihi, convenit illa tibi' ('this one befits me, this one befits you').
217. Pope's addition: in Ovid the dedication is a couplet.

But why alas, relentless Youth! ah why
To distant Seas must tender *Sapho* fly?
220   Thy Charms than those may far more pow'rful be,
And *Phoebus* self is less a God to me.
Ah! canst thou doom me to the Rocks and Sea,
O far more faithless and more hard than they?
Ah! canst thou rather see this tender Breast
225   Dash'd on sharp Rocks, than to thy Bosom prest?
This Breast which once, in vain! you lik'd so well;
Where the *Loves* play'd, and where the *Muses* dwell. —
Alas! the *Muses* now no more inspire,
Untun'd my Lute, and silent is my Lyre,
230   My languid Numbers have forgot to flow,
And Fancy sinks beneath a Weight of Woe.
Ye *Lesbian* Virgins, and ye *Lesbian* Dames,
Themes of my Verse, and Objects of my Flames,
No more your Groves with my glad Songs shall ring,
235   No more these Hands shall touch the trembling String:

***218*. Youth:** MS: *Phaon*
219. MS: To those steep Cliffs, that Ocean, must I fly?
219^20. MS: If You return, thy *Sapho* too shall stay,
　　　　Not all the Gods shall force me then away:
220–1. MS: Nor *Love*, nor *Phoebus* then invok'd shall be,
　　　　For You alone are all the Gods to me.
***225*. sharp:** *1717–1736a:* those; *1736b–51:* these
***226*. in vain:** MS: ah once
***235*. No more these Hands:** MS: These hands no more

218-20 MS. One of the most worked-over sections of the MS, with annotation about what Pope has left out here from Ovid (187-8), what he should restore, and many deleted lines and ideas.

223. *TE* compares Scrope, 93, p. 7: 'one more hard than rocks, more deaf than seas'. Ovid (189) has 'scopulis undaque ferocior omni' ('more fierce than cliffs and every wave').

224-5. *TE* compares Scrope, 90-1, p. 6: 'Thou couldst not see this naked breast of mine | Dasht against Rocks, rather than joyn'd to thine'.

227. Loves: Cupids.

230-1. Pope's expansion of more literal lines in Ovid, 197-8.

230. languid: One of the meanings of the Latin 'languidus' is 'with gentle current', perhaps suggesting 'flow'.

Numbers: cf. 5 and Commentary.

231. Weight of Woe: a common phrase in elegy, e.g. those by Pope's friends William Walsh, *A Funeral Elegy Upon the Death of the Queen* (1695), p. 9; Congreve, *The Tears of Amaryllis for Amyntas*, 43 (1703), p. 5; 'The Lamentations of Hecuba . . .', 5-6, *Examen Poeticum* (1693), p. 216: 'The Mules, beneath the mangled Body go, | As bearing (now) unusual weight of Woe'.

233. Flames: desires.

234-5. Mostly Pope's addition.

Since *Phaon* fled, I all those Joys resign,
Wretch that I am, I'd almost call'd him mine!
Return fair Youth, return, and bring along
Joy to my Soul, and Vigour to my Song:
240 Absent from thee, the Poet's Flame expires,
But ah! how fiercely burn the Lover's Fires?
Gods! can no Pray'rs, no Sighs, no Numbers move
One savage Heart, or teach it how to love?
The Winds my Pray'rs, my Sighs, my Numbers bear,
245 The flying Winds have lost them all in Air!
Oh when alas! shall more auspicious Gales
To these fond Eyes restore thy welcome Sails?
If you return — ah why these long Delays?
Poor *Sapho* dies while careless *Phaon* stays.

236–7. MS: *Phaon* (*My Phaon* I almost had said!)
 Is fled, with *Phaon* your Delights are fled.
 1717–51: My *Phaon*'s fled, and I those arts resign,
  (Wretch that I am, to call that *Phaon* mine!)
243. or: MS: and
245. Air!: MS: Air;
246–7. MS: And shall at last more kind auspicious Gales
 Waft to these Eyes thy long expected Sails!

236–7 variants. The MS shows further that Pope was reminded, not very accurately, of the Latin text of Ovid, 203, at this point.

240–1. Mostly Pope's addition, perhaps in part recalling Rochester's lyric, 'Absent from thee, I languish still'. Ovid (203–6) says nothing about the 'Lover's Fires' but does say that Phaon has both bestowed 'ingenio vires' ('strength to my genius'), and removed it. 'Exclam: Paraphr:-Pulchra' ('exclamation: paraphrase:-beautiful'), MS.

240. Poet's Flame: perhaps recalling (and removing the irony from) Tate, *Panacea: A Poem upon Tea*, II (1700), p. 22: ''Tis Tea sustains, *Tea* only can inspire | The Poet's Flame, that feeds the Hero's Fire'.

244–5. An expansion of Ovid's much simpler image (208), of the Zephyrs bearing off Sappho's frail words. Cf. Scrope, 96, p. 7: 'The flying Winds bear thy Complaints away'. Pope parodies this classical trope in 'The Rape of the Locke', I.63–4.

246. auspicious Gales: a common phrase in epic discourse, e.g. Dryden, *Aeneid*, III.607, *Works of Virgil*, p. 285; cf. also 'Arrival of Ulysses in Ithaca', 156. Less common in this amorous context, but cf. Richard Duke's version of 'Paris to Helena' in *Ovid's Epistles*, p. 120, where Venus 'with a kind and an auspicious gale | Drove the good Ship, and stretch't out ev'ry Sail'.

246–7 MS. 'Pleonasm', MS comment, with 'kinder & more auspicious, too much', deleted, by way of explanation.

249. Pope's addition. Pope omits here Ovid's 210, in which Sapho says 'hoc te, si saperes, lente, decebat opus' ('this business would befit you, slow one, if you were wise'). On the MS Pope is further reminded of omissions from Ovid's 211, about making votive gifts for the stern of the ship.

250 O launch thy Bark, nor fear the watry Plain,
   Venus for thee shall smooth her native Main.
   O launch thy Bark, secure of prosp'rous Gales,
   For thee shall *Cupid* spread the swelling Sails.
   If you will fly — (yet ah! what Cause can be,
255 Too cruel Youth, that you shou'd fly from me?)
   If not from *Phaon* I must hope for Ease,
   Ah let me seek it from the raging Seas:
   From thee to those, unpity'd, I'll remove,
   And either cease to live, or cease to love!

---

251. **Venus for thee shall:** MS: For thee shall *Venus*
253. 1717–51: Cupid for thee shall spread the swelling sails.
253^4. MS: The God shall sit upon the painted Prore,
   And steer thy Ship to this deserted Shore.
256. MS: From you more cruel if I find no ease.
257. **Ah:** *1712b:* And
258. MS: Forsaken *Sapho* shall to these remove,
  1717–1736a, 1741–51: To raging seas unpity'd I'll remove,
259. MS: And cease to live at least, if not to love!

250-3. The pair of couplets mimics repetition in Ovid, but Ovid begins and ends one pair of lines (213–14) with 'solve ratem' ('launch the boat').

250. fear . . . Plain. Not in Ovid (213).

251. native Main: the ocean from which Venus was born, according to one version of her myth. Cf. 'Arrival of Ulysses in Ithaca', 2.

253 MS. *Prore:* prow of a ship, from Latin 'prora': 'a poetical word, used for a rhyme' (*SJ*).

255-9. The MS shows much reworking of phrases at this point, apparently Pope's own unprompted revisions.

256. In Ovid (219) Phaon is requested to let Sapho know her fate by letter, an invitation retained by Turberville and Sherburne (but not Saltonstall or Scrope) and taken up by later poets (see Headnote).

258-9. Pope's addition; once again (cf. 119) the 'live/love' wordplay is Pope's. The 'cease . . . cease' repetition itself recurs in 'The Fable of Dryope', 100, as *TE* notes.

7

MESSIAH

(1712)

Editors' Headnote

Composition and publication

'Messiah' was first published on 14 May 1712. At the very end of his life, in April 1744, Pope estimated that the verse of his *Pastorals* was more 'laboured' than anything else; Spence noted: 'The last (the *Messiah*) his own favourite of them all' (*OAC*, I.175, no. 400). On the same occasion Pope observed, 'Though Virgil in his pastorals has sometimes six or eight lines together that are epic, I have been so scrupulous as scarce ever to admit above two together, even in the *Messiah*' (*OAC*, I.176, no. 401). There is no other substantial evidence that the 'Messiah' was produced over a long period of thoughtful care in the way the *Pastorals* were (see Headnote); even the relatively detailed statement of method outlined in the 'Advertisement' to the poem in the 1717 *Works* contains very little of substance about timing and process, acting rather as a gloss on how it ought to be read. The poem seems to have been composed very shortly before its anonymous publication in the *Spectator*, no. 378, on 14 May 1712. On 23 May, John Caryll wrote to Pope asking him about his planned imitation of Virgil's fourth *Eclogue* (addressed to Gaius Asinius Pollio and commonly known as 'Pollio'; see 'Models' below): 'I hope your health permitted you to execute your design of giving us an imitation of *Pollio*' (*Corr.*, I.142), and on 28 May Pope replied, saying that

> the eclogue on the Messiah in imitation of Pollio, I had transcribed a week since with design to send it to you; but finding it printed in the *Spectator* of the fourteenth (which paper I know is constantly sent down to you) I gave it to Mr Englefield.
>
> (*Corr.*, I.144; Anthony Englefield was a neighbour of Pope's at Binfield)

The first printing introduced the poem with the following note:

> I Will make no Apology for entertaining the Reader with the following Poem, which is written by a great Genius, a Friend of mine, in the Country; who is not ashamed to employ his Wit in the Praise of his Maker.

The 14 May *Spectator* was signed 'T', signalling Steele's responsibility this particular issue, and, on 1 June, Steele, having compared the poem with its sources, wrote to Pope praising it lavishly ('Your Poem is already better than the *Pollio*'), citing lines 29 and 75 as particular beauties, and offering advice for its revision at line 46:

> you have preserv'd the sublime heavenly spirit throughout the whole, especially at – *Hark a glad voice* – and – *The lamb with wolves shall graze* – There is but one line which I think below the original,
>
> > He wipes the tears for ever from our eyes.
>
> You have express'd it with a good and pious, but not with so exalted and poetical a spirit as the prophet ... If you agree with me in this, alter it by way of paraphrase or otherwise ...
>
> (*Corr.*, I. 146).

Pope acted on Steele's suggestion, and when the poem was reprinted in later collections of the *Spectator* the line (46) becomes 'From ev'ry Face he wipes off ev'ry Tear' – a reading retained, along with other revisions, in the text of *Works* (1717) and subsequent editions (see the textual apparatus at 45–8). In the *Spectator* of 12 November (no. 534), Mr Spectator answered the purported enquiry of a reader – Abraham Dapperwit – as to the authorship of 'Messiah' with the statement that 'that excellent Piece is Mr. *Pope's*.'

Text

The text presented here is taken from the first edition of 1712. The correction of one obvious misprint at line 6 has been noted in the textual apparatus. In the *Works* of 1717 Pope expanded what were originally marginal cues to passages in Isaiah into footnotes more specifically cued to particular words or phrases. In 1717 he first added the quotations from Isaiah and Virgil's fourth Eclogue, together with the prose 'Advertisement', setting out a view of his method of composition. On these paratextual aspects see McLaverty (2001: 75–81). The various extant texts of 'Messiah' are referred to in the apparatus as follows:

1712: The Spectator, No. 378 (Griffith 5)

1713: The Spectator, vol. 5 (ESTC T097943)

1717: Works, quarto (Griffith 79)

1720: Windsor-Forest, fourth edition, octavo (Griffith 125)

1727: Miscellany Poems, vol.I, duodecimo (Griffith 192)

1732: Miscellany Poems, vol.I, duodecimo (Griffith 273)

1736: Works, vol.I, octavo (Griffith 413, 414)

1751: Works, vol.I, octavo (Griffith 643)

Models and sources

For Pope's general relationship to the 'bucolica' or *Eclogues* of Virgil, see Headnote to *Pastorals*. In his 'Discourse on Pastoral Poetry', Pope had found matter to object to in the English pastorals of Spenser because he 'treats of matters of religion in a pastoral style'; similarly, Virgil was not always limited in his language to the 'simplicity' of true pastoral. By the time of the mock essay on Pastoral in *Guardian*, no. 40, 27 April 1713 (*PW*, I.97–106), Pope had decided that Virgil's *Eclogues* could be presented as in some sense outside the pastoral tradition for similar reasons, and that his own efforts were 'by no means *Pastorals*, but *something Better*'. 'Messiah' represents a clear attempt in itself to produce 'something Better', a Christian super-eclogue, based on Virgil's 'prophetic' fourth eclogue spliced with, and eventually eclipsed by, the prophecy of Messiah's coming in the book of Isaiah.

Virgil's 63-line fourth *Eclogue* was addressed to Gaius Asinius Pollio (76 BC–AD 4), a commander who played a leading role in the wars after the assassination of Julius Caesar, and a cultivated and literary man, who eventually retired from politics to pursue a literary career. He was thought to have been instrumental in helping Virgil to reclaim his farm in Cisalpine Gaul, and was also a friend of Catullus and Horace; he was consul in 40 BC, the supposed date of the *Eclogue*. Virgil's poem self-consciously transcends the limits of the form in prophetic celebration of a returning golden age of peace and justice, heralded by an as yet unborn redemptive child, variously interpretable as Pollio's own son, an heir to the recently married Octavian (later the emperor Augustus), or to Mark Anthony, also recently married (to Octavian's sister). The poem is not specific, no doubt for political reasons: the peace celebrated by Virgil erupted in new hostilities shortly afterwards, a power struggle which perhaps underlies Pope's own sense of the national situation in 1712. The mention of Sybilline (Cumean) prophecies in line 4 of Virgil's poem, and the magical 'virgo' in line 6 (Astraea, goddess of justice, to Virgil, but suggesting to certain readers the 'Virgin' mother of Christ, hence line 8 of Pope's poem) gave rise to the early tradition that Virgil had in some mystical way apprehended the coming birth of Christ in the 'nova progenies' ('new offspring') of line 7.

The 'Pollio' Eclogue had long had a special status in English versions, for this reason. Abraham Fleming, in *The Bucoliks of Publius Virgilius Maro* (1589), p. 10, introduces the poem as written to celebrate the son of Pollio:

> Wherein this is to bee marked, that such things as the prophetesse *Sybilla* of *Cuma* foretold of the coming and birth of Christ (as *Lactantius, Euseb[i]us, & Augustine* doo testifie) the poet vtterly ignorant of that diuinitie, applieth to the happinesse of *Augustus* his gouernment, and also to the child *Salonine*.

'W. L.', in his *Virgils Eclogues Translated into English* (1628), notes the early gloss on the Sybilline tradition in Virgil of Ludovicus Vives (p. 60), and in his own glosses asserts boldy that the 'descent of the Sonne of God from heaven amongst us, could not by a Christian man bee expressed more exactly, or in more absolute termes' (p. 69). He adapts his translation to reflect Christian notions of sin and redemption, and in rendering a line of Virgil as 'Deer Childe of God (p. 63) glosses it 'Nothing can bee more plainly spoken of Christ' (p. 75). His glosses on the latter half of the poem find full-scale allegorical equivalents in Virgil's prophecy for 'the course of Christs Church' (pp. 70–71). Works such as Alexander Ross's *Virgilius Evangelisans* (1634), telling religious history in Virgilian phrasing, emphasised this alignment, and in John Ogilby's *The Works of Publius Virgilius Maro translated* (1649), p. 14, the Eclogue is prefaced:

> Here *Sibill* is appli'de to *Pollio's* son,
> Her Prophesies his *Gnethliacon,*
> But *Christs* birth he by happie error sings.
> The Prince of Poets crowns the King of Kings.

There were dissentient voices, such as David Blondel, who in *A Treatise of the Sibyls* (1661), chapters 13 and 14, disputes the 'divine' content of 'Pollio' by reference to its historical circumstances. In his version, published first in the separate section of *Virgil's Eclogues. Translated by Several Hands*, in *Miscellany Poems* (1684), and afterwards in the *Works of Virgil* (1697), Dryden circumspectly remarks that '*Many of the verses are translated from one of the Sibyls, who prophesie of our Saviour's Birth*' (*Works of Virgil*, p. 17). But *Grotius, his Arguments for the Truth of the Christian Religion rendered into plain English Verse* (1686), pp. 161–8, defended the 'inspired' reading and the Earl of Lauderdale's 1709 translation of the eclogue imported touches such as Myrrh and Frankincense to emphasise the Christian link (*The Works of Virgil, translated into English Verse*, pp. 12–14). Charles Leslie explicitly linked Virgil's prophetic inspiration with the book of Isaiah, Pope's other source, including some of the same material, in *A Short and Easie Method with the Deists*, fifth edition (1711), pp. 32–6 and in his *The Truth of Christianity Demonstrated* (1711), pp. 79–82. Leslie had perhaps read another poetic model: in the same year as Dryden's full Virgil translation, a Norfolk clergyman, Daniel Baker (1654–1723), in his *Poems on Several Occasions* (1697), pp. 115–131, included 'Virgilius Evangelizans. A Poem upon Christmas Day', a long Ode expanded from 'Pollio', the text of which preceded the English version. The poem, like Pope's, Christianises the Virgilian prophecy, but in Baker's case there is a heavy emphasis on the redemption of Sin. Baker's 'Preface' sets out an orthodox position:

> The Fourth Eclogue of *Virgil,* taken by him out of *Sibylla's* Oracles, containeth a famous Prediction, concerning the Birth of our blessed Saviour (which was then at hand) and the Benefits of his Incarnation, together with the State of his Church, until the Restitution of all things. Which the Poet not understanding, nor imagining that a Person so extraordinary could arise any where but among the *Romans,* applies to *Saloninus* the Son of *Pollio,* then newly born; or as I rather think, to some young Infant of the Imperial Family: for he would hardly ascribe so great a Kingdom, and such mighty Acts to a private Person, for fear of displeasing *Augustus,* on whose Line all Power and Greatness was by the Flattery of Courtiers entailed for ever. I have here endeavoured to rectifie *Virgil's* Mistake, and restore this excellent Poem to its right owner: there

being several things in it, which cannot, with any shew of Truth, he applied to any Person, but the Son of God. And herein I have taken the Liberty (which the Poet, I suppose did with the Prophetess) to leave out some things, to add others, and by a Paraphrase to make the Sense more plain and easie. Yet the Reader will find very little in the Translation, that is not hinted in the Original, which will appear, if any Man will take the Pains to confer them together.

Tho' *Virgil* was not so happy as to understand his own Verses, yet in After times the reading of them did incline several Persons to the Christian Faith, and the Primitive Fathers made use of them, to convince the Pagans, that a *Messias,* a King from Heaven, a Restorer of all things was promised by God, and about that time expected by Men. Thus God left not himself without Witness, even amongst the *Gentiles,* tho' through their Pride and Ignorance they misapplied the Intimations given them from Heaven.

Baker also added ten marginal notes indicating extra sources and resemblances from the Bible, four New Testament and six Old Testament, including, in the third stanza, three from Isaiah; two of his passages are also cited by Pope (11.6 at line 75 and 2.4 at line 55) and the other (7.15) is adjacent to the passage cited by Pope at line 8. There is no particular evidence that Pope knew this model directly, but it is a sign of the context in which Pope was working.

More broadly, the versification of scripture, especially the Psalms, had become a well-established genre through the seventeenth century; Pope knew such things well enough to parody them in the ribald 'Roman Catholick Version of the First Psalm' (1716). Chapters of Isaiah were versified as holy exercises by, among others, John Norris, 'The 63 Chap. of Isaiah Paraphrased to the 6 Verse', in *A Collection of Miscellanies* (1692), pp. 51–3; Benjamin Keach, 'The Song of the Prophet *Isaiah.* chap. 5', in *Spiritual Songs* (1700), pp. 4–5; and Robert Gould, 'The True FAST: A Paraphrase on the 58th of Isaiah', in his *Works* (1709), pp. 408–12. Pope's future enemy Sir Richard Blackmore included four versions from Isaiah in his *A Paraphrase upon the Book of Job* (1700), based on chapters 14, 34, 40 and 52–3; 40 was one of the chapters mined by Pope (see his notes to 29 and 47). Several paraphrases of this type, including one from Isaiah 14, were published in *Miscellaneous Poems and Translations,* alongside Pope's poems 8–14 below. Brought up in a pious Catholic household, Pope adhered to a form of ecumenical Christianity throughout his life and is thought to have been experimenting with versions of Thomas à Kempis and Psalm 111 at about this time, though these were not published until much later. Alongside the obvious and already-dominant example of Milton, Pope was certainly acquainted with scripture-based poetry of Joshua Sylvester and George Sandys, whose verse paraphrases of Old Testament sources such as the Psalms and the Book of Job were much reprinted into the 1670s (see further Mack 1985: 211–12).

In addition, a religious and prophetic language of a redeemed 'golden age' or worldly state of peace and justice presided over by a benign, godlike monarch was also the common currency of political poetry from the Restoration of 1660 onwards through the War of Spanish Succession, usually in connection with a change of monarchy or birth of a future prince; Dryden's *Britannia Rediviva,* on the birth of an heir to James II in

1688, was an obvious case in point for Pope. Pope owned a volume described by Mack (1982: 434–7, item 136) as *Poems Relating to State Affairs* (1705; sometimes found as *A New Collection of Poems Relating to State Affairs*) in which he noted on p. 496 against the title of an anonymous poem, 'The Golden Age Restor'd. A Poem in Imitation of the Fourth Pastoral of *Virgil*, Suppos'd to have been taken from a *Sybilline* prophecy' that it was 'By W. Walsh, Esq', i.e. his friend and mentor William Walsh (see Headnote to *Pastorals*). Immediately after this parody of a High-Tory position came Dryden's 1697 version of the same eclogue (pp. 499–501) as if enlisted in the same kind of reading. After a small gap came two other poems, 'The Golden Age Revers'd' (pp. 505–8), a response to Walsh's poem, and 'The Golden Age, from the fourth Eclog of Virgil, &c' (pp. 508–12), the heavily pro-Stuart prophecy of Anne's reign against which Walsh's poem had itself been aimed. This quartet had already appeared in much the same arrangement in *Poems on Affairs of State, from the Reign of K. James the First, to this Present Year 1703*, 'Vol. II', pp. 422–45 (for publication history see Ellis 1970: 449–65, 487–505 and 517–29, and for additional detail see Hone 2015a 120–2). Isaiah itself could be easily co-opted for political verse of opposite alignments, as in *A Paraphrase on the Fourteenth Chapter of Isaiah, only appropriating what is there meant of the King of Babylon to Oliver the Protector* (1710) and *A Paraphrase on Part of the Fourteenth Chapter of Isaiah* (1712), a poem celebrating Marlborough's victory at Ramillies. Given the context of, and opportunity for, political innuendo, Pope's version appears relatively innocent and ecumenical, therefore, except perhaps as an unexceptionable step towards the prophetic mode of *Windsor-Forest* (on this aspect see Weinbrot 1993: 283–5). As Brower (1959) noted, certain aspects of the poem's imagery (e.g. 25–6, 34–6, 99–106) present the kind of inherited 'sublime' imagery Pope would later burlesque in the parody-apocalypse of *The Dunciad*.

Context

Pope had probably been introduced to Richard Steele by John Caryll senior around 1711, and was at this period still on good terms with him, though not at this stage close to his Whig co-adjutor Addison. More than a dozen letters between Steele and Pope survive, all from the period 1711–12 (see further Headnote to *Ode for Musick*). Addison had praised Pope's *Essay on Criticism* in *The Spectator* of 20 Dec 1711 (see Headnote to that poem). Ault suggests that Pope was already contributing to *The Spectator* from 16 Nov 1711 (*PW*, I.20); the first acknowledged contribution was no. 406, 16 June 1712 (*PW*, I.42). 'On a Fan of the Author's Design', no. 15 below, was in the issue of 4 November 1712, and a letter on the last words (in verse) of the Emperor Hadrian, apparently finding religious seriousness in the 'heathen' utterance, appeared in no. 532, 10 November 1712 (*PW*, I.72–3). Pope later published four poems in Steele's *Poetical Miscellanies* of December 1713 (nos. 19–22 below).

In the letter of 23 May 1712 already cited (*Corr.*, I.142), Caryll tells Pope, of this poem, 'I am satisfy'd 'twill be doubly *Divine* and I shall long to see it. I ever thought churchmusick the most ravishing of all harmonious compositions, and must also believe sacred subjects, well handled, the most inspiring of all Poetry'. After the problems amongst his Catholic fraternity caused inadvertently by some mildly satirical aspects of the *Essay on Criticism*, 'Messiah' returned Pope to a form of ecumenical orthodoxy which could please both Catholic friends and Whig protestants such as Steele, whose journalism included much mainstream piety in the wake of his own *The Christian Hero* (1701). As *TE* noted, and as the Commentary here mostly confirms, Pope's citations from Isaiah in the revised annotations cite the text of the 'authorised' or 'King James Bible' first published in 1611, as might be expected in a protestant context; but the actual phrasing of his own verses often appears to suggest a greater acquaintance with the Catholic translation known as the Douay-Rheims version, after the New Testament printed at Rheims in 1582 (and Antwerp in 1600) and the Old Testament, printed at Douay, 1609–10 (and Rouen in 1635). The act of placing 'Messiah' after the *Pastorals* in his *Works* of 1717 emphasises its sublime transcendence of 'classical' pastoral and also its redemptive, regenerative quality, following the death of everything in 'Winter'; 'Messiah' is the Christian pastoral of rebirth (see further Battestin 1969).

The poem was regarded in its day as at worst inoffensive, except for the suggestion made in the wake of *The Dunciad* that Pope had not written it (Guerinot 1969: 118–19) and some hair-splitting objections to the imagery of line 39 (see Commentary). It was rendered into Latin by Samuel Johnson as a college exercise in 1728 (Lonsdale, IV.288n), and again by C. Billinge in 1785; a Greek version by John Plumptre appeared in 1796. Isaac Watts, whose own *Horae Lyricae* (1706) offered many examples of Christian verse paraphrase, admired 'Messiah' and thought Pope should have done more work of this type (*Reliquiae Juveniles*, 1734, p. 73), a view echoed by Henry Brooke in a private letter to Pope of 1739 (*Corr.*, IV.198–200). Warburton's 'Remarks', appended to Pope's own notes (retitled 'Imitations' in Warburton's edition) gave the poem a further religious imprimatur. Warton, writing in 1756, found that the poem clearly surpassed Virgil's 'Pollio', but also began the tradition (most conspicuously highlighted by Wordsworth in the 'Appendix to the Preface' to the *Lyrical Ballads*) of criticising Pope's version for its poetic diction and occasional florid distractions from the 'dignity, energy and simplicity of the original' holy writ (1756: 11–14). Johnson, who had endorsed this view in his review of Warton's *Essay* in 1756, merely commented in his *Pope* (1781) 'That the *Messiah* exceeds the *Pollio* is no great praise, if it be considered from what original the improvements are derived' (Lonsdale, IV.67 and see 324n).

MESSIAH.

*A sacred Eclogue, compos'd of several
Passages of* Isaiah *the Prophet.*

Written in Imitation of Virgil's POLLIO.

    YE Nymphs of *Solyma*! begin the Song:
    To heav'nly Themes sublimer Strains belong.
The Mossie Fountains and the Sylvan Shades,
The Dreams of *Pindus* and th' *Aonian* Maids,
5   Delight no more — O Thou my Voice inspire

1717–20, 1736–51:
ADVERTISEMENT.

IN reading several passages of the Prophet *Isaiah*, which foretell the coming of Christ and the felicities attending it, I could not but observe a remarkable parity between many of the thoughts, and those in the *Pollio* of *Virgil*. This will not seem surprising when we reflect, that the Eclogue was taken from a *Sybilline* prophecy on the same subject. One may judge that *Virgil* did not copy it line by line, but selected such Ideas as best agreed with the nature of pastoral poetry, and disposed them in that manner which serv'd most to beautify his piece. I have endeavour'd the same in this imitation of him, tho' without admitting any thing of my own; since it was written with this particular view, that the reader by comparing the several thoughts might see how far the images and descriptions of the Prophet are superior to those of the Poet. But as I fear I have prejudiced them by my management, I shall subjoin the passages of *Isaiah*, and those of *Virgil*, under the same disadvantage of a literal translation.

Motto. *1713: Aggredere, O Magnos, aderit jam tempus, honoret.* Virg.
Title. *1717–51:* MESSIAH. | A | Sacred Eclogue, | *In imitation of* VIRGIL'S POLLIO.

Title note. *Wit:* intelligence, creative power (see *Essay on Criticism*, Headnote).
Epigraph. For the 'Sybilline' tradition of Virgil's fourth *Eclogue*, known as 'Pollio', see Headnote.
1–5. The 'ordinary' muse of Pope's *Pastorals* is displaced by a higher poetic authority. Wakefield compares the opening of Dryden's translation of Virgil, *Eclogues*, IV.1–2, *Works of Virgil* (1697), p. 17: 'Sicilian Muse begin a loftier strain! | Though lowly Shrubs, and Trees that shade the Plain, | Delight not all . . .'.
1. Solyma: The name is derived from the Greek version of Jerusalem (cf. 85); very commonly used in religious contexts by George Sandys, e.g. throughout his *Paraphrase vpon the Divine Poems* (1638) and his version of Grotius's *Christ's Passion* (1640), where in Act III (p. 39) Jesus addresses the 'Daughters of Solyma' (a chorus of Jewish women). The 'Nymphs' here appear to represent some kind of biblical as opposed to classical muse (the 'musae' of Virgil, 1).
2. sublimer: For the theory and contemporary meaning of 'the sublime' see Headnote to *Essay on Criticism*.
    Strains: songs. Matthew Scrivener discusses the interaction between collective

Who touch'd *Isaiah*'s hallow'd Lips with Fire!
Rapt into future Times, the Bard begun;
A *Virgin* shall conceive, a *Virgin* bear a Son!

8, n. *1717–20, 1736–51:* A *Virgin shall conceive — All crimes shall cease,* &c.
 VIRG. E. 4. V. 6. Jam redit & Virgo, redeunt Saturnia regna,
     Jam nova progenies coelo demittitur alto —
     Te duce, si qua manent sceleris vestigia nostri,
     Irrita perpetuâ solvent formidine terras —
     Pacatumque reget patriis virtutibus orbem.

6. hallow'd: *1712:* hollow'd

---

singing and the 'sublimer strains' of individual worship in *The Method and Means to a True Spiritual Life* (1688), p. 358; cf. also *To the Memory of Devereux Knightly* (1708), 2: 'And with sublimer Strains inform my Breast'.

3. TE compares 'Summer', 72; see Commentary there.

 Mossie Fountains: recalled here from Dryden's version of Virgil, *Eclogues*, VII.67, *Works of Virgil*, p. 33, translating 'muscosi fontes' from Virgil's line 45; but the same phrase is in Bidle's version (1634, p. 14) and W. L.'s version (1628, p. 127). Pope's rejection of the motif included a good deal of Virgilian tradition.

 Sylvan Shades: Dryden uses this phrase in the translation of the *Aeneid* (e.g. VII.566, *Works of Virgil*, p. 417); Lauderdale uses it in his 1709 translation of 'Pollio', 3 (see Headnote). Pope might also have remembered it from books VI and XV of Sandys's *Ovid's Metamorphosis Englished* (1632), pp. 211 and 497; it too stands for a wide spectrum of non-Christian themes.

4. Pindus: one of several mountains in Greece (Thessaly) sacred to the Muses (the '*Aonian* Maids'); Aonia or Boeotia was the site of Mount Helicon, another seat of the Muses, who were sometimes referred to as 'Aonides'. This line is quoted (without acknowledgment) in William Duff, *An Essay on Original*

Genius (1767), p. 184, as a reference to the imaginative world of classical Greece.

5. TE (p. 104) takes the long dash to emphasise the change in register from pastoral to religious sublime.

6. Isaiah: the Old Testament prophet whose book underlies the imagery of the poem. The Douay version (*DV*) of Isaiah 6:6–7, reads: 'And one of the Seraphims flewe to me, & in his hand an hote cole . . . And he touched my mouth . . . '. Wakefield compares Milton, 'On the Morning of Christ's Nativity', final line, *Poems of Mr. John Milton* (1645), p. 2: 'From out his secret Altar toucht with hallow'd fire'. Isaac Watts writes of the 'hallow'd lips' of a persuasive preacher in 'On the Reverend Mr. T. Gouge', *Horae Lyricae* (1706), p. 261. The 'hollow'd' of the first reading is most likely a simple mistake, subsequently corrected, though it could refer to the open mouth of the prophet.

7. Rapt: carried forward in spiritual imagination.
 the Bard: Virgil.
 begun: commonly used for 'began' in Pope's period.

8 Pope's note. TE notes that the constellation 'Virgo' was derived from Astraea or Justice, who had left the world at the end of the Golden Age (as mentioned in Ovid, *Metamorphoses*, I.149–50, and Virgil, *Georgics*, II.473–4. In Virgil's eclogue, the 'virgin' thus returns from exile rather than being predicted to emerge

From *Jesse*'s Root behold a Branch arise,
10   Whose sacred Flow'r with Fragrance fills the Skies.
Th' Aethereal Spirit o'er its Leaves shall move,
And on its Top descends the Mystic Dove.
Ye Heav'ns! from high the dewy Nectar pour,

9.] Cap 11. v. 1.
13.] Cap. 45. v. 8.

8, n. (cont.)
   Now the Virgin returns, now the kingdom of Saturn returns, now a new Progeny is sent down from high heaven. By means of thee, whatever reliques of our crimes remain, shall be wip'd away, and free the world from perpetual fears. He shall govern the earth in peace, with the virtues of his Father.
   ISAIAH, Ch. 7. V. 14. *Behold a Virgin shall conceive, and bear a Son* — Ch. 9. V. 6, 7. *Unto us a Child is born, unto us a Son is given; The Prince of Peace: of the increase of his government, and of his Peace, there shall be no end: Upon the Throne of David, and upon his Kingdom, to order and to stablish it, with judgment, and with justice, for ever and ever.*

---

directly from humanity. *Virgils Eclogues* (1620) has a note, p. 40, on the identification of the 'virgo' with Mary. Pope's quotation from Isaiah in his note is almost entirely from the Authorised Version (*AV*).

9 Pope's note. *TE* adds that Pope's imagery appears to derive from *DV* rather than the *AV*: 'And a rod shal come forth of the roote of Iesse, and a flowre shal rise vp out of his roote'; *AV* has 'branch', however (where *DV* has 'flowre'). 'Jesse's *Root*' is the line of David from which Jesus's family was derived; the imagery to line 16 presents Christ as the mystical flower and fruit of that family 'tree'. In Virgil, and all translations, the divine son is sent down from heaven, in a line glossed explicitly as unconsciously Christian by 'W. L.' in 1628; see Headnote.

10. sacred Flow'r: Saffron is twice described as a 'sacred Flow'r' in Nahum Tate's version of book IV of Cowley's *Of Plants*, in *The Third Part of the Works of Mr Abraham Cowley* (1689), pp. 101–2; Pope recalled the phrase in his *Iliad*, XI.770.

11. Aetherial Spirit: a phrase normally found in alchemical and medical writing, e.g. T. Byfield, *Horae Subsecivae* (1695), pp. 2, 11, 23, transplanted to a religious context (see next note).

12. Mystic Dove: the Holy Spirit, which descends from heaven in the shape of a dove. *TE* notes that the general idea recalls Isaiah 11:2, but the specific image is closer to Matthew 3:16 (*DV*): 'And Iesvs being baptized ... he saw the Spirit of God descending as a doue, & coming vpon him'.

13 Pope's note. Neither *AV* ('Drop down, ye heavens, from above, and let the skies pour down righteousness') nor *DV* ('Droppe dew ye heauens from aboue, and let the cloudes rayne the iust') mentions 'Nectar' (for which see 'The Episode of Sarpedon', 31) but as *TE* notes, *DV* suggests Pope's 'dewy'. Warburton, the first of Pope's clergyman editors, took 'dewy Nectar' to refer to the grace of God (in 1751), an interpretation regarded as 'to the last degree forced, and fanciful, and far-fetched' by Warton, also a clergyman (*Works of Pope*, I.96). Dryden's version of the 'Pollio' eclogue predicts that oaks will secrete 'show'rs of Honey', 35 (translating 'roscida mella', 'dewy honeys'). The phrase is not uncommon, e.g. *Anacreon Done Into English* (1683), p. 35: 'When every verdant *Rose Tree* still | Of *dewie-Nectar* drinks it's fill'. See Commentary to 14.

And in soft Silence shed the kindly Show'r!
15 The Sick and Weak the healing Plant shall aid;
From Storms a Shelter, and from Heat a Shade.
All Crimes shall cease, and ancient Fraud shall fail;
Returning Justice lift aloft her Scale;

15.] Cap. 25. v. 4.
18.] Cap. 9. v. 7.

---

14. *soft Silence:* cf. Pope's 'On Silence'. The phrase is common in religious verse, e.g. Milton, 'Upon the Circumcision', 5, *Poems* (1645), p. 25: 'Through the soft silence of the list'ning night'.

kindly Show'r: Wakefield compares Dryden, *Don Sebastian*, V (1690), p. 130: 'But shed from nature, like a kindly shower'; and the 'laeto . . . imbri' or 'pleasing shower' in which Jupiter descends in Virgil, *Eclogues*, VII.60 ('kindly Rain' in Dryden's version, 83, *Works of Virgil*, p. 33). The phrase already had religious connotations, as in Matthew Poole, *Annotations on the Holy Bible*, vol. 2 (1685), note to Philippians 1:9, where knowledge of God's grace 'is not onely an empty cloud in the Air, but becomes effectual by falling down in a kindly showre upon the Heart warmed with the love of God'.

15-16 Pope's note. *TE* suggests that here Pope is closer to *AV*: 'For thou hast been a strength to the poor, a strength to the needy in his distress, a refuge from the storm, a shadow from the heat'; *DV* has 'Because thou art become a strength to the poore, a strength to the needie in his tribulation: an hope against the whirlwinde, a shadow against the heate'.

15. *healing Plant:* Congreve twice laments the lack of a suitable 'healing Plant' in *The Tears of Amaryllis for Amyntas*, 69-71 (1703), p. 4; here the healing agent is Christ.

17. *ancient Fraud:* perhaps Original Sin, inflected by Milton's frequent use of 'fraud' in relation to Satan in *Paradise Lost*, as Warburton suggests (e.g. IX.55, 89, 285, 287). Cf. also *Paradise Regain'd*, IV.3. It is prompted by Virgil's 'sceleris vestigia', quoted and translated by Pope in his note to 8 above as 'reliques of our crimes', and *Eclogues*, IV.31: 'priscae vestigia fraudis', translated by Dryden, as Wakefield notes, as (37) 'of old Fraud some footsteps', a phrase then all but absorbed into 'The Golden Age, from the fourth Eclog of Virgil, &c', a Stuart version of the prophecy in *A Collection of Poems relating to State Affairs* (1705), p. 510 (see Headnote). Several earlier versions of the eclogue have closer instances, e.g. Bidle, *Virgil's Bucolicks Engl[l]ished* (1634), sig. B2[r]: 'few Seeds of Ancient Fraud'; W. L., *Virgils Eclogues translated into English* (1628), p. 62: 'some small track, | Of ancient fraud', and Ogilby, *Works of Publius Virgilius Maro* (1649), p. 15: 'some steps of ancient fraud'. Baker has 'Footsteps of Orig'nal Sin', 'Virgilius Evangelizans', *Poems on Several Occasions* (1697), p. 125; Samuel Wesley, *The Life of our Blessed Lord & Saviour Jesus Christ* (1693), p. 243 has 'Yet still some Signs of antient *Fraud* remain', keyed in Wesley's notes to this line of Virgil's eclogue. In the political version of 'Pollio' identified as Walsh's by Pope (see Headnote), the 'ancient Crimes' are supposedly those of the Duke of Marlborough, disguised by dashes.

18. *Justice . . . Scale:* *TE* suggests that *DV* is Pope's source: 'he shal sit vpon the throne of Dauid . . . that he may confirme it, and strengthen it in iudgement and iustice'. But *AV* also has the key elements of 'judgment and . . . justice'. Cf. also the quotations in Commentary to 8.

Pope parodies the classical idea of the Scales of Justice in 'The Rape of the Locke', II.126, and *The Dunciad Variorum*, I.50.

Peace o'er the World her Olive-Wand extend,
20 And white-roab'd Innocence from Heav'n descend.
Swift fly the Years, and rise th' expected Morn!
Oh spring to Light, Auspicious Babe, be born!
See Nature hastes her earliest Wreaths to bring,

23, n. *1717–20, 1736–51: See Nature hastes*, &c.
   VIRG. E. 4. V. 18 At tibi prima, puer, nullo munuscula cultu,
                      Errantes hedaeras passim cum baccare tellus,
                      Mixtaque ridenti colocasia fundet acantho —
                      Ipsa tibi blandos fundent cunabula flores.

   For thee, O Child, shall the earth, without being tilled, produce [*1736–51: her*] *early offerings; winding Ivy,* [*1736–51: mixed*] *with* Baccar, *and* Colocasia *mixed* [*1736–51: mixed omitted*] *with smiling* Acanthus. *Thy Cradle shall pour forth pleasing flowers about thee.*

   ISAIAH, Ch. 35. V. 1. *The wilderness and the solitary place shall be glad, and the desert shall rejoice and blossom as the rose.* Ch. 60.V.13. *The glory of* Lebanon *shall come unto thee, the firr-tree, the pine-tree, and the box together, to beautify the place of thy Sanctuary.*

---

19. Olive-Wand: cf. *Windsor-Forest*, 427–8, and Commentary.

21. Wakefield cites Virgil, *Eclogues*, IV.46–7: '"Talia saecla" suis dixerunt "currite" fusis | concordes stabili fatorum numine Parcae', '"Run on, ages of such a kind", said the Fates to their spindles, concurring as to the fixed will of the Fates'. Pope's image, if it refers to this at all, is a drastically Christianised version.

22. Auspicious Babe: 'Auspicious' is 'having omens of success; prosperous; fortunate; propitious' (*SJ*). Dryden uses the adjective twice in his version of Pollio, 13 ('auspicious Face') and 73 ('auspicious Boy'), in neither case translating anything directly from Virgil. 'Auspicious' was applied in 1688 to the new heir to James II in Dryden's *Britannia Rediviva*, 17, and the birth of the heir prompted much golden-age prophecy: 'From thee, auspicious babe, when Time shall show | His pleasing youthful face, and England grow | As free from Guilt, as far from Fear as thou'; John Spencer, 'Sereniss. Principis Walliae', in *State-Amusements, Serious and Hypocritical, Fully Exemplified in the Abdication of King James the Second* (1711), p. 68. The actual phrase was also used by Charles Gildon in arguing that the spirit of poetry 'must be born, and grow up with the *auspicious Babe*', 'An Apology for Poetry', in Gildon, *Miscellaneous Letters and Essays* (1694), p. 14.

be born: Wakefield suggests a 'palpable imitation' of Callimachus, 'Hymn to Delos', 214: γείνεο, γείνεο κοῦρε ('Be born, be born young man...'), but 'where our poet fell upon it, I cannot discover'. There were apparently no versions of the 'Hymn to Delos' before Pope's poem; a version of the 'Hymn to Jupiter', was available in Matthew Prior's *Poems on Several Occasions* (1709). Pope certainly knew of Callimachus as the author of a poem on Berenice, preserved in a translation by Catullus, and referenced in 'The Rape of the Locke', II.174. Around the time he was recalling 'Messiah', Pope told Spence he once had 'a design of giving a taste of all the most celebrated Greek poets by translating one of their best short pieces...a hymn of Homer, another of Callimachus,...and so on' (*OAC*, I.82, no. 192, 5–7 April 1744).

23. Wreaths: normally associated with poetic achievement by Pope, e.g. 'Summer', 10, 57; here a signal of coronation by nature. Cf. Commentary to 'Sapho to Phaon', 25–6.

With all the Incense of the breathing Spring:
25   See lofty *Lebanon* his Head advance,
     See nodding Forests on the Mountains dance,
     See spicy Clouds from lowly *Saron* rise,
     And *Carmel*'s flow'ry Top perfumes the Skies!
     Hark! a glad Voice the lonely Desert chears:

25.] Cap. 35. v. 2.
29.] Cap. 40. v. 3. 4.

29, n. *1717–20, 1736–51: Hark! A glad Voice,* &c.
   VIR. E. 4. V. 46. Aggredere ô magnos, aderit jam tempus, honores,
           Cara deum soboles, magnum Jovis incrementum —
           Ipsi laetitia voces ad sydera jactant

---

24. Incense: often used of a flower's perfume (e.g. 'Winter', 48) as well as in religious observance (e.g. 'The First Book of Statius his Thebais', 371).

   breathing: cf. 'Spring', 32. For the idea as a whole *TE* cites Milton, *Paradise Lost*, IX.193–5 (1674), p. 220: 'the humid Flours, that breathd | Thir morning incense, when all things that breathe | From th' Earth's great Altar send up silent praise'.

25–8. *TE* suggests that Pope is closer here to the *DV* text of the verse he cites as his source: 'Springing it shal spring, & shal reioyce ioyful and praising: the glorie of Libanus is geuen to it, the beautie of Carmel, & Saron, they shal see the glorie of the Lord'. *AV* has: 'It shall blossom abundantly, and rejoice even with joy and singing: the glory of Lebanon shall be given unto it, the excellency of Carmel and Sharon, they shall see the glory of the LORD'. *TE* cites also Isaiah 2:11–13, where cedars are among other 'lofty' things laid low by God's power.

25. lofty Lebanon: i.e. *Cedrus Libani*, cedar of Lebanon. Pope might have known the phrase from Sandys, *A Paraphrase vpon the Song of Solomon*, Canto V (1641), p. 21: 'His Looks, like Cedars planted on | The Brows of loftie Lebanon'; and cf. 'Run like a youthful Hart upon | The tops of lofty *Lebanon*', last line of canto II of the same poem as revised in Tate's *Poems by Several Hands, and on Several Occasions* (1685), p. 303.

26. nodding: waving, but perhaps here suggesting the godlike 'nod' of assent, here from the natural world. Wakefield cites Dryden's version of Virgil, *Eclogues*, VI.44–5, *Works of Virgil*, p. 27: 'And Sylvan Fauns, and Savage Beasts advanc'd', | And nodding Forests to the Numbers danc'd'. The line was held to be 'an improper and burlesque image' by Warton (*Works of Pope*, I.99). But the image is not very far from Psalm 29:6: 'the LORD breaketh the cedars of Lebanon. He maketh them also to skip like a calf' (*AV*), and the mountains themselves 'dance' in some metrical versions of the psalms, e.g. William Barton, *The Book of Psalms in Metre* (1644), Psalm 114. Cf. also 'Summer', 81–4.

27. spicy Clouds: cf. the description of a sacrifice in Charles Hopkins, *Neglected Virtue*, II. ii. (1696), p. 13: 'Let smoaking Altars Loads of Incense waste, | Forrests of perfumed Trees be rooted up; | Whence hallow'd Herds in spicy Clouds, shall mount'.

   lowly Saron: Sharon (*AV*) or Saron (*DV*) is the northern region of modern Israel's coastal plain.

28. Carmel: mountain region in the north of modern Israel; the 'flow'ry Top' signals vegetation. Cf. Francis Bragge, *The Passion of our Saviour* (1694), p. 3: 'When on the Flow'ry top of *Olivet* . . . '.

29–32. Pope's revised note to 29 actually quotes from Virgil, *Eclogues*, IV.48–9 and V.62–4; McLaverty (2001: 79) suggests that

30   Prepare the Way! a God, a God appears.
       A God, a God! the vocal Hills reply,
       The Rocks proclaim th' approaching Deity.
       Lo Earth receives him from the bending Skies!
       Sink down ye Mountains, and ye Vallies rise:
35   With Heads declin'd, ye Cedars, Homage pay;
       Be smooth ye Rocks, ye rapid Floods give way!

29, n. (cont.)
Intonsi montes, ipsae jam carmina rupes,
Ipsa sonant arbusta, Deus, deus ille Menalca! E. 5. v. 62

Oh come and receive the mighty honours: The time draws nigh, O beloved offspring of the Gods, O great encrease of Jove! *The uncultivated mountains send shouts of joy to the stars, the very rocks sing in verse, the very shrubs cry out, A God, a God!*

ISAIAH, Ch. 40. V. 3, 4. *The voice of him that crieth in the wilderness, Prepare ye the way of the Lord! make strait in the desert a high way for our God! Every valley shall be exalted, and every mountain and hill shall be made low, and the crooked shall be made strait, and the rough places plain.* Ch. 4. v. 23. *Break forth into singing, ye mountains! O forest, and every tree therein! for the Lord hath redeemed* Israel.

---

the lines from the fifth *Eclogue* presented themselves as nearer to Isaiah's image. Blackmore provided versions of Isaiah 40 in his *Paraphrase on the Book of Job* (1700). Steele signalled his particular approval of Pope's preservation of 'the sublime heavenly spirit' of his original here; to Pope, 1 June 1712, *Corr.*, I.146, and see Headnote. *AV* (which Pope quotes from) begins the relevant passage of Isaiah in a manner slightly closer to Pope's scenario than *DV*: 'The voice of one crying in the desert'.

31. vocal Hills: TE cites Milton, *Paradise Lost*, V.203–4 (1674), p. 123: 'Hill, or Valley, Fountain, or fresh shade | Made vocal by my Song', i.e., in echo.

32. Rocks proclaim: cf. Thomas Adams, *The Happines of the Church* (1619), p. 70: 'the *Disciples* hold their peace, the stones speake: they forsake Christ, the *rockes* proclaime him'.

33. bending Skies: Wakefield cites Virgil, *Eclogues*, IV.50: 'aspice convexo nutantem pondere mundum' ('behold, the world nodding with weighty dome'). In his version of Psalm 144, Sandys has the phrase 'Great God, stoope from the bending Skies'; *A Paraphrase vpon the Divine Poems* (1638), p. 166.

35. declin'd: bowed down. The line as a whole is compared by Wakefield with Milton, *Paradise Lost*, V.193–4 (1674), p. 122: 'wave your tops, ye Pines, | With every Plant, in sign of Worship wave'.

36. smooth . . . Rocks: Wakefield suggests the influence of Henry Cromwell's translation of Ovid, *Amores*, II.16: 'Then, as you pass, let Mountains Homage pay, | And bow their Tow'ring Heads to smooth your way'; this appeared in *Miscellaneous Poems and Translations* (see 'The First Book of Statius his Thebais', Headnote), which appeared after 'Messiah' was published, but it is possible Pope saw it in advance (or that Cromwell was influenced by Pope).

rapid Floods: normally themselves overpowering, as in Thomas Heyrick, 'The Submarine Voyage', IV.20, *Miscellany Poems* (1691), p. 63, of the Trojan river Scamander: 'Whose rapid Floods whole Armies bore away'.

The SAVIOR comes! by ancient Bards foretold;
Hear him ye Deaf, and all ye Blind behold!
He from thick Films shall purge the visual Ray,
40   And on the sightless Eye-ball pour the Day.
'Tis he th' obstructed Paths of Sound shall clear,
And bid new Musick charm th' unfolding Ear.
The Dumb shall sing, the Lame his Crutch foregoe,
And leap exulting like the bounding Roe.

38.] Cap. 42. v. 18.
39.] Cap. 35. v. 5. 6.

---

37. ancient Bards: cf. [Walsh], 'The Golden Age Restor'd', 5, *A New Collection of Poems Relating to State Affairs* (1705), p. 496: 'The time is come, by Ancient Bards foretold, | Restoring the *Saturnian* Age of Gold'. Walsh's lines are parodic.

38 Pope's note. *DV*, 42:18 reads: 'Heare ye deafe, and ye blind behold to see', whereas *AV* reads 'Hear, ye deaf; and look, ye blind, that ye may see'.

39 Pope's note. The sources apply up to 44. *DV*, 35:5–6 reads: 'Then shal the eies of the blind be opened, and the eares of the deafe shal be open. Then shal the lame leape as an hart, and the tongue of the dumme shal be opened'; *AV* has 'Then the eyes of the blind shall be opened, and the eares of the deaf shall be unstopped. The shall the lame man leap as an hart, and the tongue of the dumb sing'.

39. thick Films . . . visual Ray: *EC* compares Milton, *Paradise Lost*, III.619–21 (1674), p. 79: 'the Aire, | No where so cleer, sharp'nd his visual ray | To objects distant farr'; and *Samson Agonistes*, 163–4 (1671), p. 17, 'inward light alas | Puts forth no visual beam'. There is a collocation of similar phrasing at *Paradise Lost*, XI.411–15, where Michael purges Adam's sight in order to reveal the future. Pope recalled his own phrase in *Odyssey*, VIII.59: 'With clouds of darkness quench'd his visual ray' (of Demodicus, the blind poet). As *EC* notes, the image was challenged by Concanen in *A Supplement to the Profund* (1728), p. 23; Pope noted 'Milton' in his copy (Mack 1982: 403). The sense is: 'he shall purify the visual ray from the thick films which obscure it'. The phrase 'thick Films' was often used in scientific tracts, e.g. Nicholas Culpeper, *The English Physitian* (1652), p. 195, recommending a cure for 'cloudy mists, or thick Films which grow over' the eyes of the blind; and also in the story of the conversion of St Paul (the blind Saul, in Acts 9:18), e.g. Jeremy Taylor, *Antiquitates Christianae* (1675), p. 49: 'thick films like scales fell from his eyes, and his sight returned'. 'Visual Ray' was also a technical term in aesthetics and natural philosophy; cf. Joseph Moxon, *Practical Perspective* (1670), pp. 10, 11, 15, 43, etc.

42. unfolding: opening, receptive (because healed).

44. *TE* compares further The Song of Solomon 2:8–9: 'The voice of my beloued! behold! hee commeth leaping vpon the mountaines, skipping vpon the hils. My beloued is like a Roe, or a yong Hart' (*AV*). The phrase 'bounding Roe' is found in John Hanbury's 'The Mosaic Story of the Creation', *Poetical Miscellanies: The Fifth Part* (1704), p. 501.

45 Before him Death, the grisly Tyrant, flies;
    He wipes the Tears for ever from our Eyes.
    As the good Shepherd tends his fleecy Care,
    Seeks freshest Pastures, and the purest Air,
    Explores the lost, the wand'ring Sheep directs,
50 By Day o'ersees them, and by Night protects;

45.] Cap. 25. v. 8.
47.] Cap. 40. v. 11.

45–7. *1713–51: No Sigh, no Murmur the wide World shall hear,*
From ev'ry Face he wipes off ev'ry Tear.
In Adamantine Chains shall Death be bound,
And Hell's grim Tyrant feel th' eternal Wound.

50. Pastures: *1717–51:* pasture

---

45. grisly Tyrant: Milton's personification of Death in *Paradise Lost*, II.704 (1674), p. 48, is called 'the grieslie terrour'. Death as a tyrant is common from the Elizabethan period onwards, but as specifically a 'grisly Tyrant' features in Joseph Browne, *Albion's Naval Glories, or Britannia's Triumphs* (1705), p. 12. Cf. the variant at 48.

46. EC compares Milton, 'Lycidas', 181, *Poems*, p. 64: 'And wipe the tears for ever from his eyes'. For Steele's objections to this passage, see Headnote, and Pope's variants. The revision follows *AV*, 25:8: 'He will swallow vp death in victorie, and the Lord God wil wipe away teares from off al faces'. *DV* has here 'He shal cast death downe headlong for euer: and ... take away teare from al face'. Pope recalled the phrasing in 'Epilogue to the Satires: Dialogue I', 102: 'All Tears are wip'd for ever from all Eyes'

47. Pope's source reads (in *AV*): 'He shall feed his flock like a shepherd: he shall gather the lambs with his arm, and carry them in his bosom, and shall gently lead those that are with young' and in *DV*: 'As a shepheard shal he feede his flocke: in his arme shal he gather together the lambes, and in his bosome shal he lift them vp, and them with yong himself shal carie'. Blackmore included a version of this chapter in *A Paraphrase on the Book of Job* (1700).

47. fleecy Care: his flock, as in 'Spring', 20; recalled in *Iliad*, XIII.622. The phrase is found in e.g. *Rapin of Gardens ... English'd by Mr. Gardiner* (1706), p. 71: 'Beneath her Covert may the Shepherds share, | A cool Refreshment with their fleecy Care'.

47 variant. Adamantine Chains: Wakefield cites Milton, *Paradise Lost*, I.48 (1674), p. 4: 'In Adamantine Chains and penal Fire' (of the punishment of the fallen angels). Cf. *Ode for Musick*, 52 variant.

48 variant. Wakefield cites Lucretius, *De Rerum Natura*, II.638: 'aeternumque daret matri sub pectore volnus' ('he would give an eternal wound under the chest of the mother').

Hell's grim Tyrant: Milton's Sin refers to '*Grim Death*' in *Paradise Lost*, II.804 (1674), p. 51, and Wakefield points to Cowley's depiction of death as '*Hells* black *Tyrant*', *Davideis*, I.17, *Poems ... Written by A. Cowley* (1656), p. 4.

49. Explores: searches for; *OED* sense 3a, 'to search for; to find by searching'.

  The tender Lambs he raises in his Arms,
  Feeds from his Hand, and in his Bosom warms:
  Mankind shall thus his Guardian Care ingage,
  The promis'd Father of the future Age.
55 No more shall Nation against Nation rise,
  Nor ardent Warriors meet with hateful Eyes,
  Nor Fields with gleaming Steel be cover'd o'er;
  The Brazen Trumpets kindle Rage no more:
  But useless Lances into Scythes shall bend,
60 And the broad Faulchion in a Plow-share end.

54.] Cap. 9. v. 6.
55.] Cap. 2. v. 4.

---

55. Mankind shall thus: *1717–51:* Thus shall mankind
58. Nor: *1727–32:* Or
59. Nor: *1727–32:* Or

---

52. Bosom: Wakefield asserts that the original suggests 'the capacious flow of the eastern garments', rather than a part of the body; both versions of Isaiah use the word, however (above, 47–52).

53. ingage: secure, have as guaranteed.

54 Pope's note. *TE* suggests that *DV* is closer: 'and his name shal be called Meruellous, Counseler, God, Strong, Father of the world to come, the Prince of peace'. *AV* has 'his name shall be called Wonderful, Counsellor, The mighty God, The everlasting Father, The Prince of Peace'. Warton (*Works of Pope*, I.101) approves of the orthodoxy of Pope's choice of words here.

55–70. This passage in particular anticipates the millennial language of *Windsor-Forest*, 353 ff.; cf. Rogers (2004: 208 and 2005a: 71–2). At the point when the poem was published, the War of Spanish Succession was still being waged.

55 Pope's note. The same passage of Isaiah is cited in Baker, 'Virgilius Evangelizans', *Poems on Several Occasions*, p. 122. See 59 below.

56. ardent: 'hot, burning, fiery' (*SJ*); Pope recalled the phrase in his *Iliad*, VIII.708.

 hateful Eyes: literally, eyes full of hatred; the usage is probably modelled on similar instances in Dryden, *Aeneid*, IX.806, or 'Palamon and Arcite', I.214, and III.656.

58. Brazen Trumpets: Wakefield cites Dryden's *Aeneid*, VI.245 (165 in the original), *Works of Virgil*, p. 369: 'With breathing Brass to kindle fierce Alarms'. Pope's exact phrase (which is not uncommon) occurs also in Dryden, 'The Cock and the Fox', 750, in the context of a fox-hunt, but also in Dryden's version of Virgil, *Georgics*, II.789–90, *Works of Virgil*, p. 95, in reference to an age of peace 'E're hollow Drums were beat, before the Breath | Of brazen Trumpets rung the Peals of Death'. Rogers (2005a: 72) suggests this line presages *Windsor-Forest*, 371.

59. Scythes: *TE* points out that *DV* (for Pope's cited source, Isaiah 2:4) has 'they shal turne . . . their spears into siethes', rather than the 'they shall beat their . . . spears into pruninghooks' of *AV*.

60. Faulchion: 'a short crooked sword' (*SJ*), much used by Pope in the *Iliad* translation. *TE* notes that here Pope is closer to *AV*, 'they shal beat their swords into plow-shares', whereas *DV* has 'they shal turne their swords into culters'. Lauderdale's version of Virgil, *Georgics*, I, has a reverse image: 'The bending Sythes to killing *Fauchion*'s turn'; *Annual Miscellany: For the Year 1694*, p. 253.

        Then Palaces shall rise; the joyful Son
        Shall finish what his short-liv'd Sire begun;
        Their Vines a Shadow to their Race shall yield;
        And the same Hand that sow'd, shall reap the Field.
65   The Swain in barren Desarts with surprize

61.] Cap. 65. v. 21, 22.
65.] Cap. 35. v. 7.

65, n. *1717–1720, 1736–51: The Swain in barren deserts, &c.*
  VIRG. E. 4. V. 28. Molli paulatim flavescet campus arista,
                    Incultisque rubens pendebit sentibus uva.
                    Et durae quercus sundabunt roscida mella.

The field [1736–51: fields] shall grow yellow with ripen'd ears, and the red grape shall hang upon the wild brambles, and the hard Oaks shall distill honey like dew.
  ISAIAH, Ch. 35. V. 7 *The parched ground shall become a pool, and the thirsty land springs of water: In the habitations where dragons lay, shall be grass, and reeds and rushes. Ch. 55. V. 13. Instead of the thorn shall come up the firr-tree, and instead of the briar shall come up [1736: the firr-tree . . . come up* omitted] *the myrtle-tree.*

61–4. McLaverty (2001: 80) suggests a biographical background to this image of a restored patrimony, from the perspective of a Catholic dispossessed after 1688.

61 Pope's note. *AV* reads: 'And they shall build houses, and inhabit them; and they shall plant vineyards, and eat the fruit of them. [22]. They shall not build, and another inhabit; they shall not plant, and another eat'; *DV* uses similar phrasing.

62. short-liv'd Sire: a father who had not been able to live a natural term of life. For the line as a whole Wakefield compares Dryden, *Britannia Rediviva*, 40 (1688), p. 2: 'And finish what thy Godlike Sire begins'. Hone (2015a: 121) sees Pope's line as a reference to James II's brief reign as monarch.

64. Wakefield compares Callimachus, *Hymns*, VI.137 (to Demeter): φέρβε καὶ εἰράναν, ἵν' ὅς ἄροσε τῆνος ἀμάσῃ ('And nurture peace, that he who sows may also reap'); Dryden's version of Virgil, *Eclogues*, I.101, *Works of Virgil*, p. 4: 'The Fruit is theirs, the Labour only mine' (there is no real source in Virgil); and John 4:37, 'And herein is that saying true, One soweth and another reapeth'. There is a similar contrast in Dryden's *The Hind and the Panther*, III.100–1 (1685), p. 79: 'The labour'd earth your pains have sow'd and till'd: | 'Tis just you reap the product of the field'. Cf. also *Windsor-Forest*, 408.

65–8. Rogers (2004: 208–9) notes these images of a redeemed landscape presage a similar effect in *Windsor-Forest*, 87–90.

65 Pope's note. *TE* suggests the further influence of *DV*, 35:1, which Pope does not quote in his revised note: 'The desert and the land without passage shal be glad, & the wilderness shal reioyce & shal florish as the lilie' (where *AV*, which Pope quotes in his note to 23, translates 'blossom as the rose'); *DV* for 35:7 reads, in contrast to the *AV* which Pope quotes in his note, 'And that which was drie land, shal be as a pool, and the theirstie ground as fountains of waters. In the dennes wherein dragons dwelt before, shal spring vp the greenes of reede and bulrush'. *DV* for 55:13 is: 'For the shrubbe shal come vp the firre tree, and for the nettle, shal grow the myrtle tree'.

Sees Lillies spring, and sudden Verdure rise;
And Starts, amidst the thirsty Wilds, to hear
New Falls of Water murm'ring in his Ear:
On rifted Rocks, the Dragon's late Abodes,
70   The green Reed trembles, and the Bulrush nods.
Waste sandy Vallies, once perplex'd with Thorn,
The spiry Firr and shapely Box adorn;
To leaf-less Shrubs the flow'ring Palms succeed,
And od'rous Myrtle to the noisome Weed.

71.] Cap. 41. v. 19 and Cap. 55. v. 13.

---

68. Sees: *1717–51:* See

---

66. sudden Verdure: cf. Elizabeth Singer, 'A Pastoral on the Nativity of our Saviour', in *A Collection of Divine Hymns and Poems on Several Occasions* (1707), p. 35: 'And in the Depth of Winter Spring appears, | For lo! the Ground a sudden Verdure wears'. But Pope may be rather recalling the sequence of the first Creation, in Milton, *Paradise Lost*, VII.313–19, which contains similar images.

67. Starts: is startled; Wakefield says 'the effect of an unexpected circumstance is admirably pointed out by the word *starts*'.

69–70. The rhyme is rare, but occurs in Cantos I and VI of Garth, *The Dispensary*, sixth edition (1706), pp. 5, 104.

69. rifted Rocks: In Milton, 'A Mask', 517, a Spirit refers to ancient poetic tales of 'rifted Rocks whose entrance leads to Hell'; Drayton also uses the phrase of a landscape feature, in the fourteenth song of *Poly-Olbion* (1613), p. 234. *SJ*, citing Pope's lines here, explains 'rifted' as 'split'.

71 Pope's note. See Pope's note to 65, and Commentary, for quotations from Isaiah 55:13.

AV for 41:19 reads: 'I will plant in the wilderness the cedar, the shittah tree, and the myrtle, and the oil tree; I will set in the desert the fir tree, and the pine, and the box tree together'; *DV*: 'I wil geue into the wildernes the cedar, and the thorne, and the myrtle and the oliue tree: I wil set in the desert the firretree, the elme, and the box tree together'; the presence of 'thorn' suggests a *DV* echo.

71. perplex'd with Thorn: tangled, made impassable by thorny bushes. *TE* compares Dryden, 'Sigismonda and Guiscardo', 143, *Fables Ancient and Modern* (1700), p. 128: 'the Wood perplex'd with Thorns'. Cf. also 'The False Morning', *Poetical Miscellanies: The Fifth Part* (1704), p. 512: 'A bushy Thicket, pathless and unworn, | O'er-run with Brambles, and perplex'd with Thorn'.

72. spiry: 'pyramidal' (*SJ*, citing this passage), i.e. by allusion to the spire-like shape of the tree. Cf. the 'Fir, whose spiry Branches rise' in Pope's *Iliad*, XIV.325 and the 'spiry Turrets' of 'Eloisa to Abelard', 142.

shapely Box: more normally 'shapely' because of the fashionable topiary to which the box tree was subjected and which Pope ridicules in his essay on gardens, *Guardian*, no. 173, 29 September 1713, *PW*, I.150.

74. Myrtle: *SJ* calls the myrtle bush 'a fragrant tree sacred to Venus'. Cf. 'Winter', 23; 'To a Young Lady', 73, *Ode for Musick*, 79, and Commentary.

noisome: 'offensive; disgusting' (*SJ*). The phrase 'noisome Weed' is common in both botanical and religious writings of the seventeenth century: e.g. John Gerard, *The Herball, or General History of Plantes* (1633), p. 615 (describing Germander Chickweed); William Pardoe, *Antient Christianity Revived* (1688), p. 51 (describing Heresy).

75   The Lambs with Wolves shall graze the verdant Mead,
      And Boys in flow'ry Bands the Tyger lead;
      The Steer and Lion at one Crib shall meet;
      And harmless Serpents lick the Pilgrim's Feet.

75.] Cap. 11. v. 6, 7, 8.

75, n. *1717–20, 1736–51: The lambs with wolves* &c.
  VIRG. E. 4. V. 21 Ipsae lacte domum referent distenta capellae
              Ubera, nec magnos metuent armenta leones —
              Occidet & serpens, & fallax herba veneni
              Occidet. —

The goats shall bear to the fold their udders distended with milk: nor shall the herds be afraid of the greatest lions. The serpent shall die, and the herb that conceals poison shall die.
  ISAIAH, Ch. 11. V. 16. &c. *The wolf shall dwell with the lamb, and the leopard shall lie down with the kid, and the calf and the young lion and the fatling together; and a little child shall lead them* — *And the lion shall eat straw like the ox. And the sucking child shall play on the hole of the asp, and the weaned child shall put his hand on the den of the cockatrice.*

---

75. For Steele's approval of this line see Headnote and *Corr.*, I.146.

  Mead: meadow. Pope had added the (fairly common) phrase 'verdant Mead' to a poem of Wycherley's in his revisions to the older man's work, 1706–10; *TE*, VI.58. Cf. also *Alarbas. A Dramatick Opera* (1709), p. 31, on the golden age when: 'Tygers and Lambs promiscuously did feed | With Kids and Panthers in the verdant Mead'.

75 Pope's note and variants. Pope quotes from the *AV*, 11:6–8 (leaving gaps). *TE* suggests the influence of *DV*: 'The wulfe and the lambe shal feede together, the lion and the oxe shale ate straw: & to the serpent dust shal be his bread: they shal not hurt'. The same passage of Isaiah is cited by Baker, 'Virgilius Evangelizans', *Poems upon Several Occasions*, p. 122. Pope's quotation from Virgil is actually lines 21–2, 24–5 in most modern editions.

76. *flow'ry Bands:* *TE* (p. 106) finds the syntax can be read two ways: flowery bands of youth leading tigers, youths leading tigers with flowery bands. In 'To a Young Lady, with the Works of Voiture', 65, the 'flow'ry Bands' are clearly a form of adornment. McLaverty (2001: 81) points out that the illustrated initial for the poem in the *Works* of 1717 depicts a small boy leading a tiger with a floral chain.

77. *Crib:* manger, stall at which animals eat.

78. *harmless Serpents:* In *AV*, the verse cited in Pope's note, a near-repetition of that just cited at 75 but also in reference to 77, reads: 'the lyon shall eate straw like the bullocke: and dust shalbe the serpents meat' and in *DV*, 'the lion and the oxe shal eate straw: & to the serpent dust shal be his bread'. The licking of the feet suggests reversal of the biblical sentence passed on the serpent in Genesis 3:15, that the serpent would bruise the heel of mankind. The washing of feet was a Christian ceremony (e.g. John 13:4–12). *EC* suggests a reminiscence of Ovid's transformation of Cadmus and his wife into peaceable serpents (*Metamorphoses*, IV.569–603), though Ovid's narrative is erotic in aspect. 'Harmless serpents' are described in the chapter 'Of Innocent Serpents', in Topsell's *The History of Four-Footed Beasts and Serpents* (1658), p. 737.

The smiling Infant in his Hand shall take
80 The crested Basilisk and speckled Snake;
  Pleas'd, the green Lustre of the Scales survey,
  And with their forky Tongue, and pointless Sting shall play.
  Rise, crown'd with Light, Imperial *Salem* rise!
  Exalt thy Tow'ry Head, and lift thy Eyes!

83.] Cap. 60. v. 1.

83, n. 1717–20, 1736–51: Rise crown'd with light, &c.
  The thoughts [*1736–51:* of *Isaiah,* which compose the latter part of the poem] that follow to the end of the Poem, are wonderfully elevated, and much above those general exclamations of *Virgil* which make the loftiest parts of his *Pollio.*

  Magnus ab integro saeclorum nascitur ordo!
  — toto surget gens aurea mundo!
  — incipient magni procedere menses!
  Aspice, venturo laetentur ut omnia saeclo! &c.

  The reader needs only [*1751:* to] turn to the passages of *Isaiah,* [*1736–51:* here cited.] as they are cited in the margins of the preceding Eclogue.

84. Tongue, and pointless Sting shall play: *1736–51:* tongue shall innocently play

80. crested Basilisk: 'a kind of serpent, called also a cockatrice, which is said to drive away all others by his hissing, and to kill by looking' (*SJ*); cf. the 'fiery Basilisk', line 29 of a version of Psalm 91, ascribed to Pope by Ault (*TE.,* VI.70). The word appears also in the *DV* text of Isaiah 30:6, where *AV* uses 'serpent'.

82. An Alexandrine; cf. *Essay on Criticism,* 359 and Commentary. Wakefield suggests that Pope's revision was prompted by the discovery that a snake's venom is not lodged in its tail. *TE* compares the image to Dryden, *Aeneid,* XI.1092, *Works of Virgil,* p. 571, 'And shoots her forky Tongue, and whisks her threat'ning Tail'; cf. also II.650, of a 'crested Snake' which 'brandishes by fits his forky Tongue', and his version of *Georgics,* II.666. Wakefield compares the variant to Dryden, 'Palamon and Arcite', III.98, *Fables,* p. 53: 'And Troops of Lions innocently play', but the phrase is relatively common: cf. Behn, 'The Golden Age', 46-7, *Poems upon Several Occasions* (1684), p. 4 (of snakes): 'With whom the Nymphs did Innocently play, | No spightful Venom in the wantons lay'. Pope returned to it himself in *Iliad,* IV.633, and in the version of Psalm 91 (16) attributed to him by Ault (see previous note).

83 Pope's notes and variants. In *AV,* Isaiah 60:1 reads 'Arise, shine, for thy light is come, and the glory of the Lord is risen vpon thee; *DV* reads: 'Arise, be illuminated Ierusalem: because thy light is come, & the glorie of our Lord is risen vpon thee'. The lines of Virgil quoted by Pope are 5, 9, 12, and 52: 'the great series of centuries is born afresh'; 'a race of gold rises in the world'; 'the great months begin to process'; 'see, how all things rejoice in the age just coming'.

83. Imperial Salem: an abbreviation for Jerusalem, mentioned in the *DV* but not the *AV* source text. *AV* uses 'Salem' in Psalm 76:2 and it was commonly used in versions of the Psalms by e.g. Sandys, in his *Paraphrase vpon the Divine Poems* (1638), pp. 93, 98, 123 etc. The 'Imperial' is perhaps suggested by the proximity of Virgil's praise of the Roman empire.

84. Tow'ry Head: an architectural image from religious verse, e.g. Joseph Beaumont, *Psyche, or, Love's Mysterie,* VII.233 (1648),

85   See, a long Race thy spatious Courts adorn;
     See future Sons, and Daughters yet unborn
     In crowding Ranks on ev'ry Side arise,
     Demanding Life, impatient for the Skies!
     See barb'rous Nations at thy Gates attend,
90   Walk in thy Light, and in thy Temple bend.
     See thy bright Altars throng'd with prostrate Kings,
     And heap'd with Products of *Sabaean* Springs!

85.] Cap. 60. v. 4.
89.] Ibid. 60. v. 3.
92.] Ibid. v. 6.

---

p. 113: 'till *Salem's* towrie head | Had met their eyes'. Also occasionally in political or allegorical verse, such as George Stubbes, *The Laurel, and the Olive* (1710), p. 11: 'And *Rome* once more uprear'd her Tow'ry Head'.

thy Eyes: *TE* observes, in response to Wakefield's censure of the 'open vowel' here, that both versions of Isaiah 60:4 have 'thine eyes' (see Pope's note to next line). For Pope on hiatus see *Essay on Criticism*, 348 and Commentary. He had already used 'my Eyes' and 'thy Eyes' in 'January and May', 91, 258, 504; cf. 'Eloisa to Abelard', 122.

85-94. Rogers (2005a: 72) suggests this vision of a celestial city constitutes a forward glance to the praise of a redeemed British court in *Windsor-Forest*, 375-82.

85 Pope's note. *TE* says Pope is closer to *DV*: 'Lift vp thine eies round about, and see al these are gathered together, they are come to thee: thy sonnes shal come from a farre, & thy daughters shal rise from the side', but the only real difference is in the final phrase, where *AV* has 'thy daughters shalbe nourced [nursed] at thy side'. The resemblance is soon eclipsed by Pope's own idea (see next note).

86-8. Cf. the image of unborn souls parodied at the start of *The Dunciad Variorum*, III.15-22. Wakefield cites Virgil, *Aeneid*, VI.749-51: 'Letheum ad fluvium deus evocat agmine magno, | scilicet immemores supera ut convexa revisant, | rursus et incipiant in corpora velle reverti.' ('the god calls [them] to the river Lethe in a great crowd, in order that, without memory, they shall revisit the vaulted upper regions and start to wish to go back into the body').

86. future Sons: cf. Pope's 'The First Book of Statius his Thebais', 578.

87. crowding Ranks: cf. Dryden's version of 'Pollio', 64, *Works of Virgil*, p. 19: 'And joyful Ages from behind, in crowding Ranks appear'; Dryden's image is without direct source in 'Pollio'.

89 Pope's note. *TE* suggests Pope is closer (at 90) here to *DV*: 'And the Gentiles shal walke in thy light, and kings in the brightnes of thy rising' than to *AV*: 'And the Gentiles shall come to thy light, and kings to the brightnesse of thy rising'.

90. bend: bow or kneel.

91. prostrate: in submission.

92 Pope's note. *TE* suggests *DV* is the closer source: 'al of Saba shal come, bringing gold and frankincense'; *AV* has 'all they from Sheba shall come: they shal bring gold and incense'. Wakefield notes the resemblance to Dryden, *Aureng-Zebe*, IV (1676), p. 51: 'What Sweets soe'er *Sabean* Springs disclose'. *EC* adds Milton, *Paradise Lost*, IV.162 (1674), p. 90: '*Sabean* Odours from the spicie shoare'. Dryden used the adjective 'Sabaean' or 'Sabean' in several other places, e.g. in the version of Virgil, *Georgics*, II.164,

For thee, *Idume*'s spicy Forests blow;
And Seeds of Gold in *Ophyr*'s Mountains glow.
95   See Heav'n its sparkling Portals wide display,
And break upon thee in a Flood of Day!
No more the rising *Sun* shall gild the Morn,
Nor Evening *Cynthia* fill her silver Horn,

97.] Ibid. v. 19. 20.

Works of Virgil (1697), p. 76: 'And od'rous Frankincense on the *Sabaean* Bough', and of *Aeneid*, IV.86, *ibid.*, p. 299: 'She feeds their Altars with *Sabaean* Smoke'; it was associated particularly with incense and altars. Saba is usually thought to be modern Yemen.

93. For thee: cf. *Windsor-Forest*, 391 ff.

Idume: TE identifies this with the biblical Edom in southern Palestine, indicating there is no biblical basis for the spicy forests, but that Pope probably remembered Virgil, *Georgics*, I.57, 'molles sua tura Sabaei', translated by Dryden (86, *Works of Virgil*, p. 52) as 'And soft *Idume* weeps her od'rous Tears' (in a passage listing various natural products of the world's regions). Cf., however, Dryden's *Annus Mirabilis*, 11–12 (1667), p. 2: 'For them the *Idumaean* Balm did sweat, | And in hot *Ceilon* Spicy Forrests grew'.

94. Seeds of Gold: an alchemical idea: cf. Daniel Sennert, *Thirteen Books of Natural Philosophy* (1660), p. 155. Patrick Hume draws on this in annotating Milton's 'Potable Gold', *Paradise Lost*, III.608: 'that aimed at by Philosophers, is a living Gold, like red Powder, or granulated Saffron, extracted from the most pure Seeds of Gold, and so heightened, that by meer Contact, it will not only turn the impurer Metals into the finest Gold, but multiply, even that so made and transmuted, into Mountains'; *Annotations on Milton's Paradise Lost* (1695), p. 128.

Ophyr: Ophir is mentioned in several books of the bible as a place of riches, especially of gold; e.g. Isaiah 13:12: 'I will make a man more pretious then fine gold; euen a man then the golden wedge of Ophir' (*AV*).

For the ripening of gold in the earth see Commentary to *Windsor-Forest*, 394.

95–6. Rogers (2005a: 72) aligns this couplet with the images in *Windsor-Forest*, 389–94.

97 Pope's note. The versions are similar: *AV* reads: '[19] The Sunne shall be no more thy light by day, neither for brightnesse shall the moone giue light vnto thee: but the Lord shall be vnto thee an euerlasting light, & thy God thy glory. [20] Thy Sunne shall no more goe downe, neither shall thy moone withdraw it selfe: for the Lord shall bee thine euerlasting light, and the dayes of thy mourning shall be ended.' *DV*: '[19]. Thou shalt haue the sunne no more to shine by day, neither shal the brightnes of the moone lighten thee: but the Lord shal be vnto thee for an euerlasting light, and thy God for thy glorie. [20]. Thy sunne shal goe downe no more, and thy moone shal not be diminished: because the Lord shal be vnto thee for an euerlasting light, and the daies of thy mourning shal be ended'.

97. gild the Morn: a conventional figure, e.g. 'On the Untimely Death of Lord Hastings', *Lachrymae Musarum*, ed. Richard Brome (1649), p. 85: 'when fair *Phoebus* 'gins to gild the Morn'.

98. Evening Cynthia: i.e. the moon, as 'Cynthia' is one of the alternative names for moon goddess; cf. Commentary to *Windsor-Forest*, 198. Wakefield finds a source in Ovid, *Metamorphoses* I.10–11: 'nullus adhuc mundo praebebat lumina Titan, | nec nova crescendo reparabat cornua Phoebe' ('as yet no Titan showed light to the world, nor did Phoebe repair her new horns by growing'),

But lost, dissolv'd in thy superior Rays;
100 One Tyde of Glory, one unclouded Blaze,
O'erflow thy Courts: The LIGHT HIMSELF shall shine
Reveal'd; and *God*'s eternal Day be thine!
The Seas shall waste; the Skies in Smoke decay;
Rocks fall to Dust, and Mountains melt away;
105 But fix'd *His* Word, *His* saving Pow'r remains:
Thy *Realm* for ever lasts! thy own *Messiah* reigns.

103–4.] Cap 51. v. 6. and Cap. 54. v. 10.

---

and Sandys' translation of 10, 'Nor waxing *Phoebe* fill'd her wained horns' (*Ovids Metamorphosis Englished*, 1632, p. 1). Pope probably knew Congreve's 'The Birth of the Muse', which contains at 52–3, in the midst of a creation narrative, some elements of Pope's apocalypse here: 'Nor yet, did Golden Fires the Sun adorn, | Or borrow'd Lustre silver *Cynthia*'s Horn'; *Works* (1710), III.862. Warton (*Works of Pope*, I.104) objected to the use of Cynthia as 'classical' and therefore 'improper', but Pope no doubt conceived it as part of the splicing of classical with Christian, the classical playing here a subordinate role, giving way to a sublime Christian future; the issue is further explored in McLaverty (2001: 81).

99. superior Rays: cf. Oldmixon, *Amores Britannici*, II.i.137–8 (1703), p. 9 of second sequence: 'With Envy from the East the Sun surveys | A Mortal shining with Superior Rays'.

100. Tyde of Glory: perhaps recalling Cowley, 'Hymn. To Light', 5, *Works of Mr. Abraham Cowley* (1668), p. 35 of additional sequence: 'Thou Tide of Glory which no Rest dost know'.

101. LIGHT HIMSELF: Jesus describes himself as the 'light of the world' in John 8:12 and the identification of God with Light was orthodox.

102. eternal . . . thine: Wakefield compares Dryden, 'To the Pious Memory of Mrs Anne Killigrew', 15, *Poems by Mrs Anne Killigrew* (1686), sig. A2ʳ: 'Since Heav'ns Eternal Year is thine'. Pope returned to the thoroughly orthodox image of 'eternal Day' in 'Eloisa to Abelard', 222.

103–4 **Pope's note.** *TE* suggests Pope is closer to *DV*, 51:6: 'the heauens shal melt as smoke, and the earth shal be worne away as a garment', whereas *AV* has 'the heavens shall vanish away like smoke, and the earth shall wax old like a garment'. For 54:10, *AV* has: 'For the mountaines shall depart, and the hilles be remoued', and *DV*: 'the mountaines shal be moued, and the little hilles shal tremble'. Cf. also Psalm 97:5: 'The hilles melted like waxe at the presence of the Lord' (*AV*).

105. saving: redemptive. The idea of God's 'saving Pow'r' is common in religious verse paraphrase, e.g. Tate and Brady's *A New Version of the Psalms of David* (1696), pp. 15, 23, 104.

106. A further Alexandrine, here suggesting epic elongation.

thy . . . reigns: *TE* compares Virgil, *Eclogues*, IV.10: 'tuus iam regnat Apollo' ('thy own *Apollo* reigns'; Dryden's translation, 12, *Works of Virgil*, p. 17); in Virgil, 'thy' refers only to Artemis, Apollo's sister. Cf. also Luke Milbourne, *The Psalms of David in English Metre*, Psalm 97 (1698), p. 210: 'The Lord, the Great Messiah, reigns'.

8
THE FIRST BOOK OF STATIUS HIS THEBAIS
(1712)

Editors' Headnote

Composition and publication

'The First Book of Statius his Thebais' was published on 20 May 1712. As with many of his early poems, there is conflicting evidence about the date of composition of Pope's translation of Statius – or rather, evidence to suggest that he revised an earlier version of the poem at a significantly later date, and over several years. Pope's copy of *Publii Papinii Statii Sylvarum libri V, Thebaidos libri XII, Achilleidos libri II*, edited by Johanne Veenhusen (Leiden, 1671), now at Hartlebury Castle, is described in Mack (1982: 442, item 155). It is not annotated and the date when Pope acquired it is not known. There is, however, ample testimony to the importance of Statius as an element in Pope's 'great reading period ... from about thirteen or fourteen to about twenty-one', i.e. roughly from 1701 to 1709 (*OAC*, I.20, no. 44, March 1743). Late in life Pope told Spence that he had first read Statius, in a natural sequence after Ogilby's Homer and Sandys's Ovid, not long after he was 'about eight years old' in a partial translation 'by some very bad hand' – most probably Thomas Stephens' 1648 *An Essay upon Statius* (*OAC*, I.14; no. 30). Mack (1985: 848) suggests that Pope encountered Statius as part of his clandestine Catholic schooling, on the grounds that it was not in the English curriculum (see also Shugrue 1957); but this earlier translation was done by a schoolmaster explicitly to help his students, and in any case Statius was hardly an obscure author (see 'Models' below). Pope also told Spence that it was in the course of 'the scattererd lessons' he used to set for himself in his early teens that he translated 'that part of Statius which was afterwards printed with the corrections of Walsh' – the only suggestion that Walsh, who died on 15 March 1708, had any involvement with the translation (*OAC*, I.14, no. 31), and perhaps a mistake for a different literary advisor such as Cromwell. Spence's judgement reflects the relatively low standing that Statius had in the early eighteenth century:

> There were some few marks besides of a mistaken taste in Mr. Pope, from that early and unguided reading of his. He met with Statius very early, liked him much, and translated a good deal from him, and to the last he used to call him the best of all the Latin epic poets after Virgil.
>
> (*OAC*, I.232, no. 551, 21–25 February 1743)

Pope's general view was confirmed several times (e.g. *OAC*, I.233, no. 552), and we know that Statius was one of the poets imitated in Pope's early epic *Alcander* (*OAC*, I.18, no. 40, March 1743). In 1730, he told Jonathan Richardson that in 1701 he 'applyd himself so Diligently as to be able to Translate into Verse, within 2 or 3 Years, many Passages of Homer, Virgil, Ovid, Statius, and the most eminent Latin & Greek Poets, some of which (tho since corrected) have been printed' (Sherburn 1958a: 346). In the 'Argument' at the head of the first printing of the poem, Pope stated that the translation 'was made almost in his Childhood', but that 'finding the Version better, upon Review, than he expected from those Years, he was easily prevail'd upon to give it some Correction', while the half-title in the 1717 *Works* specifies that the poem was 'Translated in 1703.' In 1735, when he printed the letter to Cromwell in which he first discusses the revision of the poem, Pope added the following note: 'This was the Translation of the first book of *Statius*, done when the Author was but 14 Years old' (*Corr.*, I.36), i.e. in 1702. In the 1735 edition of his correspondence, this letter to Cromwell – in which Pope asks his friend to attend to the attached papers and to 'Let them go no farther than your Chamber & to be very free of your remarks in the Margins, not only in regard to the Accuracy, but to the fidelity of the Translation: which I have not had time to Compare of Late with its Original' – is dated 22 January 1708-9. However, Sherburn (*Corr.*, I.36) suggests that the cancelled date on the contemporary transcript of the letter in the Bodleian Library – 19 January 1707-8 – is more likely to be correct, and this earlier date would lend further support to the suggestion that Pope was engaged on the revision of a piece of work which he had begun some time in his mid-teens. The version sent with this first letter was incomplete: Pope warns Cromwell that he has omitted two passages of Statius (128-44 and 168-312 in modern numbering), the latter on the grounds that it contains

> a Noble Description of the *Council* of the *Gods*, & a *Speech* of *Jupiter*; which Contain a peculiar beauty & Majesty; & were Left out for no Other reason but because the Consequence of this Machine [supernatural epic device] appears not till the 2d Book.

Pope later relented and included versions of both passages (approximately 178-99 and 224-443 of the poem as it stands). He tells Cromwell that he has omitted a further passage (408-81 of Statius, in modern numbering) containing

> an Unmannerly Batle at fistycuffs between the *two Princes* on a Very slight Occasion. . . . This I had actualy translated but was Very ill satisfied with it ev'n in my own Words to which an Author cannot but be partial enough of Conscience. It was therefore Omitted in this Copy[.]

Pope continued to exclude this section (see Commentary at 559-62) and his initial version has not survived. The letter contains several apologetic remarks about the poet:

Statius was none of the Discreetest poets tho he was the best Versifyer Next Virgil ... I should not have insisted so much on the fault[s] of this *Poet* if I did not hope you would take the same freedom with and revenge it upon his *Translator*.

On 7 May 1709, Pope wrote once again to Cromwell, re-sending him the revised and enlarged manuscript and asking him once again to 'improve [the] Translation':

I had I know not what extraordinary Flux of Rhyme upon me for three days together, in which time all the Verses you see added, have been written; which I tell you that you may more freely be severe upon them ... If you will please to begin where you left off last, & mark the Margins as you have done in the pages immediately before, (which you will find corrected to your Sense since your last perusal) you will extreamly oblige me.

(*Corr.*, I.56–7)

On 10 June, Pope thanked Cromwell for returning 'part of the Version of *Statius*' with his 'remarks ... which I think to be just, except where you cry out ... *Pulchrè, benè, recté!* [beautiful, well, correct] There I have some fears, you are often, if not always, in the wrong' (*Corr.*, I.63). He went on to correct elaborately what he sees as an error by the French theorist René Le Bossu, which criticised the *Thebaid*'s faults in 'unity of action', then listed several aspects of Statius which he considered faulty; these are noted in the Commentary at the appropriate points. On 31 October 1709, Trumbull wrote to Ralph Bridges that Pope was 'copying fairly his Translat[n]. of the 1st. Book of Statius' Theb.' (*TE*, I.348; Sherburn 1958a: 345). Trumbull had apparently attempted to find a French version for Pope's use, in October 1708 (Sherburn 1958a: 344). Further letters to Cromwell, 30 November and 15 December 1709 (*Corr.*, I.76–7), may refer either to 'Sapho to Phaon' or the Statius version, then both in hand. On 10 April 1710 Pope wrote once again to Cromwell, enclosing the 'Arguments in Prose to the Thebaid', and on 24 June asked him to return them 'with any Remarks you may have made on that Author' (*Corr.*, I.82, 91).

TE suggests that because it contains thirteen expletives and nine Alexandrines, in contravention of the 'rules' formulated in a letter to Cromwell of 25 November 1710 (*Corr.*, I.107), it is likely that 'The First Book of Statius' was substantially completed before that date; ten of the expletives and three of the Alexandrines were removed from texts of *1717* onwards (see textual apparatus). Pope had already voiced similar objections in an earlier letter to Walsh on 22 October 1706 (*Corr.*, I.23), a letter which may, on the other hand, be partly or wholly fabricated. In any case the exact date of final composition remains conjectural. The translation was evidently finished early in 1712; on 19 February Lintot paid Pope £16 2s 6d for the copyright together with that of 'The Fable of Vertumnus and Pomona'; at fourpence a line it was at the cheaper end of Pope's productions for the volume (McLaverty 2001: 17). 'The First Book of *Statius* his Thebais' was published in *Miscellaneous Poems and Translations*, occupying pp. 5–56 (B1[r]–E4[v]);

it opens the volume, the first of Pope's seven acknowledged contributions, and has a divisional title page, as it does in the 1717 *Works*.

Text

The text presented here is taken from the first edition of 1712. Significant revision is confined to the *Works* of 1717 and 1736. It is possible that some of the variant readings from the second state of the 1736 *Works* are misprints rather than authorial revisions. From the 1736 *Works* on, the original Latin text was printed with the translation. The various extant texts of 'The First Book of Statius' are referred to in the apparatus as follows:

> *1712*: *Miscellaneous Poems and Translations*, octavo (Griffith 6)
>
> *1717*: *Works*, quarto (Griffith, 79)
>
> *1736a*: *Works*, vol.III, octavo (Griffith 417)
>
> *1736b*: *Works*, vol.III, octavo (Griffith 418)
>
> *1741*: *Works*, vol.I, part ii, octavo (Griffith 521)
>
> *1751*: *Works*, vol.II, octavo (Griffith 644)

Models and sources

Publius Papinius Statius was born at Naples soon after AD 45 and is thought to have died before the assassination (in 96) of Domitian, under whose autocratic rule he had lived his entire poetic career. The 12-book *Thebaid* (as it is conventionally known in modern times) dates from about AD 92, before five books of 'occasional' poems, *Silvae*, including further panegyrics on the emperor, and an unfinished epic, the *Achilleid*. The *Thebaid* was published as a whole by its own author, and carries with it an air of epic aspiration, clearly adopting the mantle of Virgil. It was very popular in the middle ages in England, forming a key source for Chaucer's *Troilus and Criseyde*, *Hous of Fame* and 'The Compleynt of Feire Anelida and Fals Arcite'. In Chapter X of Henry Peacham's *Complete Gentleman* (1622), p. 90, Statius is 'a smooth and a sweete Poet, comming neerest of any other to the state and Maiestie of *Virgils* verse, and *Virgil* onely excepted, is the Prince of Poets as well Greekes as Latine; for he is more flowery in figures, and writeth better lines then *Homer*'. Statius is mentioned as a standard reference point in Sir William Davenant's preface to *Gondibert* (1651) and in the notes to Cowley's epic *Davideis*.

There was no substantial English version before *An Essay upon Statius, or, The five first books of Publ. Papinius Statius his Thebais done into English verse by T. S., with the Poetick History Illustrated* (1648), by Thomas Stephens, who went on to edit *Publii Papinii Statii Sylvarum libri V* (Cambridge, 1651). The translation begins with a short 'Preface', explaining that the 'metaphrased' version was performed to help his students (he was a schoolmaster at Bury), though its publication at the end of the Civil War was suggestive, at least: alongside Cowley's *Davideis* (*Poems*, 1656) came numerous translations from war epics, such as Sir Richard Fanshawe's version of Camoens' *Lusiad* (1655) and Thomas Ross's translation from Silius Italicus (1661) that might also have influenced Pope. Stephens supplies about 185 footnotes to book 1, mostly of a simple explicatory kind, and his his own not entirely reliable line-numbering, used in our Commentary for ease of reference, alongside page numbers. The translation was not reprinted and there was no full translation into English of the poem before that by William Lillington Lewis, elegantly produced at the Clarendon Press at Oxford in 1767. Sir Robert Howard's *Poems* of 1660 contained a version of Statius' unfinished *Achilleid*; Dryden's commendatory poem 'To my Honoured Friend, Sir Robert Howard', 67–98, praises this as an improvement on its original, further illuminated with Howard's notes.

The critical reputation of Statius began to fade in the seventeenth century, as Dryden's poem itself confirms. Rymer's translation of Rapin's *Reflections on Aristotle's Treatise of Poesy* (1674), p. 24, placed Statius among 'those who place the essence of *Poetry* in big and pompous words'. Dryden said that Statius, though 'the best Versificator next to *Virgil*, knew not how to Design after him, though he had the Model in his Eye' ('A Discourse concerning the Original and Progress of Satire', prefacing *Satires of Juvenal*, 1693, p. vii). In 'A Parallel Betwixt poetry and Painting', Dryden compares the soberness of Virgil with the excess 'fustian' of Statius, who 'was always in a Foam at his setting out'; '*Statius* never thought an expression could be bold enough; and if a bolder could be found, he rejected the first' (*De Arte Graphica* (1695), pp. l, lv). In the prefatory essay to his translation of the *Aeneid* he says that Statius was 'noted for want of Conduct and Judgment' throughout; he had a 'bladdered greatness... full of Humours, and swell'd with Dropsie' (*Works of Virgil*, 1697, sig. e3ᵛ-e4ʳ). Statius was among the would-be sublime poets downgraded by Dennis in his *Reflections, Critical and Satyrical* (1711), p. 4. Just before Pope's version came out, Addison had noted Statius's faults in similar terms in *The Spectator* (nos. 279, 19 January 1712, and 285, 26 January 1712), though Statius is given a slightly better press, after Pope's version, in *The Guardian*, no. 122, 31 July 1713.

Statius was not latterly among the most imitated of Latin poets. 'A translation out of Statius. To Sleep', apparently by John Potenger, appears on pp. 53–4 of *Poems by Several Hands, and on Several Occasions*, edited by Nahum Tate (1685); this was Statius's most popular short poem, V.4 of *Silvae*. *A Pacquet from Parnassus* (1702), p. 23, has 'The Dawn: *Done out of Latin*. Statius lib.1.', initialled 'H. D.'. Addison quotes and translates an extract from the *Silvae* in *Remarks on Several Parts of Italy* (1705), pp. 257–8, and Statius was much referenced in the notes to the collective *Ovid's Art of Love* (1709), a volume which Pope owned. Laurence Eusden translated two sections of book IV of the *Thebaid* in Steele's *Poetical Miscellanies* (late 1713, dated 1714), to which Pope also contributed.

Pope's poem thus stands in a slightly insecure tradition of imitation and reference to the lesser epics of the classical tradition (which also included Lucan and Silius Italicus). He made no further versions of Statius. In the Preface to the *Iliad* (*PW*, I.225) he refers to Statius' 'sudden, short, and interrupted Flashes' of poetic fire, with other features of his poetic character; the notes to the *Iliad* translation make sporadic reference to Statius as a comparative literary and historical source, and example of non-Homeric attempts at the sublime (e.g. III.219; IV.430 and 508; V.1033). In the final note to book XXIII, Pope commends the sixth book of the *Thebaid* as the best part of the poem; this was translated by Pope's friend Walter Harte, with notes, in his *Poems on Several Occasions* (1727), pp. 109–225. Thomas Gray experimented with lines from the same book (and from book IX) around 1736. Later, around the time he was recalling his early enthusiasm to Spence, Pope mentions Statius among those (like Blackmore) who falsely propose themselves immortality through epic (note to *Dunciad*, IV.6); he had used the example of Statius in constructing his mock-epic title to *The Dunciad* on its first appearance in 1728 (see Rumbold 2007: 14–15). For further comment on versions of Statius up to and beyond Pope see Gillespie (1999).

Context

This poem, with other conributions to the volume, constituted Pope's first commercial venture with Barnaby Bernard Lintot or Lintott (1675–1736), and a further move, following the *Essay on Criticism*, away from Tonson. Lintot was a bookseller-publisher who had come through the regular system of Stationers' Company apprenticeship and set up shop in Fleet Street, London. In *Examen Miscellaneum* (1702) he had attempted to institute a series of *Miscellanies* to rival those published between 1684 and 1709 by Tonson, initially under the editorship of Dryden, who had died in 1700: Pope's first published poems (1–3 of this volume) had appeared in the *Sixth Part* of Tonson's series (1709). McLaverty (2007: 188) suggests that Pope may have known Lintot, who was from Horsham in Sussex, through the Caryll family (of West Grinstead). Lintot would be the publisher of Pope's *Windsor-Forest* (1713), the *Ode for Musick* (1713), the extended version of *The Rape of the Lock* (1714), *The Temple of Fame* (1715), Pope's *Works* of 1717, and the Homer translations (1715 onwards). Lintot also published work by members of Pope's circle such as Gay, Parnell, and Fenton.

Lintot had advertised for contributions to the collection in the *General Post* of 8–10 October 1711, and subsequently. Pope was named as one of the authors involved. *Miscellaneous Poems and Translations* (1712), was, according to a loose phrase of Addison, 'published by Mr. *Pope*, in which there are many excellent Compositions of that ingenious Gentleman' – slightly toxic praise, immediately supplanted by strong commendation of Tickell's poem on the Peace of Utrecht, a serious rival to Pope's *Windsor-Forest* (*Spectator*, no. 523, 30 October 1712). Ault (1949: 29–32) presents an extended case for Pope as editor, which is broadly accepted by Foxon (1991: 34–8) and somewhat modified by McLaverty (2001: 15–20). That Pope had a considerable part in the organisation of the volume, in contributing seven acknowledged poems, including the first version of *The Rape of the Lock*; that he was variously connected with at least eight of the other contributors (including Prior, Gay, Cromwell, Fenton and Broome), and prepared for press two 'Chaucerian' contributions from his dead friend the actor Thomas Betterton, is not in dispute. Ault's contention (1949: 38–48) that he also contributed 'The Story of Arethusa', from Ovid, which lies just before 'Vertumnus and Pomona' in the volume, is possible but far from certain: Ault's case rests heavily on verbal parallels between the anonymous poem and versions of Ovid acknowledged by Pope, but in an imitative genre this is a perilous form of evidence, and there is also vocabulary in the piece which is not so easily paralleled elsewhere in Pope. Ault offers no cogent reason why Pope should never have claimed as his own such a competent and inoffensive poem, which was also not absorbed into the rival collective translations of the *Metamorphoses* issued in 1717, in both of which Pope appeared (see Headnote to 'Vertumnus and Pomona). It is therefore not included in this volume. The two poems ascribed to Betterton have also been regarded by some, including his contemporaries, as Pope's work (see discussion in Mack 1985: 92–3, Foxon 1991: 34, and McLaverty 2001: 17), and he no doubt at the very least revised and retouched them; but Betterton's widow was paid (via Pope) five guineas for them and there is no conclusive evidence that they are substantially Pope's rather than his friend's work. They are likewise not included here. On Pope's relations with Lintot see further Headnote to 'Verses design'd to be prefix'd to Mr. Lintott's Miscellany', which might be taken to bespeak the confidence of a poet in control, or as disengaging ridicule of the publisher. The verses were not 'prefix'd' to the volume as they might have been if Pope were its controlling editor, and there is no contractual evidence that Pope was paid to do anything editorial to the volume, whereas payments for the individual poems are in most cases recorded. The volume was not in this first form advertised as under Pope's special care, though his name occurs more prominently in promotional material for the second edition of 1714.

The first book of Statius' *Thebaid* consists of 720 lines of hexameter verse. Pope's version runs to 864 lines of pentameter couplets, roughly comparable to Stephens' 872 lines of the same verse, except that Stephens does not omit lines 408–81 of Statius, as Pope does, so Pope's 864 lines are based on 646 of Statius, not counting several other omissions. Lewis's 1767 translation takes 990 lines of couplets for the full book, which is in line with Pope's level of expansion. As usual with Pope's translations, his use of end-stopped couplets rather than enjambed lines produces some areas of omission and addition and a more pointed use of antithesis, as well as additional adjectives and periphrasis. There was at once 'low' material to excise, and 'high' hyperbole to tone down (Gillespie 1999: 164–7). Pope clarified obscure aspects of mythology by adding (or dropping) names (e.g. 8–10, 35–9, 90, 243, 338–9, 373–7, 547). He cut anything he regarded as undignified (e.g. 59–60, 100, 150, 154–5, 166, 206–9, 221, 297, 354–7, 470–3, 490–1, 559–62, 688, 733–4, 765–8, 777) and freely expanded to generate 'sublime' effects (e.g. 23, 24, 120–3, 212–15, 437–42, 841–9) or political allusion (e.g. 228–33).

Pope's poem comes in the first phase of his imitative career, and involves further forms of imitation; Statius was imitating Virgil, who was imitating Homer, while Pope was modelling his own translation skills on those of Dryden, and was working towards a 'Homeric' sublimity and turn of phrase. The poem contains a lot of echoes, and pre-echoes of Pope's own Homer translations, and the retention of some Latinisms particularly inflects the vocabulary of this poem (e.g. 1, 6, 83, 178, 240, 487, 758). For careful comparative study of the stylistic effects of Pope's translation see Sowerby (2006). Mack (1985: 160–2) suggests Pope's boyhood interest in Statius was moved by the excitement, pathos, horror, passion and darkness of the original; and that as a writer he was inspired by the 'virtuosity of the Statian style ... more figural, hyperbolic, and "conceited"'. There are also links to the 'public' declamation and political allegory of *Windsor-Forest*.

Lee (2010: 133–8) contends that Statius was a useful model for Pope in his popularity, mastery of style, and aspiration towards epic in the shadow of dominant predecessor (i.e. Virgil; Dryden in Pope's case).

The date of publication has led some readers to detect a strong political context to the poem. Even apart from its flattering address to Domitian, the story of violent and sexually depraved internecine struggles for a long-established throne might have had political significance for Statius, writing in a period of relative stability, while for Pope, in the temporary safety of a Tory ministry under Queen Anne, but with uncertainty on the horizon, Statius provided a suitably distant context to explore dynastic tensions and rival claims to sovereignty. Aden (1973: 728–38, revised in Aden 1978: 84–90) suggested that some parts of the the poem, particularly 224–72, constituted Pope's first experiment at covert political satire against the line of Protestant kings stemming from the Glorious Revolution and strengthened by measures to promote the Hanoverian succession during the years of its composition. The possible political correspondences are multiple, however, and certainly not clear enough to enact any simple propagandist purpose, as Erskine-Hill (1982: 53) argues. A further specific slant is given by Daly (2013), which aligns Juno's complaints against Jove (348–53, and 400–2) with Queen Anne's frustration at Marlborough and his resistance to ending the war. One additional oddity is the lavish praise of the martial successes of Domitian (24ff), which Pope renders even more flagrantly obsequious than Statius. In the context of a proliferating genre of battle poetry during the War of Spanish Succession, most of it devoted to Marlborough in a way Pope steadfastly refused to comply with (see Headnote to *Windsor-Forest*), the experiment with panegyric looks almost ironic: Marlborough, some of whose successes lay in the same areas as Domitian's, had been dismissed by the Queen from his military positions at the end of 1711 after a campaign by Pope's Tory friends. This may, however, be a consequence of the type of experimental intensification of style identified by Sowerby rather than any active political undercurrent.

Aden insists that no audience in the thick of political strife in 1712 could have missed Pope's pointed parallels, but nobody, not even Whig partisans like Addison and Dennis, said anything at all about this aspect. 'The First Book of Statius his Thebais' was only occasionally cited in Pope's day (see Commentary to 39, 43–6). Lewis's 1767 translation carefully deferred to Pope's (I.ix, xxi, 4, 12, 24, etc.). Warton (1782: 84–8), concurring with Spence, thought Statius a very 'injudicious' choice for a 'youth of genius', exhibiting a vitiated, false sublime that tended to 'dazzle, or to mislead inexperienced minds'; he cited Pope's 705–13 and 109–14 by way of exhibiting the unnatural extravagance (and thus moral badness) of the horrors in Statius. In his 1797 edition of Pope's *Works* (II.169–239), Warton continued the critique of Statius's 'bloated magnificence of description, gigantic images, and pompous diction' (II.174), compared with the chastity and propriety of Virgil, but added a more refined appreciation of the strengths (and weaknesses) of Pope's own version. He comments on Pope's 132–83, and especially 150–60: 'Great is the force and the spirit of these lines . . . a surprising effort in a writer so young'. Johnson more soberly comments: 'He must have been at this time, if he had no help, a considerable proficient in the Latin tongue' (Lonsdale, IV.3).

THE
FIRST BOOK
OF
STATIUS
HIS
THEBAIS.

Translated By Mr. *POPE.*

Title. *1751:* THEBAIS of STATIUS. | BOOK I.
  Translated by Mr. *POPE: 1717–41:* Translated in the Year 1703.

The Argument.

OEdipus *King of* Thebes *having by mistake slain his Father* Laius, *and marry'd his Mother* Jocasta, *put out his own Eyes, and resign'd the Realm to his Sons,* Etheocles *and* Polynices. *Being neglected by them, he makes his Prayer to the Fury* Tisiphone, *to sow Debate betwixt the Brothers. They agree at last to Reign singly, each a Year by turns, and the first Lot is obtain'd by* Etheocles: *The Murmurs of the People on this occasion are describ'd in an excellent Speech.* Jupiter, *in a Council of the Gods, declares his Resolution of punishing the* Thebans, *and* Argives *also, by means of a Marriage betwixt* Polynices *and one of the Daughters of* Adrastus *King of* Argos. Juno *opposes, but to no effect; and* Mercury *is sent on a Message to the Shades, to the Ghost of* Laius, *who is to appear to* Etheocles, *and provoke him to break the Agreement.* Polynices *in the mean time departs from* Thebes *by Night, is overtaken by a Storm, and arrives at* Argos; *where he meets with* Tydeus, *who had fled from* Calydon, *having kill'd his Brother.* Adrastus *entertains them,*

The Argument: *1751:* ARGUMENT
6–7. The Murmurs ... Speech: *1717–51: omitted*

---

1. OEdipus: The story was widely known from classical sources, including dramatisations by Sophocles and Seneca, and from Dryden and Lee's tragedy *Oedipus* (1679), which, however, ends in the suicide of the main character before the point reached in the current story. Observations on Homer's version of the legend, which appears in Pope's translation of the *Odyssey*, XI.317–40, are given in a note to XI.319.

Thebes: major Greek city of Boeotia, the region to the north-west of Attica on mainland Greece, site of Oedipus' abdication and the contested throne. Other classical sources for the story possibly known to Pope were the plays *Seven against Thebes*, by Aeschylus, and *The Phoenician Women*, by Euripides.

4. Fury Tisiphone: The Furies (or 'Erinyes' or 'Eumenides') were semi-deities in female form dedicated to the avenging of family crimes; cf. 'Sapho to Phaon', 159; *Ode for Musick*, 68. 'Tisiphone' is one of the individual Furies named in sources such as Virgil.

6–7. Murmurs of the People ... excellent Speech: The removal of this comment in 1717 was perhaps prompted by its political suggestiveness after the 1715 Jacobite rising. The section referred to is 224–72.

7. Jupiter: king of the classical gods, also known as Zeus (Greek) and Jove (Latin).

9. Argos: capital of the Argolis or region of Greece immediately south-west of the isthmus at Corinth.

Juno: Jupiter's wife and half-sister, the Roman equivalent of Hera.

10. Mercury: the messenger god, the Roman equivalent of Hermes.

the Shades: the underworld.

13. Tydeus: son of Oeneus, king of Calydon; see 555.

15   *having receiv'd an Oracle from* Apollo *that his Daughters shou'd be marry'd to a Boar and a Lion, which he understands to be meant of these Strangers by whom the Hydes of those Beasts were worn, and who arriv'd at the time when he kept an annual Feast in honour of that God. The Rise of this Solemnity he relates to his Guests, the loves of* Phoebus *and* Psamathe, *and the Story of*
20   Coraebus. *He enquires, and is made acquainted with, their Descent and Quality; The Sacrifice is renew'd, and the Book concludes with a Hymn to* Apollo.

The Translator hopes he needs not Apologize for his Choice of this Piece, which was made almost in his Childhood. But finding the Version
25   better, upon Review, than he expected from those Years, he was easily prevail'd upon to give it some Correction, the rather, because no Part of this Author (at least that he knows of) has been tolerably turn'd into our Language.

23–28. **The Translator . . . into our Language:** *1717:* omitted.
24–28. **Version . . . our Language:** *1736a–51:* Version better than he expected, he gave it some Correction a few Years afterwards.

---

15. Apollo: son of Jove by Leto (Latona in Latin); god of prophecy, archery, music, the sun, and of medicine.
19. Phoebus: alternative name for Apollo.
  Psamathe: daughter of Crotopus, king of Argos; cf. 669.
20. Coraebus: or Coroebus or Choroebus; see 714–89.
24. almost . . . Childhood: see Headnote.
26-7. no Part . . . Author: For Pope's knowledge of at least one version, see Headnote.

THE
FIRST BOOK
OF
STATIUS his Thebais.

F Raternal Rage, the guilty *Thebe's* Alarms,
Th' Alternate Reign destroy'd by Impious Arms,
Demand our Song; a sacred Fury fires
My ravish'd Breast, and All the Muse inspires.
5   O Goddess, say, shall I deduce my Rhimes
From the dire Nation in its early Times,
Europa's Rape, *Agenor's* stern Decree,

1. Thebe's: 1717–51: Thebes

---

1. Closely modelled on 'Fraternas acies' ('brotherly battles'), Statius, 1.
2. Alternate Reign: i.e. the pattern of exchanging the throne of Thebes each year, as set out in 'The Argument'. Stephens, *An Essay upon Statius,* I.3 (1648), p. 1 (see Headnote), has 'alternate Crown'.

   Impious Arms: cf. *Essay on Criticism,* 712 and Commentary; and 198 and 211 below.
3-4. Statius, 3, has 'Pierius menti calor incidit' ('Pierian heat of mind incites').
3. sacred Fury: Stephens, *Essay,* 1, p. 1: 'A Sacred heat inflames me'. Cf. 'sacred Rage' for poetic inspiration in *Windsor-Forest,* 289 and Commentary.
5. deduce: 'to draw in a regular connected series, from one time or event to another' (*SJ*, citing this passage). Maxwell (1964: 56) suggests a model in Dryden, 'The First Book of Ovid's Metamorphoses', 5–6, *Examen Poeticum* (1693), p. 1: 'And add perpetual Tenour to my Rhimes, | Deduc'd from Nature's Birth, to *Caesar's* Times'. In his letter to Cromwell, 19 Jan 1708, *Corr.,* I.36, Pope cites this opening passage as one of the author's faults: 'In the Very beginning he Unluckily betrays his Ignorance in the rules of Poetry (which *Horace* had already taught the Romans) when he asks his Muse *where to begin his* THEBAID & seems to doubt whether it should not be, *ab Ovo Ledaeo*?'
6. dire: 'dreadful; dismal; mournful; horrible; terrible; evil in a great degree' (*SJ*). A Latinism, based on Statius, 4, 'gentisne ... dirae' ('of the cruel [or terrible] people'). *EC* states that it means 'ill-omened'. 'Dirae' is a name for the 'Furies' (see Commentary to 73–6). Pope uses 'dire' or 'direful' nine times in the poem; cf. the parodic usage in 'The Rape of the Locke', I.1.
7. Europa's Rape: Statius, 5, refers to the 'Sidonios raptus' ('Sidonian rape'), because of Europa's origin in the Phoenician city

And *Cadmus* searching round the spacious Sea?
How with the Serpent's Teeth he sow'd the Soil,
10   And reap'd an Iron Harvest of his Toil;
Or how from joyning Stones the City sprung,
While to his Harp Divine *Amphion* sung?
Or shall I *Juno*'s Hate to *Thebes* resound,
Whose fatal Rage th' unhappy Monarch found;

---

of Sidon, but Stephens, *Essay*, 6, p. 1, has 'Europa's rape'. For the Latin significance of 'rape' see Headnote to 'The Rape of the Locke'. Some versions of the story make Europa the mother of Sarpedon (see Commentary to Pope's preface to the 'Episode of Sarpedon').

stern Decree: Agenor, king of Tyre commanded his son Cadmus to find Europa, his daughter, abducted by Jupiter in the likeness of a bull, telling him not to return if he failed. Pope recalled the phrase in his *Iliad*, XVI.1038. The story is also told in Ovid, *Metamorphoses*, III, translated by Addison in *Poetical Miscellanies: The Fifth Part* (1704), pp. 509-92.

8-10. Cadmus went into Boeotia, slew a dragon which had killed his men, and sowed the dragon's teeth; these sprouted as armed men, who killed each other until five were left; with these five Cadmus founded the city which later became Thebes. Pope's lines clarify a more obscure reference to the story in Statius, 7-8.

10. Iron Harvest: TE cites Virgil, *Aeneid*, XII.663-4 'seges ... horret | ferrea', and Dryden's translation, XII.964, *Works of Virgil* (1697), p. 607: 'An Iron Harvest mounts'. Dryden had previously used the phrase (of Luther) in *The Hind and the Panther*, III.643 (1687), p. 109: 'He sow'd the *Serpent*'s teeth, an iron-harvest rose'. It was current in the militaristic poetry of Pope's era, e.g. Samuel Wesley, *Marlborough: or, the Fate of Europe* (1705), p. 3: 'The *Dragons Teeth* fierce New-born *Armies* yield, | An *Iron Harvest* round the moisten'd Field'.

11-12. The city walls of Thebes were built, in one version of the story, by Amphion and Zethus, sons of Jupiter and Antiope, Amphion using the power of music to move the stones; see Commentary to 'January and May', 324; *Ode for Musick*, 35^6 variant; and the long note to Pope's *Odyssey*, XI.319, in which it is observed that the story is not found in Homer.

13. Juno: wife of Jupiter. Her antipathy to Thebes is traced back to her jealousy of Europa. Pope omits here Statius' reference (11) to Bacchus, whose mother Semele, a daughter of Cadmus, was killed because of Juno's jealousy; see next note and below, 361.

14-18. Athamas (the 'unhappy Monarch' of 14, named in Statius, 13), one of the kings of Thebes, had two sons with Ino, another daughter of Cadmus; they fostered Semele's son Bacchus, and Juno caused the fury Tisiphone (see 85) to drive both Athamas and Ino mad. Athamas killed one son and Ino jumped with the other, Melicertes, into the sea; they were metamorphosed into sea gods, Leucothea and Palaemon. Cf. 167-8, 324. Pope omits the names, most of which Statius gives and Stephens retains, but adds other details.

15   The Sire against the Son his Arrows drew,
     O'er the wide Fields the furious Mother flew,
     And while her Arms her Second Hope contain,
     Sprung from the Rocks, and plung'd into the Main.

     But wave whate'er to *Cadmus* may belong,
20   And fix, O Muse! the Barrier of thy Song,
     At *Oedipus* — from his Disasters trace
     The long Confusions of his guilty Race.
     Nor yet attempt to stretch thy bolder Wing,
     And mighty *Caesar*'s conqu'ring Eagles sing;

---

17. **her Second:** *1741–51:* a second

---

15. **Sire:** father.
17. **Second Hope:** i.e. Melicertes. For the phrasing, cf. *Windsor-Forest*, 81–3. Not in Statius.
18. **Sprung... Rocks:** not in Statius.
   Main: ocean.
19. **wave:** i.e. waive, pass over.
20. **Barrier:** translating Statius' 'limes' ('boundary line'), 16. *SJ* cites this passage (under 'Barrier') as an illustration of the sense 'boundary; limit'. *TE* cites Dryden, *Aeneid*, XII.1301, *Works of Virgil* (1697), p. 617: 'Barrier of the Ground'. Pope quotes Statius, 16–17, in his letter to Cromwell, 10 June 1709, *Corr.*, I.64, as an example of Statius' confusion of purpose in the early lines.
22. **long Confusions:** extended history of trouble. Statius, 17, has 'Oedipodae confusa domus' ('the disorderly house [or family] of Oedipus').
   guilty Race: cf. 340. Pope recalled this phrase in his *Iliad*, VIII.684, and had perhaps observed it in religious verse, e.g. the Tate and Brady, *A New Version of the Psalms of David*, XXI.10 (1696), p. 38: 'Ravage all their guilty Race, | And to their Seed descend'.

23. **bolder Wing:** recalling Milton, *Paradise Lost*, III.14 (1674), p. 61: 'Thee I re-visit now with bolder wing'. Not in Statius; it represents the 'flight' of sublime verse, as in *Essay on Criticism*, 151 and Commentary.
24. **Caesar:** For Statius this was Domitian, emperor of Rome from AD 81 until he was assassinated in 96; an authoritarian figure latterly driven by lust, cruelty and paranoia, with a strong but unreliable interest in poetry and an unpredictable inclination to censorship, according to his early biographer, Suetonius (*De Vita Caesarum*, c. 120 AD), though modern historians are more inclined to credit his relatively long reign with stable government. He was celebrated, perhaps ironically, in the epigrams of Martial and attacked in the satires of Juvenal (e.g. IV). Statius (17–31) does not mention 'Caesar' directly at all, referring to these triumphs in a series of passive constructions; Pope follows Stephens in this more direct usage. Pope's 'conqu'ring Eagles' are likewise merely 'signa' ('standards'), in Statius, 18; cf. *Essay on Criticism*, 687. Pope significantly strengthens the tone and elaborates the detail of the panegyric in this section; see Headnote: Context.

25 How twice the Mountains ran with *Dacian* Blood,
And trembling *Ister* check'd his rapid Flood;
How twice he vanquish'd where the *Rhine* does roll,
And stretch'd his Empire to the frozen Pole;
Or long before, with early Valour strove
30 In youthful Arms t'assert the Cause of *Jove.*
And Thou, great Heir of all thy Father's Fame,
Encrease of Glory to the *Latian* Name;
Oh bless thy *Rome* with an Eternal Reign,

25–7. 1717–51: How twice he tam'd proud *Ister*'s rapid flood,
While *Dacian* mountains stream'd with barb'rous blood;
Twice taught the *Rhine* beneath his laws to roll,

---

26. Ister: the Danube (cf. *Windsor-Forest*, 366), along with the Rhine a constant battle ground as the northern border of the Empire in Domitian's time. He visited the disputed area on three campaigns between 82 and 89, with mixed success; having defeated in 83 the Chatti he received one formal 'triumph' at Rome, taking the title 'Germanicus' in celebration. But he was defeated by the Germanic tribes the Quadi and the Marcomanni in Dacia, north of the Danube; unusually, peace was made in AD 90 at the cost of paying annual tribute to the Dacian general Decebalus. Statius is supposed to have composed a poem, *De Bello Germanico*, now lost, as propaganda for the emperor on the occasion.

26 variant. barb'rous blood: cf. Sir Richard Fanshawe's translation of *The Lusiad, or, Portugals Historicall Poem*, Canto III. st. 85 (1655), p. 63: 'he with barb'rous blood made BETIS swell'.

27. Domitian annexed the Taunus district between the Rhine and the Main.

28. frozen Pole: as TE notes, an expansion of Statius' 'Arctoos ... triumphos' ('Northern ... triumphs'). Cf. *Windsor-Forest*, 388.

29–30. During the last fighting between the adherents of Vespasian and Vitellius, AD 69, Domitian hid in the temple on the Capitol at Rome. After his father's accession Domitian built a small temple to 'Jupiter the Saviour' with an altar on which a marble relief told of the adventure; in his own reign he built an enormous temple to 'Jupiter the Guardian', with a statue of himself sitting in the god's lap (Tacitus, *Histories*, III.74).

31. thy Father's Fame: Vespasian, emperor of Rome AD 69–79, regarded by Suetonius as a moderate and capable figure (*De Vita Caesarum*). Named by Stephens, *Essay*, 27, p. 2, but not by Statius. Domitian was his younger son; the elder, Titus, ruled first, providing Statius (and Pope) with a model of brotherly rule which faintly mirrors the action of the poem.

32. Latian: the area along the coast south of Rome, site of the pre-Roman civilisation and hence an archaising term for Rome's ancient history.

33–4. The couplet is expanded from Statius, 24: 'aeternum sibi Roma cupit' ('Rome desires [you] forever her own').

Nor let desiring Worlds intreat in vain!
35 What tho' the Stars contract their Heav'nly Space,
And crowd their shining Ranks to yield thee place;
Tho' all the Skies, ambitious of thy Sway,
Conspire to court thee from our World away;
Tho' *Phoebus* longs to mix his Rays with thine,
40 And in thy Glories more serenely shine;
Tho' *Jove* himself no less content wou'd be,
To part his Throne and share his Heav'n with thee;
Yet stay, great *Caesar*! and vouchsafe to reign
O'er the wide Earth, and o'er the watry Main,
45 Resign to *Jove* his Empire of the Skies,
And People Heav'n with *Roman* Deities.

The Time will come, when a diviner Flame

---

34. **vain!:** *1736a–51:* vain.

35–8. Much expanded and rephrased from Statius, 24–8, including a cut, 26, referring to skies 'Pleiadum Boreaeque et hiulci fulminis expers' ('unaware of the Pleiades, Boreas and the shattering thunderbolt').

36. A reference to the customary deification of an emperor at his death, whereby he became 'divus', or divine, and potentially embodied in a constellation. Domitian was reported to have adopted divine honours during his lifetime, an exceptional move. After his actual death his memory was condemned to oblivion by the Senate (Suetonius, chapters 13 and 23). The transformation of Belinda's lock into a constellation in 'The Rape of the Locke' (II.172–3) is in part a parody of this process.

39. Phoebus: not named in Statius (Stephens, *Essay*, 32, p. 2, has '*Apollo*'); implied by 'ignipedum frenator equorum' ('the bridler of fire-footed horses'), 27. Pope has cut this and deepened the extent of respect for the emperor; in Statius, 28–9, the god would 'ipse tuis alte radiantem crinibus arcum | imprimat' ('himself place the high radiant band on your hair'). Addison quotes this and the next line of Pope in his posthumous *Dialogues upon the Usefulness of Ancient Medals* (1726), p. 112.

40. Pope's addition.

43–6. These lines were also quoted by Addison in his *Dialogues upon the Usefulness of Ancient Medals*, p. 89. They were, conversely, cited by Concanen as examples of Pope's 'Florid' and 'Unmeaning' false sublimity in his *Supplement to the Profund* (1728), pp. 7–8; Mack (1982: 403) records that Pope responded in the margins of his copy with a comment (too cropped to be fully legible) about Concanen's ignorance of the deification custom.

46. A large expansion of Statius, 31, 'et sidera dones' ('and give stars'), i.e. create constellations in the name of the Imperial family.

47–8. Expanded from Statius, 32–3, 'cum Pierio tua fortior oestro | facta canam' ('when bolder with Pierian frenzy I shall sing your deeds').

47. Cf. Stephens, *Essay*, 39, p. 2: 'The time may come, when a diviner rage'. Statius, 32, has 'tempus erit', 'the time will be'.

diviner Flame: cf. 'To the unknown Author of this Admirable Poem', in Dryden, *Absalom and Achitophel* (1681), sig. A4[r]: 'Scarce a Diviner flame inspir'd the King'.

Shall warm my Breast to sing of *Caesar*'s Fame:
Mean while permit that my preluding Muse
50   In *Theban* Wars an humbler Theme may chuse:
Of furious Hate surviving Death, she sings,
A fatal Throne to two contending Kings,
And Fun'ral Flames, that parting wide in Air,
Express the Discord of the Souls they bear:
55   Of Towns dispeopled, and the wandring Ghosts
Of Kings unbury'd, on the wasted Coasts;
When *Dirce*'s Fountain blush'd with *Grecian* Blood,
And *Thetis*, near *Ismenos*' swelling Flood,
With Dread beheld the rolling Surges sweep
60   In Heaps his slaughter'd Sons into the Deep.

---

56. on: *1736b–51:* in

---

49. More deferential than in Statius, 33–4, 'nunc tendo chelyn; satis arma referre | Aonia' ('at present I stretch sufficiently my lyre to recount Aonian wars').

preluding Muse: i.e. this epic is a prelude to the greater epic (of Domitian's glories) to follow, though this phrase has no direct equivalent in Pope's source. Statius left an epic of Achilles unfinished at his death; see Headnote.

50. Theban: a clarification of Statius' 'Aonian'; the Aonians were the inhabitants of Boeotia before the arrival of Cadmus.

51–4. Though (eventually) burned on adjoining funeral pyres, the smoke from the bodies of Eteocles and Polynices remained separate; Statius presents the story at XII.429–46.

52. contending Kings: The phrase is in Shakespeare's *Rape of Lucrece*, 939, and, more politically, in *An Idyll on the Peace* (1697), p. 4; it is also the opening phrase of Tickell's 'To the Lord Privy-Seal', *On the Prospect of Peace* (see *Windsor-Forest*). Pope used it again in the 1730 variants to *Ode for Musick*, 35^6. In Statius, 34, they are 'geminis... tyrannis' ('twin tyrants'). Aden (1978: 84) sees this as the opening of Pope's covert political agenda in the poem.

53–4. *EC* contends that Pope's lines are closer to Stephens, *Essay*, 47–8, p. 3: 'funeral flames | Divided, like the soules they carry', than to Statius: 'flammasque rebelles | seditione rogi' ('the rebel flames in the unrest of the funeral pyre').

55. Towns dispeopled: cf. *Windsor-Forest*, 47; Defoe, *The True-Born Englishman*, 183 (1701), p. 14, has 'dispeopled Towns'; in Milton, *Paradise Lost*, VII.151 (1674), p. 178, Heaven has been 'dispeopl'd'.

wandring Ghosts: not in Statius.

56. wasted Coasts: coastlines laid waste by war. Not in Statius. Cf. Thomas Ross's translation from Silius Italicus, *The Second Punick War between Hannibal, and the Romanes* (1661), p. 440: 'By whom my wasted Coasts invaded are'.

57–8. Dirce...Ismenos: respectively a spring, and a river of Thebes into which the spring flowed.

57. Cf. Stephens, *Essay*, 51, p. 3: 'When *Dirce* blush'd, being stain'd with *Graecian* bloud'.

58. Thetis: sea-nymph, daughter of Nereus, mother of Achilles.

59–60. Pope has cut the description (39) of the Ismenos as 'arentes adsuetum stringere ripas' ('accustomed to graze arid banks'), and enhanced the image of the slaughter; 60 in particular is his addition.

>   What Hero, *Clio*! wilt thou first relate?
>   The raging *Tydeus*, or the Prophet's Fate?
>   Or how with Hills of slain on ev'ry side,
>   *Hippomedon* repell'd the hostile Tyde?
> 65   Or how the Youth with ev'ry Grace adorn'd,
>   Untimely fell, to be for ever mourn'd?
>   Then to fierce *Capaneus* thy Verse extend,
>   And sing, with Horror, his prodigious End.
>
>   Now wretched *Oedipus*, depriv'd of Sight,
> 70   Led a long Death in everlasting Night;
>   But while he dwells where not a chearful Ray
>   Can pierce the Darkness, and abhors the Day;

65, n. Parthenopaeus.

---

62. The raging: *1736a–51:* The Rage of

61–7. The Seven who fought against Thebes in Polynices' campaign to seize the throne, the subject of Statius' poem as a whole.

61. Clio: the muse of History.

62. raging Tydeus: At his death, related by Statius at VIII.751–62, Tydeus bites into the severed head of his dead enemy Melanippus, an incident used by Pope in his note to his version of *Iliad*, XXII.437, as an instance of the greater horror indulged in by Statius.

Prophet's Fate: One of the Seven, Amphiarus foretold that all the seven would die except Adrastus (king of Argos). In the later version of the story in book VIII, Jove causes the earth to swallow Amphiarus and his chariot rather than allow him to be killed by the Thebans: Statius alludes to the 'subitos hiatus' ('sudden gaps') here (42), but Pope keeps his 'Fate' vague.

63–4. Hippomedon: One of the Seven, he slew so many that the bodies blocked the river Ismenos, which was rising in answer to the prayer of the mother of one of his victims. The death of Hippomedon is described in book IX of Statius' poem.

63. Hills of slain: not in Statius. Perhaps recalled from Addison, *The Campaign*, 16 (1704), p. 2; reused by Pope in his *Iliad*, X.356.

65–6. Parthenopaeus, one of the Seven, son of Atalanta of Calydon; killed at Thebes (book IX of Statius). In Statius (45), referred to as an unnamed Arcadian; the name is given in Stephens, *Essay*, 60, p. 3.

67–8. Capaneus: another of the Seven, was killed as he climbed over the walls of Thebes by a thunderbolt from Jove, whose power he had boastingly insulted (this action concludes book X of Statius).

68. prodigious: 'astonishing...portentous...such as may seem a prodigy' (*SJ*), because caused by a divine act.

69–70. Pope cuts Statius' clear statement that Oedipus had blinded himself out of guilt (46–7), transferring it to 78. For further analysis on Pope's version of this section see Sowerby (2006: 223–5).

73–6. Statius, 52, refers to the 'saeva dies animi' ('savage daylight of mind'), and the 'scelerumque in pectore Dirae' ('avenging Furies of his crimes in his heart').

The clear, reflecting Mind, presents his Sin
In frightful Views, and makes it Day within;
75   Returning Thoughts in endless Circles roll,
And thousand Furies haunt his guilty Soul.
The Wretch then lifted to th' unpitying Skies
Those empty Orbs, from whence he tore his Eyes,
Whose Wounds yet fresh, with bloody Hands he strook,
80   While from his Breast these dreadful Accents broke.

Ye Gods that o'er the gloomy Regions reign
Where guilty Spirits feel Eternal Pain;
Thou, sable *Styx*! whose livid Streams are roll'd
Thro' dreary Coasts which I, tho' Blind, behold:
85   *Tisiphone*! that oft hast heard my Pray'r,
Assist, if *Oedipus* deserve thy Care!
If you receiv'd me from *Jocasta*'s Womb,
And nurst the Hope of Mischiefs yet to come:
If leaving *Polybus*, I took my Way

---

73. reflecting: punning, according to Sowerby (2006: 225), on mirror-type reflection and thoughtful pondering.

77. unpitying Skies: not in Statius.

78. Orbs: eye-sockets.

79. strook: struck. *TE* note that Statius' lines 54–5: 'manibusque cruentis | pulsat inane solum' could mean 'and with hands dripping blood beats the hollow earth' or 'and with hands dripping blood beats the empty eye-socket'. Pope takes the latter line (Stephens interprets it the other way, *Essay*, 73–4, p. 3). Beating the earth would be a means of invoking underworld gods. Lewis, in his 1767 *Thebaid* (see Headnote), sides with Pope (I.71), giving a note on the problem.

80. Accents: 'language or words' (*SJ*), signalling this as a 'poetical' usage).

81. gloomy Regions: specifically Tartarus, a region of Hell, in Statius, 56. For the phrase cf. Blackmore, *Prince Arthur*, VI (1695), p. 178: 'From all their gloomy Regions to his Court, | At his Command, th' Infernal Lords resort'.

83. sable Styx: main river of Hades, the underworld; 'sable', black, is Pope's addition. Pope uses 'sable flood' in for 'dark river' in *Iliad*, II.1000, and ironically for the Thames in *The Dunciad Variorum*, II.331.

livid: 'discloured, as with a blow; black and blue' (*SJ*), the Latin sense; Statius (57) has 'livida'.

84. dreary Coasts: cf. *Ode for Musick*, 54. Not in Statius.

85. Tisiphone: see Argument, 4; one of the *Erinyes* or 'Furies' responsible for punishing crimes within the family. Pope omits here Statius, 59: 'perversaque vota secunda' ('following perverse [or 'unnatural'] vows').

87. Jocasta: mother and wife of Oedipus, not named in Statius (60) or Stephens.

88. Pope's invention, replacing the detail in Statius (61) that Tisiphone is supposed to have nurtured and healed Oedipus (specifically the wound in his feet, inflicted by his father in response to the oracle which predicted he would kill his father; hence his Greek name, 'swollen foot').

89. Polybus: the King of Corinth who brought up the abandoned Oedipus; 'falso' ('false'), in Statius, 63; 'my supposed Father', Stephens, *Essay*, 82, p. 4.

90 To *Cyrrha's* Temple on that fatal Day,
    When by the Son the trembling Father dy'd,
    Where the three Roads the *Phocian* Fields divide:
    If I the *Sphynxe's* Riddles durst explain,
    Taught by thy self to win the promis'd Reign:
95 If wretched I, by baleful Furies led,
    With monstrous Mixture stain'd my Mother's Bed,
    For Hell and Thee begot an impious Brood,
    And with full Lust those horrid Joys renew'd:
    Then self-condemn'd to Shades of endless Night,
100 Tore from these Orbs the bleeding Balls of Sight.
    Oh hear, and aid the Vengeance I require;
    If worthy Thee, and what Thou might'st inspire!
    My Sons their old, unhappy Sire despise,
    Spoil'd of his Kingdom, and depriv'd of Eyes;

---

100. **Tore:** *1717–51:* Forc'd

---

90. Cyrrha's Temple: at the Castalian spring north-east of Delphi, site of the oracle consulted by Oedipus; see 831. Statius, 62–3, locates the scene more obscurely near 'the lake of Cirrha'.

91. Son ... Father: the antithesis is less marked in Statius, 65–6, where Oedipus claims to have cut the face of the trembling old man (Laius) while 'quaero patrem' ('I seek my father').

92. three Roads ... Phocian Fields: 'trifidaeque in Phocidos arto' ('in the strait of three-forked Phocis'), Statius, 64: site of the parricide. Phocia is north-west of Boeotia in central Greece.

93. Sphynxe's Riddles: Oedipus became king of Thebes (and husband of Jocasta) after solving a riddle set by the Sphinx, a monster which preyed on Cadmus' people.

95. Statius' Oedipus is not led to his mother's bed by 'baleful Furies', though the phrase might be suggested by the 'dulces furias' ('sweet furies', i.e. passions) he enjoyed there.

96. monstrous: 'deviating from the stated order of nature ... shocking, hateful' (*SJ*).

Mixture: sexual intercourse (*OED*, sense 6). Dryden uses the same combination of words to refer to father-daughter incest in 'Cinyras and Myrrha', 84.

stain'd ... Bed: TE notes that Stephens, *Essay*, 89, p. 4, also translates 'stain'd my Mothers bed'. Statius, 68–9, speaks of 'lamentabile matris | conubium gavisus' ('having enjoyed the deplorable marital bed of [my] mother').

97. Statius, 70: 'natosque tibi ... paravi' ('prepared children for you'). Pope's enhanced description is perhaps coloured by the allegory of Sin and Death (another incest narrative) in Milton, *Paradise Lost*, II.746–814.

98. horrid Joys: a phrase also used to denounce incest in Lee, *Constantine the Great*, III.i.(1684), p. 30.

99. Shades ... Night: Pope's addition; cf. 137.

100. bleeding Balls of Sight: cf. John Hopkins, 'To Amasia', *Amasia* (1700), p. 138, 'Hurl, hurl the Bleeding Balls ...'. In Statius, 72, Oedipus literally places the torn-out eyes on his mother.

101. aid ... require: Pope's addition.

103. Sire: father.

105	Guideless I wander, unreguarded mourn,
	While These exalt their Scepters o'er my Urn;
	These Sons, ye Gods! who with flagitious Pride
	Insult my Darkness, and my Groans deride.
	Art thou a Father, unregarding *Jove*!
110	And sleeps thy Thunder in the Realms above?
	Thou *Fury*, then, some lasting Curse entail,
	Which shall o'er long Posterity prevail:
	Place on their Heads that Crown distain'd with Gore,
	Which these dire Hands from my slain Father tore;
115	Go, and a Parent's heavy Curses bear;
	Break all the Bonds of Nature, and prepare
	Their kindred Souls to mutual Hate and War.

112. 1717–51: Which o'er their childrens children shall prevail:

---

105. unreguarded: an unusual but not unexampled spelling of 'unregarded'; e.g. Dryden, 'Theodore and Honoria', 238, *Fables Ancient and Modern*, p. 266: 'My vain pursuit of unreguarded Love'. There is apparently no influence on pronunciation.

106. TE compares Stephens, *Essay*, 99, p. 4: 'Grown proud, they raise their Scepters from my urne'. Statius (77) has 'nostro iamdudum in funere reges' ('being kings, with us already long in the grave').

107. ye Gods!: In Statius (77) the address is 'pro dolor!' ('o anguish!'; 'O grievous smart!' Stephens, *Essay*, 98, p. 4).

flagitious: 'wicked; villainous; atrocious' (*SJ*); cf. *Essay on Criticism*, 530.

108. Insult: triumph over; cf. 337, and the usage in 'Episode of Sarpedon', 115, 316.

109. Father: Statius, 79–80, has Oedipus call Jove 'deorum | ignavus genitor' ('of gods the idle father'); Pope's rephrasing aligns Jove's position with Oedipus' own parental wrath.

unregarding: 'not regarding or taking heed; indifferent', *OED*. Pope uses it again at *Iliad*, XX.202. Cf. Behn, *The Widdow Ranter*, V.i (1690), p. 51: 'ye unregarding Gods is't possible?'

110. Pope's addition.

111. TE compares Stephens, *Essay*, 104, p. 5: 'Entaile a Curse'. 'Entail' has a slightly legal resonance, referring to the means normally adopted to ensure a line of male inheritance; the suggestion is not in Statius.

112 variant. EC compares Dryden's version of the *Aeneid*, III.132, *Works of Virgil*, p. 271: 'And Childrens Children shall the Crown sustain'. Statius (81) has 'totos … nepotes' ('all their offspring').

113–14. EC compares Stephens, *Essay*, 105–6, p. 5: 'Put on that Diadem besmeard with gore, | Which from my fathers head these fingers tore'.

113. distain'd with Gore: cf. 'Episode of Sarpedon', 294; the phrase is several times recalled in Pope's *Iliad*, e.g. V.447. To 'distain' is literally to stain, but also metaphorically to 'blot; to sully with infamy' (*SJ*).

114. dire Hands: cf. Thomas Ross, *An Essay Upon the Third Punique War* (1671), p. 11: 'her dire Hands the Lungs divide' (of a mother killing her child).

115. Statius, 83, has 'votis … paternis' ('prayers of a father').

116. Break … Nature: Pope's additional emphasis. EC compares Dryden, *Aeneid*, III.78, *Works of Virgil*, p. 269: 'Broke ev'ry Bond of Nature, and of Truth'.

Give them to dare, what I might wish to see,
Blind as I am, some glorious Villany!
120 Soon shalt thou find, if thou but arm their Hands,
Their ready Guilt preventing thy Commands:
Cou'dst thou some great, proportion'd Mischief frame,
They'd prove the Father from whose Loins they came.

The Fury heard, while on *Cocytus'* Brink
125 Her Snakes, unty'd, Sulphureous Waters drink;
But at the Summons, roll'd her Eyes around,
And snatch'd the starting Serpents from the Ground.
Not half so swiftly shoots along in Air
The gliding Lightning, or descending Star.
130 Thro' Crouds of Airy Shades she wing'd her Flight,
And dark Dominions of the silent Night;
Swift as she past, the flitting Ghosts withdrew,

---

118. Pope omits Oedipus' invocation (Statius, 85) of 'Tartarei regina barathri' ('Queen of the abyss of Tartarus'), and inserts 'to dare' as a means of producing an antithesis with 'to see'.

119. Blind as I am: Pope points up the contrast between Oedipus' wish to see the results of his prayer with his state of actual blindness, a contrast not noted in Statius; similarly, Pope's 'glorious Villainy' invents a dramatic oxymoron which is not in Statius (86), who has merely 'vidisse nefas' ('to have seen the crime').

120-3. Greatly expanded from Statius, 86-7, in the interests of balanced antithesis.

120. arm . . . Hands: Pope's addition.

121. preventing: anticipating. Pope's addition; in Statius, 86-7, 'nec tarda sequetur | mens iuvenum' ('and the mind of the young men will follow, not slow').

122. proportion'd: proportional, suitable. One of Pope's additions to the curse; in Statius, 87, Oedipus promises: 'modo digna veni, mea pignora nosces' ('only come in worthy form, you shall recognise my pledges'), punning on the senses of 'pledge' as 'promise' and 'pledge of love', i.e. children.

124. Cocytus: one of the rivers of the underworld.

126. roll'd . . . around: Pope's addition.

127. starting: startled. This image is Pope's addition; in Statius (92) the picking up of the loose snakes is not mentioned.

128-9. The awkward rhyme is uncommon (Dryden does not appear to use it) but not unexampled: e.g. J. S., *The Innocent Epicure: or, the Art of Angling. A Poem* (1697), p. 24.

129. Lightning: In Statius, 92, this is specifically 'igne Iovis' ('Jove's fire').

131. dark Dominions: perhaps recalled from II.652 of Dryden's 'Palamon and Arcite', *Fables*, p. 48, but Dryden had earlier used the phrase of the underworld in the second act of *The Indian Emperour* (1667), p. 17, and it was used of the world of the dead in Blackmore's *Prince Arthur*, III (1695), p. 71. Pope recalled it in the Homer translations, e.g. *Iliad*, XX.86. Pope's line replaces Statius, 95: 'et caligantes animarum examine campos' ('fields darkened with a crowd of souls').

132-3. Expanded from Statius, 92-3; the 'flitting Ghosts' and 'pale Spectres' are more vividly precise than Statius' 'inane | vulgus' ('empty crowd'). Cf. *Ode for Musick*, 49-61.

And the pale Spectres trembled at her View:
To th' Iron Gates of *Taenarus* she flies,
135   There spreads her dusky Pinions to the Skies.
The Day beheld, and sick'ning at the Sight,
Veil'd her fair Glories in the Shades of Night.
Affrighted *Atlas*, on the distant Shore,
Trembl'd, and shook the Heav'ns and Gods he bore,
140   Now from beneath *Malea*'s airy Height
She mounts aloft, and steers to *Thebes* her Flight,
Does with glad Speed the well-known Journey go,
Nor here regrets the Hell she left below.
A hundred Snakes her gloomy Visage shade,

139. **bore,:** *1736a–51:* bore.
141–3. *1717–51:* Aloft she sprung, and steer'd to *Thebes* her flight;
   With eager speed the well-known journey took,
   Nor here regrets the hell she late forsook.

133. **at her View:** 'at the sight of her'; or possibly, 'on her looking at them'.

134. **Taenarus:** or Taenarum, the south-central promontory at the end of the Peloponnese in south-western Greece, with a cave sometimes regarded as a portal to the underworld, hence the 'Iron Gates' ('Iron gate' in Stephens, *Essay*, 121, p. 5). Statius, 96, does not specify the material of the gate but calls it 'inremeabile' ('from which there is no return'). Pope is probably influenced by the 'gates of burning Adamant' at the limits of Hell in Milton, *Paradise Lost*, II.436 (1674), p. 40.

135. **Pinions:** wings. Not in Statius.

136–7. In Statius, 97–8, Day feels the presence of the Fury, and Night intrudes a dark cloud, startling the 'lucentes ... equos' ('shining horses').

137. **Shades of Night.** The final words of Milton, *Paradise Lost*, IV.1015.

138. **Atlas:** the Titan who holds up the heavens as a punishment for revolt; supposedly turned to rock (hence Mount Atlas) by Perseus, who showed him the Gorgon's head (see 637–8). In Statius, 98, he is 'procul arduus' ('far off and steep'); there is no 'Shore'.

139. **and Gods:** Pope's addition.

140–1. Mason (1987) suggests an alignment with Satan's flight in Milton, *Paradise Lost*, I.225–6 (1674), p. 9: 'Then with expanded wings he stears his flight | Aloft, incumbent on the dusky Air'.

140. **Malea:** promontory at the south-eastern extremity of the Peloponnese, known as a danger to shipping; in Statius, 100, she rises from Malea's 'valle', a 'vale', or 'plaines' in Stephens, *Essay*, 127, p. 5. Commentators such as Bowles found that Pope's positioning of the word forced an incorrect emphasis on the second syllable of the name.

142. **well-known Journey:** For Tisiphone's previous trip, see 14.

144–5. Statius, 104–5, mentions a hundred (horned) snakes, as does Stephens, *Essay*, 130, p. 5, but neither duplicates the image. Cf. John Harrington, 'Ode to Mercury', 17–18, *The Odes and Epodon of Horace* (1684), p. 64 (of Cerberus): 'though hundred *Snakes* | His Fury's head did *Guarding* throng'.

145   A hundred Serpents guard her horrid Head,
In her sunk Eye-balls dreadful Meteors glow,
Such Light does *Phoebe*'s bloody Orb bestow,
When lab'ring with strong Charms, she shoots from high
A fiery Gleam, and reddens all the Sky.
150   Blood stain'd her Cheeks, and from her Mouth there came
Blue steaming Poisons, and a Length of Flame;
From ev'ry Blast of her contagious Breath,
Famine and Drought proceed, and Plagues, and Death:
A Robe obscene was o'er her Shoulders thrown,
155   A Dress by Fates and Furies worn alone:
She tost her meagre Arms; her better Hand
In waving Circles whirl'd a Fun'ral Brand;
A curling Serpent from her left did rear

---

147. 1717–51: Such rays from *Phoebe*'s bloody circle flow,
158. 1717–51: A serpent from her left, was seen to rear

---

145. hundred Serpents: Pope recalls the detail for Jove's shield in *Iliad*, II.528; a similar image is in Dryden's *Aeneid*, VII.911.

   horrid: bristling, from the Latin 'horridus' (as in Statius, quoted in Commentary at 154 below; cf. the quotation from Milton in Commentary at 841–4 below.

146. In Statius, 105, the image is of 'ferrea lux' ('iron light'). *TE* cites Garth, *The Dispensary*, VI, sixth edition (1706), p. 105: 'In her parch'd Eye-balls fiery *Meteors* reign'.

147–9. Much expanded from Statius, 105–6, where the 'strong charms' are specifically 'Atracian'.

148. *TE* compares Milton, *Paradise Lost*, II.665–6 (1674), p. 47: 'while the labouring Moon | Eclipses at thir charms'. Cf. also Dryden, *Threnodia Augustalis*, 150–1 (1685), p. 8: 'like the labouring Moon, | By Charms of Art was hurried down'.

150. In Statius the poisoned blood ('sanie', 107) is causing the whole body to swell rather than being visible on the cheek.

152. contagious: infected. The line is Pope's addition.

154. obscene: 'offensive; disgusting; inauspicious; ill-omened' (*SJ*); cf. 735 below. Statius (109–10) has 'horrida ... palla' ('rough cloak'); Stephens calls the cloak 'tattered', *Essay*, 139, p. 6. In Dryden's *Aeneid*, VI.750–1, *Works of Virgil*, p. 384, 'dire *Tisiphone*' is 'Girt in her sanguine Gown, by Night and Day'. Pope has dropped Statius' 'et caerulei redeunt in pectora nodi' ('and blue knots join again on her chest').

155. In Statius, 111, the robe is said to be made anew by Proserpine, goddess of the underworld, and by Atropos, the 'Fate' who cuts the thread of life.

156. meagre: 'twin' ('geminis') in Statius, 112.

   better Hand: i.e. the right (the 'left' is in 158). Statius, 112–13, has simply 'haec ... haec' ('this hand ... that hand'). *EC* compares Dryden, *Aeneid*, X.582, *Works of Virgil*, p. 515: 'And from *Strimonius* hew'd his better Hand'. Cf. also II.984, X.772, XII.450.

157. Brand: burning torch.

158. did: the first of several expletives in the poem (cf. 170, 198, 204, 460, 510, 554, 668), some later removed, as here. Pope had mocked the use of such 'low' helps in *Essay on Criticism*, 349, and *TE* uses their presence here as evidence of early composition; but see Headnote, 'Composition and publication'.

His flaming Crest, and lash'd the yielding Air.

160 But when the Fury took her Stand on high,
Where vast *Cythaeron*'s Top salutes the Sky,
A Hiss from all the Snaky Tire went round;
The dreadful Signal all the Rocks rebound,
And thro' th' *Achaian* Cities send the Sound.
165 *Oete*, with high *Parnassus*, heard the Voice;
Eurota's Banks remurmur'd to the Noise;
Again *Leucothoë* shook at these Alarms,
And press'd *Palaemon* closer in her Arms.

---

159. **lash'd:** *1717–51:* lash

---

159. flaming Crest: In Statius, 113, the 'vivo ... hydro' is a 'live water-snake'. *TE* attributes the added crest to the inflationary influence of Dryden's habit of adding such features to snakes in his translations from Virgil, e.g. *Aeneid*, II.515, 643. But Milton's Satanic serpent also has a distinctive crest in *Paradise Lost*, IX.525 and 634.

yielding: Pope's addition. In Statius the Fury lashes the air with the snake, while in Pope the snake adopts the active role.

161. Cythaeron's Top: Cithaeron or Kithairon, a mountain range between Athens and Thebes; cf. 466.

salutes: greets or hails.

162. Snaky Tire: the serpents forming the headgear of the Fury; *SJ*, citing this passage, derives this form of 'tire' from 'tiara', or 'attire'; *OED*, 'tire', senses 1-3. Statius, 115, has 'crine virenti' ('from green hair').

163. rebound: echo; adapted from Statius, 116, 'congeminat' ('redouble').

164. Achaian: of the region of Greece on the north-east of the Peloponnese, sometimes used as a shorthand reference to Greece as a whole. The 'cities' are Pope's addition; in Statius the image is of the Achaian coastline. Pope omits Statius' reference, 117, to the 'Pelopea ... regna' ('realm of Pelops'), son of Tantalus and father of Atreus and Thyestes.

165. **Oete:** mountain south of Thessaly.

Parnassus: mountain in central Greece, just north of Delphi, associated with Apollo and the muses; cf. 739, and *Essay on Criticism*, 94.

166: **Eurota:** 'Eurotas' in Statius, 119, the main river in Laconia (Sparta).

remurmur'd: cf. 'Winter', 64. *OED*, referring to the word as 'chiefly poetical', cites nothing earlier than Dryden's Virgil translations of 1697; *TE* cites the version of *Aeneid*, VI.964, *Works of Virgil*, p. 391: 'The Rivers and the Rocks remurmur to the Sound'. Pope omits the rest of Statius, 119–20, in which the mountain Oete staggers with the noise and Isthmus (cf. 470–3) is scarcely able to withstand the seas on either side. In his letter to Cromwell, 10 June 1709, *Corr.*, I.64, he cites these two lines of Statius as 'most extravagantly hyperbolical', and one of the 'numberless particulars blame-worthy in our Author, which I have try'd to soften in the version'.

167–8. Referring to the part of the story already mentioned, 14–18; Palaemon is mentioned in Statius, 122, but Leucothoë is referred to (121) not by name but as his 'genetrix' (mother); in Statius (and Stephens, *Essay*, 150–2, p. 6) she snatches him from a wandering dolphin he is riding on.

Headlong from thence the Fury urg'd her Flight,
170 And at the *Theban* Palace did alight,
Once more invades the guilty Dome, and shrouds
Its bright Pavilions in a Veil of Clouds.
Strait with the Rage of all their Race possest,
Stung to the Soul, the Brothers start from Rest,
175 And all the Furies wake within their Breast.
Their tortur'd Minds repining Envy tears,
And Hate, engender'd by suspicious Fears;
And sacred Thirst of Sway; and all the Ties

173, n. 1717–51: Gentilisque animos subit furor, *seems to me a better* [*1751: seems a better*] *reading than* Gentilesque.

169–70. 1717–51: Headlong from thence the glowing fury springs,
  And o'er the *Theban* palace spreads her wings,
175. **the Furies:** *1736b–51:* their furies

---

169 variant. glowing: Pope's addition. Of the variant couplet as a whole, Warton (*Works of Pope*, II.187) declares: 'A great image, and highly improved from the original, assuetâ nube!' (for the Latin tag see next note).

171–2. TE draws attention to Pope's variations on Statius, 123–4: 'Atque ea Cadmeo praeceps ubi culmine primum | constitit adsuetaque infecit nube penates' ('then she descended at once upon the Cadmean roof-ridge and struck the household with customary cloud'). TE suggests that 'Dome' means 'mansion' (carrying something of the Latin sense of 'domus' as 'house and family') and that the 'pavilions' are prompted by illustrations to Ogilby's translation of Homer, one of Pope's favourite early books (see Headnote to the 'Episode of Sarpedon'). Ogilby does not use the actual word. Cf. Dryden, 'Theodore and Honoria', 257, *Fables*, p. 266: 'proud Pavilion'; and Defoe, *A Hymn to Peace*, 344 (1706), p. 22, the 'bright Pavilion' of Peace.

173. Rage: madness.

173 Pope's note. Modern editions retain 'gentilesque' at Statius, 126; in the context of Pope's rendering, the difference is not significant.

174. Pope's addition.

176–83. Aden (1978: 84) emphasises the possible allusion to the contemporary political situation of Pope's day here.

176. repining: vexed, resentful.

178–99. According to his letter to Cromwell, 19 January 1707/8, Pope's first draft did not contain a version of this section (Statius, 128–43); see Headnote.

178. sacred Thirst of Sway: TE glosses 'sacred' as 'accursed' on the score of the Latin, 'sacer', which can mean 'devoted to an infernal deity'; e.g. Virgil, *Aeneid*, III.57, 'auri sacra fames' ('cursed hunger for gold'). Cf. *Essay on Criticism*, 522 and Commentary. A similar phrase is found in similar contexts in Fanshawe, *Lusiad*, III.32 (1655), p. 52: 'sacred Thirst of *Raign*', and in the final scene of Thomas Southerne, *Oroonoko* (1696), p. 79: 'burning with the sacred Thirst of Sway'. Aden (1978: 84) suggests that Pope heightens the political language of the moment indicating both James II and William III, but Statius, 127–8, does have 'regendi | saevus amor' ('savage love of ruling').

Of Nature broke; and Royal Perjuries;
180 And impotent Desire to Reign alone,
That scorns the dull Reversion of a Throne;
Each wou'd the sweets of Sovereign Rule devour,
While Discord waits upon divided Pow'r.

As stubborn Steers by brawny Plowmen broke,
185 And join'd reluctant to the galling Yoke,
Alike disdain with servile Necks to bear
Th' unwonted Weight, or drag the crooked Share,
But rend the Reins, and bound a diff'rent way,
And all the Furrows in Confusion lay:
190 Such was the Discord of the Royal Pair,
Whom Fury drove precipitate to War.
In vain the Chiefs contriv'd a specious way,

178-9. Ties ... broke: In his 1838-9 entry, 'Pope', in *Encyclopaedia Britannica*, De Quincey views this line as a mistranslation, taking 'vices' ('alternations') to indicate the formal agreement to reign alternately (*Works*, XIII.250). Aden (1978: 84) views it as an addition, Pope thinking of the 'Ties of Nature' broken in the Glorious Revolution of 1688.

179. Royal Perjuries: Statius, 128, does not mention the specifically 'Royal' nature of the broken promises.

180. impotent Desire: Pope's addition, perhaps alluding to the frustrations of both James II and William III.

181-2. De Quincey, despite his objections to Pope's failures as a linguist, identified this couplet as an example of the 'perfectly astonishing' felicity sometimes reached by Pope's translation: here Pope 'most judiciously, by reversing the two clauses [in Statius, 128-30], gains the power of fusing them into connection' (*Works*, XIII.250).

181. Reversion: 'The right of succeeding to the possession of something, or of obtaining something at a future time; the action or process of transferring something in this way' (*OED*, sense 3a). There is a Latinate suggestion of something 'reverting' to a legal or political right. Cf. 'Is there no bright Reversion in the Sky', 'Verses to the Memory of an Unfortunate Lady', 9. Cf. also 'To the Author of a Poem, intitled, Successio', 23-4.

183. Discord: Statius, 130: 'sociisque comes discordia regnis' ('discord, companion of shared rule'). The goddess 'Eris', 'strife', known from Homer and Hesiod, lies behind the image; cf. *Windsor-Forest*, 412.

184-5. Cf. 'Vertumnus and Pomona', 36.

184. stubborn Steers: for Statius, 131, 'delectos per torva armenta iuvencos' ('young bullocks chosen from the wild herd').

brawny Plowmen: Pope's substitution for 'agricola' ('farmer'), Statius, 132.

broke: broken in, tamed.

187. crooked Share: ploughshare.

188. Reins: As Bowles notes, this word implies the use of horses, not oxen (Statius, 135, uses 'vincula', 'chains'). The point is that mutual conflict destroys intended order and direction.

190. Royal Pair: Statius, 137: 'indomitos ... fratres' ('untamed brothers').

192. Pope's substitution for Statius' emphasis on the legal process ('sub legibus', 138).

specious: 'superficially, not solidly right' (*SJ*).

To govern *Thebes* by their Alternate Sway;
Unjust Decree! while This enjoys the State,
195   That mourns in Exile his unequal Fate;
And the short Monarch of a hasty Year
Foresees with Anguish his returning Heir.
Thus did this League their impious Arms restrain,
But scarce subsisted to the Second Reign.

200   Yet then no proud aspiring Piles were rais'd,
Whose fretted Roofs with polish'd Metals blaz'd,
No labour'd Columns in long Order plac'd,
Nor *Grecian* Stone the pompous Arches grac'd;

---

198. **this:** *1736a–51:* the
201. **Whose:** *1736a–51:* No
203. **Nor:** *1717–51:* No

194–7. Pope emphasises the emotional state of the participants; Statius is more concerned with the abstract legal position (139–41), though he does indicate that the 'novus heres' ('new heir') will make the holder anxious: 'sceptra tenentem ... angeret'. Aden (1978: 84) sees 194–5 in particular as an unequivocal invocation of the contemporary political scene.

196. **short Monarch:** i.e. the reign is short-lived.
   hasty Year: a year that passes quickly.

200. **aspiring Piles:** towers and other ostentatious buildings; mostly Pope's addition. Cf. *Windsor-Forest*, 412.

201. **fretted Roofs:** TE compares *Temple of Fame*, 138; but Pope is there, and probably here, recalling Milton, *Paradise Lost*, I.717 (1674), p. 23: 'The Roof was fretted Gold', part of a description of Pandemonium; 'fretted' indicates ornamental raised metalwork. Statius, 144, has metal ceiling panels. The phrase is commonly associated in seventeenth-century literature with needless pomp and expense, e.g. in George Chapman's dedication to Sir Francis Bacon of his *The Georgicks of Hesiod* (1618), sig. A3ʳ, speaking of a humble cottage: 'wherein your Lordship may finde more honour, than in the fretted Roofes of the Mighty'; Jonson praises Penshurst for not having a 'roofe of gold'; 'To Penshurst', 3, *Workes* (1616), p. 819. Statius might have been thinking of Domitian's extraordinarily self-aggrandising palace on the Palatine hill, and Pope might have been glancing at the neoclassical palace under construction at Blenheim; cf. Commentary to *Windsor-Forest*, 375.

202. **labour'd:** laboriously constructed. Cf. Pope's later attack on the architectural vanity project of 'Timon's Villa', 'The whole, a labour'd Quarry above ground; *Epistle to Burlington*, 110.

202–8. Pope's rhetorical use of 'no' openings to these lines is based on Statius' use of 'nondum' and 'nec', 144–9, but in Statius the words are not so conspicuously placed. 202–3 is much expanded from Statius, 145; Pope omits Statius' image, 146, of the halls full of thronging 'clients' (dependants in the Roman social system).

202. **Columns in long Order:** a colonnade; not in Statius. Warton (*Works of Pope*, II.188) notes approvingly Pope's omission of Statius' image of 'montibus' ('mountains'), to describe the stonework.

No nightly Bands in glitt'ring Arms did wait
205 Before the wakeful Tyrant's guarded Gate;
No Chargers then were wrought in burnish'd Gold,
Nor Silver Vases took the forming Mold,
Nor Gems on Bowls emboss'd were seen to shine,
Blaze on the Brims, and sparkle in the Wine —
210 Say, wretched Rivals! what provokes your Rage?
Say to what End your impious Arms engage?
Not All bright *Phoebus* views in early Morn,
Or when his Evening Beams the West adorn,
When the South glows with his Meridian Ray,
215 And the cold North receives a fainter Day;
Not all those Realms cou'd for such Crimes suffice,

---

204. **No:** *1717:* Nor
Arms did wait: *1717–51:* armour wait
205. **wakeful:** *1717–51:* sleepless
216. 1717–51: For crimes like these, not all those realms suffice,

---

204-5. In Statius, 147-8, the guards are 'gementes' ('groaning'), at this duty.
204. TE compares Milton, *Paradise Lost*, IV.684-5 (1674), p. 105: 'oft in bands | While they keep watch, or nightly rounding walk' (speaking of guardian angels).
   nightly Bands: recalled in *Iliad*, IX.117.
206-9. Much expanded from Statius, 149-50. Pope then cuts most of Statius 151-5, in which, having stated that the fight was simply about 'nuda potestas' ('naked power'), Statius outlines the view that the kingdom was in itself too poor to be worth the fight, and that in the meantime all sense of law and honour is lost. In his letter to Cromwell, 19 January 1707/8, *Corr.*, I.37, Pope comments: 'when [Statius] Comes to the scene of his Poem & the *Prize* in Dispute between the *Brothers* he gives us a Very Mean Opinion of it — *Pugna est de paupere Regno*. Very diffr[ent] from the Conduct of his Master Virgil who at the Entrance of his Poem informs his reader of the Greatness of its Subject'. He goes on to quote from lines 156-62 as hyperbolic to the point of bathos ('I do not remember to have met with so great a fall in any ancient Author whatsoever'), hence the omissions and reorderings of his own version up to 217. *EC* censures Pope for weakening the moral force of Statius here, and other commentators, including Gillespie (1999), have suggested that Pope obscures the critical irony of Statius, 150-1.
206. **Chargers:** large dishes (*SJ*).
210-11. In Statius, 155, the question is rather 'quo tenditis iras' ('to where will you extend your wrath'; or 'wither does passion bear you', Stephens, *Essay*, 195, p. 8). Mason (1987) suggests that the repetition of 'Say' recalls the syntax of *Paradise Lost*, I.27-9.
211. **impious Arms:** cf. 2. Statius has rather 'crimine tanto' ('with so much guilt'), 156.
212-15. A symmetrical rendering of less strictly ordered details in Statius, 157-61.
214. **Meridian Ray:** the midday sun.
216-17. Statius, 161-2, adds that the combined wealth of Phrygia and Tyre would have been insufficient justification; Pope cuts this, and the rest of 162-4 (retained by Stephens) which again compares the poverty of the kingdom with the violence of the hatred, and finds the cause of the desire to sit in Oedipus' throne in 'furiis ... immanibus' ('monstrous rages').

Were all those Realms the guilty Victor's Prize!

But Fortune now (the Lots of Empire thrown)
Decrees to proud *Etheocles* the Crown:
220 What Joys, oh Tyrant! swell'd thy Soul that Day,
When all were Slaves thou cou'dst around survey,
Pleas'd to behold unbounded Pow'r thy own,
And singly fill a fear'd and envy'd Throne!

But the vile Vulgar, ever discontent,
225 Their growing Fears in secret Murmurs vent,
Still prone to change, tho' still the Slaves of State,
And sure the Monarch whom they have, to hate;
Madly they make new Lords, then tamely bear,

---

228. 1736a–51: New lords they madly make, then tamely bear,

218-19. Statius, 164-5, presents instead Polynices losing the turn, as does Stephens.

221. EC compare Stephens, *Essay*, 206-8, p. 8: 'How was thou lost | In thine own joyes, proud Tyrant then? when all | About thee, were thy slaves?' Statius, 167, uses the word 'minores', 'lower' or 'lesser', where the translators use 'slaves'. Pope to Cromwell, 10 June 1709, *Corr.*, I.64, observes of Statius' 166-8: 'Nor did I ever read a greater piece of Tautology', which his own 221-3 attempts to untangle.

223. fill . . . Throne: Pope's addition; Statius, 168, has 'nusquam par stare caput' ('no head to stand equal').

224-443. This section, corresponding to 168-311 in Statius, was omitted in Pope's first attempt; see Headnote, 'Composition and publication'.

224-72. Aden (1978: 84-90) reads this section as a series of Dryden-inflected glances at William III's agitation for the crown in 1688 and the Hanoverian monarchs in waiting since the Act of Settlement, 1701.

224. vile Vulgar: Statius, 169-70, uses three names for the populace, 'plebis', 'vulgus' and 'populis'; Stephens, *Essay*, 210, p. 8, has 'the commons'; 'vile' is Pope's addition. Cf.

Dryden's hostile account of popular political agitation at the beginning of the 1680s in *Absalom and Achitophel*, e.g. 45-66, 210-19, which underlies Pope's enhancement of the political importance of the seditious speaker, up to 233.

discontent: Warton (*Works of Pope*, II.191) declares that it 'should be discontented', but *SJ* lists 'discontent' as an adjective without comment.

225. growing Fears: Pope's addition.

226. Pope's addition. TE compares Dryden's *Aeneid*, VII.62, *Works of Virgil*, p. 580: 'Still unresolv'd, and still a Slave to Fate?' Cf. Dryden's description of 'Adriel' (Pope's friend, the Jacobite Earl of Mulgrave) in *Absalom and Achitophel*, 879 (1681), p. 27: 'True to his Prince; but not a Slave of State'.

227. In Statius, 170, this is rather 'venturus amatur' ('the one to come is loved').

228-9. EC comments that this couplet has no source in Statius and 'seems to have been suggested by [Pope's] hostility to the revolution of 1688'. The reference to the making of new lords was perhaps risky in the light of the twelve new peers created earlier in 1712 to ensure a Tory majority in the House of Lords.

And softly curse the Tyrants whom they fear.
230 And one of those who groan beneath the Sway
Of Kings impos'd, and grudgingly obey;
(Whom Envy to the Great, and vulgar Spight
With Scandal arm'd, th' Ignoble Mind's Delight,)
Exclaim'd — O *Thebes*! for thee what Fates remain,
235 What Woes attend this inauspicious Reign?
Must we, alas! our doubtful Necks prepare,
Each haughty Master's Yoke by turns to bear,
And still to change whom chang'd we still must fear?
These now controul a wretched People's Fate,
240 These can divide, and these reverse the State;
Ev'n Fortune rules no more: — Oh servile Land,
Where exil'd Tyrants still by turns command!
Thou Sire of Gods and Men, Imperial *Jove*!
Is this th' Eternal Doom decreed above?
245 On thy own Offspring hast thou fix'd this Fate,
From the first Birth of our unhappy State;
When banish'd *Cadmus* wandring o'er the Main,

230-3. Expanded from Statius, 171-3; 'Kings impos'd', 'Envy to the Great', 'vulgar Spight', and all of 232, are largely Pope's addition. In Statius it is clear that the speaker is malign and intends 'laesisse' ('to harm').

232. vulgar: of the people; cf. 224.

234. This is the beginning of the 'excellent Speech' referred to in Pope's 'Argument', 6-7.

234-5. Pope's substitution for Statius, 173-4: 'hancne Ogygiis ... aspera rebus | fata tulere vicem' ('is this the lot the rough fates have imposed on the Ogygian [Boeotian] land').

235. inauspicious: ill-starred; not in Statius.

236. doubtful: i.e. doubting, uncertain; literally from Statius, 175: 'dubitantia ... colla' ('doubting necks').

237. haughty Master: not in Statius.

238. The elaborate verbal turn here is not based on Statius' syntax.

239. controul ... wretched: Pope's additions.

240. reverse: based on Statius, 176, 'versant' ('they turn round'); it can also mean 'they direct'), but in Statius it is the 'populorum fata' ('fates of people') which get 'turned', not the 'State' itself, which Statius does not identify.

241. servile: based on Statius, 178, 'servire' (to serve), but Statius' speaker is talking about his own personal submission, not that of the whole country.

243. Imperial Jove: not named in Statius, 178-9; Pope's addition is part of a general enhancement of tone in these lines.

244. Eternal Doom: irrevocable judgment.

245-6. Pope's substitution for Statius, 180, which asks whether the 'vetus ... omen' ('ancient augury') still holds from the early days of Thebes; the question about 'offspring' is perhaps influenced by Statius,185, speaking of Cadmus: 'augurium seros dimisit ad usque nepotes' ('an omen he sent out even to his later offspring').

247. banish'd Cadmus: alluding to the claimants of the exiled Stuart line, according to Aden (1978: 88).

Main: ocean; described as 'Carpathian' in Statius, 182, i.e. the sea around Carpathus, an island in the Aegean.

For lost *Europa* search'd the World in vain,
And fated in *Boeotian* Fields to found
250 A rising Empire on a foreign Ground,
First rais'd our Walls on that ill-omen'd Plain
Where Earth-born Brothers were by Brothers slain?
What lofty Looks th' unrival'd Monarch bears!
How all the Tyrant in his Face appears!
255 What sullen Fury clowds his scornful Brow!
Gods! how his Eyes with threatning Ardour glow!
Can this Imperious Lord forget to Reign,
Quit all his State, descend, and serve again?
Yet who, before, more popularly bow'd,
260 Who more propitious to the suppliant Crowd,
Patient of Right, familiar in the Throne?

---

248. Europa: see 7; not named in Statius, 181–2, who uses the periphrasis 'Sidonii . . . blanda iuvenci | pondera' ('the pleasing burden of the Sidonian bull'). See Commentary to 682.

249. Boeotian: See note to Argument, 1; 'Hyantean' in Statius (183); 'fields of *Hyas*' in Stephens, *Essay*, 227, p. 9.

250–1. Mainly Pope's addition.

252. Cf. 8. Statius' line, 184, 'fraternasque acies fetae telluris hiatu' ('fraternal battles from the chasm of the pregnant earth'), recalls the opening of the whole poem and the sowing of the dragon's teeth (8–10).

253. unrival'd: i.e. without a competitor.

255–6. The brow/glow rhyme is not common before Pope, but cf. Blackmore, *Eliza*, I (1705), p. 3: 'Thus fir'd and swoln with Rage, did *Satan* glow, | Like a hot Furnace on a Mountain's Brow'.

255. sullen Fury: recalled in Pope's *Iliad*, IV.623; Achilles is accused of 'sullen Fury' in Yalden's 'Patroclus's Request to Achilles for his Arms', *Annual Miscellany: For the Year 1694* (1694), p. 263.

256. Mostly Pope's addition, substituting for Statius, 188: 'quanto premit omnia fastu' ('with how much pride he suppresses [or 'conceals'] all').

257–8. Much expanded from Statius, 189, 'hicne umquam privatus erit' ('will this one ever be [content to be] deprived').

259. Pope appears to take Statius' 'ille', 'he' (or 'that one', in 189, as the same as 'hicne', 'this one', i.e. the present tyrant (Eteocles) used to behave (falsely) like an ideal ruler; the 'ille' could however refer to the absent brother, as some modern translations take it. Stephens (*Essay*, 236, p. 9) interprets it the same way as Pope, as does Lewis in 1767 (I.257–8), and Aden (1978: 88).

259–62. Aden (1978: 88) compares this sketch of political fawning with the public behaviour of the manoeuvring claimant (the Duke of Monmouth) in Dryden's *Absalom and Achitophel*, 686–91, and suggests recollection of William's calculatedly ingratiating behaviour before his accession.

260. propitious: 'favourable; kind' (*SJ*); used especially of oracles and gods, and used four times in this poem (see 788, 802, 855) and very commonly in the Homer translations; in mock-heroic vein in 'Rape of the Locke', I.52.

261. familiar . . . Throne: not in Statius.

What Wonder then? he was not then Alone.
Oh wretched we, a vile submissive Train,
Fortune's tame Fools, and Slaves in ev'ry Reign!

265   As when two Winds with Rival Force contend,
This way and that, the wav'ring Sails they bend,
While freezing *Boreas* and black *Eurus* blow,
Now here, now there, the reeling Vessel throw:
Thus on each side, alas! our tott'ring State
270   Feels all the Fury of resistless Fate,
And doubtful still, and still distracted stands,
While that Prince Threatens, and while this Commands.

And now th' Almighty Father of the Gods
Convenes a Council in the blest Abodes:

---

263. vile: from Statius, 191, 'vilis' ('worthless').

264. Fortune's ... Fools: stronger than Statius, 192, 'prompta ... casus' ('ready for all chances'). Romeo calls himself 'fortune's fool' in Shakespeare, *Romeo and Juliet*, III.i.135.

  Slaves ... Reign: Aden (1978: 89) suggests that Pope is again emphasising political critique in these lines.

265-72. Pope has elaborated Statius, 193-6, to form a perfectly symmetrical eight-line simile.

265. TE compares Dryden, *Aeneid*, X.496, *Works of Virgil*, p. 512: 'As wint'ry Winds contending in the Sky'.

267. Boreas: classical name for the north wind; cf. 'Winter', 87, and 'Lines from *The Critical Specimen*', I.3.

  Eurus: classical name given to the east or south-east wind. Eurus is described as 'black' in Chapman's completion of Marlowe's *Hero and Leander*, VI.49 (1598), sig. M4; in Statius, 193, Eurus is 'nubifer' ('cloud-bringing'). These winds are both mentioned in Pope's ironic 'Receit to make an Epick Poem', *Guardian*, no. 78, 10 June 1713.

269. tott'ring State: a commonplace of seventeenth-century political discourse, found as early as Shakespeare, *Richard III*, III.ii.37. Cf. also 'Prologue to *Cato*', 22.

In Statius, 196, however, the speaker refers to the insecurity of 'peoples' ('populis').

270. resistless: irresistible, as elsewhere in Pope e.g. 'Episode of Sarpedon', 203; *Essay on Criticism*, 215, 633, etc. Statius, 195, has rather 'toleranda ... nullis', 'to be borne by none'.

271. TE compares Stephens, *Essay*, 241-2, p. 9: 'such fate | Hangs o're this doubtfull, this distracted State'. The 'distracted' element is not in Statius.

272. Pope has reversed the order of Statius, 196: 'hic imperat, ille minatur', 'this one orders, that one threatens'.

273-83. This passage was singled out for praise in Lewis's 1767 translation, I.261 and note; it is also the subject of analysis in Sowerby (2005: 158 and 2006: 217-18), which shows how Pope has enhanced the epic dignity of the scene. Mason (1987) suggests it draws on God's oversight of the world in Milton, *Paradise Lost*, III.56-9 and 69-71.

273. Almighty ... Gods: Jove only, in Statius, 197.

274. blest Abodes: Pope's addition; a common phrase, perhaps recalled from Sandys, *Ouid's Metamorphosis Englished*, I (1632), p. 2: 'Bright Constellations, and faire figured Gods, | In heauenly Mansions fixt their blest abodes'.

275 Far in the bright Recesses of the Skies,
     High o'er the rowling Heav'ns, a Mansion lyes,
     Whence, far below, the Gods at once survey   ⎫
     The Realms of rising and declining Day,   ⎬
     And all th' extended Space of Earth, and Air, and Sea. ⎭
280 Full in the midst, and on a Starry Throne,
     The Majesty of Heav'n superior shone;
     Serene he look'd, and gave an awful Nod,
     And all the trembling Spheres confess'd the God.
     At *Jove*'s Assent, the Deities around
285 In solemn State the Consistory crown'd:
     Next a long Order of Inferior Pow'rs

282, n. 1717–41: Placido quatiens tamen omnia Vultu, *is the common reading; I believe it should be* Nutu, *with reference to the word* quatiens.

---

278. Realms: Sowerby (2005: 158) notes that this translation of 'domus' (Statius, 200), normally indicating 'house' or 'family', lends Jupiter additional epic splendour.

279. As *TE* notes, an Alexandrine; in this case, concluding a triplet, a device rare in later Pope but common in this poem (there are over 20 of them). In the *Essay on Criticism*, 359, Pope mocks the effects of the Alexandrine; but *TE* suggests recollection of Cowley's 'Nor can the glory contain it self in th' endless space', *Davideis*, I.354, *Poems ... Written by A. Cowley* (1656), p. 11, and his note indicating that 'it is to paint in the number the nature of the thing which it describes'. There is also more in Pope's description than Statius' ('and Air' is an addition). The day/sea rhyme appears acceptable in Pope's day; see e.g. 58–9 of Congreve's version of book III of *Ovid's Art of Love* (1709), p. 183.

281. Pope's addition.

282 Pope's note. 'Nutu' is 'nod', normally the divine signal of assent from Jove, as in e.g. Pope's *Iliad*, I.680–1 and note; 'vultu' ('countenance') is retained in modern editions (202). 'Quatiens' ('causing to shake') is registered by Pope in the 'trembling' of the spheres, 283.

282. awful: awe-inspiring. In Statius, Jove makes everything tremble, yet is 'placido ... vultu' ('calm of face').

283. confess'd: acknowledged, showed awareness of. Sowerby (2005: 158) points out that in Statius it is the other Gods who tremble, but in Pope the whole universe does.

284–5. *TE* compares Pope's *Iliad*, X.231–2, describing the Greek kings: 'The Trenches past, th'assembl'd Kings around | In silent State the Consistory crown'd'. A consistory (stressed on the first and third syllables here) is a religious court or 'any solemn assembly' (*SJ*, citing the present passage). Satan summons his peers to a 'gloomy Consistory' in Milton's *Paradise Regain'd*, I.42 (1671), p. 3. Statius, 204–5, describes how the heaven-dwellers do not dare to sit until Jove, having arrived at his throne, has signalled that they may, similarly with 'tranquilla ... manu' ('tranquil hand'); Stephens retains the sequence, but in Pope, the actual motion of sitting down in order is obscured, a move which suggested to De Quincey (*Works*, XIII.250) that Pope had misunderstood his source; but it seems rather an attempt to enhance the august aspect of the proceedings.

286. In Statius simply 'turba vagorum | semideum' ('a crowd of wandering demigods'), 205–6.

	Ascend from Hills, and Plains, and shady Bow'rs;
	Those from whose Urns the rowling Rivers flow,
	And those that give the wandring Winds to blow,
290	Here all their Rage, and ev'n their Murmurs cease,
	And sacred Silence reigns, and universal Peace.
	A shining Synod of Majestick Gods
	Gilds with new Lustre the divine Abodes,
	Heav'n seems improv'd with a superior Ray,
295	And the bright Arch reflects a double Day.
	The Monarch then his solemn Silence broke,
	The still Creation listen'd while he spoke,
	Each sacred Accent bears eternal Weight,
	And each irrevocable Word is Fate.

300	How long shall Man the Wrath of Heav'n defy,
	And force unwilling Vengeance from the Sky?
	Oh Race confed'rate into Crimes, that prove
	Triumphant o'er th' eluded Rage of *Jove*!

---

287. Pope's addition.

288–91. Much expanded from Statius 206–8.

288. Urns ... rowling: cf. *Windsor-Forest*, 335–6 and Commentary.

291. Pope's addition. *TE* compares Dryden's version of the *Aeneid*, XI.370–1, *Works of Virgil*, p. 549: 'the murmuring Sound | Was hush'd, and sacred Silence reign'd around'. 'Sacred silence' is common in seventeenth-century poetry, and cf. the prophecy of peace in 'Messiah', 13–20, though here the argument between Jupiter and Juno does not bear out the promise.

292. Pope's addition.

   shining Synod: recalled by Pope in similar contexts in *Iliad*, I.690 and XXIV.130; probably from Shakespeare, *Cymbeline*, V.iv.90, where it is similarly used of Jupiter's council of Gods. A 'synod' is 'an assembly called for consultation', particularly in church government; it can also mean 'conjunction of the heavenly bodies' (*SJ*).

294. Heav'n ... improv'd: Pope's addition.

295. double Day: Pope's addition.

296. Cf. Milton, *Paradise Lost*, IX.895 (1674), p. 240: 'First to himself he inward silence broke'.

297. Pope's substitution for Statius 211, in which the terrified universe falls silent at Jove's command.

299. On Jove's power in relation to Fate, cf. 'Episode of Sarpedon', 232 and Commentary.

300–47. Aden (1978: 90) suggests a general reminiscence of the commanding speech of David at the end of Dryden's *Absalom and Achitophel*, 939–1031.

301. unwilling Vengeance: Pope's addition. In Statius, 214, Jove complains that mankind 'nec exsaturabile Diris' ('cannot be satiated by Furies').

303. Pope's addition. Statius' Jove complains (215–16) that he must continually drive criminals into punishment, not that anyone eludes it or triumphs over it.

This weary'd Arm can scarce the Bolt sustain,
305 And unregarded Thunder rolls in vain:
Th' o'erlabour'd *Cyclop* from his Task retires;
Th' *Aeolian* Forge exhausted of its Fires.
For this, I suffer'd *Phoebus'* Steeds to stray,
And the mad Ruler to misguide the Day,
310 When the wide Earth to Heaps of Ashes turn'd,
And Heav'n it self the wand'ring Chariot burn'd.
For this, my Brother of the watry Reign
Releas'd th' impetuous Sluices of the Main, —
But Flames consum'd, and Billows rag'd in vain.
315 Two Races now, ally'd to *Jove*, offend;
To punish these, see *Jove* himself descend!

---

316. **descend!:** *1751:* descend.

---

304. Bolt: thunderbolt, the traditional weapon of Jove. TE points out that in Statius, 217-18, the muscle fatigue is that of the Cyclopes (306), one-eyed giants who make the thunderbolts (cf. 307) and whose 'operosa ... bracchia ... fatiscunt' ('hardworking arms become tired'), and suggests Pope is following Stephens, *Essay*, 270, p. 10: 'This arme is tir'd with thundering'. But Jove does say (216-17) 'taedet saevire corusco | fulmine' ('It is wearying to be furious through flashing thunder').

305. Largely Pope's addition.

307. Th' Aeolian Forge: Stephens, *Essay*, 272, p. 10, names it as the forge of Vulcan, the fire-god, supposedly situated on the volcanic island of Hiera near Sicily; Stephens's note identifies this as 'Aetna'. EC suggests that 'exhausted' (Statius, 218: 'desunt ... ignes', 'the fires are lacking') was a reference to the extinction of the volcano in that area.

308, 312. For this: Pope adds this rhetorical repetition; for its epic effect, cf. Pope's *Iliad*, I.135-7, and the parody of the formulation in *Rape of the Lock*, IV.97-101.

309. mad Ruler: Phaeton, son of Helios the sun god (sometimes identified with Phoebus Apollo, as here in Pope but not in Statius, who uses 'Sol' as the name of the sun god), who attempted to drive the sun chariot but had to be killed by Zeus as he was too weak to control it. Pope's addition, substituting for Statius, 219, 'falso rectore' ('false driver'). Cf. Commentary to 'Spring', 62.

310-11. Pope has reversed the order of Statius' narrative (220-1) and greatly extended the amount of ash involved: in Statius, the earth is made dirty ('squalere') by the funeral ashes ('favilla') of Phaeton.

312-14. TE sees this as a reference to the flood, as described in Ovid, *Metamorphoses*, I.262-92. In Statius, 223, Jove addresses his 'germane' ('brother'), directly; this is Neptune, god of the sea, so named in Stephens, *Essay*, 276, p. 10.

312. Statius does not have anything corresponding to 'watry Reign' or 'impetuous sluices'; instead the sea is allowed to go over 'inlicitum' ('forbidden'), land (223).

watry Reign: a common periphrasis for 'ocean', e.g. Dryden, *Aeneid*, I.52, 178; and Pope, *Iliad*, I.469.

314. Pope's invention, loosely based on 'nil actum' ('nothing was done'), Statius, 222.

315. ally'd: Statius' Jove claims (224-5) that 'sanguinis auctor | ipse ego' ('I myself am author of their blood').

  The *Theban* Kings their Line from *Cadmus* trace,
  From God-like *Perseus* those of *Argive* Race.
  Unhappy *Cadmus*' Fate who does not know?
320 And the long Series of succeeding Woe:
  How oft the Furies from the deeps of Night
  Arose, and mix'd with Men in Mortal Fight:
  Th' exulting Mother stain'd with Filial Blood;
  The Savage Hunter, and the haunted Wood;
325 The direful Banquet why shou'd I proclaim,
  And Crimes that grieve the trembling Gods to name?
  E'er I recount the Sins of these Profane,
  The Sun wou'd sink into the Western Main,
  And rising gild the radiant East again.
330 Have we not seen (the Blood of *Laius* shed)
  The murd'ring Son ascend his Parent's Bed,

---

317. **Cadmus:** Statius refers to 'Aonias ... Thebas' ('Aonian Thebes') at this point (226); see notes to 49–50.

318. **God-like Perseus:** Jove's son by Danae (see 357), and thus in the line of kings of Argos; see also 637; 'Godlike' is Pope's addition.

319. **Fate:** In Statius, 227, the word is 'funera', 'destruction' or 'ruin'.

320. **succeeding Woe:** cf. Waller and Godolphin, *The Passion of Dido for Aeneas* (1658), sig. C1ʳ: 'The pregnant spring of all succeeding woe'. The line is Pope's addition, perhaps substituting for Statius, 227: 'mens cunctis imposta manet' ('the character once instilled remains for all'), i.e. bad character plays out over succeeding ages.

321. **deeps of Night:** Pope's substitution for 'sedibus imis' ('the very lowest seats'), i.e. of Hell, 228.

323. **Mother:** Agave, daughter of Cadmus, who with other Maenads (female devotees of Bacchus) tore apart her own son, Pentheus, in a frenzy, a story dramatised in Euripides, *Bacchae*; see 463–5. Statius' reference, 229, to 'mala gaudia matrum' ('the evil joys of mothers'), is more obscure. Pope would also have known of the comment in Juvenal, VII.82–7, indicating that Statius wrote a pantomime libretto on the theme of Agave.

324. **Savage Hunter:** Athamas, as in 14. Again Statius (230) does not spell this out: 'erroresque feros nemorum' ('the wild wanderings of the groves'). The 'haunted' is Pope's addition.

325. **direful:** 'dire; dreadful; dismal' (*SJ*, who reports that the word 'is frequent among the poets', but regarded as ungrammatical).

Banquet: Tantalus tested the divinity of the gods by serving up his own son Pelops (see 164) to see if they could detect the impiety and was punished in Tartarus (Homer, *Odyssey*, XI.582–92). EC claims the 'direful Banquet' is Pope's invention, but he has rather duplicated it from the 'saevae ... mensae' ('savage dinner-table') at the end of Statius' verse paragraph, 247; cf. 347 below.

326. **grieve ... Gods:** Statius 230–1: 'reticenda deorum | crimina' ('crimes against the gods that must be kept quiet'). Stephens, note to *Essay*, 288, p. 11, suggests it refers to crimes elsewhere mentioned in the poem: Niobe (see 849), Pentheus (323), Semele (14–18).

327–9. a visionary expansion of Statius, 231–2.

330. Pope's addition.

331. **murd'ring:** Pope's addition.

> Thro' violated Nature force his way,
> And stain the sacred Womb where once he lay?
> Yet now in Darkness and Despair he groans,
> 335 And for the Crimes of guilty Fate attones;
> His Sons with Scorn their Eyeless Father view,
> Insult his Wounds, and make them bleed anew.
> Thy Curse, oh *Oedipus*, just Heav'n alarms,
> And sets th' avenging Thunderer in Arms.
> 340 I from the Root thy guilty Race will tear,
> And give the Nations to the Waste of War.
> *Adrastus* soon, with Gods averse, shall join
> In dire Alliance with the *Theban* Line;
> Hence Strife shall rise, and mortal War succeed;
> 345 The guilty Realms of *Tantalus* shall bleed;
> Fix'd is their Doom; this all-remembring Breast
> Yet harbours Vengeance for the Tyrant's Feast.
>
> He said; and thus the Queen of Heav'n return'd;
> (With sudden Grief her lab'ring Bosom burn'd)

332-3. Statius, 234-5: 'immeritae gremium incestare parentis | appetiit, proprios – monstrum! – revolutus in ortus' ('he sought to defile the womb of his innocent parent, and reverted – o monstrous! – to his own origins'). Warton (*Works of Pope*, II.198) complained that Statius' image was 'insufferably gross, unnatural, and offensive; and the translation . . . is equally so'.

336. Pope's addition.

337. Statius, 238-9: 'at nati – facinus sine more! – cadentes | calcavere oculos' ('but the sons – an action without moral sense – trampled his eyes as they fell'); *TE* compares Stephens, *Essay*, 299, p. 11: 'Triumphing o're his blindnesse'.

338-9. TE compares Addison, 'Account of the Greatest English Poets', 62-3, *Annual Miscellany* (1694), p. 321: 'Shakes Heav'ns Eternal Throne with dire Alarms, | And sets the Almighty Thunderer in Arms'. Cf. the parody in 'Rape of the Locke', II.108. Statius, 239-40, has Jove say rather that Oedipus has earned the right to hope for Jove as his avenger. Jove does not name Oedipus, but calls him 'dire senex' ('terrible old man'; 'Old Mischief', Stephens, *Essay*, 300, p. 11).

342. **Adrastus:** king of Argos, one of the Seven against Thebes, and the only one to escape, on a magical horse. Jove uses this wedding of Adrastus' daughters Argeia and Deipyle as the occasion for sowing disorder, as Pope explains, without direct basis in Statius, at 344. See also the 'Argument'.

345-7. See Commentary to 325.

348. **He said:** epic formulation borrowed from Homer, replacing Statius, 248, 'Sic', 'thus'. Cf. 'January and May', 139; 'Episode of Sarpedon', 53.

Queen of Heav'n: Pope's periphrasis for Juno, named directly in Statius, 250. Daly (2013: 340) suggests that Juno's complaint can be aligned with Queen Anne's frustrations with the Duke of Marlborough's military intransigence; cf. also 400-2.

350   Must I whose Cares *Phoroneus'* Tow'rs defend,
      Must I, oh *Jove!* in bloody Wars contend?
      Thou know'st those Regions my Protection claim,
      Glorious in Arms, in Riches, and in Fame:
      Tho' there the fair *Aegyptian* Heifer fed,
355   And there deluded *Argus* slept and bled;
      Tho' there the Brazen Tow'r was storm'd of old,
      When *Jove* descended in Almighty Gold.
      Yet I can pardon those obscurer Rapes,
      Those bashful Crimes disguis'd in borrow'd Shapes;
360   But *Thebes*, where shining in Coelestial Charms
      Thou cam'st Triumphant to a Mortal's Arms,

---

350. Phoroneus' Tow'rs: Phoroneus was the son of Inachus, a river-god and early king of Argos, and had himself the reputation of a city founder. Statius, 252, has Juno refer to the towers as 'Cyclopum', 'of the Cyclopses', presumably to indicate their colossal structure.

351. oh Jove: 'o iustissime divum' ('o most just of the gods') in Statius, 250.

354-7. In Statius, Juno more directly accuses 'improbus' ('depraved' or 'shameless') Jove of crimes relating to his sexual exploits.

354. Aegyptian Heifer: Io, daughter of Inachus, and a priestess of Hera at her Argive shrine; she was transformed into a white cow when Zeus' impregnation of her was discovered. The many-eyed creature Argus (355), not named in Statius, was set as her guard, but was duped and killed by Hermes, at Jove's command, after which she was driven to Egypt, transformed back into human shape, and gave birth to Epaphus, ancestor of the Argive king Danaus (see 458). 'Aegyptian' is Pope's addition.

357. Jove . . . Almighty Gold: Danae, a princess of Argos, imprisoned by her father Acrisius in a tower, but seduced by Jove who visited her in a shower of gold; Perseus (318) was the result of the union. In Statius, 255, Juno reminds Jove more simply that 'aureus intres', 'you enter, golden'. Cf. also 'The Wife of Bath her Prologue', 64-5, Commentary.

358-9. An elaboration of Statius, 256, 'mentitis ignosco toris', 'I ignore [or 'pardon'] deceitful beds', i.e. sexual unions performed in disguise; 'obscurer Rapes' and 'bashful Crimes' are Pope's addition.

359. bashful: showing some shame (by the use of disguise).

borrow'd Shapes: the practice of seducing or raping mortal women in the guise of animals or other fictitious identities; also in Pope's mind from the shape-shifting attempts of Vertumnus, in the next poem. Stephens, *Essay*, 319, p. 12, has: 'a borrow'd shape offended'.

360-3. expanded, to explain Juno's wrath, from Statius 257-8, where Juno complains less specifically that Jove has used the thunder and lightning associated with their marriage without disguising himself.

360. Coelestial Charms: Not in Statius. The phrase occurs, in that spelling, but of a godlike woman, in John Dennis's *Appius and Virginia* (1709), p. 18. Pope recalled it as 'Celestial Charms' in the *Iliad*, III.205 (referring to Helen of Troy).

361. Mortal's Arms: those of Semele, daughter of Cadmus, and mother of Bacchus by Jove (above, 14-18). In some versions of the story, Semele was killed by the appearance of Jove in the full majesty of his thunder and lightning, a manifestation deliberately arranged by Juno.

> When all my Glories o'er her Limbs were spread,
> And blazing Lightnings danc'd around her Bed;
> Curs'd *Thebes* the Vengeance it deserves, may prove, —
365 Ah why shou'd *Argos* feel the Rage of *Jove*?
> Yet since thou wilt thy Sister-Queen controul,
> Since still the Lust of Discord fires thy Soul,
> Go, rase my *Samos*, let *Mycenè* fall,
> And level with the Dust the *Spartan* Wall:
370 No more let Mortals *Juno*'s Pow'r invoke,
> Her Fanes no more with Eastern Incense smoke,
> Nor Victims sink beneath the Sacred Stroke;
> But to your *Isis* all my Rites transfer,
> Let Altars blaze and Temples smoke for her;
375 For her, thro' *Aegypt*'s fruitful Clime renown'd,
> Let weeping *Nilus* hear the Timbrel sound.
> But if thou must reform the stubborn Times,
> Avenging on the Sons the Father's Crimes,
> And from the long Records of distant Age
380 Derive Incitements to renew thy Rage;
> Say, from what Period then has *Jove* design'd
> To date his Vengeance; to what Bounds confin'd?

---

364. prove: experience, undergo. Rhyming 'prove' with 'Jove' was apparently acceptable; examples include Dryden, 'The First Book of Ovid's Metamorphoses', 293–4, *Examen Poeticum* (1693), p. 20.

366. Sister-Queen: Juno and Jove were the offspring of Kronos and Rhea; cf. 'Episode of Sarpedon', 226. The whole line is Pope's addition.

367. In Statius, 260, Juno's point is rather 'si tanta est thalami discordia sancti' ('if the discord of the sacred marriage-bed is so great').

368. rase: destroy completely.

368–9. In Homer (*Iliad*, IV.51–2) Juno (Hera) favours Mycenae, Sparta and Argos; she had a temple sanctuary on the island of Samos.

371. Fanes: temples; Statius, 263, has 'ara' (altars).

372. Pope's addition.

373–6. An expansion of Statius 264–5, which refers much less directly to this story, via a more obscure allusion to Mareotic Copts.

373. Isis: Egyptian goddess of maternity and reincarnation; sometimes identified with Io (see 354) with whom she shared bovine iconography; not named in Statius.

376. Nilus: the Nile.

Timbrel: a sort of gong, cymbal or tambourine; normally used in biblical or oriental contexts, translating Hebrew 'toph' (*OED*), but here standing for 'aerisoni' ('bronze-sounding').

378. Father's: the Latin 'auctorum crimina' ('crimes of ancestors'), 266, suggests the whole family history rather than that of Oedipus alone.

Begin from thence, where first *Alphëus* hides
His wandring Stream, and thro' the briny Tydes,
385 Unmix'd, to his *Sicilian* River glides.
Thy own *Arcadians* there the Thunder claim,
Whose impious Rites disgrace thy mighty Name,
Who raise thy Temples where the Chariot stood
Of fierce *Oenömaus*, defil'd with Blood;
390 Where once his Steeds their savage Banquet found,
And Human Bones yet whiten all the Ground.
Say, can those Honours please? and can'st thou love
Presumptuous *Crete*, that boasts the Tomb of *Jove*?
And shall not *Tantalus* his Kingdoms share

---

394. Tantalus **his:** *1751:* Tantalus's

383–5. EC compares Dryden, *Eclogues*, X.6–7, *Works of Virgil*, p. 45: 'So may thy Silver Streams beneath the Tide, | Unmix'd with briny Seas, securely glide'. 'Unmix'd' is Pope's addition.

383. **Alphëus:** river of the Peloponnese which flows from south Arcadia, past Olympia and into the Ionian Sea; commonly personified as a river god.

385. **Sicilian *River*:** Arethusa, turned into a well or spring in Ortygia, Sicily, to avoid rape by Alpheus, who nonetheless contrives to mingle with her by flowing under the sea. The story, told in Ovid, *Metamorphoses*, V, is one of the myths underlying the 'Lodona' episode in *Windsor-Forest*; see Commentary at 183–6 of that poem. Cf. Milton, 'Arcades', 30–1, *Poems of Mr. John Milton* (1645), p. 53: 'Divine *Alpheus*, who by secret sluse [sluice], | Stole under Seas to meet his *Arethuse*'.

386. **Arcadians:** inhabitants of the central region of the Peloponnese.

the Thunder claim: i.e. align themselves with Jove; Pope's addition.

387. **impious Rites:** *EC* suggests reference to worship of Jupiter by human sacrifice, but *TE* points out that Statius, 273–7, refers to establishment of temples to Jove on defiled ground ('nefastis . . . locis'). See next line.

389. **Oenömaus:** King of Pisa (in the Peloponnese) who challenged all suitors to Hippodamia, his daughter, to a chariot race, the losers being killed; the challenge was designed to avoid a prophecy that his son-in-law would kill him. In Statius, 275, the horses are likened to the man-eating mares of Diomedes, tamed by Hercules, hence Pope's 'savage Banquet', 390, but in Statius, Oenomaus' horses do not eat people; Juno complains rather that the mutilated corpses lie unburied (cf. Pope's 391).

393. Jove was born (in some accounts) on Mount Ida, on Crete. Statius, 278, also mentions 'Ida nocens' ('criminal Ida'), perhaps because, as Stephens suggests, *Essay*, 345n, p. 13, this was the traditional site of Paris' judgement in favour of Aphrodite (Venus) and against Hera (Juno) and Athena (Minerva). Callimachus' *Hymn to Zeus* complains about Cretan allegations of Zeus' death, hence Pope's line.

394–5. See Commentary to 325. Statius' Juno implies rather that Jove is jealous of her attachment to her lands. 'Wife and Sister's Tutelary Care' is a further invention (cf. 366).

395   Thy Wife and Sister's Tutelary Care?
         Reverse, O *Jove*, thy too severe Decree,
         Nor doom to War a Race deriv'd from thee;
         On Impious Realms, and barb'rous Kings, impose
         Thy Plagues, and curse 'em with such Sons as those.

400   Thus, in Reproach and Pray'r, the Queen exprest
         The Rage and Grief contending in her Breast;
         Unmov'd remain'd the Ruler of the Sky,
         And from his Throne return'd this stern Reply.
         'Twas thus I deem'd thy haughty Soul wou'd bear
405   The dire, tho' just, Revenge which I prepare
         Against a Nation thy peculiar Care:
         No less *Dione* might for *Thebes* contend,
         Nor *Bacchus* less his Native Town defend,
         Yet these in Silence see the Fates fulfil
410   Their Work, and rev'rence our Superior Will.
         For by the black infernal *Styx* I swear,

399, n. *Tydeus* and *Polynices*.

399, n. 1736a–51: Etheocles *and* Polynices

---

395. Tutelary: protective.
396. Pope's addition.
397. deriv'd from thee: via Perseus, his son (see 357).
398. barb'rous Kings: Pope's addition to Statius' more general point, 281–2, and thus potentially political (Aden 1978: 90).
399 **Pope's note and variant.** Pope did not correct his own mistake about the names of the sons until 1736.
400–2. Daly (2013: 340) suggests that here, as at 348–53, Juno represents Queen Anne, bitterly opposing her general, the Duke of Marlborough.
401. Pope's addition.
402–3. Largely Pope's addition. In Statius, Jove responds 'non ... gravis dictis, quamquam aspera motu' ('not in severe words, although harsh in import').
404. haughty: Pope's addition.

405. dire ... Revenge ... prepare: Pope's substitution for 'quodcumque ... consulerem' ('whatsoever I would devise').
406. peculiar Care: particular or personal responsibility; in Statius, 286, 'tuos ... Argos' ('your Argos'). Cf. 'January and May', 468; 'Arrival of Ulysses in Ithaca', 91, and Commentary there. The phrase is common in Pope's full Homer translations, e.g. *Iliad*, I.494 and XV.260, as in Dryden's version of the *Aeneid*, e.g. I.617, normally in reference to a God's care for a particular mortal or region.
407. **Dione:** consort of Jove and (in Homer) mother of Aphrodite (Venus), whose daughter Harmonia married Cadmus.
408. **Bacchus:** cf. Commentary to 13, 323; son by Jove of Semele (above, 14–18), and thus associated with Thebes.
409. Pope's invention.
411–14. Expanded from Statius, 290–2.

(That dreadful Oath which binds the Thunderer)
'Tis fix'd; th' irrevocable Doom of *Jove*;
No Force can bend me, no Persuasion move.
415 Haste then, *Cyllenius*, thro' the liquid Air,
Go mount the Winds, and to the Shades repair;
Bid Hell's black Monarch my Commands obey,
And give up *Laius* to the Realms of Day,
Whose Ghost yet shiv'ring on *Cocytus*' Sand
420 Expects its Passage to the farther Strand:
Let the pale Sire revisit *Thebes*, and bear
These pleasing Orders to the Tyrant's Ear;
That, from his exil'd Brother, swell'd with Pride
Of foreign Forces, and his *Argive* Bride,
425 Almighty *Jove* commands him to detain
The promis'd Empire, and Alternate Reign:
Be this the Cause of more than mortal Hate;
The rest, succeeding Times shall ripen into Fate.

---

415. **Cyllenius:** epithet of Mercury (below, 429), born on Mount Cyllene in Arcadia; so named in Statius, 293; '*Mercury*' in Stephens, *Essay*, 362, p. 13.

liquid Air: a favourite phrase of Dryden, especially in translations, e.g. *Aeneid*, III.571; *Georgics*, I.557, etc.; the Latin 'liquidus' can mean 'flowing', 'clear', 'bright'. Cf. *Windsor-Forest*, 184; '*Rape of the Locke*', II.172.

417. **Hell's black Monarch:** Hades or Pluto, king of the underworld (referred to merely as Mercury's 'patruo', 'uncle' in Statius, 295).

419. **yet shiv'ring:** Pope's simplification of Statius, 297-8, which indicates that the further bank of Lethe (cf. 420) had not yet received him 'lege Erebi' ('by the law of Erebus'). TE explains this as meaning that he had been killed by his own son; Stephens notes (*Essay*, 368n, p. 14) that the tradition was that slaughtered bodies had to wander a hundred years before crossing.

Cocytus: see 124.

422. **Tyrant's Ear:** 'diro ... nepoti' ('to the evil grandson'), Statius, 298; i.e. Eteocles, the current ruling brother.

424. **Argive Bride:** not quite in Statius, who has 'Argolis... hospitiis' ('Argive friendships'); but see Argument.

425. **Almighty ... commands:** simply 'mea iussa' ('my commands'), Statius, 298.

426. **promis'd Empire:** Pope's addition.

427. **more than mortal:** Pope's addition.

428. Statius, 302: 'certo reliqua ordine ducam' ('what remains I shall lead out in due order').

In his letter to Cromwell, 10 June 1709, *Corr.*, I.63, Pope mentions a previous state of this line, to which Cromwell had objected:

One of your objections, namely on that passage,

The rest, resolving years shall ripen into Fate,

may be well grounded, in relation to its not being the exact sense of the words —*Caetera reliquo ordine ducam*. But the duration of the Action of *Statius*'s poem may as well be excepted against, as many things besides in him ... For instead of confining his narration to *one year*, it is manifestly exceeded in the very first two books,

as Pope goes on to calculate.

        The God obeys, and to his Feet applies
430   Those golden Wings that cut the yielding Skies;
        His ample Hat his beamy Locks o'erspread,
        And veil'd the Starry Glories of his Head:
        He seiz'd his Wand that causes Sleep to fly,
        Or in soft Slumbers seals the wakeful Eye;
435   That drives the Dead to dark *Tartarean* Coasts,
        Or back to Life compells the wondring Ghosts.
        Thus, thro' the parting Clouds the Son of *May*
        Wings on the whistling Winds his rapid way,
        Now smoothly steers through Air his equal Flight,
440   Now springs aloft, and tow'rs th' Ethereal Height,
        Then wheeling down the Steep of Heav'n he flies,

---

433. **his:** *1736a–51:* the
436. **wondring:** *1741–51:* wand'ring

429-33. The traditional accoutrements of Mercury, the Roman equivalent of the messenger god Hermes, son of Zeus and Maia, daughter of Atlas, and hence referred to as 'Atlantiades' in Statius, 303.

430. TE compares Dryden, *Aeneid,* I.413, *Works of Virgil,* p. 213: 'And cleaves with all his Wings the yielding Skies', an image also of 'Cyllenius' or Mercury; 'yielding Skies' occurs at least three further times in Dryden's *Aeneid.*

431. **beamy:** radiant; otherwise only used by Pope in the Homer translations, on the model of Dryden, who uses it to describe e.g. the 'Temples' of 'Young *Caesar*' in the *Aeneid,* VIII.904, *Works of Virgil,* p. 461.

432. **Starry Glories:** i.e. his radiant hair. TE compares Stephens, *Essay,* 379, p. 14: 'starry head'. Statius (305) has 'obnubitque comas et temperat astra galero' ('and clouds his hair and shades the stars with a fur cap').

433. **Wand:** the 'caduceus' or herald's sign, 'virgam' in Statius, 306, 'charming rod' in Stephens, *Essay,* 380, p. 14.

434. TE compares Dryden, *Aeneid,* IV.358, *Works of Virgil,* p. 307: 'With this he seals in Sleep, the wakeful sight' (Hermes).
    seals ... Eye: Pope's addition.

435. In Statius, Mercury uses the wand to conjure slumbers, to enter Tartarus, and to recall the dead to life; he does not use it to drive the dead to hell. The antithesis with 436, modelled on the pattern of sleep in 433–4, is Pope's.

436. **wondring:** Pope's addition, as is the substituted 'wand'ring'; Statius' adjective is 'exsangues' ('without blood').

437-42. Luxuriantly expanded from Statius, 309–11, in the interests of greater sublimity.

437. **Son of May:** cf. Commentary to 429–33; 'May' for 'Maia'.

438. **whistling Winds:** TE compares Dryden, *Aeneid,* IX.927, *Works of Virgil,* p. 491 (of trees): 'Dance to the whistling Winds', and also XII.404, and *Georgics,* IV.287. The phrase was already in fairly wide circulation, e.g. Fanshawe, *Lusiad,* IV.i (1655), p. 75: 'After the whistling winds have spent their spight'. Pope recalled it in *Iliad,* XXIII.285. The image here is his addition.

441. TE compares Milton, *Paradise Lost,* III.741 (1674), p. 83: 'Throws his steep flight in many an Aerie wheele', and Dryden, *Aeneid,* I.413, *Works of Virgil,* p. 213: 'Down from the Steep of Heav'n *Cyllenius* flies'. Pope's addition.

And draws a radiant Circle o'er the Skies.

    Mean time the banish'd *Polynices* roves
(His *Thebes* abandon'd) thro' th' *Aonian* Groves,
445   While future Realms his wandring Thoughts delight,
His daily Vision, and his Dream by Night;
Forbidden *Thebes* appears before his Eye,
From whence he sees his absent Brother fly,
Enjoys an airy Empire, all his own,
450   And swells on an imaginary Throne.
Fain wou'd he cast a tedious Age away,
And live out all in one triumphant Day.
He chides the lazy Progress of the Sun,
And bids the Year with swifter Motion run.
455   With anxious Hopes his craving Mind is tost,
And all his Joys in length of Wishes lost.

    The Hero then resolves his Course to bend
Where ancient *Danaus*' fruitful Fields extend,
And fam'd *Mycene*'s lofty Tow'rs ascend,

---

449. 1717–51: With transport views the airy rule his own,

443–4. In Statius, Polynices wanders 'furto', 'stealthily'.

444. Aonian: i.e. Boeotian; see 50.

445–56. Pope has reordered much of the material in Statius, 316–23, in order to emphasise the delusional quality of Polynices' thought.

445. wandring Thoughts: Mason (1987) compares Milton, *Paradise Lost*, VIII.182–7 (1674), p. 199, where the 'wandring thoughts' are Adam's theological enquiries.

446. TE compares 'Sapho to Phaon', 143–4; see Commentary on those lines. In Statius, it is less a 'vision' than 'una cura', 'one concern'.

447–50. Statius governs Polynices' thought with a verb of seeing, 'cerneret' ('he should see'), 319, but Pope's expanded phrasing is much closer to dreamlike fantasy. Mack (1985: 160–1) suggests this passage represents a hit at William III and his agitation to succeed to the English throne in the 1680s; 'fly' (448) could refer to the flight of James II in 1688.

449. airy: imaginary, visionary; Pope's addition.

450. Pope's addition.

455. craving: Pope's addition.

458. Danaus: an earlier ruler of Argos; Inachus (Statius, 324), whom Pope omits, was the ancestor of the Argive kings. Cf. 354.

    fruitful Fields: Pope's addition; cf. *Windsor-Forest*, 26.

459. Mycene: cf. 368; Mycenae, a hill on the north-east edge of the Argive plain, site of an elaborate early civilisation.

460   (Where late the Sun did *Atreus*' Crimes detest
      And disappear'd, in Horrour of the Feast.)
      And now by Chance, by Fate, or Furies led,
      From *Bacchus*' consecrated Caves he fled,
      Where the shrill Cries of frantick Matrons sound,
465   And *Pentheus*' Blood enrich'd the rising Ground.
      Then sees *Cythaeron* towring o'er the Plain,
      And thence declining gently to the Main.
      Next to the Bounds of *Nisus*' Realm repairs,
      Where treach'rous *Scylla* cut the Purple Hairs:
470   The hanging Cliffs of *Scyron*'s Rocks explores,
      And hears the Murmurs of the diff'rent Shores:
      Passes the Strait that parts the foaming Seas,

---

470. **Rocks:** *1717–51:* rock

---

460. In mythology, the region was made dark by 'abrupto sole' ('withdrawal of the sun'), Statius 325, to signal the anger of the gods at the impiety committed when Atreus killed and cooked the sons of his brother Thyestes and then served them to the father, as Pope explains in his extra lines 460–1. The story was well known from Seneca's tragedy *Thyestes*. Pope comments on Statius' line as inconsistent with the chronology suggested by details of the story in IV.305 (to Cromwell, 10 June 1709, *Corr.*, I.64), though this requires no particular adjustment in Pope's own lines.

462. A condensation of Statius, 326–8, in which Erinys (a Fury) and Atropos (a Fate) are both named.

463–5. See 323 and Commentary. Pentheus was the grandson of Cadmus, and a king of Thebes; he was torn to pieces by the Maenads (Pope's 'frantick Matrons') after he had banned their rites. The caves are not 'consecrated' in Statius and he does not mention Pentheus and the Maenads, just Bacchic blood sacrifice in general. Pope omits the location, 'Ogygia', given in Statius, and Stephens, *Essay*, 410, p. 15.

466. **Cythaeron *towring*:** see 161. Pentheus is said to have been killed on the mountainside.

466–7. The same rhyme is in Stephens, *Essay*, 413–14, p. 15.

468–9. Scylla, daughter of Nisus, king of Megara, between Corinth and Athens, fell in love with Minos when he besieged the town; to help him, she plucked out the purple hair which magically protected her father. The story was well known from Ovid, *Metamorphoses*, VIII.1–151; see Commentary to 'Rape of the Locke', I.102–4. Pope supplies explanatory detail to fill out Statius' oblique reference.

470–3. As *TE* notes, Pope reorders the route of Statius, 332–5, where Polynices passes the cliffs of Sciron (also near Megara) and Scylla's country, and Corinth before reaching the middle of the isthmus, where he can hear the waves on either shore. Pope to Cromwell, 10 June 1709, *Corr.*, I.64, writes 'In the Journey of *Polynices* is some geographical error, "— In mediis audit duo litora campis" could hardly be; for the *Isthmus* of *Corinth* is full five miles over'; hence his muffling of what he takes to be an absurdity. *EC* points out that at its narrowest the isthmus is 3.5 miles; in any case this is an epic poem, not geography. The detail did not trouble Stephens, *Essay*, 418, p. 15: 'Two neighbour seas made musick in his eare'.

And stately *Corinth*'s pleasing Site surveys.

      'Twas now the Time when *Phoebus* yields to Night,
475   And rising *Cynthia* sheds her silver Light,
      Wide o'er the World in solemn Pomp she drew
      Her airy Chariot, hung with Pearly Dew;
      All Birds and Beasts lye hush'd; Sleep steals away
      The wild Desires of Men, and Toils of Day,
480   And brings, descending thro' the silent Air,
      A sweet Forgetfulness of Human Care.
      Yet no red Clouds, with golden Borders gay,

---

473. stately: in Statius, 334, the adjective is 'mitem', 'gentle' ('quiet' in Stephens, *Essay*, 417, p. 15). Pope has added 'pleasing Site' to the image.

474-87. Perhaps the most excerpted passage in the poem. Warton (*Works of Pope*, II.209), states of 474-81: 'We have scarcely in our language eight more beautiful lines than these'; expanded from six of Statius (336-41). *TE* (p. 350) uses 477-81 of this passage as a sample of Pope's skill in comparison with Stephens. Gillespie (1999) suggests that at 478-81 Pope is recalling a passage from Dryden's *The Indian Emperour*, III.ii.1-5 (1667), p. 29: 'All things are hush'd, as Natures self lay dead, | The Mountains seem to Nod their drowsie head; | The little Birds in dreams their Songs repeat, | And sleeping Flowers, beneath the night-dew sweat; | Ev'n Lust and Envy sleep'. Rymer, in the 'Preface' to his translation of Rapin's *Reflections* (1674), sig. b1, had pointed to these lines to show the superiority of Dryden to their source in Statius, *Silvae*, V (see Headnote), a point later discussed in a note to Pope's *Odyssey*, XIV.510. Sowerby (2006: 212-15) provides a detailed commentary on this passage (to 487) alongside Statius, 336-46, and suggests the general influence of Milton's description of the evening, *Paradise Lost*, IV.598-609.

475. **Cynthia:** alternative name for Diana or Artemis, the moon goddess, sister of Apollo the sun god; cf. 'Sapho to Phaon', 99; '*Rape of the Locke*', II.8; *Windsor-Forest*, 198; etc. Statius does not name her, and this line is largely Pope's addition.

476. Largely Pope's addition; Statius, 337-8, emphasises the drop in temperature as the moon rises.

477. Stephens, *Essay*, 422, p. 15: 'Her Ayery charriot, pearld with drops of dew'.

479. **wild Desires:** Pope's addition; Statius, 339-40, emphasises rather the 'avaris ... curis' ('greedy worries') of the day.

    Toils of Day: cf. Oldham, 'The Dream', 2, *Poems, and Translations* (1683), p. 122: 'in soft sleep forgot the Toils of Day'; the phrase is recalled by Pope in e.g. *Iliad*, X.111 and *Odyssey*, XXIII.371.

480-1. TE observes that Pope returned to this couplet in *Iliad*, IX.841-2 (i.e. 426-7); some aspects of his own phrasing here recur also in *Odyssey*, XII.365-6 and XXIII.370.

481. Cf. Stephens, *Essay*, 426, p. 15: 'A sweet forgetfulnesse of labour past'. Statius, 341, has 'grata laboratae ... oblivia vitae' ('a pleasing forgetting of hardworking life').

482-3. Statius, 342-3: 'sed nec puniceo rediturum nubila caelo | promisere iubar' ('but no clouds gave promise by the red sky that light would return').

Promise the Skies the bright Return of Day;
No faint Reflections of the distant Light
485 Streak with long Gleams the scatt'ring Shades of Night;
From the damp Earth impervious Vapours rise,
Encrease the Darkness and involve the Skies.
At once the rushing Winds with roaring Sound
Burst from th' *Aeolian* Caves, and rend the Ground,
490 With equal Rage their airy Quarrel try,
And win by turns the Kingdom of the Sky:
But with a thicker Night black *Auster* shrouds
The Heav'ns, and drives on heaps the rowling Clouds,
Then down on Earth a ratling Tempest pours,
495 Which the cold North congeals to haily Show'rs.
From Pole to Pole the Thunder roars aloud,
And broken Lightnings flash from ev'ry Cloud.
Now smoaks with Show'rs the misty Mountain-Ground.
And floated Fields lye undistinguish'd round:
500 Th' *Inachian* Streams with headlong Fury run,
And *Erasinus* rowls a Deluge on:

***494*. Then down on Earth:** *1717–51:* From whose dark womb
***498*. Mountain-Ground.:** *1717–36b:* mountain-ground,; *1741–51:* mountain-ground

---

486-7. impervious . . . Skies: Pope's addition; Statius, 345-6, emphasises total blackness more straightforwardly.

487. involve: 'enwrap' (*SJ*), from the Latin, 'involvo', 'to roll up' or 'to wrap up'; cf. Tate, *On the Memory of our Late Sovereign* (1685), p. 4: 'eternal night seem'd to involve our Skies'.

489. Aeolian Caves: where, in Greek mythology, the winds were kept under control by Aeolus.

490-1. EC compares Dryden, *Aeneid*, II.567-8, *Works of Virgil*, p. 251: 'Thus, when the Rival Winds their Quarrel try, | Contending for the Kingdom of the Skie . . .' and IV.638, p. 315: 'As when the Winds their airy Quarrel try', in response to Warton's contention (*Works of Pope*, II.211) that Pope's phrase constitutes a 'very faulty expression'. The political reflection of the power struggle between the two brothers is clearer in Pope than in Statius, though prompted by 350, 'caelum sibi quisque rapit' ('each seizes the sky for itself'). Stephens also uses a political language, *Essay*, 435-6, p. 16: 'Each holding | Heav'n by a proper title, for his owne'. Pope has dropped Statius 349, which describes how the winds dislodge the world from its axial point (Stephens retains this).

492. Auster: Roman equivalent of Notus, the south wind. Cf. 'Lines from *The Critical Specimen*', I, 3; and Pope's *Iliad*, V.1058.

495. cold North: specifically Boreas, the north wind, in Statius, 353.

496. Pope's addition.

498-9. Pope's substitution for the more specific geographical list in Statius, 355-6, involving Nemea, Arcadia and the woods of Taenarus.

500-1. Inachian *Streams* . . . Erasinus: rivers (and river gods) of the Argos region. Statius, 357, specifies that the floods of the latter are 'gelidas' ('freezing'). Cf. also 'Summer', 84.

　　　　The foaming *Lerna* swells above its Bounds,
　　　　And spreads its ancient Poysons o'er the Grounds:
　　　　Where late was Dust, now rapid Torrents play,
505　　Rush thro' the Mounds, and bear the Dams away:
　　　　Old Limbs of Trees from crackling Forests torn,
　　　　Are whirl'd in Air, and on the Winds are born;
　　　　The Storm the dark *Lycean* Groves display'd,
　　　　And first to Light expos'd the Venerable Shade.
510　　The Prince with Wonder did the Waste behold,
　　　　While from torn Rocks the massy Fragments roll'd;
　　　　And heard astonish'd from the Hills afar
　　　　The Floods descending and the watry War,
　　　　That driv'n by Storms, and pouring o'er the Plain,
515　　Swept Herds, and Hinds, and Houses to the Main.
　　　　Thro' the brown Horrors of the Night he fled,
　　　　Nor knows, amaz'd, what doubtful Path to tread,

---

509. **Venerable:** *1717–51:* sacred
510–11. 1717–51: Th' intrepid *Theban* hears the bursting sky,
　　　　　　　　　　Sees yawning rocks in massy fragments fly,
512. **heard:** *1717–51:* views

---

502. **Lerna:** lake near Argos, lair of the multi-headed and venomous water serpent, the Hydra, killed by Herakles as one of his twelve labours. The poison of the lake is mentioned by Pope in his note to his translation of Homer, *Iliad*, XI.968.

505. The 'Dams' are Pope's addition.

506. **crackling Forests:** cf. Pope's *Iliad*, XVI.770. The 'crackling' is Pope's addition.

507. **whirl'd in Air:** Pope's addition.

508. **dark Lycean Groves:** these are not 'sacred' in Statius, 363, just 'shady summer retreats' ('umbrosi... aestiva'); but Mt Lycaeus was the site of a mystery cult of Zeus, which may be in Pope's mind here. Alternatively, Stephens, *Essay*, 453n, p. 16, notes that the god Pan 'kept his summer Court of residence' there.

510 variant. **intrepid Theban:** Polynices; merely 'ille', 'he', in Statius, 364.

511. **massy:** heavy.

512–13. EC compares Dryden, *Aeneid*, II.415–16, *Works of Virgil*, p. 246: 'The Shepherd climbs the Cliff, and sees from far, | The wastful Ravage of the wat'ry War'. There is no equivalent for 'watry war' in Statius.

515. EC compares Dryden, *Georgics*, I.652, *Works of Virgil*, p. 68: 'Bore Houses, Herds, and lab'ring Hinds away'. The alliteration is perhaps motivated by Statius' phrasing, 367: 'pastorum pecorumque domos' ('houses of shepherds and flocks'). The 'main' (ocean) is not mentioned in Statius.

516. TE compares Dryden, *Aeneid*, VII.40–1, *Works of Virgil*, p. 401: 'a wood | Which thick with Shades, and a brown Horror, stood.' See further 'Eloisa to Abelard', 170. Statius, 368, has Polynices take his way through 'nigra silentia' ('black silences').

His Brother's Image to his Mind appears,
Inflames his Heart with Rage, and wings his Feet with Fears.

520 So fares a Sailor on the stormy Main,
When Clouds conceal *Boötes*' golden Wain,
When not a Star its friendly Lustre keeps,
Nor trembling *Cynthia* glimmers on the Deeps;
He dreads the Rocks, and Shoals, and Seas, and Skies,
525 While Thunder roars, and Lightning round him flies.

Thus strove the Chief on ev'ry side distress'd,
Thus still his Courage, with his Toils, encreas'd;
With his broad Shield oppos'd, he forc'd his way
Thro' thickest Woods, and rouz'd the Beasts of Prey.
530 Till he beheld, where from *Larissa*'s Height
The shelving Walls reflect a glancing Light;
Thither with haste the *Theban* Hero flies;
On this side *Lerna*'s pois'nous Water lies,
On that, *Prosymna*'s Grove and Temple rise:

518–19. The couplet is expanded from a chiasmus in Statius, 369, 'pulsat metus undique et unique frater' ('fear impels him on each side and on each side his brother [impels him]'); 'Fear and's brother, spur him faster', Stephens, *Essay*, 462, p. 17.

519. An Alexandrine.

521. Boötes' golden Wain: in Statius, 371, 'Temo piger' ('the slow Plough'). Boötes, 'the ox-driver', a constellation resembling an ox-drawn wagon ('wain'), is referred to as a navigational reference point in Homer, *Odyssey*, V.272. Cf. 'Autumn', 72; *Windsor-Forest*, 119.

523. trembling Cynthia: 'Luna', the moon, in Statius, 372.

524. TE compares Milton, *Paradise Lost*, II.947–50 (1674), pp. 55–6 (Satan's journey): '. . . So eagerly the fiend | Ore bog or steep, through strait, rough, dense, or rare, | With head, hands, wings, or feet pursues his way, | And swims or sinks, or wades, or creeps, or flyes.' The phrasing is closer to Milton than to Statius (373–5), and Pope has omitted some of Statius' images of the ship.

Shoals: shallows or sandbanks.

525. Pope's addition.

526–7. Mostly Pope's invention; Statius has Polynices hurry more straightforwardly through the dark woods (376–7), and adds that 'dat stimulus animo vis maesta timoris' ('the sober force of fear gave spurs to his spirit').

526. the Chief: Statius, 376, 'Cadmeius heros' ('the Cadmean hero').

530. Larissa: the hill at the foot of which stands Argos.

532. with haste: 'spe concitus omni' ('spurred on by every hope'), Statius, 382.

533–4. Pope has reversed Statius' order, 383–5, basing a symmetrical couplet on Statius' repetition of 'hinc ... hinc' ('on this side ... on that side'). He drops a reference to Hercules in relation to Lerna (see 502).

534. Prosymna's Grove: the Argive temple of Juno (Hera) or Heraion; Statius (383) states this specifically.

535   He pass'd the Gates which then unguarded lay,
        And to the Regal Palace bent his way;
        On the cold Marble spent with Toil he lies,
        And waits 'till pleasing Slumbers seal his Eyes.

        Adrastus here his happy People sways,
540   Blest with calm Peace in his declining Days,
        By both his Parents of Descent divine,
        Great *Jove* and *Phoebus* grac'd his noble Line;
        Heav'n had not crown'd his Wishes with a Son,
        But two fair Daughters heir'd his State and Throne.
545   To him *Apollo* (wondrous to relate!
        But who can pierce into the Depths of Fate?)
        Had sung —'Expect thy Sons on *Argos*' Shore,
        A Yellow Lyon and a bristly Boar.'
        This, long revolv'd in his Paternal Breast,
550   Sate heavy on his Heart, and broke his Rest;
        This, great *Amphiaraus*, lay hid from thee,
        Tho' skill'd in Fate and dark Futurity.
        The Father's Care and Prophet's Art were vain,
        For thus did the Predicting God ordain.

---

537. cold Marble: a 'dura cubilia' ('hard bed'), in Statius, 389, who specifies that the hall is 'ignotae' ('unknown').

538. pleasing Slumbers: Pope used the phrase again in 'The Arrival of Ulysses in Ithaca', 6, and *Iliad*, XXIV.4.

540. declining Days: also in 'January and May', 171.

541–2. Statius mentions that the genealogy stretches back to Jove on both sides ('utroque', 392) but does not mention Phoebus (Apollo). Stephens notes (*Essay*, 486, p. 17) that Adrastus was 'Son to *Talaus* the grandchild of *Jupiter*, and *Eurynome* daughter to *Apollo*'.

543. a Son: In Statius, 393, Adrastus is 'sexus melioris inops' ('lacking the better sex').

544. heir'd: EC compares Dryden, *Aeneid*, VII.79, *Works of Virgil*, p. 402: 'One only Daughter heir'd the Royal State'; the usage is repeated at VII.367.

546. Pope's substitution for Statius, 396, 'mox adaperta fides' ('soon the truth became open'). Statius has Phoebus give his message 'fato ducente' ('at Fate's instigation'), however.

547. thy Sons: not in Statius, where Apollo's message is thus more obscure.

548. Yellow: translating 'fulvum' ('tawny'), Statius, 397.

    bristly Boar: The phrase (translating 'saetigerum suem', 'bristle-bearing pig', Statius, 397) recurs in Pope's *Iliad*, XVI.994, and might have been learned from Dryden's version of Virgil, *Georgics*, IV.589.

549. revolv'd: turned over, meditated. TE compares Dryden, *Aeneid*, VI.454, *Works of Virgil*, p. 375: 'Revolving anxious Thoughts within his Breast'.

550. Pope's addition, partly based on Statius, 400, out of sequence.

551. Amphiaraus: See 62 and Commentary. Pope has greatly expanded what Statius addresses to Amphiaraus, 398–9.

554. Predicting God: named as Apollo in Statius, 399, and in Stephens, 494.

555   Lo hapless *Tydeus*, whose ill-fated Hand
         Had slain his Brother, leaves his Native Land,
         And seiz'd with Horror, 'midst the Shades of Night,
         Thro' the thick Desarts headlong urg'd his Flight:
         Now by the Fury of the Tempest driv'n,
560   He seeks a Shelter from th' inclement Heav'n,
         Till led by Fate, the *Theban*'s Steps he treads,
         And to fair *Argos* open Court succeeds.

         When thus the Chiefs from diff'rent Lands resort
         T' *Adrastus*' Realms and Hospitable Court,
565   The King surveys his Guests with curious Eyes,
         And views their Arms and Habit with Surprize.
         A Lyon's yellow Skin the *Theban* wears,
         Horrid his Mane, and rough with curling Hairs;
         Such once employ'd *Alcides*' youthful Toils,

---

557. **'midst:** *1717–51:* in
559. **Tempest:** *1717–36a:* tempests
562. **Argos:** *1717–51: Argos'*

---

555. **hapless:** luckless. Pope's substitution for 'Olenius' ('Olenian', i.e. from Olenos), Statius, 402.

  Tydeus: son of Oeneus, king of Calydon. Stephens, *Essay*, 499n, p. 18, reports the tradition that he killed his brother in a hunting accident. Statius names Calydon as the 'Native Land' (Pope, 556) that he leaves.

557–8. In Statius, 403–4, Tydeus is said to traverse 'eadem ... lustra' ('the same wild boglands', or 'the same desert wood', Stephens, *Essay*, 500, p. 18), as Polynices.

559–62. Statius concentrates more directly on how cold and wet Tydeus is; 562 is Pope's substitution for Statius' image of Polynices lying on the floor. Stephens retains more of Statius' detail. Unlike Stephens, Pope omits 408–81 of Statius, a description of a fierce fight between Tydeus and Polynices, prompted only by a desire to possess what little shelter there is, which is stopped by Adrastus himself, woken by the clamour. For Pope's omission of this 'Scuffle' as inappropriate to the situation of the princes, see Headnote. Lewis, while retaining the passage in 1767, admits that it is 'an unseasonable Insertion' (note to I.559).

563–4. Pope's couplet, which has no basis in Statius, is an attempt to bridge the missing portion of the narrative.

566. **Habit:** clothing, attire.

567. **Theban:** Polynices; identified only as 'huius' ('of this one') in Statius, 483.

568. **Horrid:** shaggy, bristling; see Commentary at 145.

  curling: 'impexis', 'uncombed', in Statius, 484.

569. **Alcides:** Herakles or Hercules, son of Jove by Alkmene; named more obscurely in Statius, 485–6, as the son of Amphitryon, but named in Stephens, *Essay*, 597, p. 21; Stephens explains the reference, using detail in Statius that Pope has cut: '*Hercules* whilst a child slew a Lion neer *Teumessus*, whose skin he always used as a mantle'.

570   E're yet adorn'd with *Nemea*'s dreadful Spoils.
      A Boar's stiff Hyde, of *Calydonian* Breed,
      Oenides' manly Shoulders overspread,
      Oblique his Tusks, erect his Bristles stood,
      Alive, the Pride and Terror of the Wood.

575   Struck with the Sight, and fix'd in deep Amaze,
      The King th' accomplish'd Oracle surveys,
      Reveres *Apollo*'s vocal Caves, and owns
      The guiding Godhead, and his future Sons.
      O'er all his Bosom sacred Transports reign,
580   And a glad Horror shoots through ev'ry Vein:
      To Heav'n he lifts his Hands, erects his Sight,
      And thus invokes the silent *Queen* of *Night*.

      Goddess of Shades, beneath whose gloomy Reign

---

579. **sacred:** *1717–51:* secret

---

570. **Nemea:** a valley in the northern Argive region, the scene of Hercules' defeat of the famed lion as his first 'labour'. Statius, 487, refers more obscurely to the 'Cleonaei … proelia' ('battles of Cleonae'), a village in the region of Nemea.
571. **Calydonian:** see 574.
572. **Oenides:** Tydeus; cf. 555. His ordinary name is used in Statius, 489, and Stephens, 603.
573. **Oblique … Tusks:** Pope used 'tusks oblique' of a boar in his *Odyssey*, XIX.525, probably recalling Dryden, 'Palamon and Arcite', II.206, *Fables*, p. 32 (comparing the two warriors to fighting boars): 'Their adverse Breasts with Tusks oblique they wound'. Statius, 488, has 'dente recurvo' ('with backward-curving tusk').
574. Pope's addition, expanding Statius, 490, 'Calydonis honos' ('ornament of Calydon'). The goddess Artemis (Diana) sent a great boar to attack Calydon when Oeneus omitted a sacrifice to her; it was killed by another son of Oeneus, Meleager. See also 793. The story was better known from Ovid, *Metamorphoses*, VIII.269–525.

577. **Reveres:** in Statius, 492, the verb is 'agnoscens' ('recognising as genuine').
   vocal Caves: literally from Statius, 'vocalibus antris' (492); 'speaking Den', Stephens, *Essay*, 606, p. 21.
578. **future Sons:** Pope cuts Statius 495–7, in which Apollo's prophecy is characterised as ambiguous and deceptive.
579. **sacred Transports:** cf. 'January and May', 576, and Pope's variant here; also *Windsor-Forest*, 90. Statius' Adrastus is merely frozen in silence ('gelida ora premit'), 493.
580. **glad Horror:** literally from Statius, 493–4, 'laetusque … horror'; Latin 'horror' can mean 'trembling' or 'religious awe'.
581. **erects . . . Sight:** Pope's addition.
582. **Queen** *of* **Night:** simply 'nox' ('night'), in Statius, 498; 'Thou sacred power of Night', Stephens, *Essay*, 613, p. 22.
582-3. Largely Pope's addition.
583-7. Sowerby (2006: 215–16) reads this passage as a characteristic 'Miltonic magnification' of the scene, bringing out in the last two lines of the triplet the dual senses of Statius' 'ortus' (501), i.e. 'sunrise' and 'new birth'.

Yon spangled Arch glows with the starry Train,
585 Who dost the Cares of Heav'n and Earth allay,
Till Nature quicken'd by th' Inspiring Ray,
Wakes to new Vigor with the rising Day.
Oh thou who freest me from my doubtful State,
Long lost and wilder'd in the Maze of Fate!
590 Be present still, oh Goddess! in our Aid;
Proceed, and firm those Omens thou hast made!
We to thy Name our Annual Rites will pay,
And on thy Altars Sacrifices lay;
The Sable Flock shall fall beneath the Stroke,
595 And fill thy Temples with a grateful Smoke:
Hail, faithful *Tripos*! Hail ye dark Abodes
Of awful *Phoebus*: I confess the Gods!

---

585. Who dost : *1717–51:* You who
591. made!: *1736a–51:* made.

---

584. spangled Arch: perhaps modelled on Ogilby's translation of Virgil, *Aeneid*, VIII, *Works of Publius Virgilius Maro* (1649), p. 36: 'the night falls from heavens spangled arch', but the phrase is fairly common in this connection. Stephens, *Essay*, 615, p. 22, has 'sky . . . spangled by thy hand'.
    starry Train: Mason (1987) notes that Milton has a similar description of the night sky at *Paradise Lost*, IV.648–9, including this phrase.
586. Nature: not in Statius, 500–1, where it is the 'proximus . . . Titan', 'the next Titan' (i.e. Sun) which awakens 'aegris animantibus' ('weak living things').
589. wilder'd: to wilder is 'to lose or puzzle in an unknown or pathless tract' (*SJ*, citing this passage).
Maze of Fate: possibly recalling the words of the title character in Dryden and Lee's *Oedipus: A Tragedy*, III.i (1679), p. 47: 'wandring in the maze of Fate I run'.
591. firm: literally from Statius, 504 'tuaque omina firmes' ('confirm your omens'). *EC* compares Dryden, *Aeneid*, VIII.107–8, *Works of Virgil*, p. 437: 'But oh! be present to thy Peoples Aid; | And firm the gracious Promise thou hast made'. *SJ* cites Pope's lines 588–91 in his definition: 'to settle; to confirm; to establish; to fix'.
594. Sable Flock: For 'sable' see 83. Statius, 506–7, has 'nigri . . . greges' ('black herds'). Pope omits some of Statius' detail of the proposed sacrifices, 507–8; Stephens, *Essay*, 622–4, retains them.
595. grateful: 'pleasing; acceptable; delightful; delicious' (*SJ*); 'grateful Smoke' recurs in a similar context at Pope's *Iliad*, VI.383.
596. faithful Tripos: the three-legged chair on which the Pythoness sat to give oracular utterance.
596–7. *TE* compares Stephens, *Essay*, 625–6, p. 22: 'Haile faithfull *Tripos*, and ye close aboads | Of the dark Oracle. I've found the gods', a more literal version of Statius, 509–10. Phoebus is not named in Statius. Dryden uses the phrase 'dark abodes' at least six times in the translation of Virgil's *Aeneid*, indicating sacred caves, the underworld, and the interior of the Trojan horse (e.g. I.91; II.337; IV.874, etc.).

Thus, seiz'd with Sacred Fear, the Monarch pray'd;
Then to his Inner Court the Guests convey'd;
600 Where yet thin Fumes from dying Sparks arise,
And Dust yet white upon each Altar lies;
The Relicks of a former Sacrifice.
The King once more the solemn Rites requires,
And bids renew the Feasts, and wake the sleeping Fires.
605 His Train obey; while all the Courts around
With noisie Care and various Tumult sound.
Embroider'd Purple cloaths the Golden Beds;
This Slave the Floor, and That the Table spreads;
A Third dispels the Darkness of the Night,
610 And fills depending Lamps with Beams of Light;
Here Loaves in Canisters are pil'd on high,
And there, in Flames the slaughter'd Victims fry.
Sublime in Regal State, *Adrastus* shone,
Stretch'd on rich Carpets, on his Iv'ry Throne;
615 A lofty Couch receives each Princely Guest;

---

604. **the sleeping Fires:** *1717–51:* the fires
612. **fry:** *1736b–51:* fly

---

598. In Statius, 510, merely 'sic fatus' ('having spoken thus').

Sacred Fear: reverential dread; a common image in seventeenth-century religious poetry. The phrase is also used by Pope in *Iliad*, VI.204.

601–2. TE compares Stephens, *Essay*, 628–30, p. 22: 'Where th' Altars still look'd white | With their late fires; I'th ashes yet there fumed | Some sparkes alive ...' Stephens explains in a note that the ashes and sparks are from a previous day's sacrifice to Apollo.

604. EC compares Dryden, *Aeneid*, VII.725, *Works of Virgil*, p. 455: 'And on his Altars wak'd the sleeping Fires'. Until the variant was substituted in 1717, the line was an Alexandrine.

605. Train: in Statius, 515, the 'ministri', 'attendants', obey 'certatim' (516), 'emulously'.

607. Purple: the royal or imperial colour.

608. The linking of one verb ('spreads') with two objects ('floor', 'table') is Pope's addition: in Statius the floor is not mentioned.

The slaves ('ministri') are all plural in Statius, not singular as in Pope; Sowerby (2006: 218–20) shows how Pope has enhanced the grandeur of Adrastus in this passage.

610. depending: suspended, hanging down: a Latinism, but not based on Statius; cf. however 719–20.

611. Canisters: A canister was 'a small basket' (*SJ*), as well as a tin; literally from Statius, 523, 'canistris'. Perhaps modelled on Dryden's version of Virgil's description of Dido's feast, *Aeneid*, I.981, *Works of Virgil*, p. 230: 'Then Canisters with Bread are heap'd on high' (and cf. VIII.241). Pope uses the word several times in the Homer translations, but nowhere else.

613. Pope has omitted Statius, 524–5, in which Adrastus happily watches his house bustling with obedient activity.

615–16. Pope's substitution for Statius, 527–9, in which the two young men, healed of the wounds sustained in the fight Pope has omitted, forgive each other their mutual injuries.

Around, at awful Distance, wait the rest.

 And now the King, his Royal Feast to grace,
Acestis calls, the Tutress of his Race,
Who first their Youth in Arts of Virtue train'd,
620 And their ripe Years in modest Grace maintain'd.
Then softly whisper'd in her faithful Ear,
And bad his Daughters to the Rites repair.
When from the close Apartments of the Night,
The Royal Nymphs approach'd divinely bright,
625 Such was *Diana*'s, such *Minerva*'s Face;
Nor shine their Beauties with superior Grace,
But that in these a milder Charm indears,
And less of Terror in their Looks appears.
As on the Heroes first they cast their Eyes,
630 O'er their fair Cheeks the glowing Blushes rise,
Their down cast looks a decent Shame confest,
Then, on their Father's rev'rend Features rest.

---

618. **Tutress:** *1717–51:* guardian
622. **to the Rites repair:** *1717–51:* at the rites appear
624. **approach'd:** *1736a–51:* approach

616. at awful Distance: in due deference to awe-inspiring majesty; not in Statius.
617. The second half of the line is Pope's addition.
618. Acestis ... Tutress: i.e. nurse of the two daughters.
621. faithful Ear: Pope recalled the phrase (of Hector) in his *Iliad*, VII.51 The ear is 'tacita', 'silent', in Statius, 532, indicating that Acestis can be trusted with secrets.
622. Pope's addition, based on what then happens.
623. close Apartments: 'arcano ... thalamo' ('secret bed-chamber'), Statius, 534.
624. Royal Nymphs: Pope's addition.
625. **Diana:** Roman version of the Greek Artemis, goddess of chastity and hunting (cf. *Windsor-Forest*, 160).

Minerva: Roman version of the Greek Athena, goddess of wisdom and skill; given a Greek epithet, 'Pallas' (epithet of Athena) in Statius, 535, where both are described as armed.
626–8. Much expanded from Statius, 536: 'aequa ferunt, terrore minus' ('they bear themselves equally, with less terror').
627. Charm: perhaps a more forceful word in Pope's time, connoting quasi-magical power; cf. 671.
630. Pope's less pointed substitution for Statius, 537–8, 'pariter pallorque ruborque | purpureas hausere genas' ('paleness and redness equally consumed their bright cheeks').
631. decent: 'becoming; fit; suitable' (*SJ*), close to Latin 'decens', though not based on Statius at this point; cf. *Essay on Criticism*, 322.

>   The Banquet done, the Monarch gives the Sign
>   To fill the Goblet high with sparkling Wine,
> 635   Which *Danaus* us'd in sacred Rites of old,
>   With Sculpture grac'd, and rough with rising Gold.
>   Here to the Clouds victorious *Perseus* flies;
>   *Medusa* seems to move her languid Eyes,
>   And, ev'n in Gold, turns paler as she dies.
> 640   There from the Chace *Jove*'s tow'ring Eagle bears
>   On golden Wings, the *Phrygian* to the Stars;
>   Still as he rises in th' Aethereal Height,
>   His native Mountains lessen to his Sight;
>   While all his sad Companions upwards gaze,
> 645   Fix'd on the Glorious Scene in wild Amaze,
>   And the swift Hounds, affrighted as he flies,
>   Run to the Shade, and bark against the Skies.
>
>   This Golden Bowl with gen'rous Juice was crown'd,

---

644. **upwards:** *1717–51:* upward

---

633. **Monarch:** 'Iasides', 'son of Iasus', i.e. of an earlier king of Argos, in Statius, 541.

635. **Danaus:** king of Argos whose race, the Danaans, was used by Homer and other poets to designate the Greeks in general; cf. 354, 458. Pope has here cut Statius' reference (542) to 'seniorque Phoroneus' ('the elder Phoroneus': see 350 above), one of a number of condensations and clarifications (see Sowerby 2006: 220–2).

636. **rising Gold:** i.e. embossed work. TE compares Dryden, *Aeneid*, V.704, *Works of Virgil*, p. 348: 'Accept this Goblet rough with figur'd Gold', but there is a closer match in Dryden's translation of 'The Twelfth Book of Ovid his Metamorphoses', 330–1, *Fables*, p. 431: 'An ample Goblet stood, of antick Mold: | And rough with Figures of the rising Gold'. Cf. Pope's 'Spring', 37–8.

637–8. **Perseus ... Medusa:** the legendary hero Perseus (cf. 318) killed Medusa, the snake-haired Gorgon or female monster of Greek mythology. Pope has omitted Statius' image of Perseus holding the severed head (543–4). Stephens, *Essay*, 661n, p. 23, explains that Perseus was thought to have wings because he was the first to use a ship with sails.

640. **Chace:** chase, hunt.

Jove's ... Eagle: Pope's addition, to clarify the reference (see next line).

641. **the Phrygian:** the young Trojan prince Ganymede, abducted to be the cup-bearer of the gods, by means of an eagle; named in Stephens, *Essay*, 665. Sowerby (2006: 220–2) comments on Pope's enhancement of the emotional aspects of the scene and on its liberal use of words indicating upward motion, compared with Statius, 547–51.

644. **sad Companions:** Pope revisited the phrase in his *Iliad*, XVIII.276; XXIII.313.

645. Pope's addition. For the phrasing and rhyme cf. Creech's translation of Horace, *Epistles*, II.1: 'And if the *Vulgar* with a wild amaze ... | ... on an *Elephant* or a *Panther* gaze'; *The Odes, Satyrs and Epistles of Horace* (1684), p. 535.

648. **Golden Bowl:** Pope's addition, perhaps recalling a detail of the feast in Dryden, *Aeneid*, I.1013, *Works of Virgil*, p. 231: 'The Golden Bowls with sparkling Wine are

The first Libations sprinkled on the Ground;
650 By turns on each Celestial Pow'r they call;
With *Phoebus* Name resounds the vaulted Hall.
The Courtly Train, the Strangers, and the rest,
Crown'd with chast Laurel, and with Garlands drest,
(While with rich Gums the fuming Altars blaze)
655 Salute the God in num'rous Hymns of Praise.

Then thus the King: Perhaps, my Noble Guests,
These honour'd Altars, and these annual Feasts,
To bright *Apollo*'s awful Name design'd,
Unknown, with Wonder may perplex your Mind.
660 Great was the Cause; our old Solemnities
From no blind Zeal or fond Tradition rise;

651. Phoebus: 1717–51: *Phoebus'*
654. 1736a–51: no parentheses

---

crown'd'; almost duplicated at III.455, and common in like circumstances in Pope's *Iliad*, e.g. XV.96; XXIII.273; and XXIV.351-4.

gen'rous Juice: cf. 'The Arrival of Ulysses in Ithaca', 127; the phrase is probably recalled from similar moments in Dryden's version of the *Georgics*, III.761, and *Aeneid*, XII.263. Tate's 'Pomona', 184, in *The Third Part of the Works of Mr. Abraham Cowley* (1689), p. 109, translating book V of Cowley's *Plantarum Libri Sex*, has Bacchus, god of wine, refer to his 'gen'rous Juice'; 'gen'rous' here is 'rich' or 'strong'.

649. Libations: a ritual offering of wine to the gods. Pope's addition. TE compares Dryden, *Aeneid*, I.1031, *Works of Virgil*, p. 232: 'Sprinkling the first Libations on the Ground'.

653. chast Laurel: an allusion to Daphne, turned into a laurel to avoid rape by Apollo; in Statius, 554-5, the celebrants are garlanded with 'pudica .. fronde' ('a modest branch'). Stephens has 'chast unspotted baies', *Essay*, 671, p. 24, with a note on Daphne.

654. rich Gums: perhaps recalling Dryden, 'Of the Pythagorean Philosophy', 584, *Fables*,

p. 525: 'the rich Gums *Arabia* bears'. Pope's substitution for Statius, 555-6, 'largo ... ture' ('with abundant incense').

655. Salute: greet, address, pay homage to.

num'rous: 'harmonious; ... melodious; musical' (*SJ*), after the 'numbers' or metre of verse (*Essay on Criticism*, 340). TE compares Milton, *Paradise Lost*, V.150 (1674), p. 121: 'in Prose or numerous Verse'.

656. TE notes that Pope's phrasing is close to Stephens, *Essay*, 675, p. 24: 'Then saies the King: Perhaps my noble guests'. TE further compares the whole of 656-63 with Dryden's version of the *Aeneid*, VIII.246-61.

658. awful: cf. 282.

659. Pope omits Statius, 561, 'animos advertite, pandam' ('give your attention, I will explain').

661. blind Zeal: cf. Milton, *Paradise Lost*, III.452 (1674), p. 74: 'painful Superstition and blind Zeal'. Statius, 559-60, has 'non inscia... relligio' ('no ignorant superstition', or 'no vain religion', Stephens, *Essay*, 678, p. 24); 'blind Devotion' and 'heady Zeal' are among the things denied in a similar context in Dryden, *Aeneid*, VIII.248-9, *Works of Virgil*, p. 441.

But sav'd from Death, our *Argives* yearly pay
These grateful Honours to the God of Day.

When by a thousand Darts the *Python* slain
665   With Orbs unroll'd lay stretch'd o'er all the Plain,
(Transfix'd as o'er *Castalia*'s Streams he hung,
And suck'd new Poisons with his triple Tongue)
The Victor God did to these Realms resort,
And enter'd old *Crotopus*' humble Court.
670   This *Argive* Prince one only Daughter blest,
That all the Charms of blooming Youth possest;
Fair was her Face, and spotless was her Mind,
Where Filial Love with Virgin Sweetness join'd.

---

665. **stretch'd o'er:** *1717–51:* covering
668–69. *1717–51:* To *Argos*' realms the victor God resorts,
                And enters old *Crotopus*' humble courts
670. ***Argive:*** *1717–51:* rural

---

662. **Argives:** inhabitants of Argos. The line is Pope's addition, based on the story that follows.

664-9. The 'Python' is the dragon-like animal guarding the oracle at Delphi; killed by Apollo, to whom the oracle then became sacred. Warton (*Works of Pope*, II.223) chides Pope for his omission of several 'forcible expressions' of Statius relating to the death throes.

664. **thousand Darts:** TE finds a source for this image in Ovid's version of the story, *Metamorphoses*, I.443, where Apollo uses 'mille ... telis' to destroy the monster. Statius mentions 'absumptis numerosa in vulnera telis' ('with darts having inflicted many wounds'), 567.

665. **Orbs:** coils; Pope's word is suggested by 'septem orbibus atris' ('seven black rings') of Statius, 563.

666. **Castalia:** the spring where the nymph Castalia threw herself to avoid Apollo's pursuit; hence a shrine and washing place on the route to the Delphic oracle, associated with purification (and with poetic inspiration); here, the site of Apollo's killing of the Python (cf. 90, 831); later referred to ironically by Pope in *Dunciad Variorum*, III.144, and *Epistle to Arbuthnot*, 230.

667. **triple Tongue:** 'ore trisulco' ('threefold mouth'), Statius, 565. Cf. the crested serpent who 'dares at *Phoebus* shake his triple tongue', in Ogilby's version of Virgil, *Georgics*, III, *Works of Virgil*, p. 89. EC explains, on the basis of slightly clearer imagery in Statius, that 'the water was not itself poisonous, but it turned to venom in the serpent'.

668. In Statius, 569–70, Apollo comes to Argos (as clarified in Pope's variant) in search of further expiatory sacrifice for the dead: 'nova ... piacula caedis | perquirens', rendered by Stephens 'To cleanse the guilt of bloud'; *Essay*, 690 and note, p. 24.

669. **Crotopus:** an earlier king of Argos; the daughter is named as Psamathe in some sources (see Argument).

672. **spotless ... Mind:** cf. Pope's more developed version of this image in 'Eloisa to Abelard', 209. Shakespeare's raped Lucretia proclaims, *Rape of Lucrece*, 1656: 'Immaculate, and spotlesse is my mind'.

Happy! and happy still She might have prov'd;
675 Were she less beautiful, or less belov'd!
But *Phoebus* lov'd, and on the Flow'ry Side
Of *Nemea*'s Stream the yielding Fair enjoy'd:
And e'er ten Moons their Orb with Light adorn,
Th' illustrious Off-spring of the God was born.
680 The Nymph, her Father's Anger to evade,
Now flies from *Argos* to the Sylvan Shade,
To Woods and Wilds the pleasing Burden bears,
And trusts her Infant to a Shepherd's Cares.

How mean a Fate, unhappy Child! is thine?
685 Ah how unworthy those of Race divine?
On flow'ry Herbs in some green Covert laid,
His Bed the Ground, his Canopy the Shade,
He mixes with the bleating Lambs his Cries;
While the rude Swain his rural Musick tries,
690 To call soft Slumbers on his infant Eyes.
Yet ev'n in those obscure Abodes to live,

---

678. And: *1736a–51:* Now,
681. Now flies: *1736a–51:* Retires

---

675. Statius' emphasis, 574, is rather on her furtive trysts with Apollo ('furta nec occultum ... amorem').

677. Nemea's Stream: river of the Nemean valley, flowing between Corinth and Sicyon; cf. 570.

  yielding Fair: In Statius, 575, she is said to have 'passa deum' ('suffered' or 'allowed the god'); in Stephens, *Essay,* 695–6, p. 24: 'giving way | To th' sportfull god'. At 578 Statius refers to the union as 'coactis' ('enforced').

678. Moons: personified as Cynthia, Statius 577.

679. Statius, 577, says rather that she gave a grandson to Latona (Apollo's mother).

682. pleasing Burden: Pope's addition ('natum', 'son', in Statius, 580), but see quotation in Commentary to 248. Pope used it again in *Iliad,* VI.617, of Andromache's baby son, and perhaps recalled Ovid, *Metamorphoses,* IX.339, where 'dulce ... onus', 'sweet burden', is used of Dryope's baby; Sandys translates this as 'pleasing burden' in *Ouid's Metamorphosis Englished* (1632), p. 308.

684. Pope's addition.

686. Mason (1987) suggests that Pope draws on Milton, *Paradise Lost,* VIII.253–4 (1674), p. 201, where Adam describes his first memory: 'As new wak't from soundest sleep | Soft on the flowrie herb I found me laid'.

688. Pope's addition, perhaps recalling Statius, 580, where the infant is laid furtively amongst the sheep-pens. Pope has dropped several images of the construction of the infant's lodging and protection from Statius, 583–5.

689. rude Swain: uncultivated peasant. The music is Pope's expansion of Statius, 585, 'cava fistula' ('hollow pipe') i.e. the oaten reed of pastoral.

Was more, alas! than cruel Fate wou'd give!
For on the grassie Verdure as he lay,
And breath'd the Freshness of the rising Day,
695 Devouring Dogs the helpless Infant tore,
Fed on his trembling Limbs, and lapt the Gore.
Th' astonish'd Mother when the Rumour came,
Forgets her Father, and neglects her Fame,
With loud Complaints she fills the yielding Air,
700 And beats her Breast, and rends her flowing Hair;
Then wild with Anguish, to her Sire she flies;
Demands the Sentence, and contented dies.

But touch'd with Sorrow for the Dead, too late,
The raging God prepares t' avenge her Fate.
705 He sends a Monster, horrible and fell,
Begot by Furies in the Depths of Hell;
The Pest a Virgin's Face and Bosom bears;
High on her Crown a rising Snake appears,
Guards her black Front, and hisses in her Hairs:

---

694. rising: *1736a–51:* early
708. her: *1741–51:* a

---

695. helpless Infant: Pope's addition.
696. trembling Limbs: Pope's addition.
698. The neat antithesis is Pope's substitution for Statius, 591–2, followed closely by Stephens, *Essay*, 714, p. 25: 'But she forgot both father, shame, and fear'.
700. The 'Hair' detail is Pope's.
702. In Statius, 595, Adrastus exclaims that the father's command is 'infandum' ('unspeakable' or 'abominable'). Stephens also omits this.
704. raging God: named as Phoebus in Statius, 597.
705–13. In his *Essay* (1782: 87–8), Warton prints this passage as evidence of what Pope has done with what is bad in Statius. In his edition (*Works of Pope*, II.227) Warton says this line is 'Much superior to the original', which reads (597–8) 'paras monstrum infandis Acherone sub imo | conceptum Eumenidum thalamis' ('you prepare a monster conceived in the unspeakable beds of the Furies, below lowest Acheron'). For the imagery cf. *Essay on Criticism*, 557.
705. fell: cruel, savage.
706. EC compares Sandys, *Ouids Metamorphosis Englished*, VI (1632), p. 215: 'And calls the Furies from the depth of hell'.
707. Pest: *SJ* cites this description in his definition of 'pest' as 'anything mischievous or destructive'. The term was stronger term in Pope's day by its Latin connection with 'plague'. Statius refers to the monster as 'lues' ('pestilence'), in 601. In some versions of the story the monster is known as 'Poene' ('punishment').
709. Front: forehead (Latin 'frons'). In Statius, 600, the snake 'ferrugineam frontem discriminat' ('divides the rust-coloured forehead'; or 'parts her cloudy brow', Stephens, *Essay*, 725, p. 25).

710 About the Realm she walks her dreadful Round,
    When Night with sable Wings o'erspreads the Ground,
    Devours young Babes before their Parent's Eyes,
    And feeds and thrives on Publick Miseries.

    But gen'rous Rage the bold *Choraebus* warms,
715 *Choraebus*, fam'd for Virtue as for Arms;
    Some few like him, inspir'd with Martial flame,
    Thought a short Life well lost for endless Fame.
    These, where two Ways in equal Parts divide,
    The direful Monster from afar descry'd;
720 Two bleeding Babes depending at her Side;
    Whose panting Vitals, warm with Life, she draws,
    And in their Hearts embrues her cruel Claws.
    The Youth surround her with extended Spears;
    But brave *Choraebus* in the Front appears,
725 Deep in her Breast he plung'd his shining Sword,
    And Hell's dire Monster back to Hell restor'd.
    Th' *Inachians* view'd the Slain with vast Surprize,

---

712. **Parent's:** *1736a–51:* parents
723. **Youth:** *1751:* youths
727. **view'd:** *1736a–51:* view

---

711. **sable Wings**: a common formulation, but perhaps closest to the final line of Dryden, *Aeneid*, XI, *Works of Virgil*, p. 577: 'While Night with sable Wings o'respreads the Sky'. Pope's addition; for 'sable' see 83, 594.

712–13. Cf. Stephens, *Essay*, 728–30, p. 25: 'devouring some | With rav'nous jaws, before their Parents eyes, | And fats herself with publike miseries'; 'before their Parent's Eyes' is a substitution for Statius, 603, 'abripere altricum gremiis' ('ripped from the breasts of nursing mothers').

714. **gen'rous Rage**: cf. 'The Episode of Sarpedon', 21–2, and Commentary. Pope's addition.

 Choraebus: normally Coroebus or Coraebus (see Argument).

716. Martial flame: cf. 'Episode of Sarpedon', 5.

719. Pope's addition.

720. depending: cf. 610, and the parody of this image in *Dunciad Variorum*, II.150.

721. panting Vitals: cf. Charles Cotton, 'The Battaile of Yvry', XCIX, *Poems on Several Occasions* (1689), p. 720: 'Th' unpitying Steel his panting Vitals tore'. The 'panting' and 'warm with life' are Pope's addition.

726. A neater antithesis than Statius, 615–16: 'sua monstra profundo | reddit habere Iovi' ('gave back his monster to underworld Jove to have').

727. **Inachians**: descendants of Inachus; cf. 350.

 vast Surprize: a favourite phrase of Dryden's, e.g. 'Meleager and Atalanta', 206–7; *Aeneid*, VIII.202` and IX.1096; remembered by Pope in his *Odyssey*, IV.154 and XIX.532. In Statius, 616, 'iuvat' ('it pleases') them to view the dying monster; ''Twas a joy', Stephens, *Essay*, 743, p. 26.

Her twisting Volumes, and her rowling Eyes,
Her spotted Breast, and gaping Womb imbru'd
730 With livid Poyson and our Infant's Blood.
The Crowd in stupid Wonder fix'd appear,
Pale ev'n in Joy, nor yet forget to fear.
Some with vast Beams the squallid Corps engage,
And weary all the wild Efforts of Rage.
735 The Birds obscene, that nightly flock'd to Tast,
With hollow Screeches fled the dire Repast;
And ravenous Dogs, allur'd by scented Blood,
With starving Wolves, ran howling to the Wood.

But fir'd with Rage, from cleft *Parnassus*' Brow
740 Avenging *Phoebus* bent his deadly Bow,
And hissing flew the feather'd Fates below;

---

730. **Infant's:** *1736a–51:* childrens
736. **hollow:** *1736b–41:* hallow
738. **With:** *1717–51:* And

---

728. twisting Volumes: coils. Not in Statius at this point, but Pope may recall the description of the dying Python, 562, 'caerulei sinuosa volumina monstri' ('twisted coils of the dark-blue monster'). Cf. *Windsor-Forest*, 143, and Commentary.

729. spotted: 'squalentia' ('filthy'), in Statius, 618, where the breast is thick with decaying matter ('crasso ... tabo').
    imbru'd: soaked.

730. livid Poyson: Pope's addition, in part recalling the 'liventes in morte oculos' ('eyes lead-coloured in death'), of Statius, 617. Cf. 83. In Statius the womb has a 'nefandum | proluvium' ('an unspeakable flood').

731. stupid Wonder: prompted by 'stupet' ('is stupefied'), Statius, 619. Cf. 'Sapho to Phaon', 128.

733–4. Pope glosses over some of the more brutal details in Statius, 621–3, such as the bashing out of teeth from the jaws of the monster with staves; Stephens retains this, 748–50.

733. squallid: prompted by an earlier part of Statius' description; see 729.

735. Birds obscene: a common formulation, e.g. Cowley, *Davideis*, II.818, *Poems* (1656), p. 62: 'The *birds obscene* far from his passage fly', and Dryden's version of Virgil, *Georgics*, I.635. For 'obscene' see 154 above and for the combination, cf. *Windsor-Forest*, 71, and Pope's jocular mention of 'owls and obscene animals' in his letter to Caryll, 19 November 1712 (*Corr.*, I.154).

738. In Statius, 626, the wolves and dogs gape with dry mouths.

739. cleft Parnassus: cf. 165. Parnassus is 'biverticis' ('twin-headed'), in Statius, 628 ('double top' in Stephens, *Essay*, 757, p. 26). Cf. 'Proud, as *Apollo* on his forked hill', *Epistle to Arbuthnot*, 231.

740. Avenging Phoebus: in Statius, 627–8, Apollo is 'saevior ... Delius' ('the more savage Delian'), suggesting comparison with the wild wolves of the previous line. Pope's 'avenging' is transferred from Statius' adjective for the dead monster, 'ultricis'.
    deadly Bow: see next note.

741. feather'd Fates: arrows. Statius, 630, has 'pestifera arma' ('plague-bearing weapons');

A Night of sultry Clouds involv'd around
The Tow'rs, the Fields, and the devoted Ground:
And now a thousand Lives together fled,
745 Death with his Scythe cut off the fatal Thread,
And a whole Province in his Triumph led.

But *Phoebus*, ask'd why noxious Fires appear,
And raging *Sirius* blasts the sickly Year,
Demands their Lives by whom his Monster fell,
750 And dooms a dreadful Sacrifice to Hell.

Blest be thy Dust, and let Eternal Fame
Attend thy *Manes*, and preserve thy Name;
Undaunted Hero! who, divinely brave,
In such a Cause disdain'd thy Life to save;
755 But view'd the Shrine with a superior Look,
And its upbraided Godhead thus bespoke.

---

the hissing is Pope's addition. TE compares Dryden, *Iliad*, I.73-4, *Fables*, p. 192, speaking of Apollo: 'Then with full Force his deadly Bowe he bent, | And Feather'd Fates among the Mules and Sumpters sent'. Pope recalled his version of that version in *Iliad*, I.67-8: 'he twang'd his deadly Bow, | And hissing fly the feather'd Fates below'.

742. involv'd: cf. 487.

743. devoted: doomed, fated. Pope has omitted Statius' detail that the city was 'Cyclopum', 'of the Cyclopes', the original builders.

744. thousand: Statius, 632, gives no number to the 'dulces animae' ('sweet souls') which fall.

745. Statius, 632, has Mors (Death) cut the threads of the Sororum (Sisters, i.e. the three Fates) with 'ense', a sword, rather than a scythe.

746. TE compares Stephens, *Essay*, 762, p. 26: 'and captive townes in triumph led'. In Statius, 633, Death rather bears the city 'manibus' ('to the Shades').

748. Sirius: the main star in the constellation Canis Major, its rising associated with the 'dog days' of summer, and thereby with illness brought on by excessive heat; cf. 'Summer', 21, and *Epistle to Dr Arbuthnot*, 3-4.

749-50. TE compares Stephens, *Essay*, 765-6, p. 26: 'The same Power bids, their lives should pay to hell | A sacrifice, by whom his monster fell'. Stephens is closer to Statius, 636-7, but omits 'cruento' ('gory'), in relation to the monster.

752. Manes: normally the shade or spirit of a dead person (see quotation in Commentary to 746, from which perhaps Pope transfers it). Statius does not use this word for Coroebus, the 'Undaunted Hero' of 753.

755. Shrine: specifically the temple of Cirrha (cf. 90) in Statius, 641, i.e. the Delphic shrine.

superior Look: not in Statius, where Coroebus gives vent to 'sacras ... iras' ('sacred rages'), 642. Dryden's King Theseus regards his contending knights with a 'superiour Look' from his throne in 'Palamon and Arcite', III.490, *Fables*, p. 67.

756. Mostly Pope's addition, based on the general import of Coroebus' speech (e.g. he calls Phoebus 'inique', 'unjust', 648).

>   With Piety, the Soul's securest Guard,
>   And conscious Virtue, still its own Reward,
>   Willing I come; unknowing how to fear;
> 760   Nor shalt thou, *Phoebus*, find a Suppliant here:
>   Thy Monster's Death to me was ow'd alone,
>   And 'tis a Deed too glorious to disown.
>   Behold him here, for whom, so many Days,
>   Impervious Clouds conceal'd thy sullen Rays;
> 765   For whom, as Man no longer claim'd thy Care,
>   Such Numbers fell by Pestilential Air!
>   But if th' abandon'd Race of Human-kind
>   From Gods above no more Compassion find;
>   If such Inclemency in Heav'n can dwell;
> 770   Yet why must un-offending *Argos* feel
>   The Vengeance due to this unlucky Steel?
>   On me, on me, let all thy Fury fall,
>   Nor err from me, since I deserve it all:
>   Unless our Desart Cities please thy Sight,
> 775   And Fun'ral Flames reflect a grateful Light.
>   Discharge thy Shafts, this ready Bosom rend,

---

775. **And:** *1736a–41:* Our; *1751:* Or

757–79. Much extended from Statius, 643–61, apparently to render Coroebus' civic heroism more loftily uncompromising.

757. **Piety . . . Guard:** 'pietas' in Statius, 644, is closer to 'patriotic duty' than the religious sense, and the rest of the line is Pope's invention.

758. **conscious Virtue:** literally from Statius, 644, 'conscia virtus'. Cf. 'Prologue to Cato', 3.

759. **unknowing how:** cf. the phrasing at 'Gardens of Alcinous', 12; 'Vertumnus and Pomona', 3.

762. Pope's addition.

764. **Impervious:** Pope's adjective; Statius calls the clouds 'atris' ('black'), 646.

765–8. A very free paraphrase of Statius, 648–50, omitting a taunt about the fondness of the gods for savage monsters and the direct address to 'inique' ('unjust') Apollo (both retained by Stephens, *Essay*, 779–80).

771. **Steel:** i.e. his sword; Pope's addition.

772. TE compares Milton, *Paradise Lost*, III.236–7 (1674), p. 68: 'Behold mee then, mee for him, life for life | I offer, on mee let thine anger fall' (Christ's offer to stand substitute for humanity), and Dryden, *Aeneid*, IX.571–2, *Works of Virgil*, p. 481: 'Me, me, he cry'd, turn all your Swords alone | On me; the Fact confess'd, the Fault my own'. The repetition is however in Statius, 651, 'me, me . . . solum' ('me, me alone').

773. **err:** wander, divert gaze. The line is Pope's addition.

774. **Desart Cities:** Statius' Coroebus mentions also agricultural land in flames, 654–5.

775. **grateful:** cf. 595.

776. Pope omits some details of Coroebus' challenge to Phoebus, 655–8, including mention of the town's mothers and the final prayers uttered on his own behalf.

  And to the Shades a Ghost Triumphant send;
  But for my Country let my Fate attone,
  Be mine the Vengeance, as the Crime my own.

780 Merit distress'd impartial Heav'n relieves;
  Unwelcome Life relenting *Phoebus* gives;
  For not the vengeful Pow'r, that glow'd with Rage,
  With such amazing Virtue durst engage.
  The Clouds dispers'd, *Apollo*'s Wrath expir'd,
785 And from the wondring God th' unwilling Youth retir'd.
  Thence we these Altars in his Temple raise,
  And offer Annual Honours, Feasts, and Praise;
  These solemn Feasts propitious *Phoebus* please,
  These Honours, still renew'd, his antient Wrath appease.

790 But say, Illustrious Guest (adjoin'd the King)
  What Name you bear, from what high Race you spring?
  The noble *Tydeus* stands confess'd, and known
  Our Neighbour Prince, and Heir of *Calydon*:

---

777. Triumphant: contrasting Death's triumph in 746; Statius' adjective is 'insignem' ('distinguished'). Stephens, *Essay*, 793, p. 27, has 'Send a triumphing soul to th' grave'.

778–9. This model of civic virtue and self-sacrifice, strongly associated with the later work of Pope, is inserted in place of Statius 659–61, where Coroebus reminds Phoebus to discharge the plague-cloud as he kills him.

780. impartial Heav'n: In Statius, 661–2, it is 'Sors aequa' ('impartial fate'; a 'sors' is technically a 'lot' or chance fortune) which 'merentes | respicit' ('regards the deserving'). Stephens omits this.

783. In Statius, 662, Phoebus is deterred by 'reverentia caedis' ('awe of killing'); the 'amazing Virtue' too great for Apollo's daring is Pope's addition.

785. An Alexandrine, with a further one in 789, apparently underlining the end of a narrative segment. This four-line conclusion is expanded from portions of Statius, 666–8; Adrastus changes tack and addresses the youths in the middle of a line (668).

unwilling: EC censures Pope for adding this to Coroebus' character, on the grounds that it lessens his heroism in offering his life if he was weary of it; but Statius prompts the sense by having Apollo grant him 'tristemque ... honorem | ... vitae' ('the sad blessing of life'), 663–4. He subsequently founded a temple to Apollo on Mt Geraneia.

788. propitious: cf. 260.

790–1. Loosely based on Statius, 668–9, with a much higher degree of expectation.

790. Illustrious Guest: Mason (1987) compares Milton, *Paradise Lost*, VII.109, where these words apply to the angel Raphael, visiting Adam.

792. confess'd: acknowledged. His identity was divulged in the section Pope omitted, which requires him to remove Statius' reference, 670, to that moment and rationalise the recognition with 'Our Neighbour Prince'.

793. Calydon: Greek city in Aetolia, west-central Greece; see 574.

Relate your Fortunes, while the friendly Night
795 And silent Hours to various Talk invite.

The *Theban* bends on Earth his gloomy Eyes,
Confus'd, and sadly thus at length replies:
Before these Altars how shall I proclaim
(Oh gen'rous Prince) my Nation or my name,
800 Or thro' what Veins our ancient Blood has roll'd?
Let the sad Tale for ever rest untold!
Yet if propitious to a Wretch unknown,
You seek to share in Sorrows not your own;
Know then, from *Cadmus* I derive my Race,
805 *Jocasta's* Son, and *Thebes* my Native Place.
To whom the King, (who felt his gen'rous Breast
Touch'd with Concern for his unhappy Guest)
Replies — Ah why forbears the Son to Name
His wretched Father, known too well by Fame?
810 Fame, that delights around the World to stray,
Scorns not to take our *Argos* in her Way.
Ev'n those who dwell where Suns at distance roll,
In *Northern* Wilds, and freeze beneath the Pole;
And those who tread the burning *Lybian* Lands,
815 The faithless *Syrtes* and the moving Sands;

---

795. silent Hours: Mason (1987) notes that Milton uses this phrase during the story of creation in *Paradise Lost*, VII.444.

various Talk: literally from Statius, 672, 'variis sermonibus'; but cf. 'Rape of the Locke', I.75.

796. Theban: Polynices. Statius, 673, calls him 'Ismenus', after the Theban river Ismenos; Stephens calls him 'noble *Thebane*', *Essay*, 808, p. 28.

797. Pope has here omitted Polynices' sidelong glance at Tydeus, whom he has wounded, Statius, 674–5 (Stephens, *Essay*, 809–10); Polynices also says, in Statius, 676, that it is not appropriate that he be questioned ('non sum ... quaerendus') about his origins in the holy context of Apollo's feast; Stephens retains this.

799. Oh gen'rous Prince: Pope's addition; for 'gen'rous' cf. 714.

802–3. A generous interpretation of Statius, 679, 'sed si praecipitant miserum cognoscere curae' ('but if your cares press you to know a wretch').

806–7. Statius' Adrastus, 681–2, is more simply 'motus ... hospitiis' ('moved by hospitable friendliness').

808–9. Son ... Father: more explicit than in Statius, 682, 'quid nota recondis' ('why hide known things?').

814. Pope's addition; he reorders the detail of Statius, 685–7, in these lines.

815. faithless Syrtes: shifting sandy shallows of the coastal gulfs to the north of modern Libya and Tunisia, widely referred to as a dangerous area for ships in Latin poetry.

Who view the *Western* Sea's extreamest Bounds,
Or drink of *Ganges* in their *Eastern* Grounds;
All these the Woes of *Oedipus* have known,
Your Fates, your Furies, and your haunted Town.
820 If on the Sons the Parents Crimes descend,
What Prince from those his Lineage can defend?
Be this thy Comfort, that 'tis thine t' efface
With Virtuous Acts thy Ancestors Disgrace,
And be thy self the Honour of thy Race.
825 But see! the Stars begin to steal away,
And shine more faintly at approaching Day;
Now pour the Wine; and in your tuneful Lays,
Once more resound the Great *Apollo*'s Praise.

Oh Father *Phoebus*! whether *Lycia*'s Coast
830 And snowy Mountains thy bright Presence boast;
Whether to sweet *Castalia* thou repair,
And bath in silver Dews thy yellow Hair;
Or pleas'd to find fair *Delos* float no more,
Delight in *Cynthus* and the Shady Shore;
835 Or chuse thy Seat in *Ilion*'s proud Abodes,

---

823. **Ancestors:** *1717–51:* ancestor's
832. **bath:** *1717–51:* bathe

---

817. **Ganges:** also in *Windsor-Forest*, 363. The latter half of the line is Pope's invention.
818–19. Replacing, out of sequence, Statius, 684: 'regnum et furias oculosque pudentes' ('the reign, the rages, and the shamed eyes').
820–1. Statius, 688–9, has Adrastus advise Polynices to stop lamenting the crimes of his family, and tells him that his own lineage has many crimes to deface it. Pope's pointed and quotable couplet is based on Statius, 690, 'nec culpa nepotibus obstat', rendered by Stephens, *Essay*, 830–1, p. 28: 'that blot | Don't prejudice their off-spring'.
822–4. The triplet enacts a conspicuous extension of Statius, 691–2.
825–6. Pope simplifies a complicated reference to the movements of the constellations in Statius, 692–3.

829–54. Cited by Warton (*Works of Pope*, II.237) as 'Some of the most finished lines [Pope] has ever written'.
829. **Lycia:** region of south-west Asia Minor of which Apollo was the patron god. In the prayer, Pope reorders some of the geographical details of Statius, 696–702.
831. **Castalia:** cf. 666.
832. **silver Dews:** Pope's addition; in Statius, 697, Castalia is 'pudico' ('chaste').
833. **float no more:** Delos was in legend a floating island, anchored by Jupiter as a safe place for Leto (Latona) to avoid the wrath of Hera and give birth to Apollo and Artemis/Diana.
834. **Cynthus:** mountain on Delos, sacred to Apollo; most of the ancient temples were on the west or 'shady' side of the island.
835. **Ilion:** Troy.

The shining Structures rais'd by lab'ring Gods!
By thee the Bow and mortal Shafts are born,
Eternal Charms thy blooming Youth adorn:
Skill'd in the Laws of Secret Fate above,
840   And the dark Counsels of Almighty *Jove*,
Thou dost the Seeds of future War foreknow,
The Change of Scepters, and impending Woe;
When direful Meteors spread thro' glowing Air
Long Trails of Light, and shake their blazing Hair.
845   Thy Rage the *Phrygian* felt, who durst aspire
T' excel the Musick of thy Heav'nly Lyre;
Thy Shafts aveng'd lewd *Tityus*' guilty Flame,
Th' Immortal Victim of thy Mother's Fame;
Thy Hand slew *Python*; and the Dame who lost

---

836. Gods!: *1736a–b:* Gods.; *1741–51:* Gods,
841. *1717–51:* 'Tis thine the seeds of future war to know,

---

836. lab'ring Gods: The walls of Troy were built by Apollo and Poseidon; cf. 'Rape of the Locke', I.137. Statius' Adrastus makes more of Apollo's labour and its unfitness for a god, 699–700, retained in Stephens, *Essay*, 844–5; the 'shining Structures' are Pope's addition.

840. dark Counsels ... Jove: in Statius, 707, 'placitura Iovi' ('things that will be pleasing to Jove').

841–4. Pope's lines lavishly expand Statius, 708, 'quae mutent sceptra cometae', 'which comets shall change sceptres'. Warton (*Works of Pope*, II.237), commends the passage as 'far superior to the original'. TE compares Milton, *Paradise Lost*, II.708–11 (1674), p. 48, where Satan: '... like a Comet burn'd, | That fires the length of *Ophiucus* huge | In th' Artick Sky, and from his horrid hair | Shakes Pestilence and Warr.'

Pope might also have recalled Blackmore, *King Arthur*, VI (1697), p. 166: 'Dragons of Fire flew swiftly thro' the Air, | And ruddy Meteors shook their blazing Hair'. Since 'comet' comes from the Greek word for 'hair' such images are mostly derived from classical sources; Pope has very similar images in *Temple of Fame*, 453 and *Iliad*, IV.106, and he parodied it at the end of 'The Rape of the Locke', II.172–3. There is perhaps some contemporary political nuance to the lines, especially the 'Change of Scepters'.

845. the Phrygian: in this instance (cf. 641) Marsyas, a satyr who challenged Apollo to a music contest and was flayed by Apollo upon his defeat; the story was located by Herodotus at Celaenae in southern Phrygia (Asia Minor); *Histories*, II.26. 3. Pope adds 846 to explain the allusion.

847. lewd ... Flame: The giant Tityus was killed by Apollo (in some versions, by Artemis, or Jupiter) for his attempt to rape their mother Leto; in Tartarus two vultures fed continually on his liver (Homer, *Odyssey*, XI.576–81; 709–14 in Pope's version). Again, 848 is added to explain what in Statius, 709–10, is a simple allusion, but Pope has also changed the detail: in Statius Apollo stretches Tityus out on the Stygian sands, and he is 'terrigenam' ('earth-born'), rather than 'leud'.

849. Python: see 664.

the Dame: Niobe, daughter of Tantalus and wife of Amphion of Thebes, who boasted of her extensive family at the expense of Leto;

850   Her num'rous Off-spring for a fatal Boast.
       In *Phlegias'* Doom thy just Revenge appears,
       Condemn'd to Furies and Eternal Fears;
       He views his Food, wou'd taste, yet dares not try;
       But dreads the mouldring Rock that trembles from on high.

855   Propitious hear our Pray'r, O Pow'r Divine!
       And on thy Hospitable *Argos* shine.
       Whether the Style of *Titan* please thee more,
       Whose Purple Rays th' *Achaemenes* adore;
       Or great *Osyris*, who first taught the Swain
860   In *Pharian* Fields to sow the Golden Grain;

853–54. 1717–51: He views his food, but dreads, with lifted eye,
          The mouldring rock that trembles from on high.

Apollo and Artemis then killed all her children. The story was referred to in Homer, *Iliad* (Pope's translation, XXIV.757 and note) and Ovid, *Metamorphoses*, VI.146–312. Pope refers to it further in 'On the Statue of Cleopatra', 56–9, and *The Dunciad* (1743), II.311 and note. Pope's 850 is again an addition to clarify the allusion in Statius, 711–12. Stephens calls her 'The *Thebane* dame', *Essay*, 860, p. 30.

851–4. Phlegyas burned down Apollo's temple at Delphi after Apollo raped or seduced his daughter Coronis. In Statius, 713–15, the scene is Megaera. He was presented with a feast which lay under unstable rocks, threatening to crush him if he ate: Statius, 713, 'subter cava saxa iacentem', 'lying under hollow rocks'. In Statius it is also clear that Phlegyas cannot eat the food because it has been profaned. *EC* suggests the influence of Dryden, *Aeneid*, VI.817–18, *Works of Virgil*, p. 386, describing the punishment of Pirithous and Ixion (the latter a son of Phlegyas): 'High o're their Heads a mould'ring Rock is plac'd, | That promises a fall; and shakes at ev'ry Blast'. *TE* compares Stephens, *Essay*, 862–3, p. 30:

'hungry Phlegias, who does fear | The ever-falling stone'.

856. **Argos:** 'Iunoniaque arva', 'fields of Juno', Statius, 716.

857. **Style:** mode of address, name.

Titan: of the order of gods preceding the Olympian family; Hyperion was the Titan sun-god corresponding to Apollo.

858. **Purple:** transferred from 'roseum', 'rose-coloured', applied to 'Titan' in the previous line, Statius, 717.

Achaemenes: the tribal descendants of Achaemenes, legendary ancestor of the Persian king Darius; the reference is to Persian worship of the sun, as in 861.

859. **Osyris:** Osiris, Egyptian god of death, rebirth, and agriculture; 'frugiferum' ('harvest-bringing'), in Statius, 719, hence Pope's explanatory addition, 860.

860. **Pharian:** Egyptian (after the famous lighthouse island at Alexandria, or by allusion to 'Pharaoh'); cf. Milton, 'A Paraphrase on *Psalm* 114', 3, *Poems of Mr. John Milton* (1645), p. 12: 'And past from *Pharian* fields to *Canaan* Land'.

Golden Grain: cf. 'Vertumnus and Pomona', 31.

Or *Mitra,* to whose Beams the *Persian* bows,
And pays in hollow Rocks his awful Vows,
Mitra, whose Head the Blaze of Light adorns,
Who grasps the strugling Heifer's Lunar Horns.

The End of the first Book.

The End of the first Book.: *1717-51:* omitted

***861*. Mitra:** Mithras, an Indo-Iranian god of the dawn light and of cattle-herding, identified by the Romans as a bull-killing sun-god, worshipped in underground caves or grottoes. Most of the line is Pope's addition, as are the 'Vows' in 862, the whole of 863, and 'Lunar' in 864. Stephens, *Essay,* 871–2, p. 30, is closer to Statius: 'Or, as the *Persians* in their caves below, | *Mitra,* which drawes by th' hornes a stubborn Cow'. The horns of the cow or bull represent the horned moon and the struggle is that between night and day.

862. awful: solemn, awe-inspiring, reverential.

***864.* Lunar Horns:** cf. Dryden, 'The Fable of Isis and Ianthe', 185-6, *Examen Poeticum,* p. 81: 'the Lunar Horns that bind | The brows of *Isis*'.

9

THE FABLE OF VERTUMNUS AND POMONA

(1712)

Editors' Headnote

Composition and publication

'Vertumnus and Pomona' was first published on 20 May 1712. Spence records Pope's early enthusiasm for Ovid's *Metamorphoses*: 'When Mr. Pope first got into the way of teaching himself and applied so close to it in the Forest, some of his first exercises were imitations of the stories that pleased him most in Ovid' (*OAC*, I.12, no. 25, 1743). The language of this recollection echoes the 'Advertisement' with which Pope prefaced his translations in collected editions from the 1736 *Works* on:

> THE following Translations were selected from many others done by the Author in his youth; for the most part indeed but a sort of *Exercises*, while he was improving himself in the Languages, and carried by his early Bent to *Poetry* to perform them rather in Verse than Prose.

Pope told Spence that in his early youth he had translated 'above a quarter of the *Metamorphoses*' (*OAC*, I.14, no. 31, March 1743); if so, all but the present poem, the 'Fable of Dryope' and 'Polyphemus and Acis' are now lost, unless the version of the Arethusa story (see Headnote to previous poem) is by Pope. While there is no evidence for a precise date of composition, the present story was clearly in his mind in 1708, as in a letter of 25 April of that year (*Corr.*, I.47) Pope teased his rakish friend Henry Cromwell about his ascendancy 'over all the Sex': 'I guess that your Friend *Vertumnus* among all the Forms he assum'd to win the good Graces of *Pomona*, never took upon him that of a Slovenly Beau'. This letter was one of several which remarked on Cromwell's relationship with 'Sappho' (see Headnote to 'Sapho to Phaon'). *TE* suggests that because it contains a number of expletives of the kind which Pope set his face against in the *Essay on Criticism* (see 349 and commentary), it is likely that 'Vertumnus and Pomona' was substantially completed before 1711; there are three instances in the poem, all of which were removed from texts of *1717* onwards (9, 27–8, 122). However, Pope had voiced similar objections in earlier letters (the possibly fabricated letter to

Walsh, 22 October 1706, and to Cromwell, 25 November 1710, *Corr.*, I.23 and 107) and the date of composition remains conjectural. The translation was evidently finished early in 1712: on 19 February 1712 Lintot paid Pope £16 2s 6d for the copyright of this poem combined with that of 'The First Book of Statius' (McLaverty 2001: 17). 'Vertumnus and Pomona' was the first of Pope's translations from the *Metamorphoses* to be printed, and was first published in *Miscellaneous Poems and Translations, By Several Hands*, occupying pp. 129–36, at the start of a group of his contributions to the volume (for which, see Headnote to 'The First Book of Statius his Thebais').

Text

The text presented here is taken from the first edition of 1712. Revision is largely confined to the *Works* of 1717. All editions from the *Works* of 1736 onwards include an edited (i.e. truncated to fit) Latin text on the lower half of each page; this was altered to a facing-page arrangement in 1751.

Pope's lines were incorporated as part of book XIV of *Ovid's Metamorphoses. In Fifteen Books. A New Translation. By Several Hands*, a composite version edited by George Sewell and published by (among others) Edmund Curll in 1716 (dated 1717; Griffith 59b); book XIV is ascribed to 'Mr. *Pope* and Mr. *Theobald*', i.e. Lewis Theobald, a future enemy, who presumably supplied everything in the book outside Pope's lines. Pope is not known to have made any comment about this, but it seems very unlikely to have had his authorisation. The volume was apparently designed to pre-empt the more famous version edited by Garth, which included Pope's 'Fable of Dryope' in book IX, later in 1717: *Ovid's Metamorphoses in Fifteen Books. Translated by the Most Eminent Hands* (Griffith 88). Sewell's version was reissued several times. The text follows Pope's 1712 version, but lacks the later authorised changes; it has some minor variants, quite possibly errors of transcription; they appear to have no authority and are not included in the collation. The various extant texts of 'Vertumnus and Pomona' are referred to in the apparatus as follows:

1712: *Miscellaneous Poems and Translations*, octavo (Griffith 6)

1717: *Works*, quarto (Griffith 79)

1736: *Works*, vol.III, octavo (Griffith 417, 418)

1741: *Works*, vol.I, part 2, octavo (Griffith 521)

1751: *Works*, vol.II, octavo (Griffith 644)

Models and sources

For Pope's early reading of and association with the Roman poet Ovid, see Headnote to 'Sapho to Phaon'. As that poem was modelled on the collective versions of Ovid's *Heroides*, and especially on Dryden's practice, so the selection of an episode from the *Metamorphoses* was sanctioned by Dryden's model in the various *Miscellanies* of which he was the editor, and on his individual contributions in *Fables Ancient and Modern* (1700); Pope's title, 'The Fable of . . . ', suggests a specific link to the latter (cf his 'Fable of Dryope', 1717). Dryden had extracted from various books of the *Metamorphoses* the variously amorous stories of Meleager and Atalanta (VIII); Baucis and Philemon (VIII); Pygmalion (X); Cinyras and Myrrha (X); and Ceyx and Alcyone (X), as well as one entire book (XII) and some less erotically focused material: Ajax and Ulysses (XIII); and 'Of the Pythagorean Philosophy' (XV). Pope based his poem on Ovid's narrative in a relatively untouched book of the *Metamorphoses*, XIV.623–771, omitting 693–762, a lugubrious inset story of the love-suicide of Iphis and transformation to stone of the cold princess Anaxorete, told by Vertumnus to Pomona as part of his attempt to seduce her. *Miscellaneous Poems and Translations* contained other Ovidian translations, including two short pieces from the *Amores* by Cromwell, the story of Arachne from the sixth book of *Metamorphoses* by Pope's future friend John Gay, and an unascribed version of the 'Story of Arethusa' from book V, positioned suggestively immediately before Pope's poem. Pope was also certainly aware of at least the major earlier translations: *The .xv.bookes of P. Ouidius Naso, entytuled Metamorphosis, translated oute of Latin into English meeter* by Arthur Golding (1567); and *Ovid's Metamorphosis Englished* (1626) and *Ouid's Metamorphosis Englished, Mythologiz'd, and Represented in Figures* (1632), both by George Sandys. Pope told Spence that Golding's was 'a pretty good one, considering the time when it was written' (*OAC*, I.181, no. 416, May 1730), and he recorded that he 'liked extremely' Sandys (*ibid.*, I.14, no. 30, March 1743); it is likely that he had access to both versions, but there is little to suggest that one or other was foremost in his mind in this poem; in the Commentary we quote from the 1632 version unless otherwise stated.

The material used by Pope occupies pp. 182^v–5 of the Golding version and (respectively) pp. 407–12 and 469–72 of the 1626 and 1632 versions of Sandys. Golding takes roughly 100 fourteen-syllable lines to translate 79 of Ovid; Sandys takes 92 lines of heroic couplets, Pope's own form. Pope might conceivably have been aware of the oddly repetitive version by Abraham Fraunce of the whole tale, including a drastic summary of the inset narrative, in *The Third Part of the Countess of Pembroke's Yuychurch* (1592), pp. 51–3; this takes 132 unrhymed fourteen-syllable lines. More recently there had been a version by John Hopkins, 'The Metamorphosis of Love', in his *Amasia* (1700), III.1–5, an 87-line version in decorously erotic loose couplets, which also omits the inset story. The strongest verbal echoes, however, are from Sandys.

Pope's 1–107 corresponds to Ovid's XIV.623–92, and his 108–23 to Ovid's 763–71. Thus 123 lines of Pope are derived from 79 lines of Ovid. The expansion is mainly in terms of small detail, the addition of epithets and other modifiers, and the generation, from relatively enjambed hexameters, of symmetry and antithesis to fill out end-stopped couplets. Pope's line 28, 'With greater Passion, but with like Success', is a much neater antithesis than that in Ovid's 641–2; his couplet at 41–2 is based on a single line in Ovid; the couplets at 108–11 are constructed out of two contrasting lines in Ovid (763–4). The biggest expansion comes in the final six lines; some 25 or so other points of significant addition are noted in the Commentary.

Vertumnus was an obscure god of Roman mythology, thought by some to have an Etruscan origin. His status as shape-shifter (equivalent to the Greek Proteus) was derived from a pun on the name, alluding to the Latin verb *vertere* or 'turn', hence his usefulness to Ovid's theme of metamorphosis, and his designation as 'sly' by Golding (p. 182ᵛ, with the marginal note '*Turner*') and 'slippery turnecoate' by Fraunce (p. 52). He was mentioned by Propertius as a god of horticulture (e.g. the opening of *Elegies*, IV.ii). Ovid is however thought to have invented this particular story, the version that became well known, and which came to have some importance in Roman history and culture (see Littlefield 1965; Lindheim 2010). Sandys, in his notes to the 1632 version, pp. 485-6, presents Vertumnus as an emblem of the changing seasons of the year and of the roles adopted by labourers (ploughman, reaper, winemaker); the old woman signifies 'when in the declination of the yeare he marries with *Pomona*; in that all fruits then come to maturity; and then his festivals were celebrated in October'. Vertumnus is also 'taken for the inconstant mutability of our humane affections'. William King, in his *Historical Account of the Heathen Gods and Heroes* (1710), p. 118, summarises contemporary understanding:

> *Vertumnus* is an Emblem of the Year, which turns it self into Variety of Shapes, according to the Multitude of its Productions in different Seasons, but is at no time more graceful than when *Pomona* the Goddess of ripe Fruits submits to his Embraces.

King records the tradition that Vertumnus was an early king of the Tuscans, who taught orchard husbandry to his people.

Pomona had an independent status as a minor goddess of tree-fruits, sometimes conflated with Flora, and the name was often invoked in botanical or georgic literature, e.g. John Evelyn's appendix on cider-making in *Sylva* (1664). Pope mentions her again in *Windsor-Forest* (37). In *Paradise Lost*, IX.393-5, Milton makes a comparison between Eve and Pomona and, in turn, Pope's Pomona, especially at 9-16, much resembles Milton's horticulturalist Eve. The subject was recommended for paintings in fountains and gardens in John Elsum, *The Art of Painting after the Italian Manner* (1703), p. 85, but the erotic motif of the disguised god attempting to seduce Pomona was also a very common subject of paintings in the European baroque.

Context

In the immediate wake of Pope's poem, Abel Evans addressed *Vertumnus*, a poem on the coming peace, to Jacob Bobart, professor of botany at Oxford (1713); Henry Carey wrote a short cantata on the erotic aspects of the theme (*Poems on Several Occasions*, 1713, pp. 75-6). These aspects were both no doubt in Pope's mind. The story might have appealed as a further exploration of the 'hortus conclusus' or enclosed garden or orchard image from 'January and May' (and leading on to the 'beauteous Order' of 'The Gardens of Alcinous') but the reference in the letter to Cromwell suggests that its erotic potential was certainly present, putting it alongside the sexual theme of 'January and May', 'Sapho to Phaon', 'The Rape of the Locke' and 'On a Fan of the Author's Design'. Pope had probably met the Blount sisters, Martha and Teresa, around 1707 (see Headnote to 'To a Young Lady with the Works of Voiture') and much of his correspondence and some of the verse of this period has a strong sexual slant, with perhaps a certain amount of wishful thinking: Rumbold (1989: 91) comments that Pomona is more consciously complicit with the seduction (or assault) than Belinda in *Rape of the Lock*. The same applies in relation to the Lodona episode of Ovidian pursuit in *Windsor-Forest* (see Headnote to that poem), where a huntress leaves a protected zone and is immediately subject to the aggressive sexual pursuit of a nature-god. Ault (1949: 39) connects the poem to another seduction-transformation scene from Ovid, the story of Arethusa (a clear influence on the Lodona episode) which appears immediately before 'Vertumnus and Pomona' in the 1712 anthology (pp. 123–8) and which is argued by Ault to be in fact by Pope (the attribution remains unconfirmed). Pomona's fortified garden, having kept out the wild 'Sylvans', eventually admits more willingly a god of cultivation, with no 'Force' required (see Commentary to the final six lines). The sense of a transcendent order of nature resulting from a mixed economy of desire and resistance, of the kind shortly to be glorified in *Windsor-Forest*, e.g. 11–16, perhaps also underlies Pope's selection of the episode.

THE
FABLE
OF
Vertumnus and *Pomona*;
FROM
The Fourteenth Book of OVID's
METAMORPHOSES.
Rege sub hoc Pomona fuit — &c.
By Mr. *POPE*.

THE fair *Pomona* flourish'd in his Reign;
Of all the Virgins of the Sylvan Train,
None taught the Trees a nobler Race to bear,

Title. THE | FABLE | OF: *1717–51:* omitted
Epigraph. 1717–51: omitted

Title. For the use of 'Fable' see Headnote. The Latin is quoted from Ovid, *Metamorphoses*, XIV.623, the start of the passage Pope is translating.

1. *flourish'd:* a generous expansion of Ovid's 'fuit', 'was'; but the versions in Abraham Fraunce, *The Third Part of the Countess of Pembroke's Yuychurch* (1592), p. 51ᵛ, George Sandys, *Ouids Metamorphosis Englished, Mythologiz'd, and Represented in Figures* (1632), p. 469, and John Hopkins, 'The Metamorphosis of Love', *Amasia* (1700), III.1, all have versions of this word.

  his Reign: that of Proca (Ovid, *Metamorphoses*, XIV.622), king of Alba Longa in Central Italy (cf. 76 below).

2. *Virgins . . . Train:* i.e. the wood nymphs who hunt with Artemis (Diana); explicitly a 'hamadryad' in Ovid, XIV.624, and translated as such in Sandys, p. 469. Cf. Tate, *Panacea: A Poem upon Tea*, II (1700), p. 27: '*Diana* thus—and, with her Sylvan Train | Of Nymphs attended . . .'. Cf. also 9 below, and *Windsor-Forest*, 160 and 198. Pope recalled his phrasing in his *Odyssey*, VI.119: 'A sylvan train the huntress Queen surrounds'.

3. *taught:* cf. 'teach' in 12, and 'The Gardens of Alcinous', 12; 'trained' in the modern horticultural sense.

  nobler Race: Pope's addition, perhaps looking towards the grafting which takes place in 14. In Shakespeare's *The Winter's Tale*, IV.iv.95, Polixenes uses the same phrase to describe high-status grafts on low-status stock, in a discussion about breeding more generally.

Or more improv'd the Vegetable Care.
5   To her the shady Grove, the flow'ry Field,
The Streams and Fountains, no Delights cou'd yield;
'Twas all her Joy the ripening Fruits to tend,
And view the Boughs with happy Burthens bend.
No Dart she wielded, but a Hook did bear,
10 To lop the Growth of the luxuriant Year,
To decent Form the lawless Shoots to bring,
And teach th' obedient Branches where to spring.
Now the cleft Rind inserted Graffs receives,
And yields an Off-spring more than Nature gives;

---

8. **view:** *1717–51:* see
9. 1717–51: The hook she bore, instead of *Cynthia*'s spear,

---

4. **Vegetable Care:** horticulture. *TE* cites Dryden's version of Virgil's *Georgics*, IV.178, *Works of Virgil*, p. 127: 'To teach the vegetable Arts'. Pope omits here 'unde tenet nomen', 'hence she held her name', i.e. Ovid (626) explains that she was named after 'poma', 'fruit' or 'fruit-tree', a word which appears several times in Ovid in this section (e.g. 627). The element is lost in English.

5. **flow'ry Field:** Pope's addition, recalled by him in 'Polyphemus and Acis', 57.

8. **happy Burthens:** i.e. burdens, Ovid's 'felicia poma', 'abundant fruits', translated by Sandys, p. 469, as 'generous burdens'; the phrase suggests pregnancy (cf. 'The First Book of Statius', 682), perhaps prompted by Ovid's 'fetus' (625), 'productive' or 'pregnant'.

9. **Hook:** a pruning hook ('adunca ... falce', 'curved pruning-hook', Ovid, 628), as in 37, rather than the hunting weapon, 'Dart', or '*Cynthia*'s spear' in the variant, associated with the nymphs of Diana (cf. 2); 'iaculo', 'spear', in Ovid, 628, translated as 'dart' by Arthur Golding, *The .xv. Bookes of P. Ouidius Naso, entytuled Metamorphosis* (1567), p. 182ᵛ. Ovid and the earlier translators do not mention Cynthia.

10. **lop ... Growth:** cf. Milton, *Paradise Lost*, IX.208–11 (Eve speaking): 'our Labour grows | Luxurious by restraint; what we by day | Lop overgrown, or prune, or prop, or bind, | One night or two with wanton growth derides'. The 'Year' is Pope's addition, perhaps recalling Dryden, *Georgics*, II.568–9, *Works of Virgil* (1697), p. 88: 'Twice in the Year luxuriant Leaves o'reshade | The incumber'd Vine', from the section on pruning.

11. **decent:** in the Latinate sense of 'becoming; fit; suitable' (*SJ*).

lawless: cf. 20: another humanisation, along with 'obedient' in 12. Ovid has (629–30): 'luxuriem premit et spatiantia passim | bracchia conpescit', 'she pushed back the luxuriant growth and pruned the branches spreading everywhere'. Sandys, p. 469, translates: 'luxurious twigs, and boughes that dare | Transcend their bounds'.

13. **Rind:** bark.

Graffs: grafts; the process whereby a slip from one tree is inserted into a small slit in the bark of another to produce hybrid effects. There is a long section on grafting in book II of Virgil's *Georgics* (in Dryden's translation, II.37–74).

14. **more than Nature:** Ovid, 631, has 'sucos alieno praestat alumno', 'she provides sap to a foreign foster-child'. Pope's phrase is not often used in this positive sense.

15   Now sliding Streams the thirsty Plants renew,
     And feed their Fibres with reviving Dew.

     These Cares alone her Virgin Breast imploy,
     Averse from *Venus* and the Nuptial Joy;
     Her private Orchards wall'd on ev'ry side,
20   To lawless Sylvans all Access deny'd.
     How oft the *Satyrs* and the wanton *Fawns*,
     Who haunt the Forests or frequent the Lawns,
     The *God* whose Ensign scares the Birds of Prey,
     And old *Silenus*, youthful in Decay,

---

18. Joy;: *1736–51:* joy.

---

15. sliding Streams: TE cites Sandys's version, p. 469: 'soft-sliding Springs'. Ovid, 633, has 'labentibus ... undis', 'with slipping waters'.

18. Nuptial Joy: marriage and sex: Pope's addition. He recalled this locution in his translation of Homer, *Odyssey*, XIX.146.

19. wall'd on ev'ry side: Cf. 'January and May', 450–1, and 'The Gardens of Alcinous', 3–4 and Commentary. In Ovid, 635, Pomona builds her walls 'vim ... agrestum metuens', 'fearing rustic force', i.e. sexual violence, the 'rapefull Ruralls' of Sandys, p. 469.

20. Sylvans: woodland dwellers, specifically 'viriles', 'masculine', in Ovid, 636. Cf. 'Winter', 22.

21. Satyrs ... Fawns. Satyrs were wild human-like male creatures of the woods, associated with sexual desire, and companions of the God of wine, Bacchus, and, in the later classical period, of Pan, the horned and goat-legged Nature god (cf. *Windsor-Forest*, 37 and 181). At this point Ovid (638) has 'Panes', Pans, i.e. horned avatars of the god Pan, as does Golding, p. 182ᵛ: 'the Pannes that wantonly doo praunce, | With horned forheads'. Fraunce, Sandys and Hopkins all feature Pan himself. A fawn is normally a young deer, as in Dryden's 'Sylvan Fauns' in his version of Virgil, *Eclogues*, VI.44, *Works of Virgil*, p. 27, and Pope's *Essay on Man*, III.29, also rhyming 'wanton fawn' with 'lawn'. Pope might have been recalling Jonson, 'To Penshurst', 16–18, *Workes of Beniamin Ionson* (1616), p. 820, which has 'many a SYLVANE', 'ruddy *Satyres*' and 'lighter *Faunes*' in succession.

wanton: for the senses see Commentary to 'Spring', 35 and 53–6.

22. Pope's addition; Ovid 637, mentions the dances of the Satyrs, which Pope omits. Conventional pastoral imagery; cf. Oldmixon, *A Pastoral Poem on the Victories at Schellenburgh and Blenheim* (1704), p. 2: 'the generous Swains | Who haunt the Forest, or frequent the Plains'.

23. Ensign: emblem. The emblem of Priapus was a large phallus, as he was a fertility figure, but he was also a god of gardens (cf. 'January and May', 452–3) who threatened invaders with violence. Ovid says that Priapus, whom he also does not name, 'fures vel falce vel inguine terret', 'scares thieves with either sickle or groin'. Also mentioned in the 'Fable of Dryope', 32. TE cites Dryden's description from his version of Virgil, *Georgics*, IV.167–8, *Works of Virgil*, p. 127: 'Besides, the God obscene, who frights away, | With his Lath Sword, the Thiefs and Birds of Prey'. Golding calls him a 'feend' and uses the phrase 'priuy part' (p. 182ᵛ), Sandys refers to his 'member' (p. 469); Fraunce (p. 52) and Hopkins (p. 2) name Priapus but gloss over the detail.

24. Silenus: regarded as father of the satyrs (21), and a habitual drunkard ('old staggring Tospot', in Fraunce, p. 52); he features prominently in Virgil, *Eclogues*, VI. Ovid, 639: 'suis semper iuvenilior annis, 'still more youthfull then his years', in Sandys, p. 469.

432   THE FABLE OF VERTUMNUS AND POMONA (1712)

25   Imploy'd their Wiles and unavailing Care,
         To pass the Fences, and surprize the Fair?
         But most *Vertumnus* did his Love profess,
         With greater Passion, but with like Success;
         To gain her Sight, a thousand Forms he wears,
30   And first a Reaper from the Field appears,
         Sweating he walks, while Loads of golden Grain
         O'ercharge the Shoulders of the seeming Swain.
         Oft o'er his Back a crooked Scythe is laid,
         And Wreaths of Hay his Sun-burnt Temples shade;
35   Oft in his harden'd Hand a Goad he bears,

27–28. 1717–51: Like these, *Vertumnus* own'd his faithful flame,
         Like these, rejected by the scornful dame.

---

youthful in Decay: cf. William Shippen, *Faction Display'd* (1704), p. 12: 'A batter'd Beau, yet youthful in Decay'.

25–6. Pope's addition, based on slighter suggestions in Ovid, 637–41, that they are plotting 'ut poterentur ea', 'in order that they should possess her'.

25. unavailing Care: a phrase Pope remembered in *Iliad*, XIX.31, and perhaps echoed from Congreve, 'To Sir Godfrey Kneller', 5, *Works* (1710), III.999: 'Oft have I try'd, with unavailing Care . . .', a line itself probably modelled on Dryden, *Aeneid*, XI.239, *Works of Virgil*, p. 545: 'Vain Vows to Heav'n, and unavailing Care'.

28 variant. scornful dame: an addition. A common phrase in this context, e.g. in the story of Iphis and Anarexete translated by Thomas Uvedale in his Ovidian *The Remedy of Love* (1704), p. 89, and Pope's rival Ambrose Philips's 'First Pastoral', *Poetical Miscellanies. The Sixth Part* (1709), p. 5. Pope reused the phrase for the goddess Athena in his translation of Homer, *Iliad*, XXI.476.

31. Sweating: Pope's addition; Ovid's reaper (643) is 'duri', 'rough'.

   golden Grain: Cf. 'The First Book of Statius his Thebais', 860 and Commentary. In Ovid, 643–4, Vertumnus more modestly 'aristas | corbe tulit' 'has brought barley ears in a basket'; Pope exaggerates the rough labourer look, perhaps following Golding's 'bundells' of corn (p. 182ᵛ); Fraunce also has 'sheaues of corne in a bundell', p. 52, and Sandys 'Laden with weightie sheafes', p. 469.

32. seeming Swain: figure disguised as an agricultural labourer, 'verique . . . messoris imago', 'the image of a real reaper', Ovid, 644.

33. crooked Scythe: an addition; cf. Fraunce's 'crookt sithe' (p. 52).

34. Wreaths: cf. Sandys, p. 469: 'Oft wreathes of new-mow'd grasse his browes array'. In Ovid (645), his temples are 'faeno religata recenti', 'bound with fresh hay'.

   Sun-burnt: Pope's addition, but based on Ovid's hint (646) that he looked as if he had been turning the new hay, i.e. in a sunny period of harvest, a detail otherwise omitted by Pope.

35–6. TE cites Sandys's version, p. 469: 'A gode now in his hardned hands he beares, | And newly seemes to haue vnyok't his Steeres'.

35. harden'd Hand: Ovid (647) uses the adjective 'rigida', 'stiff' or 'hard'; Golding elaborates, 'in hand made hard with woork extreeme', p. 182ᵛ.

   Goad: cattle-prod.

Like one who late unyok'd the sweating Steers.
Sometimes his Pruning-hook corrects the Vines,
And the loose Straglers to their Ranks confines.
Now gath'ring what the bounteous Year allows,
40   He pulls ripe Apples from the bending Boughs.
A Soldier now, he with his Sword appears;
A Fisher next, his trembling Angle bears.
Each Shape he varies, and each Art he tries,
On her bright Charms to feast his longing Eyes.

45   A Female Form at last *Vertumnus* wears, ⎫
With all the Marks of rev'rend Age appears, ⎬
His Temples thinly spread with silver Hairs: ⎭
Prop'd on his Staff, and stooping as he goes,
A painted Mitre shades his furrow'd Brows.

---

42. **bears.:** *1717–51:* bears;

---

36. sweating Steers: in Ovid, 648, 'fessos... iuvencos', 'weerye Oxen' (Golding, p. 183). Cf. Dryden's version of Virgil, *Eclogues*, II.96, *Works of Virgil*, p. 9: 'The sweating Steers unharness'd from the Yoke'. Cf. also 'The First Book of Statius his Thebais', 184–5.

37. TE cites Sandys, p. 469: 'Oft vines and fruit-trees with a pruning hooke | Corrects'. King, *Historical Account of the Heathen Gods* (1710), p. 118, says that Vertumnus is depicted with a 'Pruning Hook in one Hand, and ripe Fruits in the other'. Ovid's Vertumnus, 649, has a 'falce', pruning-hook, like Pomona, in 628 (see 9 above), but does nothing with it.

38. An addition, perhaps echoing the gardening scenes in *Paradise Lost* (see 10 above) or Shakespeare, *Richard II*, III.iv.29–39, where a gardener instructs a servant: 'Go, bind thou up young [or 'yon'] dangling apricocks'.

39. Mostly Pope's addition.

   bounteous Year: cf. Behn, 'Song to Ceres', 1, *Poems upon Several Occasions* (1684), p. 68: '*Ceres*, Great Goddess of the bounteous Year'; Dryden, *Britannia Rediviva*, 266 (1688), p. 11: 'The timely product of the bounteous Year'.

40. Ovid (650): 'lecturum poma putares'; 'you would think he was going to pick fruits'; Ovid equips him with a ladder.

41–2. Based on a single line of Ovid (651): 'miles erat gladio, piscator harundine sumpta', 'he was a soldier with a sword, an angler with a rod picked up'. Translated by Golding (p. 183) and Sandys, p. 469, as one line, but extended into two by Hopkins (p. 2) and generously expanded by Fraunce (p. 52).

42. trembling Angle: cf. *Windsor-Forest*, 137–8 and Commentary.

44. TE cites Sandys's version, p. 469: 'To winne excesse ['accesse', in the 1626 version], and please his longing eyes'. Ovid, 653, has 'ut caperet spectatae gaudia formae', 'to gain the joys of her watched form'.

46. rev'rend Age: Pope's addition.

49. painted Mitre: literally from Ovid's 'picta... mitra', 654, and rendered the same way by Sandys (p. 469). Pope reorders the description to culminate in this, where Ovid begins with it. The Latin word was a transliteration of the Greek one, meaning variously a headband, wig, snood, or turban. Sandys glosses it: 'A head attire which old women wore with labels hanging downe at their eares'. Dryden associates the

50   The God, in this decrepit Form array'd,
     The Gardens enter'd, and the Fruits survey'd,
     And *happy You*! (he thus address'd the Maid)
     Whose Charms as far all other Nymphs out-shine,
     As other Gardens are excell'd by thine!
55   Then kiss'd the Fair; (his Kisses warmer grow
     Than such as Women on their Sex bestow.)
     Then plac'd beside her on the flow'ry Ground,
     Beheld the Trees with Autumn's Bounty crown'd;
     An Elm was near, to whose Embraces led,
60   The curling Vine her swelling Clusters spread;
     He view'd their twining Branches with Delight,

---

58. crown'd;: *1717–51:* crown'd.
61. their: *1741–51:* her

'painted Mitre' with corrupt Eastern wear in the translation of Juvenal, *Satires of Juvenal*, III.116–17, p. 37 (III.66 in the original). TE declares that the headdress was exclusively female; but Pope has '*Oresbius*, in his painted Mitre gay' in *Iliad*, V.870. Golding (p. 183) has 'womans wimple gay'; Fraunce (p. 52) a 'red thrumbd hat'.

furrow'd Brows: Pope's substitution for Ovid's repeated 'tempora', 'temples' (654 and 655); Fraunce (p. 52), has 'wrinckled browes'.

50. decrepit Form: Pope's addition. William Oldisworth uses the phrase in relation to deformed children in his translation of Claude Quillet's *Callipaedia*, II (1710), p. 22.

52–4. Greatly expanded from Ovid (657).

56. Women: in Ovid, specifically old women: 'vera...anus', 659, rendered 'trew old women', by Golding (p. 183), and with similar acknowledgement to age by all the other translators. EC compares Sandys's 1632 version of *Metamorphoses*, II, p. 54: 'His kisses too intemperate grow; | Not such as Maids on Maidens doe bestow', during a similar episode in which Jupiter seduces Calisto. Hopkins (p. 2), invents some extra amorous psychology in Vertumnus at this point.

59–66. A proverbial model widespread in English literature. TE cites Milton, *Paradise Lost*, V.215–19 (1674), p. 123: '...or they led the Vine | To wed her Elm; she spous'd about him twines | Her mariageable arms, and with her brings | Her dowr th' adopted Clusters, to adorn | His barren leaves.' Milton was probably himself recalling Ovid, 663–9.

59. Embraces: essentially an addition, but cf. Fraunce, p. 52^v, 'Mutual imbracements', and Sandys, p. 470, 'amorous foldings'.

60. curling Vine: In Ovid (662) the vine is 'socia', 'companionate'. Cf. John Banks, *The Destruction of Troy*, V.ii (1679), p. 68: 'My longing Arms about her I will twine, | Like Woodbine, Jessamin, or the curling Vine'.

swelling Clusters: cf. 'Spring', 36 and Commentary. In Ovid (661), the grapes are 'nitentibus', 'shining', or 'glistring' (Golding, p. 183); Sandys, p. 470, has 'with purple clusters shin'd'.

61. twining Branches: cf. Pope's note to 'Spring', 99. Tate's version of book V of Cowley's *Sex Libri Plantarum*, subtitled 'Pomona', has the phrase at 47; *The Third Part of the Works of Mr. Abraham Cowley* (1689), p. 106. Cf. also Shaftesbury, 'The Moralists', II.iv, in *Characteristicks of Men, Manners, Opinions, Times*, vol. II (1711), p. 287 (Theocles speaking): 'as the strong and upright Trunk of the *Oak* or *Elm* is fitted to the twining Branches of the *Vine* or *Ivy*'.

And prais'd the Beauty of the pleasing Sight.

    Yet this tall Elm, but for his Vine (he said)
Had stood neglected, and a barren Shade;
65   And this fair Vine, but that her Arms surround
Her marry'd Elm, had crept along the Ground.
Ah beauteous Maid, let this Example move
Your Mind, averse from all the Joys of Love.
Deign to be lov'd, and ev'ry Heart subdue!
70   What Nymph cou'd e'er attract such Crowds as you?
Not she whose Beauty urg'd the *Centaur*'s Arms,
Ulysses' Queen, nor *Helen*'s fatal Charms.
Ev'n now, when silent Scorn is all they gain,
A thousand court you, tho' they court in vain,
75   A thousand Sylvans, Demigods, and Gods,

---

71. Centaur's: 1717–51: Centaurs

---

64. barren Shade: Dryden has the phrase at II.80 of his translation of Virgil, *Georgics, Works of Virgil*, p. 73, speaking of infertile trees; Pope recalled it phrase in describing a tomb precinct in *Iliad*, VI.532-3: 'Jove's Sylvan Daughters bade their Elms bestow | A barren Shade, and in his Honour grow'. Ovid (664), says that without the vine the elm 'should haue nothing (sauing leaues) too bee desyred', Golding (p. 183).

66. marry'd Elm: Ovid (666), 'si non nupta foret', 'if it [the vine] were not married'.

    crept ... Ground: TE compares Sandys, p. 470: 'would creepe vpon the ground'. Ovid (666) says 'terrae acclinata iaceret', 'it would lie flat on the earth'.

71-2. Pope has changed Ovid's order of sought-after beauties (Helen, Hippodamia, Penelope, 669-71).

71. she ... Centaur's: Hippodamia (also not named in Ovid, 670-1); drunken centaurs attempted to rape her at her wedding to the Lapith Pirithous, causing a bloody battle; Ovid had already given the story at *Metamorphoses*, XII.210-535. Ovid has 'Lapitheia ... proelia', 'Lapithian battles', rather than Centaurs, but Sandys names the Centaurs only, naming Hippodamia in a note p. 470.

72. Ulysses' Queen: Penelope, who resisted the band of suitors who descended upon Ithaca during Odysseus' 20-year absence, as described in Homer's *Odyssey*. Pope drops Ovid's adjective' 'nimium tardantis', 'too much delaying' from the description of Ulysses (671).

    Helen: of Troy, whose abduction precipitated the Trojan war in which Homer's *Iliad* is set.

    fatal Charms: a commonplace, but '*Hellen's fatal Charms*' occurs in the opening line of the Prologue to Farquhar's *The Recruiting Officer* (1706).

73. silent Scorn: an addition, perhaps recalling Sir John Denham, *The Sophy*, V.i.79, *Poems and Translations with the Sophy* (1668), p. 73: 'Thou could'st not hear't with such a silent scorn'.

75. Demigods: uncertain category of classical deity, literally from Ovid's 'semidei' (673); 'Demi-gods' in Fraunce, Sandys and Hopkins. Cf. *Ode for Musick*, 42.

That haunt our Mountains and our *Alban* Woods.
But if you'll prosper, mark what I advise,
Whom Age, and long Experience render wise,
And one whose tender Care is far above
80   All that these Lovers ever felt of Love,
(Far more than e'er can by your self be guest)
Fix on *Vertumnus*, and reject the rest.
For his firm Faith I dare ingage my own,
Scarce to himself, himself is better known.
85   To distant Lands *Vertumnus* never roves;
Like you, contented with his Native Groves;
Nor at first sight, like most, admires the Fair;
For you he lives; and you alone shall share
His last Affection, as his early Care.
90   Besides, he's lovely far above the rest,
With Youth Immortal and with Beauty blest.
Add, that he varies ev'ry Shape with ease,
And tries all Forms, that may *Pomona* please.
But what shou'd most excite a mutual Flame,
95   Your Rural Cares, and Pleasures, are the same.
To him your Orchards early Fruits are due,

---

95. same.: *1736–51*: same:

---

76. Alban Woods: The Alban hills ('Albanos... montes', Ovid, 674) are a few miles south east of Rome, and an ancient sacred site; Sandys refers to '*Alba's* high and shadie hills' (p. 470).

80. An addition.

81. guest: i.e. guessed; Ovid (677), has 'plus, quam credis', 'more, than you would believe'.

82. Pope softens Ovid's phrase (678), 'tori socium tibi selige', 'select him as the companion of your bed'.

83. firm Faith: a common phrase, but perhaps here recalling Eve's protests about her own 'firm Faith' in Milton, *Paradise Lost*, IX.286 (1674), p. 222.

84. himself, himself: cf. Shakespeare, *The Rape of Lucrece*, 157: 'And for himself himself he must forsake' (and similarly 160 and 998). The effect is less striking in Ovid's phrasing (679–80): 'neque enim sibi notior ille est, | quam mihi', 'for he is not better known to himself, than to me'. Cf. Sandys, p. 470: 'by himselfe not better knowne'.

86. Like you: an addition.

   Native Groves: for Ovid (681), 'haec loca', 'these places'; cf. *Windsor-Forest*, 407.

87. *TE* cites Sandys, p. 470: 'Nor loues, like common louers, at first sight'; close to Ovid's 'quam modo vidit, amat', 'as soon as he sees, he loves' (682).

   the Fair: women.

91. An addition; Ovid says only that Vertumnus is 'iuvenis', 'a young man'; Sandys, p. 470, makes this 'youth perpetuall', however.

96–7. *TE* cites Sandys's version, p. 470, which has the same rhyme: 'The first-fruits of your Hort-yard are his due; | Which ioyfully he still accepts from you'. Ovid (688) has rather 'primus habet laetaque tenet tua munera dextra', 'he first has and holds your gifts in his happy right hand'.

>   (A pleasing Off'ring when 'tis made by you;)
>   He values these; but yet (alas) complains,
>   That still the best and dearest Gift remains.
> 100   Not the fair Fruit that on yon' Branches glows
>   With that ripe red th' Autumnal Sun bestows,
>   Nor tastful Herbs that in these Gardens rise,
>   Which the kind Soil with milky Sap supplies;
>   You, only you, can move the God's Desire:
> 105   Oh crown so constant and so pure a Fire!
>   Let soft Compassion touch your gentle Mind;
>   Think, 'tis *Vertumnus* begs you to be kind!
>   So may no Frost, when early Buds appear,
>   Destroy the Promise of the youthful Year;
> 110   Nor Winds, when first your florid Orchard blows,
>   Shake the light Blossoms from their blasted Boughs!
>
>   This when the various God had urg'd in vain,
>   He strait assum'd his Native Form again;

98-9. An addition.

101. An addition.

102. tastful: flavourful; 'high-relished; savoury' (*SJ*, citing this instance). An addition.

103. kind Soil: an addition, perhaps echoing Joseph Trapp, *A Prologue to the University of Oxford* (1703), 17-18: 'As Plants their fading Vigor will renew | From that kind Soil, in which at first they Grew'.

milky Sap: Ovid (690), 'sucis mitibus', 'mild juices'.

104. God's Desire: Ovid lays no stress on Vertumnus' divine status.

105. An addition.

107-8. At this point Ovid's Vertumnus tells Pomona a tale of the love-suicide of Iphis and transformation to stone of the indifferent princess Anaxarete; this section is supplied, presumably by Theobald, when Pope's 'Vertumnus and Pomona' is incorporated in Sewell's 1717 version. Pope's 108 picks up seamlessly from Ovid's 763, the closing monitory line of the inset story.

107. kind: sexually compliant.

108-11. Pope's neatly symmetrical pair of couplets is expanded from a slightly less formal contrast in a pair of lines in Ovid (763-4); much of the detail is Pope's.

109. youthful Year: Cf. *Rapin of Gardens... English'd by Mr. Gardiner* (1706), p. 31: ''Tis the gay Month of all the youthful Year'; also Garth, *The Dispensary*, sixth edition (1706), p. 69, 'crowns the youthful Year'.

110-11. Not a common rhyme, but evidently acceptable: Edward Sherburne, 'Phaedrus and Hippolyta', II.i.172-3, *The Tragedies of L. Annaeus Seneca the Philosopher* (1702), p. 157.

110. florid: 'productive of flowers' (*SJ*), Ovid's 'florentia', 'flowering', 764.

112. various: appearing in different shapes; cf. 'On Silence', 8. TE refers to Pope's *Odyssey*, IV.524, where Proteus is called 'the various God'; at IV.521 Pope has a long note on the cultural and historical significance of this Greek version of the shape-shifting deity. In Ovid, Vertumnus is still 'formae aptus anili', 'joined to the form of an old woman'.

113. Native Form: natural shape. Probably recalling Milton, *Paradise Lost*, III.603-5 (1674), p. 79: '... call up unbound | In various shape old *Proteus* from the Sea, | Draind through a Limbec to his Native forme.'

Such, and so bright an Aspect now he bears,
115 As when thro' Clouds th' emerging Sun appears,
And thence exerting his refulgent Ray,
Dispels the Darkness and reveals the Day.
Force he prepar'd, but check'd the rash Design;
For when, appearing in a Form Divine,
120 The Nymph survey'd him, and beheld the Grace
Of charming Features and a youthful Face,
A sudden Passion in her Breast did move,
And the warm Maid confess'd a mutual Love.

120. **survey'd ... beheld:** *1717–51:* surveys ... beholds
121. **Face,:** *1751:* face!
122. 1717–51: In her soft breast consenting passions move,

114. **Aspect:** 'look; air; appearance' (*SJ*).
116. **refulgent:** 'bright; shining; glittering; splendid' (*SJ*); no specific equivalent in Ovid, where the sun shines rather 'nullaque obstante', 'with nothing to obscure'. The phrase 'refulgent Ray' is common in seventeenth-century verse, e.g. Waller, 'Of the Danger His Majestie (being Prince) escaped at the rode at St Andere', 121, *Poems, &c.* (1645), p. 8: 'Like bright *Aurora*, whose Refulgent Ray'.
117. An addition.
118–23. As *TE* notes, Pope generates this six-line flourish from Ovid's two-line conclusion (770–1): 'vimque parat: sed vi non est opus, inque figura | capta dei nympha est et mutua vulnera sensit', 'and force he prepares; but there is no need for force, and the nymph is caught by the person of the god and feels mutual wounds' (i.e. of desire). Pope's 'check'd the rash Design' is a conscious additional reining-in of the rape impulse, therefore. Ovid uses the same word, 'vim' for Vertumnus' prepared force and for the Satyrs' planned rape of Pomona (625, 770); Golding (p. 185) and Sandys (p. 472) both use 'force' here. Hopkins suppresses the idea of force altogether in his version.
118. **rash Design:** Pope returned to this phrase in more epic contexts in his *Iliad*, VII.129 and VIII.254. In *The Rape of the Lock*, III.121, the Baron is addressed as a 'rash Youth' and his 'design' on Belinda is associated with 'force', a word used six times in the poem. Cf. also 'The Rape of the Locke', I.48, 50, 101, 142.
122 **variant.** This was probably designed to remove the expletive 'did', in accordance with the earlier prescriptions of *Essay on Criticism*, 349.
123. **warm:** amorous, sexually excited; cf. *Windsor-Forest*, 19.
   confess'd: acknowledged.

10
TO A YOUNG LADY, WITH THE WORKS OF VOITURE
(1712)

Editors' Headnote

Composition and publication

'To a Young Lady, with the Works of Voiture' was first published on 20 May 1712. The title in the 1735 *Works* states that the poem was 'Written at 17 years old', which would place it around 1705, when a new translation of Voiture was published by Samuel Briscoe and others, perhaps constituting the gift of the title (see further below). One of Pope's earliest letters, based on one by Voiture and dating from 1704 (*Corr.*, I.4), is addressed to an unnamed woman, supposedly to accompany the gift of a book. However, there is no other evidence for composition at this early date, and it appears more likely (Ault 1949: 49–56) that versions of the poem were in Pope's mind somewhat later than this, particularly in 1709–10. Pope was perhaps encouraged in his reading of the French writer by Wycherley, who alludes to Voiture in letters to Pope of 6 December 1707 and 13 November 1708 (*Corr.*, I.34 and 53). Pope's extended comparison of life to a play in his letter to Cromwell of 29 August 1709 (*Corr.* I.70–1) appears like a prose summary of lines 21–8 of the poem (see Commentary). On 24 June 1710 Pope sent Cromwell a suggestive 'Rondeau' based (without identification) on a short poem of Voiture's, and this evidently enjoyed a certain manuscript circulation amongst Pope's male acquaintance, though it did not appear in print until 1726 (*Corr.*, I.90). (The poem is a short act of witty revenge against a woman, perhaps Teresa Blount, who had mocked his diminutive stature.) Cromwell identified the source in his letter of 3 August 1710, and Pope's reply, 12 October 1710, offered further Voiture-inspired persiflage (*Corr.*, I.95, 98). On 5 December 1710 (*Corr.*, I.109) Cromwell wrote to Pope in response to what is evidently a circulated version of the present poem, since it quotes from line 8:

> Your Poem shews you to be, what you say of *Voiture, with Books well-bred*: The state of the Fair, tho' satirical, is touch'd with that delicacy and gallantry, that not the Court of *Augustus*, nor — But hold, I shall lose what I lately recover'd, your opinion of my Sincerity; yet I must say, 'tis as faultless as the Fair to

whom 'tis address'd, be she never so perfect. The M.G. ['major-general', John Tidcombe] . . . transcrib'd it by lucubration: From some discourse of yours, he thought your inclination led you to (what the men of fashion call Learning) Pedantry; but now he says he has no less, I assure you, than a Veneration for you.

Additionally, Pope's letter to Cromwell, 24 July 1711 (*Corr.*, I.130–1) appears to anticipate line 4 of the poem (see Commentary).

By the *Works* of 1735, the 'Miss Blount' of the revised title could only mean Martha Blount (1690–1763), by then Pope's pre-eminent female friend and concealed addressee of the *Epistle to a Lady* (1735). If the poem were indeed first composed around 1705 and then revised with one of the Blount sisters (whom Pope probably met around 1707) in mind, Teresa might have been the more likely original recipient (see Rumbold 1989: 52–3 and chapter 3 *passim*). In 1717 Pope placed the poem next to the poem now known as 'Epistle To Miss Blount, On her Leaving the Town, after the Coronation', and indicated that the same young lady was addressed in each case; but that poem could also have been addressed to Teresa rather than Martha, and there is no finally definitive evidence of the identity of the addressee. Cromwell's response to the draft, quoted above, does not suggest that a particular woman was being addressed at that stage, and when Pope sent a copy of the *Miscellaneous Poems* in which it was published to Martha Blount, he made no special mention of this poem (see further below).

Lintot paid Pope £3 16s 6d for the poem together with 'On Silence' and 'To the Author of a Poem, intitled, Successio', on 9 April 1712 (McLaverty 2001: 17), making it one of Pope's more lucrative early pieces. It appeared on pp. 137–42 of *Miscellaneous Poems and Translations*; for the context of the anthology, see Headnote to 'The First book of Statius his Thebais'.

Text

The text presented here is taken from the first edition of 1712. Revision is confined to the *Works* of 1717 and 1735. In a copy of the *Works*, vol.II (1736) in the British Library (C.122.e.31, pp.71–4), there are several corrections, in Pope's hand, to punctuation – removing commas at lines 9, 35, 38, 60, and 62 – and capitalisation – restoring capitals from earlier editions for 'Graces' (line 1), 'Thing!' (line 54), 'Hearts' (line 64) and 'Care' (line 69). It is not known why these changes were not implemented in subsequent editions. The various extant texts of 'To a Young Lady' are referred to in the apparatus as follows:

1712: *Miscellaneous Poems and Translations*, octavo (Griffith 6)

1717: *Works*, folio (Griffith 79)

1726: *Miscellany Poems*, vol.I, duodecimo (Griffith 164)

1735: Works, vol.II, folio (Griffith 370)

1743: Works, vol.II, part I, octavo (Griffith 583)

1751: Works, vol.VI, octavo (Griffith 648)

Models and sources

Vincent de Voiture (1597–1648) was a French writer of light poetry and particularly of witty and 'gallant' letters to female members of a courtly salon run by Catherine de Vivonne, the Marquise de Rambouillet (1558–1665) (see line 76 of the poem). An English translation, *Letters of Affaires Love and Courtship*, appeared in 1657, and translated extracts from his letters, often in combination with other French writers of similar vein, appeared periodically thereafter, e.g. in *The Lover's Secretary* (1692). Voiture was the first listed source in *Choice Letters French and English* (1701), a dual-language book of letter-writing templates by Abel Boyer and others with instructions for imitation. A translation of some of Voiture's letters was appended to John Dennis's collective *Letters upon Several Occasions* (1696), which involved also Dryden, Wycherley and Congreve, and a second collection, *Familiar and Courtly Letters*, numbering Dryden and Henry Cromwell among the translators, was published in 1700 with a second volume in 1702, dated 1701 (see Hopkins 2005 for Dryden's role in these enterprises). The publisher, Samuel Briscoe, issued a two-volume collection of *The Works of Monsieur Voiture* in 1705; an edition in French had appeared at Paris in 1678 and another came out in Amsterdam in 1709. Any of these could be the 'Works of Voiture' mentioned in Pope's title. Edmund Curll and two of his associates put out a further two-volume edition of the *Works*, translated by John Ozell, in 1715, brazenly co-opting Pope's poem as 'A Character of his WRITINGS' (I.i–iv).

Voiture was well-known in the Restoration as a literary model, described as 'one of the most delicate Wits of these latter Ages' in Thomas Rymer's translation of Rapin, *Reflections upon Aristotle's Treatise of Poesie* (1674), p. 94, and as 'a very gallant Writer' in Dennis' *The Impartial Critick* (1693) ('A Letter to a Friend', sig. a2^v). English poets had begun to derive wit and gallantry from the French model; Oldham's coarsely humorous 'Upon a Lady' (*Poems, and Translations*, 1683) was supposedly 'Out of *Voiture*', and Oldmixon used Voiture as a reference point in impersonating Edmund Waller in his *Amores Britannici* (1703), Epistle II.vii. As a poet, Voiture was often compared with Waller (see Kaminski 2000), and his genteel and urbane 'raillery' had complex ramifications in Swift (see Sheehan 1978).

Voiture's letters represented the kind of lightly rakish, elegant wit that Pope was often aiming for in his tentative relations with women and his more robust discussions of women with male friends, as recorded in the early letters, themselves obviously influenced by Voiture's style (see Winn 1979). Pope's other French reading, in critics (Rapin and and Fontenelle), essayists (Montaigne) and poets (Boileau), was less libertine in character (see Audra 1931: 315–46 for the French perspective). The poem reflects Pope's youthful enthusiasm for the French writer. He made a more jocular reference in his self-portrait as Dick Distick, a short poet, in his essays on 'The Club of Little Men', Voiture also being a model of shortness (*PW*, I.128; *Guardian*, no. 92, 26 June 1713). Writing to Baroness Harvey around 1720 he intimated that letters in the Voiture style could be too 'pretty', and in 1730, he told Spence 'Voiture in his letters wants sentiments. He wrote only to divert parties over their tea' (*OAC*, I.218–19, nos. 514–15). However, in 1736 he also said 'The style in letters, as in all other things, should be adapted to the subject. Many of Voiture's letters on gay subjects are excellent' (*OAC*, I.177, no. 406). There are brief mentions of the pleasure, and the artificiality, of Voiture's letters, in correspondence with Swift and Bolingbroke in the 1730s (*Corr.*, III.92, 102, 505); in the imbroglio surrounding the publication of Pope's letters in 1735, Curll somewhat desperately described four of Voiture's letters as the work of Pope, supposedly writing to Martha Blount (*Corr.*, III.487, 495).

This was the first of Pope's published poems to be addressed to a woman, or indeed to any single person, and it thus prefigures one of Pope's favourite later forms, the 'epistle'. Pope's implication in 1717 that it was addressed to Teresa Blount, and in 1736 that it was addressed to Martha Blount, does not accord with his dating of the poem to 1705. Pope's earliest surviving letter to Martha Blount dates from 25 May 1712, and evidently accompanied a copy of *Miscellaneous Poems and Translations*, the volume containing this poem, 'The Rape of the Locke' and several other items of his likely, according to the self-consciously gallant poet, to cause her to 'Blush' fetchingly (*Corr.*, I.143). Ault (1949: 49–59) records finding a copy of the volume at Mapledurham, the Blount family home, with an amorous inscription from Pope to Martha Blount, but no special mention of or annotation to the present poem; he did not find a copy of the 'Works of Voiture' which could have been given with a separate copy of the poem, though there was a copy of Curll's 1715 edition.

The courtly gesture of the poem–book-gift combination was itself instanced by the letter Voiture sent to Madam Saintot with a copy of Ariosto's *Orlando Furioso* (*Familiar and Courtly Letters*, II, 1702, dated 1701, 52). The gesture might also have been influenced by efforts such as Charles Tooke's 'To a Young Lady, with the first edition of these *Miscellanies*', which fronts *A Collection of Poems, viz. The Temple of Death: by the Marquis of Normanby* [. . .] (1701), a much more openly amorous overture; Pope's language at 59–68, substituting good humour as the way to keep a man beyond the transient bonds of sexual allure, may constitute a response to the conventional gallantry of that poem. That miscellany contains several other instances of the poem–book-gift combination, such as 'To a Lady, with Milton's Paradise Lost' (for a study of the volume, including matters of authorship, see Batt 2011). Earlier examples include 'To a Fair Lady, with a Miscellany of Poems', 'Sent with Ovid's Epistles, to a Fair Lady', and 'Sent with Cowley's Works, to Astrea', in Behn's *Lycidus* (1688). The poem-gift has some currency in Pope's early work, as with 'On a Fan of the Author's Design', 'To a Lady with the Temple of Fame' and 'To Belinda with the Rape of the Lock'.

Context

As a poem which begins as a discussion of writing, art, the ethics of living, and friendship, 'To a Young Lady' clearly shows allegiances with the *Essay on Criticism*; one of Pope's main themes is 'well-bred' writing, reading and behaviour, unconstrained by too rigorous a commitment to social form, and free of oppressive restraints. Passages such as those at 7–10 and 27–30 sound like more informal versions of aspects of the larger verse treatise. Addressed to a woman as it is, the poem also has a relatively substantial statement of sympathy for the rule-bound life lived by even well-to-do women, which is at odds with Voiture but appears aligned rather with poems and complaints by women (see particularly 31–48). Pope might have been influenced by politely well-meaning documents such as *A Dialogue concerning Women, being a Defence of the Sex written to Eugenia* (1691), by his mentor William Walsh, which in fact mentions Voiture's admiration for certain intellectual women (p. 92); but the language of the passage is closer to the verse protests of poets like Lady Mary Chudleigh and Sarah Fyge Egerton. This aspect has been the focus of a certain amount of modern critical attention, alongside Pope's well-intentioned if now rather paternalistic-looking efforts on behalf of unhappily married women in his Catholic circle during the 1710s. Mack (1985: 247–8) summarises the case for Pope's self-identification with Voiture in his approaches to women, stressing the proto-feminism of the poem; Rumbold (1989: 48–53) discusses the poem in the context of Pope's other early exercises in sexual politics and amatory gesture. As Cromwell's letter, quoted above, indicates, the representation of the social position of women in the poem includes aspects (e.g. the micro-fable of Pamela's cripplingly empty marriage at 49–56) which were at least gently satirical, and a number of the issues and ideas raised in raillery here return in more confidently satiric form in poems such as the *Epistle to a Lady* (1735). There are a number of features in common with Clarissa's speech in Canto V of the revised *Rape of the Lock* (1717); see Commentary at 61.

TO A
Young Lady,
WITH THE
Works of *VOITURE*.
By the same Hand.

IN these gay Thoughts the Loves and Graces shine,
And all the Writer lives in ev'ry Line;
His easie Art may happy Nature seem,
Trifles themselves are Elegant in him.

Title. *1735:* EPISTLE V. | TO | Miss BLOUNT, | With the Works of *VOITURE.* | Written at 17 years old.; *1743:* EPISTLE IX. | TO | Miss BLOUNT, | With the Works of *VOITURE.*; *1751:* EPISTLE | To Miss BLOUNT. | With the WORKS of VOITURE.
By the same Hand.: *1717–51:* omitted

---

1. gay Thoughts: 'Gay' is 'airy; cheerful; merry; frolick'; also 'fine; showy' (*SJ*); cf. *Essay on Criticism*, 317. Pope uses the word further in the poem at 11, 16 and 25. His comment on the 'gay subjects' of Voiture's letters (*OAC*, I.177, no. 406) is quoted in the Headnote. The word could also indicate rakish behaviour; Pope's physician, William Cheselden, told Spence in 1744 that Pope 'had been gay, but left it on his acquaintance with Mrs Blount' (*OAC*, I.111, no. 252). In 'A Farewell to London in the Year 1715' Pope mock-regretted his pursuit of 'girls' and called himself 'The gayest Valetudinaire, | Most thinking Rake alive' (39–40). The precise phrase recalls similar usages in Denham's *Cato Major Of Old Age. A Poem*, IV.25–6 (1669), p. 43: 'vigorous Youth may his gay thoughts erect | To many years, which Age must not expect', or Tom Brown, 'The xxvi. Ode in Hor. L. 3. Paraphras'd', 2, *A Collection of Miscellany Poems, Letters, &c* (1699), p. 23: 'And vigorous Youth gay thoughts inspire'.

Loves: Cupids; cf. 'Winter', 23, and 'Sapho to Phaon', 227.

Graces: species of minor classical goddess, the '*charites*', associated with female charm and beauty; very commonly paired with 'Loves' in the ornamental scenery of Restoration drama and poetry, e.g. the character list in Dryden, *Albion and Albanius* (1685), 'A Grand Chorus of Hero's, Loves and Graces'. In a translated letter of flattery to a woman, Voiture asks 'M. D. B.' 'And was not all that the Poets say of Smiles, Graces, and Loves, visibie discovered about you at that time?'; Letter XXIX, *Letters of Affaires Love and Courtship* (1657), p. 118.

2. Perhaps echoing Dryden, *Religio Laici*, 153 (1682), p. 10: 'It speaks no less than God in every Line'; and cf. 'The Wife of Bath Her Prologue', 105.

5	Sure to charm all was his peculiar Fate,
	Who without Flatt'ry pleas'd the Fair and Great;
	Still with Esteem no less convers'd than read;
	With Wit well-natur'd, and with Books well-bred;
	His Heart, his Mistress and his Friend did share;
10	His Time, the Muse, the Witty, and the Fair.
	Thus wisely careless, innocently gay,
	Chearful, he play'd the Trifle, Life, away,
	'Till Death scarce felt did o'er his Pleasures creep,
	As smiling Infants sport themselves to Sleep:
15	Ev'n Rival Wits did *Voiture*'s Fate deplore,
	And the Gay mourn'd who never mourn'd before;

---

13. **Death:** *1735–51:* fate
   did o'er his Pleasures creep: *1717–51:* his gentle breath supprest
14. **Sleep::** *1717:* rest:; *1735–51:* rest.

---

3. easie Art . . . happy Nature seem: the apparent result of accident and grace rather than of painstaking work; cf. *Essay on Criticism*, 75 and Commentary; a distant echo perhaps of Milton, *Paradise Lost*, IX.23–4 (1674), p. 215: 'inspires | Easie my unpremeditated Verse'. Pope recalled 'easy Art' for his description of Ulysses' eloquence in the *Iliad*, III.285. Cf. 'To a Young Lady, with the First Edition of these Miscellanies', *A Collection of Poems: viz. The Temple of Death* . . . (1701), p. 2: 'Here *just Roscommon* with full lustre shines, | And easy Art informs his flowing Lines'. SJ defines 'happy' as 'lucky; successful; fortunate'.

4. Trifles: cf. Pope to Cromwell, 24 July 1711, 'It deserves an Elegy but who besides Catullus & Voiture can write agreably upon Triffles?' (*Corr*, I.130–1). Cf. also Rymer's translation of Rapin's *Reflections upon Aristotle's Treatise of Poesie* (1674), p. 146: '*Voiture* and *Sarazin* have *gay* things in their *Odes*; for they have the art of drolling pleasantly on mean Subjects, and they sustain this Character well enough, but they have not vigour and sublimity for high matters'.

5. peculiar: particular.

7. convers'd: talked about, discussed; an anomalous usage in this passive sense. Cf. the '*Gen'rous Converse*' of the ideal critic in *Essay on Criticism*, 644.

8. Much in accordance with the values of *Essay on Criticism*, e.g. 638. See also Headnote to the present poem for Cromwell's comment in relation to this line.

9. did: an expletive of the kind Pope disowned in the *Essay on Criticism*, 349, as pointed out by William Benson in 1739 (Guerinot 1969: 280).

10. the Witty, and the Fair: revisited by Pope in the *Epistle to Dr Arbuthnot*, 311: 'Whose Buzz the Witty and the Fair annoys'.

11. innocently gay: a phrase more often used of women, e.g. Nahum Tate, *A Consolatory Poem to the Right Honourable John Lord Cutts* (1698), p. 4 (describing Cutts's dead wife): 'All Mildly Bright, and Innocently Gay'. Ward, in *Female Policy Detected* (1695), p. 36, uses it to describe the appearance of natural virtue.

12. Trifle, Life: cf. Mary Chudleigh, 'On the Vanities of this Life', 1, *Poems on Several Occasions* (1703), p. 14: 'What makes fond Man the trifle Life desire . . . ?'

14. sport: amuse, play.

The truest Hearts for *Voiture* heav'd with Sighs;
Voiture was wept by all the brightest Eyes;
The *Smiles* and *Loves* had dy'd in *Voiture*'s Death,
20 But that for ever in his Lines they breath.

Let the strict Life of graver Mortals be
A long, exact, and serious Comedy,
In ev'ry Scene some Moral let it teach,
And, if it can, at once both Please and Preach:
25 Let mine, like *Voiture*'s, a gay Farce appear,
And more Diverting still than Regular,
Have Humour, Wit, a native Ease and Grace;
No matter for the Rules of Time and Place.
Criticks in Wit, or Life, are hard to please,
30 Few write to those, and none can live to these.

---

15. Fate: 1735–51: death
24. Preach:: 1735–51: preach.
25. like Voiture's, a: 1735–51: an innocent
28. No matter for the Rules of: 1735–51: Tho' not too strictly bound to

---

15. deplore: lament.
18. brightest Eyes: i.e., of women; cf. 77–8 below, and *Rape of the Lock*, IV.76.
19. Smiles and Loves: the combination of wit and gallantry; cf. quotation from Voiture in Commentary at 1 above. Pope denotes Venus (Aphrodite) as the 'Goddess of the Smiles and Loves' in his translation of Homer, *Iliad*, III.524.
21–8. This comparison of life to drama is elaborately prefigured in Pope's letter to Cromwell, 29 August 1709, *Corr.* I.70–1: 'for tho' Life for the most part, like an old Play, be still the same [, yet] now & then a New Scene may make it more entertaining. As for myself, [I] wou'd not have my life a very Regular Play; let it be a good merry Farce, a G—ds [name] and a figg for the Critical Unities!'. For Pope's association with the theatre, see Headnote to 'Prologue to *Cato*'. The phrasing here suggests a liking for aspects of Restoration drama regarded as suspect by moralists such as Jeremy Collier; for that controversy see Headnote to *Essay on Criticism*.

24. Please and Preach: the well-known prescription of Horace (*Epistola ad Pisones* or *Ars Poetica*, 343) that literature should mix 'dulce' with 'utile', 'useful' with 'pleasing'. Cf. *Essay on Criticism*, 125 and Commentary.
25. gay Farce: short, light comedy. Pope's friend John Gay produced his 'tragi-comical farce' *The Mohocks* in 1712, and would write another farce, *The What D'Ye Call It*, perhaps with help from Pope, in 1715.
26. Regular: ostensibly in the sense appropriate to literary criticism (*Essay on Criticism*, 243, 255), the 'Rules' being cited in 28. It could also mean 'governed by strict regulations' (*SJ*), and hence 'morally restricted'; see the quotation from Pope's letter to Cromwell, note to 21–8 above.
27. native: inborn, natural (i.e. unaffected).
   Ease and Grace: qualities also much prized in the *Essay on Criticism*, e.g. 145, 156, 177.
28. Time and Place: two of the 'unities' of drama, according to the neoclassical rules based on Aristotle's *Poetics*; see Headnote to *Essay on Criticism*, and 278–9 of that poem, and the reference in Pope's letter quoted

Too much *your Sex* is by their Forms confin'd,
Severe to all, but most to Womankind;
Custom, grown blind with Age, must be your Guide;
Your Pleasure is a Vice, but not your Pride;
35 By nature yielding, stubborn but for Fame;
Made Slaves by Honour, and made Fools by Shame.
Marriage may all those petty Tyrants chace,
But sets up One, a greater, in their Place;
Well might you wish for Change, by those accurst,
40 But the last Tyrant ever proves the worst.
Still in Constraint your suff'ring Sex remains,
Or bound in formal, or in real Chains;
Whole Years neglected for some Months ador'd,
The fawning Servant turns a haughty Lord;

---

in the note to 21–8 above. Pope might also perhaps be remembering Rochester, 'Upon Nothing' (see 'On Silence'), 4, *Poems on Several Occasions* (1696), p. 101: 'E're time and place were, time and place were not'.

29. Criticks: For contemporary characterisations of critics, see Headnote to *Essay on Criticism*.

30. Few write with critics in mind, and nobody can live up to the precepts of moralists.

31. Forms: social conventions; cf. 42. The 'forms' were laid down in standard guidebooks like Hannah Woolley's *The Gentlewomans Companion; or, A Guide to the Female Sex containing Directions of Behaviour, in all Places, Companies, Relations, and Conditions, from their Childhood down to Old Age* (1673), the final page (247) of which, however, recommends Voiture's 'incomparable' letters, 'translated into *English*', as a guide for female letter-writing. Another popular guide to female behaviour was Halifax's *The Lady's New-years Gift: Or, Advice to a Daughter* (1688).

33–6. i.e. women are guided towards certain restrictive modes of behaviour, preventing pleasure, in order to remain marriageable, and their own 'pride', normally a sin, is used to diminish sexual adventure. Here the argument is politely sympathetic, but cf. the later satiric assertion that 'ev'ry Woman is at Heart a Rake' (*Epistle to a Lady*, 216).

35. yielding, stubborn: compliant with or resistant to external pressure, either sexual invitation, or the blandishments of a marriage-offer.

but: only.

Fame: reputation, a persistent theme for Pope (cf. *Essay on Criticism*, 46, 171 etc. for literary senses); often particularly the unblemished reputation of chastity, required of women, equivalent to 'Honour' in the next line; cf. 'On Silence', 26–7, and 'Rape of the Locke', II.29.

36. Similar phrasing recurs in more openly satirical accounts of women's situation, e.g. Pope's fragment, 'Sylvia' (published 1727), 10, 'A Fool to Pleasure, yet a Slave to Fame', and almost the same line in the character of Narcissa in the *Epistle to a Lady*, 62.

37. chace: i.e. chase away.

40. Tyrant: cf. *One Thousand Seven Hundred and Thirty-Eight*, Dialogue II, 135: 'And was, besides, a Tyrant to his Wife'; *Epistle to Cobham*, 202: 'a Tyrant to the Wife his heart approves'.

42. Or: either.

formal ... Chains: marriage, 'formal' meaning 'legal', 'socially binding'. Cf. also 64 below.

45   Ah quit not the free Innocence of Life!
       For the dull Glory of a virtuous Wife!
       Nor let false Shows, or empty Titles please;
       Aim not at Joy, but rest content with Ease.

       The Gods, to curse *Pamela* with her Pray'rs,
50   Gave the gilt Coach and dappled *Flanders* Mares,
       The shining Robes, rich Jewels, Beds of State,
       And, to compleat her Bliss, a Fool for Mate.
       She glares in *Balls*, *Front-boxes*, and the *Ring*,
       A vain, unquiet, glitt'ring, wretched Thing!
55   Pride, Pomp, and State but reach her outward Part,
       She sighs, and is no *Dutchess* at her Heart.

---

45. Life!: *1717–51:* life,

43–4. i.e. the appearance of subservient adoration lasts only during courtship, after which the husband is in absolute control.

44. haughty Lord: cf. Chudleigh's anti-marriage poem, 'To the Ladies', 19, *Poems on Several Occasions*, p. 40: 'And nothing act, and nothing say, | But what her haughty Lord thinks fit'. The presentation of marriage here has much in common with Chudleigh's short diatribe, and with proto-feminist verse by Sarah Fyge Egerton, e.g. 'The Emulation', in *Poems on Several Occasions* (1703).

45. free Innocence: the life of a spinster, or (less likely) unmarried sexual activity; the sentiment of 46 is close to Eloisa's passionate devotion to the state of mistress ('Eloisa to Abelard', 85–92), but 47–8 suggest something more retired. Pope's compensatory lines to Martha Blount in the *Epistle to a Lady*, 287–8, celebrating the fact that she is too poor to have attracted a husband, retrospectively suggests the first interpretation.

47. empty Titles: cf. Oldham, 'A Satyr touching Nobility', 9–10, *Poems, and Translations* (1683), p. 128: 'Who besides empty Titles of high Birth, | Has no pretence to any thing of Worth'.

49. Pamela: a romance name, from Sir Philip Sidney's *Arcadia* (1590), accented in Pope's time on the second syllable. Pope's Pamela evidently prays for worldly advantage, not, like Sidney's, for divine protection.

50. Supposedly the ideal equipage of a showy woman, as in Robert Gould's anti-feminist 'The Sketch, A Satyr', I, *Works* (1709), p. 337, in which a coach with 'New *Harness*, and a Brace of *Flanders Mares*' is used to seduce and ruin a woman; here, Pamela is 'ruined' by socially eligible but emotionally empty marriage.

51. Beds of State: an example of pointless ostentation in Behn, 'A Paraphrase upon Ovid's Epistle of Oenone to Paris', 60, *Ovid's Epistles, Translated by Several Hands* (1680), p. 107: 'Nor can thy Beds of State so gratefull be, | As those of Moss, and new fall'n Leaves with me!'; and cf. Dryden, 'Lucretius The Beginning of the Second Book', 39, *Sylvae* (1685), p. 58: 'Nor will the rageing Feavours fire abate, | With Golden Canopies and Beds of State'.

53. glares: dazzles ostentatiously (cf. *Essay on Criticism*, 217); but probably also indicating her facial expression and hostile mood. Cf. also 'The Wife of Bath Her Prologue', 105.

Front-boxes: theatre boxes in the most conspicuous position. The theatre as a place for audience display (and assignation) was a commonplace of restoration comedy, e.g. Farquhar, *The Inconstant*, V.i. 2 (1702), p. 87:

> But, Madam, if the Fates withstand, and you
> Are destin'd *Hymen*'s willing Victim too,
> Trust not too much your now resistles Charms,
60   Those, Age or Sickness, soon or late, disarms;
> *Good Humour* only teaches Charms to last,
> Still makes new Conquests, and maintains the past:
> Love, rais'd on Beauty, will like That decay,
> Our Hearts may bear its slender Chain a Day,
65   As flow'ry Bands in Wantonness are worn;
> A Morning's Pleasure, and at Evening torn:
> *This* binds in Ties more easie, yet more strong,
> The willing Heart, and only holds it long.
>
> Thus *Voiture*'s early Care still shone the same,
70   And *Montausier* was only chang'd in Name;
> By this, ev'n now they live, ev'n now they charm,

69.] Madamoiselle Paulet.

'the Lady, the rich Beauty in the front Box had my attention'. Pope returned to the image in Clarissa's speech, added to the *Rape of the Lock* in 1717 (V.17 of that version).

the Ring: a circuit in Hyde Park for the riding of horses and for social display and observation; also associated with theatrical visibility in Garth's 'Epilogue' to Addison's *Cato* (1713), 25: 'At plays you ogle, at the ring you bow', and in *The Rape of the Lock*, I.44.

55–6. Cf. *Epistle to a Lady*, 67–8: 'A very Heathen in the carnal part, | Yet still a sad, good Christian at her heart'.

57. withstand: 'to offer resistance or opposition' (*OED* sense 3, intransitive). Here perhaps 'remain obstinate'.

58. Hymen's willing Victim: Hymen was the Greek god of marriage. Neither Martha nor Teresa Blount married, probably because they had insufficient dowries to attract suitable offers within the limited marriage market of the Catholic community; Martha became Pope's closest female friend and benefited from his will.

59. resistless: irresistible. Cf. 'The Episode of Sarpedon', 203, and Commentary; Pope normally uses the word in epic contexts.

61. Good Humour: a virtue also recommended for women as more lasting than beauty in Clarissa's speech, *Rape of the Lock*, V.30–1 of the 1717 version; and in the final line of the *Epistle to a Lady* (addressed to Martha Blount).
only: alone.

62. Still: constantly.

64. Cf. 'Rape of the Locke', I.40. An embellishment on the argument of Tooke's 'To a Young Lady, with the First Edition of these Miscellanies' (see Headnote), where the young lady is encouraged to '... improve | The Charms of Beauty, with the Charms of Love: | 'Tis that alone enslaves the willing Mind, | And makes our Chains more sure, yet softer bind.'

65. flow'ry Bands: garlands; cf. 'Messiah', 76.

67. This: the '*Good Humour*' of 61.

69 Pope's note. Cf. the explanatory note from *Works of Voiture* (1715), I.i: 'She was the Daughter of *Charles Paulet*, Secretary of the King's Bed-Chamber: This Lady was one of those who had the strongest Passion for Monsieur *Voiture*, who was not insensible to the fair One, for she was rich and deserving; She was call'd the *Lyoness*; on account of her high Spirit, and yellow Hair'.

Their Wit still sparkling, and their Flames still warm.

    Now crown'd with Myrtle, on th' *Elysian* Coast,
    Amidst those Lovers, joys his gentle Ghost,
75   Pleas'd while with Smiles his happy Lines you view,
    And finds a fairer *Ramboüillet* in you.
    The brightest Eyes of *France* inspir'd his Muse,
    The brightest Eyes of *Britain* now peruse,
    And dead as living, 'tis our Author's Pride,
80   Still to charm those who charm the World beside.

---

74. Amidst: *1726–51:* Amid

Several of the letters in the various English collections are addressed to her. See also next note.

70. Montausier: Julie Lucine d'Angennes (1607–1671), daughter of the Marquise de Ramboüillet (see 76), married the Duc de Montausier in 1645, hence the change of name. Oldmixon, *Amores Britannici*, II.vii. 79–98 (1703), pp. 136–7 (Waller to the Countess of Carlisle), in a passage on Voiture's celebrated beauties, has the same pairing: '*Montausier* Cruel, as he says She's Fair. | And *Paulet* gentle, as her Friend's severe'.

73. Myrtle: fragrant shrub, normally associated with Aphrodite (Venus); in the *Ode for Musick*, 78–9, however, Pope links it with an 'Elysian' zone of love-suicides. Cf. also 'Winter', 23, and 'Messiah', 74.

    Elysian Coast: Elysium was a paradise for the dead in classical mythology. It was normally characterised as a field or plain, but the coastal image (and exact phrase) is not uncommon in the seventeenth century, e.g. Shackerley Marmion, *A Morall Poem, intituled the Legend of Cupid and Psyche*, 'The last section' (1638), sig. L2[r].

76. Ramboüillet: the mother of the lady celebrated in 70, also a celebrated salon hostess; a letter of Voiture's to her formed the model for a very early letter of Pope's (Audra 1931: 330–2).

77. brightest Eyes: cf. 18.

79. our Author: Mack (1985: 248) sees this as a sudden self-identification on Pope's part with Voiture as likewise a 'charming small poet' addressing a reigning beauty such as Teresa Blount; but ostensibly it maintains a fiction that the dead Voiture is pleased to have a 'Young Lady' reading his *Works*.

11
ON SILENCE
(1712)

Editors' Headnote

Composition and publication

'On Silence' was first published on 20 May 1712. Pope probably first composed his imitation of Rochester's 'Upon Nothing', in the period between 1702 and 1703 during which he wrote his first imitations of short pieces by various other English poets of the seventeenth century – Waller, Cowley and Dorset – alongside Chaucer and Spenser. As Pope told Spence: 'In these rambles of mine through the poets, when I met with a passage or a story that pleased me more than the ordinary, I used to endeavour to imitate it' (*OAC*, I.20, no. 45). Three contemporary manuscripts of the poem survive, representing two distinct states of the text: an undated autograph fair copy of a 16-stanza poem, 'Upon Silence in Imitation of a Modern Poem on Nothing', in the William Andrews Clark Memorial Library; a transcript of this poem in the hand of Ralph Bridges, in the Percy collection of the Bodleian Library; and a transcript, in an unidentified hand, of a significantly different state of the poem (also consisting of sixteen stanzas), in the British Library. The relationship between the two manuscript states of the poem is discussed by Howard Erskine-Hill (1966: 274–7), who supports *TE*'s 1702 date for the Clark manuscript and suggests that the British Library manuscript probably belongs to 1703. In his 'Advertisement' to the *Imitations of English Poets*, with which the poem was included in the *Works* of 1736, Pope says that the poems were written 'some of them at fourteen or fifteen years old', while a note to a letter to Cromwell of 17 May 1710 in the 1737 edition of Pope's *Letters* (*Corr.*, I.87n) identifies 'a paper enclos'd' as '*Verses on* Silence *in imitation of the Earl of* Rochester's *poem on* Nothing; *done at* 14 *years old*', which repeats the description of the poem when it was reprinted in the 1726 edition of *Miscellany Poems*: 'Writ at Fourteen Years of Age.' Sherburn (1934: 99) gives the poem a biographical slant, aligning it with 'Pope's struggle for faith in the wisdom of silence in the months after Dennis's fulminations', that is, in relation to the controversy over the *Essay on Criticism*; but there is no evidence that composition or rewriting was prompted by those events. On 9 April 1712 Lintot paid Pope £3 16s 6d for this poem together with the previous one and the one that follows in the present edition, making it one of his better-paid efforts (McLaverty 2001: 17). 'On Silence' was published in *Miscellaneous Poems and Translations* as the first (the second being 'To the Author of a Poem, Intitled, Successio') of 'TWO |

COPIES *of* VERSES, | WRITTEN | Some Years since in Imitation of the Style of | Two Persons of Quality. | *By the same Hand.*' For further discussion of the possible extent of Pope's role in the publication of *Miscellaneous Poems* see Headnote to 'The First Book of Statius his Thebais'.

Text

The text presented here is taken from the first edition of 1712. Apart from the title and half-title, Pope made only minor revisions to the poem, in the editions of 1717 and 1736. The various extant texts of 'On Silence' are referred to in the apparatus as follows:

MS: 'Upon Silence in Imitation of a Modern Poem on Nothing' (William Andrews Clark Memorial Library, PR3620 .D40; *IELM* PoA 264; and Bodleian Library, MS Eng.lett.d.59 ff. 86-7; *IELM* PoA 265)

MS2: 'Upon Silence. In imitation of a late Author upon nothing' (British Library, Add. MS 28253 ff. 135-6; *IELM* PoA 266)

1712: *Miscellaneous Poems and Translations*, octavo (Griffith 6)

1717: *Works*, quarto (Griffith 79)

1726: *Miscellany Poems*, duodecimo (Griffith 164)

1736: *Works*, vol.III, octavo (Griffith 417, 418)

1751: *Works*, vol.II, octavo (Griffith 644)

Models and sources

Pope started his publication career with a version of Chaucer's 'Merchant's Tale'. The present poem is one of Pope's several 'Imitations of English Poets' (that is, Donne, Waller, Cowley and Dorset), later grouped together as evidence of his poetic apprenticeship (and supposed precocity). This, one of only two plucked out for publication at this stage, is avowedly based on one by John Wilmot, second Earl of Rochester (1647–80). His 'Upon Nothing' was unusually widely circulated in manuscript (see Love 1985) and much reprinted in collections and separately, in part because it exemplified a (mostly) non-obscene example of Rochester's wit. It had appeared as recently as 1711 in a single-poem luxury issue by Pope's future enemy Edmund Curll as a sample of a proposed full edition (Curll had been issuing volumes of Rochester coupled with other poets since 1707). At some point, Pope owned and annotated with some attention a copy of Tonson's edition of Rochester's *Poems, (&c.) on Several Occasions* (1696; Mack 1982: 437–8, item 144), marking 'Upon Nothing' (at pp. 101–5) amongst several other lyrics and satires, with a cross, a sign of appreciation; he also emended the text of the poem at two points (see line 12 of the present poem). (Quotations from Rochester's poem in the Commentary are from this text, as the version most likely to have been Pope's source.) Pope had certainly read Rochester from an early age and continued to draw on him throughout his career, Rochester's 'Allusion to Horace' standing as one of the models for his own later series of Horatian imitations); Rochester's *Satyr against [Reason and] Mankind* (also marked with a cross in the 1696 volume) additionally inflected Pope's youthful disrespect for conventions and institutions. Apart from the present poem, Pope does not otherwise refer substantially to Rochester in his verse, and tends to do so somewhat cheekily as 'Wilmot' (e.g. *The Sixth Epistle of the First Book of Horace, Imitated*, 126).

By 1712 Pope probably had some intermediate knowledge of Rochester via friends such as Wycherley, Betterton, Walsh, and John Sheffield, the latter one of Rochester's courtly antagonists and hardly likely to pass on the best of impressions. Pope had in later life a mixed opinion of Rochester, describing him to Spence as 'of a very bad turn of mind, as well as debauched'. As a writer, Pope thought he and the Earl of Dorset should be classed as 'holiday writers – as gentlemen that diverted themselves now and then with poetry, rather than as poets', though Spence regards this as designed 'rather to excuse their defects than to lessen their characters'. He thought Rochester had 'very bad versification sometimes' and he weighed him on the score of 'delicacy' against Dorset and Oldham (see *OAC*, I.201–2, nos. 469–73; cf. Headnote to the next poem).

Nonetheless Rochester was a major, if disreputable, satiric talent, and 'Upon Nothing', with its parody of creation and extended paradoxical mind game, offered a gallery of satiric targets, and a short but powerful model for the uncreation that Pope would mock-celebrate in *The Dunciad* (see further Aden 1978: 58–61). 'Upon Nothing' was in the tradition of the 'paradoxical encomium' (Colie 1966) and exemplified Rochester's irreverent view of more orthodox uses of wit to explore the creation story, such as Cowley's 'Hymn. To Light'. Pope at least affected to be repelled by the obscenity with which Rochester was particularly associated; he was at this stage however attracted to 'Rebel Wit' against conformity, and affected a slightly rakish pose in his correspondence with Wycherley and Cromwell, though not to so flamboyant an extent (see Winn 1979).

This is one of Pope's few poems fully in triplets, and it follows Rochester's form (two 10-syllable lines followed by an Alexandrine of 12) exactly, if more smoothly. At 42 lines, it is slightly shorter than Rochester's (51 lines), though the alternative version is almost the same length (48 lines). Pope adopts several of Rochester's satiric targets, not necessarily following the same sequence, and uses the same type of oxymoron to produce satiric effects (e.g. at lines 25–6, 37–41). Pope's targets are in some ways similar to Rochester's, but he does not insult other nations in the way Rochester does, and he introduces new satiric figures, such as lawyers. In general Pope's poem, in centring on language as the reverse of silence (as opposed to the something/nothing dichotomy of Rochester), moves closer to the opening of the gospel of St John, with its mystical creation narrative of God's 'word', and away from Genesis, which underlies Rochester's more parodic images of a creation out of nothing (for further detailed comparison see Baines 1995). Much reference to and poetic invocation of silence was actually along orthodox religious lines; see McCullough (2013) for a full history. There were apparently reverential poems such as Richard Flecknoe's 'Still-born Silence' (*Love's Kingdom*, 1664, p. 38), a magical invocation of silence, as well as witty explorations such as Cowley's amorous lyric 'Silence' (*Poems... Written by A. Cowley*, 1656, p. 61). Silence sometimes featured as the subject of witty epigrams, and its potential for encomium tinged with paradox had already been mined somewhat in W. A.'s poem 'Upon Silence', published in Mary Mollineux, *Fruits of Retirement* (1702). Pope himself invokes the holiness of silence in 'Messiah', 14, and 'The First Book of Statius', 291; elsewhere he associates it with melancholy deprivation ('Winter', 78; 'Sapho to Phaon', 175-6). In the present poem, with speech and silence equally being sometimes useful and sometimes not, the theme offers Pope slightly different kind of satiric opportunity than the 'nothing' of his model, which however recurs more strongly in the apocalyptic negations of the 'uncreating Word' in *The Dunciad* (IV.654)

Context

The poem was not controversial and did not attract much comment in Pope's lifetime. In 1756, Samuel Johnson claimed that 'On Silence' had 'much greater elegance of diction, music of numbers, extent of observation, and force of thought' than the 'Ode on Solitude', which had been praised by Joseph Warton in his *Essay* on Pope that year (Johnson, review of Warton's *Essay*, *Literary Magazine*, I, April–May 1756). Johnson, however, pays virtually no attention to the poem in his *Life* of Pope, whereas he grants Rochester's 'Upon Nothing' extended discussion in his life of the Earl (Lonsdale, II.13–14). In his edition of Pope's *Works* (II.292), Warton calls the poem a 'sensible imitation' and writes: 'Pope ... has discovered a fund of solid sense, and just observation upon vice and folly, that are very remarkable in a person so extremely young as he was at the time of composing it'; disgusted as he was by most of Rochester's work, Warton found Pope had 'excelled' his model.

On SILENCE.

I.

*S*ilence! Cooeval with Eternity;
Thou wert e'er Nature first began to be,
'Twas one vast Nothing, All, and All slept fast in thee.

Title. MS: Upon Silence in Imitation of a Modern Poem on Nothing; MS2: Upon silence. An imitation of a late Author upon Nothing.; *1717:* On *SILENCE, in imitation of the style* | *of the late E. of* R.; *1726:* SILENCE, | *In Imitation of the late E. of* R.; *1736–51:* V. | E. of ROCHESTER. | *On* SILENCE.
1. Nature first: *1736–51:* Nature's self
1–3. MS, MS2: Silence! thou primitive parent even to thought
 Thy work er'e Nature was begun was wroght
 Behind, and just behind; thy Elder Brother nought
3^4. MS, MS2: Yet o're that mighty nothing thou didst reign
 (Before rude Chaos broke thy easy chain)
 And held'st o're chaos self a short liv'd Sway again.

---

1. Cooeval: a word not used elsewhere by Pope; cf. Dryden, 'Meleager and Atalanta', 87, *Fables Ancient and Modern* (1700), p. 108, of an untouched forest: 'Coeval with the World, a venerable Sight'. Dryden had also used the phrase in a discussion of creation stories ('coaeval *with the World*') in the 'Preface to the Pastorals', *Works of Virgil* (1697), sig. ***2ᵛ.

2–3. Cf. 'W. A.', 'Upon Silence', 5–6, in Mary Mollineux, *Fruits of Retirement* (1702), p. 173: 'For before any thing, thou hadst thy Place | Extended through the wide and empty Space'.

3. Nothing: For the implications of the concept as set out in Rochester's poem, see Headnote. Rochester and Pope are both utilising the creation story set out in Genesis 1:2 at this point: 'And the earth was without forme, and voyd, and darkenesse was vpon the face of the deepe' (*AV*). The use of sexual and familial imagery is modelled on orthodox uses of wit to praise the processes of creation, such as Cowley's 'Hymn. To Light', *The Works of Mr. Abraham Cowley* (1668), p. 35 of final sequence, which opens: 'First born of Chaos, who so fair didst come | From the old Negro's darksome Womb!'

3 MS. Elder Brother: cf. Rochester, 'Upon Nothing', 1, *Poems on Several Occasions* (1696), p. 101: 'thou elder Brother ev'n to Shade', itself a parody of Cowley, 'Life and Fame', *Poems . . . Written by Mr. A. Cowley* (1656), p. 39 of separate sequence: 'Oh Life, thou *Nothings younger Brother!*'

3^4 MS. mighty nothing: Pope's transformation of Rochester's 'Great Negative' ('Upon Nothing', 28); the phrase does occur in earlier poetry, e.g. Katherine Philips, 'To the Lady E. C.', 74, *Poems* (1667), p. 63: 'Yet wonder'd what the mighty nothing meant'.

rude Chaos: a standard label for what God transformed by creation, e.g. Roscommon, 'A Paraphrase on the CXLVIIIth Psalm', 23, *A Collection of Poems by Several Hands* (1693), p. 51: 'Who did all Forms from the rude Chaos draw'. Pope's later allusions to Chaos in *The Dunciad* mostly parody the extensive

II.

Thine was the Sway, e'er Heav'n was form'd or Earth,
5   E'er fruitful *Thought* conceiv'd Creation's Birth,
Or Midwife *Word* gave Aid, and spoke the Infant forth.

III.

Then various Elements against thee join'd,
In one more various Animal combin'd,
And fram'd the clam'rous Race of busie Human-kind.

---

4. MS, MS2: Great breathing space! er'e time commenc'd with Earth,
6^7. MS2: When Thought, thy captive offspring, thou didst free,
        Whisper, a soft diserter, stole from thee,
    And Rebell noise disturb'd thy midnight Majesty.
7. **Then various:** MS, MS2: Opposing
8. MS, MS2: And a long Race to break thy sway combin'd,
9. MS, MS2: (Whom Elements compos'd) [MS2: Whom Elements compound,] the Race of human kind
9^10. MS: When thought thy captive offspring thou didst free
        Whisper a soft Desrter stole from thee
        And rebell Speech disturb'd thy Midnight Majesty

---

description in Milton, *Paradise Lost*, II.890–1055 (Milton does not use this exact phrase).
4. Sway: power, empire.
5. fruitful: suggested by Rochester's more paradoxical 'fruitful Emptiness's hand', 'Upon Nothing', 11. For the normal and positive associations of 'fruitful' in Pope cf. 'Spring', 102, 'Winter', 47, *Windsor-Forest*, 26, 338, etc.; these usages are more in line with Dryden's throughout his translations from Virgil's *Eclogues* and *Georgics*.
6. Midwife **Word:** cf. Pope to Wycherley, 10 April 1706 (*Corr.*, I.16), discussing the production of poetry: 'I can no more pretend to the Merit of the Production, than a Midwife to the Virtues and good Qualities of the Child she helps into the Light'. For the oblique biblical alignment here, see John 1:1: 'In the beginning was the Word, & the Word was with God, and the Word was God' (*AV*); the 'uncreating word' which returns civilisation to the empire of Chaos at the end of the final version of the *Dunciad* (IV.654) is a parody of this idea. Pope might have found similar images in religious verse, e.g. John Quarles, 'The Second Book of God's Love, and Man's Unworthiness', 73–5, *Divine Meditations* (1655), p. 56: 'that the Earth | May (like a Midwife) hug the joyful birth | Of every word'.
8. various: cf. 'Vertumnus and Pomona', 112, and Dryden, *Absalom and Achitophel*, 545.
9. busie: 'meddling ... troublesome' (*SJ*), as in Rochester, 'Satyr against [Reason and] Mankind', 80, *Poems* (1696), p. 91: 'This busie puzling stirrer up of doubt'.

IV.

10   The tongue mov'd gently first, and Speech was low,
        'Till wrangling *Science* taught it Noise and Show,
        And wicked *Wit* arose, thy most abusive Foe.

V.

        But Rebel Wit deserts thee oft in vain;
        Lost in the Maze of Words, he turns again,

10–11. MS, MS2: Then wanton Sence began abroad to go
                    And [MS2: In] gawdy Science drest himself [MS2: her self] to shew
13. **Rebel:** MS, MS2: noisy
14. **Lost in the Maze of Words:** MS: And in the wilds of speech; MS2: Lost in ye Wilds of speech

---

11. wrangling: to wrangle is to 'dispute peevishly; to quarrel perversely' (*SJ*). Cf. Pope to Caryll, 8 June 1711 (*Corr.*, I.118): 'the heat of these disputants who I'm afraid, being bred up to wrangle in the schools . . . '; and to the same, 18 January 1717/18, (*Corr.*, I.462): 'the unrighteous labours of wrangling statesmen'. Sir William Trumbull had 'a Scorn of wrangling, yet a Zeal for truth', according to Pope's 'Epitaph' for him (1716), 8; Pope has Odysseus attack the 'wrangling Talents' of Thersites at *Iliad*, II.307.

Science: 'any art or species of knowledge' (*SJ*). Cf. Pope to Caryll, 20 September 1713 (*Corr.*, I.190): 'What we call science here, and study, is little better: the greater number of arts to which we apply ourselves, are mere groping in the dark, and even the search of our most impatient concerns in a future being, is but a needless, anxious, and uncertain haste to be knowing sooner than we can, what without all this solicitude we should know a little after.' The theme was taken up particularly in his *Essay on Man* (1733-4), and see Pope to Swift, 26 March 1736 (*Corr.*, IV.5), for Pope's later ideas on the matter.

12. wicked Wit: a common literary phrase (e.g. Shakespeare, *Hamlet*, I.v.44), but here an indirect praise of the capacity for thought, imagination, and verbal facility; see note to next line.

Foe: cf. Rochester, 'Upon Nothing', 17: 'Body, thy Foe, with thee did Leagues combine'; and 19. In his copy of Rochester's 1696 *Poems*, Pope emended 'thee' to 'them' in this line (see Headnote); modern editors read either 'these' or 'those'.

13. Rebel Wit: cf. the 'Rebel Light' of 'Upon Nothing', 15. The phrase is recalled by Pope in *Dunciad* (1743), IV.158; for Pope wit was from the *Essay on Criticism* onwards a 'rebel' against conformity and mediocrity, 'wicked' (12) only ironically; cf. *Essay on Criticism*, 53. Pope might have remembered a less ironic use of the phrase in Waller, 'In Answer to One who Writ against a Fair Lady', 22, *Poems &c.* (1686), p. 28: 'So shall thy Rebel wit become her prize'. Though Pope is capable of using 'rebel' as a mock-political allusion (e.g. *Rape of the Lock*, III.59: 'The Rebel-*Knave*, who dares his Prince engage'), its use here appears only to emphasise the intellectual freedom of 'Wit'; in the variants at 6^7 and 9^10, the opposition to 'Majesty' suggests a slightly more politicised image.

14. Maze of Words: Pope writes to Cromwell, 12 November 1711, of his creative endeavours as 'a wandring *Maze* of Thought'. Cf.

15   And seeks a surer State, and courts thy gentler Reign.

VI.

Afflicted *Sense* thou kindly dost set free,
Oppress'd with Argumental Tyranny,
And routed *Reason* finds a safe Retreat in thee.

VII.

       With thee in private modest *Dulness* lies,
20   And in thy Bosom lurks in *Thought*'s Disguise;
Thou Varnisher of *Fools*, and Cheat of all the *Wise*.

---

15. gentler: *1736–51:* gentle
16. Afflicted: MS, MS2: Opressed
17. Oppress'd: MS, MS2: Fatigu'd
21. Wise.: *1717–51:* wise!

---

the anonymous ('A. B.') commendatory poem, 'On Mr. *Clieveland* and his Poems', 30, in *Clievelandi Vindiciae, or, Clieveland's Genuine Poems, Orations, Epistles, &c* (1677), sig. a5ᵛ, contrasting Clieveland's wit with those 'Who in a Maze of words the wandring sense do loose'. Cf. also the devils debating theology in Milton, *Paradise Lost*, II.561 (1674), p. 44, who 'found no end, in wandring mazes lost'.

15. Cf. the 'peaceful Realm' of 'Upon Nothing', 18.

16. *Afflicted* **Sense:** For 'Sense' see Headnote to *Essay on Criticism*. The collocation generally refers to emotional affliction such as grief, not intellectual confusion as here: cf. Charles Cotton, 'Eclogue', *Poems on Several Occasions* (1689), p. 110: 'And give thee o'er to an afflicted Sense, | As void of Reason as of Patience'.

17. Argumental: 'belonging to argument' (*SJ*, citing only this example). An uncommon word, but used previously in satire by Thomas D'Urfey, *Butler's Ghost* (1682), p. 69: 'Argumental froth'; Edward Ward, *The Poet's Ramble after Riches* (1691), p. 13: 'Argumental Fire'.

Tyranny: cf. *Essay on Criticism*, 690.

19. Dulness: a key category for Pope, not only in its more malign manifestation in *The Dunciad* (1728 onwards) but as early as the *Essay on Criticism*, 51, 394, 416 ('*proud Dulness*'), 533; see Commentary to 51 of that poem.

20. Thought's Disguise: cf. Rochester, 'Upon Nothing', 43: '*Nothing*, who dwell'st with Fools in grave disguise'.

21. Varnisher of Fools: i.e. silence provides a superficially convincing cover for idiocy; cf. quotation in previous note, and Edmund Elviden, 'On Silence', 3–4, *The Closet of Counsells* (1569), fol. 61ᵛ.: '*silence vsed in a foole | doth make him witty seeme*'.

Cheat of all the Wise: cf. Oldmixon, *Amores Britannici*, II.i.129 (1703), p. 8: 'To cheat the foolish, and amuse the wise'.

VIII.

Yet thy Indulgence is by both confest;
Folly by thee lies sleeping in the Breast,
And 'tis in thee at last that *Wisdom* seeks for Rest.

IX.

25   *Silence*, the Knave's Repute, the Whore's good Name,
The only Honour of the wishing Dame;
Thy very want of Tongue makes thee a kind of Fame.

X.

But could'st thou seize some Tongues that now are free,
How Church and State wou'd be oblig'd to thee?

---

22. MS, MS2: Yet on both sides thy kindness [MS2: Mildnes] is confest
25. MS, MS2: Thou Cloak of Vice that hid'st the Rascals name
26. The: MS: Thou; MS2: Though
29. wou'd: *1736–51:* should

---

22. Indulgence: kindness, forbearance; also, in one sense, a 'grant of the Church of Rome, not defined by themselves' (*SJ*). In a line with 'confest' (here meaning 'acknowledged') there is perhaps a faint play on the language of Pope's church.
23. Breast: cf. Rochester, 'Upon Nothing', 24: 'Into thy Bosom, where the Truth in private lies'.
25-6. The oxymora here mimic those in Rochester, 'Upon Nothing', 46–50.
25. Repute: reputation. The MS variant clarifies the satiric possibilities of the idea.
   Whore's good Name: suggested by Rochester, 'Upon Nothing', 50: 'Whores Vows'. Cf. 'January and May', 596.
26. wishing Dame: amorously inclined woman, able to preserve 'Honour' only by not speaking of her desires. Rumbold (1989: 19) notes Pope's awareness here of the sexual constraints in force against women, a matter more extensively explored in 'To a Young Lady . . .' and *The Rape of the Lock*. Cf. also Pope's jocular remark to Teresa Blount, 7 August 1716 (*Corr.*, I.350): 'I am vain enough to conclude (like most young fellows) that a fine Lady's Silence is Consent, and so I write on'.
27. Fame: an important theme for Pope, even before *The Temple of Fame* (1715); cf. e.g. *Essay on Criticism*, 46, 171. It is not a theme in Rochester's poem. For female 'Fame', i.e. reputation for chastity, cf. 'January and May', 239 and 593; 'To a Young Lady, with the Works of Voiture', 35–6.
28-30. Perhaps a playful suggestion about political censorship in Pope's world, with 31-3 acting as a more openly satiric rejoinder about the silencing of political complaint.
29. Church and State: both elements of Rochester's 'Upon Nothing' (e.g. 23-4, 33-4).

30   At Senate, and at Bar, how welcome would'st thou be?

XI.

Yet *Speech*, ev'n there, submissively withdraws
From *Rights* of *Subjects*, and the *Poor Man's Cause*;
Then pompous *Silence* reigns, and stills the noisie Laws.

XII.

       Past Services of Friends, good Deeds of Foes,
35   What Fav'rites gain, and what th' Exchequer owes,
       Fly the forgetful World, and in thy Arms repose.

---

30. **At:** MS, MS2: In
31. **ev'n there,:** MS, MS2: thy Foe
33. MS, MS2: And Silence then in Pomp sits nodding ore the [MS2: on y^e] Laws
34–36. MS, MS2: omitted
35. **th' Exchequer:** *1736–51:* the Nation

---

30. **Senate ... Bar:** parliament and the courts of law. For the former see Rochester, 'Upon Nothing', 37-9: 'But, *Nothing*, why does *Something* still permit, | That sacred Monarchs should at Council sit, | With Persons highly thought at best for nothing fit.'

32. **Rights of Subjects:** a matter not addressed in Rochester's poem, but a fundamental question of political debate explosively renewed after the revolution of 1688, e.g. in the theories of John Locke (*Two Treatises of Government*, 1690) and others; cf. *Essay on Criticism*, 551–2 and Commentary.

Poor Man's Cause: also not an issue for Rochester. For the phrasing cf. Charles Darby, 'Psalm CXL', *The Book of Psalms in English Metre* (1704), p. 240: 'But thou wilt plead the poor man's cause'; the wording of AV, verse 12, is 'the cause of the afflicted: and the right of the poore'.

35. **What Fav'rites gain:** i.e. through bribery or corruption, later a standard element of Pope's political opposition to the post-1714 regime, here perhaps (Aden 1978: 190, n. 14) a hit at the Duke of Marlborough's supposed peculation as paymaster general during the war, or the building of Blenheim Palace as a state reward for his generalship. By 1712, Marlborough had fallen and was no longer a 'favourite'.

what th' Exchequer owes: Public debt had become a particular topic of debate in the reign of William III, with the formation of the Bank of England in 1694 and the series of subsequent loans to government to finance European wars, including the War of Spanish Succession; Swift was particularly hostile to what became known as the National Debt, in his *Examiner* papers (1710–11).

XIII.

The Country Wit, Religion of the Town,
The Courtier's Learning, Policy o' th' Gown,
Are best by thee express'd, and shine in thee alone.

---

37. Country: MS: Country's;
   Religion: MS, MS2: the Policy
38. Policy o'th' Gown: MS, MS2: Citts Religion
39^40. MS, MS2: As Sleep and Night all disproportion quitt
   So do'st thou equal sence, and art to witt
   (What nothing is to man) both source and end of it.

Thou bashfull Goddes stop'st my weak essays
Thou fo[r]cest me too, [MS2: Me too thou free'st;] and whilst my voice I raise
Thou fliest disturbd away and does avoid my [MS2: thy] Praise

---

37-8. The oxymora mimic those in Rochester, 'Upon Nothing', 46-50, e.g. '*French* Truth'.

37. Country Wit: a standard oxymoron, often embodied in rustic stage characters in comedy, e.g. John Crowne, *The Countrey Wit* (1675); cf. also the satiric story in Oldmixon, 'The Country Wit', *Poems upon Several Occasions* (1696). Pope gives a rueful view of the absence of wit in the country in 'To Miss Blount, on her Leaving the Town, after the Coronation'.

Religion of the Town: Urban profanity was often a target for satire, e.g. *A View of the Religion of the Town; or, a Sunday Morning's Ramble* (1687).

38. Courtier's Learning: cf. Rochester, 'Upon Nothing', 47: '*Hibernian* Learning'. According to the 'breef rehersall of the chiefe conditions and qualities in a Courtier' in Castiglione's handbook *The Courtier* (translated by Thomas Hoby, 1561, sig. Yy. iiii^v), it was considered necessary for a courtier 'To be more then indifferentlye well seene in learninge, in the Latin and greeke tunges', and Sir Thomas Elyot devotes much of the first book of *The Boke Named the Gouernour* (1531) to calibrating the extent of 'learning' a courtier must be able to display. In *Essay on Criticism*, 669-70, Pope cites Petronius as exceptionally able to display both 'The Scholar's Learning, and the Courtier's Ease'. For other early comments on courtiers cf.

'January and May', 156; 'Rape of the Locke', II.164; and the rare distinction of Sir William Trumbull as 'an honest Courtier, yet a Patriot too' in Pope's epitaph on him (1716), 5. See also Pope to Caryll, 29 June 1714 (*Corr.*, I.233): 'I ... could point you several who would make excellent courtiers, if the science of courts required nothing but an artful way of breaking one's word'.

Policy ... Gown: the wise counsel and statesmanship of clergymen. Cf. Rochester, 'Upon Nothing', 45: 'Lawn Sleeves, and Furrs, and Gowns, when they like thee look wise'; and 46: '*Brittish* Policy'.

38 MS. Citts: citizens, usually meaning merchant-class inhabitants of the city of London, a stock target in drama and satire.

40. Parson's Cant: empty or hypocritical discourse of a clergyman; 'Parson' indicates Anglican. Pope refers to his friend Archdeacon Thomas Parnell 1679-1718 as a 'parson' (to Martha Blount, 6 October 1714) and he described a later Anglican friend, William Warburton, as 'a sneaking Parson ... I told him he flatterd' (to Martha Blount, early August. 1743; *Corr.*, I.260, IV.464). Often slightly satirical in tone, as in *Epistle to Dr. Arbuthnot*, 15: 'Is there a Parson, much be-mused in Beer'; see also 'The Happy Life of a Country Parson', published in 1727 but probably written by 1713 (*TE*, VI.110-11).

XIV.

40 The Parson's Cant, the Lawyer's Sophistry,
    Lord's Quibble, Critick's Jest; all end in thee,
    All rest in Peace at last, and sleep eternally.

40–42. MS, MS2: omitted

Sophistry: deliberately misleading and over-complex use of reason and argument. The self-serving and empty rhetoric of lawyers was another traditional satiric target, already well established in Swift's *Tale of a Tub* (1704), extended by Arbuthnot's *Law is a Bottomless Pit* (1712) and later developed as a particular Scriblerian theme in e.g. 'Stradling *versus* Stiles', in the Pope–Swift *Miscellanies. The Second Volume* (1727). Sophistry itself returns in apocalyptic guise in *The Dunciad* (1743), IV.25.

41. **Lord's Quibble:** wordplay of punning or smutty character, inappropriate for an aristocrat; possibly by allusion to the general character of Rochester's verse, including 'Upon Nothing', which presents several questionable puns. Pope does not apparently use the word 'quibble' elsewhere in poetry. In the 'Dedication' of his translation of Virgil's *Aeneid*, Dryden associated this type of wordplay with the lower classes – 'our Upper-Gallery Audience in a Play-House; who like nothing but the Husk and Rhind of Wit; preferr a Quibble, a Conceit, an Epigram, before solid Sense, and Elegant Expression: These are Mobb-Readers' ('To the Most Honourable John Lord Marquess of Normanby . . . ', in the *Works of Virgil*, 1697, sig. e3ᵛ). There is a short essay-like account of 'the quibble' in Dennis et al., *Letters upon Several Occasions* (1696), pp. 64–8.

Critick's Jest: for characterisation of critics as humourless and spiteful, see Headnote to *Essay on Criticism*.

42. **rest in Peace:** echoing 'resquiescat in pace', a phrase from the *Missa pro defunctis* or Catholic burial service. Common as the phrase was in poetry of the seventeenth century, it was regarded as suspect by Protestants (because of its suggestion of the Catholic purgatory, for which see 'The Wife of Bath Her Prologue', 238 and Commentary) and is not in the burial service set down in the Anglican *Book of Common Prayer*. In his letter to Cromwell, 17 May 1710, Pope plays extensively on these ideas: 'Tho you are no Papist, and have not so much regard to the dead as to address yourself to them, (which I plainly perceive by your silence) yet I hope you are not one of those Heterodox, who hold the dead to be totally Insensible of the good Offices & kind Wishes of their living friends' (*Corr.*, I.87–8).

The ending of the poem mirrors both Rochester's parodic 'Upon Nothing' and the closing stanza of Cowley's orthodox 'Hymn. To Light'.

12
TO THE AUTHOR OF A POEM, INTITLED, SUCCESSIO
(1712)

Editors' Headnote

Composition and publication

'To the Author of a Poem, intitled, Successio' was first published on 20 May 1712. On 9 April of that year Lintot had paid Pope £3 16s 6d for this poem and the two previous items (Foxon 1991: 35; McLaverty 2001: 17), and it first appeared in *Miscellaneous Poems and Translations*, as the second (the first being 'On Silence') of 'TWO | COPIES *of* VERSES, | WRITTEN | Some Years since in Imitation of the style of | Two Persons of Quality. | *By the same Hand*'. (For further discussion of the extent of Pope's role in the publication of *Miscellaneous Poems* see Headnote to 'The First Book of Statius'.) The third edition of *Miscellaneous Poems* (1720), published when Pope was very much more eminent, makes explicit the attribution to him – 'By Mr. Pope' – and the poem is included in the opening section of 18 poems all by Pope, and identified as such in the Index. However, Pope did not include it among his own *Works*, and it did not appear as part of an edition of his writings until the second volume of William Roscoe's edition in 1824.

When 'On Silence' and 'To the Author of a Poem, Intitled, Successio' were reprinted in *Miscellany Poems. Vol. I. By Mr. Pope* (fifth edition, 1726) they were described as 'Writ at Fourteen Years of Age'. 'To the Author of a Poem' is identified as '*In Imitation of the late E. of* D.', i.e. Charles Sackville, sixth Earl of Dorset, although Pope did not include the poem alongside his two specific imitations of Dorset in his group of *Imitations of English Poets* in the *Works* of 1736. In his note to *Dunciad Variorum* (1729), I.177, Pope says the poem was 'of a very early date [. . .] writ at Fourteen Years old and soon after printed'. Pope was fourteen in 1702, which matches the date of the poem he was attacking, but there is no sign of the poem being printed before 1712. Line 4 appears to derive from Wycherley's manuscript 'Panegyrick on Dulness', which Pope was revising with his friend in November 1707.

Text

The text presented here is taken from the first edition of 1712. Apart from the title and half-title, the text of poem was not subsequently revised. The various extant texts of 'To the Author of a Poem, Intitled, Successio' are referred to in the apparatus as follows:

1712: *Miscellaneous Poems and Translations*, octavo (Griffith 6)

1726: *Miscellany Poems*, duodecimo (Griffith 164)

Models and sources

Sherburn (1934: 84) remarks that this is Pope's first published satire, a debatable point if the 'Lines from *The Critical Specimen*' (1711) are counted; and there is much satiric material in 'On Silence', and, indeed, in 'January and May'. Nonetheless it is the first instance in Pope of a clearly satiric poem addressed to a rival author on the subject of one of his poems. It forms part of the Restoration tradition of witty response and topical review. Case (1928) identified Dorset's poem 'To Mr. Edward Howard, on his Incomparable, Incomprehensible Poem Called "The British Princes"' as Pope's direct model, on the strength of general style and particular verbal resemblances, the latter noted in the Commentary. Howard's *The Brittish Princes* was first printed in 1669; Dorset's poem was available to Pope in various guises, e.g. in Rochester's *Poems on Several Occasions* (1680), p. 88, under the title 'On Mr E— H— upon his B— P—', and as 'To a Person of Honour: Upon his Incomprehensible Poems' in *The Annual Miscellany: For the Year 1694* (1694), pp. 298–300. Its derisory, cavalier wit at the expense of a struggling poet and its use of bathetic images such as the poet's 'alacrity in sinking' certainly suggest a strong influence on Pope. His friend Walsh quoted part of the poem in his *A Dialogue Concerning Women* (1691), pp. 63–4, and it was also mentioned, as the work of his patron, in Dryden's dedication to *Examen Poeticum* (1693); Dryden then printed it, anonymously, in *The Annual Miscellany: For the Year 1694* (1694).

Charles Sackville, sixth Earl of Dorset (1643–1706) was the patron of Prior and of Dryden, who addressed the influential 'Discourse Concerning the Original and Progress of Satire' of 1693 to him (see further Hammond and Hopkins, III.302–8). He was regarded by Pope as one of the most gifted of the Restoration aristocratic poets, at least in terms of wit; he also rated him superior to Rochester in terms of 'delicacy' and 'exactness' (Spence's records of Pope's comments, gathered over the last 15 years of the poet's life, are at *OAC*, I.200–3, items 465–72, 474). He was also, interestingly in view of this poem, said to suffer dull company politely (item 468). In 1735 Spence (item 474) discussed with Pope Dorset's presence in the series of volumes known as *Poems on Affairs of State*, and Pope agreed that he had found several of his poems by 'dipping about' in those books, an indication of his continued interest in political verse of the period. Dorset was Pope's specific model for two 'Imitations', both lyric satires against unclean women ('Artemisia'; 'Phryne'), first published in 1727. Pope also complied with Dorset's son's request for a belated epitaph, published in 1735.

Context

In 1674, after the success of his *The Empress of Morocco*, the poet and dramatist Elkanah Settle (1648–1724) engaged Dryden in a public critical squabble; in the 1680s he joined the Whig side of the Exclusion Crisis and replied to Dryden's *Absalom and Achitophel* in *Absalom Senior* (1682); he featured in Dryden's portion of the second part of *Absalom and Achitophel* as 'Doeg'. Settle's management of Pope-burnings and political pamphlets such as *The Character of a Popish Successour* (1680, but reprinted 1712 as the succession crisis loomed once more) served to enhance his status as an inimical figure, ripe for the Catholic Pope's ridicule. But he was also a time-server, switching allegiance several times up to and beyond the arrival of William and Mary in 1688, which he celebrated in a lavish ode, *A View of the Times* (1689). In 1691 he became City Poet, responsible (at least intermittently) for producing pageants for the Lord Mayor's shows; he was also associated with displays at Bartholomew Fair, giving Pope a further handle on the corruptions of Whig cultural life (though Settle also wrote on the Tory side during the 'Church in Danger' crisis of Anne's reign). Apart from Dryden's attack, Settle had already been a target for satire in Richard Ames, *A Search after Wit* (1691), and in Tom Brown's 'To Elkanah Settle the City Poet', in *Commendatory Verses* (1702), p. 17. He appears to have given no direct personal provocation to Pope, nor indeed to have responded to Pope's satire. Indeed, the full measure of Pope's ridicule only came after his death, with a full-dress appearance in book II of *The Dunciad*, as Theobald's prophetic father; Pope supplies a witty if heavily partisan account of his career in his note to I.88 of *The Dunciad Variorum*.

Settle's poem *Eusebia Triumphans. The Hannover Succession to the Imperial Crown of England, An Heroic Poem*, celebrating in Latin and English the Act of Settlement which provided for the accession of the protestant Hanoverians in preference to closer Catholic relatives to the royal line after the death of Anne, first appeared in 1702 (although the date is altered to '1703' in some copies), giving some credibility to Pope's own dating of his poem. 'Successio' was the internal title, or part thereof, for versions of Settle's poem from 1704 onwards. *Eusebia Triumphans* was republished in 1709 and 1711, perhaps prompting the eventual publication of Pope's riposte. It was in any case one of the more obviously political versions of satire published by Pope as the end of Anne's reign came into view, and in its mapping of poetic succession onto changes of monarchy it offers an early witness to Pope's interest in Dryden's *Mac Flecknoe*, the obvious model for *The Dunciad* (1728); see further Sherburn (1934: 84, 98–9); Aden (1978: 57–8); Hone (2015b: 254).

TO THE
AUTHOR *of a* POEM,
INTITLED,
SUCCESSIO.

Begone ye Criticks, and restrain your Spite,
Codrus writes on, and will for ever write;
The heaviest Muse the swiftest Course has gone,
As Clocks run fastest when most Lead is on.

Title. 1726: TO THE | AUTHOR of a POEM | ENTITLED, | SUCCESSIO. | *In Imitation of the late E. of* D.

---

1. Spite: for literary critics as malign and spiteful, see Headnote to *Essay on Criticism* and the poem itself, 601, 636. Case (1928) cites Dorset, 'To Mr. Edward Howard, on his Incomparable, Incomprehensible Poem, called "The British Princes", 1: 'Come on you Criticks, find one fault who dares'; cited here from the version found in *The Annual Miscellany: For the Year 1694* (1694), p. 298.

2. Codrus: mentioned as an envious poet in the exchange between Corydon and Thyrsis in Virgil, *Eclogues*, VII.21-8; the name is also used as an exemplar of hopeless poverty in Juvenal, *Satires*, III.202-11. Juvenal having attacked an interminable epic poet called Cordus (sometimes taken to be an error for 'Codrus') in the first lines of his first satire, the two figures were commonly identified as a representative type of the deservedly starving poet. Cf. Garth, *The Dispensary*, sixth edition, V (1706), p. 80: 'Still Censures will on dull Pretenders fall, | A *Codrus* shou'd expect a *Juvenal*'. Pope quotes Dryden's translation of Juvenal, *Satires*, III.202-11, in his own note to *The Dunciad Variorum*, II.136; see Commentary in Rumbold (2007) and to 'A Letter to The Publisher', p. 132; also the instance in Pope to Sheffield, c. 1718, *Corr.*, I.508.

3. swiftest Course: For the idea of which this is a parody, see *Essay on Criticism*, 86-7.

4. In *The Posthumous Works of William Wycherley, Esq. . . . Vol. II* (1729), p. 26, Pope's partly-suppressed response to Lewis Theobald's edition of his old friend's *Posthumous Works* (1728), Pope quotes this line as Wycherley's original, from his 'Panegyrick on Dulness', citing a letter from himself to Wycherley, 3 April 1705, and the evidence of the present poem, which, as he puts it, 'got out in a Miscellany in 1712, three Years before Mr. *Wycherley* died, and two after he had laid aside the whole design of publishing any Poems'. There is no surviving letter of 3 April 1705. In his letter to Wycherley, 20 November 1707 (*Corr.*, I.31-2), Pope explains what he has done to the 'Dulness' poem, including the insertion of a four-line simile on the weights of a clock (printed in *TE*, VI.55, as 'Of the Weights of a

5   What tho' no Bees around your Cradle flew,
    Nor on your Lips distill'd their golden Dew?
    Yet have we oft discover'd in their stead,
    A Swarm of Drones, that buzz'd about your Head.
    When you, like *Orpheus*, strike the warbling Lyre,
10 Attentive Blocks stand round you, and admire.
    Wit, past thro' thee, no longer is the same,
    As Meat digested takes a diff'rent Name;
    But Sense must sure thy safest Plunder be,
    Since no Reprizals can be made on thee.
15 Thus thou may'st Rise, and in thy daring Flight

Clock'); the first two of these lines were then adapted in *The Dunciad* (1728), I.169–70 (see Commentary there). Spence (*OAC*, I.19, item 41) records that those two lines first appeared in Pope's early (destroyed) epic poem *Alcander*. In *The Dunciad Variorum* (1729), I.177n, Pope quoted that first formulation of this image alongside that found in 17–18 in the present poem as early versions of his more developed thought.

Lead: used as a weight in clock mechanisms, but also the base metal which alchemists were supposed to transmute into gold and thus rich in negative connotations: cf. *The Dunciad Variorum*, I.26.

5–6. Alluding to the classical idea of bees providing poets or orators with the gift of 'honeyed speech' or eloquence at birth, e.g. in the case of Pindar. Dryden refers to the tradition in his elegy 'To the Pious Memory of the Accomplisht Young lady Mrs. Anne Killgrew', 50–1.

8. Drones: unproductive bees, the habits of which are described in book IV of Virgil's *Georgics*; Dryden's translation refers to 'lazy Drones' at IV.242 and 356, *Works of Virgil*, pp. 129 and 133.

9. Orpheus: semi-divine poet and magical singer of ancient Greece; cf. 'Summer', 81 and the *Ode for Musick*.

warbling Lyre: cf. 'January and May', 324 and 466. Pope normally uses 'warbling' more seriously than here; cf. 'Spring', 26; *Ode for Musick*, 6.

10. Blocks: a block is 'a blockhead; a fellow remarkable for stupidity' (*SJ*), formed from the head-shaped block on which wigs were stored.

11. Wit: creative intelligence, or evidence of this in poetry; for the many senses of the word see the Headnote to *Essay on Criticism*.

12. Meat digested: Case (1928) cites Dorset, 'To Mr. Edward Howard', 17–18, *The Annual Miscellany: For the Year 1694*, p. 299: 'Thy Wit's the same, whatever be thy Theam, | As some digestions turn all Meat to Phlegm'. Cf. also Richard Lovelace, 'Her jealous husband an adultresse gave', 8–9, *Lucasta: Posthume Poems* (1659), p. 99: 'And straight from th'hollow stomack both retreat, | To th'slipp'ry pipes known to digested meat'. *TE* notes that the same idea, in similar wording, is in Pope's *The Second Satire of Dr. John Donne, Dean of St. Paul's, Versifyed*, 33–4; the idea, expressed differently, is in Donne's original (25–30).

13. Sense: good sense, thought, poetry; for the range of meanings see Headnote to the *Essay on Criticism*.

Plunder: material to plagiarise.

14. Because Codrus has no sense or material worth 'plundering' in a revenge attack ('Reprizals').

15–18. A parody of the imaginative flight of poetry, loosely related to the theory of the sublime; cf. *Essay on Criticism*, 93, 200, and the second set of 'Lines from *The Critical Specimen*'.

(Tho' ne'er so weighty) reach a wondrous height;
So, forc'd from Engines, Lead it self can fly,
And pondrous Slugs move nimbly thro' the Sky.
Sure *Bavius* copy'd *Maevius* to the full,
20   And *Chaerilus* taught *Codrus* to be dull;
Therefore, dear Friend, at my Advice give o'er
This needless Labour, and contend no more,
To prove a dull *Succession* to be true,
Since 'tis enough we find it so in You.

17-18. Re-used, with some variations, in *The Dunciad* (1728), I.167–8; see note to line 4 above.

17. Engines: machines; cannon. Often with mock-heroic force in Pope and his contemporaries, e.g. 'Rape of the Locke', I.112 (scissors); Parnell, *Homer's Battle of the Frogs and Mice*, II.11 (1717), p. 11 (a mousetrap).

18. Slugs: A slug was 'a cylindrical or oval piece of metal shot from a gun' (*SJ*, citing this couplet).

19. Bavius . . . Maevius: conventional satiric pairing of low poets supposedly of Augustan Rome, mentioned as a pair of interchangeably bad equals by Virgil, *Eclogues*, III.90–1. See Dennis's reference in *Remarks on a Book Entituled, Prince Arthur, An Heroick Poem* (1696), p. 40: 'I am perfectly persuaded that *Bavius* and *Maevius* had a formidable Party in ancient *Rome,* a Party, who thought them by much superiour both to *Horace* and *Virgil*', an assertion which Pope twisted wittily in his note at *Dunciad Variorum*, III.16. Behn had addressed a satirical poem 'To Poet Bavius' (John Baber) in 1689; see Commentary to *Dunciad* (1728), I.240, in Rumbold (2007). Dorset's poem 'The Duel', *Poems on Affairs of State* (1698), pp. 22–4, portrays a literary fight between 'Will Maevius' and 'Bob Bavius'. See also *Essay on Criticism*, 34–5, and *Epistle to Dr Arbuthnot*, 250.

20. Chaerilus: or Choerilus; a talentless but politically flattering poet who occasionally writes a surprisingly good line, mentioned in Horace, *Epistola ad Pisones*, 357–8, and *Epistles*, II.i. 232–4.

21. Case (1928) cites Dorset, 'To Mr. Edward Howard', 30, *Annual Miscellany: For the Year 1694*, p. 300: 'Therefore, dear rogue, at my advice forbear'. Case aligns the whole of Pope's closing passage 21–4 with Dorset's final lines, 30–4, but the other resemblances are more general.

23-4. An early version of the idea that 'Still Dunce the second reigns like Dunce the first?', *Dunciad* (1728), I.6, itself modelled on Dryden's 'For Tom *the Second reigns like* Tom *the First*' in 'To my dear Friend Mr Congreve', 48, Congreve, *The Double-Dealer* (1694), sig. a3. The alignment of dull poetic successions with monarchic ones is modelled on Dryden's *Mac Flecknoe* (published 1682). The phrase 'dull Succession' equivocates on the dullness of the poem, *Successio*, and the leaden prospect of a Hanoverian future, established by the Act of Succession and celebrated by Settle's poem. Pope may have come across the wording in non-ironic political poetry, such as John Guy's 'Pindaric Ode', *On the Happy Accession of their Majesties King William and Queen Mary* (1699), p. 8: 'No dull Succession sanctifies his Right, | Nor Conquest gain'd in Fight, | But o're the Peoples minds, and there | Does *Right Divine* Triumphantly appear.' An earlier anonymous poem, 'To the King', published in *The Gentleman's Journal*, July 1692, p. 13, suggests that William's military success guarantees his crown in a way that a 'dull Succession' would not have done; this poem was later ascribed, not very convincingly, to Swift, in John Nichols, *A Select Collection of Poems* (1780), IV.303. Cf. also 'The First Book of Statius his Thebais', 181, for 'dull' in connection with merely legal rights of kingship.

13

VERSES DESIGN'D TO BE PREFIX'D TO MR. LINTOTT'S MISCELLANY
(1712)

Editors' Headnote

Composition and publication

'Verses design'd to be prefix'd to Mr. Lintott's Miscellany' was first published on 20 May 1712. The period of composition of the 'Verses' can be established with some specificity. On 12 November 1711, Pope wrote to Cromwell: 'Pray assure Mr Gay of my Service. I shou'd be glad to see the *Verses* to *Lintott* which you mention, for methinks something very odly agreable may be produc'd from that Subject' (*Corr.*, I.136). Six weeks later, on 21 December, Pope wrote again to Cromwell: 'His [Gay's] Verses to *Lintot* have put a Whim in[to] my head, which you are like to be troubled with in the opposite p[age]. Take it as you find it, the Production of half an hour, to[ther] Morning' (*Corr.*, I.138–9). *Miscellaneous Poems and Translations* (1712) contained poems addressed to Lintot by both Gay and Pope, each offering a teasing commendation of the project. Both are anonymous, and neither is 'prefix'd' to the volume: Gay's 'ON A Miscellany of Poems. To BERNARD LINTOTT' appears at pp. 168–74 and Pope's 'Verses *design'd to be prefix'd to Mr.* Lintott's *Miscellany*' follows it at pp. 174–5. McLaverty (2001: 16) suggests that Lintot probably considered the two poems 'too undignified' to act in a prefatory capacity and that he 'sandwiched' them in the middle. Together they form a something of a bridge between the more serious first half of the volume and its more satirical second part. The 'Verses' were the sixth of Pope's seven certain contributions (for further discussion of the extent of Pope's role in the publication of *Miscellaneous Poems* see Headnote to 'The First Book of Statius his Thebais'). It is the only one for which no payment from Lintot is recorded (McLaverty 2001: 17), so it remains possible that it was inserted without Lintot's knowledge of Pope's authorship. The version of the poem printed by Edmund Curll, and attributed to Pope – 'Written, (as he says) by Mr. *Pope*' – in his *Court Poems in Two Parts Compleat* (1719), mischievously alters

Pope's reference to Thomas Rawlinson at line 10 into a hit at *'JOHNNY GAY'* – a gesture typical of Curll's fencing with Pope.

Pope revised the 'Verses' – adding a further eight lines, and altering the order of several others – at some point between its appearance in the fourth edition of *Miscellaneous Poems and Translations* (1722) and Curll's publication of the expanded version in his *Miscellanea*, published on 14 July 1726. The poem was never explicitly acknowledged by Pope, although he included the revised version, without attribution, in *Miscellanies. The Last Volume* (1728).

Text

The text presented here is taken from the first edition of 1712. The various extant texts of the 'Verses' are referred to in the apparatus as follows:

1712: *Miscellaneous Poems and Translations* (Griffith 6)

1728: *Miscellanies. The Last Volume* (Griffith 196)

1742: *Miscellanies. The Fourth Volume* (Griffith 564)

Models and sources

Gay's poem, 'On a Miscellany of Poems. To Bernard Lintott' was clearly the immediate prompt and model for Pope's. It was a genial verse letter of advice about what Lintot should seek to insert in his volume, 'Wouldst thou for Miscellanies raise thy Fame; | And bravely rival *Jacob*'s mighty Name' (11–12), and it included a tribute to Pope (80–7) as a rising genius amongst necessary contributors such as Congreve, Prior, Granville, Buckingham, Addison and Garth, most of whom were already Pope's friends, though in the event only a few actually contributed. Pope, who would go on to develop a public attitude often contemptuous of book trade personnel, could also have known Dryden's 'Lines on Tonson', an *ad hominem* satirical triplet probably occasioned by a spat about money late in Dryden's life, as a version of them appeared in William Shippen, *Faction Display'd* (1704); see Hammond and Hopkins (V.26). Earlier models of the writer-bookseller satire include John Oldham, 'Upon a Bookseller, that expos'd him by Printing a Piece of his grosly mangled, and faulty', in *Some New Pieces* (1681); Pope owned a number of Oldham's works (Mack 1982: 431–2, items 122–5).

Context

For the volume, and Pope's general relationship with its publisher, Barnaby Bernard Lintott (or Lintot from around 1716; *ODNB*), see Headnote to 'The First Book of Statius his Thebais'. For Pope, Lintot represented an opportunity to avoid Tonson's dominance, and their relationship persisted for a decade or so, but the present poem foreshadows an antagonism already in the making. Pope would have known that Lintot was also the publisher of Dennis's *Appius and Virginia* (1709) as well as of his vicious assault on the *Essay on Criticism* (1711; see Headnote to that poem), which Lintot had shown him in advance (Pope to Cromwell, 25 June 1711; *Corr.*, I.125). Despite help in that respect, repeated when Lintot sent him a copy of Tickell's rival *Iliad* translation (*Corr.*, I.294, 10 June 1715), Pope was never much impressed by his publisher's abilities, and portrays him as a comically hapless misreader of his own publications and authors in another item from the Dennis fallout, the prose squib *The Narrative of Dr. Robert Norris* (1713; *PW*, I.153–68). Pope's entertaining showpiece letter to the Earl of Burlington, November 1716, recounting a ride towards Oxford on horseback in Lintot's company, describes the bookseller as 'the redoubtable rival of Mr. *Tonson*' in business terms, but goes on to portray him as personally crass and philistine: understanding nothing of Greek, Latin, French or Italian, he manages his translators by getting any 'civil gentleman' in the shop to spot-check their versions. He is the very opposite of the learned, humanist, imaginative and bold scholar-printers with whom he is contrasted in this poem (*Corr.*, I.371–5).

Pope initially profited from Lintot's relative generosity in respect of contracts, but his attempts to get his own way with his publisher and to control his own copyrights eventually foundered badly. After the success of the *Iliad* translation, Pope tried to switch back to Tonson, but Pope's collaborator Fenton reported to William Broome, 9 January 1724, 'Tonson does not care to contract for the copy, and application has been made to Lintot, upon which he exerts the true spirit of a scoundrel, believing that he has Pope entirely at his mercy' (*Corr.*, II.214). Pope and Lintot parted company in the 1720s, Pope thereafter using his own printer and publisher wherever possible and referring to Lintot as a fool or a cheat in several letters, a view echoed by Edward Young (and accidentally transmitted to Lintot himself; Spence, *OAC*, I.342). Pope pictured an obese Lintot farcically engaged in a foot race against Edmund Curll in *The Dunciad Variorum*, II.47–100, the prize being a hapless poet. The elements introduced into later versions of the present poem (see Variants and Commentary) confirm its satirical essence; while it is possible to read this poem as in some sense playfully or optimistically setting Lintot at the culmination of a tradition of good printing (see McLaverty 2001: 16–17 and 2007: 188), there is already a strong satiric element, and it is at least as likely that it constitutes Pope's first published instance of resistance, however light, to the dominance of the literary market by publishers and booksellers at the expense of writers. For Lintot to publish it, albeit not 'prefix'd' to the volume, is a kind of self-proving critique, in that it suggests he has either not read it, or not understood it to be an insult.

Pope read very widely, across a long historical range, beginning in his father's library, but what is known of his own books does not suggest a keen bibliophilic interest: he owned some items printed by the prestigious firms mentioned in the poem (as noted in the Commentary) but made no special effort to collect fine printing. His acquaintance with Robert Harley, first Earl of Oxford and initiator of one of the great historic libraries of Britain until its sale in 1742, was just beginning at this time; Pope later used and contributed to the library, especially during its development by the second Earl. But his artistic sense of design, manifest in his control of typeface selection and page arrangements, did not extend to a love of fine printing for its own sake. However, the 'Elzevier' style of printed edition (see 4) was not antiquarian but just becoming a contemporary fixture in British book design. Foxon (1991: 23–32) concludes: 'Pope adopted the Elzevier style the moment it began to establish itself in England, and remained faithful to it all his life'.

VERSES *design'd to be prefix'd to Mr. Lintott's Miscellany.*

SOME *Colinaeus* praise, some *Bleau*
Others account them but so, so;
Some *Stephens* to the rest prefer,
And some esteem *old Elzevir.*
5   Others with *Aldus* would besot us;
I, for my part, admire *Lintottus.*

Title. *1728–42:* VERSES | To be prefix'd before | *BERNARD LINTOT's* | NEW MISCELLANY.
2. them: *1728–42:* 'em
3. Stephens: *1728–42:* Plantin

Title. Lintott: for the bookseller and publisher Bernard Lintot see Headnote.
1. Colinaeus: Simon de Colines (d. 1546), Parisian printer from about 1520; he married the widow of Henri Estienne (see note to 3), his former employer. He was respected for the modernising elegance of the typography and page design of his publications. Under the influence of Aldus (see note to 5) he developed a range of small-format editions of classic texts.

Bleau: normally Blaeu, a Dutch family of eminent printers, engravers and mapmakers in the seventeenth century, including Willem Jansz Blaeu (1571–1638) and his son Joan (1598/9–1673). The firm had recently folded (1708).

3. Stephens: the Estienne (Latinised to 'Stephanus') family of French scholar-printers, active 1502–1664, publishers of some 2000 editions of Latin and Greek classics. Henri Estienne (d. 1520) was succeeded by his son Robert (1503–59), a major force in typographic design. He was royal printer in Greek, hence the '*Heathen Greek*' reference in the variant at 14^5, though he also printed the first textually critical edition of the Greek New Testament (1550). His son, Henri (1531–98) printed monumental editions of Plato (1578) and a Greek *Thesaurus* (1572). Pope owned an Estienne Cicero of 1555 (Mack 1982: 401, item 37), and he refers to a Stephens edition of Homer at his version of the *Iliad*, XV.23n. See also note to 9 below.

4. old Elzevir: The Elzevier family was active in printing in the Netherlands from 1575 to 1712, the year of the poem's publication. The founder, Louis Elzevier (1540–1617), had worked with Plantin (see 15) in Antwerp before founding his own business in Leiden. The sons (Matthijs and Bonaventura) grandsons (Isaac and Abraham) and great-grandsons (Jean, Daniel and Louis) of the dynasty established successful printing houses in the Hague, Utrecht, and Amsterdam, and developed a huge European trading network. Their small-format 'petits Elzeviers' were sought after by bibliophiles. Pope owned an Elzevier Horace of 1629 and an Elzevier Virgil of 1636 (Mack 1982: 419,

Those printed unknown Tongues, 'tis said,
Which some can't construe, most can't read;
What *Lintott* offers to your Hand,
10   Even *R*—— may understand:
They Print their Names in Letters small,

7–10. 1728–42: omitted
7^11. 1728–42: His Character's beyond Compare,
   Like his own Person, large and fair.

459, items 90 and 170); he took the Elzevier Virgil with him on his trip in Lintot's company in 1716 (Pope to Burlington, November 1716, *Corr.*, I.372). However, the typefaces and publication style associated with the firm were becoming dominant in English publishing around the time of the *Miscellaneous Poems*: Pope's nemesis, the bookseller Edmund Curll, was fond of advertising his more aspirational publications, such as his Latin edition of Petronius (1707 and 1711) as printed in 'a neat Elzevir letter'; but Tonson and indeed Lintot did likewise (see Foxon 1991: 23–32). Gay, 'On a Miscellany of Poems', 91–2, remarks: 'While neat old *Elzevir* is reckon'd better | Than *Pirate Hill's* brown Sheets, and scurvy Letter...' (Henry Hills was a publisher of low-quality piracies).

5. Aldus: Aldus Manutius (c. 1451–1515), founder of an enormously prestigious printing firm at Venice, then Rome, from 1495 to 1597, specialising in scholarly editions of classical works, such as the colossal Aristotle edition (1495–8). The firm produced some innovative and influential type designs, including newly cut italic and cursive fonts. The commercially successful series of pocket edition of Latin works with which the firm became strongly identified began with a text of Virgil in 1501. Cf. Gay, 'On a Miscellany of Poems', 93–4: 'While Print Admirers careful *Aldus* chuse | Before *John Morphew*, or the weekly News', and Pope's parody of bibliophile connoisseurship in the *Epistle to Burlington*, 136: 'These Aldus printed...'.

6. Lintottus: comic Latinisation of Lintot, as if himself a scholarly publisher; apparently invented by Pope.

7. Those: the printers just mentioned.
   unknown Tongues: the classical languages (Hebrew, Greek, Latin).

7^11 variant. **Character:** playing on 'character' as font and typeface as well as personal reputation.
   Person: cf. the comic race in *Dunciad Variorum*, II.47–70, where Lintot is described as 'lofty' and 'huge' and compared to a waddling dab-chick. Lintot's size is obliquely confirmed in *OAC*, I.342, where Pope's occasional friend the poet Edward Young describes him as a 'great sputtering fellow'.

8. construe: 'to interpret; to explain; to show the meaning' (*SJ*), especially of school exercises in Latin translation; the metre's requirement of an accent on the first syllable is apparently normal in the eighteenth century.

9–10. Miscellanies had, since the first days of the Dryden–Tonson series, offered English versions of classical verse, a feature which Gay notes among his recommendations to Lintot (29–32); hence the two first of Pope's contributions to the volume. In his letter to Burlington, already cited, Pope alleges that Lintot has to ask a 'civil gentleman' to check the work of his translators, having no Latin or Greek himself.

10. R——: Thomas Rawlinson (1681–1725), bibliophile, antiquary, and collector of literary papers. *TE* notes the satire on 'Tom Folio', a 'learned ideot' based on Rawlinson, in *Tatler*, no. 158, 13 April 1710; he has 'a

> But *LINTOTT* stands in Capital;
> Author and he with equal Grace
> Appear, and stare you in the Face.
15   Oft in an *Aldus* or a *Plantin*,
> A Page is blotted, or Leaf wanting;
> Of *Lintott*'s Books this can't be said,
> All fair, and not so much as read.

---

14. **Face.:** *1728–42:* Face:
14^15. *1728–42: Stephens* prints *Heathen Greek,* 'tis said,
        Which some can't construe, some can't read:
        But all that comes from *Lintot*'s Hand
        Ev'n *Ra - - - - - son* might understand.
18^19. *1728–42:* Their Copy cost 'em not a Penny
        To *Homer, Virgil,* or to any;
        They ne'er gave *Sixpence* for *two Lines,*
        To them, their Heirs, or their Assigns:
        But *Lintot* is at vast Expence,
        And pays prodigious dear for - - - Sense.

---

greater esteem for *Aldus* and *Elzevir,* than for *Virgil* and *Horace.* If you talk of *Herodotus,* he breaks out into a panegyric upon *Harry Stephens'* (cf. 3).

12-14. The allegation that Lintot thought himself as just as important as his authors is taken up further in the 'episode of the Booksellers', *Dunciad Variorum,* II.47-52.

12. **Capital:** The title of Gay's poem to Lintot in the volume (p. 168) presents *LINTOTT* in italic capitals, as in this line; Pope's own title (p. 174) has 'Lintott'. The imprint of the *Miscellaneous Poems* volume has 'Lintott' in normal-sized italic, and there is no author's name on the title page for it to rival. The name appears in small capitals with larger initial letters on e.g. Lintot's 1711 printing of George Farquhar's *Love and a Bottle,* and likewise on Dennis's *Reflections Satyrical and Critical* (1711); but Tonson and others also did this. Pope mocked Lintot's title page designs as 'Lintot's rubric post' in *The Dunciad Variorum,* I.38.

14^15 variant. **Stephens:** See 3.

15. **Plantin:** Christopher Plantin (c. 1520-1589), Antwerp-based printer, typefounder and publisher from 1555, and University Printer at Leiden 1583-1585; his output was mainly theological, including the eight-volume, five-language Antwerp Polyglot Bible (1569-72); but he also published editions of classical works.

16. Damage caused by actual reading of the books over time, whereas Lintot's productions remain unopened (17-18).

18^19 variant. **Copy:** Copyright, the 'copy money' or fee paid by a publisher to a writer for copyright, a practice much developed during Pope's career, partly by his efforts, after *An Act for the Encouragement of Learning* (8 Anne c. 9), the first 'copyright act', came into force in 1710.

    Sixpence ... Lines: there was no set rate for the production of verses, but the celebrated contract between Tonson and Dryden for the *Fables Ancient and Modern* (1700),

Their Books are useful but to few,
20 A Scholar, or a Wit or two:
Lintott's for general Use are fit,
For some Folks read, but all Folks Sh–t.

---

in which Tonson paid Dryden 250 guineas for 10,000 verses, gives a rate of roughly sixpence per line (Lonsdale, II.116–17). Dryden was Tonson's most eminent author; for Tonson's payment to Pope, more like twopence a line, see the Headnote to 'January and May'. Pope's 1716 letter to Burlington, already cited, records Lintot telling Pope the details of a contract for a translation, 'agreeing to pay the author so many shillings at his producing so many lines'. McLaverty (2001: 17) shows that Pope's contributions to the volume averaged between fourpence and sixpence per line, depending on genre, though this poem does not appear to have specifically been paid for.

Heirs ... Assigns: the legal formula in contracts indicating those who would benefit from payment in the event of the death of the original party.

Sense: intelligence, wit, good writing; cf. Headnote to *Essay on Criticism*.

19. Their Books: i.e. those of the high-status printers.

20. Wit: clever person, poet; cf. *Essay on Criticism*, 31, 36, etc.; not normally aligned with scholars, but see *ibid.*, 371. Pope suggests that some higher-level Wits will, unostentatiously, have such scholarship at their fingertips.

22. A common joke about the fate of unsold sheets of printed works: cf. Dryden, *Mac Flecknoe*, 100–1: 'From Dusty Shops neglected Authors come, | Martyrs of Pies, and Reliques of the Bum', a couplet highlighted by Pope in his note to *The Dunciad Variorum*, II.71. *TE* notes that Pope made a similar joke against Colley Cibber and in a letter to Hugh Bethel, 28 September 1734 (*Corr.*, III.435).

14

THE RAPE OF THE LOCKE
(1712)

Editors' Headnote

Composition and publication

'The Rape of the Locke' was first published on 20 May 1712. In 1735 Pope told Spence that the poem was 'written fast', and, in a note added in 1736 to the later, five-canto *Rape of the Lock*, he claimed to have written this first version in under two weeks (*OAC*, I.45n). If correct, this fortnight most probably fell between the beginning of August and end of September 1711 (*TE*, II.83–7), and the 'little poetical present' which Pope mentioned to John Caryll on 21 September (*Corr*, I.133; date from Mack 1982: 461–2) was very possibly a draft of the poem, as Pope clearly thought it too important an effort to be entrusted to Lewis the bookseller; but it is not certain which poem was indicated. However, a letter Pope sent to Cromwell on 15 July of the same year (*Corr.*, I.125) suggests something of the difficulty of attempting to fix precise dates for the composition of his poems. In this letter he offers a mock-heroic tribute to Cromwell's latest 'conquest':

> The Trophy you bore away from one of 'em, in your Snuffbox, will doubtless preserve her Memory, and be a Testimony of your admiration, for ever.
>
> As long as Moco's happy Tree shall grow,
> While Berries crackle, or while Mills shall go;
> While smoking streams from Silver Spouts shall glide,
> Or China's Earth receive the sable Tyde;
> While Coffee shall to British Nymphs be dear;
> While fragrant Steams the bended Head shall chear;
> Or grateful Bitters shall delight the Tast;
> So long her Honour, Name, and Praise shall last!

Versions of these lines recur in 'The Rape of the Locke' at I.90, 93–4, 114 and 134. It is typical of Pope's compositional habits that these 'private' verses, apparently more or less improvised in the letter, should later be recycled as part of a public performance, but they can hardly be said to constitute an early draft.

The poem seems to have circulated in manuscript among a select group of Pope's intimates; his 'Dedication' to the revised, greatly expanded and illustrated version published separately in March 1714 reminds Arabella Fermor (see below) that,

> as it was communicated with the Air of a Secret, it soon found its Way into the World. An imperfect Copy having been offer'd to a Bookseller, You had the Good-Nature for my sake to consent to the Publication of one more correct.

In June 1739 Pope told Spence that 'Copies of it got about, and 'twas like to be printed, on which I published the first draught of it' (*OAC*, I.44, no. 105). On 21 March 1712 Pope was paid £7 for the poem by Lintot (McLaverty 2001: 17), and on 20 May it appeared in *Miscellaneous Poems and Translations*, at pp. 353–76, the last item in the book (apart from advertising leaves, called for by the catchword on the last page of Pope's poem). Pope's work thus bookended the volume, since his version of Statius had opened it. 'The Rape of the Locke' has its own title page, running head and sequence of signatures, evidently with a view to offprint circulation; the pagination appears to be designed to match the poem's place in the book, but effects a break with the previous item (there is no segment of pp. 321–52). A possible reconstruction of the process of printing which would explain the gap is given in Foxon (1991: 34–8; and see McLaverty 2001: 18–22 and the Editors' Headnote to *Windsor-Forest*). Advance copies of the poem on its own had been sent in the week preceding publication to friends and interested parties, including the central protagonists (see below, Context). The collection as a whole seems not to have sold well, and in 1714 unsold sheets were reissued, supplemented by the addition of *Windsor Forest*, the *Ode for Musick* and the *Essay on Criticism* (Foxon 1991: 34–8). By this time Pope had turned the two-canto poem into a five-canto one, more than doubling its length and rendering it essentially a new work (separately edited in Volume 2).

Text

The text presented here is taken from the first edition of 1712, with the correction of the obvious misprint 'There' for 'Their' at II.160. There were no subsequent revisions to this version. The extant text of the 'The Rape of the Locke' is referred to in the apparatus as follows:

1712: *Miscellaneous Poems and Translations*, octavo (Griffith 6)

Models and sources

Pope's subtitle identifies 'The Rape of the Locke' as an 'Heroi-Comical Poem', apparently an English variant of his own devising on 'mock-epic' or 'mock-heroic', presumably by imitation of 'poëme héroi-comique', a label used in a 1701 edition of Boileau's *Oeuvres* (II.413) for *Le Lutrin*, one of Pope's models. Mock-heroic was the witty literary form in which the high language of ancient epic was used to describe the occupations of modern life, and ordinary pursuits were aligned with the major episodes of ancient epic (journeys, battles, heroic deaths) to comic effect. (For a succinct account of mock-heroic in the period, see Parker 2012.) It was Pope's first venture in the genre. The newness of Pope's phrase, perhaps designed to indicate that the poem was not limited by the conventions of mock-epic but open to more positively 'heroic' readings, was denounced (along with much else) by John Dennis in his *Remarks on Mr. Pope's Rape of the Lock* (1728), sig. B1ᵛ.

Pope had been reading and translating the *Iliad* and the *Odyssey* from his boyhood (see Headnote to 'The Episode of Sarpedon') and was shortly to begin translating the *Iliad* in earnest with Lintot as his publisher. Homer was the ultimate source for epic language and incident, though Pope's sense of heroic literature was also profoundly influenced by Virgil's *Aeneid* and Dryden's 1697 translation of it, as well as Milton's *Paradise Lost*, about which Addison had been writing (in 1711–12) a series of influential essays in *The Spectator*, itself a major source of mildly satirical observation on the fashionable world portrayed in Pope's poem. The language of his version of 'The First book of Statius his Thebais', another poem of high epic intent, is also occasionally glanced at. As McLaverty (2001: 18–22) points out, the poem draws on the epic conventions but also reflects the social gestures and amorous hyperbole exemplified within the volume of *Miscellaneous Poems and Translations* as a whole. It has particular ties to Pope's own 'Vertumnus and Pomona', which privileges male desire, and 'To a Young Lady, with the Works of Voiture', which focuses on social limitations to female actions. Pope drew conspicuously on Ovid (I.102–4) and other Latin poets, such as Martial, for the epigraph, and Catullus, for the transformation of the lock into a constellation (II.174). Pope also cites the romance *Orlando Furioso* (1532) of Ludovico Ariosto as a source at II.159. He was also aware of the Cervantesque tradition of burlesque romance, e.g. in Samuel Butler's *Hudibras* (originally published in three parts, 1663–78), and some of the high, as well as some of the comic, language is influenced by the theatrical posturing of the heroes of seventeenth-century drama. Much of Pope's phrasing, having pointedly alluded to English versions of epic, was reproduced without irony in his own Homeric translations.

Mock-heroic was itself an ancient genre, as in the ancient Greek poem *Batrachomyomachia*, translated by Pope's friend Thomas Parnell as *The Battle of the Frogs and the Mice* (1717). Pope knew later European examples, such as Alessandro Tassoni's *La Secchia Rapita* (the 'stolen bucket', 1622), partially translated by John Ozell as *The Trophy Bucket* (1710), recounting violent struggles between Guelphs and Ghibellines in a manner which according to Ozell made it the first 'Mock-Heroic Poem'. Closer to Pope's mode was *Le Lutrin* ('the reading-desk'; 1674–83) by Nicolas Boileau-Despréaux, which had also been translated by Ozell, in 1708 (see Pope's 'Epigram, Occasion'd by Ozell's Translation of Boileau's Lutrin', in Volume 2). Both poems feature a disputed physical object and discord between clearly identified groups; Ozell's Anglicised *Lutrin* fed in a good deal of detail from the War of Spanish Succession as part of the 'epic' aspect. Dryden's *Mac Flecknoe* (1682) was a major English example of the form, though more of an influence on *The Dunciad* in Pope's case. The most direct English model for Pope was *The Dispensary* (1699) by Samuel Garth, an early friend and mentor (see Headnote to *Pastorals*); its key battle sequence (Canto V, pp. 89–99 of the sixth edition of 1706) comically employs phials, bedpans and medical textbooks in place of heroic weapons. The poem satirised a quarrel between the physicians (Garth was a doctor) and the apothecaries of London: it was set in and around the City, often near the Thames. It reached three editions in 1699, a fourth in 1700, a fifth in 1703 and others in 1706 and 1709, not counting piracies. Pope owned and annotated the 1703 and 1706 editions (Mack 1982: 412–13, items 67 and 68). Swift's *Battle of the Books* (1704) was a prose version of mock-epic battle, in part based on the book-throwing episode in the *Lutrin*. Pope also knew mock-Miltonic exercises as *The Splendid Shilling* (1701), by John Philips, and mock-Georgic displays such as John Gay's *Wine* (1708). Swift's short poems 'A Description of the Morning' and 'A Description of a City Shower', published in *The Tatler* in 1709 and 1710, experimented with classical vocabulary for contemporary situations. Pope's mock-theoretical 'Receit to Make an Epick Poem', in which he satirises the conventional elements of the modern would-be epic, including descriptions of battles, appeared in *The Guardian*, no. 78, 10 June 1713.

Pope's title draws explicitly on non-ironic poems about female abduction or violation. The elopement of Helen with Paris, leading to the Trojan war, was sometimes referred to as 'rape' (from Latin *rapio*, to seize), as in Pope's 'To Belinda on the Rape of the Lock', 7–8: 'Thus *Helens* Rape and *Menelaus*' wrong | Became the Subject of great *Homer*'s song'. Classical literature was densely populated with similar stories: Persephone, Philomela, the Sabine women, Lucretia (the last of these also lightly referenced in Pope's 'To Belinda'). Tate's *Poems by Several Hands, and on Several Occasions* (1685) contained 'The Rape of Philomel', translated from Ovid; *Poetical Miscellanies: The Fifth Part* (1704) included 'The Rape of the Sabines, from Ovid', by Dryden (pp. 13–15) and Addison's version of 'Europa's Rape', also from Ovid (pp. 87–91; cf 'The First Book of Statius his Thebais', 7). Shakespeare's *The Rape of Lucrece* (1594) appears to have been the first poem separately published under such a title; it was turned into a play by Thomas Heywood (1608). Both were much reprinted, and the Shakespeare poem had appeared in Lintot's 1709 collection of his poems. *The First Rape of Faire Hellen* had been 'done into poeme' in 1595; Leonard Digges had produced a *Rape of Proserpine* from Claudian in 1617. *The Rape of Europa by Jupiter* was performed as a masque in 1694. In the same year, Thomas Yalden published 'The Rape of Theutilla, Imitated from the Latin of Famian. Strada.' in *The Annual Miscellany: For the Year 1694*, in which a heroic and exonerated young woman stabs her abductor to death with a dagger which, by suggesting that revenge rather suicide is a justifiable option, perhaps prefigures the 'deadly Bodkin' Belinda wields threateningly at II.141. These texts were mostly in heroic or tragic vein, with the female figures reduced to passive victimhood or pathetic suicide (Yalden's heroine is a rare deviation from this norm). Pope's title at once diminishes the scale of the 'rape' but reminds readers that in Belinda's culture such gestures have a strong symbolic force. (For the widespread classical use of hair-cutting as a symbol of marital status, for women particularly, and for the argument that Pope uses this allusive material to suggest covertly that Belinda is, despite her protests, ripe for marriage, see Wasserman 1966, and for further discussion of the allusive weight of the epigraph from Martial in this context, Rogers 2018.) Pope's mock-heroic was unusual in focusing attention away from male conflicts, however belittled, and towards intimate female experience, however inflated; female characters are not absent in the main exemplars of mock-heroic, but the chief conflicts are all between rival factions of men, and the reconciliatory aspect of Pope's poem is unusual.

Some fashionable pastimes such as the drinking of tea had already produced quasi-panegyric verse, perhaps feeding Pope's use of polite mockery; John Ovington quoted Waller's verse praise of 'the best of Queens, and best of Herbs' ('Of Tea commended by Her Majesty') in his *Essay upon the Nature and Qualities of Tea* (1699), p. 30, and Nahum Tate's *Panacea* (1700), a two-canto 'Poem upon Tea', was followed in 1701 by Peter Anthony Motteux's poem on the same subject, republished by Tonson in 1712 as both *A Poem Upon Tea* and *A Poem in Praise of Tea* (by which time Motteux had become an actual tea-merchant, celebrated in *Spectator*, no. 552, 3 December 1712). The social world of Pope's poem, particularly its obsession with objects and accoutrements, is lightly satirised in periodical papers such as *The Tatler* and *The Spectator*, on which Pope clearly drew for many details.

Context

For Pope's relationship with Lintot and the volume, see Headnote to 'The First Book of Statius his Thebais'.

The immediate occasion for the poem was a request from Pope's close friend John Caryll senior (1667–1736), with whom Pope had been corresponding since 1710 (Erskine-Hill 1975: 42–102) to patch up a quarrel between the Fermor and Petre families. Caryll was something of a figurehead amongst the Catholic community of Pope's early manhood; in their beleaguered internal exile, Catholic families tended to associate and intermarry. Caryll had been guardian to Robert, seventh Baron Petre (1690–1713), until he came of age in 1710; they were also related by marriage, since Caryll's grandfather had married Petre's great-aunt Catherine. Her brother, William Petre, had married in 1628 Lucy Fermor, sister of Arabella Fermor's great-grandfather (for further genealogical information see Rogers 2007b). In the summer of 1711 Caryll was staying at Lord Petre's family seat at Ingatestone in Essex, and it is probable that during that visit he learned of an incident in which Petre had cut off a lock of hair from a well-known society beauty, Arabella Fermor (c. 1689–1738), leading to a serious estrangement between the two families. (The actual location of the incident has never been established; it is thought more likely to have taken place at Ingatestone or at one of the London houses of either family, than as the poem has it, at Hampton Court.) Pope referred to Lord Petre in a letter to Caryll of 25 June 1711 as 'one of those young Lords that have wit in our days' (*Corr.*, I.123), apparently basing his view on the judgment of others 'who have ye happiness to know him'. He seems to have known Arabella Fermor scarcely at all; Mack (1985: 248 and 257) plausibly contends that the sexual attractiveness of the poem's heroine draws rather on Pope's fascination with Teresa Blount, possible addressee of 'To a Young Lady, with the Works of Voiture': contemporary portraits of her display dark curling shoulder-length hair. Pope's relationships with these 'reigning beauties' (the Blount sisters and their 'Cosen Belle' as she is known in their letters) and the poem's significance within a contemporary circuit of sexual exchange, are described in searching detail in Rumbold (1989: 48–82). Such an emblematic heroine requires no single biographical model, of course.

Pope's family was a relative newcomer to the faith amid the other, long-established Catholic dynasties, and he had no blood ties to any of them. According to Pope's later account, 'The stealing of Miss Belle Fermor's hair was taken too seriously, and caused an estrangement between the two families, though they had lived long in great friendship before'. Caryll asked him 'to write a poem to make a jest of it, and laugh them together again' (*OAC*, I.43–4, no. 103, June 1739). Caryll is acknowledged, not quite openly, as the sponsor of the poem at I.3–6; his uncle, John, Lord Caryll (c. 1626–1711), a Jacobite courtier and poet, who died in September of the year in which the poem was composed (for Pope's 'Epitaph' on him see *Corr.*, I.133), is covertly remembered in the opening lines. Much of Pope's correspondence with Caryll in these years concerns literary projects and their reception (see in particular Headnote to *Essay on Criticism* for Caryll's management of the Catholic response to that poem in 1711–12). While Pope later remembered that the poem 'was well received and had its effect in the two families' (*OAC*, I.44, no. 104, June 1739), he acknowledged that the immediate outcomes were more ambiguous.

On 16 May 1712, another Catholic friend, and Caryll's maternal uncle, Edward Bedingfield, wrote to Pope, apparently in reply to a lost letter of 11 May, indicating that he had 'enclosed the Copys for Lord Petre and that for Mrs. Belle Fermor – she is out of Towne and therefore all I can do is to leave her pacquet at her lodgeing' (*Corr.*, I.141–2). These were offprint segments from the volume, circulated pre-publication to its protagonists. Caryll himself was asking about publication on 23 May 1712, shortly after it had in fact been published (*Corr*, I.142): 'where hangs the *Lock* now?' He told Pope he had written to Lord Petre 'upon the subject of the Lock', probably meaning the poem rather than the incident, but had not received an answer. His letter also notes with some alarm that 'rather than draw any just reflection upon your self, of the least shadow of ill-nature, you would freely have suprest one of the best of Poems', indicating that there had been some anxiety about whether or not the poem could or should be published at all. Pope responded on 28 May (*Corr.*, I.143–5), to say that the bookseller Lewis (the Catholic publisher of the *Essay on Criticism*) had been entrusted with 'the *Rape of the Lock*, [and] what other things of mine are in Lintot's collection; the whole book I will put into your hands when I have the satisfaction to meet you'. On 25 May Pope had sent one of the first copies of the volume to Martha Blount and her sister Theresa, accompanied by a jauntily flirtatious letter (*Corr*, I.143):

> At last I do myself the honour to send you the Rape of the Locke; which has been so long coming out, that the Ladies Charms might have been half decay'd, while the Poet was celebrating them, and the Printer publishing them.

Pope highlighted the poem as the main reason for sending the volume, but since the Blount family was within the circle of Catholic gentry involved in attempts at reconciliation among the original participants, he acknowledged that 'you and your fair Sister must needs have been surfeited already with this Triffle' and directed her attention to 'the rest of this Booke, wherein (they tell me) are some things that may be dangerous to be lookd upon'. Pope's contribution to the volume thus constituted an element in the socially coded game of flirtation and suggestion that the poem itself dramatises.

While the poem's roots in generic mock-epic, its witness to Pope's social and sexual interests and relations and its witty caricature of the habits of a contemporary beau monde have dominated discussion of the poem (itself rapidly occluded by the expanded versions from 1714 onwards), this first version has been aligned with something like the same political narrative that underlies 'The First Book of Statius his Thebais', i.e. the internecine political struggles during the Tory ministry of 1710–14, particularly in relation to the War of Spanish Succession. Daly (2013) suggests that the poem, while in no sense a straightforward political allegory of the type that Pope himself parodied in *A Key to the Lock* (1715), does draw on the bitter and widely satirised political struggle between Queen Anne (who appears in her own person briefly at I.71–2, amidst her 'Statesmen', but who would in this reading be represented by Belinda as a justifiably enraged avenger of affronts to her power) and the Duke of Marlborough and his wife Sarah, each of whom had been dismissed from the Queen's service on grounds of arrogance, insults of various kinds and, in the Duchess's case, theft of items from the royal household. The Baron's military triumph (I.125–6) is opposed by Belinda's 'deadly Bodkin', under the influence of Thalestris, who might be taken to represent the influential Abigail Masham (1670–1734), successor to the Duchess of Marlborough as Keeper of the Privy Purse and the dominant female figure in the Queen's household. There is no evidence, however, of anyone's having read the poem this way in Pope's own day.

In public, the poem was with Pope's other contributions warmly received by Addison in *Spectator*, no. 523, 30 October 1712, though Pope might have found the praise poisoned by its proximity to warm notice of work by his rivals, Ambrose Philips and Thomas Tickell. Addison acknowledged the 'graceful' benefits of 'Heathen Mythology' in 'Mock-Heroic' poetry – and in that genre only – a comment no doubt suggested by 'The Rape of the Locke'. On 8 November 1712 (*Corr.*, I.151), however, Pope wrote to John Caryll junior. 'Sir Plume blusters, I hear', indicating that Sir George Browne (d. 1719), a first cousin of Arabella Fermor's mother with family connections to the Carylls and the Blounts (see Rogers 2007b), had been offended by what was evidently a maliciously accurate portrait of him in the character of Sir Plume at II.39–48. (Martha Blount, confirming to Spence several identities in the story that Pope appears not to have specified himself, remarked that 'what is said of Sir George Browne ... was the very picture of the man'; *OAC*, I.45, no. 106, 27 May 1749.) Browne was angry enough to threaten violence (Pope to John Caryll, junior, 5 December 1712, *Corr.* I.163–4). In *A Key to the Lock* (1715), pp. 9–10, *PW*, I.184, Pope represented two separate Catholic gentlemen claiming to be the original of Sir Plume, perhaps an attempt to obscure the identification. In June 1739 Pope told Spence: 'Nobody but Sir George Browne was angry, and he was so a good deal and for a long time. He could not bear that Sir Plume should talk *nothing* but nonsense' (*OAC*, I.44, no. 104).

Ostensibly, the poem sought to transform the suggestion (unspoken, but implicit) that Arabella Fermor's private sexual reputation might be damaged by the public assault on her hair into a triumphant glorification of her poetic 'fame' as Belinda – while the Baron, having proclaimed at I.134 that his 'Honour, Name, and Praise shall live!', is never given a name at all. Lord Petre's reactions are not recorded, but Pope noted that 'the celebrated lady herself is offended, and, which is stranger, not at herself, but me' (Pope to Caryll, 8 November 1712, *Corr.*, I.151). After her return in 1704 from the Paris convent at which she was educated, she had been widely celebrated for her beauty in verse: the anonymous *St. James's Park: A Satyr* (1708), p. 13, devotes six lines to 'Farmer' (indicating the way the surname was pronounced); she rates eight lines of similar rapture in *The Mall: or, the Reigning Beauties* (1709), p. 11, and a further six in 'The Celebrated Beauties', published in the 1709 *Poetical Miscellanies* in which Pope's own first works appeared (p. 525). But 'The Rape of the Locke' was a different kind of poem, less a testimony to her status in what could be seen as catalogues of potential wives than a perhaps insufficiently tactful reminder of the original breach of decorum, with considerably enhanced sexual symbolism. Perhaps some of the covertly scandalous suggestions about the heroine's motivations and desires – to be greatly increased in the revised version – or her hyperbolic reaction to a prank, had become clear enough to offend Arabella, or perhaps in the particularly closely knit world of the Catholic gentry, she felt her prospects dented by public exhibition of a humiliation known originally only to those within a fold to which Pope had no access by rank. Petre himself had married Catherine Walmsley, a younger (and much richer) woman in March 1712, just before publication of the volume, and the timing may not have seemed auspicious. (Walmsley was just over 15, and from a known recusant family; as a young widow, from 1713, she was apparently considered a possible bride for the Jacobite 'Old Pretender'; Rogers 2007b: 14.) The revision and expansion of the poem, with its flattering dedication, may have been undertaken in part to try to smooth over some of these difficulties (Lord Petre died of smallpox on 22 March 1713, so was no longer in question). Pope wrote to Caryll, 15 December 1713 (*Corr.*, I.203):

> I have been employed, since my being here in the country, in finishing the additions to the *Rape of the Lock* . . . I have some thoughts of dedicating that poem to Mrs Fermor by name, as a piece of justice in return to the wrong interpretations she has suffered under on the score of that piece.

Further negotiations were complete by 9 January 1714, when Pope reported that she had approved of the chosen text of the 'Dedication' (*Corr.*, I.207). Advance copies of the revised poem went out in late February and it was published as a separate octavo item on 4 March. Later that year Arabella Fermor married Francis Perkins, another Catholic from a prominent family of recusants. Pope appears not to have approved (see his letter to Martha Blount, *post* 24 November 1714; *Corr.*, I.268–9); his apparently gracious letter to Mrs Perkins on the occasion, *Corr.*, I.271–2, may be a later fabrication. She had six children, and died in 1738; there is some evidence, derived from family tradition, that she was in later life rather vain of being the heroine of the poem; equally, that the family regarded it as a sort of insult. See further Headnote to *The Rape of the Lock* in Volume 2.

TE reprints the present poem, with light annotation, at II.127–37, immediately before the 1717 version with much fuller annotation. In our Commentary '*TE*' indicates reference to relevant material in both versions.

THE *RAPE* of the *LOCKE*.
AN
HEROI-COMICAL
POEM.

Nolueram, Belinda, *tuos violare capillos,*
Sed juvat hoc precibus me tribuisse tuis.
MART. Lib. 12. Ep. 86.

Title. For the significance of 'Rape' see Headnote: Sources.

Epigraph. 'I did not wish, Belinda, to violate your hairs, but it is pleasing to have granted this thing to your prayers'.

MART. Marcus Valerius Martialis (c. 41–c. 104 AD), Roman poet, known for twelve books of *Epigrams*, in this case XII.84 (86 in Pope's time) with 'Belinda' substituted for 'Polytime' (Polytimus, a man). The epigraph was dropped from the 1714 version in favour of some lines from Ovid, but restored in the *Works* text of 1717. 'Hoc', 'this thing', could in this context refer either to the poem (compensating Belinda for the loss of her hair), or to the action of cutting the hair (Belinda's covert wish to have her hair symbolically violated). Wasserman (1966), noting that the rest of the epigram explains that Polytimus requested the cutting of the hair to reveal his beauty for his wedding day, suggests that Pope implies the 'violation' was necessary or invited; Rogers (2018) suggests Pope was alluding also to Martial's mention of the artificial ivory shoulder of Pelops, likewise displayed by cutting hair (cf. Belinda's 'Iv'ry Neck' beneath the locks at I.38). Warburton in the 1751 *Works* attributes to Pope a note in which the epigraph is used as evidence that Arabella Fermor had requested publication of the poem, but this does not conform to the statement in I.3 and is not regarded as authoritative.

THE
Rape *of the* Locke.

CANTO I.

WHAT dire Offence from Am'rous Causes springs,
What mighty Quarrels rise from Trivial Things,
I sing —This Verse to C—l, Muse! is due;

CANTO. 'Book, or section of a poem' (*SJ*), widely used by Renaissance poets with whom Pope was familiar, such as Ariosto, in *Orlando Furioso* (1532) (cf. Pope's note to II.159) and Spenser, in *The Faerie Queene* (1590–6). Tassoni's *La Secchia Rapita*, Boileau's *Le Lutrin* and Garth's *Dispensary* (see Headnote: Models and sources) were also divided into Cantos; Pope does not use the term for his own work outside the *Rape of the Lock* texts.

1. The poet sings (line 3) the 'dire Offence' which springs from amorous causes; when the hostile critic John Dennis failed to understand this, in *Remarks on Mr. Pope's Rape of the Lock* (1728), p. 36 of second sequence, Pope noted on his copy of the attack that the structure of his opening was based on that of the opening of Virgil's *Georgics* (Mack 1982: 410). It also imitates the opening formula of the *Aeneid*, 'arma virumque cano', 'arms and the man I sing', though less obvious in uninflected English syntax. Cf. the delayed main verb (also 'sing') in the opening of Milton's *Paradise Lost*, I.1–6. Erskine-Hill (1975: 68) suggests plausibly that Pope alludes to a line in a translation of Virgil's first Eclogue, 'What dire effects from Civil Discord flow!', by the Jacobite poet and diplomat John Lord Caryll (d. 1711), uncle of Pope's friend mentioned in the note to I.3; the poem appeared in *Miscellany Poems* (1684), p. 8 of second sequence. The line was retained in Dryden's full translation (*Works of Virgil*, p. 4), and it would be repeated five lines from the end of Addison's *Cato* (1713). Another Royalist model is Denham, *Cooper's Hill*, 151, *Poems and Translations* (1668), p. 8: 'Tell me (my Muse) what monstrous dire offence...' For the Latinate 'dire' see 'The First Book of Statius his Thebais', 6. Pope's handling of these sources, however, is mock-heroic rather than simply 'royalist'.

2. Trivial Things: Roscommon used the phrase in *Horace's Art of Poetry*, 159 (1680), p. 10: 'But then you must not Copy trivial things' and Oldham was evidently fond of it ('The Thirteenth Satyr of Juvenal', 160 and 250; 'Horace his Art of Poetry', 771). More recently Robert Gould had used the exact rhyme pair in 'Myrtillo and Aminta', 145, *Works* (1709), p. 410: '*Amynta* is above such Trivial Things, | And moves the Lover by Sublimer Springs'.

3. C—l: John Caryll, senior (c. 1666–1736), Catholic landowner and a close friend of Pope's since about 1704; see Headnote. The name was not fully printed out until 1751. In a letter of 25 February 1714, Pope told Caryll that he thought of putting the name in 'at length' in the enlarged edition, but 'I remember'd your desire you formerly expressed to the contrary' (*Corr.*, I.210). The verse is 'due' to him because he requested the poem be written.

Muse: one of the nine goddesses of the arts in Greek mythology, conventionally invoked at the beginning of an epic poem.

This, ev'n *Belinda* may vouchsafe to view:
5   Slight is the Subject, but not so the Praise,
If She inspire, and He approve my Lays.

Say what strange Motive, Goddess! cou'd compel
A well-bred *Lord* t' assault a gentle *Belle?*
Oh say what stranger Cause, yet unexplor'd,
10 Cou'd make a gentle *Belle* reject a *Lord?*
And dwells such Rage in *softest Bosoms* then?
And lodge such daring Souls in *Little Men?*

---

4. Belinda: poetic codename for Arabella Fermor, the young woman humiliated by the cutting of the lock (see Headnote: Context); she was familiarly known as 'Belle' (see Commentary to I.8). The name was in wide poetic use, not least in the volume in which Pope's poem appeared, as McLaverty (2001: 19) observes; e.g. Broome's 'On a Flower which Belinda gave me from her Bosom', p. 116, and the pastoral 'sent to Belinda', p. 225.

vouchsafe: condescend, deign.

5. Slight . . . Subject: borrowing mock-dignity from Dryden's version of the opening of book IV of Virgil's *Georgics, Works of Virgil*, p. 122: 'Slight is the Subject, but the Praise not small, | If Heav'n assist, and *Phoebus* hear my Call'; *TE* also cites the model of Sedley's version: 'The Subjects humble, but not so the Praise, | If any Muse assist the Poets Lays', *Miscellaneous Works* (1702), p. 174. Addison's version, in *Annual Miscellany: For the Year 1694*, p. 59, has the same rhyme: 'A trifling Theam provokes my Humble Lays, | Trifling the Theam, not so the Poet's Praise'.

6. Lays: songs.

7. Say: in line with epic invocations such as the first line of Homer's Odyssey, ἄνδρα μοι ἔννεπε, μοῦσα ('tell me, Muse, of the man'), or the 'Say first' of Milton, *Paradise Lost*, I.27–8, and similarly at I.376 and VII.40 (see further Mason 1987).

Goddess: the 'Muse' of I.3.

8. Belle: fashionable young lady; a word recently imported from France, and close to the short form of Arabella Fermor's name. *TE* (II.143) states that Pope does not use the word apart from in this poem; in fact he uses it once, in *Sober Advice from Horace* (1734), 108–9: 'And *secondly*, how innocent a *Belle* | Is she who shows what Ware she has to sell'.

9. unexplor'd: *SJ* cites this line to illustrate the definition 'Not searched out'; he also gives 'Not tried; not known'. Cf. 'Messiah', 49.

10. There is nothing in the story to indicate that Belinda does reject a formal advance from the Baron at any point (and nothing is certainly known of any such approach in the family squabble underlying the poem), apart from in the general rejection at I.28.

11–12. Pope eventually (1736) revised this couplet to avoid ending line 11 with 'then', after Concanen cited it as an instance of Pope's own definition of bathos, in *Supplement to the Profund* (1728), pp. 19–20.

11. Rage: passion, as well as anger; cf. 'Prologue to Cato', 44.

Bosoms: 'the breast; the heart' (*SJ*), i.e. the emotional centre of the individual; 'softest' indicates female here, as at II.62; cf. I.20.

12. Little Men: Lord Petre (see Headnote) was short, as was Pope, whose two facetious essays on 'The Club of Little Men' appeared in *The Guardian*, nos. 91 and 92, 25 and 26 June 1713 (for the attribution to Pope, see *PW*, I.lvii). The phrase also signals mockheroic diminution. For the line as a whole *TE* suggests a source in Virgil, *Georgics*, IV.83 (speaking of bees): 'ingentis animos angusto in pectore', translated by Addison as 'Their little Bodies lodge a mighty Soul', *Annual Miscellany* (1694), p. 65, and notes that Pope returned to the idea in his *Iliad*,

   Sol thro' white Curtains did his Beams display,
   And op'd those Eyes which brighter shine than they;
15 *Shock* just had giv'n himself the rowzing Shake,
   And Nymphs prepar'd their *Chocolate* to take;
   Thrice the wrought Slipper knock'd against the Ground,
   And striking Watches the tenth Hour resound.
   Belinda rose, and 'midst attending Dames
20 Launch'd on the Bosom of the silver *Thames*:

V.999: 'Whose little Body lodg'd a mighty Mind'. Milton imitated the idea in *Paradise Lost*, VII.486 (1674), p. 188, speaking of ants, which 'in small room large heart enclos'd'.

13. Sol: Latin for 'sun'; see Commentary to *Essay on Criticism*, 469–70.

 white Curtains: suspended round the bed.

14. op'd: opened.

 brighter: the eyes of young women shine more brightly than the sun; a mockingly conventional piece of praise, as in I.29.

15. Shock: conventional name for a shaggy-coated lapdog. There is a suggestively flirtatious discussion of 'Shock-Dogs' in II.i of Wycherley's *The Gentleman Dancing-Master* (1673), pp. 25–6. *OED*, dating the term from 1638, cites *Tatler*, no. 70, 20 September 1709: 'a little French Shock that belongs to the Family'. Arabella Fermor's lapdog was called Fidelle ('faithful'); see Rumbold (1989: 73).

16. Nymphs: in Greek mythology, female nature spirits associated with woodland and rivers, as in 'Spring', 96, etc.; here, and throughout the poem, used for young women of fashion.

 Chocolate: in drinkable form, a fashionable and very expensive breakfast dish from the Restoration onwards, and like coffee and tea (also newly imported) the subject of much controversy and satire. Pope does not mention it in the literary works other than the *Rape of the Lock* texts, but he writes to Martha Blount, 6 October 1714 (*Corr.*, I.260), from Bath: 'My whole Day is shar'd by the Pump-Assemblies, the Walkes, the *Chocolate* houses, Raffling Shops, Plays, Medleys, &c'.

17. wrought Slipper: highly ornamented house shoe, used to hit the floor in order to summon a servant.

18. striking Watches: a relatively recent (and very expensive) invention: the watchmaker Daniel Quare (1628–1724) helped the Clockmakers' Company win a patent dispute in 1687 over the relevant technology; see also the details in William Derham, *The Artificial Clock-maker* (1696). Pope apparently referred to a 'Tompion' watch in his juvenile epic *Alcander* in lines salvaged for the mock-treatise 'Peri Bathous', in *Miscellanies. The Last Volume* (1728), p. 45. Cf. *Essay on Criticism*, 9.

 tenth Hour: Late rising was a conventional object of satire; *TE* cites the third satire of Persius and Horace, *Epistles*, I.ii.30, particularly in relation to the 1714 version which puts the time back to midday (I.16).

19. Dames: Pope uses the term commonly in the Chaucer imitations (e.g. 'January and May', 258). Belinda is accompanied by women of her own social class, who nonetheless 'attend' or wait on her.

20. Bosom: 'the embrace of the arms holding any thing to the breast', 'any receptacle close or secret' (*SJ*); cf. I.11.

 silver: sparkling; cf. *Windsor-Forest*, 202, and, ironically, *The Dunciad* (1728), II.252, where Pope will besmirch his own glittering images of London, which, as *TE* observes, obscured the actual filth of the river's edge. The river voyage itself is common to both epic (Virgil, *Aeneid*, VII) and mock-epic (Dryden, *Mac Flecknoe*, 38–50).

A Train of well-drest Youths around her shone,
And ev'ry Eye was fixed on her alone;
On her white Breast a sparkling *Cross* she wore,
Which *Jews* might kiss, and Infidels adore.
25 Her lively Looks a sprightly Mind disclose,
Quick as her Eyes, and as unfixt as those:
Favours to none, to all she Smiles extends;
Oft she rejects, but never once offends.
Bright as the Sun her Eyes the Gazers strike,
30 And, like the Sun, they shine on all alike.
Yet graceful Ease, and Sweetness void of Pride,
Might hide her Faults, if *Belles* had Faults to hide:

---

21. Train: group of followers or attendants.

23. white Breast: pale (upper) chest; Belinda's dress is (as was fashionable) low-cut. Arabella Fermor's 'Snowey Breasts' (and neck) are the subject of considerable attention in *The Mall: or, the Reigning Beauties* (1709), p. 11; Broome's poem to a different Belinda in the same volume (see Commentary to I.4) studies her 'Bosom' closely.

sparkling: bejewelled.

24. Jews would conscientiously refuse to kiss the sign of the Christian faith, and 'infidels' (atheists or heathens) would not 'adore' it; they might do so here because the cross is on Belinda's 'Breast'. A portrait of Arabella Fermor wearing a cross in this position was painted c. 1714 (reproduced in Mack 1985: 249). TE notes that Tassoni's *La Secchia Rapita*, III.xlv, contains an ensign illustrating a Jew forced to kiss the cross.

25. sprightly: 'gay; brisk; lively; vigorous; airy; vivacious' (*SJ*).

26. Quick: lively, active.

unfixt: SJ cites this line to underscore the definition 'wandering; erratick; inconstant; vagrant'. Pope may have had slightly less pejorative connotations in mind, especially since the unfixedness of Belinda's eye is in contrast to 22; he does not use this word elsewhere.

27-8. Cf. the representation of Arabella Fermor in the anonymous 'The Celebrated Beauties', from *Poetical Miscellanies: The Sixth Part* (1709), p. 525: 'Obliging with Reserve, and Humbly Great, | Tho' Gay, yet Modest, tho' Sublime, yet Sweet; | Fair without Art, and graceful without Pride'.

27. Favours: i.e. a special favour, kindness, or appointment, or 'something given by a lady to be worn' (*SJ*), of the kind a lady in romance might give a knight (cf. I.55 below); in other contexts 'favours' might more strongly suggest sexual willingness.

28. rejects: i.e. she turns down offers and invitations from the 'Youths' of I.21.

30. Perhaps, following the faintly blasphemous hints of I.24, a deliberate echo of Matthew 5:45: 'your father ... in heauen ... maketh his sunne to rise on the euill and on the good'. Wakefield suggests recollection of the description of Henry in Shakespeare, *Henry V*, Chorus to Act IV.43-4: 'like the sun, | His liberal eye doth give to every one ...', as well as Quintilian, *Institutio Oratoria*, I.ii.14: 'ut sol, universis idem lucis caloriisque largitur' ('as the sun, it imparts to everyone light and heat'). See also Shakespeare, *The Winter's Tale*, IV.iv.445-7: 'The selfsame sun that shines upon his court | Hides not his visage from our cottage, but | Looks on alike'.

31. graceful Ease: an ideal of politeness already proposed in the *Essay on Criticism* (e.g. 658-61), albeit for gentlemen rather than young ladies; cf. Dryden, 'Cymon and Iphigenia', 223, *Fables Ancient and Modern* (1700), p. 549: 'He Rode, he Fenc'd, he mov'd with graceful Ease'.

If to her share some Female Errors fall,
Look on her Face, and you'll forgive 'em all.

35   This Nymph, to the Destruction of Mankind,
Nourish'd two Locks, which graceful hung behind
In equal Curls, and well conspir'd to deck
With shining Ringlets her smooth Iv'ry Neck.
Love in these Labyrinths his Slaves detains,
40   And mighty Hearts are held in slender Chains.
With hairy Sprindges we the Birds betray,

---

33. **Female Errors:** foibles and vanities routinely associated with the 'fair sex' by periodicals such as *The Spectator*.

34. **forgive:** this became 'forget' in the 1714 *Rape of the Lock*, II.18.

35. **Destruction:** a mock-epic inflation of the damage Belinda's beauty does to the men around her; 'destruction of mankind' was a very common phrase in seventeenth-century religious discourse, and cf. Addison's comment on the epic quality of *Paradise Lost*, in *The Spectator*, no. 267, 5 January 1712: '*Milton*'s Subject was still greater... it does not determine the Fate of single Persons or Nations, but of a whole Species. The united Powers of Hell are joyned together for the Destruction of Mankind'. Cf. also Caryll's *The English Princess*, I.iv.(1667), p. 8: 'When Nature form'd this Monster, she design'd | No less, then the destruction of Mankind'. TE cites Dryden, *The Conquest of Granada by the Spaniards*, Part One, Act III (1672), p. 28: 'You bane, and soft destruction of mankind'.

37. **conspir'd:** agreed, worked together; see Commentary to *Essay on Criticism*, 342; here punning on the 'spiral' effect of the wound lock of hair.

38. **shining Ringlets:** Pope recalled this phrase in his version of *Iliad*, XIV.205 (Hera dressing up to impress Zeus).

39–44. As *TE* shows, Pope combines a long classical tradition of the imprisoning power of female hair with a specifically English association between hair and fishing nets. For the former, see e.g. Dryden, 'The Fifth Satire of Persius', 246–7, *Satires of Juvenal* (1693), p. 70: 'She knows her Man, and when you Rant and Swear | Can draw you to her, with a single Hair'; and Sandys, *Paraphrase vpon the Song of Solomon*, Canto IV (1641), p. 15: 'One Haire of thine in Fetters tyes'. For the latter, see e.g. Butler, *Hudibras*, II.iii.21–2 (1684), p. 326: 'And though it be a two-foot *Trout*, | 'Tis with a single hair pull'd out'. Milton, in wondering 'Were it not better [for a poet]... To sport... with the tangles of *Neaera*'s hair', 'Lycidas', 67–9, *Poems of Mr. John Milton* (1645), p. 60, shows that the image was already a poetic cliché to be parodied.

39. **Love... Labyrinths:** 'Love' invokes the classical god Eros, or Cupid; the labyrinth, a legendary underground maze on the island of Crete, with the monstrous minotaur at the centre, was designed by the engineer Daedalus; a mock-heroic reference to the imprisonment of lovers in the coils of Belinda's hair. Pope may recall Oldham's erotic 'The Dream', 23–4, *Poems, and Translations* (1683), p. 123: 'A while my wanton hand was pleas'd to rove | Through all the hidden Labyrinths of Love'.

40. Cf. 'To a Young Lady, with the Works of Voiture', 64.

41. **hairy Sprindges:** wire traps for birds, but here with an obscene suggestion. The exact phrase was occasionally in scientific use, e.g. to indicate the hair which prevents insects from entering the nasal cavity, in Helkiah Crooke, *Mikrokosmographia. A Description of the Body of Man* (1615), p. 614.

CANTO I

Slight Lines of Hair surprize the Finny Prey,
Fair Tresses Man's Imperial Race insnare,
And Beauty draws us with a *single Hair*.

45   Th' Adventrous *Baron* the bright Locks admir'd,
He saw, he wish'd, and to the Prize aspir'd:
Resolv'd to win, he meditates the way,
By Force to ravish, or by Fraud betray;
For when Success a Lover's Toil attends,
50   Few ask, if Fraud or Force attain'd his Ends.

For this, e'er *Phoebus* rose, he had implor'd
Propitious Heav'n, and ev'ry Pow'r ador'd,

---

42. Lines of Hair: fishing lines were made with horsehair.
    Finny Prey: epic periphrasis for fish; cf. Addison's 'The Third Book of Ovid's Metamorphoses', in *Poetical Miscellanies: The Fifth Part* (1704), p. 552: 'With Lines and Hooks he caught the finny Prey'.
43. Imperial: powerful, regal; the phrase 'Man's Imperial Race' is found in Dryden's translation of Virgil's *Georgics*, III.377, *Works of Virgil*, p. 107, in a section on the irresistible power of sexual desire.
44. draws: leads, attracts.
45. Baron: the male hero of the poem, based on Robert, seventh Lord Petre, of Ingatestone in Essex (1690–1713; see Headnote).
    admir'd: carrying a wider range of meanings then than now: see Commentary to *Essay on Criticism*, 392.
46. Prize: carrying the epic sense of 'spoils of war', a constant feature of the Homeric poems; it occurs 16 times in the first book of Pope's translation of *The Iliad* alone, mostly in the quarrel between the Greek generals over possession of Trojan women abducted as 'prizes'. The main action of the *Iliad* turns less on the 'rape' of Helen (see Headnote) than on this quarrel.
47. meditates: considers, plans carefully; cf. 'Episode of Sarpedon', 23.
48. Force...Fraud: commonly paired in epic, e.g. Blackmore, *King Arthur*, II (1697), pp. 38, 51; the collocation of the two nouns occurs at least five times in Dryden's translation of Virgil, *Aeneid* (e.g. I.401, 942, etc.) and three times in Pope's translation of the *Odyssey*: I.385; IV.871; XX.306. *TE* finds the source of the idea in *Aeneid* II.390: 'dolus an virtus, quis in hoste requirat?'; 'deceit or strength, who would ask in battle?' These usages are all to do with military success, not seduction as here. Cf. also 'Vertumnus and Pomona', 118.
    ravish: 'to take away by violence' (*SJ*). See note on title, and Headnote: Sources.
51–4. In addition to classical examples of sacrificial prayers, e.g. at *Aeneid*, XI. 785–93 (similarly addressed to Apollo), Pope may be drawing on part three of Geoffrey Chaucer's *Knight's Tale*; Dryden's modernised version of the story, 'Palamon and Arcite', in *Fables*, has Palamon's prayer to Venus for possession of Emily at III.129–88. Garth, *The Dispensary*, III, sixth edition (1706), pp. 35–7, has an extended sequence of altar-building and mock-prayer. Cf. 'January and May', 418–19. Pope would parody the scene more extensively in *The Dunciad* (1728), I.125–202.
51. Phoebus: Apollo, Greek god of the sun.
    implor'd: prayed.
52. Propitious: 'favourable; kind' (*SJ*, citing this line); often used of omens. Cf. 'The First Book of Statius his Thebais', 260, and Chryses' prayer to Apollo, *Iliad*, I.51–60 (in Pope's translation). 'Propitious heav'n' was a phrase much used by Blackmore in his epics; e.g. *Prince Arthur* (1695), I, p. 16; IV, p. 207.

But chiefly *Love* — to *Love* an Altar built,
Of twelve vast *French* Romances, neatly gilt.
55   There lay the Sword-knot *Sylvia*'s Hands had sown,
With *Flavia*'s Busk that oft had rapp'd his own:
A Fan, a Garter, half a Pair of Gloves;
And all the Trophies of his former Loves.
With tender *Billet-doux* he lights the Pyre,
60   And breaths three am'rous Sighs to raise the Fire.

Here used proleptically: the Baron prays heaven to be propitious.

ev'ry Pow'r: celestial beings.

ador'd: worshipped religiously (as in I.24).

54. twelve . . . gilt: early French novels of sexual adventure, in expensive 'gilt' bindings. See Commentary to 'January and May', 455. The bulk of these is the subject of humour in Ozell's *Lutrin*, pp. 96-8. Pope is not known to have read widely in such material but in November 1716 (*Corr.*, I.375) he sent Martha Blount the five volumes of Madame de Scudéry's *The Grand Cyrus* (1649-53); on 6 October 1714 (*Corr.*, I.261) he had promised her his own adventures as 'better than reading Romances'. On her appetite for such fiction and the use of romance names amongst the coterie of Pope's Catholic friends see Rumbold (1989: 53-4).

55-8. *The Tatler*, no. 113, 29 December 1709, reproduces the inventory of a deceased beau, which contains among other miscellaneous objects a garter, some fans, and a lock of hair.

55. Sword-knot: ornamental ribbon or cord tied to the handle of the sword that the Baron was entitled to wear as a sign of rank. Dryden mocks the sword-knot and cravat of the overdressed beau in his 'Epilogue' to Etherege's comedy *Sir Fopling Flutter*, 23, and Pope returns to the idea in *The Dunciad*, II.36.

Sylvia: conventional name in love poetry; cf. 'Spring', 49. Here, a former lover of the Baron's; the sword-knot is a 'favour' (see I.27) or lover's gift.

sown: sewn.

56. Busk: 'a piece of steel or whalebone, worn by women to strengthen their stays [corsets]' (*SJ*), as in the poem 'On a Juniper Tree, cut down to make busks', formerly attributed to Rochester, but actually by Aphra Behn. They could also be made of horn or wood, and in some designs were detachable, fitting into a busk-pocket or slot, hence their availability as a sexual trophy. In John Phillips's *Maronides: or, Virgil Travestie* (1678), p. 61, Proserpine uses her busk as a weapon, and in Cotton's 'To Chloris', *Poems on Several Occasions* (1689), p. 439, the speaker must exchange 'a *Ladies* busk' for the sword of war. *TE* reads the line as suggesting that the Baron himself is wearing busks, and presents some Elizabethan evidence that men wore stays, but the sense could be that Flavia, another former idol of the Baron's affections, has often flirtatiously 'rapp'd' his hands ('his own', in 56, referring back to 'Hands' in 55) with this item of intimate apparel, whether worn (in which case the Baron's hands would be involved in an erotic approach) or held separately. Either way this prefigures the mock-epic combat of II.92-103. 'Flavia' is the heroine of the poem by Atterbury cited as a source to 'On a Fan of the Author's Design' (Headnote to that poem).

57. Garter: ribbon to hold a stocking up.

58. Trophies: by analogy with 'Prize', I.46 and 62; the Baron sacrifices objects associated with previous amorous conquests to gain the supreme prize, Belinda's lock.

59. Billet-doux: love letters.

Pyre: sacrificial fire, usually associated with funerals, as in *Iliad*, XXIII, the funeral of Patroclus.

CANTO I 493

Then prostrate falls, and begs with ardent Eyes
Soon to obtain, and long possess the Prize:
The Pow'rs gave Ear, and granted half his Pray'r,
The rest, the Winds dispers'd in empty Air.

65   Close by those Meads for ever crown'd with Flow'rs,
Where *Thames* with Pride surveys his rising Tow'rs,
There stands a Structure of Majestick Frame,
Which from the neighb'ring *Hampton* takes its Name.
Here *Britain's* Statesmen oft the Fall foredoom

61-2. *TE* cites Dryden's version of *Aeneid*, XI.1124-5, *Works of Virgil*, p. 572: 'Him, the fierce Maid beheld with ardent Eyes; | Fond and Ambitious of so Rich a Prize'.

63. Pow'rs . . . half: Cf. 'Sapho to Phaon', 244-5. An indication that the Baron will not get everything he asks for, and itself an allusion to epic: see Pope's translation of *Iliad*, XVI.306-9: 'Great *Jove* consents to half the Chief's Request, | But Heav'ns eternal Doom denies the rest; | To free the Fleet was granted to his Pray'r; | His safe Return, the Winds dispers'd in Air.' In his note to that passage, and in a later note (1736) to the revised *Rape of the Lock*, Pope pointed to Virgil's version of the half-successful prayer in *Aeneid* XI.794-5; in Dryden's translation, 1145-6, *Works of Virgil*, p. 573: '*Apollo* heard, and granting half his Pray'r, | Shuffled in Winds the rest, and toss'd in empty Air'. As Wasserman (1966) notes, this prayer was uttered by a male warrior seeking to slay the chaste and warlike virgin athlete Camilla.

65-8. *TE* notes Pope's models in Dryden, *Mac Flecknoe*, 64-9 (describing the Barbican); Garth, *Dispensary*, sixth edition, pp. 1-2 (the Old Bailey and the Royal College of Physicians), and p. 38 (Apothecaries' Hall); and Blackmore, *The Kit-Cats*, (1708), pp. 3-5 (the tavern frequented by Jacob Tonson and the 'Kit-Cat Club'). Cf. also John Tutchin's satire *The Tribe of Levi* (1691), p. 3: 'Close by those Banks, the Banks where Silver Theams | Still glides along with unpolluted Streams, |

A Fabrick stands, no Storm of Fate molests, | From its Foundation was possest by Priests'.

65. Meads: meadows.

66. Thames: personified (cf. I.20) as a river-god as in *Windsor-Forest*, 328.

 rising Tow'rs: buildings in the process of construction, in the sense used by Dryden, 'Dido to Aeneas', 11, *Ovid's Epistles Translated by Several Hands* (1680), p. 216: 'Nor can my rising Tow'rs your flight restrain'; and similarly in his *Aeneid*, IV.123. Cf. *Windsor-Forest*, 349-50, and 138 below.

67. Frame: design.

68. Hampton: Hampton Court Palace, on the banks of the Thames, a few miles upstream from Twickenham, where Pope would build his own villa from 1719 onwards. Built by Cardinal Wolsey for his own use but gifted in 1526 to Henry VIII and extended by Charles II and William III and Mary alongside much work on the gardens. It is much more likely that the historical offence took place at Ingatestone or in London; see Headnote: Context.

69-70. *TE* compares two lines from a similar scene in the 'Conclusion of the Bill of Fare' (part of Pope's attempts to help Wycherley edit his poems, not published until 1729), 3-4: 'Some, over each Oracl'lous Glass, foredoom | The Fate of Realms, and Conquests yet to come'. See *TE*, VI.59-60.

69. Statesmen: politicians, who might meet at Hampton Court to discuss foreign policy and government business. The politicians Pope was closest to were Robert Harley and

70   Of Foreign Tyrants, and of Nymphs at home;
      Here Thou, great *Anna*! whom three Realms obey,
      Dost sometimes Counsel take — and sometimes *Tea*.

      Hither our Nymphs and Heroes did resort,
      To taste awhile the Pleasures of a Court;
75   In various Talk the chearful hours they past,

Henry St John (see Headnote to *Windsor-Forest*), but in 1712 his acquaintance with them was fairly slight. Of the two, the latter was more interested in 'Nymphs at home'.

Fall foredoom: plan the downfall (political or sexual) of.

70. Foreign Tyrants: i.e. the French king, Louis XIV, with whom Britain and her allies had been fighting the War of Spanish Succession, which Harley and Bolingbroke were working to bring to the end celebrated in *Windsor-Forest*; see also II.181–2. The syntax by which Pope joins two widely differing objects to one verb in two senses is known as syllepsis and is characteristic of mock-heroic: the statesmen plot victory in international politics and in their sex lives without distinction of scale.

71. great Anna: Queen Anne (1665–1714, reigned 1702–14), last of the Stuart monarchs and often the recipient of Pope's praise (see Headnote to *Windsor-Forest*); here subject to gentle irony. Her political and martial skills are praised (without a direct identification) in Ozell's *Lutrin*, p. 38, and in Canto II of Garth's *Dispensary*, sixth edition (1706), pp. 19–20. Notwithstanding I.71–2, the palace was not much used by Anne, though this could not be, as *TE* (II.399) suggests, because her son the Duke of Gloucester died there; he was born there in 1689 but died at Windsor Castle in 1700. Possibly it was too closely associated with her predecessor William III. Daly (2013: 343) points out that Anne had been using Hampton Court more often in 1710–11, partly as a way to avoid the Duchess of Marlborough.

three Realms: *TE* (II.169) suggests that this refers to the ancient claim of the English crown to France; see Commentary to 'Spring', 89–90. But Pope could simply mean England, Scotland and Ireland. The phrase was extremely common in seventeenth-century political verse, e.g. D'Avenant, *A Panegyrick to his Excellency the Lord General Monck* (1660), p. 1: 'How farre three Realms may on your strength rely', and his reworking of the idea for the returned King Charles II in his *Poem, Upon His Sacred Majesties Most Happy Return to his Dominions* (1660), p. 6, where 'three Nations' is equivalent to 'three Realms'. Cf. the poem attributed to Pope's mentor Walsh, 'The Golden Age Restor'd', 100, *A New Collection of Poems Relating to State Affairs* (1705), p. 498: 'See his three realms by vile U[surpe]rs sway'd'.

72. Counsel . . . Tea: another figure of syllepsis. Wasserman (1966) suggests the influence of Ovid, *Metamorphoses*, II.146: 'consiliis, non curribus, utere nostris', translated by Addison as 'not my Chariot, but my Council [counsel] take', in 'The Story of Phaeton', *Poetical Miscellanies: The Fifth Part* (1704), p. 55. At p. 73 Addison provides a note on Ovid's fondness for the figure, which he regards as '*a very low Kind of Wit*, [which] has always in it a mixture of Pun'. 'Tea' appears to have been sounded to rhyme with 'obey' in Pope's time; in the 1714 version (I.22) he rhymes it with 'away'.

73. Heroes: a comic inflation of the men of fashion into noble men of strength, appropriate to epic action such as that of the *Iliad*.

did resort. Pope removed the 'did' expletive in his 1714 revision; cf. *Essay on Criticism*, 349 and Commentary.

75. various Talk: cf. 'The First Book of Statius his Thebais', 795. *TE* cites Dryden, *Aeneid*, VI.721, *Works of Virgil*, p. 383: 'While thus, in talk, the flying Hours they pass'. Wasserman (1966) suggests a Latinate echo of Virgil's 'varia . . . sermone' ('various conversation'); *Aeneid*, VIII.309.

Of, who was *Bitt,* or who *Capotted* last:
This speaks the Glory of the *British Queen,*
And that describes a charming *Indian Screen*;
A third interprets Motions, Looks, and Eyes;
80   At ev'ry Word a Reputation dies.
Snuff, or the *Fan,* supply each Pause of Chatt,
With singing, laughing, ogling, and all that.

---

76. Bitt: cheated or tricked ('low and vulgar language', *SJ*), in this context indicating a card game; for the word in wider senses cf. *Epistle to Dr. Arbuthnot,* 369: '*Sapho* can tell you how this Man was bit'.

Capotted: a figure from a card game: 'When one party has won all the tricks of cards at picquet, he is said to have *capotted* his antagonist' (*SJ*). Pope dropped this reference in the expanded version of 1714, where the full-dress card game of Ombre is introduced.

78. Indian Screen: item of fashionable furniture, usually intended to act as a fire-screen, imported by the East India Company; already the subject of smart repartee, e.g. in William Walker's comedy, *Marry, or do Worse,* I (1708), p. 8, where 'Betty' responds to a young man's vanity by comparing him to 'a Figure at large, upon an *Indian* Screen'. TE cites a later letter of Atterbury to Pope, 28 September 1720 (*Corr.,* II.56), indicating his distaste for the 'Odd Paintings' on such screens.

80. Reputation dies: The interpreter of 'Motions, Looks, and Eyes' in I.79 engages in gossip based on the signals given off in elite conversation (cf. the effect of 'Lady Blast' in *The Spectator,* no. 457, 14 August 1712, attributed to Pope; Ault, *PW,* I.61). This rumour-mongering sets the stage for Thalestris' later fears about Belinda's reputation, at II.28. There appears to have been a whispering campaign about Arabella Fermor, which the poem did not succeed in quashing, and which it may have stimulated: see Headnote: Context.

81–2. TE compares Pope's earlier but then unpublished lines: 'At length the Board, in loose disjointed Chat, | Descanted, some on this Thing, some on that', from 'Conclusion of the Bill of Fare', 1–2.

81. Snuff ... Fan: Snuff is 'powdered tobacco taken by the nose' (*SJ*); an aristocratic pastime, recently popular, with its own rituals and accessories; cf. II.44–8. Snuff-boxes formed objects of comic business in late Restoration comedy, e.g. Farquhar, *The Recruiting-Officer,* III (1706), p. 32. The beau of *Tatler,* no. 113, 29 December 1709, who expired on the removal of his snuff-box, possessed 'Four pounds of scented snuff, with three gilt snuff-boxes; one of them with ... a looking-glass in the lid'. See Pope to Cromwell, 15 July 1711, quoted in the Headnote, about the latter's success with the ladies and his snuff-box trophy. *The Spectator,* no. 138, 8 August 1711, mock-advertised the teaching of 'The Exercise of the Snuff-Box, according to the most fashionable Airs and Motions, in opposition to the Exercise of the Fan', the rules for which the paper had mockingly supplied in no. 102, 27 June 1711, supplementing previous mockery in *The Tatler,* no. 52, 9 August 1709, and no. 239, 19 October 1710. High-status women carried decorated fans to keep themselves cool and as an aid to modesty but also for purposes of display and the accentuation of gesture. Cf. II.99; *Essay on Criticism,* 543; and 'On a Fan of the Author's Design'. Gay's mock-heroic poem *The Fan* appeared in 1713.

82. ogling: to ogle is 'to view with side glances, as in fondness' (*SJ*), in a gesture of sexual admiration.

Now, when declining from the Noon of Day,
The Sun obliquely shoots his burning Ray;
85   When hungry Judges soon the Sentence sign,
And Wretches hang that Jury-men may Dine;
When Merchants from th' *Exchange* return in Peace,
And the long Labours of the *Toilette* cease —

83-4. Nearly a straightforward epic formula; cf. Pope's translation of the *Odyssey*, XVII.687-8: ''Till now declining tow'rd the close of day, | The sun obliquely shot his dewy ray'. *TE* suggests an echo of Philips, *Pastorals*, V.7-8, *Poetical Miscellanies: The Sixth Part* (1709), p. 33: 'The Sun, now mounted to the Noon of Day, | Began to shoot direct his burning Ray'.

83. declining: beginning to set.

84. obliquely: the rays of the sun become more horizontal than vertical.

85-6. In parody of epic sequences where heroic actions mark the time of day, Pope alludes to courtroom scenes where judges and juries hasten trials to conviction, regardless of justice, so that they can get to dinner. Cf. *Odyssey*, XII.519-20, in Pope's translation: 'What-time the Judge forsakes the noisy bar | To take repast, and stills the wordy war'; Pope added a note to the translation defending the propriety of the image, a version of which had already appeared in his *Iliad*, XVI.468-9. Cf. also Pope's note to *Dunciad Variorum*, II.258. Law and lawyers form part of the satiric world of Boileau's *Lutrin*, esp. in Canto V, and Garth inserted several satiric mentions of the Old Bailey in *The Dispensary*, e.g. I, sixth edition (1706), pp. 1-2: 'Where little Villains must submit to Fate, | That great Ones may enjoy the World in State', and further, Canto III, p. 41: 'The Laws were but the hireling Judge's Sense, | Juries were sway'd by venal Evidence'. Cf. also Thomas Shipman, 'The Gossips', *Carolina; or, Loyal Poems* (1683), p. 113: 'A Buck, you know, oft' stops the fury | Both of an hungry *Judge* and *Jury*'. *TE* cites further Wycherley, *The Plain Dealer*, I.i (1677), p. 11: 'I shall no more mind you, than a hungry Judge does a Cause, after the Clock has struck One'; and Congreve, *Love for Love*, I.i (1695), p. 5: 'I have dispatch'd some half a Dozen Duns with as much Dexterity, as a hungry Judge do's Causes at Dinner-time'.

87-8. As Wasserman (1966) indicates, this parodies images of real labour, such as that of the ploughman in *Odyssey*, XIII.39-43 in Pope's translation.

87. Merchants ... Exchange: the Royal Exchange in the City district of London, between Cornhill and Threadneedle Street, near Pope's place of birth; Pope's father was a 'Merchant' (a dealer in linen) until 1688. The building Pope and his contemporaries knew had been built in 1669 following the Great Fire. Its busy interchanges between commercial men of many nations had attracted both caustic censure, e.g. Ned Ward, *The London Spy* (1698), no. 3, and fervent praise, e.g. Addison, *Spectator*, no. 69, 19 May 1711.

88. long Labours: cf. 'Arrival of Ulysses in Ithaca', 169.

Toilette: dressing table; the ceremony of cosmetic adornment. 'The Toilet is their great Scene of Business, and the right adjusting of their Hair the principal Employment of their Lives', complains Addison, in *The Spectator*, no. 10, 12 March 1711, in an effort to encourage women to greater achievements. Pope added the famous 'toilet scene', in which Belinda puts on her make-up, to the revised version of the poem (1714), I.121-48.

89-96. A parody of epic feasting, based on e.g. *Iliad*, I.599-621 in Pope's translation; *Aeneid*, I.893-908, in Dryden's translation (Dido's welcome feast for Aeneas). *TE* notes that Pope's ritual coffee-drinking

CANTO I

      The Board's with Cups and Spoons, alternate, crown'd;
90   The Berries crackle, and the Mill turns round;
      On shining Altars of *Japan* they raise
      The silver *Lamp*, and fiery Spirits blaze;
      From silver Spouts the grateful Liquors glide,
      And *China*'s Earth receives the smoking Tyde:
95   At once they gratifie their Smell and Taste,
      While frequent Cups prolong the rich Repast.
      Coffee, (which makes the Politician wise,
      And see thro' all things with his half shut Eyes)

---

scene resembles the tea ceremony in Tate's *Panacea: A Poem upon Tea* (1700), p. 3; see I.92 and 99.

89. Board's: tables or sideboards; or perhaps a single one is intended, since in the 1714 version (III.105), 'the Board' is clearly singular. For Pope's light-hearted description of Swift making coffee at a sideboard, see his letter to Arbuthnot, 11 July [1714], *Corr.*, I.234.

90–4. Pope had experimented with versions of many of these images in commemoration of a social visit from Henry Cromwell; see Headnote: Composition and publication.

90. Berries crackle: The coffee beans are roasted and then ground in the 'Mill'.

91. Altars of Japan: 'japanned' or lacquered stands for a spirit-burner to heat the coffee in a pot, with 'Altars' supplying the mock-heroic sense of something sacred, as in a church or sacrifice. Japanning was a relatively new practice: *OED* cites nothing earlier than John Stalker and George Parker, *A Treatise of Japaning and Varnishing* (1688), which exhibits several typical patterns.

92. silver Lamp ... blaze: the burner which heats the coffee. Cf. Tate, *Panacea*, p. 3: 'On burning Lamps a Silver Vessel plac'd'.

93. silver Spouts: of the coffee pots.

    grateful: 'pleasing; acceptable; delightful; delicious' (*SJ*).

    Liquors: liquids; more normally associated with alcohol or other intoxicants.

94. China's Earth: porcelain or 'china' cups, still in 1712 an expensive imported commodity, as alternative manufacturing processes for it were only just being discovered in Germany and France.

    smoking Tyde: steaming liquid.

96. Repast: normally signifying a meal of food rather than drink.

97. Coffee: popular in the Restoration with the founding of many coffee-houses after 1660; see Cowan (2005). It was the subject of much ephemeral verse, e.g. *The Character of a Coffee-House* (1665) and *The Coffee-House, or News-Mongers Hall* (1672); its physiological effects were analysed in *Philosophical Transactions*, no. 256, September 1699, pp. 311–15. Coffee was often mentioned in Pope's letters to Cromwell, e.g. 21 December 1711 (*Corr.*, I.137). Pope's refers here to a 'coffee-house politician', i.e. a man who spends his time talking politics in a coffee house, as satirised in e.g. *Tatler*, no. 178, 30 May 1710, and *Spectator*, no. 403, 12 June 1712. Charles Johnson's comedy *The Generous Husband* (1711) has the subtitle 'The Coffee-House Politician'. For the process Pope is alluding to, cf. John Ayloffe, 'Nulla manere diu neque vivere carminant possum, que scribuntur aque notoribus', *State-Poems* (1697), p. 191: 'As easily may Water Poets make, | As Coffee Politicians does create, | The Two Grand Whigs of Poetry and State.'

98. half shut Eyes: Coffee counteracts the drowsiness brought on by the 'rich Repast' as well as providing a suitable prop for pretensions to thoughtfulness.

Sent up in Vapours to the *Baron*'s Brain
100 New Stratagems, the radiant Locke to gain.
Ah cease rash Youth! desist e're 'tis too late,
Fear the just Gods, and think of *Scylla*'s Fate!
Chang'd to a Bird, and sent to flitt in Air,
She dearly pays for *Nisus*' injur'd Hair!

105 But when to Mischief Mortals bend their Mind,
How soon fit Instruments of Ill they find?
Just then, *Clarissa* drew with tempting Grace
A two-edg'd Weapon from her shining Case;
So Ladies in Romance assist their Knight,
110 Present the Spear, and arm him for the Fight.

103.] Vide Ovid. Metam. 8.

---

99. Vapours: fumes. In being driven by fluids, the Baron acts in a manner reminiscent of the mock-theory of psychology in Swift's *A Discourse Concerning the Mechanical Operation of the Spirit* (published with *A Tale of a Tub*, 1704); but cf. also Tate's description of the effects of tea, *Panacea* (1700), p. 3: 'About their Heart enliven'd Spirits danc'd, | Then to the Brains sublimer Seat advanc'd'.

100. Stratagems: See Commentary to *Essay on Criticism*, 182, and 'The Wife of Bath Her Prologue', 163.

101. Cf. 'Vertumnus and Pomona', 118.

102-4 and Pope's note. Scylla: daughter of Nisus, legendary king of the Greek city of Megara, who was protected by a magical lock of purple or red hair. Pope cites the version by Ovid (*Metamorphoses*, VIII.1-151): Scylla fell in love with King Minos, who was besieging their city, and cut her father's lock of hair off. After attempting to cling to Minos' ship, she was changed into a bird and pursued by her implacable father, himself turned into an osprey or sea-eagle. In early editions of the 1714 *Rape of the Lock* the epigraph was from this section of Ovid. Lauderdale's version of Virgil, *Georgics*, I, *Annual Miscellany: For the Year 1694*, p. 244, has the phrase 'Poor Scylla dearly pays his fatal Hair'; cf. also 'The First Book of Statius his Thebais', 468-9.

103. flitt: 'to flutter; to rove on the wing' (*SJ*, citing this line).

106. Instruments of Ill: 'Instrument' can refer either to the scissors which Clarissa hands the Baron, or to Clarissa herself as the agent of the crime. (Clarissa is not known to be identifiable with any historical figure.) *TE* notes that 'instrument of ill' is in Shakespeare, *I Henry VI*, III.iii.65, and that the idea is suggested by Dryden's *Absalom and Achitophel*, 79-80 (1681), p. 3: 'But, when to Sin our byast Nature leans, | The carefull Devil is still at hand with means'. In *Paradise Lost*, II.871-2 (1674), p. 53, Sin unlocks the gate of Hell with 'the fatal Key, | Sad instrument of all our woe'.

108. two-edg'd Weapon: scissors, kept in a personal 'Case'. Rogers (2006) suggests an allusion to the biblical two-edged sword (Hebrews 4:12).

shining Case: similar to the tweezer-cases of II.160-1. The phrase is used to refer to armour in Dryden, *The Indian Emperour*, II.iii (1667), p. 21.

110. Spear: in romances (I.154 above), the lance would be the more appropriate weapon; 'spear' suggests the epic weaponry of the *Iliad*.

He takes the Gift with rev'rence, and extends
The little Engine on his Finger's Ends,
This just behind *Belinda*'s Neck he spread,
As o'er the fragrant Steams she bends her Head:
115   He first expands the glitt'ring *Forfex* wide
T' inclose the Lock; then joins it, to divide;
One fatal stroke the sacred Hair does sever
From the fair Head, for ever, and for ever!

    The living Fires come flashing from her Eyes,
120   And Screams of Horror rend th'affrighted Skies.
Not louder Shrieks by Dames to Heav'n are cast,
When Husbands die, or *Lap-dogs* breath their last,

---

112. little Engine: an oxymoron, since 'engine' in the context of warfare normally suggests large-scale weaponry: 'a military machine' (*SJ*, who however cites this present couplet under the meaning 'any instrument'). Cf. 'To the Author of a Poem, intitled, Successio', 17. *TE* sees this moment as a miniaturisation of the massive boxing gauntlets of epic games, e.g. *Aeneid*, V.543-4, in Dryden's version, *Works of Virgil*, p. 343: 'Astonish'd at their weight the Heroe stands, | And poiz'd the pond'rous Engins in his hands'.

114. fragrant Steams: of coffee. See Pope's letter to Cromwell of 15 July 1711 (quoted in Headnote: Composition and publication).

115. expands: opens the scissors.

Forfex: not in *SJ*: a Latin word meaning a pair of shears or scissors.

117. sacred Hair: Dryden uses this phrase in his version of Juvenal, *Satires*, VI.632, of a women's hairdressing session.

119. living Fires: cf. the 'lightning' of Belinda's eyes at II.131. Lovelace uses this phrase of a woman's eyes in 'The Triumphs of Philamore and Amoret', 29, *Lucasta* (1659-60), p. 50. *TE* notes a resemblance to the eyes of the angry Saul in Cowley's *Davideis*, I.644-5, *Poems... Written by A. Cowley* (1656), p. 17: 'A violent *Flame* rolls in his troubled brest, | And in fierce *Lightning* from his *Eye* do's break'.

120. Screams of Horror: an epic inflation of Belinda's complaint, alluding to the complaints of female victims; cf. 'January and May', 758-61. *TE* compares the scene to Pope's version of the *Iliad*, XIV.456-60; cf. also the phrases from Denham's *Destruction of Troy*, in Commentary to II.14 below.

122. Husbands... Lap-dogs: The syllepsis mockingly suggests the death of a husband or a dog as equivalent disasters for some women. Though it has a long history (e.g. Juvenal, *Satires*, VI.654, where wives, in Dryden's version, 853, *Satires of Juvenal*, p. 122, 'Wou'd save their Lapdog sooner than their Lord'), love and grief for lapdogs and other pets constituted a particular kind of 'female Error' (I.33) much satirised in contemporary journals, e.g. *Tatler*, no. 40, 12 July 1709; no. 47, 28 July 1709; no. 121, 17 January 1710. Cf. 'The Wife of Bath Her Prologue', 308-12. Pope added a note from Dacier to his translation of the *Iliad*, XI.212, 'More grateful, [pleasing] now, to Vulturs than their Wives', defending Homer's representation of the authentic grief of wives for their slaughtered husbands. *TE* finds a comic model for the actual phrasing in Farquhar, *Sir Harry Wildair*, I.i (1701), p. 2: 'A fine Lady can laugh at the Death of her Husband, and cry for the loss of a Lap Dog'.

Or when rich *China* Vessels fal'n from high,
In glittring Dust and painted Fragments lie!

125   Let Wreaths of triumph now my Temples twine,
(The Victor cry'd) the glorious Prize is mine!
While Fish in Streams, or Birds delight in Air,
Or in a Coach and Six the *British* Fair,
As long as *Atalantis* shall be read,
130   Or the small Pillow grace a Lady's Bed,
While *Visits* shall be paid on solemn Days,
When num'rous Wax-lights in bright Order blaze,

---

123. China Vessels: porcelain vases, another luxury item (see I.94). As Williams (1962) shows, the fragility of China was much associated in Restoration literature with female habits of collecting and display.

125. Wreaths: victory wreaths, as in classical celebrations, invoking the 'triumphs' of successful generals (see Commentary to *Essay on Criticism*, 513). *TE* compares Horace's self-crowning with Delphic laurel in *Odes*, III.xxx. 14–16.

Temples: head, brow.

127–34. As *TE* (II.180–1) shows, Pope is drawing on a long tradition of such prophetic utterances, e.g. Aeneas' promise to Dido, Virgil, *Aeneid*, I.854–7 in Dryden's translation, *Works of Virgil*, p. 227: 'While rowling Rivers into Seas shall run, | And round the space of Heav'n the radiant Sun; | While Trees the Mountain tops with Shades supply, | Your Honour, Name, and Praise shall never dye.' Another instance is *Eclogues*, V.76–8. *TE* further notes parody of similar epic-based promises in Philips, *Pastorals*, III.105–8. In all Pope's sources the prophecy is that the name of someone else (host, hero, loved one) will be preserved, whereas the Baron vaingloriously transfers the fame to himself. Cf. 'Winter', 83–4, and Commentary, which gives the source of the Baron's words.

127–8. The verb 'delight' (127) governs all the clauses here: 'while Fish delight in Streams . . . While British women delight in a Coach and Six . . .'. The 'Coach and Six' (i.e. a coach drawn by three pairs of horses) is the sign of a rich husband.

128. Fair: the fair one or the fair sex, i.e. women in general.

129. Atalantis: *Secret Memoirs and Manners of Several Persons of Quality, of Both Sexes, From the New Atalantis*, a scandalous *roman-à-clef* published initially in two volumes in 1709, by Delarivier Manley, a Tory-inclined writer and associate of Pope's friend Swift. Full of lightly disguised and politically biased portraits of contemporary nobles, and spiced with sexual adventure, it got Manley into immediate trouble with the authorities.

130. small Pillow: *TE* cites Rochester, 'Timon: A Satyr', 81, as evidence that the small pillow was a fashionable accessory for ladies of the period; but since the pillow in Rochester's poem is failing to conceal a duchess's large dildo, there is probably a deliberately smutty suggestion here. The phrase appears otherwise only to be used in surgical or obstetric contexts, not in poetry, and very rarely to indicate furnishings.

131. Visits . . . solemn Days: conventional exchanges of polite visits between women, a source of amusement for *The Tatler*, e.g. no. 109, 20 December 1709, and no. 262, 12 December 1712. Millamant stipulates the 'liberty to pay and receive visits to and from whom I please' in her marriage negotiations in Congreve's *Way of the World*, IV.i. (1700), p. 57. Cf. also 'The Wife of Bath Her Prologue', 283–5; 'solemn' here suggests (ironically) a religious regularity of observance.

132. Wax-lights: candles, carried by servants, illuminating a lady's evening visits.

> While Nymphs take Treats, or Assignations give,
> So long my Honour, Name and Praise shall live!

135   What Time wou'd spare, from Steel receives its date,
       And Monuments, like Men, submit to Fate!
       Steel did the Labour of the Gods destroy,
       And strike to Dust th'aspiring Tow'rs of *Troy*;
       Steel cou'd the Works of mortal Pride confound,
140   And hew Triumphal Arches to the ground.
       What Wonder then, fair Nymph! thy Hairs shou'd feel
       The conqu'ring Force of unresisted Steel?

---

133. Treats: entertainments, or delicacies given at an entertainment; cf. 'The Wife of Bath Her Prologue', 115.

Assignations: 'an appointment to meet; used generally of love appointments' (*SJ*).

134. So long ... live: The Baron proclaims his fame like a victor in an epic battle. See Pope's 15 July letter to Cromwell, cited in Headnote: Composition and publication. Thalestris' speech, II.35-8, is the female answer to this vaunting.

135. Steel (the scissors, and more generally, weaponry) assigns the end-date to something (the lock, and more generally human achievement) that time would have left immortal.

136. The ruins of classical civilisations of Greece and Rome often inspired a non-ironic version of this sentiment: cf. Pope's 'Epistle to Addison, Occasion'd by his Dialogues of Medals'. Wakefield suggests an allusion to Juvenal, *Satires*, X.146: 'quandoquidem data sunt ipsis quoque fata sepulchris' ('since fates are assigned even to tombs themselves').

137. Labour ... Gods: Troy was supposedly constructed by the Greek gods Apollo and Poseidon; cf. 'The First Book of Statius his Thebais', 835-6.

138. aspiring Tow'rs of Troy: as in Thomas Heywood, *The Brazen Age*, II (1613), sig. F2ʳ: ''Til thy aspiring Towers of *Illium* | Lye leuell with the place on which we stand'; 'aspiring' here means 'reaching upwards' (cf. I.66), though the element of ostentation is not absent. Pope was about to begin translating *The Iliad*, which tells the story of Troy from the anger of Achilles to the death of Hector. The actual fall of Troy is described in Virgil's *Aeneid*, book II; and cf. Denham's poem, *The Destruction of Troy* (1656).

139. confound: reduce to confusion, destroy.

140. Triumphal Arches: as built in Rome to celebrate imperial triumphs in war; by Pope's day largely in ruins, but illustrated in some of the nine large-scale works by Andrea Mategna known as 'Triumphs of Caesar', which had been acquired by Charles I and were installed at Hampton Court. The Baron's own 'triumph' may be subject to the same rule of decay and defeat. For the line as a whole, Wakefield compares Addison's version of Horace, *Odes*, III.iii.121; *Poetical Miscellanies: The Sixth Part* (1709), p. 270 (speaking of Troy): 'And hew the shining Fabrick to the Ground'.

141. TE compares Catullus, *Carmina*, LXVI, 47: 'quid facient crines cum ferro talia cedant?' ('What should hairs do when such things yield to iron?'). Catullus' comparison is with the cutting of a channel through a mountainous region.

142. unresisted: irresistible. Cf. e.g. Pope's translation of the *Iliad*, V.777: 'Urg'd by the Force of unresisted Fate', and XXI.671-2, where Pope uses the same rhyme words. Pope uses 'unresisted' at least five further times in the *Iliad* translation.

Steel: TE notes the mock-heroic usage of 'Steel' as a synonym for 'ferrum' (iron, but signifying a sword in Latin epics) in Garth, *Dispensary*, IV, sixth edition (1706), p. 55.

THE
Rape *of the* Locke.

CANTO II.

But anxious Cares the pensive Nymph opprest,
And secret Passions labour'd in her Breast.
Not youthful Kings in Battel seiz'd alive,
Not scornful Virgins who their Charms survive,
5   Not ardent Lover robb'd of all his Bliss,
Not ancient Lady when refus'd a Kiss,
Not Tyrants fierce that unrepenting die,
Not *Cynthia* when her *Manteau*'s pinn'd awry,
E'er felt such Rage, Resentment, and Despair,
10 As Thou, sad Virgin! for thy ravish'd Hair.

While her rackt Soul Repose and Peace requires,

1–2. As Pope later indicated (from 1736), this alludes to Virgil, *Aeneid*, IV.1–2, where Dido finds herself reluctantly in love with Aeneas; in Dryden's version, *Works of Virgil*, p. 296: 'But anxious Cares already seiz'd the Queen; | She fed within her Veins a Flame unseen'. The phrase 'anxious cares' is also in Milton, *Paradise Lost*, VIII.185, where Adam acknowledges that God has kept him and Eve free of such things.

1.   pensive: 'sorrowfully thoughtful; ... mournfully serious; melancholy' (*SJ*, citing this passage); cf. 'January and May', 394, and 'The Arrival of Ulysses in Ithaca', 68–9, for contrasting reasons to be pensive.

3. youthful Kings: Pope is perhaps thinking of the staged passions of such heroes in the heroic drama of the Restoration period.

4–10. For the type of display of female emotion which Pope is parodying here, cf. 'Sapho to Phaon', 130–4.

4.   scornful Virgins: women who reject offers of marriage. Cf. Cobb, 'The Desperate Lover', 118, *Poems on Several Occasions* (1710), p. 104: 'Ye scornful Virgins, *be forewarn'd by Me*'.

  survive: outlive.

7. Tyrants fierce: another mainstay of drama, but cf. also *Essay on Criticism*, 590.

8. Cynthia: conventional female distraught because her Mantua (loose outer gown) is crookedly pinned; there is also a faint suggestion of the goddess Artemis, for whom 'Cynthia' is another name (cf. 'Sapho to Phaon', 99; *Windsor-Forest*, 198; etc.).

10. ravish'd Hair: As *TE* notes, Sandys used this phrase in concluding his version of Ovid's story of Nisus (see Commentary to I.102–4).

11. rackt: tormented, as on a rack; cf. Satan in Milton, *Paradise Lost*, I.126 (1674), p. 6: 'rackt with deep despare'. This is one of the very few lines of the 1712 poem completely dropped in the 1714 version, to be replaced (IV.93) by '*Belinda* burns with more than mortal Ire'.

  requires: implying the Latin sense 'seeks'.

The fierce *Thalestris* fans the rising Fires.
O wretched Maid (she spread her hands, and cry'd,
And *Hampton*'s Ecchoes, wretched Maid! reply'd)
15   Was it for this you took such constant Care,
Combs, Bodkins, Leads, Pomatums, to prepare?
For this your Locks in Paper Durance bound,

---

12. Thalestris: one of the Queens of the Amazons, legendary race of female warriors. Ozell's *The Trophy Bucket* (p. 20) and *Lutrin* (p. 96) both feature bands of 'Amazonian' warriors. The first 'novel' in William Painter's *The Second Tome of the Palace of Pleasure* (1567) includes the story of Thalestris' encounter with the Greek commander Alexander the Great, which also features in Anne Killigrew's poem 'Alexandreis'; the character had appeared in John Weston's *The Amazon Queen* (1667), and (played by Nell Gwyn) in Samuel Pordage's play *The Siege of Babylon* (1678). Warton identified Thalestris with Elizabeth Morley, sister of Sir George Browne (i.e. Sir Plume, II.39, and see Headnote), but *TE* (II.376) argues that the context suggests his wife Gertrude Morley (d. 1720). For the suggestion that there is a political allusion here to Abigail Masham, Queen Anne's new confidante, see Headnote: Context.

rising Fires: of emotion.

13-38. *TE* compares Thalestris' speech with Nestor's combined lament and call to arms, in *Iliad*, VII.145-94 in Pope's translation, and notes that this had already been parodied in canto III of Boileau's *Lutrin*.

13. spread her hands: a theatrical gesture.

14. Ecchoes: perhaps, as Wakefield suggests, in parody of the 'echo poems' of the seventeenth century, e.g. Cowley's 'The Eccho'. Cf. 'Spring', 44 variant, and 'Summer', 16, for non-parodic versions of the idea. *TE* notes also Denham's *Destruction of Troy*, 474-5 (1656), p. 24: 'The womens shrieks and cryes, | The Arched Vaults re-eccho to the skyes'.

15. Was it for this: standard syntax for female complaint, e.g. Thomas Collins, *The Teares of Loue* (1615), p. 42: 'Was it for this, that I would go so trim, | To gaine his loue, then be beguild of him? | Was it for this, that I did tricke my hayre, | And sought all meanes to make me supreme fayre?'

16. Bodkins: 'Bodkin' can mean: 'an instrument with a small blade and sharp point used to bore holes ... an instrument to draw a thread or riband through a loop ... an instrument to dress the hair' (*SJ*, citing this line); cf. II.141. The role of the bodkin is much enhanced in Canto V of the revised 1714 version of the poem. Pope does not use the word, which was probably most famous as the instrument of 'quietus' by suicide in Hamlet's 'To be, or not to be' speech, outside the *Lock* texts, but Garth, *Dispensary*, VI, sixth edition (1706), p. 99, writes of 'Bodkin Spears' during a description of mock-heroic battle. See also Headnote: Models and sources for the possibility that Belinda's threat here is modelled on Yalden's 'Rape of Theutilla'. A five-inch silver bodkin inscribed 'Keep Vertue Ever' and dated 1660 is shown in Tracy (1974: 70).

Leads: Small pieces of lead were used to seal the curl papers (next line).

Pomatums: ointments, originally derived from apples; cf. Margaret Cavendish, 'The First Part of the Lady Contemplation', Scene 24, *Playes* (1662), p. 208: 'embalm your hair with *Gessimond Pomatums*'.

17. Paper Durance: Belinda has bound her hair in 'curl papers'; 'durance' means imprisonment. This section balances the images of imprisonment by hair in I.39-44. Congreve's *Way of the World*, II.i, contains a humorous exchange between Millamant and her servant Mincing about the different effects of binding up hair with paper according to whether the contents are in prose or verse.

>   For this with tort'ring Irons wreath'd around?
>   Oh had the Youth but been content to seize
> 20 Hairs less in sight — or any Hairs but these!
>   Gods! shall the Ravisher display this Hair,
>   While the Fops envy, and the Ladies stare!
>   *Honour* forbid! at whose unrival'd Shrine
>   Ease, Pleasure, Virtue, All, our Sex resign.
> 25 Methinks already I your Tears survey,
>   Already hear the horrid things they say,
>   Already see you a degraded Toast,
>   And all your Honour in a Whisper lost!
>   How shall I, then, your helpless Fame defend?

---

18. tort'ring Irons: heated rods, used to produce curls.

20. Hairs less in sight: an innuendo suggesting actual sexual conquest, as opposed to the symbolic but visible 'rape' of the lock. In the 1714 version lines 19–20 are spoken by Belinda herself in a different context (IV.175–6). In Pope's 'To Belinda on the Rape of the Lock', published in 1717, Belinda is advised to face down those critical of her reputation: 'Who censure most, more precious hairs would lose, | To have the *Rape* recorded by his Muse' (29–30). McLaverty (2001: 20) draws attention to the end of Fenton's smutty poem 'The Fair Nun', in *Miscellaneous Poems and Translations* (pp. 219–20), in which the devil tries and fails, as part of a bargain with a pregnant woman, to straighten a hair 'curl'd like a Bottle-Scrue' [corkscrew], i.e. a pubic hair. Cf. also Commentary to 'January and May', 286.

21. Ravisher: cf. II.10, and Commentary to I.48; but the suggestion that the hair is a sexual trophy is intensified here. For the line, Wakefield compares *Aeneid*, II.577–8, in which Aeneas tells of his fury that Helen, the cause of the war, can go back to Sparta and parade in triumph.

22. Fops: A fop is 'a man fond of show, dress, and flutter' (*SJ*); cf. *Essay on Criticism*, 571, 625. In his letter to Caryll, 8 November 1712, Pope hoped that his writings would meet with no worse enemies than 'beaus and fops, who are the fools of women' (*Corr.*, I.151).

23–4. Honour: the reputation of chastity, which women ('our Sex') regard as more important than Ease, Pleasure and (actual) Virtue. *TE* compares the speech on Honour in Garth, *Dispensary*, III, sixth edition (1706), p. 47: 'Bigotted to this Idol, we disclaim | Rest, Health, and Ease, for nothing but a Name'.

25–9. Thalestris' vision parodies epic moments such as *Iliad*, XXII.53–4 in Pope's translation, where Hecuba forsees the death of her son, the Trojan hero Hector: 'Methinks already I behold thee slain, | And stretch'd beneath that Fury of the Plain'.

27. degraded Toast: A toast is 'a celebrated woman whose health is often drunk' (*SJ*); the term is derived from the piece of toast put in the drinking cup. A recent usage, according to *OED*, which cites Congreve, *Way of the World*, III.i.40 (1700), p. 40, as its earliest witness: 'more Censorious, than a decay'd Beauty, or a discarded Tost' (Millamant speaking). Thalestris means that Belinda will be regarded by men in general as sexually 'fallen'.

28. Honour . . . Whisper: see Commentary to I.80. On 21 December 1712 Pope wrote to Caryll, 'More men's reputations I believe, are whispered away, than any other ways destroyed' (*Corr.*, I.168).

29. Fame: reputation; particularly, the reputation for sexual chastity, crucial for women,

CANTO II

30   'Twill then be Infamy to seem your Friend!
     And shall this Prize, th'inestimable Prize,
     Expos'd thro' *Crystal* to the gazing Eyes,
     And heighten'd by the *Diamond*'s circling Rays,
     On that Rapacious Hand for ever blaze?
35   Sooner shall Grass in *Hide*-Park *Circus* grow,
     And Wits take Lodgings in the Sound of *Bow*,
     Sooner let Earth, Air, Sea, to *Chaos* fall,
     Men, Monkies, Lap-dogs, Parrots, perish all!

     She said; then raging to *Sir Plume* repairs,

---

as opposed to the (male) literary reputation that the word designates in the *Essay on Criticism* (46, 171, etc.) and in *The Temple of Fame* (1715). Cf. 'To a Young Lady, with the Works of Voiture', 35.

30. Infamy: detrimental to reputation.

32-4. The Baron will wind the lock in a ring of crystal or diamond and wear it as a trophy; for a contemporary example of such an arrangement, see Tracy (1974: 57).

34. Rapacious: 'Given to plunder; seizing by violence' (*SJ*, citing this line). *TE* compares Dryden, *Don Sebastian*, IV.i (1690), p. 105: 'From those rapacious Hands', but a nearer prompt is probably Achilles' accusation that Agamemnon has 'rapacious Hands' in stealing the woman he has secured as a prize in the Trojan war: 'The First Book of Homer's Ilias', 247, *Fables* (1700), p. 198.

35-8. Thalestris' speech answers the Baron's boasting at I.127-34 and parodies the high language of e.g. Virgil, *Eclogues*, I.59-63, translated by Dryden, 79-84, *Works of Virgil*, p. 4: 'Th' Inhabitants of Seas and Skies shall change, | And Fish on Shoar and Stags in Air shall range... | E're I, forsaking Gratitude and Truth, | Forget the Figure of that Godlike Youth.' *TE* notes that Garth had already parodied this section in *Dispensary*, III, sixth edition (1706), p. 43: 'The tow'ring *Alps* shall sooner sink to Vales, | And *Leaches*, in our Glasses, swell to *Whales*'.

35. The grass did not grow in Hyde Park circus (in the West End of London) because the gentry rode their horses there for daily exercise.

36. Wits . . . Bow: 'Wits' are writers and men of fashion; cf. Commentary to *Essay on Criticism*, 17. They did not take lodgings within the sound of the bells of St Mary le Bow church in Cheapside (modern EC2; not St Mary, Bow, in modern E3) because that was in the mercantile City and Wits congregated nearer the fashionable West End around St James's Park. Pope was himself born within the sound of the bells.

37. Chaos: the ancient state of the universe according to most creation myths, familiar particularly from Milton's descriptions in *Paradise Lost*, books II and X, whence Pope borrowed it for the mock-mythology of *The Dunciad*. See also *Essay on Criticism*, 295, and *Windsor-Forest*, 13. Thalestris adopts a pose of tragedy cursing, similar to the protagonist of Shakespeare's *Macbeth* (IV.i.58-60): 'Though the treasure | Of Natures germens tumble all together, | Euen till destruction sicken'.

38. Men . . . Parrots: Thalestris does not distinguish between men and the animals that women keep as pets; cf. I.122. *TE* cites a comment from *Letters of Wit, Politicks and Morality* (1701), p. 112: 'to keep a Monkey[,] Dog, Cat, Parrot or Thrush, has no harm in it self... but the Heart is never to be made use of on so contemptible an Occasion' ('Don Guevara, to a Lady... who fell sick for the Death of a little Bitch').

39. She said: she finished speaking (an epic formula).

Sir Plume: 'Plume' suggests lightweight self-adornment and foppish vanity; it was

40 And bids her *Beau* demand the precious Hairs:
   (*Sir Plume*, of *Amber Snuff-box* justly vain,
   And the nice Conduct of a *clouded Cane*)
   With earnest Eyes, and round unthinking Face,
   He first the Snuff-box open'd, then the Case,
45 And thus broke out — 'My Lord, why, what the Devil?
   Z—ds! damn the Lock! 'fore Gad, you must be civil!
   Plague on't! 'tis past a Jest — nay prithee, Pox!
   Give her the Hair' — he spoke, and rapp'd his Box.

   It grieves me much (reply'd the Peer again)

---

the name of a character in Farquhar's comedy *The Recruiting Officer* (1706). Pope's Sir Plume was readily identifiable as Sir George Browne (d. 1730), a first cousin of Arabella Fermor's mother (see Headnote), but Pope's characterisation here draws on stage fops such as Sir Fopling Flutter in Etherege's *The Man of Mode* (1676), to whom allusion is made at II.118. His speech is a parody of the conciliatory efforts of the elder statesman Nestor in Homer, *Iliad*, I.247–84 (329–75 in Pope's version).

repairs: takes herself, goes.

41. Amber Snuff-box: see Tracy (1974: 59) for a contemporary example. In the mock-advertisement for lessons in snuff etiquette in *The Spectator* (cf. Commentary to I.81) it was declared: 'There will likewise be Taught The Ceremony of the Snuff-box, or Rules for offering Snuff... with an Explanation of the Careless, the Scornful, the Politick, and the Surly Pinch, and the Gestures proper to each of them'. Cf. also Gay, *The Fan* (1713) I.122, where the use of the snuff-box in emphasising 'smart replies' is noted. In *Memoirs of Martinus Scriblerus*, XI, 'gold Snuff-boxes' are among the conventional 'Love-toys', along with repeating watches and tweezer-cases.

42. nice Conduct... clouded Cane: 'Nice' indicates fastidiously correct adherence to trivial rules, here governing the use of an ornamental walking-stick. *The Tatler*, no. 103, 6 December 1709, satirises use of canes, one of them 'curiously clouded, with a transparent amber head', from which the obsessed owner has to be gradually parted. The deceased beau of *Tatler*, no. 113, 29 December 1709, also possessed 'an amber-headed cane', and an expert on canes possessed several 'finely clouded' examples in *Tatler*, no. 142, 7 March 1710. *SJ* defines the verb 'cloud' as 'variegate with dark veins'; cf. Pisander's pole-axe, *Iliad*, XIII.767 in Pope's translation: 'An Olive's cloudy Grain the Handle made'. There may be a suggestion of parody of the 'sacred Sceptre' of epic; cf. the passage cited in Commentary to II.51.

43. unthinking: a recent coinage; *OED*'s first citation is from 1676.

44. The figure of syllepsis again: Sir Plume opens his (literal) box and then his (metaphorical) 'case' or argument.

45–8. A sample of 'polite' discourse, containing several impolite and blasphemous features: 'Devil', 'Z—ds!' ('God's wounds'), 'fore Gad' (before God), 'damn', and 'Pox!' (sexually transmitted disease, used here as a swearword). Most of these words occur in a parody of upper-class bad language in *Tatler*, no. 13, 10 May 1709, drawing on comic characters in Restoration drama.

46. civil: polite: an ironic requirement, as noted by 'the Peer' in 50, given Sir Plume's own incoherent swearing.

48. rapp'd... Box: a ridiculous gesture of challenge; cf. the gentleman who swears like Sir Plume and 'began to beat his snuff-box with a very saucy air' in *Tatler*, no. 110, 22 December 1709. For 'rapp'd' cf. also I.56.

49. Peer: the Baron.

50   Who speaks so well shou'd ever speak in vain.
        But by this Locke, this sacred Locke I swear,
        (Which never more shall join its parted Hair,
        Which never more its Honours shall renew,
        Clipt from the lovely Head where once it grew)
55   That while my Nostrils draw the vital Air,
        This Hand, which won it, shall for ever wear.
        He spoke, and speaking in proud Triumph spread
        The long-contended Honours of her Head.

        But see! the *Nymph* in Sorrow's Pomp appears,

51.] *In allusion* to Achilles's *Oath in* Homer. *Il.* I.

---

51 Pope's note. *Iliad*, I.309-12, in Pope's translation: 'Now by this sacred Sceptre, hear me swear, | Which never more shall Leaves or Blossoms bear, | Which sever'd from the Trunk (as I from thee) | On the bare Mountains left its Parent Tree'. Cf. the moment when Achilles cuts off his own hair at the funeral of Patroclus: 'On his cold Hand the sacred Lock he laid', *Iliad*, XXIII.191, in Pope's translation. *TE* further compares Dryden's version of the *Aeneid*, IX.402, *Works of Virgil*, p. 476: 'Now by my Head, a sacred Oath, I swear'.

52. parted Hair: the hair it has been cut from; but cf. the sexual suggestion of 'parting Hair' in the 'Lodona' episode of *Windsor-Forest*, 194, and the Baron's suggestive gesture at II.57-8.

53. Honours: For the classical and masculine usage of 'honours' for 'hair cf. 'January and May', 132. Daphne 'shook the shady Honours of her Head', her hair having become leaves, having avoided rape by transformation into the laurel tree, in Dryden's version of 'The First Book of Ovid's Metamorphoses', 768, *Examen Poeticum* (1693), p. 49; for female characters the word normally carries the connotation of sexual 'honour' (see II.21-3).

55-6. The Baron's oath balances Thalestris' at 35-8.

55. vital: life-giving. The line, as *TE* notes, imitates epic periphrasis, e.g. *Aeneid*, IV.336: 'dum memor ipse mei, dum spiritus hos regit artus' ('while I have memory of myself, while spirit rules these limbs'). Dryden has 'Vital Air' at his *Aeneid*, I.770 and at least six more times in that poem.

56. Hand: cf. II.32-4; Thalestris is proved right about the Baron's intentions.

57. spread: The gesture perhaps has a sexual component; cf. II.52 above.

58. long-contended: fought for over a long period of time, ironic in this case; in parody of epic phrasing such as Dryden, 'To Mr. Granville, on his Excellent Tragedie, call'd Heroick Love' in Granville's *Heroick Love*, 7-8 (1698), sig. A4ᵛ: 'With better Grace an Ancient Chief may yield | The long contended Honours of the Field'. *TE* notes that Pope uses 'long-contended' in later epic contexts, e.g. of Troy itself, in his *Iliad*, IV.6; the corpse of Sarpedon, *Iliad*, XVI.777, is 'long-disputed'; that of Patroclus, *Iliad*, XVIII.274, 'long-contended'; Odysseus' wife Penelope is 'the long-contended prize' in Pope's *Odyssey*, XX.400.

59. Sorrow's Pomp: 'Pomp' is normally an ostentatious ceremony or procession (*Essay on Criticism*, 74-5 variant); in *Windsor-Forest*, 272, it indicates a funeral. Here Pope suggests that Belinda adopts formal positions of grief like those in epic: cf. *Iliad*, XXIV.959: 'Sad *Helen* next in Pomp of Grief appears' (Pope's translation). The phrase was dropped from the 1714 version (IV.143).

60   Her Eyes half languishing, half drown'd in Tears;
        Now livid pale her Cheeks, now glowing red;
        On her heav'd Bosom hung her drooping Head,
        Which, with a Sigh, she rais'd; and thus she said.

        For ever curs'd be this detested Day,
65   Which snatch'd my best, my fav'rite Curl away!
        Happy! ah ten times happy, had I been,
        If *Hampton-Court* these Eyes had never seen!
        Yet am not I the first mistaken Maid,
        By Love of Courts to num'rous Ills betray'd.
70   Oh had I rather un-admir'd remain'd
        In some lone *Isle*, or distant *Northern* Land;
        Where the gilt *Chariot* never mark'd the way,

---

60. half languishing: a sign of suffering, which Pope often associates with the eye: cf. 'Eloisa to Abelard', 332: 'See the last sparkle languish in my eye!', and *Iliad*, XVIII.50: 'And the blue Languish of soft *Alia*'s Eye'; cf. III.516.

61. livid: *SJ* takes this to mean 'discoloured, as by a blow', that is, black and blue, bruised: cf. 'The First Book of Statius his Thebais', 83, 730. But Pope seems to associate it with an intense paleness, as in *OED*, sense 1c, 'unnaturally pale in colour; ashen, pallid (esp. as a result of anger or other strong emotion', supposedly not found earlier than 1728. Pope dropped this line from the 1714 version, perhaps in line with his decreasing use of the triplet.

62. heav'd: heaving, because sobbing and sighing.

64-89. Belinda's speech is partly in parody of Achilles' lament for his dead friend Patroclus, *Iliad*, XVIII.107-62 in Pope's translation, but also recalls the classical tradition of wronged women, especially Dido (*Aeneid*, IV.651-62) and the complaints of Ovid's *Heroides*, as translated in 'Sapho to Phaon' and imitated in 'Eloisa to Abelard'. Pope may also have in mind the guilty speeches of lament given to young women in 'she-tragedies' such as Nicholas Rowe's *The Fair Penitent* (1703). The image of (dull) rural retirement for young women, to avoid the temptations of London, is treated comically in Pope's 'Epistle to Miss Blount, on her Leaving the Town, after the Coronation', but see also his letter to Mrs Marriot, 28 February 1714, with a copy of the extended *Rape of the Lock*: 'I am so vain as to fancy a pretty complete picture of the life of our modern ladies in this idle town from which you are so happily, so prudently, and so philosophically retired' (*Corr*, I.211).

71. lone Isle: i.e. an uninhabited island, devoid of temptation.

    Northern Land: for the classical view of lands in Northern Europe see Commentary to *Essay on Criticism*, 401-2. To a metropolitan lady such as Belinda, Northern England appears uncultivated but safe.

72. gilt Chariot: A chariot was 'a lighter kind of coach, with only front seats' (*SJ*), that is, a horse-drawn vehicle used for pleasure trips, 'gilt' or coloured gold to display wealth, but also here punning on 'guilt'. 'Chariot' contrasts the ancient vehicle of warfare and the lightweight modern convenience, built merely for pleasure and show. In Motteux's *Love's a Jest*, III (1696), p. 27, 'Gaymood' promises a young woman to 'keep thee a Footman and a gilt Chariot, and make thee outshine a Lord's public Mistress'.

    mark'd the way: with ruts left by the wheels. *TE* compares Pope's *Iliad*, XII.128: 'Those Wheels returning ne'er shall mark the Plain'.

> Where none learn *Ombre*, none e'er taste *Bohea*!
> There kept my Charms conceal'd from mortal Eye,
75 Like Roses that in Desarts bloom and die.
> What mov'd my Mind with youthful Lords to rome?
> O had I stay'd, and said my Pray'rs at home!
> 'Twas this, the Morning *Omens* did foretel;
> Thrice from my trembling hand the *Patch-box* fell;
80 The tott'ring *China* shook without a Wind,
> Nay, *Poll* sate mute, and *Shock* was *most Unkind*!
> See the poor Remnants of this slighted Hair!
> My hands shall rend what ev'n thy own did spare.
> This, in two sable Ringlets taught to break,

---

73. **Ombre:** fashionable card-game, subject of an extended additional narrative segment of the 1714 version of the poem (III.25–100). The rules of *The Royal Game of the Ombre* were published in 1660, and the game was a common reference point of subject of social comedy, e.g. throughout Act II of Shadwell's *A True Widow* (1679), and in lyric, e.g. Waller's 'Written on a Card that her Majesty Tore at Omber'.
   Bohea: 'A species of tea, of higher colour, and more astringent taste, than green tea' (*SJ*); then a very new and expensive aristocratic preserve. OED lists the first occurrence of the word in 1702, and several broadsides advertising *The Volatile Spirit of Bohea Tea* date from around 1710; there is jocular reference to it in combination with snuff in *The Tatler*, no. 78, 8 October 1709. For tea-drinking see also I.72, and Tate, *Panacea* (1700), and Motteux's *A Poem Upon Tea* (1701).
75. **Desarts:** deserts, here indicating waste or uncultivated places without population (and temptation); cf. *Windsor-Forest*, 26. For the line as a whole *TE* cites Waller, 'Go Lovely Rose', 6–10, *Poems &c* (1645), p. 89: 'Tell her that's young, | And shun's to have her grâces spide, | That hadst thou sprung | In deserts where no men abide, | Thou must have uncommended dy'd.'
76. **rome:** roam, wander.

78. **Omens:** Belinda's examples (II.79–81) trivialise the 'dire Portents' observed by Dido, *Aeneid*, IV.655–60 of Dryden's translation; cf. also Trapp's 'A Description of the Prodigies which attended the Death of Julius Caesar', from Virgil, *Georgics*, I, in *Poetical Miscellanies: The Sixth Part* (1709), pp. 379–80.
79. **Patch-box:** the box in which Belinda keeps her 'patches'; a patch is a 'small spot of black silk put on the face' for decorative purposes (*SJ*, citing this line). Designs for 'japanned' patch-boxes are given in the treatise noted in Commentary to I.91.
80–1. The rhyme was very common (though not used outside the *Rape of the Lock* texts by Pope) and appears to have been heard as a perfect one in Pope's time; cf. e.g. Oldham, 'The Parting', 16–17.
81. **Poll:** a pet parrot (cf. II.38), here refusing to engage in talk with Belinda.
82. **slighted:** dishonoured, disregarded; it can also refer to the technical destruction of a fortification.
84. **sable:** black: a term in heraldry (see Commentary to *Windsor-Forest*, 28). Arabella Fermor's hair appears to have been light auburn, but *TE* observes that black hair was fashionable and that lighter hair was sometimes artificially darkened.
   taught to break: made to divide (in two ringlets) by styling.

85   Once gave new Beauties to the snowie Neck.
          The Sister-Locke now sits uncouth, alone,
          And in its Fellow's Fate foresees its own;
          Uncurl'd it hangs! the fatal Sheers demands;
          And tempts once more thy sacrilegious Hands.

90   She said: the pitying Audience melt in Tears,
          But *Fate* and *Jove* had stopp'd the *Baron*'s Ears.
          In vain *Thalestris* with Reproach assails,
          For who can move when fair *Belinda* fails?
          Not half so fixt the *Trojan* cou'd remain,
95   While *Anna* begg'd and *Dido* rag'd in vain.
          To Arms, to Arms! the bold *Thalestris* cries,
          And swift as Lightning to the Combate flies.

---

85. snowie: white; cf. I.23.

86. Sister-Locke: i.e. the Baron has cut off one lock of the pair but not the other, which balanced it. *TE* cites Catullus, LXVI.51–2 (the lock of Berenice speaking): 'abiunctae paulo ante comae mea fata sorores | lugebant' ('cut off a little before, sister hairs were lamenting my fate').

    uncouth: 'odd; strange; unusual' (*SJ*).

88. fatal Sheers: scissors used to cut hair, but here with a suggestion of Atropos, one of the three 'Moirai' or 'Fates' in Greek mythology, who cut the thread of people's lives once it had been measured out.

    demands: calls for.

89. thy: the Baron's; Belinda sees the remaining lock as offering him a further temptation, but the passage is also open to the suggestion that Belinda conspires in her own fate by promising to cut off the remaining lock.

    sacrilegious Hands: TE compares Dryden's version of the *Aeneid*, II.548, *Works of Virgil*, p. 250, where 'sacrilegious Hands' are in the process of abducting the Trojan princess Cassandra; Dryden had already used it in a similar context in *Tyrannick Love*, IV.I.(1670) p. 41, and satirically in his version of Juvenal, V.101, *Satires of Juvenal*, p. 77. Cf. also *Essay on Criticism*, 185.

91. Fate . . . Jove: loose invocations of figures of authority from Greek mythology; see II.108. This passage is modelled (as Pope signals at 94–5) on the encounter between the pleading Dido's sister Anna and the resolute Aeneas, Virgil, *Aeneid*, IV.404–652 in Dryden's translation, and particularly 636–7, *Works of Virgil*, p. 315: 'His harden'd Heart nor Pray'rs nor Threat'nings move; | Fate, and the God, had stop'd his Ears to Love'.

94. the Trojan: Aeneas, determined to abandon his lover, Dido, at the command of the Gods, making explicit the Virgilian allusions in play since 64.

96. To Arms: Thalestris declares war. The 'arms' are, in the poem's comic mode, items of fashionable apparel, miniaturising the spears and shields of warfare in *The Iliad*. This episode was put forward by Pope in his annotations to Dennis's *Remarks on Mr. Pope's Rape of the Lock* (1728) as an example of the mock-heroic humour that Dennis contended was missing from the poem (Mack 1982: 408). Pope may recall the clichés of the war poetry of his period, e.g. the image of Queen Anne in Joseph Harris, *Anglia Triumphans* (1703), p. 3: 'To Arms, to Arms, She cry'd ! | To Arms, To Arms, The Brittish Youth reply'd'. On the miniaturising of political struggles in the passage to 123, see Winn (2014: 588).

CANTO II

All side in Parties, and begin th'Attack;
Fans clap, Silks russle, and tough Whalebones crack;
100   Heroes and Heroins Shouts confus'dly rise,
And base, and treble Voices strike the Skies.
No common Weapons in their Hands are found,
Like Gods they fight, nor dread a mortal Wound.

So when bold *Homer* makes the Gods engage,
105   And heavn'ly Breasts with human Passions rage;
'Gainst *Pallas, Mars, Latona, Hermes* Arms;
And all *Olympus* rings with loud Alarms.

104.] Homer. *Il.* 20.

---

98. side in Parties: a faintly political allusion, as divisions hardened during negotiations for the end of the War of Spanish Succession; cf. *Essay on Criticism*, 457–8. The deleterious effects of party divisions were lamented by political activists of all sides; cf. Pope's allusion to 'giddy Factions' in the *Ode for Musick*, 35.

99. Whalebones: used for structure in the 'hoop petticoat', for which see the expanded version (1714), II.120. The 'crack' is the noise they make, like the 'clap' of the fan, both suggesting gunfire. Cf. the quasi-military 'Exercise of the Fan' in the mock-advertisement in *The Spectator*, no. 102, 27 June 1711: 'Upon my giving the Word to *discharge their Fans*, they give one general Crack that may be heard at a considerable Distance'. For the line TE cites Garth, *Dispensary*, V, sixth edition (1706), p. 89 (in the mock-battle): 'Tough Harness rustles, and bold Armour clangs'.

101. base: bass, i.e. male, contrasted with the treble or 'high' voices of the women.

103. mortal: combining the sense of 'human' and 'fatal'; Gods cannot normally be wounded by human weapons.

104 Pope's note. The reference is to the battle of the gods in *Iliad*, XX.91–100 in Pope's translation, which also included a note from the commentator Eustathius treating the passage as a concealed allegory of human passions, as suggested in the following line. Pope may also be thinking of the 'Amazon' wars, mentioned in e.g. *Iliad*, VI.229 in his translation.

105. heav'nly Breasts: cf. Milton, *Paradise Lost*, IX. 729–30 (1674), p. 235: 'can envie dwell | In heav'nly brests?' and Ozell's version of the *Lutrin*, p. 2: 'How *Heavenly* Breasts with *Human* Passions beat!'

106. Pallas: Athena, Greek goddess of wisdom, often depicted in military costume.

Mars: Roman version of Ares, the Greek god of War.

Latona: Roman version of Leto, a minor goddess, mother by Zeus of Apollo and Artemis.

Hermes: Greek god of communication. The syntax is: Mars [takes] arms against Pallas, Hermes [takes] arms against Latona. There are examples of this kind of clustering of names in Virgil, *Aeneid*, IX.574, 767 and X.749, but in inflected Latin the potential for confusion is much diminished.

107. Olympus: the mountain in Greece where the Gods were supposed to live; cf. *Windsor-Forest*, 33, 232.

Alarms: literally, calls to arms, shouts of battle (*SJ*). TE compares Dryden, 'Cymon and Iphigenia', 399, *Fables*, p. 556: 'The Country rings around with loud Alarms'. But cf. also Blackmore, *Prince Arthur*, X (1695), p. 271: 'And all the Field resounds with loud Alarms', where the rhyme word is 'Arms', as here. Pope used similar phrasing in his *Iliad*, XVI.771.

>   *Jove*'s Thunder roars, Heav'n trembles all around;
>   Blue *Neptune* storms, the bellowing Deeps resound;
> 110 *Earth* shakes her nodding Tow'rs, the Ground gives way,
>   And the pale Ghosts start at the Flash of Day!
>
>   While thro' the Press enrag'd *Thalestris* flies,
>   And scatters Deaths around from both her Eyes,
>   A *Beau* and *Witling* perish'd in the Throng,
> 115 One dy'd in *Metaphor*, and one in *Song*.

108-9. Perhaps, as Mason (1987) suggests, drawing on elements of God's vengeful storm in Milton, *Paradise Lost*, I.174-7 (1674), p. 7: 'the Thunder . . . ceases now | To bellow through the vast and boundless Deep'.

108. Jove: one of the names of Zeus, king of the Gods in Greek mythology; cf. above, II.91, and below, II.126. He was known as 'the thunderer'; see Commentary to *Essay on Criticism*, 558, and 'The First Book of Statius his Thebais', 339.

109. Blue Neptune: Neptune is the Roman version of Poseidon, Greek god of the ocean (hence 'Blue'); Pope uses the phrase in his *Iliad* translation, e.g. XV.195. Rowe had used this phrase in his play *Ulysses*, II.i (1706), p. 28, in a line singled out for ridicule in *Critical Remarks on Mr. Rowe's Last Play* (1706), p. 16.

bellowing Deeps: of the ocean; again, Pope uses the phrase in his *Iliad*, XIV.457.

110. Earth: conceived here as a goddess, like the primordial goddess Ge or Gaia in Hesiod's creation myth poem, *Theogony*.

nodding Tow'rs: falling buildings; cf. I.66 and 138.

111. start: are startled by.

Flash of Day: TE cites several non-ironic classical examples of this idea, e.g. Virgil, *Aeneid*, VIII.246: 'trepident immisso lumine manes' ('the spirits tremble at the light sent in'); Sandys' *Ouid's Metamorphosis Englished*, V (1632), p. 179: 'For feare the ground should split above their heads, | And let-in Day, t' affright the trembling Ghosts'; and Addison's version of lines from Silius Italicus in *Remarks on Several Parts of Italy, &c* (1705), p. 248: 'That pale with Fear the rending Earth survey, | And startle at the sudden Flash of Day'.

112. Press: throng, crowd.

113. scatters Deaths: an inflation of the lyric convention that a woman's eyes are 'killing' (as in II.119 below, and cf. I.14), based on allusion to epic moments such as Aeneas' actions, 'Thus rag'd the Prince, and scatter'd Deaths around', *Aeneid*, X.851 in Dryden's translation, *Works of Virgil*, p. 523; and Paris' boast, 'I scatter'd Slaughter from my fatal Bow', *Iliad*, XIII.980, in Pope's translation.

114. Beau: 'A man of dress; a man whose great care is to deck his person' (*SJ*). Cf. II.22.

Witling: see Commentary to *Essay on Criticism*, 40.

115. dy'd . . . Song: For 'die' see also II.133. For the literal deaths on the battlefield of epic, Pope here substitutes the clichés of pain and death in amorous lyrics. *The Tatler*, no. 110, 22 December 1709, poked fun at the easy use of 'die' in love letters, and *The Spectator*, no. 377, 13 May 1712, listed a mock 'Bill of Mortality' listing the various causes of lovers' 'deaths' and wounds, including sight of '*Zelinda*'s Scarlet Stocking', glances, frowns, smiles, hair, the tap of a fan and the 'brush of a Whalebone Petticoat'. EC notes that one of Pope's models for the *Essay on Criticism*, Sheffield's *An Essay on Poetry* (1682), p. 13, mocks the speeches of tragic heroes: 'Men dye in Simile, and live in Rime'. Dennis had attacked poems in which the lover is seen to 'dye by Metaphor' in his 'Preface' to *The*

CANTO II 513

    O cruel Nymph! *a living Death I bear,*
    Cry'd *Dapperwit*, and sunk beside his Chair.
    A mournful Glance Sir *Fopling* upwards cast,
    Those Eyes are made so killing — was his last:
120   Thus on *Meander*'s flow'ry Margin lies
    Th'expiring Swan, and as he sings he dies.

    As bold Sir *Plume* had drawn *Clarissa* down,
    Chloë stept in, and kill'd him with a Frown;
    She smil'd to see the doughty Hero slain,
125   But at her Smile, the Beau reviv'd again.

    Now *Jove* suspends his golden Scales in Air,

126.] Vid. Homer Iliad. 22 & Virg. Aen.12.

Passion of Byblis (1692), sig. B2ʳ. *TE* compares further Garth, *Dispensary*, V, sixth edition (1706), p. 93, in the mock-battle, where a 'batter'd Bard ... Sunk down, and in a *Simile* expir'd'. Pope imitated such conventional ideas in his pastiche of Waller, 'On a Fan of the Author's Design'.

117. Dapperwit: the beau and witling combined; the name is from 'a brisk conceited, half-witted fellow of the Town' in Wycherley's *Love in a Wood* (1672). Pope was satirically represented as 'Sawney Dapper' in Gildon's *A New Rehearsal* (1714).

118. Sir Fopling: with the connotation of 'fop', II.22; based on the title character of Etherege's *Man of Mode, or Sir Fopling Flutter* (1676).

119. Pope's later note to this line in V.64 of the 1714 version signals that the italicised words are a direct quotation from a song in *Camilla*, an opera by Mar' Antonio Buononcini, first performed in London in 1706 and highly popular thereafter. The song confirms the general sense of the clichés that Pope is guying: 'These Eyes are made so killing, | That all who look must dye' ... '"Tis fatal to come near me, | For death is in my Eyes'. As *TE* notes, the song had already been parodied in Ozell's version of Boileau's *Lutrin* (1708), p. 100: 'Here, At his Head Fair *Afra*'s Works let fly; | And may they prove as killing as her Eye'.

120. Meander: sometimes 'Maeander', 'a river in Phrygia, remarkable for its winding course' (*SJ*); hence its normal connotations of maze-like wandering, e.g. *Ode for Musick*, 99. Cf. also Milton, 'A Mask', 231, *Poems of Mr. John Milton*, p. 85: 'By slow *Meander's* margent green'. It is mentioned in *Iliad*, II.1056 (in Pope's translation), and occurs in the 'low' context of the pissing contest in some versions of *The Dunciad* (e.g. the 1736 text, II.168). A 1736 note by Pope to the extended *Rape of the Lock* signals an allusion to Ovid, *Heroides*, VII (Dido to Aeneas), 1-2: 'Sic ubi fata vocant, udis abiectus in herbis, | ad vada Maeandri concinit albus olor' ('So, when the fates summon, the white swan, cast down in damp grasses, sings by the shallows of the Maeander'); hence the 'expiring Swan' of the next line, for which see also Commentary to 'Winter', 39-40, and *Windsor-Forest*, 273.

Margin: verge, bank.

123. kill'd ... Frown: a comic inflation of the literary convention already exploited at 113; hence the automatic revival at her smile in II.125. Cf. 'The Wife of Bath Her Prologue', 66-7.

124. doughty: 'brave; noble; illustrious; eminent ... now seldom used but ironically, or in burlesque' (*SJ*, citing this line).

126 Pope's note. *Iliad*, XXII.271-6 (in his translation): '*Jove* lifts the golden Balances, that show | The Fates of mortal Men,

Weighs the Mens Wits against the Lady's Hair;
The doubtful Beam long nods from side to side;
At length the Wits mount up, the Hairs subside.

130   See fierce *Belinda* on the *Baron* flies,
With more than usual Lightning in her Eyes;
Nor fear'd the Chief th' unequal Fight to try,
Who sought no more than on his Foe to die.
But this bold Lord, with manly Strength indu'd,
135   She with one Finger and a Thumb subdu'd:
Just where the Breath of Life his Nostrils drew,
A Charge of *Snuff* the wily Virgin threw;
Sudden, with starting Tears each Eye o'erflows,
And the high Dome re-ecchoes to his Nose.

---

and things below: | Here each contending Hero's Lot he tries, | And weighs, with equal Hand, their Destinies. | Low sinks the Scale surcharg'd with *Hector*'s Fate; | Heavy with Death it sinks, and Hell receives the Weight.' Pope's other citation was translated by Dryden, *Aeneid*, XII.1054–7, *Works of Virgil*, p. 609: '*Jove* sets the Beam; in either Scale he lays | The Champions Fate, and each exactly weighs. | On this side Life, and lucky Chance ascends: | Loaded with Death, that other Scale descends.'

126. golden Scales: symbol of fate and of justice, as in 'Messiah', 18. Milton's God displays the 'golden Scales' of divine wisdom to weight the consequences of actions for the fate of the universe in *Paradise Lost*, IV.996–1005. Daly (2013: 343) points out that Pope's political epigram 'The Balance of *Europe*', 'Now Europe's balanc'd, neither Side prevails, | For nothing's left in either of the Scales', though not published until 1727, was sent in a letter to Caryll, 19 July 1711, i.e. just before the present poem was written (*Corr.*, I.130).

129. Wits ... subside: Milton's usage suggests the hair outweighs the wits and the women should win; but see the classical examples in the previous note.

131. Lightning: see Commentary to I.14 and II.113. 'Lightning' perhaps acquires something of the force of 'thunder', II.108.

132. Chief: the Baron, conceived as an epic warrior (cf. II. 153).

    unequal: because she is stronger. The phrase 'unequal Fight' here inverts the military occurrence at 'Episode of Sarpedon', 94; see Commentary there. The phrase 'Unequal Match' occurs in the disputed quatrain of 1705, 'On the Death of the Queen and Marshall Luxemburgh', ascribed to Pope in Nokes (1977).

133. on his Foe to die: a 'threadbare innuendo ... renewed' by its context in a battle (*TE*): 'to die' implies sexual climax, parodying heroic (actual) death on the battlefield. For the innuendo in action, cf. e.g. the 'Song' in IV.ii, Stanza II of Dryden's *Marriage a-la-Mode* (1673), p. 57: "Tis unkind to your Love, and unfaithfully done, | To leave me behind you, and die all alone'. This itself recalls Ovid, *Ars Amatoria*, II.725–6. Pope does not appear to use it outside these texts.

134. indu'd: endowed.

135. *TE*, II.111, sees Belinda's stratagem as drawn from a hand gesture by the 'trésorier' during the battle in Boileau's *Lutrin*, but the gesture of blessing is at some remove from Belinda's accurate discharge of powder.

136. Breath ... Nostrils: recalling the Baron's boast at II.55.

139. re-ecchoes ... Nose: The Baron sneezes loudly, in comic disparity with the 'high Dome' which suggests epic grandeur (cf.

140   Now meet thy Fate, th' incens'd Virago cry'd,
            And drew a deadly *Bodkin* from her Side.
            Boast not my Fall (he said) insulting Foe!
            Thou by some other shalt be laid as low.
            Nor think, to dye dejects my lofty Mind;
145   All that I dread, is leaving you behind!
            Rather than so, ah let me still survive,
            And still burn on, in *Cupid*'s Flames, *Alive.*

            Restore the Locke! she cries; and all around
            Restore the Locke! the vaulted Roofs rebound.

Essay on Criticism, 250); cf. also II.14. As *TE* points out, sneezing could be considered a lucky omen in classical times (e.g. *Odyssey*, XVII.624–5) in Pope's version.

140. Virago: Latin word meaning 'a female warriour; a woman with the qualities of a man' (*SJ*, citing this passage). *SJ* also notes: 'It is commonly used in detestation for an impudent turbulent woman'. Pope does not use the word outside the *Rape of the Lock* texts. Dryden uses the phrase 'fierce Virago' at least three times in the *Aeneid* translation, e.g. of the goddess Athena and of the warrior queen Camilla (whose speed Pope mentions in the *Essay on Criticism*, 373): Dryden, *Aeneid*, III.716; VII.1098 and XI.768.

141. Bodkin: see Commentary to II.16.

142. Boast not my Fall: an allusion to the dying speeches of warriors throughout the *Iliad*; see especially the exchanges at the death of Patroclus at the hands of Hector, *Iliad*, XVI.999–1021 in Pope's translation.

    insulting Foe: a common phrase in epic, re-used in Pope's version of the *Odyssey*, VIII.577–8; also close in verbal detail to Sandys' version of Psalm 13:13–14, *A Paraphrase vpon the Divine Poems* (1638), p. 15: 'Lest my insulting Foe | Boast in my overthrow' (and cf. p. 14 for a virtually identical formulation from Deuteronomy); but closer in tone to Dryden's 'To my Dear Friend Mr. Congreve', 74, in Congreve, *The Double Dealer* (1694), sig. a3ᵛ: 'Let not the Insulting Foe my Fame pursue'. Cf. also 'Episode of Sarpedon', 115 and 316, and Commentary.

145. *TE* cites the song from Dryden, *Marriage a la Mode*, quoted in Commentary at 133.

147. Cupid's Flames: the metaphorical flames of love.

148–9. Wasserman (1966) suggests a parody of Ovid, *Ars Amatoria*, III.449–50: 'Redde meum', clamant spoliatae saepe puellae, | 'Redde meum', toto voce boante foro' ('"Give me back my [cloak]", often the robbed girls cry, "Give me back my [cloak]"), their voice sounding over the whole forum'. The cloaks have been stolen by lovers. Wakefield sees the pattern of the couplet as modelled on Dryden, *Alexander's Feast*, 36 (1697), p. 2: 'A present Deity, they shout around: | A present Deity the vaulted Roofs rebound'; later itself echoed at Pope's *Ode for Musick*, 47–8.

148. Restore: give back; see Commentary to *Essay on Criticism*, 725. The political resonances of the word, in the light of the 'Restoration' of Charles II in 1660 and the 'Glorious Revolution' of 1688, which supplanted Charles's brother James, place special stress on Belinda's demand for the return of the sign of her power and integrity. Pope's own diversionary *A Key to the Lock* (1715), in which he posed as a zealous Whig, finding twisted examples of 'Popery' and Jacobite propaganda in the poem, parodied in advance the political readings of the poem which have pursued it ever since.

150   Not fierce *Othello* in so loud a Strain
      Roar'd for the Handkerchief that caus'd his Pain.
      But see! how oft Ambitious Aims are cross'd,
      And Chiefs contend 'till all the Prize is lost!
      The Locke, obtain'd with Guilt, and kept with Pain,
155   In ev'ry place is sought, but sought in vain:
      With such a Prize no Mortal must be blest,
      So Heav'n decrees! with Heav'n who can contest?

      Some thought, it mounted to the Lunar Sphere,
      Since all that Man e'er lost, is treasur'd there.
160   There Heroe's Wits are kept in pondrous Vases,

159.] Vid. Ariosto. Canto 34.

---

150. Othello: In Shakespeare's play, Othello demands that his wife Desdemona return to him a handkerchief the loss of which he takes as proof of her adultery. The play had been the subject of fierce criticism for this and other faults in Rymer's *A Short View of Tragedy* (1693), which argued that it might plausibly have been called the '*Tragedy of the Handkerchief*' (p. 135). In his own edition of *The Works of Shakespeare* (1725), VI.551, Pope calls some of Othello's incoherent raving about the handkerchief 'trash', blaming Shakespeare's actors for much of what he saw as bombast in the text. The reference here suggests that Belinda is protesting too much.

151. Roar'd: Othello is accused of roaring by Emilia in *Othello*, V.ii.197.

152. Ambitious Aims: cf. Blackmore's epic *King Arthur*, III (1697), p. 86: 'Call home my Armys who with fruitless toyl, | Pursue Ambitious Aims in Forreign Soil'. The destructive effects of rivalry for a single realm were the subject of 'The First Book of Statius his Thebais'.

155. TE compares *Iliad*, III.302 (of Pope's translation): 'Whom long my Eyes have sought, but sought in vain'.

157. TE compares Dryden, *The State of Innocence*, III.i (1677), p. 20: "Twas Heav'n; and who can Heav'n withstand?'

158. Lunar Sphere: the moon, or its orbit; Joseph Moxon's 'The Composition of the Whole Frame of the World', in *A Tutor to Astronomy and Geography* (1699), shows the Moon occupying the first of a series of concentric circles around the earth. Pope usually rhymes 'sphere' in this way; cf. II.184.

159 Pope's note. Pope cites a passage in Ariosto, *Orlando Furioso*, Canto XXXIV, stanzas 68–9, as his source for such images as male wits kept in vases (160), the broken vows and death-bed alms (162) and the courtiers' promises (164). Pope read Ariosto in his youth, and he owned and annotated a copy of Harington's translation (1591), supplying a manuscript title page to it (Mack 1982: 396). He probably also remembers here Milton, *Paradise Lost*, III.442–96, a cosmic '*Limbo*' beyond an outer 'Crystalline Sphear', which, in ridiculing especially Catholic idolatry, contributes some mock-epic element to his poem.

160-1. Heroes have enough 'wit' or intelligence to require heavy vases to keep them in; the wits of Beaus will fit into the snuffbox on which they have prided themselves (see II.41) or a tweezer-case. The deceased beau of *Tatler*, no. 113, 29 December 1709, has a tweezer-case 'containing twelve instruments for the use of each hour in the day', but is outdone by the 'virtuoso' of *Tatler*, no. 142, 7 March 1710, whose tweezer-case contains seventeen instruments 'all necessary every hour of the day during the whole course of man's life'. TE draws attention to the pronunciation of 'Vases' implied by the rhyme.

And Beau's in *Snuff-boxes* and *Tweezer-Cases*.
There broken Vows, and Death-bed Alms are found,
And Lovers Hearts with Ends of Riband bound;
The Courtiers Promises, and Sick Man's Pray'rs,
165   The Smiles of Harlots, and the Tears of Heirs,
Cages for Gnats, and Chains to Yoak a Flea;
Dry'd Butterflies, and Tomes of Casuistry.

But trust the Muse — she saw it upward rise,

---

162. Death-bed Alms: promises of charitable donations made in fear of death, as lightweight and useless as 'broken Vows'.

163. Riband: ribbon.

164-5. TE cites Dryden and Lee, *Oedipus*, III.i (1679), p. 42: 'The smiles of Courtiers, and the Harlots tears | The Tradesmans oaths, and mourning of an Heir'; these paradoxical images are similar to Rochester's examples of 'nothingness' in 'Upon Nothing', 49–50, which Pope had imitated in 'On Silence'.

164. Courtiers Promises: The promises of politicians and courtiers are similarly of no substance; cf. 'January and May', 156; 'On Silence', 38.

Sick Man's Pray'rs: Cf. the 'Death-bed Alms' of II.162; men in sickness pray with a zeal which has more to do with fear than with piety.

165. Smiles of Harlots: false, because paid for, as in Milton, *Paradise Lost*, IV.765–6 (1674), p. 107: 'the bought smile | Of Harlots'.

Tears of Heirs: hypocritical, like the grief of widows (cf. I.122) because the heir is glad to have inherited.

166. Cages . . . Flea: types of 'virtuoso' quasi-scientific project. TE compares the locust cage in Theocritus, *Idylls*, I.52. In *John Bull Still in his Senses*, second edition (1712), Arbuthnot (soon to be one of Pope's closest friends) satirises Presbyterians for their interest in impossible subjects of this kind: 'making Chains for Flea's, Nets for Flies, and Instruments to unravel Cobwebs, and split Hairs' (p. 14). Cf. also Edward Ward, *The Cock-Pit Combat* (1699), 28: 'He hopp'd to and fro, like a Flea in a Chain', and Shadwell, *A True Widow*, V (1679), p. 77, where Stanmore reads out 'A Copy of Verses upon a *Flea*, presented to his Mistress, in a gold Chain'.

167. Dry'd Butterflies: curiosities pursued by obsessive collectors, satirised in *Tatler*, no. 216, 26 August 1710. Often the subject of Pope's scepticism (e.g. *Essay on Criticism*, MS variant to 25–6; *Peri Bathous*, VI; *Dunciad*, IV.347–458;).

Tomes of Casuistry: Casuistry was the adaptation of abstract moral rules to deal with problematic individual cases, as in Joseph Hall's *Resolutions and Decisions of Divers Practicall Cases of Conscience in Continuall Use Amongst Men* (1654), but it had become associated with hair-splitting theological debate; cf. *Dunciad*, IV.28 and 642. See also Pope to Cromwell, 27 April 1708: 'I have nothing to say to you in this Letter; but I was resolv'd to write to tell you so. Why should not I content myself with so many great Examples, of deep Divines, profound Casuists, grave Philosophers; who have written, not Letters only, but whole Tomes and voluminous Treatises about Nothing?' (*Corr.*, I.48). Cf. 'January and May', 269.

168. trust the Muse: TE cites Watts, 'To Sarissa', 4–5, *Horae Lyricae*, second edition (1709), p. 175: 'Trust the muse, | She sings experience'd truth'.

Tho' mark'd by none but quick Poetic Eyes:
170 (Thus *Rome*'s great Founder to the Heav'ns withdrew,
To *Proculus* alone confess'd in view.)
A sudden Star, it shot thro' liquid Air,
And drew behind a radiant *Trail of Hair.*
Not *Berenice*'s Locks first rose so bright,
175 The Skies bespangling with dishevel'd Light.

---

169. quick Poetic Eyes: The eyes of the poet here recall those of Belinda, I.26. *TE* cites Denham, *Cooper's Hill*, 233-4, *Poems and Translations*, p. 14 (speaking of fairies, satyrs, and nymphs): 'their aery shape | All but a quick Poetick sight escape'.

170-1. 'Rome's great Founder' was Romulus in the legend Pope is citing. In order to quieten public anger against the senators, who were suspected of killing him, Proculus Julius announced that Romulus had descended in a vision to assert that he had been removed to heaven in a storm. The story is related with much sarcasm by the historian Livy, *The History of Rome*, I.xvi.

171. confess'd in: revealed to.

172-3. sudden Star ... Trail of Hair: a comet, named from the Greek word for hair (similarly, 'crines', which occurs in many of Pope's source poems, means both 'hair' and 'tail of a comet'). Belinda's lock is transfigured into something celestial in the process known as apotheosis. Warburton cited Ovid, *Metamorphoses*, XV.849-50, referring to the apotheosis of Caesar's soul: 'flammiferumque trahens spatioso limite crinem | stella micat' ('drawing a blazing trail over a large pathway it shines as a star'). Wakefield notes Ogilby's and particularly Dryden's versions of Virgil, *Georgics*, I.503, *Works of Virgil*, p. 64: 'And, shooting through the darkness, guild the Night | With weeping Glories, and long trails of Light'. Rowe's translation of the ninth book of Lucan opens with the cosmic transformation of the soul of Pompey: *Poetical Miscellanies: The Sixth Part*, pp. 51-2. A mock-heroic model is Garth, *Dispensary*, IV, sixth edition (1706), pp. 66-7, which has a sequence of aerial voyaging including meteors and a 'Trail of Light'. Cf. also 'The First Book of Statius his Thebais', 36 and 843-4; and 'Winter', 69-72.

172. liquid Air: As *TE* notes, 'liquid' here has the Latin sense of 'clear'; cf. Dryden, *Aeneid*, III.571; VI.758; IX.636, and similar instances in the translation of the *Georgics*. See Commentary to 'The First Book of Statius his Thebais', 415, and *Windsor-Forest*, 184.

174. Berenice: Egyptian queen, born c. 273 BC, wife (and second cousin) of Ptolemy III (Euergetes). A lock of Berenice's hair, voluntarily dedicated in the Pantheon at Alexandria as a pledge for her husband's safe return from battle, subsequently lost and alleged by a priest to have been transformed into a constellation known by her name, is the subject of a poem by the Greek poet Callimachus, preserved mostly in a Latin version by Catullus (*Carmina*, LXVI); cf. I.141 and II.86 above. In Catullus' poem (a gift to Quintus Hortensius Hortalus) the lock is the speaker, narrating Berenice's emotional responses to marriage and separation (emphasising the link between the cutting of hair, marriage rituals and the submission of wives). A version of the poem, and a fanciful narrative of its creation, had appeared in 1707 in *The Adventures of Catullus*, pp. 212-63. TE (II.116) suggests Pope knew Boileau's mocking version of the idea, 'La Métamorphose de la Perruque de Chapelain en Comète' (1664).

175. Skies bespangling: cf. Sir Edward Sherburne's version of *Medea* in *The Tragedies of L. Annaeus Seneca the Philosopher* (1702), p. 36: 'Whose Fires bespangle all the Skies'.

This, the *Beau-monde* shall from the *Mall* survey,
As thro' the Moon-light shade they nightly stray,
And hail with Musick its propitious Ray.
This *Partridge* soon shall view in cloudless Skies,
180   When next he looks thro' *Galilaeo*'s Eyes;
And hence th' Egregious Wizard shall foredoom
The Fate of *Louis*, and the Fall of *Rome*.

Then cease, bright Nymph! to mourn the ravish'd Hair
Which adds new Glory to the shining Sphere!

---

dishevel'd: loose; more normally associated with the hair of women, whether in a state of high emotion (as with Barberissa, in Ozell's *Lutrin*, p. 26) or as a sexual signal, as in the image of Eve in Milton's *Paradise Lost*, IV.304-6: 'Shee as a vail down to the slender waste | Her unadorned golden tresses wore | Dissheveld, but in wanton ringlets wav'd'. Addison satirises a lady's careful efforts to appear negligently 'in ... Disorder' (in both hair and dress) in *The Spectator*, no. 45, 21 April 1711.

176. Beau-monde: young people of fashion.

the Mall: a tree-lined walk through St James's Park, in front of S. James's Palace; originally designed for 'pall-mall', a type of croquet, it had become a place for people of fashion to congregate from the time of Charles II. *The Mall; or, The Modish Lovers* (1674), a comedy sometimes attributed to Dryden, is set around it. Joseph Browne's *The British Court: A Poem* (1707) described 'the most Celebrated Beauties at St. James's, the Park, and the Mall'. The park was strongly associated with Charles, as in Waller's *A Poem on St. James's Park as Lately Improved by his Majesty* (1661). The anonymous *St. James's Park, A Satyr* (1708), p. 13, mentions Arabella Fermor as a famous beauty, as does *The Mall: or, the Reigning Beauties* (1709), p. 11.

177. One of the few lines completely omitted by Pope from the 1714 version, possibly to diminish use of the triplet (cf. II.61 above).

178. hail with Musick: serenade.

propitious: cf. I.52.

179-82. In a note to Canto V of the 1736 edition of the revised poem, Pope commented 'John Partridge *was a ridiculous Star-gazer, who in his Almanacks every year, never fail'd to predict the downfall of the Pope, and the King of* France, then at war with the English'. Pope implies that Partridge's popularity as an astrologer was due in part to his anti-Catholic propaganda. Partridge had been the hapless object of some sophisticated hoaxing from Swift, in the 'Bickerstaff Papers' of 1708-9, echoed by Pope in *The Critical Specimen, PW*, I.16-17.

180. Galilaeo's Eyes: i.e. through a telescope, as modified and developed by the Italian astronomer Galileo Galilei (1564-1642) and publicised in his accounts of newly discovered moons, planets, and stars, e.g. *Sidereus Nuncius*, or 'Stellar Messenger' (1610); also mentioned by Milton, *Paradise Lost*, V.261-2.

181. Egregious: 'eminently bad; remarkably vicious' (*SJ*, citing this line and giving this negative sense as the 'usual' meaning; as Johnson notes, it can also mean 'Eminent; remarkable; extraordinary', in keeping with the double edge of the irony here).

Wizard: because Partridge behaves as if he had supernatural powers; for other evil 'wizard' figures see *Dunciad*, IV.517.

181-2. foredoom ... Rome: cf. I.69-70.

182. Louis: Louis XIV, with whose France Britain was still at war.

184. adds new Glory: TE compares Philips, *Pastorals*, III.74, *Poetical Miscellanies: The Sixth Part* (1709), p. 21: 'And add new

185   Not all the Tresses that fair Head can boast
      Shall draw such Envy as the Locke you lost.
      For, after all the Murders of your Eye,
      When, after Millions slain, your self shall die;
      When those fair Suns shall sett, as sett they must,
190   And all those Tresses shall be laid in Dust;
      This Locke, the Muse shall consecrate to Fame,
      And mid'st the Stars inscribe *Belinda*'s Name!

FINIS.

Glories to the *British* Name', and *The Mall*, p. 5: 'Since Nature gives her such a shining Ray | That adds fresh Lustre to the Beauteous Day'.

shining Sphere: the stars of the night sky. The pronunciation implied by the rhyme is common in Pope (cf. II.158–9); but he also rhymes it with 'year' (*Epistle to a Lady*, 283–4). Cf. William Cleland, 'Effigies Clericorum', *A Collection of Several Poems and Verses* (1697), p. 75: 'The Sun had not sing'd *Phaetons* hair, | Had he not walk'd beyond his sphere'.

187–8. Murders... slain: see Commentary to II.113, and also Pope's jocular comment to Cromwell, 21 December 1711 (*Corr.*, I.138): 'Sh[all] I write of *Beauties murderd long ago*, when there are those at this [in]stant that *murder me*?'.

189. Suns: Belinda's eyes (cf. I.14), which will eventually 'sett' in death.

190. Dust: the ashes of the grave. Pope returned to this rhyme and idea in his *Iliad*, XX.385–6.

191–2. TE cites several sources for this idea, the closest of which is Cowley's version of Horace, *Odes*, IV.2, *The Poems of Horace... Rendred in English Verse by Several Persons* (1666), p. 136: 'He bids him live, and grow in fame, | Among the Stars he sticks his name'

191. This Locke: the poem by which the Muse (I.3) will 'consecrate' or convert it to a holy relic of fame or reputation.

15

ON A FAN OF THE AUTHOR'S DESIGN
(1712)

Editors' Headnote

Composition and publication

'On a Fan of the Author's Design' was first published on 4 November 1712. The poem appeared anonymously in Addison and Steele's *The Spectator*, no. 527, towards the end of the periodical's life (it ceased on 6 December). Ault (*PW*, I) ascribes to Pope twelve contributions to the periodical, of which this would be the eleventh. The authorship of the poem was acknowledged by its inclusion in Pope's *Works* of 1717. There is no direct evidence for the date of the poem's composition. In the third volume of the *Works* of 1736, Pope collected a group of nine short poems (first published separately between 1717 and 1727) together under the title 'IMITATIONS OF *ENGLISH* POETS'; in the *Works* of 1741 'On a Fan' was added to this group, whereby it acquired its identity as an imitation of Waller. The 'Advertisement' in the 1736 *Works* states that the '*Imitations* of *English Authors* [. . .] were done [. . .] some of them at fourteen or fifteen Years old', and the title page to the group adds the note 'Done by the AUTHOR in his Youth'. Five other imitations of Waller (and one of Cowley) that Pope published in his anonymous 1717 miscellany, *Poems on Several Occasions*, are there designated as '*By a Youth of thirteen*' (Ault 1935). These indications, if accurate, would place drafts of this type of prentice work in about 1701–3. Pope quotes three lines of Waller in a discussion of pauses in verse lines in a purported letter to Walsh of 22 October 1706 (*Corr.*, I.23); though the date of this is uncertain, it is certain that Pope had a strong sense of Waller's style by this time. On 21 August 1712 (*Corr.*, I.97) he sent to Cromwell 'some Verses of my Youth, or rather Childhood; which (as I was a great admirer of Waller) were intended in Imitation of his Manner'; in the next letter (12 October, *Corr.*, I.98) it appears that Cromwell has been scanning Waller for Pope's models, without success; but this exchange could refer to any of the 'Waller' set.

Text

The text presented here is taken from the first edition of 1712. Revision is confined to the *Works* of 1717. The various extant texts of 'On a Fan of the Author's Design' are referred to in the apparatus as follows:

1712: *The Spectator*, Number 527, 4 November 1712

1717: *Works*, quarto (Griffith 79)

1741: *Works*, vol.I, part II, octavo (Griffith 521)

1751: *Works*, vol.II, octavo (Griffith 644)

Models and sources

Pope's ultimate source is Ovid. He had already published 'Sapho to Phaon' from Ovid's *Heroides* earlier in 1712; see Headnote to that poem for his appreciation of the Roman poet. Cephalus, who features in 'On a Fan', is mentioned in line 97 of that poem; Procris is a mournful shade in Homer's *Odyssey* (XI.395 in Pope's version). The story which Pope summarises in 'On a Fan' is originally told, with an extensive back-narrative of mutual sexual jealousy, by the remorseful Cephalus himself in Ovid, *Metamorphoses*, VII.672–865; a translation of this section, by Nahum Tate, had appeared in *Poetical Miscellanies: The Fifth Part* (1704), pp. 389–400. A shorter version, more concentrated on the scene in the wood which is Pope's direct topic, is in Ovid's *Ars Amatoria*, III.687–746. The story was therefore well known from the Latin originals and from the many translations of Ovid, from Arthur Golding's *Metamorphoses* (1567) and the two variant versions by George Sandys (1626 and 1632) onwards. Pope in 1743 confessed to having 'liked extremely' Sandys' translations as a boy (*OAC*, I.14), though he also used him as a satiric reference point in the ballad 'Sandys Ghost'. Translations of the *Ars Amatoria* were known from about 1625, in rather clandestine versions, and from 1661 in a more overt publication by Francis Wolferston (*The Three Books of... De Arte Amandi... Translated*; the story is on pp. 76–7). Pope's friend Congreve's translation of book III of *Ars Amatoria* had recently appeared in a Tonson-published translation *Ovid's Art of Love. In Three Books* (1709), which Pope probably owned and annotated (Mack 1982: 433) There was also a burlesque version of the *Ars Amatoria* by William King (1708; see pp. 191–5), and the story had previously been mentioned comically in the mechanicals' play in Shakespeare's *A Misdummer Night's Dream* (V.i.197–8). Several contintental editions of Ovid had plates showing the death scene; it was a popular subject for artists, and there were notable sixteenth- and seventeenth-century paintings of the story by, among others, Correggio, Paolo Veronese, Rubens, Claude Lorrain and Poussin. The Mortlake Tapestry Factory, which closed in 1703, had produced a tapestry illustrating the scene. Separate poetic interpretations of the subject include Thomas Howell's 'The Lamentable Historie of Sephalus, with the Unfortunat End of Procris', in *Newe Sonets, and Pretie Pamphlets* (1568), and Thomas Edwards, *Cephalus & Procris* (1595). It formed the ninth story in George Pettie's prose collection *A Petite Pallace of Pettie his Pleasure* (1576). Charles Hopkins, *The History of Love* (1695), pp. 32–47, and John Hopkins, *Amasia, or, The Works of the Muses* (1700), pp. 47–52, both contained verse versions of the episode. There was more than one seventeenth-century opera on the subject; the most recent, by Elisabeth Jacquet de la Guerre, had been staged at Paris in 1694.

The folding fan, often with a scene painted on it, had become a popular item of female accoutrement by the end of the seventeenth century. In *The Tatler*, no. 52, 9 August 1709, the exercise of the painted fan in a system of sexual intrigue was lengthily described by 'Delamira'; in *The Spectator*, no. 102, 27 June 1711, Addison wrote a further satirical key to the use of the fan in such circumstances. Hopkins's *Amasia* has several poems such as 'To Amasia, playing with a clouded fan', which makes much the same sort of erotic play of the instrument as Pope's poem. 'To Lucinda Fanning her Self', in Tate's *Poems by Several Hands* (1685), p. 244, is an early example. (For Pope's poem in relation to the 'early eighteenth-century thing-poem' of this type, see Benedict 2007.) In *The Tatler*, no. 239, 19 October 1710, there appears an untitled set of verses, on Flavia's flirtatious use of the fan, in a vein very similar to Pope's, and probably his main model. The verses had appeared anonymously as 'Written in the Leaves of a Fan' in *Examen Poeticum* (1693), p. 377:

> *FLAVIA* the least and slightest Toy
> Can, with resistless *Art*, employ.
> This Fan, in meaner Hands, wou'd prove
> An Engine, of small Force, in Love.
> Yet she, with graceful *Air* and *Meen*,
> (Not to be told! or safely seen!)
> Directs its wanton Motions so,
> That it wounds more than *Cupid's Bow*:
> Gives Coolness to the matchless Dame,
> To ev'ry other *Breast* a Flame.

The poem was firmly identified as 'Epigram by Bp. Atterbury; Written on a White Fan borrowed from Miss Osborne, afterwards his Wife', in John Nichols's *Select Collection of Poems* (1782), V.1–3, by which time the poem had been widely attributed to the Bishop.

Atterbury had edited *The Second Part of Mr Waller's Poems* (1690), adding an important and influential Preface on the elegance of Waller's verse, especially couplets, compared with previous writing. He discussed Waller in letters to Pope of 12 September 1718 and 27 September 1721 (*Corr.*, I.503, II.84). As Pope's late addition of Waller's name suggests, the 'imitation' of the style is not particularly exact. After Waller's death, in the year before Pope's birth, Tonson bought up copyright in his *Poems*, issuing seventh, eighth and ninth editions of them in 1705, 1711 and 1712. In about 1728, Spence noted that 'Waller, Spenser, and Dryden were Mr. Pope's great favourites in the order they are named, in his first reading till he was about twelve', i.e. 1700 or so (*OAC*, I.19; Spence was not certain of the order). Pope's stated fondness for Waller often relates to his 'smooth' or 'sweet' versification, as signalled in the *Essay on Criticism*, 365. Pope made several remarks to Spence in this connection, and in the last year of his life listed Waller as one of nine 'authorities for poetical language' (*OAC*, I.171; see also I.176, 194, 196–7). Waller was also one of Pope's obvious models for a public or civic mode of poetry in *Windsor-Forest*. Pope quotes Waller in a letter to Steele, 15 July 1712 (*Corr.*, I.147) and makes several approving mentions of him in later works, as well as in the notes to the various versions of *The Dunciad*. At one point, it appears, Pope may have been asked by Tonson to edit the poet, though in the event the job was done by Pope's colleague on the Homer translations, Elijah Fenton (see Pope to Tonson, 3 September

1721, and to Edward Harley, 3 April 1726, *Corr.*, II.80, 374; and Fenton to William Broome, 12 March and 28 September 1729, *Corr.*, III.24, 55).

On 4 August 1738, Pope told Spence:

> No writing is good that does not tend to better mankind some way or other. Mr. Waller has said that 'he wished everything of his burnt that did not drive some moral.' Even in love-verses it may be flung in by the way.
>
> (*OAC*, I.196)

For the present poem, Pope claims (retrospectively, from 1741) an allegiance with the mildly erotic grace of Waller's 'love-verses', moralistic or otherwise. In 'Spring', 45–6, his 'Strephon' had appealed for the power of Waller's verse in singing the praises of his 'Delia', and his set of 'Verses in Imitation of Waller', not including this one, in his covertly edited anthology, *Poems on Several Occasions* (1717), are in much this vein. The editions of Waller that Pope had available in 1712 mingled his political and public poems with his cavalier lyrics to ideal ladies such as Phillis, Amoret and Sacharissa. These latter had been specially commended in Addison's 'Account of the Greatest English Poets' 90–3, in *The Annual Miscellany: For the Year 1694* (1694), p. 323:

> While tender Airs and lovely Dames inspire
> Soft melting Thoughts, and propagate Desires; [*sic*]
> So long shall *Waller's* strains our Passion move,
> And *Sacharissa's* Beauties kindle Love.

Waller did not mention fans, which were a later feature of amorous play, but Pope's poem is to some extent in the manner of his 'On my Lady Isabella playing on the Lute', in *Poems* (1645), pp. 78–9. Waller wrote a few other lyrics with objects and women at their centre such as 'On a Girdle' (*ibid.*, p. 95); 'To a Lady from whom he received a Silver Pen' (pp. 34–5); and 'On a brede of divers colours, woven by foure Ladyes' (p. 35). His 'The Story of Phoebus and Daphne appli'd' (p. 32) is very loosely in the tradition of the *Metamorphoses*. Pope was not the only admirer of Waller: Dryden publicly recalled being encouraged to imitate him ('A Discourse Concerning the Original and Progress of Satire', the dedicatory epistle to *The Satires of Decimus Junius Juvenalis* (1693), p. l), and John Oldmixon's *Amores Britannici* (1703), pp. 131–41, contained an epistle, 'Mr Waller to the Countess of Carlisle', supposedly in Waller's style of amorous entreaty.

Context

The 'Lady' of whom Pope is writing in the poem is sometimes (e.g. Ault 1949: 74) asserted to have been Martha Blount (for whom see Headnote to 'To a Young Lady, with the Works of Voiture', above), but there is no evidence that Pope had any particular 'Delia' in mind or that any real event is being recorded. To the extent that it has any biographical significance, the poem forms part of that phase of the 1710s in which

Pope characterised himself in private letters to Cromwell and Wycherley and in some carefully released poems as subject to 'normal' masculine pursuits and rakish desires, in part as a response to the attacks on his physical incapacity from people like Dennis (see Rumbold 1989: chapter 3). Like Chaucer, Ovid offered a relatively safe literary authority for amorous narrative or displays of erotic passion. While the pose of despairing lover is common enough, the inversion of the Ovidian story, where the woman is killed by the gift she has given her husband, to the situation in which the male lover 'dies' as a result of the 'weapon' given to and handled by the woman, is striking. Procris had been one of Diana's huntress nymphs, and the melancholy aspects of the story place it in some connection with the vulnerable sylvan world of *Windsor-Forest* (1713), in which hunting accidents are aligned with distructively misplaced sexual energies.

Pope's (anonymous) introductory letter does not say that he had painted the fan himself, but Ault (1949: 74) records the story that Sir Joshua Reynolds came into possession of an actual fan (now lost) on which, it was asserted, Pope had indeed illustrated the story. Reynolds described the artwork as 'such as might be expected from one who painted for his amusement alone; like the performance of a child'. Pope did not begin taking lessons from the professional artist Charles Jervas until 1713.

The poem attracted little attention in Pope's lifetime. Having drawn on some of the lightly satirical or gallant material in his sources in arming his nymphs with fans in 'The Rape of the Locke' (1712), the extended five-canto versions of 1714 and 1717 probably derive some small impetus from the present lyric. Pope's friend Gay, in the mock-didactic poem *The Fan* (1713), perhaps drew something from this shorter poem of Pope's, as it tells the story of Cephalus and Procris at III.83–92 (pp. 26–7). Pope apparently wrote to Gay about the progress of *The Fan* on 23 August and 23 October 1713 (*Corr.*, I.188, 195; the date of the letters is uncertain, but the poem appeared on 8 December). Pope's poem was reprinted in *The London Magazine*, X (June 1741), 304, with a translation into Latin, and on the last page of *Joe Miller's Jests*, fifth edition (1742); this anthology also printed (p. 145) the Atterbury verses noted above, signalling the status of each as a light, occasional piece. It was included with a new illustration and other material in *The Universal Magazine*, LXXI (1782), 24–6.

Mr. SPECTATOR,

YOU will oblige a languishing Lover, if you will please to print the enclosed Verses in your next Paper. If you remember the *Metamorphosis*, you know *Procris*, the fond Wife of *Cephalus*, is said to have made her Husband, who delighted in the Sports of the Wood, a Present of an unerring Javelin. In Process of Time he was so much in the Forest, that his Lady suspected he was pursuing some Nymph, under the Pretence of following a Chace more innocent. Under this Suspicion she hid herself among the Trees to observe his Motions. While she lay concealed, her Husband, tired with the Labour of Hunting, came within her Hearing. As he was fainting with Heat, he cryed out, *Aura veni*; *Oh charming Air approach.*

The unfortunate Wife, taking the Word *Air* to be the Name of a Woman, began to move among the Bushes, and the Husband believing it a Deer, threw his Javelin and killed her. This History painted on a Fan, which I presented to a Lady, gave Occasion to my growing poetical.

Come gentle Air! th' Eolian *Shepherd said,*
While Procris *panted in the secret Shade;*

Title. *1717–51: On a FAN of the Author's design, in which was painted the story of* Cephalus *and* Procris, *with the Motto,* Aura veni.

---

languishing Lover: a well-worn dramatic and romance posture, imitating e.g. Ramble in John Crowne, *The Countrey Wit*, IV.i (1675), p. 61: 'charming Creature, if you have any pity in your soul, save the life of a poor languishing Lover'.

fond: 'foolishly tender' (*SJ*).

1–2. The *shade/said* rhyme was evidently acceptable: Oldham uses it at 13–14 of 'A Satyr. The Person of Spencer is brought in . . .'; Pope reuses it at *Odyssey*, XVI.432–3.

1. Come gentle Air!: translating Cephalus' fatal 'aura, veni', Ovid, *Metamorphoses*, VII.837 and *Ars Amatoria*, III.698. The word 'gentle' is supplied from the surrounding sense of Ovid's lines, or perhaps recalls 'molles', 'soft', from another invocation by Cephalus to the breezes, *Metamorphoses*, VII.728; Pope's '*charming Air*', in his letter, is likewise an expansion.

Eolian Shepherd: The cult of Cephalus was in Attica, and in book VII of the *Metamorphoses*, where he tells his story (672–865) he is clearly an Athenian envoy; but Ovid (VI.681) introduces him as 'Aeolides', the grandson of Aeolus. The Aeolian tribe and dialect were also associated with a region of northern Greece normally referred to as Thessaly, much featured in the first part of book VII of the *Metamorphoses*. As Aeolus was also god of the winds, Pope perhaps intends an allusion to the miniature movement of the 'gales' here. Cephalus was a hunter, not a shepherd.

Come gentle Air! the fairer Delia *cries,*
While at her Feet her Swain expiring lies.
5 *Lo the glad Gales o'er all her Beauties stray,*
Breathe on her Lips, and in her Bosom play.
In Delia's *Hand this Toy is fatal found,*
Nor did that fabled Dart more surely wound.
Both Gifts destructive to the Givers prove,
10 *Alike both Lovers fall by those they love:*
Yet guiltless too this bright Destroyer lives,
At Random wounds, nor knows the Wounds she gives:
She views the Story with attentive Eyes,
And pities Procris *while her Lover dies.*

---

8. did: *1717–51:* could
12. wounds: *1717–51:* wound

---

3. Delia: conventional name for a pastoral nymph, as in 'Spring', 45–6, where she is connected with Waller; from Latin usage, e.g. the amorously despairing *Elegies* of Tibullus; also idealised in the sonnet collection *Delia* of Samuel Daniel (1592).

5. glad: 'pleasing; exhilarating' (*SJ*); perhaps also suggesting the animation of the wind as caused by the erotic pleasure of the caress.

Gales: caused, mock-epic fashion, by the fan, the 'Toy' of 7; but in the period the word had a milder suggestion than it does now: 'a wind not tempestuous, yet stronger than a breeze' (*SJ*). Milton uses the phrase 'gentle gales | Fanning', *Paradise Lost*, IV.156–7 (1674), p. 90. Cf. 'Summer', 73, and the refrain in 'Autumn', beginning at 17; *Windsor-Forest*, 101; 'Gardens of Alcinous', 11.

7–8. For the acceptability of the rhyme in seventeenth-century verse, cf. 'Episode of Sarpedon', 113–14 and 'Sapho to Phaon', 129–30, and Commentary.

7. Toy: 'plaything, bauble, petty commodity, thing of no value' (*SJ*); see the first line of the 'Flavia' poem cited in the Headnote.

8. fabled Dart: the infallible hunting spear or 'unerring Javelin' of Pope's letter; for 'Dart' in hunting cf. *Windsor-Forest*, 83, 178.

11. bright Destroyer: a phrase normally found in epic guise, e.g. Blackmore, *King Arthur*, IX (1697), p. 244: 'Realms to Destruction doom'd, th'bright Destroyer wasts'.

16
WINDSOR-FOREST
(1713)

Editors' Headnote

Composition and publication

Windsor-Forest was first published on 7 March 1713. As with several other poems, Pope gave differing accounts of the circumstances of the poem's composition. The first portion of the surviving autograph manuscript fair copy probably dating from late 1712 – consisting of the first 380 lines of the earliest extant version of the poem (held in the Washington University Library and reproduced in Schmitz 1952) – includes an autograph note (clearly written some years later) in which Pope distinguishes two principal periods of composition: the first part written 'after ye Pastorals', with the last hundred lines added 'soon after' the Treaty of Utrecht, which brought an end to the War of the Spanish Succession. The unreliability of this note is clear from the hesitation over supplying precise dates (see the variants to Pope's annotation below) and the fact that the Treaty was not ratified, and its terms not finalised, until July of 1713, by which time *Windsor-Forest* had already been published. In the version of the manuscript note that Pope added to the poem in 1736, he stated that the first part was written in 1704 and the latter in 1710. In 1751 this second date, an obvious error, was changed to read 1713. Pope had certainly completed a version of the poem by 1707, when it is mentioned by Pope's friend the Reverend Ralph Bridges in a letter of 28 October to his uncle, Sir William Trumbull, who is named in the poem and who was evidently one of its early sponsors (Sherburn 1958a: 343; *TE* I.126); Bridges writes that Pope intended that either *Windsor-Forest* or one of the *Pastorals* would be dedicated to Trumbull. Writing on 12 May 1713, Trumbull claimed to have 'put [Pope] upon this subject' and to have helped revise it, as with the *Pastorals* (Sherburn 1958a: 345–6; *TE*, I.126; Rogers 2005a: 11). However, Lansdowne (Granville as he then was) was probably also one of the early readers of the poem in manuscript. In June 1739, Pope told Spence 'Lord Lansdowne insisted on my publishing my *Windsor Forest*, and the motto shoes it (*Non injussa cano*)' (*OAC*, I, 43; see notes to Epigraph and 5 below).

A gap (between pp. 320 and 352) in the collation of Lintot's *Miscellaneous Poems and Translations* (1712) has been taken as evidence that Pope originally intended to publish *Windsor-Forest* (together with the *Ode for Musick*) in that collection (Ault 1959; *TE*, I.128). The poem was indeed subsequently included in the 1714 edition of *Miscellaneous Poems* and the crowding of lines in this text (21 to a page rather than 18 elsewhere in the volume) has again been taken as evidence of late additions to the earlier version.

However, as Foxon (1991: 34–7) has shown, this hypothesis rests on a misreading of the evidence – the catchword 'The' on signature X8^V (p. 320), which immediately precedes 'The Rape of the Locke', fits perfectly with that poem but with neither *Windsor-Forest* nor the *Ode*. It remains possible, perhaps even likely, that Pope intended to publish *Windsor-Forest* in the 1712 *Miscellaneous Poems*, but it would have occupied a different set of signatures and any inferences about the possible scale of late additions to the text are therefore without foundation.

Pope's correspondence does provide evidence about some of the later revisions he made to the poem. On 29 November 1712 he wrote to John Caryll, quoting a version of 385ff. (see textual apparatus below), and setting out the problem of possible echoes of Thomas Tickell's recent *On the Prospect of Peace*, which had been published in October 1712 (*Corr.*, I.157). A week later, on 5 December, Pope told Caryll that the poem had undergone much revision since Caryll had seen it and that the revised version had not been shown to anyone (*Corr.*, I.162); further mention is made in a letter of 21 December, when Pope is struck by the irony of writing 'a painted scene of woods and forests in verdure and beauty' (that is, some of the earlier passages in the poem) in the middle of winter (*Corr.*, I.168). On 10 January 1713 Pope wrote to Lansdowne to thank him for permission to dedicate *Windsor-Forest* to him, and to ask him to exercise a 'free correction' over the verses (*Corr*, I.172).

Eventually, on 23 February, Bernard Lintot paid Pope £32 5s for the copyright, and the poem was published as a 20-page folio on 7 March 1713, his second separately printed poem (after the *Essay on Criticism*) and the first with his name on the title page of the first edition.

Text

The text presented here is taken from the first edition of 1713. All substantive variant readings from the first version of the text embodied in the manuscript fair copy have been recorded in the textual apparatus. Beyond the first edition, significant verbal revision is confined to three later texts: the *Works* of 1717, 1736 (which also embody considerable expansions in editorial apparatus, particularly the recording of variant readings), and 1751. The various extant texts of *Windsor-Forest* are referred to in the apparatus as follows:

MSw: 'Windsor-Forest' (lines 1–390: Washington University Library, no shelfmark; reproduced in Schmitz 1952; *IELM* PoA 376)

MSh: (lines 391–434: Houghton Library, fMS Eng.1336(1); reproduced in Mack 1985; *IELM* PoA 377)

Letter from Pope to Caryll, 29 November 1712 (lines 379ff: British Library, Add. MS 28618, f. 34; *IELM* PoA 378)

1713: *Windsor-Forest*, First Edition, folio (Griffith 9)

1717: *Works*, quarto (Griffith 79)

1720: *Miscellaneous Poems and Translations*, vol.I, duodecimo (Griffith 124)

1722: *Miscellaneous Poems and Translations*, vol.I, duodecimo (Griffith 135)

1726: *Miscellany Poems*, vol.I, duodecimo (Griffith 164)

1736: *Works*, vol.I, octavo (Griffith 413, 414)

1740: *Works*, vol.I, part I, octavo (Griffith 510)

1743: *Works*, vol.I, part I, octavo (Griffith 582)

1751: *Works*, vol.I, octavo (Griffith 643)

Models and sources

As scholarly work on the poem since the late eighteenth century suggests, *Windsor-Forest* is one of Pope's most densely and consciously allusive poems, steeped in the language and mythology not only of Virgil and Ovid and their seventeenth-century translators and imitators but of Spenser and the Elizabethan poets of English nationalism, as well as Stuart masques, triumphal pageants and the more hermetic codes of alchemy, heraldry and antiquarian lore. The poem has no single source and belongs to no single genre. In its pointed closing allusion to the earlier *Pastorals*, it ought to be a georgic (or didactic poem on agriculture), since Virgil moved from pastoral to georgic and then on to epic, as Pope was soon to do with the translation of Homer's *Iliad*. Pope indeed often echoes the *Georgics* (and other poems) by Virgil; the poem's broad relation to the tradition is discussed in Chalker (1969: 72–88). The *Georgics* had appeared in Dryden's illustrated translation of *The Works of Virgil* (1697), which enjoyed the patronage of many of Pope's mentors, including Henry St John (by 1713, Viscount Bolingbroke) and Trumbull, as also the future Queen Anne. It also featured an influential essay on georgic theory by Addison, who by 1713 had become the leading Whig writer of the day, and at least notionally a friendly acquaintance of Pope's. English georgic models included John Philips's *Cyder* (1708), which combined rural detail with a directly Tory slant on history, and Gay's *Wine* (1708). Gay's *Rural Sports*, issued just before Pope's poem in 1713 (13 January) and heavily revised in the wake of it, has sections on fishing and hare-coursing similar to those in *Windsor-Forest* (and much praise of Anne's peace-giving qualities, suitable to the moment; see Rogers 2005a: 65). Pope also derived some seasonal and rural lore from Spenser's *Shephearde's Calender* (1579) as well as from guidebooks such as Izaak Walton's *The Compleat Angler* (1653, revised 1655 and several times reprinted and elaborated). Walton's book included many poems on fishing, and there were specific 'georgics' on the subject, such as *The Innocent Epicure: or, the Art of Angling* (1697) by 'J. S', with a preface by Nahum Tate. Among the extensive literature of hunting, Pope was probably aware of Nicholas Cox, *The Gentleman's Recreation, in Four Parts* (1674), which could have been a source additional to direct observation.

The aspect of georgic on which Pope draws most heavily is not that of practical agriculture or hunting practice but a mythological sense of the land as template for the national destiny. Virgil's poem and its successors provided him with models of a ravaged landscape, its tenants dispossessed and evicted, recovering from civil war under benign leadership: a golden age lost and perhaps to be restored. Georgic also proposes the virtues of hunting as a civilised channel for warlike energies, and offers pliable myths of Ceres (Demeter) as a nurturing mother-goddess celebrating the return of a ravished daughter (Rogers 2005a: chapter 7). Pope also drew on the political and prophetic aspects of Virgil's *Aeneid* to colour his poem, especially in the prophecy of Britain's future greatness uttered by the personified River Thames, which is aligned with the Tiber of Imperial Rome, lauded by Virgil in *Aeneid*, book VIII. Pope was certainly aware of later Latin authors such as Claudian (author of panegyrics on the consul Honorius; see Rogers 2004: 184–9) and Ausonius, whose poem *Mosella* celebrates the river Moselle in ways which bear on Pope's presentation of the Thames. The controversial 'Lodona' episode, which ends with the transformation of the pursued nymph into a river, is conspicuously modelled on a catalogue of similar stories in Ovid's *Metamorphoses* (especially those of Syrinx, Arethusa, Daphne, Callisto, and Acis and Galatea). These well-known episodes were given still wider currency in grand mythological paintings (Rogers 2004: 69–72). Ovid's story of the punishment of Erisichthon for destroying a sacred grove (*Metamorphoses*, book VIII) has also been presented (Rogers 2005a: 270) as a likely reference point for Pope's depiction of the vulnerability of the British forest to the incursions of an outsider. The prophecy of a restored golden age, from 279 onwards, is reinforced by the biblical weight of Isaiah 60, which Pope had already spliced with Virgil's fourth *Eclogue* in his 'Messiah', with which, as Rogers (2004: 207–9) indicates, the poem shares many aspects of phrasing (it is in some ways a second version or commentary on that prophecy). The catalogue of subjugated vices and the allegorical figures of envy, discord and so on (411–20) has several classical models, particularly in the *Aeneid* and the *Georgics*, and most of the figures had become standard artistic and iconographic images by the Renaissance.

Pope had certainly read very closely verse myths of Britishness, such as Edmund Spenser's *Faerie Queene* (1590–6) and Michael Drayton's collection of song-narratives, *Poly-Olbion* (1612), and drew on them for much scenic detail of forests, rivers, and hunting, much of it specifically involving the Thames and Windsor, as well as predominantly female monarchic mystique. The most conspicuous model for the presentation of the Thames itself, for example, is Spenser, *Faerie Queene*, IV.xi. Rogers (2004) argues that the poem works additionally like a version of the ritualistic and allegorical court masque of Stuart tradition that Anne would have remembered from her early life, and that it adopts related architectural and iconographic postures and imagery of a kind recorded from the reign of James I, in work by Ben Jonson, Thomas Carew and Inigo Jones. Rogers also aligns the poem with triumphal pageants such as the one staged for the entry of James I to London in 1604, written by Jonson, with much detail indicating the closeness of Pope's prophecy, in the mouth of the river god Thames, of Britain's future supremacy, to this form of public celebration.

A good deal of historical information, and some of the heraldic and mythological pageantry, especially regarding Windsor, the Order of the Garter, and the Norman kings, was evidently drawn from William Camden's *Britannia*, originally published in Latin in 1586 and magnificently republished by Edmund Gibson in 1695 with an English translation and various supplements. *Britannia* also includes large fragments of a long poem about rivers, *De Connubio Tamae et Isis*, in which the Thames and Isis combine as the centre of a national myth (Rogers 2004: 124–37). Rogers (2004: 88–107) makes a strong case for an underlying 'armorial narrative' or heraldic colouring to the imagery of the poem, drawn from the set codes of the College of Arms and involving strong unmixed coloration (azure, sable, and so on – but not orange, which would connote the outsider William III, of Orange). Pope's particular interest in painting also dates from 1713, when he studied with Charles Jervas, but largely post-dated the composition of the poem, and was more directed towards portraiture. The poem, however, does reflect the mythological and allegorical typologies of grand narrative art as exemplified by Rubens and Poussin; the account in Ault (1949) is greatly updated by Rogers (2004).

The poem with which Pope's has always been most often compared is Sir John Denham's *Cooper's Hill*, a topographic poem published near the opening of civil war hostilities in 1642 but much revised up to Denham's death (in 1669) as the political situation was transformed (see the variorum edition by O Hehir 1969). Pope shares with Denham the sense that the landscape is imbued with historical and political significance, a feature he noted with approval in a note to XVI.466 of his translation of the *Iliad*. Notionally based on the view from a small hill near the poet's home at Egham in Surrey, *Cooper's Hill* surveys a metaphorical landscape of English political history. Pope took unusual pains to study the revisions to Denham's poem (see *OAC*, I.194–5) and *Windsor-Forest* foregrounds this poetic model at various points, noted in the Commentary. Cooper's stag-hunt, open to reading as an allegory of political persecution, was for instance a useful point of departure for Pope's poem (though far from the only model, since there are descriptions of the hunt in Virgil, *Aeneid* IV and elsewhere). Denham uses his point of vantage in the landscape to identify the City of London as politically offensive, and gradually retreats to the politically charged site overlooking the plain of Runnymede, where Magna Carta was signed (a fact conspicuously not recalled in Pope's poem, probably because of its prominent use in Whig political discourse). Pope's poem begins with the equally freighted royal seat and preserve at Windsor, but voyages the other way, along the Thames and out into the world, moving from troubled past into an apparently secure future of *Pax Britannica*.

Pope derives images more obliquely from the republican Milton, appropriating landscape imagery from *Paradise Lost* – not least to suggest a sort of Royalist *Paradise Regain'd*. Dryden, both as translator of Virgil and exponent of pro-Stuart panegyric (*Annus Mirabilis*, *Astraea Redux*, both written in praise of the redemptive and divine qualities of Charles II, a restored king from over the water), is present as a model of phrasing and tutelary idea throughout the poem; resemblances between Pope's attitude to the war and Dryden's covert assaults on William III in several of his *Fables Ancient and Modern* (1700) have also been identified (see Miller 1979). Pope cites various poets by name during the poem, including Edmund Waller and Abraham Cowley, both royalist writers whom Pope admired and imitated in early work. Cowley's prose essay 'Of

Solitude' is one of the many texts underlying the section on virtuous retirement and study (235–56). Cowley's botanical poem *Sex Libri Plantarum* (1668) provided much symbolic Royalist lore relating to forests and the land, especially the oak. This tree also features largely in John Evelyn's book *Sylva* (1664), written to provide a survey of the strength of Britain's forest stock for the use of the navy; Evelyn associated depredations on the forests with Cromwell's commonwealth in a way which was suggestive for Pope. Other royalist verse panegyrics with topographical focus include Waller's *A Poem on St. James's Park* (1661) and Thomas Otway's celebratory poem *Windsor Castle* (1685), published as a memorial to Charles II.

As for living poets, Pope offers poet-to-patron praise of Lansdowne, himself at that point a poet of some repute, which did not outlive him much (Johnson's short biography of him witheringly despatches most of the verse as obsessed with the 'puerilities of mythology'; Lonsdale, III.107). Lansdowne was one of only three living people (the others being Queen Anne and Sir William Trumbull) mentioned in the poem, which otherwise strives to transcend the local details of political struggle in favour of mythic resolution (see Winn 2014: 602–6). But Pope was acutely aware of other rivals on the scene. There are echoes of Addison's classical tour in verse, 'A Letter from Italy' (1701), and his *Remarks on Several Parts of Italy, &c. in the years 1701, 1702, 1703* (1705) translates various pieces of relevant verse, including the panegyrics of Claudian. More particularly, however, Pope's poem was written during the ascendancy of public, declamatory verse generally known as *Poems on Affairs of State* (Pope owned and annotated closely at least one such volume: Mack 1982: 434). The wars of William III, to which Pope refers obliquely, had already produced much verse of this kind, such as Charles Hopkins's *White-hall* (1698), on the blessings of peace brought by William's victories. The decade-long War of Spanish Succession, setting France against Britain and her allies for control of the Spanish empire and much of world trade, was a visible motor for verse as every allied victory generated its clutch of celebratory poems; its coming conclusion, Addison had already warned in *The Spectator* of 30 October 1712, was certain to yield a heavy harvest. Addison himself had already contributed *The Campaign*, in celebration of the victories of the Duke of Marlborough, late in 1704 (dated 1705); it reached a fifth edition in the year of *Windsor-Forest*, pointedly reprinted to remind the ascendant Tories that their peace was based on a war won by a Whig commander. Samuel Wesley's *Marlborough: or the Fate of Europe* (1705) was another example of the scores of triumphalist tributes, to which Pope's friend William Congreve contributed *A Pindarique Ode, Humbly Offer'd to the Queen, on the Victorious Progress of Her Majesty's Arms, under the Conduct of the Duke of Marlborough* (1706). Pope's enemy John Dennis, with *Britannia Triumphans: or the Empire Sav'd, and Europe Deliver'd* (1704), and enemies to come, such as John Oldmixon, with *Iberia Liberata* (1706), and Charles Gildon, with *Libertas Triumphans* (1708, with a dedication to the future George I) had offered further models for Pope's poem to stand against, or from which to reclaim ideas and phrases for the Tory cause. These poems commonly portray Marlborough as a godlike presence, an element very conspicuously lacking in Pope's poem, which scarcely mentions the war directly at all and completely ignores the Duke.

In a mode slightly closer to Pope's own, Matthew Prior, poet and Tory agent in the Utrecht negotiations, had published in 1706 *An Ode, Humbly Inscrib'd to the Queen. On the late Glorious Success of Her Majesty's Arms*, in imitation of Spenser. (Prior's *Letter to Monsieur Boileau Depreaux* [sic] on the victory at Blenheim, had been published in 1704.) John Philips's poem *Blenheim* (1705), apparently written at the suggestion of Henry St John, to subvert with irony the praise awarded to Marlborough for his decisive victory there, was dedicated to Robert Harley, who would with St John head the ministry which brought the war to an end.

During this run of verse, Windsor Castle had become a more vexed site of poetic debate: *A Dialogue between Windsor Castle and Blenheim House* (1708), an anonymous poem, plays off the ancient glories of the castle and chapel (using material from Camden) against the modern genius of Marlborough, to be embodied in his massive palace. *Windsor-Castle. A Poem* (1708) is dedicated to the Queen and presents the castle and its decorations as the site of both ancient and modern military virtue, from Edward III to William III and thence to the saviour of the nation under Anne, Marlborough; it manages to combine many of the symbols (the paradisal park, the British oak and the Thames as the site of trading supremacy) of Pope's poem with a thoroughly Whig reading of the war. Gildon's *Libertas Triumphans* similarly links Windsor Castle, the great park, the order of the Garter, the 'peace and plenty' presided over by Anne, and the Thames, with Runnymede and Magna Carta. It was partly the task of Pope's poem to reclaim the territory of Anne's Windsor for a celebration of her peace which had no trace of these Whig gestures.

The Treaty of Utrecht, which is the unnamed subject of praise in the poem, indeed generated dozens of celebrations, including work by veterans such as Elkanah Settle (*Irene Triumphans*, 1713) and Nahum Tate (*The Triumph of Peace*, 1713). There were many pieces of avowedly Tory inclination (described by Williams 2005: 164–9; for further details of Pope's relation to this material see Hone 2015a). Thomas Parnell's 'On Queen Anne's Peace. Anno 1713' was not published (perhaps to avoid rivalry with his friend Pope's poem) until his *Posthumous Works* of 1758 but was written from a similar political perspective. (Parnell's short ballad, *The Horse and the Olive: or, War and Peace*, published in 1713, was a lighter contribution.) Much Tory verse contained overt praise of Anne and her ministers, alongside disparagement of the 'faction' which had prolonged the war. *The Triumph of Virtue* (1713) offered Oxford (as Harley had become) a hymn of praise for his role in bringing the war to an end; Marshall Smith's *On the Peace: A Poem* (1713, 28 April) was also dedicated to Oxford. Joseph Trapp's *Peace: A Poem* (1713, 9 April) was dedicated to Viscount Bolingbroke, as St John had become, but allots Oxford a starring role; Bevill Higgons's *A Poem on the Peace* (1713, 28 April), was dedicated to Oxford, while giving a key speech to Bolingbroke. Both Trapp and Higgons, the latter a Jacobite cousin of Granville's, ignored Marlborough and lauded the future of British commerce under the peace, as did Pope; Higgons also included a catalogue of national rivers, and concluded by handing the task of poetic recording of it all to Granville, as Pope did. William Waller's *Peace on Earth. A Congratulatory Poem* (1713) managed to include Marlborough, somewhat marginally, alongside its paean to

Anne and Oxford. William Diaper's *Dryades; or, the Nymph's Prophecy* ('1713', actually published by Lintot on 29 December 1712), praised both Anne and Bolingbroke, and adopted a mythological scheme of the same order as Pope's.

The most notable peace poem apart from Pope's was however the Whig-sponsored *A Poem, to his Excellency the Lord Privy Seal, on the Prospect of Peace* (published by Tonson on 28 October 1712, and reprinted several times in 1713), by Thomas Tickell (1686–1740), a protégé of Addison. This poem named Pope as a 'young spreading Laurel' amid a roll call of living British poets. Addison's *Spectator* no. 523, 30 October 1712, praised Tickell's avoidance of 'Fables out of the Pagan mythology', conceivably as a pre-emptive strike against Pope's mythologically dense work: 'the Exploits of a River-God' and the appearance of Phoebus Apollo are the subject of specific condemnations, making Pope's use of such devices all the more defiantly prominent. (Addison had already ridiculed talking rivers in his *Campaign*, 467–72.) Pope was praised for the work in *Miscellaneous Poems and Translations* of 1712, but once again Philips's pastorals were puffed, without reference to Pope's. Tickell's poem, which Williams (2015: 126–7) shows outshone Pope's by at least some measures of popularity, celebrated Anne, the triumphs of commerce, Oxford and (very briefly) Bolingbroke, while evincing some scepticism about the incomplete nature of the victory; it was carefully designed to evoke bipartisan attention by redirecting attention back towards the now out-of-favour Marlborough, whose victories had put Britain in a position to make the Peace, and it commemorates not only the battle at Blenheim but the palace of that name near Woodstock (pp. 10–13), then in the process of being built as a national tribute to the Duke, with, initially at least, Anne's fervent support. Pope did not visit Blenheim until much later (Rogers 2005a: 213–15) and his poem, by contrast, ascribes the peace to the redemptive qualities of Anne.

Context

Pope had been living with his parents at Whitehill House in Binfield, a village near the centre of the Windsor Forest area, since about 1700. The family estate contained about fifteen acres. Windsor Castle, a key site of British monarchic power, with its own 'Little' and 'Great' parks, was a few miles from his house. The scenic element of the poem, as with the *Pastorals*, is partly based on direct observation of the mixed landscape of the forest region, which occupied about 100,000 acres of Berkshire (Rogers 2010: 36). Pope had indeed seen fishermen, fowlers, deer-hunters and beaglers; he might even have seen Queen Anne hunting in the forest though he himself was, he confessed, 'no great Hunter indeed, but a great Esteemer of the noble Sport' (10 April 1710, *Corr.*, I.81). Much of the correspondence of this time alludes to the pleasures of living in the Forest. But hardly any element of Pope's rural life was untouched by the political situation unfolding around him, especially the conflict between Whig and Tory which derived from the struggles of the Restoration parliaments and especially from the 'Glorious Revolution' which brought William III and Mary to the throne in 1688-9. The reign of Anne (1702–14) was dominated by the War of the Spanish Succession, initiated under William, and generating the seemingly irresistible rise and sudden fall (late in 1711) of the Whig General the Duke of Marlborough before the Treaty of Utrecht could be brought about by the Tory ministry of 1710–14 (a detailed chronology of these events, as they affect the poem, is given in Rogers 2005a: xiv–xviii). It was also dominated by the shadow War of British Succession, since Anne had no surviving children; though the Act of Settlement (1701) was intended to ensure the accession of the Protestant Hanoverian line after Anne's death, there was some uncertainty about whether this would actually happen, particularly in the light of the operations of those sympathetic to the exiled Stuart line. Shortly after Pope's poem was published, Daniel Defoe was arrested for publishing *But What if the Queen should Die?* and other pamphlets on the question.

Because of this underlying issue, Catholics like Pope were repeatedly required to remove themselves from London under laws promulgated by William III and occasionally revived during the period of the poem's composition (e.g. in 1707 and 1710); 'retreat' into the countryside was partly a political necessity, though the Forest home was certainly tinged with a roseate sense of belonging. Binfield and the surrounding area would forever feature as an Arcadian scene in Pope's self-image, and his own later efforts in gardening owe something to his sense of the balanced landscape he recalled from childhood. But the Catholic landowners of Pope's local network and class were subject to political dispossession: the Caryll family, the most prominent of the Catholic squirearchy which formed Pope's coterie, had land sequestered because of an assault on William III. Most others had suffered some form of deprivation, and looked nervously towards the future.

In Windsor Forest Pope walked, rode and read, and found literary companions; he 'used to read there whole days under the trees' (*OAC*, I.20, 31). One of the most important of his local literary companions was Trumbull, dedicatee of 'Spring' and once considered the likely dedicatee of *Windsor-Forest*. Trumbull was a lawyer, diplomat, government official and MP; knighted in 1684, he had been Secretary of State in 1695 and a correspondent of Prior, later one of the Utrecht delegation, during his earlier role as secretary to the British ambassadors at the peace conference that led to the Treaty of Rijswijk in 1697. He had been manoeuvred into 'retiring' from these high political offices into the Forest in 1697 and lived two miles south of Binfield at the family estate of Easthampstead. His estate included a deer park, originally maintained as a royal preserve but despoiled during the Civil War, when the governing system of castle and forest had collapsed, perhaps suggesting some of the motifs of the poem (Rogers 2004: 148). In 1703 Trumbull became a Verderer of the Easthampstead Walk of the Forest, responsible for maintaining forest law in the district, but he was also a model of dignified contemplation and study, above the corruptions of office, in a manner which suited the poem. He was also at the centre of an extensive network of literary and political loyalties, including patronage of Dryden and Wycherley, which suited the poet (Rogers 2005a: 34–40). After the poem was published, Pope wrote to Trumbull a letter of elegant compliment referring to his role in the Forest and the poem: 'I shall not deny but I have made it appear very Lovely in my Poem, since I there told the World that Sir W. Trumbull was retired into it' (6 June 1713; Mack 1982: 464). Trumbull died at Easthampstead in 1716, prompting an epitaph from Pope on the calm balance of his virtues; in the list of deaths he kept in a now-lost copy of Virgil, Pope called him 'Amicus meus humanissimus a juvenilibus annis' ('My most humane friend, from early years'; *EC*, I.ix).

Pope appears to have begun by planning a large-scale topographic poem which celebrated the pleasing harmonies of rural retreat from the brutal political realities of his day, especially the War of the Spanish Succession, which had commenced soon after the Pope family moved to Binfield. The fall of the Whig ministry in 1710, however, entailed the accession of a Tory ministry under Henry St John (Viscount Bolingbroke from 1712) and Robert Harley (first Earl of Oxford, from 1711); both would become close friends of Pope, and both were dedicated to putting an end to what Tories regarded as an expensive and wasteful war, more concerned with Whig finance operations and the aggrandisement of the allied generals, particularly Marlborough, than with territorial gain or political justice. As Pope revised the poem its focus shifted towards a more open and patriotic engagement with the political situation. The dismissal of Marlborough on the last day of 1711 strengthened the Tory reading of the campaign and their effort to end it. The negotiations began in earnest in January 1712 and eventually produced a peace which was by no means universally acceptable: many Whigs felt that the French had been appeased and some of the allies deserted. While Anne was known to be in favour of the peace terms, and personally much committed to the process, the Elector of Hanover (the future George I, who would succeed her) stood out against them; Austria initially refused to sign. In Britain, while the treaty went through the Commons easily enough, the House of Lords was more problematic: in order to ensure the passage of the legislation, twelve new peers had to be created at a stroke. These included Granville, the poem's dedicatee, who became Baron Lansdowne. The main treaty, between Britain and France, was signed at Utrecht on 31 March 1713, granting Britain much North Canadian territory, together with Gibraltar and Minorca, and the '*asiento*' contract for the transport of African slaves to Spanish American territories for 30 years. There was a ceremony of ratification on 11 April, a solemn proclamation of peace on 5 May, and a thanksgiving service on 5 July. A huge celebratory campaign, including a baroque firework display, specially commissioned music and other ceremonial pageantry, was mounted in order to promote the glorious image of a unified nation. As Rogers (2005a: 109–13) points out, the symbolic images in the firework display at Dublin, on 16 June, with Anne surmounting Rebellion, Sedition and Faction, resembles the display of conquered monsters at the end of Pope's poem, and the poem as a whole reflects the kind of pageantry devised for the occasion. (Handel's grand music for the celebrations was being rehearsed in St Paul's Cathedral on the day the poem was released.)

Pope's poem appeared on 7 March, well before the treaty was signed; a 'second edition' (actually a reissue) was advertised on 9 March. The anniversary of William III's death and of Anne's accession fell on 8 March. The poem was therefore aligned with a politically selective campaign and was imbued with implicit praise for the Tory ministry responsible for ending the war, as well as explicit worship of Anne's role (see Varney 1974 for the late insertion of some of these elements). The poem conceals any awareness of the fact that the ministry was falling apart because of rivalry between Bolingbroke and Oxford, and that some features of the Utrecht agreement itself were hugely divisive and already in trouble (see Rogers 2005a: 107-9). Pope's recently formed literary friendship with the Whig writers Addison and Steele remained, on the surface, intact, and Pope supplied a prologue (below) to *Cato*, Addison's tragedy of virtuous resistance to a tyrant (premiered 14 April 1713), of studied neutrality. But there were already signs of cooling, not least because of Pope's visible swing to the Tory cause in his Utrecht poem, as compared to the ecumenical efforts of *An Essay on Criticism*.

Though the poem alludes scantily to the military success of the allied armies (106-10), Marlborough himself is not even mentioned: every opportunity for panegyric is pointedly jettisoned. Pope was about to meet, and be increasingly aligned with, Swift, who had been running the Tory ministry's propaganda campaign (e.g. the pamphlet *The Conduct of the Allies*, 1711, and the periodical *The Examiner*, 1710-11) and who had been particularly vehement in his denunciation of Marlborough's ambition and the wastefulness of the long war. (The satirical *Windsor Prophecy, found in a Marlborough Rock* was issued in 1711 and widely believed to be by Swift.) Swift and Pope may have met through Lansdowne, who was a member of a Tory club that also included Prior. Pope was also close to Anne's physician, the suspected Jacobite John Arbuthnot, author of the trenchant series of satires against the handling of the war known as *The History of John Bull* (1712), as well as *The Art of Political Lying* (1712). The closeness of Pope's poem, in political terms, to these prose satires, is strongly marked (Rogers 2005a: 57-62), and Swift and Arbuthnot were both closely associated with the Windsor locale. Swift indeed was composing what would become his *History of the Four Last Years of the Queen*, a highly partisan defence of the Tory peace, at Windsor Castle, just as Pope's poem was appearing.

These writers, together with Oxford and Parnell, would form the group of Tory wits (sometimes known as the Scriblerus Club) that began to meet privately shortly after the publication of *Windsor-Forest*. The poem's dedication nails Pope's colours to the mast. Granville, Baron Lansdowne, came from a strong royalist family with vivid recollection of sacrifices made in the Civil War; he had been a patron of Dryden during his 'retirement' (or expulsion from the laureateship) under William III. A Jacobite MP under Anne, he was Secretary at War from 1710 to 1712 under Bolingbroke and Oxford, whose differences he tried without success to reconcile; he was known to be antipathetic to Marlborough. He was disappointed with the barony granted him on 1 January 1712 (Rogers 2004: 109), as St John had been with his elevation to the relatively low rank of Viscount, and while Pope's poem was being finished, Lansdowne was actively seeking the much higher grant of an earldom to match Harley's. Lansdowne's marriage in 1712 to Mary Villiers, daughter of the Jacobite first Earl of Jersey, a major figure in the Utrecht negotiations, kept him at the centre of the Tory version of political history, and he was personally very close to Anne, as privy councillor and treasurer of the household; Pope's suggestion that he was likely to be admitted to the Order of the Garter (287-8) was plausible enough at the time. Anne stood godmother to his daughter (also Anne) in 1712, with Oxford and Bolingbroke invited to act as godfathers in a futile attempt to keep them in unity. For further study of Granville's role in the poem see Clements (1972).

Pope probably met Granville in 1706, through Wycherley, and he was one of the group of wits who saw the manuscript of Pope's *Pastorals*, in which he is celebrated ('Spring', 46).

He combined a political role with some standing as a writer: Tonson published his *Poems on Several Occasions* in 1712 (Pope had a presentation copy, Mack 1982: 413) and Lintot, the publisher of *Windsor-Forest*, reprinted several of his plays in 1713. His political 'retirement' was the subject of a poem by Elizabeth Higgons in 1712 and he was celebrated, like Pope, in Tickell's *Poem . . . On the Prospect of Peace*, as well as in Bevill Higgons's *A Poem on the Peace*. Edward Young's *An Epistle to the Right Honourable the Lord Lansdown* [sic] (1713, 10 March) trespassed on Pope's dedicatory ground and other territory (it was also published by Lintot, who advertised Pope's poem on the last page of Young's). Some of Lansdowne's own verse itself celebrated retirement and covertly attacked William III, and his version of Shakespeare's *The Merchant of Venice* had been staged by royal command, at court, on the Queen's birthday in 1711 (Rogers 2005a: 86–7, 134). His poem 'The Progress of Beauty' (in *Poems on Several Occasions*) has a list of gallant kings prefiguring Pope's, and his drama *The British Enchanters* has masque-like allegory and prophecy of a kind Pope's poem tends to adopt (Rogers 2005a: 88). As with more or less everything in Pope's visionary poem, optimistic prophecy was soon defeated by the course of events: Lansdowne was never admitted to the Order of the Garter; he was dismissed from office shortly after the Hanoverian accession and imprisoned (like Oxford) on suspicion of treason in 1715. Pardoned in 1717, he moved (like Bolingbroke) to France in 1720, where he became deeply involved in the Jacobite plot known by the name of Pope's friend Francis Atterbury in 1722. Pope would recall their early encounters in the *Epistle to Dr Arbuthnot*, published in 1735 just before Lansdowne's death.

The poem's opening celebration of the patterned order of the landscape is specifically aligned with the presence of a Stuart monarch, Queen Anne, on the throne, in what seems a startlingly clear Jacobite slogan (42). Pope's Anne is the redemptive monarch by divine and hereditary right, who restores prosperity and stability, peace, and plenty. Anne was Queen, since the union of England and Scotland in 1707, of a symbolically united 'Britain' (neither 'England' nor 'English' appears in the poem); the Peace was her Peace. She had promoted big public ceremonies and the emblematic side of court life, resuming the practice of 'touching' for the King's Evil, a ceremony which the pragmatic William III had refused to indulge (see Winn 2014 and 2015). Pope's image-making poem is therefore a contribution to a royalist cult otherwise promoted by progresses, masques, pageants and similar celebrations. Anne was identified in poetry and propaganda, as Elizabeth I had been, with virginal or nurturing goddesses such as Diana, Ceres and Astraea (Hauser 1966: 481). The 'Stuart' landscape is at once contrasted with the hideous degradation that the land suffered under the invading Norman kings, since Moore (1951) generally recognised as a covert attack on their successor in name, William III, whose accession to the throne was at the expense of Anne's father, James II. 'William' is thus seen as a foreign, invading king who embroils the land in wars and devastating internal savagery. (The threat of further incursions, by the incoming Hanoverians, lurks.) A more benign, quasi-georgic version of seasonal hunting pursuits follows, indicating a sanitised course for male energies. The episode of Lodona, pursued by Pan and turned into a weeping stream (165–216), is, however, another testimony to the vulnerability of the landscape to rapacious power, and to the danger of overstepping the protective limits of the protected forest zone of Diana/Arcadia (Anne/Windsor/Britain). Coming alongside the symbolic *Rape of the Lock*[e] (1712/1714), which offers its own artistic compensation to the victim of male violence, and just after 'On a Fan of the Author's Design', which alludes to a story in which a nymph is killed in a hunting accident in a forest, the episode strongly suggests a vulnerable feminine realm violated by an aggressive invader, and is sometimes interpreted as an allegory of illegal Williamite possession of Stuart England, conventionally allegorised as a 'rape'. ('Vertumnus and Pomona' might be considered as a benign version of this scenario.)

The episode flows into Pope's patriotic vision of the Thames as a source of national power and identity, and Pope celebrates the presence in its vicinity of national poets such as the Earl of Surrey, Abraham Cowley, Sir John Denham and the dedicatee, Lansdowne. Windsor Castle too has its symbolic role: though founded by William the Conqueror near a Saxon hunting preserve, and thus historically associated with the negative exercise of royal power that the poem deplores, the castle Pope knew was largely built by Edward III; Edward IV added the royal chapel of St George, cultic home of the Order of the Garter, founded after the English victory at Crécy in 1346 (see line 303). The Order is one of Pope's major ceremonial images, associated with Anne, who had revived it in order to promote the magical qualities of monarchy and who wore its regalia on state occasions and for high-visibility portraits. (Rogers 2005a: 188–9 points out that St George's day was in addition the anniversary of Anne's coronation and a focus of Jacobite activity.) The castle itself was strongly linked to Anne, who spent much time there, unlike William III and Mary, who preferred their renovated Hampton Court, a palace completely ignored here (it is the notional site of the 'rape' in 'The Rape of the Locke'). St George's Chapel housed the relics of various martial kings, as well as others, such as Charles I and Henry VI who were (in Pope's version of history) martyred for political ends, and for whom the poem performs 'posthumous rites' (Rogers 2005a: 98). Henry VIII is conspicuously missing from the list of kings Pope knew were buried in the chapel, perhaps because of his role in the Reformation and dissolution of the monasteries (the fate of one of which, near Chertsey, is lamented in *Cooper's Hill*). Henry's daughter, Elizabeth, features subliminally (382) as a model for Anne's imperial majesty, as indeed she did in Anne's own conscious propaganda campaign, as for instance in the adoption of her motto, *semper eadem* ('ever the same') which was included on the triumphal arch constructed as part of the peace celebrations (Rogers 2005a: 111); the comparison was common (e.g. Gildon's *Libertas Triumphans*, p. 18). But like her father Elizabeth is, for her anti-Catholic bias, excluded from Pope's national celebration. The dismal, and more recent, memory of the Civil War and revolutions in England, magically dismissed in the poem by Anne's fiat 'Let Discord cease!' (325), heralds the prophecy of Britain's future greatness, uttered in the mythologised persona of the Thames, trailing mythological resonances from classical mythology (Saturn, father of Astraea, goddess of Justice) and culture (the Tiber, the Eridanus or Po), who hails the coming Peace in terms of the increased maritime empire that will accrue to Britain, a new golden age the world over.

The Stuart panegyric was, as Pope knew it would be, a doomed prophecy: Anne had no surviving issue, was known to be in ill health and died less than eighteen months after the poem was published. The Hanoverian George I arrived; Oxford and Landsdowne, with Prior and others, were imprisoned on suspicion of treason and Bolingbroke fled to France, leaving the Tories in disarray. In 1716, because of renewed anti-Catholic pressure in the wake of the abortive Jacobite rising of 1715, Pope and his family were obliged to abandon their home in the Forest and move to Chiswick, under the protection of the Whig Earl of Burlington. The 'Windsor Blacks' brought violence once more to the Forest, with Pope at the edge of the action (Thompson 1975; Rogers 2004: 154–60). Much of the imagery relating to magical queens and rivers of empire would return, travestied and besmirched, in *The Dunciad*.

Apart from coterie readers of the poem before its publication, among whom Addison was possibly the most hostile (see Cummings 1988), the earliest firm indication of the published poem's reception is probably Swift's note to 'Stella': 'Mr. Pope has publishd a fine Poem calld Windsor Forrest; read it' (*Journal to Stella*, 9 March 1713; Swift's first known reference to Pope). George Berkeley, who read it in a presentation copy, called it a 'very ingenious new poem' (Winn 2014: 608). Bridges told Trumbull on 21 April that Henry Sacheverell and Joseph Trapp (the latter the author of a rival 'Peace' poem) agreed that the poem showed Pope to 'one of the greatest genius's that this nation has bred'. Bridges also read it to the Bishop of London 'who was much pleased with it' (Sherburn 1958a: 345; Mack 1985: 185). It is known that Pope's acquaintance, the fervently Jacobite Mary Caesar, adopted it as a source of loyal slogans (Rogers 2005a: 123–4) and Garth, Whig though he was, praised it in the 'Preface' to his poem *Claremont* (1715). An appreciative poem 'To Mr. Pope on his Windsor Forest', dated June 1715, by Francis Knapp, an Irish poet outside Pope's friendship circle, appeared among the commendatory items attached to Pope's *Works* of 1717.

Pope's poem was attacked as Jacobite as early as 1714 (Guerinot 1969: 18). Dennis was predictably the most hostile to *Windsor-Forest*, not only for its politics but for its supposed inferiority to Denham's *Coopers Hill* (a common theme amongst Pope's detractors) and for what he perceived as its rhapsodic lack of form (*Remarks upon Mr. Pope's Translation of Homer* (1717), pp. 39–44). The poem, however, survived its immediate moment, as almost none of the other Utrecht poems did. Johnson (Lonsdale, IV.66–7) disposed of Dennis's complaints, though he disliked other aspects of the poem, such as its use of quasi-classical mythology. However, despite the slighting remarks of Warton about Pope's lack of skill in landscape description (1756: 20), Johnson cited it as evidence of Pope's powers of imagination (Lonsdale, IV.78) and it occasionally found favour even in the Romantic period because of its images of the 'natural' world. In modern times, the classic reading of Wasserman (1959), focused largely on the governing principle of 'Order in Variety' (13–16) and the balancing of competing energies, political, psychological and artistic, has been widely influential, albeit modified by readings which allude to elements of personal unease and uncertainty (e.g. Morris 1973; Cummings 1987). Our Commentary is particularly indebted to Rogers (2004) and (2005a), full-length studies of the poem and its deployment of rich literary and iconographic resources in endorsing, however elegiacally, Anne's 'Peace and Plenty' (42).

WINDSOR-FOREST.

To the Right Honourable

GEORGE Lord LANSDOWN.

By Mr. POPE.

Non injussa cano: Te nostrae, Vare, *Myricae*
Te Nemus omne canet; nec Phoebo gratior ulla est
Quam sibi quae Vari *praescripsit Pagina nomen.*

Virg.

Dedication. George Granville (1666–1735), Tory MP created first baron Lansdowne in 1711 (see Headnote: Context).

Epigraph. Condensed from Virgil, *Eclogues* VI.9–12: 'I sing things which are not uncommanded: it is of you, Varus, that each grove of our tamarisk shall sing; and no page is more pleasing to Phoebus than that which has the name of Varus written at its head'. The tamarisk was sacred to Apollo (Phoebus), god of poetry. Alfenus Varus was a politicial insider in the struggle between Octavian and Mark Antony, who apparently helped Virgil after an earlier patron, C. Asinius Pollio, had assisted him in the recovery of his farm, an event close to Pope's imagination (cf. Commentary to 256); the opening of this *Eclogue* (which Pope cites in his note to 'Spring', 1) suggests that Varus had commissioned an epic poem from Virgil. Pope alludes to Lansdowne's high political standing, but also to his own closeness to the career pattern of Rome's greatest poet.

WINDSOR-FOREST.
To the Right Honourable
GEORGE Lord *LANSDOWN.*

    T HY Forests, *Windsor*! and thy green Retreats,
    At once the Monarch's and the Muse's Seats,
Invite my Lays. Be present, Sylvan Maids!
Unlock your Springs, and open all your Shades.
5   *Granville* commands: Your Aid O Muses bring!
What Muse for *Granville* can refuse to sing?

Title, n. MSw: This poem was written just after ye Pastorals as apears by ye last verse of it. That was in ye year when ye author was years of age. But the last hundred lines including ye Celebrations of ye Peace, were added in ye year 1 soon after ye Ratification of ye Treaty of Utrecht – It was first printed in folio in 1 Again in folio ye same year, & in Octavo ye next.

1736–51: This Poem was written at two different times: the first part of it which relates to the country, in the year 1704, at the same time with the Pastorals: the latter part was not added till the year 1710 [*1751:* 1713] in which it was publish'd.

3, n. 1736–51: VER. 3, &c. originally thus,

    ——— *Chaste Goddess of the woods,*
Nymphs of the Vales, and Naiads of the floods,
Lead me thro' arching bow'rs, and glimm'ring glades.
[1751: Unlock your springs]

3–5. MSw: Invite my Lays: Chast Goddess of the Woods,
        Nymphs of the Vales, and Naiads of the Floods,
        Lead me, oh lead me thro' the Bow'rs and Glades,

Title MS note. For the date of composition, see Headnote.

1–28. The scene of landscape variety has been found to resemble William Camden's description of the Windsor area in *Britannia* (1587 and much reprinted) an important source throughout the poem; see Rogers (2004: 130–4).

1. green Retreats: Wakefield notes the resemblance to the opening of Charles Hopkins, *The History of Love* (1695), p. 3: 'Ye Woods, and Wilds, serene and blest retreats, | At once the Lovers, and the Muses seats'. *TE* notes that Pope has 'Seats' rhyming with Green Retreats' in 'Summer', 71–2; see Commentary there.

3. Invite: inspire, suggest.
    Lays: songs or poems.
    Sylvan Maids: wood-nymphs.

3 MS and Pope's note. *Chast Goddess:* Diana; see 160.

4. Unlock ... Shades: make the rivers and woods open to poetic vision. Wakefield cites Dryden's translation of Virgil, *Georgics,* II.245, *Works of Virgil* (1697), p. 78: 'Once more unlock for thee the sacred Spring'; *TE* adds his version of *Aeneid,* X.241, *ibid.* p. 505: 'Now sacred Sisters open all your Spring'. The allusion to the *Georgics,* a prelude to the praise of Italy, signals the public and political direction of Pope's 'rural' poem from the start.

5. Granville: see note to Dedication.

6. refuse to sing: Warburton cites Virgil, *Eclogues,* X.3: 'neget quis carmina Gallo' ('who would refuse songs for Gallus'); Wakefield cites Milton, 'Lycidas', 10, *Poems of Mr. John Milton* (1645), p. 57: 'Who would not sing for *Lycidas*?'

>   The Groves of *Eden,* vanish'd now so long,
>   Live in Description, and look green in Song:
>   *These,* were my Breast inspir'd with equal Flame,
> 10   Like them in Beauty, should be like in Fame.
>   Here Hills and Vales, the Woodland and the Plain,
>   Here Earth and Water seem to strive again,
>   Not *Chaos*-like together crush'd and bruis'd,
>   But as the World, harmoniously confus'd:

---

10. **Beauty:** MSw: Pleasure

---

7. Groves of **Eden:** most obviously still 'green' in Milton's *Paradise Lost,* especially books IV and V. Rogers (2004: 144) points out that Pope's half-sister lived inside the forest at Hall Grove, one of several place names underscoring the seemingly mythological language of the poem.

7–8. Wakefield notes the closeness to the opening of Waller's *A Poem on St. James's Park* (1661), p. 3: 'Of the first Paradise there's nothing found, | Plants set by heav'n are vanisht, & the ground; | Yet the description lasts, who knows the fate | Of lines that shall this Paradise relate?' and Addison's 'A Letter from Italy', 31–6, on lost streams immortalised in poetry.

8. **look green:** cf. Henry Vaughan, 'Mount of Olives [II]', 22, *Silex Scintillans* (1650), p. 104: 'My wither'd leafs again look green and flourish'.

9. **These:** the landscapes of Windsor Forest, which Pope proposes to preserve in the way Milton has preserved Paradise in his epic.

   equal Flame: an imaginative fire rivalling Milton's. Wakefield notes the resemblance to Addison, 'A Letter from Italy', 51–2, *Poetical Miscellanies: The Fifth Part* (1705), p. 4: 'Oh cou'd the Muse my ravisht Breast inspire | With Warmth like yours, and raise an equal Fire . . .'. In *Cooper's Hill,* 71–2, *Poems and Translations* (1668), p. 5, Denham likens the unknown architect of Windsor-Castle to the obscure birthplace of Homer: '(Like him in birth, thou should'st be like in fame, | As thine his fate, if mine had been his Flame).'

11–20. Spence noted that these lines represented Pope's 'ideas afterwards for gardening' (*OAC,* I.251–2), on which see Martin (1984).

11.   **Hills . . . Vales . . . Woodland:** reminiscent of Aemilia Lanyer's early prospect landscape in 'The Description of Cookeham', 68, *Salue Deus Rex Iudaeorum* (1611), sig. H3ʳ: 'Hills, vales, and woods . . .'. For its political resonance as a model of self-regulating constitution, see Winn (2014: 602–3).

12. **strive:** contend (with each other), perhaps recalling the divisions of land from water, and day from night, in the first chapter of Genesis.

13. **Chaos:** cf. *Essay on Criticism,* 295; 'Rape of the Locke', II.37. Milton's description of Chaos, *Paradise Lost,* II.891–916, itself recalls the opening of Ovid's *Metamorphoses* and other classical creation myths. There had been more recent scientific work on chaos in e.g. John Ray, *Miscellaneous Discourses Concerning the Dissolution and Changes of the World* (1692).

   crush'd and bruis'd: Wakefield compares Waller, 'Of her passing through a crowd of People', 1–2, *Poems, &c.* (1645), p. 48: 'As in old Chaos Heaven with Earth confus'd, | And Stars with Rocks, together crush'd and bruis'd'. The latter phrase was perhaps recalled in *Paradise Lost,* VI.656 (1674), p. 165: 'crush't in and bruis'd'; Pope recalled it in his translation of *Iliad,* XII.84: 'In one promiscuous Carnage crush'd and bruis'd'. For political overtones, notably the association of this violence with Whig militarism, see Wasserman (1959: 108).

14. **harmoniously confus'd:** the classical concept of 'discors concordia', known especially from Ovid (*Metamorphoses* I.433) and modelled in landscape in Denham's *Cooper's Hill* (especially 203–8). Pope would later satirise landscapes too symmetrically designed: *Epistle to Burlington,* 79–84.

15	Where Order in Variety we see,
	And where, tho' all things differ, all agree.
	Here waving Groves a checquer'd Scene display,
	And part admit and part exclude the Day;
	As some coy Nymph her Lover's warm Address
20	Nor quite indulges, nor can quite repress.
	There, interspers'd in Lawns and opening Glades,
	Thin Trees arise that shun each others Shades.
	Here in full Light the russet Plains extend;
	There wrapt in Clouds the blueish Hills ascend:
25	Ev'n the wild Heath displays her Purple Dies,

25, n. 1736–51: VER. 25. *Why should I sing our better suns or air,*
  Whose vital draughts prevent the leach's care,
  While thro' fresh fields th' enliv'ning odours breathe,
  Or spread with vernal blooms the purple heath.

17. **waving . . . checquer'd:** MSw: arching . . . glimm'ring
21. **in Lawns and:** MSw: among the opening

---

16. Singled out as nonsense in Concanen, *A Supplement to the Profund* (1728), p. 28.

17. checquer'd: diversified 'in the manner of a chess-board, with alternate colours, or with darker and lighter parts' (*SJ*, citing this passage). *TE* cites Milton, 'L'Allegro', 96, *Poems*, p. 34: 'Dancing in the Chequer'd shade'. Close to the heraldic term 'chequy'; Rogers (2004: 92 and 2005a: 202), suggests that the coloration that ensues suggests the Stuart coat of arms.

18. admit: grant entrance to.

19. Nymph: female nature spirit, used in flattery for women generally.

  warm Address: amorous courtship, sexual urging.

20. indulges . . . repress: cf. *Essay on Criticism*, 93.

21. Lawns: 'an open space between woods' (*SJ*). Cf. Blackmore, *Eliza*, III.55 (1705), p. 59: 'Smooth wat'ry Lawns, and Glades of open Air'.

23. russet: 'reddishly-brown' (*SJ*). *TE* notes Milton's use of 'Russet Lawns' in Milton, 'L'Allegro', 71, *Poems*, p. 33; Blackmore, *Creation*, III (1712), p. 138, has the phrase 'Russet Plain'.

24. blueish: *TE* cites Dryden's translation of Virgil, *Aeneid*, III.684–5, *Works of Virgil*, p. 287: 'When we from far, like bluish Mists, descry | The Hills . . .'. Dryden's phrase itself reflects Guyomar's words to Montezuma, describing the first sight of colonial ships as 'Like Bluish Mists', in John Ogilby's *America* (1671), p. 15. The colours in these lines are rare within the poem in not being of unmixed heraldic clarity, and neither word appears to be used by Pope elsewhere.

25. Purple Dies: indicating the presence of heather or ling; also, through the use of the imperial colour purple, part of a pattern of imagery associating the landscape with royalty and empire.

25 Pope's note. vital: life-giving; cf. 'Rape of the Locke', II.55. *TE* cites Dryden, 'To my honour'd kinsman, John Driden', 115–16, *Fables Ancient and Modern* (1700), p. 98: 'He scapes the best, who Nature to repair, | Draws Phisick from the Fields, in Draughts of Vital Air', and the return to the idea at 239–42 below.

  draughts: breeze, but also carrying the sense of something drunk, as a medical treatment.

  leach: doctor, from the leech, parasitic worm-like creature used in medicine.

  enliv'ning: life-giving.

  vernal: of spring.

And 'midst the Desert fruitful Fields arise,
That crown'd with tufted Trees and springing Corn,
Like verdant Isles the sable Waste adorn.
Let *India* boast her Plants, nor envy we
30   The weeping Amber or the balmy Tree,
While by our Oaks the precious Loads are born,
And Realms commanded which those Trees adorn.
Not proud *Olympus* yields a nobler Sight,
Tho' Gods assembled grace his tow'ring Height,

25–29. MSw: How am I pleas'd t' imbibe th' untainted Air,
           Whose vital Draughts prevent the Leache's Care?
           While thro' fresh Fields th' enlivening Odours breath,
           Or spread with Vernal Blooms the Purple Heath!
32. **Trees:** MSw: Plants
33. **proud ... Sight:** MSw: high ... Show

---

26. Desert: desert, sometimes in the sense of uncultivated or unoccupied, rather than necessarily aridly barren, land; cf. 'Rape of the Locke', II.75. Rogers (2004: 141–2), however, cites material from Defoe's *Tour thro' the Whole Island of Great Britain* (1724–6) to suggest that 'desart' was used negatively, in the modern sense, to describe the sandy heathlands of Bagshot Heath and similar areas in Pope's time.

fruitful Fields: cf. 'The First Book of Statius his Thebais', 458.

27. tufted Trees: trees in a small cluster. Cf. Milton, 'L'Allegro', 78, *Poems*, p. 33: 'Boosom'd high in tufted Trees'.

28. verdant Isles: green patches of growth amid the wild land. Cf. *Paradise Lost*, VIII.631 (1674), p. 212: 'Beyond the Earths green Cape and verdant Isles'.

sable: black, a poetic and heraldic term derived from the animal of that name, the fur of which was worn by noblemen; giving a 'rich Fur, of Colour between Black and Brown'; Kersey, *Dictionarium Anglo-Britannicum*, 1708, under 'sable'. Cf. 408, and 'Rape of the Locke', II.84. Rogers (2004: 145) notes that some authorities in Pope's day derived the word from Latin *sabulum*, 'sandy gravel', which punningly fits the context; Rogers also points out (2004: 91) that 'verdant' suggests the heraldic colour 'vert', green, and that the line as a whole suggests a heraldic 'blazon for a dark field scattered with areas of green'.

Waste: uncultivated land.

29–42. TE suggests comparison with Virgil, *Georgics*, II.136–76.

30. weeping Amber: Amber is a fossilised sap or resin originally secreted by trees; cf. 391, and 'Spring', 62. TE cites book II of Sandys's *Ovid's Metamorphosis Englished, Mythologiz'd, and Represented in Figures* (1632), p. 53: 'From these cleere dropping trees, teares yearely flow: | They, hardned by the Sunne, to Amber grow', and Virgil, *Eclogues*, IV.30: 'et durae quercus sudabunt roscida mella' ('and tough oaks shall sweat dew-lie honey').

balmy Tree: type of Asian and north African tree yielding balm, a medicinal and fragrant substance. Cf. 391. TE cites *Paradise Lost*, IV.248 (1674), p. 92, in a place of 'Balme': 'Groves whose rich Trees wept odorous Gumms'.

31. Oaks: traditional symbol for British merchant ships, as in 383–5. See also 219 for Commentary on Stuart symbolism. For similar praise of British trade to Eastern countries, TE cites Waller, *A Panegyrick to my Lord Protector*, 57–64 (1655; last reprinted 1709).

32. Realms commanded: i.e. the British empire exerts power over realms of exotic trees such as India, in the shape of mercantile ventures such as the East India Company, incorporated in 1600.

33. proud Olympus: the highest mountain in Greece, regarded as the home of the gods in Greek mythology; cf. 'Rape of the Locke', II.107.

35 Than what more humble Mountains offer here,
    Where, in their Blessings, all those Gods appear.
    See *Pan* with Flocks, with Fruits *Pomona* crown'd,
    Here blushing *Flora* paints th' enamel'd Ground,
    Here *Ceres*' Gifts in waving Prospect stand,
40 And nodding tempt the joyful Reaper's Hand,
    Rich Industry sits smiling on the Plains,
    And Peace and Plenty tell, a STUART reigns.

---

34. MSw: When crown'd with Gods, he views the World below,
40. tempt . . . joyful: MSw: crave . . . willing

---

35. Mountains: For the usage cf. 'Spring', 21.

37–42. Rogers (2004: 190) suggests these lines derive some royalist energy from John Evelyn's *A Panegyric to Charles the Second* (1661), p. 4:

O happy, and blessed spring! not so glorious yet with the pride and enamel of his flowers, the golden corn, and the gemms of the pregnant Vine, as with those Lillies and Roses which bloom and flourish in your Chaplet this day[.]

36. Blessings: their effects, the produce the gods are supposed to look after.

37. Pan: Greek fertility god, patron of shepherds and herdsmen; cf. 'Summer', 50.

Pomona: Roman goddess of tree fruit; see 'Vertumnus and Pomona', Headnote.

38. Flora: Roman goddess of flowers and Spring, 'blushing' because highly-coloured. Cf. 'Spring', 31 and 43.

enamel'd Ground: a term borrowed from enamel painting, the 'ground' being a coating on metals prepared for painting in colours to be fired; figuratively, Flora decorates the soil with the bright, pure colours of flowers, resembling also heraldic ornamentation (see Rogers 1973 and 2004: 89). The phrasing itself is not uncommon: cf. Giles Fletcher, Sonnet XXVI, *Licia* (1593), p. 27: 'And sweetest flowres enameld have the ground'; Robert Aylett, *Susanna*, I (1622), p. 5: 'And flowers all enamelled the ground'.

39. Ceres: Roman goddess of cereal crops; cf. Pope's *Epistle to Burlington*, 176. In Roman mythology Ceres blesses the benighted earth with produce after the eventual return of her daughter, Proserpina, who had been abducted by Pluto, god of the underworld; she thus heralds the safe return of a female figure from masculine aggression, and is linked to the Lodona passage below. Rogers (2010: 59) reads this passage as an allusion to the story of Erisichthon's punishment by Ceres for desecrating groves in Thessaly, which translates into an indictment of Marlborough's unquenchable thirst for gain (and blood) by the redemptive goddess-figure, Anne. Rogers (2005a: 201, 254–5) lists the survival of various folk myths and rituals relating to Ceres; cf. 368 below.

40. nodding: waving in the breeze, but appearing to 'nod' assent to the harvesting 'reaper'.

41. Industry: productive (agricultural) labour.

42. Peace and Plenty: a ubiquitous pairing in seventeenth-century poetry, based on classical depictions of Pax (peace) with Plutus (wealth) in her lap and a cornucopia (horn of plenty) in her hand. Dryden's version of the *Aeneid*, describing the golden age of Saturn, VIII.436, *Works of Virgil*, p. 447, has 'With his mild Empire, Peace and Plenty came', perhaps a Jacobite-inflected image in its context of exile and usurpation. Rogers (2004: 23, 49 and 58) shows it was a regular iconographic feature of Tudor and Stuart allegorical painting (such as the Banqueting House ceiling celebrating the reign of James I) and courtly masque culture. The coupling also appeared in local celebrations of the peace (Rogers 2005a: 112). However, the Whig Charles Gildon, in *Libertas Triumphans* (1708), p. 18, has Anne 'Show'r Peace, and Plenty round Her *British* Lands'. For further examples see Winn (2014: 257).

STUART: Queen Anne (1665–1714), daughter of James II, and the last Stuart monarch, reigning from 1702 to her death in 1714; all of her children had died in infancy, and legislation had been passed to establish that the

> Not thus the Land appear'd in Ages past,
> A dreary Desart and a gloomy Waste,
> 45   To Savage Beasts and Savage Laws a Prey,
> And Kings more furious and severe than they:
> Who claim'd the Skies, dispeopled Air and Floods,
> The lonely Lords of empty Wilds and Woods.

45.] *The Forest Laws.*

---

46. furious and severe: MSw: boundless and more fierce
47. dispeopled: MSw: unpeopled

Protestant Electors of Hanover would succeed to the throne rather than the Catholic descendants of James II. See Headnote to 'To the Author of a Poem, intitled, Successio'. While Anne lived, it was still possible for Pope to make this bold allusion to Stuart success; Erskine-Hill (1981: 130) notes that the line as a whole was adopted as a slogan by Pope's fervently Jacobite acquaintance Mary Caesar.

43–8. A mythic history of the poor stewardship of the land under the invading Norman kings, based in part on the section of William Camden's *Britannia* which deals with Berkshire (in the 1695 edition, col. 149–50; p. 115). Extensive parallels are set out by Rogers (2004: 127–9). The matter had already been treated in verse in Drayton, *Poly-Olbion* (1612) II.157–88 (Rogers 2005a: 269). As a contrast to 'Stuart' management, this section also suggests an attack on William III, king after the revolution in 1688; William is a foreign, invading king who embroils the land in continental wars and internal disputes. Moore (1951) points out that William III was also a keen hunter who died in a hunting accident, obtained the throne by military force and destroyed the churches (metaphorically, by his support for Dissent); further evidence from contemporary pamphleteering is cited in Wasserman (1959). Erskine-Hill (1981) likens this 'myth of usurpation' to a less obviously political version in *Essay on Criticism*, 684–95.

44. *EC* compares Dryden, 'The First Book of Ovid's Metamorphoses', 472, *Examen Poeticum* (1693), p. 31: 'A dismal Desart, and a silent Waste'.

45–6. Wakefield cites Waller, 'Upon the Death of My Lady Rich', 3–4, *Poems, &c.*, p. 59: 'Prove all a Desart, and none there make stay | But savage Beasts, or men as ill as they'. Pope may also be recalling Roscommon, *Horace's Art of Poetry* (1680), p. 27: Orpheus 'Did not (as Poets feign) tame savage Beasts | But Men as lawless, and as wild as they'. Pope revisited the idea in *Essay on Man*, III.167–8.

45. Savage Laws: cf. the anonymous *Short History of the Kings of England* (1692), p. 19, on 'these cruel and savage Laws of the Forest' of William I and his sons. 'Savage' is possibly derived from Latin 'silvaticus', 'of woodland', and connected to 'sylvan' (*OED*).

45 Pope's note. 'Forest' is from Latin 'foris', 'outside', not necessarily connected to woodland: forest land was land subject not to the Common Law of England but governed by special royal prerogatives, in particular the 'Forest Laws' which preserved game animals such as deer, boar and hares for the king's private hunting. The measures were unpopular and were in part addressed by Magna Carta, and more particularly by the Carta de Foresta of 1217, which took several areas out of Forest law. Rogers (2004: 144–51) details the varying levels of enforcement applied through to Pope's period and in Pope's local region, and see further Thompson (1975) for the violence of the later struggles.

46. Kings: the Norman kings, as in 63–84, but also suggesting non-Stuart monarchs.

46 MS. boundless: in the sense of unbounded, free of any restraint.

47. dispeopled: emptied of inhabitants; more commonly used of towns as in 'The First Book of Statius his Thebais', 55.

 Air and Floods: i.e. birds and fishes, as in 52, though the eviction of landworkers is also implied.

48. Wilds and Woods: cf. Milton, *Paradise Lost*, IX.910 (1674), p. 241: 'these wilde Woods forlorn'.

Cities laid waste, they storm'd the Dens and Caves
50 (For wiser Brutes were backward to be Slaves)
    What could be free, when lawless Beasts obey'd,
    And ev'n the Elements a Tyrant Sway'd?
    In vain kind Seasons swell'd the teeming Grain,
    Soft Show'rs distill'd, and Suns grew warm in vain;
55 The Swain with Tears to Beasts his Labour yields,
    And famish'd dies amidst his ripen'd Fields.
    No wonder Savages or Subjects slain

57, n. 1736–51: VER. 57, &c. *No wonder savages or subjects slain ——*
But subjects starv'd while savages were fed.
It was originally thus, but the word Savages is not so properly [*1751:* not properly] apply'd to beasts as to [*1751:* but to] men; which occasion'd the alteration.

50. Slaves): *1717–51:* slaves.)
51. lawless Beasts: MSw: Savages
52. ev'n: MSw: o'er
54. Suns grew warm: MSw: Phoebus shone
55. to Beasts his Labour: *1736–51:* his frustrate labour
56. MSw: And dies for Want amidst his fruitful Fields.
57. *1736–43:* What wonder then, a beast or subject slain

49–50. Recalling the malcontent Whiggish plotters in Dryden, *Absalom and Achitophel*, 55–6 (1681), p. 2: 'They led their wild desires to Woods and Caves; | And thought that all but Savages were Slaves'; Pope's kings have destroyed even that illusion of wild freedom.

49. storm'd: entered aggressively.

Dens and Caves: perhaps recalling Milton, *Paradise Lost*, IX.118 (1674), p. 217: 'Rocks, Dens, and Caves'.

50. wiser Brutes: i.e. animals, 'wiser' than the human beings reduced to brutishness by power. Cf. Samuel Wesley, 'A Tobacco Pipe', *Maggots* (1685), p. 45: 'Since wiser *Brutes* have often tutor'd *Man*'.

Slaves: politically powerless subjects, as in 64. The point that tyranny generates subjects who are in effect animals is made in several political poems, e.g. Gildon's tribute to Anne's benign reign, *Libertas Triumphans* (1708), p. 18: *Her PRIDE's to Rule, not SERVILE BEASTS, but MEN*'.

52. Elements: water, earth and air, presumably understood here as habitats (cf. 47).

Sway'd: ruled.

53. The crops are ruined by animals which the farmers cannot kill because of the forest laws.

kind: nurturing, conferring fertility.

teeming Grain: cf. 'Autumn', 72 and Commentary.

54. distill'd: rained, watered.

54 MS. Phoebus: see Commentary to 147.

55. Swain: rural labourer, 'pastoral youth' (*SJ*).

55 variant. frustrate: frustrated, thwarted (in that he reaps no benefit because the protected beasts eat the crop).

56. Wakefield cites the narrative of the Italian peasant starving amidst abundance in Addison's 'A Letter from Italy', 113–18, *Poetical Miscellanies: The Fifth Part* (1705) p. 9, concluding: 'Starves in the midst of Nature's Bounty curst, | And in the loaden Vine-yard dies for Thirst.' These lines come immediately before a section on liberty admired by Pope; see 91 below.

ripen'd Fields: TE cites Tickell's *A Poem ... On the Prospect of Peace* (1712), p. 6: 'Curst by the Hind, when to the Spoil he yields | His Year's whole Sweat, and vainly ripen'd Fields'.

57 Pope's note. TE notes that Pope uses 'savage' to mean 'wild beast' in his *Iliad* translation, e.g. XIII.144, XVII.815 and XVIII.373. But all the instances are singular; it appears only once as a plural noun, at *Iliad* XIV.321, not clearly applied either to animal or human.

550   WINDSOR-FOREST (1713)

>   Were equal Crimes in a Despotick Reign;
>   Both doom'd alike for sportive Tyrants bled,
> 60 But Subjects starv'd while Savages were fed.
>   Proud *Nimrod* first the bloody Chace began,
>   A mighty Hunter, and his Prey was Man.
>   Our haughty *Norman* boasts that barb'rous Name,
>   And makes his trembling Slaves the Royal Game.
> 65 The Fields are ravish'd from th' industrious Swains,

65.] Alluding to the New Forest, *and the Tyrannies exercis'd there by* William *the First.*

65, n. MSw, *1751:* Alluding to the destruction made in the New Forest, and the Tyrannies exercis'd there by Willian the Conqueror [*1751:* William I].
65–6, n. *1751:* VER. 65. The fields were ravish'd from th' industrious swains, From men their cities, and from Gods their fanes:] Translated from,
 Templa adimit divis, fora civibus, arva colonis,
an old monkish writer, I forget who.

60. *1736–51:* But that [*1751:* while] the subject starv'd, the beast was fed.
63. haughty: MSw: godless
64. the: MSw: his

---

59. sportive: addicted to sports (hunting).
61–2. Nimrod: 'a mighty hunter before the Lord', Genesis, 10:8–12; conventionally associated with a fallen world or 'brazen' age. *TE* cites evidence from biblical commentary that Nimrod was regarded as a type of the tyrannical ruler or military butcher, treating subjects like animals for hunting. *TE* further cites Waller, 'Of the late Invasion and Defeat of the Turks', 1–4, *The Maid's Tragedy Altered* (1690), p. 60, where the 'modern *Nimrod*' chases after Christians rather than game. Milton identified the ruthless hunting of Nimrod with his invention of patriarchal monarchy in *Eikonoklastes* (1649), pp. 108–9, and outlined (without naming him) Nimrod's role in history in *Paradise Lost*, XII.13–113 (1674), pp. 314–16, where it is said (30) that 'Men not Beasts shall be his game'. The same point is emphasised in Defoe, *Jure Divino*, II (1706), p. 20 and note; cf. Gildon, *Libertas Triumphans* (1708), p. 18, where tyrants 'make their People not their *Care*, but *PREY*'. Both William III, as a 'hunter' of catholics, and the Duke of Marlborough, whose military prowess was construed by some as bloodthirsty ambition, are possible targets here. See also 162, and 'Prologue to *Cato*', 7.
61. Chace: hunting.

63. haughty Norman: William I, 'the Conqueror', king of England 1066–87.
65 Pope's note. The New Forest in south-west Hampshire was created in 1079 as a royal hunting preserve by William; this was treated as an example of tyranny and oppression as early as the account by the twelfth-century historian William of Malmesbury and in Camden's *Britannia* (1695 edition), p. 115, which explicitly stated that the deaths in the Forest of William's sons (see 81–4) constituted 'divine vengeance' for the crime. *TE* cites also Drayton, *Poly-Olbion*, XVII.120n (1612), p. 268, which relates that the deaths of Richard and William Rufus 'have been thought as diuine reuenges on *William* the first, who destroy'd in *Hantshire* xxxvi. parish Churches to make dens for wild beasts'.
65. Fields are ravish'd: 'ravish'd' means 'seized violently', but probably carries with it the intensity suggested by the political use of 'rape'; cf. the story of Lodona, below, and Commentary to 'Rape of the Locke', Title, and I.48.
65–6 Pope's note. Camden, *ibid.*, has verses by John White (1510–1560), Bishop of Winchester: '*Templa adimit Divis, fora civibus, arva colonis | Rufus, & instituit Beaulensi in rure forestam: | Rex cervum insequitur, Regem vindicta, Tirellus | Non bene provisum transfixit acumine ferri. |* Towns, Fields, and

From Men their Cities, and from Gods their Fanes:
The levell'd Towns with Weeds lie cover'd o'er,
The hollow Winds thro' naked Temples roar;
Round broken Columns clasping Ivy twin'd;
70   O'er Heaps of Ruins stalk'd the stately Hind;
The Fox obscene to gaping Tombs retires,
And Wolves with Howling fill the sacred Quires.

72, *variant, n. 1736–51: And wolves with howling fill, &c.*] The Author thought this an error, wolves not being common in *England* at the time of the Conqueror.

67. lie: MSw: are
70. Ruins: *1717–51:* ruin
72. Wolves with Howling: *1736–51:* savage howlings

Churches, took from God and Men, | A spatious forest made in *Beaulieu*-plain: | The King a Hart, Vengeance the King pursu'd, | And *Tirrel*'s arrow drunk his guilty blood.'

66. Fanes: temples, churches; particularly the monasteries dissolved under Henry VIII, about which Denham complains in *Cooper's Hill*, 115–56, locally exemplified in the ruination of Reading Abbey and Chertsey Abbey (see 270). Pope is probably also suggesting the ruination to faith begun by William III, a vision given enormous political publicity in the cry of 'the Church in danger' from the High Anglican Henry Sacheverell and his subsequent impeachment and trial in 1709–10; see Commentary to *Essay on Criticism*, 551–2. Granville had been returned to parliament in the 1710 Tory landslide partly on pro-Sacheverell connections (Rogers 2005a: 36).

67. *TE* compares Addison, *The Campaign*, 91–2 (1705), p. 5: 'O'er prostrate Towns and Palaces they pass, | (Now cover'd oe'r with Weeds, and hid in Grass).'

68. *TE* compares Donne, *Satyres*, II.60, *Poems, by J. D.* (1633), p. 331: 'Then when winds in our ruin'd Abbeyes rore'. Pope later 'versify'd' this poem, omitting that image. Rogers (2004: 33) cites Thomas Carew's court masque *Coelum Britannicum* (1634), p. 16: 'Your Temples, Shrines, Altars, and Images | Vncovered, rifled, rob'd and disarray'd | By sacrilegious hands.' Rogers (2005a: 272) cites also Spenser's 'The Ruines of Time', 127–33, for similar images of destruction. *TE* (I.138) locates a biblical model of desolation underlying this vision in Isaiah 13.

69. clasping Ivy: familiar in landscape scenery from e.g. Sandys, *Ovid's Metamorphosis Englished*, IV and VI (1632), pp. 121 and 204, and Milton, *Paradise Lost*, IX.217; Pope's usage is less usual in associating the ivy with ruins, which he also does at 'Eloisa to Abelard', 243.

70. *TE* cites Virgil, *Georgics*, III.539–40: 'timidi dammae cervique fugaces | nunc interque canes et circum tecta vagantur' ('shy hinds and fleet-footed stags now wander among the dogs and round the homes').

70. Hind: female deer.

71. obscene: 'offensive; disgusting' (*SJ*, who also says that Pope uses it to mean ill-favoured or ill-omened). *TE* compares Virgil, *Georgics*, I.470–1, 'obscenaeque canes importunaeque volucres | signa dabant', translated by Trapp in *Poetical Miscellanies: The Sixth Part* (1709), p. 380, as 'And dogs obscene, and ill-presaging Birds | Gave dire Portents' [at the death of Julius Caesar]. Cf. 'The First Book of Statius his Thebais', 154, 735.

   to gaping Tombs retires: sleeps in desecrated graves.

72 Pope's note. See Pope's note to 'Summer', 79–80, and Commentary. Rogers (2004: 152) notes information about the habits and hunting of wolves in Nicholas Cox, *The Gentleman's Recreation*, fourth edition (1697), I.112–16. Wolves were actively exterminated by royal decree from pre-Norman times. *TE* suggests an echo of Virgil, *Georgics*, I.485–6, 'et altae | per noctem resonare lupis ululantibus urbes' ('and lofty cities resounded at night with the howling of wolves').

72. Quires: 'the part of the church where the service is sung' (*SJ*), now normally 'choir'.

Aw'd by his Nobles, by his Commons curst,
Th' Oppressor rul'd Tyrannick where he *durst,*
75   Stretch'd o'er the Poor, and Church, his Iron Rod,
And treats alike his Vassals and his God.
Whom ev'n the *Saxon* spar'd, and bloody *Dane,*
The wanton Victims of his *Sport* remain.
But see the Man who spacious Regions gave
80   A Waste for Beasts, himself deny'd a Grave!
Stretch'd on the Lawn his second Hope survey,
At once the Chaser and at once the Prey.

81.] Richard, *second Son of* William *the Conqueror.*

81, n. Richard: *1720–26:* William Rufus

76. treats: MSw, *1736–51:* serv'd
78. The wanton Victims of his: MSw: In Peace, sad Victims to thy
79. who: *1726:* whose
79–81. MSw: What were thy Gains? Who mighty Regions gave
   To Beasts, scarce find'st a poor, precarious Grave!
   Slain by a Stag, thy second Hope survey!

---

73. *Nobles:* the barons and other high-ranking men of William I's court.
   Commons: the common people rather than the lower house of parliament, which did not exist in the eleventh century; the Commons was not constituted as a separate entity until 1341.
74. durst: dared. The italicisation disappeared from editions after 1713, perhaps because it emphasised too obviously contempt for certain kings. The sentiment perhaps derives something from the paradox in Rochester, 'A Satyr against [Reason and] Mankind', 158, *Poems on Several Occasions* (1696), p. 95: 'For all Men would be Cowards if they durst'.
75. Iron Rod: a biblical allusion, normally signalling God's power at its most uncompromising, e.g. Psalms 2:9, Revelation 2:27; cf. also Milton, *Paradise Lost,* V.886–7.
76. Vassals: tenants, followers of a feudal lord.
77. Saxon: Germanic invaders of Britain after the collapse of the Roman empire in 410 AD; Harold, defeated by William at the Battle of Hastings in 1066, was the last Saxon claimant to the throne.
   bloody Dane: the Vikings who raided and sometimes settled in Saxon Britain from the eighth century onwards.

78. wanton: i.e. they are the victims of his 'wanton' (capricious, random) violence.
79. spacious Regions: cf. Blackmore, *Creation,* III (1712), p. 134: 'Of many spacious Regions Man defraud, | For Beasts and Birds of Prey a desolate Abode'.
80. deny'd a Grave: William of Malmesbury, making a general point about the fall of mighty princes, relates that the church at Caen chosen for William I's burial was built on land claimed by a knight named Fitz-Arthur, who had to be bribed to relinquish it (see Rogers 2005a: 98). Some early sources suggest that William I's death in 1087 was caused in part by the impact of an accident on horseback; William III's death in 1702 was caused by his horse's stumbling over a molehill while hunting in Richmond Park, suggesting a neat parallel, reinforced over the next three lines.
81. second Hope: for the phrase cf. 'The First Book of Statius his Thebais', 17. Richard was killed in a hunting accident in the New Forest between 1069 and 1074. See further Commentary to 83.
82. Wakefield cites Denham, 'The Destruction of Troy', 58, *Poems and Translations,* p. 34: 'At once the Taker, and at once the Prey'.

Lo *Rufus,* tugging at the deadly Dart,
Bleeds in the Forest, like a wounded Hart.
85   Succeeding Monarchs heard the Subjects Cries,
Nor Saw displeas'd the peaceful Cottage rise.
Then gath'ring Flocks on unknown Mountains fed,
O'er sandy Wilds were yellow Harvests spread,
The Forests wonder'd at th' unusual Grain,
90   And secret Transports touch'd the conscious Swain.

---

83. MSw: See Rufus bleeding by th' avenging Dart
84. **Bleeds:** MSw: Falls
86. **Nor saw displeas'd:** MSw: And bade secure
88. MSw: O'er sable Heaths were golden Harvests spread:
90. **Transports:** *1717–51:* transport

---

83. **Rufus:** William Rufus (c.1060–1100), third son of William the Conqueror, who ruled England as William II from 1087 to 1100. He was the second (surviving) son by the time of his father's death, which enables Pope to recast 'second Hope' as a reference to Rufus rather than his elder brother Richard in the later *Miscellany* editions (see variant to Pope's note at 81 and Rogers 2004: 130). Rufus was killed by a stray arrow from Walter Tyrell while hunting in the New Forest on 2 August 1100, in circumstances obscure enough to promote conspiracy theories about possible assassination. Pope's sources (see Commentary to 65) interpreted the deaths as divine vengeance for the perceived injustices of the establishment of the New Forest.

  deadly Dart: lethal arrow, but 'dart' could also mean 'spear' and Pope went on to use this phrase at least four times in his translation of *The Iliad*; it is also used by Spenser, *Faerie Queene*, III.xii.21, among others. Cf. 'On a Fan of the Author's Design', above, for another 'fabled Dart'.

84. **Hart:** deer, perhaps punning on 'heart', where the arrow entered his body. Wasserman (1959: 128) and Rogers (2005a: 261) suggest the passage recalls the myth of Actaeon, turned into a stag and destroyed by his own hounds as a punishment for viewing Diana bathing (Ovid, *Metamorphoses,* III.138–252); Actaeon was sometimes linked with Nimrod.

85–6. An emblem for small-scale tenant farmers, signalling the return of productive agriculture to forest regions. Pope implies that post-Norman kings turned a blind eye to encroachments on the forest out of pity for their subjects' condition. Magna Carta, signed in 1215 at Runnymede (near the site of Denham's *Cooper's Hill*), included some modifications of forest law, but Pope pays little attention to this document of Whig constitutionalism.

87–90. Rogers (2004: 208) relates these lines to the prophecy of returning plenitude in Virgil, *Eclogues* IV.18–20, and Pope's 'Messiah', 65–8.

87. **unknown Mountains:** hills (cf. 35) not previously used for pasture; *TE* cites Roscommon's 'Virgil's Sixth Eclogue. Silenus. Translated', *Miscellany Poems* (1684), p. 47 of second sequence: 'wandring Beasts on unknown Mountains fed'. Pope uses the phrase again at 'The Arrival of Ulysses in Ithaca', 67.

88. **yellow Harvests:** cereal crops; cf. the prophecy in *Epistle to Burlington*, 175. Pope used the phrase again in *Iliad*, V.120.

90. **Transports:** 'rapture; ecstasy' (*SJ*). Cf. the phrasing of 'January and May', 576, and 'The First Book of Statius his Thebais', 579.

  conscious: knowing, aware (*OED* sense 2b), perhaps in a heightened sense of self-conscious observation.

Fair *Liberty, Britannia*'s Goddess, rears
Her chearful Head, and leads the golden Years.

Ye vig'rous Swains! while Youth ferments your Blood,
And purer Spirits swell the sprightly Flood,

91, n. 1736–51: VER. 91. *Oh may no more a foreign master's rage*
With wrongs yet legal, curse a future age!
Still spread, fair Liberty! thy heav'nly wings,
Breath plenty on the fields, and fragrance on the springs.

91–94. MSw: Oh may no more a foreign Master's Rage
With Wrongs yet Legal, curse a future Age!
Still spread, fair Liberty! Thy heav'nly Wings,
Breathe Plenty on the Fields, and Fragrance on the Springs.

Ye sprightly Youths! While vig'rous Health remains,
While purer Blood dilates your active Veins,

---

91. Liberty ... Goddess: another of Queen Anne's manifestations in the poem. There was an allegorical painting of the 'Liberty of Europe' at Windsor Castle (Rogers 2005a: 183). 'Liberty' was a major focus of political debate in Pope's period and a byword for English identity; see Commentary to *Essay on Criticism*, 718-21, and the issues presented by Addison's play *Cato* in 1713. Pope recommended a verse passage on 'liberty that crowns Britannia's isle', from Addison's 'Letter from Italy', to Charles Jervas (27 August 1714, *Corr.*, I.245), and many of the 'public' poems on the war and the peace dealt with it much more extensively (e.g. Gildon, *Libertas Triumphans*, 1708).

91 Pope's note. The plea against 'a foreign master's rage', an obvious reference to (at least) William III, and expression of discontent about the line of succession, was clearly seditious. For Pope to display the manuscript passage in 1736 was a hit at the Hanoverian establishment in the high period of his satirical attacks upon it.

92. Rogers (2005a: 253) identifies this line as a 'golden' line, following the classical verse structure adjective–noun–verb–adjective–noun.

93–104. In his letter to Caryll, 5 December 1712, Pope contrasts his own studious life at Binfield to Caryll's vigorous pursuit of the 'Sprightly Delights of the Field ... rouzing a whole Country with Shouts and Horns, & inspiring Animalls & Rationals with like Fury and Ardor' (*Corr.*, I.163). On 10 April 1710 Pope told Cromwell that he was locally reckoned 'no great Hunter indeed, but a great Esteemer of the noble Sport, & only unhappy in my Want of Constitution for that' (*Corr.*, I.81).

Cf., however, his comments on hunting in his essay on animal welfare, *Guardian*, no. 61, 21 May 1713 (*PW*, I.107–14), and Rogers (2005a: 50–2). Rogers (2004: 153) notes a description of the feelings of hunters at the start of Cox, *Gentleman's Recreation*, I.1–4; and further, 307, cites *Spectator*, no. 116, 13 July 1711, on the 'cheerfulness' of hunting. He also notes (2004: 152), that Pope's section on rural sports adheres to the traditional seasons allotted to different prey. Some classical underpinning is supplied from Virgil, *Aeneid*, IV.130–59.

93. ferments: warms, ripens. SJ quotes Pope's lines here in defining the sense as 'to exalt or rarify by intestine motion of parts'. *TE* cites Kersey, *Dictionarium Anglo-Britannicum* (1708), under 'Fermentation': 'In *Physick* [medicine], any gentle Motion of the Parts of the Blood or Juices in the Body, a kind of bubbling up, rais'd by the Spirits that endeavour to get out of a Mixt Body'.

94. purer Spirits ... sprightly Flood: the 'animal spirits' supposed to dwell and move in the bloodstream, driving activity. *EC* cites Addison, *The Campaign*, 107–8 (1705), p. 6: 'Their Courage dwells not in a troubl'd Flood | Of mounting Spirits, and fermenting Blood'. Wasserman (1959: 130) illustrates the line with early physiological descriptions of these spirits, but also notes that Pope uses 'purer spirits' again in 'Verses to the Memory of an Unfortunate Lady', 25, in relation to the soul. The phrase also occurs in Blackmore, *Creation*, VI (1712), p. 287, in relation to the flow of blood: 'From this o'erflowing Tyde the curious Brain | Does thro' its Pores the purer Spirits strain'.

95   Now range the Hills, the thickest Woods beset,
      Wind the shrill Horn, or spread the waving Net.
      When milder Autumn Summer's Heat succeeds,
      And in the new-shorn Field the Partridge feeds,
      Before his Lord the ready Spaniel bounds,
100   Panting with Hope, he tries the furrow'd Grounds,
      But when the tainted Gales the Game betray,
      Couch'd close he lyes, and meditates the Prey;
      Secure they trust th' unfaithful Field, beset,
      Till hov'ring o'er 'em sweeps the swelling Net.
105   Thus (if small Things we may with great compare)

97, n. 1736–51: VER. 97. *When yellow autumn summer's heat succeeds,*
  And into wine the purple harvest bleeds,
  The partridge feeding in the new-shorn fields
  Both morning sports and ev'ning pleasures yields.
  MSw, *1751:* quaere if [*1751:* Perhaps the Author thought it not] allowable to describe the season by a circumstance not proper to our climate, The Vintage.

95. **thickest:** MSw, *1751:* gamefull
97. **milder:** MSw: yellow
97^8. MSw: And into Wine the purple Harvest bleeds,
98. MSw: The Partridge feeding in the new-shorn Fields
98^9. MSw: Both Morning Sports and Evening Pleasures yields.
103. MSw: Who trust th' unfaithful Field, with Foes beset,
104. **hov'ring:** MSw rushing

---

95 MS. **gamefull:** full of game (birds and other prey animals).

96. **Wind . . . Horn:** blow the hunting horn.
  spread . . . Net: used in hunting partridges with dogs (cf. 104).

97 **Pope's note.** Cf. Pope's translation of Homer, 'The Gardens of Alcinous', 17–25; Pope later created a vineyard in his garden at Twickenham, and wine was successfully produced in southern Britain at this period.

98. **new-shorn Field:** cereal crop trimmed to stubble by harvest, amongst which the partridges feed on dropped grain.

99. **Spaniel:** 'a dog used for sports in the field, remarkable for sagacity and obedience' (*SJ*); used to locate the shot birds.

100. furrow'd: ploughed into ridge and furrow.

101. **tainted Gales:** wafts of animal scent on the wind. Cummings (1988: 143–58) notes that the phrase 'tainted Dews' appears in Addison's pro-Marlborough poem, *The Campaign*, 122 (1705), p. 7, in a simile comparing a stag hunt with British troops' pursuit of the enemy. Pope re-used his own phrase in his translation of Homer, *Odyssey* XII.434. For the diminished sense of 'gale', cf. 390 below and 'Summer', 73.

102. **Couch'd:** lying down 'in secret; or in ambush' (*SJ*); it also suggests 'couchant', a heraldic term for recumbent animals on coats of arms (Rogers 2004: 101).
  meditates: watches closely or intently, perhaps with the sense of making a plan; *TE* cites Dryden, 'Sigismonda and Guiscardo', 245, *Fables*, p. 132: 'With inward Rage he meditates his Prey'. See also Pope's usage in *Essay on Criticism*, 126; 'Rape of the Locke', I.47; 'Episode of Sarpedon', 23.

103. **unfaithful:** treacherous, because it seems innocent but will not protect them.
  beset: besieged; preparing for the military analogy in 105–10.

104. **swelling Net:** more normally used of fishing, e.g. William Diaper, *Nereides*, XII (1712), p. 58. *TE* cites, however, a long description of the practice of hunting partridges with dogs and nets from Cox, *Gentleman's Recreation*, III.39–45. Nets are part of the equipment for the hunt in Virgil, *Aeneid*, IV.131.

When *Albion* sends her eager Sons to War,
Pleas'd, in the Gen'ral's Sight, the Host lye down
Sudden, before some unsuspecting Town,
The Young, the Old, one Instant makes our Prize,
110 And high in Air *Britannia*'s Standard flies.

See! from the Brake the whirring Pheasant springs,
And mounts exulting on triumphant Wings;

107–9. 1736–51: Some thoughtless Town, with ease and plenty blest,
    Near, and more near, the closing lines invest;
    Sudden they seize th' amaz'd, defenceless prize,
109. **The Young, the Old:** *1717–26:* The captive Race
110. **high in Air:** MSw: o'er their Captive Heads
111. **Brake:** MSw: Copse
112. MSw: Exults in Air, and plies his whistling Wings.

---

105. TE cites Virgil, *Georgics*, IV.176, 'si parva licet componere magnis', translated by Dryden (256), *Works of Virgil*, p. 130, as 'If little things with great we may compare'; Milton, *Paradise Lost*, II.921–2 (1674), p. 55: 'to compare | Great things with small', and VI.310–11, p. 155: 'to set forth | Great things by small'. Addison's version of the Georgics line reads: 'Thus, if great things we may with small compare'; *Annual Miscellany: For the Year 1694* (1694), p. 73. The inverted perspective has the effect of converting Britain's war efforts to the safe occupation of hunting; see Winn (2014: 604).

106. Albion: ancient name for Britain, often used as a dignified or mythic identity for England or Britain in patriotic poems; cf. 'Spring', 6.

eager ... War: a lightweight allusion to the War of Spanish Succession, about to be concluded by the Treaty of Utrecht (see Headnote).

107. Host: army.

108. some unsuspecting Town: sometimes taken specifically to represent Gibraltar, captured by the Tory admiral Sir George Rooke in July 1704, a naval victory which could be cited in the balance against Marlborough's land-based claims. Siege warfare was still common: the siege of the French fortress of Bouchain (August–September 1711) was Marlborough's last significant military success in the war. Cf. also *Essay on Criticism*, 435.

109. Prize: see Commentary to 'Rape of the Locke', I.46.

107–9 variants. Pope's substitution diminishes the sense of human victims in the MS and first edition, but introduces an echo of 'peace and plenty' (42). The removal of the 'General' diminishes any possible reference to Marlborough (Rogers 2005a: 102).

closing lines invest: ranks of soldiers encircle and besiege.

110. Britannia's Standard: British flag, raised in token of victory. Pope's only mention of an actual battle, making it look effortless, compared to Whig versions of hard-won military glory; Rogers (2005a: 309) suggests the line twists Addison's triumphalist *The Campaign*, 48 (1705), p. 3: '*Brittania*'s Colours in the Zephyrs fly'.

111–18. Singled out as an emotive reminder of the consequences of hunting in Francis Knapp's poem 'To Mr. Pope on his Windsor-Forest' in Pope's *Works* (1717), sig. e1ᵛ: 'Ah! how I melt with pity, when I spy | On the cold earth the flutt'ring Pheasant lie'. It found favour on the same grounds with Warton (1756: 33).

111. Brake: 'a thicket of brambles, or of thorns' (*SJ*).

whirring: 'a word formed in imitation of the sound expressed by it' (*SJ*, quoting this passage). Not used anywhere else by Pope. *OED*, 'whirr', sense 2, cites the glossary in Cox, *Gentleman's Recreation*, second edition (1677), II.168: 'Whur, is the rising and fluttering of Partridge or Pheasant'.

Pheasant: Rogers (2004: 37, 94, 101) notes resemblances to a masque costume and heraldic device, with the rising motion suggesting the heraldic posture 'rousant'. Rogers also (2004: 111) refers to Randle Holme's heraldic

Short is his Joy! he feels the fiery Wound,
Flutters in Blood, and panting beats the Ground.
115 Ah! what avail his glossie, varying Dyes,
His Purple Crest, and Scarlet-circled Eyes,
The vivid Green his shining Plumes unfold;
His painted Wings, and Breast that flames with Gold?

Nor yet, when moist *Arcturus* clouds the Sky,
120 The Woods and Fields their pleasing Toils deny.
To Plains with well-breath'd Beagles we repair,
And trace the Mazes of the circling Hare.

119, n. 1736–43: VER. 119. *When hoary winter cloaths the year in white,*
The woods and fields to pleasing toils invite.

114^5. MSw: Stretch'd out in all his Plumy Pride he lies!
115. **Ah!:** MSw: Now
119–20. MSw: When hoary Winter cloaths the Year in White,
The Woods and Fields to pleasing Toils invite:
121. **well-breath'd:** *1720–22:* well-bred
122. MSw: To trace the Circle of the tim'rous Hare,

---

manual *The Academy of Armory* (1688) for a description of the colours of the pheasant very similar to Pope's. For the colouring, TE cites Jonson, 'To Penshurst', 28, *Workes* (1616), p. 820: 'The purpled pheasant with the speckled side'. Rogers (2005a: 223) suggests the pheasant's fall from 'triumphant' ascent may allegorise the dismissal of Marlborough in late 1711.
112. **triumphant Wings:** perhaps a faint reminiscence of the classical winged figure of victory, as in Charles Cotton, 'The Battle of Yvry', *Poems on Several Occasions* (1689), p. 723: 'Now Conquest, who on her triumphant wings...'.
115. **what avail:** what use are; cf. 'Winter', 35.
    Dyes: colours, suggesting quasi-heraldic use of symbolic tints (purple, scarlet, green, gold). See Commentary to *Essay on Criticism*, 64–5. Brower (1959: 53) finds a source in the description of a dying ox, Virgil, *Georgics*, III.515–25.
118. **painted Wings:** Wakefield cites Virgil, *Georgics*, III.243: 'pictaeque volucres' ('and painted birds'); EC finds the exact phrase used of birds in Milton, *Paradise Lost*, VII.434.
119–20 variant. **hoary:** 'white with frost' (*SJ*).
119. **moist Arcturus:** cf. 'Autumn', 72; based on Virgil, *Georgics*, I.67–8. Rogers (2005a: 249) finds Pope closer in cadence to Dryden's version, 102, *Works of Virgil*, p. 52: 'When cold *Arcturus* rises with the Sun' than to the original. Arcturus is the brightest star in the constellation Boötes (the Herdsman) and its rise (anciently in September, latterly in October) is associated in classical literature with a period of rain, signalling a change of season. Rogers (2005a: 304) further recovers a link in the underlying myth to Callisto (see 176 below). Cf. also 'The First Book of Statius his Thebais', 521.
120. **pleasing Toils:** a slightly greater degree of awareness of rural labour than Pope felt appropriate to the *Pastorals*: see Commentary to 'Spring', 30.
121. **well-breath'd Beagles:** fit, trained hunting dogs. TE cites Dryden, 'To my honour'd Kinsman, John Driden', 52, *Fables*, p. 95: 'With well-breath'd Beagles, you surround the Wood'. Pope repeated the phrasing in his translation of Homer, *Iliad* XV.697 and XXII.244.
122. **trace ... Hare:** follows the sport of hare-coursing. TE cites Cowley's translation of Horace, *Epodes*, II, 'Horat. Epodon' in his Essay 'Of Agriculture', 35, *Works of Mr. Abraham Cowley* (1668), p. 108 of separate sequence: 'He runs the *Mazes* of the nimble Hare'. For 'tracing' a maze cf. also Blackmore, *A Paraphrase upon the Book of Job* (1700), p. 34: 'the Maze Divine he cannot trace'.

(Beasts, taught by us, their Fellow Beasts pursue,
And learn of Man each other to undo.)
125   With slaught'ring Guns th' unweary'd Fowler roves,
When Frosts have whiten'd all the naked Groves;
Where Doves in Flocks the leafless Trees o'ershade,
And lonely Woodcocks haunt the watry Glade.
He lifts the Tube, and levels with his Eye;
130   Strait a short Thunder breaks the frozen Sky.
Oft, as in Airy Rings they skim the Heath,
The clam'rous Plovers feel the Leaden Death:
Oft as the mounting Larks their Notes prepare,
They fall, and leave their little Lives in Air.

135   In genial Spring, beneath the quiv'ring Shade

129, n. 1736–51: VER. 129. *The fowler lifts his level'd tube on high.*

123. taught: *1736–51:* urg'd
125–6. MSw: Or, arm'd with slaughtring Guns, unweary'd rove
   O'er rustling Leaves around the naked Grove;
129. MSw: The Fowler lifts his levell'd Tube on high,
132. Plovers: MSw, *1751:* Lapwings
133. MSw: The mounting Larks, as they to sing prepare,
134. They fall: MSw: Drop down
135. In genial Spring: MSw: At Spring's Return

---

125. Fowler: 'a sportsman who pursues birds' (*SJ*).
126. naked: leafless.
127. Doves ... o'ershade: The image is of the doves shading the trees, not the other way around.
128. lonely Woodcocks: The bird is normally solitary.
129. Tube ... Eye: aims the hunting rifle. EC notes Dryden's translation of Virgil, *Georgics*, II.774, *Works of Virgil*, p. 94: 'And bends his Bow, and levels with his Eyes', a line Pope marked with a comma in his copy (now in the British Library).
130. Strait: at once, suddenly.
   Thunder: the firing of the gun.
131–3. TE cites Philips, *Cyder*, II.174–6 (1708), p. 59: '... the tow'ring, heavy Lead | O'er-takes their Speed; they leave their little Lives | Above the Clouds, praecipitant to Earth'. Warburton compares Virgil, *Georgics*, III.547: 'praecipites alta vitam sub nube relinquunt', ('falling headlong they leave life under a high cloud'). Cf. Pope's version of Homer, *Iliad*, XXIII.1041 (of a wounded bird): 'Then sudden dropt, and left her Life in Air'.
131. Airy Rings: circling flight.
132. clam'rous Plovers: alluding to the particular cry of the plover; there appears to be no literary model for this, and Pope mentions the bird (generally regarded as a game bird) nowhere else.
   Leaden Death: gun pellets, as in Oldmixon, *Iberia Liberata*, 440 (1706), p. 27: 'in his Bowels lodge the leaden Death'.
132 MS Lapwings: a slightly larger relative of the plover; in Pope's time both were still regarded as a source of food. The 'peewit' cry garnered considerably more literary attention than the similar call of the plover.
133. mounting: ascending; a normal poetic adjective for larks, as e.g. in Spenser, *Faerie Queene*, I.xi.51.
   Larks ... Notes: skylarks. Cf. 'Autumn', 45; 'Winter', 53.
135. genial: 'cheerful' (*SJ*), implying warmth; but also perhaps 'generative' (*OED* sense 1).
   quiv'ring Shade: cf. 'Summer', variant line 4.

Where cooling Vapours breathe along the Mead,
The patient Fisher takes his silent Stand
Intent, his Angle trembling in his Hand;
With Looks unmov'd, he hopes the Scaly Breed,
140   And eyes the dancing Cork and bending Reed.
Our plenteous Streams a various Race supply;
The bright-ey'd Perch with Fins of *Tyrian* Dye,
The silver Eel, in shining Volumes roll'd,
The yellow Carp, in Scales bedrop'd with Gold,
145   Swift Trouts, diversify'd with Crimson Stains,

---

143. **shining:** MSw: slimy
144. **in:** MSw: with

---

136. ***Mead:*** meadow; 'a word chiefly poetical' (*SJ*).

138. ***Angle trembling:*** fishing rod vibrating. Wakefield cites the literal 'tremula ... arundine' ('trembling fishing-rod') of Ovid, *Ars Amatoria*, II.77; *TE* notes the more euphemistic opening lines of the political poem 'Windsor', dubiously attributed to Rochester, in *A Collection of Poems Relating to State Affairs* (1705), p. 186: 'Methinks I see our Mighty Monarch stand, | His pliant Angle trembling in his Hand'. The same satire and attribution had appeared as 'Flatfoot the Gudgeon Taker', the name by which it was widely known in Restoration manuscript anthologies, in *State Poems* (1697), p. 43, and it was reprinted as 'The Royal Angler' in Curll's edition of *The Works of ... Rochester, and Roscommon* (1709), I.149; see further Mengel (1965), 189–91. Cf. a similar phrase in a literal sense in 'Vertumnus and Pomona', 42.

139. ***hopes:*** hopes to catch.
    Scaly Breed: poetic periphrasis for fish.

140. ***dancing Cork:*** the fishing float on the surface of the water. Cf. Walter Pope, 'Another Parafrase of the Same', *Moral and Political Fables* (1698), p. 6: 'Dancing upon the Billows like a Cork'.

141–6. *TE* suggests Pope's brief catalogue of fish is modelled on Ausonius, *Mosella*, 85ff., and Drayton, *Poly-Olbion*, XXVI.240ff. Walton's *Compleat Angler* (1653) contains individual discussion of all five fish mentioned by Pope.

142. ***Perch ... Tyrian:*** Tyrian, from Tyre, a major Phoenician port in the ancient world, where a rare red-purple dye used on the togas of roman senators and other high-status officials was prepared from the shells of various molluscs; cf. Pope's 'The Fable of Dryope', 24. The perch is striped in various shades, but does not usually have purple fins.

143. ***silver Eel:*** a specific type of eel, according to Walton, *Compleat Angler*, X, p. 191, and several seventeenth-century recipe books, but also with heraldic implications once more (see 167).

    Volumes: coils or convolutions 'as a fold of a serpent, a wave of water' (*SJ*). Cf. Blackmore, *Prince Arthur*, II (1695), p. 40: 'The shining Volumes of his Spiral Train', and 'The First Book of Statius his Thebais', 728. Rogers (2004: 102) suggests Pope recalls the heraldic term 'voluted', used of the coils of a serpent.

144. ***bedrop'd:*** sprinkled. Wakefield cites Milton, *Paradise Lost*, VII.406 (1674), p. 185: 'coats dropt with Gold'; *TE* compares Fenton's *Cerealia* (1706), p. 5, of a snake: 'Spires bedropt with Gold'. Tickell's 'A Description of the Phaenix', *Poetical Miscellanies: The Sixth Part*, p. 421, has a bird 'bedropt with Gold'.

145. ***diversify'd ... Stains:*** streaked with colours; 'crimson stains' normally indicate blood and bleeding, as in Pope's own *Iliad*, V.420: 'the transparent Skin with Crimson stain'd'. *TE* notes that Drayton describes the Trout as 'markt with many a Crimson spot' in *Poly-Olbion*, XXVI.240, *The Second Part* (1622), p. 120. Rogers (2004: 102) sees an allusion to heraldic 'stains', or mixed colours.

And Pykes, the Tyrants of the watry Plains.

Now *Cancer* glows with *Phoebus*' fiery Car;
The Youth rush eager to the Sylvan War;
Swarm o'er the Lawns, the Forest Walks surround,
150 Rowze the fleet Hart, and chear the opening Hound.
Th' impatient Courser pants in ev'ry Vein,
And pawing, seems to beat the distant Plain,

147, n. *1736–43:* VER. 147.   *But when bright* Phoebus *from the twins invites*
  Our active genius to more free delights,
  With springing day we range the lawns around.

147–9. MSw: But when the Summer's fav'ring Reign invites
  Our active Genius to more free Delights,
  With springing Day we range the Lawns around,

---

146. Pykes . . . Tyrants: Wakefield notes that Drayton calls the pike 'Tyrant' in *Poly-Olbion*, XXVI.244–5, *The Second Part*, p. 120. Walton comments that the pike is held to be the '*Tyrant*' of freshwater rivers, because pikes are the fiercest predators; *Compleat Angler*, VII (1653), pp. 142–3. The image recalls the tyranny of the Norman kings, 43–84, 'Plains' suggesting lands. Wasserman (1959: 132) notes that the republican group The Calves-Head Club used to celebrate the execution of Charles I by eating, amongst other things, a pike as an emblem of tyranny; Pope might have known this from Edward Ward, *The Secret History of the Calves-head Club* (1706), p. 18.

watry Plains: Wakefield cites Virgil, *Aeneid*, VI.724, 'terras camposque liquentis' [*sic*, for 'liquentes'] ('lands and the watery plains'); *TE* finds the phrase in Dryden's *Georgics*, II.625; and see Commentary to 387 below. Cf. also 'The Arrival of Ulysses in Ithaca', 196.

147–58. See Commentary to 93–104. *TE* suggests the hunt passage is based on the hunting episode in *Aeneid*, IV.129–35. Rogers (2004: chapter 5) explores the influential model of Drayton, *Poly-Olbion*, XIII.

147. Cancer . . . Car: the star sign Cancer (beginning around 22 June), warmed with the sun, supposedly the chariot of Phoebus Apollo, Greek god of the sun; indicating a change to summer. Cf. 'Summer', 14.

147 Pope's note. the twins: Gemini. The sun is in Gemini from about 21 May to the summer solstice, 22 June.

active Genius: spirit, inclination to vigorous activity.
more free Delights: more wide-ranging pleasures.
With springing Day: at daybreak.
range: 'rove at large' (*SJ*), cf. 206.

148. Sylvan War: hunting in the woods; cf. Pope, *Iliad*, XI.122.

150. Rowze the fleet Hart: flush out the swift deer (from hiding); *TE* cites Kersey, *Dictionarium Anglo-Britannicum*, 'Rouse', for the technical definition in hunting.

chear the opening Hound: encourage the barking of the hunting dog. 'Open' in this sense is 'a term of hunting' (*SJ*), meaning the cry of dogs picking up a scent. Cf. Dryden, 'The Pythagorean Philosophy', 701, *Fables*, p. 529: 'Nor opening Hounds the trembling Stag affright'. There are relevant descriptions of stag-hunting in Virgil, *Aeneid*, IV; Drayton, *Poly-Olbion*, XIII; and Denham, *Cooper's Hill*, 247–325, in the latter case clearly freighted with political significance. Pope begins the hunt, but no stag is actually killed.

151–4. *TE* notes a resemblance to the simile in *Essay on Criticism*, 228–31.

151–2. Warburton stated that these lines were translated from Statius (*Thebais*, VI.400–1) after Dryden had commended them in his 'Preface' to his translation of Du Fresnoy's *De Arte Graphica* (1695), p. li; *TE* contends that the influence of surrounding lines in Statius can also be felt. Wakefield finds a more obvious source in Virgil, *Georgics*, III.83–4: 'tum, si qua sonum procul arma

Hills, Vales, and Floods appear already crost,
And ere he starts, a thousand Steps are lost.
155 See! the bold Youth strain up the threatning Steep,
Rush thro' the Thickets, down the Vallies sweep,
Hang o'er their Coursers Heads with eager Speed,
And Earth rolls back beneath the flying Steed.
Let old *Arcadia* boast her spacious Plain,
160 Th' Immortal Huntress, and her Virgin Train;
Nor envy *Windsor*! since thy Shades have seen
As bright a Goddess, and as chast a Queen;

---

155. **threatning:** MSw: pendant
158. **And Earth rolls back:** MSw: And the Ground rolls
158^9. MSw: They stretch, they sweat, they glow, they shout around;
   Heav'n trembles, roar the Mountains, thunders all the Ground.
159. MSw: new paragraph
   spacious: MSw, *1717–51:* ample
160. **Virgin:** MSw: buskin'd

---

dedere, | stare loco nescit, micat auribus et tremit artus', translated (expansively) by Dryden, III.130-3, *Works of Virgil*, p. 100, as 'The fiery Courser, when he hears from far, | The sprightly Trumpet, and the shouts of War, | Pricks up his Ears; and, trembling with Delight, | Shifts place, and paws; and hopes the promis'd Fight'. Rogers (2005a: 306) finds a further echo of Dryden's translation of Virgil, *Aeneid*, IV, 190-2, *Works of Virgil*, p. 302, where the 'lofty Courser' (horse) of Dido 'paws the Ground' in impatience.

154. **ere . . . lost:** The horse could have gone that distance in the time taken to get ready.

155. **threatning Steep:** dangerously steep slope. Cf. the 1643 text of Denham, *Cooper's Hill*, p. 2: 'Where no stupendious Cliffe, no threatning heights | Accesse deny, no horrid steepe affrights'.

155 MS. **pendant:** overhanging; cf. 211.

158^9 MS. Pope's unusual syntax perhaps emphasises that the roaring of the mountains is caused by the shouts of the hunters.

159. **old Arcadia:** remote inland plateau region of central Greece, long regarded as the site of ideal pastoral landscape, both in classical poetry and in later prose romance, such as the *Arcadia* of Sir Philip Sidney (1590).

160. **Immortal Huntress:** Diana, Roman version of the Greek goddess Artemis, dedicated to chastity (hence the 'virgin-train') and hunting, especially in woodland; cf. 198; 'Spring', 66; 'The First Book of Statius his Thebais', 625.

162. Anne (cf. 42), celebrated as Diana, protective goddess of woods, chastity, and women, with perhaps some hint of Astraea, goddess of justice, identified with the star Virgo, whose return to earth is prophesied in Virgil's fourth eclogue, the model for 'Messiah'; see Rogers (2005a: 138–40 and 256–8). Swift told 'Stella' that Anne 'hunts in a chaise with one horse, which she drives herself, and drives furiously, like Jehu, and is a mighty hunter, like Nimrod' (*Journal to Stella*, 31 July 1711). For the phrasing, EC compares Congreve, 'Prologue to the Queen', 9-10, *Annual Miscellany: For the Year 1694* (1694), p. 101: 'For never was in Rome, nor Athens, seen | So Fair a Circle, and so bright a Queen'. Congreve's Queen was Mary, consort of William III. Rogers (2004: 192 and 179) links the imagery to the more acceptable (to Pope) version of royal panegyric in Jonson's *Cynthia's Revels*, V.vi (opening of the Hymn to Diana), *Workes* (1616), p. 254: 'Queene, and Huntresse, chaste, and fair' and to the royalist evocation of Diana as Queen of the Forest in Drayton, *Poly-Olbion*, XIII.98–108.

>   Whose Care, like hers, protects the Sylvan Reign,
>   The Earth's fair Light, and Empress of the Main.
>
> 165   Here, as old Bards have sung, *Diana* stray'd,
>   Bath'd in the Springs, or sought the cooling Shade;
>   Here arm'd with Silver Bows, in early Dawn,
>   Her buskin'd Virgins trac'd the Dewy Lawn.
>   Above the rest a rural Nymph was fam'd,
> 170   Thy Offspring, *Thames*! the fair *Lodona* nam'd,
>   (*Lodona*'s Fate, in long Oblivion cast,

165, n. *1736–43:* VER. 165. *Yet here, 'tis sung, of old* Diana *stray'd:*
  And Cynthus' *top forsook for* Windsor *shade.*
  Here was she seen o'er sunny heaths to rove,
  Seek the clear spring, or haunt the pathless grove.

160^7. MSw, *1751* [*1751:* new paragraph]:
  Here too, tis sung, of old Diana stray'd,
  And Cynthus Top forsook for Windsor Shade.
  Here was she seen o'er airy Wastes to rove,
  Or tir'd with Hunting sought the closer Grove;
  [*1751:* Seek the clear spring, or haunt the pathless grove;]
166. Springs: *1726:* spring
168. Buskin'd: MSw: Quiver'd
169. MSw, *1736–51:* new paragraph
170. Lodona: MSw: Lodone
171. Lodona's: MSw: Whose wondrous

---

163. Sylvan Reign: woodland territory.
164. Earth's fair Light: the moon, another symbol of Diana (see 174).

  Empress of the Main: queen of the oceans, a reference to the increased empire Britain had acquired as a result of the Treaty of Utrecht.
165. sung . . . stray'd: apparently a fulfilment of the possibility raised by Damon in Pope's 'Spring', 65–8.
167. Silver Bows: associated with the huntress Diana, e.g. by Milton, 'A Mask', 440–1; perhaps because of the crescent moon. Cf. Pope, *Iliad*, XX.54: 'And the chast Huntress of the silver Bow'. Silver is also the heraldic colour 'argent', suggesting chastity (Rogers 2005a: 259).
168. buskin'd: wearing boots, appropriate for hunting.

  trac'd: trod, walked across. Rogers (2005a: 141) points out that Anne was greeted on some ceremonial occasions by young women dressed in this manner.

  Dewy Lawn: recalled by Pope in his version of Homer, *Iliad*, VIII.2 and XXIV.1000.

168 MS. Quiver'd: i.e. equipped with a quiver of arrows; cf. 177.
170. Lodona: Pope's invention for the spirit of the river Loddon, a tributary of the Thames, here a daughter of that river god. The Loddon joins the Thames at Henley, after passing a few miles from Pope's Binfield. For the view that the episode is an allegory of illegal Williamite possession of Stuart England, see Rogers (2005a: 2, 302). Rogers (2004: 143) describes the course of the river and cites Defoe's approval, in his *Tour*, on its industrial applications, an aspect not present in Pope's rural vision. The episode is modelled on several similar stories of nymphs fleeing from amorous gods in Ovid, *Metamorphoses*, including Arethusa, Callisto and Syrinx. Rogers (2005a: 272) finds another analogue in the 'Molanna' episode among the 'Mutabilitie' cantos of the *Faerie Queene*.
171. long Oblivion: Pope suggests that her story has been long forgotten and that his Muse is bringing it to light, rather than inventing it. Wakefield notes the phrase 'longa oblivia' in Virgil, *Aeneid*, VI.715.

         The Muse shall sing, and what she sings shall last)
         Scarce could the Goddess from her Nymph be known,
         But by the Crescent and the golden Zone,
175   She scorn'd the Praise of Beauty, and the Care;
         A Belt her Waste, a Fillet binds her Hair,
         A painted Quiver on her Shoulder sounds,
         And with her Dart the flying Deer she wounds.
         It chanc'd, as eager of the Chace the Maid
180   Beyond the Forest's verdant Limits stray'd,
         Pan saw and lov'd, and furious with Desire
         Pursu'd her Flight; her Flight increas'd his Fire.
         Not half so swift the trembling Doves can fly,
         When the fierce Eagle cleaves the liquid Sky;
185   Not half so swiftly the fierce Eagle moves,
         When thro' the Clouds he drives the trembling Doves;

173. **her:** MSw: the
174. **the ... the:** MSw: her ... her
176. **Fillet binds:** MSw: Ribband ty'd
181. **furious:** *1717–51:* burning

173. ***Goddess:*** i.e. Diana; the likeness of the pursued nymph to Diana herself is borrowed from the Syrinx episode, *Metamorphoses*, I.689–712.

174. ***Crescent ... Zone:*** signs of Diana's identity, the moon (Crescent) and girdle (Latin, 'zona').

175. TE likens the attitude to that of Arethusa, in Ovid, *Metamorphoses*, V.580–2.

176. ***Fillet:*** 'a band tied round the head or other part' (*SJ*). These details, as Warburton suggested, are modelled on the story of Jupiter's pursuit of the nymph Callisto, in Ovid, *Metamorphoses*, II.412–13.

177. ***painted Quiver:*** EC compares Dryden's translation of Virgil, *Aeneid*, XI.1120, *Works of Virgil*, p. 572: 'A guilded Quiver from his Shoulder sounds'; 'painted Quiver' is fairly common, e.g. Dryden, 'Palamon and Arcite', II.648, *Fables*, p. 48.

   sounds: rattles (because of the arrows).

180. ***verdant:*** green, flourishing, as in line 28.

181–2. EC compares Dryden's translation of *Aeneid*, XII.108–9, *Works of Virgil*, p. 581: 'The Lover gaz'd, and burning with desire, | The more he look'd, the more he fed the Fire'.

181. ***Pan:*** See 37. Pan was notoriously given to sexual pursuit; the nymph Syrinx escapes by being turned into a reed which Pan then made into pan-pipes.

183–6. The antithesis is based on the pursuit of Arethusa by Alpheus the river god, Ovid, *Metamorphoses*, V.572–641; EC cites Sandys, *Ovid's Metamorphosis Englished*, V (1632), p. 187: 'As trembling Doues the eager Hawkes eschew; | As eager Hawkes the trembling Doues pursew'. Wasserman (1959: 137) suggests that Pope's substitution of eagle for the 'accipiter' or hawk of Ovid, aligns the pursuit with a symbol of war (the Roman eagle). For the version of the Arethusa story published in Lintot's *Miscellaneous Poems and Translations* (1712) next to Pope's 'Vertumnus and Pomona' and attributed to Pope on the bases of stylistic similarity by Ault (1949: 38–48) see Headnote to 'The First Book of Statius his Thebais'.

184. ***cleaves:*** cuts through.

   liquid: 'soft, clear' (*SJ*); transparent, from Latin 'liquidus'. *TE* cites Dryden's translation of Virgil, *Georgics*, III.377–8, *Works of Virgil*, p. 107: 'but they | That wing the liquid Air'. Cf. 'Rape of the Locke', II.172; 'The Arrival of Ulysses in Ithaca', 14. Pope used the phrase 'liquid skies' at least three times in the *Iliad* translation, and cf. 'The First Book of Statius his Thebais', 415.

As from the God with fearful Speed she flew,
As did the God with equal Speed pursue.
Now fainting, sinking, pale, the Nymph appears;
190 Now close behind his sounding Steps she hears;
And now his Shadow reach'd her as she run,
(His Shadow lengthen'd by the setting Sun)
And now his shorter Breath with sultry Air
Pants on her Neck, and fans her parting Hair.
195 In vain on Father *Thames* she calls for Aid,
Nor could *Diana* help her injur'd Maid.
Faint, breathless, thus she pray'd, nor pray'd in vain;
'Ah *Cynthia*! ah — tho' banish'd from thy Train,
Let me, O let me, to the Shades repair,
200 My native Shades — there weep, and murmur there.'
She said, and melting as in Tears she lay,

---

187. **fearful:** MSw: headlong
187–8. 1717–51: As from the God she flew with furious pace,
    Or as the God, more furious, urg'd the chace.
192. 1736–51: no parentheses
195. **calls:** *1736–43:* call'd
197. **Faint:** MSw: Spent

---

188 **variant. urg'd the chace:** pursued the hunt; punning on 'chase' in the modern sense and 'chace' as hunt as in 61 and 179.

189–94. Wakefield compares Sandys's translation of the Arethusa episode from Ovid, *Metamorphoses*, V, in *Ovid's Metamorphosis Englished* (1632), p. 187: 'The Sunne was at our backs: before my feet | I saw his shadow; or my feare did see't. | How-ere his sounding steps, and thick drawne breath | That fann'd my haire...'.

190. **sounding:** resounding.

191. **run:** ran; a fairly common grammatical looseness, here required by the rhyme.

193. **sultry:** hot, from exertion and desire. The phrase 'sultry air' appears in Addison's *Remarks on Several Parts of Italy* (1705), p. 229, and Blackmore's *Creation*, II (1712), p. 64, among other instances, normally connoting disease.

194. **Pants:** with desire; cf. 'Winter', 80, and 'On a Fan of the Author's Design', 2.

parting Hair: cf. 'Rape of the Locke', II.52. Rogers (2004: 202) compares the image to the hunting of the hare in Dryden, *Annus Mirabilis*, st. 132 (1667), p. 34: 'With his loll'd tongue he faintly licks his prey/ | His warm breath blows her flix up as she lies'.

196. **injur'd:** morally wronged.

197 **MS. Spent:** exhausted.

198–200. Similar prayers are uttered by Daphne and Arethusa (*Metamorphoses*, I.545 and V.618); but Arethusa is helped by Diana to avoid the intended rape, and Daphne's transformation into laurel also protects her from Apollo's assault. Cf. 'Sapho to Phaon', 28.

198. **Cynthia:** one of Diana's names, because of her supposed birth on Mt Cynthus, on Delos (cf. 165 variant and 'Spring', 66), a detail mentioned by Ovid in the *Metamorphoses*, e.g. VI.204. Cf. also 'Sapho to Phaon', 99; 'The First Book of Statius his Thebais', 475; 'The Rape of the Locke', II.8.

banish'd ... Train: because no longer virginal; cf. the moment in *Metamorphoses* II.464–5 where Diana expels a nymph raped by Jove.

199. **Shades:** sheltered woodland, perhaps with a hint of the deathly region known as the Shades.

repair: go, retire.

In a soft, silver Stream dissolv'd away.
The silver Stream her Virgin Coldness keeps,
For ever murmurs, and for ever weeps;
205   Still bears the Name the hapless Virgin bore,
And bathes the Forest where she rang'd before.
In her chast Current oft the Goddess laves,
And with Celestial Tears augments the Waves.
Oft in her Glass the musing Shepherd spies
210   The headlong Mountains and the downward Skies,
The watry Landskip of the pendant Woods,
And absent Trees that tremble in the Floods;
In the clear azure Gleam the Flocks are seen,
And floating Forests paint the Waves with Green.
215   Thro' the fair Scene rowl slow the lingring Streams,
Then foaming pour along, and rush into the *Thames.*

205.] The River Loddon.

209, n. 1751: Oft in her glass, etc] These six lines were added after the first writing of this poem.

205–6. MSw: The Flood retains the Name the Virgin bore,
        And bathes the Forests which she lov'd before.

202-6. Arethusa is transformed into a stream in Ovid, *Metamorphoses*, V.632–6.

202. silver: sparkling; cf. 'Rape of the Locke', I.20.

205. Name: see Commentary to 170. *TE* suggests a coincidence with the river Ladon, where Syrinx is transformed into reeds to avoid the pursuit of Pan (Ovid, *Metamorphoses*, I.702).

   hapless: 'unhappy; unfortunate; luckless; unlucky' (*SJ*); cf. 'Winter', 39.

206. rang'd: wandered in hunting.

207. chast: pure, untouched by sexual pursuit, perhaps with another pun on chace/chased.

   laves: washes, bathes.

208. Celestial Tears: EC cites Dryden's 'The Meeting of Bacchus with Ariadne', *Poetical Miscellanies: The Fifth Part*, p. 34: 'Her briny Tears augment the briny Flood'. Pope reused the phrase, of Thetis, in his translation of the *Iliad*, I.541. Cf. also 'Sapho to Phaon', 185.

209-14. TE finds an extended model for this passage in Ausonius, *Mosella*, 189–99.

209. Glass: the mirror-like surface of the water. Pope would later make several experiments in setting up reflections from the Thames inside his grotto.

   musing: thoughtful.

210. headlong ... downward: The scene appears upside-down in reflection. Wakefield compares Dryden, *The State of Innocence*, II (1677), p. 13: 'another Firmament below, | Spread wide, and other trees that downward grow', itself recalling Eve looking into the 'Lake, that to me seemd another skie' in Milton, *Paradise Lost*, IV.459 (1674), p. 98. *TE* locates a source in Ausonius, *Mosella*, 223–4: 'reddit nautales vitreo sub gurgite formas | et redegit pandas inversi corporis umbras' ('reflects sailor-like forms under the glassy flood and throws back crooked pictures of the inverted body').

211. Landskip: landscape.

   pendant: hanging or 'jutting over' (*SJ*), as in a 'hanging wood'; but also a heraldic term (Rogers 2004: 103).

212. absent Trees: i.e. present only virtually, by reflection. *TE* cites particularly 'tremit absens | pampinus' ('the absent vine-tendril trembles'), from Ausonius, *Mosella*, 194–5.

213. azure: pure blue; originally made from lapis lazuli. The term also indicates the heraldic colour blue (Rogers 2004: 90). Cf. 349.

214. floating: seen in reflection in the water.

Thou too, great Father of the *British* Floods!
With joyful Pride survey'st our lofty Woods,
Where tow'ring Oaks their spreading Honours rear,
220 And future Navies on thy Banks appear.
Not *Neptune*'s self from all his Floods receives
A wealthier Tribute, than to thine he gives.
No Seas so rich, so full no Streams appear,

---

218. survey'st: *1717–26:* survey
219. spreading: *1751:* growing
220. Banks: *1736–51:* shores
221. his Floods: *1736:* his streams; *1740–51:* her streams
223. so full no Streams appear: *1736–51:* so gay no banks appear

---

217. Father ... Floods: the Thames, a symbol here for Britain's national identity and maritime trading prowess. Wakefield cites Dryden's translation of Virgil, *Aeneid*, VIII.46: 'the Father of the *Roman* Flood'.

218. lofty: high, well-grown, signalling here a plentiful supply of wood for the 'future Navies' (220) to be built in London's shipyards.

219. tow'ring Oaks: symbolising British character and sturdiness, as well as naval prowess and protection (as in 31 and 385–8). See also 'Spring', 86. The oak, sacred to Zeus in classical times, was strongly linked with the Stuart line, especially after the future Charles II escaped his pursuers after the battle of Worcester, 1651, by hiding in the 'Boscobel Oak', a 'precious Load' (31) in Pope's conception. In 1662 Charles had decreed 29 May as 'Royal Oak Day' and he commissioned coinage with the Royal Oak on it; see Evelyn, *Numismata* (1697), p. 122. Cowley had expatiated on these associations in book VI of his botanical poem *Sex Libri Plantarum*; see e.g. pp. 159–60 of the English version by Aphra Behn, in *The Third Part of the Works of Mr. Abraham Cowley* (1689). According to *The Queen's Famous Progress* (1702), p. 7, Anne was greeted on her early post-coronation tour by the pupils of the Free School at Marlborough with a masque celebrating the Royal Oak. Wasserman (1959: 109) cites Ogilby's description of triumphal arches for the coronation of Charles II, decorated with 'the ROYAL OAK bearing Crowns, and Scepters, instead of Acorns'. Rogers (2005a: 147–8) points out the oak was the clan badge of the Stewarts, from which Anne's line descended, and (297–302) explores Pope's debt to Evelyn's *Sylva* (1664), a Royalist treatise of the forest specifically dedicated to restoring loss after the depredations of the Civil War. The Boscobel Oak had, however, been slily mocked in Dryden's *Mac Flecknoe*, 27, *Miscellany Poems* (1684), p. 2: 'Thoughtless as Monarch Oakes ...'.

spreading Honours: foliage, following the Latin usage of 'honores' to indicate leaves as a sort of distinction or decoration; cf. 'Episode of Sarpedon', 291; 'Spring', 73; 'Winter', 32; *Iliad*, IV.557 in Pope's translation. See also the passage from Dryden's 'First Book of Ovid's Metamorphoses' quoted in Commentary to 'Rape of the Locke', II.53.

220. future Navies: Pope returned, satirically, to this idea in the *Epistle to Burlington*, 188.

221. Neptune: Roman god of the ocean, equivalent to the Greek Poseidon.

222. Tribute: payment made by one nation to another in token of subjection, but punning on 'tributary'. Neptune awards a greater honour to Thames than he receives from all the rivers in the world.

223 variant. gay: bright with flowers and other natural decorations.

223–4. *TE* compares Denham's famous description of the Thames, *Cooper's Hill*, 191–2, *Poems and Translations*, p. 12: 'Though deep, yet clear, though gentle, yet not dull, | Strong without rage, without ore-flowing full'.

                No Lake so gentle, and no Spring so clear.
225   Not fabled *Po* more swells the Poets Lays,
            While thro' the Skies his shining Current strays,
            Than thine, which visits *Windsor*'s fam'd Abodes,
            To grace the Mansion of our earthly Gods.
            Nor all his Stars a brighter Lustre show,
230   Than the fair Nymphs that gild thy Shore below;
            Here *Jove* himself, subdu'd by Beauty still,
            Might change *Olympus* for a nobler Hill.

225–6. MSw: Not fabled Poe a nobler Journey goes,
             While thro' the Skies his shining Current flows,
   1751: Nor Po so swells the fabling Poet's Lays,
             While led along the skies his current strays,
227. Than: *1751:* As
229–30. MSw: Nor yield his Stars above a fairer Show,
             Than the bright Beauties on thy Side below:
   1751: Nor all his stars above a lustre show,
             Like the bright Beauties on thy banks below;
230. gild . . . Shore: *1736–43:* grace . . . side
230^1. MSw: Whose pow'rful Charms enamour'd Gods may move
             To quit for this the radiant Court above;
231. MSw: And force great Jove, if Jove's a Lover still,
   1751: Where Jove, subdu'd by mortal Passion still,
232. Might: MSw: To

225-9. The Po, a river running through Northern Italy into the Adriatic, celebrated by Virgil and Ovid under the name Eridanus (*Georgics*, IV.371-3; *Metamorphoses*, II.372). It was also sometimes identified as an underworld river, and the name was also applied to a constellation with the shape of an undulating river, hence 'skies' in 226 and 'stars' in 229. See also 'Spring', 62, and *Dunciad* (1728), II.164. EC compares Denham, *Cooper's Hill*, 193–6, *Poems and Translations*, p. 12: 'Heaven her *Eridanus* no more shall boast, | Whose Fame in thine, like lesser Currents lost, | Thy Nobler streams shall visit *Iove*'s aboads, | To shine amongst the Stars, and bath the Gods'. Rogers (2004: 186) finds a propagandist model in Claudian's panegyric on the sixth consulship of Honorius, 159-68; Hauser (1966: 475-8) explores the mythology of the Eridanus in Virgil, Claudian and Pope, and see material cited in Commentary to 330.

225. swells . . . Lays: fills, forms a subject for praise in songs (poems), as in 3.

227. fam'd Abodes: magnificent villas built along the riverbanks; cf. 373.

228. Mansion . . . Gods: Windsor Castle, the royal palace originally built in the 1070s by William the Conqueror (see Headnote).

230. fair Nymphs: nature spirits in classical mythology used as a flattering label for women generally (see 19). Clements (1972: 48) takes these lines to refer to the women celebrated by Lansdowne in his poems; Rogers (2004: 169–71) suggests that Pope was thinking of local 'nymphs' in his Catholic circle such as the Blount sisters and Arabella Fermor, hidden heroine of *The Rape of the Lock*. For the mythology of Thames nymphs, see Ackroyd (2007: 83–4).

232. Olympus: see Commentary to 33.

   nobler Hill: i.e. a hill near the Thames.

233. The phrase 'Happy the man' is normally a translation of Horace, *Epodes* II.1, 'beatus ille' ('blessed is he'), a description of the joys of rural retirement, as here at 235–56 and in Pope's early 'Ode on Solitude' (published in the *Works* of 1717). Horace's poem ends with an ironic twist, absent from Pope's early conceptions of such things.

Happy the Man whom this bright Court approves,
His Sov'reign favours, and his Country loves;
235 Happy next him who to these Shades retires,
Whom Nature charms, and whom the Muse inspires,
Whom humbler Joys of home-felt Quiet please,
Successive Study, Exercise and Ease.
He gathers Health from Herbs the Forest yields,
240 And of their fragrant Physick spoils the Fields:
With Chymic Art exalts the Min'ral Pow'rs,
And draws the Aromatick Souls of Flow'rs.

233, n. 1736–51: VER. 233.   *Happy the man who to the shades retires,*
  But doubly happy, if the Muse inspires!
  Blest whom the sweets of home-felt quiet please;
  But far more blest, who study joins with ease.
235–8. MSw: Happy the Man who to the Shades retires,
  But doubly happy, if the Muse inspires!
  Blest whom the Sweets of home-felt Quiet please,
  But far more blest who Study joins with Ease!
239. **He:** MSw: Or

233–4. The statesman approved at the court of Queen Anne, such as the dedicatee Lansdowne, made Treasurer of the Household in 1713.

235–56. The 'man' of these verses derives features from both Lansdowne (see Headnote and Commentary to Dedication) and Sir William Trumbull (named at 256; see Headnote), both of whom went into 'retirement' under William, albeit for different reasons. Trumbull claimed no inspiration from the 'Muse' of poetry, unlike Lansdowne, whose retirement verse (including some 'Happy the Man' phrasing) indicts the 'guilty courts' of William III; see Rogers (2005a: 86–7), and Clements (1972: 50). Edward Young's *An Epistle to the Right Honourable the Lord Lansdown* (1713) contains a long section of praise for Lansdowne's course of study among 'Sylvan Scenes' (pp. 15–16). Clements argues that Lansdowne is the main figure, but the local context perhaps fits Trumbull's known role in the actual Forest better. The passage is partly based on the section ('O fortunatos nimium') on the peaceful blessings of rural life in Virgil, *Georgics*, II.458–540, translated by Cowley in his Essay 'Of Agriculture'; *Works* (1668), pp. 105–7 of separate sequence. Pope had also worked with Wycherley on a poem, 'Lines on Solitude and Retirement', on a similar theme; *TE*, VI.57–9. *TE* cites also a section on virtuous study in Philips, *Cyder*, I.754–64; Rogers (2004: 179–81) locates further extensive models in Drayton, *Poly-Olbion* XIII.164–80.

235–6. who . . . inspires: the poet who lives and works in this landscape; Cowley (270 below) is one possible model here, though equally Pope may be thinking of himself.

240. fragrant Physick: medicinal drugs found in flowers; cf. the passage of Dryden cited in Commentary to 25 Pope's note above.

spoils: despoils, i.e. robs, extracts. Brower (1959: 55) observes that the scientific pursuits detailed here are not far removed from those Pope would later satirise in *The Dunciad*, IV.

241. Chymic: chemical, pharmaceutical; or alchemical.

exalts . . . Pow'rs: produces a purer form of a substance; to exalt is to 'refine by fire, as in chymistry' (*SJ*), or to distil; see Wasserman (1959: 150). Rogers (2005a: 128) associates the image with the mystical power of Stuart monarchy.

242. Extracts fragrant essences, perhaps by distillation.

Now marks the Course of rolling Orbs on high;
O'er figur'd Worlds now travels with his Eye.
245 Of ancient Writ unlocks the learned Store,
Consults the Dead, and lives past Ages o'er.
Or wandring thoughtful in the silent Wood,
Attends the Duties of the Wise and Good,
T' observe a Mean, be to himself a Friend,
250 To follow Nature, and regard his End.
Or looks on Heav'n with more than mortal Eyes,
Bids his free Soul expatiate in the Skies,
Amidst her Kindred Stars familiar roam,
Survey the Region, and confess her Home!

251–2. MSw: His Kindred Stars he watches in the Skies,
  And looks on Heav'n with more than mortal Eyes.
253. **Amidst:** *1727–51:* Amid

---

243. Watches the movements of the planets. For 'rolling Orbs' in this context, see Blackmore, *Creation*, II (1712), p. 79, and Bevil Higgons, *A Poem on the Peace* (1713), p. 14. Pope himself later took a course of astronomy lectures, in London, with William Whiston, and his friend John Arbuthnot was a close contact of the astronomer Edmund Halley, whose *Historia Coelesti* was published in 1712 (*Corr.*, I.185; Rogers 2005a: 47, 57). See Commentary to 'Spring', 102, and 'Rape of the Locke', II.179–92. Ackroyd (2007: 297) notes that several observatories were erected along the Thames, by scientists such as Francis Bacon; Greenwich Observatory was founded in 1675.

244. Travels in imagination, by looking at maps, globes, or the Zodiac. Rogers (2004: 214) notes that 'figure' was an astrological term for 'horoscope' and contrasts the serious observer here with the kinds of astrological prediction common in contemporary popular culture.

245–6. Reads ancient literature and history.

247–8. EC cites Thomas Creech's translation of Horace, *Epistles*, I. iv, *Odes, Satyrs and Epistles of Horace Done into English* (1684), p. 484: 'Or dost thou gravely walk the healthy Wood, | Considering what befits the Wise and Good?'

249. Mean: an average, indicating here moderate behaviour, avoiding extremes, as in the classical idea of the 'golden mean' discussed by Aristotle in his works on Ethics.

250. follow Nature: cf. *Essay on Criticism*, 68. Brower (1959: 55) locates the source in the stoic tag 'sequere Naturam', associated with the Roman poet Lucan.

regard his End: be mindful of death and the need to prepare for it, translating the Latin proverb 'respice finem' ('regard the end'), as in e.g. the poem of that title in John Davies' *Wittes Pilgrimage* (1605).

251–4. Meditates on religious matters and imagines his liberated soul finding its appropriate home. Rogers (2005a: 128) suggests the passage may have a specifically hermetic and occult meaning associated with the magical powers of the Stuart monarch.

252. expatiate: 'To range at large; to rove without any prescribed limits' (*SJ*, quoting this passage). Pope returned to this idea in his *Essay on Man*, I (1733) 97–8.

253. Kindred Stars: i.e. the soul is celestial, not earthly; cf. the last lines of 'The Rape of the Locke'. Wakefield compares Ovid, *Metamorphoses*, I.81, 'cognati ... caeli', 'of kindred sky', but cf. also Samuel Cobb's loyal ode to military success, *The Female Reign* (1709), p. 5: '*True Virtue* to Her *kindred Stars* aspires'.

254. confess: acknowledge.

255 Such was the Life great *Scipio* once admir'd,
Thus *Atticus*, and *Trumbal* thus retir'd.

Ye sacred Nine! that all my Soul possess,
Whose Raptures fire me, and whose Visions bless,
Bear me, oh bear me to sequester'd Scenes
260 Of Bow'ry Mazes and surrounding Greens;
To *Thames*'s Banks which fragrant Breezes fill,
Or where ye Muses sport on *Cooper*'s Hill.

---

259. MSw: Oh bear me Gods! To Windsor's pleasing Shades,
260. **Of:** *1726:* To; *1736–51:* The
  surrounding Greens: MSw: the glimm'ring Glades
262. **ye:** MSw: the

---

255. Scipio: Publius Cornelius Scipio Africanus (236–183 BC), Roman general who defeated Hannibal and the Carthaginians in the second Punic War, 202 BC. He declined honours and advancement and, when prosecuted for bribery at the instigation of his enemies, retired to his estate in dignified aloofness. Cowley's essay 'Of Solitude', in *Works* (1668), pp. 91–5, celebrates him; Cowley was himself a model of conspicuous retirement near Chertsey (Rogers 2005a: 286). Perhaps an oblique slighting of Marlborough, who had fallen from supreme military power in late 1711 but did not behave like Scipio. Pope returned to Scipio in *The Temple of Fame*, 163–4.

256. Atticus: Titus Pomponius Atticus (109 or 110–32 BC), wealthy friend of the Roman orator and politician Cicero, and recipient of many of Cicero's letters, who refused to engage in public politics and instead pursued wide-ranging studies in Athens, hence the toponym 'Atticus', from the region of Greece of which Athens is part. Pope later used the name as an ironic soubriquet for Addison, in the *Epistle to Dr. Arbuthnot*, 193–214.

Trumbal: Sir William Trumbull (1639–1716), lawyer, diplomat, resident of the Forest and Pope's most important early patron; see Headnote. Pope wrote an epitaph on him and in his own editions of his letters asserted that Trumbull was the model of rural retirement celebrated in the poem (*Corr.*, I.328, n. 3).

Rogers (2005a: 244) suggests that Pope was also thinking of C. Asinius Pollio, Virgil's patron, in these images of dignified retreat from politics.

257. sacred Nine: the Muses. Wakefield compares Dryden's translation of Virgil, *Georgics*, II.673–4 (Virgil 475), *Works of Virgil*, p. 91: 'Ye sacred Muses, with whose Beauty fir'd, | My soul is ravish'd, and my Brain inspir'd'.

259–62. TE compares Virgil, *Georgics*, II.486–9, and Dryden's translation (692–5), *Works of Virgil*, p. 92: 'Some God conduct me to the sacred Shades, | Where Bacchanals are sung by *Spartan* Maids. | Or lift me high to *Hemus* hilly Crown; | Or in the Plains of *Tempe* lay me down.'

259. sequester'd: removed, remote, separated 'from others for the sake of privacy' (*SJ*, quoting this passage). The term was also used of estates forfeited to the state for political crimes or Catholicism (as with the Pope's friends the Carylls).

260. Bow'ry Mazes: zones of woodland with intricate paths and secret recesses, as in John Harington, *The History of Polindor and Flostella* (1657), p. 5: 'He view'd (transported) | The Bowry *Maze*'.

262. Cooper's Hill: site of Denham's famous poem of that title, hence the sporting Muses. It is not a mountain (264) but a small hill about 65 metres above sea level, near Englefield Green, overlooking Runnymede.

(On *Cooper*'s Hill eternal Wreaths shall grow,
While lasts the Mountain, or while *Thames* shall flow)
265 I seem thro' consecrated Walks to rove,
And hear soft Musick dye along the Grove;
Led by the Sound I roam from Shade to Shade,
By God-like Poets Venerable made:
Here his first Lays Majestick *Denham* sung;
270 There the last Numbers flow'd from *Cowley*'s Tongue.
O early lost! what Tears the River shed

270.] Mr. *Cowley died at* Chertsey *on the Borders of the Forest, and was from thence convey'd to* Westminster.

263–5. MSw: On Cooper's Hill, and Thames's Banks below,
        Eternal Bays and living Greens shall grow,
        While lasts the Mountain, or the Stream shall flow!
265–7. MSw: Methinks around your Holy Scenes I rove,
        And hear your Music ecchoing thro' the Grove:
        With Transport visit each inspiring Shade,
266. **And:** *1736–51:* I

---

263. **Wreaths:** of laurel or 'bays', signifying poetic achievement; cf. 'Summer', 10, and *Essay on Criticism*, 184, 709.

263–5 MS. Triplets are rare in Pope's verse and he appears to have suppressed the extra line to avoid one here.

265–6. Pope perhaps recalls images of solitary wandering from Marvell, 'Upon Appleton House', st. lxxiv, *Miscellaneous Poems* (1681), p. 97, where the speaker compares himself to 'some great *Prelate of the Grove*'. This passage was singled out for its 'poetic enthusiasm' by Warton (1756: 24).

265. **consecrated:** made sacred, as in a church; in opposition to the desecration of the landscape under the Normans.

266. **dye along:** i.e. the music fades as he passes through the grove.

267. **Shade:** shaded area, but perhaps with a sense of the ghosts (shade) of poets associated with the forest (cf. 199, 277).

268. EC compares Philips, *Cyder*, II.7–8 (1708), p. 49, 'Unrival'd Authors by their Presence, made | For ever venerable, rural Seats'.

269. **Denham:** Sir John Denham (1615–69), poet knighted after the Restoration for his royalist sympathies; already praised by Pope in the *Essay on Criticism*, 364. Denham's *Cooper's Hill* (1642, subsequently much revised) was a major model for Pope's *Windsor-Forest* (see Headnote); his other 'first Lays Majestick' include a play, *The Sophy* and a translation of the second book of Virgil's *Aeneid*, called *The Destruction of Troy*, not published until 1656.

270. **Numbers:** verse, poetry, as in *Essay on Criticism*, 340.

Cowley: Abraham Cowley (1618–67), lyric poet and essayist, focus of some of Pope's early imitations, including 'The River', 'The Garden' (with much detail suggestive of the paradisal Forest landscape), and the 'Ode on Solitude'. Cowley also wrote royalist epics such as *Davideis* (1656) and *The Civil War* (published 1679). He was latterly a gentleman farmer at Chertsey, near the site of the Abbey dissolved by Henry VIII in 1536.

271. **early lost:** TE cites Walsh, 'Delia', 87, *Poetical Miscellanies: The Fifth Part*, p. 615: 'Oh, early lost!'. Cowley was 49 when he died at Chertsey in 1667. Pope told Spence (*OAC*, I.192–3, item 449) that Cowley had contracted a fever after losing his way home while drunk and sleeping in a damp meadow, but his earliest biographer (Thomas Sprat, 'An Account of the Life and Writings . . .' in

When the sad Pomp along his Banks was led?
His drooping Swans on ev'ry Note expire,
And on his Willows hung each Muse's Lyre.

275   Since Fate relentless stop'd their Heav'nly Voice,
No more the Forests ring, or Groves rejoice;
Who now shall charm the Shades where *Cowley* strung
His living Harp, and lofty *Denham* sung?
But hark! the Groves rejoice, the Forest rings!
280   Are these reviv'd? or is it *Granville* sings?

273, n. 1736–51: VER. 273. *What sighs, what murmurs fill'd the vocal shore!*
  His tuneful swans were heard to sing no more.

272. Pomp: MSw: Pomps
273–4. MSw: What Sighs, what Murmurs filld the vocal Shore?
  His tuneful Swans were heard to sing no more.
278. Harp: MSw: Lyre
279^80. MSw: What Bard, what Angel tunes the warbling Strings?

---

the *Works* of 1668, sig. e1ʳ) records that he caught a fatal chill while supervising labourers on his farm.

272. sad Pomp: funeral ceremony, 'Pomp' indicating a 'procession of splendour and ostentation' (*SJ*). Rogers (2005a: 272) cites the mourning rivers witnessing the 'sad pomp funerall' of Sir Philip Sidney in Spenser, 'A Pastorall Aeglogue', *Colin Clouts Come Home Againe* (1595), sig. H3ᵛ. Cf. also 'Rape of the Locke', II.59; and Pope's version of the *Iliad*, XXIV.898. Cowley's coffin was taken by boat down the Thames from Chertsey to London for a lavish burial in Westminster Abbey; the presence of many 'noblemen and persons of quality' was recorded by the diarist John Evelyn, a friend of the poet, who was also present (3 August 1667). Rogers (2005a: 132) points out that Anne's son, and heir to the throne, Prince William of Gloucester, died (1700) at Windsor shortly after his eleventh birthday (also 'early lost') and his body was ferried along much the same route.

273 variant. vocal: i.e. the shore is 'vocal' with the sound of people mourning.

273. drooping Swans: cf. Thomas Stanley, 'A Paraphrase upon Psalme CXLVIII', 235, *Poems and Translations* (1647), p. 13 of separate sequence: 'You drooping swans by age dyde white'. The 'swan song' is traditionally sung by a swan just before it dies, and thus signifies elegy. Cf. 'Winter', 39–40; *Essay on Criticism*, 452^3 MS; and 'Rape of the Locke', II.121. Swans on the Thames were also associated with royal power; see Ackroyd (2007: 238–41).

274. Willows: see 'Winter', 14.

  each Muse's Lyre: symbols of the various types of poetry Cowley had written, hung up as a sign of mourning, in imitation of the exiled Israelites in Psalm 136 (or 137 in the Anglican Bible); Wakefield compares the Douay Bible version of verse 2: 'On the willowes ... we hanged up our instrvmentes'; the King James version (Psalm 137) reads: 'Wee hanged our harpes vpon the willowes'.

277–8. strung ... Harp: wrote poetry.

278. living Harp: TE sees the phrase as a pointed recollection of Cowley's own 'The Resurrection', stanza 2, *Poems ... Written by A. Cowley* (1656), p. 21: 'Begin the *Song*, and strike the *Living Lyre*'.

  lofty: high-minded, noble, as at 285; also figuratively on top of Cooper's Hill.

279. rings: resounds.

280. these: Cowley and Denham.

  Granville: Granville's (by then Lansdowne's) *Poems on Several Occasions* had been published

'Tis yours, my Lord, to bless our soft Retreats,
And call the Muses to their ancient Seats,
To paint anew the flow'ry Sylvan Scenes,
To crown the Forests with Immortal Greens,
285 Make *Windsor* Hills in lofty Numbers rise,
And lift her Turrets nearer to the Skies;
To sing those Honours you deserve to wear,
And add new Lustre to her Silver *Star*.

288, n. *1736–51:* All the lines that follow till within eight of the conclusion, [*1751:* All the lines that follow,] were not added to the poem till the year 1710. The 425th verse, *My Humble Muse in unambitious strains,* &c. immediately follow'd this. [*1751:* What immediately followed this, and made the Conclusion, were these,

My humble Muse in unambitious strains
Paints the green forests and the flow'ry plains;
Where I obscurely pass my careless days,
Pleas'd in the silent shade with empty praise,
Enough for me that to the list'ning swains
First in these fields I sung the sylvan strains.]

281. our: MSw: the

---

by Tonson in 1712 and he is flatteringly invited to fill the job vacancy created by the deaths of the earlier Windsor poets.

281. soft Retreats: Behn, 'To Mr. Creech, Under the Name of Daphnis', 59–62, *Poems upon Several Occasions* (1684), p. 53, has Wadham College, Oxford, offering a 'soft retreat' to the Muses.

282. Seats: places of abode, thrones (cf. 2).

284. Immortal Greens: cf. 8, and Dryden's 'To the pious memory of... Anne Killigrew', 4, *Examen Poeticum*, p. 351: 'Rich with Immortal Green above the rest'.

286. Turrets: of Windsor Castle.

288 Pope's note. For composition history, see Headnote.

288. Silver Star: of the Order of the Garter, a chivalric order of knighthood which had only 24 members at any one time. Founded by Edward III on St George's Day, 1349, it was strongly associated with Edward's rebuilt Windsor Castle; the star itself was an emblem introduced by Charles I and was thus specifically Stuart in significance. The Order was personally sponsored by Anne, who wore its regalia on state occasions. Denham had celebrated it in praising Edward in *Cooper's Hill* (93–104), and so, aspirationally, did Lansdowne, in 'The Progress of Beauty', *Poems on Several Occasions* (1712), p. 30. Rogers (2005a: 59) cites Henry St John's 'A Pindarick Ode', *A New Miscellany of Original Poems, on Several Occasions* (1701), p. 106: 'One more bright Star shall in that field appear, | And *Granville*'s Pen adorn the glitt'ring Sphere'. But Lansdowne was not created a Knight of the Garter, though Oxford, architect of the peace, had been, in 1712.

289 Pope's note. Henry Howard, Earl of Surrey (c. 1516–47), courtier, soldier, and poet. Some of his poems were set in or around Windsor Castle, where he was imprisoned in 1537 for striking a courtier; he had also lived at Windsor from 1530 to 1532, and was admitted to the Order of the Garter in 1541. Surrey was executed for treason in 1547, a fact which, for Pope, reflects badly on Henry VIII and establishes Windsor as a scene for martyrs. Henry VIII is conspicuously missing from the list of kings Pope knew were buried in St George's Chapel, Windsor, probably because of his role in the Reformation and dissolution of the monasteries.

Here noble *Surrey* felt the sacred Rage,
290 *Surrey,* the *Granville* of a former Age:
Matchless his Pen, victorious was his Lance;
Bold in the Lists, and graceful in the Dance:
In the same Shades the *Cupids* tun'd his Lyre,
To the same Notes, of Love, and soft Desire:
295 Fair *Geraldine,* bright Object of his Vow,
Then fill'd the Groves, as heav'nly *Myra* now.

Oh wou'dst thou sing what Heroes *Windsor* bore,
What Kings first breath'd upon her winding Shore,

289.] Henry Howard, *E. of* Surrey, *one of the first Refiners of the* English *Poetry; famous in the Time of* Henry *the* VIIIth *for his Sonnets, the Scene of many of which is laid at* Windsor.

289, n. *famous* . . . **Windsor:** *1717–51:* who flourish'd in the time of Henry the VIIIth.

297. MSw: Your Muse shall tell the God-like Race she bore,

---

289. sacred Rage: the holy frenzy of poetical inspiration, or 'furor poeticus'. A common usage, often in heroic or religious contexts. For Pope's unusual uses of 'sacred' see Commentary to *Essay on Criticism*, 522; 'The First Book of Statius his Thebais', 3. For 'Rage' cf. 'Sapho to Phaon', 34; 'Prologue to *Cato*', 44. See also Commentary to 'The First Book of Statius his Thebais', 755.

291–2. *TE* points out that Granville's military and courtly prowess had been celebrated together in a poem, 'Sent the Author into the Country', apparently by his cousin Elizabeth Higgons, printed in his *Poems upon Several Occasions* (1712), pp. 94–6; this also summons him back to public life from retirement.

291. Lance: symbol of his military prowess, as the pen is of his poetic talent.

292. Lists: jousting tournaments. Granville had apparently taken part in such an event in Paris, in his youth. Rogers (2004: 40) suggests Pope was aligning Granville with the court culture of Edward III, who appears at 301.

293. Cupids: Cupid was the Roman god of love, usually represented in art as a playful infant and thus easily turned into a decorative cherub.

295. Geraldine . . . Vow: the ideal woman of Surrey's poetry, usually identified in Pope's day with Lady Elizabeth Fitzgerald (c. 1528–89). A fictitious exchange of verse letters between Surrey and Geraldine is given in Oldmixon's *Amores Britannici* (1703), II.iii, pp. 43–73 of second sequence.

296. Cf. 'Autumn', 4 variant. *TE* points out that Surrey's poem 'Prisoned in Windsor', *Songes and Sonnettes* (1557), fol. 7, refers to 'The secret groues, which oft we made resound | Of pleasaunt plaint, and of our ladies praise'.

296. Myra: poetic name used by Granville in his poems. An anagram of Mary (of Modena, consort of James II), later used for Granville's mistress, Frances Brudenal, Countess of Newburgh. Pope more likely intends a reference to Granville's wife, Lady Mary Thynne, a member of the Villiers family, whom he married in December 1711. Her father, the Jacobite Earl of Jersey, was a major figure in peace negotiations; see Rogers (2004: 108–9 and 2005a: 80–1).

297. thou: Granville. Pope suggests Granville should produce a Windsor epic, to outlive the ceiling paintings by Antonio Verrio at the Castle (305). *TE* cites the model of Virgil, *Georgics*, II.167–72, a roll-call of past Roman heroes, and Denham, *Cooper's Hill*, 60–3, *Poems and Translations*, p. 5: 'The Gods great Mother . . . cannot boast . . . More *Hero's* than can *Windsor*'.

298. winding Shore: curved river bank, but possibly connected with the etymology of

Or raise old Warriors whose ador'd Remains
300   In weeping Vaults her hallow'd Earth contains!
With *Edward*'s Acts adorn the shining Page,
Stretch his long Triumphs down thro' ev'ry Age,
Draw Kings enchain'd; and *Cressi*'s glorious Field,
The Lillies blazing on the Regal Shield.

301.] Edward III. *born here.*

---

299. MSw: And sing the Heroes, whose ador'd Remains
301. **With *Edward*'s Acts:** MSw: Let Edward first
303. **Kings enchain'd;:** *1717–51:* Monarchs chain'd,
304. **The Lillies:** MSw: With Iris
304^5. MSw: When Brass decays, when Trophies lye o'erthrown,
      And mouldring into Dust drops the proud Stone,

Windsor as given in Camden, *Britannia* (1695), p. 151, from Old English words meaning 'winding shore'. Cf. Hugh Holland, *Pancharis: The First Booke* (1603), sig. B1ᵛ–B2ʳ: 'From *London* Westward doth a Castle stand | Along the Thames, which of the winding shore | Is called *Windsore*, knowne by sea and land'. Pope re-used the phrase 'winding shore' at least four times in the *Iliad* translation, and cf. 'Summer', 3. *TE* cites Dryden's translation of Virgil, *Aeneid*, I.809, *Works of Virgil*, p. 225: 'The Ports and Creeks of ev'ry winding shore'; the phrase had also appeared in Dryden's *Satires of Decimus Junius Juvenalis*, XIV.110 (1693), p. 280.

300. **weeping Vaults:** burial vaults in St George's Chapel at Windsor Castle, damp and condensation rendered here as a symbolic 'weeping' in mourning for the dead kings; Wakefield cites Virgil, *Georgics* I.480, 'et maestum inlacrimat templis ebur aeraque sudant' ('the sad ivory wept in the temples, and the bronzes sweated'). Cf. 'Eloisa to Abelard', 22.

301. **Edward:** Edward III (1312–77), as Pope's note indicates, born at Windsor; founder of the Order of the Garter, he also remodelled the Castle in the 1340s.

shining Page: history, imagined as an illuminated or glorious book, or, according to Rogers (2004: 95–6), a heraldic shield. Cf. also Oldmixon's address to Marlborough, *Iberia Liberata* (1706), p. 36: 'Thou *Churchill!* wilt the shining Page adorn, | Like our Third *Edward* or his Eldest Born'. Pope pointedly refers to the victories of Edward III, rather than those of Marlborough.

302. **long Triumphs:** pageants and other rituals celebrating military successes, as well as the successes themselves (Rogers 2004: 40).

303. **Kings enchain'd:** David II of Scotland, captured at the battle of Neville's Cross in 1346, released in 1357; Jean II (Jean le Bon) of France, captured by the Black Prince, Edward of Woodstock (1330–76, eldest son of Edward III), at the battle of Poitiers in 1356, and likewise imprisoned at Windsor. The events are alluded to in *Cooper's Hill*, 81–2, and the latter featured among the scenes painted at Windsor by Antonio Verrio (305 below), described in Thomas Otway's poem *Windsor Castle* (1685), pp. 17–18. Neither was in fact subject to very severe restraint, pending ransom; Rogers (2004: 40) points out that Jean le Bon was allowed to hunt in the forest and both he and David were invited to court pageants. Rogers (2005a: 267) notes another account of the matter in Camden, *Britannia* (1695), p. 145.

Cressi's glorious Field: Edward III's military triumph over the French at the battle of Crécy, 1346, following which the Order of the Garter was founded at Windsor Castle. 'Field' is also a heraldic term (Rogers 2005a: 174).

304. **Lillies:** Lilies or *fleurs de lys* were the heraldic emblem of the French king, appropriated by Edward III on his assumption of the title of King of France in 1340 and still part of Anne's royal arms at her accession,

305   Then, from her Roofs when *Verrio*'s Colours fall,
        And leave inanimate the naked Wall;
        Still in thy Song shou'd vanquish'd *France* appear,
        And bleed for ever under *Britain*'s Spear.

        Let softer Strains Ill-fated *Henry* mourn,
310   And Palms Eternal flourish round his Urn.

309.] Henry VI.

---

305. Then, from her: MSw: From Windsor's

---

her claim to sovereignty over France not having been renounced; see Commentary to 'Spring', 89–90. The event is alluded to in Denham, *Cooper's Hill*, 77–8, and *TE* notes that the King's Bedchamber at Windsor featured a ceiling painted by Verrio portraying Charles II receiving the submission of 'France', adorned with '*Flower-de-luces*'.

    Blazing: punning on heraldic 'blazon' and the quartering of arms on Edward's 'Shield'; see Rogers (2004: chapter 3).

304 MS. *Iris*: a member of the lily family.

304^5 MS. Pope alludes to the decay of monumental plaques, sculptures and inscriptions; cf. the opening lines of Pope's 'To Mr. Addison, Occasioned by his Dialogue on Medals', and Commentary to *Essay on Criticism*, 132 and 'Rape of the Locke', I.136.

305. Verrio: Antonio Verrio (1639–1707), Italian artist who with his assistants painted this sequence of historical events in St George's Hall, Windsor Castle, for Charles II's restoration of the state apartments. Some 20 ceilings, 3 staircases, the hall and the chapel of the castle were decorated with historical, mythological and allegorical scenes (Rogers 2005a: 181–5). The paintings had been celebrated as a witness to '*England*'s Triumphs' in Otway's *Windsor Castle*, in terms which as *TE* points out were perhaps a source for Pope, but mineral deposits in the plaster were beginning to show through by the early eighteenth century. The state of the (still impressive) paintings was noted by Defoe in his *Tour*, II.81–2. Cf. *Essay on Criticism*, 493–4, for the fading of painted colours, and *Epistle to Burlington*, 146, where Pope is more disparaging about the artist. Verrio is addressed in Bainbrigg Buckeridge's verse epistle 'On Her Majesty's Grant of Woodstock Park, &c. To His Grace the Duke of Marlborough, 1704', in *Poetical Miscellanies: The Sixth Part* (1709), pp. 554–57, on the assumption that he would be decorating Blenheim Palace.

306. inanimate: not animated by painted historical scenes.

307–8. vanquish'd . . . Spear: Pope puns on the heraldic 'impalement' of French arms (304), but the 'Spear' also reminds readers of the local patron saint, St George defeating the dragon, and St Michael mastering Satan (McWhir 1981: 296). The phrase 'vanquish'd France' appears in Otway, *Windsor Castle*, p. 19, in a description of Verrio's painting of the Black Prince's triumph.

    bleed for ever: Wakefield cites *An Epistle to the Right Honorable Charles, Earl of Dorset and Middlesex* (1690), p. 9, by Charles Montagu, later Earl of Halifax, a Whig panegyrick on William III's prowess which ridicules the supposed tendency of the French to glorify the exploits of their king; had he been wounded in battle, the tapestry makers would have ensured 'The wounded Arm wou'd furnish all their Rooms, | And bleed for ever Scarlet in the Looms'. See also Commentary to 'Gardens of Alcinous', 26, and the travesty of the idea in the *Dunciad* (1728), II.136.

309. Strains: melodies, tunes: i.e., poetry.

    ***Ill-fated* Henry:** Henry VI (1421–71), born at Windsor, 'ill-fated' because he was twice deposed before being murdered in the Tower of London on the orders of Edward IV (see 312), his rival for the throne.

310. Palms Eternal: signifying martyrdom; also associated with St George.

    Urn: funeral casket or memorial.

Here o'er the Martyr-King the Marble weeps,
And fast beside him, once-fear'd *Edward* sleeps:
Whom not th' extended *Albion* could contain,
From old *Belerium* to the *German* Main,
315 The Grave unites; where ev'n the Great find Rest,
And blended lie th' Oppressor and th' Opprest!

Make sacred *Charles*'s Tomb for ever known,
(Obscure the Place, and uninscrib'd the Stone)
Oh Fact accurst! What Tears has *Albion* shed,

312.] Edward IV.

315, n. MSw: Charles I.

313. **th' extended:** MSw: th' Extent of
314. ***German:*** *1717–51:* Northern
315. MSw: Now in long Peace beneath one Roof they rest;
319. MSw: Oh Fact accurst! oh sacrilegious Brood
          Sworn to Rebellion, principl'd in Blood!
          Since that dire Morn what Tears has Albion shed,

---

311. *Martyr-King:* Henry was regarded as a saint by some of his supporters; in 1479 his statue on the rood screen of York Minster was removed in an attempt to suppress such veneration. There is perhaps some suggestion of a later 'martyr King', Charles I (see 317).
Marble: tombstone or grave slab.
weeps: cf. 302. TE cites Congreve, *The Mourning Muse of Alexis*, 85 (1695), p. 5: 'The Marble weeps', but the phrase is standard in seventeenth-century elegy, e.g. Henry King, 'An Elegy upon my Best Friend L. K. C.', *Poems, Elegies, Paradoxes, and Sonets* (1664), p. 3 of second sequence: 'in moist Weather when the Marble weeps'.
312. *fast:* close.
Edward: Edward IV (1442–83), died at Westminster and was buried at St George's Chapel, Windsor. Henry VI's body, originally buried at Chertsey Abbey, was transferred by Richard III to a new shrine in St George's Chapel in 1484.
313–14. Wakefield compares Dryden's translation of Juvenal, X.236–7, *Satires of Juvenal*, p. 200 (speaking of Hannibal): 'Whom *Affrick* was not able to contain, | Whose length runs Level with th' Atlantick main'.

313. extended Albion: the whole land mass of Britain.
314. Belerium: Latin name for Land's End in Cornwall; see e.g. Milton, 'Lycidas', 159–60.
314. German Main: the sea north of the European continent.
317. sacred Charles: Charles I, buried at Windsor, without formal funeral, after his execution, 30 January 1649; regarded as a martyr by Jacobites and by some Tories. He had, like Surrey, been imprisoned in Windsor Castle, captured by parliamentarian forces early in the Civil War (the Chapel was despoiled). A colossal mausoleum for Charles was planned in 1678 but never built. In 1696 a bare inscription identifying the coffin was found when the vault was opened for the burial of one of Anne's stillborn children. Pope's lines supply the kind of obsequies missing at his actual funeral. See Rogers (2005a: 198–9).
319. *Oh Fact accurst!*: TE compares Philips, *Cyder*, II.508–9 (1708), p. 79: 'O Fact | Unparallel'd! O *Charles*! O Best of Kings!' 'Fact' is here a deed or action, perhaps specifically 'crime'.
***319ff.* MS.** The omitted lines constitute a more powerful and specific indictment of

320   Heav'ns! what new Wounds, and how her old have bled?
      She saw her Sons with purple Deaths expire,
      Her sacred Domes involv'd in rolling Fire.
      A dreadful Series of Intestine Wars,
      Inglorious Triumphs, and dishonest Scars.
325   At length great *ANNA* said — Let Discord cease!
      She said, the World obey'd, and all was *Peace*!

---

320. **Heav'ns!:** MSw: Gods!
322. **Fire.:** *1726–51:* fire,
323. **Intestine:** MSw: successive
325–6. MSw: Till ANNA rose, and bade the Furies cease;
    Let there be Peace – She said; and all was *Peace.*

---

the parliamentarian court that condemned Charles I, emphasising the religious component of Charles's identity as king.

319–24. References to the Civil War and political strife after the Restoration of Charles II, Charles I's son, in 1660. Cf. 'The First Book of Statius his Thebais', 319–26.

321. **purple Deaths:** perhaps suggesting victims of the plague in 1665. In Pope's *Iliad*, V.108, 'the Purple Hand of Death' indicates more straightforwardly a violent and bloody death, as does 'purple Death' (a literal translation from the Greek) at XX.552, and 415 below; so the idea may include the Civil War. In Dryden's version of Virgil, *Aeneid*, XII.1090, *Works of Virgil*, p. 610, 'Purple Death' indicates the death of a hunted stag.

322. **Domes:** buildings, perhaps specifically churches, but not necessarily 'domed' in shape as the word invokes the Latin 'domus' ('house' or 'building').

   involv'd: engulfed, encircled; again calling on a Latinate sense, here also suggesting 'rolling'. The reference is to the Great Fire of London, 1666.

323. ***Intestine Wars:*** internal or domestic conflicts; cf. Milton, *Paradise Lost*, VI.258–9, and Pope, *Ode for Musick*, 34. The couplet is directed against the Civil War, and the Glorious Revolution of 1688, and perhaps reflects on more recent divisions (see Winn 2014: 605–6), but is expressed with sufficient vagueness to evade censorship.

324. ***Inglorious:*** perhaps also a hit at Marlborough's triumphs. Erskine-Hill (1996: 69) argues that it may also disparage the 'Glorious Revolution' of 1688.

   dishonest: 'disgraceful; ignominious' (*SJ*, quoting this passage and commenting, 'these two senses are scarcely English, being borrowed from the Latin idiom'). 'Honestus' means 'honourable' or 'distinguished by virtue'. EC compares Creech, translation of Horace, *Odes* I.xxxv, *Odes . . . of Horace Done into English* (1684), p. 48: 'I blush at the dishonest show, | I die to see the Wounds and Scars, | Those Glorys of our Civil Wars'. Pope more likely recalled Dryden, *Absalom and Achitophel*, 71–2 (1681), p. 3, where the 'sober' citizens, 'looking backward with a wise affright, | Saw Seams of wounds, dishonest to the sight'. The honourable scar of the defeated soldier should appear on his front, showing that he was facing the enemy; see Shakespeare, *Macbeth*, V.ix.12: 'Had he his hurts before?' 'Ay, on the front', and Pope's *Iliad*, VIII.120.

325. **great ANNA:** Queen Anne, Charles II's niece, whose reign, which began in 1702 after the death of William III, Pope presents as ending the political infighting and the European war vaguely blamed on William. Her fiat, 'Let Discord cease!' is aligned with God's word of creation, 'Let there be light', Genesis, 1:3. As *TE* points out, the MS phrasing is closer to the biblical model. But as Rogers (2005a: 159) notes, it is also a summary of Anne's official proclamations concerning the war and peace negotiations, helping to establish her as superior to parliament. Pope had used the phrase 'great *Anna*'

In that blest Moment, from his Oozy Bed
Old Father *Thames* advanc'd his rev'rend Head.
His Tresses dropt with Dews, and o'er the Stream
330   His shining Horns diffus'd a golden Gleam:

328^9, n. 1736–51: Between Verse 328 and 329 originally stood these lines,

> From shore to shore exulting shouts he heard,
> O'er all his banks a lambent light appear'd,
> With sparkling flames heav'ns glowing concave shone,
> Fictitious stars, and glories not her own.
> He saw, and gently rose above the stream;
> His shining horns djffus'd a golden gleam:
> With pearl and gold his tow'ry front was drest,
> The tributes of the distant East and West.

329–30. MSw: From Shore to Shore exulting Shouts he heard,
O'er all his Banks a Lambent Light appear'd,
With sparkling Flames Heav'n's glowing Concave shone,
Fictitious Stars, and Glories not her own.
He saw, and gently rose above the Stream;
His shining Horns djffus'd a Golden Gleam:
With Pearl and Gold his Tow'ry Front was drest,
Old Ocean's Presents from [   ] East and West.

---

with light irony in 'Rape of the Locke', I.71, and in the revised *Rape of the Lock*, III.46, would parody a female fiat with 'Let Spades be Trumps!'. TE compares Philips, *Cyder*, II.639-40 (1708), p. 87: 'till prudent ANNA said, | LET THERE BE UNION', i.e. the Act of Union between England and Scotland, 1707. Hone (2015a: 112-13) lists other panegyric models, including Henry Waring, *The Coronation* (1702), p. 16, where the 'Great *England*'s Genius' declares '*Let fatal Discord and Contention cease*', and Joseph Harris, *Anglia Triumphans* (1703), p. 3: 'Her Productive Voice, *Let it be so*'. For similar ideas in Ambrose Philips's text for Handel's 1713 birthday ode for the Queen, see Winn (2014: 513-15). For the more protracted and complex processes underlying the as yet unratified Treaty of Utrecht, see Headnote.

325 MS. *Furies:* see Commentary to 420.

327-8. Wakefield cites Spenser, *Faerie Queene*, IV.xi.25, describing the Thames: 'With head all hoary, and his beard all gray, | Deawed with siluer drops, that trickled downe alway'. TE aligns the image with Dryden's *Annus Mirabilis*, st. 232 (1667), p. 59: 'Old Father Thames rais'd up his reverend head...| Deep in his *Ooze* he sought his sedgy bed, | And shrunk his waters back into his Urn'. Rogers (2004: 105) likens the posture to the heraldic image '*assurgeant*'.

327. Oozy Bed: the muddy river bed. Wakefield finds Pope's direct source in Dryden, *Threnodia Augustalis*, 513–14 (1685), p. 25: 'While starting from his Oozy Bed, | Th' asserted Ocean rears his reverend Head'. The 'Reverend Thames' lifts his 'dropping Head' from his 'Green Oozy Bed' in D'Urfey's *Gloriana* (1695), an elegy on Queen Mary; cf. another instance in Congreve's poem on the Anglo-French peace of 1697, *The Birth of the Muse*, 121 (1698), p. 5. Johnson (Lonsdale, IV.67) thought it 'strange' that Pope should insert this episode soon after Addison had in *The Campaign*, 467-72 (1705), p. 23, deplored the falsity of having 'Rivers from their Oozy Beds arise' to declaim national events, but the defiance is probably deliberate.

328. Father Thames: cf. 217, and 'Rape of the Locke', I.66. For the image, which draws on many classical sources, and resembles

Grav'd on his Urn appear'd the Moon, that guides
His swelling Waters, and alternate Tydes;
The figur'd Streams in Waves of Silver roll'd,
And on their Banks *Augusta* rose in Gold.
335 Around his Throne the Sea-born Brothers stood,
That swell with Tributary Urns his Flood.

---

331. MSw: His Urne in Sculpture shows the Moon that guides
335. **Sea-born Brothers:** MSw: blue-hair'd Rivers
336. **That:** *1736–51:* Who

---

the Baroque statues of seventeenth-century fountains, see also *Essay on Criticism*, 703 and Commentary.

328^9 **Pope's note. shore to shore:** The 'echo' effect is found also in 'Winter', 41–2, and 'Rape of the Locke', II.14 and 149.

lambent: 'playing about; gliding over without harm' (*SJ*).

glowing concave: the 'arch' of the heavens, the skies.

Fictitious stars: extravagant firework displays marking the peace, which would also supply the 'lambent light'. *TE* cites records of the Utrecht fireworks from William Maitland, *History of London* (1756), I.512, but also points out that fireworks were used to celebrate the accession of Anne in 1702 (*ibid.* I.503–4) and that the variant lines may predate Utrecht; Rogers (2005a: 110–11) supplies further contemporary descriptions of the scene.

tow'ry: 'adorned or guarded with towers' (*SJ*); used at least five times to describe Troy in Pope's translation of the *Iliad*. Pope's juvenile imitation of Spenser, 'The Alley', 54, has '*Windsor*'s tow'ry pride'.

front: forehead. Cf. Congreve, *A Pindarique Ode, Humbly Offer'd to the Queen*, 43–4 (1706), p. 4, in praise of Marlborough's victories: 'Rise, Fair *Augusta*, lift thy Head, | With Golden Tow'rs thy Front adorn'; and Pope, *Temple of Fame*, 261: 'Till to the roof her tow'ring Front she rais'd'.

tributes . . . East and West: see Commentary to 222.

329. ***dropt:*** dripped.

330. ***shining Horns:*** a conventional classical sign of power attributed to river gods in classical mythology. Wakefield cites Virgil, *Georgics*, IV.371–2: 'gemina auratus taurino cornua voltu | Eridanus' ('Eridanus, with golden twin horns on his bull-like forehead'); and Addison's translation of Claudian's lines on the Eridanus in *Remarks on Several Parts of Italy* (1705), p. 440: 'And as he rose his golden Horns appear'd, | That on the Forehead shone divinely bright, | And o'er the Banks diffus'd a yellow Light'.

331. ***Grav'd:*** engraved.

Urn: Thames appears with an urn from which the waters flow.

333. ***figur'd:*** pictured on the urn.

335–46. *TE* cites as general models for Pope's river catalogue Ausonius, *Mosella*, 349–74; Spenser, *Faerie Queene*, IV.xi; Drayton, *Poly-Olbion*, XVII; and Milton, 'At a Vacation Exercise', 91–100.

334. **Augusta**: one of the early Roman names for London, later adopted by poets, e.g. Dryden, *Annus Mirabilis*, st. 296, and (ironically) *Mac Flecknoe*, 64–5. Used here and at 375 by Pope, but not otherwise.

335–46. Warton (1756: 25–6) judged this catalogue of rivers to be superior to Milton's in 'At a Vacation Exercise', 91–100.

335. **Sea-born Brothers:** The offspring of the early Greek deities Oceanus and Tethys all become rivers; *TE* cites Spenser, *Faerie Queene*, IV.xi.18 as an example of the myth, and Denham, *Cooper's Hill*, 161–2, *Poems and Translations*, p. 10: '*Thames*, the most lov'd of all the Oceans sons, | By his old Sire'. Here, the tributaries of the Thames, hence 'tributary urns' in 336; cf. 'The First Book of Statius his Thebais', 288.

First the fam'd Authors of his ancient Name,
The winding *Isis*, and the fruitful *Tame*:
The *Kennet* swift, for silver Eels renown'd;
340   The *Loddon* slow, with verdant Alders crown'd:
Cole, whose clear Streams his flow'ry Islands lave;
And chalky *Wey*, that rolls a milky Wave:
The blue, transparent *Vandalis* appears;
The gulphy *Lee* his sedgy Tresses rears:

---

341. **clear:** MS, *1751:* dark

337-8. The Isis, the river running through Oxford, now thought of as a section of the Thames (cf. 'Summer', 25), and the Thame, which joins it just below Dorchester in Oxfordshire, were thought by some antiquaries to have combined to form the Latin name 'Thamesis' or 'Thames'. The idea was fruitful in terms of mythology (for Isis see 'The First Book of Statius his Thebais', 373) and iconography (a symbolic marriage) for poets such as Spenser (*Faerie Queene*, IV.xi.24) and Drayton, *Poly-Olbion* (1612), XIV, XV and XVII. Camden's *Britannia* includes threads of a Latin poem, *De Connubio Tamae et Isis*, on the theme with (in 1695) English translation by Basil Kennet: for detailed study of the influence of this on Pope's design see Rogers (2004: 124–37). Rogers (2004: 29–32) cites Samuel Daniel's *Tethys' Festival* (1610), a masque of rivers performed to celebrate the investiture of Henry Prince of Wales, as a further possible source. The Thames rises near Cirencester, in Gloucestershire; for the tributary rivers and the Thame-Isis link see Ackroyd (2007: xviii–xxi, 24–9, 43–51).

339. **Kennet:** river which flows into the Thames at Reading, Berkshire. Its swiftness was remarked by Josuah Sylvester, *Du Bartas: His Diuine Weekes, and Workes ... Translated*, 'The Sixt Day of the First Week', 652 (1621), p. 161. TE notes that Spenser called it 'chaulky' (*Faerie Queene*, IV.xi.29), and Drayton 'cleere' (*Poly-Olbion*, XV.290). It was 'smooth' in William Diaper's *Dryades* (1712), p. 2.

340. **Loddon:** see Commentary to 170.

verdant Alders crown'd: EC cites Addison, *Remarks on Several Parts of Italy* (1705), p. 191: 'Where Silver Lakes, with verdant Shadows crown'd'.

341. **Cole:** normally identified as the Colne, a river that flows through Hertfordshire and into the Thames at Staines; one section flows in several channels through a flat valley, giving the appearance of 'islands'. Rogers (2004: 133) notes that Camden describes 'several pleasant Islands' in the Cole, *Britannia* (1695), p. 279. Two smaller tributaries, the Coln and the Cole, run into the Thames at Lechlade. TE suggests the variant reading 'dark' was suggested by its name, and points out that it was described as 'Crystall' and 'transparent' by Drayton, *Poly-Olbion*, XVI.3 and 9.

342. **Wey:** river in Surrey which joins the Thames near Weybridge. TE remarks that Drayton calls it 'cleere', *Poly-Olbion* XVII.21, and suggests that Pope's 'chalky' was transferred from Spenser's comment on the Kennet (Commentary to 339 above).

343. blue, transparent: EC suggests a source in Addison's translation from Claudian, in *Remarks on Several Parts of Italy*, p. 56: 'The blue transparent *Adda* next appears'.

Vandalis: the Wandle, which flows north into the Thames at Wandsworth in London; described by Drayton in *Poly-Olbion*, XVII.73–80, and Camden, *Britannia* (1695), p. 158.

344. gulphy: 'full of gulphs or whirlpools' (*SJ*).

Lee: or Lea, river which joins the Thames near Blackwall in London.

sedgy Tresses: overgrown with sedge, imagined as a kind of hair. EC notes that Milton uses the adjective 'gulphie' of the river Dun and describes the Lee as 'Sedgie' in 'At a Vacation Exercise', 92 and 97, *Poems, &c.* (1673), p. 68.

345 And sullen *Mole,* that hides his diving Flood;
And silent *Darent,* stain'd with *Danish* Blood.

High in the midst, upon his Urn reclin'd,
(His Sea-green Mantle waving with the Wind)
The God appear'd; he turn'd his azure Eyes
350 Where *Windsor-*Domes and pompous Turrets rise,
Then bow'd and spoke; the Winds forget to roar,
And the hush'd Waves glide softly to the Shore.

Hail Sacred *Peace*! hail long-expected Days,
Which *Thames*'s Glory to the Stars shall raise!

---

348. **with:** MSw: to
350. MSw: Where Windsor-Turrets steal into the Skies;
352. **glide:** MSw: roll
354. **Which:** *1717–51:* That

---

345. **sullen:** 'flowing sluggishly' (*OED*, sense 5). Milton uses the phrase 'sullen Mole that runneth underneath', 'At a Vacation Exercise', 95, *Poems, &c.* (1673), p. 68.

Mole: river which periodically disappears into swallow holes, a source of imagery for Spenser, *Faerie Queene,* IV.xi.32, and Drayton, *Poly-Olbion* XVII.59-60. Rogers (2004: 133) draws attention to a long description of the Mole in Camden, *Britannia,* pp. 155–6. It joins the River Ember and the merged river flows into the Thames near Hampton Court.

346. **Darent . . . Blood:** river in Kent that flows into the Thames estuary near Dartford; it runs past Otford, site of a defeat of the Danes by the Saxons in 1016, as Pope could have learned from Camden, *Britannia,* p. 190. There is a similar idea in 'The First Book of Statius his Thebais', 57–8. Rogers (2004: 102) finds the 'stain' here a possible allusion to the heraldic ceremony of disgrace, fitted to Pope's view of Marlborough's warmongering.

347–420: Rogers (2004: 35–6) links the description of Thames as river god to the early Stuart culture of flamboyant masque and pageant, and specifically to Jonson's entertainment for the entry of James I to London, 1604.

348. **Sea-green Mantle:** *TE* compares Virgil's description of the Tiber, *Aeneid,* VIII.33-4: 'eum tenuis glauco velabat amictu | carbasus' ('a fine robe wrapped his limbs in a sea-green fold'), and of the Juturna, XII.885: 'tantum effata caput glauco contexit amictu', translated by Dryden, XII.1281, *Works of Virgil,* p. 616, as 'But in her Azure Mantle wrap'd her Head'. Warton (1756: 25) thought Pope's detail 'highly picturesque', compared to the 'trite and obvious insignia' otherwise assigned to the river god.

350. **pompous:** 'splendid; magnificent; grand' (*SJ*).

351. **bow'd:** as to a superior god; *TE* cites the gesture of Apollo, Ovid, *Metamorphoses,* XII.597 in Dryden's version.

Winds . . . roar: Wakefield cites Dryden's version of Virgil, *Aeneid,* X.157-8, *Works of Virgil,* p. 502: 'the Winds their Breath restrain; | And the hush'd Waves lie flatted on the Main'; *EC* compares Hopkins, *White-hall* (1698), p. 9: 'Unrowling waves steal softly to the shore, | They know their Soveraign, and they fear to roar'.

353–420. *TE* suggests the pervasive presence of the redemptive prophecies of Isaiah 60–1, already hybridised with Virgil's fourth *Eclogue* in 'Messiah', behind this vision; see especially 55–70 of the latter. Pope also draws on the vision of *Pax Romana* and the coming age of Augustus in *Aeneid,* I.257-96.

353. ***Sacred*** **Peace:** in particular, the Treaty of Utrecht: see Headnote.

355   Tho' *Tyber*'s Streams immortal *Rome* behold,
       Tho' foaming *Hermus* swells with Tydes of Gold,
       From Heav'n it self tho' sev'nfold *Nilus* flows,
       And Harvests on a hundred Realms bestows;
       These now no more shall be the Muse's Themes,
360   Lost in my Fame, as in the Sea their Streams.
       Let *Volga*'s Banks with Iron Squadrons shine,
       And Groves of Lances glitter on the *Rhine*,

---

355. **immortal:** MSw: Majestick
358. **Realms:** MSw: Lands
360^1. MSw: The Sea which not from all his Floods receives
   A nobler Tribute than to mine he gives.
   Let Venice boast her Tow'rs amidst the Main,
   Where the rough Adrian swells and roars in vain;
   Here, not a Town, but spacious Realm may have
   A sure Foundation on the rolling Wave.

355-6. cf. 'Spring', 61-4.
355-60. *TE* cites a section in Ausonius, *Mosella*, 374-7, and the opening four lines of Horace's Ode in praise of the Tiber (I.vii), as models.
355. **Tyber:** Tiber, the river running through Rome.
   ***immortal* Rome:** cf. *Essay on Criticism*, 131.
356. **Hermus:** river in Lybia described in Virgil's *Georgics*, II.137, as 'auro turbidus', 'frothing with gold'.
357. **sev'nfold Nilus:** the Nile, whose inundations over the flood plain give the soil fertility; 'sevenfold' in ancient sources, because it was supposed to discharge through seven mouths into the Mediterranean. It is called 'septemfluus' ('seven-flowing'), by Ovid, *Metamorphoses*, I.422-3, and 'septemgeminus' ('seven-fold'), by Catullus, *Carmina*, XI.2.
358. **hundred Realms:** Wakefield compares 'R. B. T.', 'On the Death of the learned Mr. John Selden', in *Examen Poeticum* (1693), p. 109: 'As when old *Nilus* who with bounteous flows | Waters an hundred Nations as he goes'.
360^1 **MS. *The Sea ... gives:*** i.e. the ocean gives a greater tribute to Thames than it receives from all the rivers of the world.
   Venice ... Adrian: Venice, constructed out of many linked islets in the Adriatic, formerly the centre of a huge trading empire; cf. *Essay on Man*, IV.292: 'From dirt and sea-weed as proud Venice rose'.
   Here: i.e. in London.
361. **Volga:** The Volga runs from north of Moscow to the Caspian Sea. Charles XII of Sweden had been at war with Russia until 1709, but, as *TE* points out, he was defeated 500 miles west of the Volga, at Poltova. *TE* also cites a description of that war from Philips, *Blenheim*, 405-10 (1705), p. 18.
   Iron Squadrons: Wakefield compares Virgil, *Aeneid*, VII.703, 'aeratas acies' ('bronze-equipped battle lines'). Iron is a base metal, associated with crude militarism (cf. 75), as opposed to the 'gold' of Anne's peace (Brooks-Davies 1985: 141-2).
362. **Groves ... Rhine:** the Rhine runs from Switzerland through Germany and the Netherlands, flowing into the North Sea. It was a strategic marker through much of the war and the scene of much skirmishing; cf. 'The First Book of Statius his Thebais', 27. Rogers (2005a: 224) suggests an oblique hit at Marlborough's inconclusive campaign in the area in 1704-5. *TE* cites Dryden's translation of Virgil, *Aeneid*, X.1009, *Works of Virgil*, p. 528: 'And shakes a Grove of Lances from his Side', and the 'Episode of Sarpedon', 181. Pope has the phrase 'Groves of Lances glitter' in his translation of Homer, *Iliad*, II.991.

Let barb'rous *Ganges* arm a servile Train;
Be mine the Blessings of a peaceful Reign.
365 No more my Sons shall dye with *British* Blood
Red *Iber*'s Sands, or *Ister*'s foaming Flood;
Safe on my Shore each unmolested Swain
Shall tend the Flocks, or reap the bearded Grain;
The shady Empire shall retain no Trace
370 Of War or Blood, but in the Sylvan Chace,

---

366. Iber's . . . Ister's foaming: MSw: Ister's . . . Iber's guilty
369. MSw: O'er all the Forests shall appear no Trace

363–4. TE compares Dryden, *Absalom and Achitophel*, 331–2 (1681), p. 11: 'Let Haughty *Pharaoh* Curse with such a Reign | His Fruitfull *Nile*, and Yoak a Servile Train'.

363. barb'rous **Ganges**: river running from the Himalayas through northern India to the Indian Ocean; 'barb'rous' because of the wars of the Moghul emperor Aurangzeb (d. 1707). Rogers (2004: 188) suggests this may be influenced by a mention of the 'Ganges's servile banks' in Claudian's panegyric on the second consulship of Honorius. The Ganges also appears (as 'pulcher', 'beautiful') in Virgil, *Georgics*, II.136–9. Cf. 'The First Book of Statius his Thebais', 817.

366. Red **Iber**: the river Ebro, running through northern Spain into the Mediterranean, and scene of an allied victory under Stanhope at Saragossa (Zaragoza), 1710; 'red' may indicate the sandy terrain or the blood of the battle.

Ister: the Danube, the river running from Germany through Austria, Hungary and Romania before discharging into the Black Sea; cf. 'The First Book of Statius his Thebais', 26. The 'Ister' is referred to as 'turbidus' ('disturbed' or 'frothing') by Virgil, *Georgics*, III.350. Marlborough's definitive victory, at Blenheim, took place near the Danube in 1704, as did another victory in the same year (Schellenberg). *TE* notes a reference to 'th' ensanguin'd *Ister*'s reeking Flood' in Fenton's *Cerealia* (1706), p. 2. Blackmore's *Advice to the Poets* (1706), p. 4, expatiates on the heroics of the Danube battle; as Tickell put it, '*Who hath not read of . . . Danube choak'd with Slain!*', *A Poem . . . On the Prospect of Peace* (1712), sig. A2ʳ; he later replays the scene of '*Danube*'s raging Flood', p. 4. Pope's line is another oblique slight to the general, who appears as an indiscriminate butcher.

367. **unmolested**: not persecuted by anyone in power (cf. the Norman oppressions of 43–78); probably a hopeful thought towards relaxed treatment of the Catholic minority, much harassed and dispossessed under William III. Rogers (2005a: 249) compares Philips, *Cyder*, II.657–9 (1708), p. 88: 'mean while the Swains | Shall unmolested reap, what Plenty strows | From well stor'd Horn, rich Grain, and timely Fruits'.

368. **bearded Grain**: ears of corn 'having sharp prickles' (*SJ*, s. v. 'Bearded'). *TE* compares Milton, *Paradise Lost*, IV.981–2 (1674), p. 114: '. . . *Ceres* ripe for harvest waving bends | Her bearded Grove of ears', and Dryden, translation of Virgil, *Georgics*, II.746, *Works of Virgil*, p. 93: 'A full return of bearded Harvest yield'; Dryden had used 'bearded Harvest' already in *Satires of Juvenal*, Persius, II.89, p. 24. Cf. also the Duchess of Newcastle, 'A Morall Description of Corne', 1, *Poems, and Fancies* (1653), p. 104: 'The *yellow* Bearded *Corne* bowes downe each *Head*'. Rogers (2004: 109–10) suggests an allusion to the Granville family crest, a *garb vert* or green wheatsheaf.

369. **shady Empire**: i.e. woods, as the MS reading 'O'er all the Forests' indicates.

370. **Sylvan Chace**: woodland hunting, as already described in 93–164 (especially 148). *TE* finds a source for this idea in 41–2 of Cowley's imitation of Horace's second epode in 'Of Agriculture', *Works*, pp. 107–8

The Trumpets sleep, while chearful Horns are blown,
And Arms employ'd on Birds and Beasts alone.
Behold! th' ascending *Villa*'s on my Side
Project long Shadows o'er the Chrystal Tyde.
375   Behold! *Augusta*'s glitt'ring Spires increase,
And Temples rise, the beauteous Works of Peace.

376, n. 1751: VER. 376. *And Temples rise,*] The fifty new Churches.

371. **Trumpets:** *1743–51:* trumpet

of separate sequence: 'And all his malice, all his craft is shown | In innocent wars, on beasts and birds alone'.
371. **Trumpets:** bugles used as signalling devices in war, contrasted with the 'chearful Horns' of hunting. Cf. 'Messiah', 58 and Commentary, and Montagu, *Epistle to Dorset*, p. 5: 'The Drums and Trumpets sleep' (as William III ends the Battle of the Boyne in Ireland).
373. **ascending Villa's:** Pope would build his own villa on leased land at Twickenham, facing the Thames, from 1719 onwards. For earlier uses of the Italian-Latin term see Dryden's version of Juvenal, XIV.108, *Satires of Juvenal*, p. 280: 'costly *Villa*'s'. OED cites nothing earlier in English than Shaftesbury, *Characteristicks*, vol. III. Misc. III.ii. (1711), p. 184n (in a discussion of taste): 'Behold the Disposition and Order of these finer sorts of Apartments, Gardens, *Villa*'s!' The building of new mansions in the period of William III, especially along the Thames in Middlesex and Surrey (and at '*Twittenham*') was noted with approval by Defoe in his *Tour*, I.123-7 (Letter II). Wakefield notes that Drayton, *Poly-Olbion*, XVII.81-6 (1612), p. 259, has the Thames observing 'Kingly houses . . . of more than earthly pride, | Upon his either Banks, as he along doth glide'.
374. **Chrystal:** 'bright; clear; transparent' (*SJ*); cf. 'January and May', 459; 'Summer' 27-8; 'Winter', 21; and *Essay on Criticism*, 355.
375-8. Wakefield finds echoes in the opening of Hopkins, *White-hall* (1698), p. 1: 'Above that Bridge, which lofty Turrets Crown, | Joyning two Cities; of it self a Town, | As far as fair *Augusta*'s Buildings reach, | Bent like a Bow, along a peaceful beach.' Cf. also 'Messiah', 85-94.
375. **glitt'ring Spires:** Rogers (2004: 204) discerns an echo of the prophecy of London's rebuilding in Dryden, *Annus Mirabilis*, st. 295; there is perhaps also something from Satan's visionary prophecy of the future architectural glory of Rome in Milton, *Paradise Regain'd*, IV.54 (1671), p. 81, signalled by 'Turrets and Terrases, and glittering Spires'. Pope re-uses the phrase, of Troy, in *Iliad*, XIII.23. An optimistic reference, as Pope's note to 376 indicates, to the legislative measure of 1711 (9 Anne c. 17), which ordered the building of 50 new churches in London and Westminster, using funds from coal duties at the port of London. The measure had Anne's personal support and was in part a Tory answer (under the leadership of the future Jacobite plotter and friend of Pope's, Francis Atterbury) to the magnificent Blenheim palace built for Marlborough; Swift made the point about relative costs in *The Examiner*, no. 42, 24 May 1711. The rebuilding symbolically counters the earlier destruction of churches (66-72). Work had begun in 1712, but less than a quarter of the project was eventually completed. See Commentary to *Essay on Criticism*, 706. St Paul's Cathedral, also a notable work of post-Fire regeneration, had been completed by Sir Christopher Wren in 1710. Young also alludes to the new churches in the context of the peace in his *Epistle to . . . the Lord Lansdown* (1713), p. 7.

I see, I see where two fair Cities bend
Their ample Bow, a new *White-Hall* ascend!
There mighty Nations shall inquire their Doom,
380   The World's great Oracle in Times to come;
There Kings shall sue, and suppliant States be seen
Once more to bend before a *British* QUEEN.

---

382. **bend:** MSw: bow

---

377. **two fair Cities:** London and Westminster were administratively distinct and culturally divided between the centre of commerce in the City of London and the centres of political and fashionable life around the royal palaces at Westminster.

378. **ample Bow:** broad curve of the river Thames between Westminster and the City of London.

new White-Hall: The palace of Whitehall, between Westminster and the City, had served as a royal residence until it burned down in 1698, leaving just the banqueting hall, outside which Charles I had been executed in 1649. The palace had been celebrated as representing 'the Court of England' in Hopkins's peace poem, *White-hall*, in 1698. Reconstruction was planned but never executed. Pope saw Inigo Jones's original Whitehall designs on a visit to Oxford in 1717 (*Corr.*, I.376).

379. **Doom:** fate, judgement, judicial sentence. EC compares Addison, *Remarks on Several Parts of Italy*, p. 334, translating Claudian's lines on Rome: 'Thither the Kingdoms and the Nations come, | In supplicating Crouds to learn their Doom; | To Delphi less th' enquiring Worlds repair'. TE suggests further Waller, *A Panegyrick to my Lord Protector*, 15–16 (1655), p. 4: 'The seat of Empire, where the *Irish* come, | And the unwilling *Scotch* to fetch their doome'.

380. **Oracle:** 'Any person or place where certain decisions are obtained' (*SJ*, citing this passage), but classically the oracle at Delphi, as in the source cited at 379.

381. **sue:** 'beg, entreat, petition' (*SJ*).

suppliant: 'an humble petitioner; one who begs submissively' (*SJ*). For the phrasing and idea Rogers (2004: 204) compares Dryden, *Annus Mirabilis*, st. 298 (1667), p. 75: 'Now, like a Maiden Queen, she will behold, | From her high Turrets, hourly Sutors come: | The East with Incense, and the West with Gold, | Will stand, like Suppliants, to receive her doom'. The defeated Louis is a 'sceptred Suppliant' to Anne in Tickell's *A Poem . . . on the Prospect of Peace*, (1712), p. 1.

382. **British QUEEN:** After the Union of England and Scotland in 1707 'British' took on extra meaning, but the point is also to emphasise that the incoming Hanoverian monarch would be German. The previous example was Elizabeth I, whose aid against Philip of Spain had been solicited by the Dutch in 1575 and 1585. Anne partly modelled herself on Elizabeth as a strong British Queen (see Headnote), but Elizabeth is virtually missing from Pope's national celebration, by comparison with her role in Spenser and Drayton, probably because of her anti-Catholic bias.

383. i.e. to form navies, as in 218–20, and as in Pope's negative fable of 'Young Cotta' in the *Epistle to Bathurst*, 209–10: 'The woods recede around the naked seat, | The Sylvans groan – no matter – for the Fleet'. In the MS Pope wrote 'if obscure?' against this line. TE finds a source for the idea in Ovid, *Metamorphoses*, I.94–5, and an echo of phrasing from Waller, *A Panegyrick to My Lord Protector*, 41–2 (1655), p. 4: 'Lords of the Worlds great Waste, the Ocean, wee | Whole Forrests send to Raigne upon the Sea'. Hone (2015a: 116–18) finds several more sources for the prediction in the Tory panegyrics of Anne's reign, such as Heneage Finch's *The Queen's Famous Progress* (1702),

> Thy Trees, fair *Windsor*! now shall leave their Woods,
> And half thy Forests rush into my Floods,
385 Bear *Britain*'s Thunder, and her Cross display,
> To the bright Regions of the rising Day;

383–87, n. 1736–51: VER. 383, &c. were originally thus;
> Now shall our fleets the bloody Cross display
> To the rich regions of the rising day,
> Or those green isles, where headlong Titan *steeps*
> His hissing axle in th' Atlantic *deeps.*
> Tempt icy seas, &c.

384. **my:** *1740, 1751:* thy
385–90. Pope to Caryll, 29 November 1712 (*Corr.* I, 157):
> Now shall our fleets the bloody cross display
> To the rich regions of the rising day,
> Or those green iles, where headlong Titan steeps
> His hissing chariot in th' Atlantick deeps,
> Temp[t] icy seas, where scarce the waters roll,
> Where clearer flames grow round the frozen pole,
> Or under southern skies exalt their sails,
> Led by new stars, and born by balmy gales.

386^7. MSw: Or those green Iles where headlong Titan steeps
> His hissing Chariot in th' Atlantick Deeps;

---

and the anonymous *Windsor-Castle: A Poem* (1708). Cf. also *Ode for Musick*, 40.

385. Thunder: military force (cf. 130), here perhaps with the sense of Zeus-like epic power; cf. *Essay on Criticism*, 558; 'Rape of the Locke', II.108.

Cross: the red cross on white background of St George, the English emblem partially subsumed within a combined English/Scottish flag from the time of James I, who held both thrones. It was linked to the Order of the Garter, which had its home in St George's Chapel, Windsor. Rogers (2005a: 249) finds an extended source for the idea here in the closing section of Philips, *Cyder*, II.645–69 (1708), p. 88. Pope's local parish church at Binfield had stained glass depicting George and the Dragon (Rogers 2005a: 176). The Pretender was known as 'the Chevalier de St George', which may have been in Pope's mind also, along with Rosicrucian associations (Rogers 2004: 97). St George's Day was the anniversary of Anne's coronation, and a focus for Jacobite activity (see Headnote).

385–90 variants. On 29 November 1712, Pope asked John Caryll's opinion of these lines in relation to a segment from Tickell's *A Poem ... On the Prospect of Peace* (1712), p. 9: 'Fearless our Merchant now may fetch his Gain, | And roam securely o'er the boundless Main. | Now o'er his Head the Polar Bear he spies, | And freezing Spangles of the *Lapland* Skies, | Now swells his Canvas to the sultry Line, | With glitt'ring Spoils where *Indian* Grottoes shine, | Where Fumes of Incense glad the Southern Seas, | And wafted Citron scents the balmy Breeze.'

386. i.e. the east.

386^7 MS. green Iles ... Atlantick Deeps: The Titan is Atlas, charged with holding up the pillar (the 'axle') that separates earth from sky, and supposedly resident near the Hesperides ('green isles'), conceived of as lying at the Western boundary of the ocean. Cf. 'The First Book of Statius his Thebais', 138. There is some resemblance to Comus's lines in 'A Mask', 96–7, 'His glowing Axle doth allay | In the steep *Atlantick* stream', but the reference there is to Apollo.

>   Tempt Icy Seas, where scarce the Waters roll,
>   Where clearer Flames glow round the frozen Pole;
>   Or under Southern Skies exalt their Sails,
> 390 Led by new Stars, and born by spicy Gales!
>   For me the Balm shall bleed, and Amber flow,
>   The Coral redden, and the Ruby glow,
>   The Pearly Shell its lucid Globe infold,
>   And *Phoebus* warm the ripening Ore to Gold.

390. **spicy:** MSh: balmy
391. MSh: For me shall Gums congeal, and Spices blow,

---

387. ***Tempt Icy Seas:*** attempt or venture into the arctic seas, to extend maritime knowledge and mercantile profit. Wakefield cites Dryden, 'The First Book of Homer's Ilias', 86, *Fables*, p. 192: 'once more we tempt the watry Plains'. Rogers (2004: 194) reflects that by the Treaty of Utrecht Britain gained trading rights in Newfoundland and the Hudson Bay area.

388-9. EC finds a similarly extended prospect of globally dominant travel in Addison, *A Poem to his Majesty*, 115–22 (1695), p. 6. Rogers (2004: 32) finds an earlier source in Carew's *Coelum Britannicum* (1634), in a long speech voiced by 'Plutus' (Wealth).

388. ***clearer Flames:*** the Aurora Borealis, or Northern Lights.

  frozen Pole: cf. 'The First Book of Statius his Thebais', 28.

389-94. Cf. 'Messiah', 95–6, and Commentary.

389. ***Southern Skies:*** The South Sea Company, Robert Harley's answer to the Whig financial institutions such as the Bank of England and the East India Company, was set up in 1711 with the promise of trading and mining operations in South America, still dominated by the Spanish; it was also latterly, in theory, responsible for administering the 'Asiento' or slave trade concession (see 406). Its mercantile potential was associated with Harley's Tory peace, supposedly recouping the financial losses of the 'Whig' war. In practice, it turned into a finance operation with the disastrous consequence known as the South Sea Bubble, 1720, in which Pope and several of his associates, including Lansdowne and Gay, lost money. Swift and Arbuthnot were among the original shareholders. See Rogers (2005a: 231–7) for an extended gloss on these lines.

exalt: hoist, raise.

390. ***spicy Gales:*** the winds driving the ships along trade routes; spices were a major trading commodity from the East especially. Rogers (2004: 206) cites the final couplet (st. 305) of Dryden, *Annus Mirabilis*, p. 77: 'A constant Trade-wind will securely blow, | And gently lay us on the Spicy shore'. Milton, *Paradise Lost*, IV.157–71 (1674), p. 90, compares Satan's voyage to Paradise with marine adventures driven by 'odoriferous' winds from the 'spicie shoare' (157, 162).

391. ***Balm ... bleed:*** because the bark of the balm tree (as in 30) will be pierced to allow the liquid to flow out for collection. The 'Amber' (also in 30) flows for the same purpose; cf. 'Spring', 82. TE compares Dryden, *Annus Mirabilis*, st. 3 (1667), p. 2 (of the Dutch merchant adventurers): 'For them the *Idumaean* Balm did sweat, | And in hot *Ceilon* Spicy Forrests grew'. Cf. also 'Messiah', 93.

393. The formation and ripening of the pearl in a shell, associated with the South Seas.

394. ***Phoebus:*** See 147.

  warm ... Gold: gold and gems were supposed in alchemical theory to have been formed by the heat of the sun; cf. e.g. Trapp, *Aedes Badmintonianae* (1701), p. 1: 'When pointed Beams through Earth's deep Caverns pass, | Ripen thick Beds of Ore, and form the sluggish Mass'. EC compare Tickell, *A Poem ... On the Prospect of Peace*, p. 9: 'Here nearer Suns prepare the rip'ning Gemm ... | And here the Ore'. Dryden's note to st. 3 of *Annus Mirabilis* (on the lines cited in Commentary to 391 above), witnesses such ripening process in '*Eastern Quarries,*

395 The Time shall come, when free as Seas or Wind
Unbounded *Thames* shall flow for all Mankind,
Whole Nations enter with each swelling Tyde,
And Oceans join whom they did first divide;
Earth's distant Ends our Glory shall behold,
400 And the new World launch forth to seek the Old.
Then Ships of uncouth Form shall stem the Tyde,
And Feather'd People crowd my wealthy Side,
While naked Youth and painted Chiefs admire
Our Speech, our Colour, and our strange Attire!

396, n. 1751: VER. 396. *Unbounded Thames, etc.*] A wish that London may be made a FREE PORT.

398. **Oceans:** MSh: Seas but
   whom they did first divide: *1717–51:* the regions they divide
403. **While naked Youth:** *1717–26:* Whose naked youth; *1736–51:* And naked youths

---

&c'. Rogers (2005a: 6, 128, and 260), considers these lines as the centre of an alchemical transformation being wrought by the power of Stuart monarchy. For the phrasing see also 'The Gardens of Alcinous', 6.

395. Wakefield compares Denham, *Cooper's Hill*, 179–80, *Poems and Translations*, p. 11: 'Nor are his Blessings to his banks confin'd, | But free, and common, as the Sea or Wind', and *TE* suggests further influence on Pope's prophecy from the succeeding lines, 181–8. Rogers (2004: 205–6) finds many resemblances between the expression here and Dryden, *Astraea Redux* (1660), 298–305, where the returning Stuart monarch guarantees free-roaming commercial expansion.

396 **Pope's note.** The Treaty of Utrecht determined control of international trade; see Headnote. *TE* cites as evidence for support for the idea of a free port, i.e. one without customs duties, Addison's naming of the Whig merchant member of his Spectator Club 'Sir Andrew Freeport' (*Spectator*, no. 2, 2 March 1711). Various attempts to abolish certain duties at the Port of London had been made but none was carried through. For the political divisions surrounding these issues see Hudson (2016).

397–8. Wakefield compares Waller, *A Panegyrick to my Lord Protector*, 99–100 (1655), p. 6: 'While by your Valour, and your Courteous mind | Nations divided by the Sea are joyn'd'.

401. **uncouth:** 'odd, strange, unusual' (*SJ*).
   stem: block, crowd, 'oppose a current' (*SJ*). Hone (2015a: 120) suggests this line contains a brief coded reference to the future arrival of the foreign ships of the Hanoverians, replacing the native 'Oaks' of the exiled Stuarts.

402–3. **Feather'd People ... painted Chiefs:** native Americans or 'Indians' as Pope knew them. Four so-called Iroquois chiefs (one not actually an Iroquois and three of no great rank) visited London as part of a propaganda exercise, largely organised and supported by Tory partisans, on behalf of the colonial governors on 20 April 1710, and were granted a somewhat theatrical audience with Queen Anne; their speech on the occasion, requesting protection against the French in Canada, was printed shortly afterwards, along with much other material (e.g. *The Four Kings of Canada*, 1710, *The History and Progress of the Four Indian Kings*, 1710). *TE* notes that Addison's essay on Londoners as supposedly seen from their point of view (cf. 403–4 here) appeared in *The Spectator*, no. 50, 27 April 1711, and that Tickell's *A Poem ... On the Prospect of Peace*, 180–1 (1712), p. 8 also alluded to their submission to Anne. A further prose satire following Addison's lead appeared as *Royal Remarks* (c. 1711). See Rogers (2005a: 226–31) for a summary of the political and literary responses.

403. **admire:** wonder at; cf. *Essay on Criticism*, 101.

405   Oh stretch thy Reign, fair *Peace*! from Shore to Shore,
        Till Conquest cease, and Slav'ry be no more:
        Till the freed *Indians* in their native Groves
        Reap their own Fruits, and woo their Sable Loves,
        Peru once more a Race of Kings behold,
410   And other *Mexico's* be roof'd with Gold.
        Exil'd by Thee from Earth to deepest Hell,
        In Brazen Bonds shall barb'rous *Discord* dwell:

---

406. Slav'ry: By a special measure of the Treaty of Utrecht, signed by Britain and Spain on 13 July 1713, Britain acquired the 'Asiento des Negros', a license to trade in slaves to the Spanish colonies for 30 years. The grant was administered by the South Sea Company (above, 389). For discussions of Pope's position in relation to issues of contemporary slavery, see Erskine-Hill (1998); Richardson (2004); and Rogers (2005a: 237–9).

407. freed Indians: in the Spanish colonies in South America. Cf. Pope to Caryll, 5 December 1712, *Corr.*, I.162, on 'poor naked Indians' facing European weaponry. Pope annotated a section of his copy of Charles Cotton's 1685–6 translation of Montaigne's *Essais* with the words 'Of the Indian World and the Cruelty of ye Spaniards from hence to ye end of ye chapter' (Mack 1982: 430). He returned to a similar image in *Essay on Man*, I.105–8.

    native Groves: cf. 'Vertumnus and Pomona', 86.

408. Reap ... Fruits: cf. *Messiah*, 64.

    Sable: black, with a suggestion of heraldic richness and value: 'a word used by heralds and poets' (*SJ*). Cf. 28. For use in relation to skin colour, cf. Pope's translation of the *Odyssey*, XIX.279.

409. Peru ... Kings: South American country devastated by invasions of early Spanish conquistadores; a byword for the destructive effects of colonisation, as e.g. in William D'Avenant's play *The Cruelty of the Spaniards in Peru* (1658). A similar story was dramatised by Dryden in the two parts of *The Conquest of Granada by the Spaniards* (1672).

410. other Mexico's: The colonisation of Mexico was similarly treated in Dryden's play *The Indian Emperour: or, the Conquest of Mexico* (1665). Its wealth was a matter of common reference; *TE* cites Dryden, *Annus Mirabilis*, st. 294, p. 74: 'Rich as the Town which gives the *Indies* name, | With Silver pav'd, and all divine with Gold'. Defoe's verse often connects the two realms of plundered riches, 'the Golden Mines of *Mexico*' and 'the Silver Mountains of *Peru*'; e.g. *The True-Born Englishman* (1701), p. 6. Rogers (2005a: 233n) remarks that Peru and Mexico were both specifically mentioned as a source of vast riches in Harley's plan for the South Sea Company.

    roof'd with Gold: *TE* cites Dryden's version of *Aeneid*, VI.17, *Works of Virgil*, p. 362: 'the Temple roof'd with Gold' (translating Virgil's 'aurea tecta', 'golden roofs'). The roof of Milton's Pandemonium (*Paradise Lost*, I.717) is 'fretted Gold'.

411–20. Wakefield finds sources for this passage in Virgil, *Georgics*, III.37–9 and *Aeneid*, I.293–6, both prophetic passages foretelling the future glory of Rome. Morris (1973) cites the personified spectres (including Furies with snakes) that greet Aeneas in the underworld in *Aeneid*, VI, especially in Dryden's translation (VI.384–93). Rogers (2004: 43, 56–7) locates relevant imagery in Stephen Harrison's design for a triumphal entry for James I to London, and in the allegorical painting in the ceiling of the Banqueting House at Whitehall, by Rubens, for which Trumbull's grandfather was the British agent. Rogers (2005a: 291) suggests also recollection of the allegorical depiction of Sedition in Cowley, *Civil Wars*, I.221–4, and (2005a: 63) cites a letter of Swift to the Archbishop of Dublin, almost contemporary with the poem, in which 'Faction, Rage, Rebellion, Revenge, and Ambition' are specifically identified with

Gigantick *Pride*, pale *Terror*, gloomy *Care*,
And mad *Ambition*, shall attend her there.
415   There purple *Vengeance* bath'd in Gore retires,
Her Weapons blunted, and extinct her Fires:
There hateful *Envy* her own Snakes shall feel,
And *Persecution* mourn her broken Wheel:
There *Faction* roars, *Rebellion* bites her Chain,
420   And gasping Furies thirst for Blood in vain.

---

419. **roars, . . . bites:** *1736–51:* roar, . . . bite

---

opponents of the Queen's peace. The unbuilt tomb of Charles I, planned in 1678, would have displayed a similar sequence of defeated abstractions (Rogers 2005a: 199).

412. ***Brazen:*** brass or bronze. Cf. Dryden's version of *Aeneid*, I.405, *Works of Virgil*, p. 213, 'Imprison'd Fury, bound in brazen chains' (translating Virgil's 'aënis . . . nodis', 'bronze fetters', 295–6).

Discord: an allegorical figure, 'Discordia' in Latin, under the command of Jupiter. Cf. Anne's dismissal of discord, 325, and 'The First Book of Statius his Thebais', 183. Pope uses both 'Discord' and the Greek equivalent 'Eris' in his *Iliad*. Rogers (2004: 76–8) notes that among Poussin's allegorical paintings there is one pairing Discord with Envy (below, 417), with similar visual attributes. Parnell's poem 'On Queen Anne's Peace, Anno 1713', *Posthumous Works* (1758), pp. 257–9, associates Discord with Whig factionalism and sedition.

414. mad **Ambition:** perhaps, as with Pride in the previous line, a hit at Marlborough; cf. 'Prologue to *Cato*', 12. Pope recalled the phrase in *Iliad*, I.520 and XIII.458, in martial contexts.

415. ***purple . . . Gore:*** Vengeance is purple with bloodshed (cf. 321).

417. ***Envy . . . Snakes:*** Envy (Invidia) is threatened with snakes in Virgil, *Georgics*, III.37–9 (Dryden, II.62–3, *Works of Virgil*, p. 98: Envy 'Shall . . . fear the curling snakes | Of lashing Furies'); she is made to eat poisonous snakes in Ovid, *Metamorphoses*, II.768–9, and subjected to her own torments at 781–2; she is equipped with snakes in the prologue to Jonson's play *Poetaster* (1602), and in 'To the Queen', from Defoe's *Jure Divino*, XII (1706), p. 20. Pope returned to the image of Envy's snakes in *Ode for Musick*, 34, and see *Essay on Criticism*, 467–70. Rogers (2005a: 182) points to a similar allegorical painting at Windsor Castle.

418. ***broken Wheel:*** Breaking on the wheel was a widely reported form of punishment in certain European countries, especially France; the convict was tied to the wheel and beaten to death. Pope alludes to the practice again in the *Epistle to Dr Arbuthnot*, 308.

419–20. EC compares Sir John Beaumont, *Bosworth-Field* (1629), p. 5: 'Beneath his feete pale Enuie bites her chaine, | And snaky Discord whets her sting in vaine'. The poem had been reprinted in 1710.

419. **Faction:** political infighting; see Commentary to *Essay on Criticism*, 457–8; *Ode for Musick*, 35. Pope means the Whigs specifically.

420. **Furies:** the Erinyes, in Greek mythology, implacable semi-divine females who pursued vengeance especially for crimes against kin or family; cf. 'The First Book of Statius his Thebais', 111, 124ff, and *Ode for Musick*, 68, 105. Morris (1973) links Pope's image to the Virgilian concept of 'furor impius', an excessive and irrational energy. Bloodthirstiness was a charge frequently levelled at Marlborough by Swift and other Tories, and Rogers (2004: 59–61) suggests that he and the Duchess could have been part of Pope's idea here; cf. 325 MS.

Here cease thy Flight, nor with unhallow'd Lays
Touch the fair Fame of *Albion*'s Golden Days.
The Thoughts of Gods let *Granville*'s Verse recite,
And bring the Scenes of opening Fate to Light.
425 My humble Muse, in unambitious Strains,
Paints the green Forests and the flow'ry Plains,
Where Peace descending bids her Olives spring,
And scatters Blessings from her Dove-like Wing.
Ev'n I more sweetly pass my careless Days,
430 Pleas'd in the silent Shade with empty Praise;
Enough for me, that to the listning Swains
First in these Fields I sung the Sylvan Strains.

FINIS.

---

421. **Flight,:** MSh: Flight!

---

421. **thy Flight:** the imaginative 'flight' of poetry (cf. *Essay on Criticism*, 93, 151, 200, 737–8). Pope hands the task of recording '*Albion*'s Golden Days' or reclaimed alchemical future to the court insider Granville.

423. **Gods:** the Queen and her officers. Warburton suggests a source in Horace, *Odes* III.iii. 70–2: 'quo, Musa, tendis? desine pervicax | referre sermones deorum et | magna modis tenuare parvis' ('where are you going, Muse? cease, obstinate, to reveal the conversations of gods and to belittle great matters in small measures'). *EC* notes Addison's expanded translation of this poem, supposedly written by Horace in relation to a plan of Augustus to rebuild Troy, 124–5, *Poetical Miscellanies: The Sixth Part* (1709), p. 270: 'But hold, my Muse, forbear thy tow'ring Flight, | Nor bring the Secrets of the Gods to Light'.

424. **opening:** in the process of being revealed.

425. **unambitious:** There are numerous classical sources for this deferential pose, e.g. Horace, *Odes*, I.vi. *EC* notes the resemblance of the conclusion to Addison's deference to his patron Halifax at the end of his 'A Letter from Italy', *Poetical Miscellanies: The Fifth Part*, p. 12: 'My humble Verse demands a softer Theme, | A painted Meadow or a purling Stream, | Unfit for Heroes; whom immortal Lays, | And Lines like *Virgil*'s, or like yours shou'd praise'.

427–8. **Olives ... Wing:** invoking the olive branch and dove as symbols of peace, from the story of Noah's ark (Genesis 8:11); the olive was also a royal tree of peace in heraldic lore (Rogers 2005a: 202). Cf. 'Messiah', 19–20. In the New Testament the descending dove represents the Holy Spirit (Matthew 3:16); see also Milton's invocation to the 'Dove-like' Holy Spirit, *Paradise Lost*, I.17–26.

429. **careless:** without anxiety.

431–2. recalling the opening of 'Spring', the first of Pope's *Pastorals*, in allusion to Virgil's conclusion of his *Georgics* with an echo of the first line of his *Eclogues* (with the implication that an *Aeneid* might be next). The 'list'ning Swains' are Pope's early mentors, among them Granville and Trumbull.

17
PROLOGUE TO *CATO*
(1713)

Editors' Headnote

Composition and publication

Pope's 'Prologue' to Addison's play *Cato* was first published on 18 April 1713. It appeared, together with an 'Epilogue' written by their mutual friend Samuel Garth, in *The Guardian*, no. 33, at the end of an essay advertising the dramatic, moral and political virtues of the play. The two poems are introduced in the following terms:

> Mr. *Pope* has prepared the Audience for a new Scene of Passion and Transport on a more noble Foundation than they have before been entertained with, in the *Prologue*. I shall take the Liberty to gratifie the Impatience of the Town by inserting these two excellent Pieces, as Earnests of the Work it self, which will be Printed within few Days.

Cato had opened at Drury Lane on 14 April, and was in print on 27 April, complete with Pope's 'Prologue'. It is likely that the poem was composed in February or March of 1713. In (probably) February, Pope wrote to Caryll that he had 'lately the entertainment of reading Mr Addison's tragedy of *Cato*'; he did not mention his own possible contribution, apparently unsure whether the play would actually reach the stage, but his discussion of the central character looks towards 17–22 of the 'Prologue' (*Corr.*, I.173 and see below, Context). The hostile suggestion, in *Characters of the Times* (1728), p. 26, that Pope received help from Addison in writing it is not to be taken seriously, though some verbal changes were no doubt considered; see Commentary to 37. Pope's subsequent letter to Caryll of 30 April (see below) declares that the text of the play had sold out already, and that the 'town is so fond of it, that the orange wenches and fruit women in the Park offer the books at the side of the coaches, and the Prologue and Epilogue are cried about the streets by the common hawkers'; this latter point seems to have been an exaggeration, as there is no evidence that such broadsheet piracies (a hypothetical Griffith 15a) were actually produced. There is no record of any payment; the 'Prologue' was probably requested as a favour, during the last phase of Pope's short and uneasy friendship with Addison.

Text

The text presented here is taken from the first edition of 1713. Revision of the poem is confined to the *Works* of 1751, and is unlikely to be authorial. The Prologue continued to be printed with the play, separately and in editions of Addison's *Works*, but only versions authorised by Pope have been collated. The various extant texts of 'Prologue to Cato' are referred to in the apparatus as follows:

1713: *Guardian*, No. 33 (Griffith 13)

1751: *Works*, vol.I, octavo (Griffith 643)

Models and sources

Prologues and Epilogues, performed by one of the lead actors in a play, had become a standard feature of theatrical practice since the reopening of the theatres at the Restoration in 1660 and often acquired some independent popularity (such as Garth's 'Prologue' to Nicholas Rowe's *Tamerlane*, a much-performed Williamite drama of 1702). They were normally contributed by fellow writers rather than by the dramatist and acted as a sort of commendatory poem to the play. Prologues were, however, sometimes paid for at a commercial rate; Joseph Warton, writing about Pope's 'solemn and sublime' effort in the present case, records the anecdote that while the usual price of a prologue was four guineas, Dryden asked six on the grounds that 'the players have had my goods too cheap' (1756: 257–60).

Pope's connection with the theatre of his time is described in Goldstein (1958). He was on close personal terms with the older generation of Restoration dramatists, including Wycherley, Congreve and Southerne, and the actor Thomas Betterton (who had died in 1710), and was obviously well read in other playwrights of the era; Dryden's example, as a poet who was also a working dramatist, was always before him. By the time of the 'Prologue', he also knew emerging contemporary dramatists such as Rowe, Steele and Gay. Some of his earliest writing was in dramatic form: late in life he told Spence that at school he had written a 'something toward a tragedy' based on speeches from the *Iliad*, and at the age of thirteen, another tragedy based on 'a very moving story in the legend of St. Genevieve' (*OAC*, I.15–16, items 33–5, 1739–43). He went on,

> After I had got acquainted with the town I resolved never to write anything for the stage, though I was solicited by several of my friends to do so, and particularly by Betterton who (among other things) would have had me turn my early epic poem into a tragedy. I had taken such strong resolutions against anything of that kind, from seeing how much everybody that did write for the stage was obliged to subject themselves to the players and the town.

Martha Blount was recorded by Spence as saying 'have often heard him say so'. Some confirmation of the position comes from the correspondence. On 24 June

1706 (assuming Pope's date is correct), his mentor Walsh wrote to suggest that Pope undertake a 'Pastoral Comedy' on the Italian model, there being no rival in the field in England; on 2 July Pope responded with a genteel demurral on grounds of public taste, while showing his knowledge of that class of drama (*Corr.*, I.18–19). In a verse letter of 12 or 13 July 1707, he joked fleetingly to Cromwell about a possible tragedy (*Corr.*, I.27). After the easy hit at John Dennis's tragedy in the *Essay on Criticism* (588), Cromwell wrote facetiously to Pope on 7 December 1711 (*Corr.*, I.136):

> Think on the Dignity of Tragedy, which is of the greater Poetry, as *Dennis*, says, and foil him at his other weapon, as you have done in Criticism. Every one wonders that a Genius like yours will not support the sinking *Drama*; and Mr. *Wilks* . . . has express'd a furious ambition to swell in your Buskins.

Pope responded on 21 December (*Corr.*, I.137–8) in high rakish humour, exhibiting some mock-tragedy lines of amorous complaint with the tag 'Am I not fit to write a Tragedy?' and mocking the acting style of the suggested speaker:

> And wou'd not these Lines sound admirably in the Mouth of *Wilks*, especially if he humourd each period with his Leg, & stamp'd with just alacrity at the Cadences?

If these exchanges suggest a sceptical detachment from the theatre, the 'Prologue to *Cato*', as the first thing he had written expressly for a theatrical context, appears nonetheless to represent a dutiful attempt to adopt a conventional dramatic style, and it did allow Wilks (c. 1665–1732), the actor-manager who played the Numidian prince Juba in the drama, to 'swell' in Pope's 'Buskins' (the footwear of the classical actor).

Pope wrote other Prologues, usually of a more satirical kind, including one for the farce *Three Hours After Marriage* (1717), on which he collaborated with Gay. His 'Prologue, Design'd for Mr. D—'s last Play' is poem 21 below. It is possible that he wrote or contributed to an 'Epilogue' to Gay's *The Wife of Bath*, a play which failed (not least because of competition from *Cato*) in 1713; see Headnote to 'The Wife of Bath Her Prologue, from Chaucer'. Pope's mildly salacious 'Epilogue' to Rowe's *Jane Shore* was drafted for the play's run in February 1714 but appears to have been rejected by the actress (Anne Oldfield, who also appeared in *Cato*) and was not printed until Pope's 1717 *Works* (Ault 1949: 138–44). An anonymous 'Prologue' to Rowe's *Tragedy of the Lady Jane Gray* (1715) has been ascribed to Pope (Ault 1949: 138–44) on grounds of verbal parallels with Pope's other work; like many of Ault's ascriptions, it awaits supporting documentary evidence. Pope contributed 'Two Chorus's to Julius Caesar' for his friend the Duke of Buckinghamshire's version of *Julius Caesar*, published in his own *Works* of 1717. Pope's later satires, including *The Dunciad*, were much informed by antagonism towards the professional theatre and its writers and performers; he often refused to write Prologues or Epilogues for other poets (see e.g. letters to Broome, 18 September 1722; to Aaron Hill, 29 September 1738; *Corr.*, II.134; IV.131–2; and Ault 1949: 209), and he referred drily to the importunity of such requests in the *Epistle to*

Dr Arbuthnot (48, and see 55–60). Nonetheless he did contribute a 'Prologue' to James Thomson's *Sophonisba* (1730) and one for Dennis's benefit night (1733).

Context

The 'Cato' of Addison's title was Marcus Porcius Cato, or Cato of Utica (95–46 BC), not to be confused with his great-grandfather of the same name, 'Cato Censor' (234–149 BC) mentioned in the 'Prologue' at 39 (and, more jocularly, in a verse letter to Cromwell, 12 or 13 July 1707; *Corr.*, I.28). The elder Cato, a prominent soldier and orator, had a reputation for unbending application of the Roman virtues of self-discipline and self-sacrifice. Cato of Utica was also an eminent politician and soldier, who sided with Pompey in the Civil Wars, governed Utica (on the North African coast, in what is now Tunisia) after Pompey's defeat, and committed suicide rather than accept a demeaning pardon from the victorious Julius Caesar. He was regarded as a model of stoic martyrdom and resistance to tyranny from his own time onwards, and his reputation probably played a part in the assassination of Caesar himself two years later. In Shakespeare's *Julius Caesar*, Brutus and the other conspirators are shown as highly conscious of Cato's death and 'Young Cato', his son, appears as a character. The Cavalier poet Richard Lovelace summarised his reputation in one of his two epigrams 'Of Cato', in *Lucasta* (1659–60): 'The World orecome, victorious *Caesar*, he | That conquer'd all; great *Cato*, could not thee'. Pope's Jacobite friend Lord Lansdowne referred to the example of Cato in several poems, most notably in a long passage explaining his own political retirement; the poem supposedly dates from 1690, just after the advent of William III, but was certainly available to audiences of 1713 as it was published in his *Poems Upon Several Occasions* in 1712 (p. 98), the year in which Lansdowne was made a peer to assist the passage of the Utrecht treaty:

> Had *Cato* bent beneath the conquering Cause,
> He might have liv'd to give new Senates Laws;
> But on vile Terms disdaining to be great,
> He perish'd by his Choice, and not his Fate:
> Honours and Life th' Usurper bids, and all
> That vain mistaken Men good Fortune call,
> Virtue forbids, and sets before his Eyes
> An honest Death, which he accepts, and dies:
> O glorious Resolution! Noble Pride!
> More honour'd than the Tyrant liv'd, he dy'd,
> More prais'd, more lov'd, more envy'd in his Doom,
> Than *Caesar* trampling on the Rights of *Rome*.

(See also Commentary to 23–4.) The story of Cato's resistance and suicide was well known from Plutarch's biography (translated by Stephen Waller in the fourth volume of *Plutarch's Lives*, published by Tonson in 1685); Pope refers to this in the 'Epilogue to

Jane Shore', 31. It was perhaps even better known from Lucan's incomplete *Pharsalia* (c. AD 65), a poem highly resonant in Pope's day as a lament for political liberties lost under an imperial system. Cato was a highly malleable political icon; as well as Lansdowne's Jacobite interpretation, Pope could have found references to him in anti-monarchical treatises such as Algernon Sidney's *Discourses Concerning Government* (1698; e.g. pp. 125, 147) and Whiggish moralising such as Steele's *The Christian Hero* (1701), pp. 5-12. He certainly knew that the Whig Rowe had published versions of two extracts from Lucan's poem, each involving Cato, one of them in the same volume of *Poetical Miscellanies* which had launched his own career (1709). An extract by Charles Hopkins on Cato's character had appeared in Lintot's *Oxford and Cambridge Miscellany Poems* in 1708. Rowe's full version of *Pharsalia* (1718) probably benefited from the momentum of Addison's play. Pope and Cromwell discussed Rowe's translation, including a passage on Cato, in terms which indicate something of the heightened context of these years; as Cromwell put it (5 November 1710): 'He is so errant a Whig, that he strains even beyond his Author, in passion for Liberty, and aversion to Tyranny' (5 November 1710, *Corr.*, I.102-3; Pope to Cromwell, 11 November, *ibid.* 103-4).

Joseph Addison (1672-1719) had, as a poet, written one of the most prominent pro-Marlborough poems during the long war, *The Campaign* (1704; cf Headnote to *Windsor-Forest*); as a politician, he had held government office as Under-Secretary of State and had been Secretary to Lord Wharton in Ireland. He had also written an 'English' opera, *Rosamund*, for which Walsh appears to have supplied a 'Prologue' (according to Curll's *The Works of... Rochester, and Roscommon*, 2 vols, 1709, II.156-8). By 1713, however, Addison was a Whig apologist out of place; after the fall of the Whigs in the wake of the Sacheverell crisis of 1710, Addison spent more time with Steele on periodical endeavours, becoming a critical arbiter and the centre of Whig literary operations. Addison's play on the subject of Cato was probably first drafted when he was a student at Magdalen College, Oxford, and it may have been read by Dryden (who is said by Edward Young to have thought it would not succeed as a stage play; *OAC*, I.64-5, note to no. 153) among others. Addison took a draft with him on his European tour (1699-1703); at Venice, in 1701, he was amused by the anachronisms and incongruities in an opera on the subject, Pollarollo's *Catone Uticenze* (Hammond 2006: 602-5). He returned in 1704 with a complete version of the first four acts, which were received warmly by Steele, already heavily involved in theatre, and Colley Cibber (1671-1757), a prominent comic actor and writer (later one of Pope's major antagonists) and one of the managers at Drury Lane by the time Addison completed the play. Pope alleged that the success of Ambrose Philips's *The Distrest Mother* in 1712 was a trial run for the 'packed house' performance of *Cato*, and its success (from 17 March 1712) was certainly encouraging to Addison's circle; Addison was thought to have a considerable hand in drafting of that play and its popular 'Epilogue', notionally by Eustace Budgell (*OAC*, I.66-7; items 155-7, 28 or 29 November 1730). Heightened political tension in the run-up to the Treaty of Utrecht (signed on 31 March 1713) is another possible reason for Addison's completion of the play. As Tickell put it, 'his friends of the first quality and distinction prevailed with him to put the last finishing to it, at a time when they thought the doctrine of Liberty very seasonable' ('Preface' to *The Works of... Addison*, 1721, I.xiv). Steele (unashamedly recounting his own assiduousness in ensuring the rapturous reception of the play) recorded that the final act was written in 'less than a Week's time' ('Dedication' to Addison's *The Drummer*, 1722, p. xvi) and not long before it was staged. The Utrecht agreement was regarded as an insult to their fallen hero, the Duke of Marlborough, who was in turn regarded as a dangerous egomaniac by Tories like Swift. But Addison was keen to present the play as non-partisan and Swift, the most brilliant of the Tory propagandists, attended rehearsals; in the *Journal to Stella*, Swift records dining amicably enough with the political opponents Addison and Bolingbroke on 3 April 1713, not long before the first performance.

Addison had praised (and mildly reproved) Pope's *Essay on Criticism* in *The Spectator*, as well as the first 'Rape of the Locke' (see Headnotes to those items). It is generally assumed that the two men met through Steele at some point in 1712; an unpublished letter apparently from Addison to Pope, dated 11 February 1713, may be the first record of their correspondence (Harvard MS Eng. 1336, fol. 1). Pope told Jonathan Richardson in 1730 that Addison's benevolent critique of the *Essay on Criticism* in *Spectator*, no. 253, had 'Occasiond their Acquaintance, & he had an Opportunity of returning the Compliment by Writing the Prologue to Cato' (Sherburn 1958a: 347). Addison's request that Pope contribute the Prologue was perhaps a last attempt to keep within his sphere of influence an emerging writer, clearly heading in a Tory direction, against the Whig coterie at Buttons, as the War ended. The 'Epilogue' was by Samuel Garth, a genial Whig physician and poet long on friendly terms with Pope (see Headnote to *Pastorals*), and spoken by Mary Porter, who played Lucia. Addison probably considered that bracketing his play in this way helped preserve an official neutrality about its politics. For further commentary on the play in its context, see Kelsall (1966) and Winn (2014: 610–14); for a modern edition, with supporting material, see Henderson and Yellin (2004).

Pope gave Spence a number of anecdotes about his early friendship with Addison and the apparently non-partisan nature of his encouragement (*OAC*, I.60–3, items 145–51). He was also evidently involved in the careful preparations for the play's launch. In the already-mentioned letter to Caryll, conjecturally dated to February 1713, Pope, who had just sent *Windsor-Forest* to the press, outlines with some care his view of the play in draft:

> I have had lately the entertainment of reading Mr Addison's tragedy of *Cato*. The scene is in Utica, and the time, the last night of his life. It drew tears from me in several parts of the fourth and fifth acts, where the beauty of virtue appears so charming that I believe (if it comes upon the theatre) we shall enjoy that which Plato thought the greatest pleasure an exalted soul could be capable of, a view of virtue itself great in person, colour, and action. The emotion which the mind will feel from this character and the sentiments of humanity which the distress of such a person as Cato will stir up in us, must necessarily fill an audience with so glorious a disposition, and so warm a love of virtue, that I question if any play has ever conduced so immediately to morals as this.
> (*Corr.*, I.173)

His account of his first contact with *Cato*, given to Spence in June 1739 (*OAC*, I. 64), gives slightly different detail:

> When Mr. Addison had finished his *Cato*, he brought it to me, desired to have my sincere opinion of it, and left it with me for three or four days. I gave him my opinion sincerely, which was that 'I thought he had better not act it, and that he would get reputation enough only by printing it.' This I said as thinking the lines well writ, but the piece not theatrical enough.

Spence also recorded that Pope had objected to some lines and expressions which Addison duly altered, and had supplied some alterations himself (*OAC*, I.75; items 174 and 175, 9 August 1735). Warton (*Works of Pope*, I.345) says that Pope contributed the last line of the play. Addison is said to have agreed with Pope's scepticism about performance but to have deferred to the opinions of others who wanted the play performed. Pope also recalled being asked to show the play to Bolingbroke and Oxford 'and to assure them that he never in the least designed it as a party-play, etc. They approved of it...' (*OAC*, I.64, item 153).

Pope claimed that 'The love-part was flung in after, to comply with the popular taste; and the last act was not written till six or seven years after he came home', which would indicate revisions in about 1710 or 11 (*OAC.*, I.65; item 154, 28 or 29 November 1730). While Pope's comment in the 'Prologue' (10) that the play eschews the vulgar trope of 'the Hero's Glory' draws attention to the non-martial form of triumph that Cato gains, his suggestion that it also avoids 'the Virgin's Love' as a source of pathos strikes an odd note: as Johnson pointed out (Lonsdale, III.12), it is hard to view the love interest as 'extrinsick and adventitious', so interwoven is it into the texture of the play as completed. Cato's daughter Maria, is in love with Juba, while Lucia, the daughter of a senator, is in love with one of Cato's sons, and more or less all the male characters except Cato experience some conflict between martial duty and marital desire. Steele's essay on the play in *The Guardian*, no. 33, 18 April 1713, describes the lovers as 'more warm, though more discreet, than ever yet appeared on the Stage', and love was also the subject of Garth's 'Epilogue', which, as Steele put it, 'very agreeably rallyed the Mercenary Traffic between Men and Women of this Age'. Pope's views on the love interest might derive from recollection of a much earlier state of the play than we know of, but this seems unlikely; his misdirection in the 'Prologue' probably suggests a wish that audiences should concentrate only on the character of Cato's private virtue, the aspect he had found most moving in his letter to Caryll. (For further details of this aspect see Freeman 1999.) He might have hoped this feature would transcend party alignments, about which he seems to have been nervous, perhaps from a sense of being politically manoeuvred by Addison. There is no reason to doubt his literary admiration of the portrayal of Cato as embodiment of self-mastery, an abiding theme of Pope's own work, and the 'Prologue' derives much of its imagery from the play itself, alongside a relatively austere set of classical witnesses (Seneca, Cicero, Plutarch). It can be aligned with other work by Pope: aloofness from military posturing was part of the framework of

Windsor-Forest; suicide as a virtuous response to oppression would shortly recur as a theme in Pope's 'Verses to the Memory of an Unfortunate Lady'; British cultural aspirations had been a theme of the *Essay on Criticism*. In the event, however, there could be no escaping a political skirmish.

There was unusual pre-performance interest, stoked in part by the dual activities of Steele in his role as theatrical manager and journalist; he ensured that the house was 'packed' with supporters (*OAC*, I.66; item 155, 28 or 29 November 1730). The first night, at Drury Lane on 14 April 1713, was marked by noisy political contention, with Whigs and Tories each claiming heroic individual resistance to tyranny as the mark of their own political ethos: 'Liberty' under the rule of law was supposedly a fundamental component of British character (cf. *Essay on Criticism*, 718–21). It is probable from Pope's account of the premiere, given in a letter to Caryll, 30 April 1713 (*Corr.*, I.174–6), that he was actually present on the night. Presenting himself as immersed in the study of painting, he says that as to 'poeticall affairs I am content at present to be a bare looker on'. The first part of the letter maintains a dignified neutrality about the success of the play:

> Cato was not so much the wonder of Rome itself, in his days, as he is of Britain in ours; and tho' all the foolish industry possible has been used to make it a party play, yet what the author once said of another may be the most properly in the world applied to him on this occasion.
> Envy it self is dumb, in wonder lost,
> And factions strive, who shall applaud him most.

(Pope quotes from Addison's *Campaign*, 45–6). Politics, however, inculpates him:

> The numerous and violent claps of the Whig party on the one side the theatre, were echoed back by the Tories on the other, while the author sweated behind the scenes with concern to find their applause proceeded more [from] the hand than the head. This was the case too of the prologue-writer, who was clapped into a stanch [sic] Whig sore against his will, at almost every two lines. I believe you have heard that after all the applauses of the opposite faction, my Lord Bullingbrooke [Bolingbroke] sent for Booth who played Cato, into the box, between one of the acts and presented him with 50 guineas; in acknowledgment (as he expressed it) for his defending the cause of liberty so well against a *perpetuall dictator*: the Whigs are unwilling to be distanced this way, as 'tis said, and therefore design a present to the said Cato very speedily; in the meantime they are getting ready as good a sentence as the former on their side. So betwixt them, 'tis probable that Cato (as Dr Garth expressed it) may have something to live upon, after he dies.

In one of Gay's earliest letters, he confirms that some passages of the 'Prologue' were applauded as attacks on the Tories (see Commentary to 13–14). Likewise George

Berkeley, who attended the premiere with Addison, wrote to Sir John Percival on 16 April that 'Some parts of the prologue, which were written by Mr Pope, a Tory and even a Papist, were hissed, being thought to savour of whiggism'; nonetheless Harley, sitting in the next box, 'was observed to clap as loud as any in the house' (quoted in Mack 1985: 221). Pope and Tonson told Spence that the political rivalry, embodied in Bolingbroke's conspicuous gesture, 'was an incidental piece of good luck, and carried the success of the play much beyond what they ever expected' (*OAC*, I.66, item 156; 28 or 29 November 1730); a decade later, Colley Cibber recalled the circumstances of the ostentatious gifts to the lead actors in his *Apology* (1740), pp. 267–70, though he has uncharacteristically little to say of Pope's role.

The play had an exceptional run and was also successfully performed at Oxford (Goldstein 1958: 6–12). The publishing industry produced about 15 editions of *Cato* in 1713, nearly half of them piracies; Addison apparently gave Pope a copy of the seventh as a gift (Mack 1982: 395, item 1). There were many spin-off elements including a short *Life and Character of Marcus Cato of Utica, the Great Assertor of Liberty*, written by Pope's future enemy Lewis Theobald and published by Lintot, with a plot summary of the play. Theobald and Lintot further contributed a translation of Plato's *Dialogue of the Immortality of the Soul* (generally referred to as *Phaedo*), the book Cato reads before committing suicide. Apart from Steele's essay in the *Guardian*, already mentioned, there were several literary critiques: the anonymous *Cato Examin'd* (1713) drew out some reasons for approving of the play, as did George Sewell's *Observations on Cato* (1713), published by Curll, who also issued an English translation of a French play on the subject. There was also widespread political allegorising: the Duke of Marlborough, supposedly infallible military hero of the Whigs during the War of Spanish Succession, who had petitioned to be made Captain General for life and who had been dismissed at the end of 1711 and gone into exile, could be read into the character of Cato or Caesar, according to allegiance. *The Unfortunate General* (1713) offered a 'key' (iii–iv) identifying Cato with Marlborough and Lucius and Sempronius (coward and turncoat respectively) with Harley and Bolingbroke. Mack (1985: 856n) notes a further ultra-Whig reading in *The Flying Post*, 2 May 1713. The prince Juba could be seen as the king-in-waiting, the Electoral Prince of Hanover, and Sempronius as the embodiment of Jacobitism. Tory responses included *Mr. Addison Turn'd Tory: or, The Scene Inverted* (1713), which sees the overweening Caesar and the villain Syphax as types of Marlborough, with Harley more in the Cato role. Cato could also stand for the exiled Stuart claimants to the British throne. When George I arrived in 1714, Addison offered the play as a testimony of his Hanoverian loyalism in a formal panegyric, *To her Royal Highness the Princess of Wales, with the Tragedy of Cato* (1714). *Cato's Ghost*, however, a broadside by William Meston, who fought in the 1715 Jacobite rising, was in some ways a parody of Pope's 'Prologue', an unexpected inflection of Pope's studied neutrality.

The most sustained critique of the play was Dennis's *Remarks upon Cato, A Tragedy*, published by Lintot on 9 July 1713. Dennis, whose most successful play was called *Liberty Asserted* (1704), might have been expected to be on Addison's side of the political divide, but was outraged by almost everything in the play, not least the moral logic, in which the Stoic defender of liberty kills himself without actually being defeated. Pope's 'Prologue' was not much singled out in discussion of the play: even Dennis let this aspect lie. (See however Ault 1949: 141 for a snide contemporary remark by Philip Horneck on Pope's concealed '*Roman* bigottry', i.e. Catholicism, in this connection.) Pope is, however, almost certainly the author of *The Narrative of Dr. Robert Norris, Concerning the strange and deplorable Frenzy of Mr. John Denn—* (28 July 1713; *PW*, I.153–172), which lampoons the old critic as a crazed, jealous has-been, who is nonetheless deliberately given the opportunity to vent some telling critique of the play in the course of his ravings. In *A True Character of Mr. Pope* (1716), p. 6, Dennis asserted that Pope had 'teaz'd' Lintot into publishing the *Remarks*, prompting the further accusation that Pope '*Cato*'s Muse with faithless Sneer belied, | The Prologue father'd, and the Play decried' (see Guerinot 1969: 191). Addison ignored these developments with ostentatious high-mindedness and gave Pope to understand that this sort of defence was not welcome (Steele to Lintot, 4 August 1713; *Corr.*, I.184; Mack 1985: 222–5).

Despite the apparent good faith of the 'Prologue', there were signs that Pope was already separating himself from the play's high seriousness (see Aden 1978: 140–2 and da Silva 2005; and for further commentary on Pope's relations with Addison, political and literary, see Rogers 2010: chapters 3 and 4). The letter to Caryll, 30 April 1713 (*Corr.*, I.174–6), already quoted, was written two days after publication of his spoof essay on Pastoral in *The Guardian* (no. 40; see Headnote to *Pastorals*) in which he burned another bridge with Addison's circle. (It was published on the same day as the play was, and the coincidence is, at least, striking.) The letter continues with an anecdote about an Oxford student obsessed with the play, culminating in a bawdy epigram on the subject, involving the actress Anne Oldfield, which it is hard to imagine he did not write himself; *TE*, VI.410, regards the authorship as doubtful, but Mack (1985: 234–5 and 859n), noting the duality of Pope's response to the play, regards it as genuine. It is of a piece with the ribald item known as 'On a Lady who P–st at the Tragedy of *Cato*', probably co-written with Rowe (*TE*, VI.99–100; it appeared 18 February 1714), a sniggering riposte to Eusden's substantial poem 'To a Lady, that wept at the hearing *Cato* read' (published, with items 19–22 below, in Steele's *Poetical Miscellanies* of December 1713, dated 1714). The 'Epilogue' for Rowe's *Jane Shore*, which Pope apparently wrote in February 1714, but which was not spoken or printed with the play (it was published in his *Works* of 1717) devotes a substantial section to light mockery of Cato's domestic arrangements (29–44). Cato became something of a reference point in the breakdown of relationships with Addison over the next few years. Writing to Addison, 10 October 1714, during the early days of the Homer subscription, Pope declares pointedly: 'As to what you have said of me, I shall never believe that the Author of *Cato* can speak one thing and think another' (*Corr.*, I.263; the genuineness of the letter is not certain). Pope referred without irony to the stoicism of Cato in *The Temple of Fame* (1715), 176: 'Unconquer'd *Cato* shews the wound he tore'. But that poem had been drafted in 1712, and several letters from 1715 make sardonic reference to the play (e.g. the letter written with Gay to Caryll, April 1715, *Corr.*, I.288–9, and that to Jervas, c. 15 July 1715, *ibid.*, I.303–4). Pope's letter to Craggs of 15 July 1715 (*Corr.*, I.306–7), in the midst of what Pope regarded as Addison's treachery in sponsoring a rival translation of the *Iliad*, shows a witty subversion of the political norms underlying the rivalry:

> For they tell me, the busy part of the nation are not more divided about *Whig* and *Tory*, than these idle fellows of the Feather about Mr. *Tickel*'s and my Translation. I (like the *Tories*) have the town in general, that is the mob, on my side; but 'tis usual with the smaller Party to make up in industry what they want in number, and that's the case with the little Senate of *Cato*. However if our Principles be well consider'd, I must appear a brave *Whig*, and Mr. *Tickel* a rank *Tory*; I translated *Homer* for the publick in general, he to gratify the inordinate desires of One man only.

Pope clearly already had in mind the main element of the wounding satiric fragment, based on lines from the play (see commentary to 23), and later woven into the 'Atticus' sketch in the *Epistle to Dr Arbuthnot* (193–214), which sees Addison 'Like *Cato* give his little Senate laws, | And sit attentive to his own applause'. The lines first appeared, apparently without Pope's cognisance, in *The St. James's Journal*, 15 December 1722, after Addison's death, causing some ill-will towards the author. The lines were tinkered with through a number of versions before the final crystallisation in 1735. See further *OAC*, I.73, item 168, and more generally I.67–75, items 160–73, on the gradual break-up of the friendship. Pope's private estimates of Addison as a writer can be found in *OAC*, items 169–91. His major public testimony, 'To Mr. Addison, Occasion'd by his Dialogue on Medals', appears to have been a last attempt to patch things up; but though composed in 1715, it too remained unpublished until after Addison's death. Ultimately, 'Old *Cato*' featured in the *Epistle to Bathurst* (65–8) as a corrupted 'Patriot', and Pope sought alternative figures of beleaguered independence to serve as models of disinterested civic virtue.

PROLOGUE to *CATO*.

By Mr. *POPE*.

Spoken by Mr. *Wilks*.

    *T*O *wake the Soul by tender Strokes of Art,*
      To raise the Genius, and to mend the Heart;
    To make Mankind in conscious Virtue bold,
    Live o'er each Scene, and be what they behold:
5   *For this the Tragic-Muse first trod the Stage,*
    Commanding Tears to stream thro' every Age,

Title. 1751: PROLOGUE | TO | Mr. ADDISON's Tragedy | OF | CATO.

Title. *Wilks*: Robert Wilks (c. 1665–1732), actor, successful in both comic and tragic roles; one of the managers, with Colley Cibber, at Drury Lane Theatre. In the play he was Juba, 'Prince of Numibia'. For Pope's joking with Cromwell about him, see Headnote: Context.

1. wake the Soul: perhaps recalled from Thomas Otway, *The Orphan*, II.i (1680), p. 23): 'rouse up drowsie thoughts, and wake the Soul'.

    Strokes of Art: a phrase sometimes found in critical discourse, e.g. Rymer's translation of Rapin's *Reflections on Aristotle's Treatise of Poesie* (1674), p. 155: 'these draughts are the strokes of Art'. See also Halifax's advice on writing, in *An Epistle to the Right Honorable Charles, Earl of Dorset and Middlesex* (1690), p. 10: 'Tender the Stroaks must be, and nicely writ'.

2. Genius: spirit, character.

    mend the Heart: normally a religious phrase, e.g. Thomas Brooks, *A Cabinet of Choice Jewels* (1669), p. 207: 'to change the heart, to reform the heart, to mend the heart, to purifie the heart'; Pope also uses it in the 'First Chorus of Athenians' added to his friend the Duke of Buckinghamshire's *Tragedy of Marcus Brutus*, 10.

3. conscious Virtue: self-assured rectitude. A fairly common phrase, perhaps remembered from Dryden, *Annus Mirabilis*, st. 190 (1667), p. 48: 'Rouze conscious vertue up in every heart'. See however 'The First Book of Statius his Thebais', 758 and Commentary. Pope's letter to Caryll of February 1713, quoted in the Headnote: Context, concentrates on the presentation of virtue in ways which correspond to these verses.

5–6. Pope's dramatic history and aesthetic theory derive ultimately from Aristotle's *Poetics*, much of which describes the emotional effects of drama; see Headnote: Context to *Essay on Criticism*.

6. Commanding Tears: Pope commented publicly on the emotional effects of poetry in *Essay on Criticism*, 375–84; his letter to Caryll of February 1713 (see Headnote: Context) indicates that Addison's play 'drew tears' from him at several points in the last

> *Tyrants no more their Savage Nature kept,*
> *And Foes to Virtue wonder'd how they wept.*
> *Our Author shuns by vulgar Springs to move*
> 10 *The Hero's Glory, or the Virgin's Love;*
> *In pitying Love we but our Weakness show,*
> *And wild Ambition well deserves its Woe.*
> *Here Tears shall flow from a more gen'rous Cause,*
> *Such Tears as Patriots shed for dying Laws:*

two acts of the play. Dennis, however, was outraged by Cato's lack of personal emotion; *Remarks upon Cato* (1713), p. 39.

7. Tyrants ... Savage Nature: for the connection between tyranny and savagery see *Windsor-Forest*, 51–76 and Commentary. Caesar is called an 'Insulting Tyrant' in the play, I.i, p. 2. There are several examples of tyrants of the classical world being moved more by dramatic representations than by actual suffering, e.g. Plutarch's story of Alexander of Pherae, in *Moralia*, 334, 'On the Fortune of Alexander', 2.

9. shuns: resists the temptation.

vulgar Springs: the clichés of contemporary popular drama. Pope envisages poetry overcoming the shackles of vulgar conventions in *Essay on Criticism*, 153–6 and 425.

10. Hero's Glory: the kind of military valour lavishly celebrated in heroic drama and the nationalistic poetry of Pope's day. As a whole, the line dispenses with the classic opposition in Restoration heroic drama between military duty and private desire. Addison's Cato is moved by civic duty at the expense of all other considerations; his son Portius, however, declares in III.iii (1713), p. 49, 'my Heart | Leaps at the Trumpet's Voice, and burns for Glory'. For the 'love interest' in the play see Headnote: Context and note to next line.

11. In the play itself, however, Lucia complains 'Pity and Love, by turns, oppress my Heart', and 'Was ever Virgin Love distrest like mine'; I.vi, pp. 18 and 20.

12. wild Ambition: a common phrase, but perhaps recalling particularly Dryden, *Absalom and Achitophel*, 198 (1681), p. 7: 'But wild Ambition loves to slide, not stand'. Dryden's Ulysses speaks against the destructiveness of 'wild Ambition' in the first scene of *Troilus and Cressida* (1679), p. 2. Cf. also *Cato* itself, I.i, p. 2, referring to Caesar, 'what Havock does Ambition make'. The line is probably a hit, from Pope's point of view, at the now-fallen and exiled Duke of Marlborough, repeatedly censured for reckless egomania by Swift in the *Examiner*.

13–14. Gay, writing to Maurice Johnson, Jr., 23 April 1713, comments on the popularity with audiences of lines in the play deemed to reflect on the Tories, continuing 'some passages in the Prologue were strained that way too', including this couplet; Burgess (1966), 2–3.

13. gen'rous: disinterested, noble; cf. the quotation from the play in the next note.

14. Patriots: a prominent theme of the play; at the end of Act IV, p. 69, Cato points to his dead son and says: 'The firm Patriot there | (Who made the Welfare of Mankind his Care) | Tho' still, by Faction, Vice, and Fortune, crost, | Shall find the gen'rous Labour was not lost.' Until the era of *The Dunciad*, 'patriotism' was normally not ironised by Pope; cf. the 'Epitaph on Sir William Trumbull', 5–6: 'An honest Courtier, yet a Patriot too, | Just to his Prince, yet to his Country true'. In the later satires, it was often a suspect term indicating hypocritical populism: 'Old *Cato*' features as a corrupt 'Patriot', specifically from the reign of William III, in the *Epistle to Bathurst*, 65–8.

dying Laws: a common 'patriot' complaint, but perhaps recalling a pro-Stuart inflection: cf. Wycherley's approval of

15   *He bids your Breasts with Ancient Ardor rise,*
And calls forth Roman *Drops from* British *Eyes.*
Virtue confess'd in human Shape he draws,
What Plato *thought, and God-like* Cato *was.*
No common Object to your Sight displays;
20   *But what with Pleasure Heav'n itself surveys.*
A brave Man struggling in the Storms of Fate,

Charles II's methods against the Exclusionist plotters, 'To the King', *Epistles to the King and Duke* (1682), p. 33: 'And Justice done reprieves near dying Laws'.

15. Ancient Ardor: classical heroism, reimagined as appropriate to British national feeling at the end of the war.

16. Roman Drops: tears inspired by civic rather than private concerns. The first scene of the play contains an emotional exchange between Cato's sons, culminating in Portius' 'Behold my Eyes | Ev'n whilst I speak.—Do they not swim in Tears?' (p. 5).

17–18. The rhyme pair is not common, but cf. 'Prologue, Design'd for Mr. D—'s last Play', 15–16.

17. confess'd: revealed, made known. Wakefield cites the opening of the 'Prologue' to Dryden's *Troilus and Cressida*: 'See, my lov'd *Britons,* see your *Shakespeare* rise, | An awfull ghost confess'd to human eyes!'

18. Plato: Athenian philosopher, c. 429–347 BC. Act V of the play begins with Cato reading '*Plato's book on the immortality of soul*', by which Addison probably intends the dialogue known as *Phaedo*. Pope refers lightly to this in the jocular 'Epilogue to Jane Shore', 44. The coincidence of phrasing ('What *Plato* thought') with Pope's letter to Caryll of February 1713, cited in the Headnote: Context, suggests however that Pope is thinking in these lines of a different aspect, perhaps the one identified by Wakefield (in truncated form) as derived from Cicero, *De Officiis,* I.v.15: 'Formam quidem ipsam . . . et tamquam faciem honesti vides, "quae si oculis cerneretur, mirabiles amores," ut ait Plato, "excitaret sapientiae"' ('you see here the very form and so to speak face of virtue, "which if it could be seen with eyes', says Plato, "would excite a remarkable love of wisdom"'). Cicero's source is Plato's *Phaedrus*. Wakefield suggested a medial source in Waller, 'Upon Ben Jonson', 21–4, *Poems, &c.* (1645), pp. 154–5: 'But Vertue too as well as Vice, is clad | In Flesh and Blood so well, that *Plato* had | Beheld what his high fancy once embrac't, | Vertue with colours, speech, and motion grac't:'.

God-like Cato: Cato is twice termed 'Godlike' in the play by Juba (I.iv and v; pp. 12, 17), and once by Lucius (V.i, p. 75).

20. Warburton notes in *1751*: 'This alludes to a famous passage of Seneca which Mr. Addison afterwards used as a motto to his play, when it was printed'. The passage on the title page of the play is from Seneca, *De Providentia,* II.9, and concludes (in modern text): 'Ecce . . . vir fortis cum fortuna mala compositus . . . Non video, inquam, quid habeat in terris Iuppiter pulchrius, si eo convertere animum velit, quam ut spectet Catonem iam partibus non semel fractis stantem nihilo minus inter ruinas publicas rectum' ('Behold . . . a strong man pitched against bad fortune . . . I do not see, I say, what Jupiter has in his worlds more beautiful [than this], if he wishes to turn his mind that way, than that he should watch Cato, his forces shattered more than once, still standing upright among the public ruins').

21–2. Mack (1985: 221) suggests that these lines might have been hissed by Tories under the impression that they referred to the Duke of Marlborough (see Headnote: Context). Wakefield cites Dryden, 'Upon the Death of the Earl of Dundee', 7–8, *Poetical*

And greatly falling with a falling State!
　　　While Cato *gives his little Senate Laws,*
　　　What Bosom beats not in his Country's Cause?
25　*Who sees him act, but envies ev'ry Deed?*
　　　Who hears him groan, and does not wish to bleed?
　　　Ev'n when proud Caesar, *'midst triumphal Cars,*

Miscellanies: The Fifth Part (1704), p. 76: 'Farewel, who dying didst support the State, | And could'st not fall but with thy Country's Fate'. The images were echoed by the William Meston's Jacobite broadside *Cato's Ghost* (1715), 13-14: 'Griev'd for a King, struggling in Storms of Fate, | And greatly falling with a falling State'.

21. Storms of Fate: The day on which the play's action is set is described in the first speech of the play as 'big with the fate | Of *Cato* and of *Rome*'. Fate, as part of the system of Roman mythology, is one of the keywords of the play. Pope's phrase is common in drama, e.g. Dryden, *All for Love*, V (1678), p. 78 (almost the closing image of the play): 'While all the Storms of Fate fly o'er your Tomb', and John Caryll, *The English Princess*, IV. vii (1667), p. 45: 'All other Storms of Fate my Soul could bear'. This Caryll (c. 1626-1711) was the Jacobite uncle of Pope's close friend of the same name.

22. greatly falling: dying nobly. Cf. *Cato*, IV.iv, p. 65, on the death of Cato's son: 'Opprest with Multitudes, he greatly fell'. Cf. also Pope, 'Verses to the Memory of an Unfortunate Lady', 10: 'For those who greatly think, or bravely die'. Wakefield cites Ovid, *Heroides*, III.106 (Briseis to Achilles): 'Qui bene pro patria cum patriaque iacent' ('those who have fallen well for their country lie well with it'), but this refers to specifically to death in battle.

　falling State: One of Rowe's translations from the ninth book of Lucan (see Headnote: Models and sources), reads: 'O happy *Pompey!* happy in thy Fate, | Happy by falling with the falling State'; *Poetical Miscellanies: The Sixth Part* (1709), p. 72. Cf. 'The First Book of Statius his Thebais', 269-70 and Commentary.

23-4. Cf. Lansdowne, 'Occasion'd by the Foregoing', in his *Poems upon Several Occasions* (1712), p. 98: 'Had *Cato* bent beneath the conquering Cause, | He might have liv'd to give new Senates Laws'.

23. Cato's son Portius refers to his father's 'little Roman Senate', I.ii, p. 6, and Cato is reminded by Caesar's envoy that he is 'at the Head of your own little Senate' in II.ii of the play, which depicts the 'senate' in session; Cato responds "Tis *Caesar*'s Sword has made *Rome*'s Senate little' (p. 27). On 15 July 1715, Pope wrote to James Craggs, mocking the opposition to his *Iliad* from 'the little Senate of *Cato*'; in the fragment known as 'Atticus', drafted about 1716, Pope would transform this image to a hostile one of Addison himself, with his critical 'senate' at Buttons Coffee House, later incorporating it into the *Epistle to Dr Arbuthnot* of 1735 (see Headnote: Context).

25-6. Aden (1978: 141) suggests this couplet could be read by Tories as a reference to Robert Harley's triumphs (the Treaty of Utrecht) and disasters (the assassination attempts by Guiscard and others in 1711).

26. groan . . . bleed: normal political language of resistance to tyranny, e.g. in Defoe, *Jure Divino*, II.264-5 (1706), p. 11: 'From Whence does all their *sordid Crimes* proceed, | Which makes *Fate Groan*, and *ruin'd Nations bleed?*', and Defoe's note to I.48 of the same poem: 'Tyranny can never be describ'd by Art; the People that feel the Burthen, that Groan under the Wrongs, and that Bleed under the Sword of a Tyrant, know what it is, but can't express it'.

27. proud *Caesar:* Gaius Julius Caesar (100-44 BC), victor over the forces of his rival Pompey at the battle of Pharsalus, 48 BC. Caesar is 'the

The Spoils of Nations, and the Pomp of Wars,
Ignobly Vain, and impotently great,
30   *Show'd* Rome *her* Cato's *Figure drawn in State,*
As her dead Father's rev'rend Image past,
The Pomp was darken'd, and the Day o'ercast,
The Triumph ceas'd — *Tears gush'd from ev'ry Eye,*
The World's great Victor past unheeded by;
35   *Her last good Man dejected* Rome *ador'd,*
And honour'd Caesar's *less than* Cato's *Sword.*
      Britains *attend: Be Worth like this approv'd,*
And show you have the Virtue to be mov'd.
With honest Scorn the first fam'd Cato *view'd*
40   Rome *learning Arts from* Greece, *whom she subdu'd.*

---

proud victor' in the second speech of the play itself. Cato himself is accused of pride by his enemy Syphax (I.iv, p. 10).

triumphal Cars: chariots processing in a formal Roman triumph after a military victory (33), an image drawn from *Cato* itself (Sempronius, speaking of Cato): 'He'll make a pretty Figure in a Triumph, | And serve to trip before the Victor's Chariot', II.vi, p. 39. Pope returned to the phrase in *Odyssey*, IV.714-15: 'A train of coursers, and triumphal cars | Magnificent he leads'.

28. Pomp of Wars: a very common phrase in the poems of the War of Spanish Succession, but Pope is probably drawing once more on the play itself: *Cato*, I.v, p. 17: 'The war shall stand ranged in its just Array, | And dreadful Pomp'.

29. Cf. Rowe's version of Lucan, IX, *Poetical Miscellanies: The Sixth Part* (1709), p. 78: 'Ignobly Innocent, and meanly Good'.

30. In 'On the Statue of Cleopatra', which dates from 1717, Pope has Cleopatra relate how she resisted Caesar as 'victor' by suicide and was thereafter paraded in Rome in effigy (19-22).

drawn in State: i.e. in formal procession, as in a Triumph.

31. Wakefield cites Dryden's translation of Virgil, *Aeneid*, VI.171-2, *Works of Virgil* (1697), p. 367, where the ghost of Aeneas' father appears nightly as a 'reverend Image'.

33-6. Mack (1985: 221) suggests that these lines might have been regarded by Tories as sympathetic to Marlborough. They also echo, however, Lansdowne's Jacobite interpretation of the story; see the section of verses cited in the Headnote: Sources.

33. Triumph: see 27.

34. World's great Victor: Caesar, whose military dominance is repeatedly stressed in the play itself, e.g. IV.iv, p. 63: 'the conquer'd World | Is *Caesar*'s'; I.iii, p. 9: 'Lord of half the burning Zone'. Pope had referred to Alexander the Great as 'the *World's Victor*' in *Essay on Criticism*, 382.

36. The sword of the virtuous suicide carries more honour than that of the military victor. Caesar's sword is described as 'destructive' in the first speech of the play (p. 1). Pope would soon explore further (and controversially) the idea of suicide (by sword) as a virtuous response to oppression in the 'Verses to the Memory of an Unfortunate Lady'.

37. Britains attend: According to Warburton, 'Mr Pope had written it *arise*, in the spirit of Poetry and Liberty; but Mr. Addison frighten'd at so *daring an expression*, which, he thought, squinted at rebellion, would have it alter'd, in the spirit of Prose and Politics, to *attend*'. Cf. however 15.

39. first . . . Cato: see Headnote: Context. The elder Cato ('the great *Censor*') is mentioned by the younger Cato in the play itself at IV.iv, p. 68; he features in Pope's jocular verse letter to Cromwell, 12-13 July 1707; *Corr.*, I.28.

40. Cf. Horace, *Epistles*, II.i.156-7: 'Graecia capta ferum victorem cepit et artis | intulit agresti Latio' ('Captive Greece captured her brutal conqueror and brought arts into rural Latium' [the district of Italy in which Rome was founded]). Pope's later version of this

Our Scene precariously subsists too long
On French *Translation, and* Italian *Song:*
Dare to have Sense your selves, assert the Stage,
Be justly warm'd with your own Native Rage.
45 *Such Plays alone should please a* British *Ear,*
As Cato's self had not disdain'd to hear.

---

41. Our: *1751:* Your
45. please: *1751:* win

---

epistle, *The First Epistle of the Second Book of Horace Imitated* (1737), 263–4, translates the relationship to that of England (the conqueror) and France (the cultivated nation).
41. Scene: theatre and theatrical tradition.
42. The implication, by analogy with 40, is that Britain has subdued France and should not imitate French theatre, though Addison's play is obviously much influenced by the neoclassical drama of Racine and Corneille and French dramatic theory, as was Philips's *The Distrest Mother* (1712).
   Italian Song: probably indicating opera, which had recently begun to be fashionable in London; see Commentary to *Essay on Criticism*, 452^3 MS, and Headnote to *Ode for Musick*. Dennis, in his *Essay on the Opera's After the Italian Manner* (1706) had explicitly linked Italian opera with an effeminate falling-away from the Roman character, and had sounded an alarm about its foreign, insidious character, damaging to English national fibre. Addison, whose attempt at an English opera, *Rosamund*, had failed in 1707 (see Hammond 2006), published essays against foreign opera in *The Spectator*, nos. 18 and 29, 21 March and 3 April 1711). *TE* cites Pope's 'Prologue' to Thomson's *Sophonisba* for an expanded version of this patriotic cultural call, which is also present in Pope's 'To Mr Addison, Occasioned by his Dialogue on Medals', 53–72; cf. *Essay on Criticism*, 715–25.
43. Sense: for the shades of meaning of this word in Pope's usage, see Headnote: Context to *Essay on Criticism*.
   assert: defend, promote.
44. justly warm'd: appropriately enthused.
   Native Rage: Wakefield glosses 'Rage' as 'empassion'd fancy, poetic fury, enthusiastic rapture', by analogy with Latin 'furor', associated with poetry by Cicero, citing the opinion of Plato (*De Divinatione*, I.37). He finds a possible source in Drayton's lines on Shakespeare: 'As strong conception, and as cleere a rage, | As any one that traffiqu'd with the stage'; 'To my most dearely-loued friend Henry Reynolds Esquire *of Poets and Poesie*', in *The Battaile of Agincourt* (1631), p. 293. For a similar sense of poetic 'Rage' cf. *Windsor-Forest*, 289. 'Native' in this context suggests both 'British-born', and 'natural', as when Thomas Ross writes of the 'Native Rage' of lions in his version of Silius Italicus, *The Second Punic War*, XVI (1661), p. 462; cf. Dryden, *Don Sebastian*, II.i (1690), p. 35: 'Thou hast restor'd me to my native Rage'.
45 variant. *TE* argues plausibly that the 1751 change of 'please' to 'win' was probably done by Warburton to avoid the aural clash with 'plays', Pope having had plenty of opportunity to alter it himself without doing so.
46. Warburton states that this alludes to 'the famous story of his going into the Theatre, and immediately coming out again', for which *TE* cites the prefatory epigram of Martial's first book, addressed to Cato, which concludes 'cur in theatrum, Cato severe, venisti? | An ideo tantum veneras, ut exires?' ('Why, stern Cato, did you come into the theatre? Did you only come in, in order to go out?') Wakefield finds a closer match to the line in Martial, *Epigrams*, IX.29, in which an actor says, 'Qui spectatorem potui fecisse Catonem', which he translates as 'Me, whom e'en Cato had not blush'd to view' (literally, 'I who could have made Cato a spectator'). The story refers to Cato the Censor (39), and had been recently told by Addison in *Spectator*, no. 446, 1 August 1712.

18

ODE FOR MUSICK
(1713)

Editors' Headnote

Composition and publication

The *Ode for Musick* was first published on 16 July 1713. In the *Works* of 1736, the *Ode* follows a title page designating it in the following terms: 'ODE | ON | St. *CECELIA*'s Day, 1708.' In 1735 Pope told Spence that it 'was at the request of Mr. Steele' that he wrote the poem (*OAC*, I.28; no. 65). However, Pope had been first introduced to Steele by John Caryll only in 1711. In a letter, dated 26 July of that year, Steele wrote to Pope asking him whether he was 'at Leisure to help Mr Clayton, that is, Me to some words for Musick against Winter' (*Corr*., I.131). This was with reference to the opera composer Thomas Clayton (1673–1725), whose concerts took place at the Music Room in York Buildings (see Headnote to 'Sapho to Phaon'). On 2 August Pope wrote to Caryll saying that he had now received 'two letters from Mr. Steele, the subject of which is to persuade me to write a musicall interlude to be set next winter by Clayton, whose interest he espouses with great zeal' and expressing the reluctance he had felt in accepting the comission: 'The desire I have to gratify Mr Steele has made me consent to his request, tho' 'tis a task that otherwise I'm not very fond of' (*Corr*., I.132). It is possible that Pope had finished work on the poem and sent it to Steele by the winter of 1711: the evidence is a letter dated 6 December 1712, missing but described in a 1920 Tregaskis sale catalogue as referring to 'the Ode left with Steele last winter' (*Corr*., I.165). While it is probable that this correspondence relates to the *Ode for Musick*, it is not actually certain. The missing letter formed part of a sequence of exchanges about several projects in the winter of 1712–13 for which Steele was soliciting Pope's contributions and interest; see the letters of 12, 16 and 29 November and 4 December, *Corr*., I.152–60), concerning *The Temple of Fame*, which was written by 1712 but not published until 1715, and 'The Dying Christian to his Soul', another 'Ode' requested by Steele as an item for music, not published until 1730.

There is, however, some evidence to suggest that Pope did indeed turn to work extant in 1708 when he came to compose the *Ode* at Steele's behest. Lines from the verse portion of a letter to Cromwell of 25 April of that year are strikingly similar to those that later appear at lines 72–4 of the *Ode* ('O'er th' *Elysian* Flowers, | By those happy Souls who dwell | In Yellow Meads of *Asphodel*'):

(Not those which thin, unbody'd Shadows fill,
  That glide along th' Elysian Glades,
  Or skim the flow'ry Meads of *Asphodill*:)
              (*Corr.*, I.46).

This does not, however, amount to the 'quotation' of the lines suggested by *TE* (VI.35), and it is not possible to ascribe an earlier date of composition for the *Ode* with any certainty.

There is no evidence that the poem was in fact set to music by Clayton for the concert series. Ultimately, the *Ode for Musick* was first published (without music) by Lintot on 16 July 1713, as a 12-page folio pamphlet, the format suggesting a certain importance to the exercise; many 'Cecilia' poems were published in separate format, probably for distribution at performances; in Pope's case the format appears as more of a mark of ceremony or dignity. (Pope's earlier separately-published poems, the *Essay on Criticism* and *Windsor-Forest*, are considerably longer in themselves.) Unusually, it was not until the following week, on 23 July, that Lintot paid Pope the sum of £15 for the poem (McLaverty 2001: 18). A gap in the collation of Lintot's *Miscellaneous Poems and Translations* (1712) has been taken as evidence that Pope originally intended to publish the *Ode* (together with *Windsor-Forest*) in that collection (Ault 1959; *TE*, I.128; but see the counter-argument in Foxon 1991: 34–7 and the Headnote to *Windsor-Forest*). In 1730 Pope revised the *Ode* for the composer Maurice Greene (1696–1755), later Master of the King's Musick, whose setting was performed in Cambridge on 6 July at a 'Publick Commencement' to mark the official opening of the new Senate House. While the revisions Pope made for this version of the poem do not form part of its subsequent textual history, they have been collated as part of the apparatus below. There is a full modern edition of the setting by H. Diack Johnstone (1991).

Text

The text presented here is taken from the first edition of 1713. Beyond the first edition, and the version rewritten for Greene, significant verbal revision is largely confined to the text of 1717. The various extant texts of the *Ode for Musick* are referred to in the apparatus as follows:

1713: *Ode for Musick*, folio (Griffith 20)

1714: *Miscellaneous Poems and Translations*, octavo (Griffith 32)

1717: *Works*, quarto (Griffith 79)

1730: *An Ode Compos'd for the Publick Commencement, at Cambridge*, octavo (Griffith 240)

1736: *Works*, vol.I, octavo (Griffith 413, 414)

1751: *Works*, vol.I, octavo (Griffith 643)

Models and sources

A detailed if understandably incomplete account of St Cecilia's Day festivals, together with an anthology of the poems then known, is given in Husk (1857); supplementary details for some years are given in Hopkins (1994). Further information is recorded in unpublished doctoral dissertations, Luckett (1971) and Biklé (1982).

Luckett (1973) gives a concise history of of the early Cecilia iconography. In early accounts she was a Christian martyr under the Roman empire; the association with music came later. Pope would have known particularly Chaucer's 'Second Nunnes Tale', which draws on standard martyrology in relating the story of her marriage to a Roman, Valerian, her persuasion of him not to consummate the marriage and his conversion and execution, along with hers; but the only mention of music is very brief, during the marriage service, 'while the organs maden melodie, | To God allone in her heart thus sang she' (134–5). Nonetheless the apparent mention of 'organs' in source texts ('cantatibus organis', taken to mean 'while the organs were singing', in the source from which Chaucer draws, though 'organum' is also a form of early plainchant) appears to have prompted an association with music and with the organ in particular. Cecilia the musician became a common subject of painting from the Renaissance through to the Baroque (e.g. Raphael's 1514 painting of her with a portative organ). Musical festivals associated with the saint, sometimes including religious services, prize-giving and feasting, on the patronal day (22 November) are recorded in France from 1570 onwards; a British tradition did not emerge until the last years of Charles II's reign. In 1684 the composer Henry Purcell published the first fully recorded British experiment as *A Musical Entertainment Perform'd on November XXII. 1683*

> It being the Festival of St. Cecilia, a great Patroness of Music; whose Memory is annually honour'd by a public Feast made on that Day by the Masters and Lovers of Music, as well in England as in Foreign Parts.

The words were by Christopher Fishbourne or Fishburn. The series of events was organised by The Musical Society, an obscure body which thereafter elected annual 'stewards' to commission an ode for performance, together with a banquet (usually at Stationers' Hall) and a church service (usually, from the mid 1690s, at St Bride's), with a sermon on the theme of music in divine worship (one of these, 'On the Usefulness of Church Musick', was given in 1698 by Francis Atterbury, later a close friend of Pope's). The odes composed for the occasion were performed by members of the choirs of St Paul's Cathedral and Westminster Abbey; the orchestra was drawn from the King's Band of Music with supplementary musicians from theatre orchestras. Celebrations of this type were then held fairly regularly in London and intermittently in Oxford, for about the next twenty years, with similar occasional events taking place in Edinburgh and in cathedral cities such as Winchester.

In 1684 John Blow set John Oldham's 'An Ode for an Anniversary of Musick' for *A Second Musical Entertainment Perform'd on St. Cecilia's Day. November XXII. 1684* (published 1685). Nahum Tate's *A Song for St. Caecilia's Day* was set by William Turner in 1685, the same year in which Tate published Mr Wilson's 'A Pindarick Essay on Musick' in much the same vein in *Poems by Several Hands*, pp. 398–402; Thomas Flatman's 1686 *Song for St. Caecilia's Day* was set by Isaac Blackwell. Thomas Fletcher's 'On the Feast of Cecilia. 1686. An Ode', later printed in his *Poems on Several Occasions* (1692), pp. 21–5, was for the Oxford Cecilian festival. Dryden's first *Song for St. Cecilia's Day* was set by Giovanni Battista Draghi (1687), and republished in *Examen Poeticum* (1693), pp. 242–6; a later setting by Handel was peformed in 1739. (For context see further Hammond and Hopkins, III.181–5.) The revolution year (and year of Pope's birth), 1688, apparently produced nothing, no doubt in part because of political uncertainty during William's manoeuvres (he landed in early November). About 1689, otherwise also a blank year, the composer William Croft (or Crofts) published *A Poem, in Praise of Beauty and Musick* which he had 'set ... after the manner of a St. Caecilia's Song'.

Dryden's rival Shadwell produced 'A Song for St. Cecilia's Day', set by Robert King in 1690, while Thomas D'Urfey, subject of Pope's 'Prologue' (item 21 below), had an 'Ode' set by Blow in 1691; one by Samuel Wesley, printed in the *Gentleman's Journal* for 1694, was probably from an Oxford celebration of about 1690. Nicholas Brady produced an example (set by Purcell) in 1692; he also preached a sermon, *Church-Musick Vindicated*, for St Cecilia's Day in 1697. Dryden and Tonson published two Oxford examples, Thomas Yalden's 'An Ode, for St. Cecilia's Day, 1693' (set by Daniel Purcell) and Addison's 'A Song. For St. Cecilia's Day, at Oxford', in *The Annual Miscellany: For the Year 1694* (1694), pp. 128–38. The 1693 'Ode' by Theophilus Parsons, a friend of Dryden's, was set by Godfrey Finger. Details of the 1694 ceremony are uncertain, but the anonymous 'Welcome, welcome, ev'ry guest', printed by Husk (p. 173) as 'prior to 1700', set by Blow, could have been the item. In 1695 Blow set Peter Anthony Motteux's *Words for an Entertainment at the Music-Feast, on St. Cecilia's Day*; the following year an anonymous *Ode on St. Cecilia's Day* was set by Nicola Matteis. In 1697 Purcell's widow published a *Te Deum and Jubilate* which had been produced by the composer for 22 November 1694. The same year saw Dryden's *Alexander's Feast; or The Power of Musique. An Ode, in Honour of St. Cecilia's Day*, set by Jeremiah Clarke; this was probably the most important of Pope's models (for the context see Hammond and Hopkins, V.3–9, and for the legacy of the poem, Mason and Rounce 2000). It was also set by Charles King, Clarke's apprentice and later brother-in-law; and by the Italian composer Benedetto Marcello, as well as Handel (in 1736). The 1698 Ode was by Samuel Wesley, set once again by Daniel Purcell (also by William Norris, probably for a performance at Lincoln), with the words having already appeared in *The Gentleman's Journal* for April 1694, pp. 75–7 (see Charteris 2007, an edition of the setting). Daniel Purcell also set Addison's *Ode on St. Cecilia's Day, November 22. 1699*, with contributions from Tate, performed at an Oxford celebration. D'Urfey published another *Ode for the Anniversary*

Feast, set by Blow, in 1700. Vaughan Richardson, organist at Winchester Cathedral, included 'A Song in Praise of St. Cecilia' in his *Collection of New Songs* (1701), pp. 20–31. Congreve's *Hymn to Harmony*, for the feast day of 1701, was set by John Eccles and published by Tonson in 1702 (dated 1703), and reprinted in Congreve's *Works* (1710). John Hughes' *An Ode in Praise of Musick* was set by Philip Hart and published by Lintot in 1703, after which there was apparently a hiatus in the tradition.

A further *Ode in Praise of Musick*, possibly by Edmund Smith, set by Charles King for a performance at Oxford, dates from 1707, but was written for a degree ceremony, not a St Cecilia's Day festival. A looser 'Poem on the Power of Musick' appeared in *Moral Reflections and Pleasant Remarks* 'by a Gentleman of St. Peter's College in Cambridge' in 1707, and an 'Ode. To St. Cecilia, Patroness of Musick' appeared in *Oxford and Cambridge Miscellany Poems* (1708), pp. 132–5; this was subsequently identified by John Nichols, in vol. 4 of *A Select Collection of Poems* (1780), pp. 28–30, as the work of Thomas Bishop. Samuel Cobb's 'Love and Musick ... An Ode for the Entertainment of the Musical Club in *Cambridge*, 1700' (not strictly a Cecilia Ode, as it was dedicated to Venus), was reprinted in his *Poems on Several Occasions* (1710), pp. 134–40; this includes a section on Orpheus's musical pursuit of Eurydice in Hell which perhaps influenced Pope's work. Pope's was the next *Ode* in the sequence, chronologically, and thus came some years after the regular annual performances had ceased. Intermittent examples followed through the century, prompting settings by eminent composers such as Handel and William Boyce. Pope mocks the tradition of 'soft sing-song on Cecilia's day' in *The Dunciad Variorum* (1729), I.40–1, just before Greene's public setting of his own poem, and Swift refers ironically to the Dublin celebrations in a comic poem of about the same date, 'The Dean to Himself on St. Cecilia's Day'.

Dryden's and Pope's were the Cecilia poems most reprinted through the century. Most poems in the tradition include a formal Chorus or Grand Chorus, which Pope eschews, though Greene set some verses for chorus. The lyric form varied widely, in an effort to imitate or stimulate musical effects. But certain thematic continuities had emerged for Pope to run variations on: the divine power of music as a feature of God's regular, harmonious creation (a theme explored in other texts, such as Milton's account of creation in *Paradise Lost*, VII.243–60); the psychological power of music to calm or inflame emotions, whether amorous or military; the emotional 'affect' of particular rhythms, modes, or instruments, especially the organ (because of its use in church music); the power of particular legendary musicians (Apollo, Amphion, Orpheus, Timotheus, David, Jubal); and the role of music in divine contemplation. Pope makes little of the first of these aspects, but the others are all present in some degree. The first two stanzas experiment with the varying psychological 'affects' of musical instruments and rhythms, in a manner which draws on the whole tradition, but particularly on Dryden's *Alexander's Feast*, where the master-poet Timotheus (see *Essay on Criticism*, 375–84) directs Alexander's moods from martial exultation, through melancholy, love and sleep, before waking him in a mode of martial revenge, by the stimulus of variant musical techniques. The centrepiece of Pope's poem, however, the narrative of Orpheus in the underworld, is relatively unusual. The classical story was well known from Virgil,

Georgics, IV.453–527, and Ovid, *Metamorphoses*, X.1–105 and XI.1–43; there was a post-classical version in Boethius, *De Consolatio Philosophiae*, III.xii.31–51, as Johnson noted (*Rambler*, no. 143, 30 July 1751), and an allegorical interpretation of the 'fable' in Bacon's *Wisedome of the Ancients* (1619), pp. 54–60 (the music in hell represents 'natural philosophy'; that which moves animals and trees represents civil discipline). Pope would also have known Milton's several self-referential mentions of the story of the defeated archetypal poet (e.g. 'Lycidas', 58–63); in *Paradise Lost*, VII.30–9, Milton refers to the death of Orpheus at the hands of a violent pagan mob and implores the protection of a celestial muse in a way which perhaps prefigures the substitution of a pagan by a Christian musician in Pope's poem. Ode-like retellings in the context of the 'Cecilia' period include stanza IV of 'A Pindarique Essay upon Musick', by 'Mr. Wilson', in *Poems by Several Hands*, ed. Tate (1685), pp. 400–1, and Cobb's 'Love and Music', mentioned above. Normally Orpheus features in Cecilia odes (e.g. those by Dryden in 1687 and Addison in 1693) as the musician whose lyrical magic conjures beasts to listen and forests to move, whereas for Pope he demonstrates an extreme emotional state, the poet who regains and then loses his wife and dies violently, singing but despairing, to be supplanted in the final stanza by the redemptive figure of the Saint and her divinely aspirational musical ethos. (Wilson's poem does not describe Orpheus's death, and Cobb's ends with Orpheus's success; in Ovid, *Metamorphoses*, XI.66, Orpheus is happily reuinted with Eurydice.) There appears however to be no particular biographical application in play for Pope. The displacing of a pagan with a Christian figure of worship aligns the poem with 'Messiah', also written for Steele. The most substantial modern reading of the poem, Wasserman (1961), links Renaissance theories of musical form with post-classical attempts to identify Orpheus with Christ.

Context

Thomas Clayton was originally a violinist in the 'Royal Private Musick' and subsequently composer of *Arsinoe, Queen of Cyprus* (1705), the first all-sung Italian opera in England, and a signal success for two seasons; he also set Addison's English-opera libretto *Rosamund* (1707), which failed. His opera career was largely derailed by Handel's spectacular successes, from *Rinaldo* (1711) onwards (see McGeary 1988). Strongly associated with Whig grandees such as the first Earl of Wharton, Clayton ran a series of concerts at York Buildings which were advertised in *The Tatler* (e.g. no. 163, 25 April 1710) and later in *The Spectator*. Clayton also set work by Matthew Prior (in July 1711, around the time Steele was requesting Pope's *Ode*). He published through Tonson a setting of *The Passion of Sappho, and Feast of Alexander* (see Headnote to 'Sapho to Phaon') as performed at his house in York Buildings on 24 May 1711, and Steele republished the first poem (by William Harrison) in *Poetical Miscellanies* (late 1713, dated 1714), a volume to which Pope also contributed. The 'Feast of Alexander' was a version of Dryden's *Alexander's Feast* altered at Steele's request by John Hughes, who then criticised Clayton's music (which appears not to have survived) in a knowledgable and detailed letter to Steele of 1711 (Blanchard 1941: 45–7). *The Spectator*, no. 258

(26 December 1711) published an open letter from Clayton and others soliciting support for a new series of subscription concerts at York Buildings, which were likewise heavily advertised in the periodical. The request which led to the *Ode for Musick* was perhaps in keeping with the attempt by Addison in 1713 to keep Pope onside by requesting a 'Prologue' to *Cato*.

Despite his admiration for Cowley, who had been responsible for some of the popularity of the so-called 'Pindaric Ode' in the Restoration, the ode form was not one Pope was usually drawn to. The ode performed with music was strongly associated with patriotic royal celebrations, particularly the 'Birthday Ode' provided by poets laureate such as Shadwell (and apparently much promoted by Queen Anne: see Murphy 2015, and for the general context, Trowles 1992). Increasingly during the war years, the Ode was the default literary form for Whig military triumphalism (see Commentary at 37). It had been exemplified and defended by writers such as Dennis, and Pope's friend William Congreve had prefaced his *Pindarique Ode, Humbly Offer'd to the Queen, On the Victorious Progress of Her Majesty's Arms, under the Conduct of the Duke of Marlborough* (1706) with a 'Discourse' promoting as regular a form which had come to represent a patriotic sublime. Pope's reluctance to engage with Steele and his composer might have been partly caused by this additional factor; his other odes resemble the metrically tight lyrics of Horace. Pope also had no great love for operatic composition, at least in its recently arrived Italian form. Johnson stated that 'Pope, with all this labour in the praise of Musick, was ignorant of its principles, and insensible of its effects' (Lonsdale, IV.67–8), a view restated by Warton, in his 1797 edition of Pope's *Works* (I.142–53); the assumption that Pope lacked insight into music has, however, been challenged in modern times. He stated to Spence, late in life, that although he had never studied music formally, 'I had naturally a very good ear, and have often judged right of the best compositions in music by the force of that' (*OAC*, I.174–5, no. 398, 5–7 April 1744; see further Brownell 1978: 368–71, and Mack 1985: 380–2). His friendship with Arbuthnot, the most musically accomplished of his close friends and probably the one who supplied the well-informed burlesque music theory for chapter VI of *The Memoirs of . . . Martinus Scriblerus*, appears to postdate slightly the publication of the *Ode*. Dryden, who had already worked with musicians before writing his 'Cecilia' poems, made several public statements about the relations between poetry and music, e.g. his 'Preface' to *Albion and Albanius: an Opera* (1685, with Louis Grabu), and the 'Dedication' (in Purcell's name) to *The Vocal and Instrumental Musick of the Prophetess* (1691). Pope certainly knew of Dryden's close association with Purcell. He laid down no critical testimony on the matter himself, but music features as a source of pleasure, a form of emotional release, or a sign of cultural value, in many early poems, such as 'January and May' (320–27), the 'Episode of Sarpedon' (32), the *Pastorals* ('Spring' 24, 'Winter' 1–4), 'Messiah' (41–4), the *Essay on Criticism* (375–84), and 'The First Book of Statius his Thebais' (689–90). In the *Ode*, Pope was certainly also drawing on his own previous experiments with aural effects, including those of music, in the *Essay on Criticism* (e.g. 340–74). His letters to Cromwell are often occupied with discussions of the sound effects of verse; that of 25 Nov 1710 (*Corr.*, I.105–8) constitutes a miniature essay on sound and harmony. His next letter discusses the effects of Crashaw's 'Musicks Duell', including its potential for 'musical' rhythm (to Cromwell, 17 December 1710; *Corr.*, I.109–10). Additionally, while he probably knew nothing of standard music textbooks such as Thomas Mace's *Musick's Monument* (1676), he would certainly have been aware of religious music as it was represented in poems such as Milton's 'At a Solemn Music' and 'On the Morning of Christ's Nativity', and Cowley's discussion of the psychological effects of music and 'numbers' (rhythm) in the figure of David the harpist in *Davideis*, I.435–82.

While Pope's *Ode* was probably available for a 22 November performance in 1711 or 1712, it appears not in the event to have been set or performed by Clayton. Seventeen years after its first appearance it was adapted by Pope and set by Maurice Greene, not for a Cecilia's Day celebration but for performance on 6 July 1730 at the opening of the new Senate House at Cambridge, designed by James Gibbs. Greene had been organist of St Paul's Cathedral since 1718 and had succeeded as principal organist and composer to the Chapel Royal in 1727; he was thus already an eminent court musician, possibly known to Pope via Arbuthnot, who was on friendly terms with many contemporary composers. The singer Anastasia Robinson, covert wife since 1722 of the Earl of Peterborough, has also been suggested as a go-between (Johnstone 1991: xix). Greene had previously set Pope's 'Verses on the Death of an Unfortunate Lady' (Mack 1985: 316). Having dropped the two final stanzas of the 1713 text, thus omitting the defeat and death of Orpheus and triumph of Cecilia, Pope added a strophe (see 35^6 variants) for the Cambridge performance which bears a striking resemblance to his later imagery of ecumenical political harmony, e.g. *Essay on Man*, III.283–302, apparently in response to the barbed political images in the original version (e.g. lines 34–5, which are, however, retained in softened form). Aden (1978: 77–8) considers it possible that the additional stanza existed as early as 1708, on the grounds that some of the language resembles the version of Statius, but there is no positive evidence that it existed before 1730, and the argument that it might have been withheld in 1713 because of 'proximity' to the other poem is not very convincing; it looks rather as though Pope was attempting to depict resolution of internecine conflict as he prepared a platform for the exploration of God's cosmic harmony in the *Essay on Man*.

The score was not published, but the alto-tenor duet setting of lines 70–81 with a four-part instrumental accompaniment was transcribed by Sir John Hawkins in his account of Greene in *A General History of the Science and Practice of Music* (1776), IV.331–41. Three manuscript scores from the period survive: one, copied by William Boyce, is in the Royal College of Music (MS 228); one is in the Naki Music Library, Tokyo (MS N-3/23); one is in the Bodleian (MS Mus. d. 35). Although there is a modern edition (Johnstone 1991), there does not appear to have been a modern performance or recording. The setting begins with an overture in two sections, the first for full and the second for reduced orchestra; after which the text is set in sections of recitative, aria, duet and chorus. (Significant details are recorded in the Commentary.) The singers were apparently drawn from Greene's regular choirs at St Paul's Cathedral and the Chapel Royal, with local musicians also drafted in, at a total cost of £170, and the event was successful enough to cause Greene to be elected almost immediately to a vacant music professorship at Cambridge. The setting was performed again in London on 19 November, near to St Cecilia's Day, by members of the Academy of Vocal Music, at the Crown and Anchor Tavern in the Strand (Johnstone 1991: xxi). It is not known whether Pope attended either performance.

A Latin translation of the original poem was published by Christopher Smart in 1743, in part as a gesture of homage to Pope, who responded appreciatively to Smart's overtures (*Corr.*, IV.478, 483-4). A further choral setting of the original 1713 *Ode*, by the organist and composer William Walond (1719-68), appears to have been performed at Oxford as a BMus exercise in about 1757; his score was published without date (c. 1759) as *Mr. Pope's Ode on St. Cecilia's Day*. This setting, also largely in D major, used an orchestra of the normal stringed instruments, with trumpets, oboes, timpani and a standard four-part choir; the continuo instrument was specifically the organ, suiting the status accorded that instrument in the poem (there was no organ in the Senate House at Cambridge for Greene to use).

The *Ode for Musick* was one of the works attacked by Dennis in *A True Character of Mr. Pope* (1716), on the score of its mimicry of Dryden (p. 7), and it featured periodically among attacks thereafter (Guerinot 1969: 162, 189-91, 287-8).

Pope was aware that his poem was generally regarded as inferior to Dryden's *Alexander's Feast*, a poem he had himself praised as the best example of sound in accordance with sense in a (possibly fabricated) early letter to Walsh, 22 October 1706 (*Corr.*, I.23), and again in the letter already cited to Cromwell, 25 November 1710 (*Corr.*, I.108); he had also passed on an anecdote from Bolingbroke about its dauntingly rapid composition (Warton's edition of Pope's *Works*, 1797, I.147). He might have heard from his friend Nathaniel Hooke of the novelist Samuel Richardson's specific preference for Dryden's effort (Barnard 1973: nos. 61 and 95). 'Many people would like my ode on music better if Dryden had never written on that subject', he told Spence in 1735, while denying that his was an attempt to rival his model (*OAC*, I.28, no. 65). (Comparisons were normally made with *Alexander's Feast* rather than the 1687 *Song*, but see Ames (1998) for a comparison of the restrained 'neoclassical' aesthetics of Pope's poem with the 'baroque' style of Dryden's earlier poem.)

Spence himself had praised Pope's opening stanza as almost a 'perfect consort' (i.e. of instruments) in his *Essay on Pope's Odyssey* (1726-7), p. 151. Warburton valiantly called the poem 'one of the most artful as well as sublime of our Poet's smaller compositions' in the *Works* of 1751 (I.71), but it never escaped comparison with Dryden, though Warton did reckon it 'indisputably the second of the kind' (1756: 52). Warton particularly approved of the opening lines (again it was 'amost a perfect concert in itself; every instrument is described, and illustrated, in numbers that represent, and correspond to its different qualities and genius'; *ibid.*, 53), and he praised Pope's decision to substitute the pathos-driven story of Orpheus in the underworld for the cliché of his magical effect on animals and trees. But Warton thought that the final lines of the sixth stanza were in a 'burlesque and ridiculous' rhythm, more suited to a comic drinking-song than the pathetic situation Pope was trying to invoke, and he felt that Pope had missed some opportunities to reproduce the pathos and melancholy of his source in Virgil's fourth *Georgic* (*ibid.*, 57–60). Warton's critique was partially endorsed by Pope's first biographer, Ruffhead (*Life of Pope*, 1769, pp. 46–9). The poem meanwhile gained a certain currency in discussions of rhetoric and aesthetics because of its overt attempts at sonic effects. Lord Kames, in *Elements of Criticism*, third edition (1765), II.174–6, cited 96–108 as demonstrating a frequency of rhyme incommensurate with the seriousness of the subject; conversely, Joseph Priestley, in *A Course of Lectures on Oratory and Criticism* (1777), pp. 295–6, discussing 'the Resemblance between Sound and Sense', cited almost the same passage (96–111) as an illustration of the virtues of the poem, of which he asserted 'A great variety of just expression of sense by sound, or at least intervals of sound, may be observed in various parts of Pope's Ode ... particularly at the beginning, where he describes several instruments of music'. Johnson, sceptical about the supposedly musical effects of verbal sounds, as well as out of sympathy with the ode form and the 'dark and dismal regions of mythology' visited by Pope's Orpheus, observed in his 1781 biography that Pope was 'generally confessed to have miscarried', in the *Ode*, though he still judged it second only to Dryden's *Alexander's Feast*. Johnson conceded that the third stanza was 'not unworthy the antagonist of Dryden' (Lonsdale, IV.67–8).

ODE
FOR
MUSICK.

I.

DESCEND ye Nine! descend and sing;
    The breathing Instruments inspire,
  Wake into Voice each silent String,
    And sweep the sounding Lyre!
5   In a sadly-pleasing Strain

Title. 1714–51: ODE for MUSICK, | ON | St. *CECELIA*'s Day,; *1730:* AN | ODE

1-21. For Joseph Priestley's citation of this first stanza in a lecture on the relation of sound to sense, see Headnote; it also drew high praise from Spence, *Essay on Pope's Odyssey* (1727), I.151), and Warton (1756: 53).

1. Nine: the nine muses of poetry and other arts; cf. Congreve, *A Hymn to Harmony*, 60 (1703 [1702]), p. 4: 'Begin the pow'rful Song, yee Sacred Nine'. Cf. also the reference to Longinus and the Muses in *Essay in Criticism*, 678. The opening line was set by Greene as a bass recitative with strings, followed by a chorus setting of 1-4 with strings and oboes.

2. breathing . . . inspire: blow into the wind instruments (for 'inspire' in this sense cf. 'January and May', 325, and 'Spring', 11). Cf. the 'breathing Flute' of Timotheus in Dryden's *Alexander's Feast*, 158 (1697), p. 7, and 'inspire the Flute', in Tate's *Song for St. Caecilia's Day*, 2 (1685), p. 1. Flutes were associated with softening of passions, e.g. Dryden, *A Song for St. Cecilia's Day 1687*, st. 4, *Examen Poeticum* (1693), p. 244; Addison, *Ode on St. Cecilia's Day*, 12 (1699), p. 1; D'Urfey, *An Ode, for the Anniversary Feast* (1700), st. 6. Greene's setting uses two wind instruments, oboes and flutes.

4. sounding Lyre: classical harp, used as symbol of lyric poetry in particular in e.g. 'Sapho to Phaon', 35, 215, 229; cf. also 62 here. In the elaborate engraved headpiece for this poem in the 1717 *Works* (p. 371, reproduced Foxon 1991: 84), the central figure (probably Apollo) holds a lyre (the same headpiece was used for the *Essay on Criticism* in that volume). Dryden, *Alexander's Feast*, 159, also has 'sounding Lyre'. Congreve devotes a segment of the *Hymn to Harmony* (32-7) to the origins of the lyre, and it features likewise in Yalden, 'An Ode, for St. Cecilia's Day, 1693', *Annual Miscellany: For the Year 1694* (1694), p. 131. For the line as a whole, Wakefield compares Milton, 'Lycidas', 17, *Poems of Mr. John Milton* (1645), p. 57: 'Begin, and somewhat loudly sweep the string'. The second stanza of Cowley's 'The Resurrection' opens 'Begin the *Song*, and strike the *Living Lyre*'; *Poems . . . Written by A. Cowley* (1656), p. 21.

5-6. Greene combined these lines with 10-11 in a setting, marked 'affetuoso' ('with feeling'), for tenor (the lute) and bass (the organ) with strings.

5. sadly-pleasing: a phrase reused in Pope's *Odyssey*, I.449; perhaps remembered from

    Let the warbling Lute complain:
    Let the loud Trumpet sound,
    Till the Roofs all around
    The shrill Ecchos rebound:
10   While in more lengthen'd Notes and slow,
   The deep, majestick, solemn Organs blow.
    Hark! the Numbers, soft and clear,
    Gently steal upon the Ear;
    Now louder, and yet louder rise,
15   And fill with spreading Sounds the Skies;
   Exulting in Triumph now swell the bold Notes,
   In broken Air, trembling, the wild Musick floats;

7–17. 1730: In more lengthen'd Notes and slow,
  The deep, majestick, solemn Organs blow.
    Hark! the Numbers, soft and clear,
    Gently steal upon the Ear;
     Now louder, they sound,
     Till the Roofs all around
     The shrill Ecchos rebound:

Dryden, *The Hind and the Panther*, III.35, or *Aeneid*, X.1167, but the instance in Dudley Digges, 'An Ode to my Worthy Kinsman Mr. George Sandys', in Sandys's *A Paraphrase vpon the Divine Poems* (1638), 'sadly-pleasing tones', is closer in context.
 Strain: melody.
6. warbling Lute: a common phrase, no doubt recalled from Dryden's *Song for St. Cecilia's Day 1687*, 36, *Examen Poeticum*, p. 244, where the 'warbling Lute' represents the woes of lovers. Dryden had used the same phrase mock-heroically in *Mac Flecknoe*, 35. Cf. the 'warbling Lyre' of Pope's 'January and May', 324 (and 466), and its parody instance in 'To the Author of a Poem, intituled, Successio', 9. Pope uses 'warbling' and variants seriously in 'Spring', 26 and 'Winter', 4 and the word is very common in these odes and not open to a comic sense (e.g. Addison, *Ode*, 4).
 complain: lament.
7–9. Wakefield compares Dryden, 'Lucretius the Beginning of the Second Book', 32–3, *Sylvae* (1685), p. 58: 'If well tun'd Harps, nor the more pleasing sound | Of Voices, from the vaulted roofs rebound'; and cf. 47 below. For Greene's setting, see 12–14; 'rebound' is much repeated in the setting.
11. deep, majestic, solemn Organs: see below, 125. Wakefield compares Milton, 'On the Morning of Christ's Nativity', 130, *Poems* (1645), p. 7: 'Let the Base of Heav'ns deep Organ blow'.
12–14. Greene combined these lines with 8–9 for a tenor then bass aria with strings, the bass entering to emphasise 'Now louder'.
12. Numbers: versification, as explored in *Essay on Criticism*, 340–84.
15. spreading Sounds: Dryden uses this phrase during a description of the palace of Fame in 'The Twelfth Book of Ovids Metamorphoses Wholly Translated', 68, *Fables Ancient and Modern* (1700), p. 422.
16 Exulting ... Triumph: cf. Belinda's reaction in *The Rape of the Lock* (1714 version), III.99: 'The Nymph exulting fills with Shouts the Sky'.
17. broken Air: Wasserman (1961) suggests reference to the sound-theory of Chaucer, *Hous of Fame*, II.765: 'soun is noght but air

Till, by degrees, remote and small,
   The Strains decay,
20   And melt away
   In a dying, dying Fall.

II.

By Musick, Minds an equal Temper know,
   Nor swell too high, nor sink too low.
   If in the Breast tumultuous Joys arise,
25   Musick her soft, assuasive Voice applies;
   Or when the Soul is press'd with Cares
   Exalts her in enlivening Airs.
Warriors she fires with animated Sounds;
Pours Balm into the bleeding *Lover*'s Wounds:

---

26. press'd with: *1730:* sunk in
27. in: *1730:* with
28. with animated: *1730:* by sprightly
29–35. *1730:*   Pours Balm into the Lover's Wounds:
         Passions no more the Soul engage,
         Ev'n Factions hear away their Rage.

---

y-broken'. Dryden uses the phrase in *Annus Mirabilis*, st. 108 (1667), p. 28, but the context there is of a flying eagle. Oldham, 'Ode for an Anniversary of Musick, 13, *A Second Musical Entertainment* (1685), sig. a1ᵛ, has 'break the yielding Air'. Wakefield points out that Pope recollected the image of music floating on the air in *The Temple of Fame*, 372.

18–21. Set by Greene as a gentle Tenor aria with strings, which ends with voice accompanied only by continuo.

21. dying Fall: cf. Orsino's words in Shakespeare, *Twelfth Night*, I.i.4: 'That strain again, it had a dying fall'. The 'fall' is the cadence at the end of a musical phrase.

22–3. Ruffhead (1769: 60) defended Pope's lines, which Warton (1756: 54) had found 'a little flat' by pointing out that a calmer mood was the subject of the lines, which constituted 'a proof of our poet's skill in adapting his numbers to the sentiment'. This section, to 27, was set by Greene as a recitative for alto, perhaps signalling the shift to reflective calm.

22. equal Temper: a balanced, even temperament. The effects of music on mood were amply explored in Dryden's *Alexander's Feast* and Congreve's *Hymn to Harmony* (esp. st. 5) and were mentioned in most of the 'Cecilia' festal poems; see Headnote.

24. tumultuous Joys: probably recalled from Dryden, 'Canace to Macareus', 41, *Ovid's Epistles Translated by Several Hands* (1680), p. 11: 'Then with Tumultuous Joyes my Heart did beat', or the similarly delicate erotic periphrasis of Carr Scrope's 'Sapho to Phaon', *ibid.* p. 3. Cf. also the 'tumultuous Passions' of Congreve's *Hymn to Harmony*, 70. The same adjective occurs in similar context in Fletcher's 'On the Feast of Cecilia. 1686', st. 1, *Poems on Several Occasions* (1692), p. 20; and Yalden's 'Ode', st. 4.

25. assuasive: 'softening; mitigating' (*SJ*, citing this line only).

28–9. Greene combined these lines with a version of 34–5 in a lively alto aria with strings.

28. animated Sounds: cf. *Essay on Criticism*, 365–82.

29. Balm: 'any thing that soothes or mitigates pain' (*SJ*).

30   At Musick, *Melancholy* lifts her Head;
         Dull *Morpheus* rowzes from his Bed;
         Sloath from its Lethargy awakes,
         And list'ning *Envy* drops her Snakes;
         Intestine War no more our *Passions* wage,
35   Ev'n giddy *Factions* hear away their Rage.

---

30. **At Musick,** *Melancholy:* *1717–51:* Melancholy
31. **Dull** *Morpheus:* *1717–51: Morpheus*
32. **from its Lethargy awakes:** *1717:* unfolds her arms and wakes
33. **And list'ning:** *1717–51:* List'ning
35. **Ev'n:** *1736–51:* And
       giddy: *1730:* omitted
35^6. 1730: Amphion thus bade wild dissention cease,
         And soften'd mortals learn'd the Arts of Peace.
             Amphion taught contending Kings,
             From various discords to create
             The Musick of a well-tun'd State,
             Nor slack nor strain the tender Strings;
             Those useful Touches to impart
             That strike the Subjects answ'ring Heart;
         And the soft, silent Harmony, that springs
         From Sacred Union and consent of Things.

---

bleeding Lover: metaphorically, not literally as in 'Eloisa to Abelard', 100. Wakefield compares Dryden's elegy for Charles II, *Threnodia Augustalis*, st. x (1685), p. 15: 'For all the healing Balm thy Mercy pour'd | Into the Nations bleeding Wound'. Greene uses longer melodic notes and a softer accompaniment to imitate the effect.

30. **Melancholy:** The classic account of the condition was Robert Burton's *Anatomy of Melancholy* (1621); Pope would shortly explore the theme in 'Eloisa to Abelard', esp. 165–70, and more humorously in *Rape of the Lock*, Canto IV. For the musical connection, cf. *Alexander's Feast*, 73–4, where Timotheus 'chose a Mournful Muse, | Soft Pity to infuse', inducing Alexander's melancholy reflections on the defeated Darius. In Congreve's *Hymn to Harmony*, 64, music is said to 'Revive the melancholy drooping Heart'.

31. **Morpheus:** In Ovid, *Metamorphoses*, XI.633–8, a son of the god of Sleep (cf. 'Episode of Sarpedon', 248), who generates dreams. In *Alexander's Feast*, Timotheus charms Alexander to sleep, then wakes him again (116–25).

32. **Sloath:** i.e. Sloth, a personification of apathy; a deadly sin.

33. **Envy ... Snakes:** cf. *Windsor-Forest*, 417 and Commentary.

34. **Intestine War:** cf. *Windsor-Forest*, 323 and Commentary; the phrase was very common in the previous century as a description of internal strife or civil war, e.g. Milton, *Paradise Lost*, VI.258–9.

35. giddy **Factions:** a barbed remark in the context of the peace treaty of 1713; see Headnote to *Windsor-Forest* and Commentary to *Essay on Criticism*, 457–8, and 'The Rape of the Locke', II.98. The word 'Rage' is set by Greene (Movement 5, bars 39–40) to a huge semiquaver run before coming to rest on a minim.

35^6 variant. **Amphion:** cf. 'January and May', 324, and 'The First Book of Statius his Thebais', 11–12. The added section was

III.

But when our Country's Cause provokes to Arms,
How martial Musick every Bosom warms!
So when the first bold Vessel dar'd the Seas,
High on the Stern the *Thracian* rais'd his Strain,
40   While *Argo* saw her kindred Trees

38–9. 1730: When the first Vessel dar'd the Seas,
         The *Thracian* rais'd his Strain,
40. **While:** *1730:* And

---

set by Greene as bass recitative and aria, followed by a duet with tenor, to string accompaniment.

wild dissention ... contending Kings: close to the language of 'The First Book of Statius his Thebais', 52.

various discords: in his *Poem, to the King's Most Sacred Majesty* (1663), p. 10, D'Avenant praises the king's ability to 'an harmonious World create | Out of the various discords of your State'.

Musick of a well-tun'd State: cf. *Essay on Man*, III.294: 'Th' according music of a well-mix'd State'.

Nor slack nor strain: neither under- or over-tune a stringed instrument.

tender Strings: cf. *Essay on Man*, III.290: 'nor to slack, nor strain its tender Strings' (the 'string's of 'Pow'r', in the latter instance'.

silent Harmony: The idea is paralleled in Henry King, 'An Essay on Death and a Prison', 41–2, *Poems, Elegies, Paradoxes and Sonnets* (1664), p. 131: 'There lives a silent harmony, no jar | Or discord can that sweet soft consort mar'.

Sacred Union: a phrase with political currency in Pope's time, e.g. Tate uses it to describe political arrangements in 1701 in *A Congratulatory Poem on the New Parliament Assembled* (1701), p. 12.

consent of Things: cf. *Essay on Man*, III.296. 'From Order, Union, full Consent of things'.

36–48. This stanza is set by Greene with increasing volume: lines 36–7 are sung as bass recitative with strings, oboes doubling violins; 38–41 is a bass aria with full orchestra, including trumpets and (probably) drums; 42–4 adds an alto voice; 45–8 is a trio; 47–8 is sung again by full chorus.

36. Country's Cause: a standard phrase in the poetry of patriotism, e.g. Blackmore, *Prince Arthur*, IV (1695), p. 104, adopted without apparent irony in Pope's 'Prologue to *Cato*', 24, and in the Homer translations (e.g. Hector's speech in *Iliad*, XII.284); but heavily ironised in the *Epistle to Bathurst*, 206.

37. martial Musick: The phrase is very common, especially in the battle poetry of the period e.g. Congreve, *A Pindarique Ode, Humbly Offer'd to the King, on his Taking Namure*, 147 (1695), p. 10. The emotional effect of martial music is a common motif in the Cecilia ode tradition, e.g. in both Dryden's contributions; Congreve, *Hymn to Harmony*, st. 6; D'Urfey, *Ode, for the Anniversary Feast*, st. 5; Motteux, *Words for an Entertainment* (1695), p. 1: 'So, when the Trumpet sounds to Arms, | Britons, whom Native Valour warms, | Are doubly fir'd, and doubly run to Arms.'

38. dar'd the Seas: Wakefield (*Observations*, p. 41) compares this to Dryden's 'once more we tempt the watry Plains', 'The First Book of Homer's Ilias', 86, *Fables*, p. 192, but it is common in Dryden, e.g. the version of Virgil's *Georgics*, II.625, *Works of Virgil* (1697), p. 90: 'that scour the watry Plains'.

39. Thracian: the bard Orpheus.

40. Argo: the ship in which Jason sailed with the Argonauts to find the Golden Fleece, a story well known from the *Argonautica* of

Descend from *Pelion* to the Main.
Transported Demi-Gods stood round,
And Men grew Heroes at the Sound,
　　Enflam'd with Glory's Charms:
45　　Each Chief his sevenfold Shield display'd,
And half unsheath'd the shining Blade;
And Seas, and Rocks, and Skies rebound
　　To Arms, to Arms, to Arms!

IV.

　　But when thro' all th' Infernal Bounds
50　　Which flaming *Phlegeton* surrounds,

Apollonius Rhodius and of Valerius Flaccus, as well as from Homer's *Odyssey* (cf. Pope's *Odyssey*, XII.83–4 and note). In some versions of the story, Orpheus was among the crew.

　kindred Trees: i.e. as ships, cf. *Windsor-Forest*, 383 and Commentary.

41. Pelion: mountain in Thessaly; there is a note on the mountain in mythology at Pope's version of the *Odyssey*, XI.388–9.

　Main: ocean.

42–3. Johnson, reviewing Warton's 1756 *Essay on Pope* (*Literary Magazine*, I, April–May 1756, p. 36) stated (without giving a reason) that these were the best lines in the poem.

42. Transported: enraptured; cf. Pope's *Odyssey*, VIII.87: 'Transported with the Song, the list'ning train . . .'.

　Demi-Gods: cf. 'Vertumnus and Pomona', 75.

44. Glory's Charms: cf. 'Episode of Sarpedon', 143.

45. sevenfold Shield: a phrase from epic, based on the massive shield of Ajax, covered with seven oxhides (Homer, *Iliad*, VII.266). Cf. Dryden, 'The Speeches of Ajax and Ulysses', 2, *Fables*, p. 453; also the parodic version (a hoop-petticoat) in *Rape of the Lock* (1714), II.119.

46. shining Blade: Pope re-used the phrase in his *Iliad*, I.292 and XI.42; Wakefield suggests he derived it from 'shining Steel' in Dryden's version of Virgil, *Aeneid*, VI.404, *Works of Virgil*, p. 374, one of several instances in that translation.

47. rebound: echo, as in 9; cf. 'the vaulted Roofs rebound', *Alexander's Feast*, 36 (1697), p. 2; the image is parodied in 'Rape of the Locke', II.148–9.

49–61. Greene's setting marks the descent into Hell with a key change from D major to G minor, with much angular chromatic phrasing; an alto recitative is overwhelmed by full chorus at the barring of the gates, 52. The short phrases at 55–60 were set as alternating call and response figures, between soprano and alto, and split tenor and bass configurations, in the most daring harmonies of the piece, coming to full choral resolution at 61.

49. Infernal Bounds: regions of Hell, as also envisaged in Dryden, *Aeneid*, VI.200, *Works of Virgil*, p. 368, as Aeneas prepares to venture into the underworld; Pope repeats Dryden's rhyme word in 50. In *Alexander's Feast*, 131–45 (1697), p. 6, Timotheus makes Alexander 'see' a 'ghastly Band' of 'Grecian Ghosts', i.e. soldiers killed by the Persians, in a lugubrious sequence which no doubt influenced Pope's.

50. flaming Phlegeton: Phlegethon, a river of the classical underworld, commonly thus described, e.g. Spenser, *Faerie Queene*, II.vi.50; Milton, *Paradise Lost*, II.580–1; Dryden's version of Virgil, *Aeneid*, VI.741–2.

           Sad *Orpheus* sought his Consort lost;
        Th' Inexorable Gates were barr'd,
   And nought was seen, and nought was heard
           Around the dreary Coast,
55   But dreadful Gleams,
            Dismal Screams,
            Fires that glow,
            Shrieks of Woe,
            Sullen Moans,
60   Hollow Groans,
       And Cries of tortur'd Ghosts.
    But hark! he strikes the golden Lyre;
    And see! the tortur'd Ghosts respire,
        See shady Forms advance!

51–55. 1736–51:   Love, strong as Death, the Poet led
                     To the pale nations of the dead,
            What sounds were heard.
            What scenes appear'd,
               O'er all the dreary coasts!
            Dreadful gleams,
52. Th' Inexorable: *1730:* The Adamantine

---

51. Orpheus descends to Hades in search of his dead wife. This version of the story was known from Virgil, *Georgics*, IV.453–527 and Ovid, *Metamorphoses*, X.1–11; Warton (1756: 55) takes it to be 'elegantly translated' from the former here, though actually the resemblances are mostly rather general; Warton himself reproves Pope for omitting some 'striking circumstances' and 'natural and pathetic exclamations' from Virgil's version. Johnson (*Rambler*, no. 143, 30 July 1751) suggested a medial source in Boethius, *De Consolatio Philosophiae*, III. xii. 31–51. Dryden makes a witty conceit out of the idea of Orpheus in Hell in his *Ode, on the Death of Mr. Henry Purcell*, 16–22 (1696), sig. A1ᵛ; Cobb's 'Love and Music' is closer to the Virgilian idea and language (for this and other post-classical sources, see Headnote). The presence of Orpheus in the Cecilia tradition was often more focused on his magical ability to make beasts listen and trees move.

51–5 variants. *Love, strong as Death:* a phrase from the Song of Solomon 8:6, and thence often in religious poetry, e.g. Waller, 'Of Divine Love', V.39, *Divine Poems* (1685), p. 17.

52. *Inexorable:* 'not to be moved by entreaty' (*SJ*, citing this line).

52 variant. *Adamantine:* cf. 'Messiah', 47 variant.

54. *dreary Coast:* cf. 'The First Book of Statius', 84.

60. *Hollow Groans:* perhaps influenced by the underworld scene in Dryden's version of Virgil, *Aeneid*, VI.427; the phrase also occurs previously, at VI.73 (*Works of Virgil*, pp. 364, 375).

62–9. Greene imitates the effect of Orpheus' lyre by setting this section as an alto aria with violins playing light arpeggio figurations.

62. *golden Lyre:* cf. 4, and *Alexander's Feast*, 123: 'Now strike the golden Lyre again'; Alcinous' bard Demodicus has a 'golden Lyre' in Pope's *Odyssey*, VIII.107.

63. *respire:* breathe again or 'to take rest from toil' (*SJ*, citing this line).

65   Thy stone, O *Sysiphus*, stands still;
         Ixion rests upon his Wheel,
             And the pale Spectres dance!
         The Furies sink upon their Iron Beds,
         And Snakes uncurl'd hang list'ning round their Heads.

V.

70   By the Streams that ever flow,
         By the fragrant Winds that blow

65–66. *1730:* omitted
69. Heads: *1730:* Head

---

65. Sysiphus: normally 'Sisyphus', founder of Corinth, one of the tormented souls seen by Odysseus in Hades (*Odyssey*, XI, 593–600; in Pope's version, 733–40, with a note); he was punished for, among other crimes, cheating death, by being made to push a boulder up a hill (or, in some versions, the sun up the sky), which then immediately rolled down again, requiring him to repeat the process eternally. Warton (*Works of Pope*, I.148) stated that the line was 'taken from an ode of Cobb', i.e. Samuel Cobb, 'Love and Music', 81, *Poems on Several Occasions* (1710), p. 140: 'The Stone of *Sisiphus* stood still'; but the idea is in the classical sources (see next note). For Cobb's poems as a possible source see Headnote.

66. Ixion: parricide and would-be rapist of Zeus' wife, punished by Zeus with crucifixion on a fiery wheel (in some versions, the sun) revolving for eternity. In Virgil's telling of the story, *Georgics*, IV.484, 'Ixionii . . . rota constitit', 'Ixion's wheel stood still'. The story is parodied in *Rape of the Lock* (1714 version), II.133. In 1767 Goldsmith (see Barnard 1973: 456) claimed Pope's source for the pairing was 'A Pindarique Essay upon Musick', in *Poems by Several Hands*, ed. Tate (1685), pp. 400–1, presumably the lines in stanza IV, 'The Wheel stood still . . . The rolling stone was gathering Moss'. But Pope more likely draws on Ovid, *Metamorphoses*, X.42–4, where Ixion's wheel stands still ('stupuit') while Sisyphus sits on his stone.

67. pale Spectres dance: cf. 'The First Book of Statius his Thebais', 132–3; and *Rape of the Lock* (1714 version), IV.44. Cf. Anne Finch, 'The Spleen, A Pindarique Ode', 17, *A New Miscellany of Original Poems, on Several Occasions* (1701), p. 61: 'Antick Spectres dance'. Warton (*Works of Pope*, I.148) objected to the image as 'most improper, because ludicrous'.

68. Furies: cf. *Alexander's Feast*, 132–3, where Timotheus invokes Furies with snakes in their hair; for the mythology in relation to Orpheus' spellbinding music in the underworld see Virgil, *Georgics*, IV.482–3; in Ovid, *Metamorphoses*, X.46, the Furies weep at Orpheus' appeal. Cf. also 'The First Book of Statius his Thebais', Argument, 4, and the poem, 85, and Commentary.

Iron Beds: Dryden's version of *Aeneid*, VI.392–3, *Works of Virgil*, p. 374, refers to 'The Furies Iron Beds' during Aeneas' visit to the underworld.

70–81. Greene set this stanza as an alto-tenor duet, again in G minor, marked 'siciliana' (a slow pastoral dance) accompanied by strings and flutes. This was the only section of the setting widely known in the eighteenth century; it appeared in Sir John Hawkins's *General History of the Science and Practice of Music* (1776), IV.331–41.

71. fragrant Winds: cf. Lee, *Nero*, I.ii (1675, p. 8): 'At my command the fragrant Winds do blow'.

    O'er th' *Elysian* Flowers,
   By those happy Souls who dwell
    In Yellow Meads of *Asphodel*,
75   Or *Amaranthine* Bowers:
   By the Heroe's armed Shades
   Glitt'ring thro' the gloomy Glades,
   By the Youths that dy'd for Love,
   Wandring in the Myrtle Grove,
80   Restore, restore *Eurydice* to Life;
  Oh take the Husband, or return the Wife.

   He sung, and Hell consented
    To hear the Poet's Pray'r;
   Stern *Proserpine* relented,
85   And gave him back the Fair.
    Thus Song could prevail
   O'er Death and o'er Hell,

---

72. Elysian: Elysium, a paradisal zone for the souls of the distinguished or morally good, contrasted with the gloomier and more punitive underworld of Hades. Cf. 'To a Young Lady, with the Works of Voiture', 73, and Pope's note on the Homeric source, in his *Odyssey*, IV.765. Pope parodied the idea in *The Rape of the Lock*, IV.45, and in *The Dunciad* (1728), III.14.

73-8. This section was perhaps in Pope's mind earlier, if the passage in his letter to Cromwell, 25 April 1708 (*Corr.*, I.46) is taken as a parody of something already extant; see Headnote.

74. Meads: meadows.

 Asphodel: among the flowers from which Adam and Eve make a bed in Milton, *Paradise Lost*, IX.1040, but often associated with the underworld, as when Achilles strides away through meadows of asphodel in Homer, *Odyssey*, XI.539; and cf. XXIV.13.

75. Amaranthine: cf. 'Winter' 73-4; the immortality of the flower is emphasised in Milton, *Paradise Lost*, III.352-6.

79. *Myrtle Grove:* see Commentary to 'Spring', 65-9; 'Winter', 23; 'Messiah', 74; and 'To a Young Lady, with the Works of Voiture', 73. Ovid explains the association between myrtle and Venus at *Fasti*, IV.139-44, and the link was commonly made: e.g. Dryden, 'Palamon and Arcite', II.459-61. The soldiers wear myrtle in *Alexander's Feast*, 7.

80. Eurydice: the dead wife of Orpheus.

82-5. Greene set this as a short bass recitative.

84. Stern Proserpine: Latin form of Persephone, wife of Hades (Pluto), king of the underworld. Pope refers to 'ruthless *Proserpine*' in his *Iliad*, IX.585; in Virgil's version (*Georgics*, IV.487) it is Proserpine who imposes the condition that Eurydice must not look back on the way out of Hell; in Ovid, *Metamorphoses*, X.15, it is to Proserpine that Orpheus initially appeals.

86-91. Warton (1756: 56-7) found the rhythm of these lines 'burlesque and ridiculous' because the metre was normally used in comic drinking songs, a point contested by Johnson in his review (see above, 42-3), on the grounds that such metre could represent joy of various kinds, the specific kind being determined by the words. Greene set these lines (which concluded the 1730 version) as an extended full chorus, ending the piece on an unequivocal note of grand triumph (the death of Orpheus is omitted).

87. Cf. Hughes, *Ode in Praise of Musick* (1703), p. 9, where Musick descends 'to conquer Death and Hell'; and Milton, 'Il Penseroso',

A Conquest how hard and how glorious?
    Tho' Fate had fast bound her
90   With *Styx* nine times round her,
Yet Musick and Love were Victorious.

VI.

But soon, too soon, the Lover turns his Eyes:
Again she falls, again she dies, she dies!
How wilt thou now the fatal Sisters move?
95   No Crime was thine, if 'tis no Crime to love.
    Now under hanging Mountains,
    Beside the Falls of Fountains,
    Or where *Hebrus* wanders,

92–133. 1730: omitted

108, *Poems* (1645), p. 41: 'And made Hell grant what Love did seek'.

90. Styx: river of the underworld; cf. 'The First Book of Statius his Thebais', 83. Pope prints a composite note on the mythology of Styx in his *Iliad*, XV.43. Cf. also the parody at *Dunciad Variorum*, II.314. The 'nine times' detail is from Virgil, *Georgics*, IV.480, where it is part of the general description of the river.

92. In Virgil, *Georgics*, IV.488-91, Orpheus looked back ('respexit') because of a sudden moment of madness ('subita . . . dementia'), but in Ovid, *Metamorphoses*, X.56-7, 'ne deficeret, metuens avidusque videndi | flexit amans oculos' ('the lover fearing that she might fail, and eager to see her, turned his eyes'). Pope does not give a reason.

94. fatal Sisters: the 'Moirai' or Fates; Dryden used this phrase to describe them in 'Meleager and Atalantis', 255, *Fables*, p. 114.

95. Crime . . . love: The idea is suggested by the classical sources: Virgil's description of Orpheus' madness as 'ignoscenda quidem, scirent si ignoscere Manes' ('something to be pardoned, if the infernal regions knew how to pardon'), or Eurydice's refusal to complain on the grounds that she could only complain that she was loved (*Metamorphoses*, X.61: 'quid enim nisi se quereretur amatam'). Pope's phrasing is reminiscent of Dryden's 'Dido to Aeneas', 176, *Ovid's Epistles Translated by Several Hands* (1680), p. 225: 'Who know no Crime, but too much Love of thee', and the image was more commonly used in relation to female sexual transgression. Pope returned to the idea shortly afterwards: cf. 'Eloisa to Abelard', 68, and 'Verses to the Memory of an Unfortunate Lady' 6. Cf. also 'On the Statue of Cleopatra', 61: 'I knew no crime, if 'tis no crime to love'; the last example could predate the present poem, but it was not published until 1717, and then not acknowledged as Pope's.

96–108. A passage cited by Lord Kames as demonstrating a frequency of rhyme inappropriate for its subject, but also by Joseph Priestley as matching sound to sense; see Headnote.

96. hanging: overhanging, precipitous.

98. Hebrus: the river down which Orpheus' severed head eventually floated, still speaking, according the version of the story in Virgil, *Georgics*, IV.523-4, and Ovid, *Metamorphoses*, XI.44-66 (see 111-16 below).

	Rolling in *Maeanders*,
100	All alone,
	Unheard, unknown,
	He makes his Moan;
	And calls her Ghost
	For ever, ever, ever lost!
105	Now with Furies surrounded,
	Despairing, confounded,
	He trembles, he glows,
	Amidst *Rhodope*'s Snows:
	See, wild as the Winds, o'er the Desart he flies;
110	Hark! *Haemus* resounds with the *Bacchanals* Cries —
	— Ah see, he dies!
	Yet ev'n in Death *Eurydice* he sung,
	Eurydice still trembled on his Tongue,

---

99. Maeanders: Maeander was a long Phrygian river, mentioned in Homer (Pope's *Iliad*, II.1056), proverbial for its wandering course. Pope had used the name parodically in 'Rape of the Locke', II.120; and cf. *The Dunciad Variorum*, I.62, II.168 (later texts).

101. Unheard, unknown: cf. John Norris, 'The Choice', 11–12, *A Collection of Miscellanies* (1692), p. 29: 'Let my soft minutes *glide obscurely* on | Like *subterraneous* streams, *unheard, unknown*'.

106. confounded: perplexed.

108. Rhodope's Snows: For Rhodope see 110; in Addison's 'Song', st. 3, Rhodope is left 'without a shade', as the trees follow Orpheus on his wanderings. Ovid, *Metamorphoses*, X.11–12, describes Orpheus as 'Rhodopeius ... vates', 'Rhodopian poet'; also mentioned in Virgil, *Georgics*, IV.461 (and in Milton, *Paradise Lost*, VII.35); but Pope may be recalling rather IV.517–18, where Orpheus wanders among 'Riphaean snows'.

109. Desart: wasteland, as in *Windsor-Forest*, 26.

110. Haemus: Thracian king, son of Boreas; turned into a mountain with his wife Rhodope by Zeus after he impiously compared their status with that of Zeus and Hera (Ovid, *Metamorphoses*, VI.87–9); mentioned with Rhodope as a scene of Orpheus' wandering in *Metamorphoses*, X.77.

Bacchanals: female worshippers of the Greek god Dionysus (Bacchus; in *Alexander's Feast*, 47–60, Bacchus is celebrated as the god of wine).

111–16. Orpheus was supposedly torn to pieces by women for his refusal to remarry after the death of Eurydice: see Ovid, *Metamorphoses*, XI.1–60 and (more compactly) Virgil, *Georgics*, IV.520–7; in each case, the details are more violent and explicit than Pope's. Cf. also Milton, 'Lycidas', 58–63. Dryden's version of Virgil (at 762–4) offers Pope a model for Orpheus' last words: 'Ev'n then his trembling Tongue invok'd his Bride; | With his last Voice, *Eurydice*, he cried. | *Eurydice*, the Rocks and River-banks reply'd.' Warton (1756: 60) felt Virgil's 'vocabat' ('cried', in Dryden) was more suitable and pathetic than Pope's 'sung'. He also complained (*Works of Pope*, I.151) that in English the repetition of the name 'hurts the ear' as it is not 'harmonious enough to suffer repetition'.

111–12. Spence (*Essay on Pope's Odyssey*, II.44) praised the emotionally convincing effect of the break in sense here; Warton concedes that the 'death is expressed with a brevity and abruptness suitable to the nature of the ode' (*Works of Pope*, I.151).

>   *Eurydice* the Woods,
> 115   *Eurydice* the Floods,
>   *Eurydice* the Rocks, and hollow Mountains rung.
>
>   VII.
>   Musick the fiercest Griefs can charm,
>   And Fate's severest Rage disarm:
>   Musick can soften Pain to Ease,
> 120   And make Despair and Madness please:
>   Our Joys below it can improve,
>   And antedate the Bliss above.
>   This the divine *Cecilia* found,
>   And to her Maker's Praise confin'd the Sound.
> 125 When the full Organ joins the tuneful Quire,
>   The Immortal Pow'rs incline their Ear;
>   Born on the swelling Notes our Souls aspire,

---

117. **Griefs:** *1736–51:* grief

---

116. hollow Mountains: i.e. resounding, like a hollow instrument. Cf. Cotton, 'Winter', st. 42, *Poems on Several Occasions* (1689), p. 652: 'Or, else go whistle to the Shoar, | And make the hollow Mountains roar'.
  rung: echoed.
122. antedate: anticipate; or 'to take something before the proper time' (*SJ*, citing only this line). Cf. Oldham, 'Ode', 22, 'And seem to antedate our future Bliss on high!'
123. divine Cecilia: cf. *Alexander's Feast*, 161: 'At last Divine *Cecilia* came'. Pope follows this later model of Dryden in introducing the patron saint quite late in the poem, where other instances feature her much earlier. Though saints were largely regarded as a relic of Catholic superstition by the Anglican church, the divinity of Cecilia's music is stressed by almost all writers of Odes in the tradition from Fishbourne in 1683 onwards, and for Catholics such as Dryden and Pope there was less inhibition about the matter.
125. full Organ: D'Urfey, *Ode, for the Anniversary Feast*, st. 3, particularly associates the revival of music with Cecilia's playing on the 'Noble Organ', in part because the organ was associated with Christian church worship; Dryden's *Song for St. Cecilia's Day*, 42–4, emphasised the link, which was followed by Yalden's 'Ode', 63–4, and Congreve's *Hymn to Harmony*, 118. Motteux, *Words for an Entertainment*, p. 2, and Addison, *Ode*, 17 (1699), p. 1, both mention her 'solemn...Organ'. Luckett (1973) discusses the textual sources and iconographic representations of the link, which is more literary and playful than musicologically serious; and see Headnote. Cf. also 'Eloisa to Abelard', 272: 'And swelling organs lift the rising soul', with (in that case) possibly an erotic suggestion.
  tuneful Quire: Timotheus at *Alexander's Feast*, 21 (1687), p. 2, is 'Amid the tuneful Quire' [choir].
127. swelling Notes: cf. the image in 'Eloisa to Abelard', cited in Commentary to 125. The phrase itself appears in the same context in Congreve's *Hymn to Harmony*, 119.

  While solemn Airs improve the sacred Fire;
   And Angels lean from Heav'n to hear!
130 Of *Orpheus* now no more let Poets tell,
  To bright *Cecilia* greater Pow'r is giv'n;
   His Numbers rais'd a Shade from Hell,
   Hers lift the Soul to Heav'n.

FINIS.

---

129. TE notes that Pope recalled the phrasing in *The Temple of Fame*, 375: 'Ev'n list'ning Angels lean'd from Heaven to hear'. Wakefield notes that Dryden, 'Palamon and Arcite', III.442, *Fables*, p. 65, has gods 'leaning from their Stars' to view a battle on earth. In the legend of Cecilia, she tells her husband Valerian that she is watched over by an angel, whom he can only see once he is converted to Christianity.

130-3. In the final stanza and 'Grand Chorus' at the end of *Alexander's Feast* Dryden writes: 'Let old *Timotheus* yield the Prize, | Or both divide the Crown; | He rais'd a Mortal to the Skies; | She drew an Angel down.' In Pope, there is no dividing the honours: Cecilia is a more authentically religious figure, in the same way as 'Messiah' privileges Isaiah over Virgil, while honouring the classical forbear. In Dryden's earlier *Song*, 48-54, *Examen Poeticum*, pp. 245-6, Orpheus' magical powers over landscape and animals are celebrated, but finally Cecilia is superior: 'But bright CECILIA rais'd the wonder high'r; | When to her ORGAN, vocal Breath was giv'n | An Angel heard, and straight appear'd | Mistaking Earth for Heav'n.' In Congreve's *Hymn to Harmony*, 117-19, p. 7, Cecilia drowns out the 'soft enervate Lyre' with the 'more majestick Sound' of the organ, and Urania and Apollo yield to her. Warton (1756: 62) censured both Pope and Dryden for ending with 'an epigram . . . a species of wit as flagrantly unsuitable to the dignity, and as foreign to the nature, of the lyric, as it is of the epic muse', a point reinforced in Johnson's review (see Commentary to 42-3).

19

THE GARDENS OF ALCINOUS
(1713)

Editors' Headnote

Composition and publication

'The Gardens of Alcinous' was first published on 29 September 1713. It was printed as part of Pope's essay on gardens in *The Guardian* (no. 173), the eighth and last of Pope's acknowledged contributions to that periodical, and possibly his last periodical essay of any kind. (For Pope's relations with Addison and Steele, and his contributions to their periodicals, see Headnote to 'Messiah'.) There it is introduced in the following terms:

> The two most celebrated Wits of the World have each of them left us a particular Picture of a Garden [...] The Pieces I am speaking of are *Virgil*'s Account of the Garden of the old *Corycian*, and *Homer*'s of that of *Alcinous*. The first of these is already known to the *English* Reader, by the excellent Versions of Mr. *Dryden* and Mr. *Addison*. The other having never been attempted in our Language with any Elegance, and being the most beautiful Plan of this sort that can be imagined, I shall here present the Reader with a Translation of it.

There is no record of the period of composition, and no reference to it in surviving correspondence. In the 1717 *Works*, Pope included the poem as the last in the group of translations, at pp. 365–7, after 'The Arrival of Ulysses in Ithaca', and in 1725 it was incorporated into the *Odyssey* translation, VII.142–75, in a book otherwise largely the responsibility of Elijah Fenton, and made no subsequent separate appearance in collections of Pope's poetry.

Text

The text presented here is taken from the first edition of 1713. There is no substantive revision in subsequent texts. The various extant texts of 'The Gardens of Alcinous' are referred to in the apparatus as follows:

1713: *The Guardian*, No. 173 (Griffith 21)

1717: *Works*, quarto (Griffith 79)

1727: *The Works of Mr. Alexander Pope*, octavo (Griffith 193)

Models and sources

For Pope's early reading of Homer, and his certain and possible knowledge of other translations, see Headnote to 'The Episode of Sarpedon'. The passage can be found in place within earlier translations: George Chapman, *Homer's Odysses. Translated according to ye Greeke* (1615), pp. 101–2; John Ogilby, *Homer, His Odysses translated* (1665), p. 90; and Thomas Hobbes, *Homer's Odysses Translated* (1675), p. 78; reference is made to these versions, as here cited, in the Commentary. There were, as Pope noted, no separate models for the segment he chose.

Context

The gardens of Alcinous, as described by Homer, constituted a standard reference point in Western literary history along with the Hesperides, the gardens of Adonis and the biblical garden of Eden. Alcinous' enclosed garden was a stock model for the beautifully designed small-scale estate of a benign patriarch, an instance of 'well contrived order' as Sir Thomas Browne has it in the first chapter of 'The Garden of Cyrus'; *Hydriotaphia... Together with the Garden of Cyrus* (1658), p. 99. For Browne it was 'anciently conceived an originall phancy, from Paradise', and it was certainly a constitutive element of the conception of Paradise in Christian literature. Milton decks his description of Paradise with Homeric sources: Alcinous is mentioned specifically in *Paradise Lost*, V.341, as a point of comparison for Eve's food-gathering, and again at IX.440–2 as the architect of a 'feignd' poetic garden. Milton's early commentator, Patrick Hume, quoted liberally from Homer in establishing these and other links (e.g. IV.329, V.394) between Paradise and Alcinous's horticulture; *Annotations on Milton's Paradise Lost* (1695), pp. 147, 180, 182, 254. Poetical gardening theory often cited Alcinous: *Rapin of Gardens. A Latin Poem. English'd by Mr. Gardiner* (1706), book IV, 'The Orchard', comments on Alcinous as the genius of orchard organisation, and John Philips, *Cyder* (1708), a poem which influenced Pope's *Windsor-Forest*, reflects on Alcinous' apple orchard in book I.

Pope's immediate and acknowledged source for garden wisdom, including the selection of this passage as a model, was Sir William Temple's prose essay 'Upon the Gardens of Epicurus, or of Gardening in the year 1685', in his *Miscellanea. The Second Part* (1690), pp. 99–100:

> The Garden of *Alcinous* described by *Homer*, seems wholly Poetical, and made at the pleasure of the Painter, like the rest of the Romantick Palace, in that little barren Island of *Phaeacia* or *Corfu*. Yet as all the pieces of this

transcendent Genius, are composed with excellent Knowledge, as well as Fancy, so they seldom fail of Instruction as well as Delight to all that read Him. The Seat of this Garden, joyning to the Gates of the Palace, the Compass of the Inclosure, being Four Acres, the tall Trees of Shade as well as those of Fruit, the two Fountains, one for the use of the Garden, and the other of the Palace, the continual Succession of Fruits throughout the whole Year, are, for ought I know, the best Rules or Provisions, that can go towards composing the best Gardens[.]

Pope's father gardened on a gentlemanly estate of some 15 acres at Whitehill House, near Binfield, between 1700 and 1716, and the setting of that garden in the general area of Windsor Forest provided Pope with models of outdoor aesthetics also explored in the poem of that title, published earlier in the year. Pope's essay itself came in the wake of Addison's *Spectator*, nos. 414, 25 June 1712, and 477, 6 September 1712, each of which called for a naturalistic and productive style of gardening, against reliance on artificial patterning. Pope was later known, from his own gardening at Twickenham, his practical advice to estate owners and friends and his verse epistles to large-scale landowners such as Bathurst and Burlington, as a proponent of the 'natural' style of gardening, a forerunner of the curvilinear plantations associated with country houses of the later eighteenth century. Mack (1969: 51–7) takes the essay and the Alcinous passage seriously as the basis of Pope's own later sense of garden aesthetics, but as Martin (1984: 4–7) notes, the 1713 essay offers little sign of the practical knowledge he was later to acquire. (See also Brownell 1978, and Liu 2008, which studies Pope's classical-geometric inheritance in the essay alongside his possible knowledge of non-regular forms of design derived from Chinese gardening.) At this point, his idea of the garden can be linked to the 'hortus conclusus' tradition of medieval gardening, as reflected in his 'January and May', as well as the fortified fruit-garden in his 'Vertumnus and Pomona'. (Pope's Cowleyesque 'The Garden', written before 1709 but not published until 1736, represents a more luxuriant and pleasure-filled imaginary space for solitary wandering.)

In his prose essay, Pope, posing as the owner of a small country house, praises, like Addison, the 'amiable Simplicity of unadorned Nature'. After an epigram from Martial on the virtues of the simple country estate of Faustinus, Pope cites the garden models of Virgil and Homer, 'wherein those great Masters, being wholly unconfined, and Painting at Pleasure, may be thought to have given a full Idea of what they esteemed most excellent in this way'. In practice, Pope observes, 'These . . . consist intirely of the useful Part of Horticulture, Fruit Trees, Herbs, Water, &c.' (Pope's own later garden at Twickenham had a vineyard, fruit-trees, an orangery, and a kitchen garden.) One example is Virgil's 'Account of the Garden of the old *Corycian*', from *Georgics*, IV.127–46, lines which as Pope noted were well known from recent versions by Addison, whose translation of most of the fourth *Georgic* appeared in *The Annual Miscellany: For the Year 1694*, with the 'Corycian' vignette at pp. 68–70, and Dryden, in the *Works of Virgil* (1697), p. 128. Homer's lines on Alcinous's garden form the other example. After pointing out its significant qualities, Pope lambasts current horticultural taste as given to vulgar displays of art, especially in the form of topiary, further citing seven lines of late Latin verse, from an astrological poem, *Uraniae Libri*, III.1058-64, by Giovanni Pontano (1426-1503). (It is not known how Pope had come across this, but he later owned an 11-volume edition of Italian poets containing work by Pontano, and included some shorter pieces by him in his own anthology of neo-Latin verse, *Selecta Poemata Italorum qui Latine Scripserunt* (1740); cf. Mack 1982: 460n.) The 'Catalogue' of topiarised trees begins with a grotesquely comic '*Adam* and *Eve* in Yew', signalling the corruptions of the paradisal garden (*PW*, I.150).

Pope's Alcinous lines were reprinted (as the work of Laurence Eusden) in Stephen Switzer's *The Nobleman, Gentleman and Gardener's Recreation* (1715), p. 7, indicating rapid incorporation into formal garden design theory. By 1725 the poem had been incorporated into the wider design of the *Odyssey* translation for which it was, with the other Homer translations ('The Episode of Sarpedon' and 'The Arrival of Ulysses in Ithaca') a form of calling card. Pope's diction is the heightened 'epic' style which he was cultivating for his Homer project, and which also sometimes foreshadows his own mock-heroic inversions.

The original passage in Homer's *Odyssey* (VII.112-31) occurs at the point where the shipwrecked Odysseus has been directed by the goddess Athena to the court of Alcinous (King of the Phaeacians, on an island identified in Pope's time with Corfu) for refuge. Before entering, he stands and looks at the garden outside; the description is his particular vision before encountering his host, but is presented by Pope, removing the frame of the observing hero, as a general image of ideal aesthetic order. In Homer the passage contains 20 lines of hexameters. Chapman allots 28 lines of pentameter couplets to the translation; Ogilby trims it to 14 of the same; Hobbes has 19 lines of alternately rhyming pentameter; Pope gives it 34 lines of heroic couplets. Pope's version is therefore comparatively free, but the point of the expansion is not luxuriance but a higher level of order: Pope processes Homer's lists into fuller, more patterned clauses (mostly in well-balanced, end-stopped couplets, as opposed to Chapman's enjambed lines). In lines 6-10, Pope allots to each fruit an attribute expanded through a full line, whereas Homer (115-16) simply says: 'good-fruiting pear-trees and pomegranates and apples and sweet figs and olive trees flourish'. The concluding lines on irrigation (28-34) are similarly reconfigured on a more diagrammatic scale, perhaps to make a political point about Alcinous's wise governance. Though in context its purpose was to illustrate something about garden aesthetics, it is nonetheless a harbinger of Odysseus' return to a place of monarchical civilisation, as, more pointedly, in 'The Arrival of Ulysses in Ithaca', which it precedes in narrative terms. In another respect, Deutsch (1996: 92-4) sees the independent verses as presenting a classical literary ideal of nature and usefulness as if it constituted a real and achievable order of landscape design in which aspects of power and labour are hidden from view: 'an example whose emblematic wholeness mimics the self-sufficiency it describes ... In the garden labour is superfluous'. Pope's unnamed garden labourers, however, though present (19-21) only as implied subjects of active verbs, are actually slightly more prominent than Homer's (at VII.123-5).

The Gardens of *Alcinous,* from *Homer*'s Odyss. 7.

Close to the Gates a spacious Garden lies,
From Storms defended and inclement Skies:
Four Acres was th' allotted Space of Ground,
Fenc'd with a green Enclosure all around.

Title. 1717–27: THE | GARDENS | OF | *ALCINOUS.* | From the SEVENTH BOOK of | *HOMER*'s *ODYSSES.*

---

1. spacious Garden: Homer, VII.112, calls it: μέγας ὄρχατος ('big orchard'), rendered by Chapman, *Homer's Odysses. Translated according to ye Greeke* (1615), VII.153, pp. 101–2 as 'goodly Orchard'; by Ogilby. *Homer, His Odysses Translated* (1665), p. 90, as 'stately Orchard' and by Hobbes, *Homer's Odysses Translated* (1675), p. 78, as 'dainty Orchard'. Cf. the general resemblance to Milton, *Paradise Lost,* V.367, where Adam welcomes Raphael to 'This spacious ground', and the proprietorial 'spacious Garden' in 'January and May', 450.

2. Largely Pope's addition.

inclement Skies: cf. Milton, *Paradise Lost,* III.425–6: 'storms | Of *Chaos* blustring round, inclement skie'.

3. Four Acres: Homer's word (113), τετράγυος, designates four 'γυαι', but the precise area indicated by this term is unknown. Chapman translates it as 'neare ten Acres', 154, p. 101; Ogilby has 'four Acres', p. 90; Hobbes translates 'Four-square', p. 78. In his own prose commentary, Pope states, following Temple, 'Its Extent was four *Acres,* which, in those times of Simplicity, was look'd upon as a large one, even for a Prince...' (*PW*, I.147). Chetwood, in the 'Preface to the Pastorals', in Dryden's *Works of Virgil,* sig. ***ᵛ, mentions Cincinnatus, *'whose whole Estate was but of Four Acres; too little a spot now for the Orchard, or Kitchin-Garden of a* Private *Gentleman'.* Pope's own later garden at Twickenham was roughly five acres, that of his paternal estate at Whitehill House about 15. Dryden likens the size and design of his patron Sir William Bowyer's five-acre orchard at Denham-Court to that of Alcinous in a note on Virgil, *Georgics,* II, *Works of Virgil,* p. 627. There is no equivalent for 'allotted Space of Ground' in Homer.

4. green Enclosure: cf. Milton, *Paradise Lost,* IV.133, where Paradise is fenced in with 'enclosure green', the various increasingly wild levels of which are described in the subsequent lines (to 139). Pope's other walled gardens include that in 'January and May' (esp. 450–1) and 'Vertumnus and Pomona', 3–4. Homer's word here (113), ἕρκος, can mean wall, fence, or hedge; Chapman has 'a loftie Quickset', 155, p. 101; Ogilby calls it 'well-hedg'd', p. 90; Hobbes has 'hedge and pale', p. 78.

5   *Tall thriving Trees confest the fruitful Mold;*
The red'ning Apple ripens here to Gold,
Here the blue Figg with luscious Juice o'erflows,
With deeper Red the full Pomegranate glows,
The Branch here bends beneath the weighty Pear,
10   *And verdant Olives flourish round the Year.*
The balmy Spirit of the Western Gale
Eternal breathes on Fruits untaught to fail:
Each dropping Pear a following Pear supplies,
On Apples Apples, Figs on Figs arise:

---

5. confest: revealed, proved, bore witness to.

   fruitful: fertile. Ogilby has 'pregnant Trees' (p. 90); Homer's adjective (114), τηλεθόωντα, means 'luxuriant'.

   Mold: mould, soil; Homer does not mention the earth or its quality. In his essay, Pope writes that Homer 'mentions next the Trees, which were Standards, and suffered to grow to their full height' (*PW*, I.148).

6-10. On the reordering and expansion of Homer's 115–16 here, see Headnote.

6. ripens . . . to Gold: The imagery recalls the ancient idea that metallic gold is ripened by the heat of the sun, as in *Windsor-Forest*, 394, but also suggests the magical golden apples of the Hesperides, a common subject of art and poetry in the seventeenth century; Homer (VII.115) has simply μηλέαι ἀγλαόκαρποι ('apples with shining fruit').

8. Pomegranate: so in Homer, who lists pears, shining apples, sweet figs and olives, at 115–16. The metre requires that the word be pronounced as trisyllabic.

11. Western Gale: the Zephyr, gentlest of the classical winds (named in Homer, and in Chapman and Hobbes, and also by Pope in the 1713 essay); Ogilby has 'Western Breizes', p. 90; 'balmy Spirit' is Pope's addition. For 'Gale' see Commentary to 'On a Fan of the Author's Design', 5; *Windsor-Forest*, 101.

12. untaught to fail: an epic-sounding formulation without origin in the Greek. Similarly, Pope invents 'untaught to fear', in his *Iliad*, X.259, then parodies it in *The Dunciad Variorum*, II.53. Perhaps modelled on Shakespeare, *Henry VI, Part Two*, IV.i.125: 'untaught to plead'. Cf. 'The First Book of Statius his Thebais', 759; 'Vertumnus and Pomona', 3.

13-14. Homer, 120–1: ὄγχνη ἐπ' ὄγχνῃ γηράσκει, μῆλον δ' ἐπὶ μήλῳ, | αὐτὰρ ἐπὶ σταφυλῇ σταφυλή, σῦκον δ' ἐπὶ σύκῳ ('pear on pear matures, apple on apple, | now on grape-cluster [ripens] grape-cluster, fig on fig'). Pope's syntax reflects the Homeric ordering, but in the Greek the words are grammatically inflected, and not quite identical as in English. Of the other translators, Chapman ('Peare grew after Peare; | Apple succeeded apple; Grape, the Grape; | Fig after Fig came', 164–6, p. 101) and Hobbes ('Pears after Pears, Apples to Apples come; | Grapes are by Grapes, Figs by Figs followed', p. 78) come closest to Pope's formulation, though they retain the grapes, which Pope drops. Deutsch (1996: 93) comments 'Pope's translation credits Alcinous's fruit-trees with a self-perpetuating power of generation', but the basic idea is certainly there in Homer. Deutsch notes that Pope would parody such noun clusters in the revised *Rape of the Lock* (1714), I.101–2: 'Where Wigs with Wigs, with Sword-knots Sword-knots strive, | Beaus banish Beaus, and Coaches Coaches drive'.

14. Apples Apples: The syntax is not without example: cf. George Turberville, 'Yet ere I die', *Tragical Tales* (1587), p. 181: 'As by the art of hande | Of apples apples spring'.

   Figs on Figs arise: cf. *Essay on Criticism*, 235.

15   *The same mild Season gives the Blooms to blow,*
      The Buds to harden, and the Fruits to grow.

      Here order'd Vines in equal Ranks appear
      With all th' United Labours of the Year,
      Some to unload the fertile Branches run,

15-16. much expanded from Homer's VII.118: χείματος οὐδὲ θέρευς, ἐπετήσιος ([the fruits do not fail] 'winter nor summer, year round'). This aspect of Alcinous' garden was much imitated in English, e.g. Waller, 'The Battle of the Summer Islands', Canto I, *Poems, &c.* (1645), p. 97: 'Ripe fruits and blossoms on the same trees live, | At once they promise what at once they give'; and Milton, *Paradise Lost*, IV.147-8: 'goodliest Trees loaden with fairest Fruit, | Blossoms and Fruits at once of golden hue'. Patrick Hume suggests that the seasonal conflations of *Paradise Lost*, V.394-5, were influenced by Homer in the same way; *Annotations on Milton's Paradise Lost* (1695), p. 182. Cf. Pope's own parody of abnormal seasonal anomalies of this type in *The Dunciad Variorum*, I.71-6. Here it represents, according to Pope's essay, 'a more noble and poetical way of expressing the continual Succession of one Fruit after another throughout the Year' (*PW*, I.148). In his note to the full translation, Broome answers the question 'what reality there is in the relation, and whether any trees bear fruit all the year in this Island' by way of various classical authorities for extended seasons in other parts of the world, 'So that what *Homer* relates is in it self true, tho' not entirely of *Phaeacia*. Or perhaps it might be only intended for a more beautiful and poetical manner of describing the constant succession of one fruit after another in a fertile climate'.

15. gives: permits, encourages.
    blow: 'to bloom; to blossom' (*SJ*).

17. order'd Vines: Pope may recall Ogilby's version of Virgil's advice on vineyards in *Georgics*, II, *The Works of Publius Virgilius Maro* (1649), p. 66, where the same phrase is used.
    equal Ranks: more normally a military phrase (cf. *Essay on Criticism*, 179, and Commentary). Homer places no stress on the symmetry of the planting. In the essay, Pope asserts that the '*Vineyard* seems to have been a Plantation distinct from the *Garden*' (*PW*, I.148), hence the visual separation of the section in his verse. Homer introduces this aspect (122) with ἔνθα δέ ('there'), indicating a slight separation from what has gone before.

18. United Labours of the Year: Pope's addition. Dryden refers to 'the long Labours of the Year' in his translation 'From the First Book of Ovid's Metamorphoses', *Examen Poeticum* (1693), p. 24; in the same anthology, p. 417, Henry Sacheverell's translation 'From Virgil's First Georgick' ends with the phrase 'long expected Labours of the Year'. Gay, in his georgic *Rural Sports* (dedicated to Pope, and published in January 1713), writes of 'the revolving Labours of the Year' (I.38). Pope parodied the phrase 'united labours' in *The Dunciad Variorum*, III.324.

19-25. In the full translation, the long note (at VII.142) cites Dacier's authority to explain the variant states and colours of the grapes: '*Homer* distinguishes the whole into three orders: First, the grapes that have already been expos'd to the sun are trod; the second order is of the grapes that are exposed, while the others are treading; and the third, of those that are ripe to be gather'd, while the others are thus ordering. *Homer* himself thus explains it, by saying, that while some vines were loaded with black and mature grapes, others were green, or but just turning to blackness'. Pope bases his account on Homer, 123-6, omitting details about the drying floor and its location (123) and reordering or expanding other aspects of the scene.

19. Expanded from Homer, 124, 'ἑτέρας δ' ἄρα τε τρυγόωσιν' ('they gather the harvest

20   *Some dry the black'ning Clusters in the Sun,*
     Others to tread the liquid Harvest join,
     The groaning Presses foam with Floods of Wine.
     Here are the Vines in early Flow'r descry'd,
     Here Grapes discolour'd on the sunny Side,
25   *And there in* Autumn'*s richest Purple dy'd.*

     Beds of all various Herbs, for ever green,
     In beauteous Order terminate the Scene.

     Two plenteous Fountains the whole Prospect crown'd;
     This thro' the Gardens leads its Streams around,
30   *Visits each Plant, and waters all the Ground:*

---

of other [grapes]'). Cf. Ogilby, p. 90: 'ripe clusters load | The yielding Branches'.

21. liquid Harvest: recalled from Dryden's translation of Virgil, *Georgics*, II.753, *Works of Virgil*, p. 93: ''Tis then the Vine her liquid Harvest yields'; Pope reused the phrase at *Iliad*, XIV.139. There is no equivalent in Homer.

22. Floods of Wine: cf. 'Autumn', 74.

23. early Flow'r: In Homer (126), the flowers are actually shed, leaving immature grapes.

24. discolour'd: SJ understands 'discolour' to mean 'to change from the natural hue; to stain'. In the Greek, the grapes ὑποπερκάζουσιν ('begin to turn dark').

sunny Side: cf. Sandys's translation of Ovid, *Metamorphoses*, IV, *Ovid's Metamorphosis Englished* (1632), p. 120: 'So Apples shew vpon the sunny side';

25. Pope's addition.

26. for ever green: another phrase which would come back as parody, in *The Dunciad Varorium*, II.148: 'And the fresh Vomit run for ever green', though Pope's note to that line suggests a parody of the lines cited in Commentary to *Windsor-Forest*, 308. Homer's adjective γανόωσαι (128) means 'gleaming; bright; luxuriant'. Hobbes has 'Green beds of Herbs' here.

27. beauteous Order: Pope used this phrase of the zodiac decoration on Daphnis's bowl in 'Spring', 39–40, and may intend an allusion to 'cosmic' ordering; Homer's phrase at VII.127 is: κοσμηταὶ πρασιαί ('well laid-out garden beds'), but the first word tends to relate rather to decorative or martial ordering in Homeric Greek. Chapman's phrasing, 'the King did aime | To the preciseist order he could claime', 173–4, p. 102, also an addition to Homer, perhaps influences Pope's aesthetics here.

terminate the Scene: slightly indicated by Homer's 127, παρὰ νείατον ὄρχον ('by the lowest row of vines'), i.e. at the end of the vine section of the garden; Pope stresses rather the ordering of the visual prospect within the enclosed garden. In the essay, he states that the '*Beds of Greens . . .* at the Extremity of the Inclosure, in the Nature and usual Place of our *Kitchen Gardens*' (*PW.*, I.148), are, like the vineyard, distinct from the garden, and hence the visual separation once more of the verses, prompted by Homer's repeated 'ἔνθα δέ' (127; 'there').

28–34. Much expanded from Homer's looser formation (129–31): ἐν δὲ δύω κρῆναι ἡ μέν τ' ἀνὰ κῆπον ἅπαντα | σκίδναται, ἡ δ' ἑτέρωθεν ὑπ' αὐλῆς οὐδὸν ἵησι | πρὸς δόμον ὑψηλόν, ὅθεν ὑδρεύοντο πολῖται. ('Inside there are two water-sources: one disperses through the whole garden, the other on the other side takes a path under the courtyard to the lofty dwelling, whence the townspeople drew water'.)

28. Two plenteous Fountains: Homer's κρῆναι can mean fountains, springs, or wells. Ogilby, p. 90 and Chapman, 175, p. 102 both translate 'fountains'; Hobbes, 'Springs', one of which becomes a fountain in the town.

30. Visits: in the sense suggested by Milton, *Paradise Lost*, IV.238–40 (1674), p. 92: 'the

While that in Pipes beneath the Palace flows,
And thence its Current on the Town bestows;
To various Use their various Streams they bring,
The People one, and one supplies the King.

---

crisped Brooks . . . Ran Nectar, visiting each plant'; but Milton is describing (241–2) a natural Paradise, explicitly not ordered by 'nice Art | In Beds and curious Knots'.

33. Pope's addition.

34. The People . . . the King: In his essay, Pope understands the arrangement slightly differently from Temple (see the passage of Temple cited in the Headnote): 'The two Fountains are disposed very remarkably. They rose within the Inclosure, and were brought by Conduits or Ducts, one of them to water all Parts of the Gardens, and the other underneath the Palace into the Town, for the Service of the Publick' (*PW*, I.148). The antithetical or chiastic verse phrasing in the poem suggests some sort of mutually supportive political balance between Alcinous and his people which is not so neatly implied in Homer's looser practical formulation. Ogilby's phrasing, p. 90 may have influenced the image: 'First serves his House, and after serv'd the Town'. Homer's 'πολῖται', which Pope renders 'the People', means 'townspeople' or 'citizens'; Hobbes refers to 'the people'; Ogilby 'the Town'; Chapman 'the Citie', 179, p. 102.

20
EPIGRAM UPON TWO OR THREE
(1713)

Editors' Headnote

Composition and publication

The 'Epigram Upon Two or Three' was first published on 3 December 1713. There is no evidence of the period of composition, beyond the fact that it must have been circulating amongst Pope's acquaintance before publication, because it was alluded to by 'Alexis' (Henry Moore) in flirtatious correspondence with Teresa Blount on 30 September 1713 (see Mack 1985: 865n and Rumbold 1989: 61). The poem first appeared anonymously in the second edition of *Miscellaneous Poems and Translations*, which is dated '1714' on the title page but was advertised as 'Published this day' in *The Englishman* on 3 December 1713. The poem occupies the verso of a duplicate leaf with the page numbers 321 and 322 (the first page of the text of *Windsor-Forest*, also added to this edition, is also numbered 321); on the recto is printed a further poem 'Upon a Girl of Seven Years Old'. Neither carries an indication of authorship. In several surviving copies the leaf has been removed, leaving a stub (Ault 1949: 34; *TE*, VI.104–7); the reasons for this are not clear. In April 1714 the 'Epigram' was included and ascribed to Pope by John Oldmixon in his *Poems and Translations. By Several Hands*. Presumably in response to a query about the appearance of the poem in this collection, Pope wrote to Caryll on 19 November 1714, transcribing it and explaining its inclusion in the following terms: 'The thing they have been pleased to call a Receipt to make a Cuckold, is only six lines which were stolen from me, as follows'. Caryll's transcript of Pope's letter is preserved in the British Library (Add. MS 28618, fol. 41[r]; *Corr.*, I. 267).

The poem on the other side of the leaf, 'Upon a Girl of Seven Years Old', is attributed to Pope by Ault on the grounds that the other poems added to the second edition of *Miscellaneous Poems and Translations* (i.e. *Windsor-Forest*, *Ode for Musick*, *Essay on Criticism*, as well as the present 'Epigram') were by Pope and that his editorial influence was more obvious than in the first edition, and therefore the simplest way for him to fill any gap would have been to write something or supply material he had to hand. While this is true, and while it is also the case that the oblivion that succeeded this first and only printing of the poem does not necessarily invalidate an attribution to Pope, it is also the case that there is no external evidence linking the poem to him, as there is in the case of the present 'Epigram'. The 'Girl' of the title has not been identified, and the courtly compliment to her Athena-like wisdom and Venus-like beauty, while neat, is too conventional a conceit to be distinctive. In the absence of firm evidence of Pope's authorship, it has not been included in this volume.

Text

The text presented here is taken from the first edition of 1713. The various extant texts of the 'Epigram' are referred to in the apparatus as follows:

TS: (British Library, Add. MS 28618, f. 41; *IELM* PoA 338)

1713: Miscellaneous Poems and Translations, Second Edition, octavo (Griffith 32)

1714: Poems and Translations. By Several Hands, octavo (Griffith 31)

1726: Miscellany Poems, duodecimo (Griffith 164)

1727: Miscellanies. The Last Volume, octavo (Griffith 196)

1742: Miscellanies. The Fourth Volume, octavo (Griffith 564)

Models and sources

Originally the term 'epigram' simply denoted verse 'written on' something, such as an inscription on a monument, and it was therefore generally a short piece of verse with a clear point, not necessarily satirical. By Pope's time, however, it had come to mean a short poem with a sharp point, a miniature satire displaying barbed wit on a single subject, person or event: as Gay put it in the poem which prompted Pope's 'Verses design'd to be prefix'd to Mr. Lintott's Miscellany', 'Let short-breath'd Epigram its Force confine, | And strike at Follies in a single Line' ('On a Miscellany of Poems', 27–8; *Miscellaneous Poems and Translations* (1712), p. 169). The main model for this type was the Latin poet Martial (Marcus Valerius Martialis), author in the first century AD of over 1,100 examples published in twelve books. Martial's poems were by no means exclusively satiric, but he characterised the form himself, in the 'Praefatio' to book I, as abusive and coarse, devoted to commentary on actual details of everyday life. There were several editions of Martial in the seventeenth century, including a much-reprinted edition for the use of boys at Westminster School, first published in 1661, and it was a popular text for imitation and the display of wit: Cowley produced versions of several epigrams. At some point Pope owned a copy of an edition by Cornelius Schrevel published at Leiden in 1656 (Mack 1982: 424, item 113); the epigraph for the original 'The Rape of the Locke' was drawn from Martial, and his version of Martial, X.23 was published anonymously in the covertly edited *Poems on Several Occasions* (1717).

Martial's own model was Catullus (c. 84–c. 54 BC), many of whose poems of obscene invective were and are regarded as epigrams. Among the poems of Martial and Catullus are many on the subject of illicit sexual behaviour, such as adultery and cuckoldry, generally expressed in coarser terms than Pope uses here (or even in his later, more bitter usage of the form). Translations of epigrams by Catullus, perhaps by Matthew Prior, appeared in *Examen Poeticum* (1693), but classical epigram was not otherwise a form particularly highlighted by the Dryden–Tonson series of *Miscellanies*. There were no poems labelled 'epigram' in *Poetical Miscellanies: The Sixth Part*, in which Pope began his publishing career, or in Lintot's *Miscellaneous Poems and Translations* of 1712; there were no original epigrams and just one translation from Martial in Steele's *Poetical Miscellanies* of December 1713. Notable English exponents of the form included, however, Ben Jonson, whose book of *Epigrammes*, included in the *Workes* of 1616, contained 133 examples.

Context

Pope had included 'The Balance of Europe. An Epigram' in a letter to John Caryll, 19 July 1711 (*Corr.*, I.130). Much of his less sober verse was circulated in this private way, in particular those in short and perhaps damaging epigrammatic form, as in the smirking epigram of uncertain authorship, on the subject of Addison's *Cato*, that he sent Caryll on 30 April 1713 (*Corr.*, I.176), or 'On a Lady who P–st at the Tragedy of *Cato*' which was soon permitted to escape into print (see Headnote to 'Prologue to *Cato*'). Pope would go on to write at least twenty poems called 'epigram', of which the present example was the first certainly by him to appear in print, and several others which are epigrams in all but name.

The lightly satiric attitude towards contemporary sexual mores probably reflects comedies such as Wycherley's *Country-Wife* and Congreve's *Way of the World* as much as any actual social observation: in *Spectator*, no. 446, 1 August 1712, Addison complained: 'Cuckoldom is the Basis of most of our Modern Plays'. Resistance to stories of intrigue and adultery is made explicit in the same periodical (e.g. nos. 8, 9, 16, 34; 9, 10, 19 March, 9 April 1711), which might have reminded Pope, the author of 'January and May', that such items were not considered by everyone to be in good taste, at least in public. The pose of worldly-wise tolerance is of a piece with much of the verse that Pope shared with Cromwell and to a lesser extent with Caryll in the correspondence of these years; often Pope did not publish such items, at least until they could be safely mingled with the work of Swift in the *Miscellanies* of 1727–32. But the excising of the leaf on which the poem stands seems unlikely to have been simply an act of self-censorship on Pope's part, since the poem was anonymous and less objectionable on moral grounds than the acknowledged 'January and May'.

As noted, the poem was reprinted with Pope's name attached, under the title 'A Receipt to Make a Cuckold. By Mr. Pope', in *Poems and Translations. By Several Hands* (1714), p. 211, in a volume edited by Oldmixon and published by Curll's coadjutor John Pemberton. This was a hostile environment, as is confirmed by the inclusion of the epigrammatic 'Advice to Mr. Pope, On his intended Translation of Homer's Iliads' (anonymous; by John Hughes) at p. 245 (see Guerinot 1969: 15; the publication date was probably 13 April 1714, according to an advertisement in *The Post-Boy* of that date, not 7 April as Guerinot has it). In the 'Preface', p. 3, Oldmixon writes with obvious disingenuousness of the collection:

> *I know but of one* Poem *that has crept into it, which I would have had kept still in* Manuscript. *'Tis a very little One, and will be easily slipt over in so great a Number of Others that seem intended for the Press; which certainly that never was. Thus much was due to Justice, considering the Company it is in.*

Ault plausibly assumes that this is a hit at Pope's poem; the 'Company' otherwise includes a fairly Whiggish crowd of Oldmixon's acquaintance: Hughes, Rowe, Arthur Maynwaring and Garth, though Pope was on friendly terms with most of these and the book also includes work by the Tory Prior and by Pope's (dead) friend William Walsh. In fact, the allusion in the 'Preface' does not explicitly identify Pope's poem at all. Curll's involvement in this piece of espionage is also not explicit. He had already made significant inroads into the literary property of Prior, Swift and Rowe; if he were behind the volume it would constitute the first instance of his appropriation of Pope's work. Many of Pope's less salubrious pieces would find their way into Curll's collections, sometimes perhaps with Pope's connivance, from 1714 onwards.

It is possible that the excision was made to some stock copies after the poem was 'stolen' from him, as Pope put it to Caryll, and published under its more ribald title (which he quotes with either amusement or distaste) in order to render it more deniable in public even if he was prepared to own up to it in private. (It is also possible that the leaf was excised in the binding of some copies simply because of the duplication of numbering.) Pope's inclusion of the 'Epigram', with its Curllean title intact but with its authorship once more veiled, in the Pope–Swift *Miscellanies: Volume the Last*, was partly an act of reclamation, since Curll had reprinted it in 1726, and partly an opportunity to display, as if forced into it by Curll, some of his more unbuttoned wit in the company of Swift, another exponent of the form: Pope placed the poem in a group with six other epigrams (pp. 174–8), at least one of them by Swift.

Despite its risqué content and Curll's best endeavours to highlight the sexual aspects of Pope's oeuvre, the poem did not attract any further critical attention, hostile or otherwise, in Pope's lifetime. Its presence in *Miscellanies*, however, seems to have prompted an elaborate imitation of it by George Woodward in his 'Two or Three; or, A Receipt to make a French Beauty', *Poems on Several Occasions* (1730), pp. 79–80.

Epigram upon Two *or* Three.

TWO or *Three* Visits, *Two* or *Three* Bows,
Two or *Three* civil Things, *Two* or *Three* Vows,
Two or *Three* Kisses, *Two* or *Three* Sighs,
Two or *Three* Jesus's — and let me dyes —

Title. *1714:* A Receipt *to make a* CUCKOLD.; *1726–42:* Two or Three; | OR, A RECEIPT to make a CUCKOLD.
1. Visits, Two: TS: Visits, with two; *1714–42:* visits, and two
2. Things, Two: *1714:* Things, and two
3. Kisses, Two: TS, *1714–26:* kisses and two; *1727–42:* kisses, with two

---

Title. Epigram: This was the first of Pope's many exercises in this form to appear in print; see Headnote: Models.
Two or Three: perhaps a faintly blasphemous recollection of the words of Christ, 'For where two or three are gathered together in my Name, there am I in the midst of them', Matthew 18:20, relocated to a context in which the sanctified group of two becomes the adulterous group of three.
Title variant. Receipt: i.e. recipe; a common satiric device, as in *An Excellent New Receipt to Make Bad Husbands Good Ones* (1711) and *A Mess for the Devil. Or an Excellent New Receipt to Make a Junto* (1711). Pope's 'Receipt to make Soup. For the Use of Dean Swift' dates from about 1726; his comic 'Receit to make an Epick Poem' appeared in *The Guardian*, no. 78, 10 June 1713.
1. Visits: polite social calls. The unwritten rules of domestic visiting were a regular source of light satire for *The Tatler*, e.g. no. 109, 20 December 1709, and *The Spectator*, e.g. nos. 24 and 299, 28 March 1711 and 12 February 1712; but Oldham's poem 'Promising a Visit', in *Poems and Translations* (1683), Cotton's 'The Visit', in *Poems on Several Occasions* (1689) and John Hopkins's 'To a Lady, desiring a Visit', in *Amasia* (1700), suggest the word had strong amorous connotations in verse.

2. civil Things: gallant compliments. Cf. Pope to Caryll, 31 July 1710: 'the Tatler observes of women, that they are more subject to be infected with vanity than men, on account of their being more generally treated with civil things and compliments'. Pope uses the phrase again in his letter to Cromwell, 21 August 1710, *Corr.*, I.97; in both cases his main subject is epistolary compliments between men.

Vows: For the varying fates of amorous promises see 'January and May', 419 and 819; 'Autumn', 67–9; 'Sapho to Phaon', 107; *Rape of the Lock* (1717 version), V.117, 136.

3. Sighs: For sighing as a sign of desire, cf. 'January and May', 360, 417, 495.

4. Jesus's: an extravagant exclamation of passion. Because of blasphemy laws and moral censorship of the stage, 'Jesus' was rare as an expression in this sense in printed literature. Congreve's use of it in *The Double-Dealer* (1694), at I.i. (Lord Froth), II.i (Brisk); III.i. (Lady Plyant) and V.i (Brisk again), pp. 7, 16, 34, 78, was attacked by Jeremy Collier in his *Short View of the Immorality and*

5   *Two* or *Three* Squeezes, *Two* or *Three* Towses,
    With *Two* or *Three* hundred Pounds lost at their Houses,
    Can never fail Cuckolding *Two* or *Three* Spouses.

---

5. Squeezes, Two: TS, *1714–42:* Squeeses, and two
6. hundred: *1726–42:* thousand
  Pounds: *1727–42:* pound

Profaneness of the English Stage (1698), p. 64, particularly in respect of Lady Plyant, characterised in the 'Dramatis Personae' as 'Insolent to her Husband, and easie [sexually available] to any Pretender', and Congreve confessed: 'I had my self long since condemn'd it, and resolv'd to strike it out in the next Impression. I will not urge the *folly*, viciousness, or affectation of the Character to excuse it'; *Amendments of M. Collier's False and Imperfect Citations, &c.* (1698), p. 42.

  let me dyes: 'Let me die' is a cliché of overdone emotion in Restoration drama, e.g. Dryden, *Marriage a-la-Mode*, II.i (1673), p. 15: 'Let me die but he's a fine man'. Melantha, 'an affected lady' according to the 'Dramatis Personae', uses the phrase more than 30 times in the course of the play. Pope uses the phrase again, to be spoken by a sexually sinning woman in the context of a story of cuckoldry, in the 'Epilogue to Mr. Rowe's *Jane Shore*, Design'd for Mrs. Oldfield', 11.

5. Squeezes: cf. *The Rape of the Lock* (1714 version), I.97–8: 'When *Florio* speaks, what Virgin could withstand, | If gentle *Damon* did not squeeze her Hand?' Szilagyi (1986) notes that the word was not in 1713 in general use as a noun in this sense, and suggests that in accordance with the poem's increasing scale of physical intimacy it ought to indicate something more intimate than a squeeze of the hand, though *OED*'s 'close embrace' (sense 2b) dates from much later; also that it could have been an early instance of the meaning 'pressure for a bribe', prompting the monetary idea in 6. See also *Essay on Criticism*, 610, and Commentary.

  Towses: not given as a noun in *OED* before 1792. The senses of the verb make clear the sexual nature of the gesture: to towse is 'To pull (a woman) about rudely, indelicately, or in horse-play; to tousle' (1c); 'To disorder, dishevel (the hair, dress, etc.); to tumble, rumple (bed-clothes, sheets, etc.)' (2). It is often used thus in Restoration comedy, e.g. in the speeches and stage directions of Aphra Behn, *The Town-Fopp; or, Sir Timothy Tawdrey*, IV.i (1677), pp. 46–7. For further discussion of its sexual significance see Szilagyi (1986).

6. lost: i.e. at gaming, either with the husband to be cuckolded, to allay suspicion or act as compensation, or with the wife in question, as part of the process of seduction. For card games as part of a culture of flirtation and courtship see *Rape of the Lock* (1714 version), Canto III.

21
THE WIFE OF BATH HER PROLOGUE
(1713)

Editors' Headnote

Composition and publication

'The Wife of Bath Her Prologue' was first published on 29 December 1713. It is likely that both of Pope's 'Translations' from Chaucer were originally composed during the same period. For the date of the initial composition of this poem, see the Editors' Headnote to 'January and May' above. Sherburn (1934: 71) suggests that Gay's comedy *The Wife of Bath*, first performed in May 1713, might have 'suggested' Pope's translation but, as *TE* (II.5n) points out, this seems unlikely in the light of the 'Advertisement' in the third volume of the 1736 *Works*, in which Pope ascribed the translations from Chaucer to the period immediately following the publication of Dryden's *Fables* in 1700, and the note on p. 135 which specifies that 'January and May' was done at the age of 16 or 17. There is no corresponding note for the present poem, however, and it was no doubt revised for its appearance as a result of Gay's interest in the story; there is some possibility that Pope contributed to an epilogue for Gay's play (see below: Models). On 5 October 1713, Pope received 15 guineas from Jacob Tonson the younger for 'The Wife of Bath's Prologue' and 'The Arrival of Ulysses in Ithaca' (see *Corr.*, I.191n), and three months later the 'Prologue' was published in Steele's *Poetical Miscellanies*, on 29 December 1713 (the volume is dated 1714). Pope's poem was the opening item, occupying pp. 1–27.

Text

The text presented here is taken from the first edition of 1713. The two states of Steele's *Poetical Miscellanies* (Griffith 24 and 25) display minor variation in the punctuation and typography of 'The Wife of Bath Her Prologue', together with the introduction of a misprint, at line 345, retained in subsequent editions. The state identified by Griffith as Variant a. (Griffith 24) has been chosen as copy text. Substantive revision is confined to the *Works* of 1717 and 1736. The various extant texts of 'The Wife of Bath Her Prologue' are referred to in the apparatus as follows:

1713a: *Poetical Miscellanies*, octavo (Griffith 24)

1713b: *Poetical Miscellanies*, octavo (Griffith 25)

1717: *Works*, quarto (Griffith 79)

1736: *Works*, vol.III, octavo (Griffith 417, 418)

1751: *Works*, vol.II, octavo (Griffith 644)

Models and sources

For the reception, influence and status of Chaucer in Pope's day, editions and imitations of his verse from Dryden onwards, and Pope's own views on Chaucer, see Headnote to 'January and May'. As noted there, Pope used a 1598 edition of Chaucer as his source and was clearly influenced by Dryden's *Fables Ancient and Modern* (1700). Dryden had provided a modern retelling of 'The Wife of Bath her Tale' but had pointedly avoided the 'Prologue', popular as it would have been, on grounds of its lubricious character; Pope's title clearly recollects Dryden's in its phrasing. As with the earlier item, we quote from and refer to the edition of Chaucer that Pope read, but as this was unlineated we use the line-numbering of the *Riverside* edition of Chaucer (Benson 1988). In this case, the modern text differs from the 1598 text mostly in spelling and punctuation; there are no extra sections known to Pope but excluded from modern versions, though there are some significant verbal differences. One parenthetic insertion in the modern text (44a–f) was not known to Pope, but it does not affect lineation.

The 'Wife' had some literary life independent of (though always derived from) Chaucer: she is several times quoted as an authority on marital and other matters in the Third Partition (Love Melancholy) of Burton's *Anatomy of Melancholy* (see Commentary to 7, 94–7, 217–18, 327–8). In 1665 Richard Brathwait published *A Comment upon the Two Tales of our Ancient, Renowned, and Ever-Living Poet Sr Jeffray Chaucer, Knight* (1665), 'who for his rich fancy, pregnant invention and present composure deserved the countenance of a prince, and his laureat honor'. This included two of the more raucous characters, the Miller and the Wife of Bath, with a sequence of short passages from the 'Prologue' and 'Tale' of each, in black letter, with a 'comment' or expanded prose gloss, segment by segment, on Chaucer's verse; 'A Comment upon Chaucer's Prologue to the Wife of Bath's Tale' occupies pp. 60–149. (For a scholarly text of the book see Spurgeon 1901.) Brathwait seems amused at the Wife's self-presentation and unembarrassed by her sexual adventures, often entering into the character and speaking in her persona. It is possible that Pope knew the work (see Commentary at 249). *The Wanton Wife of Bath*, a broadside ballad ('to the tune of, Flying Fame') produced at about the same time and reprinted at least seven times to 1713, depicts the Wife arriving at Heaven's gate, where she proceeds to best a number of biblical figures, including Solomon and Paul, in debate about their own sins, before finally persuading Christ himself that she deserves mercy. The 'excellent old Ballad' was quoted approvingly by Addison, in *Spectator*, no. 247, 13 December 1711.

'Chaucer's Characters, or the Introduction to the Canterbury Tales', a version of the General Prologue by Pope's friend Betterton (widely believed to have been heavily revised, at least, by Pope; see Lonsdale, IV.12 and 257n), appeared posthumously in the 1712 *Miscellaneous Poems and Translations* alongside items 8–14 above; the section on the Wife of Bath occupies pp. 270-2. Gay's comedy, *The Wife of Bath*, which put the character energetically on stage, failed at Drury Lane on 12–13 May 1713 despite a puff for it in Steele's *Guardian*, no. 50, 8 May 1713. (A revised version would fail again in 1730.) Gay's play, in which 'Alison' (the Wife) appears, alongside Chaucer himself, entirely at home in a Restoration comedy of intrigue, resourcefully pursuing sexual pleasure and a sixth husband, was eclipsed by Addison's *Cato*, and passed unnoticed. There is a possibility that Pope wrote or contributed to the (unsigned) 'Epilogue' in the character of the Wife, as lines 25–8 of it bear a strong resemblance to 308–10 of this poem (see Commentary at that point). Gay and Pope had been friends since 1711 (see Pope to Cromwell, 21 December 1711; *Corr.*, I.138); Gay's *Rural Sports* had been dedicated to Pope in January 1713 (see Headnote to *Windsor-Forest*) and a return contribution to his friend's play was certainly a possibility. The manner of the Wife's delivery in the 'Epilogue' is similar in tone to Pope's version of Chaucer's 'Prologue'; but this quatrain is the only close verbal link and could as easily have been generated by sight of Pope's poem by any of Gay's friends, or included in a several-hands effort. The 'Epilogue' was never claimed by Pope. For discussion of Gay's friendship with Pope at the time of the play, see Nokes (1995: 124–7).

Context

Like 'January and May', 'The Wife of Bath Her Prologue, from Chaucer' was published in a polite verse anthology, once more under the Tonson imprint, with Steele as the editor, and, as in the earlier instance, Pope's contributions were in miscellaneous vein: nos. 21 and 22 below, and 19 above, which had already been published. The volume includes poems by several of Pope's friends, including Gay and Parnell, and also several by his emerging enemies, such as Tickell, Philips and Eusden. It was therefore an attempt at an ecumenical volume, for the most part avoiding the party divisions already in place across literary London. Warton (*Works of Pope*, II.147) notes that the librettist and poet John Hughes withdrew his contributions from the volume because of the presence of the present poem, which he deemed 'too obscene for the gravity of his character'; the story lacks corroboration, however.

The correspondence between Pope and Steele, consisting of about 14 letters, dates between July 1711 and December 1712; Pope mentioned Steele a few times after that in letters to Caryll, including an anecdote about a Jacobite acquaintance who had taken Pope to task for collaboration with the enemy (to Caryll, 12 June 1713; *Corr.*, I.177). He was enjoying Steele's company in the summer of 1713 (to Caryll, 14 August 1713; *Corr.*, I.185), but feeling the pressure of the party divide by 17 October 1713 (*Corr.*, I.193–4), when he writes to Caryll about the demise of *The Guardian*, to which he had contributed what seems to be his last periodical essay, no. 173, 29 September 1713 (see 'The Gardens of Alcinous'). Steele franked a letter for him in January 1714 (Sherburn 1958b: 401) but was increasingly engaged with Whig political journalism by this time, and Pope was more inclined to the company of the Tory propagandist Swift; Pope commented stiffly on the curse of party violence when Steele was expelled from the House of Commons on 18 March 1714, lamenting 'I am really amazed that so much of that vile and pernicious quality should be joined with so much natural good-humour as I think Mr Steele has' (to Caryll, 19 March 1714; *Corr.*, I.215; for a later comment on Steele's partisan zeal, see *OAC.*, I.60, item 146, June 1739). Though Steele subscribed to Pope's *Iliad*, they were never again close; Pope noted with amusement Steele's knighthood, in a letter to Caryll of April 1715 (*Corr.*, I.290), but he did not make him the target of any later satirical attack of the kind deployed against Addison.

In modern texts of Chaucer, the Wife of Bath's 'Prologue' occupies 828 lines, discounting the segment 44a–f; Pope's version is cut down almost to half that, at 441 lines. Pope condenses material, particularly during the first 150 lines of his poem, and rearranges elements significantly at 377–412. As might be expected, some of the work is done in the interests of epigrammatic couplet art: the section on wicked wives at 379–86 provides several examples of exact couplets generated from more casual three-line micro-narratives in Chaucer, and 86–99 shows the determination to produce antithesis from the looser formulations of Chaucer, 248–70. As with 'January and May', Pope trims much scholastic or historical citation (e.g. 17–18, 29–30, 46–55, 134–47, 344, *post* 386, 409–12); a good deal of the clerical misogyny quoted by Chaucer's Wife is cut from Pope's version (*post* 99, *post* 147, *post* 412), though plenty remains; fewer cuts are made to the Wife's defensive rebuttals. Direct references to Christ (see e.g. 221) are generally dropped or replaced with more innocuous formulations, and classical references are imported in a general heightening of tone (64–5, 343–5). The Wife's digressiveness and overt awkwardness in picking up the thread of her narrative are much diminished. Some of the animal imagery is cut (e.g. 68–73), but some is extended (e.g. the cat analogy at 140–7). Some colloquialism (hawthorn berries, old shoes, the Dunmow flitch) has disappeared (*post* 63, 351, 373), though much quasi-proverbial expression survives (49, 147, 217–18, 227–8, 239–40, 298–9). The character of marital confession is somewhat toned down (152–65, 257, 300–6) and direct bawdy is all but expunged (see Commentary at 21–2, *post* 45, 51, 136–7, 201, 328). Pope omits Chaucer's Wife's unembarrassed use of obvious euphemisms ('*belle chose*', 'queynte'), though he does risk the notorious 'quaint' pun at 259, and he retains the obscure '*Catterwaw'd*' at 147. A good deal of innuendo supplies the omission (see Commentary at 156, 169, 211, 234, 285, 371–2), along with some more modern homely phrasing ('serve our Turn', 28; 'clear my Quail-pipe', 213).

Much of what Pope adds by way of modernisation is the language of romance, consciously invoking the amorous fiction and marital-intrigue comedies of the Restoration: 'fond' (58); 'Splenatick' (90); 'Fool-Gallant' (95); 'all the Woman' (105); 'My Life! my Dear!' (109); 'cully' (161); 'Wheedling' and 'Stratagem' (163); 'Gamester' (220); 'Conquests' and 'Charms' (226); 'Miss' (230); 'knack' (257); 'Spark' (263); 'Masquerade' (284); together with the gestures of modern courtship at 66–7, 175, and 203–4. Some pithy epigrams on the subject are supplied (e.g. 103). This is the world of 'The Rape of the Locke' and its later incarnation, as much as of the Canterbury Pilgrims, and one effect of the shift is to make the Wife look less like a victim of circumstance (married off at the age of 12, in Chaucer, but 15, and apparently more deliberately, in Pope; see 7–8) and more like the sort of calculating strategist of sex and money that Defoe would develop with his (also five-times-married) heroine Moll Flanders in 1722: there is more economic and legal language in Pope's Wife's autobiography (see e.g. 205–8) and she accepts the logic of specifically female gold-digging and exploitation (171ff.) more equably than Chaucer's figure does.

Pope's updating of the 'Prologue' can be seen as another of his early attempts to occupy the adult ground of marital comedy and masculine discussion of the nature of women. Chaucer's poem was part of the set of Prologues and Tales sometimes referred to as 'the Marriage group' (involving the Wife of Bath, the Clerk, the Merchant, and the Franklin), a contribution to medieval debates about the status of women and relations between the sexes (for relevant texts and discussion see Blamires 1992 and Rigby 1996: chapter 4). 'The Merchant's Tale', Pope's source for 'January and May', stands immediately before the Wife's 'Prologue' in the 1598 Chaucer, and there was thus for Pope a natural continuity (which has disappeared in modern editions) between an externally narrated story of the adultery of a young wife boldly deceiving a foolish old husband and a personally confessed but decontextualised narrative of what might well have seemed like the afterlife of the 'May' character. The dramatic intervention of one of the Wife's listeners, the Pardoner, is cut (*post* 55), ensuring that the Wife dominates her own tale more than she does in Chaucer, where her 'Prologue' is also subject to interjections from other characters before her 'Tale' begins.

Pope was no doubt influenced by the portrayal of virago characters and cheating wives in Restoration comedy, and there was a strong tradition of masculine satires against women in the Restoration period, many of them derived from Juvenal's notorious sixth satire (for a survey of these see Nussbaum 1984). Compared to such items as Gould's *Love Given O're: or, A Satyr Against the Pride, Lust, and Inconstancy, &c. of Woman* (1682 and much reprinted; see Commentary to 1–2), Pope's poem seems relatively benign, in accordance with the Wife's comic status in popular literature. The Wife's declaration (366–8) that stories about women would be different if women wrote them meant something different in 1713 from what it had meant in the 1380s, because it had already been partially fulfilled, in the shape of defiant defences of women by Sarah Fyge Egerton, Lady Mary Chudleigh and others, as well as in calls for independent female education by Mary Astell, and a full range of 'stories' in all genres, including drama, by Aphra Behn and other women writers. Pope's Wife often appears to echo the sentiments of the fairy queen from 'January and May' and this note too sounds differently in Pope's context (see e.g. 363–4). It was perhaps part of Pope's creation of his own poetic manliness to present a knowing comic tolerance towards a robustly sexual female character, as it was part of his sense of paternalistic responsibility to attempt to intervene on behalf of women in his Catholic circle trapped in abusive or otherwise unhappy marriages (see Rumbold 1989: chapters 3 and 4). McLaverty (2001: 73) notes that there is a suggestively sexual element to the sequence of illustrations for Pope's Chaucer translations and other poems about errant women in the *Works* of 1717, covertly signalling and acknowledging the riskiness of this venture: the poem is there placed between 'January and May' and 'Sapho to Phaon', offering a transition from wanton sexual confidence, via fading sexual attractiveness, to the plangent melancholy of sexual loss, a theme shortly to be explored in 'Eloisa to Abelard' (and the 'Verses to the Memory of an Unfortunate Lady'). Pope's Wife mentions the historical Heloise and sometimes sounds like Pope's conception of her (see 223–4, 324 and 361), striking an elegiac note not present in Chaucer (see Commentary to 227–8). Caretta (2009) further examines the illustration and placing of the poem in relation to the *Rape of the Lock* in the 1717 *Works*.

Warburton reports (*Works*, 1751, I.v) that Pope had intended not to include the 'Juvenile translations' in the final edition of his *Works* 'on account of the levity of some, the freedom of others, and the little importance of any', and that only copyright issues (vaguely and unconvincingly suggested) required their reprinting. Pope otherwise expressed no regret about their presence in his oeuvre and continued to praise Chaucer's humour lovingly into his final decade (see Headnote to 'January and May'), so this is probably an instance of disingenuous clerical disapproval. Warton (1782: 69–72, and see *Works of Pope*, II.147), commented: 'One cannot but wonder at his choice, which perhaps nothing but his youth could excuse'; as noted, Dryden had declined the 'Prologue' on the score of indecency. However, Warton concedes that Pope has 'omitted or softened the grosser or more offensive passages', and that the lines are 'spirited and easy, and have, properly enough, a free, colloquial air' (see also Commentary to 359).

THE
WIFE of *BATH*
HER
PROLOGUE,
From *CHAUCER*.

Behold the Woes of Matrimonial Life,
And hear with Rev'rence an experienc'd Wife!
To dear-bought Wisdom give the Credit due,
And think, for once, a Woman tells you true.
5   In all these Trials I have born a Part;
I was myself the Scourge that caus'd the Smart;
For, since Fifteen, in Triumph have I led
Five Captive Husbands from the Church to Bed.

Half title. 1717–51: THE | WIFE of *BATH.* | FROM | CHAUCER.

1-8. Combining, very loosely, material from Chaucer, 1-8 and 172-5.

1-2. Chaucer, 1-3, fol. 32ᵛ: 'Experience, though none authoritie | Were in this worlde, is right ynow for mee | To speake of wo that is in mariage'. Pope's phrasing is close to conventional satire; e.g. Robert Gould, *Love Given O're: or, A Satyr against the Pride, Lust, and Inconstancy, &c. of Woman* (1682), p. 10: 'Are these (ye Gods) the Virtues of a Wife? | The Peace that Crowns a Matrimonial Life?' The rhyme recurs at 132-3.

3-4. Pope's addition.

3. dear-bought Wisdom: already proverbial, e.g. Roger Ascham, *The Scholemaster* (1570), p. 18: 'It is costlie wisdom, that is bought by experience'.

6. Scourge . . . Smart: Chaucer, 175, fol. 33ᵛ: 'my selfe hath ben the whippe'.

7. Fifteen: regarded by Pope as the age of sexual maturity; cf. *Rape of the Lock* (1714), IV. 58, where 'Spleen' (related to female hysteria) is said to 'rule the Sex to Fifty from Fifteen'. Chaucer (4) has the Wife married first at the age of 12, the earliest she could be married under canon law; Burton discusses the significance of Chaucer's lines in *Anatomy of Melancholy* (1621), p. 540 (Third Partition, sect. 2, Memb. 1, Subsect. 2). Gay's Alison reflects on the precocity of development in Italian females from ages 12 to 14 in *The Wife of Bath*, I (1713), p. 6.

7-8. Triumph . . . Captive: Pope's Wife mimics the actions of Roman emperors leading captive tribal kings in a Roman 'triumph' (cf. 'Prologue to *Cato*', 27-30, Commentary). Cf. also Dryden's 'The Rape of the Sabines, from Ovid', 144, *Poetical Miscellanies: The Fifth Part* (1704), p. 15: 'But nought availing, all are Captives led, | Trembling and blushing, to the Genial Bed' (meaning wives, not husbands). Chaucer's wife (5-6) merely thanks God that she has had five husbands; Pope also cuts her acknowledgement that they were all 'worthy men in her degree [according to their rank]' (8).

        Christ saw a Wedding once, the Scripture says,
10   And saw but one, 'tis thought, in all his Days;
        Whence some infer, whose Conscience is too nice,
        No pious Christian ought to marry twice.

        But let them read, and solve me, if they can,
        The Words addrest to the *Samaritan*:
15   Five times in lawful Wedlock she was join'd;
        And sure the certain Stint was ne'er defin'd.

        Encrease and multiply was Heav'ns Command,
        And that's a Text I clearly understand.
        This too, *Let men their Sires and Mothers leave,*
20   *And to their dearer Wives for ever cleave.*

9-16. Chaucer, 9-25, much condensed.

9. For the wedding at Cana see John 2:1-11. Brathwait, *A Comment Upon the Two Tales* (1665), pp. 61-2, paraphrases Chaucer's Wife's argument, which he describes as 'for her own purpose', albeit derived from Scripture. Chaucer's editors suggest the source for the wife's theological debate about marriage was Jerome, *Epistola adversus Jovinianum*, I.13-15.

11-12. Chaucer's Wife (9-13) is told that she personally should not marry more than once: Pope's makes the case general.

11. nice: 'scrupulously and minutely cautious ... fastidious' (*SJ*); much later, in this sense, than Chaucer.

13. solve me: explain to me; Pope's addition.

14. Samaritan: John 4:16-18, where Christ, having noted her five previous husbands, reproves a Samaritan woman for cohabiting outside marriage. Chaucer's wife quotes Christ's words and appears to be puzzled by the statement 'that ilke man that now hat the | Is not thine husbonde'; Brathwait (p. 62) makes it clear that the point that she is not married to the man she is currently living with. Pope's Wife quotes scripture as if it sanctioned her own history.

16. Stint: limit; for the word *SJ* cites Dryden, 'The exteriors of mourning, a decent funeral, and black habits, are the usual stints of common husbands' (from the dedicatory epistle to *Eleonora: A Panegyrical Poem*, 1692). Cf. also Dryden's note to the sixth satire of Persius: '*Chrysippus* cou'd never bring his Propositions to a certain stint'; *Satires of Decimus Junius Juvenalis* (1693), p. 87. Chaucer says the 'numbre' had no 'trew definicion', 24-5, fol. 32^v.

17-27. Chaucer, 26-48, much condensed.

17-18. Pope omits Chaucer's Wife's dismissive comments on the glossing of scriptures before her quotation here, 26-7.

17. Genesis 1:22, 28; 8:17; 9:7, etc. Pope echoes the Douay-Rheims (*DV*) version 'increase and multiply', whereas the King James (*AV*) version reads 'be fruitful and multiply'. There is no trace, in either Chaucer or Pope, of the Wife having children with her husbands, the implication being that she chooses to 'understand' (also Chaucer's word) the injunction as a license to have sex. Brathwait is amused by the Wife's transition from a difficult text to one 'far more easie and proper for her purpose' (p. 63).

19-20. Genesis 2:24: 'Therefore shall a man leaue his father and his mother, and shall cleaue vnto his wife: and they shalbe one flesh' (*AV*); the phrasing is very similar in Matthew 19:5-6. Chaucer, 31, has 'take to me' rather than 'cleave' to a generalised wife. Pope omits here Chaucer 32-4, on the question of number once more.

More Wives than One by *Solomon* were try'd,
Or else the Wisest of Mankind's bely'd.
I've had, my self, full many a merry Fit,
And trust in Heav'n I may have many yet.
25   For when my transitory Spouse, unkind ⎫
      Shall die, and leave his woful Wife behind, ⎬
      I'll take the next good Christian I can find. ⎭

Paul, knowing One cou'd never serve our Turn,
Declar'd 'twas better far to Wed, than Burn;
30   There's Danger in assembling Fire and Tow,
I grant 'em that, and what it means you know.
The same Apostle too has elsewhere own'd

21–2. Chaucer, 35–44, leaving out much of the Wife's comparison of her own with Solomon's sexual pleasures. For Solomon's many marriages see 1 Kings 11:1 and 3: 'But King Solomon loued many strange women, (together with the daughter of Pharaoh) women of the Moabites, Ammonites, Edomites, Sidonians & Hittites... And he had seuen hundred wiues, Princesses, and three hundred concubines: and his wiues turned away his heart' (*AV*).

For his wisdom, cf. 1 Kings 4:30, 5:12 and 11:43; 1 Chronicles 28, 29; 2 Chronicles 1–10, etc. Solomon features in the debate on marriage begun in 'January and May', 673–87; in the ballad *The Wanton Wife of Bath* (see Headnote: Context) the Wife makes short work of Solomon's errors and follies as a husband.

22. bely'd: misrepresented (*TE*). Not in Chaucer.

23. merry Fit: Cf. 'January and May', 750–1. In Chaucer, 41–3, fol. 33ʳ, the 'merry fitte' is Solomon's own, on the first night of each new marriage. A 'Fit' is an episode or experience, in this case sexual.

25. transitory: temporary, 'speedily vanishing' (*SJ*).

unkind: as if deliberately making the Wife suffer by his death; an irony not in Chaucer (45–8), where the Wife is more equable in welcoming number six. Chaucer's Wife appears to be speaking from a present position of widowhood (504, 826–7); Pope's 254 and final lines also imply this.

27. good Christian: cf. 'A Farewell to London in the Year 1715', 15: 'And *Garth*, the best good Christian he, | Although he knows it not', a non-ironic usage; *Epistle to a Lady*, 67–8: 'A very Heathen in the carnal part, | Yet still a sad, good Christian at her heart', an ironic usage. Chaucer, 48, fol. 33ʳ, has 'Some christen man'.

28–35. Chaucer, 49–76 and 89–90, greatly condensed, omitting much repetition and material on Old Testament polygamy at 53–61.

28–9. Paul: 1 Corinthians 7–9: 'it is better to marry than to be burnt'; this leaves out, as Chaucer's Wife does at 52, Paul's sense that sexual continence is best of all. Paul is one of the many biblical figures defeated in debate by the Wife in the ballad *The Wanton Wife of Bath*.

28. serve our Turn: cf. 295, and 'January and May' 261; a Restoration euphemism.

30–1. Relocated out of sequence from Chaucer, 89–90.

30. assembling: putting close together; also Chaucer's verb.

Tow: plant fibres prepared for spinning.

31. what ... know: 'Ye know what this ensample may resemble', Chaucer, 90, fol. 33ʳ. Brathwait glosses: 'It is good for young Folk to avoid occasion; for it is that which breeds a Contagion' (p. 68). Cf. 141. It had continued in proverbial use, e.g. John Philips, *Maronides; or Virgil Travestie* (1672), p. 140: 'What need I tell you, you well know, | She's nothing else but fire and Tow'.

32. own'd: admitted.

No Precept for Virginity he found:
'Tis but a Counsel — and we Women still
35   Take which we like, the Counsel, or our Will.

I envy not their Bliss, if He or She
Think fit to live in perfect Chastity,
Pure let them be, and free from Taint of Vice;
I, for a few slight Spots, am not so nice.
40   Heav'n calls us different Ways, on these bestows
One proper Gift, another grants to those:
Not ev'ry Man's oblig'd to sell his Store,
And give up all his Substance to the Poor;
Such as are perfect, may, I can't deny;
45   But by your Leave, Divines, so am not I.

Full many a Saint, since first the World began,
Liv'd an unspotted Maid in spite of Man:
Let such (a God's Name) with fine Wheat be fed,

---

33. Precept: 'a rule authoritatively given . . . a commandment' (*SJ*); also Chaucer's word (65, fol. 33). The scriptural source is 1 Corinthians 7:25, again omitting the corollary that celibacy is better.

34-5. This 'female' confession is Pope's, not Chaucer's.

34. 'Tis but a counsel: 'counsailing is no commaundement', Chaucer, 67, fol. 33ʳ; 'counsel' is 'piece of advice' or 'recommendation'.
 still: always.

36-45. Condensing Chaucer, 77–114, at some distance from his discussion of virginity and chastity, which was more relevant to a pre-Reformation England populated in part by nuns (as in the Wife's audience).

38. Taint of Vice: perhaps recalled from Viola's use of the phrase in Shakespeare, *Twelfth Night*, III.iv.392.

39. She is less particular about the minor sins of sexual pleasure. For 'Spots' see 47, and for 'nice', 11.

41. proper: particular, personal. The phrase is from Chaucer, 103, fol. 33ʳ: 'And ever-ich hath of God a proper gift', alluding to 1 Corinthians 7:7: 'but euery man hath his proper gift of God' (*AV*).

42-3. Chaucer, 107–10, cites as Christ's the injunction to the rich man to sell his possessions and give to the poor (Matthew 19:21, Luke 18:22, etc.).

42. Store: possessions.

43. Substance: property.

45. Divines: clergymen or theologians, cf. 55. Chaucer's Wife makes the same point in almost the same words, but to 'lordings' (112, fol. 33ʳ); in Chaucer her audience was predominantly lay, though there were several religious figures on the pilgrimage; Pope's change seems like an additional irony.
 At this point, Pope omits Chaucer's Wife's mocking discussion of the point of having sexual organs, 115–38.

46-55. Chaucer, 139–62, omitting amongst much else the Wife's mention of Christ's own virginity, 139; discussions of virginity and chastity were more intense in pre-Reformation England than in Pope's period.

47. unspotted Maid: cf. 39. Not in Chaucer. A common phrase, known from e.g. Spenser, *Faerie Queene*, I.vi.46: 'Then hunt the steps of pure vnspotted Maid'.

48. a: in.

And let us honest Wives eat Barley Bread.
50 For me, I'll keep the Post assign'd by Heav'n,
And use the copious Talent it has giv'n;
Let my good Spouse pay Tribute, do me Right,
And keep an equal Reck'ning ev'ry Night;
His proper Body is not his, but mine;
55 For so said *Paul,* and *Paul*'s a sound Divine.

Know then, of those five Husbands I have had,
Three were just tolerable, two were bad.
The three were Old, but rich and fond beside,
And toil'd most piteously to please their Bride:
60 But since their Wealth (the best they had) was mine,
The rest, without much Loss, I cou'd resign.

---

49. Barley Bread: cheap (ordinary) bread, suitable for everyday appetites. In modern texts of Chaucer, 144–5, the wives do not 'eat' the bread, they are 'hoten' (called) it, but in Pope's 1598 edition, fol. 33ᵛ, the wives do eat it. Brathwait (pp. 71–2), explains: 'Virgins are to be fed with Purest Manchet [a small fine loaf], because their Degree is Highest; Wives with Barly Bread, because their condition is lower'. The phrase was still current in the later seventeenth century, as in Shadwell, *The Woman Captain,* I (1680), p. 10: 'let us have some Wheat Bread, for I have gotten the Griping ... with Rye and Barley Bread'. Chaucer's Wife goes on, as Pope's does not, to allege that Christ refreshed 'many a man' with inferior bread (the story of the loaves and fishes story from John 6:9, with a carnal hint). For the complex theological and cultural iconography in play in Chaucer's image, see the note to Chaucer, 144–5, in Benson (1988).

51. Replacing Chaucer's Wife's more straightforward promise at 149, fol. 33ᵛ: she 'wol use myn instrument' (a word already in play for the male sexual organs at 132). Pope's version appears to allude to the parable of the talents, in Matthew 25:14–30, with a somewhat risky sexual twist.

52–3. The economic metaphor is loosely based on Chaucer, 153–5, and 130–1; the Wife interprets the theological notion of 'conjugal debt' (mutual sexual obligation) to her own advantage.

52. Tribute: form of payment signifying subjection; not in Chaucer.

53. equal Reck'ning: accurate account of what he owes her, a term from book-keeping.

54–5. Chaucer, 158–9, fol. 33ᵛ: 'I haue the power during al my life | Upon his proper body, and nat he'. The Wife quotes only her rights, not the mutual obligation set out in Paul, 1 Corinthians 7:4: 'The wife hath not power of her owne body, but the husband: and likewise also the husband hath not power of his owne body, but the wife' (*AV*). She also ignores his assertion of the subordination of wives, e.g. at Ephesians 5:22.

At this point in Chaucer (163–92) one of the listeners, the Pardoner, interrupts, to query the wife's evidence about marriage, a state he is contemplating; she warns him that worse is to come in her stories of married life, but concludes that nobody should take offence, as 'mine entent is not but to play'.

56–63. Condensed from Chaucer, 193–216.

57. 'Thre of hem were good, and two were bad', Chaucer, 196, fol. 33ᵛ.

58. fond: 'foolishly tender; injudiciously indulgent' (*SJ*); cf. 'January and May', 188. Not in Chaucer.

59. toil'd: cf. 'January and May', 386.

piteously: Chaucer, 202, fol. 33ᵛ, has the same word; but his Wife laughs openly when thinking about 'How pitously a night I made hem to swinke [labour]'.

THE WIFE OF BATH HER PROLOGUE (1713) 659

    Sure to be lov'd, I took no Pains to please,
    Yet had more Pleasure far than they had Ease.

       Presents flow'd in apace: With Show'rs of Gold,
65   They made their Court, like *Jupiter* of old.
    If I but smil'd, a sudden Youth they found,
    And a new Palsie seiz'd them when I frown'd.

       Ye Sov'reign Wives! give Ear, and understand;
    Thus shall ye speak, and exercise Command.
70   For never was it giv'n to Mortal Man,
    To lye so boldly as we Women can.
    Forswear the Fact, tho' seen with both his Eyes,
    And call *your Maids* to Witness how he lies.

       Hark old Sir *Paul* ('twas thus I used to say)
75   Whence is our Neighbour's Wife so rich and gay?
    Treated, caress'd, where-e'er she's pleas'd to roam —
    I sit in Tatters, and immur'd at home!
    Why to her House do'st thou so oft repair?
    Art thou so Amorous? Is she so fair?

---

79. *1717–51:* Art thou so am'rous? and is she so fair?

62-3. Pope uses the same rhyme words as Chaucer, 213–14, but places greater emphasis on pleasure than Chaucer, who stresses monetary gain.
    At this point Pope omits Chaucer's Wife's jocular reference (217–18) to the Dunmow flitch, a side of bacon annually awarded to a couple who have not quarrelled during the year.

64-7. Replacing simpler and more homely detail in Chaucer, 219–23.

64-5. This allusion, not in Chaucer, is to the seduction of Danae by Zeus (Jupiter), who entered the tower (in which she was immured) in a shower of gold. Jupiter mentions the story himself among his list of erotic conquests in Pope's *Iliad*, XIV.363; cf. also 'The First Book of Statius his Thebais', 356–7.

66-7. For the alternate powers of female smiles and frowns, cf. 'Rape of the Locke', II.122–5; not in Chaucer.

67. Palsie: paralysis.

68-73. Chaucer, 224–34, omitting a story of a mad talking bird (a chough), which reveals wifely adulteries, 232.

68. *Ye Sov'reign Wives:* 'Ye wise wiues', Chaucer, 225, fol. 33^v; female 'sovereignty' is, however, the theme of the Wife's eventual 'Tale'.

70-3. Cf. 'January and May', 660–72.

73. Maids *to Witness:* The notion is also in Chaucer, 233.

74-85. Chaucer, 235–47 (and 262), fairly closely, but omitting Chaucer's Wife's suggestion that her husband is having an affair with their maid.

74. old Sir Paul: 'Sir olde keynarde', Chaucer, 235, fol. 33^v; 'keynarde' or kaynard is 'dotard' (cf. 136–7, Commentary). 'Paul' is unexplained, but the apostle has been strongly present from 28 to 55, and this might constitute another gesture of control on the Wife's part.

75. gay: 'fine; showy' (*SJ*); also Chaucer's rhyme word, 236, fol. 33^v.

76. Treated: given treats; cf. 115.

77. immur'd: walled up. The line is expressed more strongly than in Chaucer, 238, fol. 33^v: 'I sitte at home, and haue no thrifty clothe'.

78. repair: go to.

79. Chaucer, 240, fol. 33^v: 'Is she so fayre? art thou so amorous?'

80	If I but see a Cousin or a Friend,
	Lord! how you swell, and rage like any Fiend!
	But you reel home, a drunken beastly Bear,
	Then preach till Midnight in your easy Chair;
	Cry Wives are false, and ev'ry Woman evil,
85	And give up all that's Female to the Devil.
	If poor (you say) she drains her Husband's Purse;
	If rich, she keeps her Priest, or something worse;
	If highly born, intolerably vain;
	Vapours and Pride by turns possess her Brain:
90	Now gayly Mad, now sow'rly Splenatick,
	Freakish when well, and fretful when she's Sick.
	If fair, then Chast she cannot long abide,
	By pressing Youth attack'd on ev'ry side.
	If foul, her Wealth the lusty Lover lures,
95	Or else her Wit some Fool-Gallant procures,

80-1. The rhyme is also Chaucer's, 243-4.

80. Cousin: 'gossip' in Chaucer, 243, fol. 33ᵛ (cf. 244 below), but evidently a male friend is implied ('his house', 245).

82. beastly Bear: 'as dronken as a Mouse', Chaucer, 246, fol. 34ʳ.

83. easy Chair: 'bench', Chaucer, 247, fol. 34ʳ.

85. Relocated out of sequence from Chaucer, 262.

86-99. Chaucer, 248-70, with wide variations in phrasing and emphasis. For similar male fears of women in marriage, see the discussion in 'January and May', 43-50. Chaucer's Wife draws on more or less the same misogynistic texts that her fifth husband reads out (355-412), including the treatise against marriage by Theophrastus.

87. High-status women in Chaucer's time sometimes 'kept' a private priest for household devotion and confession, but with 'something worse' the line implies sexual 'keeping'.

89. Vapours: hysteria, or specifically female 'nerves', generally of suspect kind; cf. *Rape of the Lock* (1714), IV.59-60, and *Epistle to a Lady*, 267. Addison, *Spectator*, no. 115, 12 July 1711, distinguishes Spleen as male and Vapours as female, but Pope assigns both forms of suspect irrationality to women in the *Rape of the Lock*. Chaucer's equivalent, 252, is 'Melancoly'.

90. gayly Mad: cf. Anne Finch, 'The Spleen', 137, *A New Miscellany of Original Poems, on Several Occasions* (1701), p. 69: 'turns thee gayly Mad'.

Splenatick: suffering from 'Spleen' (as in Finch's poem, and *Rape of the Lock*, 1714, Canto IV); 'fretful; peevish' (*SJ*). Not in Chaucer.

91. Freakish: 'capricious' (*SJ*).

93. In Chaucer, 256, fol. 34ʳ, women are 'assailed on every syde'.

94-7. Chaucer's 257-61 gives a list of reasons why women are allegedly desired; Pope omits some of these and turns all of the rest into compensations for being ugly. Chaucer's lines were quoted and discussed in Burton, *Anatomy of Melancholy* (1621), p. 580 (Third Partition, Section 2, Memb. 2, Subsect. 4).

94. foul: ugly, as in Chaucer, 264, fol. 34ʳ.

lusty Lover: not in Chaucer, but a fairly common seventeenth-century phrase, e.g. Cotton, *Scarronides*, IV. 189 (1667), p. 73: 'One while she takes her lusty Lover'; Dryden, 'The Rape of the Sabines, from Ovid', 146, *Poetical Miscellanies: The Fifth Part* (1704), p. 15: 'The lusty Lover made by Force a Bride'.

95. Wit: intelligence, cf. *Essay on Criticism*, Headnote: Context. It is not among the talents listed by Chaucer's Wife; Pope aligns 'Female Wit' with 'Vapours' in *Rape of the Lock*, IV.59. But see 159 below.

Or else she Dances with becoming Grace,
Or Shape excuses the Defects of Face.
There swims no Goose so gray, but soon or late,
She finds some honest Gander for her Mate.

100 Horses (thou say'st) and Asses, Men may try,
And sound suspected Vessels ere they buy,
But Wives, a random Choice, untry'd they take;
They dream in Courtship, but in Wedlock wake.
Then, not 'till then, the Veil's remov'd away,
105 And all the Woman glares in open Day.

You tell me, to preserve your Wife's good Grace,
Your Eyes must always languish on my Face,
Your Tongue with constant Flatt'ries feed my Ear,
And tag each Sentence with, *My Life! my Dear!*
110 If, by strange Chance, a modest Blush be rais'd,
Be sure my fine Complexion must be prais'd:
My Garments always must be new and gay,

---

101. **sound:** *1717–51:* ring

Fool-Gallant: an illicit and not very successful admirer; an identity not in Chaucer but based on the common language of Restoration comedy, e.g. Wycherley, *The Country-Wife*, III.i. (1675), p. 40: 'The Fool her Gallant, and she'.

96. Dances... Grace: cf. *Essay on Criticism*, 364^5. variant. In Chaucer, 259, fol. 34ʳ, some women attract because they can either 'sing or daunce', and the same useful ability is emphasised in the 'Epilogue' to Gay's *Wife of Bath*.

97. Shape: the same word as Chaucer, 258, but the corollary in the rest of the line is Pope's.

excuses: compensates for.

98-9. The proverb is in Chaucer, 269-70, fol. 34ʳ, though it does not crown the paragraph as here. See also Tilley G362.

At this point Pope omits Chaucer, 271-84, an increasingly enraged recital of the husband's misogynistic statements.

100-5. Chaucer, 285-92, with the omission of much detail of the animals and chattels which can be tested before purchase, and of the Wife's insult ('old dotard shrew') to her husband, 291, fol. 34ʳ.

101. sound: test by tapping.

suspected Vessels: not specifically among the household goods listed by Chaucer's Wife. 1 Peter 3:7 identifies woman as 'the weaker vessel'.

103. Not in Chaucer. This section bears close relation to the picture of Pamela in 'To a Young Lady, with the Works of Voiture', 49-56.

105. all the Woman: The image and the syntax are not in Chaucer. For the syntax cf. 'To a Young Lady, with the Works of Voiture', 2; for the exact phrase, cf. Rowe's translation of Quillet's *Callipaedia*, I (1712), p. 40: 'And all the Woman rises and rebells'.

glares: cf. the usage at 'To a Young Lady, with the Works of Voiture', 53 and Commentary.

106-17. Chaucer 293-302.

106. good Grace: not in Chaucer. Grace is 'favour; kindness' (*SJ*); probably the dominant sense is 'to stay in your wife's good graces'.

109. My Life! my Dear!: 'faire dame', Chaucer, 296, fol. 34ʳ.

110-12. Largely Pope's addition.

And Feasts still kept upon my Wedding-Day:
Then must my Nurse be pleas'd, and Fav'rite Maid;
115   And endless Treats, and endless Visits paid,
To a long Train of Kindred, Friends, Allies;
All this thou say'st, and all thou say'st are Lies.

On *Jenkin* too you cast a squinting Eye;
What? can our Prentice raise your Jealousie?
120   Fresh are his ruddy Cheeks, his Forehead fair,
And like the burnish'd Gold his curling Hair.
But clear that wrinkled Brow, and quit thy Sorrow,
I'd scorn your Prentice, shou'd you die to-morrow.

Why are thy Chests all lockt? On what Design?
125   Are not thy Worldly Goods and Treasure mine?
Sir, I'm no Fool: Nor shall you, by St. *John*,
Have Goods and Body to your self alone.
One you shall quit — in spight of both your Eyes —
I heed not, I, the Bolts, the Locks, the Spies.
130   If you had Wit, you'd say, 'Go where you will,
Dear Spouse, I credit not the Tales they tell.

---

119. **can our:** *1717–51:* can your

---

113. Wedding-Day: wedding anniversary. In Chaucer, 297–8, the 'feast' has to be on the Wife's birthday.

114. Nurse: either a wet-nurse to look after the children of a marriage or (more likely here) a woman who brought the Wife up; Chaucer, 299.

Fav'rite Maid: Pope's addition.

115. Treats: entertainments or gifts; cf. 76, and 'Rape of the Locke', I.133.

116. In Chaucer, specifically 'my fathers folke', 301, fol. 34^r.

117. Stronger in Chaucer, 302: 'Thus seist thou, old barelful of lies', fol. 34^r.

118–23. Chaucer, 303–7, where it is clearer that the details of Jenkin's attractiveness are seen directly by the husband, but also that the apprentice 'squiereth me up and doun', 305, fol. 34^r, a formal attendance prompting jealousy.

118. Jenkin: Janekyn in modern editions of Chaucer, 303, but 'Jenkin' in 1598. The name is the same as that of the Clerk whom the Wife eventually marries, but it was a standard name in medieval literature for an amorous clerk.

squinting Eye: suspicious look, as in Dryden, 'The First Book of Homer's Ilias', 753, in *Fables Ancient and Modern* (1700), p. 217, where Zeus angrily addresses his spying, interfering wife Hera as his 'other squinting Eye'. In Chaucer, 306, fol. 34^r, the husband has more prosaically 'caught a fals suspecioun'.

119. Prentice: apprentice, as in Chaucer.

121. Chaucer, 304: 'his crispe [curly] heer, shynynge as gold fine', fol. 34^r.

124–33. Chaucer, 308–20, fairly closely, but omitting the Wife's suggestion that she is being made 'an ydiot' and her fear that he wants to lock her in his treasure-chest.

124. On what Design: for what secret purpose.

126. St. John: St James, in Chaucer, 312, patron saint of the shrine at Campostella.

128. Chaucer, 315: 'maugree thin iyen', 'in spite of your eyes', fol. 34^r.

129. Spies: Chaucer, 316, fol. 34^r: 'What helpeth it of me to enquere or spien?' an idea which recurs at Chaucer, 357, omitted by Pope. Cf. 157 below.

Take all the Freedoms of a married Life;
I know thee for a virtuous, faithful Wife.'

      Lord! when you have enough, what need you care
135   How merrily soever others fare?
      Tho' all the Day I take and give Delight,
      Doubt not, sufficient will be left at Night.
      'Tis but a just and rational Desire,
      To light a Taper at a Neighbour's Fire.

140   There's Danger too, you think, in rich Array,
      And none can long be modest that are gay.
      The Cat, if you but singe her Tabby Skin,
      The Chimney keeps, and sits content within;
      But once grown sleek, will from her Corner run,
145   Sport with her Tail, and wanton in the Sun;
      She licks her fair round Face, and frisks abroad

---

136. **take and give:** *1736–51:* give and take

---

132. Pope's addition to the speech Chaucer's Wife proposes her husband should make, faintly based on 321–2, in which the Wife completes this section by stating a female preference for complete freedom.

134–9. Replacing Chaucer, 323–36, with the omissions of 323–8, a slice of proverbial wisdom from Ptolemy (Claudius Ptolemeus, an early astronomer) and 335–6, a restatement of her argument.

134–5. Very close to Chaucer 329–30.

136–7. In place of Chaucer's Wife's more robust formulation: 'For, certes, olde dotard, by youre leve, | Ye shall haue queint enow at eue', 331–2, fol. 34^r.

138–9. Chaucer, 333–4, fol. 34^r, has 'He is to great a nigard that woll werne [begrudge] | A man to light a candle at his Lanterne', a phrase almost repeated in Gay's *Wife of Bath*, I (1713), p. 6. The point is that having sex elsewhere does not diminish her energies at home.

140–7. Chaucer, 337–56, omitting a long quotation about female attire from St Paul (I Timothy 2:9) and the Wife's scornful riposte to it, 340–7, as well as her summary of the cat analogy, 355–6.

141. **gay:** also Chaucer's word, 337, fol. 34^r; cf. 75.

142. **Tabby:** a post-medieval usage; normally paired with fur rather than 'Skin', but Pope's exact phrase does occur in *The Excellent and Renowned History of the famous Sir Richard Whittington* (1690), p. 13.

143. **The Chimney keeps:** stays by the hearth; Pope's rendering of 'dwellen in his in', 'dwells in her habitation', Chaucer 350, fol. 34^r.

144. **sleek:** 'smooth ... glossy' (*SJ*); 'slicke and gay' in Chaucer, 351.

145. **Sport ... Tail:** not in Chaucer; an observed detail, like the licking of the face in 146, also not in the source; but 'Tail' often carries a sexual connotation in Pope's period. Cf. 218.

    wanton ... Sun: perhaps recalling Milton, 'On the Morning of Christ's Nativity', 36, *Poems of Mr. John Milton* (1645), p. 3, speaking of Nature: 'To wanton with the Sun her lusty Paramour'.

To show her Furr, and to be *Catterwaw'd*.

Lo thus, my Friends, I wrought to my Desires
These three right Ancient Venerable Sires.
150 I told 'em, *Thus you say*, and *thus you do* —
And told 'em false, but *Jenkin* swore 'twas true.
I, like a Dog, cou'd bite as well as whine:
And first complain'd, whene'er the Guilt was mine.
I tax'd them oft with Wenching and Amours,
155 When their weak Legs scarce dragg'd 'em out of Doors;
And swore the Rambles that I took by Night,
Were all to spy what Damsels they bedight.
That Colour brought me many Hours of Mirth;
For all this Wit is giv'n us from our Birth:

---

147. Catterwaw'd: not in *SJ*; *OED*, s.v. 'caterwaul', sense 1, gives: 'To make the noise proper to [cats] at rutting time', citing Chaucer's line here (354, fol. 34ʳ): 'Gon a Catrewawed'. It later acquired the extra sense of being in heat or acting lasciviously. The syntax remains odd, however, perhaps suggesting a burlesque sense of 'to be serenaded' (by another cat); the italics emphasise an overt archaism and bawdy suggestion.

After this Pope omits 357-78, consisting of the Wife's threats of escape, and outraged quotations from the Husband's misogynistic provocations.

148-204. Chaucer, 379-450.

149. Venerable: cf. 1-2, but here clearly ironic: merely 'old husbond' in Chaucer, 380, fol. 34ᵛ.

151. Chaucer's Wife, 351, also has the false oath of her niece to back her up. Pope then omits Chaucer's Wife's exclamatory couplet about her own guilt, 384-5.

152-65. Condensed from Chaucer, 386-408, omitting some repetitions of the Wife's guilt, and other touches such as the idea that the husband was 'tickled' by the accusations (395, fol. 34ᵛ) as evidence of his wife's affection and belief in his sexual capabilities. In this section Chaucer's Wife appears to be talking about one representative old husband, rather than all three.

152. Dog: 'hors' in Chaucer, 386, fol. 34ᵛ, likewise biting and whining.

156. Rambles: loose excursions, cf. 280, 339. It was Pope's normal word in his letters for a peripatetic holiday, e.g. to John Hughes, 7 October 1715 (*Corr.*, I.316): 'a ramble I have been taking about the country'. However, Rochester's 'A Ramble in St. James's Park' and another poem, 'Captain Ramble', attributed to him in his *Poems on Several Occasions* of 1680, suggest it had the connotation of sexual adventuring in the Restoration, and *SJ* derives the verb from a Dutch word meaning 'to rove loosely in lust'.

157. bedight: 'wenches that he dight', Chaucer, 398, fol. 34ᵛ, i.e. women the husband was (supposedly) sleeping with. 'Bedight' normally means 'to adorn, to dress; to set off: an old word, now only used in humorous writings' (*SJ*). It is possible that Pope has misread the Chaucer text, or that there is a pun on 'dight' and 'bedight' in Chaucer (as Benson 1988 suggests, 398n). *OED*, 'dight', sense 4b, 'have to do with sexually' cites Chaucer's 398 and 767; it was already becoming obsolete in the medieval period.

158. Colour: cover, excuse; Chaucer's own word, 399, fol. 34ᵛ.

Hours of Mirth: 'much mirth', Chaucer, 399, fol. 34ᵛ ('many a myrthe' in modern texts). Cf. Ariadne's words in Behn, *The Second Part of the Rover*, II.i. (1681), p. 32: 'possess she all the day thy hours of mirth'.

159. Wit: cf. 95.

160   Heav'n gave to Woman the peculiar Grace
      To spin, to weep, and cully Human Race.
      By this nice Conduct and this prudent Course,
      By Murmuring, Wheedling, Stratagem and Force,
      I still prevail'd, and would be in the right,
165   Or Curtain-Lectures made a restless Night.
      If once my Husband's Arm was o'er my Side,
      What? so familiar with your Spouse? I cry'd:
      I levied first a Tax upon his Need,
      Then let him — 'twas a *Nicety* indeed!
170   Let all Mankind this certain Maxim hold,
      Marry who will, our *Sex* is to be Sold!
      With empty Hands no Tassels you can lure,

---

160. peculiar: particular; cf. 'January and May', 52.

161. spin: 'spyinyng' is also in Chaucer's similar list, 401, fol. 34ᵛ.

   cully: more usually a noun rather than a verb: 'a man deceived or imposed upon; as by sharpers, or a strumpet' (*SJ*); *OED* dates the word in verb and noun forms from after the Restoration, and Pope does not apparently use it elsewhere.

162. nice: cf. 11, 39.

   prudent Course: a superficially straightforward phrase already commonly ironised, e.g. Oldham, 'Garnet's Ghost Addressing to the Jesuits', 171–2, *Works* (1684), p. 14: 'So Nero did, such was the prudent Course | Taken by all his mighty Successors'. The line has no equivalent in Chaucer.

163. Murmuring: grumbling, as in Chaucer, 406.

   Wheedling: a Restoration word, according to *OED*; replacing 'grutching' (complaining), Chaucer, 406.

   Stratagem: replacing Chaucer's 'slight'; 'an artifice; a trick by which some advantage is gained' (*SJ*), most famously in Farquhar's comedy, *The Beaux Stratagem* (1707). Originally it was a military word (from 1489, according to *OED*) and Pope mostly uses it elsewhere in the Homer translations, where it has epic connotations; cf., however, *Essay on Criticism*, 182, and 'Rape of the Locke', I.100.

   Force: also Chaucer's word, 405.

164. still: always.

   would be: insisted on being.

165. Curtain-Lectures: 'a reproof given by a wife to her husband in bed' (*SJ*); *OED* dates it from 1633. Brathwait, who had published a 'boulster [pillow] lecture' called *Ar't Asleep Husband* in 1640, appears to use the phrase (*Comment*, p. 79) of the Wife's bedroom strategies at 201–4. Pope's addition.

166–82. Chaucer, 409–31, with much rearrangement.

166. The gesture is the same in Chaucer, 410, fol. 34ᵛ, but the spoken response, 167, is Pope's.

168. Tax: apparently shifting the 'conjugal debt' (cf. 52–3) to more strictly economic exchange along the lines of 60; in Chaucer, 411, fol. 34ᵛ, the husband 'made his ransome vnto me' before being granted sexual favours.

169. Nicety: not in *SJ* in this sense, probably because Pope is picking up the obsolete Chaucerian sense, 412, fol. 34ᵛ: 'Than would I suffer him do his nicete' (*OED*, sense 2a, 'to satisfy one's lust'). Pope adds an emphasis suggesting the Wife is less than impressed with the husband's sexual performance.

170. certain Maxim: 'this tale', in Chaucer, 413, fol. 34ᵛ. For 'maxim' cf. *Essay on Criticism*, 127 variant and Commentary.

171. In Chaucer, 416, fol. 34ᵛ, 'Wine [succeed] who so may, all bene for to sell', i.e. not just 'our *Sex*'.

172. Tassels: tercels, or male peregrine falcons; 'hauks' in Chaucer, 415, fol. 34ᵛ.

But fulsome Love for Gain we can endure:
For Gold we love the Impotent and Old,
175 And heave, and pant, and kiss, and cling, for Gold.
Yet with Embraces, Curses oft I mixt,
Then kist again, and chid and rail'd betwixt.
Well, I may make my Will in Peace, and die,
For not one Word in their Arrears am I.
180 To drop a dear Dispute I was unable,
Ev'n tho' the Pope himself had sate at Table.
But when my Point was gain'd, then thus I spoke,
'*Billy*, my dear! how sheepishly you look?
Approach my Spouse, and let me kiss thy Cheek;
185 Thou should'st be always thus, resign'd and meek!
Of *Job*'s great Patience since so oft you preach,
Well shou'd you practise, who so well can teach.
'Tis something difficult I must allow,
But I, my dearest, will instruct you how.

---

179. **their:** *1717–51:* man's
188. **something difficult:** *1717–51:* difficult to do,

173–5. Pope's Wife makes a general claim about women selling sex for 'Gold' and pretending to enjoy it, but Chaucer's speaks only of her own strategies, tartly concluding 'yet in Bacon [dried meat] hadde I neuer delite', 416–18, fol. 34ᵛ.
173. **fulsome:** 'nauseous; offensive' (*SJ*). Cf. *Essay on Criticism*, 596.
175. **heave:** breathe heavily, as if from passion. Cf. Katherine Philips, 'Parting with Lucasia', 5–6, *Poems by . . . the Matchless Orinda* (1667), pp. 66–7: 'Our labouring Souls will heave and pant, | And gasp for one anothers breast'; and Lee, *The Princess of Cleve*, II.ii (1689), p. 22: 'Nay, and your Breasts . . . how they heave and pant now . . .'. These physical details are not in Chaucer.
176–7. Largely Pope's invention.
178. cf. 'Well, I may now receive, and die', the opening of Donne's fourth *Satire*, later imitated by Pope. Loosely based on Chaucer, 424.
179. **Arrears:** debt; the Wife has kept up 'payments' in verbal exchanges with the husbands. Chaucer, 425: 'I ne ow hem a word, but it is quit', fol. 34ᵛ.

181. The Pope is also present in Chaucer's line, 420, fol. 34ᵛ; Brathwait gives an extended gloss on the Wife's imagery here, p. 99.
After 182, Pope omits Chaucer 426–30, in which the Wife declares that even if her husband resembled a mad lion, she still always won their arguments.
183–204. Chaucer, 431–50.
183. **Billy . . . sheepishly:** 'Wilken', or Willie, in Chaucer, 432, fol. 34ᵛ, is 'oure shepe', whom the Wife offers to kiss (the modern reading 'ba' for kiss, not in 1598, indicates a still more overt show of infantilisation). After 185, Pope omits Chaucer's Wife's additional recommendation of 'a sweete spiced conscience', 435.
186. **Job:** the central figure of the book of Job, in which he refuses to curse God despite a sequence of deliberately inflicted personal disasters; his patience was proverbial, and specifically referred to in the New Testament (James 5:11). Pope's phrasing is close to Chaucer's at 436.
187. The idea derives from Chaucer, 437–8, but the phrase as Pope has it is closer to later proverbial wisdom, e.g. Tilley J59, P537a.
188. Pope's addition.

190	Great is the Blessing of a prudent Wife,
	Who puts a Period to Domestick Strife!
	One of us two must rule, and one obey,
	And since in Man right Reason bears the Sway,
	Let that frail Thing, weak Woman, have her way.
195	The Wives of all our Race have ever rul'd
	Their tender Husbands, and their Passions cool'd.
	Fye, 'tis unmanly thus to sigh and groan;
	What? wou'd you have me to your self alone?
	Why take me Love! take all and ev'ry part!
200	Here's your Revenge! you love it at your Heart.
	Wou'd I vouchsafe to sell what Nature gave,
	You little think what Custom I cou'd have?
	But see! I'm all your own — nay hold — for Shame!

---

195. **our Race have ever:** *1736–51:* my family have

190–1. Pope's addition.
190. **prudent Wife:** cf. 'January and May', 72 and Commentary.
191. 'Strife' is rhymed with 'Wife' in *Essay on Criticism*, 82–3, and *The Dunciad Variorum*, II.159–60. Cf. Dryden, 'To my Honour'd Kinsman, John Driden', 17–18, *Fables*, p. 94: 'Promoting Concord, and composing Strife, | Lord of your self, uncumber'd with a Wife'. Dryden also gives examples of marriages explicitly not affected by 'domestic Strife' in 'Baucis and Philemon', 172, and 'Palamon and Arcite', III.1149.
 Period: full stop at the end of a sentence.
192. Chaucer's Wife says one of the two must 'obeien' [submit]; 440, fol. 34^v.
193. **right Reason:** The phrase, from the *orthos logos* of Aristotelian logic, was much used in seventeenth-century moral philosophy, and in poetry; cf. *Essay on Criticism*, 214, and Commentary. Here obviously ironic, as is Chaucer's Wife's 'sith a man is more reasonable | Than woman is', 441–2, fol. 34^v.
194. An invention in the general spirit of Chaucer's Wife's irony.
195–6. Pope's addition, ironically recalling the more conventional positions, e.g. the anonymous translation of Quillet's *Callipaediae*, I (1710), p. 2: 'Good Wives, perhaps, will to my Rules attend, | By tender Husbands taught, who can't offend'.
198. Replacing the straightforward bawdy of 'Is it for ye would haue me queint alone', Chaucer, 444, fol. 34^v.
200. **Here's your Revenge:** replacing 'Peter, beshrew [curse] you', Chaucer, 446, fol. 34^v.
201. **vouchsafe:** 'to deign; to condescend; to yield' (*SJ*); not in Chaucer.
 what Nature gave: 'my belchose' ('*bele chose*' in modern editions), Chaucer, 447, fol. 34^v, a euphemism for vagina.
202. Pope's Wife suggests she could easily sell her favours; Chaucer's, 448, fol. 34^v, that by doing so she 'couth walke as fresh as is a rose'.
203–4. Pope's Wife appears to represent herself as modestly flustered by a sexual advance, a motif not in Chaucer, where the phrase 'Ye be to blame', 450, fol. 34^v, seems (ironically) to chide the husband's responsibility for her own modest deportment. Pope is thinking of the conventions of female sexual response common in Restoration erotic lyric, e.g. Behn, 'The Disappointment', st. II, *Poems on Several Occasions* (1684), p. 71: 'She wants the pow'r to say—*Ah! What d'ye do?*', and similarly throughout st. III.

What means my Dear — indeed — you are to blame.'

205   Thus with my first three Lords I past my Life;
A very Woman and a very Wife!
What Sums from these first Spouses I cou'd raise,
Procur'd young Husbands in my riper Days.
Tho' past my Bloom, not yet decay'd was I,
210   Wanton and wild, and chatter'd like a Pye.
In Country Dances most I did excell,
And sung as sweet as Evening *Philomel.*
To clear my Quail-pipe, and refresh my Soul,

---

207. first: *1717–51:* old
211. most I did excell: *1717–51:* still I bore the bell

205–20. Replacing Chaucer, 451–68, with some narrative rearrangement: Pope's Wife summarises her position, age and behaviour after the first three husbands, where Chaucer's moves directly to her situation with the fourth husband.

205–6. Pope's substitution for Chaucer's linking couplet, 451–2.

206. very: true (i.e. in confirmation of a stereotype); cf. Wycherley, *Gentleman Dancing-Master*, V.i (1673), p. 94, where 'A very Wife' is the rueful response to Mrs Flirt (a prostitute) bargaining for pin money.

207–8. Pope's addition, emphasising the switch in economic and sexual bargaining.

209–10. Chaucer, 455–6, fol. 34ᵛ, specifically on how she won the next husband: 'And I was yong and ful of ragerie, [wantonness] | Stubborne and strong, and ioly as a Pye [magpie]'. Brathwait glosses these lines, p. 102: 'She was but in the Flower of her Youth... full of Metal and Agilitie'. For the magpie, cf. 'January and May', 387, Commentary, and Pope's juvenile Spenserian imitation, 'The Alley', 33: '*Slander* beside her, like a Magpye, chatters' (not published until 1727).

210. Wanton and wild: cf. D'Urfey, *The Virtuous Wife*, II.ii (1680), p. 24, where Olivia threatens to 'let my self loose to gaiety and pleasure, wanton and wild as *Mercenary Creatures*'.

211. In Chaucer the Wife dances 'to an harpe small', 457, fol. 34ᵛ; it is possible that 'Country Dances' plays with the same bawdy pun as Hamlet's 'Do you think I meant country matters?', Shakespeare, *Hamlet*, III.ii.111.

211 variant. bore the bell: to lead the flock, like a sheep with a bell (a 'bell-wether').

212. Philomel: the (nocturnal) nightingale (Chaucer, 458, fol. 34ᵛ), melancholy songbird after the legend of Philomela, for which see 'Sapho to Phaon', 176–7, Commentary; and 'Spring', 26; 'Winter', 78. For the phrase cf. Congreve, *The Mourning Muse of Alexis*, 8 (1695), p. 1: 'By Morning Lark, or Evening *Philomel*'.

213–16. Chaucer, 459–64, in which the Wife's drinking is less salubriously phrased, and includes a violent response to a mythological figure, Metellius, who supposedly killed his wife for her drinking. After drinking, the Wife 'of Venus must I thinke' (464, fol. 34ᵛ), i.e. about sex.

213. Quail-pipe: 'a pipe with which fowlers allure quails' (*SJ*); not in Chaucer at this point, but mentioned by him in *Romaunt of the Rose*, 7259, a text Pope annotated fairly heavily (see Mack 1979). *OED* cites *A New Dictionary of the Canting Crew* (1699), where it means 'a woman's tongue'. Addison's Will Wimble invents an improved Quail-Pipe in *The Spectator*, no. 108, 4 July 1711. Dryden uses it perhaps suggestively in his translation of Juvenal, *Satires*,

THE WIFE OF BATH HER PROLOGUE (1713) 669

        Full oft I drain'd the Spicy Nut-brown Bowl
215   Of luscious Wines, that youthful Blood improve,
        And warm the swelling Veins to Feats of Love.
        For 'tis as sure as Cold engenders Hail,
        A Liqu'rish Mouth must have a Lech'rous Tail;
        Wine lets no Lover unrewarded go,
220   As all true Gamesters by Experience know.

        But oh good Gods! whene'er a Thought I cast,
        On all the Joys of Youth and Beauty past,
        To find in Pleasures I have had my Part,
        Still warms me to the Bottom of my Heart.
225   This wicked World was once my dear Delight;

214–15. **Bowl | Of:** *1717–51:* bowl; | Rich
216. **Love.:** *1736–51:* love:

VI.106-7, of a singing boy: 'The Rich, to buy him, will refuse no price: | And stretch his Quail-pipe till they crack his voice'; *Satires of Juvenal,* p. 93 (and cf. 500, p. 108).

214. Nut-brown Bowl: probably recalling Milton, 'L'Allegro', 100, *Poems* (1645), p. 34: 'Then to the Spicy Nut-brown Ale'; 'spicy' is not in Chaucer here, but at 436, fol. 34^v, the Wife instructs commends a 'spiced conscience' to the Husband, perhaps prompting the recollection of Milton here.

216. Feats of Love: a not uncommon phrase, but especially so in the sex manuals of Pope's day, e.g. Nicholas Venette, *The Mysteries of Conjugal Love Reveal'd* (1707), p. 145, and the anonymous translation of Quillet's *Callipaedia,* III (1710), p. 32.

217–18. Chaucer's version of this couplet (465-6, fol. 34^v-35^r) was quoted (as evidence of the effects of diet) by Burton, *Anatomy of Melancholy* (1621), p. 547 (Third Partition, Sect. 2, Memb. 2, Subsect. 1). In modern editions of Chaucer, the second line reads: 'A likerous mouth moste han a likerous tayl', making Pope's slightly different line look like a gloss, but in the 1598 Chaucer, and in Brathwait, p. 104, the line is virtually as Pope has it. Chaucer's 'likerous' can mean alcoholically-inclined or gluttonous, but also simply lecherous; not in *SJ*.

Tail: genitals (of either sex); cf. 145. The phrase as a whole became proverbial (Tilley T395) but is first recorded in Chaucer at this point.

219-20. Less salubrious in Chaucer, 467-8, fol. 35^r: 'In women vinolent [drunken] is no defence [resistance to sexual advances] | This knowe lechours by experience'.

220. Gamesters: 'Gamester' (a word not available to Chaucer) was proverbial for sexual adventurer by Pope's time, e.g. *Fifteen Real Comforts of Matrimony* (1683), p. 32: 'your true gamesters must generally prey where controul and tyranny are most sowre and severe' (i.e. against wives). Cf. Taverner, *The Maid the Mistress,* IV (1708), p. 18: 'So, so, if she has tricks before Marriage, She'll certainly be a true Gamester afterwards'. The initial B in the text of the poem in the *Works* of 1717 (p. 247) depicts a card table with a chess board on one side; this was also used for Canto IV of *Rape of the Lock,* however. On the illustrations see further Caretta (2009: 224).

221-8. Chaucer, 469-79.

221. good Gods!: substituted for 'lorde Christ!', Chaucer, 469, fol. 35^r.

225. The alliterative antithesis is a substitute for Chaucer, 473, fol. 35^r: 'That I haue had my world, as in my time'.

Now all my Conquests, all my Charms good night!
The Flour consum'd, the best that now I can
Is e'en to make my Markets of the Bran.

My fourth dear Spouse was not exceeding true
230　He kept, 'twas thought, a private Miss or two:
But all that Score I paid — As how? you'll say,
Not with my Body, in a filthy way —
But I so drest, and danc'd, and drank, and din'd;
And view'd a Friend, with Eyes so very kind,
235　As stung his Heart, and made his Marrow fry
With burning Rage, and frantic Jealousie.
His Soul, I hope, enjoys perpetual Glory,
For here on Earth I was his Purgatory.

---

228. **Markets:** *1717–51:* market
229. **true:** *1713b–51:* true;
237. **perpetual:** *1736–51:* eternal

---

226. **Conquests . . . Charms:** the modern language of romance, as in *Rape of the Lock*, I.119, 140; III.28, etc.

227–8. Proverbial, from Chaucer, 477–8, fol. 35ʳ. Bran is the fibrous part of the grain, normally discarded as too rough for consumption. Chaucer's Wife, at this point (479–80), endeavours to be 'right merie' [merry] in carrying on with her tale, having despatched her former life with 'Let go fare well'.

228. **make my Markets:** make the best bargain.

229–52. Chaucer, 480–502.

229–30. Chaucer had already introduced the fourth husband as a 'revelour' (profligate) who kept a 'paramour' at 453–4, fol. 34ᵛ; picking up the thread at 481–2 she tells her audience of her 'dispite' (anger) at his infidelity, a feature less strongly indicated in Pope's Wife.

230. **Miss:** post-medieval phrase for 'a strumpet; a concubine; a whore; a prostitute' (*SJ*); cf. Dryden's version of Chaucer's 'Nun's Priest's Tale' ('The Cock and the Fox'), 55–6, *Fables*, p. 225: 'This gentle Cock for solace of his Life, | Six Misses had besides his lawful Wife'.

231. **Score:** bill, debt; 'he was quit' (repaid), Chaucer, 483, fol. 35ʳ.

232. Very close to Chaucer, 485.

233–4. Making explicit and detailed the behaviour of Chaucer's Wife, 486–7.

233. Perhaps modelled on Cowley, 'The Grasshopper', 29, *Poems . . . Written by A. Cowley* (1656), p. 37: 'But when thou'st drunk, and danc'ed, and sung'.

234. **kind:** with a suggestion of amorous desire.

235–6. Chaucer, 487–8, fol. 35ʳ: 'That in his owne grece I made him frie | For anger, and for very ielousie'.

235. **Marrow:** i.e. bone marrow, innermost body, with some sexual suggestion (*OED*, sense 3c). For the phrase cf. Motteux, *The Loves of Mars & Venus*, 'Act Third and Last' (1696), p. 26 (the cuckolded Vulcan's speech): 'Prey on their Bones, their inmost Marrow fry'.

237–8. Pope uses the same rhymes and idea as Chaucer, 489–90, but the order of the couplet is reversed.

238. **Purgatory:** also in Chaucer, 489, fol. 35ʳ. 'A place in which souls are supposed by the papists to be purged by fire from carnal impurities, before they are received into heaven' (*SJ*) and thus a specifically pre-Reformation element of theology, not mentioned specifically anywhere else in Pope's poetry (but see 'On Silence', 42 and Commentary). Pope had recently joked to the Anglican clergyman Swift (8 December 1713, *Corr.*, I.199–200) about the cost of releasing the soul of the Catholic

Oft, when his Shoe the most severely wrung,
240 He put on careless Airs, and sat and sung.
How sore I gall'd him, only Heav'n cou'd know,
And he that felt, and I that caus'd the Woe.
He dy'd when last from Pilgrimage I came,
With other Gossips, from *Jerusalem,*
245 And now lies buried underneath a Rood,
Fair to be seen, and rear'd of honest Wood.
A Tomb, indeed, with fewer Sculptures grac'd,
Than that *Mausolus*' Pious Widow plac'd,
Or where inshrin'd the great *Darius* lay;
250 But Cost on Graves is merely thrown away.
The Pit fill'd up, with Turf we cover'd o'er,
So bless the good Man's Soul, I say no more.

Dryden from purgatory; it features flippantly in his letters (e.g. to Martha Blount, 3 June 1715; to Swift, 15 October 1725; *Corr.*, I.294; II.333). Benson (1988) notes (to 489–90) that the equivalence of marriage and purgatory was a common trope in Chaucer's time; see also 438–41 below.

239-40. The same rhyme words, reversed in order, are in Chaucer, 491–2, fol. 35ʳ, but the 'careless Airs' element is Pope's addition.

239. wrung: pinched. The phrase was already proverbial before Chaucer, usually in relation to marriage; cf. 'January and May', 204–5, Commentary.

241-2. Close in sense to Chaucer, 493–4.

244. Gossips: mature female companions; not in Chaucer here (but see note to 80 and 266).

Jerusalem: where, according to the 'General Prologue', the Wife has been three times, among other pilgrimages.

245. Rood: a wooden cross; in pre-Reformation churches often mounted on a screen where the nave crosses into the chancel, where high-status tombs were often located. In Chaucer (496), the husband is buried under the rood-beam, 'a place of especial Reverence in former times', as Brathwait puts it (p. 109). Conversely the Wife says it would have been wasteful to bury him 'preciously', 500, fol. 35ʳ (cf. Pope's 250). Brathwait's paraphrase suggests carefully that it would be 'but (as she thinks) lost labour: So much cost would make a poor Executor, and too much impoverish the Survivor'. Cf. also the passage of Dryden quoted above, Commentary to 16.

246. honest Wood: plain and therefore sincere (here ironic, because it is the cheapest and least lasting form of memorial). Dryden, *The Spanish Fryar*, I.i (1681), p. 13: 'the Walls are very honest Stone, and the Timber very honest Wood'.

248. Mausolus: Mausolus of Caria, a Satrap or provincial governor within the Persian Empire, died in 353 BC; the building which commemorates him ('Mausoleum') was already in progress at Halicarnassus on the Western coast of what was then Asia Minor and was finished after the death of his widow Artemisia (in 351). It was regarded as one of the Seven Wonders of the Ancient World. Not mentioned in Chaucer, but it is in Brathwait's commentary at this point (p. 109).

249. Darius: Darius I, 550–486 BC, Persian emperor, buried with other emperors at a site near Persepolis in modern Iran. He was supposed to have had his tomb constructed during his lifetime by a craftsman, Apelles, named in Chaucer, 498–9, fol. 35ʳ. The representation of this site in Aeschylus' *The Persians* was discussed by Rymer in *A Short View of Tragedy* (1692), pp. 11–13. *TE* cites John Weever's *Ancient Funerall Monuments* (1631), chapter IV, pp. 12–18, as a general source of commentary on the expenses of such tombs in ancient times.

Now for my fifth lov'd Lord, the last and best;
(Kind Heav'n afford him everlasting Rest)
255 Full hearty was his Love, and I can shew
The Tokens on my Ribs, in Black and Blue:
Yet, with a Knack, my Heart he cou'd have won,
While yet the Smart was shooting in the Bone.
How quaint an Appetite in Women reigns!
260 Free Gifts we scorn, and love what costs us Pains:
Let Men avoid us, and on them we leap;
A glutted Market makes Provision cheap.

In pure good Will I took this jovial Spark,
Of *Oxford* he, a most egregious Clerk:
265 He boarded with a Widow in the Town,
A trusty Gossip, one dame *Alison*.

253–62. Chaucer 503–24, heavily condensed.

255. hearty: 'vigorous; strong' (*SJ*). Not in Chaucer; cf. note to 257.

256. Tokens: bruises. Chaucer, 505–6, fol. 35ʳ: 'And yet was he to me the moste shrewe [greatest scoundrel] | That fele I on my ribbes all by rewe [row]': Chaucer's Wife associates the violence with his shrewishness or bad temper; Pope's with his 'hearty ... Love'.

257. Knack: 'a nice trick', 'pretty contrivance, a toy' (*SJ*). Cf. Pope's *Epistle to a Lady*, 155: 'For how should equal Colours do the knack?' Pope also uses the phrase 'knack of Versifying', about himself, in his essay in *The Guardian*, no. 40, 27 April 1713 (*PW*, I.101). Chaucer's Wife says not that her husband 'could have' won her love, but that despite his violence, he was sufficiently charming in bed to win it all the time (508–12), partly by being 'daungerous', i.e. coy, standoffish. Pope omits this element of their interaction, which is sympathetically glossed by Brathwait, p. 111.

258. Smart: pain, as in 6.

259. quaint: Chaucer's word: 'We women haue ... a queint fantasie' (515–16, fol. 35); there it means 'curious inclination', but often in Chaucer there is a pun on 'queynte' or female sexual organs, no doubt in play here for both writers. Cf. 'January and May', 307. It is said of Gay's Alison that she 'throws out as many quaint Jokes as an *Oxford* Scholar'; *Wife of Bath*, I, p. 3. Gay's character also expatiates on women's hankering after what is forbidden; III, p. 27.

261. leap: not in Chaucer here, but probably recollected from Chaucer's Wife's image of the ugly woman chasing a man at 267, fol. 34ʳ: 'she woll on him lepe'.

262. The proverb is condensed from Chaucer's 'Greet prees [crowd] at market maketh dere ware | And to great chepe [bargain] is hold to litle price', 522–3, fol. 35ʳ.

263–76. Chaucer, 525–42.

263. good Will: 'for love, and no richesse', Chaucer, 526, fol. 35ʳ.

Spark: a post-medieval word for a showy young man, 'commonly used in contempt' (*SJ*). Pope's phrase, which has no equivalent in Chaucer, is found in an anonymous ballad, *The Fairy Queene* (1648): 'Full many a joviall Sparke'.

264. egregious: 'eminent; remarkable; extraordinary'; or 'eminently bad; remarkably vicious. This is now the usual sense' (*SJ*). Not in Chaucer, who simply records the clerk's education at Oxford (527–8).

266. dame Alison: 'Dame' is 'the old title of honour to women' (*SJ*), generally used with a degree of irony by Pope; cf. 276. Not in Chaucer here, but Alisoun is a 'dame' at 576 and 583. Alisoun is a 'gossip' in Chaucer, 529–30, fol. 35ʳ, which can indicate either a godmother or child of one's godmother, or simply a close friend; cf. 244.

Full well the Secrets of my Soul she knew,
Better than e'er our Parish Priest cou'd do.
To her I told whatever did befal;
270 Had but my Husband Pist against a Wall,
Or done a thing that might have cost his Life,
She — and my Niece — and one more worthy Wife
Had known it all: What most he wou'd conceal,
To these I made no Scruple to reveal.
275 Oft has he blush'd from Ear to Ear for Shame,
That e'er he told a Secret to his Dame.

It so befell, in Holy Time of *Lent*,
That oft a Day I to this Gossip went;
(My Husband, thank my Stars, was out of Town)
280 From House to House we rambled up and down,
This Clerk, my self, and my good Neighbour *Alce*,
To see, be seen, to tell, and gather Tales;

---

269. **did:** *1717–51:* could
281. **Alce:** *1751:* Alse

---

268. **Parish Priest:** who would in Chaucer's time have heard the Wife's confession as part of regular duties (the phrase is in Chaucer, 532, fol. 35ʳ).

269 **variant.** Probably designed to take out the expletive 'did'; cf. *Essay on Criticism*, 349 and Commentary.

272. The same idea is in Chaucer, 536–7, but Pope condenses and repunctuates it for comic effect.

276. The proverbial inability of women to keep secrets: Brathwait has an expansive gloss on the idea (pp. 113–14), and cf. 'January and May', 698–9. Pope's story of Midas' wife's inability to keep the secret of her husband's asses ears, in *Epistle to Dr. Arbuthnot*, 69–72, was probably based on Dryden's version of 'The Wife of Bath her Tale', 155–6, *Fables*, p. 485, where the story is introduced by a comment by a female character on women: 'Like leaky Sives no Secrets we can hold: | Witness the famous Tale that *Ovid* told'.

277–89. Chaucer, 543–62, omitting 545–6, where Chaucer's Wife recounts her delight in walking well-dressed in Spring, and 553–4, where she protests she had no idea where her destiny was leading her.

278. **oft a Day:** 'so often tymes', Chaucer, 544, fol. 35ʳ. Pope's phrase was an archaism, but cf. Dryden's translation of Juvenal, *Satires*, I.37: 'Changed oft a day for needless Luxury'; *Satires of Juvenal*, p. 4.

279. Chaucer's Wife indicates, at another point in the narrative (550–1, fol. 35ʳ) that her current husband (the fourth one) was in London, giving her 'bettre laiser [leisure] for to pleie'; Pope's phrase is more reminiscent of the bored wives of Restoration drama.

280. **rambled:** cf. 156. In Chaucer, 546, they merely walk from house to house, but also 'into the fieldes', 549, fol. 35ʳ (and again at 564, also omitted by Pope here, but cf. 291), perhaps suggesting the verb.

281. As *TE* points out, Chaucer rhymes 'tales' with 'Ales' (Alice), because Chaucer's final 'e' makes the words disyllabic, a point not fully understood in Pope's time. 'Alce' is not otherwise recorded as an abbreviation of 'Alice'.

282. **To see, be seen:** The phrase is in Chaucer, 552, fol. 35ʳ, less concisely: 'And for to se, and eke for to be seie | Of lustie folke'.

Visits to ev'ry Church we daily paid,
And march'd in ev'ry holy Masquerade,
285   The Stations duly, and the Vigils kept;
Not much we fasted, but scarce ever slept.
At Sermons too I shone in Scarlet gay;
The wasting Moth ne'er spoil'd my best Array;
The Cause was this; I wore it every Day.

290   'Twas when fresh *May* her early Blossoms yields
The Clerk and I were walking in the Fields,
We grew so intimate, I can't tell how,
I pawn'd my Honour and ingag'd my Vow,
If e'er I laid my Husband in his Urn,
295   That he, and only he, shou'd serve my Turn.

---

291. **The:** *1736–51:* This
Fields,: *1717–51:* fields.

283-7. Pope's list of quasi-religious diversions replaces Chaucer's, 555-8, which includes pilgrimages, miracle plays and marriages.

283. Visits: 'visitaciouns' in Chaucer, 555, fol. 35ʳ; the visiting of churches is not specified at that point. Cf. 'Rape of the Locke', I.131.

284. Masquerade: normally in the late Restoration period a costumed assembly or 'diversion in which the company is masked' (*SJ*); 'march'd', however, suggests a religious procession. Masquerades were regarded as a front for illicit sexual liaisons by many commentators. Susannah Centlivre's poem *The Masquerade* had been published by Lintot earlier in 1713; cf. *Rape of the Lock* (1714), II.108. The phrase 'Holy Masquerade' often appeared in religious controversy, e.g. Henry Grenfield, *God in the Creature* (1686), p. 115: 'The only Saints, in Holy Masquerade'; the phrase indicated monkish garb in *The Prophets: An Heroic Poem* (1708), p. 4.

285. Stations: OED lists a number of religious senses, including regular Wednesday and Friday fasts (sense 26); religious services at holy places (sense 25); visits to specific holy sites (sense 24); and stopping places on pilgrimages and processions, including the Stations of the Cross (sense 19).

Vigils: Chaucer has 'vigilles' (and processions), 556, fol. 35ʳ, indicating 'a fast kept before a holiday [i.e. holy day]'; or 'service used on the night before a holiday' (*SJ*); hence 286, Pope's invention, which suggests not only that they broke the holy fasts, but that their wakefulness was not prompted by holy observance.

287. Scarlet: 'my gaie skarlet gites [robes]', Chaucer, 559, fol. 35ʳ, evidently signalling sexual availability. Chaucer's Wife does not say she listened to sermons dressed this way, but she does go to 'preaching', 557.

288-9. Chaucer, 560, fol. 35ʳ, has the Wife say that moths and other small creatures could not infiltrate her clothes 'for they were vsed well'.

290-9. Chaucer, 563-74, lightly condensed, with details from 545-6 out of sequence.

292. intimate: 'had such daliaunce', Chaucer, 565, fol. 35ʳ.

I . . . how: in Chaucer, 566, fol. 35ʳ, the Wife's deliberate intention to look out for the next husband is an aspect 'of my purueiance' (foresight); Pope's version is perhaps loosely suggested by 553-4 (see Commentary to 277-89 above).

293. pawn'd: pledged, promised against a future exchange. *SJ* reports 'it is now seldom used but of pledges given for money', and Pope is clearly suggesting an illicit bargain. Not in Chaucer.

294. Chaucer, 568, fol. 35ʳ: 'If I were wedowe [widow]'.

295. serve my Turn: cf. 28-9, once again with a sexual charge; not in Chaucer, who has 'should wedde me' (568, fol. 35ʳ).

> We strait struck Hands; the Bargain was agreed;
> I still have shifts against a Time of Need:
> The Mouse that always trusts to one poor Hole,
> Can never be a Mouse of any Soul.
>
> 300 I vow'd, I scarce cou'd sleep since first I knew him,
> And durst be sworn he had Bewitch'd me to him:
> If e'er I slept, I dream'd of him alone,
> And Dreams foretel, as Learned Men have shown:
> All this I said; but Dream, Sirs, I had none.
> 305 I follow'd but my crafty Crony's Lore,
> Who bid me tell this Lye — and twenty more.
>
> Thus Day by Day, and Month by Month we past;
> It pleas'd the Lord to take my Spouse at last!
> I tore my Gown, I soil'd my Locks with Dust,
> 310 And beat my Breasts, as wretched Widows — must.
> Before my Face my Handkerchief I spread,
> To hide the Flood of Tears I did *not* shed.

---

296. Pope's addition, expanding his 'pawn'd' image from 293.

298–9. Condensed from Chaucer, 572–4, where it is somewhat more colloquially expressed.

299. **Soul:** 'spirit; fire; grandeur of mind' (*SJ*); 'herte' in Chaucer, 572, fol. 35ʳ. See Tilley M1236: 'The Mouse that has but one hole is quickly taken'.

300–6. Chaucer, 575–84, omitting the melodramatic details of the supposed dream of her future husband.

301. **Bewitch'd:** Chaucer, 575, fol. 35ʳ, 'enchaunted'.

303. Not in Chaucer, though Chaucer provided Pope with a good deal of the poetry and theory of dreams, including *The Hous of Fame*, Pope's imitation of book 3 of which (already largely written) would appear as *The Temple of Fame* in 1715. Gay's Chaucer uses fictional dreams as part of his courtship technique in *Wife of Bath*, IV, p. 42.

305. **crafty Crony's Lore:** advice from an 'old acquaintance; a companion of long standing' (*SJ*, s.v. 'crony'); cf. 'January and May', 107 and Commentary. Chaucer uses the 'lore/more' rhyme, 583–4, fol. 35ᵛ.

307–28. Chaucer, 585–626, with many omissions, such as 617–18 and 622–6, a confession of the wide range of the Wife's sexual appetites.

307. Replacing Chaucer, 585–6, where the Wife struggles to recall her place in the narrative.

308–10. Fuller (1983, I.413) notes that these lines, which greatly expand the Wife's superficial mourning in Chaucer, resemble 25–8 of the unsigned 'Epilogue' to Gay's play *The Wife of Bath* (declared in the 1730 revision to be 'By a Friend'): 'When-ever Heav'n was pleas'd to take my Spouse, | I never pin'd on Thought of former Vows; | 'Tis true, I sigh'd, I wept, I sobb'd at first, | And tore my Hair – as decent Widows – must.' Chaucer has: 'Whan that my fourth husbond was on bere | I wept algate [continuously] and made sorie chere | As wiues moten [must], for it is vsage' [custom] (587–9, fol. 35ᵛ). Chaucer's wife also reminds us, at 591, that she was already 'purveyed of a make [mate]'.

309. **Locks:** of hair.

310. **wretched Widows:** Pope satirises the flamboyance of a widow's mourning in 'Rape of the Locke', I.122. The syntactic trick at the end of the line is Pope's. Cf. January's fear of 'crafty Widows', in 'January and May', 107 and Commentary.

312. Chaucer's Wife also hides her face, with a 'kerchefe', to hide the fact that she 'wept but small' (592, fol. 35ᵛ).

676   THE WIFE OF BATH HER PROLOGUE (1713)

> The good Man's Coffin to the Church was born;
> Around, the Neighbours, and my Clerk too, mourn.
> 315 But as he march'd, good Gods! he show'd a Pair
> Of Legs and Feet, so clean, so strong, so fair!
> Of twenty Winters Age he seem'd to be;
> I (to say truth) was twenty more than he:
> But vig'rous still, a lively buxom Dame,
> 320 And had a wond'rous Gift to quench a Flame.
> A Conjurer once that deeply cou'd divine,
> Assur'd me, *Mars* in *Taurus* was my Sign.
> As the Stars order'd, such my Life has been:
> Alas, alas, that ever Love was Sin!
> 325 Fair *Venus* gave me Fire and sprightly Grace,
> And *Mars* Assurance, and a dauntless Face.
> By Vertue of this pow'rful Constellation,
> I follow'd always my own Inclination.

---

313. good Man: an added irony, cf. 'Here Fannia, leering on her own good Man', *Epistle to a Lady*, 9; cf. also 390.

315–16. Close to Chaucer, 597–8, but Pope adds 'strong' and then omits the Wife's stated reaction from 599, fol. 35ᵛ, 'That all my hart I yaue vnto his hold'.

317–18. The ages are consistent with Chaucer, 600–1.

319. buxom: 'gay; lively; brisk'; 'wanton; jolly' (*SJ*); not in Chaucer here. The phrase 'buxom dame' is fairly common in the seventeenth century in this context, e.g. the ballad *The Scolding Wives Vindication* (1689): 'I am a young Buxome Dame, | and fain would my Ioys renew'.

320. To give sexual satisfaction. This couplet is condensed from Chaucer, 600–8, fol. 35ᵛ, in which the Wife reports her famously 'Gaptothed' appearance, sexual vitality, and her husbands' praise of her exceptional 'queynte' ('*quoniam*' in modern editions; either way, a codeword for vagina). Brathwait draws out some of the details of her sexual feelings, p. 121.

321. Conjurer: 'an enchanter; one that uses charms' (*SJ*); but also commonly an astrologer, as here, and in Gay's *Wife of Bath*, where the figures of both Chaucer and the Wife both use the term in reference to Dr Astrolabe, a mountebank astrologer (IV, pp. 35 and 37). Pope's addition: Chaucer's Wife is confident of her own interpretation of astrological signs. Her explanation (609–20) is much reduced and reordered by Pope.

322. Mars in Taurus: Benson (1988), note to 613, glosses: 'At the time of the Wife's birth the zodiacal sign of Taurus, a domicile of Venus, was ascending, and the planet Mars was in it'.

324. Identical with Chaucer's 614. Cf. 'Eloisa to Abelard', 68, where Eloisa finds that it is 'no sin to love'.

325–6. Chaucer, 611–12 and 619, fol. 35ᵛ, has the Wife make similar but less elegant distinctions between her Venus-inspired sexual feeling and the 'sturdie hardinesse' which Mars gives her to get her own way.

325. sprightly Grace: Pope's addition, recalling amongst other texts Dryden's repeated use of the phrase in his translation of Virgil's *Aeneid* (often with reference to the boy Ascanius); I.930; IV.200; V.96, 387, etc.

326. dauntless: normally a straightforward heroic epithet in Pope, especially in the Homer translations; but cf. the mock-heroic application, 'dauntless Curl' in *The Dunciad Variorum*, II.54.

327–8. Chaucer's version of this couplet, 615–16, fol. 35ᵛ (which Pope keeps close to, but transposes in the sequence) was quoted

             But to my Tale: A Month scarce pass'd away,
330   With Dance and Song we kept the Nuptial Day.
         All I possess'd I gave to his Command,
         My Goods and Chattels, Mony, House, and Land:
         But oft repented, and repent it still;
         He prov'd a Rebel to my Sov'reign Will:
335   Nay once by Heav'n he struck me on the Face:
         Hear but the Fact, and judge your selves the Case.

             Stubborn as any Lioness was I:
         And knew full well to raise my Voice on high;
         As true a Rambler as I was before,
340   And wou'd be so, in spight of all he swore.
         He, against this, right sagely wou'd advise,
         And old Examples set before my Eyes;
         Tell how the *Roman* Matrons led their Life,
         Of *Gracchus*' Mother, and *Duilius*' Wife;

---

by Burton in *Anatomy of Melancholy* (1621), p. 544 (Third Partition, Second Sect., Second Memb., Subsect. 1); it was the subject of a very long gloss in Brathwait, pp. 123-5, where he argues that Chaucer was satirising those who blame their decisions on their horoscopes.
329-36. Chaucer, 627-36.
329. But ... Tale: a nod to the several times Chaucer's Wife has to make this kind of gesture.
330. In place of Chaucer's less specific 'great solemnpnite', 629, fol. 35ᵛ.
331. In Pope's time, this transfer would have happened automatically, but Benson (1988) notes (630-3n) that Chaucer's Wife would not have been obliged to cede her property in this way.
332. Goods and Chattels: possessions; a phrase normally used in legal documents; 'londe and fee' in Chaucer, 630, fol. 35ᵛ.
333. Chaucer's Wife 'afterward repented me', her rash gesture, 632, fol. 35ᵛ, but the repentance is not current as here.
334. An enhancement of Chaucer, 633, fol. 35ᵛ: 'he nolde suffre nothing of my list [pleasure/ will]', using political language to stress the Wife's sense of grievance.
335. Chaucer's Wife proleptically tells the basic reason for his striking her at this point (635-6), adding that it caused deafness in that ear.

336. Pope's addition, using legal language.
337-54. Chaucer, 637-63, beginning with a near-identical line.
338. Chaucer's Wife declares herself a 'veray iangleresse' [chatterbox], 638, fol. 35ᵛ.
339. Rambler: cf. 156. In Chaucer, the Wife merely walks 'Fro hous to hous', 639-40, fol. 35ᵛ, ignoring the husband's prohibition.
340. swore: derived from Chaucer, 640, 'although he had it swore', i.e. 'prohibited'.
343. Roman Matrons: mothers and guardians of domestic virtue in Rome, exemplified in the following line; the term is not in Chaucer.
344. Gracchus' Mother ... Duilius' Wife: not in Chaucer. Cornelia was the mother of the tribune Tiberius Sempronius Gracchus and renowned for her devotion to the education of her children and refusal of marriage offers after the death of her husband; Bilia was the wife of the consul and naval commander Gaius Duilius, mentioned as a paragon of chastity by Chaucer in 'The Franklin's Tale', 1455. Both had been listed by Jerome as models of feminine virtue. Pope omits Chaucer's examples, from Roman history by way of 'Valerius' (see 359), of men who punished their wives for leaving the house without permission (643-9).

678   THE WIFE OF BATH HER PROLOGUE (1713)

345   And close the Sermon, as beseem'd his Wit,
        With some grave Sentence out of Holy Writ.
        Oft wou'd he say, Who builds his House on Sands,
        Pricks his blind Horse across the Fallow Lands,
        Or lets his Wife abroad with Pilgrims roam,
350   Deserves a Fool's-Cap and long Ears at home.
        All this avail'd not; for whoe'er he be
        That tells my Faults, I hate him mortally:
        And so do Numbers more, I'll boldly say,
        Men, Women, Clergy, Regular and Lay.

355   My Spouse (who was, you know, to Learning bred)
        A certain Treatise oft at Evening Read,
        Where divers Authors (whom the Dev'l confound
        For all their Lies) were in one Volume bound.
        Valerius, whole; and of St. *Jerome*, Part;

---

354. **close:** *1713b–51:* chose

345-6. Chaucer, 651-3, cites a passage in Ecclesiasticus which requires a man to forbid his wife to 'go roile about'.
345. *beseem'd:* befitted.
346. *grave Sentence:* a 'sententia' or moral tag.
347-50. Chaucer, 655-6, fol. 35^v (there with rhyme common to all four lines); the blind horse example is the same, but Pope's example of the house built on sand, drawn from the New Testament parable, Matthew 7:24-7, is substituted for 'Who so buildeth his hous all of sallowes' (sallows).
348. *Pricks:* spurs. Brathwait, p. 129, glosses Chaucer: 'Fallows are uneven grounds for a blind Horse to ride on'.
350. *Fool's-Cap:* jester's cap.
    long Ears: i.e. asses ears, a sign of stupidity; cf. the tale of Midas, cited in Commentary to 276 above. This is Pope's replacement for Chaucer's 'worthy to be honged on the gallowes', 658, fol. 35^v.
351. Replacing Chaucer's Wife's defiant 'I set not an hawe [hawthorn berry] | Of his prouerbes, ne of his old sawe [saying]', 659-60, fol. 35^v.
352. *Faults:* 'vices', in Chaucer 662, fol. 35^v.
353-4. The first of these equates to Chaucer, 663; the explanatory expansion is Pope's.

354. *Regular:* a monk or nun living according to a monastic 'rule'.
    At this point Pope cuts Chaucer's 664-8, which explain once more the husband's anger and violence.
355-76. Chaucer, 669-712, greatly condensed.
355. Pope's addition.
356. *certain Treatise . . . Evening:* 'a booke' in Chaucer, 669, read 'night and daie', and called 'Valerie and Theophraste', 671, fol. 35^v.
357-8. Pope's addition, prompted by Chaucer, 681.
359-61. Condensed from Chaucer, 671-81.
359. **Valerius:** supposed author of Walter Map, *Dissuasio Valerii ad Rufinum Philosophum ne uxorem ducat*, c. 1180 ('the argument of Valerius to the philosopher Rufinus that he should not take a wife').
    Jerome: St Jerome, an early church father (340-420), author of the *Epistola adversus Jovinianum*, source of much of the theological debate about marriage in Chaucer's 'Prologue'. Warton (1782: 73) regrets that Pope has here trimmed Chaucer's amusing 'stroke of humour' at the Wife's expense: she 'naturally' mistakes Jerome's period and rank, making him a Cardinal at Rome (673-4).

360 *Chrysippus* and *Tertullian*; *Ovid*'s Art;
　　Solomon's Proverbs, *Heloïsa*'s Loves;
　　And many more than sure the Church approves.
　　More Legends were there here, of wicked Wives,
　　Than good, in all the *Bible* and *Saint*'*s-Lives*.
365 Who drew the *Lion Vanquish'd*? 'Twas a *Man*.
　　But cou'd we Women write as Scholars can,
　　Men shou'd stand mark'd with far more Wickedness,
　　Than all the Sons of *Adam* cou'd redress.

368. cou'd: *1717:* can

360. **Chrysippus:** mentioned by Jerome in his *Epistola*; perhaps identical with the Stoic philosopher of the third century BC mentioned by Cicero in *De Diviniatione*. See also the quotation in Commentary to 16 above.
　　Tertullian: early Church father (c. 150–c. 230), author of works on chastity, monogamy and shame, which might have featured in Jenkin's book.
　　Ovid's Art: the *Ars Amatoria* of Publius Ovidius Naso; it had recently been very loosely translated as *The Art of Love* by William King (1708) and more closely by others, including Dryden and Congreve, as *Ovid's Art of Love* (1709); for Pope's knowledge of this latter version see 'January and May', 381–2, Commentary. This text was knowingly and wittily libertine in culture, in contrast to the theological books mentioned.
361. **Proverbs:** the book of Proverbs in the Old Testament, sometimes attributed to Solomon. Chaucer's Wife records the 'Parables of Salamon' here, 679, fol. 35ᵛ.
　　Heloïsa's Loves: as lavishly displayed in Pope's own 'Eloisa to Abelard', published in the *Works* of 1717, and perhaps already in preparation. Whatever the Wife's husband may intend, Eloisa at least was a model of sexual passion and devotion, as Pope's version of her would show; her (supposed) letters had been published in a translation by John Hughes from a French text earlier in 1713.
362. Pope's addition. Chaucer's Wife has also been subjected to quotations from Theophrastus, *Aureolus liber Theophrasti de Nuptiis* ('the golden book of Theophrastus of marriages', a particularly strident denunciation of women), and Trotula, an Italian female physician of the eleventh century, author of works on female physiology.
363–4. Condensed from Chaucer 683–91, missing out the pleasure that the Husband takes in his reading, and the Wife's complaint that scholars cannot write well of women, even holy saints. Cf. the response of the Queen in 'January and May', 700–3.
363. **wicked Wives:** Chaucer's phrase, 685, fol. 35ᵛ.
365. **Lion Vanquish'd:** cf. 337. Chaucer, 692, fol. 36ʳ: 'Who peinteth the Lion, tell me who?' Pope makes slightly clearer the allusion to the Aesopian fable of the lion being shown a picture of a lion defeated by a man as a sign of human superiority, only to point out that the picture would look different if it were painted by a lion. The story had been recently retold, in *The Spectator*, no. 11, 13 March 1711, by 'Arietta', responding to a series of stories of female infidelity told by a male visitor.
367–8. Chaucer, 695–6, fol. 36ʳ: 'They would haue written of men more wickednesse | Than all the marke of Adam may redresse'. *TE* suggests that Pope's 'mark'd' is a misunderstanding of Chaucer's 'marke of Adam', i.e. 'Sons of Adam' as Pope has it. Pope seems to have understood the sense well enough, while perhaps being prompted to use 'mark' as a stronger verb than 'write'.
368. **redress:** redeem, put right or counter.

680 THE WIFE OF BATH HER PROLOGUE (1713)

        Love seldom haunts the Breast where Learning lies,
370   And *Venus* sets when *Mercury* does rise:
        Those play the Scholars who can't play the Men;
        And use that Weapon which they have, their Pen;
        When old, and past the Relish of Delight,
        Then down they sit, and in their Dotage write,
375   That not one Woman keeps her Marriage Vow.
        (This by the Way, but to my Purpose now.)

          It chanc'd my Husband on a Winter's Night
        Read in this Book, aloud, with strange Delight,
        How the first Female (as the Scriptures show)
380   Brought her own Spouse and all his Race to Woe;
        How *Samson*'s Heart false *Dalilah* did move,
        His Strength, his Sight, his Life, were lost for Love.
        Then how *Alcides* dy'd, whom *Dejanire*

---

370. **when Mercury does:** *1717–51:* e're *Mercury* can
381–3. 1717–51: How *Samson* fell; and he whom *Dejanire*

369–70. Chaucer's Wife (697–705) gives a much more astrologically complete explanation of the enmity between those whose ascendant sign is Venus and those ruled by Mercury. Brathwait glosses those lines (p. 133): '*Mercury* is for Wisdom and Speculation; *Venus* for Riot and Sensual Meetings'. Line 369 is largely Pope's invention.

370 **variant.** Probably designed to take out the expletive 'does'; cf. 268 variant.

371–2. TE cites Pope to John Caryll, 8 November 1712 (*Corr.*, I.152): 'I beg you to offer him my utmost service ... with the only weapon I have, my pen'; for the underlying innuendo here cf. Shakespeare, *Merchant of Venice*, V.i.237. The idea is in Chaucer but the imagery and phrasing are Pope's.

371. **play:** act the part of.

373. **Relish:** also used to indicate sexual pleasure (by Alison herself) in Gay's *Wife of Bath*, II, p. 18; more colloquially expressed in Chaucer, 707–8, fol. 36^r: 'The clerke whan he is old, & may nought do | Of Venus werkes, not worth his old sho'.

374. **Dotage:** state of mental impairment in old age; also Chaucer's word, 709.

376. Partly based on another of Chaucer's Wife's recollections of where she is in her story, 711–12.

377–88. Chaucer, 713–26, 733–46, with much rearrangement of the second segment.

377. In Chaucer, 714, he is sitting by the fire but no season is mentioned.

378. **strange Delight:** not in Chaucer in this point, but based on the 'well good deuocion', 739, fol. 36^r, which Chaucer's Wife hears in his reading voice.

379–80. The story of Eve from chapter 3 of Genesis, enormously elaborated by Milton in *Paradise Lost*; 380 echoes Milton's opening lines particularly. Pope culls this couplet from Chaucer's 715–20, which also reminds the audience of Christ's blood redemption, a motif ignored by Pope but dramatically expanded by Milton in *Paradise Regain'd* (1671).

381–2. Chaucer, 721–3, with slightly more detail; the story of Samson's betrayal to the Philistines by Delilah was told in Judges 16:4–21, and had been expanded into a tragedy by Milton, *Samson Agonistes* (1671).

383. **Alcides:** Herakles or Hercules; he mortally wounded Nessus, a centaur, to prevent him from raping his wife Deianeira, who

        Wrapt in th' envenom'd Shirt, and set on Fire.
385   How curst *Eryphile* her Lord betray'd,
        And the dire Ambush *Clytemnestra* laid.
        But what most pleas'd him was the *Cretan* Dame,
        And Husband-bull — Oh monstrous! fie, for Shame!

        He had by Heart the whole Detail of Woe
390   *Xantippe* made her good Man undergo;
        How oft she scolded in a Day, he knew,
        How many Pisspots on the Sage she threw;
        Who took it patiently, and wip'd his Head;
        Rain follows Thunder, that was all he said.

395   He read how *Arius* to his Friend complain'd
        A fatal *Tree* was growing in his Land,
        On which three Wives successively had twin'd
        A sliding Noose, and waver'd in the Wind.

---

later gave him a shirt treated with the centaur's blood, which burned him to death; in Sophocles' *Trachiniae* she does this unwittingly, but in some versions she is deliberately treacherous. Chaucer, 724–6, tells it neutrally.

385. curst: 'peevish' or 'malignant' (*SJ*).

Eryphile: wife of Amphiarus (named in Chaucer, 740–6); at the instigation of Polynices, she persuaded her husband to take part in the war known as the Seven against Thebes, knowing he would die. Cf. 'The First Book of Statius his Thebais', 62 and Commentary. Pope refers to the story in his translation of the *Odyssey*, XI.406–7: 'There *Eriphylè* weeps, who loosely sold | Her lord, her honour, for the lust of gold'. Pope has brought this instance forward and greatly condensed it.

386. Clytemnestra: wife of Agamemnon, leader of the Greek forces at Troy; on his return from the war she and her lover killed him in his bath, a story dramatised by Aeschylus in the *Oresteia*. Chaucer 737–9. At this point Pope omits some further examples from Chaucer, 747–56, introducing them later at 403–8.

387. what most pleas'd him: 'For shreudnesse him thought that tale swete', Chaucer, 734, fol. 36ʳ.

Cretan Dame: Pasiphae, wife of Minos of Crete, mother of the Minotaur (fathered by the bull in question). The story is in Ovid, *Ars Amatoria*, I.295–326. In Chaucer, 735–6, fol. 36ʳ, the Wife seems more straightforwardly shocked than in Pope: 'Fie, speake no more, it is a grisely thing | Of her horible lust and hir likyng'.

389. Detail: 'a minute and particular account' (*SJ*); the metre requires stress on the second syllable here.

389–94. Chaucer, 727–32; Pope's Husband appears to have more details than Chaucer's.

390. Xantippe: wife of the Athenian philosopher Socrates (469–399 BC), portrayed in some sources as a jealous, shrewish woman (e.g. Xenophon, *Symposium*). The chamber pot anecdote is not classical in origin but is (in slightly more detail) in Chaucer, along with the first recorded instance of the proverb in 394 (for which see Tilley, T275). Xantippe is one of the examples in Jerome's *Epistola*, I.48.

395–402. Chaucer, 757–64, with added detail in 398 and 400. Chaucer, 761, fol. 36ʳ, has it that the wives 'Honged himself for harts dispitous'.

395. Arius: the story originates in Cicero, *De Oratore*, 2. 69, but Chaucer's editors suggest that 'Valerius' (cf. 359) was his source.

398. waver'd ... Wind: cf. 'January and May', 482. Pope's addition.

>   Where grows this Plant (reply'd the Friend) oh where?
> 400 For better Fruit did never Orchard bear:
>   Give me some Slip of this most blissful Tree,
>   And in my Garden planted it shall be!
>
>   Then how two Wives their Lord's Destruction prove,
>   Thro' Hatred one, and one thro' too much Love;
> 405 That for her Husband mix'd a Poys'nous Draught;
>   And this for Lust an am'rous Philtre bought,
>   The nimble Juice soon seiz'd his giddy Head,
>   Frantic at Night, and in the Morning dead.
>
>   How some with Swords their sleeping Lords have slain,
> 410 And some have hammer'd Nails into their Brain,
>   And some have drench'd them with a deadly Potion;
>   All this he read, and read with great Devotion.
>
>   Long time I heard, and swell'd, and blush'd, and frown'd,
>   But when no End of these vile Tales I found,

---

401. Slip: cutting, for propagation purposes.

403–8. Chaucer, 747–56; these stories were told between the Eryphile and Arius examples. In Chaucer the wives are named and more detail is given: Livia, lover of Sejanus, poisoned her husband (405); Lucia, wife of the Roman poet Lucretius, is the other example, both from the 'Valerius' source (cf. 359).

406. Philtre: love-potion.

407. nimble Juice: the phrasing is influenced by Dryden's translation of Juvenal's sixth satire, a classic location of misogynistic anecdote, recalling (802–3) the wife of Caligula, exemplifying the tendency for 'philtres' to turn a husband's brain: 'Some nimbler Juice wou'd make him foam, and rave, | Like that *Caesonia* to her *Caius* gave'; *Satires of Juvenal*, p. 120.

408. Pope's line is neater than Chaucer 754–5, fol. 36ʳ: 'She gaue him soch a loue maner drinke | That he were dedde, er it were morow'.

409–12. Chaucer, 765–71, omitting some of the more salacious details about wives' behaviour. For this section, in which Chaucer also gives no names, Brathwait (p. 138) suggests several 'Tragick Examples', mostly wives of Roman emperors suspected of poisoning their husbands, while Chaucer's editors suggest an allusion to the story of the Widow of Ephesus, in Petronius, *Satyricon*, 91.

410. Jael kills Sisera while he is sleeping, in Judges 4:20-2, but with a tent peg rather than a nail, and he is not her husband; this was probably what Chaucer had in mind, however, in his similar version of the line (769, fol. 36).

411. drench'd: treated medicinally; for 'drench' *SJ* gives 'to physic [medicate] by violence'.

412. Based on Chaucer, 739, where it applies to the story of Clytemnestra (cf. 386). Pope here omits Chaucer, 772–85, an extensive list of misogynistic proverbs read out by the Husband.

413–26. Chaucer, 786–810.

413. blush'd: Chaucer's Wife (786-7, fol. 36ʳ) does not react outwardly but speaks of 'The wo, that in mine hart was and pine'.

414–16. Expanded from details in Chaucer, 788–9. For the attitude, cf. 'January and May', 681-2.

415 When still he read, and laugh'd, and read again,
     And half the Night was thus consum'd in vain;
     Provok'd to Vengeance, three large Leaves I tore,
     And with one Buffet fell'd him on the Floor.
     With that my Husband in a Fury rose,
420 And down he settled me with hearty Blows:
     I groan'd, and lay extended on my Side;
     Oh thou hast slain me for my Wealth (I cry'd)
     Yet I forgive thee — Take my last Embrace.
     He wept, kind Soul! and stoop'd to kiss my Face;
425 I took him such a Box as turn'd him blue,
     Then sigh'd and cry'd, *Adieu my Dear, adieu*!

     But after many a hearty Struggle past,
     I condescended to be pleas'd at last.
     Soon as he said, My Mistress and my Wife,
430 Do what you list the Term of all your Life:
     I took to Heart the Merits of the Cause,
     And stood content to rule by wholsome Laws;
     Receiv'd the Reins of Absolute Command,
     With all the Government of House and Land;
435 And Empire o'er his Tongue, and o'er his Hand.

---

415. The laughter is mentioned much earlier in Chaucer, at 672.

417. *three large Leaves*: the same number as in Chaucer (790), but no mention is made there of their size. In her previous mention of the action, Chaucer's Wife had claimed only one leaf (667).

418. *Buffet*: 'a blow with the fist' (*SJ*). In Chaucer the blow knocks him backwards into the fire, 793; it is the Wife who is knocked 'in the flore' (796, fol. 36^r).

419. In Chaucer, 794, fol. 36^r, the Husband is compared to a 'wode [mad] Lion'; cf. 337.

420. *settled*: *OED*, sense 21a for 'settle': 'to quiet with a blow; to knock down dead or stunned'; in Chaucer (795, fol. 36^r) the husband 'smote me on mine hedde'.

hearty: cf. 255.

421. Chaucer's Wife 'lay as I were dedde' (796, fol. 36^v), prompting the Husband to consider fleeing.

422–3. Chaucer's Wife mentions a final kiss, but not forgiveness.

424–6. In Chaucer, 803–10, the Husband weeps, blames her, promises reform, and begs for forgiveness, before she hits him again and proclaims herself dying.

425. *took . . . Box*: hit him so hard.

427–37. Chaucer, 811–22, with much reordering of content.

428. In Chaucer, 812, the pair 'fell accorded within our seluen two', fol. 36^v.

430. *list*: please; the line is very close to Chaucer, 820.

431. *Merits . . . Cause*: Pope's language, recalling the legal terminology of 336.

433. *Reins*: 'bridell', Chaucer, 813, fol. 36^v.

***Absolute Command*:** with 'Laws' in the line before and 'Government' in the next line, this takes on a certain political colouring: 'absolute' was normally a Whig gibe against high-Tory or Jacobite reverence for the Divine Right of Kings. Here it is jocularly transferred to a woman's power (which is the theme of the Wife of Bath's ensuing Tale). Chaucer's Wife uses slightly different terms: 'gouernaunce', 'maistry' [mastery], and 'souerainte', 814 and 818.

434–5. Very close to Chaucer, 814–15.

As for the Volume that revil'd the Dames,
'Twas torn to Fragments, and condemn'd to Flames.

Now Heav'n on all my Husbands gone, bestow
Pleasures above, for Tortures felt below:
440   That Rest they wish'd for, grant them in the Grave,
And bless those Souls my Conduct help'd to save!

436-7. Elaborating the simpler fate of the book in Chaucer, 816, fol. 36ᵛ, and repositioning it as a climactic gesture; in Chaucer the Wife 'made hem brenne his booke anon tho', before arranging the terms of their new settlement.

438-41. Pope's conclusion differs from Chaucer's, 823-8, where the Wife records her happy and faithful life with the fifth husband, and prays that God will bless his soul, before announcing her tale. Pope's final couplet recalls the earlier idea (238) that the Wife had been a kind of purgatory on earth, hence saving the souls of the husbands.

22

PROLOGUE, DESIGN'D FOR MR. D —— 'S LAST PLAY

(1713)

Editors' Headnote

Composition and publication

The 'Prologue, Design'd for Mr. D—'s Last Play' was published on 29 December 1713. The poem was never formally acknowledged by Pope and was not included in any of his own editions of his *Works*. On its first appearance, at pp. 40–1 of Steele's *Poetical Miscellanies* (dated 1714), which contained three other poems by Pope (19, 20 and 22 of the present volume), it was said to be, 'Written by several hands'. It is not adjacent to the other poems of Pope's in the volume, all of which are acknowledged. However, since versions of lines 3–4 and 21–22 appear in letters from Pope to Cromwell, 10 May 1708, and to Wycherley, 20 May 1709 (*Corr.*, I.49 and 61; *TE*, VI.75), Pope must have been at least one of these 'hands'. *TE* (VI.102) makes a strong case for Pope's being the dominant author, but Rae Blanchard assigns it largely to Steele in *The Occasional Verse of Richard Steele* (1952), pp. 103–6, on the grounds of Pope's apparent detachment from D'Urfey's cause, and because the tone seemed closer to Addison and Steele's campaign on D'Urfey's behalf than to Pope's other references to him. But this ignores the lines which are obviously Pope's, worked in here without apparent effort; and the tone of the 'Prologue' is a matter of judgment and can easily seem more hostile to D'Urfey than Addison and Steele were, though their attitude was certainly less than wholly earnest. Pope was closely enough involved with Addison and Steele and *The Guardian*, in which the benefit performance of D'Urfey's *A Fond Husband* was promoted, and for which Pope was writing, for the attribution to him to be plausible. If it were Steele's one would expect it to feature in the *Guardian* campaign, which it does not. It was, however, later printed in the Pope–Swift *Miscellanies. The Last Volume* (dated 1727, published March 1728), prompting the accusation that it had been 'written at *Button's* in a publick Room by *several Hands*' and could not be claimed by either Swift or Pope (see Guerinot 1969: 119). Pope is far more likely to have produced it than Swift (see Context below). It is therefore on balance treated here as largely Pope's work, though some verbal parallels with other writers, including Addison and Steele, are also noted in the Commentary. It was first incorporated into the canon of Pope's verse in William Roscoe's edition of *The Works of Alexander Pope*, 10 vols (1824).

Text

The text presented here is taken from the first edition of 1713. The various extant texts of the 'Prologue' are referred to in the apparatus as follows:

1713: Poetical Miscellanies, octavo (Griffith 24)

1727: Miscellanies. The Last Volume, octavo (Griffith 196)

1742: Miscellanies. The Fourth Volume, octavo (Griffith 564)

Models and sources

Prologues and Epilogues had become a notable extra feature of theatrical life following the reopening of the theatres at the Restoration and many poets who were not themselves dramatists contributed examples on behalf of friends or acquaintances. The benefit performance, with accompanying star Prologue or Epilogue (or both), was also a relatively new phenomenon. Pope would certainly have known of items close to his circle such as Rowe's 'Epilogue spoken by Mrs. Barry, April the 7th, 1709. At a representation of Love for love: for the benefit of Mr. Betterton', printed with Congreve's 'Prologue Spoken by Mrs Bracegirdle' on the same occasion (1709). Pope had already written the more contentious and widely publicised 'Prologue to *Cato*' (item 17 above); he went on to contribute a prologue to the collective Scriblerian farce *Three Hours after Marriage* in 1717 and one to James Thomson's tragedy *Sophonisba* in 1730. He would return to the genre of (facetious) benefit prologue on behalf of his old enemy John Dennis in 1733, his last work for theatre. His view thereafter was tartly expressed in 1735: 'Three things another's modest wishes bound, | My friendship, and a Prologue, and ten Pound' (*Epistle to Dr. Arbuthnot*, 47–8). See further Headnote to 'Prologue to *Cato*', and for a summary of Pope's relations with the theatre, Goldstein (1958).

The phrasing of the title suggests that this example might not have been intended for actual theatrical delivery. The phrase 'Prologue, design'd for' could be an innocuous sign of a change of intention, as in Charles Johnson's *The Force of Friendship* (1710), which had in its published form a 'Prologue design'd for Mr. Betterton, spoken by Mr. Wilks'. But equally the phrasing was already established as satiric, e.g. *Prologue, Design'd for the last new Farce, call'd the Fool's Expectation, or the Wheel of Fortune* (1698), actually a satire on lotteries. *An Imitation of the Sixth Ode of Horace, apply'd to His Grace the Duke of Marlborough*, 'With a prologue design'd for the first day of Mr. Estcourt's acting, but forbid to be spoke by Mr. Rich, who thought himself reflected on in one of the verses' (1704) is one of many 'design'd for' prologues printed separately from the play it supposedly accompanied, as with Pope's own 'Epilogue to Mr. Rowe's Jane Shore, Design'd for Mrs. Oldfield' (not spoken or printed with the play, which appeared in 1714, but published in Pope's *Works* of 1717; see Ault 1949: 133–8). Warton (1756: 259–60), writing on Pope's 'Prologue to *Cato*', draws slightly disparaging attention to the 'satyrical and facetious' nature of Dryden's work of this type, indicating that Pope could have found a collection of them in the inaugural Dryden–Tonson *Miscellany Poems* (1684), pp. 263ff.; the present prologue seems more akin to this model.

Context

Thomas D'Urfey or Durfey (c. 1653–1723) had been the author of several reasonably successful comedies, such as *Madam Fickle* (1676), *The Royalist* (1682), *Love for Money* (1691) and a musical version of *Don Quixote* (1694); he was also a prolific writer of comic songs and catches. He had become something of a figure of satire as early as 1692, in the opera *The Fairy-Queen*, by Elkanah Settle and Henry Purcell; his stutter (see Pope's 'Prologue', 4) and drunkenness formed a comic focus. D'Urfey's status as an underrewarded man of a certain literary talent, forced to become a 'Sonneteer for Bread', had already been noted in the version of Juvenal VII, 'A Satyr on the Poets', ascribed to Matthew Prior in *Poems on Affairs of State* (1703), p. 138, and in Curll's unauthorised collection of Prior's *Poems on Several Occasions* (1707), pp. 14–15 (the ascription is accepted by Wright and Spears 1959). Swift mocked his 'vast Comprehension ... universal Genius, and most profound Learning' with heavy irony in the 'Epistle Dedicatory' to *A Tale of a Tub* (1704), p. 9, and had more directly referred to the 'low' tone and content of D'Urfey's in the 'Conclusion', contrasting him with Congreve and aligning '*Durfy*'s last Play' directly with '*Excrement*' (p. 217). In early January 1714 Swift published his *First Ode of the Second Book of Horace Paraphras'd*, which aligned D'Urfey with two of Pope's acquired enemies, Philips and Dennis.

While he had not personally provoked Pope, D'Urfey's shift towards the Whig cause after the revolution of 1688 put him to some extent in the enemy camp; as Addison pictures it in *The Guardian*, no. 67, 28 May 1713, he had previously been intimate with Charles II to the point of singing duets with him, and latterly 'turned a considerable part of the Pope's Musick against himself' in promoting the Protestant cause. Pope writes slightly of D'Urfey's literary abilities in a letter to Cromwell of 29 August 1709, and more genially, if still facetiously, in a later letter, 10 April 1710: 'I have not quoted one Latin Author since I came down, but have learn'd without book a Song of Mr Tho: Durfey's, who is your only Poet of tolerable Reputation in this Country'; and 'So may it be said of Mr Durfey, to his Detractors; Dares any one despise Him, who has made so many men Drink?' (*Corr.*, I.71 and 81). There is a passing hit at D'Urfey in the *Essay on Criticism*, 620, and a further joke comparing him to Dennis, in *The Critical Specimen*, *PW*, I.16. Pope told Spence that there was originally a chapter, contributed by Anthony Henley, on D'Urfey as a music teacher in the *Memoirs of Martinus Scriblerus* (*OAC*, I.56, no. 135; and I.58, no. 140). D'Urfey was latterly an easy target for the satirists of Pope's group, including Parnell, Gay and Arbuthnot (see further Ellis 1959). He was used as a model of low rustic humour in the 'Pastoral war' with Philips; Pope's parody of Philips's folkish simplicity, *Guardian*, no. 40, 27 April 1713, in which D'Urfeyesque comic rustics are used to besmirch the rustic simplicity of Philips's version of pastoral, appeared amid the succession of articles in support of D'Urfey in that periodical. Pope further mentions D'Urfey with easy contempt in *Sandys' Ghost* (1717) and *The Dunciad* (see *Dunciad Variorum*, III.138); he used him as an example of the 'Frogs' in chapter 6 of 'Peri Bathous' (1728; see Commentary to 15–16). A further set of comic 'Verses' on D'Urfey, of uncertain date, remained unpublished until 1726 (*TE*, VI.85).

From the perspective of 1713, D'Urfey's 'last' play (i.e. last *new* play) was *The Modern Prophets*, performed in 1709, but Pope's title more probably refers to the revival of *A Fond Husband: or, The Plotting Sisters*, a comedy dating originally from 1677 but reprinted twice in 1711 and performed on 15 June 1713 for the benefit night. It was not reprinted that year. The play was rated by Langbaine (see note to 14) as 'One of his best Comedies'; *An Account of the English Dramatick Poets* (1691), p. 180. Addison and Steele, more sympathetic than Pope or Swift to the drift of D'Urfey's political songs, had begun a facetious but essentially genuine support campaign on behalf of their 'Honour'd Friend' as early as the first *Tatler*, in which *The Modern Prophets* was advertised as D'Urfey's twenty-fifth play (12 April 1709; and further, no. 11, 15 May 1709). Addison had commended D'Urfey's insufficiently rewarded 'jocose labours' in an essay on laughter (*Guardian*, no. 29, 14 April 1713) and warmly promoted the benefit night in the same paper (no. 67, 28 May). The performance was again promoted on the day by either Addison or Steele in the same paper (no. 82, 15 June 1713), drawing attention to the play's popularity 'in the last Generation', an audience which had supposedly included Charles II. Pope wrote to Caryll, 23 June 1713, about his involvement with *The Guardian* and noted, neutrally, the paper's support of D'Urfey (*Corr.*, I.180). There is no record of the 'Prologue' being delivered on the night; it is not mentioned in the *Guardian* papers, and the light and dismissive tone of it might have given the play a rather inauspicious start. Steele's inclusion of it in the *Miscellanies*, however, leaves the question of its performance, as of its authorship, open. In *The Lover*, no. 40, 27 May 1714, Steele attempted, once again in jocular fashion, to sustain support for D'Urfey's dignity in advance of a further benefit performance (of *The Richmond Heiress*). The playwright received intermittent patronage in his final decade from the publisher Tonson and well-disposed aristocrats such as the seventh Earl of Dorset. For a full review of D'Urfey's career see McVeagh 2000.

PROLOGUE,

Design'd for Mr. D ──'s last Play.

Written by several Hands.

 GROWN Old in Rhyme, 'twere barbarous to discard
 Your persevering, unexhausted Bard:
 Damnation follows Death in other Men,
 But your damn'd Poet lives and writes again.
5 Th' adventrous Lover is successful still,

Title. *1727–42:* PROLOGUE, | Design'd for | *Mr. Durfy's last Play.*

---

1. GROWN **Old in Rhyme:** when the poem appeared, D'Urfey was about 60; he would survive until 1723. For the phrasing cf. Addison, 'An Account of the Greatest English Poets', *The Annual Miscellany: For the Year 1694* (1694), p. 325, speaking of Dryden: 'Grown old in Rhime, but charming ev'n in Years'. Pope's mention of the poet's age is less respectful; in *The Guardian*, no. 67, 28 May 1713, Addison spoke of D'Urfey's 'blooming old Age'.

2. **unexhausted:** not apparently elsewhere used by Pope, but commonly used of poetic inspiration in e.g. Cowley's 'Upon Mrs. K. Philips her Poems', *Poems by the Most Deservedly admired Mrs. Katherine Philips, the Matchless Orinda* (1667), 40–1: 'And there is so much room | In the unexhausted and unfathom'd womb'; and Addison, speaking of Congreve, in 'An Account of the Greatest English Poets' (p. 326): 'who's Fancies unexhausted Store | Has given already much, and promis'd more'. The usage here is only ironically a compliment.

3–4. Pope had concluded his letter about fame to Cromwell, 10 May 1708 (*Corr.*, I.49) with this exact couplet (excepting 'agen' for 'again'), at that stage applying it to himself ('If ever I seek for Immortality here, may I be d—d! for there's not so much danger in a *Poet's* being damn'd)'.

3. **Damnation . . . Death:** perhaps echoing a common theatrical oath, e.g. from D'Urfey's own *A Fond Husband*, I.i (1677), p. 4: 'Death and Damnation, must I stay and see this?'

4. **damn'd:** condemned by audience opinion; cf. *Essay on Criticism*, 414. The phrase is common in similar contexts, e.g. the 'Epilogue' to Congreve's *The Mourning Bride* (1697), 12: 'a damn'd Poet, and departed Muse'. Cf. the 'Song' in D'Urfey's own *Sir Barnaby Whigg*, III.i (1681), p. 28: 'Though I fall a damn'd Poet, I'le mount a Musician', and Henry Higden, *A Modern Essay on the Thirteenth Satyr of Juvenal* (1686), p. 19: 'Or what damn'd Poet ere would write, | That did not hope a good third Night?' D'Urfey, who had a stammer (see Headnote: Context), is reported to have said: 'The Town may da-da-damn me for a Poet, [. . .] but they si-si-sing my Songs for all that'; *The Fourth and Last Volume of the Works of Mr. Thomas Brown* (1715), p. 117.

5. **adventrous Lover:** cf. Waller, 'The Miser's Speech in a Mask', 5–6, *Poems, &c* (1645), p. 68): Venus 'could well advise | Th' adventurous Lover how to gain the prize'. D'Urfey himself used the phrase in the last scene of *Squire Oldsapp* (1679), p. 64.

Who strives to please the Fair against her Will:
Be kind, and make him in his Wishes easie,
Who in your own Despite has strove to please ye.
He scorn'd to borrow from the Wits of Yore;
10 But ever Writ as none e'er Writ before.
You modern Wits, should each Man bring his Claim,
Have desperate Debentures on your Fame;
And little would be left you, I'm afraid,
If all your Debts to *Greece* and *Rome* were paid.
15 From his deep Fund our Author largely draws;
Nor sinks his Credit lower than it was.

---

6. A common joke of the period about the insincerity of women's resistance to sexual advances; Rumbold (1989: 20) compares examples from *Windsor-Forest* (19–20) and 'Spring' (59–60). Cf. also Pope's 'Roman Catholick Version of the First Psalm', 5: 'To Please her shall her Husband strive...'.

9–16. Pope alludes to the increasingly contested balance between allusion to classical writers and a stress on originality. Swift's fable of the toxic Spider (which draws everything out of its own interior) and the nutritious Bee (which makes honey from a variety of available flowers), condenses the debate; see 'A Full and True Account of the Battel fought last Friday...' in *A Tale of a Tub* (1704), pp. 243–51, and for the context, Levine (1991). Cf. also the positions set out in *Essay on Criticism*, 184–91 and 327–8.

10. *as none e'er Writ*: idiosyncratic writing unsanctioned by any model of authority, foreshadowing satire against the outré in *The Dunciad*. Vieth (1966) points out that this is based on an ironic phrase from Rochester's 'An Epistolary Essay from M. G. to O. B. upon their Mutual Poems', 48–9, *Poems on Several Occasions* (1696), p. 82: 'Man can wish no more | Than so to write, as none e'er writ before', and that Pope later echoed himself in the epigram 'On J. M. S. Gent'.

11. *modern Wits*: contemporary writers.

12. *desperate Debentures*: Dryden's similar analogy in the 'Prologue' to *Love Triumphant* (1694), sig. a1ʳ: 'And many desperate Debentures paid'. A debenture (a word Pope does not elsewhere use; here requiring stress on the second syllable) is a 'writ or note, by which a debt is claimed' (*SJ*, citing this passage, as the work of Swift). The modern wits are 'in debt' to the ancient authors from whom they borrow ideas.

Fame: reputation; cf. 25 below.

15. Cf. *Tatler*, no. 1, 12 April, 1709, on D'Urfey's lyric style, a 'Manner wholly new and unknown to the Antient *Greeks* and *Romans*', a double-edged compliment, followed up in *The Guardian*, no. 67, 28 May 1713, with the suggestion that D'Urfey's novel (unsuited) rhyme-words 'without his good Offices, would never have been acquainted with one another'. Dramatists were much subject to the charge of plagiarism, and in his *Account of the English Dramatick Poets* (1691), pp. 179–85, Langbaine (p. 179) accuses D'Urfey of wholesale borrowing:

> He is accounted by some for an Admirable Poet, but it is by those who are ... deceiv'd by Appearances, taking that for his own Wit, which he only borrows from Others: for Mr. *Durfey* like the *Cuckow*, makes it his business to suck other Birds Eggs.

He is also accused of plagiarising songs (p. 185).

15–16. *Fund ... sinks ... Credit*: economic terms, following 'Debentures', ironically suggesting the poverty-stricken D'Urfey's self-generated poetic riches. In the 'Epistle

Tho' Plays for Honour in old Time he made,
'Tis now for better Reasons — to be Paid.
Believe him, Sirs, h' has known the World too long,
20   And seen the Death of much Immortal Song.
He says, poor Poets lost, while Players won,
As Pimps grow rich, while Gallants are undone.
Tho' *Tom* the Poet writ with Ease and Pleasure,
The Comick *Tom* abounds in other Treasure.
25   Fame is at best an unperforming Cheat;

19. **Sirs, h' has:** *1727:* he has

Dedicatory' to *A Tale of a Tub* (1704), p. 9, Swift satirically identified D'Urfey as 'A Poet of a vast Comprehension, an universal Genius, and most profound Learning'. Pope's 'deep Fund' suggests the ironic 'bathos' or 'depth' that Pope would parody in the 'Profund' section of 'Peri Bathous' (1728), where D'Urfey appears with Ned Ward and James Moore among the '*Frogs*' who 'can neither walk nor fly, but can *leap* and *bound* to admiration: They live generally in the bottom of a ditch, and make a great noise whenever they thrust their heads above water' (*PW*, II.197). The rhyme pair is uncommon, but Pope had already used it in the 'Prologue to *Cato*', 17–18.

20. Immortal Song: alluding to Dryden, *Absalom and Achitophel*, 197 (1681), p. 7: 'And Heaven had wanted [lacked] one Immortal song'. An earlier instance of the phrase is Sir Richard Fanshawe's version of Camoens, *The Lusiad, or, Portugal's Historicall Poem*, III.i. 3 (1655), p. 46: 'Breathe an immortal *Song,* and *voice* divine'. D'Urfey's songs, while plentiful and popular, are ephemeral by comparison with biblically-inspired 'song'.

21–2. Pope's letter to Wycherley, 20 May 1709 (*Corr.*, I.61), on the subject of his getting published by the eminently wealthy Jacob Tonson, concludes: 'What Authors lose, their Booksellers have won, | So Pimps grow rich, while Gallants are undone'. At this point, as with the earlier example (3–4), Pope was trying out poses of distressed authorship with his fellow wits; in the 'Prologue', these are satirically applied to the theatrical world of D'Urfey.

Players: actors and theatre managers, profiting from the underpaid work of poets; a slightly disparaging label, as in e.g. Pope's note to *The Dunciad Variorum*, I.55, throughout the 'Preface' to his edition of Shakespeare (1725) and *Epistle to Dr Arbuthnot*, 60. In *The Guardian*, no. 67, Addison claims to have sent for three theatre managers, on hearing of D'Urfey's poverty, to remind them of their profits from his labours, with the result that the benefit night was proposed.

Pimps . . . Gallants: writing as analogous to the buying of sexual services, with pimps standing in for go-betweens such as theatre managers and 'gallants' (customers at a brothel) as the deluded and disappointed dramatists.

24. Comick: comic dramatist, the 'other Treasure' being his plays.

25. Fame: reputation, cf. 12, and *Essay on Criticism*, 481; a major theme Pope would soon return to in *The Temple of Fame* (1715). Fame was conventionally a fickle and unreliable goddess, like Fortune.

unperforming Cheat: a rogue who promises more than is achieved. For 'unperforming' cf. Dryden, 'Prologue' to *The Conquest of Granada*, pt. 1 (1672), sig. I3ʸ: 'You will excuse his unperforming Play'.

But 'tis substantial Happiness to Eat —
Let Ease, his last Request, be of your giving,
Nor force him to be Damn'd to get his Living.

---

26. substantial ... Eat: In his verse letter to Cromwell, 25 April 1708, Pope had greeted his friend from a region where 'two Substantial Meals a day were made' (*Corr.*, I.46). The phrase 'substantial happiness' normally meant something more emotional and less material, as in D'Urfey's own *Intrigues at Versailles*, II.ii, and IV.i. (1697), pp. 15 and 38. The emphasis on bodily sustenance foreshadows much of Pope's later humour about the poverty of dunces and hacks, notably in *The Dunciad* (1728), e.g. I.42, where they weigh 'solid pudding against empty praise'; also *Epistle to Dr Arbuthnot*, 14, 152. For the phrasing cf. Oldham, 'Counterpart to the Satyr against Virtue', 148, *Works* (1684), p. 9: 'Oh mighty envied Happiness to eat!'

27. Ease: comfort, as opposed to fluency (cf. 23). 'He has made the World merry, and I hope they will make him easie so long as he stays among us'; Addison, *Guardian*, no. 67.

23
THE ARRIVAL OF ULYSSES IN ITHACA
(1713)

Editors' Headnote

Composition and publication

'The Arrival of Ulysses in Ithaca' was first published on 29 December 1713. While there is no direct evidence for the period of composition, *TE* (I.358–60) plausibly suggests that Pope began his translation of this passage from book XIII of the *Odyssey* in 1707–8, during the period in which he composed the 'Episode of Sarpedon'. He was evidently looking at the *Odyssey* in 1709, when he sent Cromwell a version of his lines 'Argus' (not published until 1727), on the subject of Odysseus's dog (*Odyssey*, XVII), which recognises the returning King before dying (to Cromwell, 19 October 1709; *Corr.*, I.74). The letter from Trumbull to Bridges of 31 October 1709, cited by *TE* and indicating that Pope has temporarily suspended work on Homer because of headaches, accords more directly with that known piece of translation than with the present piece, but it could refer to any of the early versions. In any event, Pope evidently completed work on the poem before 5 October 1713, when he received fifteen guineas from Jacob Tonson (junior) for it, together with 'The Wife of Bath Her Prologue'; see further *Corr.*, I.191–2, for a letter of agreement from Tonson to Pope on the same date. Both poems were first published in Steele's *Poetical Miscellanies* (see Headnote to 'The Wife of Bath Her Prologue'); the present poem occupies pp. 120–34.

Text

The text presented here is taken from the first edition of 1713. Substantive revision is confined to two later texts: the *Works* of 1717 and the incorporation of the poem into the full translation of the *Odyssey* in 1725. The text of the 1725 *Odyssey of Homer* adds notes at the foot of the page, written by Pope's collaborator William Broome, together with an additional 76 lines following line 52. Neither addition relates to the 'Arrival of Ulysses' as a separate poem and they have therefore been omitted from the apparatus, but verbal revision of lines included in the earlier poem has been recorded. The British Library manuscript of Pope's *Odyssey* translation omits almost all of the lines of the 'Arrival', including only a few lines as cues for its subsequent incorporation. These have been collated as part of the textual record. The various extant texts of 'The Arrival of Ulysses in Ithaca' are referred to in the apparatus as follows:

MS: 'The Odyssey' (British Library, Add MS 4809, ff. 116–17, and 119–20; *IELM* PoA 242)

1713: *Poetical Miscellanies*, octavo (Griffith 24)

1717: *Works*, quarto (Griffith 79)

1725: *The Odyssey of Homer*, quarto (Griffith 159)

Models and sources

For Pope's reading of, attitude towards and earlier translations from Homer, and the influence of earlier translators from Chapman to Dryden, see the Headnotes to 'The Episode of Sarpedon' and 'The Gardens of Alcinous'. As for those earlier poems, there were models available in the full translations of Chapman, Ogilby and Hobbes; it does not appear that there were any previous separate translations of this segment of the poem. It was more common to translate sections of the *Iliad* than the *Odyssey*; the four Homer translations in *Examen Poeticum* (1693) and *Annual Miscellany: For the Year 1694* (1694) are all from the *Iliad*. However, the only other Homeric version in Steele's *Poetical Miscellanies* was Pope's own republished 'Gardens of Alcinous', from the *Odyssey*, which followed this item. In the Commentary, earlier translations are quoted from the following sources, using additionally modern lineation in the case of Chapman (from Nicoll 1957): Chapman, *Homer's Odysses. Translated according to ye Greeke* (1615), pp. 198–206; Ogilby, *Homer his Odysses Translated, Adorn'd with Sculpture, and Illustrated with Annotations* (1665), pp. 179–87; Hobbes, *Homer's Odysses translated by Tho. Hobbes of Malmsbury* (1675), pp. 157–63.

Context

For Pope's relations with Steele in the period leading up to publication of the anthology, see Headnote to 'The Wife of Bath Her Prologue'.

Book XIII of the *Odyssey* begins the second half of Homer's epic; having experienced various adventures and disasters, and recounted several of them to Alcinous, ruler of Phaeacia, where he is washed up on the shore (see Headnote to 'The Gardens of Alcinous'), Odysseus has been granted a ship to return him to Ithaca. Subsequent books tell the story of Odysseus' eventually successful struggle to reclaim his island territory, palace, and wife and son, from the foreign suitors who have taken up residence. The 'Return of Ulysses', as the story was sometimes labelled ('Ulysses' being the common Latinisation of 'Odysseus') was sometimes foregrounded as a crucial example of Homer's handling of narrative in neoclassical epic theory, e.g. in book II of *Monsieur Bossu's Treatise of the Epick Poem*, translated by 'W. J.' (1695). Pope's poem begins part way through *Odyssey*, XIII.76, and at 52 breaks off part way through 125; his 53 picks up part way through Homer's 187, and his final line, 247, is equivalent to Homer's 360. The large gap, covering the return of the Phaeacians and Poseidon's implacable revenge against them for helping the loathed Odysseus, is supplied in the full translation, where the first passage is equivalent to 92–143, the omitted sequence to 144–219, and the second part to 220–414. Pope's poem therefore makes 247 lines from about 223 of Homer, a relatively modest scale of expansion (cf. items 2 and 19). In fact, the enlargement is slightly greater than this, as Pope has dropped a further 10–12 lines of Homer in passing. The other translators, in their full versions, do not make cuts of this type. Chapman converts Homer's lines into about 338 lines; Ogilby, about 309; and Hobbes, the most literal of the three, about 203. All use rhyming couplets.

Pope's major omission allows him to concentrate seamlessly on the arrival on the shore of Ithaca and Odysseus' reaction on waking alone in a region he does not recognise. Apart from incidental details (see Commentary to e.g. 43–4, 199–200), Pope mostly drops epic formulae and repeated epithets, in accordance with the principles stated in the 'Preface' to the full *Iliad* translation (1715), sig. F1^r (*PW*, I.248–9; cf. further comments on the issue in his notes to I.117 and VIII.707). He omits references to gestures which might seem less than heroic (69, 110, 161), and anything which suggests a less than high heroic character to Odysseus himself, or less than divine attributes to Athena (92–3, 116, 136–9, after 147, 149, 153, 166–9, 198, 244); Pope's Odysseus is less the improvisatory trickster of Homeric legend than the resourceful and enduring strategist bearing up against Fate. Pope consistently adds ennobling detail and adjectival enhancement (7, 8, 10, 23–4, 41–2, 48, 52, etc). Homer's 'hawk' becomes Pope's 'Eagle' (14); Ithaca is made more paradisal (122–31), Athena more obviously divine and resourceful (100–2, 198–9, 205–6). Sentiments which Homer applies to a local situation become universal moral positions (86–7, 208–12). Odysseus and Athena speak to and of each other in a high, third-person mode, eschewing Homer's more colloquial approach (75, 193, 216, 220). Odysseus' emotion is usually intensified (57, 68, 77, 79, 96, 99, 112, 135). Religious aspects are emphasised (26, 38, 74, 88–91, 93, 230). Pope stresses the role of Alcinous, benign ruler of Phaeacia, where Homer writes of the collective action of the Phaeacians (49, 177). Above all, Odysseus' status as the rightful ruler, returning from exile, is emphasised by a number of small but significant verbal changes and allusions which might appear to align him, at certain moments, with the exiled Stuart claimant to the throne of Britain (15, 61–3, 69, 82–3, 159, 182–7, 217, 223, 246). The verse, which generates antitheses more neatly than Homer's unrhymed and usually enjambed hexameters do (176, 178, 194, 219), is heavily influenced by Dryden's translations of Virgil, especially of the *Aeneid* (another epic of homecoming or homebuilding). The influence of Milton is sometimes confined to landscape descriptions, with Ithaca featuring as another Paradise, but since Milton was himself imitating and developing Homeric and Virgilian tropes of heroism, there are other complex pointers to Miltonic epic in Pope's poem. Pope also echoes a number of his own earlier poems, particularly 'The First Book of Statius' and 'Sapho to Phaon'; much of his phrasing here proved useful in the larger Homer venture that was just beginning.

The return of a king from over the water ('An hapless Exile on a foreign Shore', as he calls himself at 159), having survived much dangerous overseas wandering, under the protective aegis of a deity, in order to reclaim his island kingdom and protect his faithful queen from rapacious, power-crazed rivals, might suggest a political reading, especially after Dryden's versions of Virgil, with their glancing uses of contemporary political vocabulary such as 'restor'd' or 'succession' (see Hammond 1999 for balanced commentary on this issue). Aden (1978: 76–7) and Erskine-Hill (1996: 62–3) highlight some areas suggesting Pope's possible intentions in this connection, including the sections on uneasy reliance on foreign princes (82–3) and patriotism and rural virtue (122–31). However, published as it was eight months before the death of Queen Anne in the middle of a polite anthology edited by a Whig MP, and with no obvious overall allegorical programme, whatever fleetingly subversive signals it embodied for Pope were well buried, and nobody at the time identified any Jacobite coding. Pope had just issued, in October 1713, his proposals for a full translation of the *Iliad*, a venture which proved profitable but much more controversial as Pope's uneasy friendship with Addison finally collapsed over the covert preparation of a rival 'Whig' version. Pope's translation appeared in sequential volumes from June 1715 onwards; a serious Jacobite rising occupied national attention from November 1715 to February 1716 and Pope's *Iliad* was caught up in offensive critique, most of it overtly political in character. Pope's version of the *Odyssey* (1725–6) was a more muted affair; a substantial and largely positive critique of it was published 1726–7 by his future friend Joseph Spence under the title *An Essay on Pope's Odyssey*, and some significant references in this to the present poem (as it was incorporated in the full translation) are noted in the Commentary.

THE
ARRIVAL
OF
ULYSSES
IN
ITHACA.

Being Part of the XIIIth Book of *HOMER*'s *ODYSSES*.

By Mr. *POPE*

The Beginning of this Book describes the Parting of Ulysses *from* Phaeacia; *with the Gifts of* Alcinous *to his Guest*; *and his taking Ship for his Native Country* Ithaca.

THE Sun descending, the *Phaeacian* Train
Spread their broad Sails, and launch into the Main:
At once they bend, and strike their equal Oars,

Title. *1717:* Part of the | THIRTEENTH BOOK | OF | *HOMER*'s *ODYSSES*.
1. **The Sun descending:** MS, *1725:* Now plac'd in order
2. **Spread their broad Sails:** MS, *1725:* Their cables loose

---

Title. Ulysses: the common Latinisation of 'Odysseus' in Pope's period; so in all previous translations.
Phaeacia: a legendary region of Greece, also known as Scheria, where Odysseus is washed up alone at the end of Odyssey, book V after leaving Ogygia on a raft which is wrecked by Poseidon. Its location is not consistently identified, but see Commentary to 21 below.
Alcinous: ruler of Phaeacia; see Headnote to 'The Gardens of Alcinous'.
Ithaca: the island home and central powerbase of the domain of Odysseus (Ulysses); it is not clear whether Homer's island can be straightforwardly identified with modern Ithaca, a small Greek island in the Ionian Sea, west of mainland Greece; see Commentary to 126.
1–52. Corresponding to Homer, XIII.76–125 (finishing part-way through the line).
1–12. Homer, XIII.76–85.

1–4. Corresponding to but mostly replacing Homer's seating of the oarsmen and launching of the boat.
2. Spread . . . Sails: There are no sails in Homer: the ship is being rowed. *TE* notes that Pope revised the image, perhaps because the sails are not compatible with rowing (next line); but he did not revise 13 (which is also not in Homer). Ogilby, *Homer, his Odysses translated, adorn'd with sculpture, and illustrated with annotations* (1665), p. 181, has the mariners setting sail when they leave Odysseus, at Pope's 52.
   launch . . . Main: cf. 'Sapho to Phaon', 250–1; 'main' is an epic word for ocean, used eight times in the poem, always as a rhyme-word.
3. equal Oars: i.e. in matching rhythm; not in Homer. Cf. Dryden, *Aeneid*, V.203–4, *Works of Virgil* (1697), p. 333: 'The *Centaur*, and the Dolphin, brush the brine | With equal Oars, advancing in a Line'. The phrase later

      And leave the sinking Hills, and less'ning Shores.
5   While on the Deck the Chief in Silence lies,
      And pleasing Slumbers steal upon his Eyes.
      As fiery Coursers in the rapid Race,
      Urg'd by fierce Drivers thro' the dusty Space,
      Toss their high Heads, and scour along the Plain;
10   So mounts the bounding Vessel o'er the Main:
      Back to the Stern the parted Billows flow,
      And the black Ocean foams and roars below.

      Thus with spread Sails the winged Gally flies;
      Less swift, an Eagle cuts the liquid Skies:

---

recurred in Pope's full Homer translations: *Iliad*, II.619; *Odyssey*, IV.787 and XV.592.

4. *TE* likens this addition to Virgil, *Aeneid*, III.72: 'terraeque urbesque recedunt' ('and the lands and the cities fall back'). Spence comments on this passage as a particular beauty in *An Essay on Pope's Odyssey* (1726), p. 69. Not in Homer.

5. Odysseus' silence on deck is mentioned earlier by Homer, at 76.

6. pleasing Slumbers: a common phrase in seventeenth-century poetry, and cf. 155 and 'The First Book of Statius his Thebais', 538. Homer, 79–80, has νήδυμος ὕπνος ἐπὶ βλεφάροισιν ἔπιπτε, | νήγρετος, ἥδιστος ('deep sleep upon his eyelids fell, unwaking, sweetest').

7–10. In the full translation Broome adds a long note on the fitness of these similes in Homer (XIII.98). The Phaeacian ships were magical, as Alcinous has explained at *Odyssey*, VIII.555–63; they required no pilots or steering mechanism because they understood where the sailors wished to go.

7. fiery Coursers: a common phrase, but Pope is probably recalling Dryden's *Aeneid*, V.190–1, *Works of Virgil*, p. 333: 'Not fiery Coursers, in a Chariot Race, | Invade the Field with half so swift a Pace'; this passage, on a boat race, also lies behind the phrasing in 3 above. Simply ἄρσενες ἵπποι ('male horses') in Homer, 81. A courser is 'a swift horse; a war horse; a word not used in prose' (*SJ*).

8. dusty Space: not in Homer.

9. scour ... Plain: Pope re-used this phrase in his *Iliad*, XXI.24. For 'scour' in this sense cf. *Essay on Criticism*, 373. The plain is mentioned by Homer in 81: ἐν πεδίῳ, and Ogilby, p. 179 and Hobbes, *Homer's Odysses translated by Tho. Hobbes of Malmsbury* (1675), p. 157 both use the word; Chapman, *Homer's Odysses. Translated according to ye Greeke* (1615), XIII.127, p. 198, has 'faire field'.

10. bounding Vessel: 'bounding' is Pope's addition; Chapman, 132, p. 198, refers to the ship's 'fiery Bound'. The phrase is paralleled in Blackmore's epic *King Arthur*, V (1697), p. 124: 'The bounding Vessel ran before the Wind'.

11–12. *TE* suggests comparison with Chapman, 133–4, p. 198: 'About whom rusht the billowes, blacke, and vast; | In which the Sea-roares burst'. Homer's adjective, 85, is πορφύρεον ('purple' or 'dark-gleaming').

13–20. Homer, XIII.86–92.

13. Gally: i.e. galley, ship powered by oars.

14. Eagle: in Homer, 86, ἴρηξ, a hawk, as in Hobbes, p. 157; Chapman, 136, p. 198 and Ogilby, p. 180, have 'Faulcon' or 'Falcons'.

    cuts ... liquid Skies: cf. *Windsor-Forest*, 184 and Commentary; 'liquid' is clear or transparent, adopted from Latin 'liquidus'. Lauderdale's version of Virgil, *Georgics*, IV, has additionally (speaking of cranes) 'And cut their Airy flight through liquid Skies'; *Annual Miscellany: For the Year 1694*, p. 242. Not in Homer (88), where it is rather the vessel which ἔταμνεν ('cut') the waves, as it is in Chapman, 137, p. 198; but Ogilby, p. 180, has 'cut the yielding Skie'.

15	Divine *Ulysses* was her Sacred Load,
	A Man, in Wisdom equal to a God.
	Much Danger long, and mighty Toils he bore,
	In Storms by Sea, and Combats on the Shore:
	All which soft Sleep now banish'd from his Breast;
20	Wrapt in a pleasing, deep, and death-like Rest.
	But when the rising Star did Heav'n adorn,
	Whose radiant Fires foretell the blushing Morn,
	Like distant Clouds the Mariners survey
	Th' emerging Hills and Rocks of *Ithaca*.
25	Far from the Town, a spacious Port appears,
	Sacred to *Phorcys*' Pow'r, whose Name it bears;
	Two craggy Rocks, projecting to the Main,
	The roaring Winds tempestuous Rage restrain;

21–4. 1717–25: But when the morning star with early ray
  Flam'd in the front of heav'n, and promis'd day,
  Like distant clouds the mariner descries
  Fair *Ithaca*'s emerging hills arise.

---

15. Sacred Load: No equivalent in Homer. Perhaps aligned with the royalist moment of Waller's 'Of the danger his Majestie (being Prince) escaped at the rode at St. *Andere*', *Poems &c* (1645), p. 4: 'Yet the bold *Britans* still securely row'd, | *Charles* and his vertue was their sacred load'.

16. TE cites Hobbes, p. 157, 'Bearing a man for wisdom like a God'; 'Euen with the Gods, in counsailes', Chapman, 138, p. 198; 'Able to sit in Counsel 'mongst the Gods', Ogilby, p. 180.

20. death-like Rest: from earlier in Homer, 80, where sleep is θανάτῳ ἄγχιστα ἐοικώς ('as near as possible like death'). Ogilby, p. 179, has a note to Homer's line explaining the entire epic as an allegory of death and transfiguration in 'eternal Repose'.

21–44. Homer, XIII.93–112.

21. In the full translation Broome adds a note arguing that the timing shows that Homer's relative placing of Ithaca in relation to Phaeacia, which he identifies with Corcyra (modern Corfu) is accurate.

22. blushing Morn: Homer, 94, has Ἡὼς ἠριγενείης ('early-born Dawn').

22 variant. front: face, countenance.

23–4. Not in Homer, where the ship simply arrives at the island (95). This passage, from the full translation, was the focus of an approving commentary in Spence, *Essay on Pope's Odyssey* (1726), pp. 67–8. TE suggests analogy with Dryden's translation of Virgil, *Aeneid*, III.684–5, *Works of Virgil*, p. 287: 'When we from far, like bluish Mists, descry | The Hills, and then the Plains of *Italy*'.

25. Far ... Town: not in Homer.
  spacious: Pope's addition.

26. Sacred to: not at this point in Homer, who simply identifies the port as Phorkynos (96).

  Phorcys: sea-god, father of sea-creatures and monsters. Broome, annotating the full translation (XIII.116), explains the mythology as codified at the time (already noted by Ogilby, p. 180): '*Phorcys* was the son of *Pontus* [ocean] and *Terra* [earth] according to *Hesiod*'s genealogy of the Gods; this Haven is said to be sacred to that Deity, because he had a temple near it, from whence it receiv'd its appellation'.

28. tempestuous Rage: perhaps recalling the similar attribute of 'Cruel *Typhaon*' in Spenser, *Faerie Queene*, VI.vi.11.

                    Within, the Waves in softer Murmurs glide,
30   And Ships secure without their Haulsers ride.
                    High at the Head a branching Olive grows,
                    And crowns the pointed Cliffs with shady Boughs.
                    Beneath, a gloomy *Grotto's* cool Recess,
                    Delights the *Nereids* of the neighb'ring Seas;
35   Where Bowls and Urns were form'd of living Stone,
                    And massie Beams in native Marble shone,
                    On which the Labours of the Nymphs were roll'd,
                    Their Webs Divine of Purple mix'd with Gold.
                    Within the Cave, the clustring Bees attend

---

29. Mostly Pope's addition.

30. Haulsers: i.e. hawsers, ropes to 'haul' and moor ships with, Homer's δεσμοῖο, 100.

31. branching: Homer, 102, τανύφυλλος ('slender-leaved').

Olive: sacred to Athena, according to Ogilby's note, p. 181.

32. Pope's addition.

33-4. The rhyme appears unusual in Pope's time; he uses it again at 228-9, and in the full translation at XII.377-8. It is found in Defoe, *Caledonia* (1707), part one, p. 6 (speaking of a harbour): 'The wearied Sailors safe and true Recess, | A full Amends for wild Tempestuous Seas', and Defoe also rhymes 'Seas' with 'possess', p. 18. These are probably half-rhymes, not carrying any implication for pronunciation.

33. Grotto: here, a natural cave, of the type mentioned in 'Sapho to Phaon', 163-6; cf. also 'Eloisa to Abelard', 20 and 158, and *Rape of the Lock*, IV.21. Pope's famous grotto, an ornamental underground cavern and passage, was constructed beneath the villa he built at Twickenham from 1719 onwards. Pope no doubt recalled the phrase 'gloomy Grotto' from Dryden's version of Virgil's fifth eclogue, 26, *Works of Virgil*, p. 21, but Cotton had already used it for a natural cave in *The Wonders of the Peake*, 90 (1681), p. 6.

cool Recess: recalling Milton, *Paradise Lost*, IV.257-8 (1674), p. 93: 'umbrageous Grots and Caves | Of coole recess'; Milton has a vine rather than an olive above (see further Mason 1987). At this point in the full translation (XIII.124) Broome summarises, sceptically, allegorical interpretations of the cave drawn from earlier commentaries; cf. 228 below. Homer, 103, calls it ἄντρον ἐπήρατον ἠεροειδές ('a pleasing cloudy-grey cave').

34. Nereids: sea nymphs, daughters of Nereus (see 26): the word is only used by Pope in the Homer translations. Homer, 104, indicates Naiads (water nymphs), as do Chapman and Ogilby; but Hobbes, p. 157, has '*Nereiades*' (cf. 236-9).

neighb'ring Seas: not in Homer.

35. living Stone: simply λάϊνοι ('made of stone') in Homer, 106; 'petrifi'd', Ogilby, p. 180. *TE* cites *OED*, s.v. 'living', sense 2d (c): 'Native; in its native condition and site, as part of the earth's crust' and compares Dryden's *Aeneid*, I.78, *Works of Virgil*, p. 203: 'in a spacious Cave of living Stone'; he reuses the phrase and idea at VIII.257 (*ibid.*, p. 441).

36. Beams: here, part of a loom on which the 'warp' strands are wound before weaving begins, hence 'roll'd' in the next line. Homer mentions ἱστοὶ λίθεοι περιμήκεες ('very long stone looms'), 107; Hobbes, p. 157, has 'Long Beams of stone'.

38. Divine... Gold: not in Homer, who has φάρε' ... ἁλιπόρφυρα ('sea-purple shrouds'), 108.

39. Pope moves the bees here, from Homer's sequence (106); the following line is Pope's addition.

40   Their Waxen Works, or from the Roof depend.
     Perpetual Waters o'er the Pavement glide;
     Two Marble Doors unfold on either side;
     Sacred the South, by which the Gods descend,
     But Mortals enter at the Northern End.

45   Thither they bent, and haul'd their Ship to Land,
     (The crooked Keel divides the yellow Sand)
     Ulysses sleeping, on his Couch they bore,
     And gently plac'd him on the Rocky Shore:
     His Treasures next, *Alcinous*' Gifts, they laid
50   In the wild Olives unfrequented Shade;
     Secure from Theft: Then launch'd the Bark again,
     And tugg'd their Oars, and measur'd back the Main.

---

52. And tugg'd: MS, *1725:* Resum'd

---

40. Waxen Works: Pope's addition, perhaps recalling Addison's use of the phrase in a passage on bees in his translation of Virgil's fourth *Georgic*, in *Annual Miscellany: For the Year 1694*, p. 72.
   depend: hang down.
41. Pavement: 'stone floor' (*SJ*); not in Homer. The word had a more epic resonance in Pope's time; cf. Milton, *Paradise Lost*, I.682 (1674), p. 22: 'The riches of Heav'ns pavement, trod'n Gold'; at I.725-6, the 'smooth | And level pavement' of Pandemonium is contrasted with a brightly lit ceiling; cf. III.362-3, etc. Also Dryden, 'Of the Pythagorean Philosophy', 473-4, *Fables Ancient and Modern* (1700), p. 521, speaking of a petrifying stream: 'Whate'er it touches it converts to Stones, | And makes a Marble Pavement where it runs'.
42. Marble: Pope's addition (cf. quotation from Dryden in the previous note); in Homer, 109, there is no folding of the doors.
43-4. Pope reverses the order here and omits some of Homer's stress on the impassability of the South entry to humans (110-12).
45-52. Homer, XIII.113-25.
46. Pope harvested this line for his translation of the *Iliad*, I.631.
   crooked Keel: Pope's addition; cf. Dryden, 'Cymon and Iphigenia', 389, *Fables*, p. 555: 'The crooked Keel now bites the *Rhodian* Strand'.

divides... Sand: in Homer, 114, ὅσον τ' ἐπὶ ἥμισυ πάσης ('as much as half of all') of the ship is beached, apparently by the force of the rowers.
47. At this point in the full translation (XIII.138), Broome has a long note commenting on the absurdity of the action here, commentary on which began with Aristotle's *Poetics*; he follows this at 142 with an even longer note summarising defences of the incident.
48. gently: Pope's addition.
   Rocky Shore: ψαμάθῳ ('sand') in Homer, 119.
49. Alcinous' Gifts: The treasures are from the Φαίηκες ἀγαυοὶ ('illustrious Phaeacians') in Homer (120), not (at this point) from Alcinous personally; they are given at the instigation of Athena, a detail Pope omits.
51. Bark: ship.
52. tugg'd... Oars: apparently a recognised technique: cf. Roger Boyle, *Parthenissa* (1669), p. 726: 'Those timorous Men tugg'd at their Oars so vigorously...'. For the second half of the line, *TE* compares Dryden, *Aeneid*, X.931-2, *Works of Virgil*, p. 526: 'the Vessel plows the Sea, | And measures back with speed her former Way'. In Homer the sailors simply turn for home (125).
   Pope omits Homer, XIII.126-86, which tells of the revenge of Poseidon on the Phaeacians for helping Odysseus.

Mean while *Ulysses* in his Country lay,
Releas'd from Sleep; and round him might survey
55   The solitary Shore, and rowling Sea.
Yet had his Mind, thro' tedious Absence, lost
The dear Remembrance of his Native Coast;
Besides *Minerva* to secure her Care,
Diffus'd around a Veil of thicken'd Air:
60   For so the Gods ordain'd, to keep unseen
His Royal Person from his Friends and Queen,
Till the proud Suitors, for their Crimes, afford
An ample Vengeance to her injur'd Lord.

Now all the Land another Prospect bore,
65   Another Port appear'd, another Shore,
And long-continu'd Ways, and winding Floods,
And unknown Mountains, crown'd with unknown Woods.

---

63. **her:** *1725:* their

53–247. Homer, XIII.187–360 (entering midline).

53–63. Homer, XIII.187–93.

54–5. Mostly Pope's addition.

55. **solitary:** i.e. deserted except for him.

57. Mostly Pope's addition.

58. **Minerva:** Roman identity of Athena, Homer's goddess of wisdom, patron of Athens (and of the Greeks at Troy) and protector of Odysseus in particular.

    secure . . . Care: Pope's addition; 'Care' means an object of protection.

59. **Veil . . . Air:** ἠέρα ('fogs'), in Homer, 189; 'cloud' in Chapman, 277, p. 201; 'grosser mists', Ogilby, p. 182. Athena performs a like feat on Odysseus' behalf as he approaches the city of Alcinous in *Odyssey,* VII (53–4 in Pope's full version). Pope would come to mine these images for mock-heroic purpose in *The Rape of the Lock* (IV.39–40) and *The Dunciad* (e.g. I.67–72 of the 1728 version).

60. **unseen:** Broome, in the full translation (XIII.225), has a note discussing the meaning (literal and symbolic) of this passage, especially Homer's word ἄγνωστον ('unrecognised' or 'unrecognisable'), 191, which he concludes refers to Athena's disguising of both the country and Odysseus himself.

61–3. The reference is to the bloody revenge Odysseus and his son will eventually wreak on the foreign nobles who have been pursuing claims to Odysseus' wife Penelope and his island kingdom, on the presumption that he is dead, and who have abused laws of hospitality in the process. In Homer (192–3), Odysseus will πᾶσαν μνηστῆρας ὑπερβασίην ἀποτῖσαι ('pay back the suitors for each outrage'). Pope's 'Royal Person' and use of 'Queen' rather than Homer's more colloquial ἄλοχος ('bedfellow'), gives a faintly political colouring to the phrasing.

64–73. Homer, XIII.194–9.

66. **Floods:** rivers (an epic exaggeration, and an addition to Homer).

67. **unknown:** cf. *Windsor-Forest,* 87, and Commentary. Pope's addition, the culmination of a series of slightly altered details from Homer's 194–5.

THE ARRIVAL OF ULYSSES IN ITHACA (1713)

Pensive and slow, with sudden Grief opprest,
The King arose, and beat his careful Breast,
70   Cast a long Look o'er all the Coast and Main,
And sought around his Native Realm in vain;
Then with erected Eyes stood fix'd in Woe,
And, as he spoke, the Tears began to flow.

Ye Gods (he cry'd) upon what barren Coast,
75   In what new Region is *Ulysses* tost?
Possest by wild Barbarians fierce in Arms?
Or Men, whose Bosom tender Pity warms?
Where shall this Treasure now in Safety lie?
And whither, whither its sad Owner flie?
80   Ah why did I *Alcinous*' Grace implore?
Ah why forsake *Phaeacia*'s happy Shore?
Some juster Prince perhaps had entertain'd,
And safe restor'd me to my Native Land.

---

68. Pensive ... slow: probably a recollection of Milton, *Paradise Lost*, IV.173 (1674), p. 90: 'Satan had journied on, pensive and slow'.

Pensive: 'sorrowfully thoughtful; sorrowful; mournfully serious; melancholy' (*SJ*). A more forceful adjective in Pope's time than now; cf. 'January and May', 394, and 'The Rape of the Locke', II.1, and Commentary there.

sudden ... opprest: cf. 'Rape of the Locke', II.1-2. The whole line is Pope's addition.

69. careful: i.e. full of care. In Homer, 198-9, Odysseus beats his thighs, a detail retained by all previous translators. Pope may be recalling Dryden, *Absalom and Achitophel*, 934 (1681), p. 30, where David (Charles II) regains his royal authority: 'And long revolving in his careful Brest ... ', a phrase echoed by Pope, in relation to a trapped Odysseus, in his *Iliad*, XI.521: 'Such Thoughts revolving in his careful Breast'.

72-3. Pope's addition.

72. erected Eyes: i.e. looking up to heaven. The phrase is common in epic translation, e.g. Dryden, *Aeneid*, XII.292-3, *Works of Virgil*, p. 587: 'Then with erected Eyes and Hands, | The *Latian* King before his Altar stands'. Cf. 224, and Pope's *Temple of Fame*, 123.

74-93. Homer, XIII.200-16.

74-7. Pope reused this lament in his *Odyssey*, VI.139-42, when Odysseus is washed up on the shores of Phaeacia, and lines 76-7 also recur in Pope's *Odyssey*, VIII.627-8, spoken as a question by Alcinous to Odysseus.

74. Ye Gods: Pope's addition.

75. Replacing Homer, 200, τέων αὖτε βροτῶν ἐς γαῖαν ἱκάνω ('to the land of what people do I come?')

77. Homer, 202, ἦε φιλόξεινοι, καί σφιν νόος ἐστὶ θεουδής ('or friendly to foreigners and godly in mind').

79. Much expanded from Homer, 203-4, πῇ τε καὶ αὐτὸς | πλάζομαι; ('where am I myself to go?')

80. Pope's addition.

82-3. Homer has Odysseus imagine ἄλλον ὑπερμενέων βασιλήων ('another exceedingly great-spirited king'), who might have helped him return, 205-6. Erskine-Hill (1996: 63) suggests a glance at the exiled James (son of James II) in this couplet, strengthened by the insertion of 'restor'd', a Jacobite keyword with no close equivalent in Homer. The Stuarts were harboured by the French, who regarded them as the rightful sovereigns, but who never supplied sufficient military force to restore them.

Pope omits a repetition of the problem of the security of the treasures, Homer, 207-8.

82. juster Prince: 'kind Prince', Ogilby, p. 183.

Is this the promis'd, long expected Coast;
85 And this the Faith *Phaeacia*'s Princes boast?
Oh righteous Gods! of all the Great, how few
Are just to Heav'n, and to their Promise true!
But He the Pow'r, to whose All-seeing Eyes
The Deeds of Men appear without Disguise,
90 'Tis his alone, t' avenge the Wrongs I bear;
For still th' Opprest are his peculiar Care:
To count these *Presents*, and from thence to prove
Their Faith, is mine; the rest belongs to *Jove*.

Then on the Sands he rang'd his wealthy Store,
95 The Gold, the Vests, the Tripods number'd o'er;
All these he found, but still, in Error lost,
Disconsolate he wanders on the Coast:
Sighs for his Country; and laments again
To the deaf Rocks, and hoarse-resounding Main.

---

85. **Princes:** *1717–25:* rulers

---

84. Pope's addition.
86-7. Mostly Pope's addition, generalising the complaint: Homer's Odysseus (209) accuses only the Phaeacian leaders of not being discerning or just in all things (οὐκ ἄρα πάντα νοήμονες οὐδὲ δίκαιοι), and failing to carry out their promise to return him to Ithaca. Ogilby however also adds here: 'I will no more, You Gods, my Judgment trust', p. 183. The lines are open to a political reading amid the tensions and disputes of 1713-14.
88-91. Expanded from Homer, 213–14, largely by avoiding the name of Zeus (but see 93) and making the divine vengeance sound more like something exercised by the Jehovah of the Old Testament.
91. **peculiar Care:** object of particular protection; the same phrase is in 'January and May', 468, and 'The First Book of Statius his Thebais', 406.
92-3. In Homer, 216, Odysseus appears to check to see if the sailors have stolen anything. In the full translation (XIII.262) Broome has a long note defending Odysseus from the charge of avarice, using a passage of Plutarch to indicate that what Odysseus is doing is proving the fidelity of the Phaeacians, as emphasised here in Pope's enhanced version.
93. TE compares *Epistle to Arbuthnot*, 419: 'the rest belongs to Heav'n'.
94-115. Homer, XIII.217-35.
95. **Vests:** simply 'an outer garment' (*SJ*, who cites the phrase 'militarie Vest' from Milton, *Paradise Lost*, XI.241). Cf. 105 below, and Dryden's translation of the *Aeneid*, e.g. II.529, V.175, etc. In Homer, ὑφαντά τε εἵματα καλά ('beautiful woven cloaks'), 218; Ogilby translates 'Vests, and rich Mantles', p. 183.

Tripods: three-legged apparatus for heating water, often specially crafted as a prize and regularly listed among the spoils of war in epic; so in Homer, 217, though described as περικαλλέας ('very beautiful') there; Pope has omitted λέβητας ('cauldrons').
96. **in Error lost:** not knowing where he was. Pope's addition, perhaps recalling Miltonic phrases such as 'With Serpent errour wandring', *Paradise Lost*, VII.302, and 'in wandring mazes lost', *ibid*. II.561.
99. **deaf Rocks:** cf. Dryden, *Aeneid*, VI.637, *Works of Virgil*, p. 381: 'the deaf Rocks, when the loud Billows roar'.

100   When lo! the Guardian Goddess of the Wise,
      Celestial *Pallas*, stood before his Eyes;
      In show a youthful Swain, of Form divine,
      Who seem'd descended from some Princely Line:
      A graceful Robe her slender Body drest,
105   Around her Shoulders flew the waving Vest.
      Her decent Hand a shining Jav'lin bore,
      And painted Sandals on her Feet she wore:
      To whom the King: Whoe'er of Human Race
      Thou art, that wander'st in this desart Place,
110   With Joy to thee, as to some God, I bend
      To thee my Treasures and my self commend.
      O tell a Wretch, in Exile doom'd to stray,
      What Air I breath, what Country I survey?
      The fruitful Continent's extreamest Bound,
115   Or some fair Isle which *Neptune*'s Arms surround?

---

hoarse-resounding Main: echoing Dryden, 'The First Book of Homer's Ilias', 54, *Fables*, p. 191: 'the hoarse-resounding Shore'. Pope reused the image in his *Iliad*, I.203; *Odyssey*, I.396, etc. The whole line is in essence Pope's addition.

100. Pope's addition. This moment is shown in the illustration at the start of book XIII in Ogilby's translation (opposite p. 177).

101. Celestial **Pallas:** one of the (Greek) epithets of Athena, from earlier in Homer, 189; 'Celestial' is Pope's addition.

102. show: appearance.

   youthful **Swain:** the same phrase is given by Ogilby, p. 183.

   of Form divine: not in Homer.

105. waving: δίπτυχον ... εὐεργέα ('double-folded, well-wrought'), in Homer, 224.

   Vest: cf. 95; λώπην (a mantle), in Homer. Chapman, 328, p. 202, has 'a double Mantle'.

106. decent Hand: perhaps indicating the right hand, 'decent' in the Latinate sense of 'fitting'; cf. 'The First Book of Statius his Thebais', 156. Not in Homer.

   Jav'lin: spear.

107. painted Sandals: Homer's Athena wears sandals on her ποσσὶ ... λιπαροῖσι ('shining [or 'anointed'] feet'), 225; 'painted' is Pope's addition.

108-9. Pope's replacement for Homer, 227-9, in which Odysseus asks that the stranger conceive no bad thought of him but rather offer him protection.

108. To ... King: replacing Homer's formulaic 227, καί μιν φωνήσας ἔπεα πτερόεντα προσηύδα ('and speaking to her, addressed winged words'); Pope then used his reduced formula repeatedly in the *Iliad* translation (IV.226, X.49, etc.).

109. desart: i.e. desert, uncultivated space; commonly so spelt in Pope's time (cf. *Windsor-Forest*, 26); not in Homer.

110. bend: bow in token of subservience; in Homer, 231, Odysseus supplicates Athena by clasping her knees, the customary gesture.

112. Largely Pope's addition.

113. Homer's Odysseus, 233, asks rather who lives in the country.

115. **Neptune:** Latin version of the Greek god Poseidon, ruler of the seas and implacable enemy of Odysseus, because Odysseus had blinded his son, the cyclops Polyphemus, as Odysseus has narrated to the court of Alcinous in book IX. The periphrasis for the sea is not in Homer.

From what far Clime (said she) remote from Fame,
Arriv'st thou here, a Stranger to our Name?
Thou seest an Island, not to those unknown,
Whose Hills are brighten'd by the rising Sun.
120 Nor those, that plac'd beneath his utmost Reign,
Behold him sinking in the Western Main.
The rugged Soil allows no level Space
For flying Chariots, or the rapid Race;
Yet not ungrateful to the Peasant's Pain,
125 Suffices Fulness to the swelling Grain;
The loaded Trees their various Fruits produce,
And clustring Grapes afford a gen'rous Juice;
Woods crown our Mountains, and in ev'ry Grove
The bounding Goats and frisking Heyfers rove;

116–33. Homer, XIII.236–49.

116. Pope omits Homer's formulaic description of Athena, 236, and her playful accusation that Odysseus is νήπιός ('infantile' or 'naïve'), 237 (Chapman has 'foolish', 344, p. 202; Ogilby, 'in Experience Young', p. 184, Hobbes, p. 160, 'Simple').

Clime: 'climate; region; tract of earth' (*SJ*, where it is regarded as 'poetical').

118–21. Much expanded from Homer's 240–1.

120. utmost: furthest, most remote.

122–7. Greatly expanded from Homer's 242–4. The passage (in his own version) was cited in a note to Pope's full translation of the *Odyssey*, IV.998, to contest the scholarly tradition that Ithaca was rocky and barren. The fertile (and well-managed) island scene is also reminiscent of Pope's own 'Gardens of Alcinous' and 'Vertumnus and Pomona'. Broome, annotating the full translation (XIII.293), regards the description as a way of showing the epic importance of Odysseus' kingdom.

123. rapid Race: cf. Dryden's version of Virgil, *Georgics*, III.178, *Works of Virgil*, p. 101: 'Four Horses for the rapid Race design'd'; the phrase recurs in similar context in Pope's *Temple of Fame*, 217.

124. ungrateful: unfruitful, unresponsive; cf. Dryden, *Absalom and Achitophel*, 12 (1681), p. 7: 'A Soil ungrateful to the Tiller's care', spoken metaphorically of David's barren wife (i.e. Charles II's Queen).

Pain: labour, toil.

125–7. Mason (1987) suggests echoes of Milton's various depictions of luxuriant growth in *Paradise Lost*, IV.146–7 and 421–3; VIII.306–7; IX.576–7.

125. Suffices: affords sufficient.

swelling Grain: cf. Dryden's version of Virgil's third eclogue, 129, *Works of Virgil*, p. 15: 'The Show'rs are grateful to the swelling Grain'. Homer, 244, mentions only σῖτος ἀθέσφατος ... τε οἶνος ('limitless corn and wine').

126. Cf. Blackmore, *Creation*, II.833 (1712), p. 103: 'Hence various Trees their various Fruits produce', itself probably echoing Milton, *Paradise Lost*, V.389–91 (1674), p. 128: 'more numerous ... | Then with these various fruits the Trees of God | Have heap'd this Table'.

127. clustring Grapes: Dryden uses this phrase in his version of Virgil, *Georgics*, II.6.

gen'rous Juice: cf. 'The First Book of Statius his Thebais', 648.

129. frisking Heyfers: the phrase is in Addison's translation of Virgil's fourth Georgic, *Annual Miscellany: For the Year 1694*, p. 59; it was also in Philips's first 'Pastoral', *Poetical Miscellanies: The Sixth Part*, p. 4, and Gay's *Rural Sports*, 330, a poem published earlier in the year with a dedication to Pope. Homer mentions goats and cattle pasture, 246, but the vision here is Pope's own.

130 Soft Rains and kindly Dews refresh the Field,
And rising Springs Eternal Verdure yield.
Ev'n to those Shores is *Ithaca* renown'd,
Where *Troy*'s majestic Ruins strow the Ground.

At this, the Chief with Transport was possest,
135 His panting Heart exulted in his Breast:
Yet well dissembling his untimely Joys,
And veiling Truth in plausible Disguise;
Thus, with an Air sincere, in Fiction bold,
His ready Tale th' inventive Hero told.

140 Oft' have I heard, in *Crete*, this island's Name,
For 'twas from *Crete*, my Native Soil, I came;
Self-banish'd thence, I sail'd before the Wind,
And left my Children and my Friends behind.

---

130. kindly: nurturing, promoting growth; OED sense 9c (a) and (b). Evelyn uses 'kindly dews' in a similar sense in *Sylva* (1664), p. 115.

131. Eternal Verdure: Pope's addition; cf. the evergreen nature of Alcinous' garden. Samuel Wesley had concluded his panegyric *Marlborough* (1705), p. 12, with these words, having previously associated the concept with Christ in books I and IX of his *Life of our Blessed Lord & Saviour Jesus Christ* (1693), pp. 23 and 313. This aspect is Pope's addition.

132. Broome (note to XIII.299) regards the delay in mentioning the actual name as a psychological masterstroke. Chapman, 364, p. 203, delays mention of the name until the last word of Athena's speech; Hobbes until the last line, p. 161; in Homer, 248, it comes in the middle of the line before, as here.

133. Troy: city near the coast north-west Asia Minor, site of the Trojan war, usually now identified with Hisarlik in modern Turkey.
   strow: are strewn about. The ruins are not mentioned in Homer, 248–9.

134–9. Homer, XIII.250–5.

134. Transport: rapture.

135. The reaction is more intense than in Homer, 250–1, though Homer's Odysseus is described as χαίρων ('rejoicing'); he γήθησεν ('took pleasure').

136–9. Odysseus' main talent (in addition to conventional martial virtues) was for strategic cunning; a note to the first line of Pope's full version of the *Odyssey* refers to this passage in a long gloss on Homer's adjective for his hero, πολύτροπον, i.e. 'versatile' or 'of many turns', which Pope translates as 'for Wisdom's various Arts renown'd'. Cf. 188 and Commentary. Pope has omitted some formulaic expressions about their exchange (252–3) and intensified the visible aspects of Odysseus' dissembling.

138. in Fiction bold: confidently convincing in his invented story.

140–59. Homer, XIII.256–86.

140. Crete: island south of Greek mainland, in the Mediterranean. Homer's Odysseus passes but does not land on Crete during his journey (IX.80–2). Broome cites (at *Odyssey*, XIII.316) an alternative version of the story in which Odysseus does actually visit Crete.

141–3. Largely Pope's addition.

142. Self-banish'd: not in Homer. Perhaps recalling Dryden, 'Of the Pythagorean Philosophy', 77–80, *Fables*, p. 506: 'Here dwelt the Man divine whom *Samos* bore, | But now Self-banish'd from his Native Shore, | Because he hated Tyrants, nor cou'd bear | The Chains which none but servile Souls will wear'.

143. Homer, 258, mentions παισὶ ('children') but not friends.

From fierce *Idomeneus'* Revenge I flew,
145   Whose Son, the swift *Orsilochus*, I slew,
      (With Brutal Force he seiz'd my *Trojan* Prey,
      Due to the Toils of many a bloody Day.)
      Unseen I scap'd; and favour'd by the Night,
      In a *Phoenician* Vessel took my Flight;
150   For *Pyle* or *Elis* bound; but Tempests tost,
      And raging Billows drove us on your Coast:
      In dead of Night an unknown Port we gain'd,
      Spent with Fatigue, and slept secure on Land;
      But ere the Rosie Morn renew'd the Day,
155   While in th' Embrace of pleasing Sleep I lay,
      Sudden, invited by auspicious Gales,
      They land my Goods, and hoist their flying Sails.

---

144. **Idomeneus:** fierce leader of the Cretan contingent at Troy; he is particularly prominent in book XIII of the *Iliad*, and Pope gives a long note on his character at 278 of his version.

145. **Orsilochus:** son of Idomeneus in Odysseus' fabricated story; present at Troy, according to *Iliad*, V.541–9 (670–5 in Pope's translation). Pope drops Homer's 261, a gloss on the speed of Orsilochus.

146. **Brutal Force:** Pope's addition.

After 147, Pope omits Homer's 264–71, in which Odysseus gives a more circumstantial (and insalubrious) account of the supposed killing of Orsilochus.

148. Pope's addition.

149. **Phoenician:** from the trading nation based in the Levant at the eastern end of the Mediterranean; again, Odysseus does not go there. Pope omits Homer's details of the payment Odysseus supposedly made to the sailors, 273, and their unwillingness to default on the deal, 277.

150. **Pyle . . . Elis:** condensed from a more circumstantial account in Homer, 274–5. Elis was a city-state on the north-west plain of the Peloponnese, mentioned in the second book of the *Iliad* (Pope's version, II.747–59; he has a note on the geography at his *Iliad*, XI.818). Pylos ('Pyle') was the name of several cities, including one within Elis, and was identified as the city of the ancient Greek leader Nestor in Homer (in Pope's version, II.100, 715–16, and XI.873).

Tempests tost: The same phrase, used directly of Odysseus, is in line 2 of Pope's 'Argos', set out in the letter of 1709 to Cromwell mentioned in the Headnote. The phrase is also present earlier in the sequence of Ogilby's translation, p. 180, probably remembered from the witch's curse in Shakespeare, *Macbeth*, I.iii.25.

153. Pope omits Homer's detail, 280, that everyone is hungry.

154. **Rosie Morn:** from the famous epithet, ῥοδοδάκτυλος Ἠώς ('rosy-fingered Dawn'), *Odyssey*, II.1; Pope reuses his phrase at *Iliad*, I.623 and elsewhere. The line is Pope's addition.

155. **pleasing Sleep:** cf. 6. In Homer, 282, it is γλυκὺς ὕπνος ('sweet sleep'). Cf. Dryden, 'Ceyx and Alcyone', 309, *Fables*, p. 373: 'Sweet pleasing Sleep'.

156. **auspicious Gales:** cf. 'Sapho to Phaon', 246. Pope's addition.

157. **flying Sails:** not in Homer, where the sailors simply embark and go; but Chapman says they 'made saile', 414, p. 204, and Hobbes, p. 161, that 'they sail'.

Abandon'd here, my Fortune I deplore,
An hapless Exile on a foreign Shore.

160   Thus while he spoke, the blue-ey'd Maid began
With pleasing Smiles to view the God-like Man;
Then chang'd her Form, and now divinely bright
Jove's heav'nly Daughter stood confess'd to Sight,
Like a fair Virgin in her Beauty's Bloom,
165   Skill'd in th' illustrious Labours of the Loom.

O still the same *Ulysses*! she rejoin'd,
In useful Craft successfully refin'd;
Artful in Speech, in Action, and in Mind!
Suffic'd it not, that thy long Labours past
170   Secure thou seest thy Native Shore at last?
But this to me? who, like thy self, excel
In Arts of Counsel, and Dissembling well:
To me, whose Wit exceeds the Pow'rs Divine,
No less, than Mortals are surpass'd by thine:

---

159. **An hapless:** *1717–25:* A hapless

---

158. **deplore:** lament.
159. Pope's addition. Hobbes has earlier (p. 161) 'a man exil'd'.
160–5. Homer, XIII.287–9.
160. **blue-ey'd:** γλαυκῶπις ('bright-eyed' or 'glaring-eyed'), in Homer, 287.
161. Pope's substitution for Homer, 288, where she smiles ('laught' in Chapman, 415, p. 204) but also κατέρεξε (strokes) him; 'God-like Man' is Pope's addition.
163. **Jove:** i.e. Zeus, Athena's father.
    confess'd: revealed. This line is Pope's addition.
165. Homer, 289, describes Athena as ἀγλαὰ ἔργα ἰδυίῃ ('skilled in bright works'). The 'Loom' suggestion may be prompted by Chapman's 'expert in the frame | Of vertuous Huswiferies', 418–19, p. 204, but also by Penelope's continued ruse of unpicking her own hand-worked tapestry, on completion of which she had promised to choose a suitor. Pope omits Homer's 290, a formulaic introduction to her speech. He burlesqued this image in *The Dunciad Variorum*, II.147.
166–87. Homer, XIII.291–310.

166–9. Substituting for Homer's more colloquial address, 291–3, where she calls Odysseus σχέτλιε, ποικιλομῆτα (a 'wicked, scheming man'; these adjectives can also mean 'enduring, inventive'), who could outwit most gods. In Chapman, 'Thou still-wit-varying wretch! Insatiate | In overreaches', 424–5, p. 204.
169. **long Labours:** Pope's addition. Modelled here on the 'Long Labours' of Aeneas' fortitude and journey in Dryden's version of the *Aeneid*, e.g. I.4, *Works of Virgil*, p. 201; cf. the parody of the idea in 'Rape of the Locke', I.88.
172. **Dissembling well:** cf. 'January and May', 816, where it is associated with the deceitfulness of women, as it is in Pope's *Iliad*, XV.38. At XIII.338 of the *Odyssey* translation, Broome inserts a note defending Odysseus from the charge of behaving in a fashion unbecoming an epic hero. Cf. 136–9.
173. **Wit:** intelligence. See *Essay on Criticism*, Headnote, for the range of meaning; cf. also however the word's use for the deceitful and strategic intelligence of women in 'The Wife of Bath Her Prologue', 95.

175 Know'st thou not me, who made thy Life my Care,
   Thro' ten Years Wand'ring, and thro' ten Years War;
   Who taught thee Arts, *Alcinous* to persuade,
   To raise his Wonder, and ingage his Aid?
   And now appear, thy Treasures to protect,
180 Conceal thy Person, thy Designs direct,
   And tell what more thou must from Fate expect;
   Domestick Woes, far heavier to be born,
   The Pride of Fools, and Slaves insulting Scorn.
   But thou be Silent, nor reveal thy State,
185 Yield to the Force of unresisted Fate,
   And bear unmov'd the Wrongs of base Mankind,
   The last and hardest Conquest of the Mind.

   Goddess of Wisdom! (*Ithacus* replies)
   He who discerns thee must be truly wise,
190 So seldom view'd, and ever in Disguise.

---

175. The question format is perhaps prompted by Hobbes's version, p. 162: 'Did you not know me...?' It is not a question in Homer (299). Mason (1987) compares Satan's repeated 'Know ye not mee' response to the angels guarding Adam and Eve in *Paradise Lost*, IV.827–8.
176. Pope's addition.
177. In Homer, 302, Athena claims to have made Odysseus Φαιήκεσσι φίλον πάντεσσιν, ('dear to all the Phaeacians') rather than to Alcinous, who is not mentioned; Ogilby, however, has 'I gave Thee Favour in *Alcinous* Eys', p. 185. Homer's narrative of these events comes in books VI to VIII of the *Odyssey*.
178. Pope's addition.
180. Conceal thy Person: Pope's addition.
182–7. Much of this is Pope's invention, and closely aligned with the political burden of Addison's *Cato*, in which self-mastery is the sign of true liberty; see Headnote to 'Prologue to *Cato*'.
183. Slaves: not actual slaves but people who ought to be subservient; cf. 'The First Book of Statius', 221–6 and 264. This line is Pope's addition.
185. unresisted: irresistible; cf. *Rape of the Lock*, III.178. Pope recycled the phrase in his *Iliad*, V.777: 'Urg'd by the Force of unresisted Fate'.
186–7. These moralising lines are very much expanded from the simpler direction to suffer in silence which Homer's Athena delivers, 309–10, and 187 is wholly Pope's.
187. last and hardest: cf. 'Sapho to Phaon', 80, and Commentary.
188–206. Homer, XIII.311–328, omitting 311, a formulaic introduction to the next speech.
188. Ithacus: Ulysses, identified now with his kingdom; in Homer, 311, πολύμητις Ὀδυσσεύς ('crafty Odysseus'); 'the King', in Ogilby, p. 186. Chapman sometimes uses 'Ithacus' for Odysseus, e.g. 568, p. 207, following Latin examples such as Virgil, *Aeneid*, II.122; Homer uses the name only once (XVII.207) but rather of a founder-king of Ithaca, not of Odysseus himself.

THE ARRIVAL OF ULYSSES IN ITHACA (1713)

When the bold *Argives* did their Arms imploy
Before the Walls of well-defended *Troy*,
Ulysses was thy Care, Celestial Maid,
Grac'd with thy Sight, and favour'd with thy Aid:
195 But when proud *Ilion*'s Tow'rs in Ashes lay,
And, bound for *Greece*, we plow'd the Watry way;
Our Fleet dispers'd, and driv'n from Coast to Coast:
Thy sacred Presence from that Hour I lost;
Till I beheld thy radiant Form once more,
200 And heard thy Counsels on *Phaeacia*'s Shore.
But by th' Almighty Author of thy Race,
Tell me, oh tell, is this my Native Place?
For much I fear, long Tracts of Land and Sea
Divide this Coast from distant *Ithaca*.

191-2. 1717-25: When the bold *Argives* led their warring pow'rs
    Against proud *Ilion*'s well-defended tow'rs,
195. **proud *Ilion*'s Tow'rs:** *1717-25:* the *Trojan* piles

---

191. Argives: strictly, soldiers from Argos, main city of the Argive plain (for which see 'The First Book of Statius', Argument, 9), but used generally for the Greek side in the Trojan war. Homer, 315, has υἶες Ἀχαιῶν ('sons of Achaians'), another general term for the Greeks; Hobbes has 'the *Argive* Army', p. 162.
192. Simply ἐνὶ Τροίῃ ('in Troy') in Homer, 315.
193. Pope's addition. Homer's Odysseus does not in this section speak of himself in the third person.
194. Grac'd: Hobbes, p. 162, has 'how gracious you were': Homer, 314, reads μοι πάρος ἠπίη ἦσθα ('you were mild to me formerly').
195. TE compares Dryden, *Aeneid*, III.4, *Works of Virgil*, p. 267: 'And *Ilium*'s lofty Tow'rs in Ashes lay'.
195 variant. piles: buildings. The variant may be designed to lessen the resemblance to Dryden's line.
196. Pope's addition.
  plow'd the Watry way: probably recalling Dryden's version of the *Aeneid*, IX.118, *Works of Virgil*, p. 467: 'and plow the watry Way'; 'watery Way' is a common periphrasis in Dryden generally (cf. *ibid*., III.350; V.1, 1078, etc.). Cf. *Windsor-Forest*, 146; 'Sapho to Phaon', 250. Pope uses the exact phrase again in the full *Iliad* translation, II.685.
197. driv'n ... Coast: Pope's addition.
198. sacred Presence: Pope's addition.
  Pope omits Homer's 319-22, detailing Odysseus' uncertainties and sufferings without Athena's guidance.
199. radiant Form: Pope's addition; Mason (1987) compares Adam's extended vision of the 'radiant forms' of the celestial beings in *Paradise Lost*, V.454-9.
201. Almighty ... Race: i.e. Zeus, often referred to as the 'father' of the gods; simply πρὸς πατρὸς ('in respect of your father') in Homer, 324. Blackmore uses the phrase 'almighty Author' to indicate the Judaeo-Christian God in *Creation*, II.571 (1712), p. 67, but Pope's usage here seems merely an epic inflation of Homer's phrase.
203. long ... Sea: Pope's addition.

205　　The sweet Delusion kindly you impose,
　　　　To sooth my Hopes and mitigate my Woes.

　　　　　Thus he: The blue-ey'd Goddess thus replies:
　　　　How prone to Doubt, how cautious are the Wise?
　　　　Who vers'd in Fortune, fear the flatt'ring Show,
210　　And taste not half the Bliss the Gods bestow.
　　　　The more shall *Pallas* aid thy just Desires,
　　　　And guard the Wisdom which her self inspires.
　　　　Others, long absent from their Native Place,
　　　　Strait seek their Home, and fly with eager Pace,
215　　To their Wives Arms, and Childrens dear Embrace.
　　　　Not thus *Ulysses*; he decrees to prove
　　　　His Subjects Faith, and Queen's suspected Love,
　　　　Who mourn'd her Lord twice ten revolving Years,
　　　　And wastes the Days in Grief, the Nights in Tears.
220　　But *Pallas* knew (thy Friends and Navy lost)
　　　　Once more 'twas giv'n thee to behold thy Coast:

205–6. Much expanded from Homer's 326–7, in which Odysseus accuses Athena of κερτομέουσαν ('teasing'), in order ᾗπερ οπεύσῃς ('to deceive') his mind; Pope adds a reason for this possible 'Delusion' in 206; cf. Hobbes, p. 162, 'With comforts feign'd my sorrows to abate'. In the full translation Broome (XIII.369) added a note in which Odysseus' apparent disbelief of Athena is explained as plausible. Pope's idea is probably drawn from Swift, *Tale of a Tub* (1704), section IX, p. 171, in which happiness is defined as '*a perpetual Possession of being well Deceived*', though this itself has classical roots, e.g. in Horace, *Epistles*, II.ii.139–40, in which a hallucinating man is cured, but complains that he has been robbed of 'mentis gratissimus error', 'the most pleasing error of my mind'. On this theme see also 'January and May', 823–4 and Commentary.
207–33. Homer, XIII.329–51.
207. Thus he: i.e. thus he said; an epic formulation, modelled on Homer's ὣς φάτο (e.g. Homer, 250), but not present at this point (328–9).
　　blue-ey'd: cf. 160.
208–12. This general wisdom is Pope's addition, replacing Homer's 330–2, where Athena comments only on Odysseus' own personal circumspection; 211–12 is very loosely based on the same passage.
208. This line recurs in a speech of the nymph Calypso to Odysseus in Pope's *Odyssey*, V.237.
213–15. The triplet is generated from two lines of Homer, 333–4.
216. decrees: to decree is 'to determine; to resolve' (*SJ*). As in 193, the shift towards third-person reference is Pope's; Homer's Athena addresses Odysseus directly as σοὶ ('you'), 335.
217. Subjects Faith: Pope's addition.
　　Queen's suspected Love: Homer's Odysseus will, less grandly, σῆς ἀλόχου πειρήσεαι ('test your bedfellow'), 336.
218. Pope's addition.
　　revolving Years: on the model of Dryden's *Aeneid*, V.814 and VI.511, with the sense of a yearly cycle.
219. The antithesis between night and day is in Homer, 337–8, but less sharply epxressed.
220. Pallas: cf. 101. Homer's Athena, 339, speaks without epithet in the first person, not third.
　　Friends . . . lost: cf. Blackmore, *Prince Arthur*, I (1695), p. 16: 'Your Friends and Navy on the Ocean lost'.

THE ARRIVAL OF ULYSSES IN ITHACA (1713)　　　　713

    Yet how could I with adverse Fate engage,
    And mighty *Neptune*'s unrelenting Rage? —
    Now lift thy longing Eyes, while I restore
225 The pleasing Prospect of thy Native Shore!
    Behold the Port of *Phorcys*, fenc'd around
    With Rocky Mountains, and with Olives crown'd!
    Behold the gloomy *Grot*, whose cool Recess
    Delights the *Nereids* of the neighb'ring Seas;
230 Whose now neglected Altars, in thy Reign
    Blush'd with the Blood of Sheep and Oxen slain.
    Behold where *Neritus* the Clouds divides,
    And shakes the waving Forests on his Sides!

    So spake the Goddess, and the Prospect clear'd,
235 The Mists dispers'd, and all the Coast appear'd:
    The King with Joy confess'd his Place of Birth,
    And, on his Knees, salutes his Mother Earth;
    Then, with his suppliant Hands upheld in Air,
    Thus to the Sea-green Sisters sends his Pray'r.

---

222. *adverse Fate:* Pope's addition.
223. *Neptune:* cf. 115. Odysseus' ships and crew had been destroyed by storms raised by Poseidon, the reasons for whose grudge Homer's Athena, 342–3, explicitly reminds Odysseus of at this point; Pope omits this, and the reminder that Poseidon is her uncle.
224–5. Largely Pope's addition.
226–9. Repeating, as in Homer 345–9, details from 25–34, but in a more condensed form. Ogilby, p. 187, inserts a long note from the commentary tradition indicating that there is no such cave on Ithaca and that therefore the details are to be interpreted as an allegory on human life. On the second pass over this passage, p. 163, Hobbes uses 'Naïades'; cf. 34.
228. *Grot:* grotto or cave; cf. 33 and Commentary.
230–1. Greatly expanded from Homer, 350, which mentions hecatombs performed in the cave.
230. *neglected Altars:* not in Homer.
232. *Neritus:* Nirito or Neriton is a mountain in the north of modern Ithaca.
    Clouds divides: Pope's addition.

233. TE compares Chapman, 526–7, p. 206: 'Here, Mount *Nerytus* shakes his curled Tresse | Of shady woods'. Spence, *Essay*, p. 38, asks whether this image (in the full translation) 'is fitter for an Earthquake, than a *Metaphor*'. In Homer, 351, Neritus is merely καταειμένον ὕλῃ ('with a Forest clad', Ogilby, p. 187, or 'cloth'd with wood', Hobbes, p. 163).
236. *King:* in Homer, 353, δῖος Ὀδυσσεύς ('godlike Odysseus').
    confess'd: acknowledged.
237. In Homer, 354, Odysseus κύσε δὲ ζείδωρον ἄρουραν ('kissed the grain-bearing ploughland').
238. *suppliant:* in an attitude of prayer or petition. More specific than in Homer, where at 355 Odysseus prays with uplifted hands: ἠρήσατο, χεῖρας ἀνασχών.
239. *Sea-green Sisters:* Pope's addition. Dryden uses this phrase of river-nymphs in his version of Virgil, *Georgics*, IV.474, *Works of Virgil*, p. 136, and Pope aligns the 'circling *Nereids*' with the 'Sea-green Sisters of the Deep' in his version of the *Iliad*, XVIII.45–6.

240   All hail! Ye Virgin Daughters of the Main;
          Ye Streams, beyond my Hopes beheld again!
          To you once more your own *Ulysses* bows,
          Attend his Transports, and receive his Vows.
          If *Jove* prolong my Days, and *Pallas* crown
245   The growing Virtues of my youthful Son,
          To you shall Rites Divine be ever paid,
          And grateful Off'rings on your Altars laid.

---

240. In Homer, 356, the Naiads are addressed as κοῦραι Διός ('daughters of Zeus').

241. Homer's Odysseus does not address the streams.

242. Pope's addition.

243. Attend ... Transports: listen to his raptures; cf. 134. Pope's addition.

244. Jove ... Days: Homer's Odysseus mentions Zeus only as Athena's father, and it is Athena who is asked to preserve his life. *TE* suggests that Pope omits Homer's epithet ἀγελείη for Athena here (359) on grounds of decorum, taking it to mean 'she that drives off the spoil' (Chapman has 'mighty Pillager', 540, p. 206); it can mean more simply 'bestower of spoil'. It is probably omitted as formulaic and irrelevant at this point.

245. In Homer, 359–60, Odysseus merely makes the deferential proviso that Athena permit his dear son to live.

growing Virtues: Mezentius uses this phrase of his (dead) son Lausus in Dryden's version of the *Aeneid*, X.1214, *Works of Virgil*, p. 534.

246. Rites Divine: Pope's addition. Erskine-Hill (1996: 63) suggests a partial allusion to Dryden's version of the *Aeneid*, I.7–10, *Works of Virgil*, p. 201, where Aeneas has 'His banish'd Gods restor'd to Rites Divine | And setl'd sure Succession in his Line: | From whence the Race of *Alban* Fathers come, | And the long Glories of Majestick Rome.' The political resonance in Pope's lines, if intended at all, is more attenuated than in Dryden's however.

247. grateful: 'pleasing; acceptable; delightful; delicious' (*SJ*); cf. 124. Homer's Odysseus promises simply that δῶρα διδώσομεν ('we will give gifts'), 358.

Bibliography

Abbreviations

Corr.	*The Correspondence of Alexander Pope*, ed. George Sherburn, 5 vols (1956), Oxford.
EC	*The Works of Alexander Pope*, ed. Whitwell Elwin and William John Courthope, 10 vols (1871–86).
ESTC	The English Short-Title Catalogue, estc.bl.co.uk
Griffith	Reginald H. Griffith, *Alexander Pope: A Bibliography*, 2 vols (1922), Austin, TX.
Guerinot	J. V. Guerinot, *Pamphlet Attacks on Alexander Pope, 1711-1744: A Descriptive Bibliography* (1969), New York.
IELM	*Index of English Literary Manuscripts, vol. 3: 1700–1800*, 4 parts, compiled by Margaret M. Smith et al. (1986–92).
Lonsdale	Samuel Johnson, *The Lives of the Poets*, ed. Roger Lonsdale, 4 vols (2006), Oxford.
OAC	Joseph Spence, *Observations, Anecdotes, and Characters of Books and Men*, ed. James M. Osborn, 2 vols (1966), Oxford.
ODNB	H. C. G. Matthew and Brian Harrison, eds, *Oxford Dictionary of National Biography* (2004), Oxford; online edition, www.oxforddnb
OED	*Oxford English Dictionary Online*, oed.com
PW	*The Prose Works of Alexander Pope*, ed. Norman Ault and Rosemary Cowler, 2 vols (1936 and 1986).
SJ	Samuel Johnson, *A Dictionary of the English Language* (1755).
TE	*The Twickenham Edition of the Poems of Alexander Pope*, general editor John Butt, 11 vols (1939–69).
Tilley	Morris Palmer Tilley, *A Dictionary of the Proverbs in England in the Sixteenth and Seventeenth Centuries* (1950), Ann Arbor, MI.
Wakefield	Gilbert Wakefield, *Observations on Pope* (1796).
Warburton	*The Works of Alexander Pope, Esq. . . . Published by Mr. [William] Warburton*, 9 vols (1751).
Warton (1756)	Joseph Warton, *An Essay on the Genius and Writings of Pope*.
Warton (1782)	*An Essay on the Genius and Writings of Pope. Volume the Second.*

Certain journal titles are abbreviated:

ELH	*A Journal of English Literary History*
PMLA	*Publications of the Modern Language Association of America*
RES	*Review of English Studies*
SEL	*Studies in English Literature 1500–1900*

Works of modern scholarship and commentary have been cited by author's surname and year of publication, except in the case of those items given in the list of abbreviations above. Most literary works cited as sources, models or analogues for Pope have been cited from editions that he might conceivably have owned or seen (where there is positive evidence that he did own a particular text, this is normally noted). Reference is normally to the smallest division available in the contemporary source (act, scene, stanza, etc.), along with page number or, where un-paginated, signature. In some cases, such as Dryden's *Works of Virgil*, or Oldmixon's *Amores Britannici*, the contemporary works themselves supply line-numbers, and these have accordingly been used. However, where convenient modern editions of such works exist, additional reference is given to modern lineation, and the modern editions are cited by cross-reference in the bibliography below. Spelling from contemporary sources has largely been left unmodernised in accordance with the textual principles of the edition as a whole; in a few cases a text originally in italic (e.g. a prologue or preface) has been normalised to roman.

The Bible is cited in the Commentary by book, chapter and verse from either *AV*, familiarly known as the 'Authorised' or 'King James Bible', i.e. *The Holy Bible, Conteyning the Old Testament, and the New: Newly Translated out of the Originall Tongues* (1611) or *DV*, familiarly known as the 'Douay-Rheims' version, after the *New Testament* printed at Rheims in 1582 and the *Old Testament* printed at Douay in 1609–10. *AV* was the version 'authorised' for use in the Church of England; *DV* was used covertly by English Roman Catholics such as Pope.

Texts in Greek and Latin are cited from modern editions, normally from the *Oxford Classical Texts* or *Loeb Classical Library* series, using long-established standard referencing and divisions. All foreign-language quotations are translated, often from contemporary sources that Pope could have seen; all uncredited translations are our own and have been made as literal as possible.

Works without identified author are listed alphabetically by title or first significant word. No attempt has been made to represent the often complicated habits of anonymity in eighteenth-century publishing; we have used commonly accepted identifications from the English Short-Title Catalogue (estc.bl.co.uk) and other bibliographies such as Guerinot, sometimes noting where an attribution is particularly compromised by uncertainty. Place of publication is London unless otherwise stated.

Ackroyd, Peter (2007), *Thames: Sacred River*.
Adams, Thomas (1619), *The Happines of the Church*.
Aden, John (1973), 'The Change of Scepters, and Impending Woe: Political Allusion in Pope's Statius', *Philological Quarterly*, 52, 728–38.
—, (1978), *Pope's Once and Future Kings: Satire and Politics in the Early Career*, Knoxville, TN.
Addison, Joseph (1695), *A Poem to his Majesty, Presented to the Lord Keeper*.
— (1699), *An Ode on St. Cecilia's Day, November 22. 1699*.
— (1704, dated 1705), *The Campaign, a Poem, to His Grace the Duke of Marlborough*.
— (1705), *Remarks on Several Parts of Italy, &c. in the Years 1701, 1702, 1703*.
— (1713), *Cato. A Tragedy*.

— (1719), *Poems on Several Occasions. With a Dissertation upon the Roman Poets.*
— (1721), *The Works of the Right Honourable Joseph Addison, Esq.*, ed. Thomas Tickell, 4 vols.
— (1722), *The Drummer; or, the Haunted House*, third edition.
— (1726), *Dialogues upon the Usefulness of Ancient Medals.*
—: for a modern edition of *Cato*, see Henderson and Yellin (2004).
—: for *Miscellaneous Works*, see Guthkelch (1914).
—: for *The Guardian*, see Stephens (1982).
—: for *The Spectator*, see Bond (1965).
—: for *The Tatler*, see Bond (1987).
The Adventures of Catullus, and History of his Amours with Lesbia (1707).
Alarbas. A Dramatick Opera (1709).
Alderson, William, and Arnold Henderson (1970), *Chaucer and Augustan Scholarship*, Berkeley, LA.
Alderson, Simon (1996), 'Alexander Pope and the Nature of Language', *RES*, n.s. 47:185, 23–34.
Alexander, Peter, ed. (1951), *William Shakespeare: The Complete Works.*
Alpers, Paul J. (1996), *What is Pastoral?*, Chicago.
Ames, Clifford R. (1998): 'Variations on a Theme: Baroque and Neoclassical Aesthetics in the St Cecilia Day Odes of Dryden and Pope', *ELH*, 65:3, 617–35.
Anacreon Done into English out of the Original Greek (1683), Oxford.
The Annual Miscellany: For the Year 1694. Being the Fourth Part of Miscellany Poems (1694).
Arbuthnot, John (1712), *Law is a Bottomless Pit.*
— (1712), *John Bull Still in his Senses: Being the Third Part of Law is a Bottomless Pit.*
—: for *The History of John Bull*, see Bower and Erickson (1976).
Aristotle: for *Poetics*, see Lucas (1968).
Aristotle's Art of Poetry. Translated from the Original Greek (1705).
Ascham, Roger (1570), *The Scholemaster or Plaine and Perfite Way of Teachyng Children, to Vnderstand, Write, and Speake the Latin Tong.*
Atterbury, Francis, ed. (1690), *The Second Part of Mr. Waller's Poems.*
— (1708), *Fourteen Sermons Preach'd on Several Occasions.*
Audra, Emile (1931), *Les traductions françaises de Pope (1717–1825), étude de bibliographie*, Paris.
Ault, Norman, ed. (1935), *Pope's Own Miscellany: Being a Reprint of Poems on Several Occasions, 1717, Containing New Poems by Alexander Pope and Others.*
— (1949), *New Light on Pope with Some Additions to his Poetry hitherto Unknown.*
—, and Rosemary Cowler, eds (1936–86), *The Prose Works of Alexander Pope*, 2 vols.
Aylett, Robert (1622), *Susanna: or, the Arraignment of the Two Vniust Elders.*
Bacon, Sir Francis (1625), *The Essayes, or Counsels, Ciuil and Moral.*
— (1640), *Of the Advancement and Proficiencie of Learning*, Oxford.
—: for *The Wisedome of the Ancients*, see Gorges (1619).
Baines, Paul (1995), 'From "Nothing" to "Silence": Rochester and Pope', in *Reading Rochester*, ed. by Edward Burns, pp. 137–65, Liverpool.
Baker, Daniel (1697), *Poems upon Several Occasions.*

Banks, Theodore Howard, ed. (1969), *The Poetical Works of Sir John Denham.*
Barnard, John, ed. (1973), *Pope: The Critical Heritage.*
Barnes, Joshua (1675), *Gerania: A New Discovery of a Little Sort of People Anciently Discoursed of, Called Pygmies.*
Barton, William (1644), *The Book of Psalms in Metre.*
Basore, John, ed. and trans. (2014), *Seneca: Moral Essays, Volume 3: De Beneficiis*, Cambridge, MA.
Batt, Jennifer (2011), ''*A Collection of Poems* and Charles Tooke', *Notes and Queries*, 58:3, 394–9.
Battestin, Martin (1969), 'The Transforming Power: Nature and Art in Pope's Pastorals', *Eighteenth-Century Studies*, 2, 183–204.
Bayle, Pierre (1710), *An Historical and Critical Dictionary . . . Translated into English*, 4 vols.
Beaumont, Francis, and John Fletcher (1620), *Phylaster. Or, Love Lyes Bleeding.*
Beaumont, Sir John (1629), *Bosworth-Field: With a Taste of the Variety of Other Poems.*
Beaumont, Joseph (1648), *Psyche, or, Love's Mysterie in XX Canto's, Displaying the Intercourse betwixt Christ and the Soule.*
Behn, Aphra (1677), *The Town-Fopp; or, Sir Timothy Tawdrey.*
— (1681), *The Second Part of the Rover.*
— (1684), *Poems upon Several Occasions: With a Voyage to the Island of Love.*
— ed. (1685), *Miscellany, Being a Collection of Poems by Several Hands.*
— (1688), *Lycidus: or, The Lover in Fashion.*
— (1690), *The Widdow Ranter or, The History of Bacon in Virginia. A Tragi-Comedy.*
Benedict, Barbara M. (2007), 'Encounters with the Object: Advertisements, Time, and Literary Discourse in the Early Eighteenth-Century Thing-Poem', *Eighteenth-Century Studies*, 40, 193–207.
Benson, Larry, ed. (1988), *The Riverside Chaucer*, third edition, Oxford.
Bernard, Stephen, ed. (2015), *The Literary Correspondences of the Tonsons*, Oxford.
Berry, Reginald (1988), *A Pope Chronology*, Basingstoke.
Bidle, John, trans. (1634), *Virgil's Bucolicks Eng[l]ished.*
Biklé, Charles Henry (1982), 'The Odes for St. Cecilia's Day in London (1683–1703)', unpublished doctoral dissertation, University of Michigan.
Billingsley, Nicholas (1658), *Kosmobrephia, or, The Infancy of the World.*
Blackmore, Sir Richard (1695), *Prince Arthur. An Heroick Poem. In Ten Books.*
— (1697), *King Arthur. An Heroick Poem. In Twelve Books.*
— (1700), *A Paraphrase on the Book of Job.*
— (1700), *A Satyr against Wit.*
— (1705), *Eliza: An Epick Poem. In Ten Books.*
— (1706), *Advice to the Poets. A Poem.*
— (1708), *The Kit-Cats. A Poem.*
— (1712), *Creation. A Philosophical Poem.*
Blamires, Alcuin, ed. (1992), *Woman Defamed and Woman Defended: An Anthology of Medieval Texts*, Oxford.
Blanchard, Rae, ed. (1941), *The Correspondence of Richard Steele*, Oxford.
—, ed. (1952) *The Occasional Verse of Richard Steele*, Oxford.

Blondel, David: see D., J. (1661).
Blount, Sir Thomas Pope (1684), *De Re Poetica: or, Remarks upon Poetry*.
Blount, Thomas (1656), *The Academy of Eloquence*, second edition.
Boileau-Despréaux, Nicolas (1696), *The Second, Fourth, and Seventh Satyres of Monsieur Boileau Imitated*.
— (1701), *Oeuvres diverses*, Paris.
—: for *L'Art poétique*, see Soames and Dryden (1683).
—: for *Lutrin*, see Ozell (1708).
Boire, Gary A. (1977), 'The Context of Allusion and Pope's "Winter" Pastoral', *Concerning Poetry*, 10, 79–84.
Bond, Donald F., ed. (1965), *The Spectator*, 5 vols, Oxford.
—, ed. (1987), *The Tatler*, 3 vols, Oxford.
The Book of Common Prayer, and Administration of the Sacraments . . . According to the Use of the Church of England (1708).
Bouhours, Dominique (1705), *The Art of Criticism: or, the Method of Making a Right Judgment upon Subjects of Wit and Learning . . . Translated . . . by a Person of Quality*.
Bowden, Betsy, ed. (1991), *Eighteenth-Century Modernizations from the Canterbury Tales*, Woodbridge.
Bower, Alan W., and Robert A. Erickson, eds (1986), *John Arbuthnot: The History of John Bull*, Oxford.
Boyce, Benjamin (1962), *The Character-Sketches in Pope's Poems*, Durham, NC.
Boyer, Abel (1701), *Letters of Wit, Politicks and Morality*.
— (1701), *Choice Letters French and English*.
— (1702), *The English Theophrastus; or, the Manners of the Age*.
— (1707), *The History of the Reign of Queen Anne, Digested into Annals. Year the Fifth*.
Boyle, Roger (1669), *Parthenissa: A Romance. The Last Part. The Sixth Tome*.
Bragge, Francis (1694), *The Passion of Our Saviour*.
Brathwait, Richard (1665), *A Comment upon the Two Tales of our Ancient, Renovvned, and Ever-Living Poet Sr Jeffray Chaucer, Knight*; for a modern edition of *A Comment*, see Spurgeon (1901).
Brewer, Derek, ed. (1978), *Chaucer: The Critical Heritage*, 2 vols.
Brome, Richard, ed. (1649), *Lachrymae Musarum: The Teares of the Muses*.
Brooks, Harold F., and Raman Selden, eds (1987), *The Poems of John Oldham*, Oxford.
Brooks, Thomas (1669), *A Cabinet of Choice Jewels or, A Box of Precious Ointment*.
Brooks-Davies, Douglas (1985), *Pope's Dunciad and the Queen of the Night: A Study in Emotional Jacobitism*, Manchester.
Brower, Reuben A. (1959), *Alexander Pope: The Poetry of Allusion*, Oxford.
Brown, Tom (1699), *A Collection of Miscellany Poems, Letters, &c.*
— (1702), *Commendatory Verses, on the Author of The Two Arthurs, and The Satyr against Wit; By Some of his Particular Friends*.
— (1715), *The Fourth and Last Volume of the Works of Mr. Thomas Brown*.
Browne, Joseph (1705), *Albion's Naval Glory, or, Britannia's Triumphs: A Poetical Essay Towards a Description of a Sea Fight*.
— (1707), *The British Court: A Poem*.

Browne, Sir Thomas (1658), *Hydriotaphia, Urne-Buriall . . . Together with the Garden of Cyrus.*
— (1672), *Pseudodoxia Epidemica*, fourth edition.
Brownell, Morris (1978), *Alexander Pope and the Arts of Georgian England*, Oxford.
Buckinghamshire, John Sheffield, Duke of (1682), *An Essay upon Poetry.*
—: for *Works* see Pope (1723).
Burgess, C. F., ed. (1966), *The Letters of John Gay*, Oxford.
Burton, Robert (1621), *The Anatomy of Melancholy, What It Is.*
Butler, Samuel (1684), *Hudibras. In Three Parts*; for a modern edition, see Wilders (1967).
Butt, John, ed. (1939–69), *The Twickenham Edition of the Poems of Alexander Pope*, 11 vols.
Buxton, John, ed. (1958), *Charles Cotton: Poems.*
Byfield, T. (1695), *Horae Subsecivae.*
Camden, William: see Gibson (1695).
Canterbury Tales Composed for the Entertainment of all Ingenious Young Men at their Merry Meetings upon Christmas, Easter, Whitsontide, or any other Time (1687).
Canterbury Tales, Rendered into Familiar Verse (1701).
Caplan, Harry, ed. and trans. (2014), *Cicero: Rhetorica Ad Herennium*, Cambridge, MA.
Carew, Thomas (1634), *Coelum Britannicum. A Masque at White-Hall in the Banquetting House . . . the 18. of February, 1633.*
Carey, Henry (1713), *Poems on Several Occasions.*
Carey, John, ed. (2007), *John Milton: Complete Shorter Poems*, second edition.
Carretta, Vincent (2009), '"Images Reflect from Art to Art": Alexander Pope's Collected *Works* of 1717', in Neil Fraistat, ed., *Poems in Their Place: Intertextuality and Order of Poetic Collections*, pp. 195–233, Chapel Hill, NC.
Cartwright, William (1651), *Comedies, Tragi-Comedies, with other Poems.*
Caryll, John, Lord (1667), *The English Princess, or, The Death of Richard III.*
Case, Arthur E. (1928), 'The Model for Pope's Verses to the Author of a Poem Intitled "Successio"', *Modern Language Notes*, 43, 321–2.
Castiglione: see Hoby (1561).
Catullus: see Mynors (1963a).
Centlivre, Susannah (1713), *The Masquerade. A Poem.*
Chalker, John (1969), *The English Georgic: A Study of the Development of a Form.*
Chapman, George (1598), *Hero and Leander: begun by Christopher Marloe; and finished by George Chapman.*
—, trans. (1611), *The Iliads of Homer Prince of Poets.*
—, trans. (1615), *Homer's Odysses. Translated according to ye Greeke.*
—, trans. (1618), *The Georgicks of Hesiod.*
—: for *Chapman's Homer*, see Nicoll (1957).
Characters of the Times (1728).
Charleton, Walter (1663), *Chorea Gigantum, or, The Most Famous Antiquity of Great-Britain.*
Charteris, Richard, ed. (2007), *Daniel Purcell: Ode for St. Cecilia's Day.*
Chaucer, Geoffrey: for *Workes*, see Speght (1598).
—: for *The Riverside Chaucer*, see Benson (1988).

Chaucer's Ghoast, or, A Piece of Antiquity Containing Twelve Pleasant Fables of Ovid (1672).
Chudleigh, Lady Mary (1703), *Poems on Several Occasions*.
— (1710), *Essays upon Several Subjects in Prose and Verse*.
—: for *Poems and Prose*, see Ezell (1993).
Cibber, Colley (1740), *An Apology for the Life of Mr. Colley Cibber, Comedian*.
Cicero, Marcus Tullius: for *De Officiis*, see Winterbottom (1994).
—: for *De Oratore*, see Wilkins (1961).
—: for *De Divinatione*, see Falconer (1953).
—: for *Rhetorica Ad Herennium*, see Caplan (2014).
Clausen, W. V., ed. (1992), *A. Persi Flacci et D. Ivni Ivvenalis Saturae*, Oxford.
Cleland, William (1697), *A Collection of Several Poems and Verses, Composed upon Various Occasions*.
Clements, Frances M. (1972), 'Lansdowne, Pope, and the Unity of *Windsor-Forest*', *Modern Language Quarterly*, 33, 44–53.
Cleveland, John (1677), *Clievelandi Vindiciae, or, Clieveland's Genuine Poems, Orations, Epistles, &c.*
Cobb, Samuel (1700), *Poetae Britannici. A Poem, Satyrical and Panegyrical*.
— (1707), *Poems on Several Occasions*.
— (1709), *The Female Reign: An Ode, Alluding to Horace, B.4. Od. 14*.
— (1710), *Poems on Several Occasions*, third edition.
— (1712), *The Carpenter of Oxford, or, The Miller's Tale, from Chaucer*.
Colie, Rosalie (1966), *Paradoxia Epidemica: The Renaissance Tradition of Paradox*, Princeton, NJ.
A Collection of Divine Hymns and Poems on Several Occasions (1707).
A Collection of Poems by Several Hands (1693).
A Collection of Poems Relating to State Affairs (1705).
A Collection of Poems: viz. The Temple of Death: By the Marquis of Normanby . . . (1701).
Collier, Jeremy (1695), *Miscellanies upon Moral Subjects. The Second Part*.
— (1698), *A Short View of the Immorality and Profaneness of the English Stage*.
Collins, Thomas (1615), *The Teares of Loue: or, Cupids Progresse*.
A Comparison Between the Two Stages, With an Examen of the Generous Conqueror (1702). Possibly by Charles Gildon.
Concanen, Matthew (1728), *A Supplement to the Profund*. The authorship is uncertain.
Congleton, J. E. (1952), *Theories of Pastoral Poetry in England, 1684–1798*, Gainesville, FL.
Congreve, William, (1693), *The Old Bachelour, A Comedy*.
— (1694), *The Double Dealer, A Comedy*.
— (1695a), *Love for Love. A Comedy*.
— (1695b), *The Mourning Muse of Alexis. A Pastoral*.
— (1695c), *A Pindarique Ode, Humbly Offer'd to the King on his Taking Namure*.
— (1697), *The Mourning Bride, A Tragedy*.
— (1698), *Amendments of M. Collier's False and Imperfect Citations, &c.*
— (1700), *The Way of the World, A Comedy*.
— (1702, dated 1703), *A Hymn to Harmony, Written in Honour of St. Cecilia's Day*, M DCC I.

— (1703), *The Tears of Amaryllis for Amyntas. A Pastoral.*
— (1706), *A Pindarique Ode, Humbly Offer'd to the Queen, On the Victorious Progress of Her Majesty's Arms, under the Conduct of the Duke of Marlborough.*
— (1710), *The First* [etc] *Volume of the Works of Mr. William Congreve*, 3 vols.
—: for *Works*, see Mackenzie (2011).
Cotton, Charles (1667), *Scarronides: or, Virgile Travestie.*
— (1681), *The Wonders of the Peake.*
— (1689), *Poems on Several Occasions.*
—: for *Poems*, see Buxton (1958).
Court Poems in Two Parts Compleat (1719).
Cowan, Brian (2005), *The Social Life of Coffee: The Emergence of the British Coffeehouse*, New Haven, CT.
Coward, William (1709), *Licentia Poetica Discuss'd: or, the True Test of Poetry.*
Cowley, Abraham (1656), *Poems, viz. I. Miscellanies . . . IV. Davideis, or, a Sacred Poem of the Troubles of David, Written by A. Cowley.*
— (1668), *The Works of Mr. Abraham Cowley.*
— (1689), *The Third Part of the Works of Mr. Abraham Cowley, Being his Six Books of Plants.*
—: for *The English Writings*, see Waller (1905).
Cox, Nicholas (1674), *The Gentleman's Recreation, in Four Parts.*
— (1677), *The Gentleman's Recreation, in Four Parts*, second edition.
— (1697), *The Gentleman's Recreation, in Four Parts*, fourth edition.
Craufurd, David (1703), *Ovidius Britannicus: or, Love Epistles.*
Creech, Thomas, trans. (1684a), *The Odes, Satyrs and Epistles of Horace Done into English.*
—, trans. (1684b), *The Idylliums of Theocritus with Rapin's Discourse of Pastorals Done into English*, Oxford.
—, trans. (1700), *Lucretius his Six Books of Epicurean Philosophy: and Manilius his Five Books.*
Critical Remarks on Mr. Rowe's Last Play (1706).
Crofts, William (c.1689), *A Poem, in Praise of Beauty and Musick, set, by Mr. Will. Crofts, after the Manner of a St. Caecilia's Song.*
Crompton, Hugh, trans., (1652), *The Glory of Women, or a Looking Glass for Ladies . . . Written first in Latine by Henricus Cornelius Agrippa.*
Crooke, Helkiah (1615) *Mikrokosmographia. A Description of the Body of Man.*
Crowne, John (1675), *The Countrey Wit. A Comedy.*
Culpeper, Nicholas (1652), *The English Physitian, or An Astrologo-Physical Discourse of the Vulgar Herbs of this Nation.*
Cummings, Robert (1987), 'Windsor-Forest as a Silvan Poem', *ELH*, 54:1, 63–79.
— (1988), 'Addison's "Inexpressible Chagrin" and Pope's Poem on the Peace', *Yearbook of English Studies*, 18, 143–58.
Cutts, John (1687), *Poetical Exercises Written upon Several Occasions.*
D., J., trans, (1661), *A Treatise of the Sibyls . . . Written Originally by David Blondel; Englished by J. D.*
Daly, Patrick (2013), 'Court Politics and the Original Two-Canto *Rape of the Locke*', *Clio*, 42:3, 331–58.

Darby, Charles (1704), *The Book of Psalms in English Metre.*
Dart, John (1722), *A Poem on Chaucer and his Writings.*
Da Silva, Jorge Bastos (2005), 'Cato's ghosts: Pope, Addison, and Opposition Cultural Politics', *Studies in the Literary Imagination*, 38, 95–115.
D'Avenant, Charles (1677), *Circe, a Tragedy.*
D'Avenant, Sir William (1651), *Gondibert. An Heroick Poem.*
— (1660a), *A Panegyrick to his Excellency the Lord General Monck.*
— (1660b), *Poem, upon His Sacred Majesties Most Happy Return to his Dominions.*
— (1663), *Poem, to the King's Most Sacred Majesty.*
Dearing, Vinton A., ed. (1974), *John Gay: Poetry and Prose*, 2 vols, Oxford.
Defoe, Daniel (1701), *The True-Born Englishman. A Satyr.*
— (1704), *The Storm: Or, A Collection of the most Remarkable Casualties and Disasters which Happen'd in the Late Dreadful Tempest, both by Sea and Land.*
— (1705), *The Dyet of Poland, A Satyr.*
— (1706a), *Jure Divino: A Satyr. In Twelve Books.*
— (1706b), *A Hymn to Peace.*
— (1707), *Caledonia, A Poem in Honour of Scotland, and the Scots Nation. In Three Parts.*
— (1724–6), *A Tour thro' the Whole Island of Great Britain, Divided into Circuits or Journies*, 3 vols.
Dekker, Thomas (1609), *The Guls Horne-Book.*
Denham, Sir John (1643), *Coopers Hill. A Poëme*, Oxford.
— (1650), *Coopers Hill A Poeme*, second edition.
— (1656), *The Destruction of Troy, An Essay upon the Second Book of Virgils Aeneis.*
— (1668), *Poems and Translations, with The Sophy.*
— (1669), *Cato Major of Old Age. A Poem.*
—: for a modern edition of *Coopers Hill*, see O Hehir (1969).
—: for *Poetical Works*, see Banks (1969).
Denne, Henry (1695), *A Poem on the Taking of Namur, by His Majesty.*
Dennis, John (1692), *The Passion of Byblis, Made English.*
— (1693), *The Impartial Critick: or, Some Observations upon a Late Book, entituled, A Short View of Tragedy.*
— (1695), *The Court of Death. A Pindarique Poem, Dedicated to the Memory of Her Most Sacred Majesty, Queen Mary.*
— (1696a), *Remarks on a Book entituled, Prince Arthur, an Heroick Poem.*
—, ed., (1696b), *Letters upon Several Occasions.*
— (1699), *Rinaldo and Armida: A Tragedy.*
— (1701), *The Advancement and Reformation of Modern Poetry. A Critical Discourse.*
— (1702a), *The Monument: A Poem Sacred to the Immortal Memory of the Best and Greatest of Kings, William the Third. King of Great Britain, &c.*
— (1702b), *A Large Account of the Taste in Poetry, and the Causes of the Degeneracy of it.*
— (1704a), *Britannia Triumphans: or the Empire Sav'd, and Europe Deliver'd.*
— (1704b), *The Grounds of Criticism in Poetry, Contain'd in Some New Discoveries Never Made Before, Requisite for the Writing and Judging of Poems Surely.*

— (1706a), *The Battle of Ramillia: Or, the Power of Union.*
— (1706b), *An Essay on the Opera's after the Italian Manner.*
— (1709), *Appius and Virginia. A Tragedy.*
— (1711), *Reflections Critical and Satyrical, upon a Late Rhapsody, Call'd, An Essay upon Criticism.*
— (1713), *Remarks upon Cato, A Tragedy.*
— (1716), *A True Character of Mr. Pope, and his Writings.*
— (1717), *Remarks upon Mr. Pope's Translation of Homer.*
— (1728), *Remarks on Mr. Pope's Rape of the Lock.*
— (1729), *Remarks upon Several Passages in the Preliminaries to the Dunciad, Both of the Quarto and the Duodecimo Edition.*
—: for *Critical Works*, see Hooker (1939–43).
De Quincey, Thomas: see Lindop (2000–3).
Deutsch, Helen (1996), *Resemblance and Disgrace: Alexander Pope and the Deformation of Culture*, Cambridge MA.
A Dialogue between Windsor Castle and Blenheim House (1708).
Diaper, William (1712), *Nereides: or, Sea-Eclogues.*
— (1712, dated 1713), *Dryades; or, the Nymph's Prophecy.*
Donaldson, Ian (1982), *The Rapes of Lucretia: A Myth and its Transformations*, Oxford.
Donne, John (1633), *Poems, by J. D. With Elegies on the Authors Death.*
Downie, J. A. (1979), *Robert Harley and the Press.*
Drayton, Michael (1603), *The Barron's Warrs ... With England's Heroical Epistles.*
— (1613), *Poly-Olbion. Or A Chorographicall Description of Tracts, Riuers, Mountaines, Forests, and Other Parts of this Renowned Isle of Great Britaine.*
— (1622), *The Second Part, or a Continuance of Poly-Olbion from the Eighteenth Song.*
— (1631), *The Battaile of Agincourt.*
—: for *Works*, see Hebbel (1931–41).
Drummond, William (1623), *Flowres of Sion.*
Drury, G. Thorn, ed. (1893), *The Poems of Edmund Waller*, 2 vols.
Dryden, John (1660), *Astraea Redux. A Poem on the Happy Restoration & Return of His Sacred Majesty Charles the Second.*
— (1667), *Annus Mirabilis: The Year of Wonders, 1666.*
— (1667), *The Indian Emperour, or, The Conquest of Mexico by the Spaniards.*
— (1668a), *Of Dramatick Poesie, an Essay.*
— (1668b), *Secret-Love, or The Maiden-Queen.*
— (1670a), *The Tempest, or The Enchanted Island. A Comedy.*
— (1670b), *Tyrannick Love, or The Royal Martyr. A Tragedy.*
— (1672), *The Conquest of Granada by the Spaniards: in Two Parts.*
— (1673a), *The Assignation; or, Love in a Nunnery.*
— (1673b), *Marriage a-la-Mode. A Comedy.*
— (1676), *Aureng-Zebe: A Tragedy.*
— (1677), *The State of Innocence, and Fall of Man: An Opera.*
— (1678), *All for Love: or, The World Well Lost.*
— (1679), *Troilus and Cressida, or, Truth Found Out Too Late.*
— (1680), *The Kind Keeper; or, Mr. Limberham: A Comedy.*

— (1681a), *Absalom and Achitophel. A Poem.*
— (1681b), *The Spanish Fryar or, The Double Discovery.*
— (1682a), *Mac Flecknoe, or A Satyr upon the True-Blew-Protestant poet, T.S.*
— (1682b), *The Medall. A Satyre against Sedition.*
— (1682c), *Religio Laici or a Layman's Faith. A Poem.*
— (1685a), *Albion and Albanius: An Opera.*
— (1685b), *Threnodia Augustalis: A Funeral-Pindarique Poem Sacred to the Happy Memory of King Charles II.*
— (1687a), *The Hind and the Panther. A Poem. In Three Parts.*
— (1687b), *A Song for St. Cecilia's Day 1687.*
— (1688), *Britannia Rediviva: A Poem on the Birth of the Prince.*
— (1690a), *Amphitryon; or, the Two Socia's. A Comedy.*
— (1690b), *Don Sebastian, King of Portugal: A Tragedy.*
— (1691), *King Arthur, or, the British Worthy. A Dramatick Opera.*
— (1692a), *All for Love: or, The World Well Lost.*
— (1692b), *Eleonora: A Panegyrical Poem: Dedicated to the Memory of the late Countess of Abingdon.*
—, trans. (1693), *The Satires of Decimus Junius Juvenalis. Translated into English Verse by Mr. Dryden, and Several Other Eminent Hands. Together with the Satires of Aulus Persius Flaccus.*
— (1694), *Love Triumphant, or, Nature will Prevail. A Tragi-Comedy.*
—, trans. (1695), *De Arte Graphica. The Art of Painting, by C. A. Du Fresnoy. With Remarks.*
— (1696), *An Ode, on the Death of Mr. Henry Purcell; Late Servant to his Majesty, and Organist of the Chapel Royal, and of St. Peter's Westminster.*
— (1697a), *Alexanders Feast; or The Power of Musique. An Ode, in Honour of St. Cecilia's Day.*
— (1697b), *The Works of Virgil: Containing his Pastorals, Georgics, and AEneis. Translated into English Verse; by Mr. Dryden.*
— (1700), *Fables Ancient and Modern; Translated into Verse, from Homer, Ovid, Boccace, & Chaucer: With Original Poems.*
—, and Nathaniel Lee (1679), *Oedipus: A Tragedy.*
— (1683), *The Duke of Guise. A Tragedy.*
—: for *Letters*, see Ward (1942).
—: for *Poems*, see Hammond and Hopkins (1995–2005).
—: for *Works*, see Hooker (1956–89).
Du Bartas: see Sylvester (1621).
Duff, J. D., ed. and trans. (1928), *Lucan: The Civil War.*
Duff, William (1767), *An Essay on Original Genius; and its Various Modes of Exertion in Philosophy and the Fine Arts, Particularly in Poetry.*
Durant, David S. (1971), 'Man and Nature in Alexander Pope's "Pastorals"', *SEL*, 11, 469–85.
D'Urfey, Thomas (1677), *A Fond Husband: or, The Plotting Sisters. A Comedy.*
— (1679), *Squire Oldsapp: or, The Night-Adventurers. A Comedy.*
— (1680), *The Virtuous Wife; or, Good Luck at Last. A Comedy.*

— (1681), *Sir Barnaby Whigg: or, No Wit like a Womans. A Comedy*.
— (1682), *Butler's Ghost: or, Hudibras. The Fourth Part*.
— (1695), *Gloriana. A Funeral Pindarique Poem: Sacred to the Blessed Memory of . . . our Late Gracious Soveraign Lady Queen Mary*.
— (1697), *The Intrigues at Versailles: or, A Jilt in all Humours*.
— (1700), *An Ode, For the Anniversary Feast Made in Honour of St. Caecilia. Nov. 22. Anno Domini, 1700*.
Echard, Laurence, trans. (1699), *Terence's Comedies: Made English*.
Edgecombe, Rodney Stenning (2005), 'Horace's Odes 4. 2 and Pope's "Essay on Criticism"', *ANQ: A Quarterly Journal of Short Articles, Notes, and Reviews*, 18, 21–2.
Edwards, Thomas (1595), *Cephalus & Procris*.
Egerton, Sarah Fyge (1703), *Poems on Several Occasions*.
Elias, Richard (1977), 'Two Commendary Poems on Pope's "Pastorals"', *Notes and Queries*, CCXXII, 229–30.
Ellis, Frank, ed. (1970), *Poems on Affairs of State: Augustan Satirical Verse, 1660–1714, Volume 6: 1697–1704*, New Haven and London.
Ellis, William D., Jr. (1959), 'Thomas D'Urfey, the Pope-Philips Quarrel, and "The Shepherd's Week"', *PMLA*, 74, 203–12.
Elsum, John (1703), *The Art of Painting after the Italian Manner*.
Elviden, Edmund (1569), *The Closet of Counsells*.
Elwin, Whitwell, and William John Courthope, eds (1871–86). *The Works of Alexander Pope*, 10 vols.
Elyot, Sir Thomas (1531), *The Boke Named the Gouernour*.
Evans, Abel (1713), *Vertumnus. An Epistle to Mr. Jacob Bobart, Botany Professor to the University of Oxford, and Keeper of the Physick-Garden*.
Empson, William (1950), 'Wit in the *Essay on Criticism*', *Hudson Review* 2, 559–77.
'Ephelia' (1682), *Female Poems on Several Occasions*.
Erasmus: see Kennett (1683).
Erskine-Hill, Howard (1966), 'Alexander Pope at Fifteen: A New Manuscript', *RES*, 17, 268–77.
— (1975), *The Social Milieu of Alexander Pope*.
—, and Anne Smith, eds (1979), *The Art of Alexander Pope*.
— (1981), 'Alexander Pope: The Political Poet in his Time', *Eighteenth-Century Studies*, 15, 123–48.
— (1982), 'Literature and the Jacobite Cause', in Eveline Cruickshanks, ed., *Ideology and Conspiracy: Aspects of Jacobitism, 1689–1759*, pp. 49–69, Edinburgh.
— (1996), *Poetry of Opposition and Revolution, Dryden to Wordsworth*, Oxford.
—, ed. (1998), *Alexander Pope: World and Word*, Oxford.
An Essay upon Sublime. Translated from the Greek of Dionysius Longinus Cassius, the Rhetorician (1698).
Etherege, Sir George (1676), *The Man of Mode; or, Sir Fopling Flutter. A Comedy*.
Evelyn, John (1661), *Panegyric to Charles the Second*.
— (1664), *Sylva, or A Discourse of Forest-Trees, and the Propagation of Timber in His Majesties Dominions*.
— (1697), *Numismata. A Discourse of Medals, Antient and Modern*.

Evelyn-White, H. G., ed. and trans. (1914), *Hesiod: The Homeric Hymns and Homerica.*
Examen Poeticum: Being the Third Part of Miscellany Poems (1693).
The Excellent and Renowned History of the Famous Sir Richard Whittington (1690).
Ezell, Margaret, ed. (1993), *The Poems and Prose of Mary, Lady Chudleigh,* Oxford.
Fairer, David (1984), *Pope's Imagination,* Manchester.
— (2007), 'Pope and the Elizabethans', in Rogers, ed. (2007), pp. 89–104.
The Fairy Queene (1648). A single-sheet ballad.
Falconer, W. A., ed. and trans. (1953), *Cicero: De Senectute, De Amicitia, De Diviniatione,* Cambridge, MA.
Fanning, Christopher (2005), 'The Scriblerian Sublime', *SEL,* 45, 647–67, 783–4.
Fanshawe, Sir Richard, trans. (1655), *The Lusiad, or Portugals Historicall Poem.*
Farquhar, George (1701), *Sir Harry Wildair . . . A Comedy.*
— (1702a), *The Inconstant: or, The Way to Win Him. A Comedy.*
— (1702b), *Love and Business: in a Collection of Occasionary Verse, and Epistolary Prose, not hitherto Publish'd.*
— (1706), *The Recruiting Officer. A Comedy.*
— (1707), *The Beaux Stratagem. A Comedy.*
Fenton, Elijah (1706), *Cerealia: An Imitation of Milton.* Sometimes attributed to John Philips.
Ferraro, Julian (1993a), 'Political Discourse in Alexander Pope's *Episode of Sarpedon*: Variations on the Theme of Kingship', *Modern Language Review,* 88:1, 15–25.
— (1993b), '"Rising into Light": The Evolution of Pope's Poems in Manuscript and Print', unpublished doctoral dissertation, University of Cambridge.
Fifteen Real Comforts of Matrimony (1683).
Fisher, C. D., ed. (1951), *Cornelii Taciti Annalium Ab Excessu Divi Augusti Libri,* revised edition, Oxford.
Flatman, Thomas (1674), *Poems and Songs.*
— (1686), *A Song for St. Caecilia's Day, Nov. 22. 1686. Written by Mr. Tho. Flatman: And Composed by Mr. Isaac Blackwell.*
Flecknoe, Richard (1664), *Love's Kingdom, A Pastoral Trage-Comedy.*
Fleming, Abraham, trans. (1589), *The Bucoliks of Publius Virgilius Maro.*
Fletcher, Giles (1593), *Licia, or Poemes of Loue.*
Fletcher, John (1637), *The Elder Brother A Comedie.*
Fletcher, Thomas (1692), *Poems on Several Occasions, and Translations.*
The Fourth (and Last) Collection of Poems, Satyrs, Songs, etc. (1689).
The Fourth Volume of Plutarch's Lives. Translated from the Greek, by Several Hands (1685).
Fowler, Alastair, ed. (2007), *John Milton: Paradise Lost,* second edition.
Foxon, David (1975), *English Verse, 1701–1750,* 2 vols, Cambridge.
— (1991), *Pope and the Early Eighteenth-Century Book Trade,* rev. James McLaverty, Oxford.
France, Peter (1988), 'The French Pope', in Nicholson, ed. (1988), pp. 117–29.
Fraunce, Abraham (1592), *The Third Part of the Countess of Pembroke's Yuychurch: Entituled, Amintas Dale.*
Freeman, Lisa A. (1999), 'What's love got to do with Addison's *Cato*?', *SEL,* 39:3, 463–82.

Friedman, Arthur, ed. (1979), *The Plays of William Wycherley*.
Fuller, John, ed. (1983), *John Gay: Dramatic Works*, 2 vols, Oxford.
Gardiner, James, trans. (1706), *Rapin of Gardens. A Latin Poem, English'd by Mr. Gardiner*.
Garrod, H. W., ed. (1947), *Q. Horatii Flacci Opera*, revised edition, Oxford.
— (1962), *P. Papini Stati Thebais et Achilleis*, revised edition, Oxford.
Garth, Sir Samuel (1706), *The Dispensary. A Poem*, sixth edition.
— (1715), *Claremont. Address'd to the Right Honourable the Earl of Clare*.
— ed., (1717), *Ovid's Metamorphoses in Fifteen Books. Translated by the Most Eminent Hands*.
Gastrell, Francis (1709), *The Principles of Deism Truly Represented and Set in a Clear Light*, second edition.
Gay, John (1712a), *The Mohocks. A Tragi-Comical Farce*.
— (1712b), *The Present State of Wit, in a Letter to a Friend in the Country*.
— (1713a), *The Fan. A Poem. In Three Books*.
— (1713b), *Rural Sports. A Poem. Inscribed to Mr. Pope*.
— (1713c), *The Wife of Bath. A Comedy*.
— with Pope and Arbuthnot (1717), *Three Hours After Marriage. A Comedy*.
—: for *Dramatic Works*, see Fuller (1983).
—: for *Letters*, see Burgess (1966).
—: for *Poetry and Prose*, see Dearing (1974).
The Gentleman's Journal, or, The Monthly Miscellany (1692–4).
Gerard, John (1633), *The Herball, or General History of Plantes*.
Gibson, Edmund, ed. and trans. (1695), *Camden's Britannia, Newly Translated into English*.
Gildon, Charles (1694), *Miscellaneous Letters and Essays, on Several Subjects*.
— (1708), *Libertas Triumphans: A Poem*.
— (1714), *A New Rehearsal, or Bays the Younger*.
— (1718), *The Complete Art of Poetry. In Six Parts*.
Gillespie, Stuart (1988), 'The early years of the Dryden-Tonson partnership: the background to their composite translations and miscellanies of the early 1680s', *Restoration: Studies in English Literary Culture, 1660–1700*, 12:1, 10–19.
— (1999), 'Statius in English 1648–1767', *Translation and Literature*, 8, 157–75.
— and David Hopkins, eds (2005), *The Oxford History of Literary Translation in English, Volume 3, 1660–1790*, Oxford.
Glanvill, Joseph (1700), *Saducismus Triumphatus: or, Full and Plain Evidence concerning Witches and Apparitions*.
— (1703), *An Essay concerning Preaching*, second edition.
Golding, Arthur, trans. (1567), *The .xv. Bookes of P. Ouidius Naso, entytuled Metamorphosis, translated oute of Latin into English Meeter*.
Goldstein, Malcolm (1958), *Alexander Pope and the Augustan Stage*, Stanford, CA.
Gorges, Sir Arthur (1619), *The Wisedome of the Ancients, Written in Latin by . . . Sir Francis Bacon . . . Done into English by Sir Arthur Gorges Knight*.
Gould, Robert (1682), *Love Given O're: or, A Satyr against the Pride, Lust, and Inconstancy, &c. of Woman*.
— (1709), *The Works of Mr. Robert Gould: In Two Volumes*.

Gow, A. S., ed. (1952), *Bucolici Graeci*, Oxford.
Granville: see Lansdowne.
Greene, Maurice: see Johnstone (1991).
Greenfield, John (1706), *A Treatise of the Safe Internal Use of Cantharides in the Practice of Physick*.
Greenwood, James (1711), *An Essay Towards a Practical English Grammar*.
Grenfield, Henry (1686), *God in the Creature. Being a Poem in Three Parts*.
Griffin, Dustin (1978), *Alexander Pope: The Poet in the Poems*, Princeton, NJ.
— (1990), 'Venting Spleen', *Essays in Criticism*, 40:2, 124–35.
— (1996), *Literary Patronage in England 1650–1800*, Cambridge.
Griffith, Reginald H. (1922), *Alexander Pope: A Bibliography*, 2 vols, Austin, TX.
Grotius, Hugo (1686), *Grotius, his Arguments for the Truth of the Christian Religion rendered into plain English Verse*.
—: for *Christus Patiens*, see Sandys (1640).
The Guardian: see Stephens (1982).
Guerinot, J. V. (1969), *Pamphlet Attacks on Alexander Pope, 1711–1744: A Descriptive Bibliography*, New York.
Guthkelch, A. C., ed. (1914), *The Miscellaneous Works of Joseph Addison*, 2 vols.
Guy, John (1699), *On the Happy Accession of their Majesties King William and Queen Mary, to the Throne of England, &c.*
Halifax, Charles Montagu, Earl of (1688), *The Lady's New-years Gift: Or, Advice to a Daughter*.
— (1690), *An Epistle to the Right Honorable Charles, Earl of Dorset and Middlesex*.
Hamilton, A. C., ed. (2007), *Edmund Spenser: The Faerie Queene*, second edition.
Hammond, Brean (2006), 'Joseph Addison's Opera *Rosamond*: Britishness in the Early Eighteenth Century', *ELH*, 73:3, 610–29.
Hammond, Paul (1985), 'An Early Response to Pope's *Essay on Criticism*', *Notes and Queries*, 32:3, 198–9.
— (1999), *Dryden and the Traces of Classical Rome*, Oxford.
—, and David Hopkins, eds (1995–2005), *The Poems of John Dryden*, 5 vols, Longman Annotated English Poets.
—, eds (2000), *John Dryden: Tercentenary Essays*, Oxford.
Harington, John (1657), *The History of Polindor, and Flostella: With Other Poems*, third edition.
—, trans. (1684), *The Odes and Epodon of Horace, in Five Books*.
— (1685), *A Pindarick Ode upon the Death of his Late Sacred Majesty King Charles II*.
Harison, William (1706), *Woodstock Park. A Poem*.
— (1711), *The Passion of Sappho, and Feast of Alexander. Set to Musick by Mr. Thomas Clayton*. The *Feast of Alexander* is by Dryden.
Harris, Joseph (1703), *Anglia Triumphans. A Pindarique Ode, on his Grace the Duke of Marlborough*.
Harte, Walter (1727), *Poems on Several Occasions*.
Hauser, David R. (1966), 'Pope's Lodona and the Uses of Mythology', *SEL*, 6, 465–82.
Hawkins, Sir John (1776), *A General History of the Science and Practice of Music*, 5 vols.

Hebbel, J. W. (1931–41), *The Works of Michael Drayton*, 5 vols, Oxford.
Henderson, Christine Dunn, and Mark Yellin, eds (2004), *Cato: A Tragedy, and Selected Essays*, Indianapolis, IN.
Herodotus: see Wilson (2015).
Heseltine, Michael, ed. and trans. (1975), *Petronius*, revised edition, Cambridge, MA.
Hesiod: see Evelyn-White (1914).
Heyrick, Thomas (1691), *Miscellany Poems*.
Heywood, Thomas (1613), *The Brazen Age*.
Heyworth, S J., ed. (2007), *Sexti Properti Elegos*, Oxford.
Higden, Henry (1686), *A Modern Essay on the Thirteenth Satyr of Juvenal*.
— (1687), *A Modern Essay on the Tenth Satyr of Juvenal*.
Higgons, Bevil (1713), *A Poem on the Peace*.
Hobbes, Thomas, trans. (1675), *Homer's Odysses translated by Tho. Hobbes of Malmsbury*.
—, trans. (1676), *Homer's Iliads in English*.
Hoby, Thomas, trans. (1561), *The Courtyer of Count Baldessar Castilio Diuided into Foure Bookes*.
Holland, Hugh (1603), *Pancharis: The First Booke*.
Holland, Philemon, trans. (1603), *The Philosophie, Commonlie Called, the Morals vvritten by the Learned Philosopher Plutarch of Chaeronea*.
Homer: for text, see Monro (1896).
—: for translations, see Chapman (1611 and 1615); Hobbes (1675 and 1676); Ogilby (1660 and 1665); Pope (1715–20 and 1725–6).
Hone, Joseph (2015a), 'Pope and the Politics of Panegyric', *Review of English Studies*, 66, 106–23.
— (2015b), 'Pope's lost epic: *Alcander, Prince of Rhodes* and the Politics of Exile', *Philological Quarterly*, 94:3, 245–66.
Hooker, Edward Niles, ed. (1939–43), *The Critical Works of John Dennis*, 2 vols, Baltimore.
— (1951), 'Pope on Wit: The *Essay on Criticism*', in R. F. Jones, *The Seventeenth Century: Studies in the History of English Thought and Literature from Bacon to Pope*, pp. 225–46, Stanford, CA.
—, et al., eds (1956–89), *The Works of John Dryden*, 20 vols, Berkeley and Los Angeles.
Hopkins, Charles (1694), *Epistolary Poems: on Several Occasions*.
— (1695), *The History of Love. A Poem: in a Letter to a Lady*.
— (1696), *Neglected Virtue: or, The Unhappy Conquerour*.
— (1698), *White-hall; or, The Court of England: A Poem*.
Hopkins, David (1994), 'The London Odes on St Cecilia's Day for 1686, 1695, and 1696', *RES*, 45, 486–95.
— (2005), 'An uncollected translation from Voiture by John Dryden', *Translation and Literature*, 14, 64–70.
— (2010), *Conversing with Antiquity: English Poets and the Classics, from Shakespeare to Pope*, Oxford.
— (2012), 'Ovid', in Hopkins and Martindale (2012), pp. 197–215.
—, and I. D. MacKillop (1976), '"Immortal Vida" and Basil Kennett', *RES*, 27, 137–47.

Hopkins, John (1700), *Amasia, or, The Works of the Muses*.
Horace: for text, see Garrod (1947).
—: for translations, see Cobb (1709); Creech (1684); Harrington (1684); *An Imitation* (1704); Jonson (1640); *Poems* (1666); Roscommon (1680).
Howard, Sir Robert, (1668), *The Great Favourite, or, The Duke of Lerma*.
Howell, Thomas (1568), *Newe Sonets, and Pretie Pamphlets*.
Hudson, Nicholas (2016), 'Challenging the Historical Paradigm: Tories, Whigs, and Economic Writing, 1680–1714', *Eighteenth-Century Life*, 40.3, 68–88.
Hughes, Jabez (1721), *Verses Occasion'd by Reading Mr. Dryden's Fables*.
Hughes, John (1700), *The Court of Neptune. A Poem*.
— (1703), *An Ode in Praise of Musick, Set for Variety of Voices and Instruments by Mr. Philip Hart*.
—, ed. (1715), *The Works of Mr. Edmund Spenser. In Six Volumes*.
Hume, Patrick (1695), *Annotations on Milton's Paradise Lost*.
Husk, W. H. (1857), *An Account of the Musical Celebrations on St. Cecilia's Day*.
An Idyll on the Peace (1697).
Index of English Literary Manuscripts, Volume 3: 1700–1800 (1986–92), 4 parts, compiled by Margaret M. Smith et al.
An Imitation of the Sixth Ode of Horace, apply'd to His Grace the Duke of Marlborough (1704).
J., W., trans. (1695), *Monsieur Bossu's Treatise of the Epick Poem: Containing Many Curious Reflexions, Very Useful and Necessary for the Right Understanding and Judging of the Excellencies of Homer and Virgil*.
Jackson, Joseph (1708), *A New Translation of Aesop's Fables*.
Joe Miller's Jests (1742), fifth edition.
Johnson, Charles (1710), *The Force of Friendship. A Tragedy*.
— (1711), *The Generous Husband: or, The Coffee House Politician. A Comedy*.
Johnson, Samuel (1755), *A Dictionary of the English Language*.
— (1756), Review of Warton's *Essay, Literary Magazine*, I, April–May.
—: for *Lives of the Poets*, see Lonsdale (2006).
Johnstone, Harry Diack., ed. (1991), *Maurice Greene: Ode on St Cecilia's Day*, Musica Britannica 58.
Jones, Tom (2005), *Pope and Berkeley: The Language of Poetry and Philosophy*, Houndmills.
— (2010), 'Performing Gender in Augustan Criticism and Pope's "To a Lady"', *Journal for Eighteenth-Century Studies*, 33:1, 1–21.
Jonson, Ben (1616), *The Workes of Beniamin Ionson*.
— (1640), *The Workes of Beniamin Ionson*.
—, trans. (1640), *Q. Horatius Flaccus: His Art of Poetry. Englished by Ben: Jonson*.
— (1692), *The Works of Ben Jonson, Which were Formerly Printed in Two Volumes, are now Reprinted in One*.
Juvenal: for text see Clausen (1992).
—: for translations, see Dryden (1693); Higden (1686 and 1687).
Kames, Henry Home, Lord (1765), *Elements of Criticism*, 2 vols, third edition, Edinburgh.

Kaminski, Thomas (2000), 'Edmund Waller, English Précieux', *Philological Quarterly*, 79:1, 19–43.
Kaster, Robert, ed. (2016), *C. Suetoni Tranquilli De Uita Caesarum Libri VIII et De Grammaticis et Rhetoribus Liber*.
Keach, Benjamin (1700), *Spiritual Songs, being the Marrow of Scripture*.
Keener, Frederick (1974), *An Essay on Pope*, New York.
Kelsall, M. M. (1966), 'The Meaning of Addison's "Cato"', *RES*, 17, 149–62.
Kennett, Basil, ed. (1701), *Marci Hieronymi Vidae Cremonensis Albae Episcopi, Poeticorum Libri Tres*, Oxford.
Kennet, White, trans. (1683), *Witt against Wisdom. Or a Panegyrick upon Folly: Penn'd in Latin by Desiderius Erasmus, render'd into English*, Oxford.
Kerby-Miller, Charles, ed. (1950), *Memoirs of the Extraordinary Life, Works, and Discoveries of Martinus Scriblerus*, New York.
Kersey, John (1708), *Dictionarium Anglo-Britannicum: or, A General English Dictionary*.
Killigrew, Anne (1686), *Poems by Mrs Anne Killigrew*.
King, Henry (1664), *Poems, Elegies, Paradoxes and Sonnets*.
King, William (1708), *The Art of Love: In Imitation of Ovid De Arte Amandi*.
— (1710), *An Historical Account of the Heathen Gods and Heroes; Necessary for the Understanding of the Ancient Poets*.
L., W., trans. (1628), *Virgils Eclogues Translated into English*.
La Bruyère, Jean de (1702), *The Characters, or the Manners of the Age . . . Made English by Several Hands*, third edition.
Lacy, John (1714), *The Steeleids, or, The Tryal of Wit*.
Langbaine, Gerard (1691), *An Account of the English Dramatick Poets*.
Lansdowne, George Granville, Baron (1698), *Heroick Love: A Tragedy*.
— (1706), *The British Enchanters: Or, No Magick Like Love. A Tragedy*.
— (1712), *Poems upon Several Occasions*.
— (1732), *The Genuine Works in Verse and Prose, of the Right Honourable George Granville, Lord Landsowne*, 2 vols.
Lanyer, Aemilia (1611), *Salue Deus Rex Iudaeorum*.
Lashmore-Davies, Adrian (2009), 'Sir William Trumbull on Plain Living and the Use of Riches', *Scriblerian and the Kit-Cats*, 41:2, 189–97.
Lauderdale, Richard, Earl of, trans. (1709), *The Works of Virgil, Translated into English Verse*.
Le Bossu, René: see J., W. (1695).
Lee, Nathaniel (1675), *The Tragedy of Nero, Emperour of Rome*.
— (1676), *Gloriana, or The Court of Augustus Caesar*.
— (1684), *Constantine the Great*.
— (1689), *The Princess of Cleve*.
Lee, Anthony W. (2010), 'Samuel Johnson as Intertextual Critic', *Texas Studies in Literature and Language*, 52:2, 129–56.
Leslie, Charles (1711a), *A Short and Easie Method with the Deists*, fifth edition.
— (1711b), *The Truth of Christianity Demonstrated*.
Letters of Wit, Politicks and Morality (1701).

Levine, Joseph M. (1991), *The Battle of the Books: History and Literature in the Augustan Age*, Ithaca, NY.
Lewis, William Lillington, trans. (1767), *The Thebaid of Statius, Translated into English Verse, with Notes and Observations*.
Lindheim, Sara (2010), 'Pomona's Pomarium: The "Mapping Impulse" in *Metamorphoses* 14 (and 9)', *Transactions of the American Philological Association*, 140:1, 163–94.
Lindop, Grevel, ed. (2000–3), *The Works of Thomas De Quincey*, 21 vols.
Lindsay, W. M., ed. (1914), *T. Macci Plauti Comoediae*, 2 vols, Oxford.
—, ed. (1963), *M. Val. Martialis Epigrammata*, Oxford.
Lipking, Lawrence (1988), *Abandoned Women and Poetic Tradition*, Chicago, IL.
Littlefield, David (1965), 'Pomona and Vertumnus: A Fruition of History in Ovid's *Metamorphoses*', *Arion*, 49, 465–73.
Liu, Yu (2008), 'In the Name of the Ancients: The Cross-Cultural Iconoclasm of Pope's Gardening Aesthetics', *Studies in Philology*, 105:3, 409–28.
Lloyd Thomas, M. G., ed. (1927), *The Poems of John Philips*, Oxford.
Locke, John (1690), *An Essay Concerning Humane Understanding. In Four Books*.
The London Magazine, X (1741).
Longinus: for text, see Russell (1967).
—: for translations, see *An Essay upon Sublime* (1698); Welsted (1712).
Lonsdale, Roger, ed. (2006), *Samuel Johnson, The Lives of the Poets*, 4 vols, Oxford.
Love, Harold (1985), *The Text of Rochester's 'Upon Nothing'*, Monash.
—, ed. (1999), *The Works of John Wilmot Earl of Rochester*, Oxford.
Lovelace, Richard (1659), *Lucasta: Posthume Poems of Richard Lovelace Esq.*
The Lover, 40, 27 May 1714.
The Lover's Secretary. In Four Parts: Being a Collection of Billets Doux, Letters Amorous, Letters Tender, and Letters of Praise (1692)
Lucas, D. W., ed. (1968), *Aristotle: Poetics*, Oxford.
Lucan: see Duff (1928).
Lucian: see *Works of Lucian* (1711).
Luckett, Richard (1971), 'The Legend of St. Cecilia and English Literature', unpublished doctoral dissertation, University of Cambridge.
— (1973), 'St. Cecilia and Music', *Proceedings of the Royal Musical Association*, 99, 15–30.
Luctus Britannici: or The Tears of the British Muses; for the Death of John Dryden, Esq. (1700)
Lund, Roger D. (2009), '"The Filigree Game": Imitation and Mock-Form in Pope's *Pastorals*', *1650–1850: Ideas, Aesthetics, and Inquiries in the Early Modern Era*, 16, 97–132.
M., W. (1704), *The Female Wits: or, The Triumvirate of Poets at Rehearsal*.
Mack, Maynard (1969), *The Garden and the City: Retirement and Politics in the Later Poetry of Pope 1731–1743*, Toronto.
— (1977–8), 'Pope: The Shape of the Man in His Work', *Yale Review*, 67, 493–516.
— (1979), 'Pope's Copy of Chaucer', in *Evidence in Literary Scholarship: Essays in Memory of James Marshall Osborn*, ed. René Wellek and Alvaro Ribeiro, pp. 105–21, Oxford.
— (1980), 'Pope's Pastorals', *Scriblerian*, 12, 85–161.
— (1982), *Collected in Himself: Essays Critical, Biographical, and Bibliographical on Pope and Some of his Contemporaries*.

— (1984), *The Last and Greatest Art: Some Unpublished Poetical Manuscripts of Alexander Pope*.
— (1985), *Alexander Pope: A Life*, New Haven, CT.
McCullough, Diarmid (2013), *Silence: A Christian History*.
McGann, Jerome (1991), *The Textual Condition*, Princeton, NJ.
McGeary, Thomas (1988), 'Thomas Clayton and the Introduction of Italian Opera to England', *Philological Quarterly*, 77, 171–85.
McKenzie, D. F., ed. (2011), *The Works of William Congreve*, prepared by Christine Ferdinand, 3 vols, Oxford.
McLaverty, James (2001), *Pope, Print and Meaning*, Oxford.
— (2007), 'Pope and the Book Trade', in Rogers, ed. (2007), pp. 186–97.
MacMahon, Barbara (2007), 'The Effects of Sound Patterning in Poetry: A Cognitive Pragmatic Approach', *Journal of Literary Semantics*, 36, 103–20.
McVeagh, John (2000), *Thomas Durfey and Restoration Drama: The Work of a Forgotten Writer*.
McWhir, Anne (1981), 'Alternate tides: structure in Pope's "Windsor-Forest"', *English Studies in Canada*, 7, 296–311.
The Mall: or, The Reigning Beauties (1709).
Mallet, David (1733), *Of Verbal Criticism: An Epistle to Mr. Pope. Occasion'd by Theobald's Shakespear, and Bentley's Milton*.
Manilius: see Creech (1700).
Mannheimer, Katherine (2008), 'Echoes of Sound and Sense: Alexander Pope's *Essay on Criticism* and Ben Jonson's *Eupheme*', *Literary Imagination*, 10, 152–64.
Manley, Delarivier (1709), *Secret Memoirs and Manners of Several Persons of Quality, of Both Sexes, From the New Atalantis*.
Marmion, Shackerley (1638), *A Morall Poem, intituled the Legend of Cupid and Psyche*.
Martial: see Lindsay (1963).
Martin, Peter (1984), *Pursuing Innocent Pleasures: The Gardening World of Alexander Pope*, Hamden CT.
Marvell, Andrew (1681), *Miscellaneous Poems*.
Mason, H. A. (1972), *To Homer through Pope: An Introduction to Homer's 'Iliad' and Pope's Translation*.
— (1974), 'Dryden's "Georgic" and Pope's "Essay on Criticism"', *Notes and Queries* 21:7, 252.
Mason J. R. (1987), 'To Milton through Dryden and Pope: or, God, man and nature: *Paradise Lost* regained?', unpublished doctoral dissertation, University of Cambridge.
Mason, Tom (1975), 'Dryden's Version of the Wife of Bath's Tale', *Cambridge Quarterly*, 6, 240–56.
— (2005), 'Chaucer and Other Earlier English Poetry', in Gillespie and Hopkins, eds (2005), pp. 427–39.
— (2007), 'Dryden's *The Cock and the Fox* and Chaucer's *Nun's Priest's Tale*', *Translation and Literature*, 16:1, 1–28.
— and Adam Rounce (2000), '*Alexander's Feast; or the Power of Musique*: The Poem and its Readers', in Hammond and Hopkins (2000), pp. 140–73.

Matthew, H. C. G., and Brian Harrison, eds (2004), *Oxford Dictionary of National Biography*, Oxford; online edition, www.oxforddnb.
Maxwell, J. C. (1964), 'Pope's Statius and Dryden's Ovid', *Notes and Queries*, 11:2, 56.
May, Thomas (1628), *Virgil's Georgicks Englished*.
Melchiori, Giorgio (1963), 'Pope in Arcady: The Theme of "Et in Arcadia Ego" in his Pastorals', *English Miscellany*, 14, 83–93.
Memoirs of Scriblerus: see Kerby-Miller (1950).
Mengel, Elias F., ed. (1965), *Poems on Affairs of State: Augustan Satirical Verse, 1660–1714, Volume 2: 1678–1681*, New Haven and London.
Messenger, Ann (2001), *Pastoral Tradition and the Female Talent: Studies in Augustan Poetry*, New York.
Meston, William (1715), *Cato's Ghost*.
Milbourne, Luke (1698), *The Psalms of David, in English Metre*.
— (1698), *Notes on Dryden's Virgil. In a Letter to a Friend*.
Miller, Rachel (1979), 'Regal Hunting: Dryden's Influence on *Windsor-Forest*', *Eighteenth-Century Studies*, 13, 169–88.
Milton, John (1645), *Poems of Mr. John Milton, both English and Latin, Compos'd at Several Times*.
— (1649), *Eikonoklastes in Answer to a Book intitl'd Eikon Basilike, the Portraiture of his Sacred Majesty in his Solitudes and Sufferings*.
— (1671), *Paradise Regain'd. A Poem. In IV Books: To which is added Samson Agonistes*.
— (1673), *Poems, &c. upon Several Occasions*.
— (1674), *Paradise Lost. A Poem in Twelve Books*.
—: for *Complete Shorter Poems*, see Carey (2007).
—: for a modern edition of *Paradise Lost*, see Fowler (2007).
Miscellany Poems . . . By the Most Eminent Hands (1684).
Miscellany Poems . . . By the Most Eminent Hands (1702), third edition.
Miscellaneous Poems and Translations. By Several Hands (1712).
Miscellaneous Poems and Translations. By Several Hands (1713, dated 1714), second edition.
Mollineux, Mary (1702), *Fruits of Retirement: or, Miscellaneous Poems, Moral and Divine*.
Monk Samuel Holt (1944), 'A Grace Beyond the Reach of Art', *Journal of the History of Ideas*, 5, 131–50.
Monro, D. B., ed. (1896), *Homeri Opera et Reliquiae*, Oxford.
Montagu, Charles: see Halifax.
Moore, J. R. (1951), '*Windsor Forest* and William III', *Modern Language Notes*, 66, 451–4.
Moral Reflections and Pleasant Remarks on the Vertues, Vices, and Humours of Mankind with a Poem on the Power of Musick (1707).
Morris, David (1973), 'Virgilian Attitudes in Pope's *Windsor-Forest*', *Texas Studies in Literature and Language*, 15, 231–50.
— (1984), *Alexander Pope: The Genius of Sense*, Cambridge, MA.
Morsberger, Katharine M. (1993), 'Voices of Translation: Poet's Voice and Woman's Voice', *Pacific Coast Philology*, 28, 3–19.

Motteux, Peter Anthony (1695), *Words for an Entertainment at the Music-Feast, on St. Cecilia's Day being the 22d of November, 1695.*
— (1696a), *Love's a Jest. A Comedy.*
— (1696b), *The Loves of Mars & Venus.*
— (1701), *A Poem upon Tea.*
Moxon, Joseph (1670), *Practical Perspective; or Perspective made Easie.*
— (1699), *A Tutor to Astronomy and Geography*, fifth edition.
Mozley, J. H., ed. and trans. (1979), *Ovid: The Art of Love and Other Poems*, revised edition, Cambridge, MA.
Mr. Addison Turn'd Tory: or, The Scene Inverted (1713)
Murphy, Estelle, '"Sing Great Anna's Matchless Name": Images of Queen Anne in the Court Ode', in Reverand, ed. (2015), pp. 205-26.
The Muses Mercury: or Monthly Miscellany, I (1707).
Mynors, R. A. B., ed. (1963a), *Catulli Carmina*, Oxford.
—, ed. (1963b), *Plini Epistulae*, Oxford.
—, ed. (1967), *P. Vergili Maronis Opera*, Oxford.
Nashe, Thomas (1592), *Pierce Penilesse his Supplication to the Deuil.*
Newcastle, Margaret Cavendish, Duchess of (1653), *Poems, and Fancies.*
— (1662), *Playes Written by the Thrice Noble, Illustrious and Excellent Princess, the Lady Marchioness of Newcastle.*
A New Collection of Poems Relating to State Affairs, from Oliver Cromwel to this Present Time (1705).
A New Miscellany of Original Poems, on Several Occasions (1701).
A New Session of the Poets, Occasion'd by the Death of Mr. Dryden (1700).
Nicoll, Allardyce, ed. (1957), *Chapman's Homer*, 2 vols.
Nichols, John, ed. (1780-2), *A Select Collection of Poems: With Notes, Biographical and Historical*, 8 vols.
— (1812-15), *Literary Anecdotes of the Eighteenth Century*, 9 vols.
Nicholson, Colin, ed. (1988), *Alexander Pope: Essays for the Tercentenary*, Aberdeen.
Nicolson, M. H., and G. S. Rousseau (1968), *'This Long Disease, My Life': Alexander Pope and the Sciences*, Princeton, NJ.
Nisbet, H. B., and Claude Rawson, eds (1997), *The Cambridge History of Literary Criticism, Volume 4: The Eighteenth Century*, Cambridge.
Noggle, James (2001), *The Skeptical Sublime: Aesthetic Ideology in Pope and the Tory Satirists*, Oxford.
Nokes, David (1976), 'Pope's Chaucer', *RES*, 27, 180-2.
— (1977), 'Lisping in Political Numbers', *Notes and Queries*, CCXXII, 328-9.
— (1995), *John Gay, A Profession of Friendship: A Critical Biography*, Oxford.
Norris, John (1692), *A Collection of Miscellanies: Consisting of Poems, Essays, Discourses & Letters, Occasionally Written*, second edition.
Nussbaum, Felicity (1984), *The Brink of all we Hate: English Satires on Women, 1660-1750*, Lexington, KY.
An Ode in Praise of Musick (1707), Oxford.
Ogilby, John, trans. (1649), *The Works of Publius Virgilius Maro.*
—, trans. (1654), *The Works of Publius Virgilius Maro*

—, trans. (1660), *Homer His Iliads Translated, Adorn'd with Sculpture, and Illustrated with Annotations*.
—, trans. (1665), *Homer His Odysses Translated, Adorn'd with Sculpture, and Illustrated with Annotations*.
— (1671), *America: Being an Accurate Description of the New World*.
O Hehir, Brendan, ed. (1969), *Expans'd Hieroglyphicks: A Critical Edition of Sir John Denham's Coopers Hill*, Berkeley, LA.
Oldham, John (1681a), *Satyrs upon the Jesuits: Written in the Year 1679*.
— (1681b), *Some New Pieces Never Before Publisht*.
— (1683), *Poems, and Translations*.
— (1684), *The Works of Mr. John Oldham, together with his Remains*.
— (1685), *A Second Musical Entertainment Perform'd on St. Cecilia's Day. November XXII. 1684*.
—: for *Poems*, see Brooks and Selden (1987).
Oldisworth, William, trans. (1710), *Callipaedia: or, the Art of Getting Pretty Children. In Four Books. Translated from the Original Latin of Claudius Quilletus*.
Oldmixon, John (1696), *Poems upon Several Occasions, in Imitation of the Manner of Anacreon, with other Poems, Letters and Translations*.
— (1703), *Amores Britannici. Epistles Historical and Gallant, in English Heroic Verse: From Several of the Most Illustrious Personages of their Times*.
— (1704), *A Pastoral Poem on the Victories at Schellenburgh and Blenheim*.
— (1706), *Iberia Liberata: A Poem*.
Osborn, James M., ed. (1966), *Joseph Spence: Observations, Anecdotes, and Characters of Books and Men*, 2 vols, Oxford.
Otway, Thomas (1680), *The Orphan: Or, The Unhappy Marriage*.
— (1681), *The Souldier's Fortune: A Comedy*.
— (1685), *Windsor Castle, in a Monument to our Late Sovereign K. Charles II. of Ever Blessed Memory*.
Ovid: for the text of *Ars Amatoria*, see Mozley (1979).
—: for the text of *Metamorphoses*, see Tarrant (2004).
—: for the text of *Heroides*, see Showerman (1977).
—: for translations, see Garth (1717); Golding (1567); Saltonstall (1636); Sandys (1626 and 1632); Sewell (1717); Turberville (1567); Wolferston (1661).
Ovid's Art of Love. In Three Books . . . Translated into English Verse by Several Eminent Hands (1709).
Ovid's Epistles, Translated by Several Hands (1680).
Ovid's Epistles, Translated by Several Hands (1701), sixth edition.
Ovid's Epistles, Translated by Several Hands (1712), eighth edition.
Ovington, John (1699), *An Essay upon the Nature and Qualities of Tea*.
Oxford and Cambridge Miscellany Poems (1708).
Ozell, John, trans. (1708), *Boileau's Lutrin: A Mock-Heroic Poem . . . Render'd into English Verse*.
—, trans. (1710), *La Secchia Rapita: The Trophy-Bucket, A Mock-Heroic Poem, the First of the Kind. By Signor Alessandro Tassoni*.
A Pacquet from Parnassus: or, A Collection of Papers (1702).

Painter, William (1567), *The Second Tome of the Palace of Pleasure*.
— (1623), *Chaucer New Painted*.
Pardoe, William (1688), *Antient Christianity Revived*.
Parker, Fred (2012), 'Travesty and Mock-Heroic', in Hopkins and Martindale (2012), pp. 323–59.
Parnell, Thomas (1717), *Homer's Battle of the Frogs and Mice. With the Remarks of Zoilus. To which is Prefix'd, the Life of the said Zoilus*.
— (1758), *The Posthumous Works of Dr. Thomas Parnell*.
Patey, Douglas Lane (1997a), 'The Institution of Criticism in the Eighteenth Century', in Nisbet and Rawson, eds (1997), pp. 1–31.
— (1997b), 'Ancients and Moderns', in Nisbet and Rawson, eds (1997), pp. 32–72.
Patterson, Annabel (1987), *Pastoral and Ideology: Virgil to Valéry*, Berkeley, CA.
Peacham, Henry (1622), *The Complete Gentleman*.
Pellicer, Juan Christian (2008): 'Corkscrew or Cathedral? The Politics of Alexander Pope's *Windsor-Forest* and the Dynamics of Literary Kind', *Huntington Library Quarterly*, 71:3, 453–88.
Péti, Miklós (2012), '"Envy'd Wit" in *An Essay on Criticism*', *SEL*, 52:3, 561–83.
Petronius, see Heseltine (1975).
Pettie, George (1576), *A Petite Pallace of Pettie his Pleasure*.
Philips, Ambrose (1712), *The Distrest Mother. A Tragedy*.
Philips, John (1705), *Blenheim, a Poem*.
— (1708), *Cyder. A Poem*.
—: for *Poems*, see Lloyd Thomas (1927).
Philips, Katherine (1667), *Poems by the Most Deservedly Admired Mrs. Katherine Philips, the Matchless Orinda*.
Phillips, John (1672), *Maronides: or, Virgil Travestie: Being a New Paraphrase upon the Fifth Book of Virgils Aeneids in Burlesque Verse*.
Philosophical Transactions: Giving some Accompt of the Present Undertakings, Studies and Labours of the Ingenious in many Considerable Parts of the World (1665–).
Pick, Samuel (1639), *Festum Uoluptatis, or the Banquet of Pleasure*.
Piles, Roger de (1706), *The Art of Painting, and the Lives of the Painters . . . Done from the French*.
Plautus: see Lindsay (1914).
Pliny the Younger: see Mynors (1963b).
Plowden, G. F. C. (1983), *Pope on Classic Ground*, Athens, OH.
Plutarch: for translations, see *Fourth Volume* (1685); Holland (1603).
Poems and Translations. By Several Hands (1714)
The Poems of Horace . . . Rendred in English Verse by Several Persons (1666).
Poems on Affairs of State, From the Reign of K. James the First, to this Present Year 1703 (1703).
Poetical Miscellanies: The Fifth Part (1704).
Poetical Miscellanies: The Sixth Part (1709).
Poetical Miscellanies, Consisting of Original Poems and Translations. By the Best Hands. Publish'd by Mr. Steele (late 1713, dated 1714).
Pomfret, John (1700a), *The Choice. A Poem*.

— (1700b), *Reason. A Poem.*
— (1707), *Miscellany Poems on Several Occasions*, second edition.
Poole, Matthew (1685), *Annotations on the Holy Bible.*
Pope, Alexander (1711a), *An Essay on Criticism.*
— (1711b), *The Critical Specimen.*
— (1713), *The Narrative of Dr. Robert Norris, Concerning the Strange and Deplorable Frenzy of Mr. John Denn—, an Officer in the Custom-House.*
—, ed. (1717), *Poems on Several Occasions.* See Ault (1935).
— (1717), *The Works of Mr. Alexander Pope.*
—, trans. (1715–20), *The Iliad of Homer*, 6 vols. With contributions to the annotation by William Broome.
—, ed. (1723), *The Works of John Sheffield, Earl of Mulgrave, Marquis of Normanby, and Duke of Buckingham*, 2 vols.
—, ed. (1725), *The Works of Shakespear..., Collated and Corrected by the Former Editions, by Mr. Pope*, 6 vols.
—, trans. (1725–6), *The Odyssey of Homer*, 5 vols. With contributions to several books of the translation by Elijah Fenton and William Broome.
—, and Jonathan Swift (1722), *Miscellaneous Poems and Translations*, fourth edition.
—, and Jonathan Swift (1727), *Miscellanies in Prose and Verse*, 2 vols.
— (1728, dated 1727) *Miscellanies. The Last Volume.*
— (1732), *Miscellanies. The Third Volume.*
—: for *The Dunciad*, see Rumbold (2007 and 2009).
—: for other editions of the *Poems* and *Works*, see Butt 1939–69; Elwin and Courthope (1871–86); Rogers (2006); Southall (1988); Warburton (1751); Warton (1797).
—: for *Prose Works*, see Ault and Cowler 1936–86
Pope, Walter (1698), *Moral and Political Fables.*
Pordage, Samuel (1678), *The Siege of Babylon.*
Porter, Roy (2003), *Flesh in the Age of Reason.*
Prest, Harry (1977), 'Alexander Pope's Pastorals: A Study of their Genesis and Evolution', unpublished doctoral dissertation, McMaster University.
Pricket, Robert (1603), *A Souldiers Wish unto his Soveraigne Lord King James.*
Priestley, Joseph (1777), *A Course of Lectures on Oratory and Criticism.*
Prior, Matthew (1706), *An Ode, Humbly Inscribed to the Queen. On the Late Glorious Success of Her Majesty's Arms.*
— (1707), *Poems on Several Occasions* (unauthorised).
— (1709), *Poems on Several Occasions.*
—: for *Literary Works*, see Wright and Spears (1971).
Propertius: see Heyworth (2007).
The Prophets: An Heroic Poem. In Three Cantos (1708).
Purcell, Henry (1684), *A Musical Entertainment Perform'd on November XXII. 1683.*
— (1691), *The Vocal and Instrumental Musick of the Prophetess.*
Quarles, Francis (1643), *Emblemes*, Cambridge.
Quarles, John (1655), *Divine Meditations upon Several Subjects.*
The Queens Famous Progress: Or, Her Majesty's Royal Journey to the Bath, and Happy Return (1702).

Quillet, Claude (1710), *Callipaediae; or, An Art How to Have Handsome Children . . . Now Done into English Verse.*
—: for other translations, see Oldisworth (1710); Rowe (1712).
Quintilian: see Winterbottom (1970).
Quintero, Ruben (1992), *Literate Culture: Pope's Rhetorical Art*, Newark and London.
Radcliffe, Alexander (1681), *Ovid Travestie, A Burlesque upon Ovid's Epistles*, second edition.
Rainbolt, Martha (1997), 'Their Ancient Claim: Sappho and Seventeenth- and Eighteenth-Century British Women's Poetry', *Seventeenth Century*, 12:1, 111–34.
Ralegh, Sir Walter (1693), *Introduction to a Breviary of the History of England.*
Randolph, Thomas (1652), *Poems with The Muses Looking-Glasse*, fourth edition.
Rapin, René, (1706), *The Whole Critical Works of Monsieur Rapin . . . Newly Translated into English by Several Hands*, 2 vols.
—: for *Reflections*, see Rymer (1674).
—: for *Of Gardens*, see Gardiner (1706).
Reverand II, Cedric D., ed. (2015), *Queen Anne and the Arts*, Lewisburg.
Reynolds, Margaret (2003), *The Sappho History.*
Richarson, Jonathan (1776), *Richardsoniana: Or, Occasional Reflections on the Moral Nature of Man.*
Richardson, John (2004), *Slavery and Augustan Literature: Swift, Pope, Gay.*
Richardson, Samuel (1804), *The Correspondence of Samuel Richardson*, ed. Anna Laetita Barbauld, 6 vols.
Richardson, Vaughan (1701), *A Collection of New Songs, for One, Two, and Three Voices.*
Rigby, S. H. (1996), *Chaucer in Context*, Manchester.
Robinson, David (1963), *Sappho and her Influence*, New York.
La Rochefoucauld, François, duc de (1694), *Moral Maxims and Reflections, in Four Parts . . . Now Made English.*
Rochester, John Wilmot, Earl of (1679), *Upon Nothing. A Poem.*
— (1680), *Poems on Several Occasions.*
— (1696), *Poems, (&c.) on Several Occasions; with Valentinian, a Tragedy.*
— (1707), *The Works of the Right Honourable the late Earls of Rochester and Roscommon*, second edition.
— (1709), *The Works of the Right Honourable the Earls of Rochester, and Roscommon*, 2 vols, third edition.
—: for *Works*, see Love (1999).
Rogers, Pat (1972), *Grub Street: Studies in a Subculture.*
— (1973), '"The Enamelled Ground": The Language of Heraldry and Natural Description in "Windsor-Forest"', *Studia Neophilologica*, 45, 356–71.
— (1980), 'Rhythm and Recoil in Pope's *Pastorals*', *Eighteenth-Century Studies*, 14:1, 1–17.
— (2004), *The Symbolic Design of Windsor-Forest: Iconography, Pageant, and Prophecy in Pope's Early Work*, Newark, DE.
— (2005a), *Pope and the Destiny of the Stuarts: History, Politics, and Mythology in the Age of Queen Anne*, Oxford.

— (2005b): 'The Memory of Henrietta Tempest: Pope's "Winter" and the Great Storm', in Colin Gibson and Lisa Marr, eds, *New Windows on a Woman's World: Essays for Jocelyn Harris*, vol. 1, pp. 276–87, Dunedin, NZ.
—, ed. (2006), *Alexander Pope: The Major Works*, Oxford.
—, ed. (2007), *The Cambridge Companion to Alexander Pope*, Cambridge.
— (2007), 'What Stranger Cause? Family and Kinship in *The Rape of the Lock*', TLS, 5455, 19 October, 13–15.
— (2010), *A Political Biography of Alexander Pope*.
— (2018), 'Pope and Martial: The Myth of Pelops And Belinda's "Iv'ry Neck"', RES, 69, 76–93.
Roscommon, Wentworth Dillon, Earl of (1680), *Horace's Art of Poetry. Made English*.
— (1684), *An Essay on Translated Verse*.
— (1685), *An Essay on Translated Verse*, second edition.
Rosenmayer, Thomas (1969), *The Green Cabinet: Theocritus and the European Pastoral Lyric*, Berkeley, CA.
Ross, Thomas, trans. (1661), *The Second Punick War Between Hannibal, and the Romanes ... from the Latine of Silius Italicus*.
— (1671), *An Essay upon the Third Punique War. Lib. I. and II.*
Rowe, Nicholas (1703), *The Fair Penitent. A Tragedy*.
— (1706), *Ulysses: A Tragedy*.
—, ed. (1709), *The Works of Mr. William Shakespear*, 6 vols.
—, trans. (1712), *Callipaedia. A Poem. In Four Books*.
Rudat, Wolfgang (1984), 'Pope's "Mutual Commerce": Allusive Manipulation in "January and May" and "The Rape of the Lock"', *Durham University Journal*, 77, 19–24.
Ruffhead, Owen (1769), *The Life of Alexander Pope, Esq*.
Rumbold, Valerie (1983), 'Pope and the Gothic Past', unpublished doctoral dissertation, University of Cambridge.
— (1989), *Women's Place in Pope's World*, Cambridge.
—, ed. (2007), *The Poems of Alexander Pope, Volume 3: The Dunciad (1728) & The Dunciad Variorum (1729)*, Longman Annotated English Poets.
—, ed. (2009), *Alexander Pope: The Dunciad: In Four Books*, revised edition.
Russell, Donald A., ed. (1967), *Longinus Libellus de Sublimitate*, Oxford.
Rymer, Thomas, trans. (1674), *Reflections on Aristotle's Treatise of Poesie. Containing the Necessary, Rational, and Universal Rules for Epick, Dramatick, and the Other Sorts of Poetry ... By R. Rapin*.
— (1677), *The Tragedies of the Last Age Consider'd and Examin'd by the Practice of the Ancients, and by the Common Sense of all Ages*.
— (1692), *A Short View of Tragedy; it's Original, Excellency, and Corruption*.
—: for *Critical Works*, see Zimansky (1956).
S., J. (1697), *The Innocent Epicure: or, the Art of Angling. A Poem*.
Sacheverell, Henry (1709), *The Perils of False Brethren, Both in Church and State*.
Saint-Evremont (1700), *The Works of Mr de St. Evremont ... Translated from the French*, 2 vols.
St. James's Park, A Satyr (1708).
Saltonstall, Wye, trans. (1636), *Ovid's Heroicall Epistles. English'd by W. S.*

Sambrook, James (1997), 'Poetry, 1660–1740', in Nisbet and Rawson, eds (1997), pp. 73–116.
Sandys, George, trans. (1626), *Ovid's Metamorphosis Englished*.
—, trans. (1632), *Ouid's Metamorphosis Englished, Mythologiz'd, and Represented in Figures*.
— (1638), *A Paraphrase vpon the Divine Poems*.
—, trans. (1640), *Christ's Passion. A Tragedy*. Originally by Hugo Grotius.
— (1641), *A Paraphrase vpon the Song of Solomon*.
Santesso, Aaron (2004), 'The Conscious Swain: Political Pastoral in Pope's Epic', *Eighteenth-Century Studies*, 37:2, 253–71.
Savage, Roger (1988), 'Antiquity as Nature: Pope's Fable of "Young Maro"', in Nicholson ed. (1988), pp. 83–116.
Schenck, C. M. (1988), 'The Funeral Elegy as Pastoral Initiation. Plato, Theocritus, Virgil', *Mosaic*, 21, 93–113.
Schmitz, Robert M. (1952), *Pope's "Windsor Forest," 1712: A Study of the Washington University Holograph*, St. Louis, MO.
— (1962), *Pope's "Essay on Criticism" 1709: A Study of the Bodleian Manuscript Text with Facsimiles, Transcripts, and Variants*, St. Louis, MO.
The Scolding Wives Vindication: or, An Answer to the Cuckold's Complaint (1689).
Scrivener, Matthew (1688), *The Method and Means to a True Spiritual Life*.
Sedley, Sir Charles (1702), *The Miscellaneous Works of the Honourable Charles Sedley, Bart*.
Sellin, Paul R. (1968), *Daniel Heinsius and Stuart England: With a Checklist of the Works of Daniel Heinsius*, Leiden.
Seneca: for *De Beneficiis*, see Basore (2014).
—: for *Tragedies*, see Sherburne (1702).
Sennert, Daniel (1660), *Thirteen Books of Natural Philosophy*.
Settle, Elkanah (1702 [possibly published 1703]), *Eusebia Triumphans. The Hannover Succession to the Imperial Crown of England, An Heroic Poem*.
Sewell, George, ed (1717), *Ovid's Metamorphoses. In Fifteen Books. A New Translation. By Several Hands*.
Shadwell, Thomas (1671), *The Humorists, a Comedy*.
— (1676), *The Virtuoso. A Comedy*.
— (1679), *A True Widow: A Comedy*.
— (1680), *The Woman Captain: A Comedy*.
Shaftesbury, Anthony Ashley Cooper, Earl of (1711), *Characteristicks of Men, Manners, Opinions, Times*, 3 vols.
Shakespeare, William: for early editions of the *Works* see Rowe (1709) and Pope (1725); for a modern edition, see Alexander (1951).
Sheehan, David (1978), 'Swift, Voiture, and the Spectrum of Raillery', *Papers on Language and Literature*, 14, 171–88.
Sheffield, John: see Buckinghamshire, Duke of.
Sheppard, Samuel (1651), *Epigrams Theological, Philosophical, and Romantick*.
Sherburn, George (1934), *The Early Career of Alexander Pope*, Oxford.
—, ed. (1956), *The Correspondence of Alexander Pope*, 5 vols, Oxford.

— (1958a), 'New Anecdotes about Alexander Pope', *Notes and Queries*, CCIII, 343–9
— (1958b), 'Letters of Alexander Pope, Chiefly to Sir William Trumbull', *RES*, 9, 388–406.
Sherburne, John, trans. (1639), *Ovids Heroical Epistles, Englished by Iohn Sherburne.*
Sherburne, Sir Edward, trans. (1702), *The Tragedies of L. Annaeus Seneca the Philosopher.*
Shipman, Thomas (1683), *Carolina; or, Loyal Poems.*
Shippen, William (1704a), *Faction Display'd. A Poem.*
— (1704b), *Moderation Display'd: A Poem.* (The attribution is regarded as dubious.)
Showerman, Grant, ed. and trans. (1977), *Ovid: Heroides [and] Amores*, second edition, rev. G. P. Goold, Cambridge, MA.
Shugrue, Michael (1957), 'Pope's Translation of Statius', *Notes and Queries*, CCII, 463.
Sidney, Algernon (1698), *Discourses Concerning Government.*
Sidney, Sir Philip (1593), *The Countesse of Pembrokes Arcadia ... Now Since the First Edition Augmented and Ended.*
— (1595), *The Defence of Poesie.*
Smallwood, Philip (2003), *Reconstructing Criticism: Pope's Essay on Criticism and the Logic of Definition*, Lewisburg, PA.
— (2004), 'To "value still the true": Pope's *Essay on Criticism* and the Problem of the Historical Mode', in Smallwood, ed., *Critical Pasts: Writing Criticism, Writing History*, pp. 75–94, Lewisburg, PA.
— (2015), 'Great Anna's Chaucer: Pope's January and May and the Logic of Settlement', in Reverand, ed. (2015), pp. 99–117.
Smith, J. C., and Ernest. de Selincourt, eds (1912), *The Poetical Works of Edmund Spenser*, Oxford.
Smith, Marshall (1713), *On the Peace: A Poem.*
Soames, Sir William, and John Dryden, trans. (1683), *The Art of Poetry Written in French by the Sieur de Boileau, Made English.*
Southall, Raymond, ed. (1988), *Pope: An Essay on Criticism, The Rape of the Lock and Epistle to Several Persons (Moral Essays)*, second edition, Plymouth.
Southerne, Thomas (1696), *Oroonoko: A Tragedy.*
Sowerby, Robin (2005), 'Epic', in Gillespie and Hopkins, eds (2005), pp. 149–72.
— (2006), *The Augustan Art of Poetry: Augustan Translation of the Classics*, Oxford.
Spacks, Patricia Meyer (1970), 'Imagery and Method in *An Essay on Criticism*', *PMLA*, 85, 97–106.
The Spectator: see Bond (1965).
Speght, Thomas, ed. (1598), *The Workes of our Antient and Learned English Poet, Geffrey Chavcer, newly Printed.*
Spence, Joseph (1726–7), *An Essay on Pope's Odyssey: In which some Particular Beauties and Blemishes of that Work are Consider'd.*
—: for *Observations*, see Osborn (1966).
Spenser, Edmund (1579), *The Shepheardes Calender, Conteyning Twelue Aeglogues Proportionable to the Twelve Monethes.*
— (1590–6), *The Faerie Queene.*
— (1595a), *Colin Clouts Come Home Againe.*
— (1595b), *Amoretti and Epithalamion.*

—: (1596), *Prothalamion Or a Spousall Verse made by Edm. Spenser*.
—: for a modern edition of *The Faerie Queene*, see Hamilton (2007).
—: for *Poetical Works*, see Smith and de Selincourt (1912).
—: for *Works*, see Hughes (1715).
Spingarn, J. E., ed. (1908–9), *Critical Essays of the Seventeenth Century*, 3 vols, Oxford.
Spurgeon, C. F. E., ed. (1901), *Richard Brathwait, Comments in 1665, upon Chaucer's Tales of the Miller and the Wife of Bath*.
— (1914), *Five Hundred Years of Chaucer Criticism and Allusion, 1357–1900*.
Stalker, John and George Parker (1688), *A Treatise of Japaning and Varnishing, Being a Complete Discovery of those Arts*, Oxford.
Stanley, Thomas (1647), *Poems and Translations*.
— (1651), *Poems, by Thomas Stanley Esq*.
State-Amusements, Serious and Hypocritical, Fully Exemplified in the Abdication of King James the Second (1711).
State-Poems; Continued from the Time of O. Cromwell, to this Present Year 1697 (1697).
Statius: for text, see Garrod (1962).
—: for translations, see Lewis (1767); Stephens (1648).
Steele, Richard (1701), *The Christian Hero: An Argument Proving that no Principles but those of Religion are Sufficient to Make a Great Man*.
—: for *Correspondence*, see Blanchard (1941).
—: for *Occasional Verse*, see Blanchard (1952).
—: for *The Guardian*, see Stephens (1982).
—: for *The Spectator*, see Bond (1965).
—: for *The Tatler*, see Bond (1987).
Stephanson, Raymond (1991), 'The Love Song of Young Alexander Pope: Allusion and Sexual Displacement in the *Pastorals*', *English Studies in Canada*, 17:1, 21–35.
Stephens, John Calhoun, ed. (1982), *The Guardian*, Lexington, KY.
Stephens, Thomas, trans. (1648), *An Essay upon Statius, or, The Five First Books of Publ. Papinius Statius his Thebais Done into English Verse by T.S., with the Poetick History Illustrated*.
Stevenson, Matthew (1680), *The Wits Paraphras'd; or, Paraphrase upon Paraphrase. In a Burlesque of the Several Late Translations of Ovid's Epistles*.
Stubbes, George (1710), *The Laurel, and the Olive*.
Suckling, Sir John (1638), *Aglaura*.
Suetonius: see Kaster (2016).
Surrey, Henry Howard, Earl of (1557), *Songes and Sonettes, Written by the . . . late Earle of Surrey, and Others*.
Svetich, Kella (2000), 'Pope's "Constant Remembrance": Shakespearean Allusion in *An Essay on Criticism*', *Scriblerian*, 32, 347–8.
Swift, Jonathan (1704), *A Tale of a Tub. Written for the Universal Improvement of Mankind*.
—: see also Walsh (2010).
—: for *Journal to Stella*, see Williams (2013).
Switzer, Stephen (1715), *The Nobleman, Gentleman and Gardener's Recreation*.
Sylvae: or, The Second Part of Poetical Miscellanies (1685).

Sylvester, Joshuah, trans. (1621), *Du Bartas His Diuine Weekes, and Workes... Translated.*
Szilagyi, Stephen (1986), 'Pope's *Two or Three*', *Explicator*, 44:3, 23–6.
Tacitus: see Fisher (1951).
Tarrant, R. J., ed. (2004), *P. Ovidi Nasonis Metamorphoses*, Oxford.
Tassoni: see Ozell (1710).
Tate, Nahum (1682), *The Second Part of Absalom and Achitophel*, London.
—, ed. (1685), *Poems by Several Hands, and on Several Occasions.*
— (1685), *A Song for St. Caecilia's Day 1685 Written by Mr. N. Tate and Set by Mr. William Turner.*
—, trans. (1686), *Syphilis: or, A Poetical History of the French Disease. Written in Latin by Fracastorius.*
— (1698), *A Consolatory Poem to the Right Honourable John Lord Cutts upon the Death of his Most Accomplish'd Lady.*
— (1700), *Panacea: A Poem upon Tea: In Two Canto's.*
— (1701a), *A Congratulatory Poem on the New Parliament Assembled.*
— (1701b), *A Monumental Poem in Memory of the Right Honourable Sir George Treby Kt.*
—, and Nicholas Brady (1696), *A New Version of the Psalms of David, Fitted to the Tunes Used in Churches.*
The Tatler: see Bond (1987).
Taverner, William (1708), *The Maid the Mistress. A Comedy.*
Taylor, Jeremy (1675), *Antiquitates Christianae: or, The History of the Life and Death of the Holy Jesus.*
Temple, Sir William (1690), *Miscellanea. The Second Part.*
Terence: see Echard (1699).
Terry, Richard (1993), 'Pope's Miltonic Parody and his Feud with Dennis', *English Studies*, 74:2, 138–42.
— (1999), '"The Sound must seem an Eccho to the Sense": An Eighteenth-Century Controversy Revisited', *Modern Language Review*, 94, 940–54.
Theocritus: for text see Gow (1952).
—: for translation, see Creech (1684b).
Thompson, E. P. (1975), *Whigs and Hunters: The Origin of the Black Act*, Harmondsworth.
Tickell, Thomas (1712, dated 1713), *A Poem, to His Excellency the Lord Privy-Seal, on the Prospect of Peace.*
Tilley, Morris Palmer (1950), *A Dictionary of the Proverbs in England in the Sixteenth and Seventeenth Centuries*, Ann Arbor, MI.
Tissol, Grant, 'Ovid', in Gillespie and Hopkins, eds (2005), pp. 204–17.
Topsell, Edward (1658), *The History of Four-Footed Beasts and Serpents.*
To the Memory of Devereux Knightly ... A Poem (1708).
Tracy, Clarence (1974), *The Rape Observ'd*, Toronto.
Trapp, Joseph (1701), *Aedes Badmintonianae: A Poem most Humbly Presented to His Grace Henry Duke of Beaufort, &c.*
— (1711–19), *Praelectiones Poeticae: in Schola Naturalis Philosophiae Oxon. Habitae*, 3 vols.
— (1713), *Peace: A Poem.*

Trapp, J. B. (1958), 'The Owl's Ivy and the Poet's Bays. An Enquiry into Poetic Garlands', *Journal of the Warburg and Courtauld Institutes*, 21, 227–55.
Trickett, Rachel (1988), 'The Heroides and the English Augustans', in Charles Martindale, ed., *Ovid Renewed: Ovidian Influences on Literature and Art from the Middle Ages to the Twentieth Century*, pp. 191–204, Cambridge.
The Triumph of Virtue (1713).
Trowles, T. A. (1992), 'The Musical Ode in Britain c. 1670–1800', unpublished doctoral dissertation, University of Oxford.
Turberville, George (1567), *The Heroycall Epistles of the Learned Poet Publius Ouidius Naso, in English Verse*.
— (1587), *Tragicall Tales Translated by Turberuile in Time of his Troubles out of Sundrie Italians, with the Argument and Lenuoye to Eche Tale*.
Tutchin, John (1691), *The Tribe of Levi. A Poem*.
— (1701), *The Apostates. A Poem*.
The Unfortunate General; or, the History of the Life and Character of Cato (1713).
The Universal Magazine, LXXI (1782).
Uvedale, Thomas (1704), *The Remedy of Love, in Imitation of Ovid*.
Vanbrugh, Sir John (1702), *The False Friend, A Comedy*.
Varney, A. J. (1974), 'The Composition of Pope's "Windsor Forest"', *Durham University Journal*, 36, 57–67.
Vaughan, Henry (1646), *Poems, with the Tenth Satyre of Iuvenal Englished*.
— (1650), *Silex Scintillans: or Sacred Poems and Priuate Ejaculations*.
Venette, Nicholas (1707), *The Mysteries of Conjugal Love Reveal'd*.
Vermeule, Blakey (1998), 'Shame and Identity: Pope's Critique of Judgment in *An Essay on Criticism*', *1650–1850: Ideas, Aesthetics, and Inquiries in the Early Modern Era*, 4, 105–36.
Vida, Marco Giralomo: see Kennett (1701) and Williams (1976).
Vieth, David M. (1966), 'Pope and Rochester: An Unnoticed Borrowing', *Notes and Queries*, 13:12, 457–8.
A View of the Religion of the Town; or, a Sunday Morning's Ramble (1687)
Virgil, Publius Maro: for text, see Mynors (1967).
—: for translations, see Bidle (1634); Dryden (1697b); Fleming (1589); L., W. (1628); Lauderdale (1709); Ogilby (1649).
Voiture, Vincent de (1657), *Letters of Affaires Love and Courtship.... English'd by J. D.*
— (1700–2, dated 1700 and 1701), *Familiar and Courtly Letters, Written by Monsieur Voiture... Made English by John Dryden, Esq.* [and several others], 2 vols.
— (1705), *The Works of Monsieur Voiture... Made English by John Dryden, Esq.* [and several others], 2 vols.
— (1715), *The Works of the Celebrated Monsieur Voiture... Done from the Paris Edition by Mr. Ozell*, 2 vols.
Wakefield, Gilbert (1796), *Observations on Pope*.
Walker, William (1708), *Marry, or do Worse. A Comedy*.
Waller, A. R., ed. (1905), *The English Writings of Abraham Cowley*, 2 vols, Cambridge.
Waller, Edmund (1645), *Poems, &c*.
— (1655), *A Panegyrick to my Lord Protector*.

— (1661), *A Poem on St. James's Park as Lately Improved by his Majesty*.
— (1685), *Divine Poems*.
— (1686), *Poems, &c. Written upon Several Occasions, and to Several Persons*.
— (1690), *The Maid's Tragedy Altered*.
— and Sidney Godolphin (1658), *The Passion of Dido for Aeneas as it is Incomparably Exprest in the Fourth Book of Virgil*.
—: for *The Second Part*, see Atterbury (1690).
—: for *Poems*, see Drury (1893).
Waller, William (1713), *Peace on Earth. A Congratulatory Poem*.
Walls, Kathryn (2008), 'Pope's *Essay on Criticism*, ll. 205-6: A Source in the *Moriae Encomium* of Erasmus', *Notes and Queries*, 55:3, 315-16.
Walond, William (c. 1759), *Mr. Pope's Ode on St. Cecilia's Day*.
Walsh, Marcus, ed. (2010), *Jonathan Swift, A Tale of a Tub and Other Works*, Cambridge.
Walsh, William (1691), *A Dialogue concerning Women. Being a Defence of the Sex Written to Eugenia*.
— (1692), *Letters and Poems, Amorous and Gallant*.
— (1695), *A Funeral Elegy upon the Death of the Queen*.
Walton, Isaac (1653), *The Compleat Angler or, The Contemplative Man's Recreation*.
The Wanton Wife of Bath (c. 1665). Single-sheet ballad.
Warburton, William (1751), *The Works of Alexander Pope, Esq. . . . Published by Mr. [William] Warburton*, 9 vols.
Ward, C. E., ed. (1942), *The Letters of John Dryden with Letters Addressed to Him*, Durham, NC.
Ward, Edward (1691), *The Poet's Ramble After Riches*.
— (1692), *The Miracles Perform'd by Money; A Poem*.
— (1695), *Female Policy Detected*.
— (1698), *The London Spy*.
— (1699a), *The Cock-Pit Combat; or, The Baiting of the Tiger, on Thursday, March 9, 1698*.
— (1699b), *Modern Religion and Ancient Loyalty: A Dialogue*.
— (1700), *A Journey to H[ell]; or, a Visit Paid to, &c. A Poem: Part II*.
— (1704), *In Imitation of Hudibras. The Dissenting Hypocrite, or Occasional Conformist*.
— (1706), *The Secret History of the Calves Head Club, Complt. Or, The Republican Unmask'd*.
— (1710), *The Fourth Part of Vulgus Britannicus: or, The British Hudibras*.
Waring, Henry (1702), *The Coronation, or, England's Patroness: Being a Small Poem Dedicated to Her Sacred Majesty Queen Anne*.
Warton, Joseph (1756), *An Essay on the Genius and Writings of Pope*.
— (1782), *An Essay on the Genius and Writings of Pope. Volume the Second*.
— (1797), *The Works of Alexander Pope, Esq. . . . With Notes and Illustrations by Joseph Warton*, 9 vols.
Wasserman, Earl (1959), *The Subtler Language: Critical Readings of Neoclassic and Romantic Poems*, Baltimore, MD.
— (1961), 'Pope's "Ode for Musick"', *ELH*, 28, 163-86.

— (1966), 'The Limits of Allusion in "The Rape of the Lock"', *Journal of English and Germanic Philology*, 65, 425–44.
Watts, Isaac (1706), *Horae Lyricae. Poems Chiefly of the Lyric Kind.*
— (1709), *Horae Lyricae. Poems Chiefly of the Lyric Kind*, second edition.
— (1734), *Reliquiae Juveniles: Miscellaneous Thoughts in Prose and Verse, on Natural, Moral, and Divine Subjects.*
Weinbrot, Howard (1993), *Britannia's Issue: The Rise of British Literature from Dryden to Ossian*, Cambridge.
Welsted, Leonard, trans. (1712), *The Works of Dionysius Longinus, On the Sublime . . . With some Remarks on the English Poets.*
Wesley, Samuel (1685), *Maggots: or, Poems on Several Subjects, Never Before Handled.*
— (1693), *The Life of our Blessed Lord & Saviour Jesus Christ: An Heroic Poem.*
— (1705), *Marlborough; or, The Fate of Europe: A Poem.*
Weston, John (1667), *The Amazon Queen; or, the Amours of Thalestris to Alexander the Great.*
Whiting, Bartlett Jere (1968), *Proverbs, Sentences and Proverbial Phrases from English Writings Mainly Before 1500*, Cambridge, MA.
Wilders, John, ed. (1973), *Samuel Butler: Hudibras*, Oxford.
Wilkins, A. S., ed. (1961), *M. Tulli Ciceronis Rhetorica*, vol. 1, Oxford.
Williams, Abigail (2005), *Poetry and the Creation of a Whig Literary Culture 1681–1714*, Oxford.
—, ed. (2013), *Jonathan Swift, Journal to Stella: Letters to Esther Johnson and Rebecca Dingley, 1710–1713*, Cambridge.
— (2015), 'The Diverting Muse: Miscellanies and Miscellany Culture in Queen Anne's Reign', in Reverand, ed. (2015), pp. 119–34.
Williams, Aubrey (1962), 'The Fall of China and *The Rape of the Lock*', *Philological Quarterly*, 41, 412–25.
Williams, Ralph G., trans. (1976), *The De Arte Poetica of Marco Giralamo Vida Translated with a Commentary, and with the Text of c. 1517*, New York.
Wilmot, John, see Rochester, Earl of.
Wilson, N. G., ed. (2015), *Herodoti Historiae*, vol. 1, Oxford.
Wimsatt, William (1965), *The Portraits of Alexander Pope*, New Haven, CT.
— (1994), 'Rhyme/Reason, Chaucer/Pope, Icon/Symbol', *Modern Language Quarterly*, 55:1, 17–46.
Windsor-Castle: A Poem (1708).
Winn, James Anderson (1979), 'Plays the Rake: His Letters to Ladies and the Making of the *Eloisa*', in Erskine-Hill and Smith, eds (1979), pp. 89–118.
— (2014), *Queen Anne, Patroness of the Arts*, Oxford.
— (2015), 'Praise the Patroness of Arts', in Reverand, ed. (2015), pp. 7–39.
Winterbottom, Michael, ed. (1970), *Quintilian Institutionis Oratoriae*, 2 vols, Oxford.
—, ed. (1994), *Marci Tulli Ciceronis De Officiis*, Oxford.
Wolferston, Francis (1661), *The Three Books of Publius Ovidius Naso, De Arte Amandi. Translated, with Historical, Poetical, and Topographical Annotations.*
Womersley, David, ed. (1997), *Augustan Critical Writing.*
Woodman, Tom (1990), '"Wanting Nothing but the Laurel": Pope and the Idea of the Laureate Poet', in David Fairer, ed., *Pope: New Contexts*, pp. 45–58, New York.

Woodward, George (1730), *Poems on Several Occasions*, Oxford.
Woolley, Hannah (1673), *The Gentlewomans Companion; or, A Guide to the Female Sex: Containing Directions of Behaviour, in all Places, Companies, Relations, and Conditions, from their Childhood down to Old Age.*
The Works of Lucian Translated from the Greek by Several Eminent Hands . . . With a Life of Lucian . . . by John Dryden (1711), 4 vols.
Wotton, William (1694), *Reflections upon Ancient and Modern Learning.*
Wright, H. Bunker, and K. Monroe Spears, eds (1971), *The Literary Works of Matthew Prior*, 2 vols, Oxford.
Wycherley, William (1672), *Love in a Wood, or, St. James's Park. A Comedy.*
— (1673), *The Gentleman Dancing-Master. A Comedy.*
— (1675), *The Country-Wife, A Comedy.*
— (1677), *The Plain-Dealer. A Comedy.*
— (1682), *Epistles to the King and Duke.*
— (1704), *Miscellany Poems: As Satyrs, Epistles, Love-Verses, Songs, Sonnets, &c.*
— (1729), *The Posthumous Works of William Wycherley, Esq. . . . Vol. II.* Edited by Pope.
—: for *Plays*, see Friedman (1979).
Yalden, Thomas (1695), *On the Conquest of Namur. A Pindaric Ode, Humbly Inscrib'd to his most Sacred and Victorious Majesty.*
Young, Edward (1713), *An Epistle to the Right Honourable the Lord Lansdown.*
Zimansky, C. A., ed. (1956), *The Critical Works of Thomas Rymer*, New Haven, CT.

Indexes of Titles and First Lines

Titles

A Discourse on Pastoral Poetry 168
An Essay on Criticism 184
Autumn 144

Epigram upon Two or Three 642

January and May; Or, The Merchant's Tale: From Chaucer 1

Lines from *The Critical Specimen* 293

Messiah 329

Ode for Musick 610
On a Fan of the Author's Design 521
On Silence 451

Pastorals 103
Prologue, Design'd for Mr. D—'s Last Play 685
Prologue to *Cato* 593

Sapho to Phaon. Wholly Translated 301
Spring 116
Summer 132

The Arrival of Ulysses in Ithaca 693
The Episode of Sarpedon 60
The Fable of Vertumnus and Pomona 424
The First Book of Statius his Thebais 353
The Gardens of Alcinous 633
The Rape of the Locke 477
The Wife of Bath Her Prologue, from Chaucer 648
To a Young Lady, with the Works of Voiture 439
To the Author of a Poem, intitled, Successio 463

Verses design'd to be prefix'd to Mr. Lintott's Miscellany 469

Windsor-Forest 528
Winter 154

First Lines

A Faithful Swain, whom Love had taught to sing 132
Begone ye Criticks, and restrain your Spite 466
Behold the Woes of Matrimonial Life 654
Beneath the Shade a spreading Beech displays 144

Close to the Gates a spacious Garden lies 637
Come gentle Air! th' Eolian *Shepherd* said 526

Descend ye Nine! descend and sing 620

First in these Fields I try the Sylvan Strains 116
Fly Pegasaean *Steed, thy Rider bear* 299
Fraternal Rage, the guilty *Thebe's* Alarms 364

Grown Old in Rhyme, 'twere barbarous to discard 689

In these gay Thoughts the Loves and Graces shine 444

Say, lovely Youth, that dost my Heart command 308
Silence! Cooeval with Eternity 455
So on *Maeotis*' Marsh (where Reeds and Rushes 297
Some *Colinaeus* praise, some *Bleau* 473

The fair *Pomona* flourish'd in his Reign 429
The Sun descending, the *Phaeacian* Train 698
There liv'd in *Lombardy*, as Authors write 10
Thus *Hector*, great in Arms, contends in vain 68
Thy Forests, *Windsor*! and thy green Retreats 544
Thyrsis, the Musick of that murm'ring Spring 154
'Tis hard to say, if greater Want of Skill 204
To wake the Soul by tender Strokes of Art 604
Two or Three Visits, Two or Three Bows 646

What dire Offence from Am'rous Causes springs 486

Ye Nymphs of *Solyma*! begin the Song 336